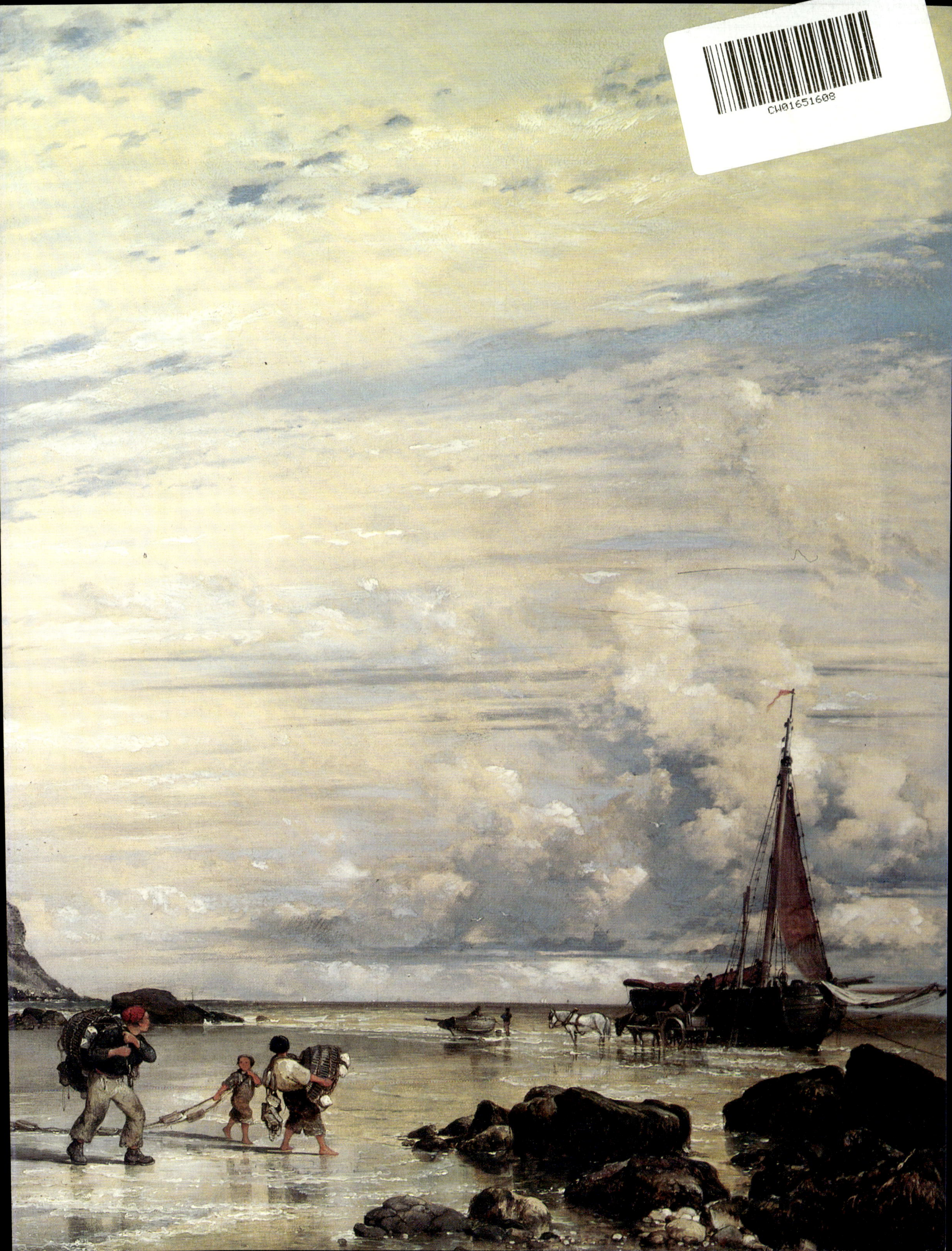

EDWARD WILLIAM COOKE

RA FRS FSA FLS FZS FGS

1811-1880

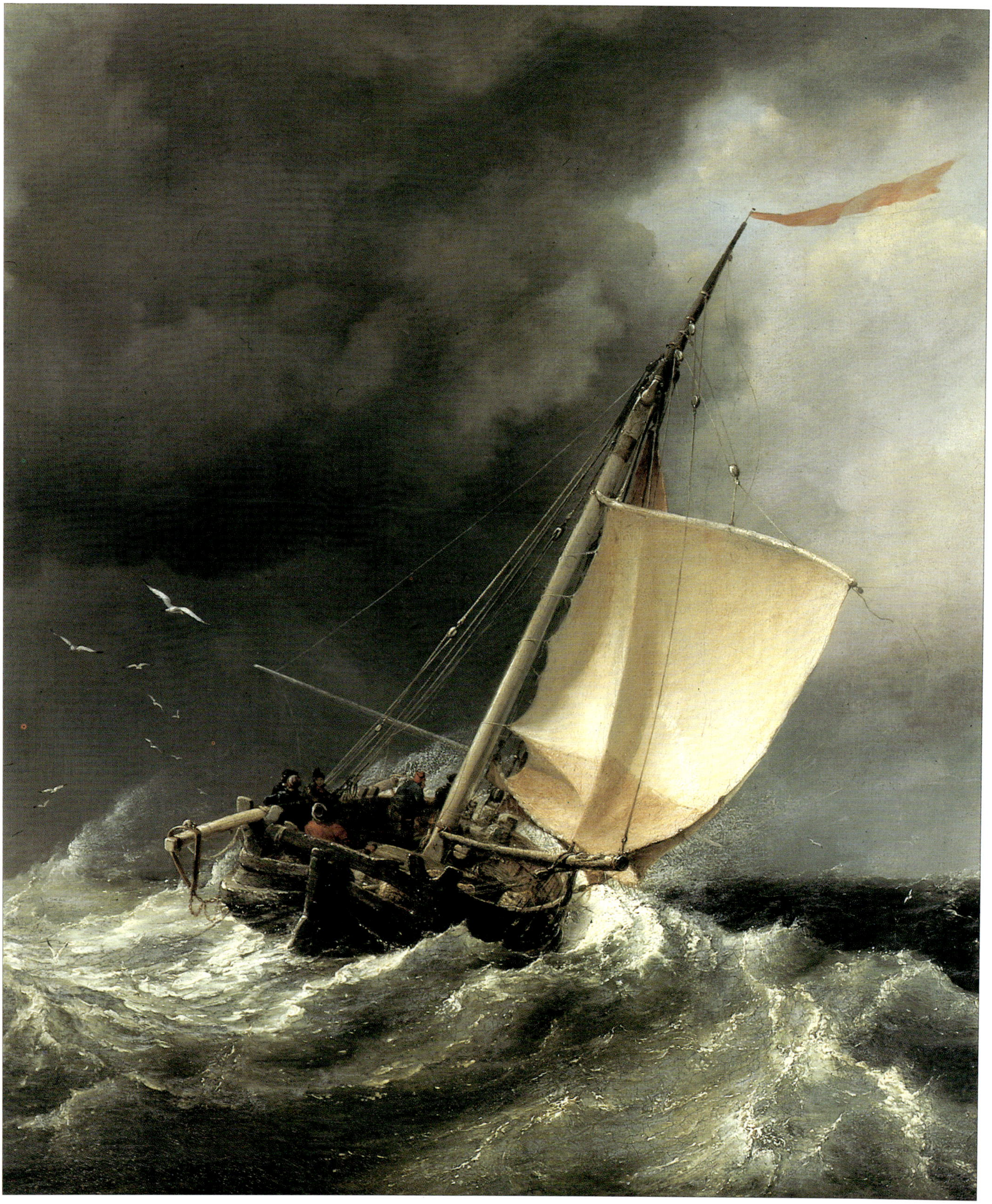

EDWARD WILLIAM COOKE

RA FRS FSA FLS FZS FGS

1811-1880

A Man of his Time

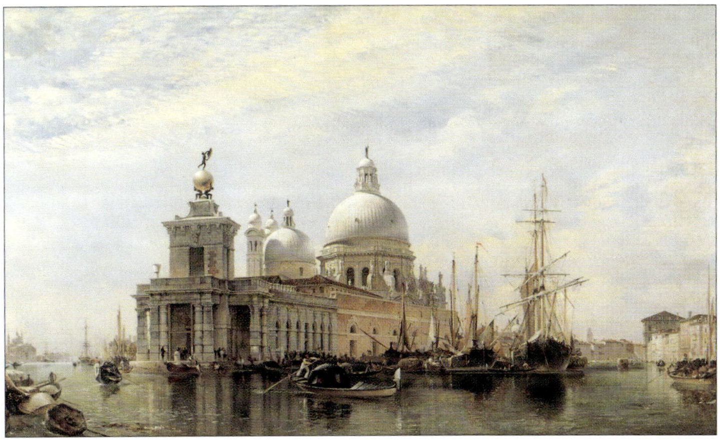

John Munday

Antique Collectors' Club

ISBN 1 85149 222 4

British Library Cataloguing-in-Publication Data
A catalogue record for this book is available from the British Library

Printed in England
by the Antique Collectors' Club Ltd., Woodbridge, Suffolk
on Consort Royal Satin paper
supplied by the Donside Paper Company, Aberdeen, Scotland

Frontispiece – *Detail of Colour Plate 39*
Title-page – *Detail of Colour Plate 122*

The Antique Collectors' Club

The Antique Collectors' Club was formed in 1966 and quickly grew to a five figure membership spread throughout the world. It publishes the only independently run monthly antiques magazine, *Antique Collecting*, which caters for those collectors who are interested in widening their knowledge of antiques, both by greater awareness of quality and by discussion of the factors which influence the price that is likely to be asked. The Antique Collectors' Club pioneered the provision of information on prices for collectors and the magazine still leads in the provision of detailed articles on a variety of subjects.

It was in response to the enormous demand for information on 'what to pay' that the price guide series was introduced in 1968 with the first edition of *The Price Guide to Antique Furniture* (completely revised 1978 and 1989), a book which broke new ground by illustrating the more common types of antique furniture, the sort that collectors could buy in shops and at auctions rather than the rare museum pieces which had previously been used (and still to a large extent are used) to make up the limited amount of illustrations in books published by commercial publishers. Many other price guides have followed, all copiously illustrated, and greatly appreciated by collectors for the valuable information they contain, quite apart from prices. The Price Guide Series heralded the publication of many standard works of reference on art and antiques. *The Dictionary of British Art* (now in six volumes), *The Pictorial Dictionary of British 19th Century Furniture Design, Oak Furniture* and *Early English Clocks* were followed by many deeply researched reference works such as *The Directory of Gold and Silversmiths,* providing new information. Many of these books are now accepted as the standard work of reference on their subject.

The Antique Collectors' Club has widened its list to include books on gardens and architecture. All the Club's publications are available through bookshops world wide and a full catalogue of all these titles is available free of charge from the addresses below.

Club membership, open to all collectors, costs little. Members receive free of charge *Antique Collecting*, the Club's magazine (published ten times a year), which contains well-illustrated articles dealing with the practical aspects of collecting not normally dealt with by magazines. Prices, features of value, investment potential, fakes and forgeries are all given prominence in the magazine.

Among other facilities available to members are private buying and selling facilities, the longest list of 'For Sales' of any antiques magazine, an annual ceramics conference and the opportunity to meet other collectors at their local antique collectors' clubs. There are over eighty in Britain and more than a dozen overseas. Members may also buy the Club's publications at special pre-publication prices.

As its motto implies, the Club is an organisation designed to help collectors get the most out of their hobby: it is informal and friendly and gives enormous enjoyment to all concerned.

For Collectors —By Collectors —About Collecting

ANTIQUE COLLECTORS' CLUB
5 Church Street, Woodbridge Suffolk IP12 1DS, UK
Tel: 01394 385501 Fax: 01394 384434
or
Market Street Industrial Park, Wappingers' Falls, NY 12590, USA
Tel: 914 297 0003 Fax: 914 297 0068

DEDICATION

To my Dear Wife
who has lived with the Artist for over thirty years;
her encouragement, forbearance and help
have seen this study accomplished.

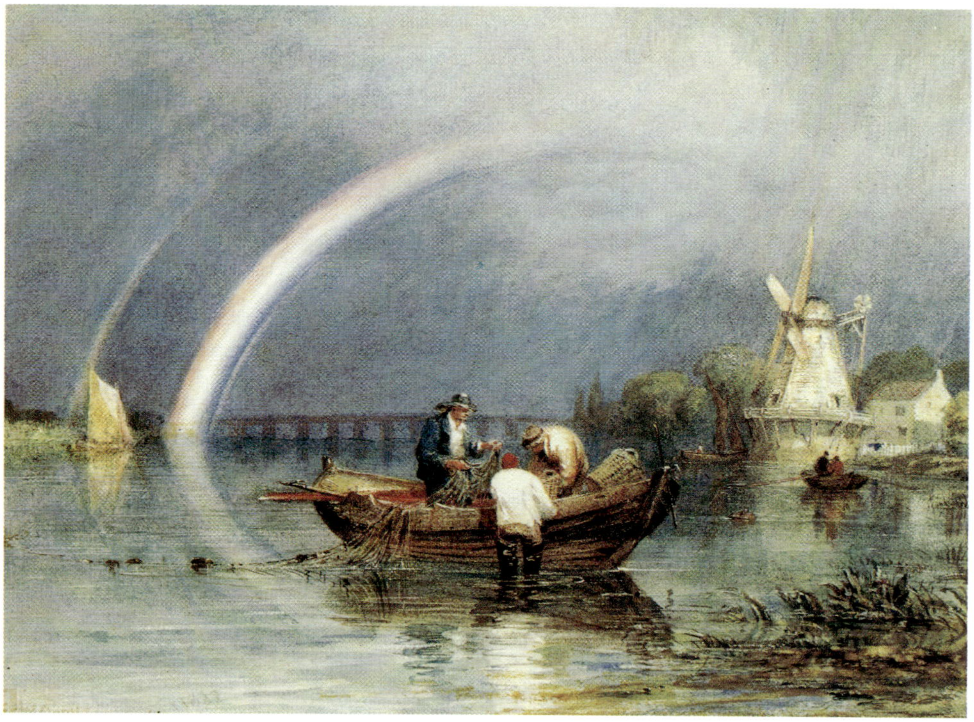

(Above)
Thames fishermen, Battersea with rainbow
Watercolour, 1837
Photo courtesy Private Collection

(Opposite) Landing fish at Egmont, coast of Holland 70/4
Van Kook at his dramatic best: with brilliant reflections the wet and windy Dutch fishery has here, in this English painter, a worthy portraitist.
Photo courtesy Private Collection

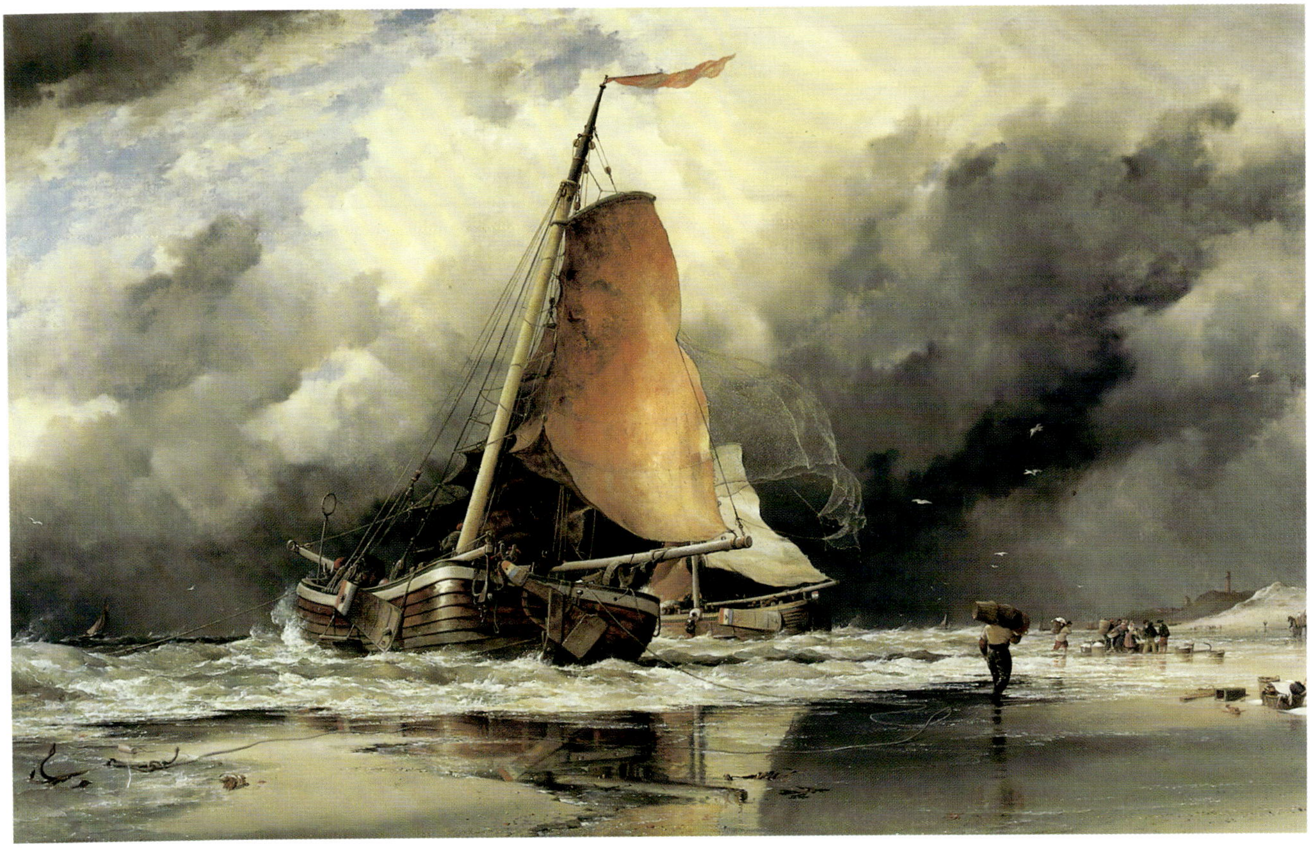

CONTENTS

ACKNOWLEDGEMENTS

The artist's great-grandson, the present owner of the diaries, Lt Col Conrad Reginald Cooke, OBE, CE, FIMechE, FIEE, has been of the greatest help and support although he has had long to wait for the results of my labours. His family here and abroad have also shown great interest and have readily supplied me with information relating to the artist's works.

I am indebted to my colleague Michael S. Robinson, MBE, the world authority on the work of great marine artists the Willem van de Veldes, father and son, for the original introduction to his friends the Cooke family and their collections, which is most appropriate. To the Trustees of the National Maritime Museum, Greenwich, for a grant from the Caird Fund towards travel and photography, I am likewise very grateful.

It is extremely gratifying that an entire alphabetical directory of picture gallery owners – from Abbott to Zwemmer – have expressed enthusiasm for the artist and have been unfailingly helpful and encouraging. *Now there's a man who knew what he was about!* declared one old stager of E.W. Cooke. Among those who have handled a considerable number of Cooke's works I must name Martyn Gregory of Bury Street who was amassing material for a study of the artist but generously allowed me to use it on discovering how far down the road this work had progressed. Peter Johnson of Ackermann & Johnson, whose firm can show a long addiction to E.W. Cooke, has given me the freedom of his records and much good advice. Thomas Agnew & Sons, whose archives stretch back to the artist's own time and who actually bought pictures from him, have readily answered endless questions. The Appleby brothers, Michael and John, both collectively and individually, have a long memory for the artist's paintings; William Drummond, with a lively interest and flair for the unexpected, must also be acknowledged. Michael Bryan, the late Owen Edgar, Richard Green, Roger Hadlee, R.A. Lee, John Morton Lee, Richard Macdougall of Clarges Gallery, Jeremy Maas, FSA, the Polak Gallery, Andrew Reid, Spink & Sons and Bill Thomson, Albany Gallery must also be specially thanked. The staff of the Royal Academy have been of the greatest help. In the United States of America Jane Studabaker of Guarisco Gallery, Washington DC, has put me in touch with owners of important pictures over there.

The benefit of conversations with the late William Gaunt and with Dr. Patrick Conner, Dr David Cordingly, Mr James S. Dearden, Dr Helen Guiterman, Mr Peter Hayden, Professor Michael Kitson, Mr Huon Mallalieu, Dr Marcia Pointon, Dr Andrew Saint, Dr Marion Spencer, Dr Pieter van der Merwe and Dr Clive Wainwright have been of enormous help.

The great London auction houses of Christie's and Phillips and Sotheby's, without whose co-operation the search for details of paintings would be well-nigh impossible, have allowed me access to their records and have supplied illustrations of Cooke's paintings which have passed under the hammer.

The many curators of public collections across the world who have answered my enquiries must be thanked in this general way – without any suggestion of perfunctoriness, I assure them.

Private individuals, some of them collectors possessing groups of works by the artist, stand nearer to him than most, being in daily contact. Although their names are not recorded here my debt to them is none the less huge and this is hereby gratefully acknowledged.

Finally, the death of an admired painter and teacher, so soon after completing a memorable term as President of the Royal Academy of Arts, has sadly deprived us of Roger de Grey's opinion of the completed book and also the chance of thanking him fully for his encouragement.

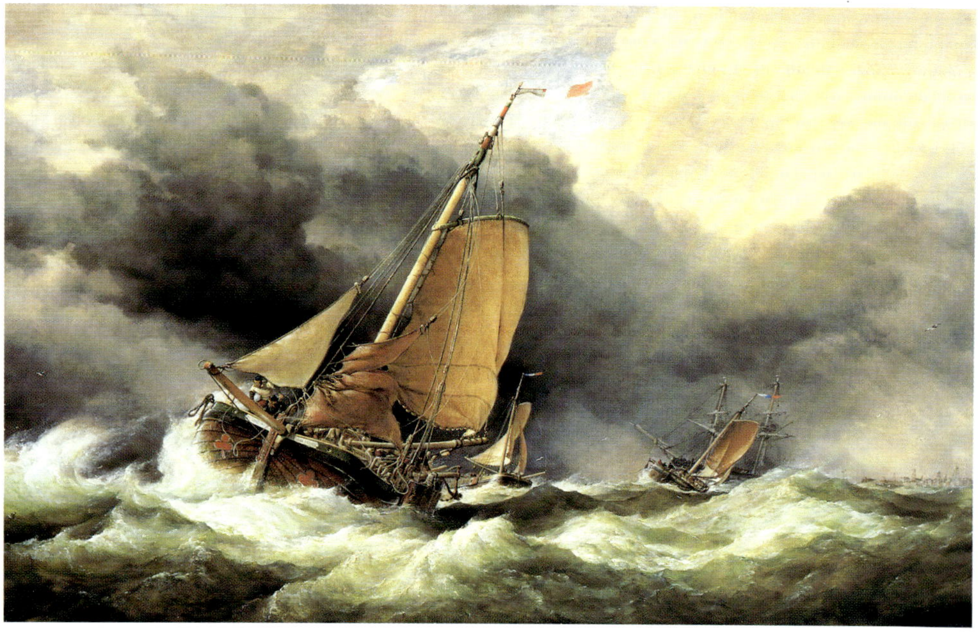

Colour Plate 1. 64/1
Scheveling Pincks running to anchor off Yarmouth
The artist's choice as his Diploma picture to represent him in the permanent collection of the RA on his election as full member. He noted: During stormy easterly gales these Dutch fishing vessels are compelled to make for the English coast. Photo courtesy Royal Academy of Arts

FOREWORD

Written by the late Sir Roger de Grey, KCVO, PPRA
1918 -1995

Motivation, the driving force, is not always easy to discover. Surviving pictures and those more intimate sketchbooks will reveal the sort of creature an artist of former times may have been. The impact of their painted rectangles apart, evidence about their thinking and their character will emerge from letters, autobiographical outpourings and from scholarly studies of the life and works. For some there remain only the paragraphs of the critics and the barometer of popularity, changing as taste changes, from which to judge.

Occasionally personal journals exist to present a valuable insight into the business of living and painting in a past age; capable of interpretation beyond the bare narrative, such sources are endlessly fascinating. The journals of Joseph Farington RA, who died in 1821, are probably the most noteworthy, full of informative gossip about the art world and its inhabitants. That later Academician Edward William Cooke has not so far attracted a full-length study but his *Diary* has survived and although his entries are brief they do reveal a complete chronicle of his occupations and travels. These and other documents which have been made available by his descendants provide a remarkable picture of a busy painter's life.

The Library at Burlington House includes another important manuscript, the artist's *Ledger* containing details of most of the larger pictures in oils which he completed in a painting career of some forty-five years; it too has been incorporated in this book. In addition to his Diploma work which portrays – and I use the word deliberately – Dutch fishing craft running to shelter under the English coast, as appropriate and typical a Cooke as one could wish for (Colour Plate 1), we possess also a collection of his pencil sketches. These are a sample from the 'library' of over 20,000 which at his own estimate

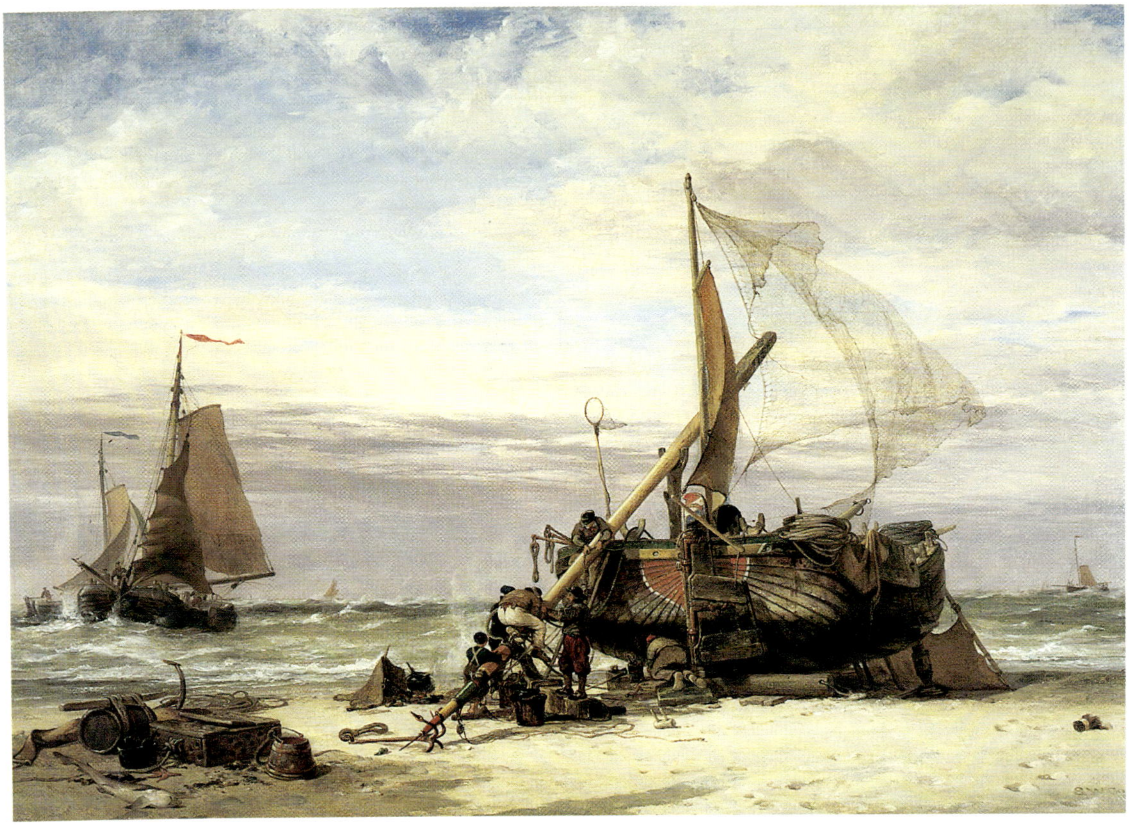

Colour Plate 2. 43/7

Mast down, Scheveling

Running repairs to one of the fleet of Scheveling fishing pincks gave the artist a subject full of tarry seashore activity and bright paint. He used this bare title, reading rather like a command, on several occasions.

Photo Martyn Gregory. Private Collection

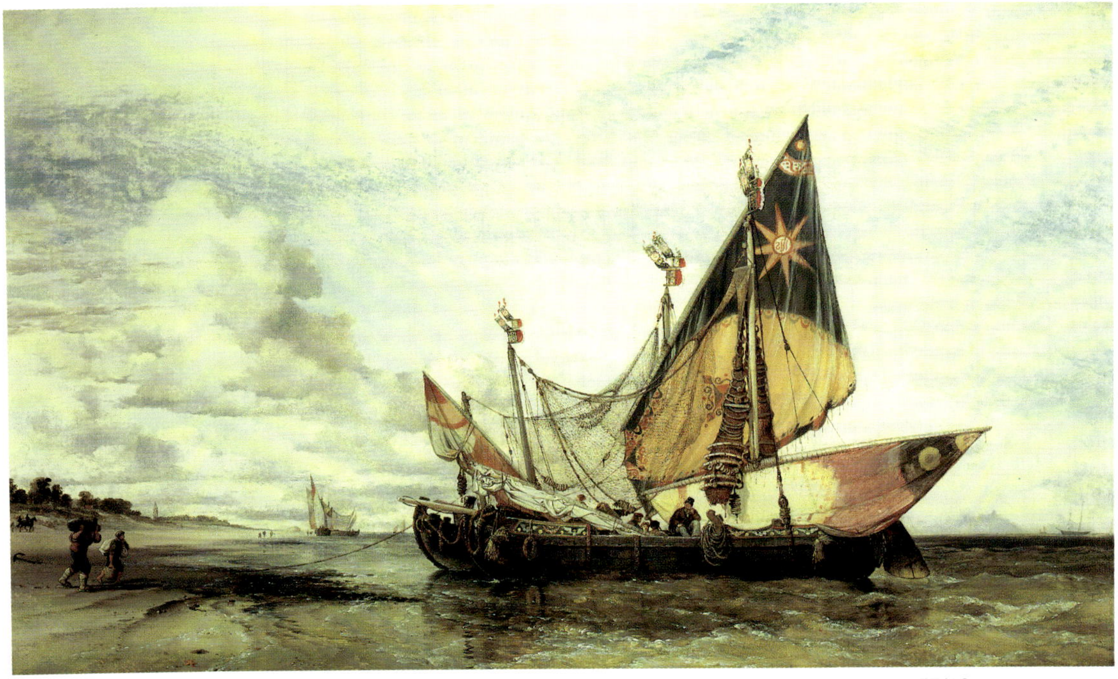

Colour Plate 3. 57/13

Venetian fishing craft on the Adriatic; shore of Lido

Photo courtesy Arthur Ackermann & Peter Johnson Ltd. Private Collection

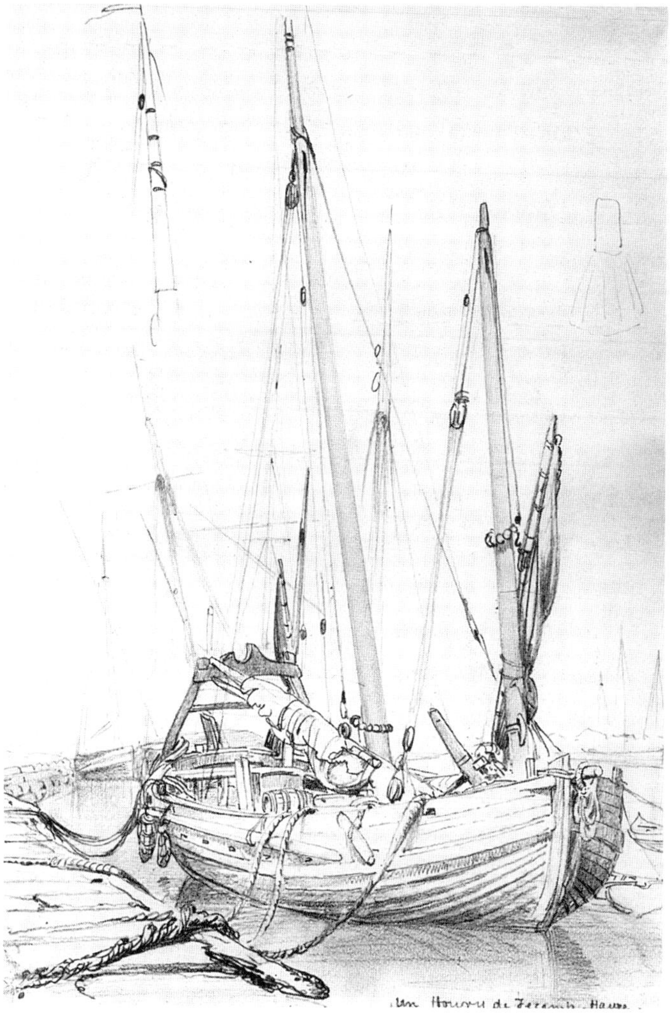

Plate 1. Pencil drawing *Un Houry de Fécamp, Havre* The name is like the English 'wherry' and, according to Admiral Smyth, from the Roman horia – and *numbers of them were notorious smugglers.*

Photo courtesy The Trustees of the National Maritime Museum, Greenwich

he had accumulated, classified and filed, containing clear evidence of his dedication as a recorder, for he had an almost obsessional interest in showing how things were made and therefore how they worked. His analytical pencil recorded sailing craft and their gear, coastal rock formations, landscape and architecture and, although he was an habitual worker *en plein air*, for studio compositions he could turn to his comprehensive boxes of drawings. Typically it was the 'highly finished' examples which were then the most prized, but in fact the quick brief notes in hasty sketches often delight us with his sure grasp of the subtle shapes of hulls and his deft clarification of a maze of rigging.

Cooke set the greatest store on becoming a member of the Royal Academy and mentions 'signing the book', in the custom of those days, more than once. His circle included the older marine painters Augustus Callcott and Clarkson Stanfield and also David Roberts, William Mulready and Edwin Landseer. In holding his course he worked hard and applied himself to developing what would nowadays be called good public relations. Successful, without having acquired a very large fortune from his paintings, he clearly had seen other artists and their families in want. In his will E.W. Cooke left monies to the Academy establishing a fund for the relief of needy painters in watercolour and oil over sixty years of age who were not Members or Associates.

His pictures were admired and collected in his time; he had the good sense to attract the notice of those patrons of modern art John Sheepshanks, Robert Vernon and William Wells. The qualities which pleased them, the understanding and attention with which he painted small working sailing craft and coastal scenery, are still the attraction for collectors today.

One is put in mind of Samuel Rogers' criticism of a painting as 'Dull prose, dull prose!' and his opponent's equally emphatic condemnation of the alternative as 'Unintelligible poetry'. One feels bound to say that Cooke is at times quite lyrical on his chosen theme and a literary parallel for most of his work would be 'lucid and scholarly exposition'.

Of course it was a time for specialists – John Philip RA, 'Philip of Spain' named from his Iberian subjects and 'Cow Cooper', the prolific painter of Kentish kine, T.S. Cooper RA, were others on whom the public could rely, season after season, for new variations on a popular if familiar theme. They were joined by *Van Kook* of the Scheveningen sands (Colour Plate 2) who later also became known as 'Venetian Cooke' (Colour Plate 3) to the dealers. In both incarnations he left many paintings which are now, at the very worst, masterly and valuable records of nautical archaeology!

The author was a student of mine, years ago, and I recall that he too chose the coast and sea-shore to paint. That he should have devoted so much work to Edward Cooke and his paintings, providing a well-rounded and intriguing portrait, seems entirely appropriate.

I am sure this book will be of lasting value as a catalogue but it is also a monument to Cooke the 'earnest art-worker', to quote one of his fellow Academicians, and illustrates another aspect of English art in the great Victorian age.

INTRODUCTION

The Cooke Diaries

To recall in some detail the varied events in the daily life of a man one has never met must seem strange. Allow a century or more to intervene, and the survey to embrace fifty years of work and travel, then the proposal becomes a little bizarre – unless one reflects that it is exactly the position enjoyed by the reader of a private diary!

Whether it was his own resolve to keep a journal we do not know; the young artist Edward Cooke was clearly going far, not only travelling in search of subjects but also in his pursuit of excellence and academic laurels. His burgeoning talent was remarked upon even in the gifted group of his father's artist friends while approval from patrons and from the critics brought encouragement from a widening circle; this perhaps suggested his keeping a record for future reference.

A small tin trunk containing some fifty assorted notebooks, pocketbooks and printed diaries has been carefully preserved by his descendants and must be the foundation of any study of the artist's life. The late Lt Col Conrad Allan Cooke OBE was collecting material for a biography of his grandfather in 1930 and had enlisted the help of a neighbour, the nautical writer Basil Lubbock, historian of sailing ships, who was a great admirer of the artist's work. The project foundered for some reason and in 1955 Allan Cooke allowed the diaries to be temporarily deposited in the National Maritime Museum at Greenwich for study, an arrangement which his son Conrad Reginald Cooke OBE most kindly continued.

In order to gain material for a dissertation[1] an edited transcript of the diaries was made

1. Durham University, MA, 1961. Unpublished.

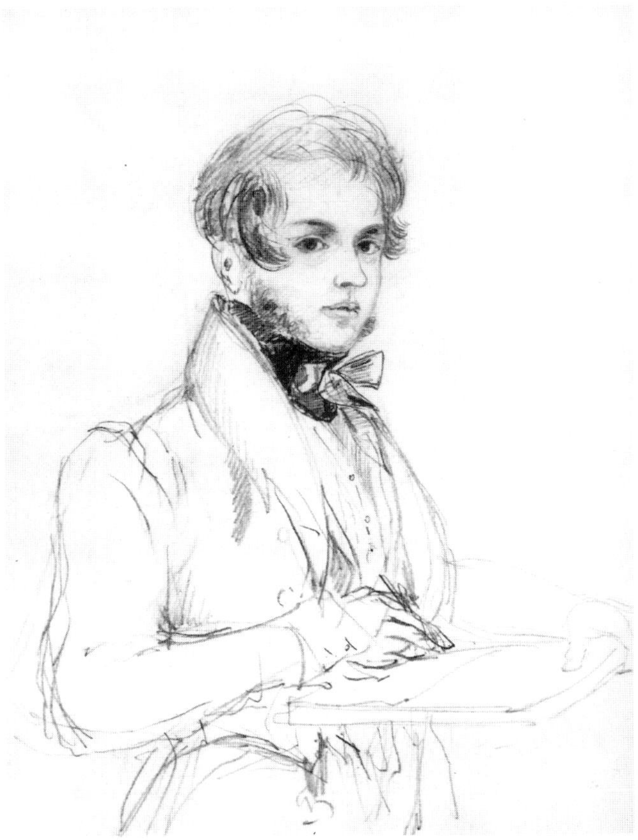

Plate 2. Pencil drawing
Self portrait, Christmas Day 1831
He drew a portrait of his sister Clarinda on the same occasion. Exhibited: 1987 *E.W. Cooke The Early Years: Drawings & Engravings,* Guildhall Library.
Photo courtesy Arthur Ackermann & Peter Johnson.
Private Collection

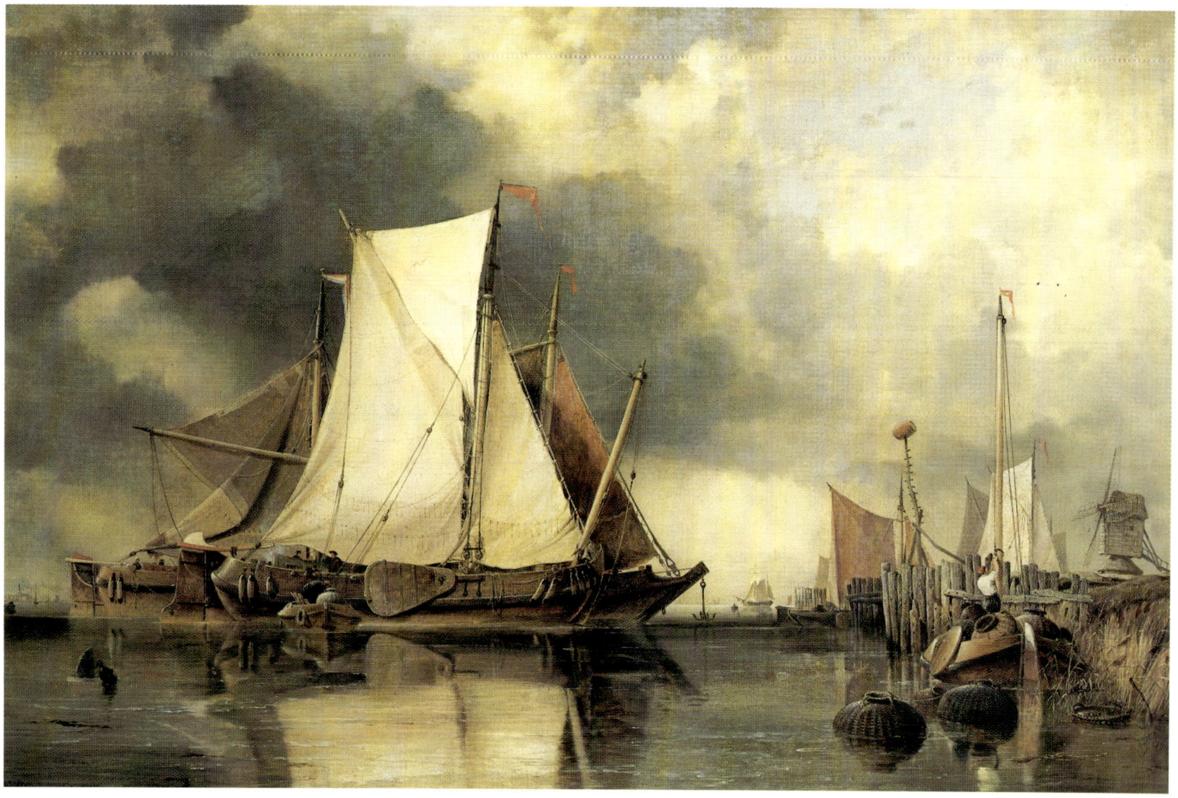

Colour Plate 4. 66/6
Fishing 'botter' aground on the Scheldt
Photo courtesy Christie's. Private Collection

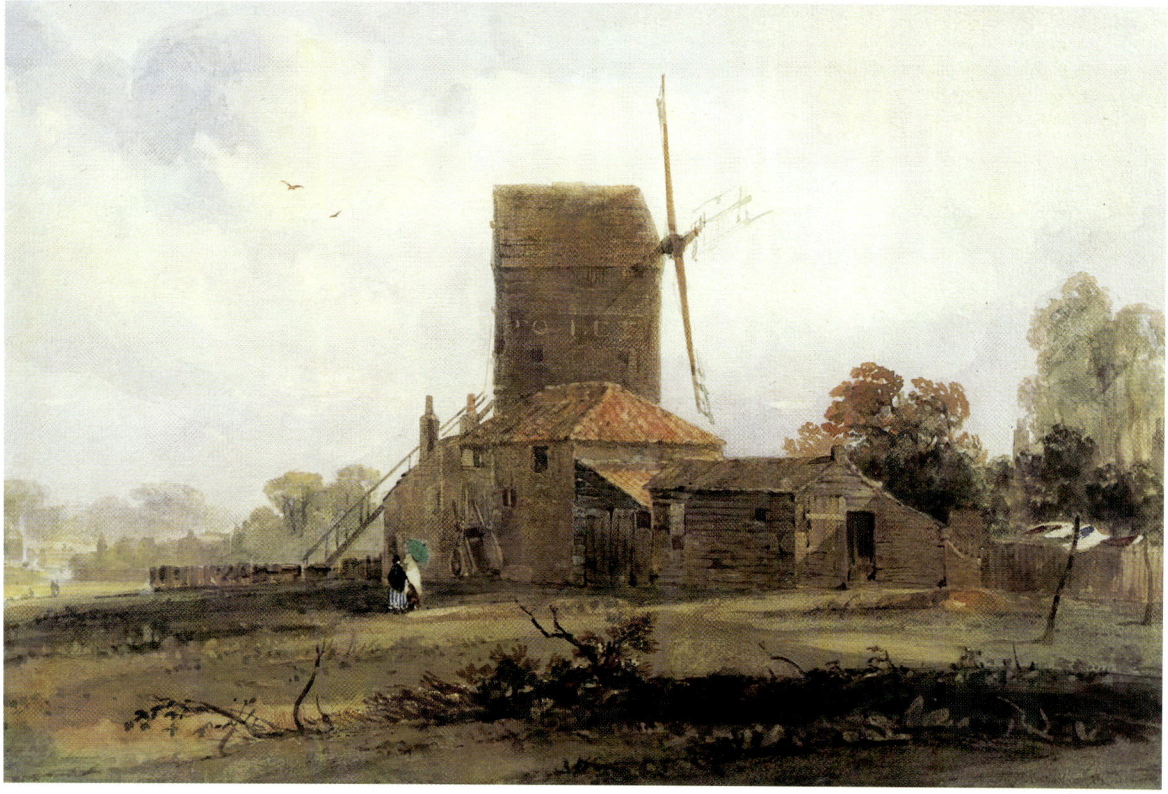

Colour Plate 5. Watercolour, 1835
Post Mill, Blackheath
Photo courtesy Private Collection

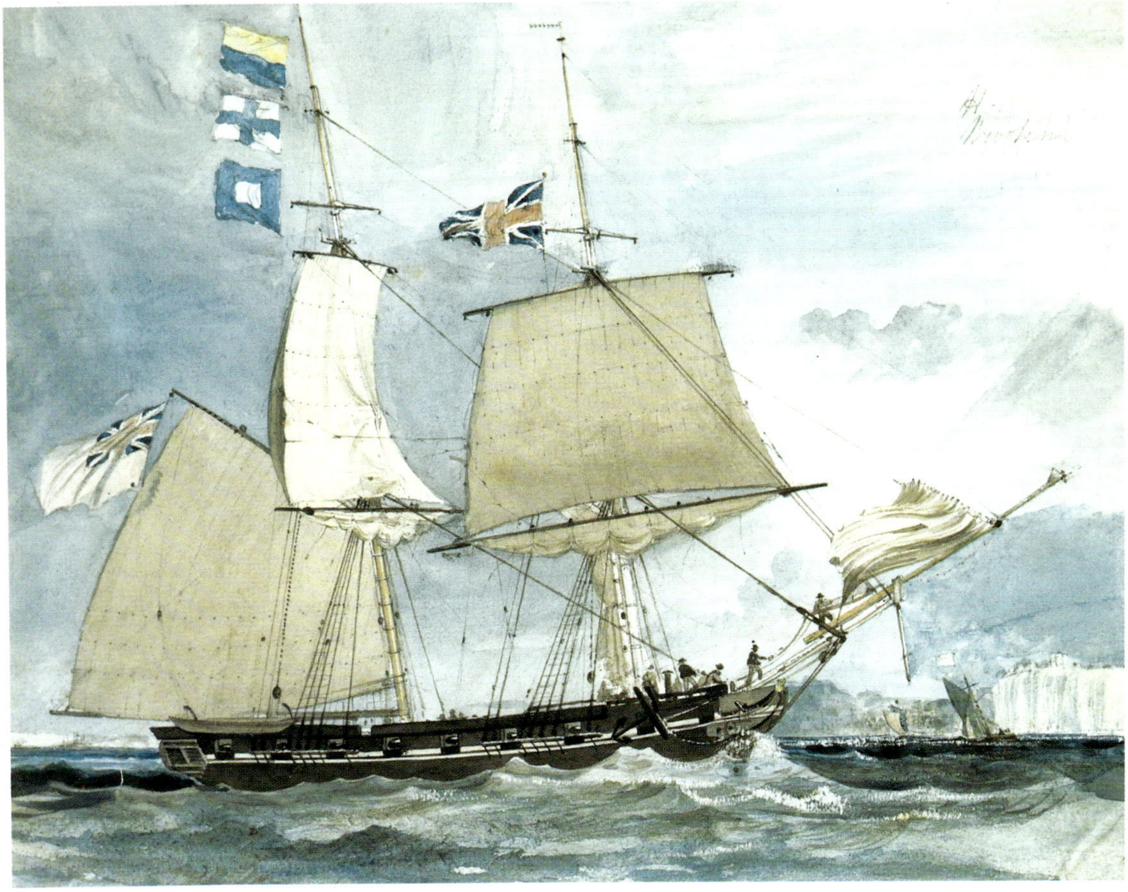

Colour Plate 6. Watercolour, 1828

The Wolf *brig of war off Dover*

The subject was etched for *Shipping & Craft* which indicates that some of those plates were based on developed studies. Photo courtesy Private Collection

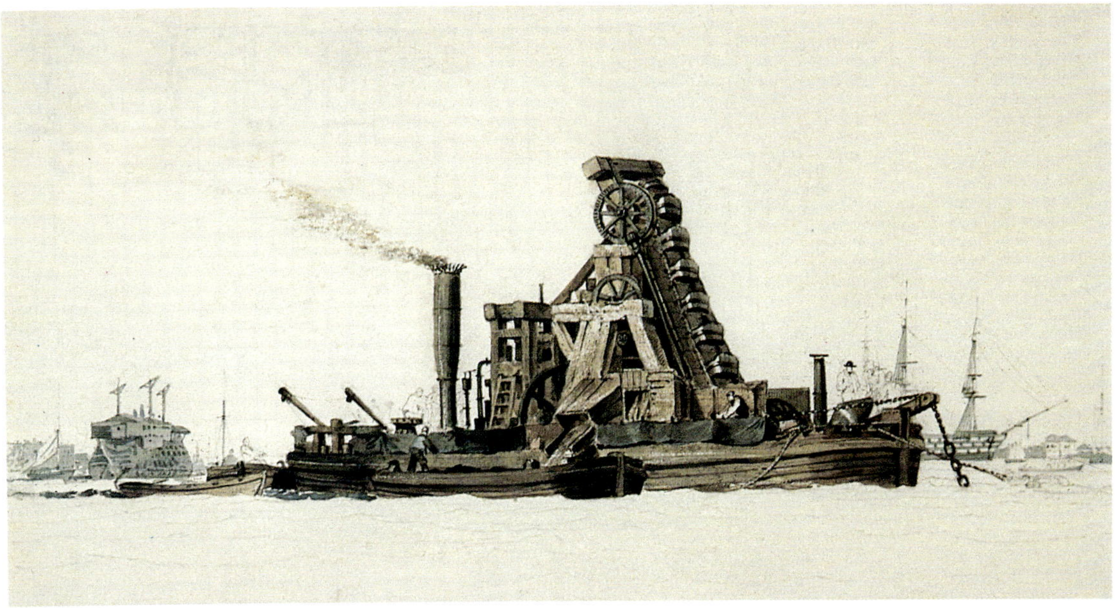

Colour Plate 7. Watercolour, 1828

Mud Dredger Portsmouth harbour

This was also etched for his book. Photo courtesy The Trustees of the National Maritime Museum, Greenwich

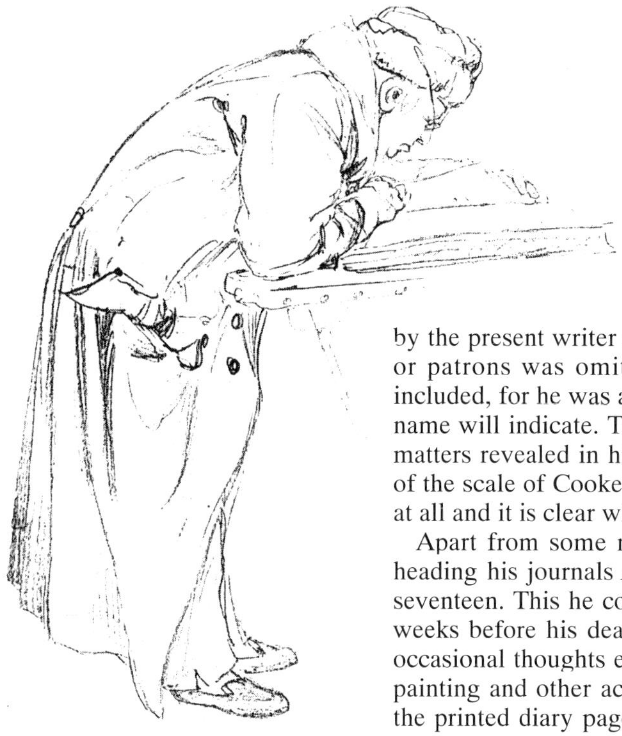

Plate 3. Pencil drawing
Grandfather reading
Thomas Eglinton, the amiable retired customs officer, lived to be eighty-seven and is here making use of the good natural light at the engraver's desk.
Photo courtesy C.R. Cooke, OBE

by the present writer from which no mention of artistic activity or of contact with artists or patrons was omitted. Much detail concerning Cooke's other interests was also included, for he was active in several fields as the imposing procession of letters after his name will indicate. The fascinating account of artistic, domestic, social and horticultural matters revealed in his minutely written pages was enthralling to read. Becoming aware of the scale of Cooke's activities one could only marvel that he found time to keep notes at all and it is clear why his entries in later years are tantalisingly brief.

Apart from some notes on trips during 1828, he first began to keep a daily record, heading his journals *A Memorandum of Passing Events*, in January 1829 when he was seventeen. This he continued with daily entries and only minor interruptions until a few weeks before his death at the age of sixty-eight. In the earlier years his comments and occasional thoughts enliven the chronicle but, as he became more and more busied with painting and other activities, he had time to complete only the few lines per day which the printed diary page allowed. There was also letter-writing and habitual sketching, as well as his chief relaxation which was gardening, so between pencil, pen, brush and trowel his hands can never have been idle!

As a diarist Edward Cooke was limited not only by the size of pocketbook and by time for composition and reflection, but daylight had to be more profitably employed in drawing and painting, although he often worked by lamplight. His notes after the first few years are unselfconscious and lack the literary mannerisms found in some of his surviving letters, so it is doubtful that he foresaw publication although he had provided himself with an unrivalled basis for an autobiography.

The Cooke family's life in the London art world was centred on the engraver's studio. The English school of engraving and etching on copper, the means of reproducing the works of painters and draughtsmen, had seen, since its imported beginnings in the sixteenth century, a low point in the 1740s but had enjoyed a renaissance from the 1770s.

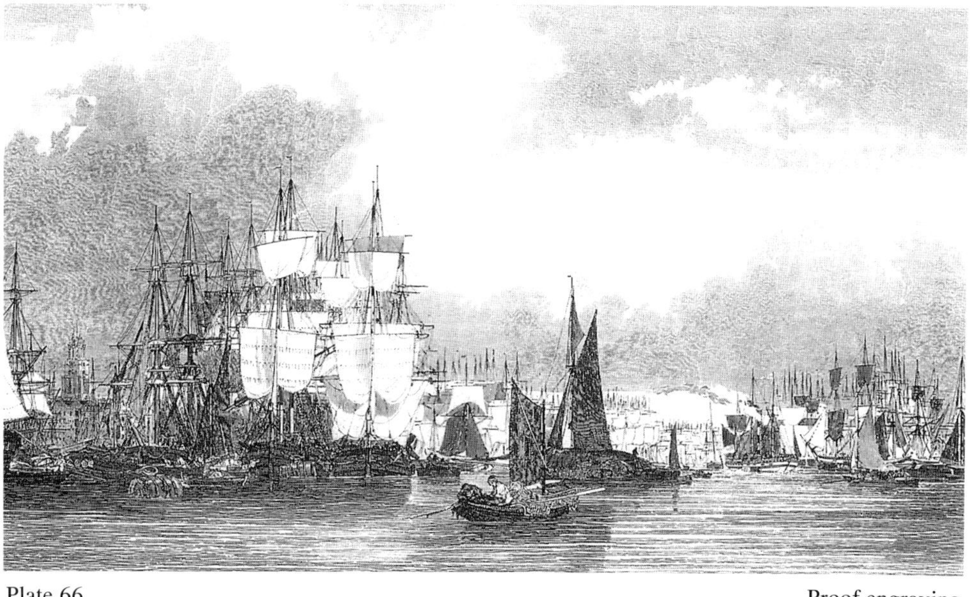

Plate 66. Proof engraving
The Pool of London
Trial proof of a plate in progress showing crowded colliers in the Thames, for George Cooke's *London...* drawn and etched by Edward in 1830. See Diary Extract for 1 January 1830.

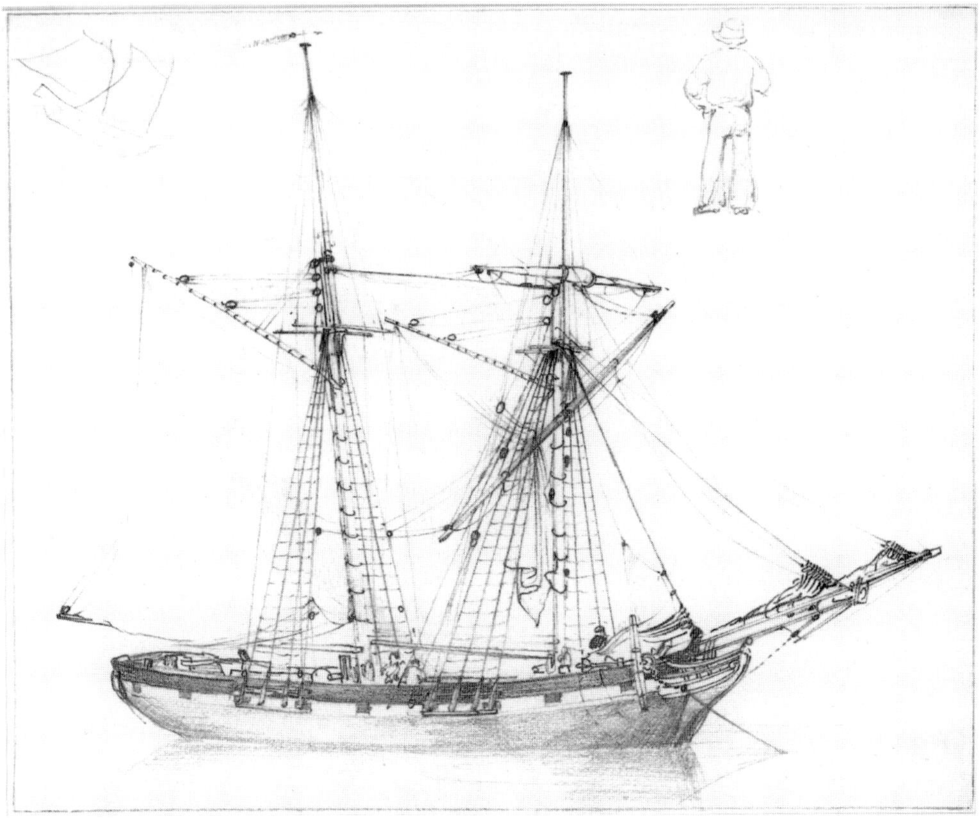

Plate 5. Pencil drawing
Schooner at anchor – c. 1830
Painted man'o'war fashion, this pretty little vessel has figurehead and rails of an earlier style. Above – a seaman, noted for good measure. Photo courtesy C.R. Cooke, OBE

Engravers were hard at work on plates for book illustrations, for published portraits, architectural views, landscapes, historical pieces, caricatures, maps, trade cards – in fact the very widest range. George Cooke and his elder brother William Bernard (Edward's father and uncle) were in the forefront of the landscape engravers and highly regarded. They were usually called 'line engravers', although there were more processes involved than that, but their work was always a collaboration with other draughtsmen and painters so they were near the centre of artistic life. Among topographical draughtsmen (and 'place drawing' can be seen as the origin of the English watercolour school) there were some who engraved their own work, but the skills of these specialist engravers were always in demand.

They published, among much else, two series of *Views on The Thames* in 1811 and 1822 which are of particular relevance to this review of the life and works of Edward William Cooke, but the quality of their topographical plates surged to a higher level when later they worked from coastal drawings by J.M.W. Turner. The river and seashore therefore were subjects with which the young Cooke became familiar and Turner was a considerable influence; his admiration of the great man's drawings and paintings is frequently stated although regrettably he never seems to have put on paper any detailed comment. Perhaps the fund of anecdote for which he was remembered by the Redgraves contained gems now lost![2]

Others from whose works the Cooke brothers engraved were artist-patrons like Lt Col Robert Batty and Sir Henry Englefield Bt, artist-colleagues like James Stark and John Sell Cotman and friends like George Loddiges, the Hackney nurseryman of international renown. They ranged across a broad field and it was into that world of sight-taxing precision that the young Cooke was launched even before his schooling was finished, with a series of plant drawings for John Claudius Loudon.

The works of Edward Cooke the marine artist, from his first virtuoso productions

2. *A Century of British Painters* by Richard & Samuel Redgrave, new edition by Ruthven Todd, Phaidon Press 1947, p 424.

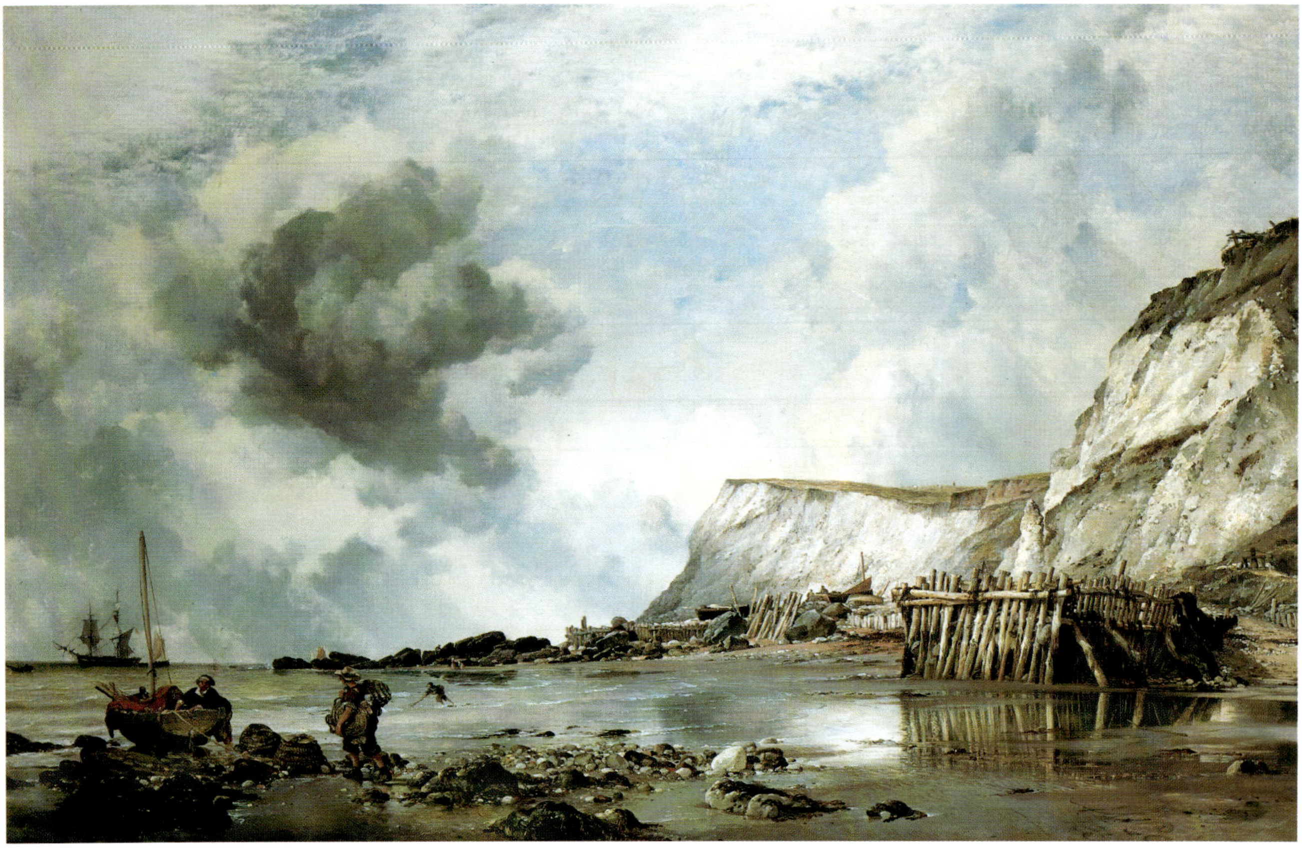

Colour Plate 8. 58/2

The Undercliff at Bonchurch

A view southward from this famous stretch of coast. Cooke's initials are painted as if drawn in the wet sand, a humorous touch executed with precision.

Photo courtesy Arthur Ackermann & Peter Johnson. Private Collection

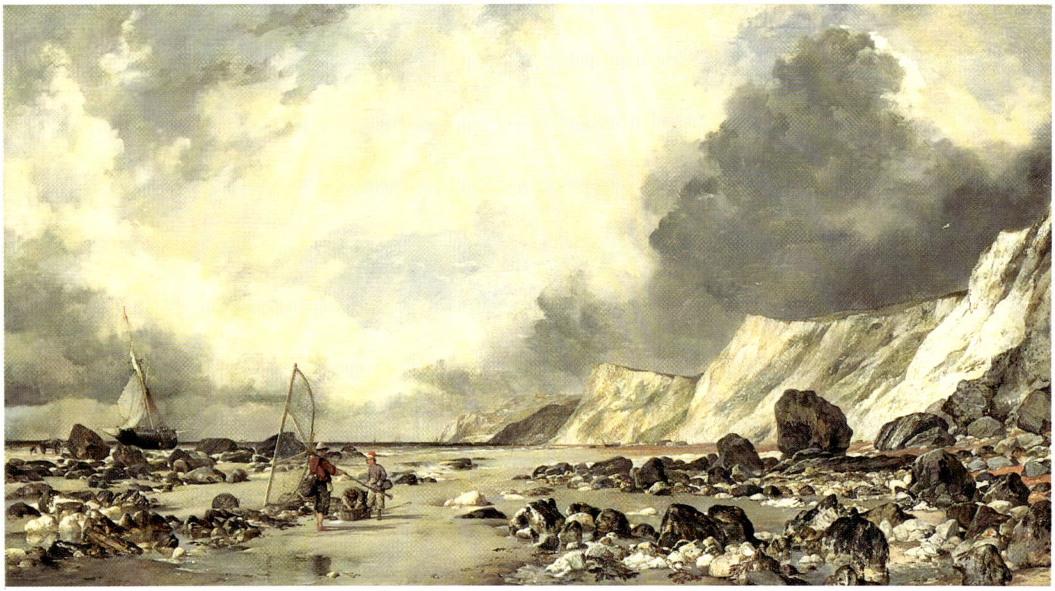

Colour Plate 9. 66/10

Bonchurch Shore looking towards Ventnor

Begun in 1856, it was not completed until sent for exhibition in the last show of the British Institution in 1867. The figures at left appear in a small sketch (56/18, Plate 264).

Photo courtesy J. Collins & Son, Bideford

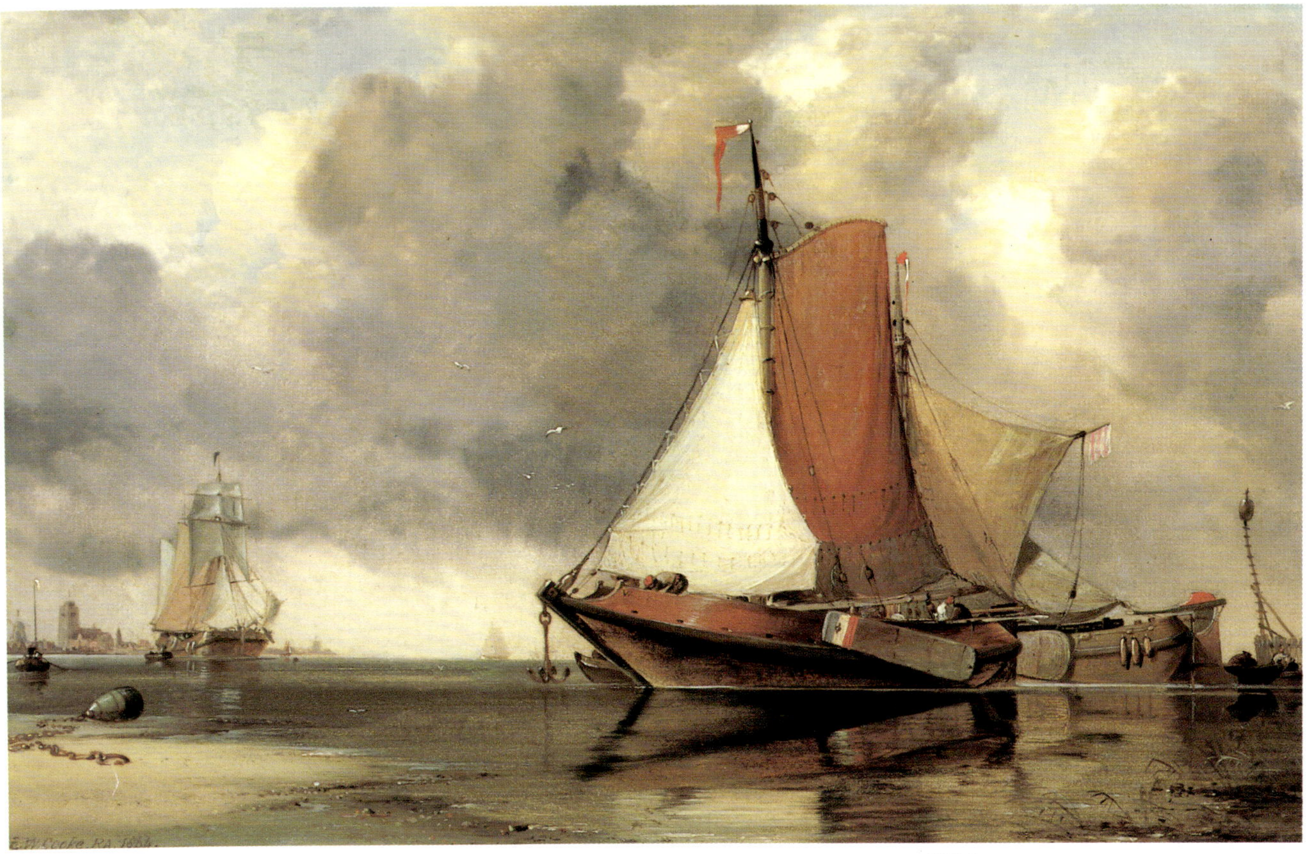

Colour Plate 10. 63/18

Dutch fishing craft on the Ij off Ransdorp, near Amsterdam

A small version of a subject which served him in all sizes up to his largest (see 76/2, Colour Plate 76). On this scale the nicely balanced lights and darks with Cooke's liquid handling are admirably shown. *Van Kook* is on the bow of the principal boat.

Photo:courtesy Arthur Ackermann & Peter Johnson.Ltd. Private Collection

which were etchings of everyday shipping scenes, have always commanded a devoted following. This is surely due to his instinctive grasp of the characteristics and behaviour of sailing craft and his determination to lose no significant detail in studies made with 'botanical' care. His later paintings of the littoral exhibit also a strong sense of atmosphere (in its meteorological meaning) and are also documents which share a feeling for the English weather and the seasons with a devotion to geological observation. The painter John Piper wrote: *This atmosphere has sunk into our souls. It has affected our art as it affects our life. But it has not resulted in a congenital softness of vision. It has inspired the sharp-outlined visions of Blake as well as the vague adumbrations of Whistler's nocturnes.*[3]

William Blake, one must remember, had earlier been an apprentice engraver with the Basire family in a similar *milieu* to the elder Cooke's. With Edward Cooke a sharpness of outline seems also to have been an important consideration in picture making, something which developing critical taste did not always endorse, although his telling draughtsmanship was applauded. It was said of Turner's early marine oil *Fishermen at Sea* of 1796 (Tate Gallery), *the boats are buoyant and swim well*[4] – he got it right and it was immediately apparent; even the bitter 'Anthony Pasquin' in 1797 pronounced on Turner's *Fishermen coming Ashore ...that singularity of perception is so adroit that it enables him to give a transparency and undulation to the sea more perfect than is usually seen on canvas....* It happens that Edward Cooke strove for the same ends; his early mentors, both artists and patrons, included several men with experience of ships and the sea and he lived, after all, in the age of sail when steam engines had only just begun to alter the scene. Londoners were used to viewing a splendid variety of sailing

3. *British Romantic Artists,* John Piper, Collins, Britain in Pictures [Series] 1942, p.7.

4. *The Critical Guide* 1796, quoted by Peter Cunningham, quoted by Redgrave, *A Century...* 1st edition 1866, Vol. II, p.99.

Plate 6.
The Fern and Edward Cooke
The diary records 8 August 1851 that *Mr Rippingham* took two photographs of him on glass. On 5 June 1854 he sat to Cundell for a *Photographic Portrait.* It is not clear whether either is the likeness shown, but his contemplation of the fern leaf is a studied pose for by that date he had named his Kensington residence *The Ferns* and was known for his fern collection. Photo courtesy Alex.Stirling Esq

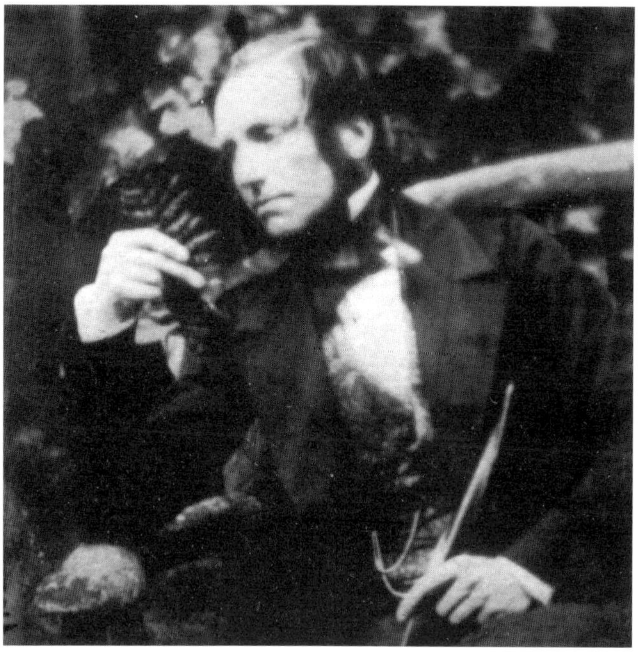

vessels of all rigs and sizes in their famous river and docks. The Thames had been for centuries London's main artery and the heavy, varied waterborne traffic in the main port of the kingdom was a source of constant interest. In fact sailing craft of all nationalities had an attraction for E.W .Cooke and in the majority of his pictures a careful study of a local type, whether in calm, storm or sunset, takes pride of place.

Throughout his life he seems to float serenely, independent of tidal 'Movements' but holding to his chosen course, successful, admired, perhaps not universally popular because of his single-minded pursuit of an ideal, but exhibiting paintings, in the words of F.T. Palgrave,[5] *rendered with Mr Cooke's well-known and always scientific accuracy* while Maurice Grant could write that *his works were an anticipation at the annual exhibitions.*[6]

In his diary Cooke was unable to set down everything he might have wished, but at his easel it was otherwise, for in paint he was able to indulge his obvious passion for significant detail, the essential characteristics which a painter with a broader training might merely have suggested and which lesser men would miss altogether with fatal results.

In recording the rig and build of working sailing craft in such detail and in painting the geological characteristics of coastlines with such fidelity, Cooke was explaining the purpose of the one and the evolution of the other. This idea was later carried abroad to France, Holland and the Venetian Lagoons. *His manner is a fine adjustment between meticulous accuracy in detail with breadth of the whole, his works therefore are interesting both at a glance or a close examination.*[7]

Paintings and drawings shed light on many things which have now disappeared, his determination to capture the fundamental aspects of construction, operation and environment leaving an immensely valuable pictorial record. His interests and natural inclination led him to choose simple subjects and to render them monumental. Small working vessels of all types, complete with their gear, were his delight wherever encountered and most often these were fishing craft, the centre of interest. Cooke's devotion to them dates from his earliest Thames-side period and it is noteworthy that after his famous etchings, *Fifty Plates of Shipping and Craft,* 1828-29, he maintained his aim of being as a recorder *superlative* and that was the word he used.

He is today recognised as one of the great marine artists of the last century, not only by reason of this precise and detailed draughtsmanship which sought to describe shipping with the care of a botanical illustration, but also by his devotion to atmosphere. When this analytical work was rendered into paint it produced detailed images as intense and totally realised as any from the brushes of the Pre-Raphaelite brethren with whom, incidentally, it can be seen he shared a fascination with sunrise and sunset, the afterglow, the moon and stars.

5. *Essays on Art* by Francis Turner Palgrave, 1863.
6. *A Chronological History of the Old English Landscape Painters* by M.H. Grant, revised edition 1957.
7. Grant op. cit.

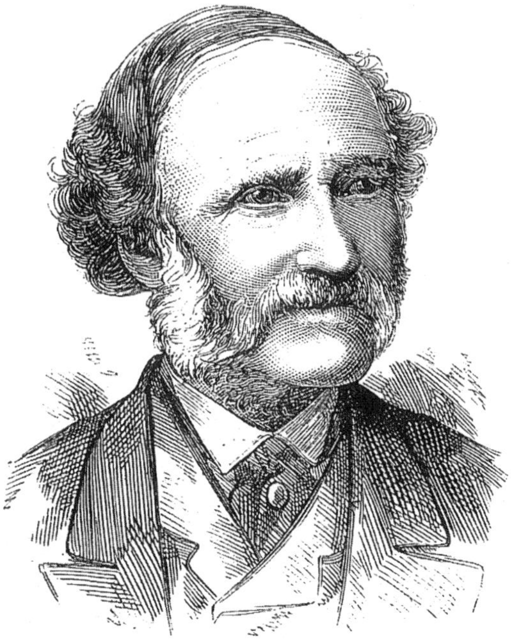

Plate 7.
E.W. Cooke RA
Engraving after a photograph by Lock & Whitfield, 1877. This appeared with the obituary notice of the painter in *The Graphic,* January 1880.

Overall, it is not surprising that Cooke's work has in the twentieth century taken on an archaeological importance. If Cooke painted or drew it, it is reliably correct; conversely, if not correct, it is manifestly not by E.W. Cooke!

The Man

To complete a picture of the man himself, filling out the surviving portraits taken at various times in his life with indications of character and behaviour, one turns to those who knew him intimately, his fellow artists and fellow gardeners, for he threw as much into his pastimes as into his profession.

The brothers Richard and Samuel Redgrave, his Kensington neighbours, recalled that *his hands were never idle and even at a party he would bring out a little sketch book and begin to take artistic notes... He was of a lively and genial disposition, restlessly active, a great talker and full of anecdote.*[8]

Frederick Goodall RA, a contemporary, remembering him long afterwards wrote: *Edward Cooke was one of the most earnest art-workers in those days. Then strenuousness was a more general note than it is in these times....*[9]

An obituary notice in *The Gardeners' Chronicle* adds a further dimension: *His zeal and enthusiasm often seemed too great for his feeble frame, but it may be that they supported him in trials which would have injured a stronger man not so endowed.*[10]

John Ruskin, writing home from Venice in 1851, said among other things: *He is the smallest clever man I ever knew... full of affection, most unselfish...* but Cooke evidently irritated Ruskin by his ceaseless activity: *with a perpetual buz from one thing to another...* as well as *Cooke who must see everything....*[11] He never painted on the Sabbath and later Ruskin noted, perhaps with a touch of gentle amusement, Cooke's *responses in a most serious and earnest manner* at Sunday morning prayers in their rooms in Venice'.

A close neighbour in later years was William Cotton Oswell, friend and colleague of David Livingstone. The artist is portrayed in his studio in the former's biography: *the children knew no greater pleasure than going to Mr Cooke's... many of his Academy pictures owe bright-coloured pebbles, fish, boats and other minor accessories to their suggestions and his good-natured readiness to gratify and amuse them... The expressive gesticulations, the alert, restless figure, the clear, wide-set blue eyes, the marvellously rapid, marvellously sure hand darting from palette to canvas, from canvas to palette, had a perfect fascination for them.*[12]

We now have a portrait more rounded and in some depth: the small, well-informed person, in whom seriousness was matched with geniality, humour, energy and enthusiasm. Above all he evidently felt a compulsion to draw, something his father had

8. Redgrave, 1947.
9. *The Reminiscences of Frederick Goodall RA,* 1902, p329.
10. *The Gardener's Chronicle,* 10 January 1880.
11. Ruskin's *Letters from Venice, 1851-1852.* Ed. J.L. Bradley, 1955.
12. *William Cotton Oswell, Hunter & Explorer – The Story of his Life* by W. Edward Oswell, 1900, Vol. II, p.961.

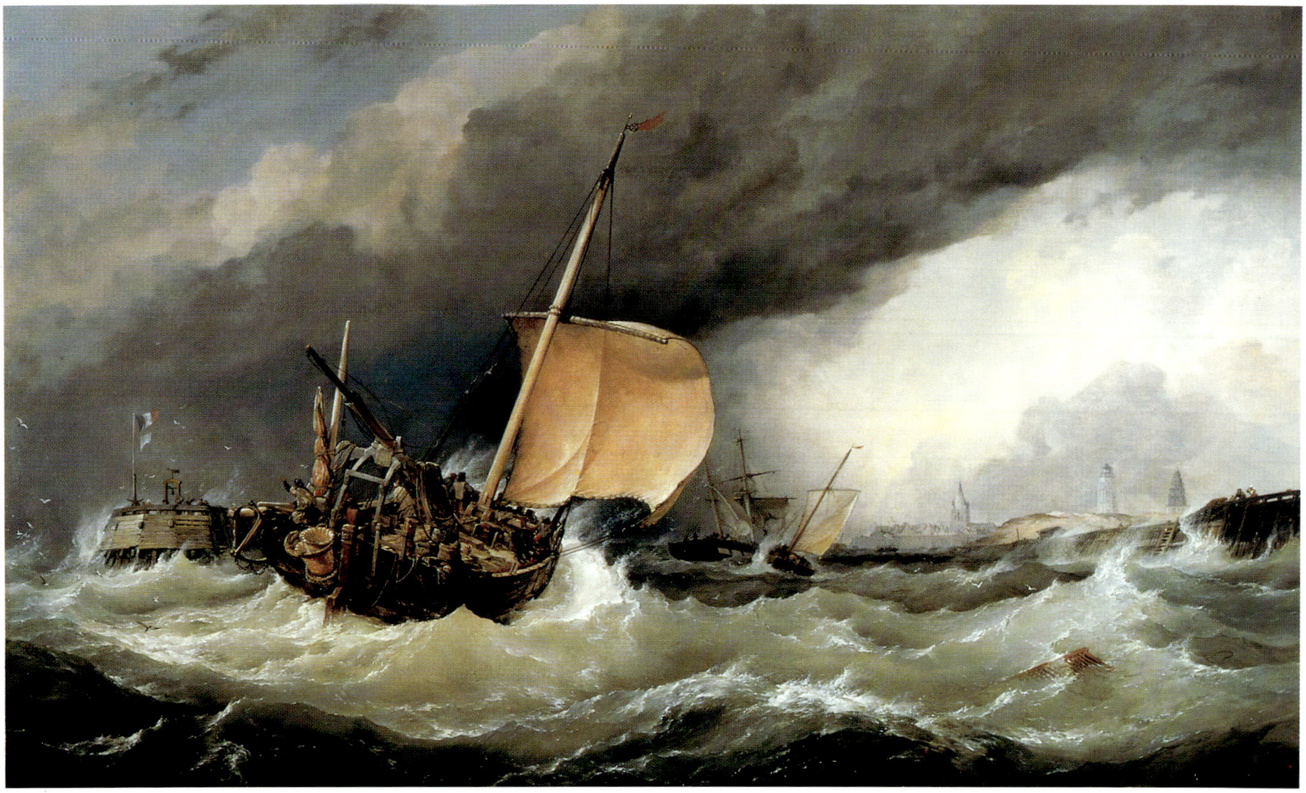

Colour Plate 11. 54/2
French lugger running into Calais
The painting must have been one of his favourites; he chose it to illustrate the *Art Journal's* biography of 1869. Photo courtesy Private Collection USA

advised at the outset of his career.[13] His architect Richard Norman Shaw RA, in a letter to Harriette Cooke, the eldest sister, when the artist lay dying in their fine country house at Groombridge, wrote: *Your account of your dear brother's patience and submission is, I feel most true, and so like him – amidst all his fun he had always a quiet dignity of manner and a profound reverence for serious things.*[14]

Edward Cooke, although in the habit of noting his state of health in the diary, did not confide what his medical advisers told him. However, entries from the middle of the year 1879 mention sleepless nights and pain, even when travelling abroad. It begins to look as if he was going on a farewell pilgrimage when in August he and his youngest sister Mary Needham visited the Normandy coast where he had made his first memorable foreign sketching tour in 1833.

In September Belgium, then Germany, land of his forebears, were followed in mid-month by Holland, to Scheveling for a last look. He was sketching a little and after a return to Belgium – Antwerp, Ghent and Bruges – they left Ostend in the steamer *Comte de Flandres* at the end of the month. In October his earliest trip into East Anglia in 1828 was in a way commemorated by visits to Yarmouth, Cromer, Norwich and Lowestoft. His last visits to London were in late November when he managed to see *HMS Pinafore* which (apart from *The Gondoliers*) must have been the most appropriate entertainment for this marine painter! Notes of his final dinner with the Royal Society Club and the onset of heavy snows, with his concern for the laden young conifers, are accompanied by the more frequent mention of sleepless nights and increasing pain.

The diary actually ends on 20 December where he had previously marked 'Irving-Lyceum' but his mind was now on a Codicil to his Will, and his strength fast going.

18th Dec. [Note] R.A. Election. ½ p. 7.
Not a wink of sleep all night. Lucy rubbed my back and removed the severe pain... attended me & read nearly all day... at 5 went into the Whale room. Lucy read to me

13. below p.29
14. Cooke MSS.

& Mother. Severe frost all day. Made lists of sketches for the different Societies. I felt easier during day. William Breffit sent us a superb Crimp'd Cod... Whitelock called to see me.

19th Dec. Had a very good night, more sleep less pain. Eatwell sent the picture back, stretched. Mr H. Willett sent a large Turkey to Mother. At 2 carriage fetched Mr Hannah who consulted with me. Mr Wallis called, also Dr Satchell. Still cold & frosty. Felt easier during day.

20th Frost continuing. Mr Wallis called in morng. Carriage fetched at 2 Con[rad} & Laura. She brought my Will from Mr Hopgood & we went through it together and consulted as to a Codicil to be added. Laura sat up all night. Had a restless night.

Footnotes can be supplied: Lucy was his Brighton cousin, the Whale room must have housed his painting of the stranded fin whale, which he never sold, and William Breffitt was from the Barnes family, the Cookes' close neighbours. Whitelock, the clergyman, friend of thirty years, was also from Barnes and Hannah, the painter, was one of his executors. Wallis was the surgeon, etc. Crimp'd Cod – a note of 1698 in the *Oxford English Dictionary* explains that its flesh was rendered firm by gashing before rigor mortis set in.

In W.C. Oswell's biography we also have news from Groombridge at the end of the year 1879:

In Mrs Oswell's diary and her husband's letters this year the references to pleasant visits to and from Glen Andred are more than usually numerous. Among many others meetings are spoken of with McClintock, Glaisher, Long, Holl, McWhirter, Bierstadt and Holman Hunt – 'A nice gentle, quiet man' Oswell calls him. But these were the last pages of a delightful chapter.

Journal Jan 4th 1880. – Alas! alas! our friend and neighbour Mr Cooke is dead. He has been hopelessly ill since Dec. 18th. We have all been frequently to see his mother and sisters and William constantly to see him during his illness. He was greatly impressed by his calm cheerfulness and collectedness and his wonderful endurance of pain...

A letter which his sister Harriette wrote to the daughter of his recently deceased friend William Wilson Saunders, the entomologist, describes how they saw the closing days of his life:

Our dear brother had intended to write to you himself, but is too weak so he dictated the few words I have written and told me to write you a line on this sheet to tell you how seriously ill he is... the medical man agreed that nothing could save him and the only thing that could be done was to alleviate his sufferings... dropsy, cough on the lungs and much inward pain... I cannot tell you how calm & peaceful he is – perfectly resigned to his fresh changes & fully prepared to meet his God...

The page with a Christmas heading is inscribed *With every good and kind wish from E.W. Cooke to Mr & Mrs Stebbing.*

The founder-editor of *The Portfolio*, Philip Hamerton, painter, critic and writer on art, published an obituary notice which is balanced and interesting:

Cooke... who died lately aged 68 was remarkable for the combination of the artistic and scientific faculties. His two distinctions of Academician and Member [Fellow] of the Royal Society exactly expressed the double nature of his talents. His paintings, though popular, offended some judges by their very precision, they were in fact too true to represent the dreams and aspirations of a poetical artist, but their qualities were not the less real for being prosaic and matter of fact. Mr Cooke painted remarkably well in his own way and expressed himself with much ability so that he may be said to have been a really successful artist if, as we believe, the most perfect success consists in the complete expression of the natural tendencies and gifts. He was admirable for the persistent industry with which he disciplined his powers and though of course he can never be classed among poetic artists who have touched the heart or awakened the imagination, there is no reason why he should not be remembered for centuries as an English equivalent to the celebrated Dutch who have painted the simple truth.[15]

The Scientific Artist and Collector

These other great interests of E.W. Cooke's life stem from an early familiarity with botany and geology, subjects which featured in his father's studio work. The cultivated friends of the Cooke family included not only artists but antiquaries, scientists, clergy, medical men, engineers and musicians.

Drawing the growing plants from the Loddiges' glasshouses and nursery gardens[16] gave young Cooke an insight which eventually became a passion. The families were linked by his marriage and his scientific education owed a great deal to his father-in-law, George Loddiges. Other interests such as collecting species of fern and devising settings for them widened his gardening into garden design which he adroitly managed to combine with his career as a painter. He brought to those buyers of his pictures whom he visited, a ready pencil and great horticultural knowledge, so helping them to improve their grounds. A special preference for rocky gardens sprang from a study of geology and his experience in painting landscape where the setting for his inshore fishing vessels sometimes dominates his picture and calls for a sub-title describing the rock formations in some detail.

He was elected a Fellow of the Linnaean Society in 1857, a Fellow of the Geological in 1862 and his election as a Fellow of the Royal Society, an uncommon distinction for a painter, came in 1863, a little before he was made an RA. His Certificate of Candidature shows him as *Distinguished for his acquaintance with the science of Natural History in its relation to Art. Eminent as a Landscape and Marine painter – and as a faithful delineator of Geological features in nature.*

His obituary notice in *The Gardener's Chronicle* began with words which indicate an Editorial attachment beyond the ordinary: *It is with a sense of irretrievable loss and deep grief that we announce the death of this accomplished gentleman... Best known to the general public as an artist, he was still more widely known in scientific and literary circles by the catholicity of his sympathies.*

The long notice concluded:

In his pictures... the work by which he achieved fame and fortune– his mental characteristics may be traced– his love of truth, his accurate observation and fidelity in reproducing them. Many of his pictures are scientific lesson-books: the dip of the strata, the grains of the sand, the shapes of the leaves, the curvature of the trunks of the Palm trees, the form of the rain-clouds, the line of the waves, and hundreds of such instances betoken, not only the artist, but the man of science.There is an amount of absolute truth about them, apart from imagination, which will give his pictures a permanent value beyond that of many of his contemporaries.[17]

Typical in his time and among his class, E.W. Cooke was an ardent collector – it was an inherited interest and in his various homes the curiosities and *objets d'art* gathered over the years were displayed for the admiration and interest of all. Venetian glass, majolica,

15. *The Portfolio,* January 1880
16. below p.35.
17. *The Gardener's Chronicle,* 10 January 1880.

animal heads, horns and skulls, spears, axes and bronzes, the acquisition of which he pursued with his usual energy, all testified to the wide interests of the man.

Biographers

The chief notice to appear in his lifetime was an illustrated article, No. 85 in a series *British Artists: Their Style and Character* in *The Art Journal* for 1869, written by James Dafforne, its Associate Editor for twenty-six years under the redoubtable Samuel Carter Hall.

Dafforne was presumably supplied by his subject with much detail, but the piece contains a number of errors indicating that Cooke did not bother to turn up his old diaries for verification. A year or so earlier or later can hardly have seemed important, but inevitably the article was a source for the *Dictionary of National Biography* in 1908 and the errors have therefore been perpetuated. We know for example that his first oil painting was not sold in 1826 but 1834 and it was not in 1830 but 1833 that he first set foot in France, although it remains difficult to check some of the pre-diary dates.

The *Illustrated London News* printed a short biographical notice and an engraved portrait soon after his election as RA, late in 1863. This is most interesting as an example of art criticism at the time when his characteristics as a painter had become well defined.[18]

Many published accounts of British art and artists include notes on E.W. Cooke RA, but many more do not. Sir Joshua Reynolds' hierarchy, the 'classification' of painters from the heights of history-painting down to landscape, was enduring. The marine specialists, with the exception of Turner, come where they always have, near the last, a surprising fact in the art of this maritime nation.

Equally strange is the omission of Cooke's work in two major shows at the Royal Academy of Arts. Both *The First Hundred Years 1769-1868* (1951) and the *Bicentenary Exhibition* (1968) were devoid of mention, but then too Dominic Serres, a founder member and consummate painter of ships and the sea, was also absent.

The present narrative, much of it using Cooke's own words, is followed by a tentative catalogue of his paintings. The itinerary, from the diary, will be useful in identifying the location of sketches which bear only a date, or in dating named subjects. Together these make not only a work of reference but also through the illustrations, it is hoped, a fitting tribute to the artist. His surviving paintings and drawings are really his memorial, with his published etchings and other works. His fine Norman Shaw house on the Kent and Sussex borders still stands and his garden design, some of which has survived there but most notably at the celebrated Biddulph Grange in Staffordshire (now under the care of the National Trust), puts us in touch with him in a very real way.

As well there remains the fascinating diary of fifty busy years – the excerpts quoted will indicate something of its value and interest, but to do justice to the whole would need further volumes!

18. below p.219.

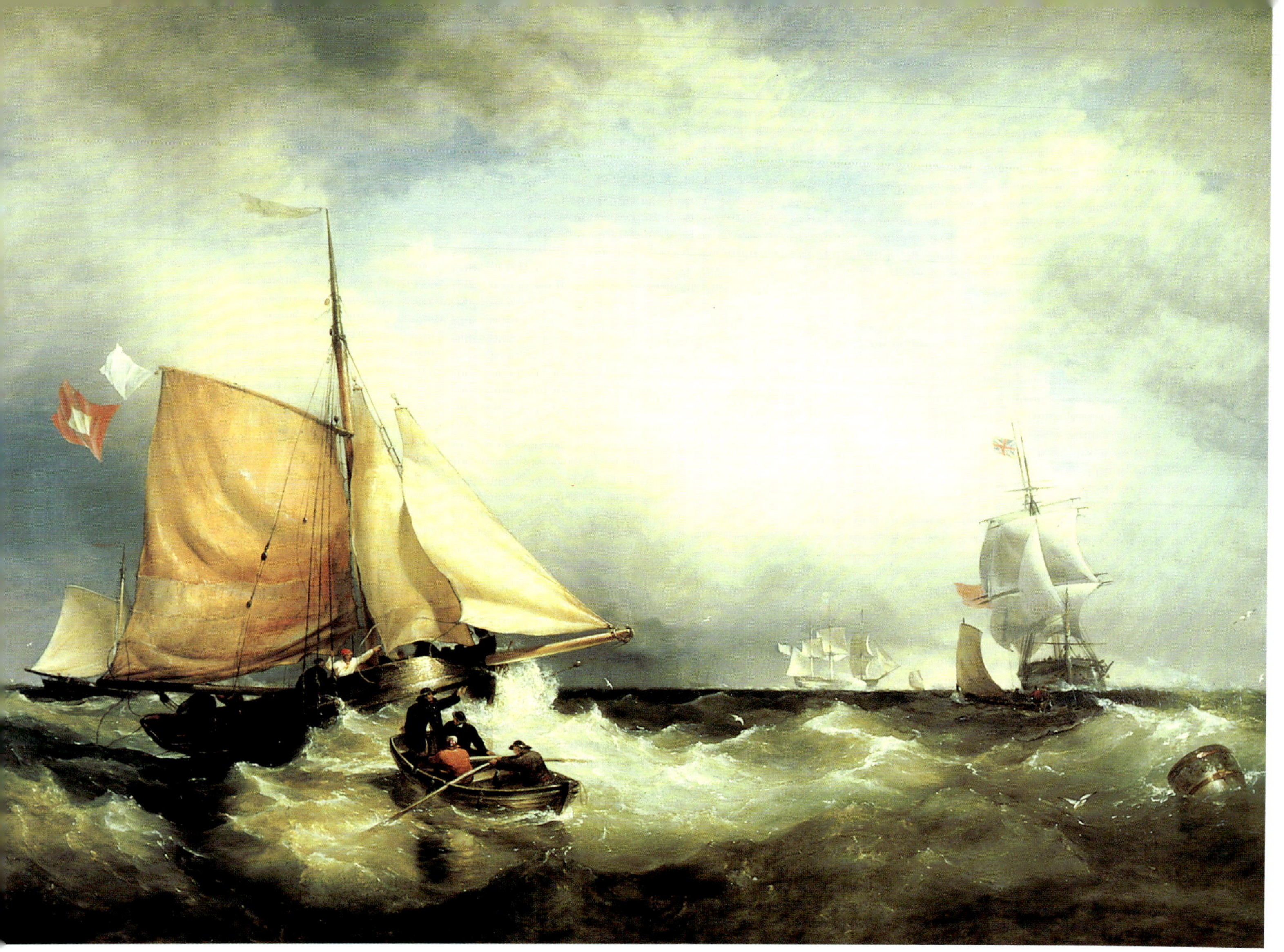

Colour Plate 12. 40/1
Pilot boat lying-to. Pilot going on board a frigate
A major early work steeped in the traditions of the British marine school; it was, however, a subject to which he does not seem to have returned.
Photo courtesy Private Collection

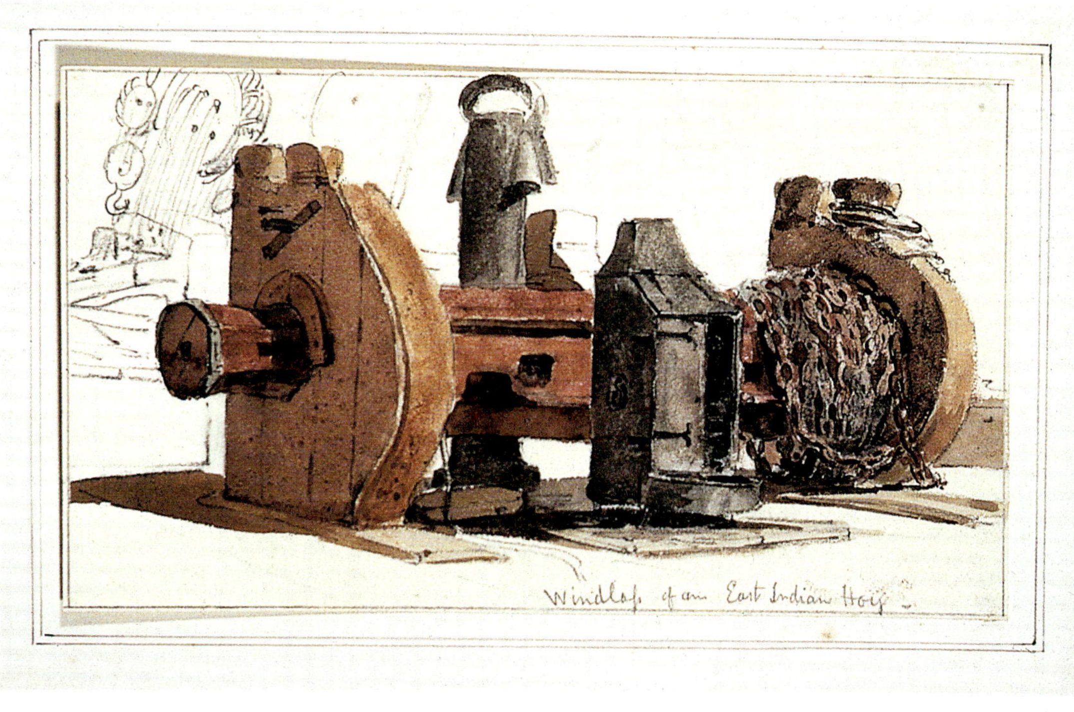

Colour Plate 13. Watercolour, 1828
Windlass of an East India Hoy
Deck fittings, even on a small work-boat, provided useful notes for a marine painter.
Photo courtesy The Trustees of the National Maritime Museum, Greenwich

Chapter 1

THE FAMILY CIRCLE

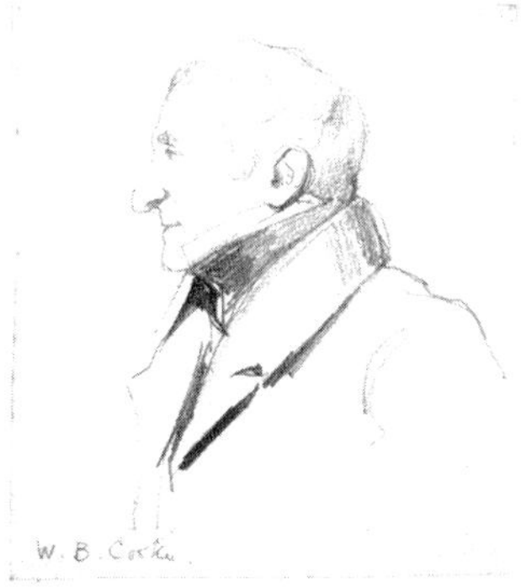

Plate 8. Pencil drawing *William Bernard Cooke (1779-1855)*
Although a painting by George Clint is known to have existed, this is the only likeness so far discovered of the celebrated engraver, publisher and proprietor of the Soho Square print gallery.
Photo courtesy C.R. Cooke, OBE

The Cookes were an industrious and talented family, Londoners but, like many of their relations and friends, of German origin on the male side. Britain under her Hanoverian monarchs from 1714 was host to thousands of immigrants and Johann Bernhard Guck from the great Free City of Frankfurt am Main was one. Already a travelled man, his passport bearing the signature of Count Mikhail Vorontzov and dated St Petersburg May 1758, is a permit to leave all the Russias of the Empress Elizabeth Petrovna and return to Germany.[1] His occupation given as *zucker-becker* is translatable as sugar-baker, of which there were numbers in the London Directories; it could mean sugar-refiner but also confectioner. In later years his occupation was rendered as *wholesale confectioner* but a family copy of *Arnold's Magazine of the Fine Arts* for April 1834 containing an obituary of his son George Cooke is altered in manuscript to 'sugar merchant' which indeed he may have become.

Known as Mr J.B. Cooke and resident with his wife Maria Anna, née White, first in Leather Lane and then in Charles Street, Hatton Garden, he was evidently prosperous and became the father of numerous sons and daughters. These included William Bernard the uncle (Plate 8) and George the father of the artist, both of whom became prominent fine art engravers.

Of incidental interest, two of the Cooke daughters married men from Germany whose names are recorded in rather different fields; Lucy became the wife of John Leonard Shuckard, otherwise Schuckardt, also from Frankfurt, a popular landlord of the famous *Old Ship Inn* at Brighton. His son William Edward Shuckard became Librarian to the Royal Society and later Editor of *Lloyds' List.*

At a time when John Constable was sketching on Brighton beach, the Cooke family took occasional seaside holidays with their inn-keeping relatives and Edward was entranced by the fishing boats and sea life of the place. Another of his aunts was the wife of Johan Christian Kramer, the Leader of the King's Private Band of Music in the Royal Household, who was also proprietor of a Brighton glass and china warehouse. He is depicted among the figures in George IV's Coronation Procession[2] and officiated likewise at the monarch's Windsor funeral, as is recorded by his nephew.

Others of their acquaintance were the family Steigenberger, colour manufacturers in Homerton who brought certain expertise and knowledge from Frankfurt and prospered. They shortened their name to Berger, which is still known in paint manufacture today, and they married into local families, Gillhams and Burnands.

Most closely linked to the Cookes is a family with the unusual name of Loddiges, the founder of the English branch of which had come from Hanover at about the same time as the grandfather Guck.

Edward William Cooke was born on 27 March 1811 in Chapel Street, Pentonville, and baptised at St James's on 19 May, the second child and second son of George Cooke and Elizabeth Harriet (née Eglinton). They had been married in 1808 at the Church of St. Mary, Islington, and produced eleven children, nine of them girls, five of whom died before reaching maturity, three of them in the same year.

The family lived until 1818 in the area where the famous City Road led to the highway north out of London, and the parish church of St Luke's, Old Street, recorded the baptism of several of the children. Then they moved eastwards, out among the nursery

1. Cooke MSS.
2. Victoria & Albert Museum: James Stephanoff.

gardens of Hackney, to No 4. Loddiges Place, Mare Street, in the precincts of the celebrated gardens and glasshouses of Conrad Loddiges & Sons. The Cooke family's uprooting was all in the cause of art, for George Cooke had embarked upon engraving the plates for a periodical publication, *The Botanical Cabinet,* which illustrated Loddiges' stock and gave instructions on cultivation.

His second son drew precociously, copying from illustrated books – the wood engravings from Barr's edition of Buffon's *Natural History* are mentioned. He attended school at Grove House, Woodford, an ancient Tudor building which contained old carvings which he drew in addition to objects from his father's 'Cabinet of Curiosities'. He also learnt the methods of engraving and etching in the company of a succession of his father's apprentices including his cousin William John Cooke and Thomas Shotter Boys.

That Edward Cooke's talents were early recognised as being of a superior order is clear and he was in this typical, for the sons of prominent engravers seem often to have become painters – Edwin Landseer, Frederick Goodall, Thomas Hartley Cromek and John Frederick Lewis were examples.

This upbringing naturally had a marked effect on his development as a painter with draughtsmanship remaining a dominant feature of his art. His first biographer, in the *Art Journal* 1869, must have consulted the artist and states that before reaching the age of nine he drew on wood several thousand plants, to be engraved as illustrations for John Claudius Loudon's *Encyclopaedia of Plants,* 1829. We have to take his word for it; they were engraved by R. Branston and the Proprietors in their Preface *...beg leave to thank, in a very particular manner Messrs. Loddiges of Hackney for original drawings of many species, made from living plants in their unrivalled collection of exotics...,* but the boy Cooke remains an unacknowledged sub-contractor!

Youthful artistic efforts are often fondly preserved; a folder of pencil drawings from 1820-1828 was cherished by his family[3] and show his copying activities. They also illustrate a lively sense of fun with his version of a coat of arms – a many sleeved jacket!

The brothers Redgrave recount a story, which they too must have had from Cooke himself,[4] that the boy was sent *up to town, from Hackney, to take perspective lessons from Augustus Pugin; but after young Cooke had paid two visits, Pugin begged his father not to send him so far again, saying with great honesty the boy knew as much as he did.*

This, told with pardonable pride, is as much a testimonial to George Cooke's tuition; his son was not sent to any School of Art but was evidently taking part in some of the studio work under his father's keen eye. It has been stated that Cooke worked in Pugin's studio, but this must be a reference to the short spell of instruction as there is no evidence of such employment in the diary, i.e. from age seventeen.

The sole surviving letter to Edward from his parent, written during what was evidently the young man's first extended absence from home, may also explain, with all its earnest exhortations, the origins of his diary-keeping.

Hackney – 20 Oct. 1828
My Dear Edward,
Your welcome and interesting letter has arrived safe & I think it does you infinite credit both as to matter and quality / it is full of pleasant detail and that detail well detail'd but above all I rejoice to find that you are well... really you are among rare good friends and before I say any more I will comment slightly on your letter. I am highly pleased to find you can write so well & I have no doubt but you have stored your book as well as head with good things. I know you love your Art– its [?] professors & I know you are industrious, be assured you will be rewarded by the

3. National Maritime Museum, Greenwich.
4. Redgrave op.cit., 1947, p.423.

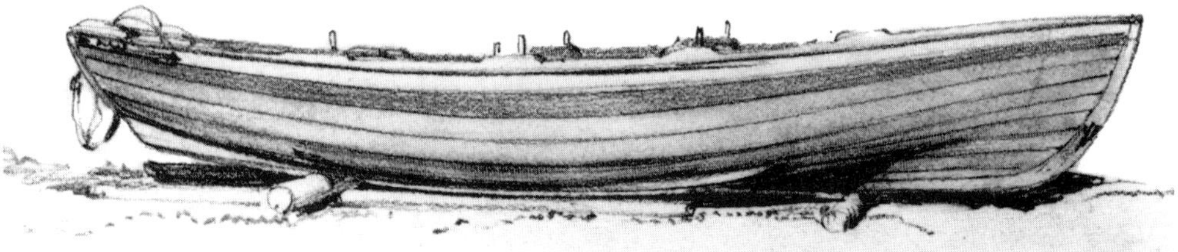

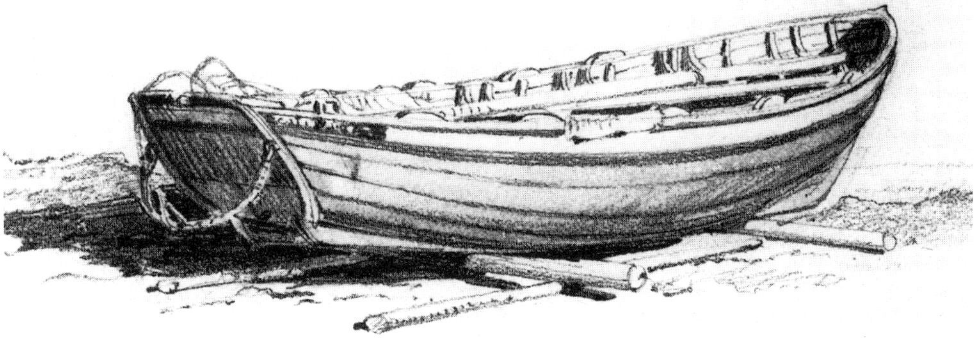

Plates 9 and 10. Pencil drawing

Cobles at Yarmouth Oct.19th 1828

The characteristic flowing shape of the east-coast fishing coble, found from Northumberland down to Norfolk, has clearly delighted the seventeen-year-old's sensitive eye and pencil. These are better in every way than the etched cobles in *Shipping & Craft* of the same date.

Photo courtesy The Trustees of the National Maritime Museum, Greenwich

love and admiration of discerning men, if you deserve it by your kindness and talent – these are stimuli sufficient I am sure for you and I shall hail your return with the delight of a gratified Parent.

Pray thank Mr Hicks in my name and also Friend Edmund and his highly respected Father & Mother for the kindness from and through them. It will be a sweet epoch in your life to recollect these early kindnesses and to bear in mind that your kind friends are sowing the rudiments of your Art by giving you the means and may your Gratitude to them prove Your sense of it. I find you are a theatrical man and applaud where applause is wisdom so it should be. I am glad you went to the Norwich Exhibition and approve of it. I wish this thing well it will encourage Home talent encourage men who are far away from the great Empire of Art. Norwich has men of talent and that they may meet with encouragement is much to be hoped if foster'd by its natural Parents. I am much pleased with Hodgsons attention to you. I think him a very worthy young man and tell him I am more than pleased to hear the good account of the Drawing as well as his kindness to you. I shall acknowledge these things by letter to him soon. Draw everything new and singular... [Editor's underlining] Kindly thank my Dear and estimable Stark, Cotman and all dear and generous friends. Tell Stark I have not forgotten him in the National Gallery. Poor Stanfield, I am much afraid he will not be a long-lived Man he is in the country and they say "better". Prout called Thursday and said he had heard he was a something

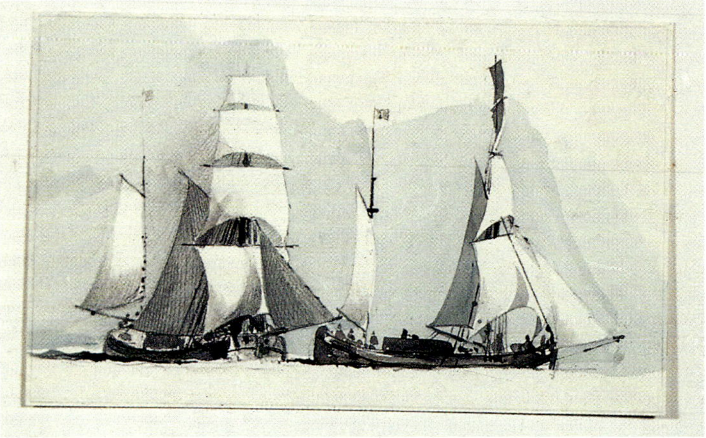

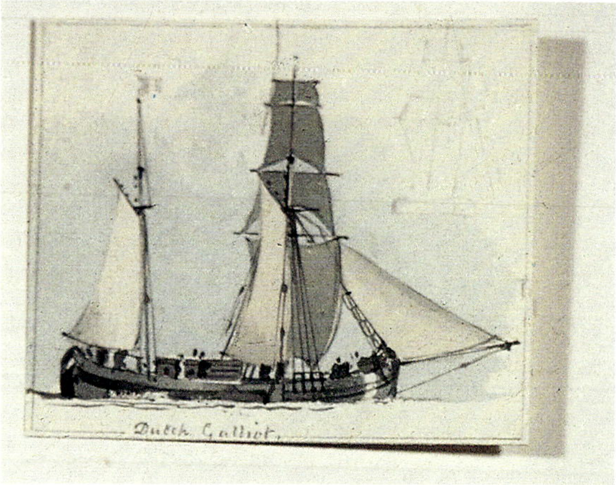

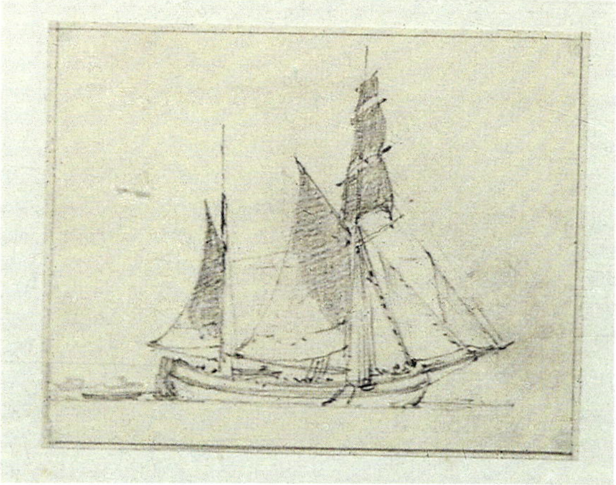

Colour Plate 14. Watercolour, 1829
Sketches of sailing craft from the artist's file
Photo courtesy The Trustees of the National Maritime Museum, Greenwich

better but I believe but trifling. Captain Burton has returned and has some fine things. He has been at Calais, St.Omer, Boulogne, Amiens &c &c, I shall see his things tomorrow I am going to drink tea with him and his Brother. He told me he only wanted his Wife on one side of him and You on the other to compleat his Happiness . Prout sends his Love to you, Mrs P. is a little better... All the Gentlemen in the Studio beg their kind regards to you esp. Lindsey & Mr Hay... spend your time with Prudence– do not be out drawing in the damp and chilly evenings they are deceitful at this time of the Year... You must not regret Edmund's engagements precluding his attentions to you, he cannot as you did not give him your whole time. Poor fellow I have much regretted our plain fare with him...
To Master Edward William Cooke at Mrs Colls Chapel St., Yarmouth. [5]

The *dramatis personae* hardly need introduction: John Sell Cotman, his son Miles Edmund, James Stark, Samuel Prout and Clarkson Stanfield are major figures. Others mentioned are Theo. Lindsey Aspland, former apprentice engraver, son of Rev. Robt. Aspland, a local Nonconformist leader; Alexander Hay, apprentice engraver; David Hodgson, painter in Norwich; John Hicks, Edmund Cotman's cousin and Capt J. Burton, master of the ship *Thetis*.

His father's advice, to extend his skill and experience by drawing *everything new and singular* was evidently heeded. For young Cooke drawing seems to have become a reaction, as it was with Turner, making him a constant recorder to judge from the large number of his pencil sketches which survive. Redgrave thought the total must have been *enormous*[6] and the artist in later life told his publisher that he had upwards of 20,000 on file![7] The friendships which existed between his father and the established marine painters would have been an added stimulus. Augustus Wall Callcott, Cotman, Prout and Stanfield were all masters of the marine, adept at coastal and shipping subjects.

The Art Journal has it that at age fourteen (1825) Edward Cooke produced a *vast*

5. Cooke MSS.
6. Redgrave, 1947, p.424.
7. John Murray Archives.

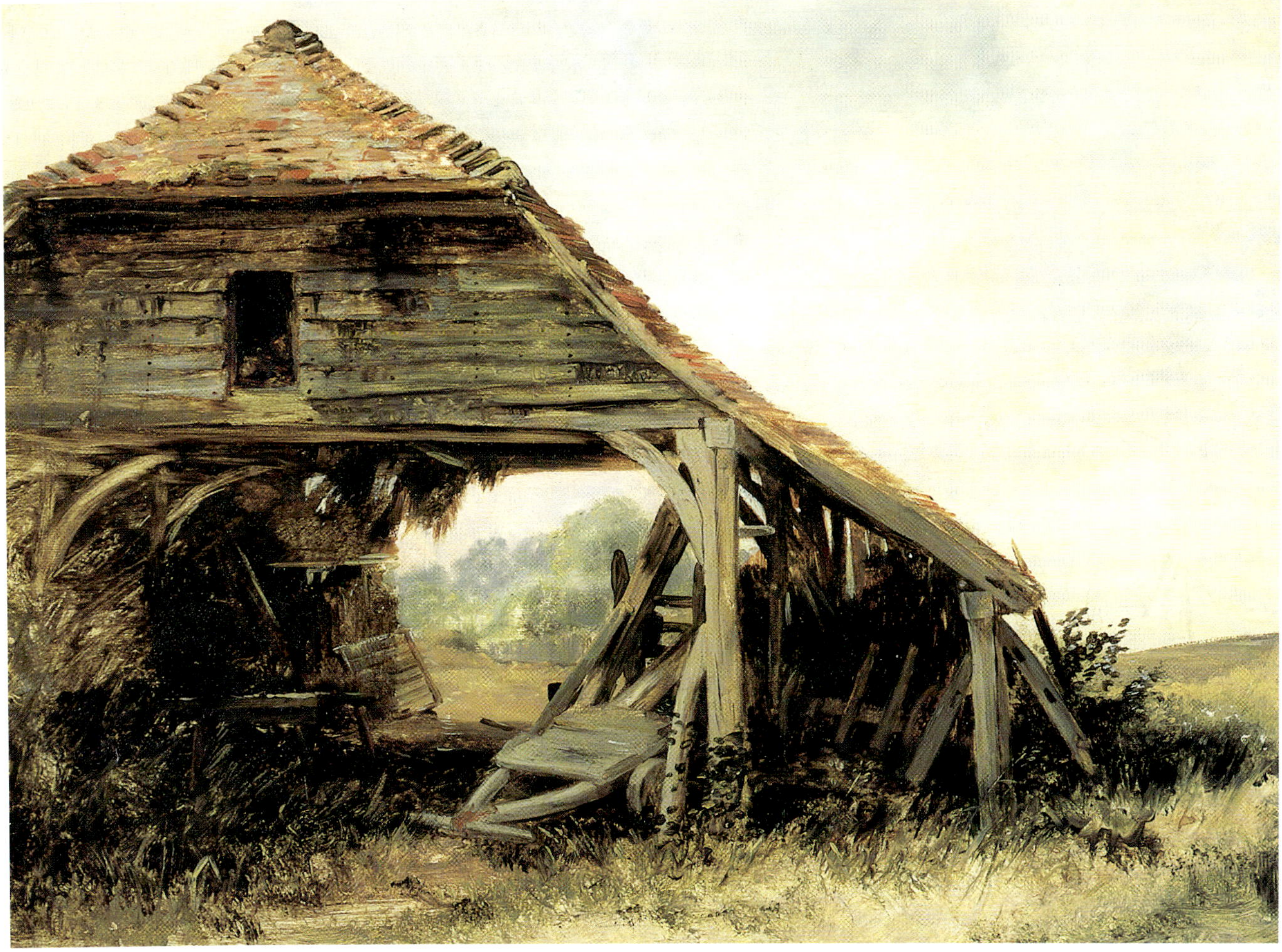

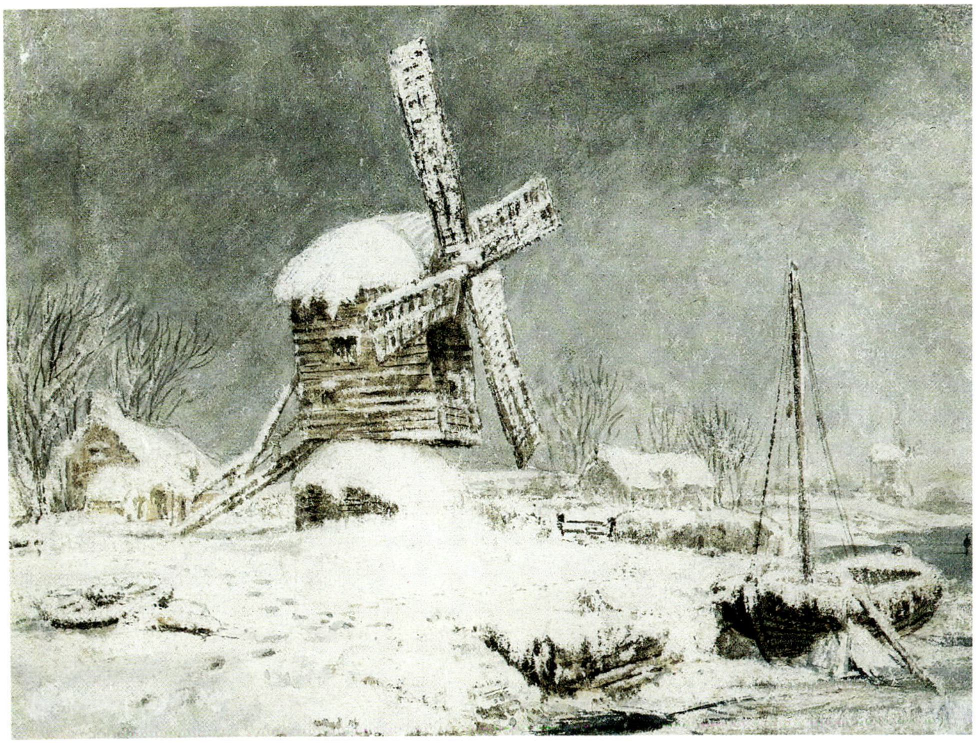

Colour Plate 15. 35/25
Old shed, Barnes
Taking subjects close to home in a country district by the Thames, Cooke began his painting in oils with riverside studies and rustic idylls.
Photo courtesy Private Collection

Colour Plate 16. Watercolour
Snow scene with windmills
December 1832.
Photocourtesy John and Joanna Meulkens, Holland

number of drawings of boats, anchors, fishing baskets and gear of all kinds for Stanfield. This has sometimes appeared in other notices as 'after Stanfield' but in 1825 the artist, ex-seaman and successful theatrical scene-painter who had already exhibited 'cabinet' pictures in London was engaged in producing a diorama for *The Adventures of a Ship of War* in *Jack of All Trades* at Drury Lane.

A reference collection of well-drawn details would have been extremely useful to him, while for the younger artist to draw for and to satisfy such a critic would have been immensely valuable training. The friendship of Capt J. Burton, commander and owner of the fine West-Indiaman *Thetis* of 460 tons, trading to Jamaica, enabled him to make hundreds of drawings on board, in the docks and on the Thames. He does not appear ever to have voyaged with his friend, who was perhaps the James Burton of Clapton Square, Hackney, amateur artist and honorary exhibitor at the British Institution known to Graves;[8] his paintings included views of Calais, Amiens and St Omer. The West-India trade – sugar – possibly indicates an association with J.B. Cooke, the sugar merchant.

All sorts of Prints and Maps...

An advertisement of 1714 by Joseph Smith offered *All sorts of Prints and Maps for Halls, Parlors, Stair-Cases, &c.* indicating the fashion.[9] By 1785 one authority could declare *Engraving was never more encouraged than at the present day, especially in England, where almost every man of taste is in some degree a collector of prints.*[10]

The brothers Cooke had in turn served their apprenticeships to master engravers. William Bernard Cooke was bound to William Angus, engraver and publisher of *Seats of the Nobility and Gentry,* 1787-97, which continued a long line of earlier works devoted to portraits of grand houses and the views from their porches and terraces. That of course was where much of the patronage lay and it has been noted that painters who made a living from views of country houses and parks were not taken seriously. Things were changing, however, with the dawn of Romanticism and two major artists contrived in different ways to raise this sort of picture to a new dignity – J.M.W. Turner, intent on elevating landscape to the poetic heights attained by the Old Masters, and John Constable with *his refusal to be more impressive than Nature... but to explore it with all the insistence and honesty* of which he was capable.[11] It was evidently Edward Cooke's inclination to follow the example of Constable, though frequently faced by the works of Turner.

George Cooke was apprenticed in 1795 to James Basire II, an association which was comparatively unproductive from Cooke's point of view. It had one redeeming feature which brought him within the orbit of Turner, of whose work he became a great admirer.

> *...during the whole term of seven years Mr Basire scarcely wrought at his desk as many months and the youth was left to make his own way... an ardent love for and seeking after excellence, saved him from the disgust which his probationary occupations were calculated to excite: one drawing by Turner came annually to Basire's to be translated to copper, as an appendage to the Oxford Almanac, and like the Angel's descent to the Pool of Bethesda this solitary visitation brought healing on its wings and wrought miracles on those within the sphere of its influence.*[12]

The brothers J. & H. Le Keux were in the same studio. When he was 'out of his time' George joined his brother who was then working on J.N. Brewer's *Beauties of England and Wales* (1813).

The elder brother appears to have possessed enterprise for in 1808 he ventured *A New Picture of the Isle of Wight... 36 Plates... in imitation of the original sketches* as artist, engraver and publisher. In 1811 he engraved drawings by Samuel Owen for *The Thames* which made two volumes and included numerous seats, thereby gaining subscribers to the publication from the owners of the villas, and there were further editions.

8. *The British Institution 1806-1867* by A.Graves, 1908.
9. *A History of the 'Old Water-Colour' Society* by J.L. Roget, 1891, Vol.I, p.11.
10. *Dictionary of Engravers,* Strutt, 1785.
11. *The Story of Art* by E.H.Gombrich,1966.
12. *Arnold's Magazine of the Fine Artss,* 1834, Vol. III No. VI (obituary by George Hollis).

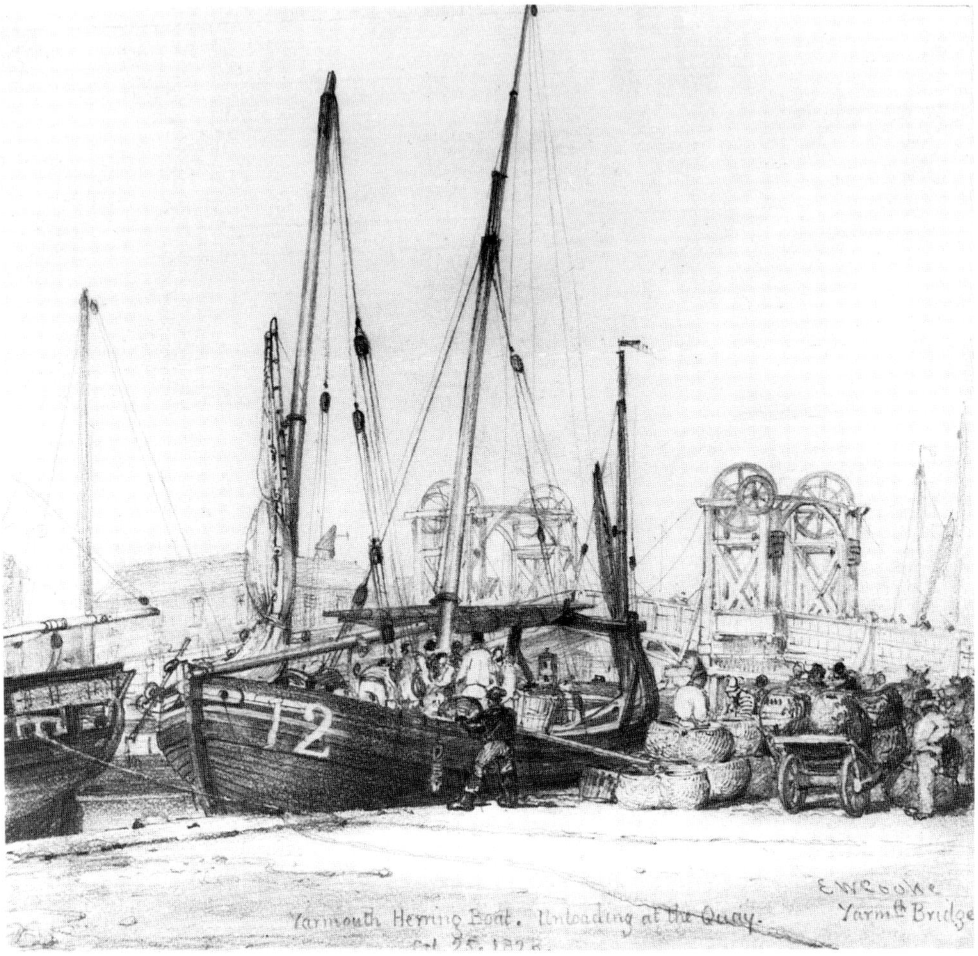

Plate 11. Pencil drawing

Yarmouth Herring boat unloading at the Quay. Oct 25th 1828

A finished drawing very near the plate in *Shipping & Craft* with the same title but with the removal of the vessel lying ahead of No 12 and the addition of a few more baskets and figures. The intricate construction of the lifting bridge takes its proper place in the background. He was staying with the Cotmans and Starks at this time, but there is a gap in his newly commenced diary.

Photo courtesy Martyn Gregory

W.B. Cooke became also an entrepreneur, operating a gallery and print shop at 9 Soho Square until the year 1830.[13] Here from 1821-24 exhibitions of the works, first of English engravers (1821) and then of watercolour painters, were held.[14] Under Royal Patronage, W.B. Cooke claimed to *present a connected view of the Progress of the Art of Drawing in the country from the time of Paul Sandby to the Present Day;* it was also, he claimed, *The most splendid collection of drawings ever exhibited.*

With his associates, for many of the exhibits were on loan from collectors and not for sale, W.B. Cooke was publicising the work of fellow engravers as well as other artists, and there were print rooms and a shop on the ground floor. Charles Stokes, Sir John Swinburne Bt, William Upcott, John Britton, Dr Thomas Munro, John Fuller of Rosehill, Stephen Rimbault and others contributed from their collections to the exhibitions.

Although it is stated that his publishing ventures did not meet with much success,[15] he was an innovator and a keen propagandist. His business relations with J.M.W. Turner in the first quarter of the century are significant and illuminating,[16] as are his contacts with John Constable.[17]

It must be noted that while the younger brother George was a family man the elder William Bernard, who married in 1804, appears to have had no surviving heirs. Their collaboration continued although George Cooke embarked in 1817 on the long *Botanical*

13. Sale: Southgate, Grimston & Wells, 7-16 July, 1830.
14. National Art Library (V & A Museum).
15. *Dictionary of National Biography* – Cooke, W.B.
16. *Turner's Rivers, Harbours & Coasts,* Eric.Shanes, 1981.
17. John Constable's Correspondence, Vol. III. Ed. R.B. Beckett, Suffolk Record Office, Ipswich, 6 vols., 1962-68.

Cabinet series and was projecting other works of his own. Uncle William, as he appears in the diary, after giving up his gallery in 1830 continued to engrave and publish on a diminishing scale with occasional valuable help from his nephew.

An undated note from the painter James Stark in Norwich to the engraver George Cooke in Hackney reads:

> *I am extremely oblig'd by your kind offer of one of your prints from Turner: anything from your hand is not only anxiously looked for, not only by myself, but by all who have any taste for the arts in this place as well as all others that have any pretensions to refinement. Your inimitable work of the Southern Coast has given a new era to the Art of Engraving and these impressions you were so kind as to place in my possession have caused much envy in the small circle of my friends in Norwich.*

He then asks for some more proofs *for Charles Turner of Pottergate St., Norwich, one of our present Sherrifs and a liberal encourager of the Fine Arts (regardless of expence).*[18]

Over this narrative of the Cooke family there broods with a pervading influence the squat, untidy figure of Joseph Mallord William Turner RA, whose eyes seem to have been his most impressive personal feature.The towering splendour of his work, known to George Cooke from his apprentice days – as most likely was the painter himself – was an important influence. Six years older than the master engraver, with whom he was eventually to have a stand-up row over *touched* proofs which ended their association,[19] Turner was practised in various forms of print-making and was able to direct the men who worked upon his drawings with an uncanny sureness.

The finest and most successful of the engraved works upon which the brothers Cooke were engaged, of which the young Edward William must have absorbed the essence, was their *Picturesque Views of the Southern Coast of England*, issued between 1814 and 1826 in twelve parts each containing three views, two vignettes and letterpress. Engraved mainly from the watercolour drawings commissioned from Turner, the series also included a wide range after Samuel Owen, William Collins, Luke Clennell, James Hakewill, Edward Blore, William Havell, Henry Edridge, Louis Francia, Peter de Wint, Joshua Cristall, William Westall, William Alexander and Samuel Prout.

The plates were unquestionably the summit of the Cookes' achievement; admitting they were excellent and perceptive craftsmen, their success owed a great deal to Turner's having himself *touched* or worked-up the trial proofs from each plate. His exacting standards and extraordinary insight brought the engravers to heights which perhaps surprised even themselves.

William Bernard and George Cooke also produced large plates from Sir Henry Englefield's drawings for his folio volume of 1816, *A Description of the Principal Beauties Antiquities and Geological Phoenomena of the Isle of Wight*. The scientific element was included in a series of letters to the author from J. Webster. Englefield used the somewhat cumbersome invention of Cornelius Varley, the Patent Graphic Telescope, a development of the *camera lucida*,[20] and gave one to J.S. Cotman for his Normandy tour in 1817. It was certainly recommended by Samuel Prout and became an item in Cooke's travelling kit.

The delineation of chalk cliffs with embedded flints and other features of coastal geology may also have kindled the young Cooke's interest, for the Isle of Wight became a favourite painting ground. Fossils featured in their family 'Cabinet of Curiosities' and their botanical neighbour George Loddiges was a firm friend and believer in the theories of the Rev Dr John Pye Smith FRS, Minister of the Gravel Pit Chapel, whose observations on the new science of Geology *created quite a panic in the Religious world*.[21] John Pye Smith also presided over the Protestant Dissenting College at Homerton, and his long standing interest in geology led to the publication of his lectures

18. Cooke MSS.
19. Goodall op.cit., p.161-2.
20. *The Camera Lucida in Art & Science* by J.H. Hammond & J. Austin,1987.
21. *Glimpses of Ancient Hackney* by Benjamin Clarke, 1893.

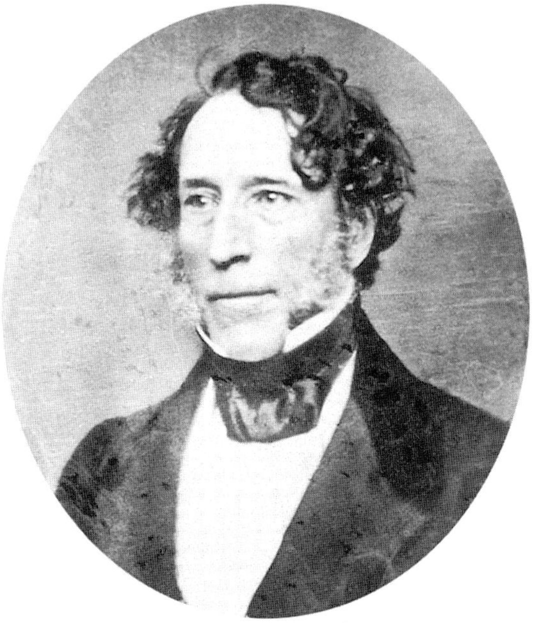

Plate 12.
Mr Loddiges of Hackney
The artist collected *carte de visite* photographs of family, friends and associates during the 1860s and his album has survived. Labelled *George Loddiges* in a later hand, this bears a strong resemblance to the painting of Cooke's father-in-law by John Renton, now belonging to the Royal Horticultural Society. However George died in 1846 and it is unclear whether this could be a photograph of a daguerrotype of him, or a portrait of his son, Conrad Loddiges II (1821-1865) – the brother of Jane Cooke.
Photo courtesy C.R. Cooke, OBE

to students as *The Relation between The Holy Scriptures and some parts of Geological Science,* 1843.

A devout and regular churchgoer, Edward Cooke lived when young in this place where there was a remarkable and long-standing concentration of religious fervour – *the surrounding district was dominated by Nonconformity of various types – their schools, colleges and institutions of various kinds, as well as with many private residences of dissenters – it was the Mecca of Nonconformity.*[22] Hassocks rather than prayer mats were surely the furnishing of the chapels of Homerton and Hackney which the Cookes attended; however the beliefs and interests of his friends and contacts naturally exerted considerable influence. The pleasant township of Hackney on the eastern outskirts of London had always been celebrated for its private schools and was also, with neighbouring Hoxton and Stoke Newington, an area of nursery and market gardens. The transitional stage in development from country into town, these nurseries were often run by men of resource who published lists of their stock, accounts of their floral achievements and treatises on gardening.

The name of Loddiges, frequently mistaken by later writers for a plural and so rendered as 'Loddige', looms large in E.W. Cooke's life and also in the history of that part of London. The firm of Conrad Loddiges and Sons, Nurserymen, was founded in Hackney by Joachim Conrad Loddiges who claimed to be already the third generation of professional gardeners. He came from near Hildesheim in Hanover, via Haarlem in Holland, to England in 1761. He had served his apprenticeship from 1754-57 in the royal gardens of King George II of Hanover and Great Britain, and worked in England for Sir J-B.Z. Silvester FRS, the physician, in Hackney.

Ten years later he acquired a nursery business there, one started by his compatriot John Busch who had departed for Russia to devise gardens for Catherine the Great. Conrad's sons William and George further developed both the installations and the scope of the business, continuing the importation of new species. Their culture of orchids began as early as 1812 and they were said to be the foremost growers in Europe for the next forty years. From the first, in 1777, their printed catalogues of plants available grew in size and range; the thirteenth edition appeared in 1823 and by the 1840s the collection of greenhouse, stove plants, orchids, palms in over two hundred varieties, hardy perennials, trees and shrubs, ferns, cacti and other items from the fifteen acre site, supports their international reputation. Their glasshouses were steam-heated by a system of their own

22. *Renton & other Hoxton Nurserymen* by W. Roberts, *Journal R.H.S.* Vol. 63, 1938.

design and their residence was warmed by the same installation. The Palm House *designed without the intervention of the architect, was erected by his own workmen*. The onset of smoke pollution and the expiration of a lease contributed to the decline of the famous nurseries by 1860. When Conrad Loddiges III died in 1898, William Robinson wrote: *...the Loddiges were greater benefactors to horticultural science than all their prototypes and rivals put together.For very many years they were, both in enterprise, and in the extent of their business, far and away the leading English firm of nurserymen and plant introducers. It would be an exaggeration to say that they revolutionised English gardening; but they developed it in a very remarkable manner.*[23]

Here is a major influence on Edward Cooke's life and interests; he married in 1840 Jane, the younger daughter of George Loddiges and Jane Creighton, a daughter of another dissenting clergyman, the Rev James Creighton of Hoxton, a Wesleyan. William Loddiges, the elder brother, had married Alice Creighton, her sister. Their brother, James Creighton Junr, married a daughter of John Renton (c.1747-1810), proprietor of a another nursery garden who is thought to have been foreman in the Loddiges nursery. His son, John Renton II, became a portrait painter who exhibited likenesses of Nonconformist celebrities which were engraved and published in the *Methodist Magazine*. He also painted the portraits of Joachim Conrad Loddiges and Mr and Mrs George Loddiges, exhibited at the Royal Academy in 1818 and 1821 respectively.[24]

23. *The Athenaeum* No.3722, 25 February 1899.
24. Roberts op.cit.

Chapter 2

THE ARCANA OF PUBLISHING: ENGRAVINGS AND ETCHINGS

The Redgrave brothers wrote that George Cooke intended his son to be an engraver *and he continued to assist him in his art until he was nearly twenty.*[1] Who assisted whom is not clear but either way it was true: E.W. Cooke's engraved and etched work owes a great deal to his father's hand, and it is clear that the son's superior talent as draughtsman was of equal value in his father's publications. Instead of attending a drawing school, his father's instruction and the close study of so much first-class work passing through the studio were his training; narrow perhaps, but concentrated.

His father's apprentices, of whom there were usually two and in the 1820s sometimes as many as four, came from very different backgrounds. Some of their Indentures have survived,[2] binding them for seven years to George Cooke, Citizen and Stationer of London. In 1808 the first was George Hollis, son of an Oxford innkeeper; in 1811 W.J. Cooke, his nephew, and also John Barnett, son of a Pentonville printer; in 1817 Thomas Shotter Boys, son of a Pentonville salesman; in 1820 John Percy Heath, son of a deceased chemist of Nottingham and in 1821 Theophilus Lindsey Aspland, son of Robert Aspland, Unitarian minister in Hackney. Alexander Hay, the last, was 'out of his time' in 1829. William Miller, a Scot who had trained under Archibald, the Edinburgh engraver of the *Encyclopaedia Britannica* plates, came to London for two years with George Cooke (1819-21), became celebrated as an interpreter of Turner and as the subject of a detailed volume of memoirs.[3] The fees paid by the parents varied from £50 in 1808 to 190 guineas in 1820. George Cooke's own fee to James Basire Junr. in 1795 had been £45.

The Botanical Cabinet

The Cooke studio, which included not only apprentices but also family, was at work on plant drawings which were then engraved in aquatint for subscribers to this work, issued in periodical parts between 1817 and 1833.

> *The Botanical Cabinet, Consisting of Coloured Delineations of Plants from All Countries: with a short account of each, Directions for management &c by Conrad Loddiges and Sons. The Plates by George Cooke.*

Ten aquatint engravings with appropriate text formed each part. These were published monthly by John & Arthur Arch of Cornhill, Longman, Rees, Orme and Brown of Paternoster Row and ten parts formed a volume. The text by the Loddiges brothers, William and George, contains not only information on origin and culture, but also frequent moral exhortations – *Horticultural notes and pious observations recall the evangelical piety that then centred on Hackney... The charming illustrations portraying little-known or new plants grown in their Nurseries.*[4]

There were twenty volumes in the completed work and thus no fewer than 2,000 plates. George Loddiges drew some 1,700 of his specimens himself, but Edward Cooke reckoned to have produced the originals of about 410 (Colour Plate 17). The arithmetic is faulty considering that other artists assisted including T.S. Boys who is credited with 194, W.J. Cooke and William Miller as well as Jane Loddiges and a Miss Rebello. The

1. Redgrave, 1947, p.423.
2. Cooke MSS.
3. *Memorials of Hope Park* by William Miller.
4. Exhibition of Flower Books from the Society of Herbalists Library [Catalogue] by Wilfrid Blunt, Arts Council, 1953.

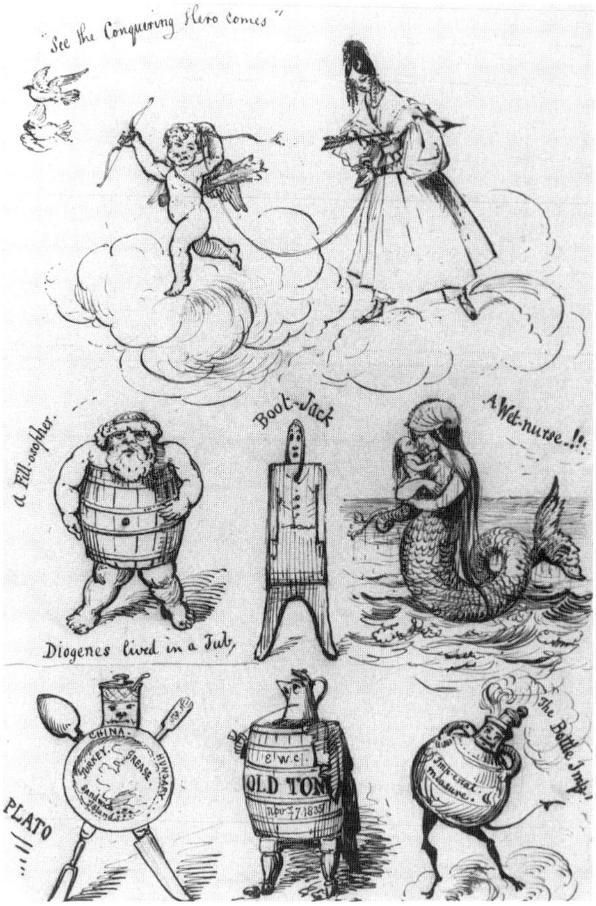

Plate 13. Ink sketch
Humorous illustrations. Nov. 1835, For a young lady's scrap-book
He noted drawing 'whimsicals' at Oxford for his Wyatt friends. Photo courtesy Martyn Gregory

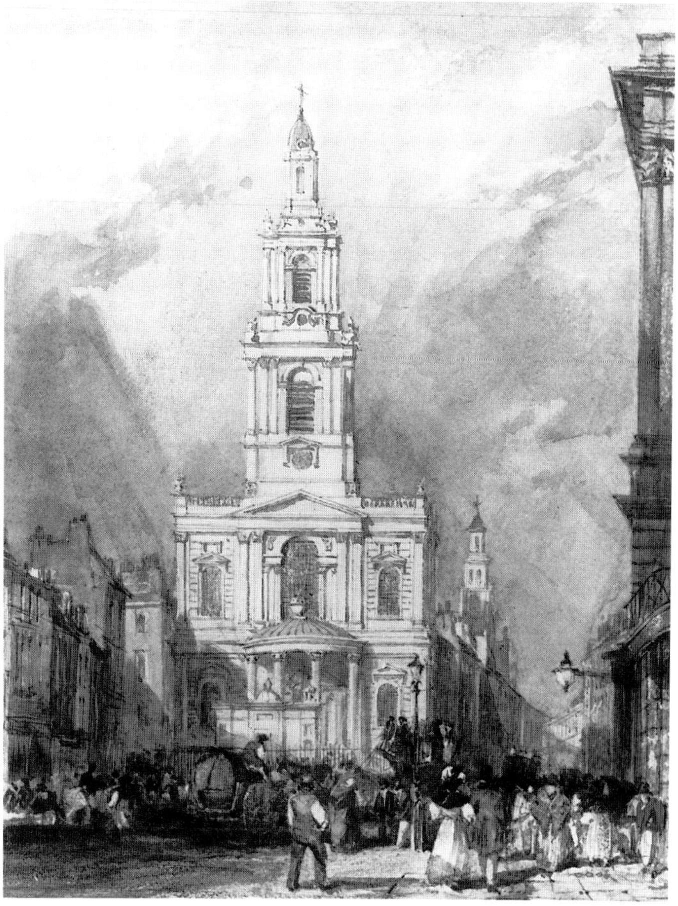

Plate 14. Watercolour
The church of St Mary le Strand
This may be a preliminary for a plate intended for George Cooke's *London.* Photo courtesy Spink & Son Ltd

Cooke family had moved to Loddiges Place adjoining the nursery proprietor's own house in about 1818, for it was essential to be on hand to draw the hothouse plants as they came into flower and some plants were actually sent into the studio. These were drawn in watercolour, then traced, transferred to the copper and engraved. The size of the plates was only about 6in. x 4in. (15cm x 10cm), but their continued production at the rate of ten each month required a discipline and application in George Cooke's studio which was clearly of no mean order. The final note printed in the last number stated: *having been enabled to complete our 20th volume and thus to place 2000 plants before the public, our labours are closed... the precarious state of our draughtsman's health not permitting him to go any farther.*

G. Cooke and G. Loddiges were both subject to indisposition according to the diary, but the former died a year later in 1834 and the latter not until 1846.

The Thames

W.B. Cooke's *The Thames or graphic illustrations of seats, villas, public buildings and picturesque scenery on the banks*, 1811, two volumes, was a series of eighty-four plates after drawings by Samuel Owen in the well established tradition of grand house portraiture but with fine river views as well.

It was followed between 1814 and 1822 by another version for which the basic material, the original drawings, could be examined in the engraver's studio by a young artist anxious to learn. John Murray was the chief publisher and seventy-five plates after Peter de Wint, William Alexander, R.R. Reinagle, Louis Francia as well as S. Owen, W.

Havell and G. Arnald were engraved by W.B. Cooke and J.C. Allen, his assistant and former apprentice, and by George Cooke. It was published by W.B. Cooke at 9 Soho Square, dedicated to Sir John E. Swinburne Bt, President of the Society of Antiquaries of Newcastle, and entitled *Views on the Thames*.

George Cooke has all the marks of a strict master, even towards his talented nine-year old son, who wrote on a scrap of paper, properly folded, addressed and sealed:

> *My dear Father, If I write a very good copy and do another sum, may I model toms ear in wax for thomas boys. He has given me wax and tools and with the other part of the wax I can model somthing for you. I Remain Your Affectionate, dutiful and Benevolent Son E.W.Cooke.*[5]

His elder brother Thomas Bernard was to 'sit' for the ear and the Redgraves recalled that *when quite a boy, he modelled a deer in high relief most correctly and accurately in black wax on a slate.*[6] A little later, in another miniature missive, he approached his parent again:

> *...As I have drawn a good many of your curiosities, may I now do what you so long promised me, that is may I etch them in a manner Superlatively well, cribbly and accurate. I remain, as I was, Your affectionate son....*[7]

The phonetic rendering of the engraver's term *criblé,* denoting a dotted surface texture, from the Latin *cribrum,* a sieve, is intriguing and is typical of the small details of their daily tasks which can be gathered from the diary. Re-covering their work boards with baize is mentioned, and in one instance they forgot a plate in the acid bath *while the aqua fortis was on and it bit outrageously black, will take several hours to repair.*

He was blessed with a sense of humour, as has been noted; fun even in serious studio work was evidently not unknown. On a small plate, *St Pancras, Old Church* from his father's *London,* with its graveyard and bent figures in the foreground, the tombstones are minutely detailed with death's head symbols and one which, under a good glass, says surprisingly 'Good Bye'! The perpetrator is unknown – it might have been a 'dare' – and there are doubtless others awaiting discovery. Brotherly affection is revealed among the hatched 'tone' on the narrow edge of a ladder in a view of a carronade on board a brig of war (Plate 22 of *Shipping and Craft*). Here is lettered, upside down, 'Clarinda Cooke', commemorating the artist's oldest sister who was to die of smallpox in 1832 at the age of nineteen.

London

A most significant publication was George Cooke's own *Views of London and Its Vicinity,* a series of forty-eight plates which was issued in bi-monthly parts, each to contain four engravings, between December 1826 and 1834. His advertisement stated that he was: *...happy to announce that he has received the most liberal assistance and offers of Drawings from the most eminent Artists. The subjects in preparation are from the works of Callcott, Prout, Stark, Stanfield...*

The printed wrapper enclosing each published part included also the names of David Roberts, J.D. Harding, J.S. Cotman and W. Havell and his *Address to Subscribers* dated Hackney 1826 refers to *subjects supplied by his own personal friends.* The time and the labour required to produce such plates, small though they were – even if no other commissions, illness or accidents interrupted the work – meant that subscribers had long to wait before they could leaf through a bound volume. *The favourite object of his life*, as his book on London was remembered,[8] took nearly eight years to complete and was curtailed by his death. Although projected as a total of eighty plates in twenty parts, only twelve parts of *London* were issued, the last posthumously.

5. National Maritime Museum, Greenwich.
6. Redgrave, 1947, p.423.
7. National Maritime Museum, Greenwich.
8. *Arnold,* op. cit.

An advertisement of 1830 had informed subscribers:

> *the great delay in this publication has been occasioned by a series of untoward circumstances and ill-health, which together with the many cheap publications that have been issued, gave a temporary check to the exertions of the Engraver, who is now anxious to complete the work and his desire to accomplish this object intends to engrave only the most interesting and beautiful of his drawings, in two or three Parts, which will quickly succeed each other, making a handsome volume of about Fifty or Fifty-five Plates.*

The title-page, after listing the names of contributors continued : *After the original sketches made on the spot by Edward W. Cooke.*

It would be interesting to know whether the youngster consulted the contributors as to the particular view and composition of his sketches, but at kerbside and quayside he formed the draughts for the established painters to work upon. Perhaps this was an inducement for busy men to take part in their friend's project. Whether they clothed the outline drawings or merely put in the finishing touches is also not clear: the captions to some plates would indicate less rather than more, *The Effect by C. Stanfield* and *The Figures and Effect by A.W. Calcott* are typical. The artist's *touching* a proof to indicate areas for the engraver's continued working was an essential stage, so it is arguable that in *London* Edward Cooke's sketches served almost as a preliminary proof. Thirteen views are in fact credited solely to him in the contents list although the plates bear only his father's name as engraver. One of them, *The Thames near Limehouse, called the Lower Pool. Tiers of Colliers, craft &c.,* is nearest to the subjects with which the young man was shortly to make his name. Ruskin referred to *That mysterious forest below London Bridge*[9] – the masts of the brigs carrying coal to the capital – an impressive sight, which is admirably shown.

George Hollis, the former apprentice, composed a long obituary notice on George Cooke for *Arnold's Magazine of the Fine Arts* which included the note:

> *The adaptation of steel plates to the purposes of Book illustration that has recently effected such extensive changes in the arcana of publishing and which it is at once conceded has greatly benefitted... by diffusing far and wide their choicest embodyings, was for a time confined to cheap and trashy ephemera. catchpenny plans to undersell not emulate, works of sterling merit. By a work of this class the "London" of George Cooke was opposed, and the usual machinery of puffs and advertisements set in motion. For a time he maintained his course with precision and cheerfulness, but one pair of hands was not equal to such a contest... and his adversary's punctuality and above all his cheapness, turned the balance.*[10]

The appearance of Charles Heath's *London and Its Environs*, 1825, is probably the rival in question although there were many others illustrating the developing metropolis. Heath's small bleak plates are undistinguished and the shipping content is third-rate, to coin a phrase. His advertisements, however, guaranteed completion of the whole within a year. Hollis' note continues:

> *[George Cooke]strongly participated in the dislike entertained by nearly all the eminent engravers to the introduction of steel plates, and, as he conscientiously believed that the consequences would be disastrous to an art which he loved above all things beside, he in common with the seniors of his profession, openly proclaimed his determination never to work on the hated metal.*

Later in the century Richard Redgrave could write that:

9. *Modern Painters,* J. Ruskin, 9 7,
10. *Arnold,* op. cit.

while the love of art has undoubtedly spread and artists have multiplied and prospered, the engraver's art alone is without encouragement. We do not impute this to lithography, photography, acierage [steel facing] or any other means by which art is diffused, but to the system of sale which has been unscrupulously adopted by the speculative publishers... The term 'proof' which formerly designated the few impressions taken off by the engraver to prove his work during its progress and was afterwards extended to a very limited number of early impressions of the finest quality now has no other meaning than the number of subscribers who can be induced to pay double....[11]

Frederick Goodall reported that Ruskin said he would *write down* line engraving but that it was dying a natural death, *it was too laborious a process for the commercial spirit of art publishing.*[12]

The question of how the output of an engraver's studio was organised, with the many complicated stages of reducing, tracing, etching and engraving, 'proving' the plates and sending them for printing, raises many problems. Time – working hours and deadlines, money – the gathering of subscriptions against the expenses of production, and the unforeseen – illness, strife and conflicting interests – all these rendered the business at times uncertain and always taxing.

A note in W.B. Cooke's 1824 exhibition catalogue indicates the duration of an engraver's labour. J.H. Robinson commenced a plate after William Mulready's *The Wolf and the Lamb* in October 1823; it measured 16in. x 19in. (40cm x 48cm) and *will have his undivided attention so there is just reason to expect it [to be] completed in two years.*

Painters may have been guided by their Muse, but engravers were led by hard economic truths; according to one artist-writer, *Engravers are proverbially more careful of their money than painters, because they find their work more laborious and their money harder earned.*[13] The Cookes appear to have either overestimated their own capabilities or underestimated the labour involved in work of the highest class, to judge by the number of publishing ventures advertised, and even begun, but which did not materialise. References to being hard pressed for time are frequent; there had been a financial 'crash' at the end of 1825, with many banks and businesses failing, and George Cooke had lost money with the collapse of the agent publishing his plate of Callcott's *Rotterdam* which meant a straitening of his circumstances. There followed an economic recession in 1826; the publishing firm of Hurst & Robinson, who may have been George Cooke's agents, went to the wall and attempts on his part to recoup meant perhaps that too many tempting commissions were agreed, without regard to studio capacity. Sir Walter Scott's labours to pay off his debts incurred by the crash of his publishing partnership at this time shows how the arts were not immune from market maladies. There are several indications that money was never easy with George Cooke. His reference to their plain fare when Edmund Cotman stayed with them bears out a note in J.S. Cotman's biography that Cooke's affairs were *in disorder.*[14] There was also his stiff-necked attitude on the Turner proofs and this conservatism about copper. William John Cooke, his nephew and former pupil, had already mastered the new material, steel, and had won a gold medal from the Society of Arts for his improvements. His engravings from Turner and R.P. Bonington and contributions to the Annuals were all on steel. T.S. Boys had left the studio in about 1823, but the project of a book of plates of London scenes had doubtless been discussed and, in view of his later works of lithography, *London as It Is* and *Paris,* marking a new generation of townscape plates, this is relevant and of some interest.

The copper plates worked by the Cookes were in great part etched, but with some line engraving to give sharpness to detail or for laying an even tone. Theirs was a school *truly indigenous, both in its style and its technical means... Analysis discloses a wriggling*

11. Redgrave, 1866, Vol. I, p.463.
12. Goodall op cit., p.123.
13. *An Art Student & his Teachers in the Sixties...,* W.S. Spanton ,1927, p.57.
14. *John Sell Cotman,* S.D. Kitson, 1937.

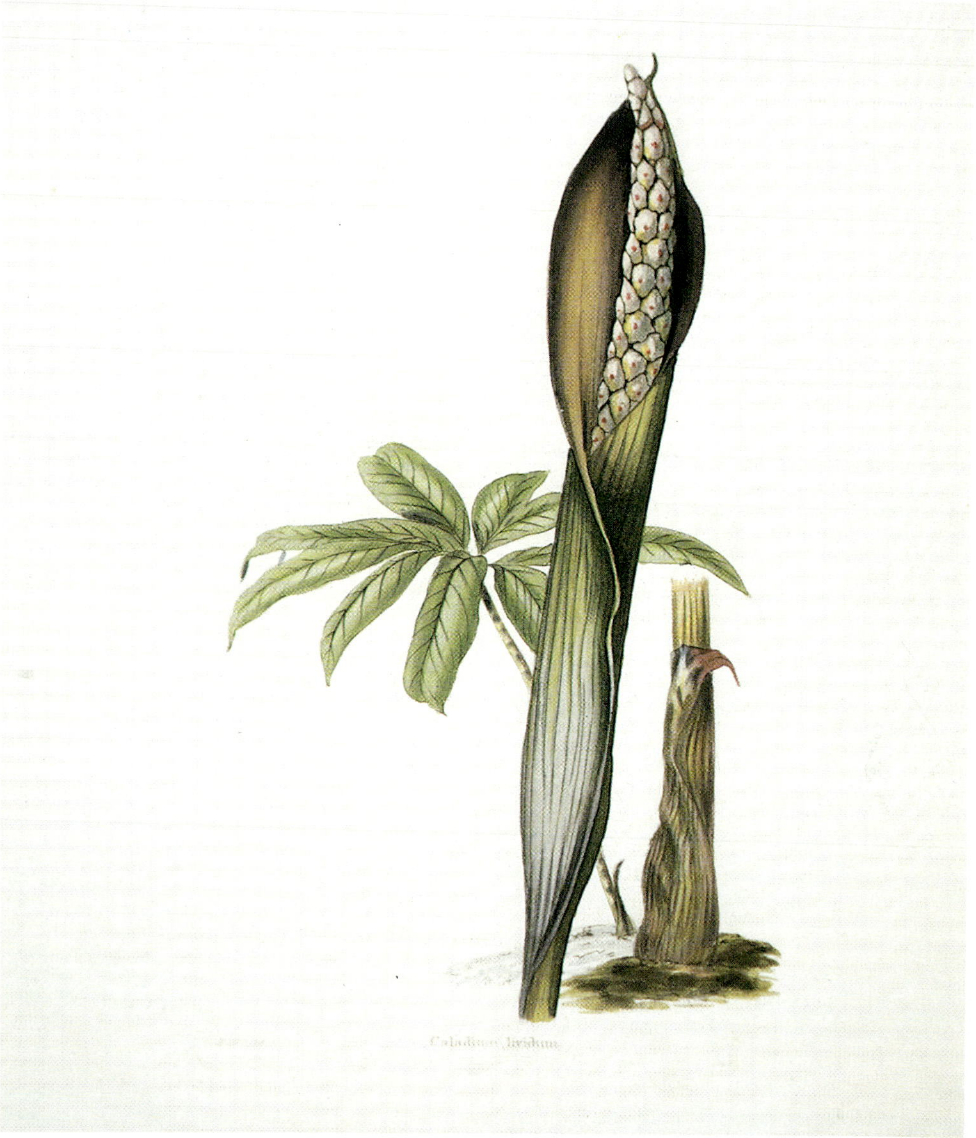

Colour Plate 17. *Caladium Lividum*
The Botanical Cabinet contained small aquatint plates from drawings by George Loddiges and members of the Cooke studio This, by Edward William, is one of the Arum family from Malaya and is typical of the treatment and presentation of the book.

worm-like line which is absolutely opposed to all the reasonable possibilities and conventions of graver work... variety of tone is achieved to a large extent by numerous bitings....[15]

The Associated Society of Engravers, known to the diary as the 'Holy Nine' (not to be confused with the Associate Engravers of the Royal Academy), were committed to engraving important pictures in the National Gallery on a commercial footing. They began in 1827 at the instigation of John Sheepshanks and under the Secretaryship of John Pye. The mystic number nine represented the signatories of a manifesto of 1826 which proclaimed their determination never to become candidates for the Academy's subordinate rank of Associate (Engraver) until that body rendered to the arts of engraving that degree of importance which the rest of Europe accorded, and recognised their worth by granting the status of full Academician to senior engravers. This was a contentious subject for some years but eventually the desired result was achieved. Now, with a committee consisting of J. Pye, J. Burnet and W. Finden, they arranged to engrave plates after some ten selected old master paintings in the Gallery. Rembrandt, Claude,

15. *A History of Engraving & Etching* by A.M. Hind, 1927.

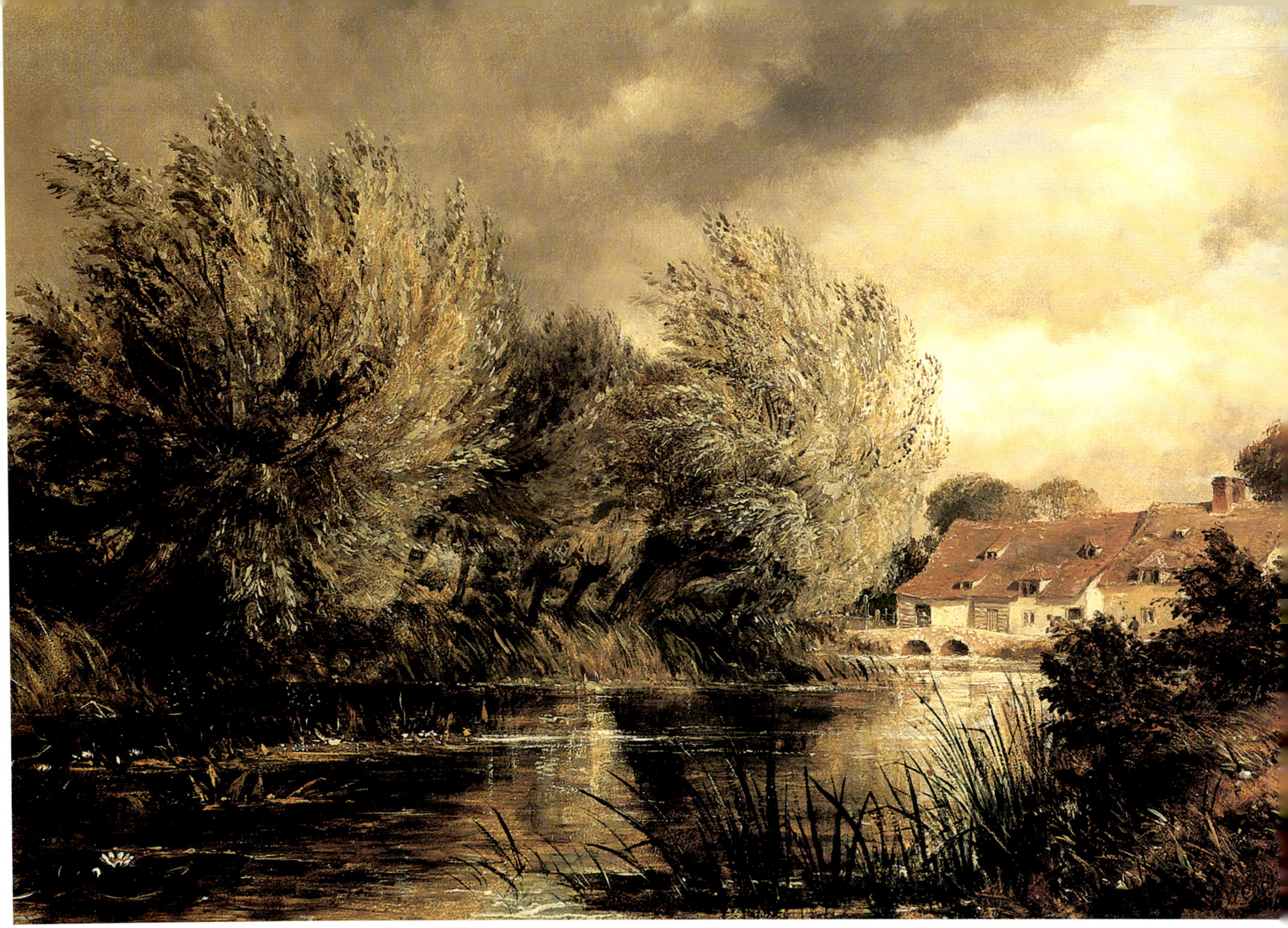

Colour Plate 18. 48/14
Beard's Mill near Oxford
A later version of one of his early (1835) paintings.
Photo courtesy Richard Green Fine Paintings. Private Collection

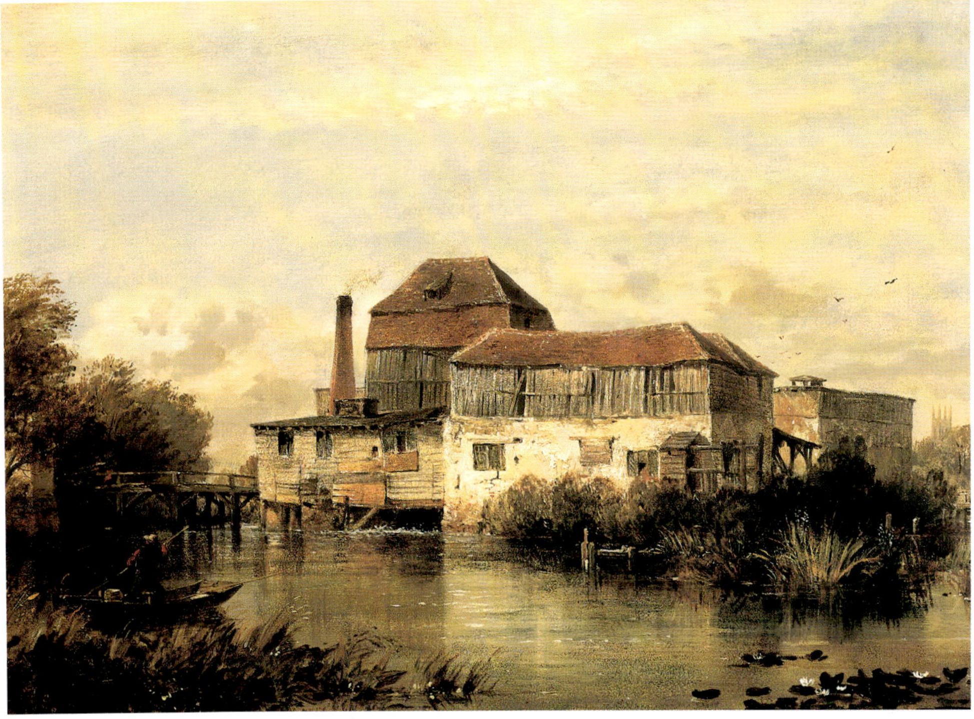

Colour Plate 19. 48/15
Wiers paper Mill near Oxford
In Oxford Cooke's attention was caught by the evidence of industry and labour, not by architectural delights. The interior of a fisherman's hut also occupied him.
Photo courtesy Agnews

the Caracci, Veronese, Rubens, Gainsborough and Reynolds are mentioned and the copper plate size was to be about 14in. x 20in. (35cm x 50cm). Royal patronage was successfully sought through Lord Farnborough and £150 was received from the King. It is interesting to note that watercolour copies of the paintings were made, of the same size as the plates, by artists including John Linnell,[16] Frederick Mackenzie and S.P. Denning at fees varying between 25 and 50 guineas, whereas the engravers contracted to do their work for between 200 and 300 guineas. The proofs were issued to subscribers in periodical numbers – the second in September 1829 – and John Sheepshanks appears to have written 'notices' for them. Other original members of this Society were G.T. Doo, J. and H. Le Keux, John Burnet, George Cooke, E. Goodall, J.H. Robinson and William Finden. Others joined in the course of time – Charles Fox, J.H. Watt, etc. The undertaking was wound up in November 1840, with a vote of thanks to Sheepshanks and a decision to destroy the plates.[17] In 1845 remaindered sets of proofs were being sold cheaply by Nattali. George Cooke's plate of a landscape by Peter Paul Rubens was unfinished at the time of his death in 1834.

The picture of a hard-pressed artist-craftsman, faced with the grim evidence of mortality, to which in the event his own family losses were to be added when three of their daughters died in the following year, is given in a letter of April 1828 from George Cooke in Hackney to his wife in Norwich:

> *My Dear Dear Harriette, Your letter, your welcome letter arrived as expected on Saty. & whilst I feel regret that you should have suffered any inconvenience by threaten'd sickness, I feel pleasure in Stark's kindness in meeting you, this excellent man is always thoughtful & good. I have just returned from attending the Funeral of poor Bonnington. Sir Thos Lawrence sent a handsome letter signifying his desire to follow this great artist as representing the Academy. He was there & Howard also as were Pickersgill the Academician, Stanfield (who is very ill) Robinson (the Architect) Robinson (the Engraver) Pugin, W.J. Cooke, W.B. Cooke, Geo. Cooke, Stanley, Robson, Lewis, S.Reynolds, Carpenter, J. Barnett, Ensom, Wm Taylor, Doo, His poor Venerable Father, Goodall, Rochard [?], Bishop, Hobday [?], Lance, Fuge and others. It was a melancholy gratification and his broken - hearted Father endeavoured to thank the Mourners for their attention to the remains of His Only Child.*
>
> *This suffering man has but one day of Mourning– but that will be lasting one. A Son at the very summit of greatness – unfolding the Doors of Wealth and Fame and sinking down in the glorious Prospect – Good God what dreadful visitations are we subject to – let me turn away from the Picture of Grief, my heart is too full to say any more....*
>
> *Ned thinks of coming on Saturday. He will come by way of Bury. We will let you know all about it. God knows when I will come – I will strive to come soon. Stark is a glorious fellow I can but thank Him/ truly I shall have a deal to thank him for when I come. Give my kindest regards to Cotman & Co., Starks All God bless them/excuse more as I am again driven for time.*

Under the same cover the son wrote:

> *I'm working hard to get my four Subjects done, two to etch by the bye before Saturday, when you may expect me. Mr Callcott has just invited us to dinner tomorrow. Father & I are going to Stanfield's tonight... Kindly remember me to Messrs Stark and Cotman etc. – Ned.*[18]

R.P. Bonington was buried in St James's Chapel, Pentonville (though later re-interred), the same church in which Edward William Cooke had been baptised.

16. Roget op. cit., 1891, Vol. I, p.413.
17. British Museum: Addl Mss. Pye.
18. Cooke MSS.

Chapter 3

SHIPPING AND CRAFT

A proof of an etched detail of sailing barges, made on the back of a discarded copper plate (printing also, in reverse, the name of Pontifex the supplier), bears his father's pencilled note: *This etching by E.W. Cooke first suggested the Idea of the work of Shipping, 1827. G.C.*[1]

Apart from its symbolic place in art, the sailing ship as an object of beauty and as evidence of man's ingenuity had always drawn the admiration of poets and artists. There had been many published series of engravings portraying those essential contrivances which enabled men to explore the oceans of the world but the earliest prints came from the Netherlands in the fifteenth century and must always have been rare. A group of nine prints by a Flemish engraver, the monogrammist WA, stand out as the probable beginning of this maritime tradition of ship portraiture, in the period 1465-1485.[2] The engraver Frans Huys, working from drawings by Peter Breughel the Elder about 1540, produced some dozen striking ship plates which are also among the earliest references for types of European sailing vessels.

The French marine atlas *Neptune françois* of 1693 included some splendid large plates of ship-types and the Venetian Padre Vincenzo Coronelli, at his Academy charmingly

1. National Maritime Museum, Greenwich.
2. *Marine Prints by the Dutch Masters* by I. de Groot & R.Vorstman,1980, p.8.

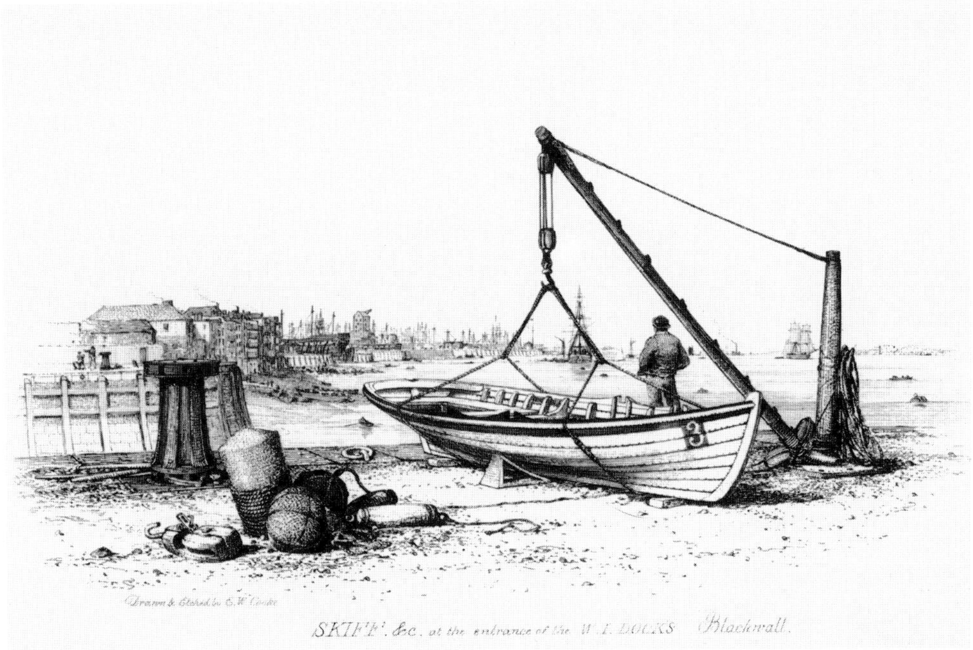

Plate 15. Engraving
Blackwall, skiff &c 1829
The East India Docks, in constant activity, were a magnet for many painters. William Wells, Cooke's patron, had owned the Blackwall Yard seen in the background.

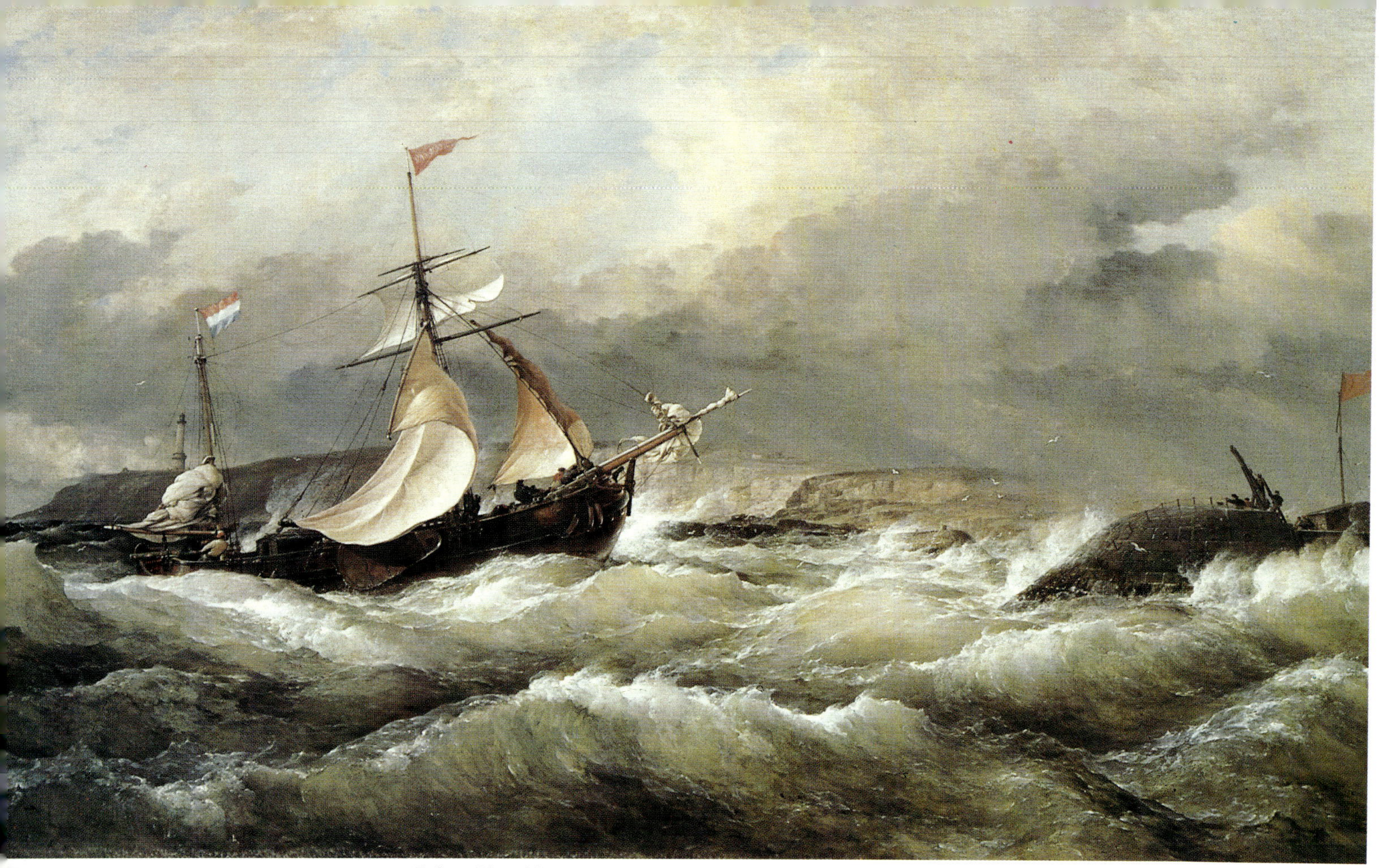

Colour Plate 20. 60/2

A Dutch Galliot running into the port of Aberdeen during a heavy gale

The artist on a visit to Scotland witnessed this dramatic entry. The picture originally belonged appropriately to Duncan Dunbar, the millionaire Scottish shipowner.

Photo courtesy Great GrimsbyMuseum & Heritage Service (Doughty Bequest)

Colour Plate 21. Watercolour

Lugger on shore near Dover. May 1829

He wasn't at Dover in 1829 but did make a drawing for the album of Miss Moffat of Mortlake, whose father owned two picures of his house by J.M.W. Turner, RA. A similar study appears in *Shipping and Craft.* Photo courtesy Private Collection.

Colour Plate 22. Watercolour, 1829

Fishing boat arrived

Very close to the etching of this title in *Shipping & Craft* 1829 and indicating his allegiance to the Bonington ideal. Photo courtesy Derek Abele. Private Collection

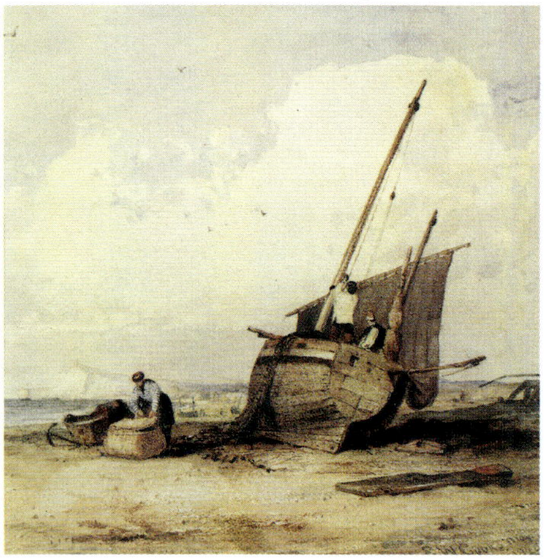

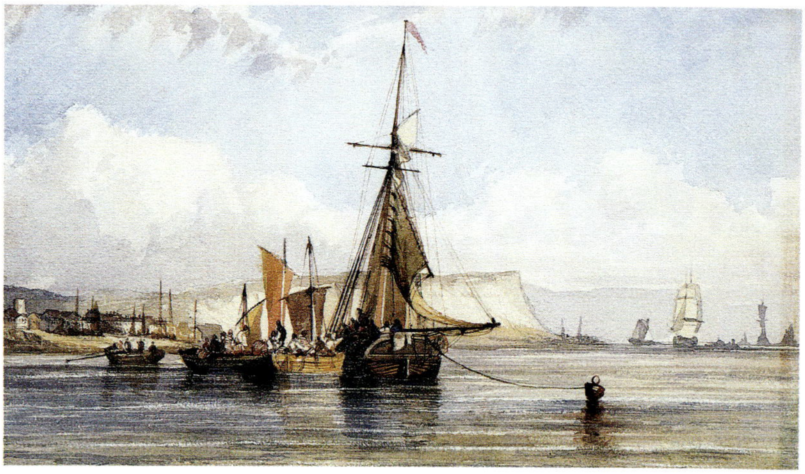

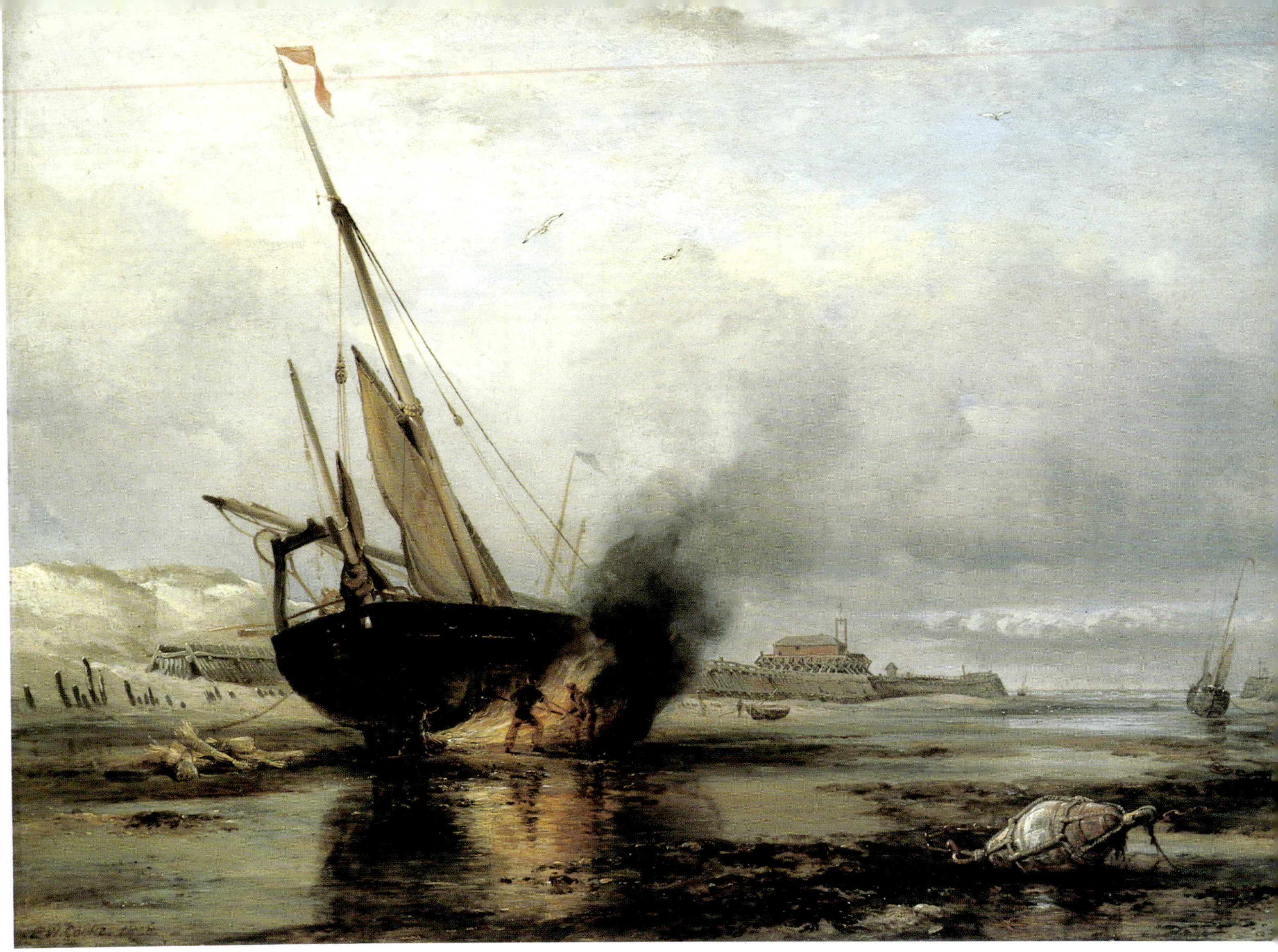

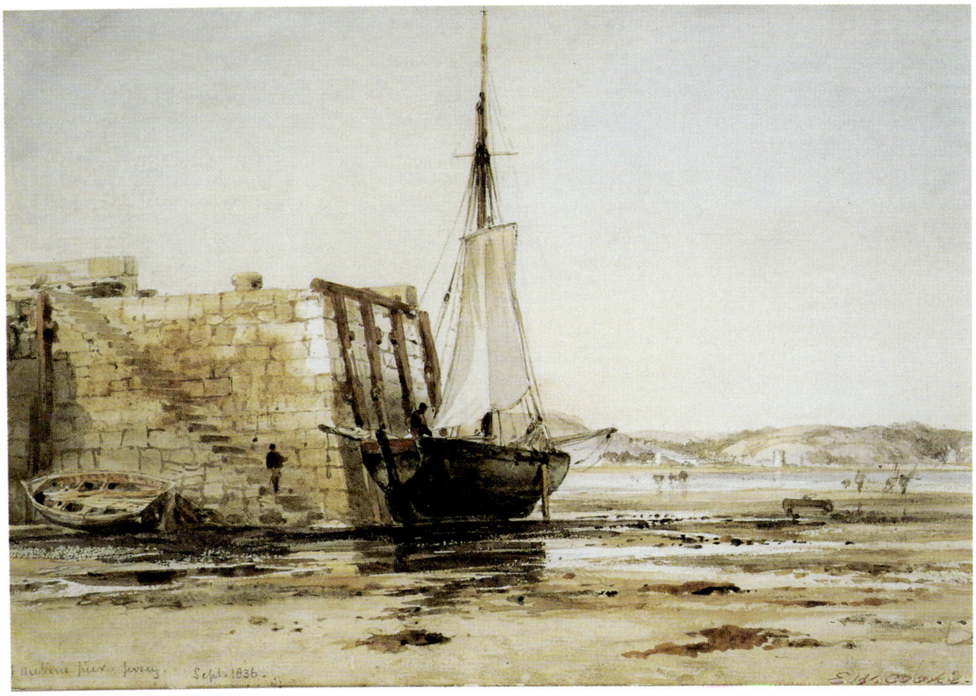

Colour Plate 23. 48/11
Breaming a Calais lugger, low tide
Work, here hard labour in a limited time, rather than picturesque repose, was Cooke's ideal, whether the subject was English, French, Dutch or Italian.

Photo courtesy Board of Trustees of the National Museums & Galleries on Merseyside, Walker Art.Gallery

Colour Plate 24. Watercolour
Gathering seaweed: pier-head St Helier's Jersey, low water

Photo courtesy Private Collection

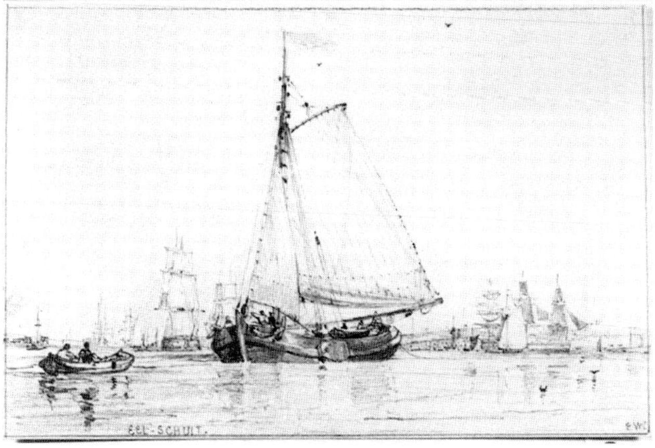

Plate 16 Pencil drawing

Eel schuyt

The Dutch trade to Billingsgate brought these beauties regularly up the Thames. With minor differences, this is a drawing for the etched plate *Dutch Schuyts Blackwall Reach (Shipping & Craft)* (Plate 64) and there is a related watercolour (Plate 65).

Photo courtesy Clarges Gallery

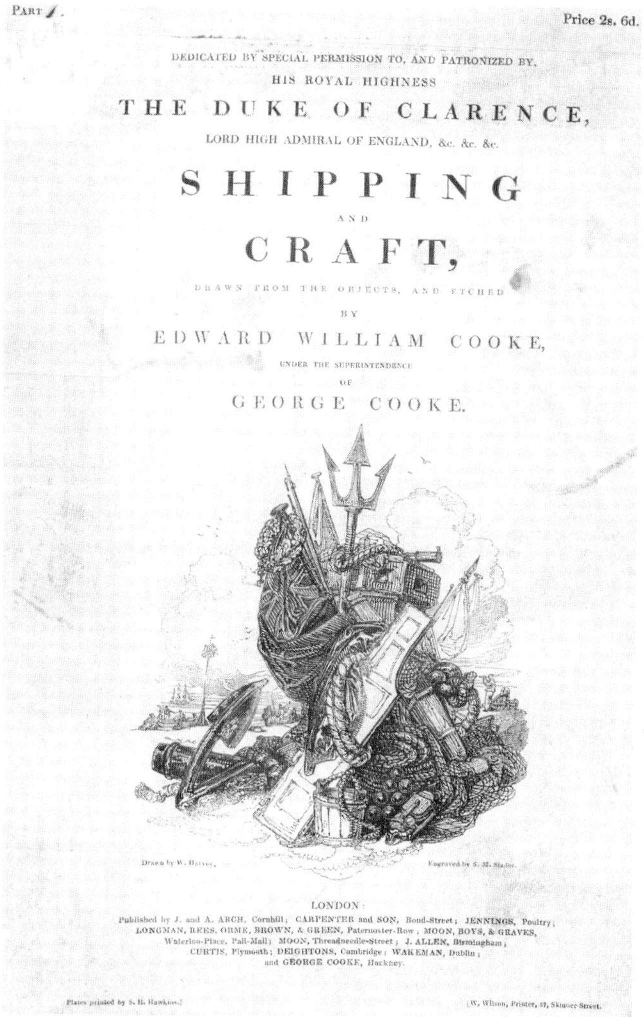

Plate 17. Engraving

Shipping & Craft

The same printed wrapper served for each Part: 1828-9. Few examples have survived as most were discarded in binding.The maritime trophy drawn by William Harvey was engraved on wood by S.M. Sladen. George Cooke, the young artist's mentor throughout, and here acknowledged, is however not named on the final title-page. Publishers and printers are fully listed.

named *Gli Argonauti,* produced a series including eastern craft in his great atlas *Atlante Veneto*, also printed at the end of the seventeenth century. In Holland plates after Jan Porcellis and other painters were engraved and published by Claes Jansz Visscher in 1627, showing small working craft; these plates enjoyed a long life and were reprinted well into the eighteenth century. Etchings by Reinier Nooms, who called himself *Zeeman* and knew his shipping, showed a similar range of everyday working craft. A later publication, Gerrit Groenewegen's *Verzameling van Vier en tachtig Stuks Hollandsche Schepen geteekend en in koper gebragt...* (Collection of Eighty-four Dutch ships drawn and engraved on copper...), Rotterdam, 1789, is a clear ancestor of Cooke's work. The Dutch artist, who had started work as a ship carpenter and was therefore very close to his subject, shows not only the craftsman's pride but also the national pleasure in their varied water-craft. Many different working boats and ships are depicted, with no conscious striving for 'effect', but simply engaged in the operations demanded by wind and tide in getting about their business – *even today they are constantly consulted by maritime historians.* [3]

The marine etchings of the painter Ludolf Backhuizen made about 1700 were a further inspiration for *amateurs* although it is not possible to say how familiar the Cookes were with any of these. Considering both their Continental family ties and their acquisitive habits, as well as the fact that their circle included a number of celebrated collectors and connoisseurs, it seems very likely that they did know them. In his *Fifty Plates of Shipping and Craft* Cooke also avoids the contrived or idealised ship portrait, although some of his plates show single vessels of some size. Grouped small-craft, aground at low

3. Ibid. p.10.

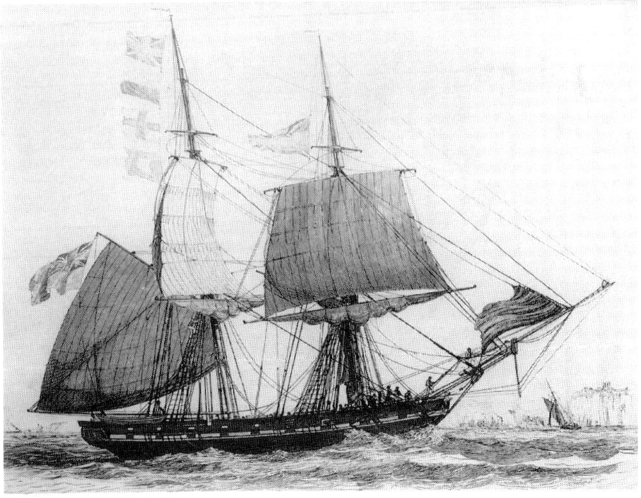

Plate 18. Engraving
Wolf *brig of war off Dover 1829* (see Colour Plate 6)

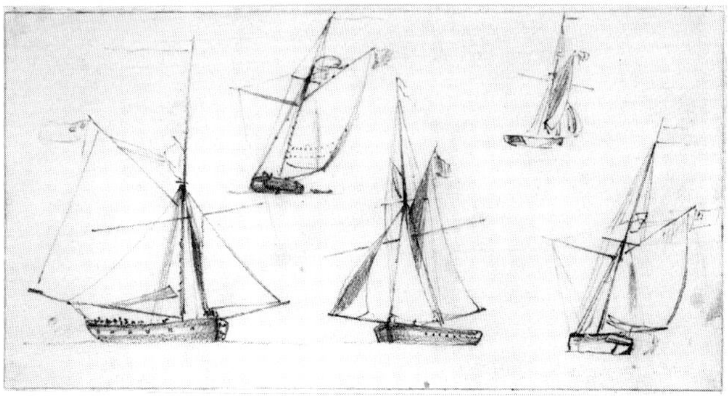

Plate 19. Pencil drawing
Man o War cutter
Memoranda of this quality stocked his sketchbooks which were later dismembered and the contents, classified and mounted, filed away. Photo courtesy Clarges Gallery

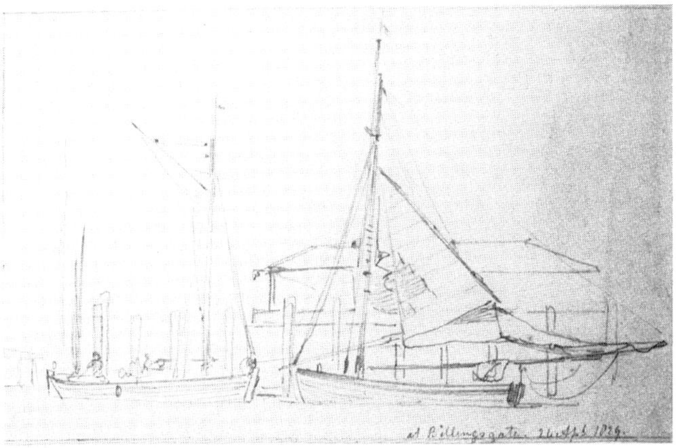

Plate 20. Pencil drawing
At Billingsgate 24th April 1829
While awaiting the arrival of the steamer *United Kingdom,* Cooke drew these smacks at the fish market; the merest outline, but everything needed to re-create the scene.
Photo courtesy Clarges Gallery

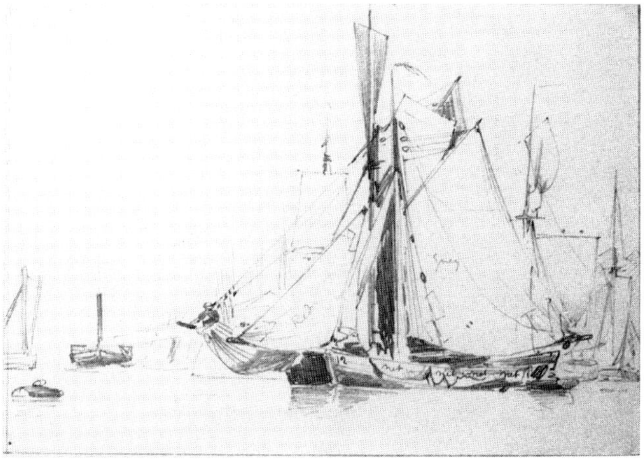

Plate 21. Pencil drawing
Fishing smacks drying nets and sails
Perhaps drawn on the same occasion as Plate 20, this study has a few colour notes added. Photo courtesy Clarges Gallery

water, alongside a wharf or moored offshore, are shown in their working disarray with all the detail relating to their particular occupations, indicating a keen appreciation of their inherent pictorial qualities. A contemporary recognised this in writing that they were *carefully drawn with a true feeling for the aspect and character of the originals as in their everyday use.*[4]

In eighteenth and early nineteenth century Britain, the hard-won sovereignty of the seas was celebrated not only in engravings of battles but also by prints illustrating the shipping of all types upon which so much depended. Men o'war and merchantmen large and small, fishing boats and pleasure craft in all varieties of weather, were popular subjects. The ship specialists came into their own: prints from paintings by Peter Monamy, Samuel Scott, Charles Brooking and others were published singly or in sets, while the *Liber Nauticus* of J.T. Serres, 1804, was practically a marine artist's handbook.

Cornelius Varley's *Etchings of Shipping, Barges, Fishing Boats and other vessels met with on the British coasts, rivers &c* of 1809 would have been familiar to the Cookes while Samuel Prout's *Studies of Boats and Coast Scenery* published by Ackermann c.1816, which were drawing and model-books for students, soft-ground etchings 'in imitation of chalk', were also widely circulated. In France the plates of the *Receuil de*

4. *Biographical & Critical Dictionary of recent & living painters & engravers* by H. Ottley, 1866.

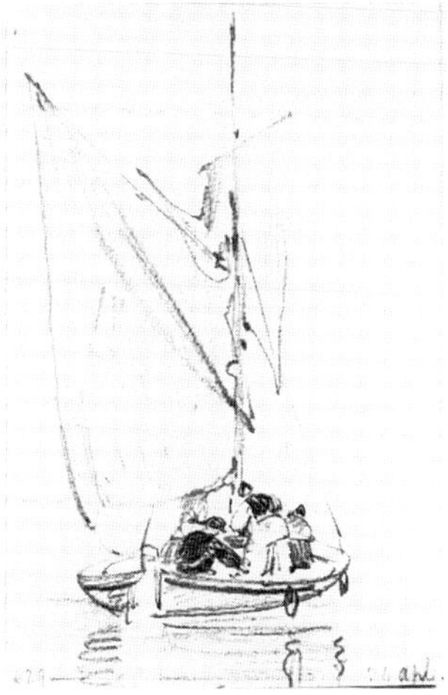

Plate 22. Pencil drawing
Fishing boat at Billingsgate.1829
Elegant craft, lowly, but drawn with understanding.
Photo courtesy Clarges Gallery

Petites Marines of J-J. Baugean, 1815, were small in scale, delicate in touch but eminently satisfying to a seaman's eye. Henry Moses, a London engraver and frequent collaborator with W.B. Cooke, published *Sketches of Shipping* 1824 and *A Marine Sketch-Book* 1825/6, consisting of small, clean etchings in outline, perhaps also meant as drawing-book examples. These are forerunners of Cooke's black and white masterpiece and were probably works which he was determined to surpass.

The Calais-born refugee François Louis Thomas Francia, a watercolour painter who had been a member of the Dr. Munro circle and was later to instruct R.P. Bonington, had when in England supplied four drawings for the Cookes' *Thames* so it is reasonable to suppose that Edward Cooke became familiar with his work although the Frenchman had returned home when the boy was only six. Francia had published four lithographed plates entitled *Marine Sketches* in 1822.

Fifty Plates of Shipping and Craft is a famous work and many of its plates have been reproduced as illustrations in other books over the years; indeed they still are, so strikingly 'right', natural and full of information are they.

The first part appeared at the beginning of March 1828 consisting of three etchings of typical small vessels to be seen on the Thames and a fourth of a group of anchors and quayside clutter with a seaman contentedly smoking his clay. There was no letterpress, the parts were advertised to appear monthly and the printed wrapper was adorned with a

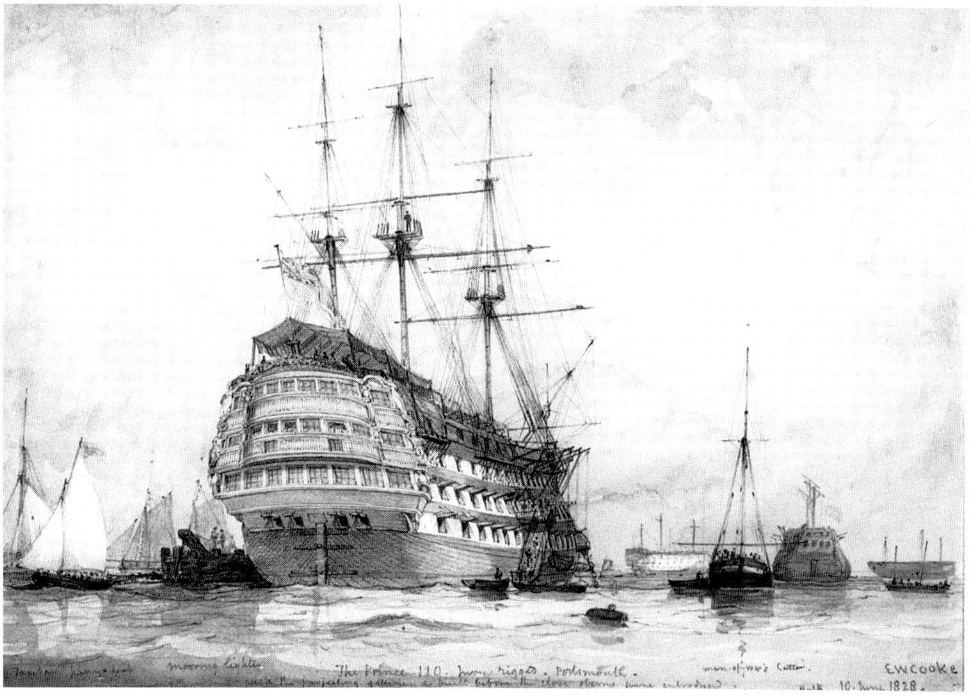

Plate 23. Watercolour
HMS Prince, *First-rate, Portsmouth harbour 10th June, 1828*
This ship, a Trafalgar veteran built in 1788, was remarkable for not having been modernised. Etched as a plate for *Shipping & Craft* (in reverse), it is impressive work for a seventeen-year-old and his notes at the foot are interesting: (left to right) Fareham passage boat. – Mooring lighter.– The Prince 110, Jury rigged, with the projecting galleries as built before the close sterns were introduced.– man of war's Cutter.– Hulk.
Photo courtesy Michael Appleby

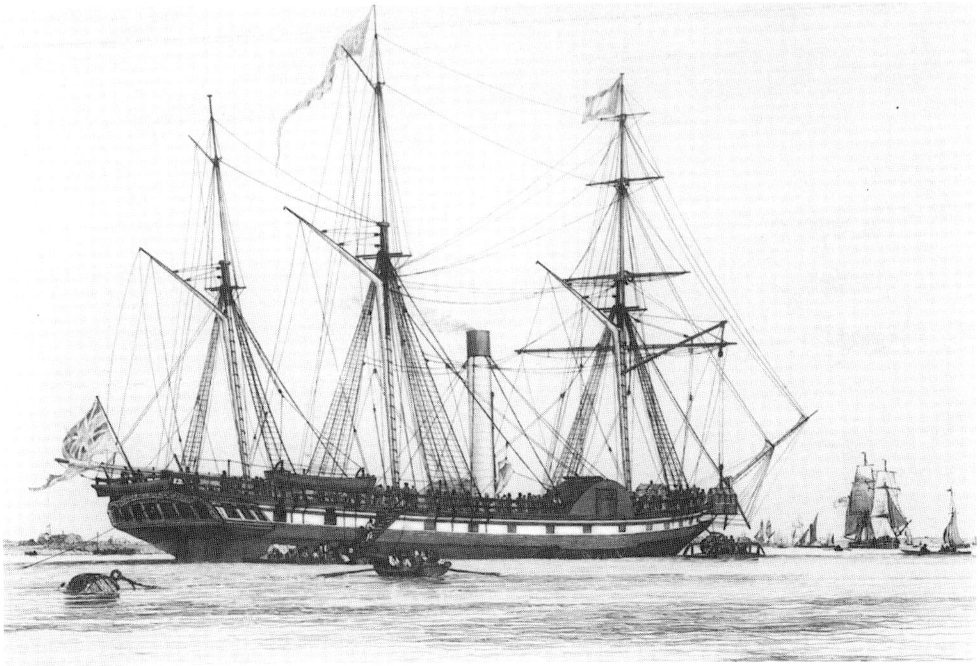

Plate 24. Engraving
United Kingdom *Steam vessel at Greenwich 1829*

grand nautical trophy of anchor, gun, capstan, rudder, ensign, trident and wreath drawn by William Harvey and engraved on wood by S.M. Sladen. It proudly announced that the work was dedicated by special permission and was under the Patronage of the Lord High Admiral, William Henry – Duke of Clarence (later King William IV). William had become heir-presumptive to the throne in 1827 on the death of the Duke of York and, having enjoyed a naval career from midshipman to Admiral of the Fleet, was appointed to the revived great Office of Lord High Admiral. This was short-lived for he entered into it with far too much enthusiasm and the Admiralty Board, whose full title was the Lords Commissioners for Executing the Office of Lord High Admiral, was re-established in August 1828!

The plates were *Drawn from the Objects and Etched by Edward William Cooke* and it was clearly stated to be *Under the Superintendence of George Cooke* (Plate 17) which fact does not appear on the engraved general title-page of the bound book and has therefore usually been ignored. It is plain from the diary however that the young man worked always under his father's eye and had a good deal of practical help on his copper plates. Pencil sketches or watercolour drawings, sometimes both, seem to have been the originals of the etched plates to judge from surviving examples (Colour Plate 6 and Plate 23). The first four parts contained, with the exception of one plate of a brig off Dover, studies of vessels in the Thames and London Docks. At the beginning of June 1828 appeared a notice:

> *Subscribers to this Work are respectfully informed that Part V will be published on August 1st. This small extension of time is required in order to afford an opportunity for obtaining drawings of vessels which are at a distance, especially the larger Ships of War &c. &c.*

The publishers were J. & A. Arch, Cornhill, Carpenter & Son, Bond Street, Longman, Rees, Orme, Brown and Green, Paternoster Row, Moon, Boys and Graves, Waterloo Place, Pall Mall, Moon of Threadneedle Street, J. Allen, Birmingham, Curtis of Plymouth, Deightons of Cambridge, Wakeman of Dublin and George Cooke of Hackney.

The twelfth and last part of *Shipping* appeared in December 1829 and the engraved title of *Fifty Plates of Shipping and Craft* bears this date.

The title-page and the table of contents were engraved, each having a vignette which counted as plates, hence the forty-eight became fifty.The cost of each part was 2s.6d.,

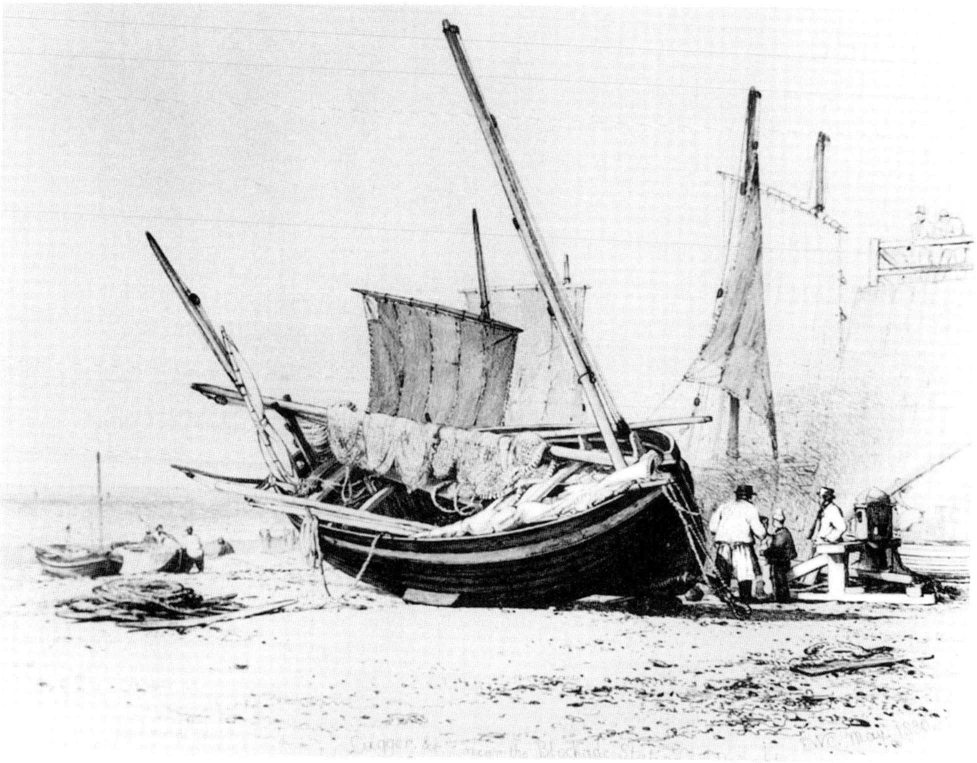

Plate 25. Engraving
Brighton lugger near the Blockade station 1830

half a crown, or as a volume bound in glazed cloth £1.16s.0d. Quarto copies at 4s.0d. each part or £2.14s.0d. a bound volume and 'large paper' versions were advertised and sets of proofs on India paper were also available.

Herbert Goodall, a grandson of Edward Goodall the engraver, writing to Sir Frank Short RA in 1907, many years after Cooke's time, claimed that the excellence of *Shipping* was due to George Cooke's engraving and etching, maintaining on Goodall family authority that Edward William's draughtsmanship was inferior to that enshrined in the prints. Professional jealousy would seem to have been at the root of that statement, for there is abundant evidence to the contrary in surviving drawings. In any case no secret was made of the father's participation in the work.[5]

Some of the appeal of this book today is due, in the words of the marine artist Roger Finch, to Cooke's faithful recording of a generation of sailing craft which, by the time photography had become possible, had largely disappeared. He *communicates a boy's enthusiastic discovery of the world of canvas, rope and wooden ships with preternatural technical skill and understanding.*[6] There were few craft which escaped the young artist's attention for the smallest fishing boats working in river or from beach had characteristics of shape, construction and gear which rendered their type highly individual. The nature of their catches and of their fishing grounds, their method of working, their markets and other factors had produced an evolution which Cooke now recorded. His images, because of this analytical drawing, have an impact which is found in the works of only a few artists. Finch continues: *One might be forgiven for feeling his subtle skill and intuitive selectivity of detail in his vast output of sketches mark him essentially as a graphic artist.* That later in his paintings the primacy of draughtsmanship is evident has been frequently noticed by the critics. The same informed writer comments on various plates from a deep understanding not only of art but also of nautical development. To take one example, *The Hatch boat, double reef'd off Gravesend* is a scene on the Thames where returning sea-going fishing smacks were met by the hatch-boats and transferred their catch. The fish were kept alive in wells in the hatch-boat where sea water flowed freely, but eventually the severe pollution of river and the expansion of the railways for carriage combined to kill the system.

5. Holograph letter, present whereabouts unknown.
6. *Shipping & Craft by E.W.Cooke. A facsimile edition with descriptive notes* by Roger Finch. Masthead Press, 1970.

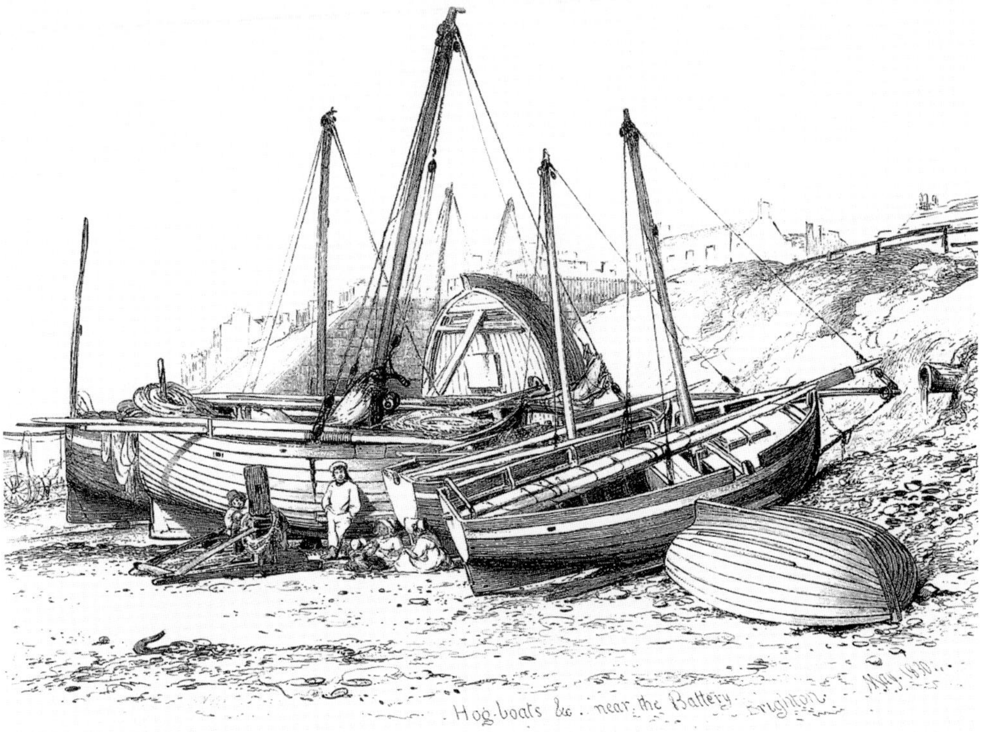

Plate 26. Engraving
Brighton Hog-boats near the Battery, May 1830
From the Coast Sketches – Brighton set No.10 later added to *Shipping & Craft* to form the second edition. The difference in these plates – a free, almost a holiday, atmosphere – does not detract from the careful recording of fishing craft.

First-Class West Indiaman (THETIS Capt. Burton) Getting under weigh off the Needles I.W. This was the vessel in which Cooke had made many drawings and the plate is doubtless a tribute to his friend the Captain. The ship at anchor with her boats alongside reveals, on close inspection, activity on deck and aloft. It is, writes Finch, *noticeable that her main and mizzen stays'ls have been replaced by trys'ls set from gaffs and that her bowsprit and jibbooms have grown to tremendous lengths in order to achieve a balanced sail plan.* This is technical comment on the fine adjustment of a crack ship in a lucrative trade, for she sailed with sugar.[7]

Coast Sketches

In the late summer of 1830 a sketching tour of the Sussex and Kent coasts produced drawings for a new series to be called at first *Marine Sketches,* and the Cookes set about planning a prospectus, a cover and the price. *This work will be continued in separate and distinct portions: each, complete in itself, will contain Twelve Plates of the most interesting features of the Marine Character of the Coast of England... The Work is uniform with E.W. Cooke's* Shipping and Craft.

A copy of Louis Francia's 1822 *Marine Sketches* was purchased by Cooke in 1830 and it is odd to find a statement in a notice on this Anglo-French artist in the *Dictionary of National Biography,* contributed by the art critic and poet Cosmo Monkhouse, suggesting that *some of his drawings were engraved to illustrate a book of sketches of shipping by E.W. Cooke.* It is difficult to detect any similarity between Francia's loose blacklead-style studies (printed by the lithographer Charles Hullmandel) and Cooke's fine little etchings. Perhaps for a landsman concerned with other matters and sparing only a cursory glance (for whom one boat could look much like the next) there might appear to be some link. However none, other than that of general subject, can possibly be discerned, so one is left speculating on the origin of the statement. Could it have been jealousy on someone's part, an expressed opinion that the critic did not trouble to verify? It may be that the clash of titles caused the Cookes to change the name of their new

7. Ibid.

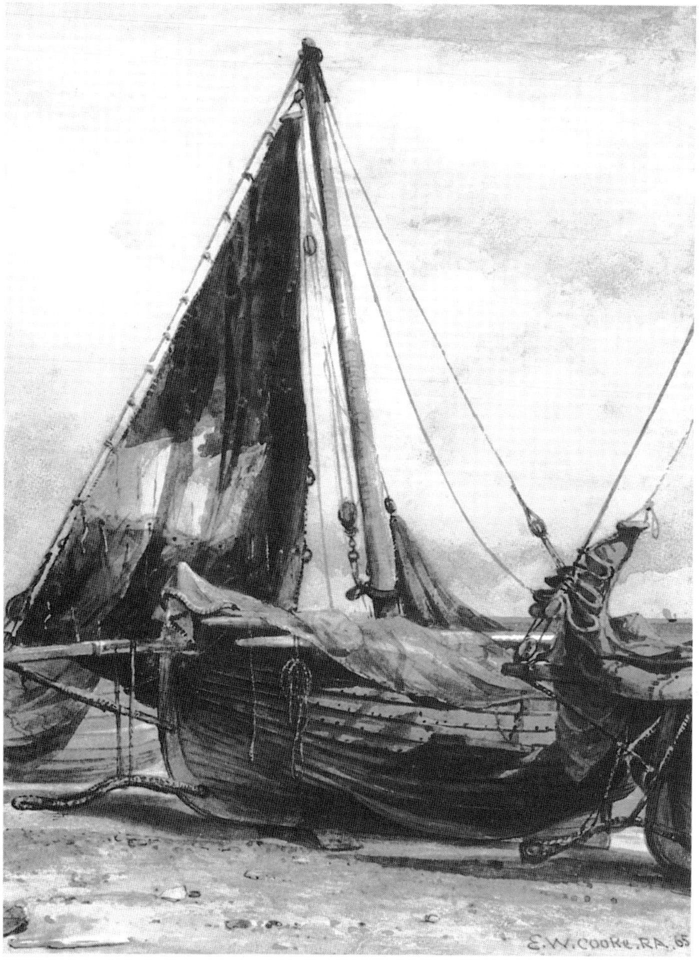

Plate 27. Watercolour
Brighton Hog-boat drying sails
Probably a drawing of the 1830s, signed for his Christie's sale of 1865 where it was Lot 14, sold Whitehead for £7.10s.0d.
Photo courtesy Martyn Gregory. Private Collection

publication, for Francia was still alive, although back in Calais, and it was henceforward referred to as *Twelve Plates of Coast Sketches – BRIGHTON – Drawn and Etched by E.W. Cooke – (Royal Quarto price 6 shillings).* Twelve plates were engraved and published in 1830 while the wrapper promised that *Hastings* was in preparation and would appear in the course of the next year.

However, the Cookes' series was abandoned, but whether from a lack of subscribers or pressure of other work, or both, does not appear. John Constable, whose visits to Brighton had been in regard to his wife's health, professed no great love of the place, but it was the sea and the boats which he mentioned to his clergyman friend at Salisbury. The ocean's *everlasting voice* had been a phrase of the Rev John Fisher's, but the painter found it drowned in the din of Piccadilly by the sea-side. His account is as graphic as a Regency caricature: *Ladies dressed and undressed – Gentlemen in morning gowns and slippers on or without them altogether about knee deep in the breakers – footmen – children – nursery maids. dogs, boys, preventive service men (with hangers and pistols) rotten fish and those hideous amphibious animals the old bathing women... nothing here for the painter but the breakers and sky... the fishing boats are picturesque but not so much so as the Hastings boats.*[8] He found the subject matter hackneyed and incapable of the *beautiful sentiment* which his pastoral art afforded. Interestingly he inveighed against hackneyed sea-shore subjects stealing the market from his landscapes but here was the young Edward Cooke looking hard at the despised hog-boats and fishing luggers on the Brighton strand (Plates 25 to 27).

The twelve plates are in style more free than *Shipping* and it has been well said that in them the artist *lost nothing of his capacity for searching observation and the finely judged feeling for scale and depth.*[9] The same critic commends Cooke's *unsurpassed creative command of the medium and powerful draughtsmanship which makes them*

8. Constable op. cit., Vol VI..
9. Finch op.cit.

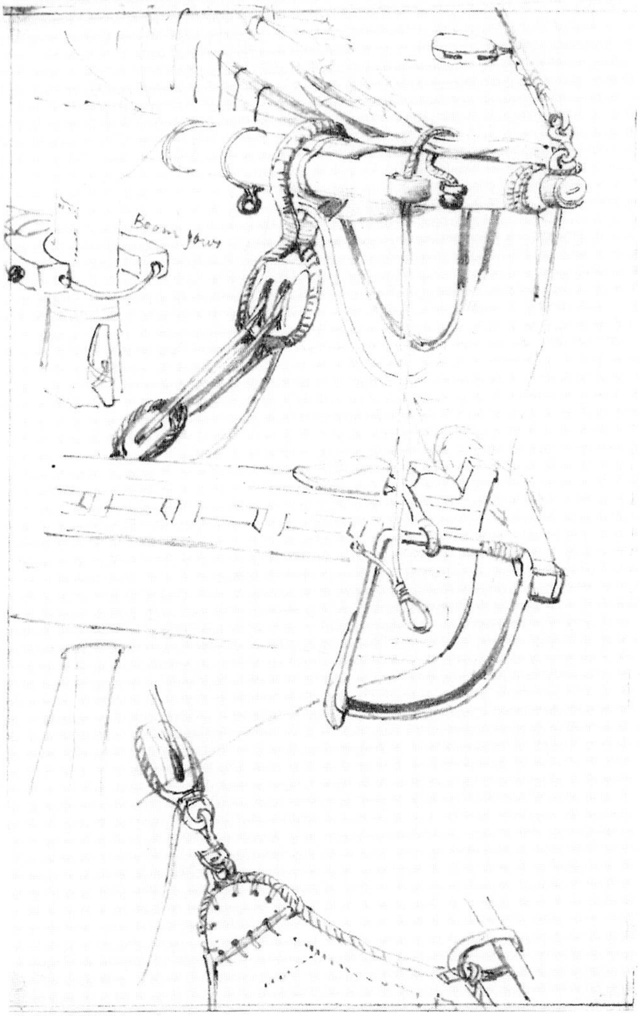

Plate 28. Pencil drawing
Details on deck and over-side Photo courtesy C.R. Cooke, OBE

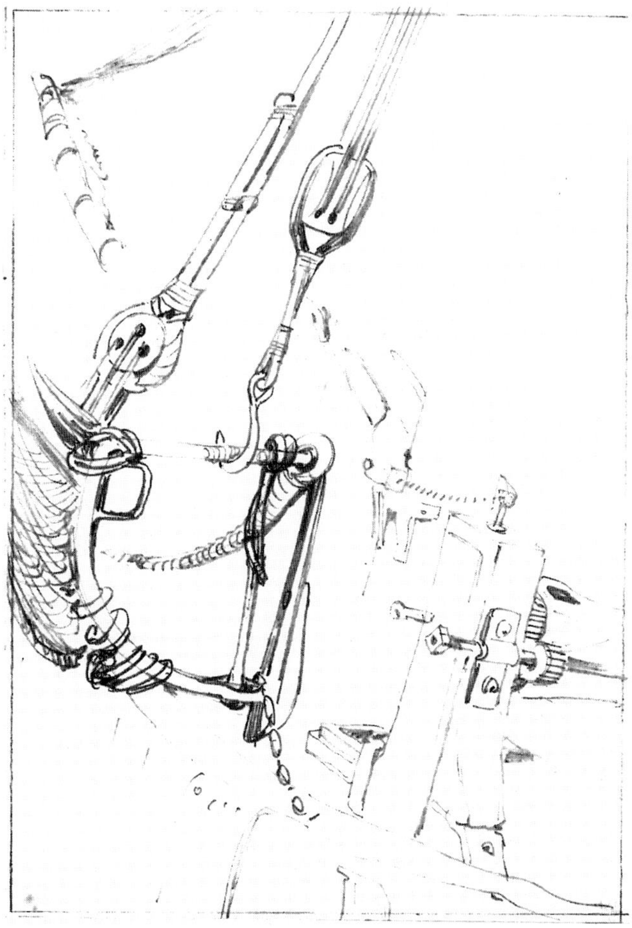

Plate 29. Pencil drawing
Some of the gear of a beam trawler
This is how it was. Photo courtesy C.R. Cooke, OBE

aesthetically the finest of the collection. It is perhaps significant that from diary entries it appears that for this set Cooke had no help from his father who was working against time to finish a plate of Gibraltar from Col Robt. Batty's drawing.

Contemporary criticism was also favourable and on the same lines. The London *Literary Gazette* reviewed Part I and pronounced *There is in our eyes much greater merit in such etchings as these in which the character of every object is marked by a light but firm hand... than in those more laboured productions where every inch of the copper or steel is covered with work that in many instances might have been advantageously spared.* Taste and feeling as an artist was demonstrated and they hoped that Mr Cooke could be induced to proceed with his work exhibiting ...*all the distinctive features which the coasts of this island presents.* It is sad to record that the proposed Hastings plates seem never to have been even started.

The British Coast

William Daniell RA had published his striking aquatints of the *Voyage Round Great Britain* between 1813 and 1825 while Turner's series of coastal views in particular had helped establish this *genre.*

Evidently still convinced of the appeal of this eternal theme, the mystery of tides and the meeting of sea and land, the Cookes planned another series of plates with a shift of emphasis, being of somewhat larger size and illustrating coastal topography rather than

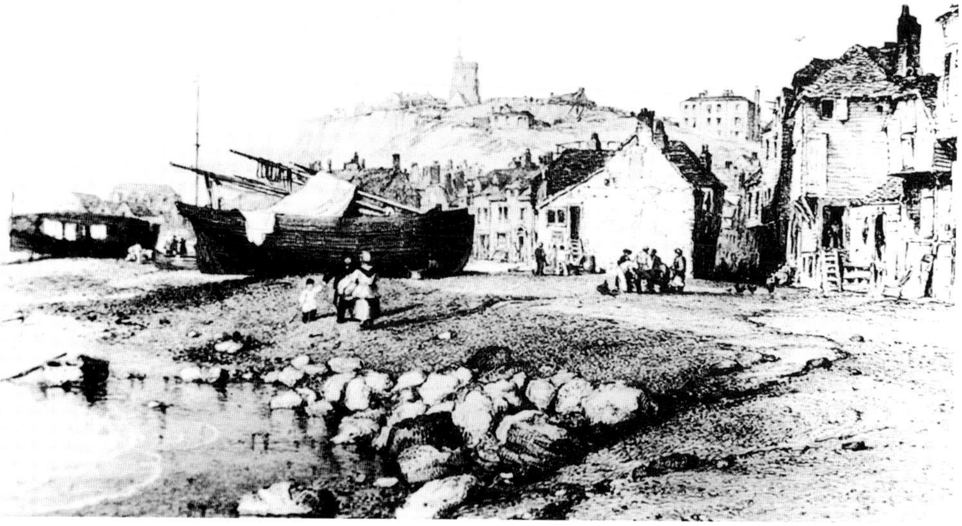

Plate 30. Engraving
Folkestone
Intended as the first of a new series, The British Coast, this was not copper but a steel plate on which he had his cousin William John Cooke's help. It was eventually put with others to form the 2nd edition of *Shipping & Craft.*

specifically boats and small craft. Having collected eighty sketches on tour, Edward began finishing several and reducing them: Ramsgate, Sandwich, Pegwell, Deal with a collier stranded, Walmer Castle and Dover. The new work was to be called *The British Coast* and three views dated 1831 of Kingsgate, Folkestone (Plate 30) and Dover were in fact published. It is curious that for these they used steel plates brought home by George Cooke in spite of his objection to the *hated metal.* Edward's cousin Bill, otherwise W.J. Cooke, the expert on steel and Society of Arts gold medallist, came to instruct and assist with *Folkestone.* Clarkson Stanfield's help was also enlisted for the drawings; he worked up the Dover drawing early in 1831 and sent down another of Ramsgate, but these are a group apart. *Stanfield's talent, used to stage scenery, overwhelmed Edward Cooke's more subtle approach, they lack involvement with the subject* wrote Finch.[10] In the event the series did not proceed and there seems little doubt that George Cooke's existing commitments and perhaps his state of health would not allow further major work, his son's part in it notwithstanding. The three steel plates may indicate a change in attitude for the elder Cooke suffered financially from his adherence to copper, but there is an intriguing side-light on the use of steel. Unlike the soft traditional copper – of which it was stated that only thirty really fine proofs could be obtained from a plate before re-working became necessary[11] – there was no appreciable wear on the hard steel plate in printing so that late impressions were as clear as the first proofs. The coveted first pulls from a copper plate – such as were demanded by Turner from his engravers, with some retained by the engravers themselves and known in the trade as *engravers' proofs* – were long sought after by collectors. These had now become a thing of the past. *Men of taste do not now care to collect engravings; the art has deteriorated, and the greatest of our living engravers are neglected* wrote the Redgrave brothers in 1866.[12]

In order to cut their losses, the Cookes conceived the idea of combining the fifteen plates of 1830-31 with *Shipping* and altered the etched title to *Sixty-five Plates of Shipping and Craft* although the original date of publication, 1829, was allowed to remain. The final chapter was written in 1840 when the copper plates were sold (for £18) to Henry Bohn, the same London publisher who acquired the plates of Cotman's soft ground etchings and was a notorious re-printer.[13] In typical commercial fashion he

10. Ibid.
11. *Reminiscences,* T.F. Dibden, 1836, quoting Thomas Lahee, printer.
12. Redgrave 1866, Vol. I, p.464.

continued to issue impressions of *Shipping* (on wove paper) until the finer passages on the copper were much worn and faint; these were sold in a brown stamped cloth publisher's binding with a gilt ship tooled on the upper cover, from a drawing specially supplied for it by the artist.

London Bridge

As early as 1826, when building works on a new London Bridge had begun, Cooke made some pencil studies for his father's *London*, Frederick Goodall noted:

> *He worked at them the whole of one winter and told me his fingers became so numb he could not cut a point to his pencils. But, strange to say, he managed to draw with his numbed fingers, and used to take two dozen pencils with him having their points already cut... Cooke must have suffered severely, as his lips in after-life showed how much they had been blistered with cold – the top lip was cut through with a deep line. But these were grand works, and the plates were splendidly engraved by his father – the finest things in their way, without doubt, that George Cooke had ever done.*[14]

Goodall was remembering his long-deceased friend and reference to photographs makes it appear that the disfigurement from frost-bite was on the lower lip. In spite of Goodall's remarks, a large part of the processes of putting the drawings on to the plates before engraving and etching was done by Edward Cooke himself. There was indeed no open acknowledgement of George Cooke's help although it is quite clear from the diary that as usual he worked on almost all the plates at some stage. Like *Shipping* it was in fact a joint venture, though doubtless the parent was intent on giving his talented son's work the highest possible degree of finish, according to the standards of the time. By 1 August 1831, when King William IV opened the new bridge, Edward Cooke had made several

13. *Steel Engraved Book Illustration in England* by B. Hunnisett,1980.
14. Goodall op. cit., p.328.

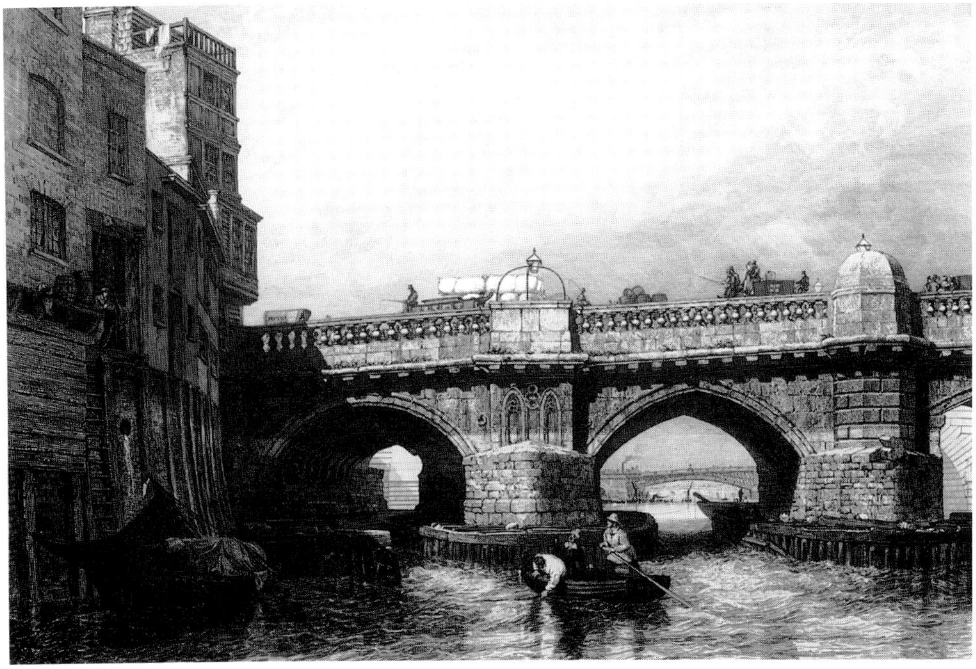

Plate 31. Engraving
Old London Bridge, Southwark end.1832

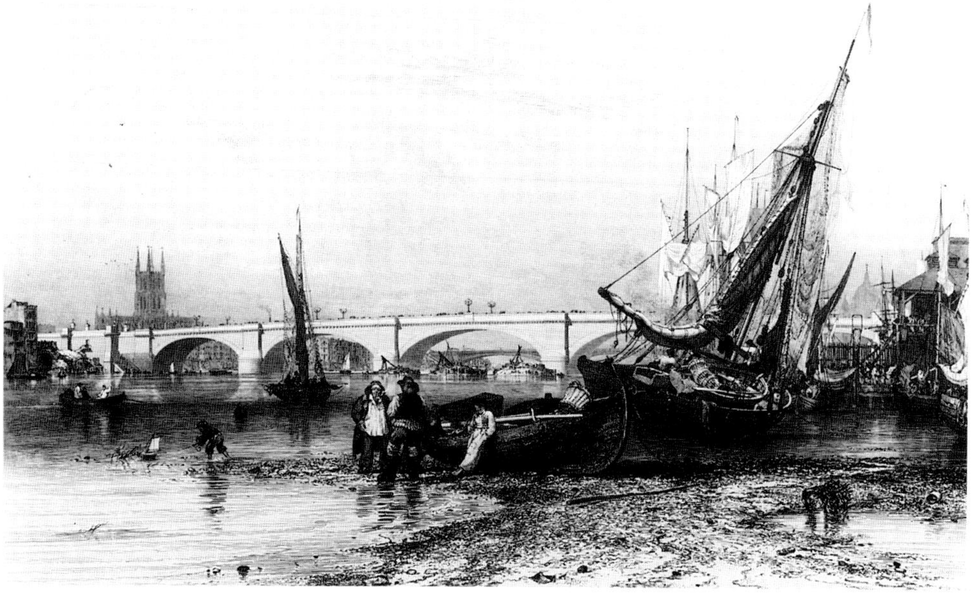

Plate 32. Engraving
New London Bridge, Billingsgate, low water.1832

detailed drawings. By September he had begun to etch the first of twelve plates and when the demolition ('delapidation' it was so properly called) of the old bridge began in the following month, he was there to record this work as well.

Views of the Old and the New London Bridges. Drawn and Etched by Edward William Cooke With Scientific and Historical Notices of the two Bridges... by George Rennie FRS. was published in April 1833 (Plates 31 to 34). The plate sizes vary from 12in. x 16in. (30cm x 40cm) down, the engraved surfaces in proportion.

A total of seventy original studies, many made with the aid of the *camera lucida*, survive as a collection presented to the City of London by Sir David Salomons Bt, MP, Lord Mayor, a later patron and friend of the artist. Reproductions published by the London Topographical Society in 1970 show eight of his pencil drawings dating between 1826 and 1832. Some of Cooke's sketches made on the day of the Royal opening of the bridge from an arranged vantage point for Clarkson Stanfield were of use in that painter's large canvas, a commission from the King to record the brilliant occasion.[15]

The *Literary Gazette* approved of *Old & New London Bridges: E.W.Cooke is the son of Mr George Cooke and is evidently a "chip off the old block". His style is precisely that which delights us: sufficiently free without being careless, sufficiently finished without being niggled. His points of view are well chosen, figures and other accessories introduced with spirit and skill.* The critic indulged in a little playful misquotation from Robert Burns' *Brig of Ayr:*

> New Brig was buskit in a brand new coat
> That he at Lon'on frae ane Adams got!.

A later notice for the work confirmed their favourable opinion *...and more than confirmed:... all strikingly picturesque and are executed with a masculine vigour and freedom which we have never seen surpassed... especially happy in the manner in which he groups and avails himself of accessories especially the Chapel Pier Demolition.* The chip and the block were working in close harmony, so Goodall was not so wide of the mark and again he was doubtless quoting common knowledge.

The last mention of etching and engraving in the diary occurs in 1834 on the completion of the *Botanical Cabinet* and *London*. He noted that he had suggested a work of shipping in lithography after a trial at the end of 1835 under the tuition of Charles Hullmandel who brought two prepared stones down to Barnes. No immediate results are recorded of

15. Royal Academy Exhibition 1832 No 313 and *The Spectacular Career of Clarkson Stanfield* by Dr. P. Van der Merwe, 1979, p.110.

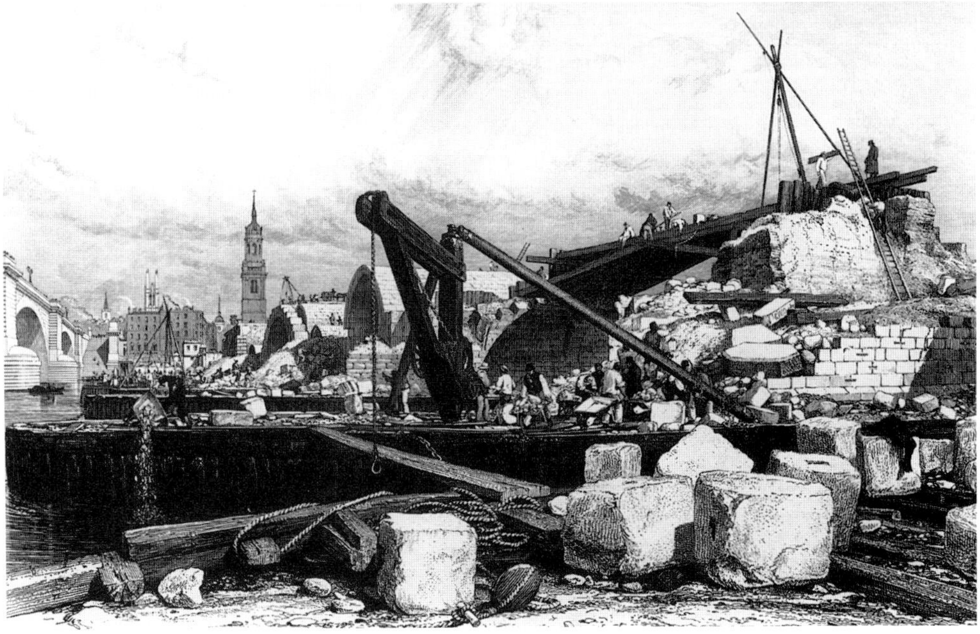

Plate 33. Engraving
Old London Bridge Demolition, low water 1832

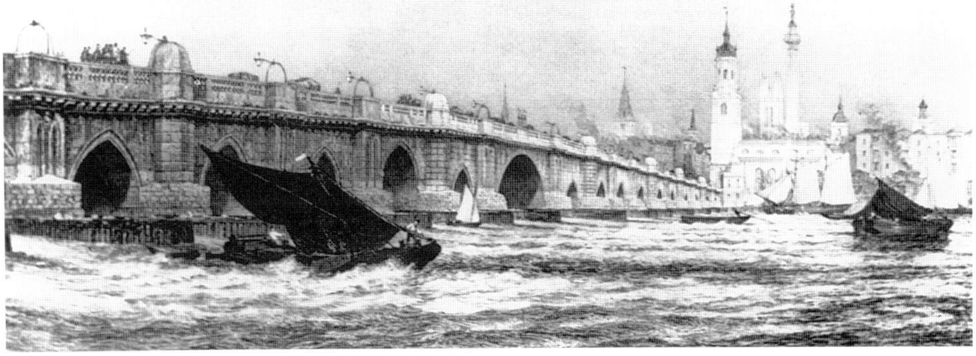

Plate 34. Engraving
Barge shooting the bridge.

this experiment although proofs of a lithographed view of Dort are mentioned a few years afterwards, when a proposal to issue some views in Holland were turned down by the publisher Moon.

Cooke continued to render valuable aid to his Uncle William by frequently touching proofs, not from plates of his own drawings but from those of others which W.B. Cooke was publishing. The superior eye and hand could pull together any weakness of drawing, particularly in perspective and the elusive shapes of boats. Putting the figures into a view of the Coliseum is mentioned and for *Richmond and its Surrounding Scenery,* 1832, with text by Mrs Barbara Hofland, Edward etched the shipping detail in his firm style for the plate of *Richmond Bridge and the Rustic Arbour,* leaving his initials on the stern of a barge.

By this time he was working in watercolour following the example and the style of Thomas Boys and through him the late Richard Parkes Bonington; as well he had already begun to try oils by 1832, though nothing so early can now be identified.

Chapter 4

WATERCOLOUR DRAWINGS

While he entered into the spirit and lively handling of the new style which he saw in the work of Bonington and the survivors of his circle, Thomas Shotter Boys, William Callow and others, a style with an exciting freshness in treating marine subjects after his own inclination, Cooke the watercolourist turns out to be chiefly the young Edward Cooke. He used the medium throughout his life, it is true, but mostly for working studies. What has come to be known as *le Boningtonisme*[1] is very evident in drawings from his first tour of the coast of northern France in 1833. Although he returned with a considerable quantity of work, to his father's great pleasure, he seems even then to have had a leaning towards oil painting.

In 1832, when he had come of age and was beginning to enjoy a reputation, he commenced keeping a record of watercolour drawings completed, sold or presented, which he continued up to 1839 (Appendix 3).[2] There are many small sepia sketches of his compositions, a *liber studiorum* done with pen, sepia ink and a finger-tip, which identify surviving drawings clearly enough (Plate 35). From the notes one can see the patronage of friends like the Rosier family, stockbrokers, dealers like Griffith and Colnaghi and a widening circle as his reputation grew; prices and sizes are noted while

1. *Bonington, Francia and Wyld* by Marcia Pointon, 1985, p.14.
2. Cooke MSS 33.

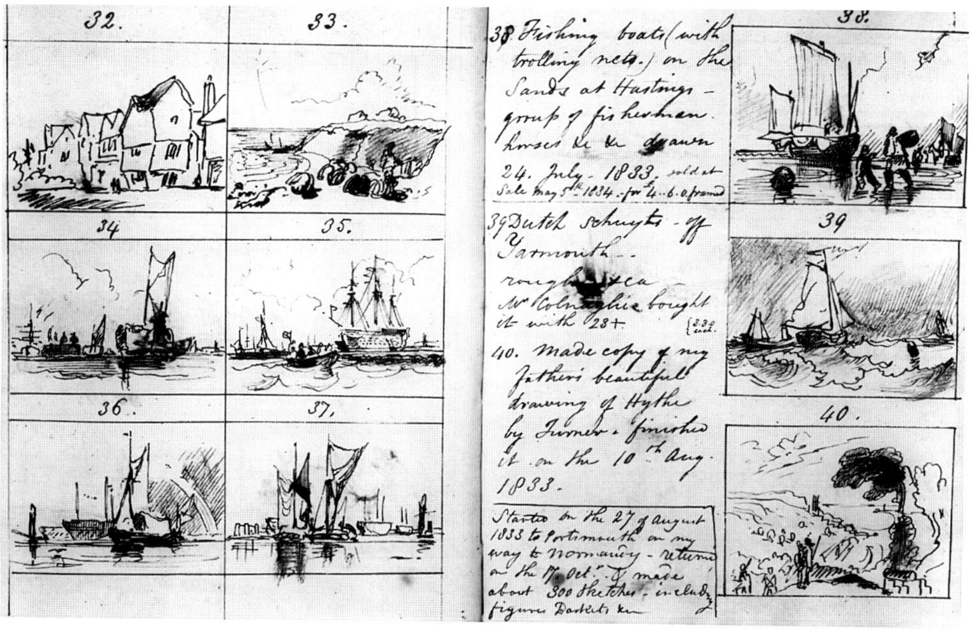

Plate 35.
Double page of the artist's *Liber* containing thumbnail sketches of many completed early watercolour drawings, and Lists (see Appendix 3)
Those indicated include Nos. 34, Private collection, 35, Victoria & Albert Museum, 36, National Maritime Museum, 37, Paul Mellon Collection and 39 Private Collection. No 40, his copy of J.M.W. Turner's Hythe, is still in the family collection.

From Cooke MSS No.33. Collection of C.R .Cooke, OBE

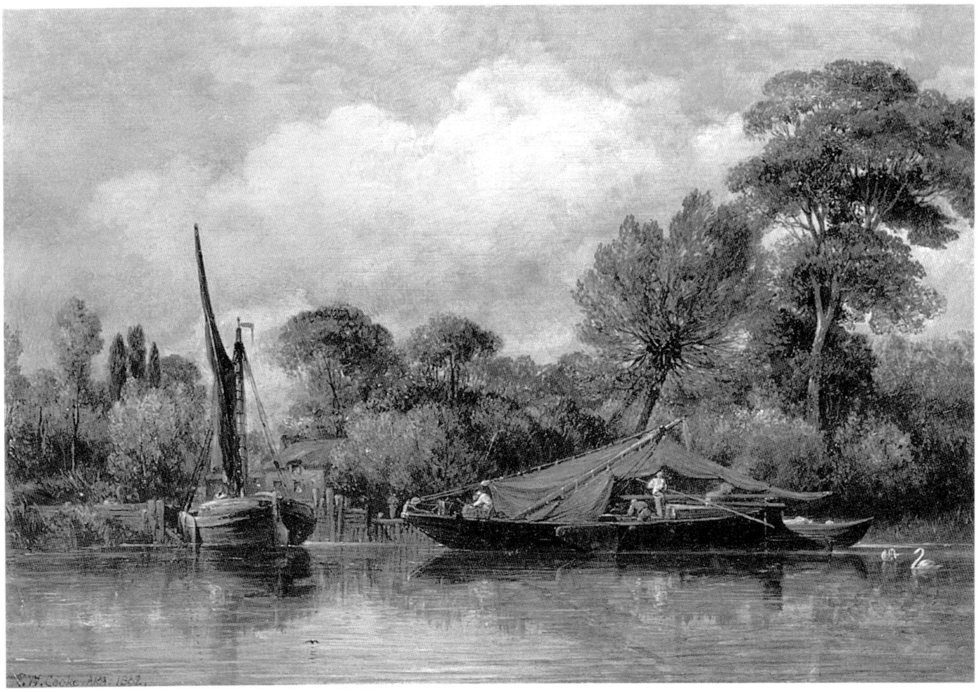

Plate 36. 47/4

Opposite my house at Barnes

Although signed and dated 1862, Cooke had removed to Kensington in 1849. His oils from 1835 included river scenes and this bears similarities to paintings at Oxford in 1848. It shows the spritsail barges which he often drew and also has an echo of John Constable, whose work he had seen with Sheepshanks. Photo courtesy Agnews

occasionally his original title gives valuable information.

No. 35, *The Temeraire 90, off Sheerness with the Admiral in his gig &c, 1st July 1833* is now in the collection of the Victoria & Albert Museum. The identity of the three-decker which was to inspire Turner in perhaps his most famous painting was hitherto unsuspected.[3] It was bought with others by Benjamin Austen. No 37, *Barges or tide-waiters – drying Sails (calm) off Bombproof battery – Medway 8th July* identifies Gillingham and the familiar spritsail barges of south-eastern England, here shown awaiting the ebb tide which will aid their passage down to the sea. It was bought by Moon, the picture dealer and print publisher, at the time and now represents Cooke in the celebrated Mellon Collection of British Art at Yale.

It is not easy to discover from diary entries which of his work was in colour, but *drawing* usually indicates watercolours while *sketches* denote pencil. Nor is the date of his first watercolour work at all certain, although the plant drawings for Loddiges certainly entailed its use.

Drawings of 1829 are listed but the majority of the larger finished works belong to the 1830s, with the British national collections each having good examples.

His use of the knife for scratching out highlights, and of gum for 'varnishing' and giving depth to colour, were devices which he would have noted in the work of others, but the characteristic of Cooke's drawings which makes him immediately recognisable is the superb grasp of the essentials of build and rig of sailing vessels. There is nothing tentative or approximate and even among expert marine draughtsmen he stands out.

The Kent coast tour of 1830 had resulted in a group of watercolours, not necessarily made on the spot, but many composed and executed in the studio from sketches. The first subject in his *liber* is of *Old Stairs Blockade Station,* the anti-smuggling post under the cliffs to the south of Kingsdown by Deal in Kent, near the South Foreland.

His experience had been broadened by handling and examining in his father's studio some of the best work to be seen in London. John Sell Cotman had spent Christmas 1828 with George Cooke and his family in Hackney. He was to contribute drawings for *London and its Vicinity* and Edward Cooke accompanied him sketching and also to show

3. *Turner Studies* Vol. 8 No. 2, p. 59

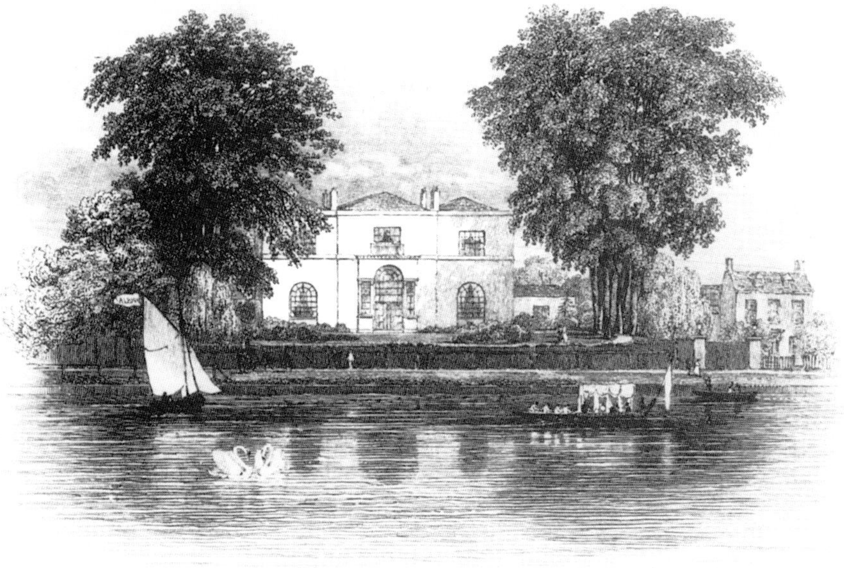

Plate 37. Engraving
Albion House, The Terrace, Barnes, Surrey.1831
The elegant house where a boarding school for young ladies was conducted by the artist's mother. The etching was used as a vignette on the scholars' Commendation awards.

him some of the sights. Turner, Cotman, Cox, Bonington, Stanfield, Prout and Stark, the list lengthens as the diary's pages are turned. It is small wonder, with such examples frequently passing before him in the studio for engraving and with such a talent as Edward Cooke possessed, if the urge to emulate was irresistible.

And it was no cursory examination that the young artist would make: close scrutiny under the best light and with the finest glass would reveal the surface and also what lay beneath the surface. The secrets of the art of watercolour must in any case be delivered up for an engraver's analysis of the artist's intention as well as his method.

In London at this time there were regular meetings for discussion and informal exhibition of works which were held in convenient premises. The Artists' and Amateurs' Conversazione dating from 1829 took place during the winter season on Saturday evenings at the Freemasons' Tavern, Great Queen Street, Lincoln's Inn Fields. Meetings of the New Conversazione which became the Graphic Society took place on Wednesdays at the Thatched House Tavern in St. James's Street. This was founded by William Brockedon early in 1833 and endured for over half a century; it is not to be confused with the Chalcographic Society to which engravers only belonged and which met at members' homes but to which apparently the Cookes did not subscribe. Rules for the Conversazioni were formulated: the composition of the first was to be 120 artists and eighty amateurs; the second was evenly divided but it boasted Rule 10: there was to be no talk of price or sale! Another group was launched to tap the wealth east of Temple Bar for there were certainly patrons among City men. At the meetings to which members, dealers and patrons as well as artists thronged, recent works were exhibited and criticised, providing a valuable exchange which embraced a wide range of talent.

J.S. Cotman recorded his impressions on seeing J.F. Lewis' drawings from Spain when he attended two Conversazioni with the Cookes in January 1834: *I saw three hundred most splendid drawings by Lewis. Words cannot convey to you their splendour. My poor reds, blues and Yellows, for which I have in Norwich been so much abused and broken hearted about, are faded fades to what I saw there.*[4]

April 1829 saw the Cooke family remove finally from Hackney to a new address – Albion House, The Terrace, Barnes, Surrey, where Mrs George Cooke was to conduct a boarding school for young ladies (Plate 37). Here the processes of engraving continued

4. Letter to Dawson Turner quoted A.P. Oppé, *Early Victorian England,* 1934, p.151.

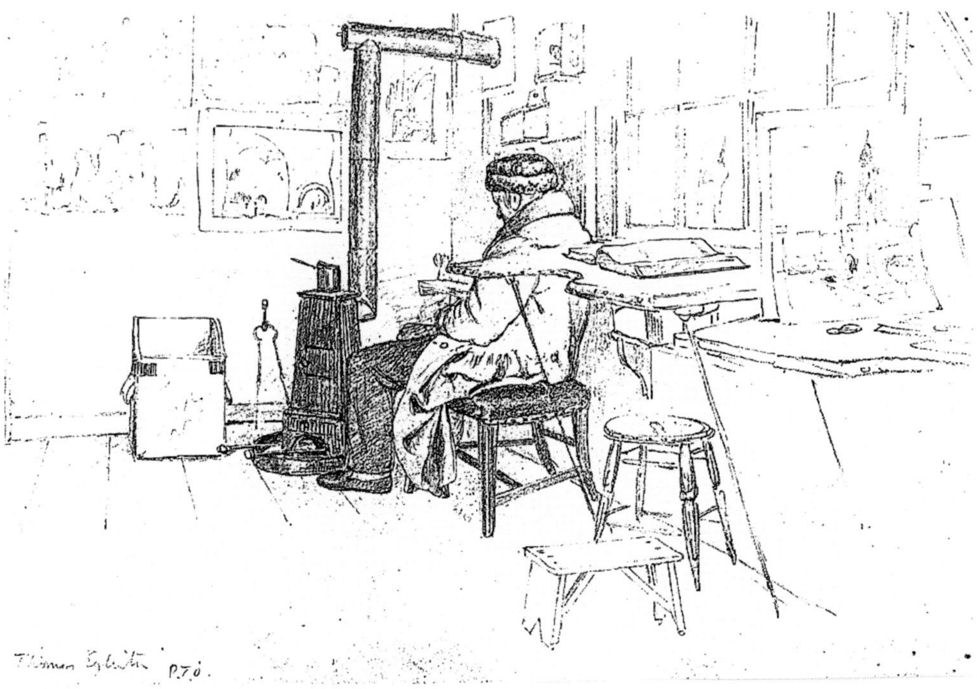

Plate 38. Pencil drawing
Grandfather dozing
In the Barnes studio where the copper plates for the various publications were etched and engraved, the old man resting in comfort by the stove was drawn by his grandson. Proofs of London Bridge plates are in evidence.

Photo courtesy C.R. Cooke, OBE

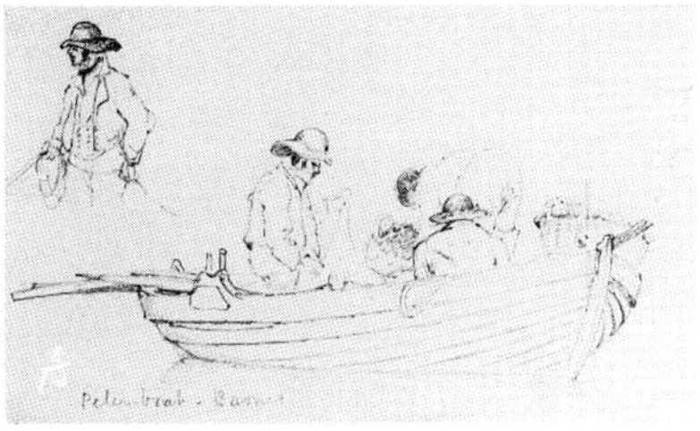

Plate 39. Pencil drawing
Peter boat Barnes
No example of this once common small Thames fishing boat has survived but, thanks to Cooke's pencil and his etched plates, its likeness is known.

Photo courtesy Clarges Gallery

and the presence of working river craft and the daily possibility of rowing oneself about gave a further dimension to a budding marine painter's experience. The pages of the diary reveal a sequence of domestic, professional and social details which it is not possible to retail in the present space – at some point they all impinge on the lives and works of a wide spectrum of painters and engravers in the London art world; if to Edward Cooke they seemed worth recording they can only be mentioned here if today they appear significant. Life on the Surrey shore is recorded, with his commitments to engraving almost in conflict with boating on the Thames, bathing, watching the fishermen, tending the garden, pruning the vines and admiring sunsets. There is always the urge to capture enchanting scenes of moving water, clouds, small craft and riverside vegetation with a predilection for early morning and evening skies; it is particularly noticeable in those Barnes days when the reflecting Thames heightened the drama of colour and clouds. but it continued throughout his painting life. It seems likely that the impact of Turner's work urged Cooke to attempt to record the light and atmosphere about his riverside home. Later in Venice and on the Spanish coast, where autumn sunsets were even more dramatic, they became compelling subjects.

He sketched fishermen working with their nets from their Peter boats off the Terrace (Plate 39); these double-ended Thames sailing and rowing fishing boats, reputedly named after St Peter the fisherman, were etched for *Shipping & Craft* which is just as well for no actual example is known to have survived. The *doble* of the River Medway still exists to represent the type, however.

The conduct of Mrs Cooke's school, where her husband found time to teach the young ladies drawing, is also indicated: the daughters of both David Roberts and Clarkson Stanfield attended. *The Botanical Cabinet* was still in progress and *Shipping* had begun, but there was still the pull of the grander art: *May 11th: ...I commenced oil painting (got in sky of small picture).* This early essay is impossible to identify since it was probably used up much later, but it is clear that he was eager to experiment. Copying, as in the black and white field, was undertaken as a means of self-instruction; he made a drawing after one of David Cox's, a mill, for Miss Margaret Moffatt, daughter of William Moffatt whose house on Mortlake Terrace was painted by Turner. A copy of his father's beautiful drawing of Hythe by the same artist was made in 1833. This watercolour from the *Southern Coast* series had been bought by George Cooke in 1824.[5] E.W. Cooke's version is in a descendant's collection in the United States, having inevitably passed for many years as an original work of the greater artist.

5. Now Corporation of London's Collection, No.1259, Guildhall, Shown No 171, Turner Exhibition, Royal Academy, 1974.

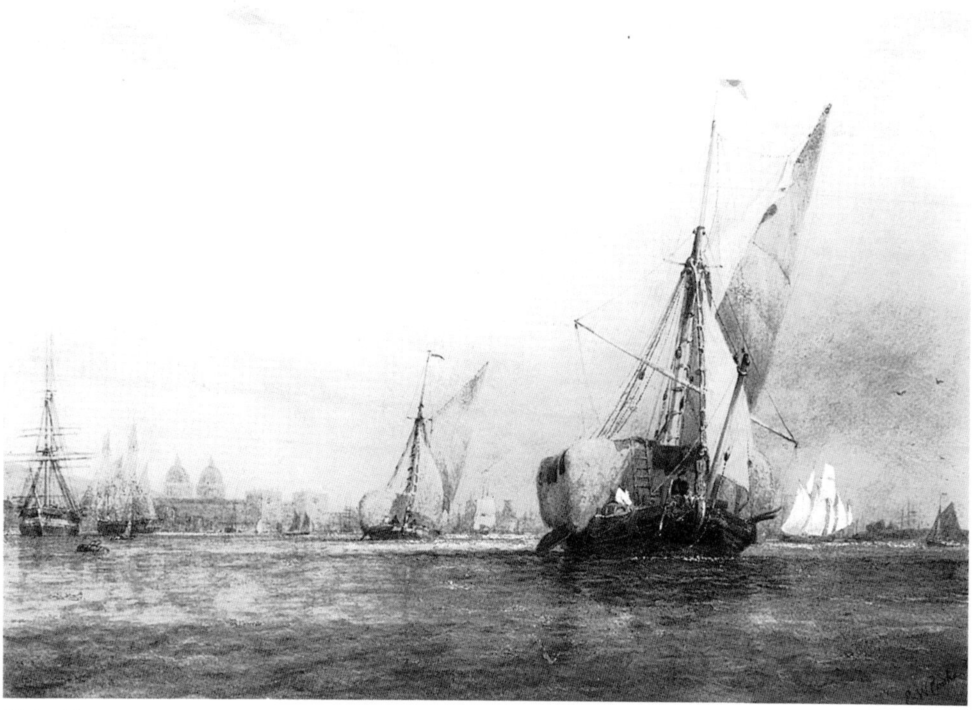

Plate 40. Watercolour
Hay barges Greenwich 1833
The nearest stretch of the Thames below bridges which offered shipping in a setting of grandeur was Greenwich, with Wren's Royal Hospital buildings. This is one of the group recorded in his *Liber* (Cooke MS 33). See No. 34, Plate 35.
Photo courtesy Martyn Gregory

One note in his *liber: [After (deleted)] recollection of a design of Bonnington's* [sic] refers to a study of two cutters off a coast in a lively sea. This was No 18, *Pilot boats,* and was noted as for Miss E. Gillham's Album.[6]

The Rosier family were close friends. William Rosier of Islington bought a dozen small watercolours of coastal and river scenes in March 1832. Richard Rosier, probably a son (a schoolfriend who shared Edward's birth date), and Rosier sisters were given drawings and albums were sent for the favour of a sketch. A drawing of boats was made for Master Wadmore's album – his father James Wadmore was a surveyor who inherited a fortune, became a connoisseur and collected modern art; he was a friend of George Cooke's and an intimate of the group called the Society of Associated Engravers.

Some notion of George Cooke's pre-eminence as an engraver is given by a note of his thirty-five year-old former apprentice and nephew, W.J. Cooke, bringing a plate of *Calais* in progress for the attention of the master. For further influences on the emerging painter one need look no further than the close family friend James Stark, pupil of John Crome and one of the Norwich painters who moved to London, attending the Royal Academy Schools. During 1827-34 Stark's *The Scenery of the Rivers of Norfolk* appeared, with young Cooke etching the shipping in Stark's plate of Yarmouth Bridge. Cooke's own plate of the Bridge in *Shipping & Craft* is based on a drawing dated 25 October 1828 (Plate 11).

Between 19 and 26 June 1833 Stark took Edward Cooke on a sketching tour of the River Medway in the Chatham and Rochester area, from which a group of the latter's more important early watercolours derive. From St Catherine's Dock they took a steamer to Chatham, met Priest – presumably Alfred Priest, Stark's pupil, so another member of the Norwich school – and after tea at the oddly named *Chest Arms* (after the Elizabethan naval charity, the Chatham Chest, founded by Sir John Hawkins) they walked over the Lines, the heights and ramparts of the defences. They made sketches all one day about Upnor on the shore opposite the dockyard and there Cooke noted making his *First picture from Nature in Oil Colours*.

Another product of that day was a watercolour, *Brick Works at Upnor,* and so

6. Mr Gillham, a Hackney resident, was proprietor of a popular chop-house in the City. (Clarke op.cit.)

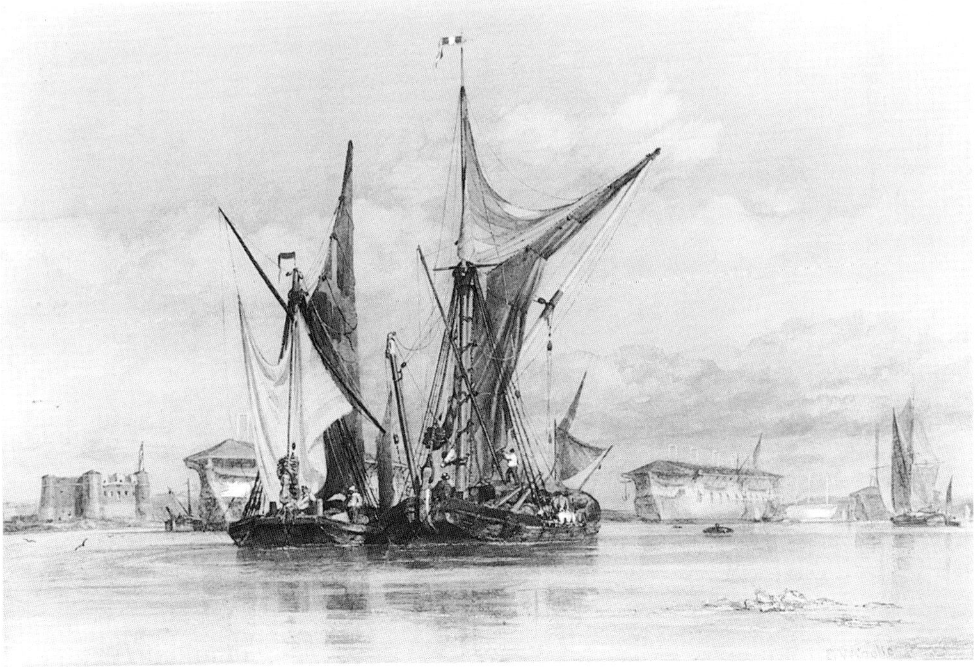

Plate 41. Watercolour
Barges or 'tide-waiters' drying Sails (calm) off Bombproof battery – Medway 8th July. [1833]
No 37 in his *Liber* (see Plate 35). The Battery was at Gillingham, below Chatham Dockyard on the River Medway. Photo courtesy Martyn Gregory. Yale Center for British Art

inscribed in pencil. It also bears his signature, E.W. Cooke RA 1864, so was signed for one of his clearance sales at Christie's in 1865 (Colour Plate 29).

Travelling Abroad

In France the whole aspect of Continental style in building, costume and colour, life and landscape, was a strong attraction, to say nothing of the delapidations caused by years of war and Revolution. With so many of their acquaintances taking inspiration from the wider European scene, it is not surprising to find Cooke looking across the Channel and in particular to the seaports of the northern coast.

Apart from J.S. Cotman, whose Normandy tours dated from 1818, their closest links were through cousin W.J. Cooke who had engraved drawings for Bonington and through T.S. Boys who worked with him in Paris and occasionally visited Barnes or sent letters via William Wyld. Turner was frequently in France at this period and in 1833 *Wanderings by the Loire* was published by Charles Heath from his accumulated sketches on previous visits. The Cookes were in a position to know what was going forward and probably to view the progress.

In Cooke's notebook also is *Sea view 6th June 1833, Mr W.Callow*. The latter's autobiography mentions an exchange of drawings with Cooke *who was then coming into prominence.*[7] They were of more or less the same age in spite of the 'Mr', but William Callow lived to become almost a centenarian. He worked in Paris with Boys and the marine watercolourist Charles Bentley who had also been apprenticed as an engraver and worked on *Excursion sur les Cotes et dans les Ports de Normandie*. However, with Edward Cooke, in spite of Professor Boase's suggestion of 'close friendship',[8] Callow seems to have had little contact in later years if the diary's pages can be relied upon. They painted in different media and exhibited in different places, although they did share a devotion to shipping and craft.

Apart from the dealers like Colnaghi, Tiffin and Griffith, buyers of his drawings seem to have been successful businessmen. He recorded that on 7 July 1833 Mr Rosier introduced him to Benjamin Austen Esq, who bought three drawings, *The Temeraire; Puckaster Cove; Hay boat, Chatham* (Colour Plate 25) for fourteen guineas. He also sold to Messrs Arch and Messrs Moon, publishers, John Sheepshanks, James Wadmore and Jeremiah

7. *William Callow, An Autobiography*, ed. H.M. Cundall,1908.
8. *English Art 1800-1870*, 1959, p.54.

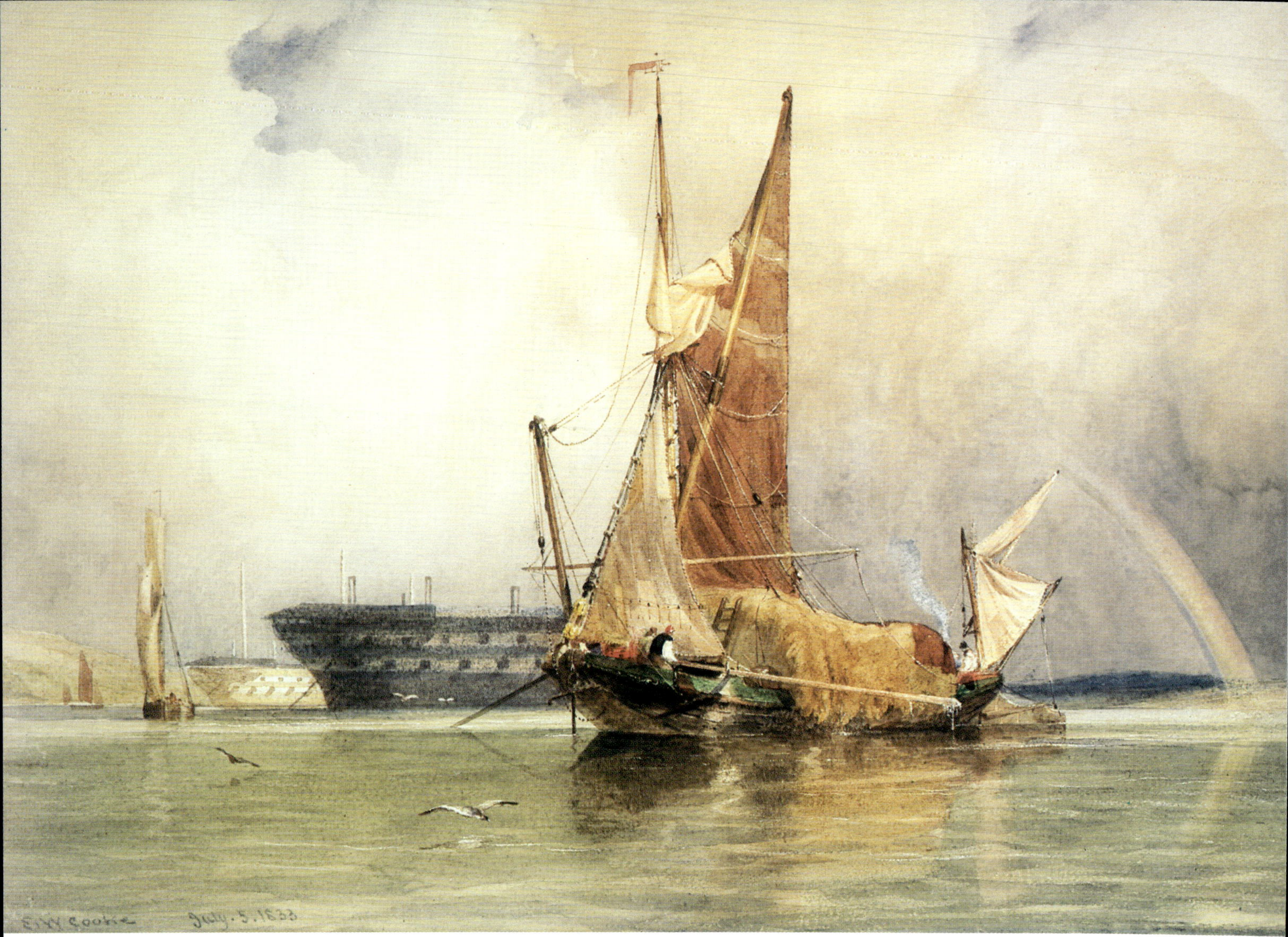

Colour Plate 25. Watercolour, 1833
Hay boat Chatham & men of war with rainbow...
Photo courtesy The Trustees of the National Maritime Museum, Greenwich

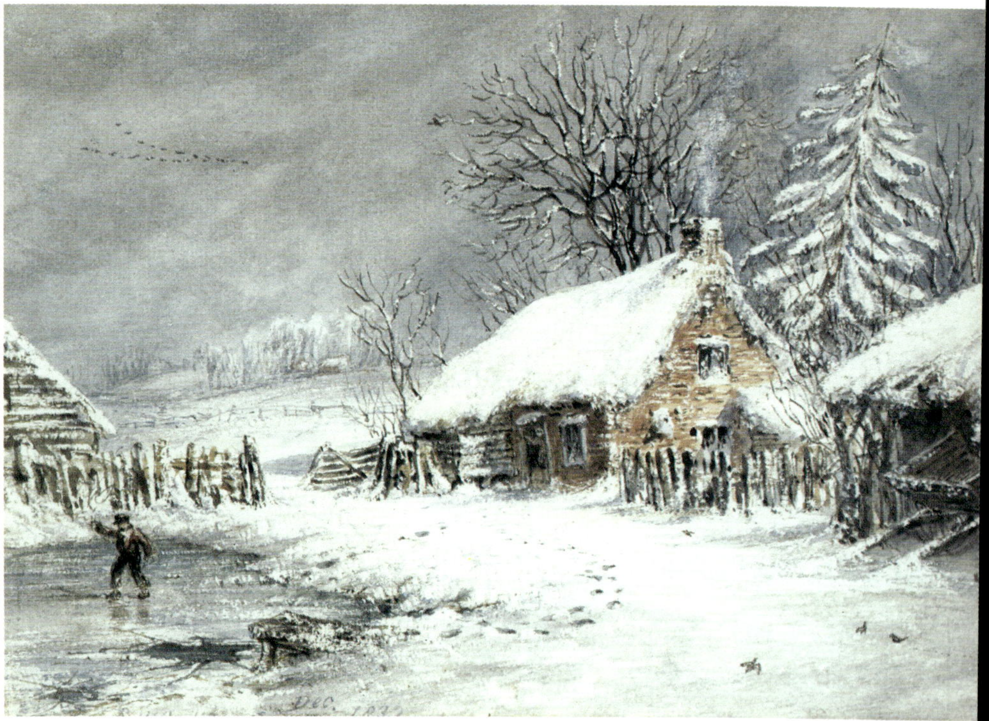

Colour Plate 26. Watercolour
Winter landscape with a boy skating
This 4½in. x 6in. (11.5cm x 15.25cm) watercolour is signed and dated December 1832. In his diary for 18 December 1832 Cooke wrote *traced, etched and bit plants all day. Cut copper also. Finished snow piece.* It is No. 6 in Appendix 3, entitled *Snow scene, ice, &c.*

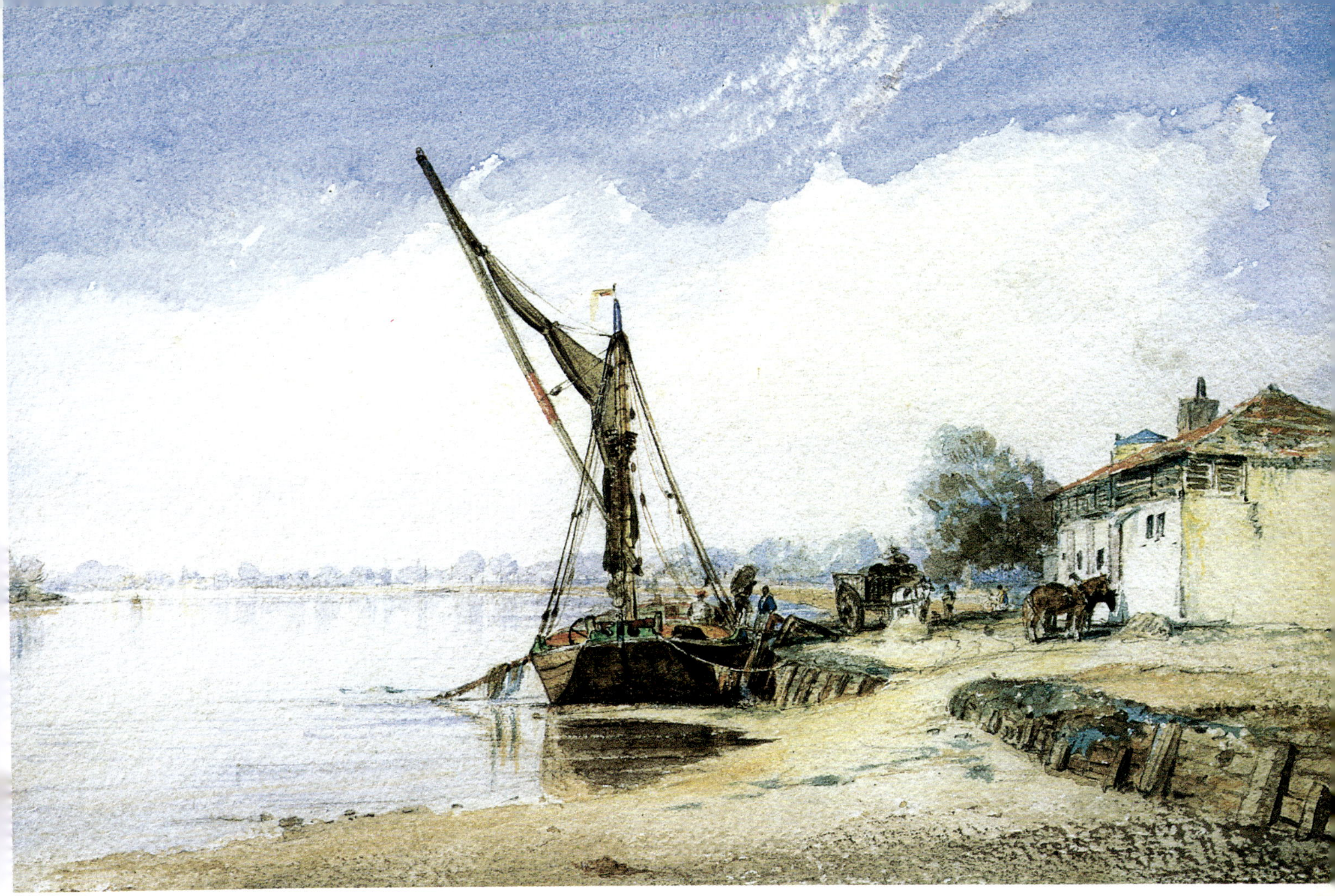

Colour Plate 27. Watercolour, 1832
Spritsail barge unloading, Barnes
Photo courtesy Private Collection

Colour Plate 28. Watercolour
Hollington Pond, nr Hastings. 1835
The artist noted this as 'Ruisdael Pond' which shows how his mind was working. Another version is known.
Photo courtesy Private Collection

Colour Plate 29. Watercolour, 1833
Brickworks at Upnor on the Medway
Photo courtesy Private Collection

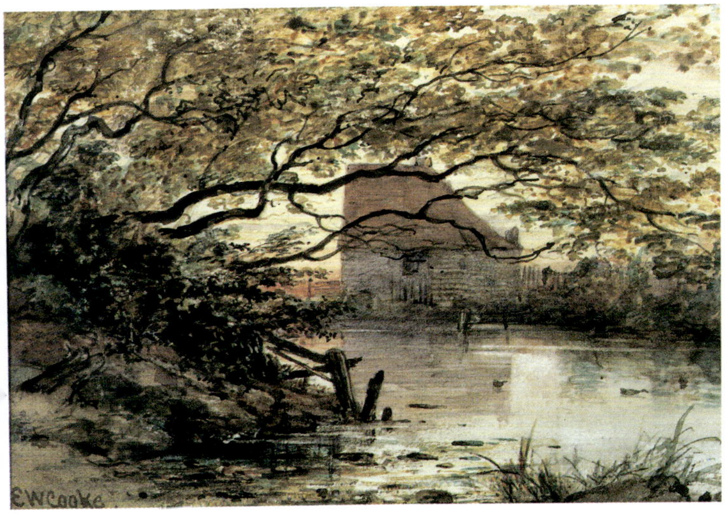

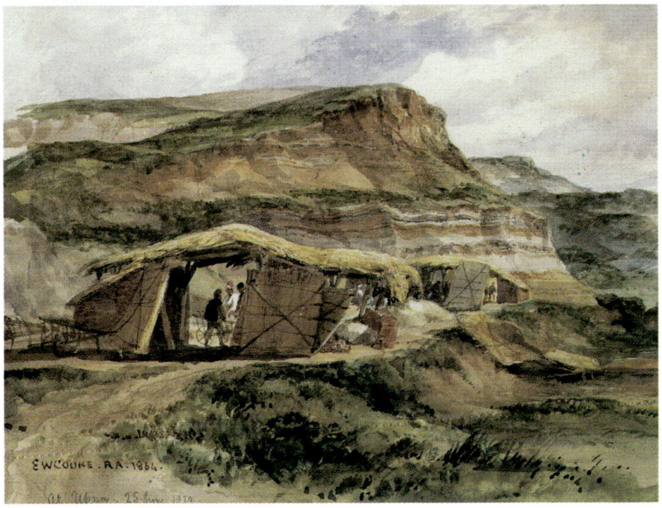

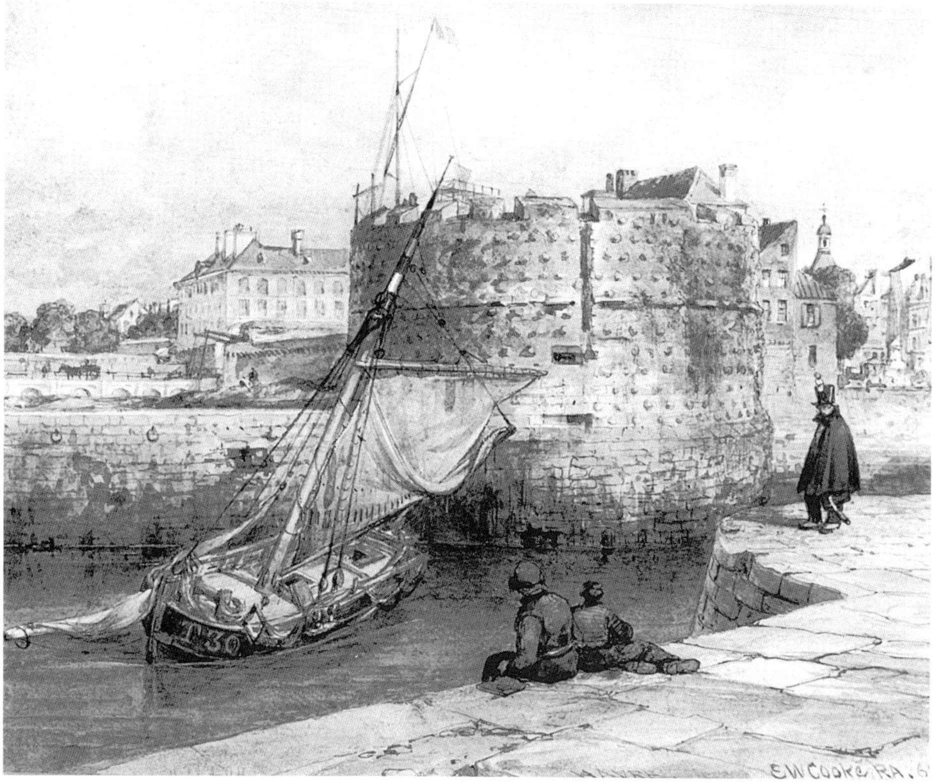

Plate 42. Watercolour
Le Havre, Tour de François Premier now demolished
Although signed and dated 1864, this drawing was made c.1833. Probably Lot 58 in Christie's sale 1865, his studio clearance. The old town was remodelled in 1856 but the delicate background here shows the old fortifications – and the Hotel de Ville, according to a faint inscription.
Photo courtesy Martyn Gregory

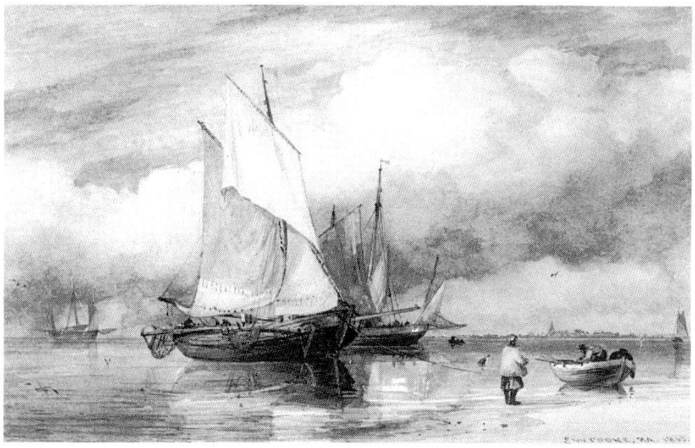

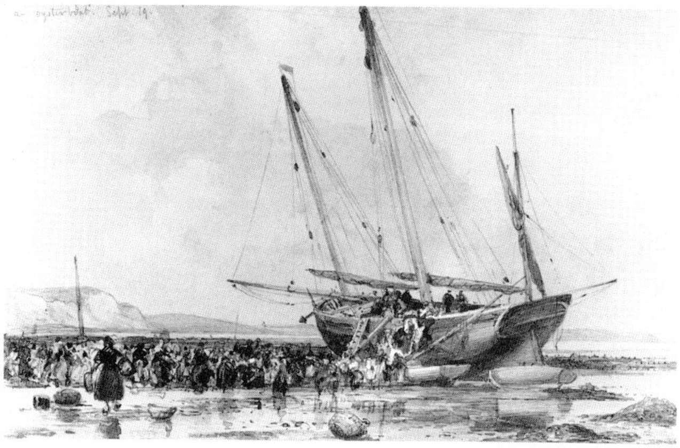

Plate 43. Watercolour
French fishing craft aground at the mouth of the Seine, waiting for wind and tide
Oil versions of this subject were painted; see 44/9 and 54/4 (Colour Plate 41).
Photo courtesy Martyn Gregory. Private Collection

Plate 44. Watercolour
Fish women of Granville unloading an oyster boat
At low water on the Normandy coast in September 1836 the artist was moved to record a scene of many women portering baskets of oysters. Photo courtesy Bill Thomson, Albany Gallery. Private Collection

Harman, who were *amateurs* and collectors. He records one rebuff, and the drawing in question is known: Mrs Benjamin Austen objected to the rainbow in a sunset view at Rouen, *the effect being too extravagant* (Colour Plate 31), so the drawing was returned.

John Piper noted in relation to a drawing of Thomas Girtin's in 1800, *The White House, Chelsea,* that *The atmosphere, the time of day, has created the whole mood of the picture; and with the mood, the form. ...Selection was the scheme of the best of the topographical draughtsmen. But Girtin and Turner set out to discover a pictorial shape... for the urge to make a particular effect of sun or rain, calm or storm ...stand as*

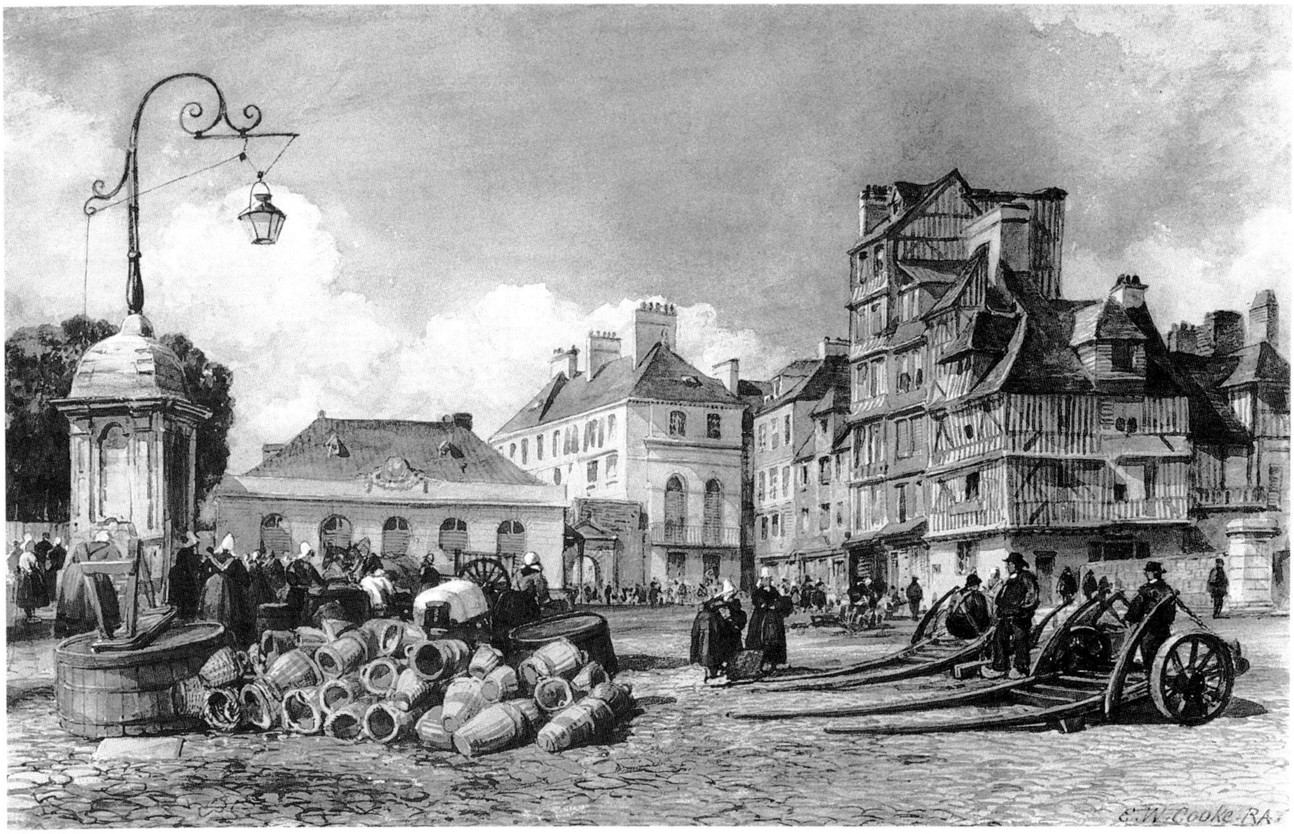

Plate 45. Watercolour
Market Place, Havre
From R.P. Bonington, T.S. Boys and Wm. Wyld he had caught the feeling for these Continental townscapes and something of their method as well. Photo courtesy Agnews. Private Collection

a symbol for something universal. They wanted to make Landscape a means of reporting not places or things, but life.[9]

F.G. Moon, partner in the important and successful fine art publishing firm of Moon, Boys and Graves (Printsellers to the Royal Family), whose gallery was in Pall Mall, bought No. 34, *Hay boats, Greenwich* (Plate 40), and No. 37, *Tide waiters* (Plate 41), for six guineas. The partner, Thomas Boys, was a cousin of T.S. Boys and Francis Graham Moon later became a baronet and Lord Mayor of London, like his predecessor the engraver and publisher John Boydell in 1790. They had absorbed the latter's successors, the firm of Hurst and Robinson, at the time of the big financial crash, 1825-26 and possibly with it some of George Cooke's hard-earned money.

Edward Cooke's progress on his first foreign tour can be traced in the Itinerary, and his diary, backed up by surviving drawings, shows his intense enjoyment of the novelty of the scene. After this French trip he noted in his book *made about 300 sketches including figures, Baskets &c.* He produced a number of quayside and street scenes at Rouen, Honfleur etc. in watercolour and studies of shipping coming and going in the port of Le Havre. Larger finished drawings were made on his return home. Subjects which appealed to him were stored up for later treatment in oils, for example, *Trouville fishing boat in a calm – distant view of Havre*. Views on the Seine at Elbeuf and Oissel, *Rainbow effect on the Seine near Canteleu* and *Quai Henri Qtier Dieppe* are subjects which he had noted other painters favouring and here again he was making his *particular* contribution. Some thirty-five French subjects are listed in his *liber* with prices and purchasers.

When there was occasion, he liked to exercise his humour in caricature style. A family trip to Oxford in 1835, when they lodged with Mr Alderman James Wyatt (Mayor of the City, picture dealer, framer, publisher and early patron of J.E. Millais), included a well-victualled aquatic picnic down river to Nuneham Courtenay. *The Kimpany on their*

9. Piper, op.cit., pp.14-16.

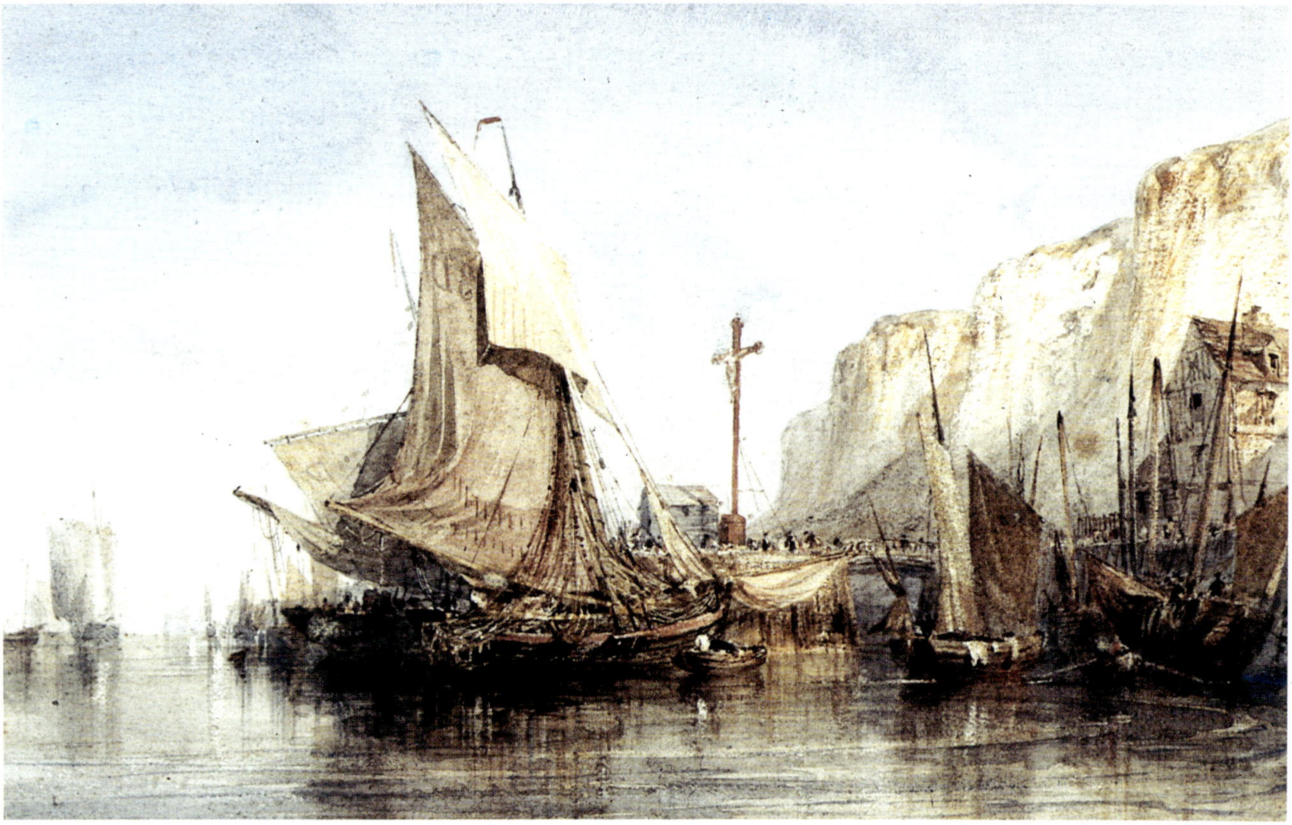

Colour Plate 30. Watercolour, 1833
Morning Dieppe harbour, fishing boats arrived
One of the series of lovely drawings made while in the first flush of enthusiasm for the novelty of the French scene. Photo courtesy J. Morton Lee

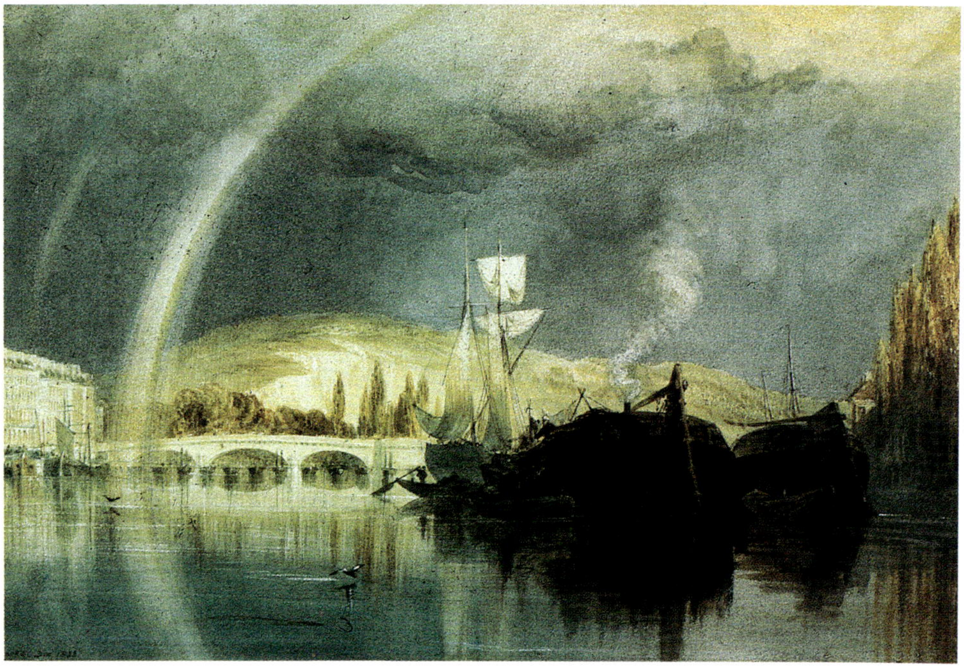

Colour Plate 31. Watercolour, 1833
Pont Neuf Rouen
The 'effect' said his patroness, *was too extravagant* – but was J.M.W. Turner RA in mind when he drew this French river scene? Photo courtesy Eric Swain. Private Collection

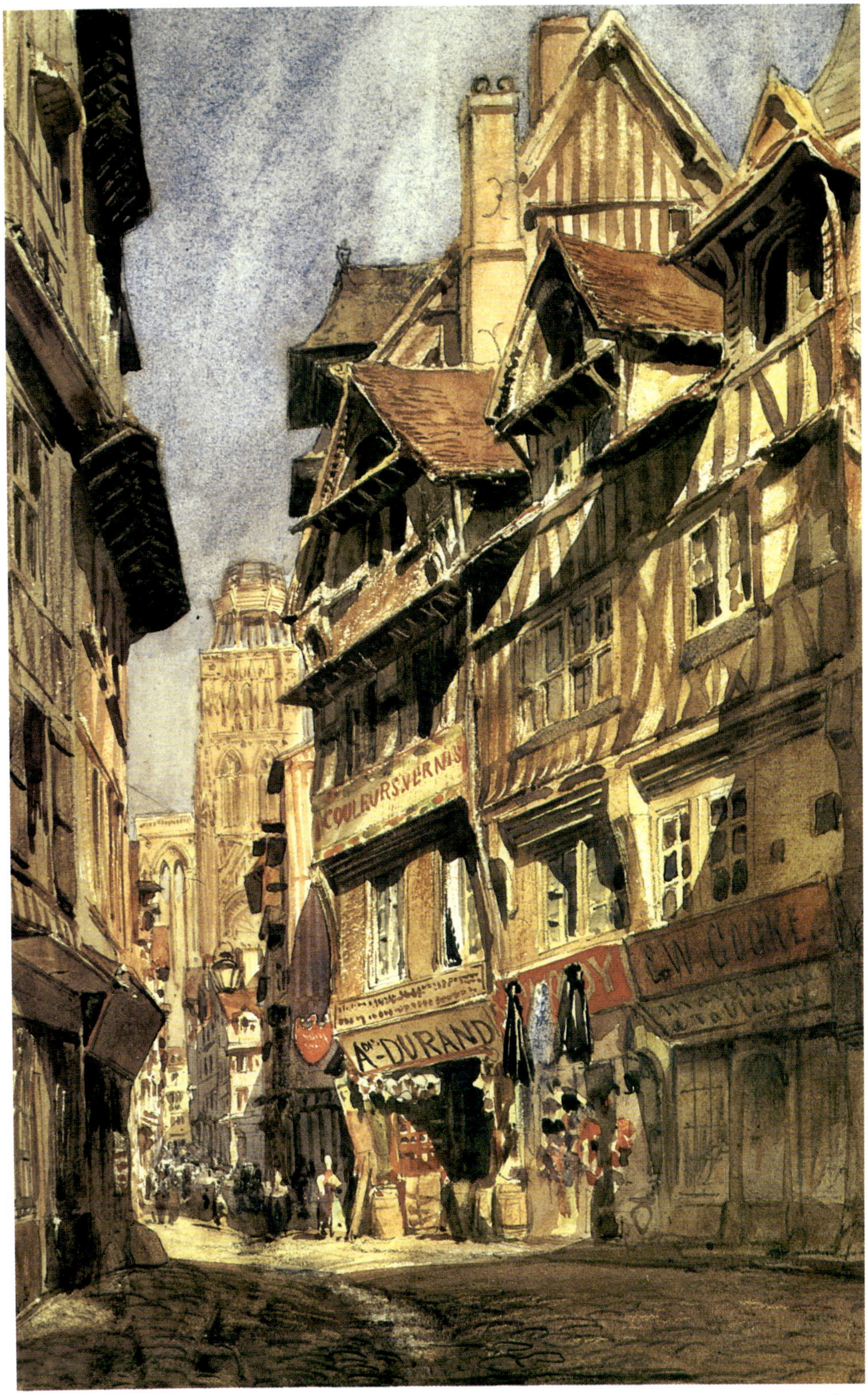

Colour Plate 32. Watercolour, 1834

Rouen. Rue de La Tuile with the Cathedral tower

Bonington, Wyld and T. S. Boys showed the way and many drawings of London street scenes had given Cooke experience. The colour and picturesque buildings delighted him. (Including the artist's name on a French shop facia board was a familiar device.)

Photo courtesy Martyn Gregory. Private Collection

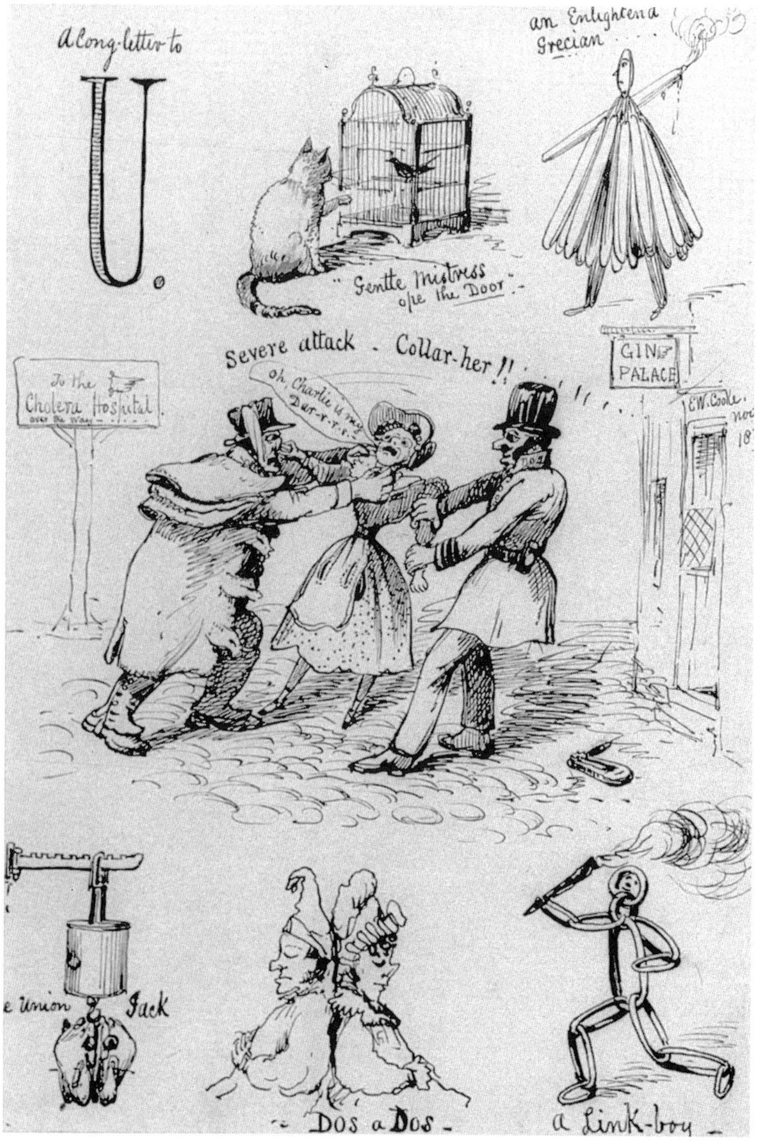

Plate 46. Ink sketch
Another page from the Elizabeth Wyatt album. Photo courtesy Martyn Gregory

Voyage to Nuneham – with <u>*part*</u> *of their provisions* (Colour Plate 35), a watercolour from an album belonging to Miss Wyatt which included a preliminary sketch, would seem to have satirised not only the preoccupation with food and drink but also someone's idiosyncratic pronunciation. The names of the participants are recorded but it is not possible to identify them in the drawings.

In later years, to raise funds when about to build a house in the country, Cooke sent a selection of drawings in pencil, in chalks, some described as 'tinted' but including over eighty watercolours, to Christie's where they occupied a half-day sale, 16 June 1865. Some of the watercolour drawings can be identified with those in his record book and some indeed bear early inscriptions. He must have ranged through his portfolios and boxes, signing everything which needed a signature, but having recently acquired full Academic honours, he of course added 'R A' and a date, usually 1864

Thus numbers of dated drawings which were in fact made some thirty years previously are to be encountered today. Doubtless he 'tickled' some of them up for the sale, but there are studies for *Shipping and Craft* – the prison-ship *York, the stern of HMS Asia* and *Hatch boats*. There are favourite subjects, perhaps duplicates from his growing

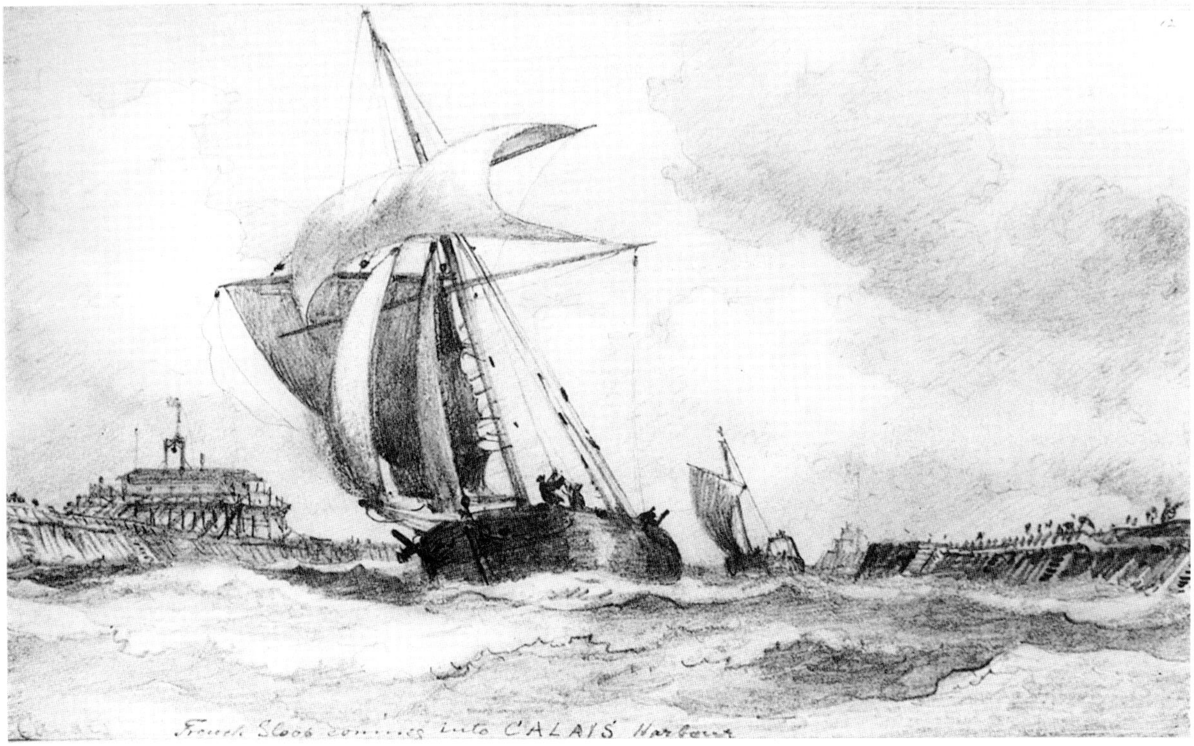

Plate 47. Pencil drawing

French sloop entering Calais

Even to the frequent cross-Channel traveller the negotiation of the narrow entrance to the harbour between the massive piers was always an excitement worth watching.

Photo courtesy Martyn Gregory. Private Collection

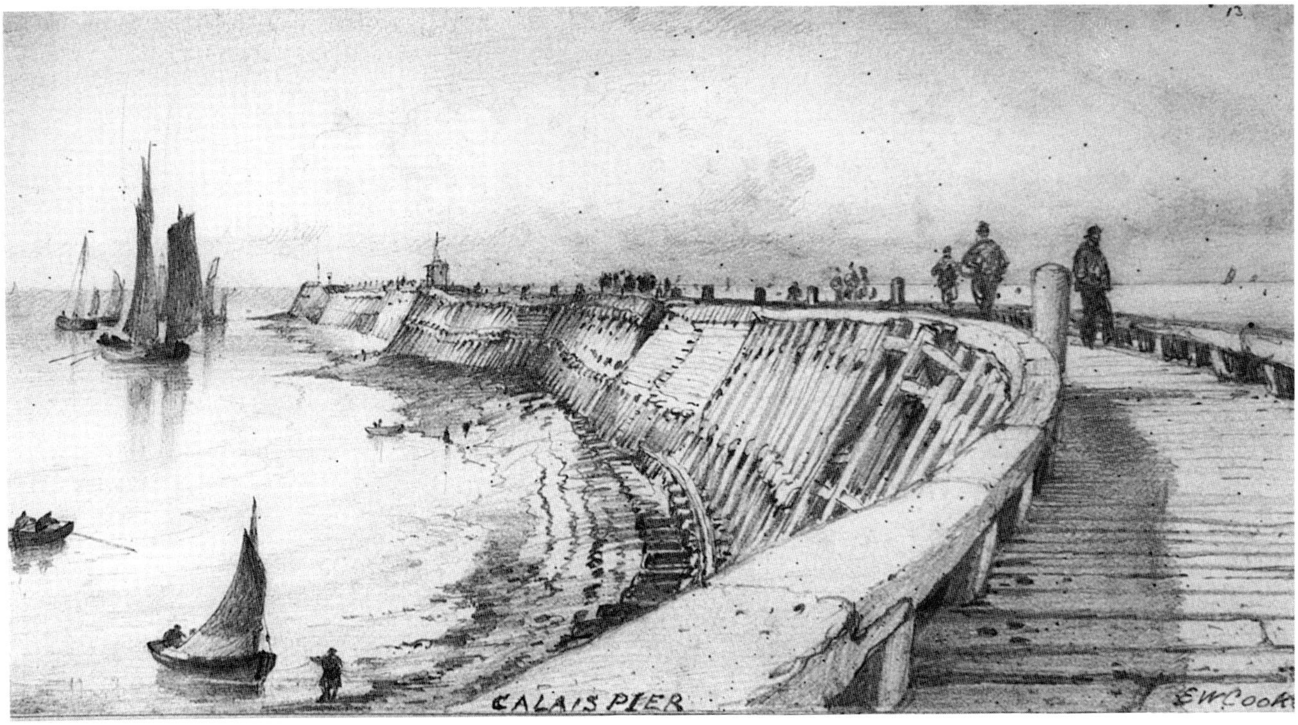

Plate 48. Pencil drawing

Calais pier, low water

In later years Cooke was to witness the steamer *Bessemer* collide with the timber pier, and he drew the resulting damage.

Photo courtesy Martyn Gregory. Private Collection

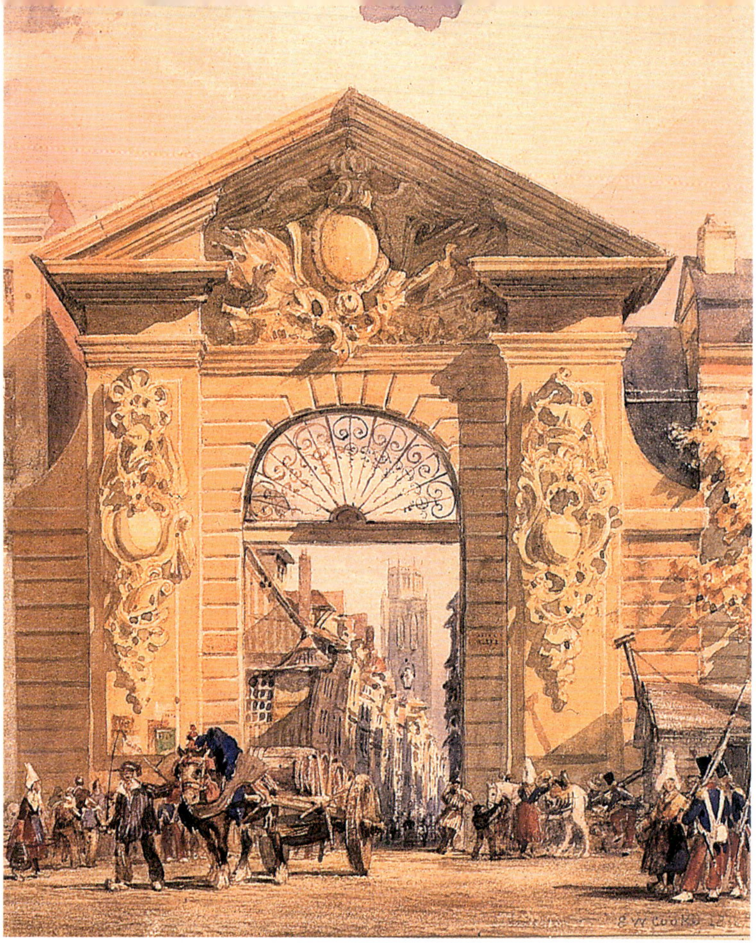

Colour Plate 33. Watercolour, 1837
Rouen Porte Guillaume Lion & Rue des Arpents
Cooke's note of this handsome drawing continued *Tower of St Ouen in the distance – soldiers & figures &c.* Another version was a commission from Arch the publisher.
Photo courtesy Private Collection

Colour Plate 34. Watercolour
Fishing house, Redleaf, on the Medway c.1840
The young river ran through William Wells' estate near Penshurst and visiting artists made use of the amenities. Photo courtesy Private Collection

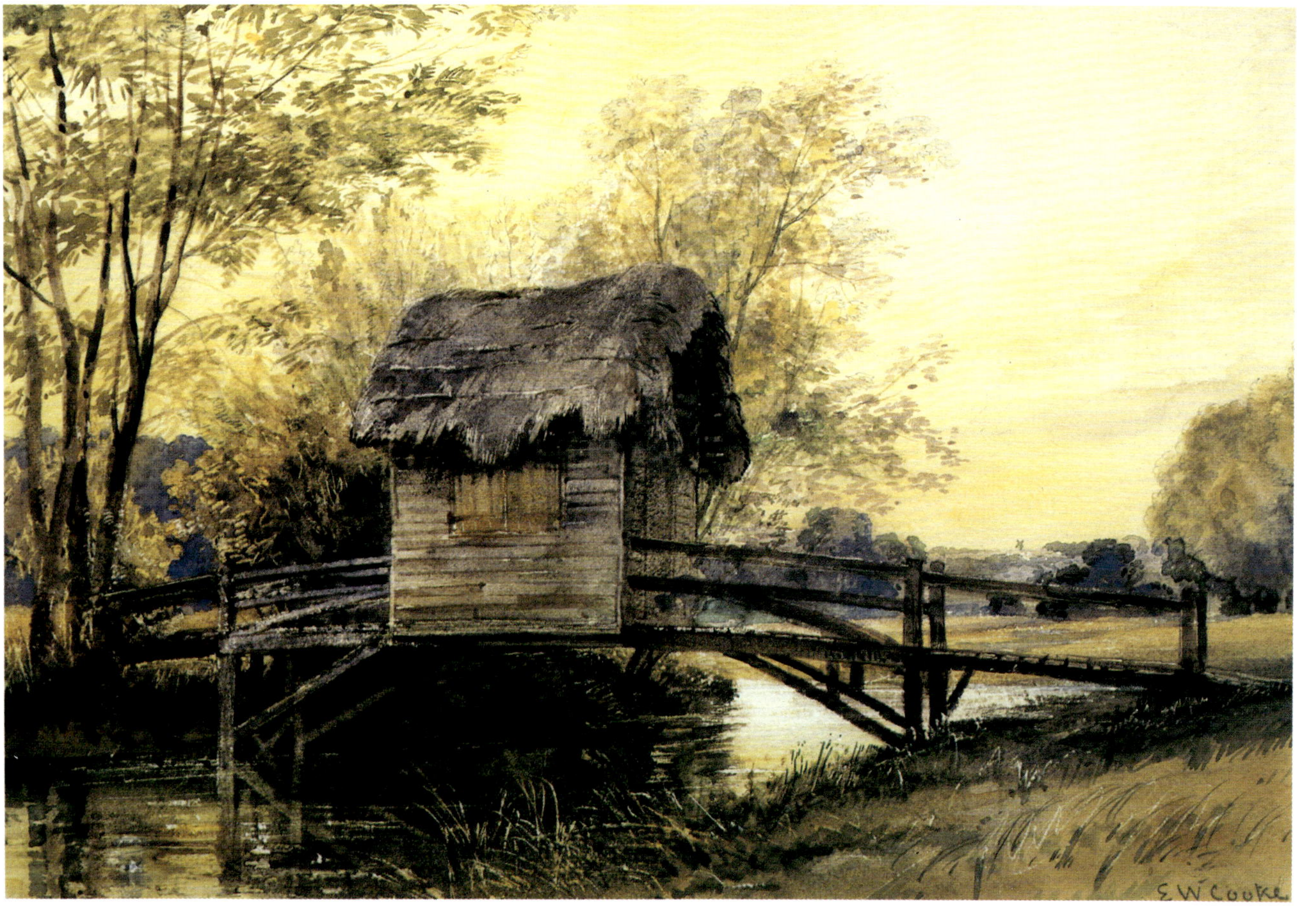

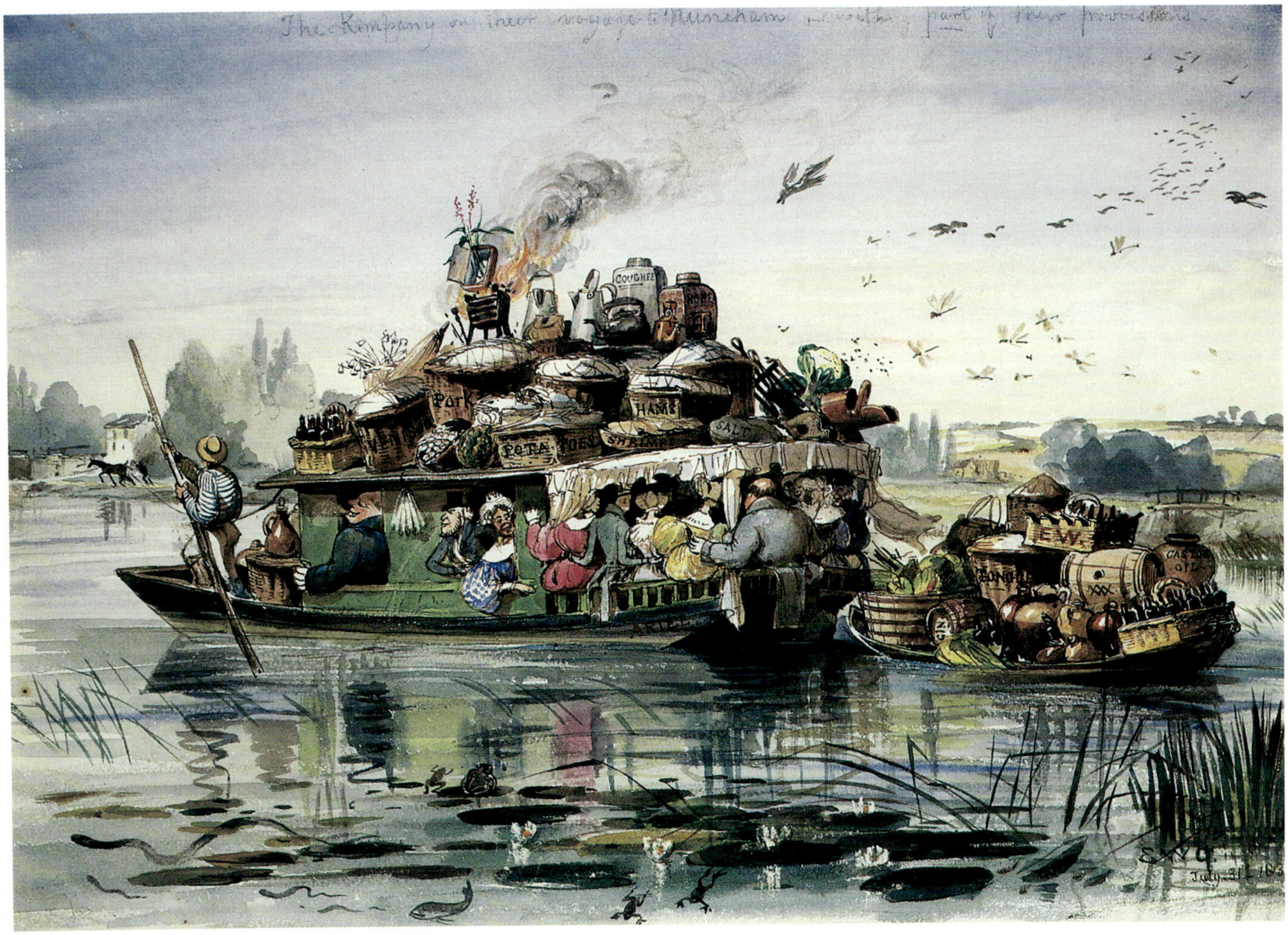

Colour Plate 35. Watercolour, 1835

Voyage to Nuneham Courtney

Hilarity in Oxford; presented to James Wyatt's daughter as a souvenir of a day afloat.

Photo courtesy Martyn Gregory. Private Collection

reference collection, studies of fish baskets, lobster pots, traps and specialist tools which always intrigued him, for example, *Rips used by Shrimpers*. The whole range of his work was represented and all the countries he had visited to date. Drawings, studies for paintings such as Lot 153, *Catalan Bay Gibraltar*, made on the spot, date from recent years as also Lot 209 *Roman Bridge, Tangier,* an 1861 chalk study for the large oil. There were comparatively few watercolours of his later life, and those that have been noted do not possess the full-bodied colour of his early days, belonging perhaps to the portfolio rather than to be framed and glazed and exposed to view. They show, however, his assured draughtsmanship and *that fidelity and vigour for which Mr Cooke is so justly esteemed* proclaimed on Christie's catalogue title.

Strangely, only a few watercolour views of Venice and its shipping, where he spent ten seasons painting between 1850 and 1877, are known, although the diary mentions several and three were in his posthumous sale at Christie's, 22 May 1880. There, only twenty-five watercolour drawings are listed (Lots 45-70), the latest being Lot 67, *Sloop Coming into Calais Harbour,* dated 1863.

The need for fast work probably dictated the use of watercolour: a shorescape and boats, with plenty of time in hand, was preferably accomplished with his oil sketching gear, but if either the subject or the artist was liable to move on, pencil and wash would be preferred (see below, Colour Plate 141).

In Blackheath as guest of John Sheepshanks in 1835, he records an early instance of taking a hand in garden design by making a plan of the garden and grounds of Park

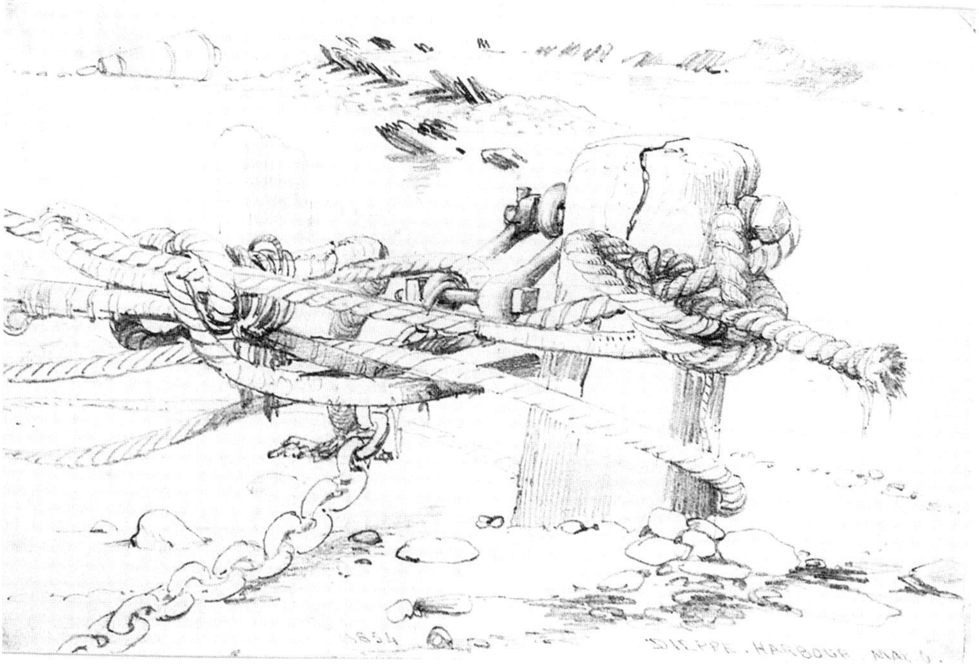

Plate 49.
Dieppe harbour 1854
A mooring bollard and a nest of cables struck Cooke as worth a memo.

Pencil drawing

Photo courtesy Clarges Gallery

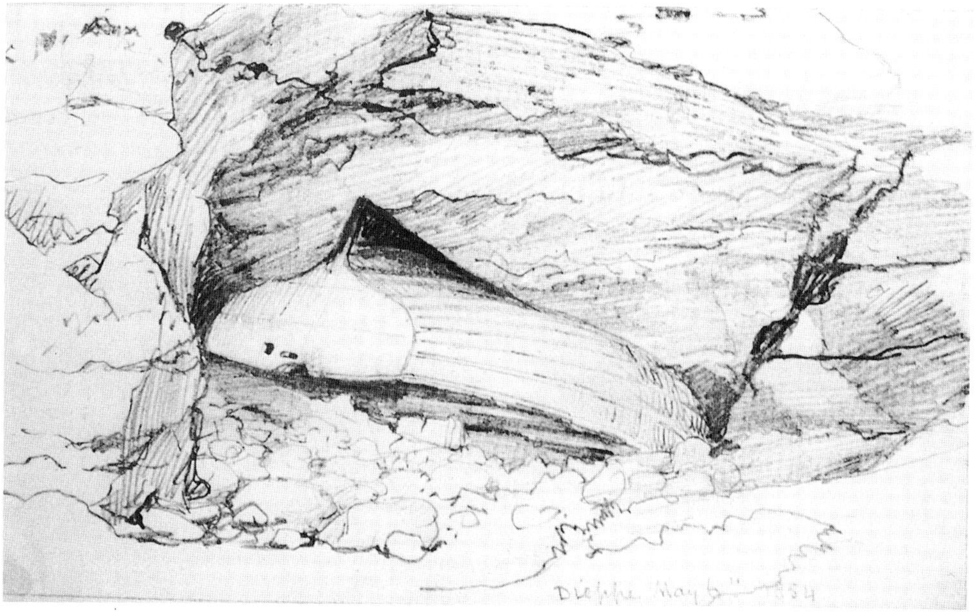

Plate 50.
Dieppe, boat under cliff

Pencil drawing

Photo courtesy Clarges Gallery

Cottage. He went to the village with Sheepshanks to buy things; John Constable wrote sarcastically that the old Yorkshireman had sold some of his fine prints and *invested in flowerpots*,[10] but Sheepshanks was a keen gardener and a Fellow of the Royal Horticultural Society. William Mulready and also James Bridges, one of the Oxford party, came to dine. Cooke was happy to note *Mr Mulready left by stage at ½ p 9 – he criticized my picture with great advantage to me: very hot day*

By this time the pictures were in oils and we have entered a new phase in the artist's development.

10. Constable op. cit. Vol. IV.

Chapter 5

THE EARLY OILS

Young men in the trades of coach, sign and house painting had occasionally advanced into the finer art of picture making as evidenced by the careers of the Scots David Roberts and John Philip. The earliest preserved painting of Edward Cooke, etcher and fine draughtsman, is, strangely enough, a sign-board for his uncle's famous *Old Ship Inn* at Brighton. He gave it the title: *The Lucy Ann 74, Running Into Portsmouth* (Plate 51). It had been returned to the artist by 1859 so he was evidently sentimentally attached to it. The *Ledger* dates it as 1829 but since there is no mention of such a work in the diary it may have been painted as early as 1825 as claimed in the *Art Journal* biography, for Cooke was at Brighton in 1824 on the evidence of an early sketchbook.[1] His cousin Lucy Ann Shuckard, the landlord's daughter, inspired the humorous naming of a mythical two-decker of 74 guns and this, another early example of Cooke's sense of fun, is certainly a competently painted image for a 'teen-age artist.

It is intriguing to trace through the diary's pages his growing interest in oil painting. Three exclamation marks must denote an important rather than a surprising event: *1833:*

1. National Maritime Museum, Greenwich.

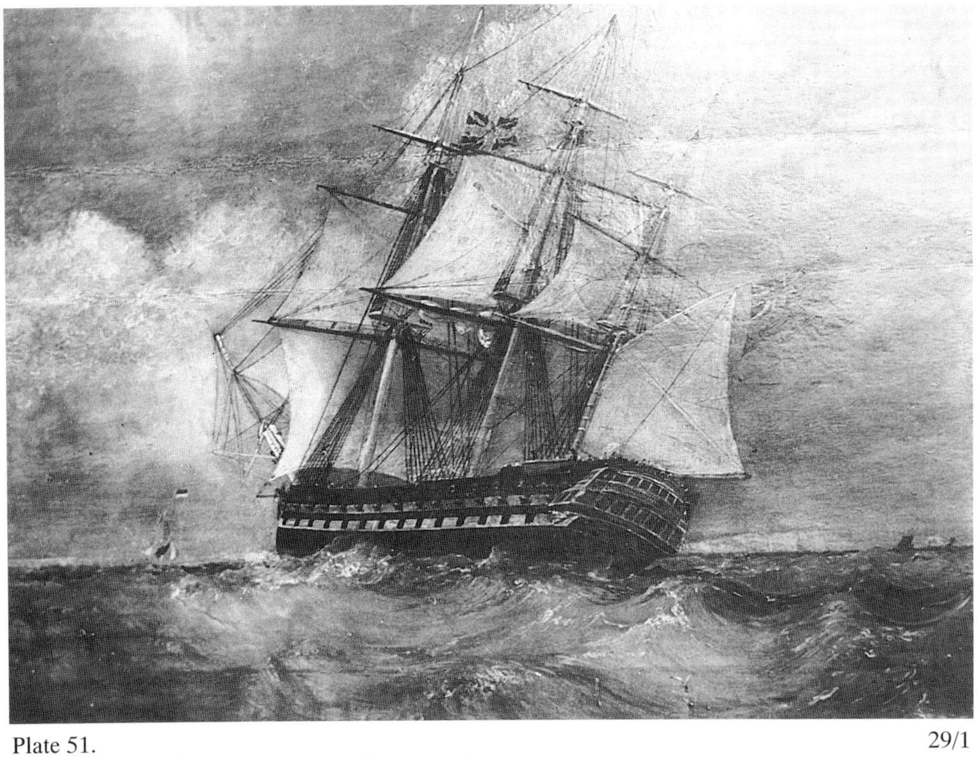

Plate 51. 29/1
The Lucy Ann *74 guns running into Portsmouth*
Painted as a sign-board for the Old Ship Inn at Brighton and hung there while Cooke's uncle, J.L. Shuckard, was landlord. Lucy was his daughter. The coastline does not look like Portsmouth.
Photo courtesy Society for Nautical Research Private Collection

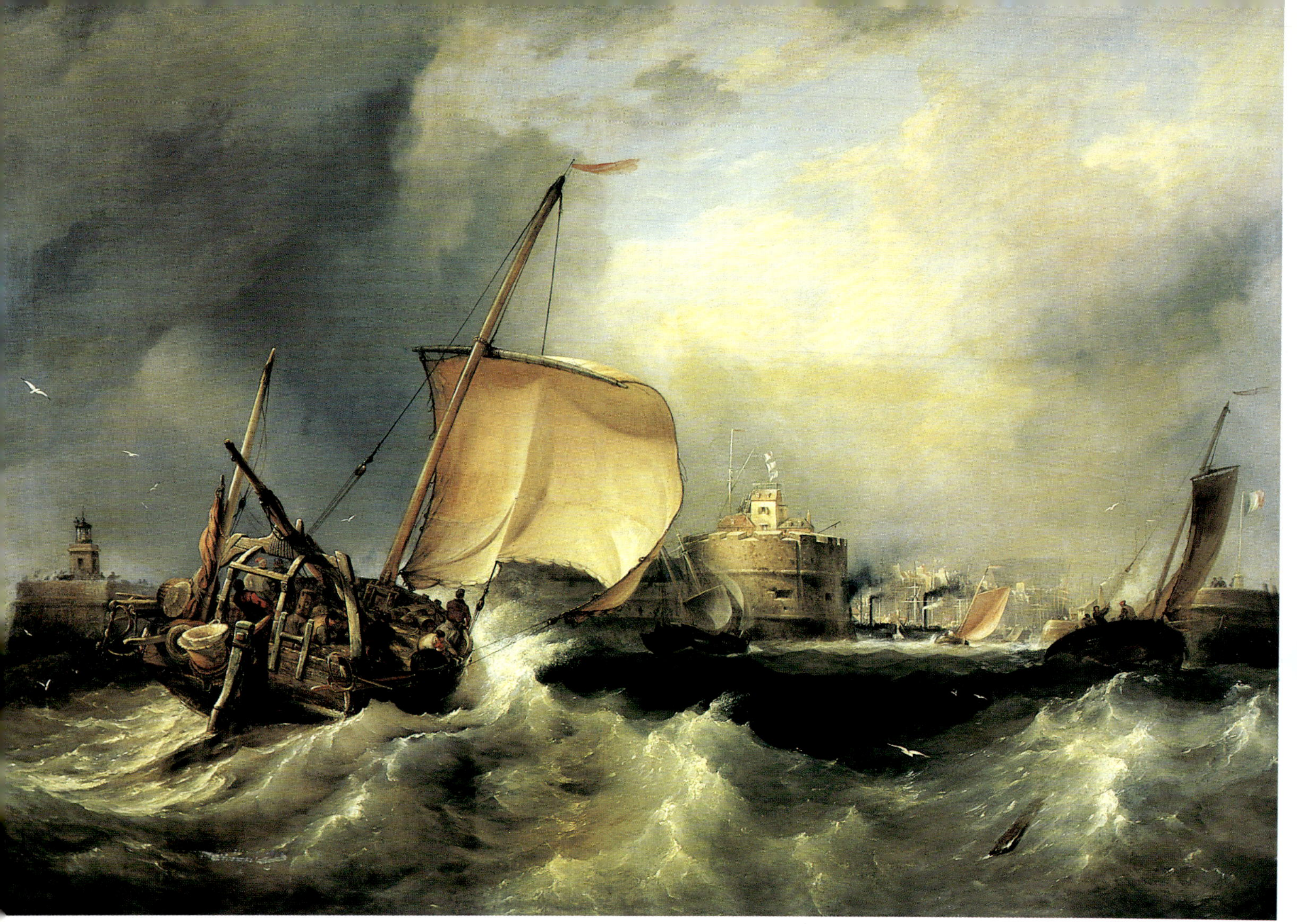

Colour Plate 36. 40/2
French Herring-boat running into the port of Havre de Grace
He had painted his first major French subject, similar to this, in 1834-5; it is not known to have survived but other versions and other harbours occupied his attention throughout his life.
Photo courtesy Bury Art Gallery & Museum, Lancashire

15th May Made first oil picture – portrait of Mr Ratcliffe's horse with Old Biggs on it!!! The *Ledger,* however, has the horse belonging to Biggs and the picture to Mr Ratcliffe, a Barnes resident.

On the 1833 Medway sketching trip with James Stark he had recorded painting his first picture *from nature in oils* around Upnor, where the ships of war lying off Chatham Dockyard were full of martial interest and were subjects favoured by Turner. Unhappily neither title nor fate of this sketch are recorded but it is significant that he had taken oils as part of his sketching kit.

An autograph note in the beginning of his *Ledger*[2] reads monumentally:

> *On the 6th of February 1834 went to Mr Stark's (Chelsea) and he gave me my first lesson in painting (a small coast scene). In evening bought colours &c and the next morning commenced my career with the oil brush upon 2 little subjects.*
>
> *On the 10th February commenced a large picture on canvas 3ft by 2ft 3 of Trouville Fishing boats entering the port of Havre. Worked 7 days on it and finished on the 19th inst.*
>
> *This was exhibited at the British Institution 1834* [sic] (in fact 1835) *and bought by Mr Walker of Nottingham at the Gallery.*

Stark lent him a palette and brushes and the following day he began three pictures of small size and laid in the dead colouring. A few days later he mentions beginning the

2. Royal Academy of Arts: MS 405.

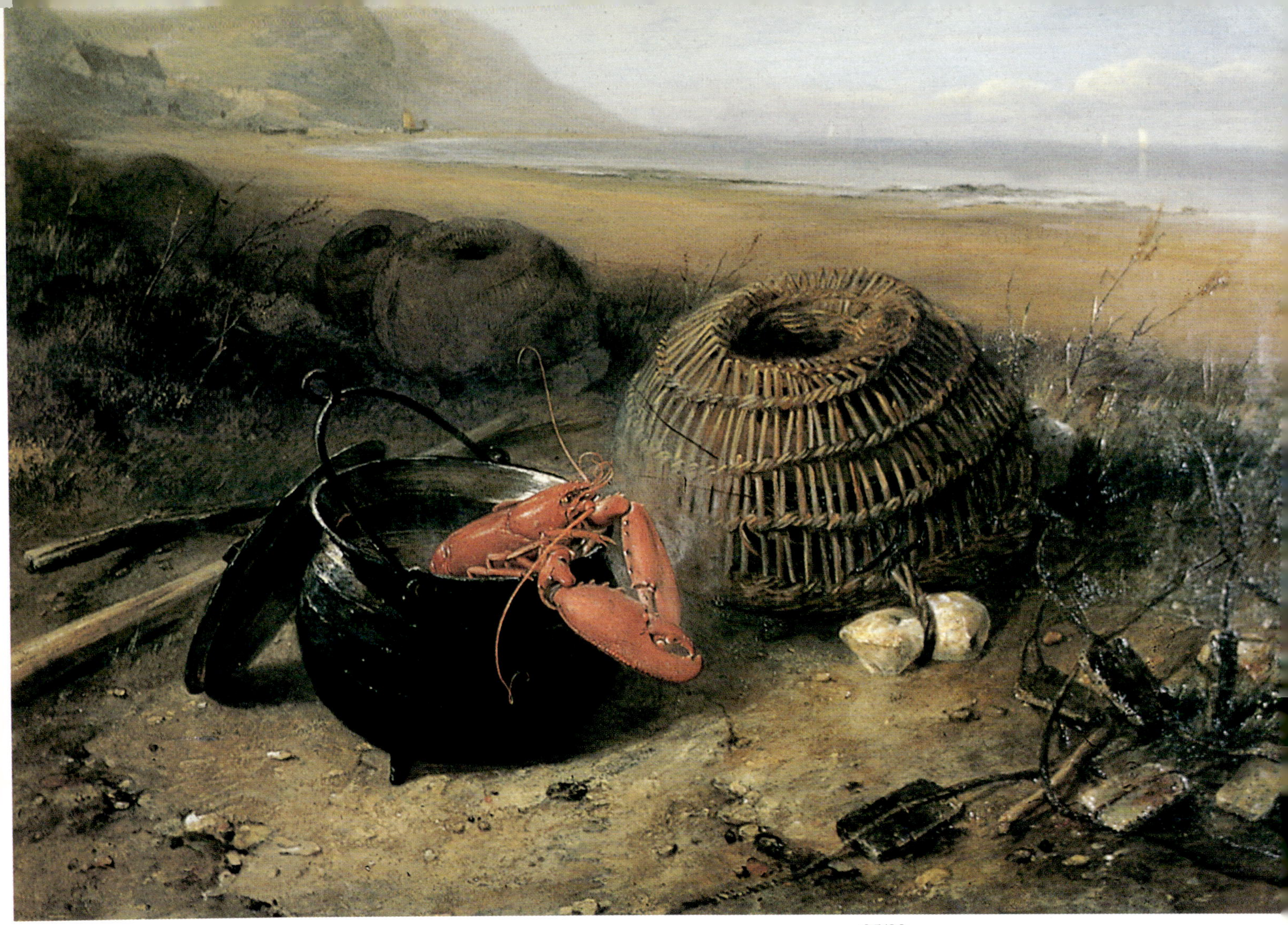

Colour Plate 37. 35/20
Lobster pots [L.]Ventnor
Professor Waagen wrote incorrectly that it was the artist's first oil painting. The attractions of the Isle of Wight took the painter there throughout his life. When development had turned fishing villages into resorts his visual reminiscence was aided by earlier sketches and models, especially of wicker baskets and pots. Photo courtesy The Board of Trustees of the Victoria & Albert Museum, No.39

large picture of Le Havre, and from that moment he can be considered launched.

He might indeed have submitted pictures for the Royal Academy in 1834, but a crisis was reached when George Cooke became ill after a late night tramp home in stormy weather from a meeting of the Conversazione. Diary entries record his last illness and the distress of his family at his death, just after midnight on 26/27 April.

The business of engraving was behind them; watercolours except for use as occasional studies were to become a secondary thing and it was to painting in oils on panel and canvas that henceforward Edward Cooke's considerable energies would be directed. A livelihood had to be won, but won by means of a more congenial occupation than that followed by his late father.

Clearance of accumulated stock, books, proofs of etchings and engravings of a lifetime were sorted, batched and marked for auction with the advice of his Uncle William. The strange circumstance of W.B. Cooke's absence from his brother's funeral was perhaps due to illness, but he was not recorded at other family gatherings and his marriage to a second wife in 1831 (noted by the diarist as a sister of Mrs Cromek) may have had some bearing on it. He sent a letter by hand of his assistant Frederick Smith on the day following his brother's death.

There was the collection of autographs to be arranged for disposal but private sales such as Turner drawings to B.G. Windus, the retired coach builder and a keen collector,

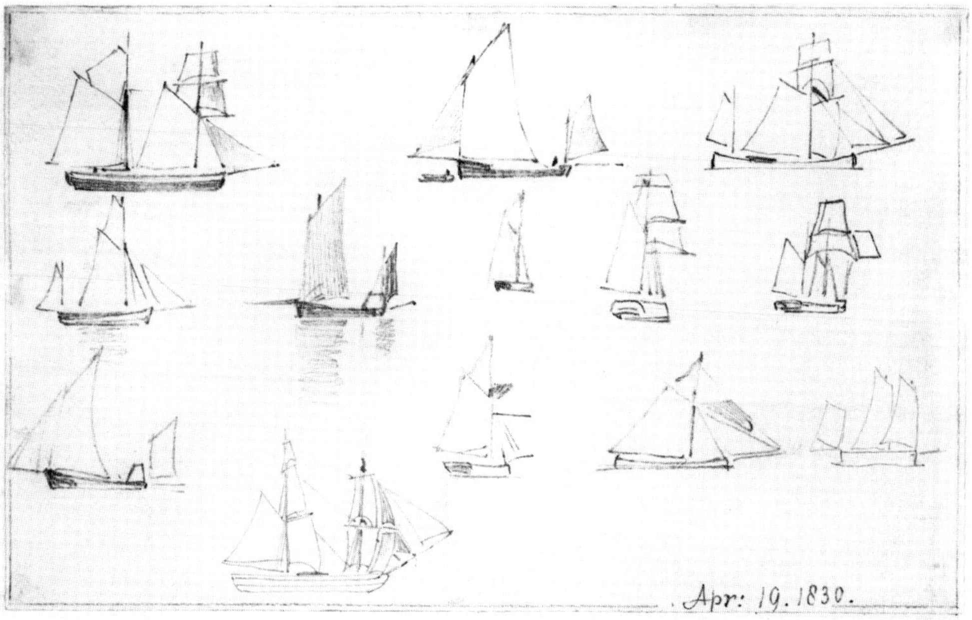

Plate 52. Pencil drawing
Studies of sailing craft Apr.19th 1830 off Hastings
A beautiful clear evening, they could see Shakespeare's Cliff Dover through the telescope *and a vast No. of vessels on the sea.* Cooke captured luggers, schooners and smacks.
Photo courtesy Martyn Gregory

were also concluded. Original drawings for *London* were unframed and sent to Christie's with a good deal more.

A high point in the young man's experience was evidently the great revelation when he viewed the exhibited collection of R.P. Bonington's drawings and pictures (see Appendix 1, Diary Extracts, 10 April 1834). That he expressed surprise seems strange; Cooke certainly had knowledge of Bonington's work, for the family owned examples and he had imitated and copied him. Perhaps it was that he had not seen a large range of that artist's powerful work, and possibly only a few oils. They knew of Bonington through his collaborators and friends T.S. Boys, W.J. Cooke and John Barnett (in whose house he died in 1828); all three were former apprentices, but there may well have been other links. Bonington's infrequent appearances in London, 1825 and 1827, probably involved a round of visits to the studios of engravers and he had been in correspondence with W.B. Cooke in the latter year[3] so George Cooke's presence at the Pentonville funeral in 1828 would indicate more than a formal gesture.

3. Pointon op.cit., p.125.

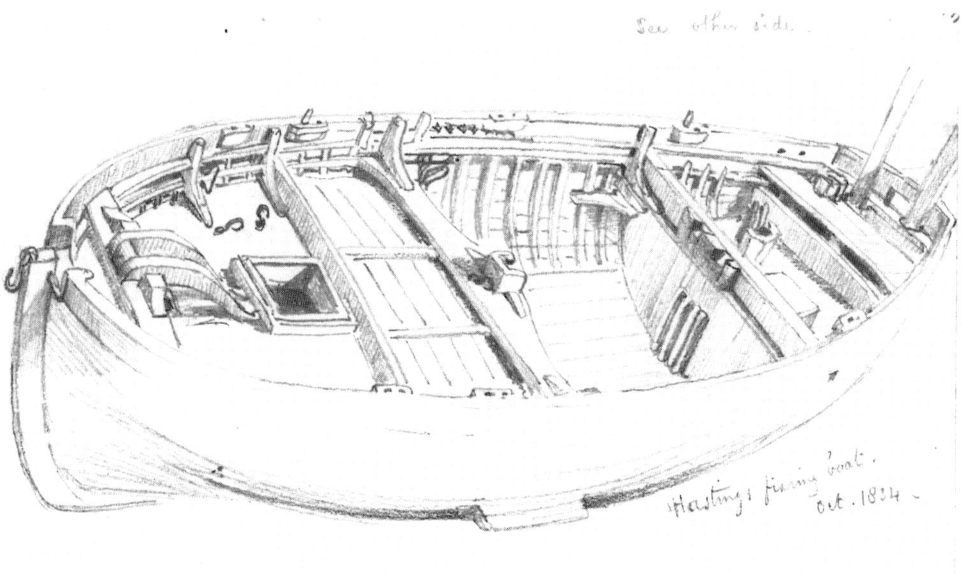

Plate 53. Pencil drawing
Hastings fishing boat 1834
Carefully considered and faithfully delineated, the hull of the fishing lugger with many of its in-board features is there for posterity. The drawing was made during a long stay with John Sheepshanks, his early patron.
Photo courtesy C.R. Cooke, OBE

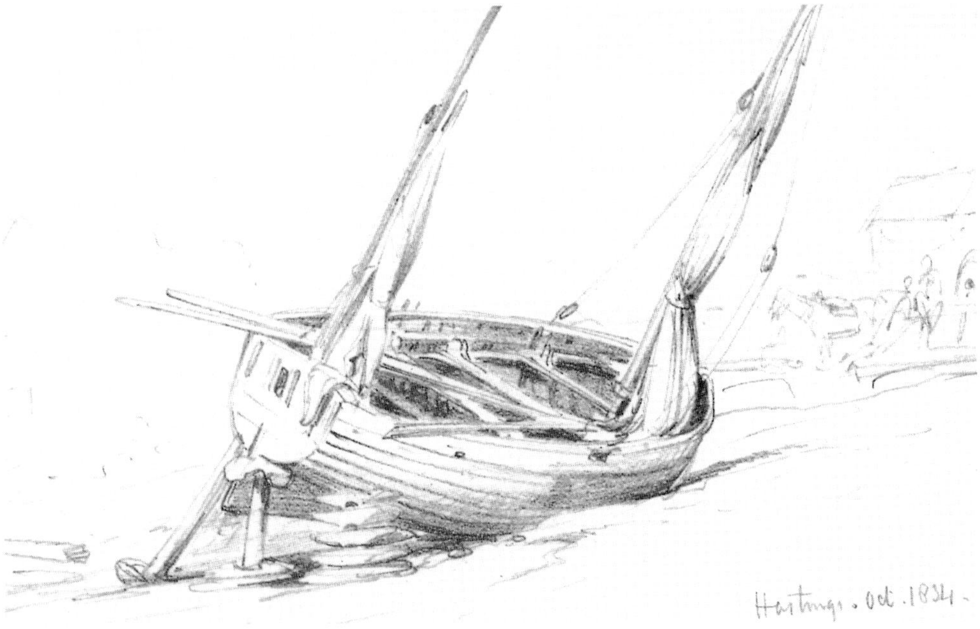

Plate 54. Pencil drawing
Hastings lugger, repairs under way
Photo courtesy C.R. Cooke, OBE

Likewise he might have expected to run across Mr.John Sheepshanks at a picture sale, so perhaps the luck on which he congratulated himself was in obtaining a commission for a picture, since he had not yet publicly exhibited, nor been subject to critical reviews.

Richard Redgrave used a phrase *a first start in the race of art* which is a typical, jolly expression of the mid-Victorian time; they talked about the Old Masters as *those grand old chaps* and there was a *cameraderie* of Art, putting all successful painters past and present on an equal footing. Cooke was in the *race* with more than a sporting chance, one might venture; he had his eye on the tape with a clear idea of how he might attain it.

John Sheepshanks' name is enshrined in the great collection at South Kensington, known since 1899 as the Victoria & Albert Museum. He gave his collection of modern pictures to the nation in 1856 and had been a generous host to artists, who stayed in his houses and painted pictures while there.

William Mulready formed a friendship with the retiring, wealthy bachelor, a Yorkshire clothier (the family fortune derived from manufacturing cloth for the uniforms of Wellington's armies). He drew Sheepshanks in home surroundings and painted his Blackheath garden in a style which foreshadowed Pre-Raphaelite aims. The collector had brothers – Richard, the astronomer, and Thomas – and a sister Ann, both of whom bought pictures. Stories of him and his lifestyle are found among the reminiscences of several painters, for example, John Callcott Horsley,[4] and Cooke seems to have become a favourite member of the circle.

John Constable recorded Sheepshanks' Yorkshire accent – 'Coooke' when speaking of his protégé.[5] A visit to Sheepshanks at his seaside place, East Hill House, Hastings, in September 1834 turned out to be memorable. There were scores of fishing boats going off and coming ashore while the power of a heavy sea, gale force winds and high tides combined to undermine houses on the cliff, all presenting subjects for Cooke to draw and paint from nature (Plates 52 to 54).

During the early part of 1835, perhaps recognising his need for a better grasp of figure drawing, he took up residence with his uncle William in Charlotte Street, Fitzroy Square, and attended evening sessions of the Drawing Academy at E.T. Parriss's in Clipstone Street, across the way (Plate 55).

Here life studies from costume figures were offered; the Rustic Academy was held on Tuesdays and Fridays while the Historical Academy took place on Mondays and Thursdays. Subjects ranged from a *Brigand* to a *Watercress man* and from a *Greek female* to a *Fireman*. Students were called on in turn to provide a pose and presumably costume; Cooke, on his evening turn, characteristically set *A Fisherman* with nets borrowed from Barnes. T.H. Cromek, who was now connected to W.B. Cooke as a result

4. *Recollections of a Royal Academician* by J.C. Horsley, 1903.
5. Constable op. cit. Vol. III.

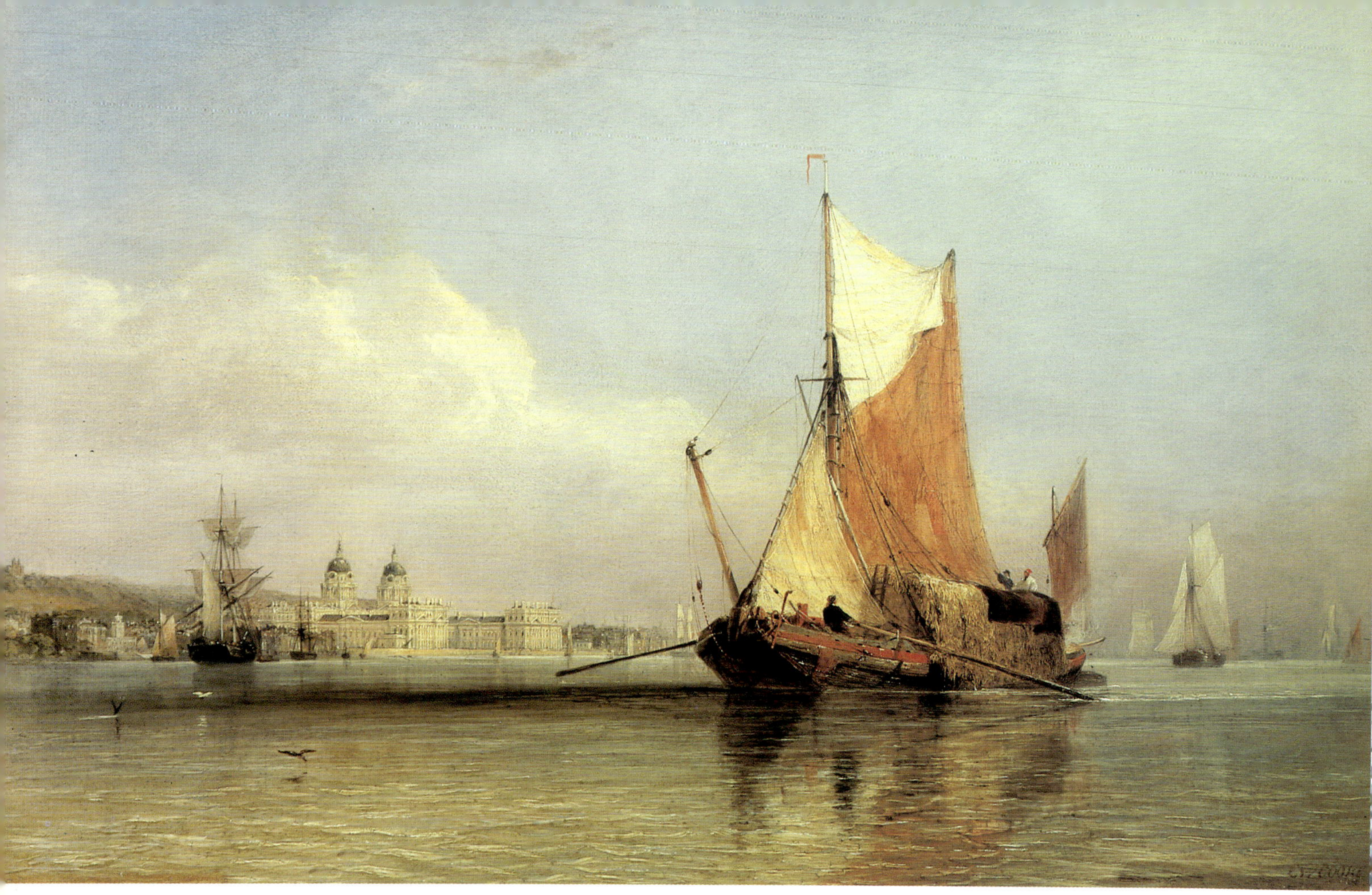

Colour Plate 38. 35/5

Hay Barge off Greenwich

Sir Christopher Wren's Royal Hospital buildings serve as a backdrop for boat-loads of horse fodder in the tideway. A practical picturesque subject, the scene not far from John Sheepshanks' home in Blackheath. Photo courtesy The Trustees of the National Maritime Museum, Greenwich

of the latter's second marriage, and Frederick Smith, engraver, the uncle's assistant, both drew with him and Edmund Cotman is also mentioned as attending.

His *début* at the London exhibitions was in 1835. The British Institution in Pall Mall held its annual show of new pictures early, with sending-in day in mid-January:

> *13th. Tues.Packed up pictures and took them outside the stage [coach] to the British Inst: the first Pictures I exhibit in London viz:*
> *Trouville Fishing Smack entering the Port of Havre,*
> *Coast Scene Normandy,*
> *Grass Boats.*

The titles for the second and third items (34/7 and 34/4) are expanded by the Institution Catalogue and by Cooke's *Ledger* entries and this comparison has been followed in compiling this Catalogue. The grass boats were presumably hay barges and the scene is on the Thames at Barnes. It was purchased by Jacob Bell, the manufacturing druggist and founder of the Pharmaceutical Society, who was of Cooke's own age and had an art collection worth the name by the time he was twenty-five. Having bought his first Cooke from the artist's first exhibition, he thereafter commissioned others. He was introduced by Edward to a meeting of the Graphic Society, the alternative Wednesday conversazione. on 8 April. Bell was friend and adviser to Edwin Landseer and was host to artistic gatherings; T.H. Hills, his business partner, succeeded to the role.

The 'Normandy' scene is located at Boulogne but none of this early group has so far been located.

Singled out for mention in several notices of E.W. Cooke is a *View of Broadstairs*

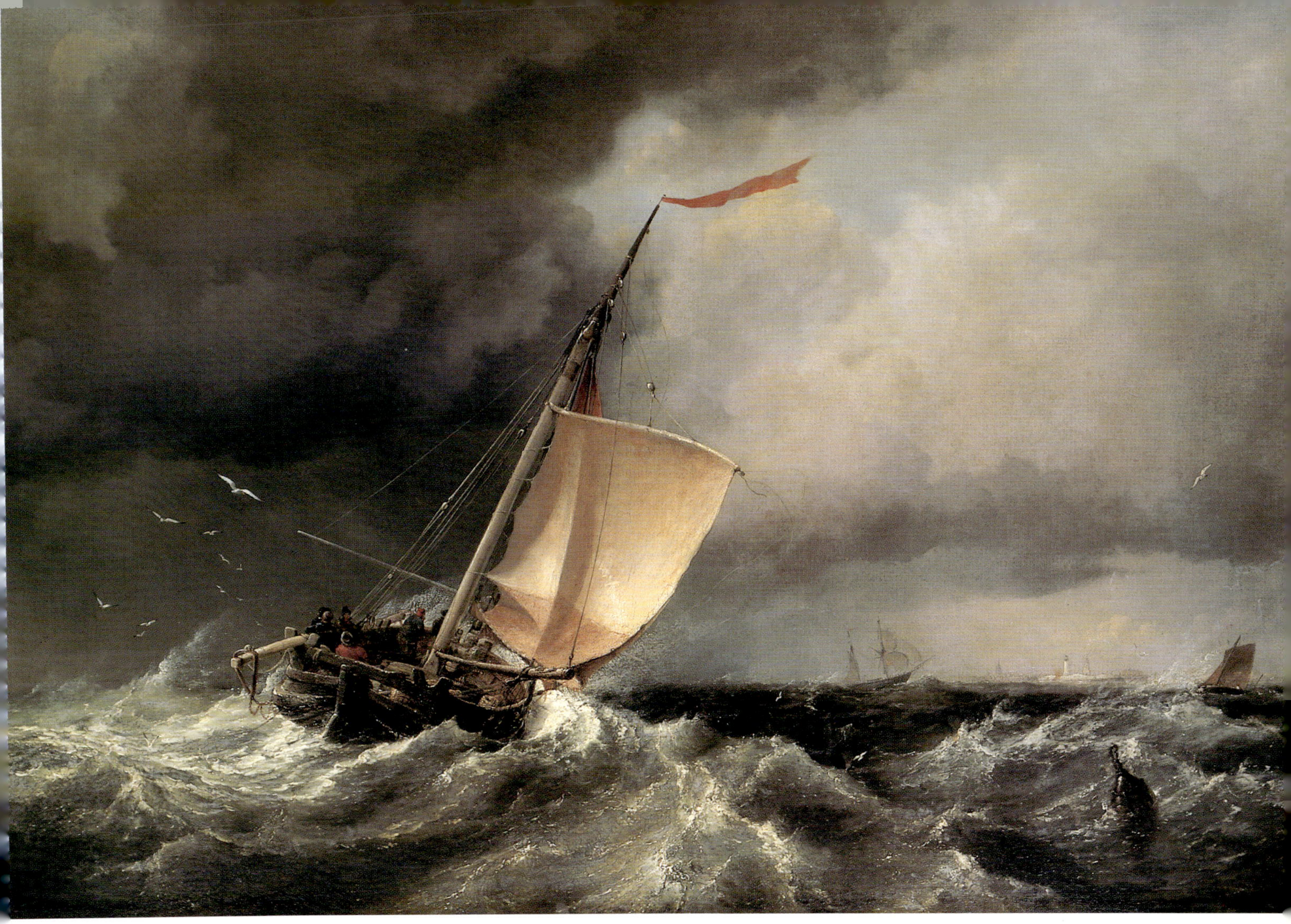

Colour Plate 39. 48/16
A squall – Trouville fishing boats making for Calais
Photo courtesy Sotheby's

(34/10), a small panel showing the pier, painted for James Wadmore at the price of twelve guineas. The *Art Journal* (1869) wrote of it, presumably because Cooke remembered it as an early commission, fetching more than six times its price twenty years later. It was not the artist's first picture from nature, nor did it date from 1826 as stated, but 1834.

The accidental burning of the Houses of Parliament in that year had been a major spectacle; equally something of a performance was the sight of J.M.W. Turner RA painting on his picture of the scene. Varnishing days at the British Institution in 1835 were well remembered by several members among the bystanders and noted also by Cooke.[6] Cousin W.J. Cooke had visited the ruins and drawn the smoking havoc. They went again and sketched and were considering etching a set of plates.They were in contact with Hodgson, the publisher, but for some reason Edward declined entering into it; perhaps having ceased his engraving he was not eager to return and now, without George Cooke's experienced hand to guide them, he possibly felt less than confident. Numerous records of so momentous a scene appeared and W.J. Cooke's drawings have also survived.[7]

Introductions at the Exhibition resulted in further commissions and Cooke also appeared at the Suffolk Street galleries of the Society of British Artists in 1835. His *Peter boat on the Thames* (35/2) was according to him badly hung, but Lord Lansdowne liked it and wrote to him. Since it was a commission for Mr. John Turner of Clapham, there was a difficulty, but the noble Marquess visited the artist at Albion House and commissioned another (35/4).

6. *Life of J.M.W. Turner RA* by A.J. Finberg, 2nd edition, 1961,.p.351.
7. 'The Palace of Westminster after the Fire of October 1834' by R.J.B. Walker, *The Walpole Society* Vol. XLIV, p.94.

Plate 55. Watercolour
The Orange seller 1835
Cooke attended Parriss' drawing Academy where models in costume, antique and current, were posed. This girl has an extraordinary resemblance to W.P. Frith's *The Sleepy Model,* also a seller of oranges, in his Diploma work of 1853.
Photo courtesy Sotheby's Pulborough

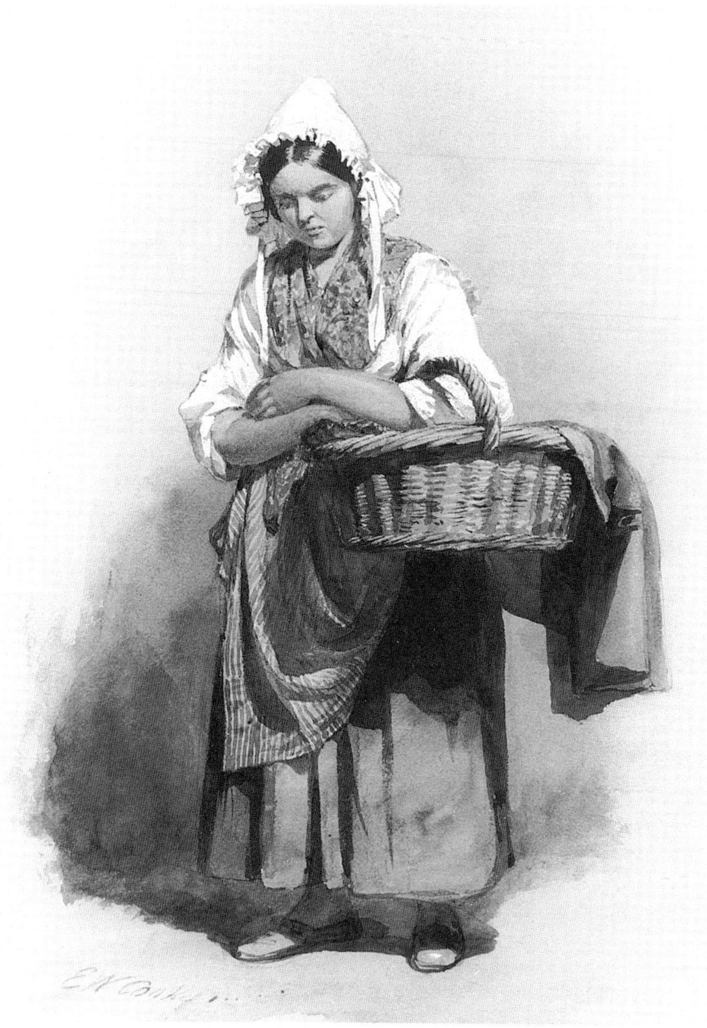

Plate 56. Pencil drawing
William Wells Esq of Redleaf, Kent
Former Hon. East India Company's Commander, shipbuilder and art collector; another version of this sketch is in Wells' *Scribblers' Book* from Redleaf, now in the British Museum.
Photo courtesy C.R. Cooke, OBE

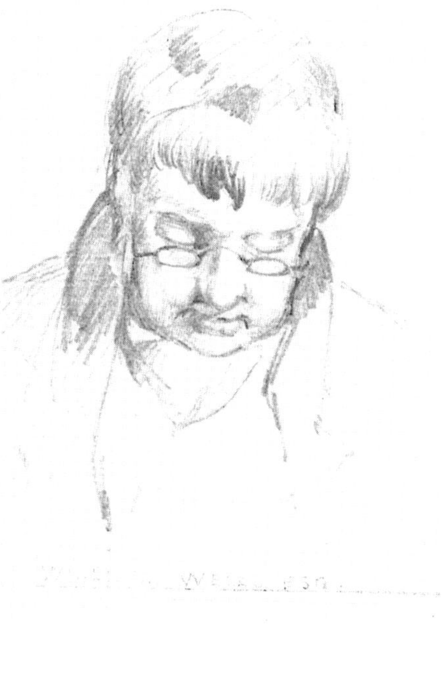

Plate 57. Watercolour
The Summerhouse, Redleaf
A rustic construction in William Wells' celebrated gardens near Penshurst.
Photo courtesy Private Collection

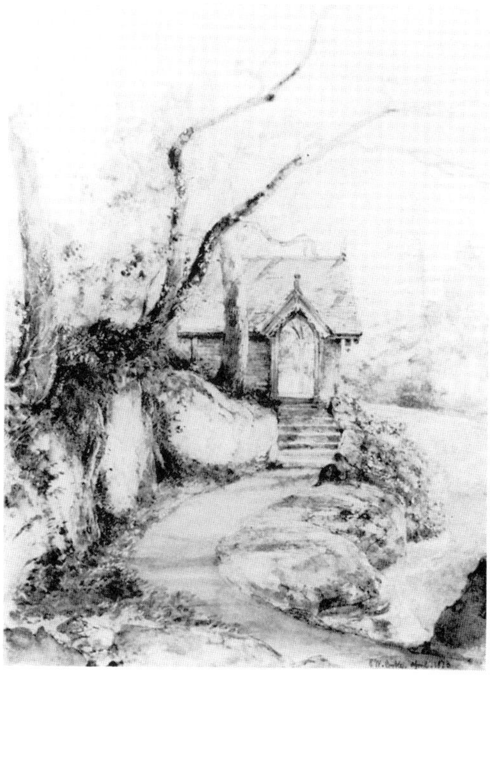

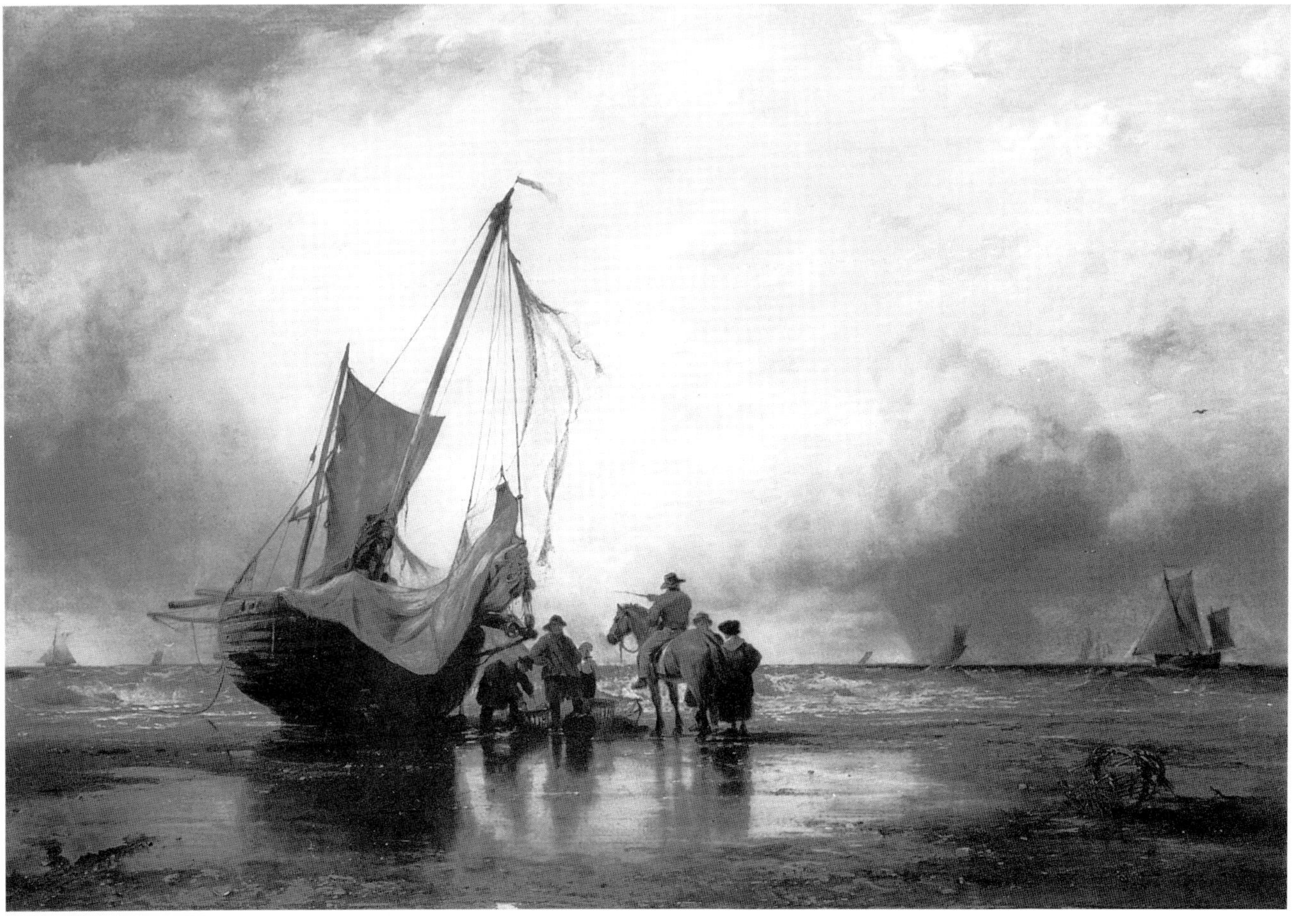

Plate 58. 37/7

Brighton hog-boat on the sands

Family ties with Brighton gave him access to the beach fishery with its distinctive tubby boats, the 'hoggies'.The horse, however, was painted in William Wells' stables at Redleaf. Professor Waagen thought it *very picturesquely conceived & carefully executed in a warm, clear & true tone... resembles a Van de Capelle in effect.*

Photo courtesy The Board of Trustees of the Victoria & Albert Museum, No.41

Cooke was about to try a subject which was to be unique in his range. Whether or not it was a remembrance of Bonington's picture *The Antiquary* or from reading Sir Walter Scott's novel of the same name, published in 1815, the idea of an elaborate still-life of antique objects was conceived.[8]

It began as 'an Antiquary's room', with 'curiosities' grouped in his own study. He made a sketch in colour in the evening by candlelight, something T.S. Boys had previously demonstrated most beautifully according to the diary. Neighbours called to see the setting and the Miss Warings lent china jars to group with the rest; he went to town taking up old pictures and old clothes to make exchanges with dealers in Princes Street, Soho. He bought from Mr. Hull *...a China jar, Carvings, a Helmet and a fine carved chair &c.* He placed a recently completed small portrait of his aged maternal grandfather in the foreground. T.H. Cromek joined him in setting up and painting the scene.

The Antiquary's Cell (35/7, Colour Plate 160), its title when exhibited in 1836, was bought by Sheepshanks. Cooke called it *Olla Podrida,* an amusing analogy with the Spanish hash, which was also used by Captain Frederick Marryat RN as the title of one of his works.

In March 1836 Cooke accompanied Sheepshanks to the Suffolk Street Exhibition and called afterwards to see Edwin Landseer's pictures. Two days later, armed with an introduction from the latter and a folio of his own drawings, he went to Fladong's Hotel

8. *The Romantic Interior* by Clive Wainwright, 1989.

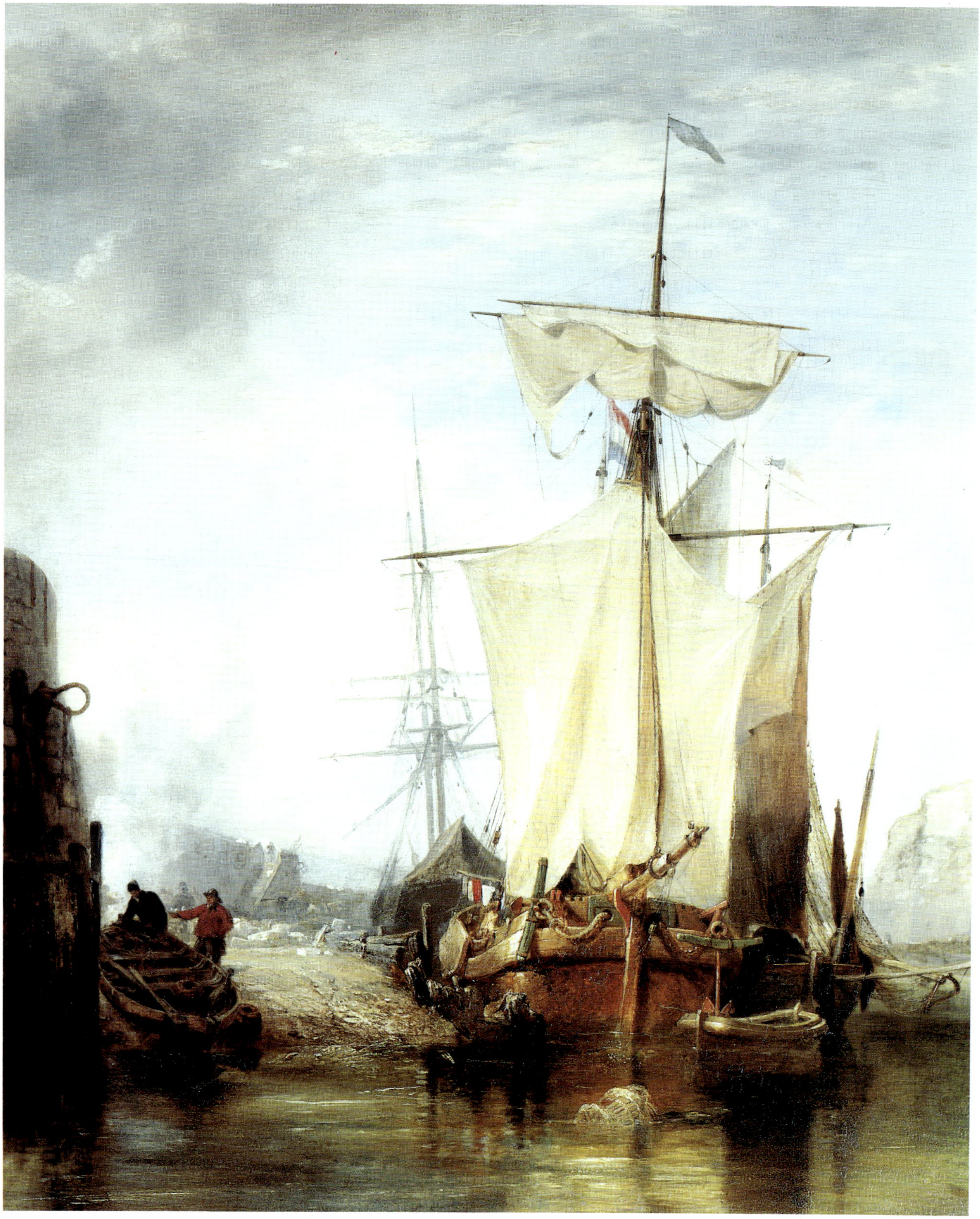

Colour Plate 40. 36/17

Dutch Galliott, St Peter Port, Guernsey

The foreign trader was observed by the artist on his visit and painted not only for her decorative qualities but also as a comment on coastwise commerce.

Photo courtesy Arthur Ackermann & Peter Johnson. Private Collection

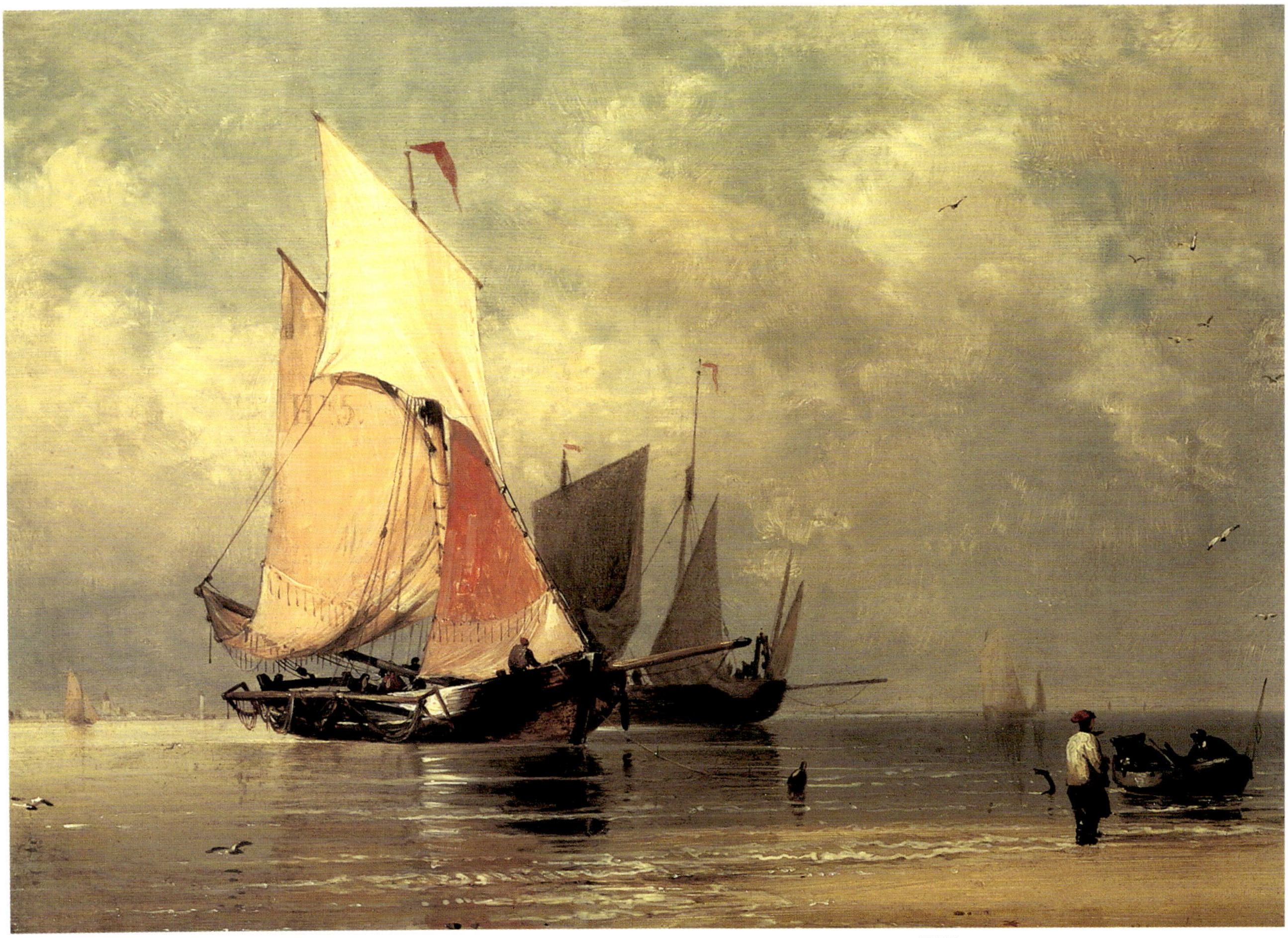

Colour Plate 41. 54/4
French craft off Quillebeuf
He had noted this basic group in watercolour on his first visit to France in 1833 and introduced it into subsequent pictures of the Seine estuary with monumental effect. The craft, he usually explained, were waiting for a wind and the tide. Photo courtesy Phillips Fine Art Auctioneers

to call upon Mr. William Wells (Plate 56) who, liking what he saw, gave a commission for a picture of an Isle of Wight coast scene.

Here we confront another collector, not only of contemporary art but also of Old Masters and one who had a special approach to marine subjects. It is a universal and timeless phenomenon that seafaring men require certain things from paintings that include ships and failing to find these things will reject pictures which others might accept without hesitation. The prerequisite is an essential *truth* in form, in build, rig and behaviour. Poetic imagination, one might say, is no substitute for seaworthiness!

William Wells belonged to a family long connected with ships, dockyards and the Thames. An ancestor, John Wells, was Queen Elizabeth's Storekeeper at the Royal Yard at Deptford. Vice-Admiral Sir Thomas Wells, a pall bearer at Nelson's funeral who lived at Holmewood, Hunts., was a brother and John Wells of Bickley Hall, Kent, was another.[9] Joseph Farington RA was an intimate of William Wells and was often at his table. In the diary which he kept[10] there is a great deal about the Wells family, their finances and their friends. William had been at sea as an officer in the Hon. East India Company's service under Captain R.A. Farington (brother of Joseph), commanding the ship *Lascelles*. Wells ended his seagoing career as Commander of the East Indiaman *Albion* 1794/95. He then bought, with his brother John, the famous Blackwall Yard on the Thames where Indiamen were built, docked and refitted, although he had retired from business by the time Cooke met him. With such a background it is not surprising to hear from his old friend Farington that Wells had *formed a design to make a collection of*

9. *Burke's Landed Gentry*
10. *The Farington Diary,* 2nd edition, 1978

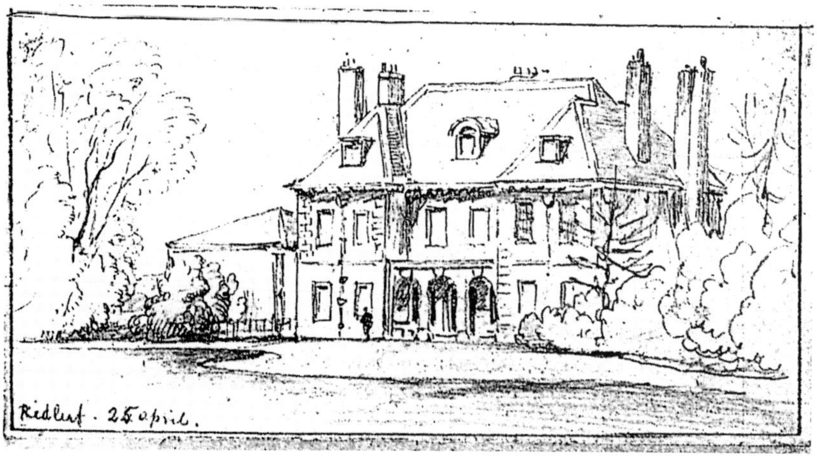

Plate 59. Pencil drawing
Redleaf
The mansion on Wells' estate near Penshurst, Kent, where he was host to many artists, both established and rising.

Photo courtesy Clarges Gallery

drawings of all the vessels, Boats, up to vessels of the largest size, used in every part of the world. He spoke highly of Pocock's excellence in drawing ships correctly and in placing properly in the water and before the wind.

How far he succeeded in his aim is not evident, but his picture collection included the marine masters Willem van de Velde and Charles Brooking, as well as Nicholas Pocock, and E.W. Cooke's work clearly measured up to Wells' exacting standards. In expectations of inheriting a fortune from his mother, Wells began collecting pictures with the help of dealers and he told Farington in 1810 that his total expenditure on his collection, which included Old Masters, had been £16,000, but its value was only about £12,000. It would be wrong, however, to suggest that he was only an investor in works of art, for he patronised coming painters who took his fancy. The three sales of his pictures from 1848-1860 realised in excess of £114,000 and there were six E.W. Cookes included.

He was known as Wells of Redleaf, from the location of his fine estate near Penshurst in Kent. A Trustee of the National Gallery and a Director of the British Institution, his connoisseurship appeared somewhat suspect to some, for we find John Constable RA saying of the young Cooke *a clever lad, better that he should be under Sheepshanks than get into old Redleaf's clutches.*[11] Was it perhaps that the requirements and taste of such a patron were calculated to stifle freedom and self expression? Certainly, in preferring F.R Lee's landscapes to those of John Constable the old mariner was declaring a conservative stance in which he was not alone.

Constable's encounters with Wells are recorded: 1833 *...but my pictures do not come into his rules or whims of the art and he said I had 'lost my way'.* 1834 *...an admirer of commonplace called to see my picture, and did not like it at all, so I am sure there is something good in it. Soon after Mr Vernon called, and bought it....*[12] F.R. Lee and Edwin Landseer, Richard Redgrave and Frederick Goodall were others who enjoyed the hospitality and convivial atmosphere in the gracious surroundings of a mansion containing a noteworthy collection of Old Masters as well as recently purchased examples of their own paintings! *The house is the most tasteful place I ever saw, old-fashioned, full of beautiful pictures and furniture. The grounds are charming and it has the most famous flower gardens in England.*[13]

Perhaps the desire to please a patron of pronounced tastes led to unthinking repetition – *he has noodled poor Lee out of what sense he had* wrote Constable[14] and Lee told Redgrave that Wells *used to bully him sadly* but he would allow that to no-one else.[15] In the Redleaf mansion was room for painting; there were opportunities for shooting and fishing and a countryside abounding in interest. This was near the mediaeval Penshurst Place, ancestral home of the Sidneys. It was sited on sandstone outcrops in the Weald of Kent, an interesting and varied landscape which included fine wooded grounds and the

11. Constable op.cit., Vol. III
12. *Memoirs of the Life of John Constable* by C.R. Leslie, RA, 1951, pp.218, 240,
13. Quoted W.T. Whitley, *Art in England 1821-1837*, 1930.
14. Constable op.cit., Vol. III
15. *Richard Redgrave CB RA, A Memoir Compiled from his Diary* by F.M. Redgrave.1891, p.309.

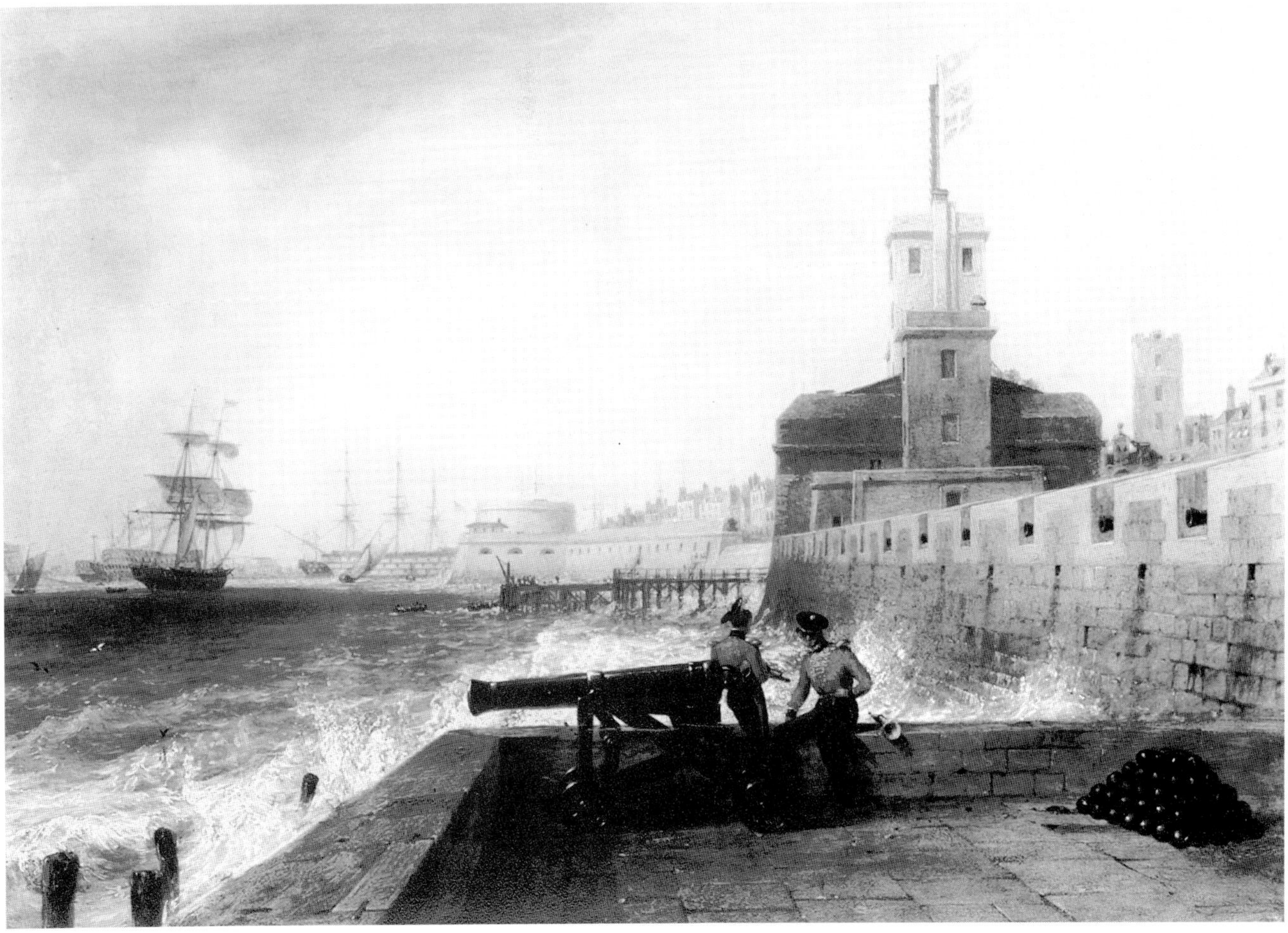

Plate 60. 36/21

Portsmouth from the Saluting Platform

Finden's engraving of this small painting was widely distributed and was itself copied by amateurs, sometimes quite well. Oil versions are therefore not unknown; on the other hand, other artists sat where he sat and the results might appear familiar.

Photo courtesy The Trustees of the National Maritime Museum, Greenwich

spectacular gardens which Wells himself had developed. There were glasshouses and ornamental rock-gardens, all of which interested Cooke. His host's keen appreciation of marine subjects, the English coast and the French ports made for a promising association.

Painting commissions for others while under Wells' roof was not unusual. Some small pictures for the Finden brothers to engrave for their *Ports, Harbours & Watering Places...* were in progress though Cooke found time to make a tracing of a Nicholas Pocock drawing of a brig on the sands. He had in hand a small painting of a similar subject (36/11), Hastings, which Wells purchased. A large Dutch subject (37/12, Plate 71), now in the Royal Holloway College Collection, is actually inscribed 'Redleaf' with the artist's signature and this has led more than one cataloguer to suppose incorrectly that it had been Wells' commission.

Cooke's enchantment with the place was complete. The terrain fascinated him and he returned to it in later years when selecting a site for his own house and gardens which owed much to the Wellsian scene. Working at Redleaf was not easy, however, for he noted having just commenced painting when neighbours Mr Glendinning and Lord DeLisle drove over with Lee and an irresistible invitation. They took fishing tackle and at Penshurst had a glorious day's sport, down one side of the river and back by the other taking pike, chubb and perch. To be on easy terms with the nobility was a sign of having achieved a certain status, but for all that there does not seem to be a Cooke among the Penshurst pictures.

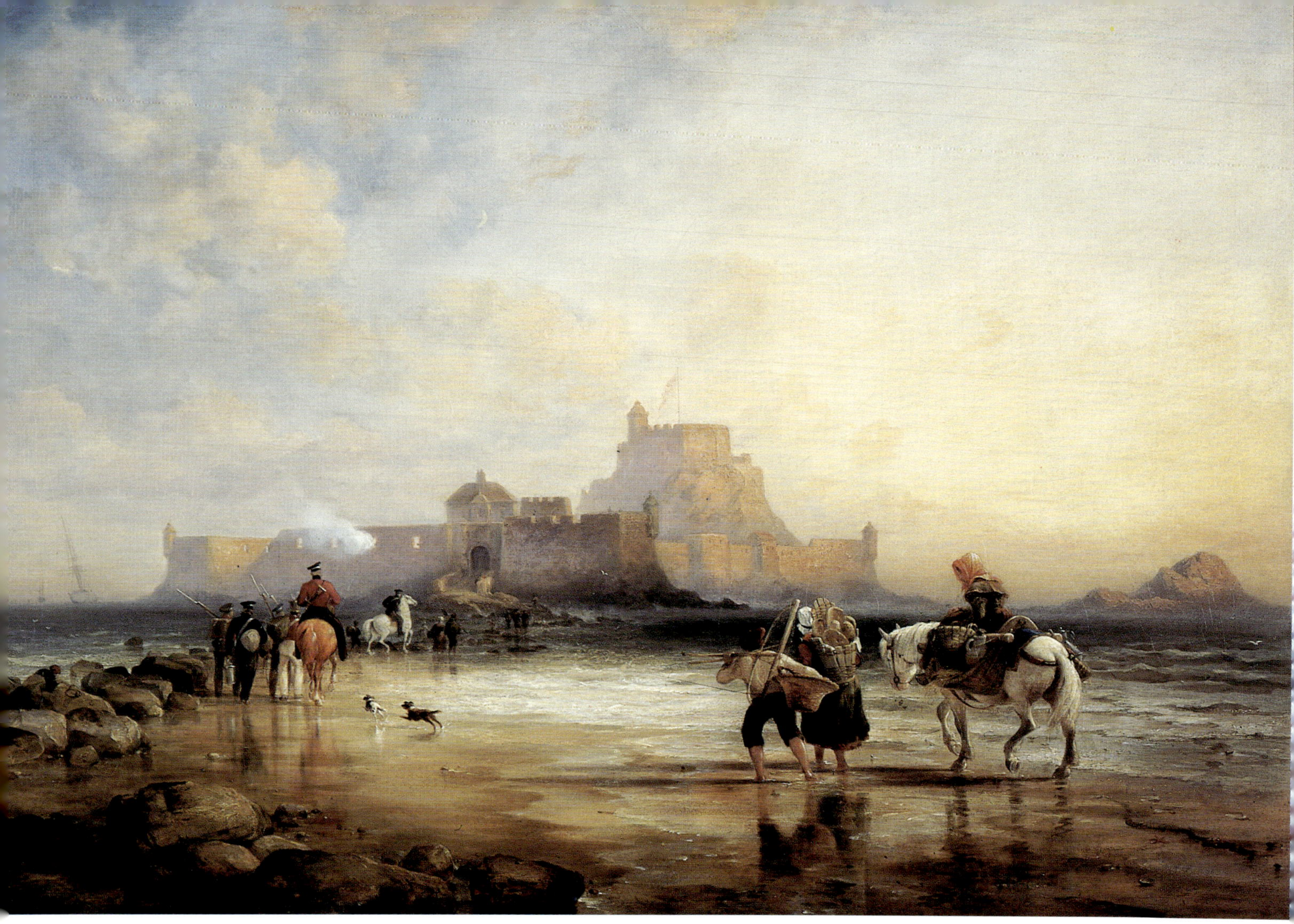

Colour Plate 42. 41/1

Elizabeth Castle, Jersey, from the Causeway; Low Water

It is evening, there is incident in the firing of a signal gun and also a reminiscence of Turner, not least in the straggling soldiery. The fisherfolk and their equipment are bound to be faithful records, not merely picturesque accessories. A commission from the Marquess of Westminster, it was viewed and approved in progress.

Photo courtesy Private Collection

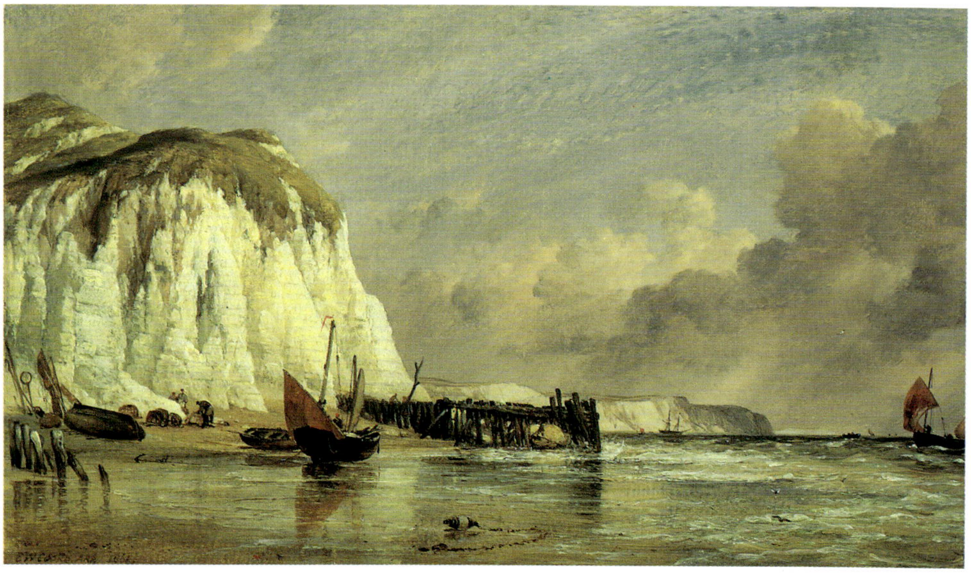

Colour Plate 43. 56/18

Little bathing bay and jetty, with Dunnose Head

This delightful Isle of Wight scene is a distillation of his Bonchurch studies and may have been a present to his friend Henry Bicknell.

Photo courtesy Spink &Son Ltd.

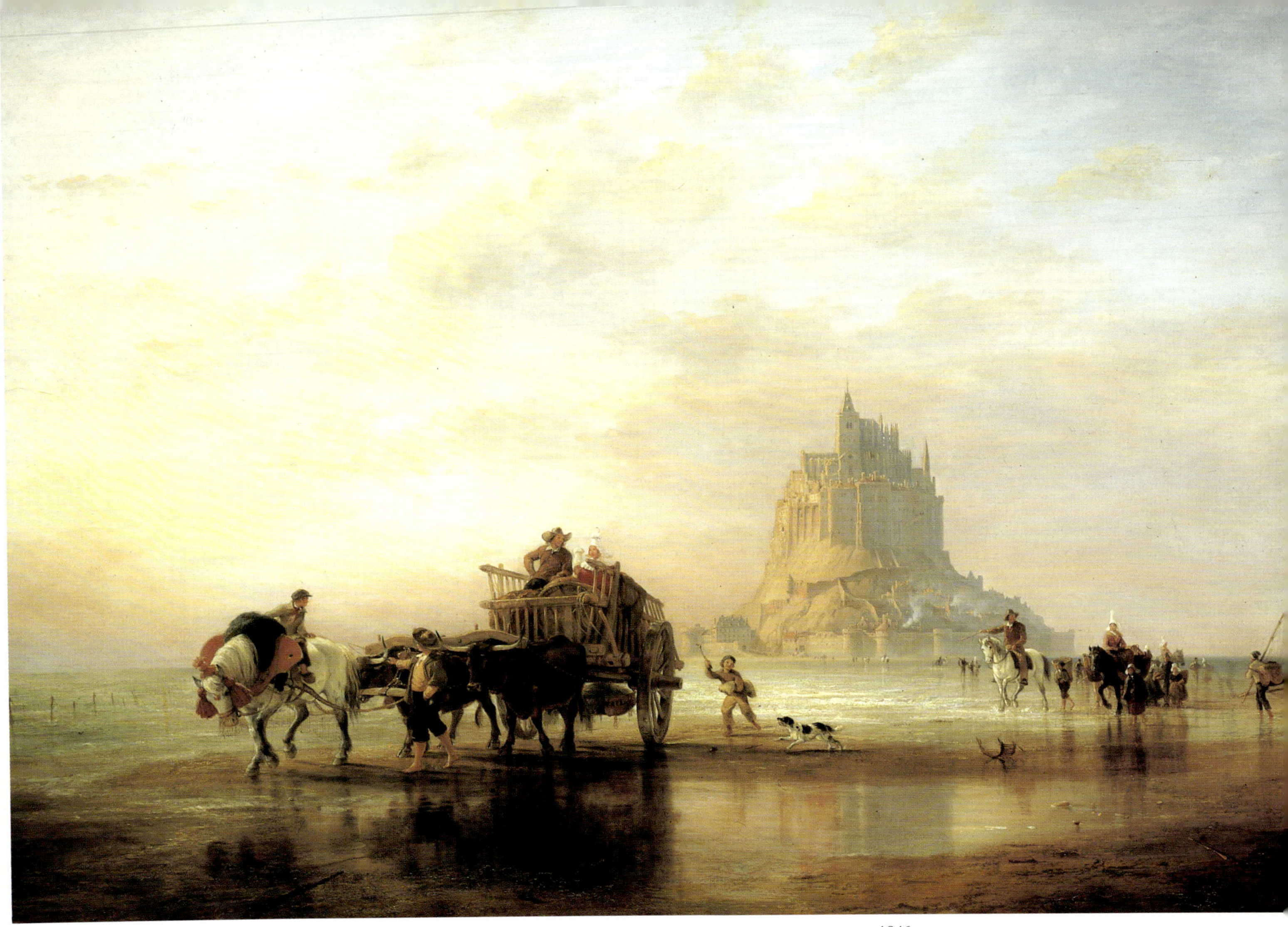

Colour Plate 44. 40/6

Mont. St. Michel, Peasants returning to Pontorson on the approach of the tide

An influential collector, the Marquess of Lansdowne, already a patron, bought the canvas at the British Institution exhibition.There is here no hint of the menace of a rapidly rising tide – in this bay it was said it could outstrip a galloping horse. The peasants are secure in their local knowledge. He painted at least six major pictures of the Mont. Photo courtesy Christie's

At home at Barnes in Surrey he began Wells' commission to be called *Tarring the Boat* (36/6), a beach scene at St Lawrence, Isle of Wight, noting *painted the sky from Nature.*

The two families of Cooke and Loddiges, now no longer in the close collaboration demanded by publishing the *Botanical Cabinet*, lived on opposite sides of London, but remained in frequent contact. On visits to art exhibitions and riverside outings to the Horticultural Society's Gardens at Chiswick, they met fellow enthusiasts, patrons and the nobility. From the notes on George Loddiges' life which Cooke compiled for his friend Dr J.S. Bowerbank in 1846,[16] it is evident that he owed much to the example and encouragement of that remarkable man. The scientific side of the painter's interests was at the outset fostered at Hackney and developed by the knowledgeable plantsman's help and advice. Demonstrations with the microscope, introduction to further aspects of collecting, music and ornithology, as well as the contacts with such figures as Dr John Pye Smith and Nathaniel Bagshaw Ward, widened his horizons. Examining ultramarines through the microscope, demonstrations of the polarisation of light and helping with large display cases of stuffed humming-birds are recorded. George Loddiges' colour-sense was evidently highly developed and his advice, we learn, was invariably accepted by the painter.

16. Cooke MSS.

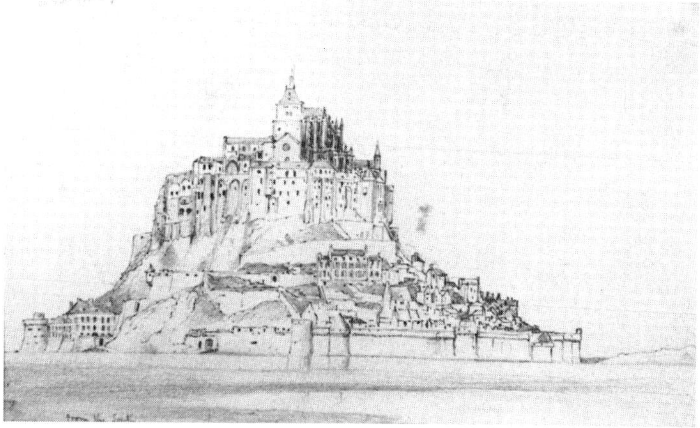

Plate 61. Pencil drawing
Mont S Michel, Normandy
From the south, September 1836. Photo courtesy Clarges Gallery

There were commissions which helped to put Cooke's name before the public: from the Finden brothers, whose *Ports, Harbours and Watering Places,* a projected series of steel engravings and text was begun in 1836-37. The originals of some were to be oil paintings (Plate 60) and others watercolours; many artists were enlisted but evidently too few copies were sold to cover costs and the publisher Charles Tilt disposed of it to George Vertue.[17] A study for this series depicting a sheer- or rigging- hulk in Portsmouth Harbour, the former HMS *Swiftsure,* was shown to Sheepshanks who bought it on the spot. The next day Cooke carried the painting to the engraver Finden and looked at the works in progress. The fate of this publication was chequered, like many another of the time. Vertue engaged William Beattie as Editor who brought in W.H. Bartlett to enlarge the range of pictures and the work in two volumes was complete by 1842 *...more for the drawing room table than the library shelf... and the octavo's of Prout, Harding and Holland gave place to the more showy quarto's of Bartlett and Allom.*[18]

All the while Cooke had paintings on the easel for the Exhibitions and they were evidently about to dispose of their lease of Albion House, the school having closed and the cottage sufficing for their needs.

A voyage to Guernsey provided new material, though not all of it to his taste. When he arrived off St Peter Port before 6 am he thought the town looked most magnificent. After breakfast at his hotel he *progged all about but found scarcely any food for the pencil, everything so tasteless and formal.* If the fashionable architecture of St Peter Port did not suit, neighbouring Jersey produced lively scenes. The smoke and fire entailed in *breaming* a collier on the shore at low water was an honest everyday maintenance job which appealed to him.

It was the next port of call, Granville on the Normandy coast, which also struck chords and the approach to his goal was equally intriguing. From Avranches, a town quite full on market day of horses and people in the most picturesque costume, he noted very fine subjects everywhere and most exquisite country all round. Then he saw the Mont St Michel at a distance. The Grève or causeway was quite dry on his arrival and he felt surprised and delighted at the magnificence of the Mont from the outside. The interior of the walls was even finer; the streets, houses and costumes of people and fishermen demanded sketches and he went all over the Prison and Chateau and round the whole place. *25th Sunday... people much alarmed for the safety of 3 Gents who were returning from Avranches in the evening across the Greve. The sea came up before they could cross and they had to run for their lives. A boat put off and rescued them.* It was well known, but evidently not well enough known, that the rising tide in the bay could outstrip a galloping horse. Sketching, buying baskets and sabots along the way, Cooke was preparing for a series of paintings of the Mont which combined atmosphere with close observation of the local fishermen and craft (Plate 61).

The marine painter almost succumbed to seasickness on board the *Ariadne* packet from

17. *Illustrated History of British Steel Engravers* by B. Hunnisett. Rev. Ed., 1989.
18. Roget op.cit., Vol. II, p.4.

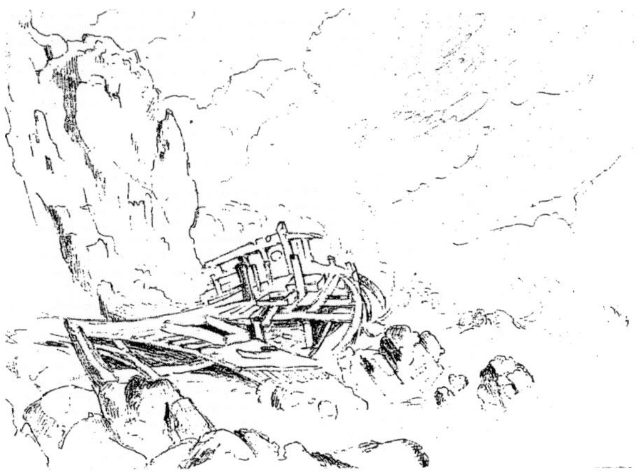

Plate 62. 43/5
Wreck of a sloop on the Hermitage rocks, Jersey
Camera lucida record of a painting exhibited in 1844 at the British Institution.

St Malo on what he described as a horrible return voyage to Jersey – it blew a heavy gale and there was an awful sea running. Storms however supplied subjects and on 12 October at about four it blew a hurricane and a Granville sloop, the *Marie Ange,* was driven ashore on the Hermitage rocks soon to become a complete wreck. Passengers and crew saved themselves on the rocks of Elizabeth Castle. Two other sloops and a brig came into port in fine style and he made sketches about the pier heads.

The following day he went over the wreck and made studies of her (Plate 62); hundreds of people were there clearing it but in the night it was driven against the walls of Elizabeth Castle. He noted buying a cap from young Le Maistre, but whether for his own wear or, like the baskets, for his collection of nautical 'props' is not recorded.

With careful attention to his patrons Cooke carried his sketches to Blackheath for John Sheepshanks' appraisal and in mid-November was at Redleaf once more. Wells it seems was anxious to smooth the way for his painters, providing *nature morte* in parcels of fish, with a lobster and a crab for Cooke and birds, golden plover, for F.R. Lee.

Landseer arrived with a stock of anecdotes and a pair of large deerhounds, Haphet and Downey. Cooke worked on his picture, altered parts possibly on the advice of Landseer who commenced his large picture of the deerhounds, making, said the young painter a 'glorious sketch'. Landseer looked over the young man's drawings and told 'capital stories'.

Cooke began a picture of Mont St Michel and F.R. Lee began a picture of pheasant. In the evening there were billiards and chess with Landseer while Cooke also found time to read Captain Frederick Marryat's *Mr.Midshipman Easy,* published in 1836.

Another wealthy patron, who was not, however, noted as a host to his painters, was Robert Vernon who made his money supplying horses to Wellington's armies and commissioned pictures from Turner, Constable, Landseer and many others including Cooke. *Dutch boats in a Calm* of 1843 (43/9, Colour Plate 57) became widely known because of the engraving of it published by the *Art Journal* in its series *The Vernon Gallery.* This was the collection by modern British masters presented to the nation three years before Vernon's death, and now in the Tate Gallery, for which S.C. Hall secured the engraving rights for his periodical.

Elhanan Bicknell, an oil merchant concerned with the sperm whale fishery who might reasonably be expected to favour marine paintings, began collecting in 1838 and at his house in Herne Hill entertained the leading artists of the time. He was a considerable patron of Turner and Stanfield and his son Henry married David Roberts' daughter Christine who had been one of the young ladies at Mrs Cooke's Albion House school.

It should not be thought that Cooke's early patrons belonged solely to the 'commercial aristocracy'. In addition to his first commission from Lord Lansdowne, The Earl of Winchilsea commissioned a sea-piece after the 1836 British Institution and had others later. Lord Wharncliffe, a keen yachtsman with whom the artist went afloat in August

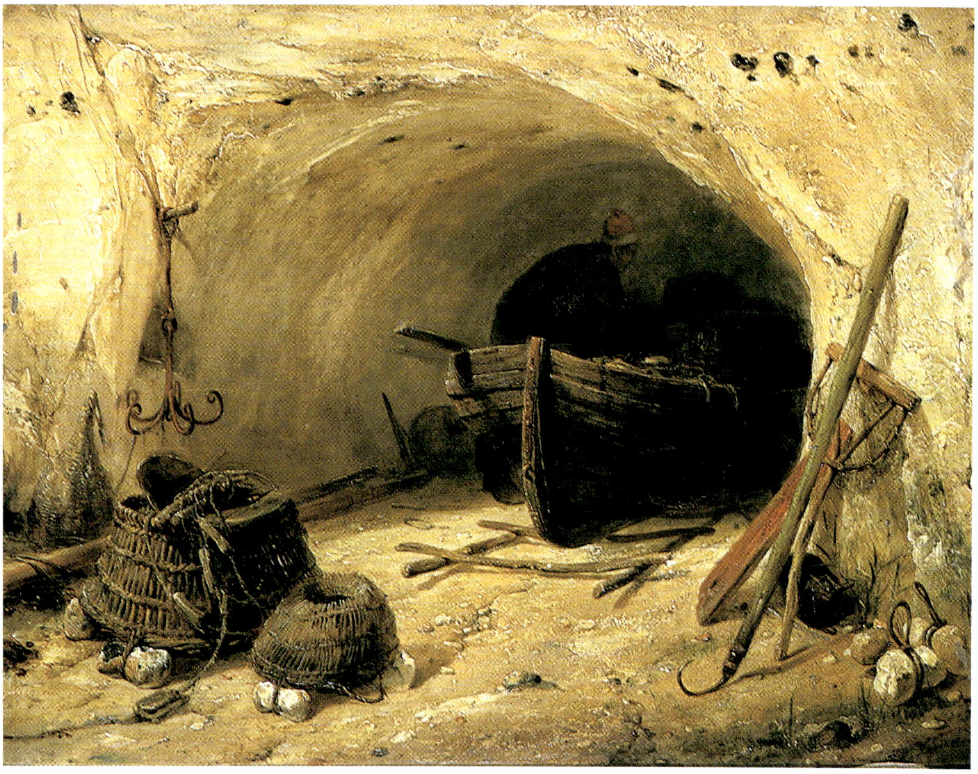

Colour Plate 45A. 35/21

Undercliff Cave, Ventnor (engraved as The Boat House*)*

Robert Vernon gave his collection to the nation and this was his second Cooke. The Wight fisherman with all his gear and his small craft in the cave intrigued Cooke greatly and he later painted another version.

Photo courtesy Tate Gallery

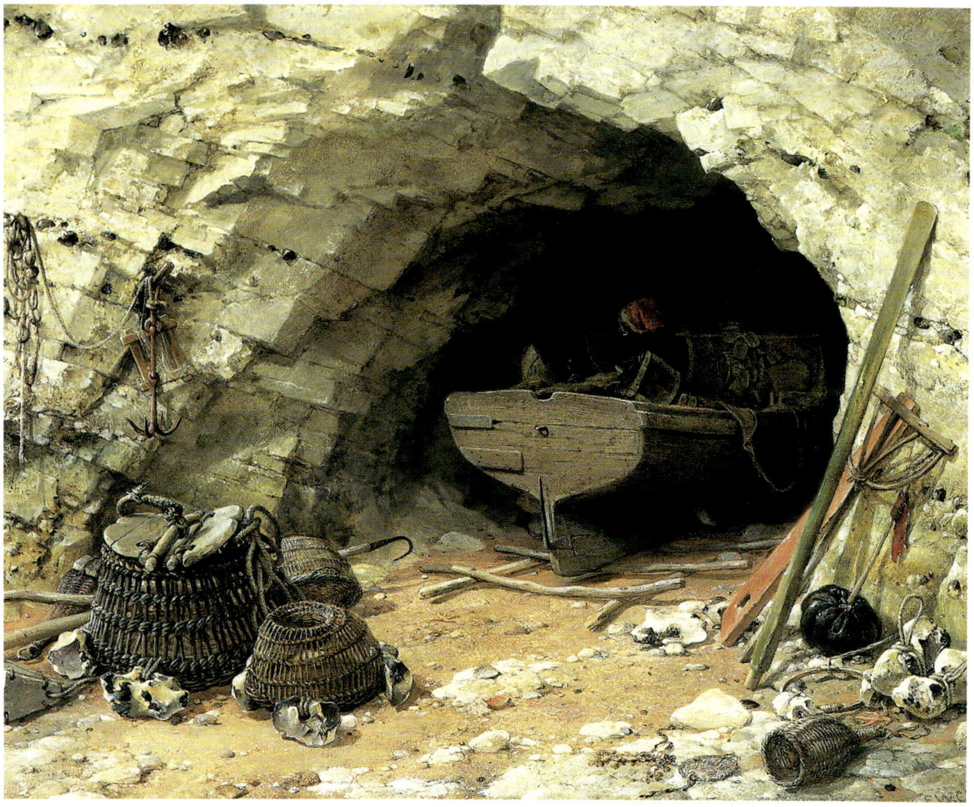

Colour Plate 45B. 66/9

Marine Stores

A more polished performance than his earlier picture; presumably the scene is still the Isle of Wight.

Photo courtesy Private Collection

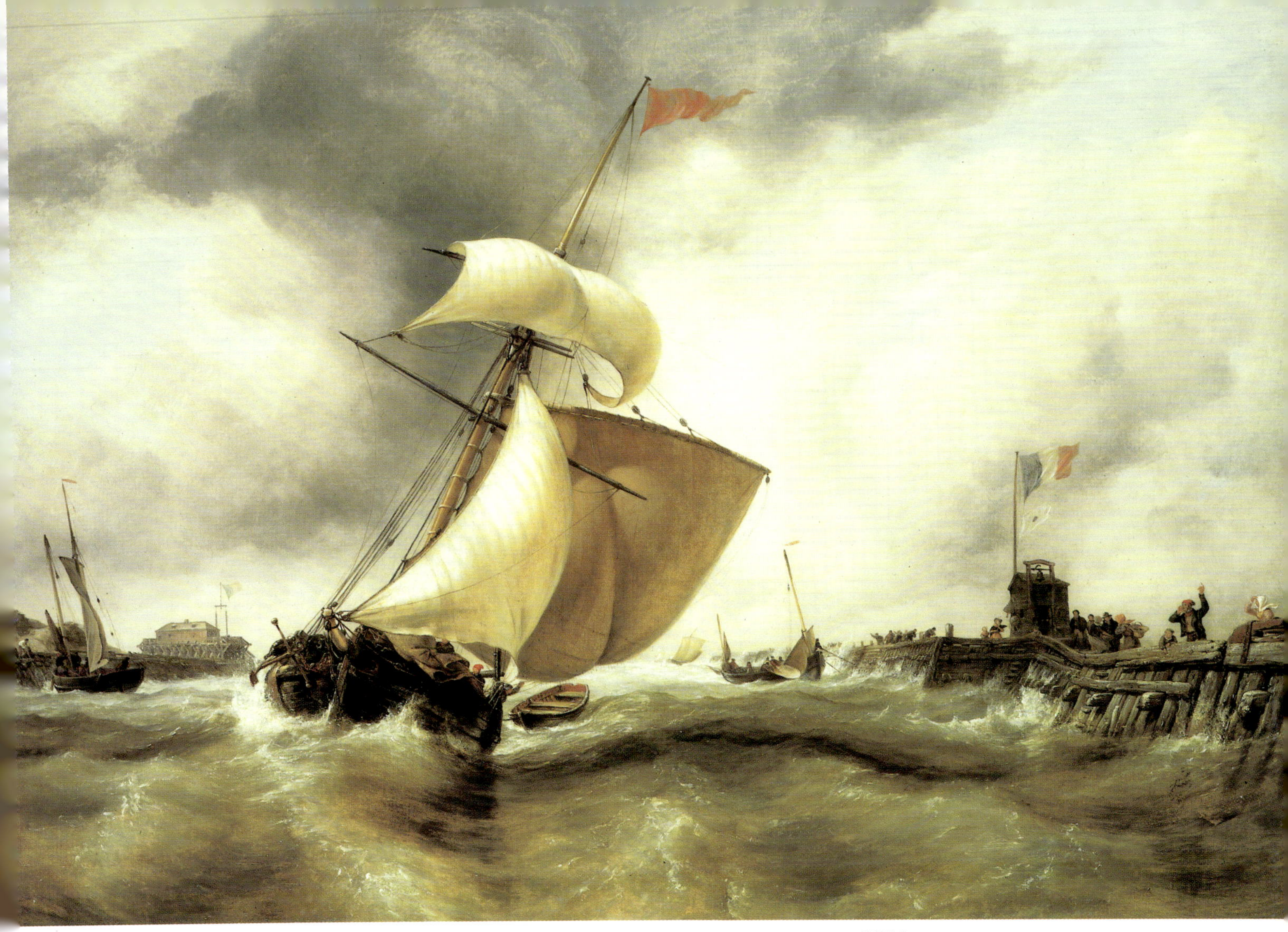

Colour Plate 46. 39/14
Calais Pier, sloop returning to port
Sailing vessels negotiating a narrow crowded channel in a breeze appealed as a subject to Cooke, as it did to those who thronged the piers to watch. Photo courtesy Martyn Gregory. Private Collection

1839, commissioned a pair of Dutch subjects. Lord Northwick, the old diplomat and a Director of the British Institution, bought several of his paintings. Sir Thomas Baring and other members of the illustrious banking family also bought representative pictures. These patrons offered the hospitality of their country seats and Cooke thus absorbed not only art but also his other favourite study – gardening – on visits to old houses and lush parklands.

Patrons, peers of the realm and merchant princes calling on the painter at his house and studio were able to view his current works in pleasant surroundings against a background of hothouse flowers, fruit and an elegant garden. Careful cultivation of a tasteful *milieu* with enterprise and a certain novelty was continued in his later Kensington residences and was undoubtedly good for the business of selling his pictures.

The *Art Union Journal* (later renamed *The Art Journal*) wrote of the British Institution 1840 show, No 44, *Calais Pier, sloop returning to port* (39/14, Colour Plate 46):

> *One of the best works in the exhibition a work of which the English school may be justly proud. It is as true to nature as Nature is to herself. Mr Cooke has this year established his reputation: he exhibits largely and without an exception all his productions are excellent. The drawing, in which so many of our artists are deficient, is faultless... They may be placed without fear beside the best works of the Old Dutch Masters.*

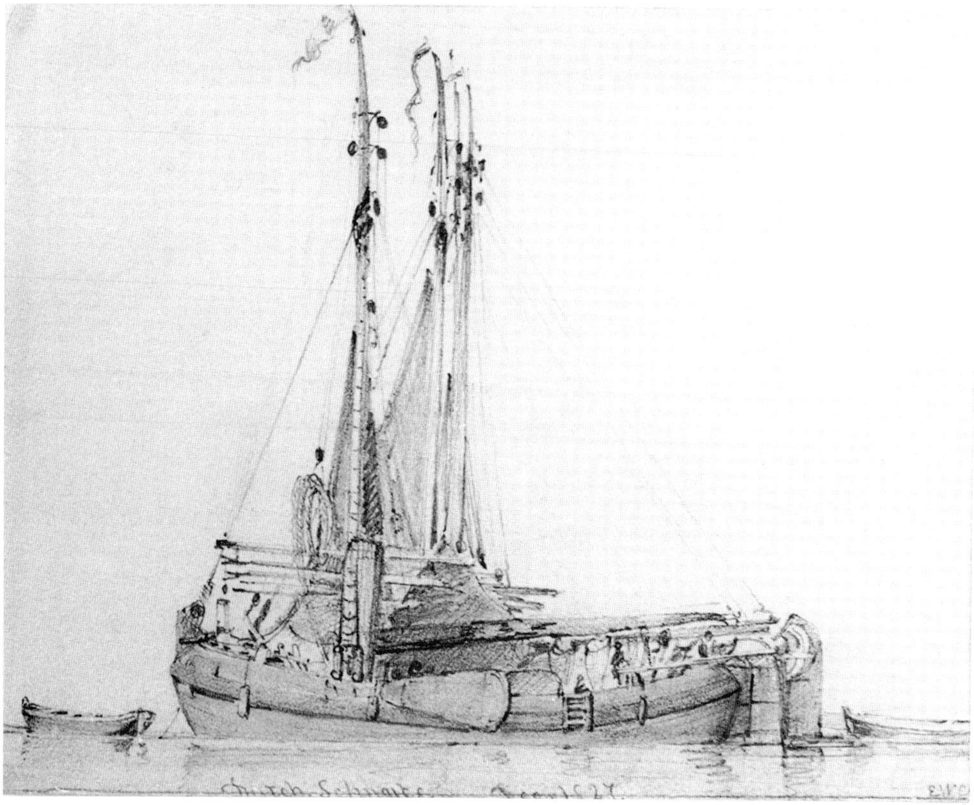

Plate 63. Pencil drawing
Dutch schuyts 1827
These are in fact Dutch visitors to the Thames and the enthusiastic sixteen-year-old Londoner collects notes on their build and rig. Photo courtesy Clarges Gallery

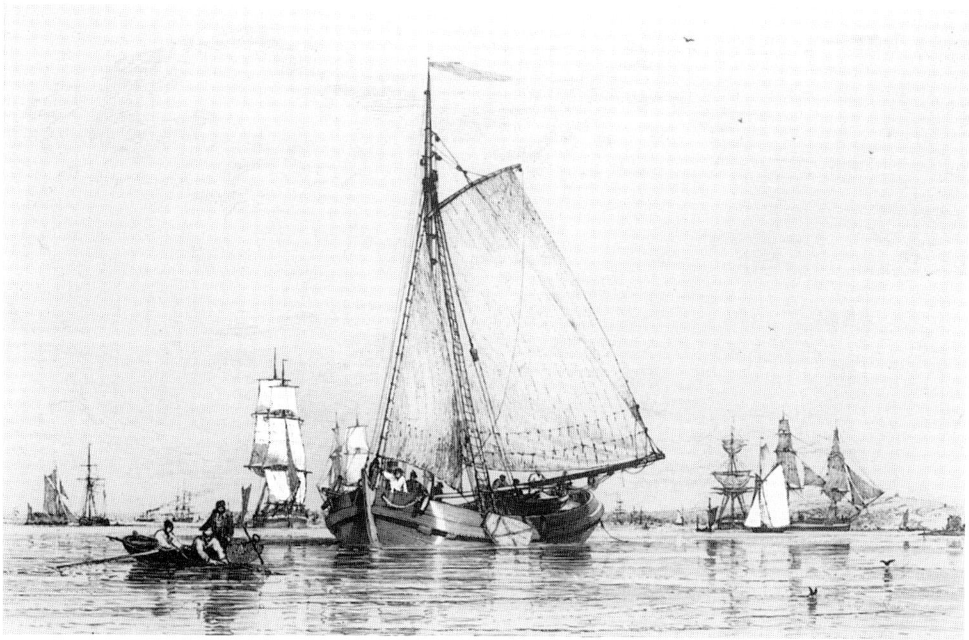

Plate 64. Engraving
Dutch schuyt Blackwall 1829
From *Shipping and Craft.* See Plate 65.

Chapter 6

DUTCH BOATS

Mr.Mayhew... sketched with curious photographic realism, the Dutch eel-boats with their bulging polished oak sides, half hidden in the river mist... You see wooden sabots and china pipes on the ledges of the boats, and the men wear tall fur caps, red shirts and canvas kilts... floating at the stern are coffin-shaped barges pierced with holes, with eel-baskets hanging over the sides.[1]

Dutch boats were always to be seen in the Thames; from the fourteenth century the eel-schuyts had been allowed moorings there and they were a colourful feature off the Billingsgate fishmarket, familiar to Cooke the Londoner (Plates 63 to 65). In four of his *Shipping & Craft* plates he had recorded Dutch galliots, even before venturing abroad: at sea [5], off Margate [15], unloading at Gt. Yarmouth [35] and a schuyt in the Thames, Blackwall [43] (Plate 64).

He had also noted their presence on his first East-coast sketching trip and a watercolour, *Dutch Schuyts off Yarmouth, rough sea,* had been in a group sold to Colnaghi in 1833.[2] The subject evidently appealed to him for its practical seagoing significance, as in 1864 his Diploma painting for the Royal Academy was entitled *Scheveling Pincks running to anchor off Yarmouth. During stormy easterly gales these Dutch fishing vessels are compelled to make for the English coast* (Colour Plate 1).

On their own coasts and in rivers and waterways the uniquely characterful Dutch

1. *Old & New London* by Walter Thornbury [1873] Vol. II, p.47, quoting Henry Mayhew, 1861.
2. Cooke MSS, 33.

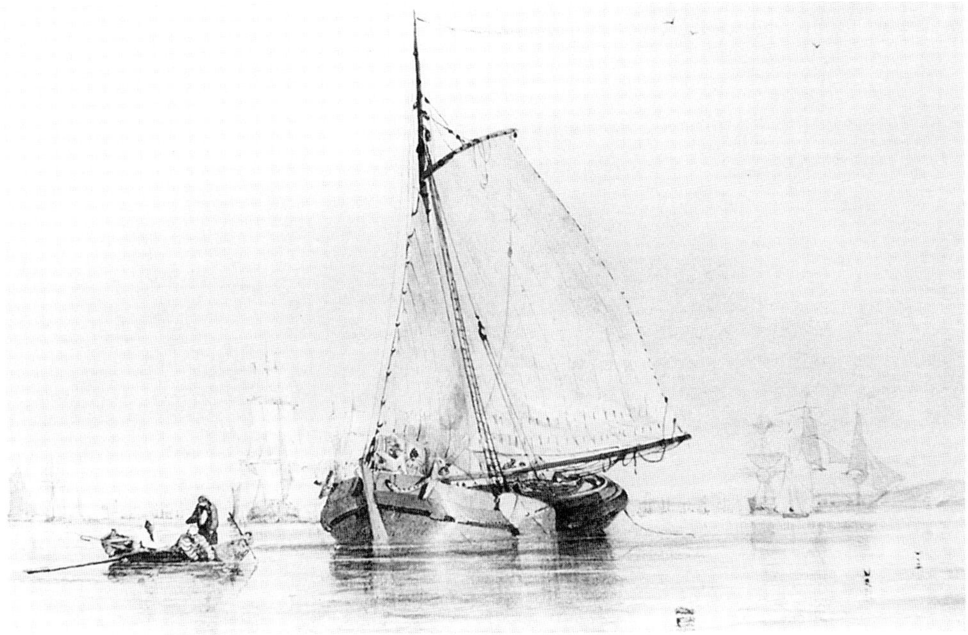

Plate 65. Watercolour
Dutch schuyt – Blackwall Reach, Thames
A study for or from his plate in *Shipping & Craft,* 1829. See Plate 16.
Photo courtesy Martyn Gregory

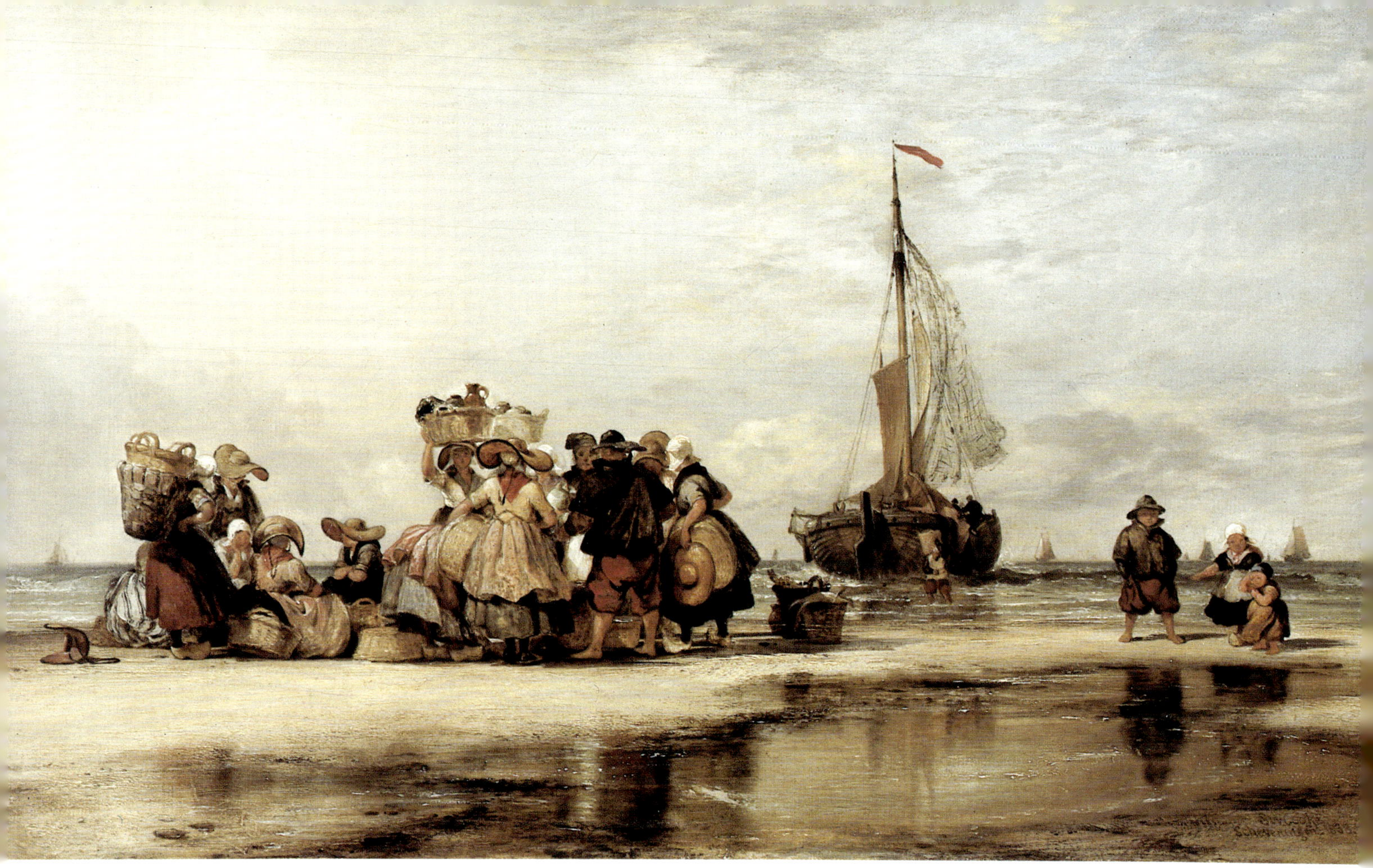

Colour Plate 47. 37/11
Dutch fishermen selling Thornback
The skate are in the basket, the fishwives bargaining with the fishermen provide a concentrated human interest which the artist seems to have avoided in later years. In the larger version (37/12, Plate 71), there are more skate, more figures, but the same group of children at right.
Photo courtesy Canon Gallery. Private Collection

vessels would be seen in their natural habitat, providing endless subjects for the recording pencil of the eager young Edward Cooke.

In 1837 he went to Holland with his sketchbooks and paintbox, accompanied by his diary, extracts from which give an account of his progress, both through the country and as an artist. The development of his interests, his contacts with Dutch collectors and painters, his studied assumption of a Dutch character – steeping himself in the nautical aspects of Dutch life and paying particular attention to the old marine Masters – are all significant aspects.

The Redleaf picture collection of William Wells contained fine Dutch marine paintings for study and he was probably urged on by the expert interest in shipping shown by that patron. Without doubt Cooke was intent on getting to grips with all the varieties of build and rig and behaviour of Dutch vessels, with the same thoroughness he had already adopted at home and in France (Plates 67 to 69).

To bring to bear his own very particular and analytical eye, to portray Dutch boats as they had rarely been shown, at least by an Englishman, was evidently his aim. It was as well a useful shift of subject, to expand his range beyond those French and English shore scenes exhibited between 1835 and 1837.

From the great wealth acquired through their seaborne trade with the Indies, the Dutch had been ready patrons of their own painters. The pictures which graced their houses were a celebration of their homeland, their coasts, their shipping and their way of life.

The marine painters in the Netherlands who emerged in the sixteenth century often portrayed the coastal fishermen landing and selling their catches and handling their stout flat-bottomed craft. It was as much an image of their national life as a village *kermes* or a

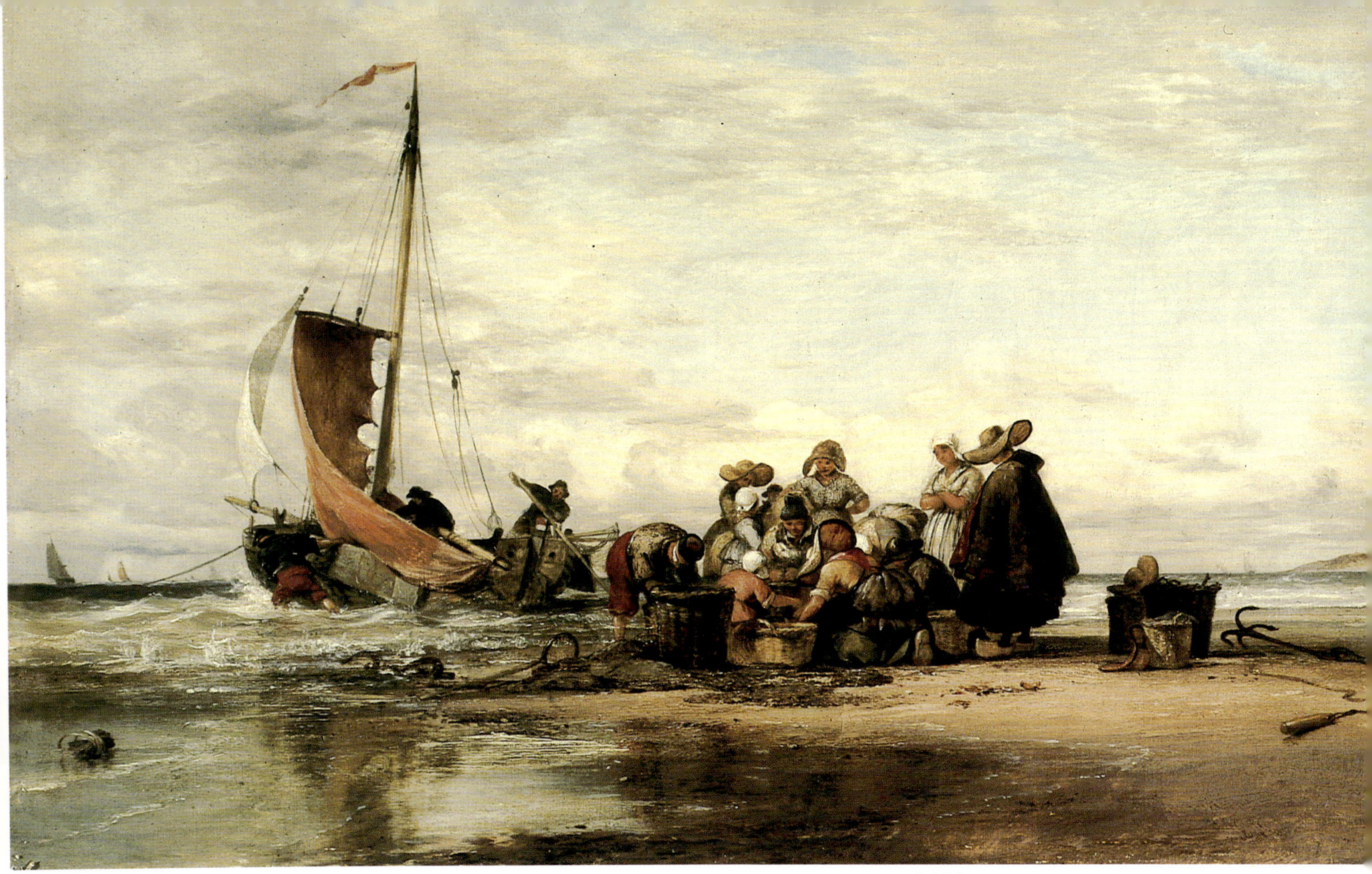

Colour Plate 48. 37/13
Sorting shrimps, Scheveling
Painted as a pair to the *Thornback* (Colour Plate 47), although no larger version is recorded.
Photo: courtesy Canon Gallery. Private Collection

canal vista with windmills. Simon de Vlieger's *The beach at Scheveningen* of 1633[3] is a perfect example; he had taught Willem van de Velde the Younger to paint from nature and the English school of marine painters began with the latter. His father Willem the elder, son of a shipmaster, was a marine draughtsman without rival; the pair emigrated to England and worked at Greenwich for the King, from 1672. Professor Gombrich compares Turner with de Vlieger *who did not only paint what he saw at a glance, but also to some extent what he knew was there. He knew how a ship was built and how it was rigged and looking at his painting we might be able to reconstruct these vessels.* No-one, he says, would be able to use a Turner steamboat for a reconstruction for one is caught up in his atmosphere and cannot notice detail.[4] It is an interesting point, for one knows that a de Vlieger in the early steam era would have produced as satisfying a model as any of his sailing ships, and Turner's earlier pictures have perfectly recognisable though somewhat perfunctory sailing ships in plenty.

There was a considerable range of *expertise* among the Dutch sea painters; some were renowned for stormy seas and some for calms, while some excelled in portraying ships and vessels of all sizes with a satisfying exactness calculated to please both shipowner and shipmaster.

Such was their devotion to nature that their 'shorescapes' have a timeless quality. The broad skies and clouds over dappled expanses of the North Sea, the sandy beaches washed by the enduring yet ever-changing ocean in all its moods and an infinite variety of lights, are the backcloth against which the hardy fisherfolk perform their daily tasks. The beamy fishing boats themselves did not alter in general appearance a great deal over the years and the working clothes of the men and women who thronged around them became a picturesque and recognisable occupational dress.

Owing much to the 'realism' of the earlier Dutch painters and their palette of softer

3. National Maritime Museum, Greenwich.
4. Gombrich, op. cit., p.373.

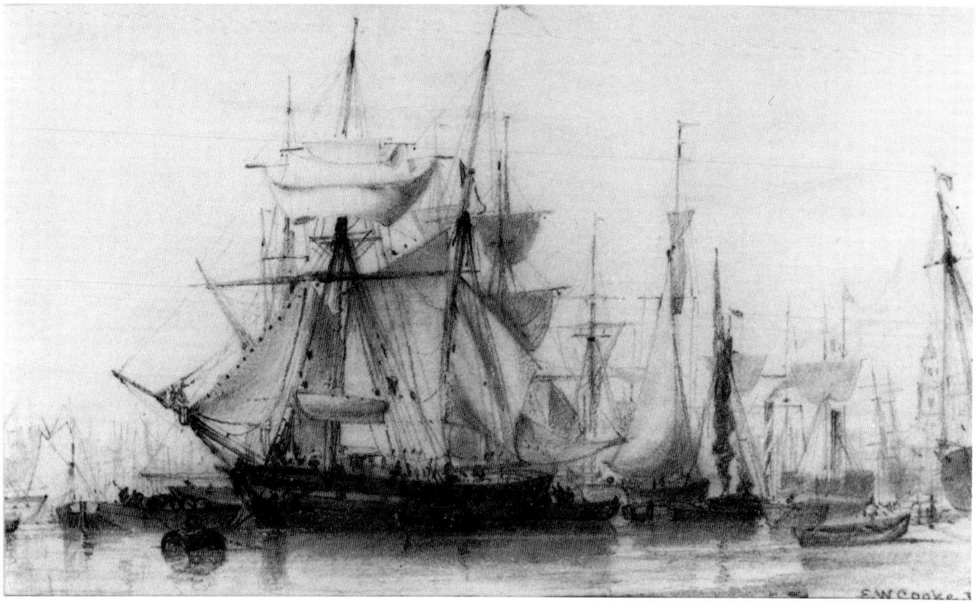

Plate 4. Pencil drawing

Sailing craft in the Pool of London c.1830 *(signed RA: inscr. to R. Cooke 1871).* Robert Cooke, no relation, was a family member of John Murray's publishing house.

Photo courtesy Martyn Gregory. Private Collection

natural colours, paintings of the 1830s could appear quite similar to scenes executed two centuries before.

Edward Cooke's detailed observation and suave style of applying paint – 'Dutch finish' the Redgrave brothers called it when noting the fashion of the pre-Constable era – accorded well with the painting of the Netherlandish masters. However Cooke, like John Constable, made his basic studies in the open air and many of his sketches are free and direct; his Dutch contemporaries the Koekkoek family, in a renascence of their landscape school, had also begun to do just that.[5]

His pictures of their boats, observed with a minuteness worthy of the school and executed with telling accuracy, were calculated to have a ready appeal to patrons seeking traditional subjects – new Old Masters at an affordable price, one might say!

A new order in the 1820s-30s was marked by *a growing piety and puritanism among artists as much as among their public... a more literal, picturesque and often prosaic realism... predilections of the growing middle class market.*[6] Cooke's *penchant* for Dutch subjects might also be traced to a familiarity with the paintings of two of his father's collaborators and friends – Augustus Wall Callcott and Clarkson Stanfield. Latterly Callcott was not an outdoor painter. *He began to rely on sketches and on his memory – to rely on his art-kowledge, his composition, his sweet execution; and his works increased in art, or what is called art, and decreased in Nature* wrote the Redgraves,[7] but he had painted many marine pictures – river and seaport scenes – and had been in Holland. His pictures of Rotterdam, one of which was engraved on a large plate by George Cooke, would have been familiar to the son.

Callcott's early work had been *painted with a full pencil and much impasto, in a crisp, large flat manner*,[8] work which was indeed popularly preferred to that of his friend J.M.W. Turner. The Cooke family were on visiting terms with the Callcotts, sending choice grapes from the Barnes hot-houses to the invalid Lady C., while her husband, as was his habit, encouraged the young painter and gave him helpful advice.

With Stanfield, who had been in Holland in 1823 and 1830, Cooke had that close relationship which, if it was not that of master and pupil, was certainly of a novice absorbing all he could from the established painter.

It was not long before he became jealous of his own Dutch 'reputation', shown by a letter to his sister Laura, commenting on news from home that Stanfield was bound for Holland in 1843: *You alarm me about Stanfield trenching on my ground – I hope he will not come to Scheveling – he ought to leave Holland for me....*[9]

5. *The Hague School. Dutch Masters of the 19th Century,* 1983.
6. Van der Merwe op.cit.
7. Redgrave op. cit., 1866, Vol. II, p 403.
8. Ibid., p.400.
9. Cooke MSS.

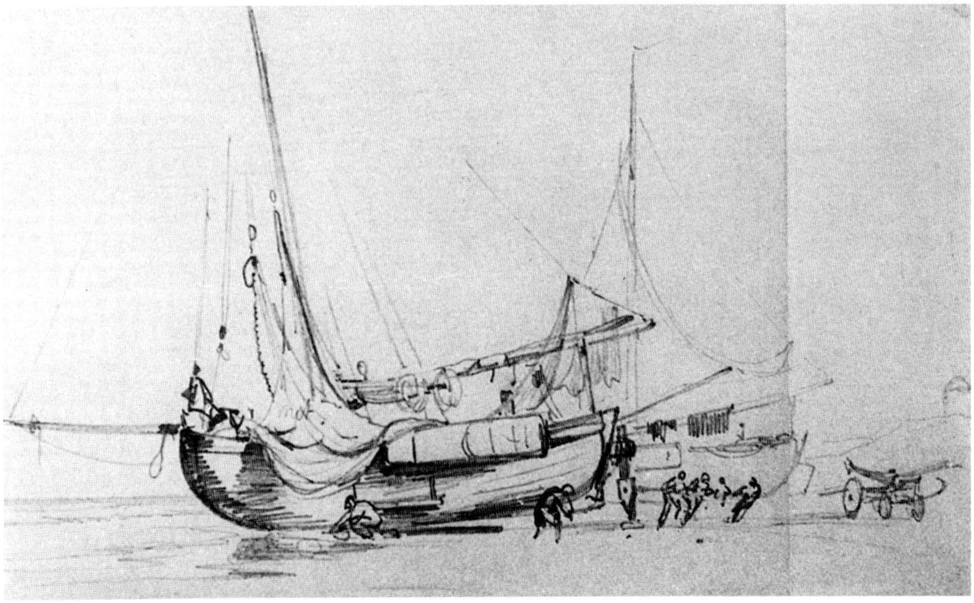

Plate 67. Pencil drawing
Hauling up a pinck
With rapid notation Cooke records a pinck being lifted on to rollers with a massive screw-jack.
Photo courtesy Clarges Gallery

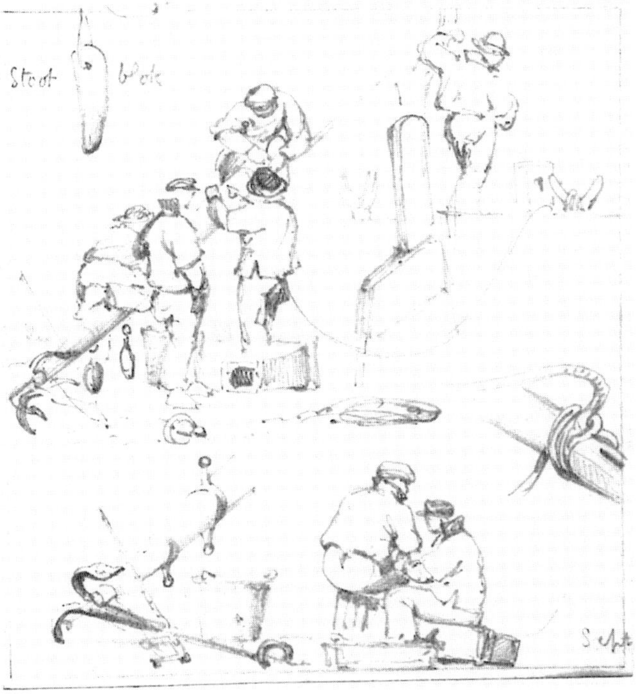

Plate 68. Pencil drawing
Men at work- & a stoot block
Photo courtesy C.R. Cooke, OBE

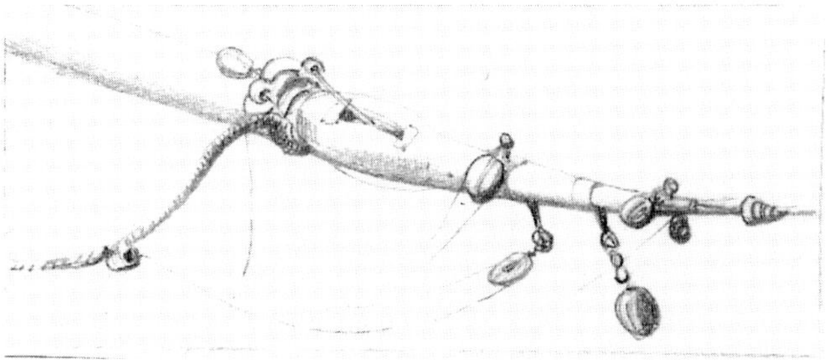

Plate 69. Pencil drawing
Masthead details for future reference
Photo courtesy C.R. Cooke, OBE

Cooke's appreciation of the old Dutch marine mastery endured. He was offered in 1857 a group of twelve drawings of W. van de Velde the Elder by his friend James Wyatt Junr., successor to the picture and print dealing business in Oxford: ...*which soon became mine,* he noted, effecting an exchange with one of his own compositions in oil of the Devon coast. The Dutch ship drawings were framed and hung in his study.

He made a series of outline drawings on small cards, probably with the *camera lucida,* of marine paintings by Dutch masters which he encountered. These were kept in a little, neat leather box-file which often travelled with him and would be exhibited to friends, guests and fellow-guests, at home and away.

To the Low Countries: Dutch subjects for the London market

His first painting tour to Holland and Belgium, for which he was well supplied with letters of introduction, began in September 1837 and the diary is all enthusiasm, the

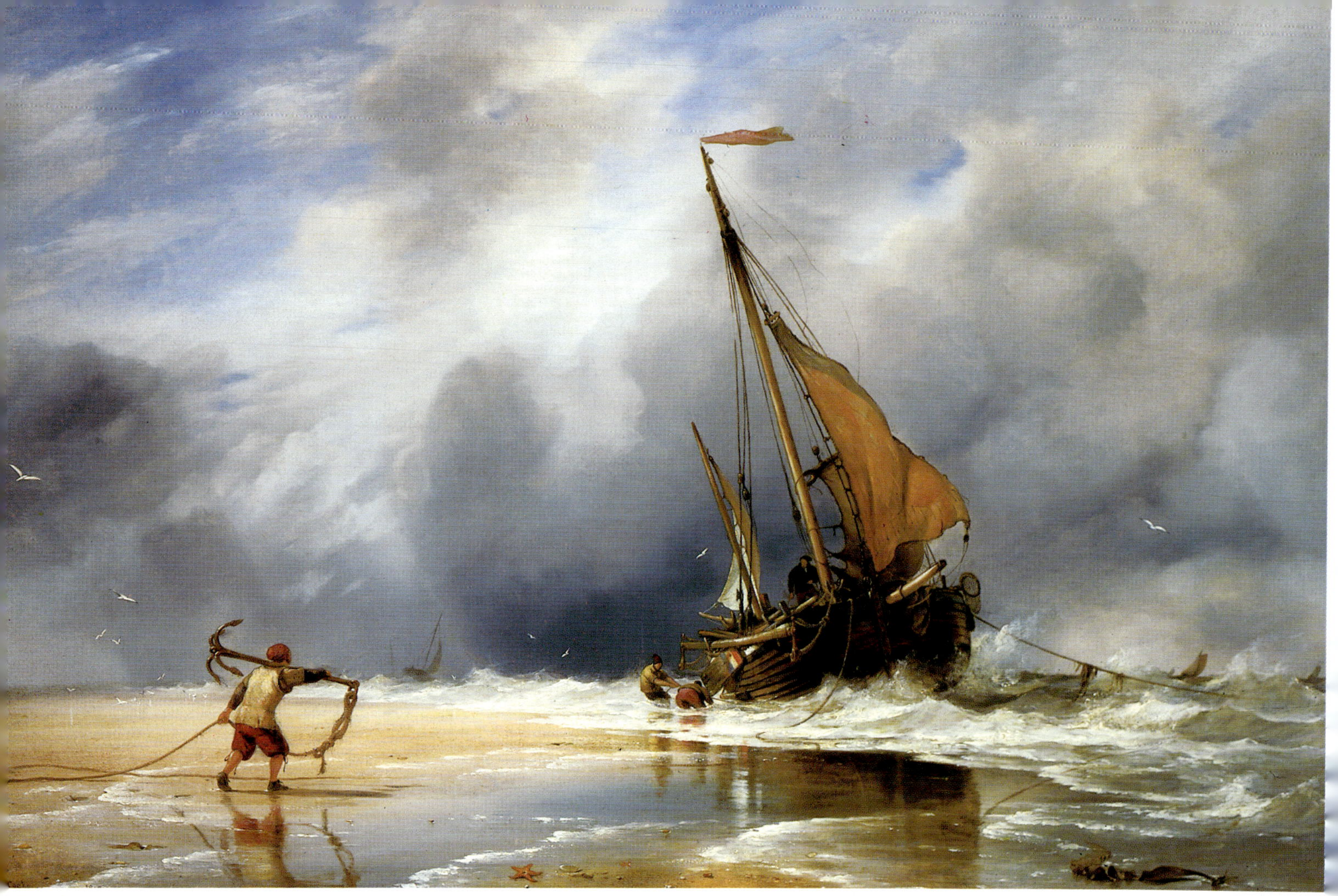

Colour Plate 49. 40/4
Scheveling Pinck getting off shore
Photo courtesy Martyn Gregory. Private Collection

excitement (and discomforts) of sea-travel providing first-rate material for a sea-painter. His contacts among artists, collectors, curators, British residents etc. provided him with a valuable base from which he could pursue his quest.

His first Dutch pictures in the London exhibitions were received with marked approval. The *Athenaeum* wrote about the British Institution, 1838:

> *We are always secure of meeting good items in these rooms. The very first item in the catalogue is by one who has made many steps towards excellence since we last encountered him, Mr E.W. Cooke. He has contributed largely: and we do not remember a beach scene arranged and wrought out, more admirably than 79, his 'Dutch Fishermen selling Thornback' – whether in right of the burly groups of merchants, the women with their floppy hats and the men with their enormous breeches – or of the moist sand, dimpled with its shallow pools of water, and the curling surf in the middle distance. There are an abundance of clever sea-pictures in the Exhibition, but, with one exception, this is the best.*

The reviewer continued: *Turner 134 ... with a striking fault or two, is still the finest work in a not very fine Exhibition.*

Turner's picture, oddly enough, was *Fishing boats, with Hucksters bargaining for fish* and it surely gave Cooke considerable satisfaction to be thus bracketed as runner-up to the Great Turner who had been in Holland twenty years before. His *Dort* sketchbook (Turner Bequest CLXII) contains notes of everyday things of exactly the sort which engaged Cooke: fisherfolk and pincks on the beach, a river scene with baskets and boats noted as *Dead Calm,* etc.

In Cooke's fish picture in the Royal Holloway College collection (Plate 71), and a

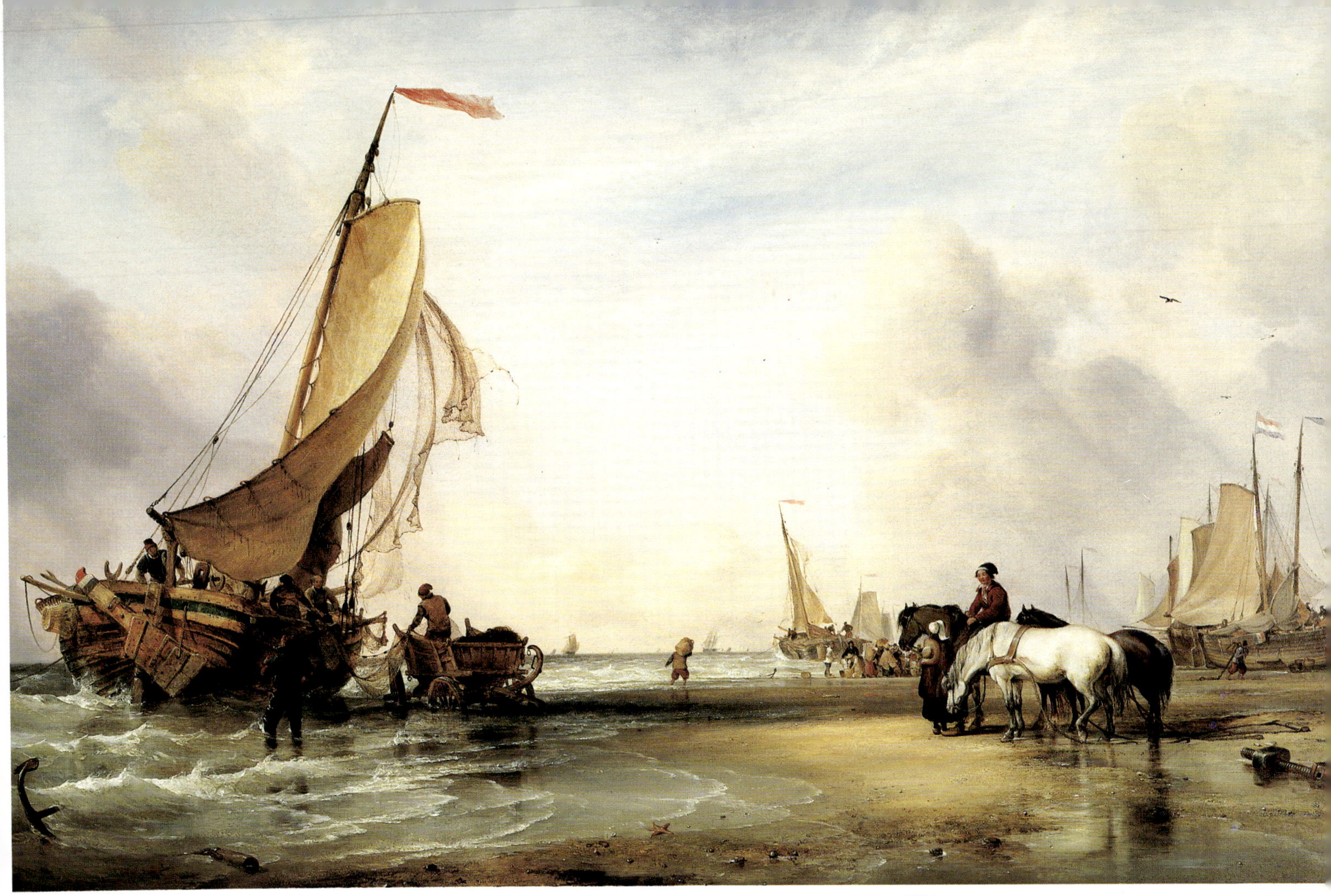

Colour Plate 50. 42/6
On the Dutch coast near Katwijk
This luminous, detailed and lively picture of the fishery was shown at the RA as Scheveling sands but failed to attract a buyer; however under its new title it was in the British Institution the following year whereupon it was bought by Sir Thomas Baring, Bt. Photo courtesy Sotheby's

smaller version (Colour Plate 47), the accent as in several of his early Dutch works is on the fishermen and women with the boats of less importance than they would later become.

However, it is clear that he was not at his happiest painting the human figure; by 1846 he was to admit it was rather late to learn and Frederick Goodall was doubtless quoting consensual opinion when he wrote that *Cooke had a remarkable facility for drawing most things but was not an accomplished figure draughtsman.*[10]

Costume, male and female, baskets and fish – the skate (thornback) – which he had noted, are however painted with his wonted clarity. It was in fact not so much man who absorbed his attention, but man's works.

Calms

Turning away from the sea, the inland waterways and their craft seem to have exerted an equal pull. Turner's *Dordrecht: the Dort Packet-boat from Rotterdam Becalmed* of 1818, owned originally by his friend and patron Walter Fawkes of Farnley Hall, now in the Mellon Collection, is a famous British example of the *genre* harking straight back to Aelbert Cuyp. The tranquil, static quality provided a welcome contrast to the usually gusty sea scenes and gave Cooke an alternative field of expression, a release from boisterous movement.

A 'Dutch Calm' became a regular feature of Cooke's exhibited work, appearing in all sizes. The Rivers Ij, or Y, and Spaarn with distant views of Amsterdam were favourite locations, while the Scheldt with the Antwerp skyline was another.

10. Goodall op.cit., p.330.

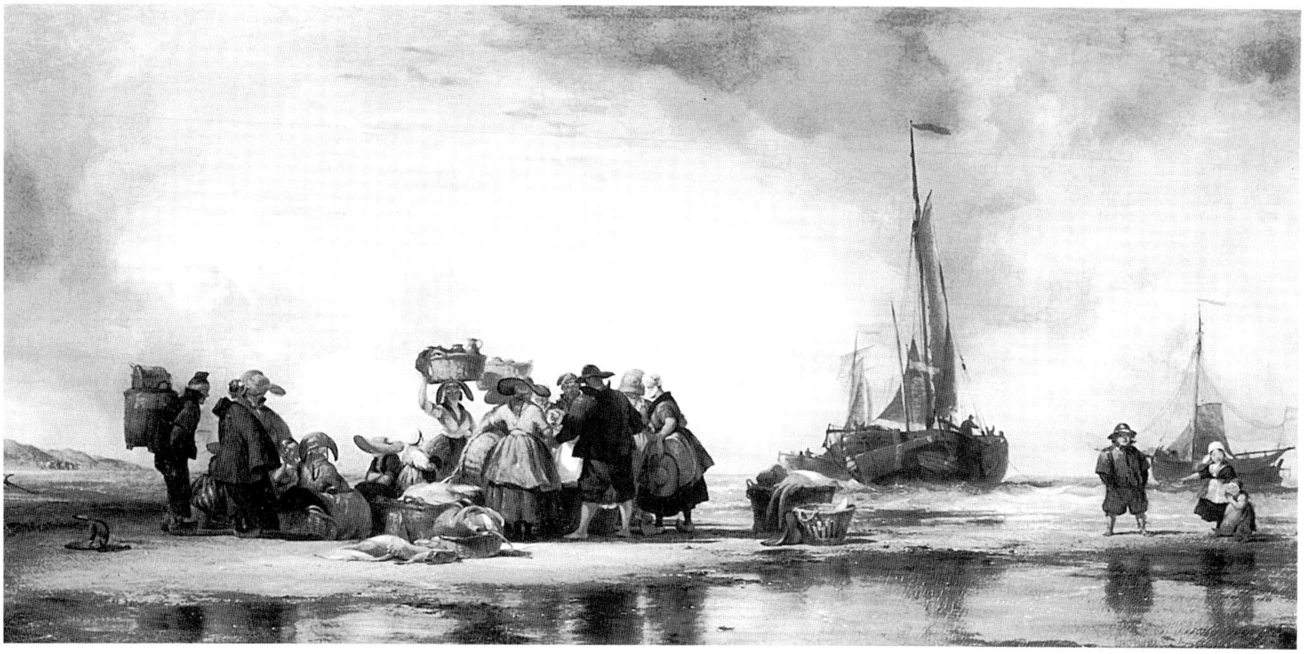

Plate 71. 37/12
Fishermen selling thornback
Photo courtesy Courtauld Institute. Royal Holloway College

Windmills at home on Barnes and Wimbledon Commons and on Blackheath had provided good subjects, for they were familiar features of the landscape. In Holland they were far more numerous, using wind power for pumping and draining, sawing timber and milling. He encountered one historic example which seems to have fascinated him, an ancient stone building beside the Old Rhine at Koukerke said to have been owned by Rembrandt's father (Colour Plates 53, 162, 163 and Plate 77). He planned an exhibition *coup* of sorts by sending in a quartet of mill paintings to the British Institution in 1839. They were hung as Nos. 131, 132, 141 and 384 and the *Athenaeum* found space to say: *Perhaps the most unique set of pictures is that by Mr E.W. Cooke, external and internal views of Rembrandt's Mill. A slight coldness and clayey tone of colouring being the only defect. The same artist has many sea and shore scenes of his usual cleverness.*

As a set of related views such a combined exhibit was unusual perhaps, but William Wells bought one of them and two went to Thomas Baring. The upstairs and downstairs views of the old working mill were recorded in a series of some dozen pictures large and small. Pleasantly broad without any undue emphasis on mechanical aspects, some bore the usual personal stamp, his initials and a date inscribed on sacks of new-ground flour. In one of them, on the easel while he was staying with Wells, his fellow guest Edwin Landseer performed an operation similar to a celebrated incident affecting Turner's *Mortlake Terrace*[11] by painting in on his friend's canvas the miller's black cat!

In 1849 John Burnet, the painter and engraver, published *Rembrandt and his Works*

11. Whitley op.cit., p.282.

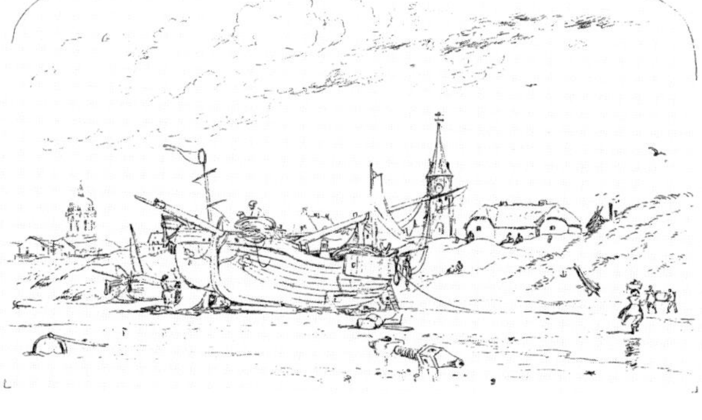

Plate 70. 48/4
Scheveling, Mast down
Camera lucida record of this Royal Academy picture of 1848.

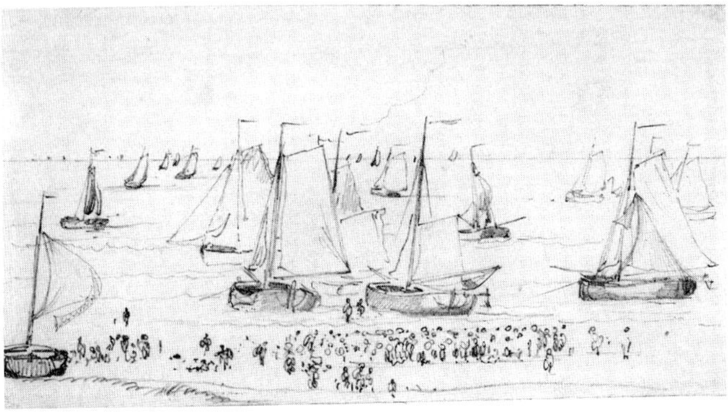

Plate 72. Pencil drawing
Scheveling, fishing fleet getting off
One of dozens of studies of the crowded beach, his sure hand giving life to the boats setting sail and a sense of urgency to the rapidly noted crowd of figures, engaged in sorting or selling fish on the shore. Photo courtesy Martyn Gregory

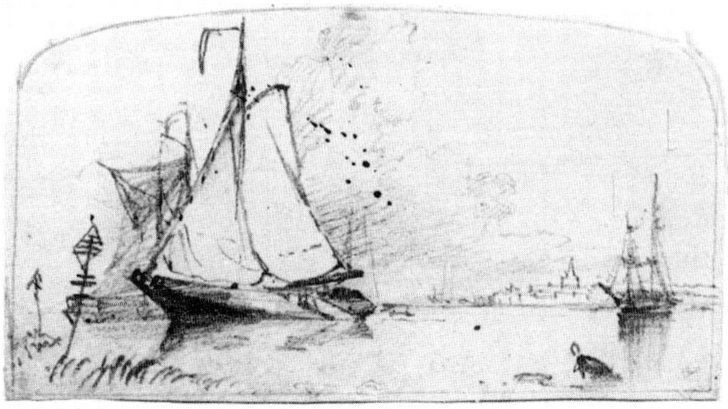

Plate 73. Pencil drawing
Botters in a calm
Probably a sketch of a completed picture, judging by the arched top. Photo courtesy Clarges Gallery

which included two plates of the mill after drawings by Cooke. Burnet also printed a very characteristic letter from him, evidence of antiquarian and technical leanings, humour, a developed sense of personal achievement and a keen desire for public acknowledgement! *My excellent young friend Mr. E.W. Cooke whose works breathe the true spirit of the best of the Dutch school... says*

> *Mr Dear Sir, I send you another sketch of the mill; the pictures, including the doorzigte, or view out of the window, I painted on the spot, and that picture is now in the possession of the King of Holland, having taken it back with me to show him.*
>
> *The mill was a magazine for powder during the Spanish invasion; it was soon after converted into a corn mill and was in the possession of Herman Geritz. Van Rhyn when his son Rembrandt was born; it is situated at Koukerk on the old Rhyn near Leyden. I hope you will correct the vulgar impression that Rembrandt was born IN a mill. There are often dwelling houses attached to water-mills such as we have in England, but in Holland not such a structure as a water-mill, with water-power; the water-mills there are only draining mills such as we have in Lincolnshire, Norfolk &c.*
>
> *Surely the noise and movement of a wind-mill would ill accord with the confinement of any lady, especially the mother of so glorious a fellow as Rembrandt. For the honour of such association I hope you will not omit my name in the work , for I painted three pictures of that precious relic. Yours etc....*

So much for the artist's impassioned interest – research has established that in fact the Rembrandt mill was in Leyden and the traditional identification, confidently based on a similarity with his etching *The Windmill* of 1641 and pointed out to tourists, was wrong. This is revealed by the catalogue of a 1991 exhibition[12] which continues:

> *Cooke had a taste for depicting accurate technical details and his Mill is at once a carefully observed record of the gearing and machinery of an old mill, and a tribute to a great artist. Employing the idiom of the picturesque in the decaying brickwork, scarred wood and deeply worn tread above the ladder, Cooke stresses the passage of time and continuity of human usage. Light comes on the scene through a single small window and is diffused over the objects inside, in a way which Cooke might have learnt from studying Rembrandt's prints.*[13] [Colour Plate 163]

One item in W.B. Cooke's exhibition of engravings of 1823, a print by Charles Turner of Rembrandt's *Mill* after the master, just published, was claimed as *being the first Landscape engraved upon Steel.*

The second Dutch tour in 1838 was extended to four months with a visit to Germany. He was armed with further letters of introduction from Sir Charles Bagot, former British Ambassador at The Hague, for Albertus Brondgeest, painter, and again for the celebrated

12. *Sunshine and Shadow,* Catalogue of an Exhibition at the National Gallery of Scotland, 1991, No 3.
13. Ibid. (Dr. Lindsay Errington.)

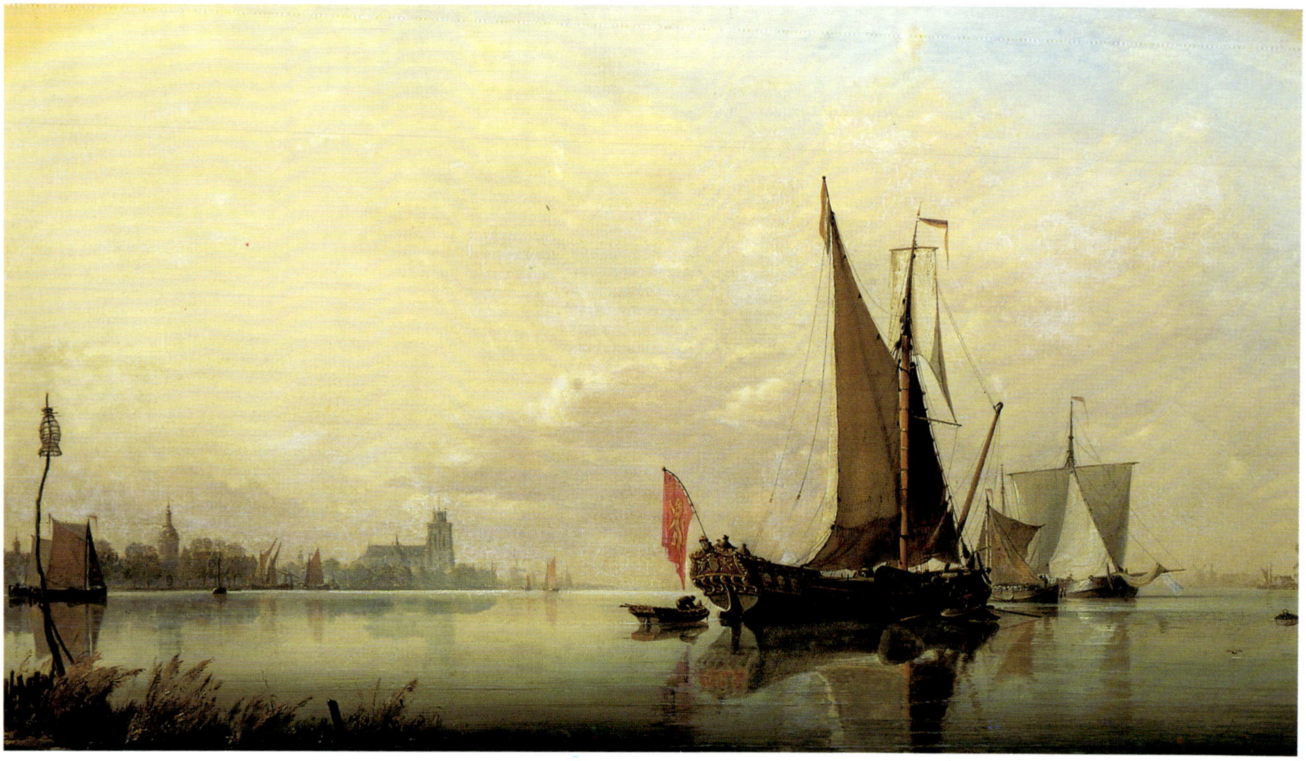

Colour Plate 51. 44/8
Dort, morning, Mijnheer's yacht becalmed
Dordrecht, otherwise Dort, home of Aelbert Cuyp, was also a famous Turner subject, so there well may be a double homage in this composition. However Cooke paints a yacht of traditional build and ornamentation, familiar in the works of the Willem van de Veldes. His ensign at the stern betrays an uncharacteristic lapse: in a wind the lion would adopt a most un-heraldic position – 'recumbent'! Photo courtesy Martyn Gregory. Private Collection

collector Baron Verstolck van Soelen whose collection was later purchased by a consortium of Jones Loyd (Lord Overstone), Thomas Baring and H. Mildmay.[14]

Marriage 1840

It is clear by the underlinings and marks of exclamation against the entry of her name in the diary that Jane, the younger daughter of George and Jane Loddiges, had become the object of Edward's affections. They had more or less grown up together: she was about a year younger, and evidently talented. Her name appears on some of the plates in *The Botanical Cabinet*, she played the harp and possessed a good singing voice. Was she also pretty? The only portrait of her that has been found shows a stylishly dressed, dark young woman with downcast eyes (Colour Plate 54). There is an ink sketch (Plate 78) of a girl with mittens and spaniel-ear curls – again she is bent over needlework or keyboard – but the sketch could be Jane or one of Edward's sisters. They had been engaged since 1838 and were married at St. John's Church, Hackney, in 1840. There were present only family and close friends; the officiating minister was the Rev Dr J. Hearn Pinckney DD, who had shown his good taste and appreciation of the young artist's work by buying several of his paintings.[15]

> 1840 June 13th: *Chariott went for Dr Pinckney at ½ p 7 and 2 coaches came for sisters. All went to Hackney Church at 10... Déjeuné at 12, most sumptuous and elegant. At 2 I and Jane left the happy circle and the rest of the party went to the Horticultural Show. We went to the Crown at Rochester, arrived at ½ p 6 to dinner. Glorious evening, made a sketch from window.*

On the honeymoon, beginning in Belgium, the sketchbook was likewise always at hand. Frankfurt, home of grandfather Guck, was visited, followed by a call on cousin William

14. *The English as Collectors* by Frank Herrman, 1972.
15. *Burke's Landed Gentry:* Pinckney of Tawstock Court, Barnstaple.

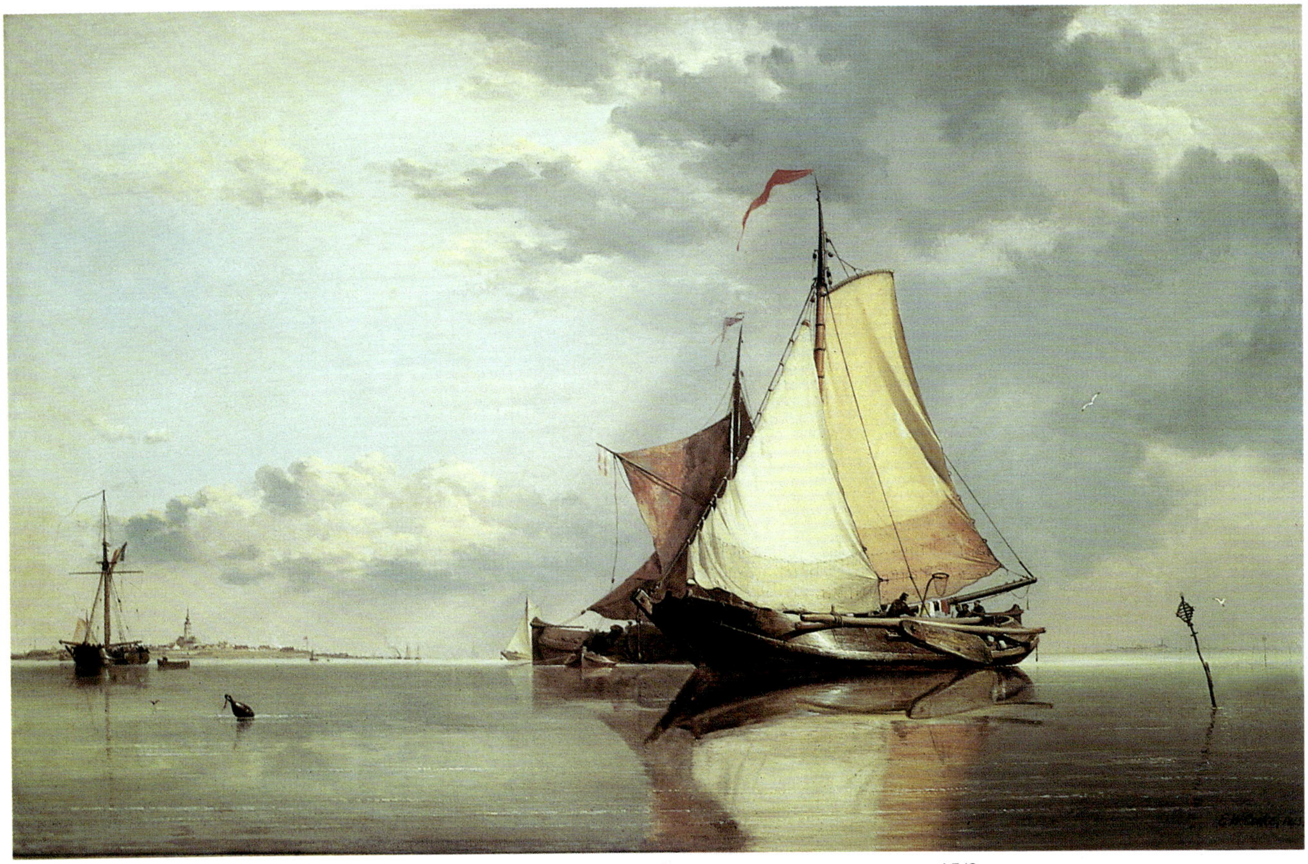

Colour Plate 52. 45/3

Dutch fishing craft off Fort Lillo, mouth of the Scheldt

Another of Cooke's masterly 'calms' this includes a distant view chosen doubtless to provide a variation on a familiar theme. Photo courtesy Private Collection. New Zealand

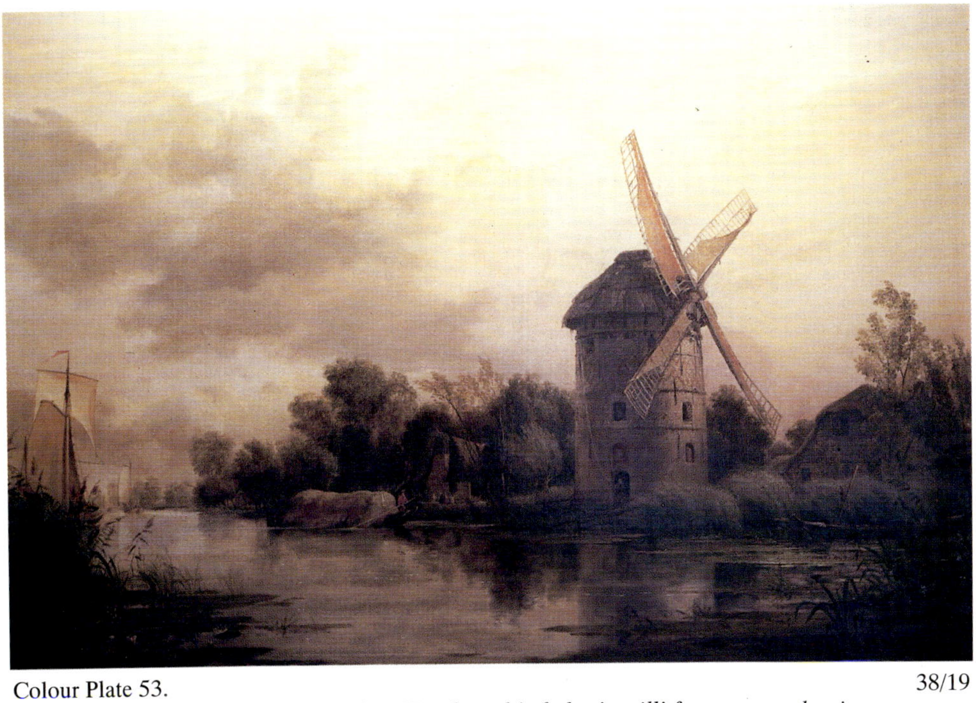

Colour Plate 53. 38/19

The Mill on the Old Rhine near Leiden; 'Rembrandt's father's mill' from across the river

Photo courtesy Guardian Royal Exchange plc

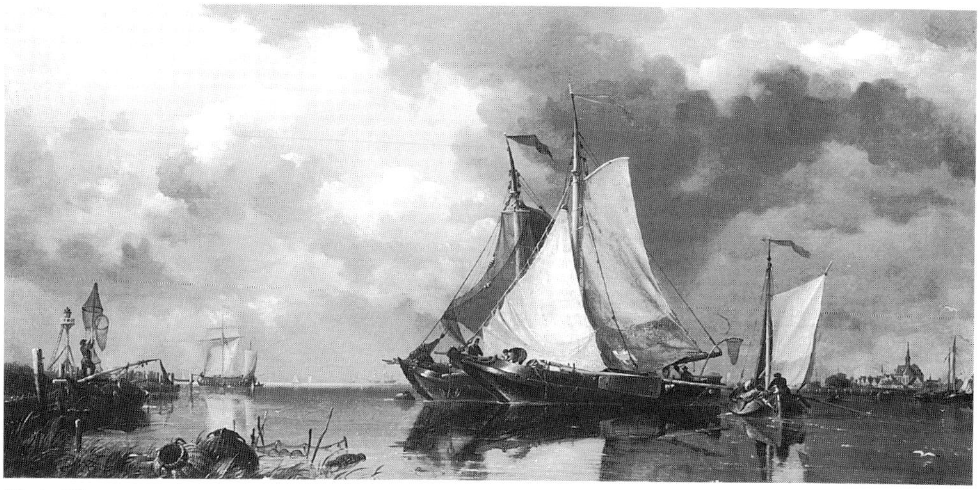

Plate 74. 49/8
Zuider Zee fishing craft drying nets in the harbour of Spaarendam Photo courtesy Thomas Agnew & Son

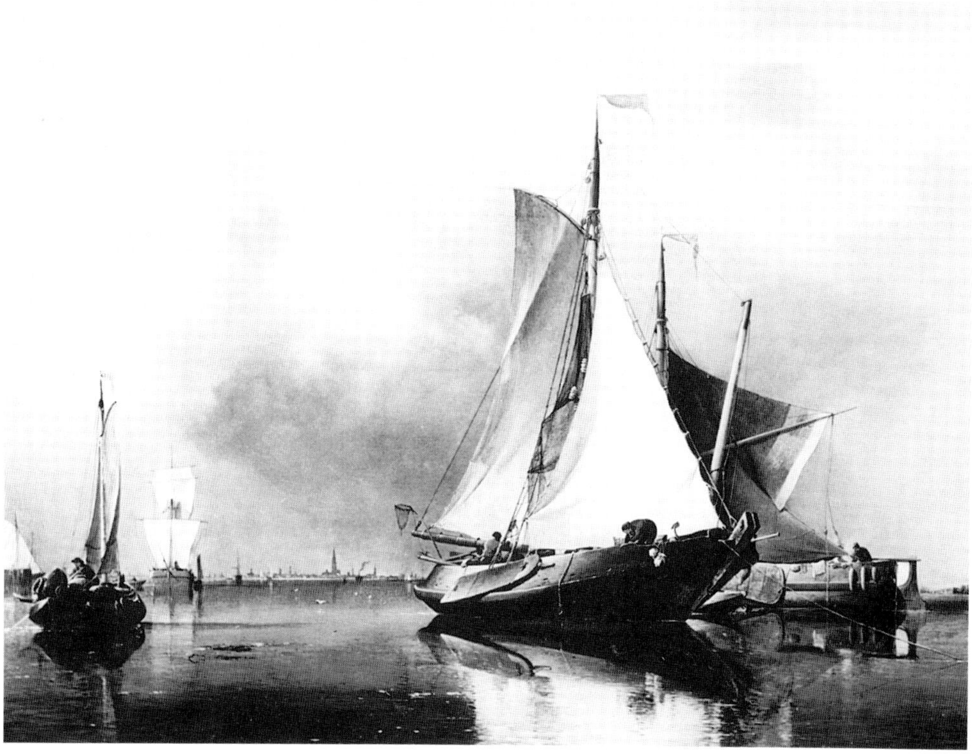

Plate 75. 70/3.
A Calm Day on the Scheldt: Antwerp in the distance Photo courtesy Martyn Gregory. Private Collection

John Cooke and his family, recently transplanted to Darmstadt. Then they travelled on to Heidelberg with time for sketching, and so to Baden-Baden, Strassbourg, Trier, Metz and finally Paris.

Once more at home, they settled down: Sept.10th: *Painted all day on large picture of Havre. The Horsleys left their cards.*

Life was naturally geared to *his* work, with extended visits to Redleaf, without wife; likewise days and nights away, but they also enjoyed some foreign travel together.

His visits to Holland in July 1841 (the diary entries are missing) and 1843 resulted in more paintings 'on the spot' to be the inspiration for further larger works. His reputation was growing: the *Athenaeum* wrote of the British Institution of 1842: *Mr Cooke is also*

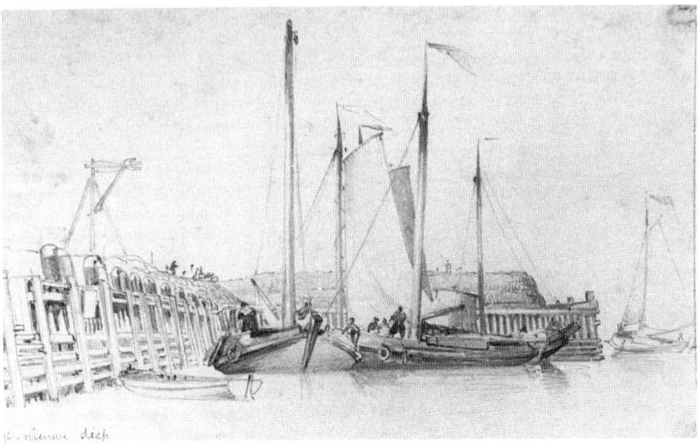

Plate 76. Pencil drawing
Hooft-Nieuw Diep
Photo courtesy Clarges Gallery

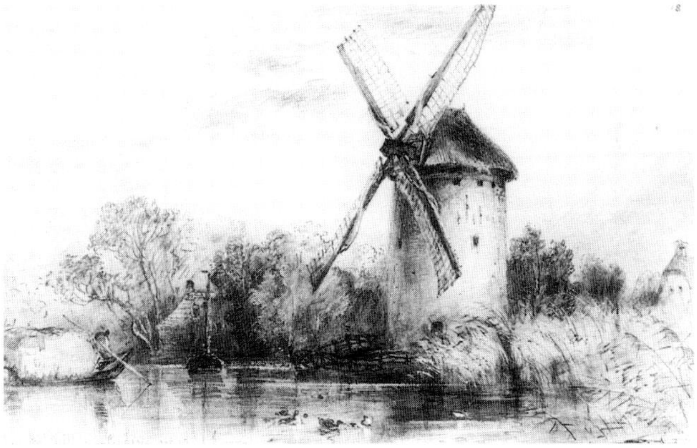

Plate 77. Pencil drawing
Rembrandt's Mill nr. Leyden 1838
Photo courtesy Martyn Gregory. Private Collection

one of our most delightful landscape painters and if he works up to his own powers will one day be our English Cuyp... he has the greatest number of pictures by any one artist, six, all of exceeding merit.

Five of these were Dutch subjects: 41/5 Mouth of the Zaan; 41/4 On the Vecht, Dutch fishing house; 38/17 Haarlemmer Meer; 38/14 Boat builders near Loenen; 38/12 Amsterdam from Buiksloot (Colour Plate 55) No blustery shore subjects disturbed the calm; two had been exhibited at Liverpool in 1839, and they were all of his larger sizes, priced according to his *Ledger* at from £168 (160 Guineas). (See Catalogue.)

A letter from this visit gives a valuable insight:[16]

...to my old quarters at Loghers, Schevg., and took possession of the little room in the roof – it commands a most perfect view imaginable, it being a corner with windows each way. We see the whole of the strand and all the bustle and doings of the fish women, boats &c... I have been working very hard at painting all the week. Mr Stokes's picture is nearly fin^{d.} besides another subject.

I have also painted a capital sky from nature, but the millboard I have got from the Hague is full of cracks, so it is nearly spoilt.

I have never before improved so much in painting from Nature, sea and sky – indeed I am glad I did not, under all circumstances go to Italy, of course now it is too late, but I am much tempted to stay here and paint several things for the Dutch market & also study skies and seas from my window, the aspect is such that I have the finest effects and not bothered by the sun– it is the same as our house, and the sunsets are glorious.

I can at home paint other subjects than Scheveling to the same skies – but of course if I think of staying here I shall return first and bring Jane, as I think she is anxious to get back to see her boy... you would be amazed at the quantity of fish that is brought in every morning by the boats... there are a hundred boats constantly employed...

The use of skies painted from one viewpoint in compositions formed on another quite different view is a device of which Cooke sometimes made use. Whether the idea was his own is not clear, but the Dutch painter J.H. Weissenbruch maintained that *the sky determines the painting.*[17]

The Charles Stokes mentioned was a collector, an amateur geologist and, incidentally, J.M.W. Turner's stockbroker. He frequented the Conversazione and had lent Turner drawings to W.B. Cooke's Soho Square exhibitions; the picture mentioned is No. 43/6, Colour Plate 56).

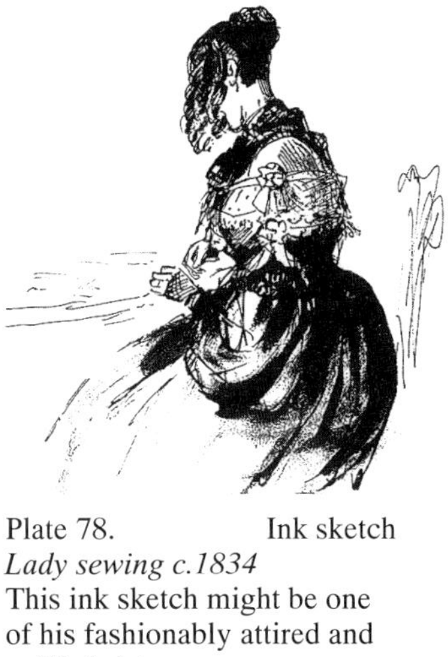

Plate 78. Ink sketch
Lady sewing c.1834
This ink sketch might be one of his fashionably attired and coiffed sisters.
Photo courtesy C.R. Cooke, OBE

To Jane and Edward William, a daughter, Florence Ada, had been born in 1841, followed by a son, George Edward, in 1842. The infant daughter, however, died, to their great distress. Jane, after accompanying her husband on that two-month tour of Holland in the summer of 1843, bore their third child, Conrad William, at snowy Christmas time.

16. Cooke MSS.
17. *The Hague School: Dutch Masters of the 19th Century,* ed. R.de Leeuw. 1983.

Colour Plate 54. 37/19

Portrait of Jane with white Lilac in her hair

Jane Loddiges became the artist's wife. Painted at Albion House, Barnes.

Photo courtesy Private Collection

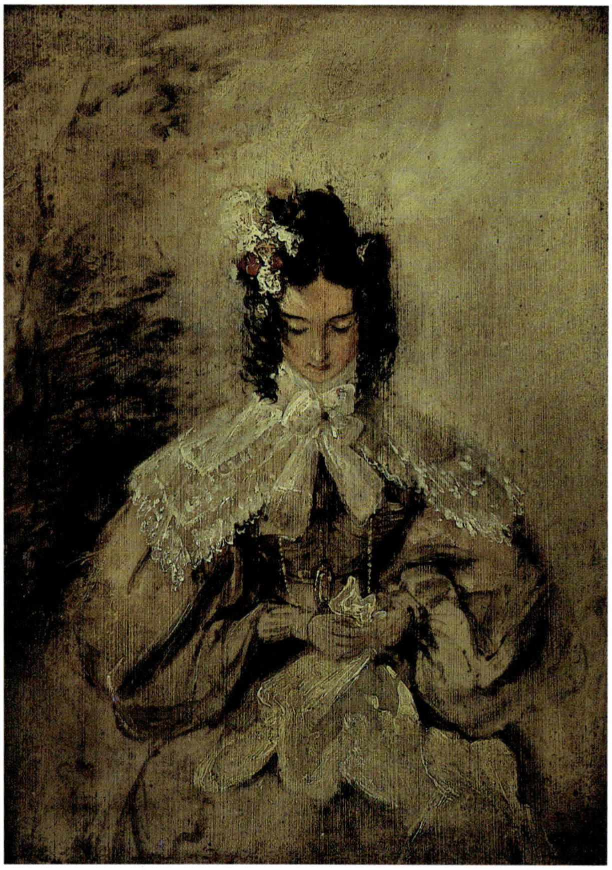

Colour Plate 55. 38/12

Amsterdam from Buiksloot Creek, looking across the Ij from the Ferry

Photo courtesy C.R.Cooke, OBE

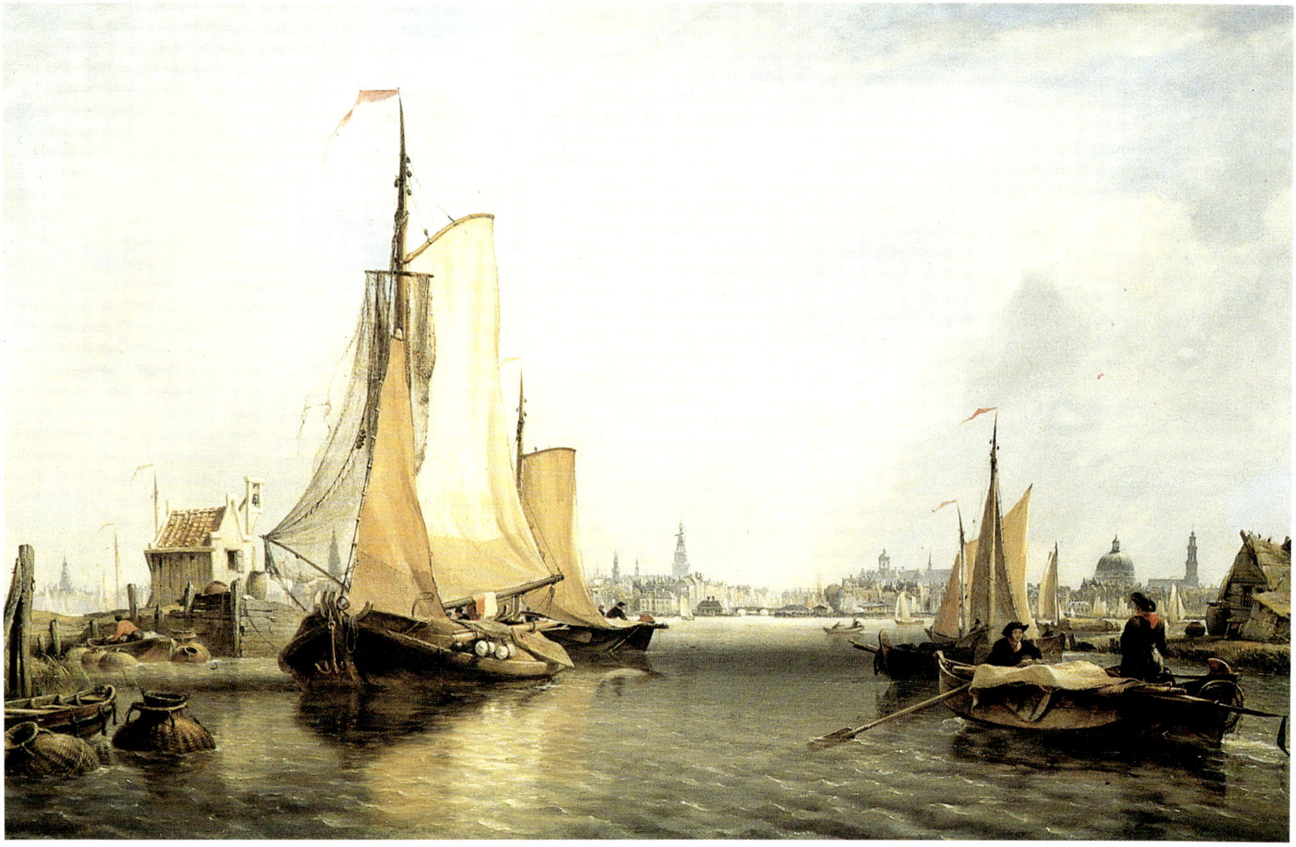

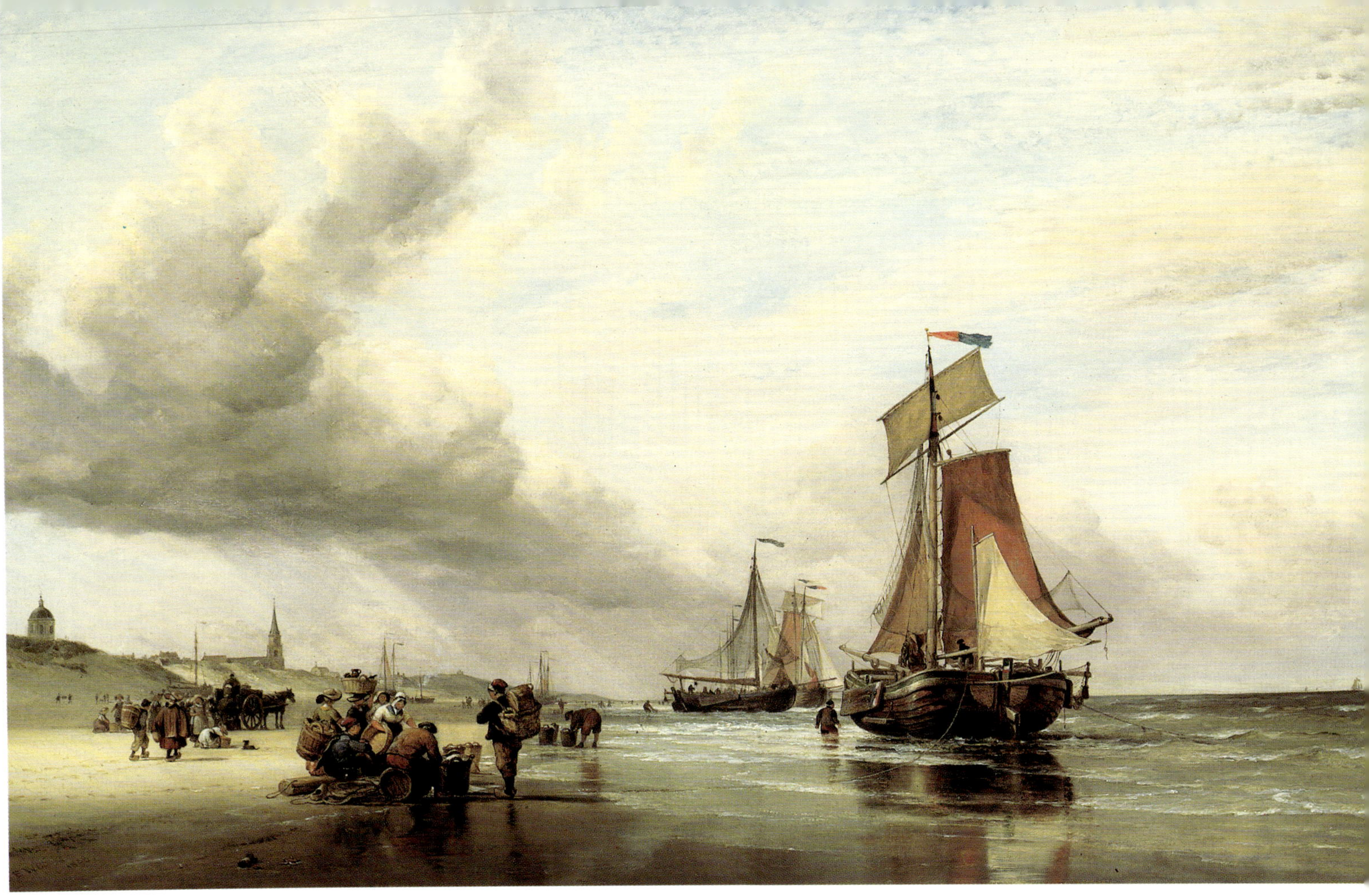

Colour Plate 56. 43/6

Scheveling sands

Painted on the spot, this was a commission from Charles Stokes, collector, antiquary and amateur geologist.

Photo courtesy Richard Green Fine Paintings. Private Collection

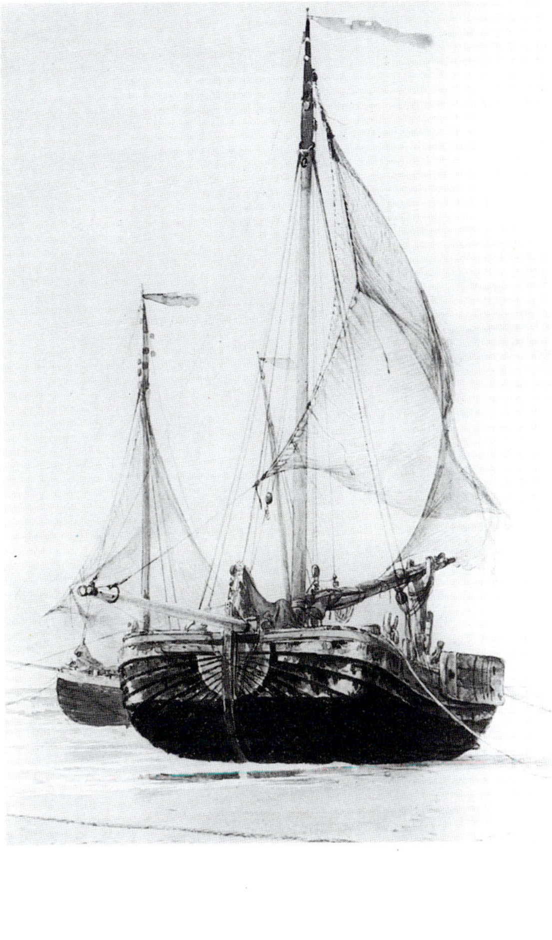

Plate 79. Watercolour

Dutch pincks ashore, drying nets

Photo courtesy Martyn Gregory. Private Collection

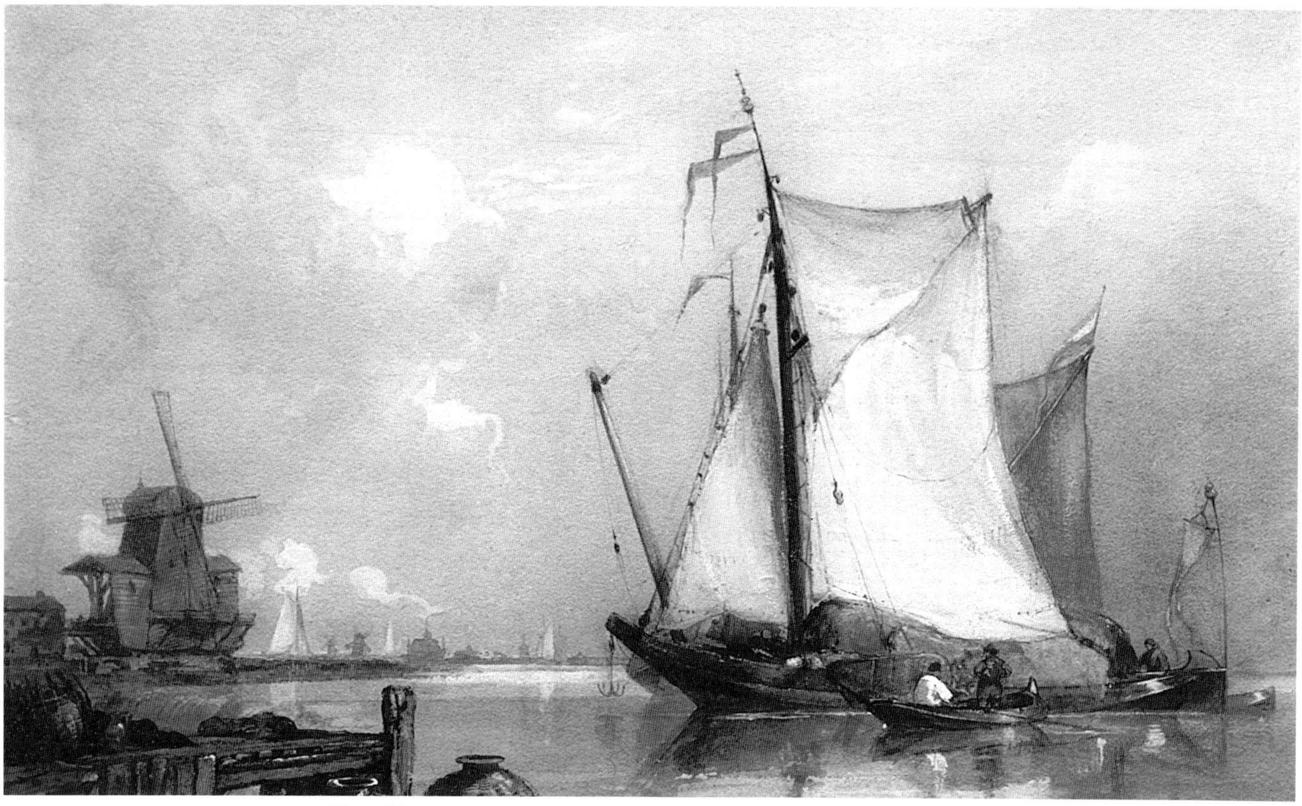

Plate 80. Watercolour
Dutch boats in a calm on the Haarlemmer Meer Photo courtesy Agnews.Private Collection

The young mother *in a very debilitated state* did not survive and a few days later, with the coffin of their daughter disinterred by a Faculty from Barnes, was laid to rest in the Loddiges' tomb in St John's churchyard, Hackney.

> *1844 Jan.5th: ...We followed in two coaches. Slowly to Hammersmith Bridge, then quicker to Hackney Turnpike, then slow through Hackney. Mr Coplestone read the*

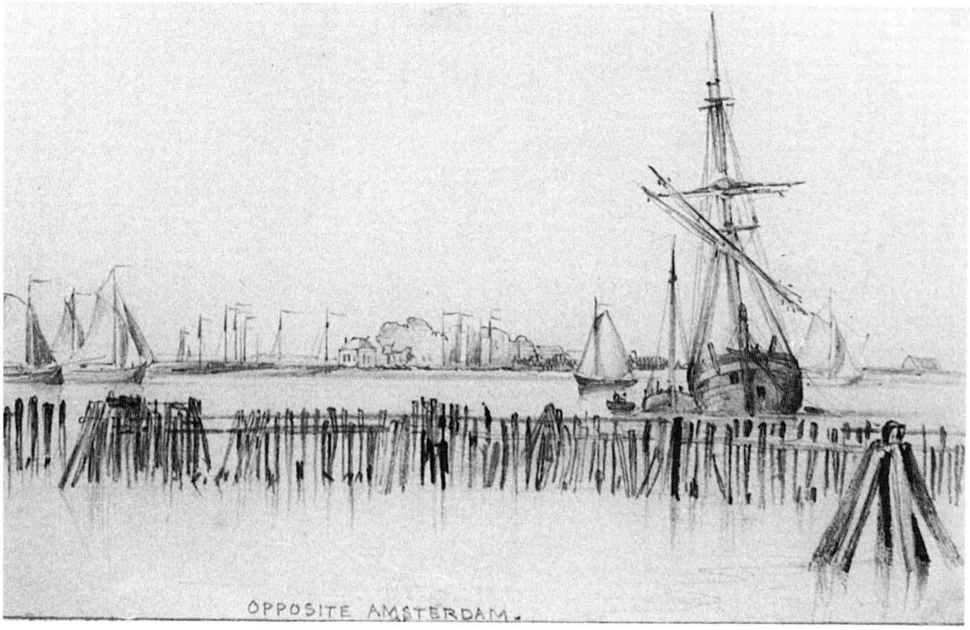

Plate 81. Pencil drawing
Opposite Amsterdam
Photo courtesy Clarges Gallery

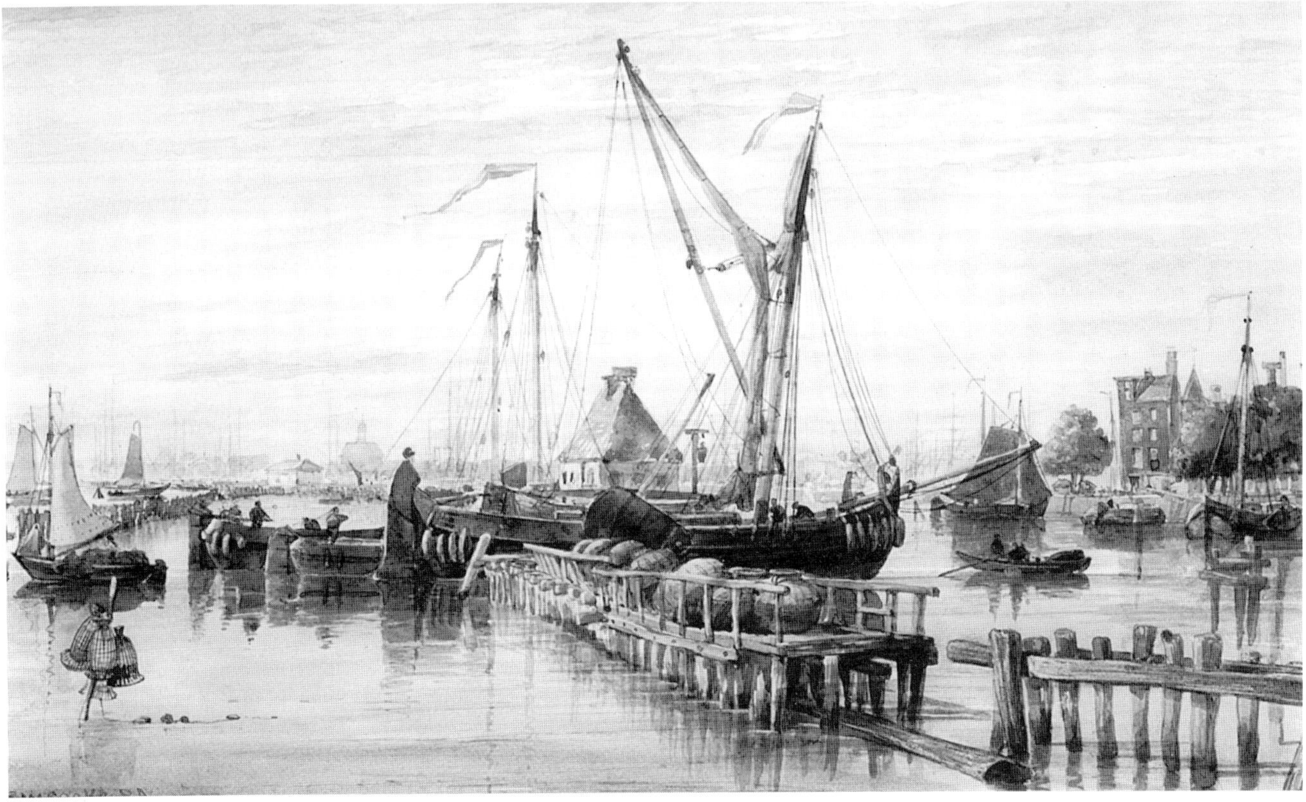

Plate 82. Watercolour
Passing the Booms, Amsterdam
Elegant and workmanlike, a drawing which relates to several oil paintings of his earlier Dutch years. Photo courtesy Rodney Todd-White. Private Collection

sublime service at ½ p 3 we committed the mortal remains of all that was so dear to me to the tomb, in the family vault...

Distractions and comfort were offered to the sorrowing husband in gifts of devotional works, volumes of sermons and visits from the local clergy and friends. Work, however, was his consolation.

1844 Jan. 8th: Left Hackney in morning, visited tomb, copied inscriptions. Home at ½ p 1, painted on Sea Piece,– Brig. Felt better.

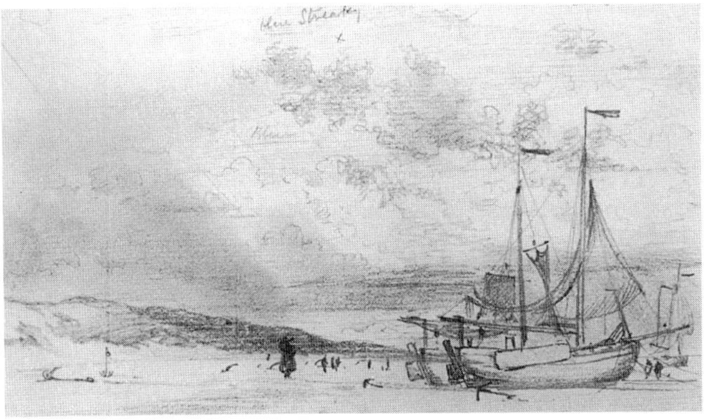

Plate 83. Pencil drawing
Scheveling, boats drying nets, evening
A soft pencil sketch with colour notes for a dramatic sky.
Photo courtesy Clarges Gallery

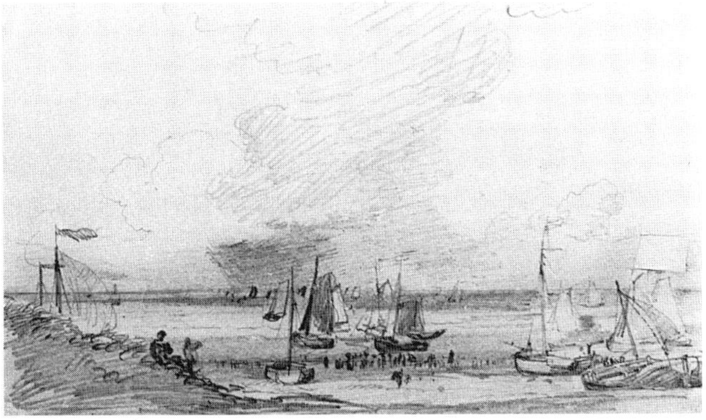

Plate 84. Pencil drawing
The Dutch Fishery
A rapid atmospheric on-the-spot study of the departing fleet.
Photo courtesy Clarges Gallery

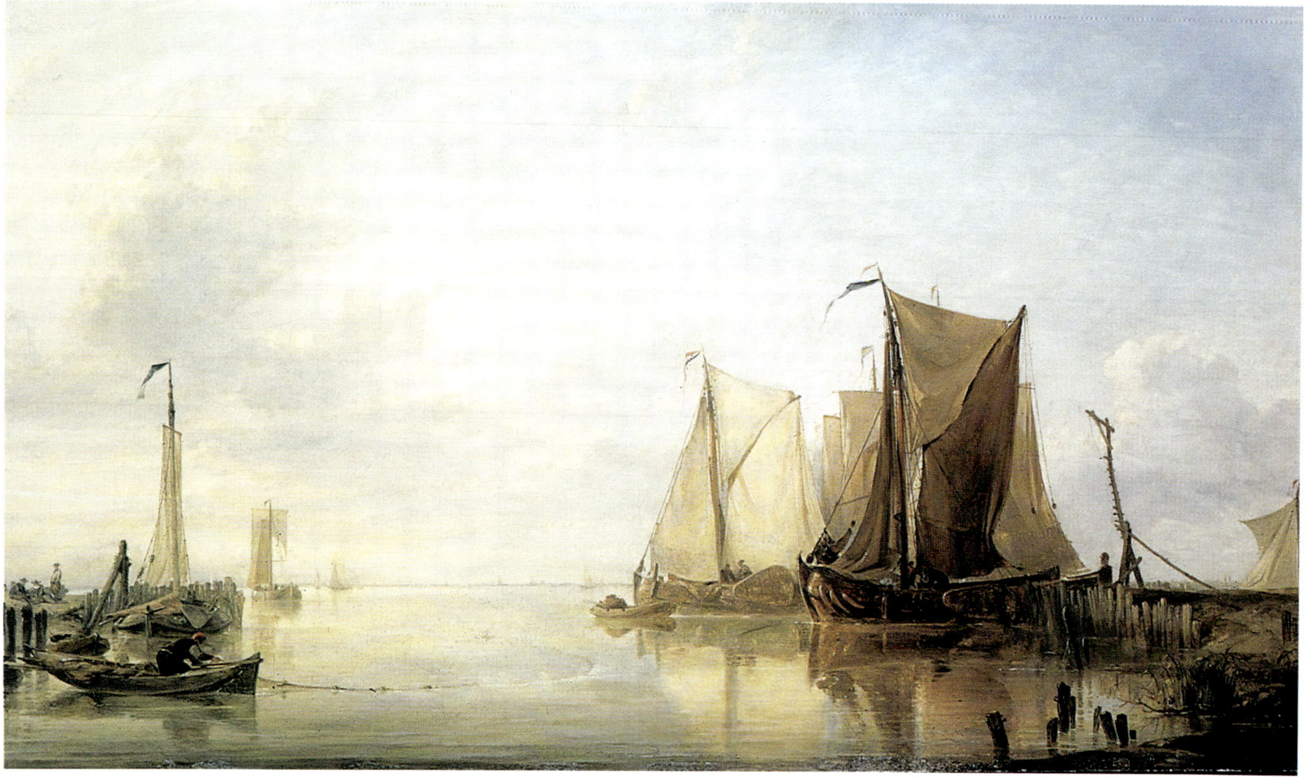

Colour Plate 57. 43/9

Dutch boats in a Calm

Well known and popular by reason of the *Art Journal* engraving (see Plate 85), this atmospheric study strongly recalled earlier Dutch masters. Photo courtesy The Tate Gallery, Robert Vernon Gift

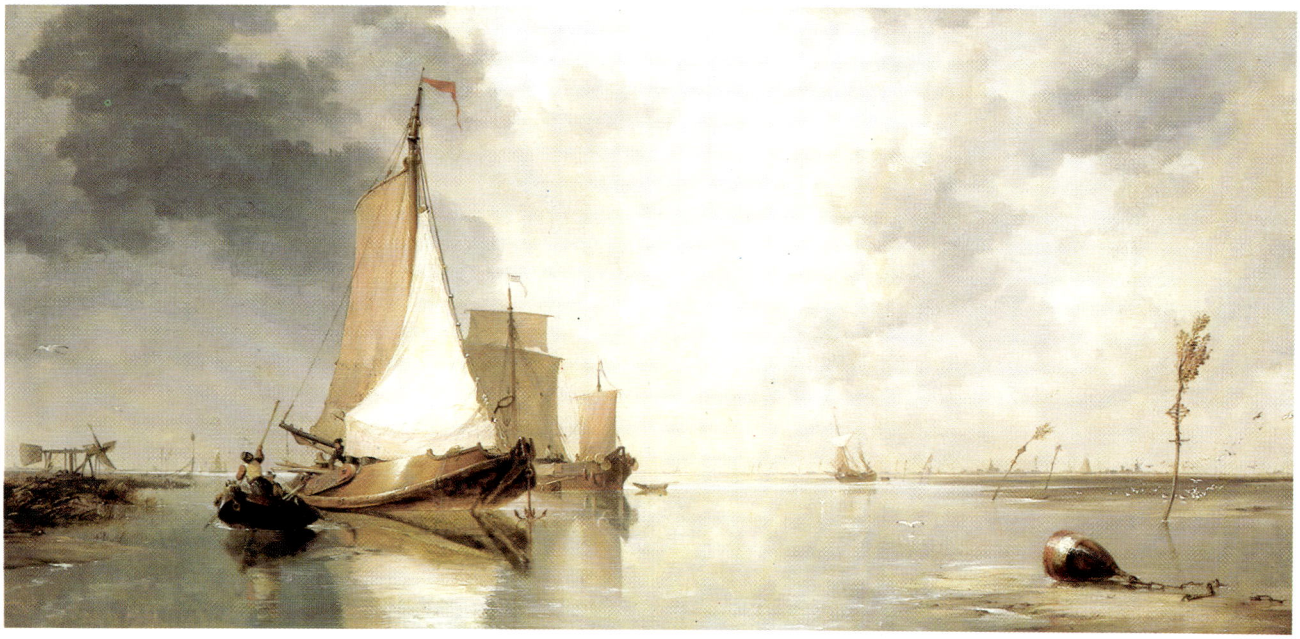

Colour Plate 58. 49/5

A Dutch Calm

Probably the picture Cooke noted as 'Dutch River' wherein he delights in painting a far distance and a statuesque group of craft, with essential working equipment.

Photo Martyn Gregory. Private Collection

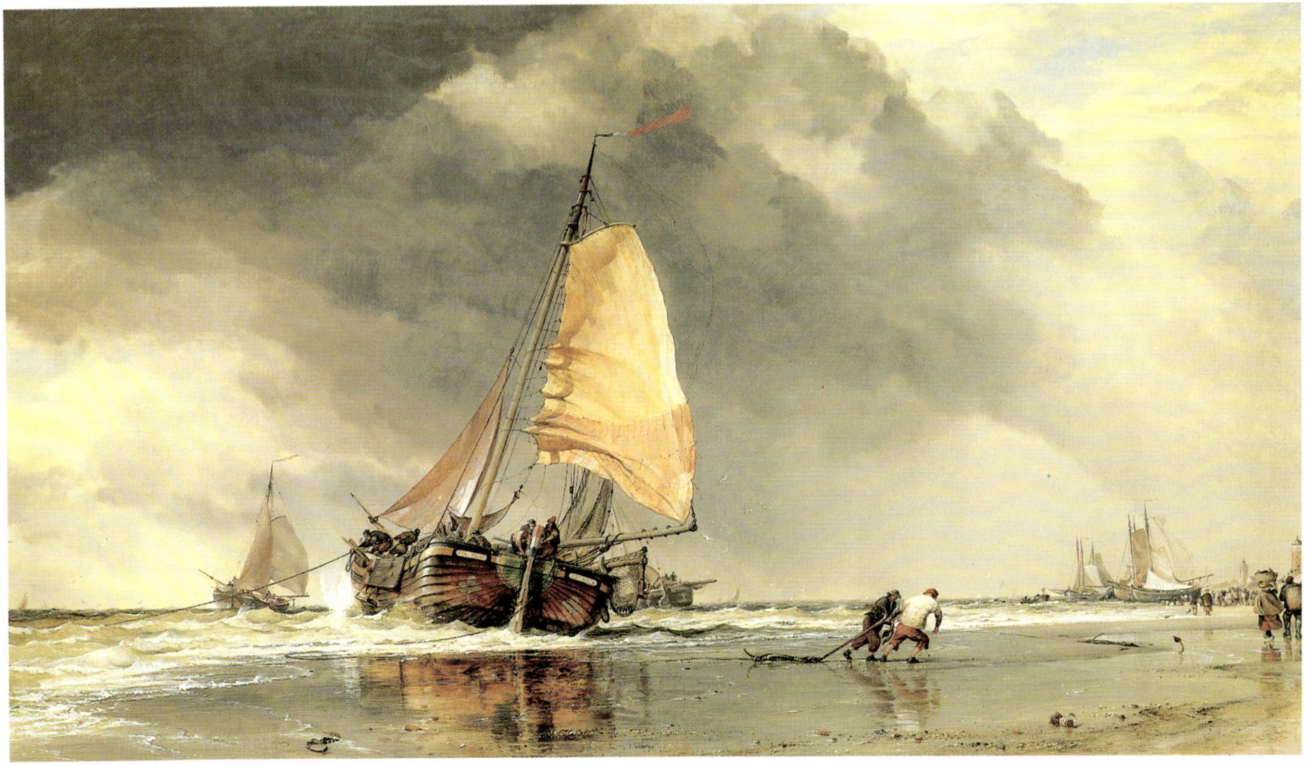

Chapter 7

VAN KOOK

As well as paintings in hand, there were other activities to absorb his attention; revived interest in fern collecting with forays to nearby country sites added choice specimens to the Albion House fernery.

Cooke's *Dutch Boats in a Calm* of 1843 is probably the most widely known of all his works (Colour Plate 57), having been illustrated in the *Art Journal's* series devoted to Robert Vernon's pictures. It was engraved on steel by Thomas Jeavons, his only plate for that publication and probably his largest.[1] Samuel Carter Hall, the founding Editor, had obtained Vernon's agreement to engrave for reproduction his entire collection given to the nation and it is possible that impressions from the plates were sold separately. Cooke was tempted to return to similar compositions, which the resident critic noticed in hearty jocular style:

1849 No 130 *A Dutch Calm*
If the group of boats were on the right instead of the left, this picture would very much resemble, in composition, the small one in the Vernon Collection. This, however, is much larger, and the light upon the water is somewhat more forced than in the other. The material is extremely commonplace, but it is impossible to praise too highly the tranquility of the whole scene. The sails hang in idle indulgence, not a whisper of the "felon winds" is heard; and the glassy surface of the tide is unruffled by a single ripple. The Dutch and their dirty water were never more worthily celebrated; the picture has only to be seen in Holland– then will the artist be immediately elected burgomaster of some place ending in dam.

1. B. Hunnisett, op. cit.

Colour Plate 59. 52/6
Dutch pincks off Katwijk, 1853
The industrious painter, having sold one picture of this long format (No. 52/5), began a companion piece, showing the same village, but here his fishing boat the *Van Kook* has just arrived.
Photo Richard Green Fine Paintings, 1996

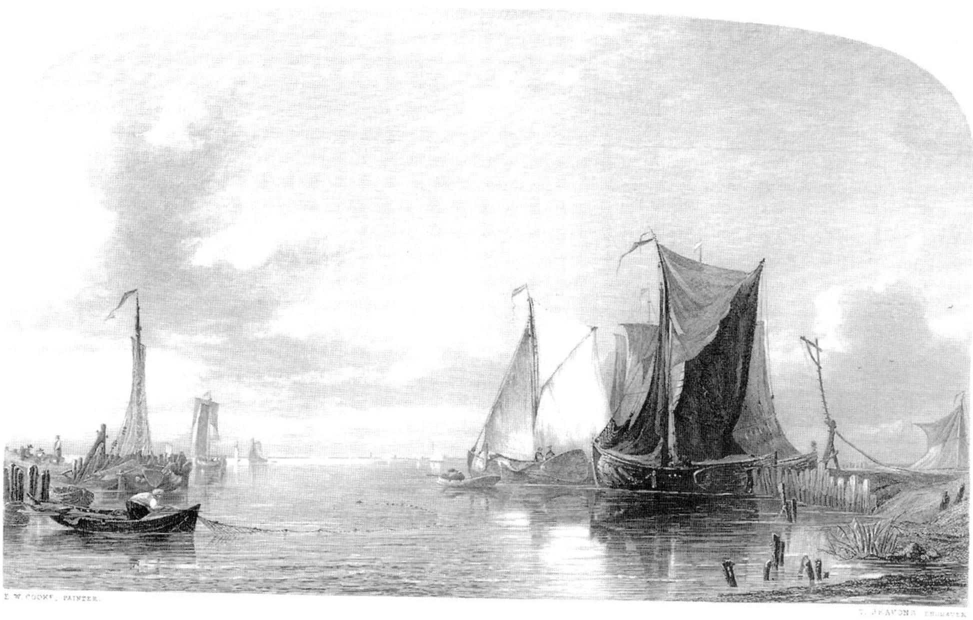

Plate 85. Engraving

Dutch boats in a Calm

The *Art Journal's* steel engraving by Jeavons, from the painting in Robert Vernon's Collection (Colour Plate 57), has rendered it probably the best known of Cooke's paintings.

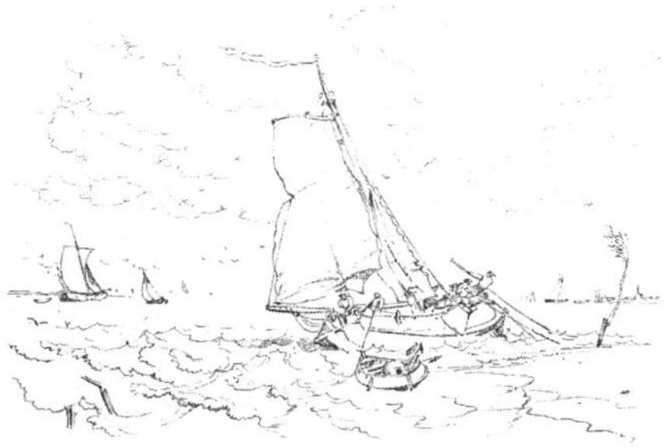

Plate 86. 47/11

Zuyder Zee botter working off a sandbank; Marken in the distance

Camera lucida record of an 1848 British Institution exhibit.

While working craft might strike a contemporary critic as extremely commonplace – presumably lacking picturesque appeal – Vernon's painting seemed to a twentieth century art writer to possess *more than a suspicion of artificiality.* A.L. Baldry, surveying British marine painting,[2] evidently failed to realise that Cooke was painting what he had recently seen. Perhaps it was the timeless appearance, particularly to a landsman, of Dutch fishing craft which seemed to Baldry merely an echo of the seventeenth century. He made an adverse comparison with Dyce's *Pegwell Bay* which, he writes, is *painted with a careful regard for reality that deserves recognition. Indeed its simple honesty makes it of more account than such a picture as Cooke's Dutch Boats in a Calm.*

One could wish that Baldry had compared like with like, for he is doubly wide of the mark. Not only was Cooke one of the best of the geologically minded shorescape painters (Colour Plate 147), but his shipping was portrayed with the 'simple honesty' which was a recognised trait of the Dutch themselves.

In 1848 Cooke showed a pair of pictures, both of which the *Art Journal's* critic was moved to mention:

> R.A. No 147 *Scheveling* (48/4, Plate 70)
> *Scheveling has been celebrated by painters of all nations and here we see the well-known sand-bank and low coast, the church and groups of unassuming houses which have been well painted every year during the last thirty years. The subject, however, is not Scheveling, but some boats which are placed in the immediate foreground; they are painted with somewhat more of sharpness than we have been accustomed to see in the North Sea subjects of the artist, but they are most faithfully detailed. These boats and the infinitely beautiful shred of sand and water near them, were enough to give value to a canvas thrice the size of this.*

2. *The Studio. British Marine Painting* Special Number, 1919, p.27.

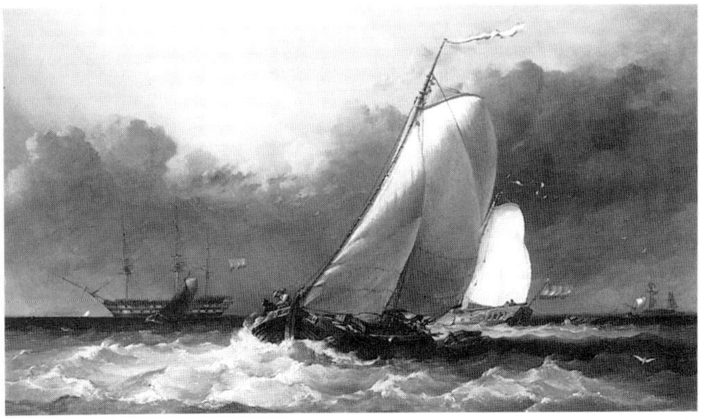

Plate 87. 48/3
Dutch Yachting on the Zuider Zee
A picture selected as an *Art Union* prize: the winner became a friend and patron of the artist.
Photo courtesy The Trustees of theNational Maritime Museum, Greenwich

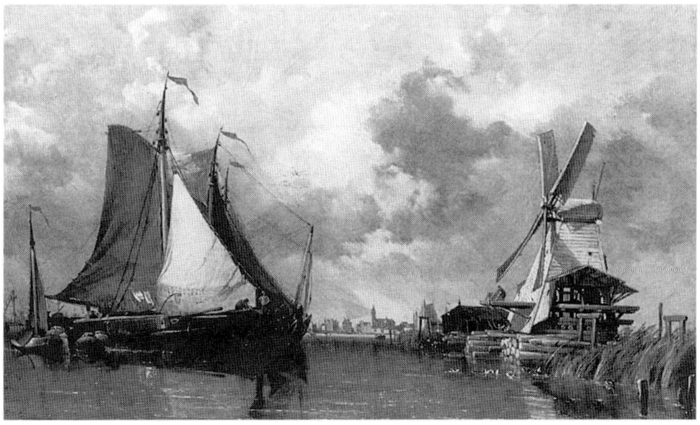

Plate 88. 50/4
Dutch sawmill & Zuider Zee craft on the Ij, Zaandam in the distance
Cooke liked to set the scene with fair precision in his titles, and there is the same quality in his painting of the boats, which had captivated him. Photo courtesy Dover Museum. W.A. Williamson Collection

Here the critic accurately identifies and acknowledges the major theme of the artist's work; his true interests are the *bomschuiten* or, as he invariably termed them, *pincks,* the fishing boats, but always with great attention to their setting, the shorescape.

If the craft were in a sharper focus than formerly they were conforming to Cooke's desire to show them not only in their truest colour but also in their utmost detail. The 'sharpness' of the image wherein Cooke delighted had begun to arouse comment and as he followed his vision the criticisms became more pointed. His smaller pictures usually escaped the strictures, in spite of the critic's remarks above.

Similar Dutch coastal scenes attracted painters from every quarter. The French marine artist Theodore Gudin was also an RA exhibitor whom Cooke met that year in London. He painted *On the Scheveningen Coast*, 1844, making a feature of the graceful tracery of the blown fishing nets, which also appealed to Cooke.

The *Art Journal* announced the result of the draw for the Art-Union Prizes and noted among those pictures selected by prizeholders was the pair to the *Scheveling*. No. 174 in the catalogue was *Dutch Yachting on the Zuider Zee* at £80, and it was chosen by George S. Marshall Esq.

They noted it also in the review of the exhibition (Plate 87):

> No 174 *Dutch Yachting:*
> *These yachts are fashioned according to the clumsy Dutch build, but they stand up well against a stiff breeze, under mainsail and foresail fully spread. The nearest boat is beating up on the larboard tack; she is beautifully set in the water and makes way bravely. The water is painted with skill and knowledge, and the work altogether is of a much higher character than the Mediterranean and Adriatic subjects which the artist has lately exhibited.*

The origin of the name *yacht* – derived from the Dutch 'jacht' which is the same for the hunt, in the sense of the chase – was perhaps unknown by the critic for whom it evidently only meant the sleek and rakish cutters of fashionable British water-sport. The 'clumsy' or rather stout-built Dutch type with its lee-boards and ornamental stern was the origin of the British royal yachts of Charles II's Restoration. Modern versions are still built and sailed.

George S. Marshall, then of Denmark Hill, later of Lee, had a picture collection and some interesting Dutch silver. He also bought the *Scheveling* so had the pair and became a friend of the artist as well as a patron.

The old master of calms, Jan van de Cappelle's *View on the Scheldt* c.1650,[3] is clearly an ancestor of a distinct group of subjects developed by Cooke – the broad expanses of the River Scheldt with usually the Antwerp skyline, but always with the local fishing craft. These are not the coastal pincks but the local botters which he painted from 1844 to 1870.

The painting of reflections in calm tidal water became a matter of much attention with

3. Toledo Museum, Ohio, USA.

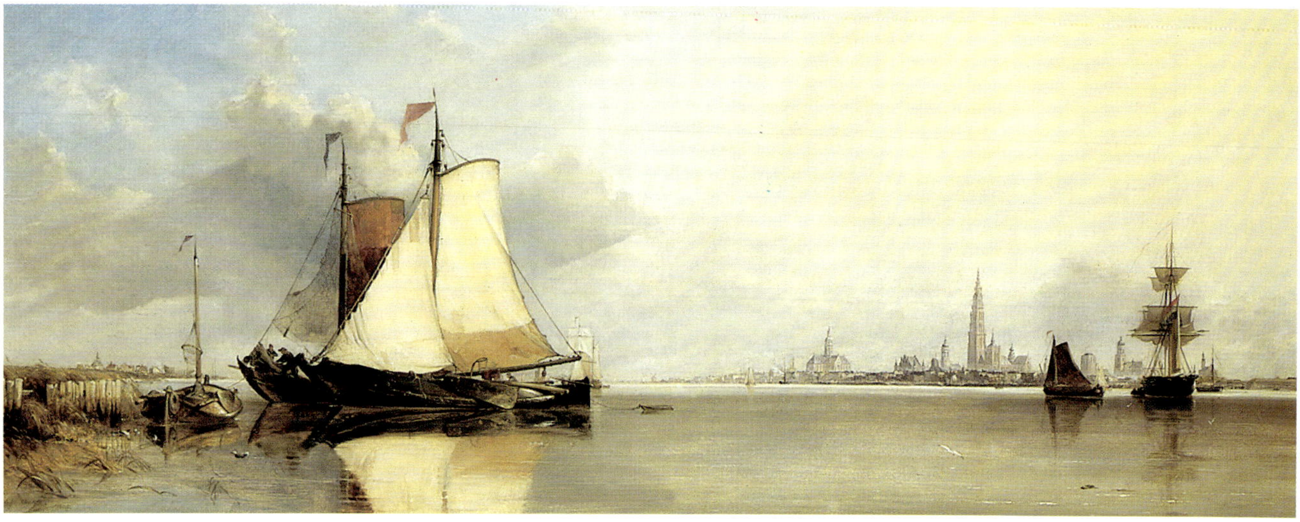

Colour Plate 60. 44/1
Antwerp from the Scheldt, morning
One of his 1844 RA pictures, this is a *tour de force* of level distance and salt atmosphere using a formula of lights and darks so convincingly.
Photo courtesy Sotheby's. Private Collection

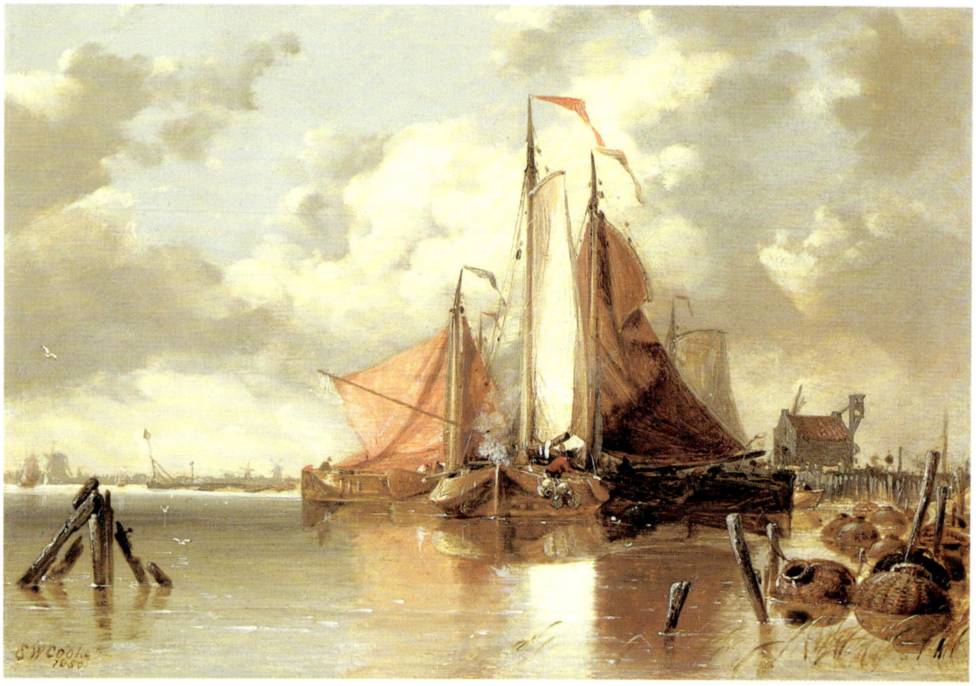

Colour Plate 61. 50/2
Dutch Fishing station
This charming small study was a New Year's gift to George S. Marshall, one of his patrons who had sent him a Dutch silver tobacco box!
Photo: courtesy Richard.Green Fine Paintings. Private Collection

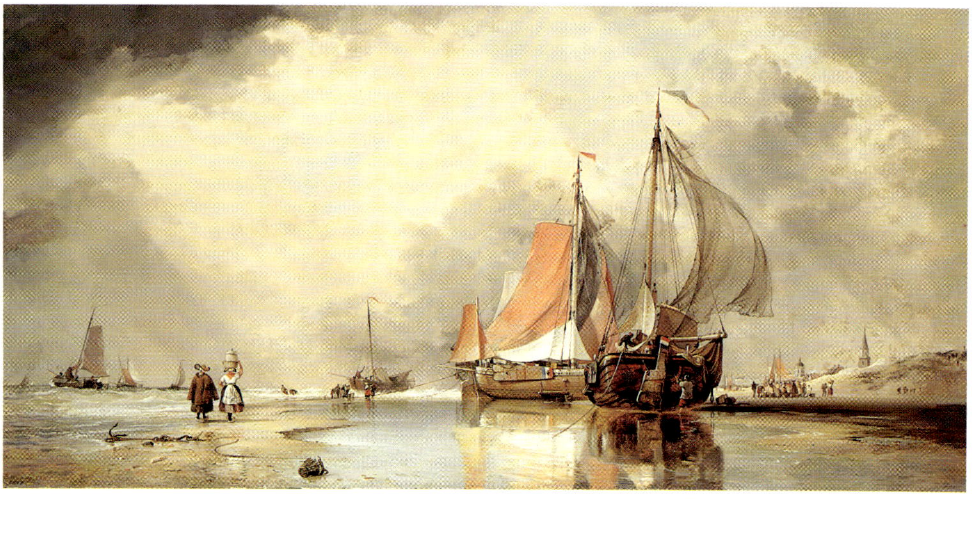

Colour Plate 62. 51/9
Scheveling shore, low water, tide coming in, pincks drying nets and sails
A favourite subject, this combines the British Institution title, 1852, with the artist's Ledger entry.
Photo courtesy Royal Exchange Art Gallery. Private Collection

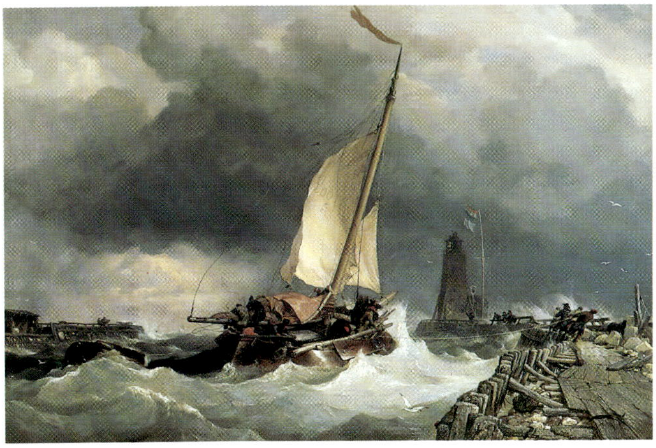

Colour Plate 63. 49/9
Dutch pilots warping their craft out of harbour in rough weather
One of his British Institution pictures of 1850, this strong dramatic piece is perhaps the counterpart of his Broekenhaven/Medemblik subjects, leaving rather than entering harbour. Photo courtesy Sotheby's. Private Collection

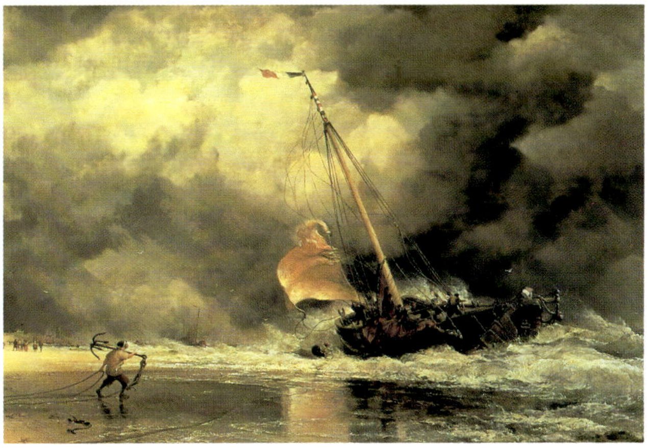

Colour Plate 64. 65/2
Rough sea with Scheveling pinck getting off shore
This spirited scene of fishermen handling their craft in typically rough conditions served Cooke as a subject for several impressive paintings over the years.
Photo courtesy Phillips Fine Art Auctioneers

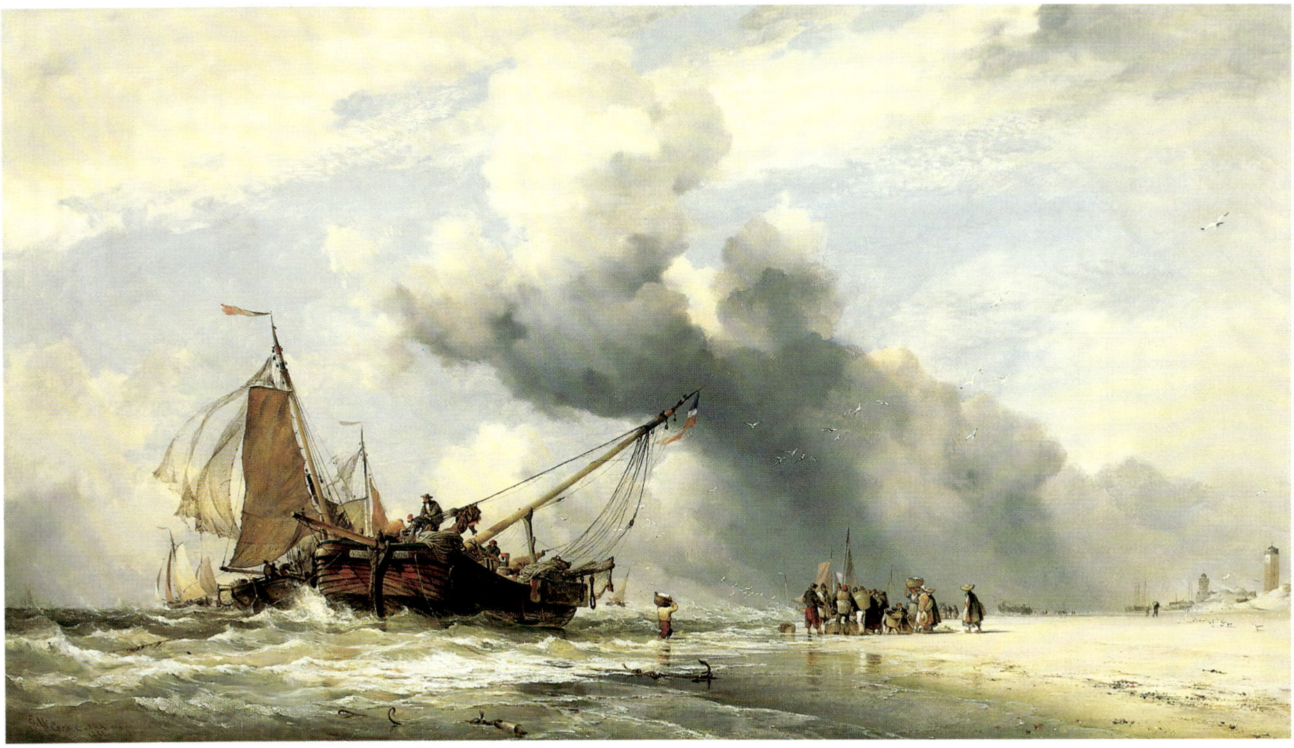

Colour Plate 65. 52/5
Dutch fishing craft, Katwijck
The towers identify the place among the dunes on the coast near Leiden.This is another subject with dramatic appeal, the mast lowered into its crutch and storm clouds approaching as the catch is landed. Photo courtesy Richard Green Fine Paintings. Private Collection

the example of the old marine masters constantly in mind. *In the Netherlands no painter could set brush to canvas without one of the Masters of the Golden Age looking over his shoulder*[4] and it was inevitable that comparisons would constantly be made. The Londoner Cooke was as aware of this as anyone and seems to have cultivated the idea.

In *Maitres d'Autrefois* the painter Eugène Fromentin perceived *in this art which has the reputation of being so down-to-earth, in these famous painters who were generally*

4. de Leeuw op..cit.

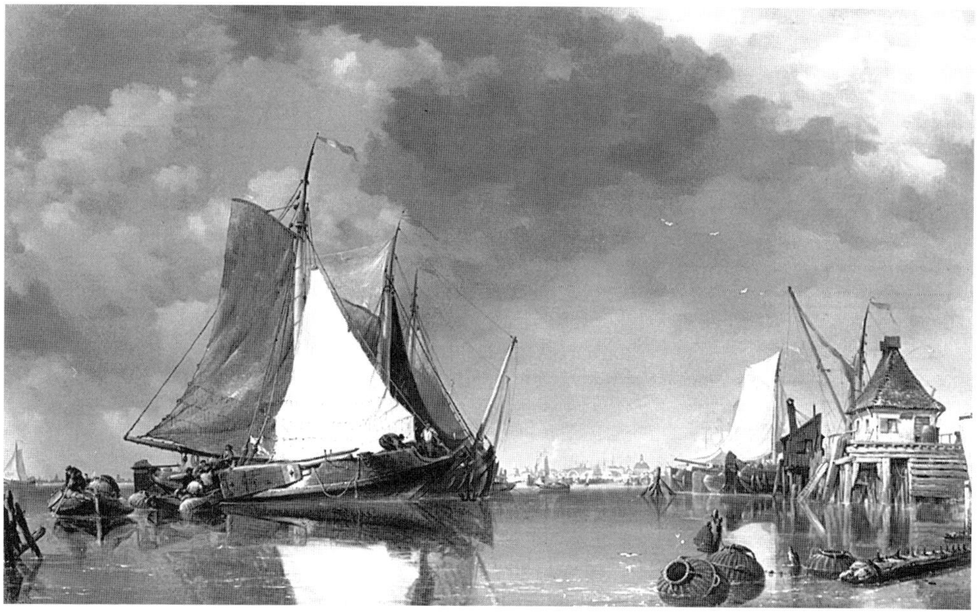

Plate 89. 49/11
Dutch fishing craft off the Booms, Amsterdam 1850
He could never exhaust the subjects round Amsterdam and this is a perfect example of his 'Dutchness'.
Photo courtesy Polak Gallery

regarded as short-sighted imitators, a grandeur and goodness of character, an affection for the truth and a warm love of reality, that lend their work a value that the things themselves do not seem to possess. While this accorded with the prevailing taste of picture buyers, artists found a ready market for their works.

The clarity of things seen at the seaside, when fogs, mists and vapours do not combine to render visibility 'soft', is well known and observed. *The atmosphere like a lens* one critic wrote, and Cooke, who had delighted in etched detail, now carried out in oil paint the exact portrayal of ordinary working boats.

It must be remarked that in such work there is today also a documentary value and, while photography was already more or less commonplace, as ever there was much a draughtsman could convey that the camera could but imperfectly achieve.

There was still the problem for a working painter inspired by his subject of how to vary his approach from year to year. *A favourite worker on the coast seas and waterways*

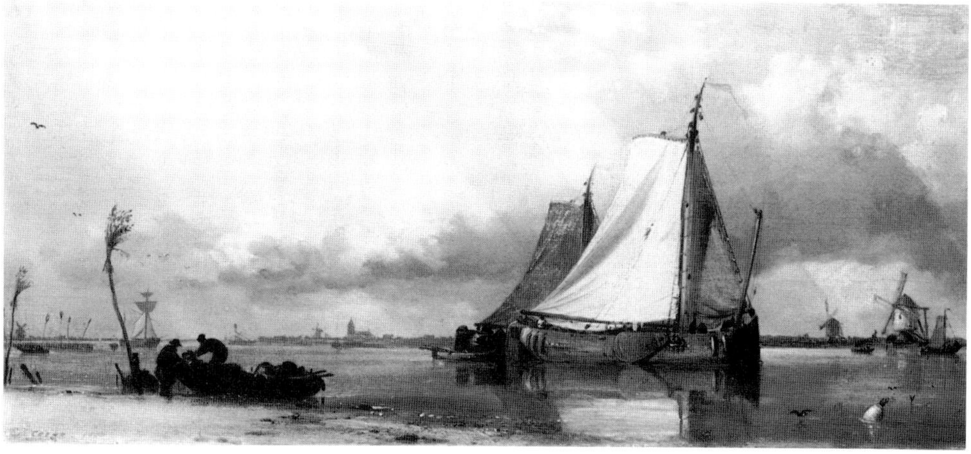

Plate 90. 50/1
A Bit of Holland
Begun as Dutch boats on a calm river, it was quickly painted for the British Institution's exhibition which opened at the end of January. It was then shown with the new title.
Photo courtesy The Trustees of the National Maritime Museum, Greenwich

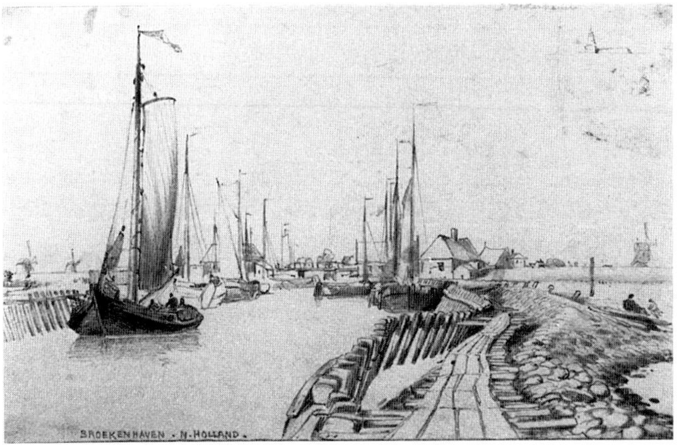

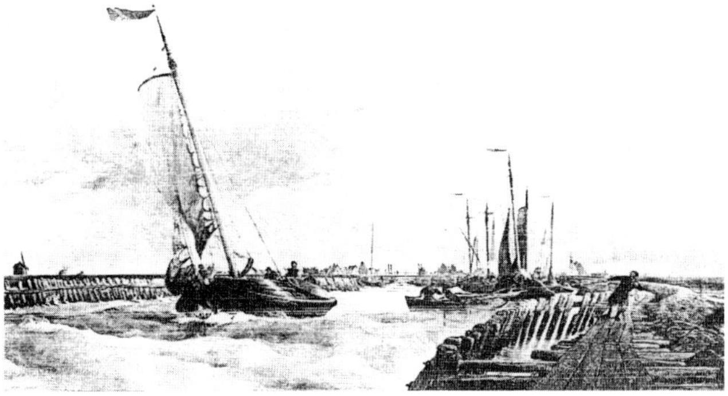

Plate 91. Pencil drawing
Broekenhaven
Photo courtesy Clarges Gallery

Plate 92 42/2
Broekenhaven, a fishing port of the Zuider Zee
He had drawn the massive timber and piled rocks of the breakwater with the planked walkway in 1838 (Plate 91) and doubtless observed the fishing botters warping in or out. He painted another version, without naming the harbour, in 1854 (see 54/3, Colour Plate 149).
Photo courtesy Arthur Ackermann & Peter Johnson. Private Collection

– in all media, whose contributions were an anticipation at the annual exhibition... wrote Maurice Grant[5] and there is abundant evidence that collectors were anxious to possess representative examples of Cooke's different subjects. It inevitably led him to duplicate, although in varying sizes, his most successful compositions.

Atmospheric effects, the time of day, location (often achieved by placing a distant tower or spire on a skyline), and incident such as 'drying nets and sails', 'hauling her head to sea', 'landing fish', 'carting off the catch', 'repairing boats & gear', these served to give the desired variety to his pictures. Drawings of details of rig and sketches of their coming ashore and putting off in all weathers were filling his sketchbooks and files (Plates 95 and 96). This use of everyday incident, such as hoisting aloft large fishing nets to dry, takes on a highly decorative function as he paints the folds of fine netting floating out on the breeze. Whilst oddly at variance with the bluff, heavy, solid boats and their massive gear, the nets in their light strength signify the means of reaping the harvest of the sea.

His scrupulous attention to the boat's gear and tackle was a characteristic of his art: his drawing and painting of baskets, pots, anchors, blocks and even the crudest utensil in use on board was of long standing. As French fish baskets differed from Dutch wicker-work, so would Edward Cooke's drawings reflect national and regional changes.

A necessary operation performed by one of the crew, shouldering the heavy iron anchor (often a four-fluked hook) and taking it either up the sandy beach or bringing it down to the boat, is frequently shown. We are then left in little doubt (whatever current title the picture may possess) whether they have arrived or are about to put off.

Another group of Cooke's pictures illustrated the manoeuvring of boats in the narrow channels between breakwaters which led to some of the harbours round the Zuider Zee. A good example was No 45, British Institution, 1850, *Dutch pilots warping...* 49/9 (Colour Plate 63) which was greeted by the critics with familiarity:

> *It is high water and the wind blows dead into the harbour mouth of one of those Dutch towns quae exeunt in 'dam'. If we read aright the legend on her stern, the craft is the good sea boat the* Eduard Van Kook *and she is being towed by her crew to the jetty head where she may at once fill away upon a tack to the galliott in the offing. This is a painting of much excellence, but we observe in the late works of this artist that matters of detail are worked out with much hardness – in smaller works this is lost and all is exquisite sweetness.*

Here the sharpness of vision has become hardness of execution and the cry was taken up

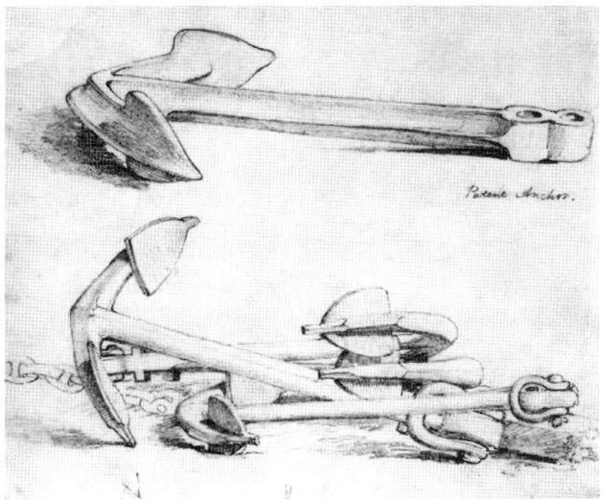

Plate 93. Pencil drawing
Patent anchor and others
The sculpturesqe group appealed to Cooke and the very 'modern' form of the unidentified patent anchor (of which there were many), with its pronounced ribs, evidently pleased his recording eye.
Photo courtesy Martyn Gregory. Private Collection

5. Grant op.cit.

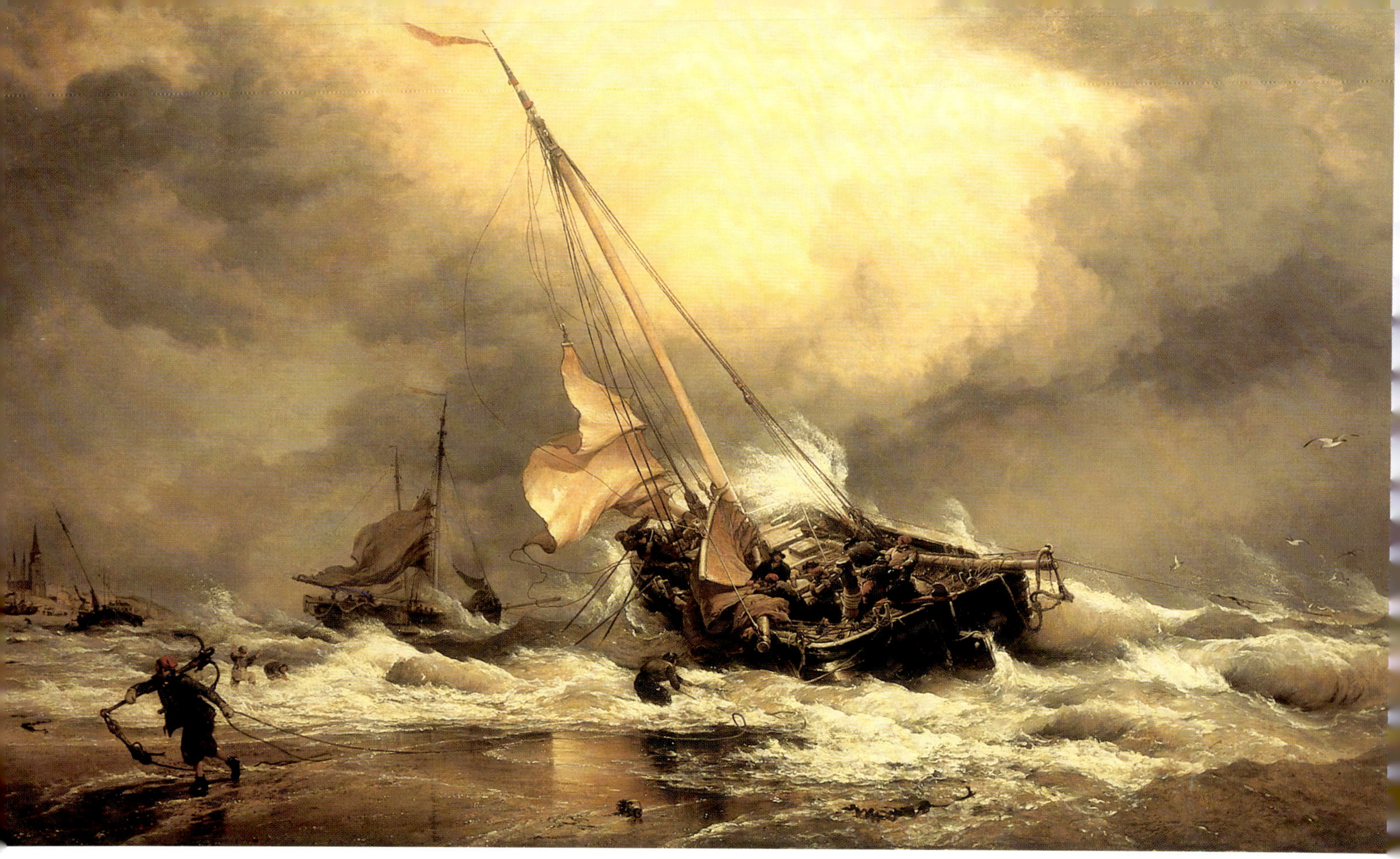

Colour Plate 66. 55/8

A North Sea Breeze on the Dutch Coast: fishermen hauling the 'pinck' out of the surf

'We have not for many years seen a sea piece so entirely satisfactory as this… it would do honour to any painter of any age.' The *Art Journal* wrote, in spite of the title, that they were trying to put to sea – but the critic's strong approbation of this spirited scene remains true today.

Photo courtesy The Trustees of the National Maritime Museum, Greenwich

Colour Plate 67. 68/6

On shore for a tide, coast of Holland

A thunderous impression of another aspect of working the heavy square-built fishing boats on the flat tidal sands.

Photo courtesy Christie's

Colour Plate 68. 52/12

Breezy Day Scheveling, landing the catch

This jewel-like picture, only 18 inches in height, is the result of careful observation and note-taking on a favourite stretch of coast which he has visited four times already. His treatment of skies continues the tradition of the Dutch school.

Photo courtesy Martyn Gregory. Private Collection

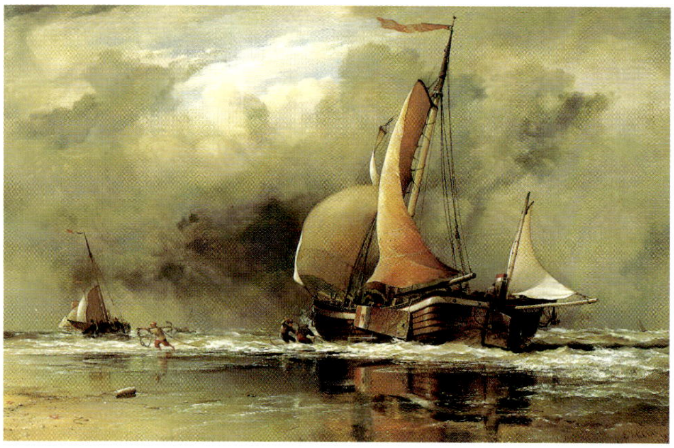

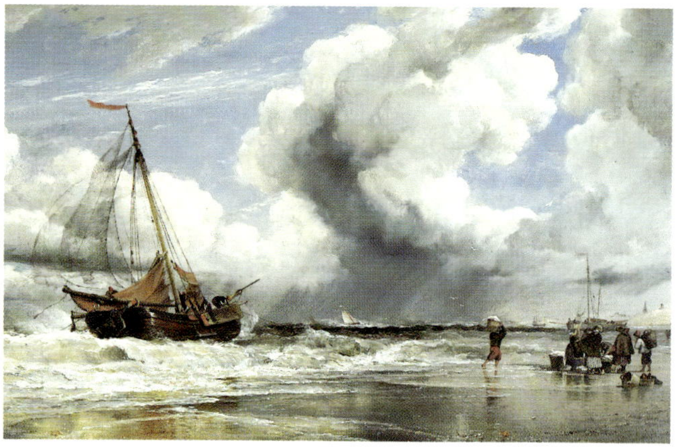

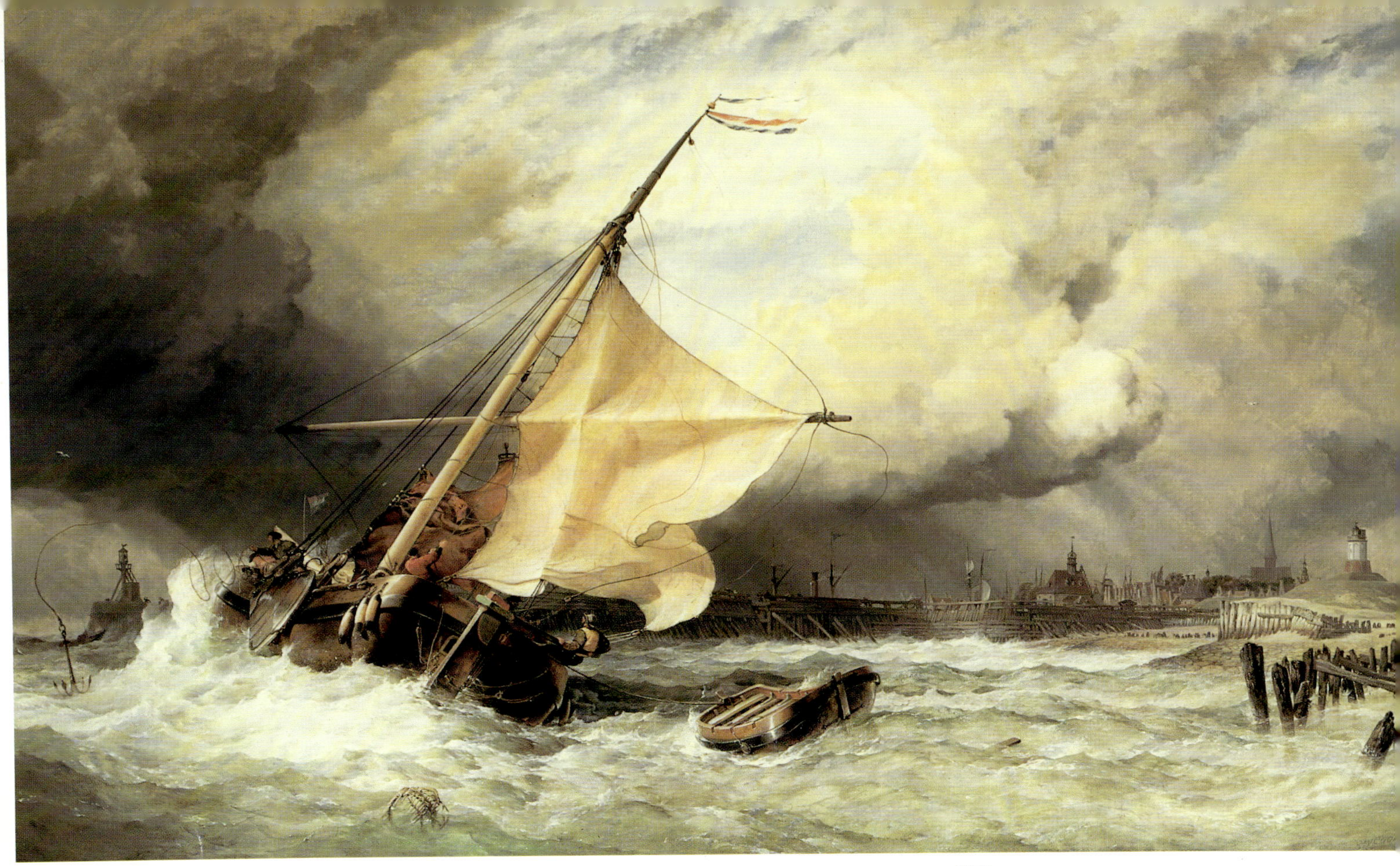

Colour Plate 70. 59/2

A Dutch peon [sic] *running for the port of Harlingen, is driven in a heavy squall outside the south pierhead*

Cooke was but once at Harlingen and was interested in its wooden piers. The art critics admired this 1859 RA picture and commented on the skipper's seamanship at some length! The Dutch boat is correctly a poon, the RA Catalogue evidently misprinted.

Photo courtesy Sotheby's. Collection Peter Gallichan, Esq

Colour Plate 69. 53/5

Scheveling beach, selling fish

Photo courtesy Bonhams. Private Collection

Colour Plate 71. 62/3

Dutch trawlers at anchor off Scheveling, waiting for the tide

The critics liked it – 'chafed by wind and wave as they wait for the flood tide... there is here the same surprising precision of touch, but certainly not the slightest want of movement and air'.

Photo courtesy Martyn Gregory

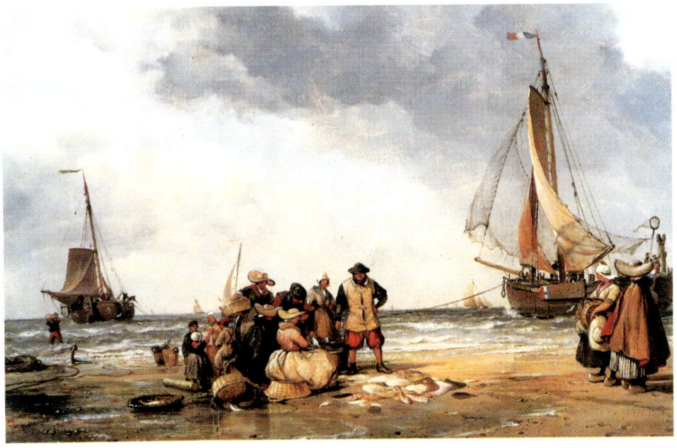

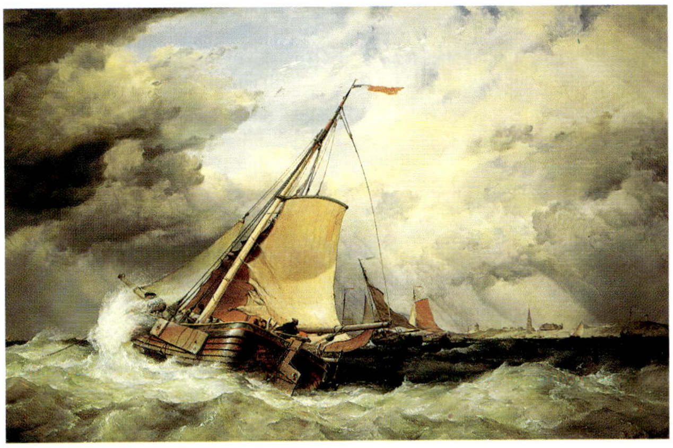

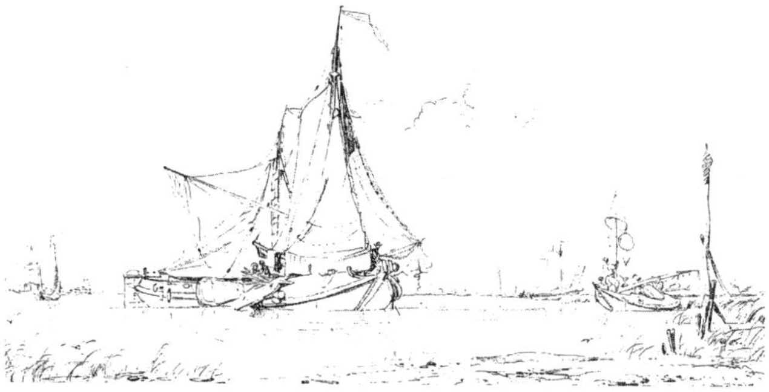

Plate 94. 49/7
Dutch Boats on the Zaan
Camera lucida record of a painting sold to a Philadelphia merchant.

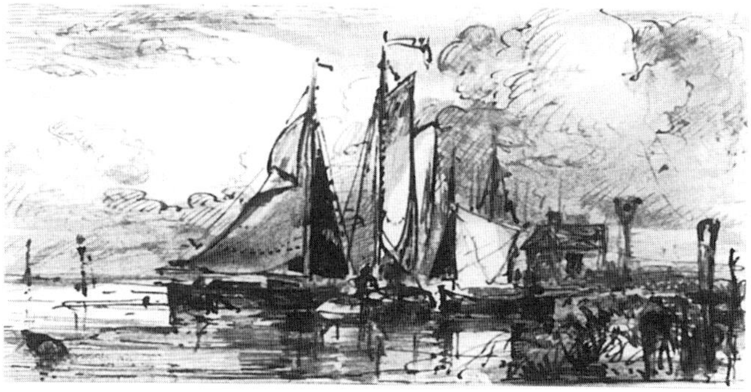

Plate 95. Ink drawing
A Calm: Dutch boats at a fishing station
An arrangement of lights and darks, possibly a sketch for or of a painting. Photo courtesy Clarges Gallery

on all sides. Freedom of brushwork and looseness in handling would not, one feels, allow E.W. Cooke to express himself adequately.

Van Kook

The device of putting one's name in a picture, apart from the signature, was common enough. T.S. Boys often inscribed his on shop facias and trade signs in his English and French street scenes, and in etchings Edward Cooke had been in the habit of putting his name on the sterns of boats where their identities might actually be found.

Van Kook appears on the bows of his Scheveningen fishing boats very frequently, a playful reminder that every Dutchman was 'van' something or other and that he wanted to be counted as one of them. The critics, as we have seen, took up the refrain, adding their own refinements!

One might speculate on whether the name of Cooke's Dutch contemporaries the Koekkoek family (sometimes rendered as Koek-Koek) was ever bandied about in these jests. The Koekkoeks were making open-air oil sketches as early as the end of the 1830s in a renascence of the Dutch school of landscape and marine painting.[6]

When working on the spot a certain looseness was an inevitable result of coping with changing light and movement. Small paintings by Cooke have survived which show dash and less than his usual detail and these are almost certainly 'on the spot' studies which have not been 'worked up' or 'finished'.

Scheveningen, the fishing village down the road from The Hague, Katwijk on the coast opposite Leiden, Zandvoort on the shore near Haarlem and, in North Holland, Egmont

6. de Leeuw op.cit.

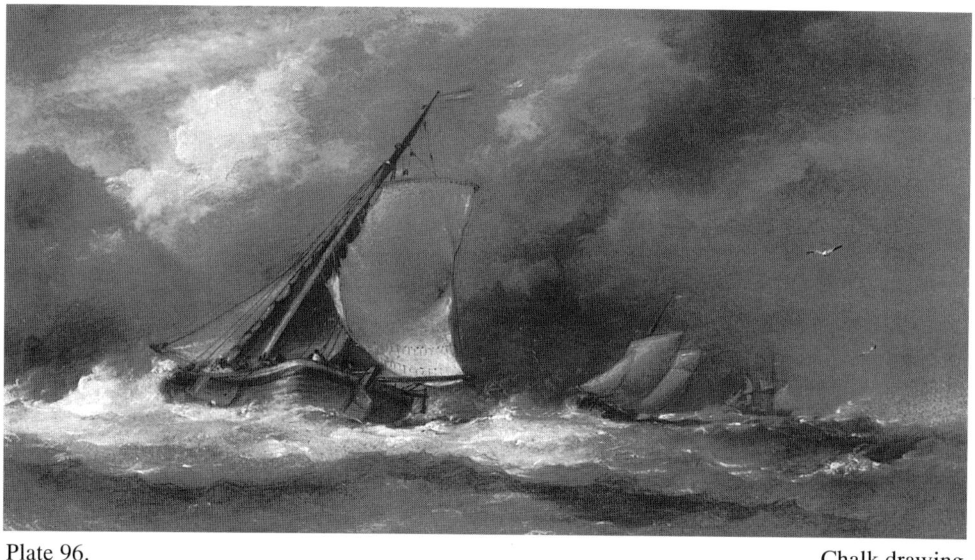

Plate 96. Chalk drawing
Dutch vessels in a strong breeze
Perhaps Lot 106 in his 1865 sale.
Photo courtesy Martyn Gregory

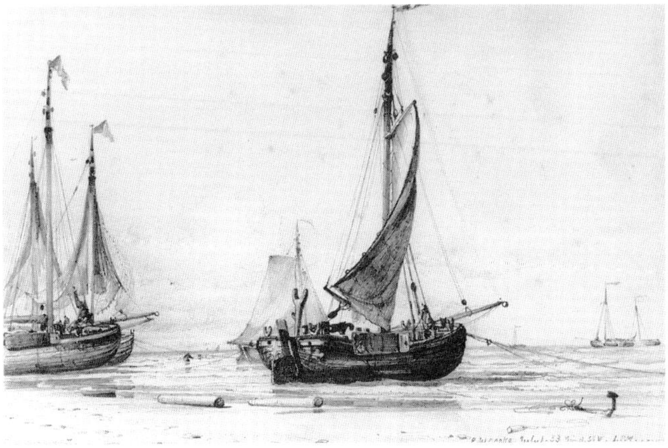

Plate 97. Pencil drawing
Scheveningen, 1st July 1853: Wind SSW, 1 PM
Photo courtesy Martyn Gregory. Private Collection

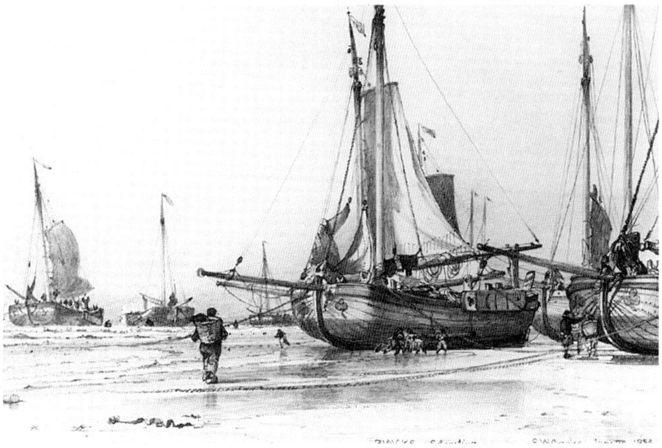

Plate 98. Pencil drawing
Dutch pincks beached at Scheveling 1853
Photo courtesy Martyn Gregory. Private Collection

aan Zee and Camperduin were coastal fishing communities among the sand dunes, all convenient settings for his North Sea pictures.

The painters of the emerging Hague school who were children when Cooke first came to Holland had, some of them, French connections and were a developing phenomenon: *a new approach in which romanticism remained as an undercurrent, but with realist and impressionist elements now playing a more important role.*[7] They gravitated to Scheveningen the fishing village and drew inspiration from both its inhabitants and from the shore scene: *it has remained what it was. Modern life has altered the details... the burghers of the past, the tourists of today, are never more than small, picturesque, moving, changing touches, fleeting dots that succeed each other century after century, between the huge sky, the great honeycomb of the immeasureable dunes and the yellow sands.*[8]

Cooke ARA

Shorter stays in Holland in 1853 and 1855 served to refresh the Dutch coast experience and resulted in a series of important pictures. Cooke, with Henry Christy the ethnologist, had evidently arranged to travel together in 1853 on what reads like an antique collector's tour in which painting took second place. In October 1855 a short visit in rough weather yielded only sketches, though there was incident in plenty.

In the middle '50s a succession of large Dutch subjects went to the London exhibitions alongside Venetian canvases with which Cooke was industriously making a new name.

Large Academy pictures by rising Associates often attracted comment: RA 1855, No.269 *A North Sea Breeze on the Dutch Coast; fishermen hauling the "pinck" out of the surf* (55/8, Colour Plate 66). The critic of the *Art Journal,* in front of one of Cooke's best and most stirring beach scenes, ignored the title and waded in, as it were:

> *This is a large composition which excites our sympathy, seeing as we do, the brave bark Van Kook, in difficulty here. The wind is off the sea and the surf is making a breach over the boat forward. It is not very clear that the stout skipper and his good crew will get their vessel off.*
>
> *As is usual in the works of this painter, the boat and all her gear are painted with an intense accuracy. Scheveningen appears on the left and on the sand are many groups of the townspeople. Scheveningen since the days of Vandervelde has been a prolific source of subject matter. Every season produces more than one Scheveningen picture. We have not for many years seen a sea-piece so entirely satisfactory as this: it blends the earlier style of the artist with his more matured experience; it would do honour to any painter of any age.*

The more than usually violent motion of the big square boat caught by a large wave makes this an impressive piece. The scrap of foresail catching the light and its reflection in the wet sand as well as the fanning waves in the shallows are among Cooke's well tried ingredients. His intention of demonstrating how the fishermen had to struggle to

7. Ibid.
8. Ibid.

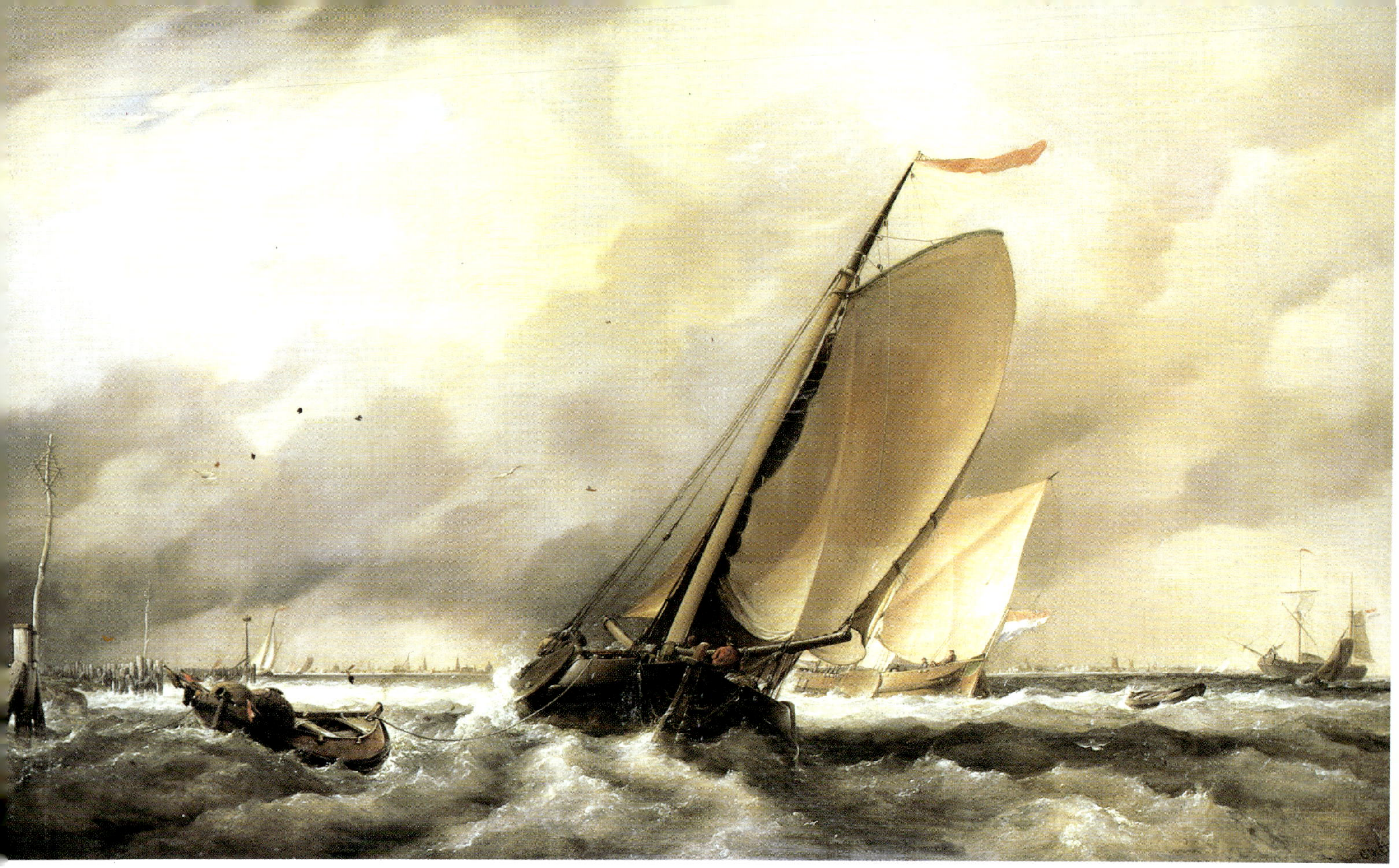

Colour Plate 73. 67/1
Dutch boats 'hugging the shore', Amsterdam in the distance
No mere arrangement of boats in a seaway, this is Cooke's observation and gleaning of local seamanship. He returned to the subject in various sizes but this at 5ft.6in. (167.5cm) is one of his largest canvases.
Photo courtesy Sotheby's. Private Collection

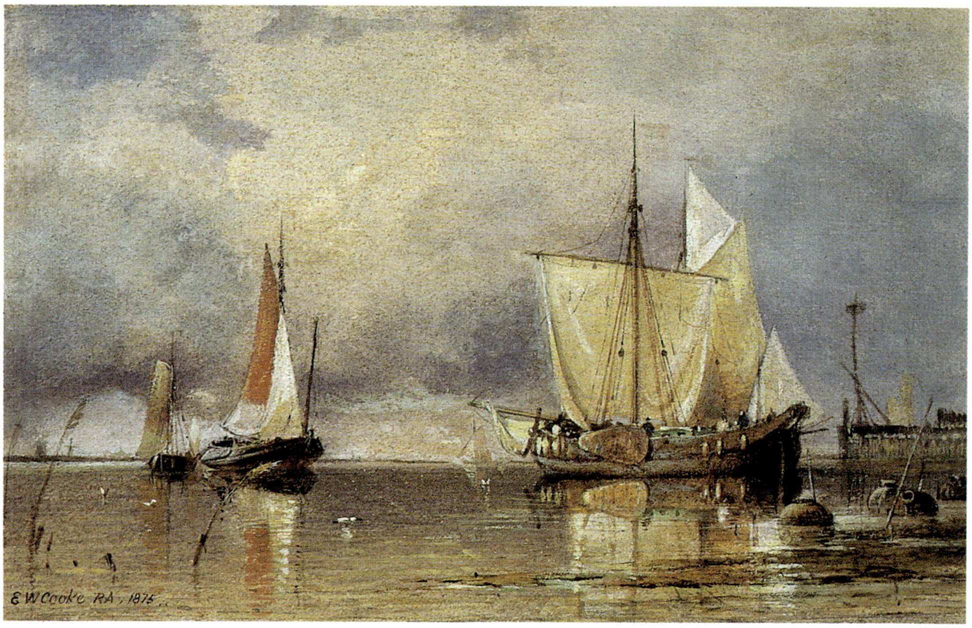

Colour Plate 72. Watercolour, 1875
Dutch boats in calm water
Photo courtesy Private Collection

beach their large craft was missed by the critic, but this hardly detracts from his approval! A mirror image would work just as well, as has been shown by its accidental reproduction in reverse.[9] Another in that year's Academy was *Dutch boats getting off, Scheveling sands, low water, tide making in.* No 323 (55/1), about which the critic enthused – *there is a reality about this picture which entirely satisfies while it greatly delights.* One is left wondering whether, in writing up his copy, the two titles for the departing and arriving boats had become mixed in his memory!

9. *Marine Painting* by William Gaunt, 1975, Plate 164.

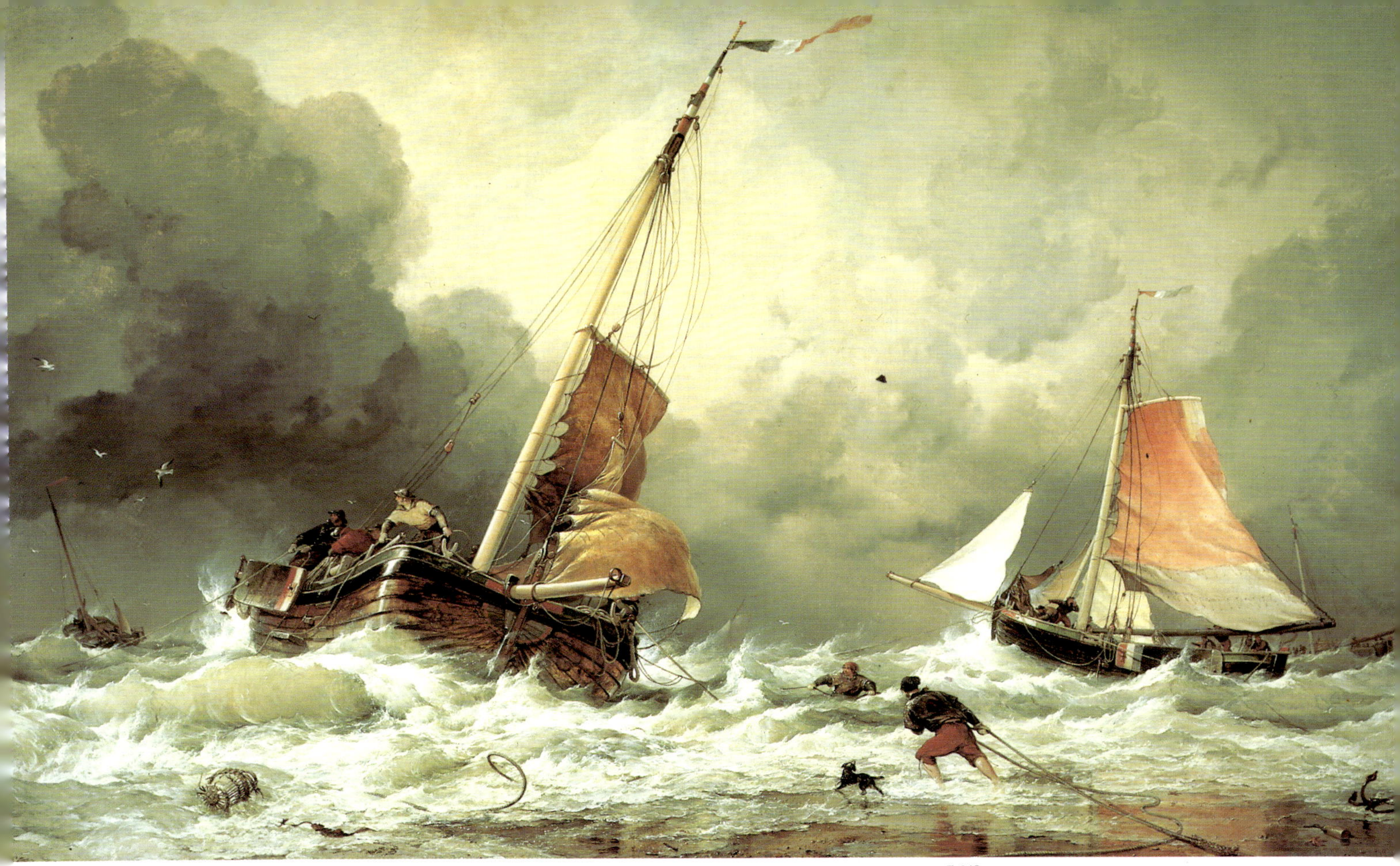

Colour Plate 74. 56/2
Dutch pincks arriving and preparing to put to sea on the return of the tide
Photo courtesy Royal Exchange Art Gallery. Private Collection

Another important canvas with human figures showing more than his usual animation was in the following year's Academy: RA 1856. No. 53 *Dutch Pinks arriving and preparing to put to sea on the return of the tide* (56/2, Colour Plate 74) The critic wrote:

> *These are the same boats that the artist has celebrated for the last two or three years; he seems as determined to make Dutch pinks as famous as Dutch tulips, but it were desirable that he should paint some other sea-flower. The skipper of the "Van Kook" (that we see is the name of the craft) is we hope too wise a man to venture to sea in such a gale. The sea is painted with a greater liberality of touch than usual, the water is not so thready as we have seen it; and this contrast gives a degree of hardness to the boats and their rigging.*

Again the light catching the varnished wooden hull, a battered basket rolling in the surf and the wet sand reflections are tried touches which one has by now come to expect .A good deal of heaving and hauling and the capering of a wet little black dog combine to give vitality to a composition in which a nice balance exists between the two boats, making this altogether one of his best rough Scheveningen scenes.

Similar compositions from the same viewpoint occur dated 1866 and 1868, the latter in chalks (Plate 100) probably one of his colour studies for a painting.

Sometimes he encountered critical snubs: 1856 No 245 *Danish Fishing Craft on the Elbe at Blankenese – The boats, as usual, are very conscientiously made out, but every thing about them is as hard as Pharoah's heart, and nothing is natural in colour – hence the commendable qualities are obtained at great sacrifice* – the justice of which, in the absence of a sight of the original painting, is difficult to judge. In 1872 the artist exhibited another much larger painting with the same title (71/10, Plate 101) which is a pleasant open scene, with fishing boats of a subtly different shape, hung nets, mirrored in calm water, wet sand, banked clouds, distant activity, all demonstrating his grasp of significant detail and his devotion to its faithful recording.

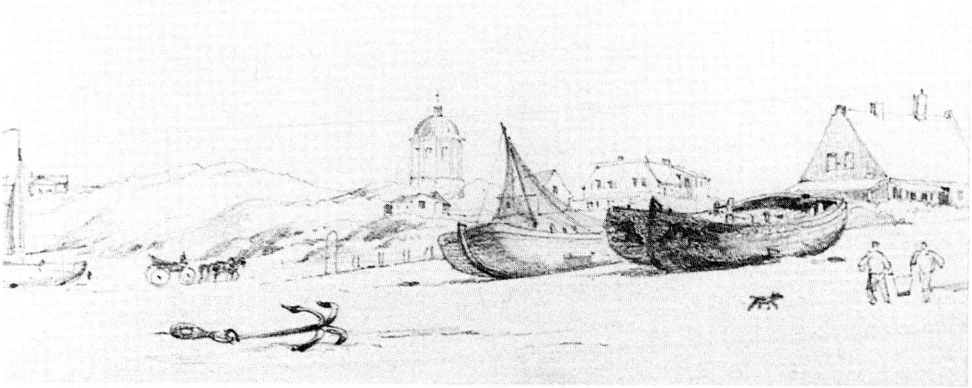

Plate 99 Pencil drawing
Scheveling beach: hulks
Photo courtesy Clarges Gallery

In 1858 the exhibition at the British Institution included two which were noticed by a critic on his mettle:

> No 23. *Dutch fishing boats, tide flowing, wind off-shore.*
> *The incident has been already frequently painted by Mr Cooke, and perhaps more faithfully than in this... the boat is painted in all her detail with the utmost precision – a nicety of finish which contrasts singularly with the water, the forms of which not only do not satisfy the eye, but they are made out with a laxity of execution which would seem to be the work of a hand less experienced than that of the author of the work.*
>
> No 121 *A Dutch shore – A Still Day after Stormy Weather.*
> *Of this identical subject Mr Cooke executes a continued series of versions – fishing boats just come in or just going out, beached on a low level shore, with the wave line on the sand running transversely into the picture. The remarks made on No 23 apply in a great measure to this work.*

While other painters were preparing their favourite subjects for the annual exhibitions and were exercised over telling sentiment, historic costume and anecdote, Edward Cooke continued his commitment to the glorification of working fishing boats, battered, massive and non-romantic. The Royal Academy exhibitions at this time have been called *the huge mouse-trap... baited with 'refined drama-pictures', with prettiness and pinafores, baited and skilfully set, precisely to catch the vulgar....*[10] Redgrave, it was, writing of C.R. Leslie's offerings, who coined the phrase 'refined drama pictures'[11] and it

10. *A Century of British Painting 1851-1951,* by Anthony Bertram, 1951, p.12.
11. Redgrave, 1947, p.340.

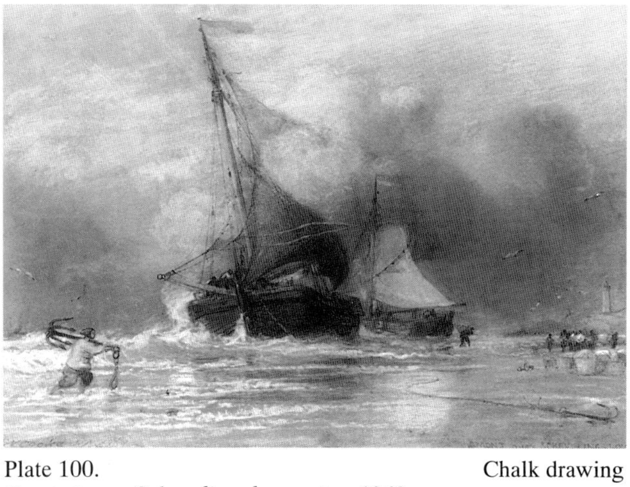

Plate 100. Chalk drawing
Egmont near Scheveling, low water. 1868
The pinck preparing to get off shore is perhaps a study for a painting. Photo courtesy Martyn Gregory

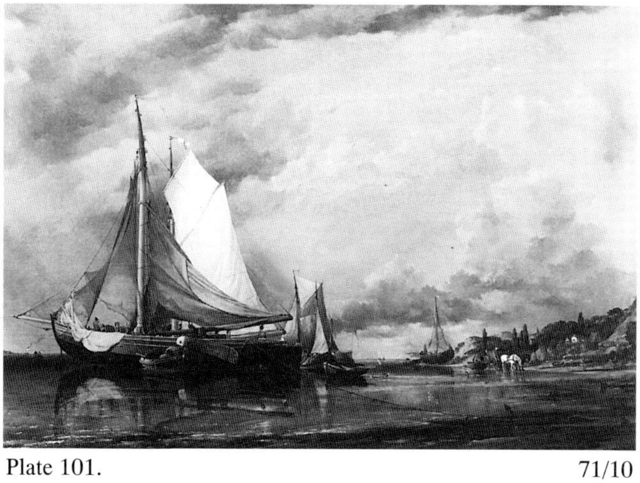

Plate 101. 71/10
Danish fishing craft on the Elbe, Blankenese
This was an Academy picture of 1872 but he had been there nearly twenty years before and painted a smaller picture, present whereabouts not known. Photo courtesy Rochdale Art Gallery

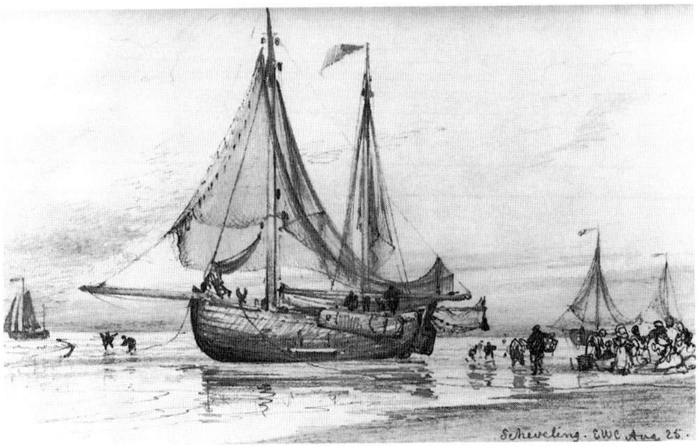

Plate 102.
Scheveling Aug 25

Pencil drawing
Photo courtesy Martyn Gregory. Private Collection

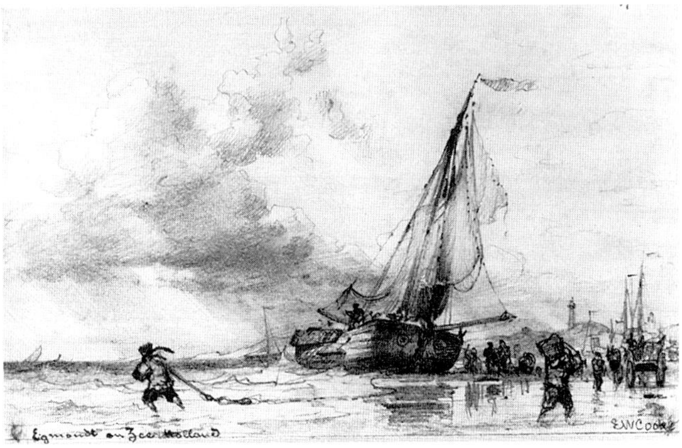

Plate 103.
Egmont aan Zee; a pinck arriving and unloading

Pencil drawing
Photo courtesy Martyn Gregory. Private Collection

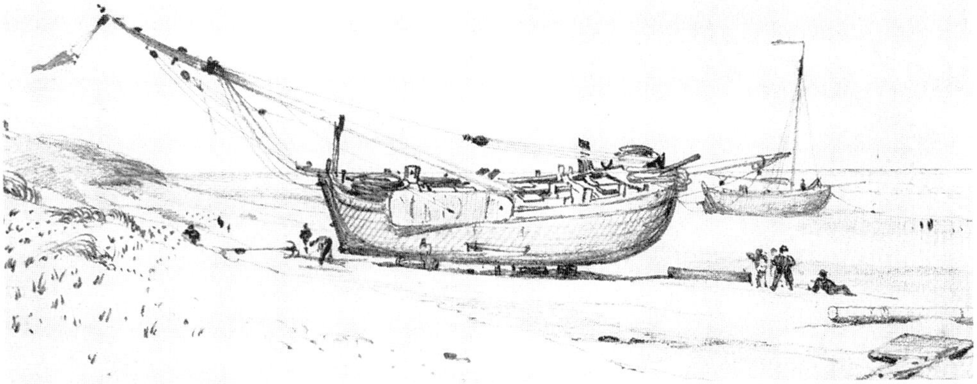

Plate 104.
Pinck ashore, mast down

Pencil drawing

High and dry at low water, the pinck with mast lowered on to the crutch is probably undergoing repairs; a rudder lies on the sand.

Photo courtesy Martyn Gregory. Private Collection

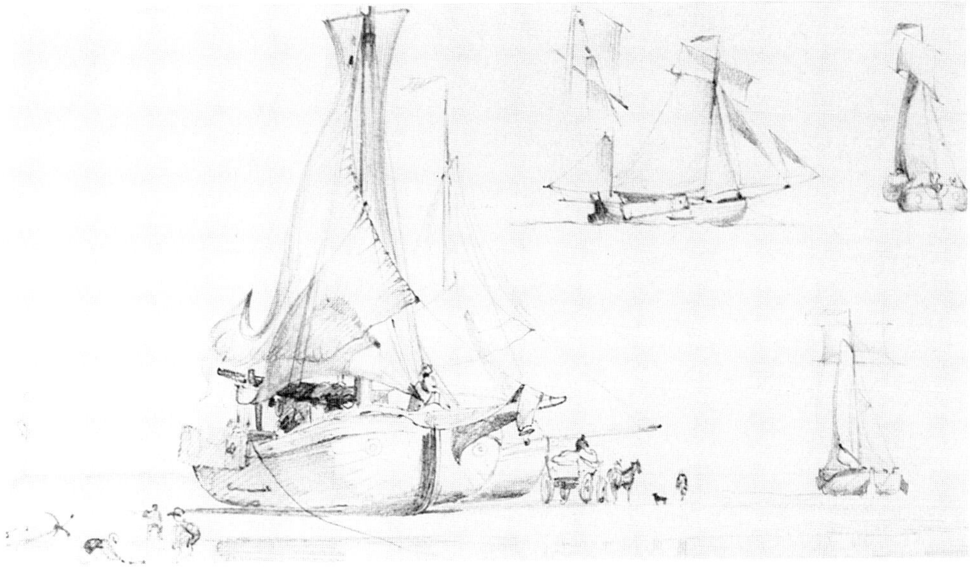

Plate 105.
Beached boat with insets

Pencil drawing
Photo courtesy Clarges Gallery

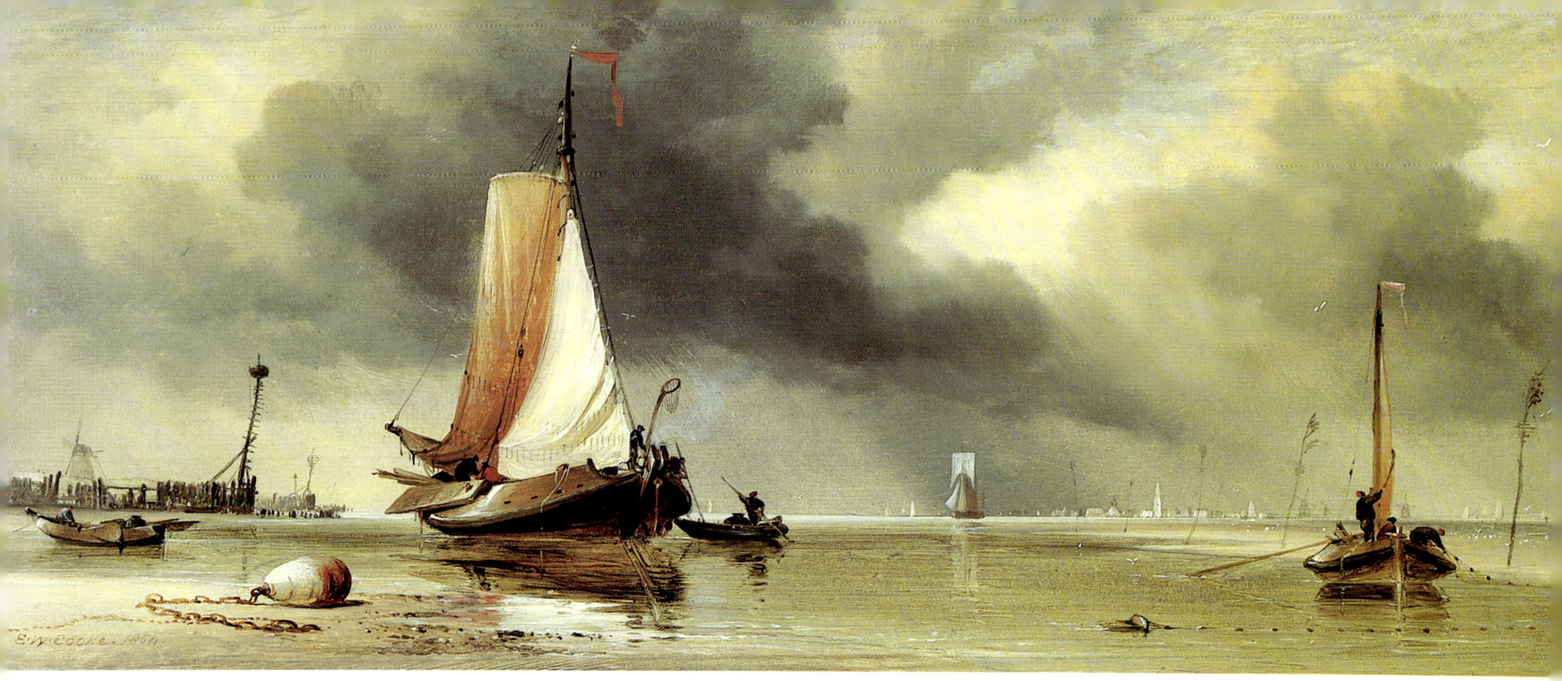

Colour Plate 75. 54/10
Still Water, a creek of the Zuider Zee
This tiny tranquil study, exhibited at the British Institution in 1855, was noted by the painter as a sketch of the larger picture (54/9) exhibited at Liverpool in the previous season of which the present whereabouts is not known.
Photo courtesy Richard Green Fine Paintings

is instructive to compare the bluff honesty of boats according to Cooke with the wardrobe pieces of some of his fellows. The critics strove to keep abreast of his subject matter, although sometimes somewhat out of their depth, as well as commenting on his technique and handling.

Occasionally a particularly dramatic incident to which he may have been an eye-witness was worked out and committed to canvas. Mr Henry Berger, the paint manufacturer, bought such an essay at the Academy in 1859 (59/2, Colour Plate 70). The *Art Journal* said of it (p.597):

> No 388 *A Dutch peon [sic], running for the port of Harlingen is driven in a heavy squall outside the South pier head.*
> *It cannot well be understood how she is to escape running foul of that same pier-head. A miserable kedge, with a whip-cord of a hawser, is thrown out, and the helm is jammed hard up, but she must go against the jetty. The craft and all her gear are very conscientiously made out. There is no artist who so completely conveys to canvas the reality of such a scene; his pictures are always true, and always evidence of intense thought and intellectual power.*

As a footnote to the title, it would appear that there was no Dutch craft called a *peon* but a *poon* (which also means *gurnard*) is recorded as a type of single masted boat. Whether this was merely a typographical error is not clear.

In the year 1860 he spent a mere weekend, yielding one sketch of a pinck, at Scheveningen on his way home from Germany whence he had taken his elder son George to stay to learn the language, just before he himself set out for Spain. Thereafter his sequence of calms and breezes continued: R.A. 1863 No 230 *Dutch Trawlers at anchor... waiting for the tide* (62/3, Colour Plate 71). This picture had lost the artist's title by the time it appeared in the saleroom in 1974 and so became *Van Kook and other fishing smacks trawling off shore*. However, the rope does not belong to a trawl from the stern but is the anchor cable, and is clearly from the bows.

His friendly critic on the *Illustrated London News* wrote of the trawlers *chafed in a stiff breeze by wind and wave as they wait for the flood tide... There is here the same surprising precision of touch, but certainly not the slightest want of movement and air....*

It should be noted that, as in this instance, the painter was not always shore-bound in his viewpoint; from seaward, in such a picture as this, he again invests the scene with an urgency well calculated to draw a response from the seaman.

Another favourite composition which enabled him to show in considerable detail the deck of a small sailing vessel, her gear and her crew, was placing the stern towards the viewer. Sailing *into* the picture presented much less tension, high wind and water apart, almost as if one is at the helm and in command!

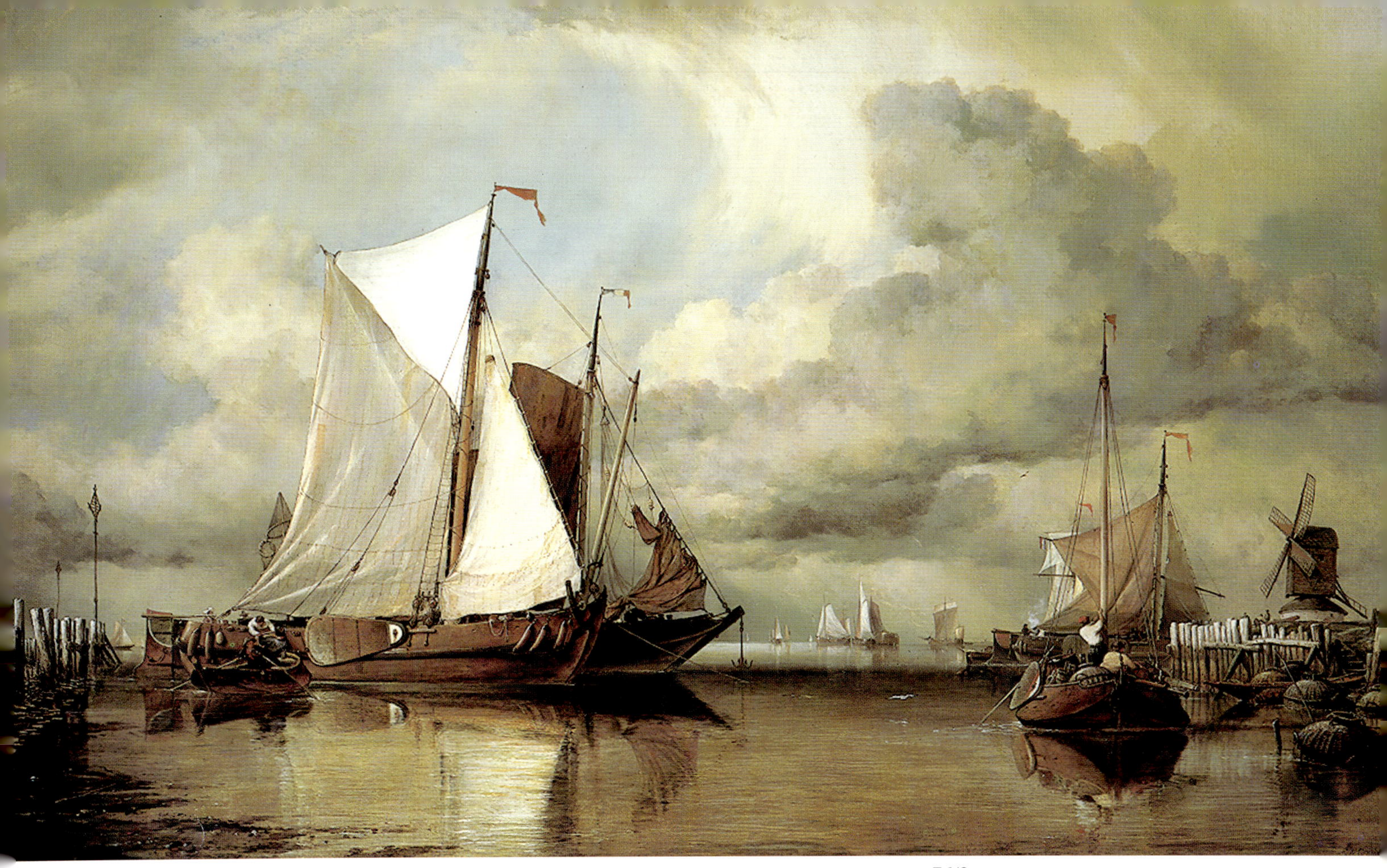

Colour Plate 76 76/2

A Zuider Zee fishing Haven

This is the last of the long and distinguished series of 'calms', a large picture which in that period of recession did not sell at the RA. *Van Kook* endures on the bow of the small boat at right. It was in Cooke's posthumous sale, 1880.

Photo courtesy Private Collection

Colour Plate 77. 71/11

Dutch pincks in a stiff breeze off the coast at Scheveling

In a way a 'miniature' at about 6 x 18 inches, this 'small very long narrow Scheveling' painted just before Christmas 1871 at his home near Groombridge is an example of Cooke's ability successfully to distil a subject which he had treated on the largest scale.

Photo courtesy Phillips Fine Art Auctioneers

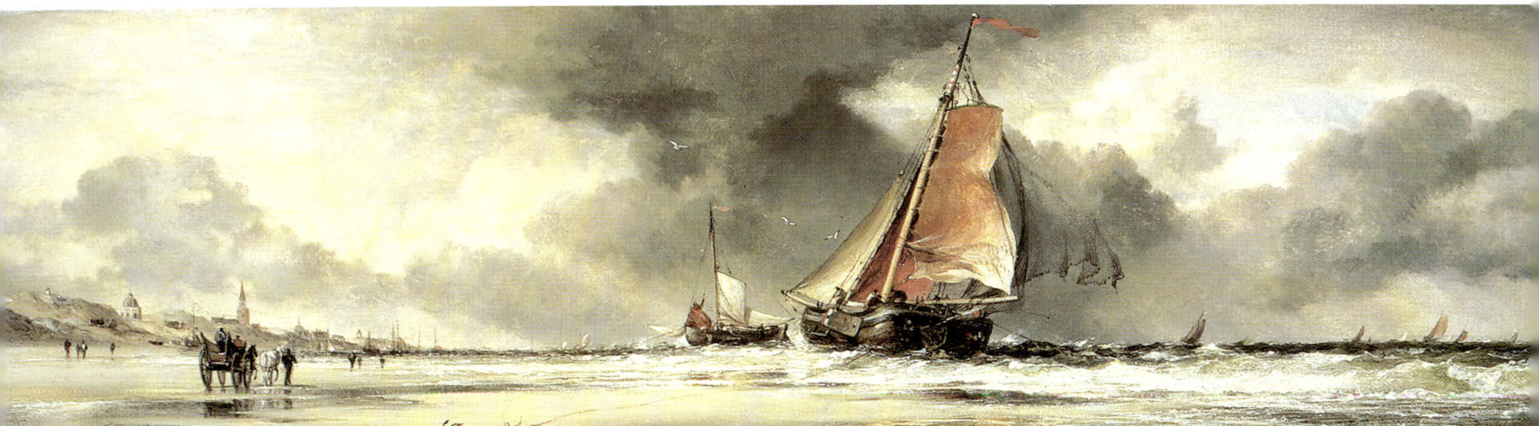

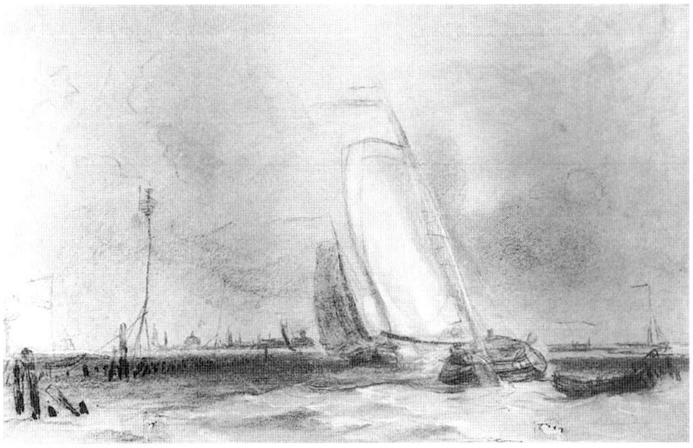

Plate 106. Chalk drawing
Hugging the shore
Preliminary studies were made in chalks; this could be for his 1867 R.A. picture, see 66/8 and 67/1 (Colour Plates 148 and 73).
Photo courtesy Martyn Gregory

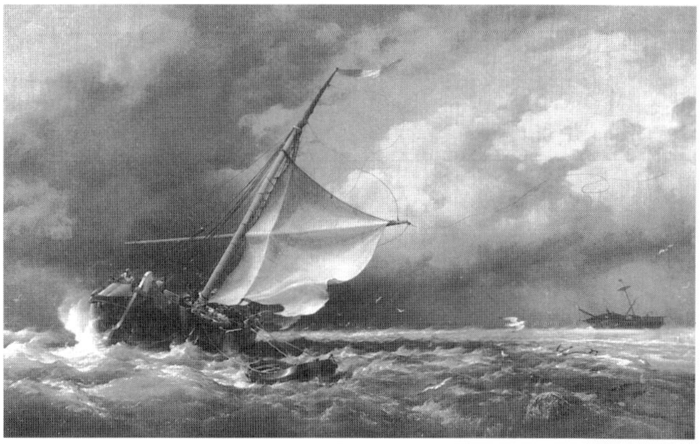

Plate 107. 65/1
A Dutch Beurtman aground on the Terschelling sand (North Sea) after a snowstorm
One of his RA pictures for 1865, the craft in difficulties was a recurring theme and provided an energetic variation from his 'calms' and sandy shores.
Photo courtesy Courtauld Institute. Royal Holloway College,University of London

His Academy Diploma picture 64/1, presented on his election to full membership, brings the Dutch pincks with which he had made a reputation, over to the English coast (Colour Plate 1). It is an example of one of his favourite compositions, with a dramatic placing of the principal vessel which surges forward into and almost out of the picture. Of undoubted impact this is a somewhat uncomfortable device on so large a scale but his 'collision-course' compositions appear spread through his British, French, Dutch and Venetian paintings: 39/14 *Calais, Sloop returning...* (Colour Plate 46), 47/9 *Dumbarton* (Plate 263), 66/2 *Dutch boats in a breeze on the Dollart Zee* (Colour Plate 146) and 73/2 *Venetian... craft caught in a Borasca* (Plate 290).

One of his Academy pictures of 1865 was at length acquired by Thomas Holloway and has thus been for many years publicly visible at the Royal Holloway College, Egham (Plate 107). It belongs to another group of subjects, vessels aground, for minor mishaps in tidal waters provided him with more varied incident.

65/1 *A Dutch Beurtman aground on the Terschelling Sand (North Sea) after a snow storm.* The title would not lead one to suspect that the composition would be strikingly similar to his Harlingen poon mishap, 59/2 (Colour Plate 70). Apart from the boat's being viewed from the starboard quarter rather than the port, the sail manoeuvre in each is the same, the loosened sprit forming a dramatic 'X' with the mast, echoed by the shadow on the mainsail which is blown against them.

This picture was shown at Greenwich in 1982[12] which acknowledged Cooke as *perhaps the most acomplished and versatile of the marine painters working in England in the second half of the nineteenth century* and as one of the Dutchmen's English followers.

Critical approval was forthcoming in 1869, Royal Academy No.116, 68/6 *On shore for a tide... Once again we have to admire not only a firm true hand in the delineation of a Dutch built craft, but great delicacy and beauty in the study of the sandy shore with bright and soft reflections on its wet, smooth surface.* [Colour Plate 67.]

It was not until 1876 that he again visited Holland for a ten-day tour. That year his Academy subjects had included two Dutch pieces: *Zuider Zee Fishing haven*, No.223, (Colour Plate 76) and *A Port on the Zuider Zee,* No.573, and it was noted in the Catalogue *This Inland sea is about to be drained by the Dutch Government.* Changes were coming inevitably to the old scenes but he continued to show his devotion to craft and shore as in the R.A. 1877, No.288 *A Scheveling pinck preparing for sea* (76/9). *One of the best painted marine pictures which has come from the hand of E.W. Cooke for years. Not only in the colour & build of the grounded craft, but in the sands, the sea, & the sky, full of local and as one might say of geographic truth.*

Keeping not only to the old place-name spelling, he pursued his habitual style though he was by now competing with younger painters of all nations and of a new persuasion.

12. *The Art of the Van de Veldes,* National Maritime Museum, 1982, No.153.

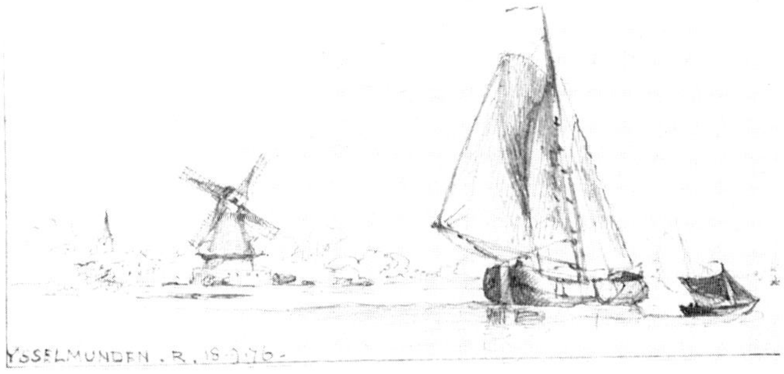

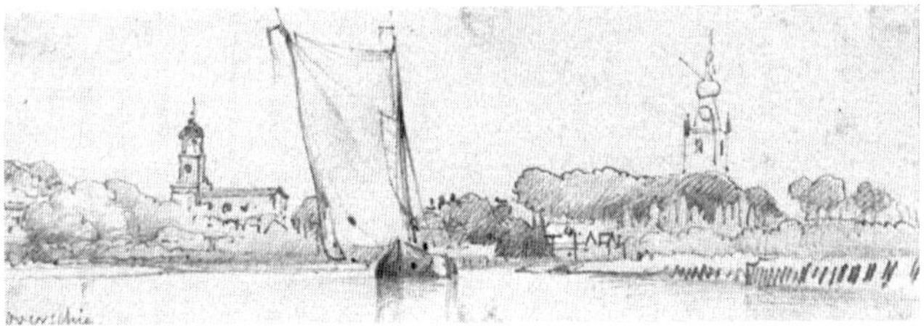

Plate 108 (Left). Pencil drawing
Ysselmunden 1876
Photo courtesy Clarges Gallery

Plate 109. Pencil drawing
Overschie
A miniature, eloquent and graceful, of an everyday river scene.
Photo courtesy Clarges Gallery

'Dutch finish' had long gone and in its place appeared a handling of paint which the ageing Edward Cooke probably regarded as unacceptably wild. Just as his father had set his face against steel plates for engraving, there can be little doubt, although there is no documentary proof, that E.W. Cooke saw only a sad deterioration in modern painting.

Finally, as part of what may have been a farewell visit to old haunts, in September 1879 the now ailing painter again saw Scheveningen. 15th: *...to the Hague – steam tram to the Great Bathhouse – Porter brought luggage on Truck to the Hotel Zeerust, found 2 good rooms opposite the sea. Washed and Table d'Hote at 5. Stroll on Sands – Boats preparing for the Herring Fishery... Lovely day The Hague en fete.*

All shows that Scheveningen was now indeed a resort. The fishing craft were there still and he went out on the shore to sketch two pincks getting off, while the next evening he noted *The long ripples of the calm sea Phosphorescent* – a natural phenomenon which, for all his love of evening skies, he did not attempt to paint. It conjures up an image suited to a Caspar David Friedrich canvas, and is intriguing. Belonging to an earlier generation, the German Friedrich, whose strange, romantic shore scenes may have been familiar to the much-travelled Cooke, used sailing vessels, boats and items of fishing gear in an elaborate religious and spiritual symbolism. The Englishman we know was a devout churchgoer and although anchors, nets, wrecked boats and other similar objects occur frequently in his paintings, nothing has been found to suggest that his thoughts had turned to their use in such a way. Rather, his scientific leanings and lifelong devotion to natural history denote a deep seated practicality at odds with mysticism.

By this date the Hague School painters had established themselves about Scheveningen, but he does not mention seeing anyone at work. His view of modern schools like Barbizon and the movement of Impressionism itself was not confided to his diary. He visited modern art shows, he was in Paris in 1878 at the great international *Exposition,* the World's Fair, looking at all the national picture galleries and it is inconceivable that he saw nothing of the modern movement, yet he left no note, perhaps having averted his eyes!

His last pictures of Holland to be exhibited were 78/1 *Dutch Galliott aground on a sandbank in the Bies-Boshe* RA 1878/182 (Colour Plate 150), returning to a theme which he had favoured in the 1840s, the exertions of a crew in getting a grounded boat afloat, and 79/3 *On the Dutch Coast at Camperdown; a squally day, tide out* RA 1879/262. The *Art Journal* said of this, *Camperdown with its large rolling clouds is full of that close observation and minute detail...* and while the painter's hand and eye had lost nothing of their cunning, the picture buying public at a time of economic depression were falling away from Van Kook and this was yet another of his large paintings to be returned to the studio.

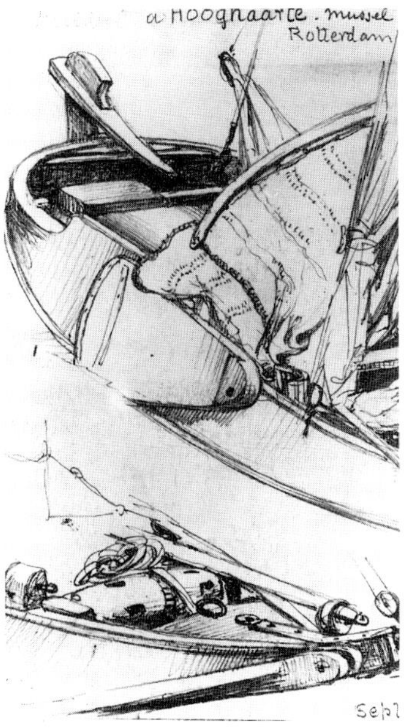

Plate 110. Pencil drawing
Details of a Mussel boat 1876.
The sharp image is produced by a metallic point on prepared surfaced paper.
Photo courtesy The Trustees of the National Maritime Museum, Greenwich

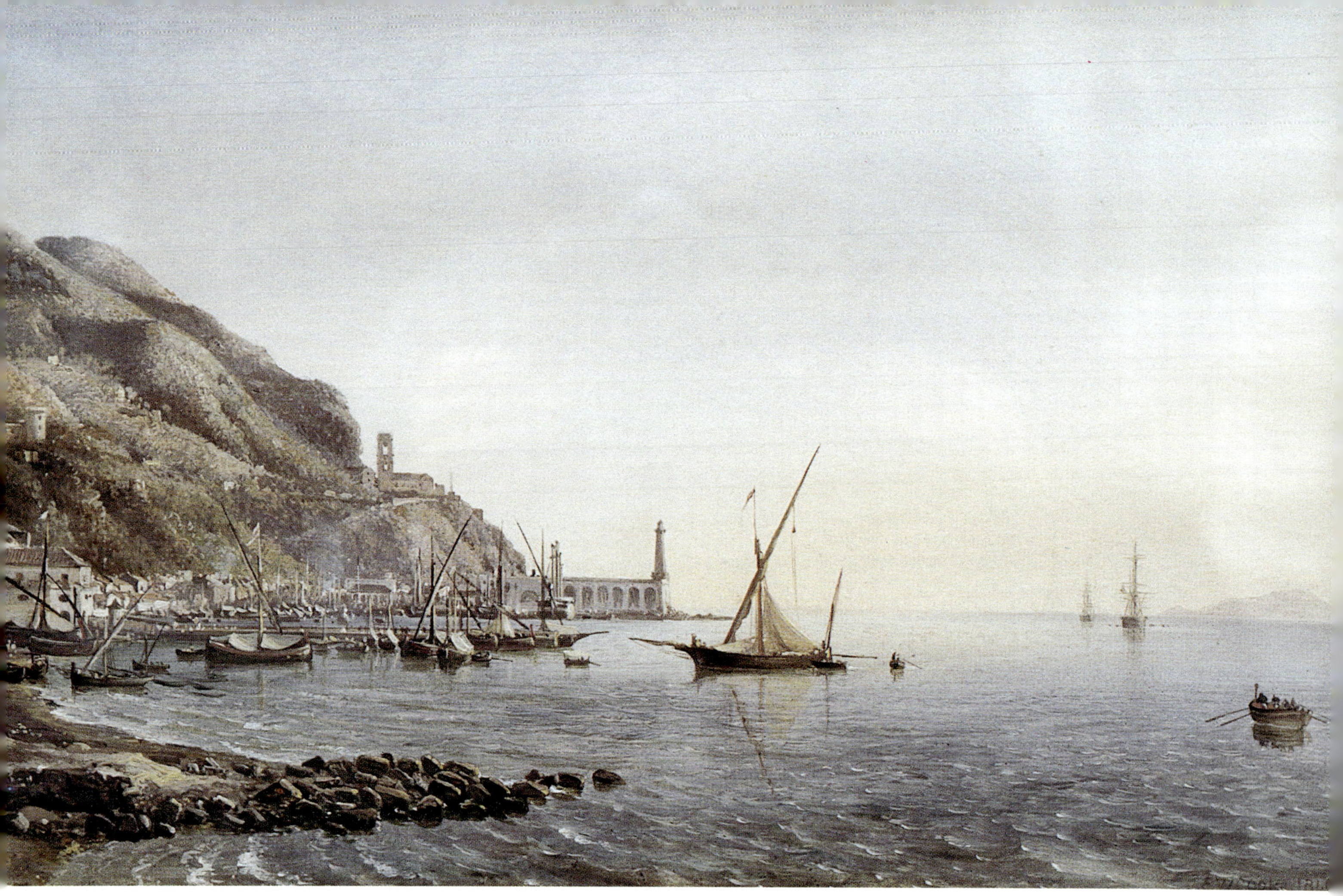

Colour Plate 79. 45/23A
Alassio – the island of Gallinaria in the distance famed among the ancients for its breed of fighting cocks
Cooke wrote the long title for a Christie's catalogue of a sale of ninety of his Mediterranean studies in 1863.
Photo courtesy Russell Cotes Art Gallery, Bournemouth

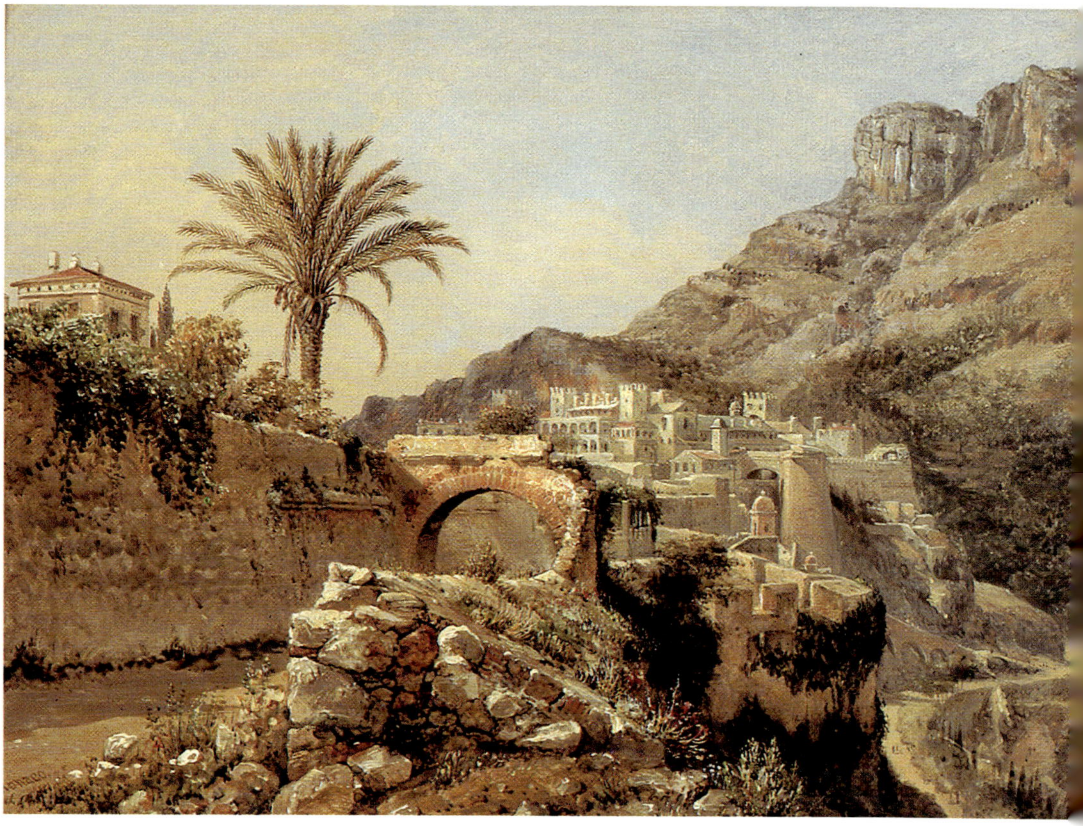

Colour Plate 78. 45/10
Monaco, the Palace of the Prince
The recently bereaved Cooke in a leisurely progress along the Riviera painted scenes which he had hoped to explore with Jane, his wife.
Photo courtesy Private Collection

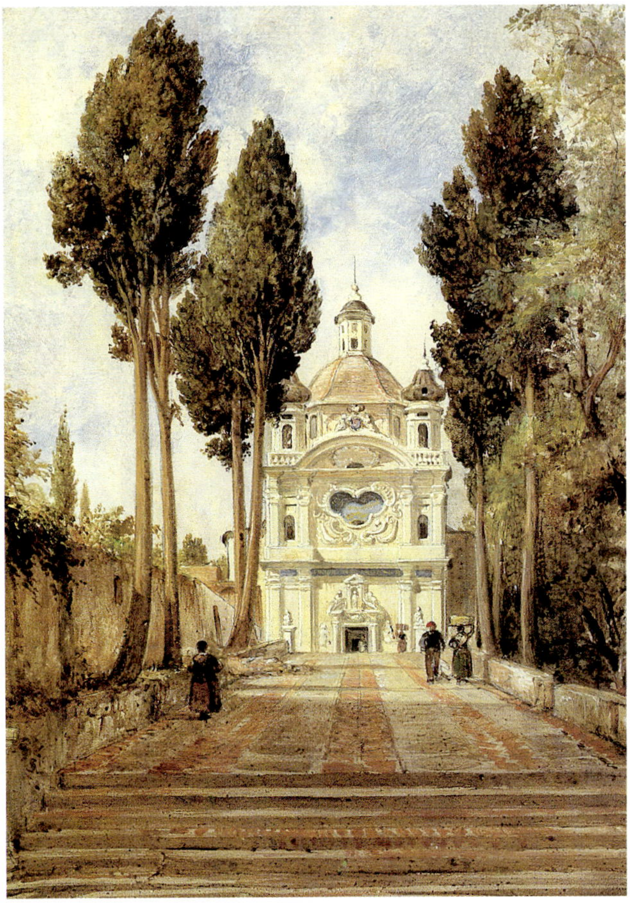

Chapter 8

ITALIAN STUDIES: THE MEDITERRANEAN TOUR OF 1845-6

He had purchased a *Handbook for Italy* and Jane his wife had read from it while he painted. Now, alone, he would make the tour which they had perhaps planned together, but for company he would take his sister Laura. The desirability – even the necessity – of a spell among the works of art and monuments of Italy was for a painter obvious, although for a marine painter perhaps less so. For a man with antiquarian leanings and a desire to join the ranks of the Royal Academicians, however, it must have seemed highly appropriate.

His friend Thomas Hartley Cromek had worked in Italy and was now back again in Rome. Hay, his father's last apprentice, had spent three years in Italy and had shown them his drawings. Robert McInnes, his painter friend, was in Florence with his Italian wife and her family. In addition, the drawings and paintings of Turner and Stanfield, of J.D. Harding, of Bonington and of Prout would have determined Cooke to see for himself and apply his *particular* vision to subjects already well-used.

Colour Plate 80. 45/18
Madonna dell' Costa with tall cypresses
The church on the summit of the City Hill, San Remo, was a landmark; the fine trees, as usual with Cooke, are an equal point of interest. Photo courtesy Private Collection

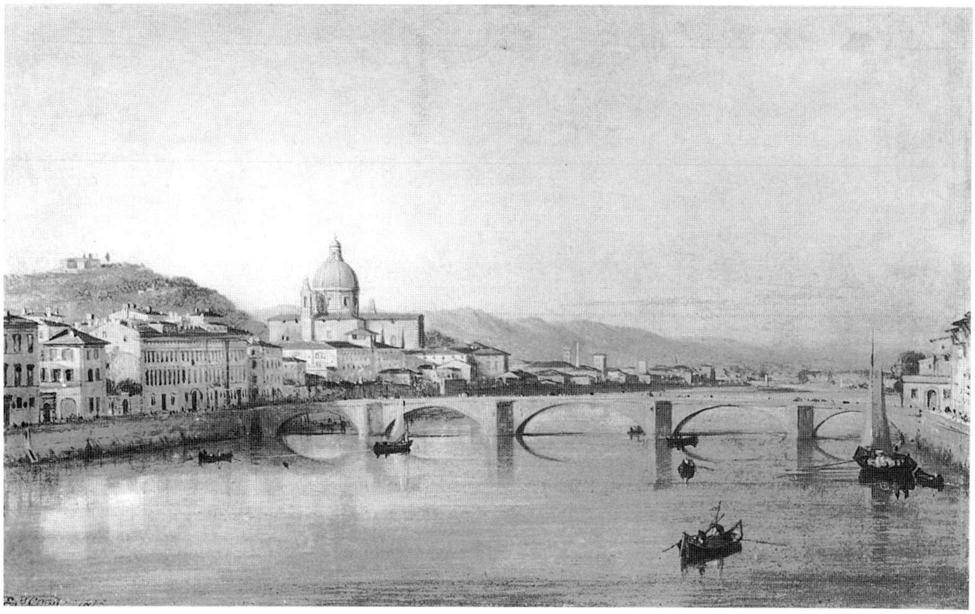

Plate 111. 45/34
Florence, San Frediano & the Ponte della Trinita over the Arno
From his hotel room, one of only three oil studies which Cooke found time for on his first visit to Florence. Photo courtesy Spink & Son Ltd

As to marines, the Mediterranean coast, new scenes, new colours, with new shipping and craft were the lure. They travelled to the South of France in the summer of 1845; he was equipped for a long painting tour and from Avignon onwards made oil sketches as well as many pencil and some watercolour drawings. His equipment included oil sketching paper in blocks as well as millboard and his notes show that both whole size and half-size of each were used.

His comments on historic buildings visited and fine scenery viewed are mixed with other interests such as fern collecting and accounts of their daily state of health. As always there was no painting on the Sabbath, which gave them welcome respite.

They were away for a year and a few weeks and the diary records their progress through France and western Italy. He was fascinated by almost everything, the geology, the flora, the architecture and the shipping, and it is hard to decide in which order, for his picture titles and their sub-titles often include all three. Their leisurely way can be plotted by the Itinerary and the diarist's comments are amplified by Laura Cooke's journal for part of the tour, which has survived. The ancient little ports of the French Riviera, no less than Marseilles and the grand arsenal of Toulon, provided good subjects. Pencil drawings were made daily and frequent oil sketches on his prepared paper blocks, revealing his method of working.

After basking in sunshine they encountered floods and found Florence enveloped in fogs. The search for suitable rooms up and down the Lung'Arno was a long one with Robert McInnes. *Saw his clever pictures* noted Cooke who forthwith plunged into the round of visits to galleries, churches and gardens.

The total of his oil sketches mounted up, and he kept a record in the back of his diary which has been included in the Catalogue, but the painter was beset by doubts of one sort or another and from one of the few surviving letters to his family, from Rome, we can gather something of his thoughts:

> *I believe I have been right in taking it coolly, as I shall probably do more hereafter... I long to be at work again from Dear Nature. I am rubbing up tools for new campaigns. I much regret losing two months work and think how much I might have got through at home at the same period, but I could not help it, and I shall do more when in good spirits again, for I have learnt a vast deal in one way or another, amidst the multitudinous objects of Art in this wonderful place... I had intended to*

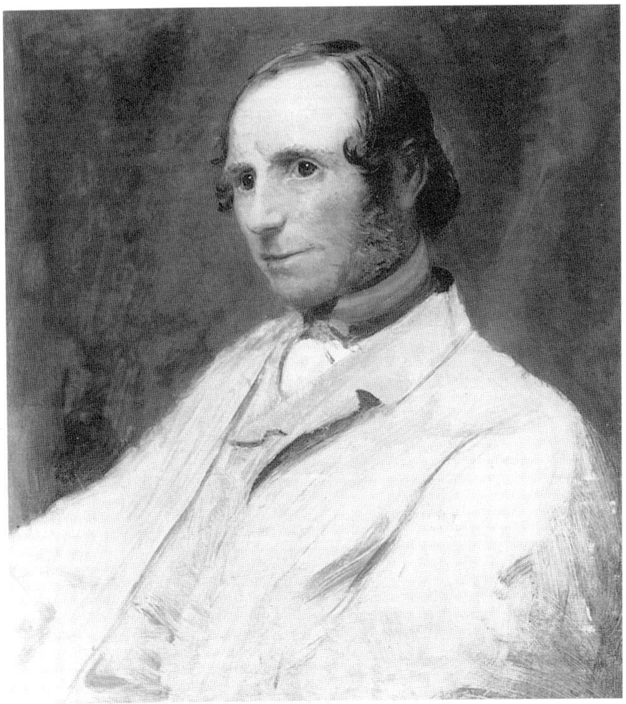

Plate 112.
E.W. Cooke. Oil sketch by Robert Hannah 1 August 1848
Cooke was staying overnight at his friend's house and recorded sitting for his portrait all day until 4 pm. Hannah, who exhibited at the RA, was one of his executors.

paint one or two pictures for the [Royal] Academy whilst here but it was impossible – 1st because I have been out of spirits and poorly, 2ndly the multitude of objects of intense interest have so completely seized all my thoughts since I left Genoa and the sea, that I seem for a time to have lost all my impressions of marine subjects and effects, so that I cannot easily bring my mind to bear on such subjects the most suited to my pencil.

3rdly I scarcely feel emboldened to come out at the Academy under my new colours till I have properly matured all my studies, and there is so much reason to

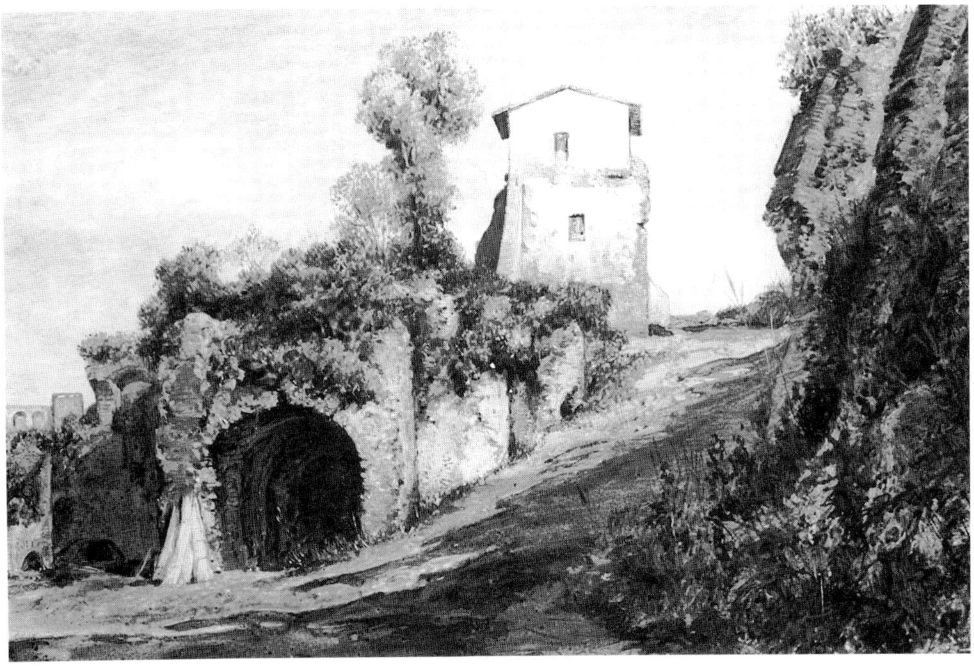

Plate 113.
Rome, ruins of the Neronian aqueduct
46/8
Photo courtesy Martyn Gregory

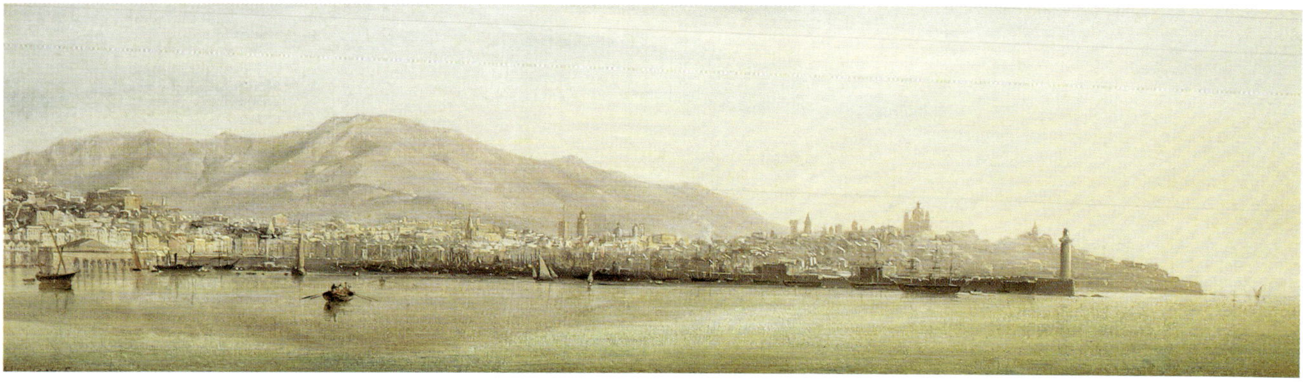

Colour Plate 81.
Genoa, early morning 45/27

Photo courtesy Guarisco Gallery, Washington DC

fear that my pictures might be injured or too late in their transmission to England... the only objection to not sending anything is the loss of the sale of them, as I shall sadly feel this want of supplies and scarcely know how to act and what to advise, but perhaps other works will sell, or I shall begin to recover lee-way when I begin to paint at home. I think you have done wisely in your management of accounts, but I now regret having returned the 50£ to Mr.W[ells], as it might have helped me... I find that two people, and particularly a Lady's expenses have exceeded my calculations...

Colour Plate 82. 45/30
La Spezzia, view of port and town from loggia of the Capuchin monastery
While Cooke painted, the monks sat round conversing.

Photo courtesy Private Collection

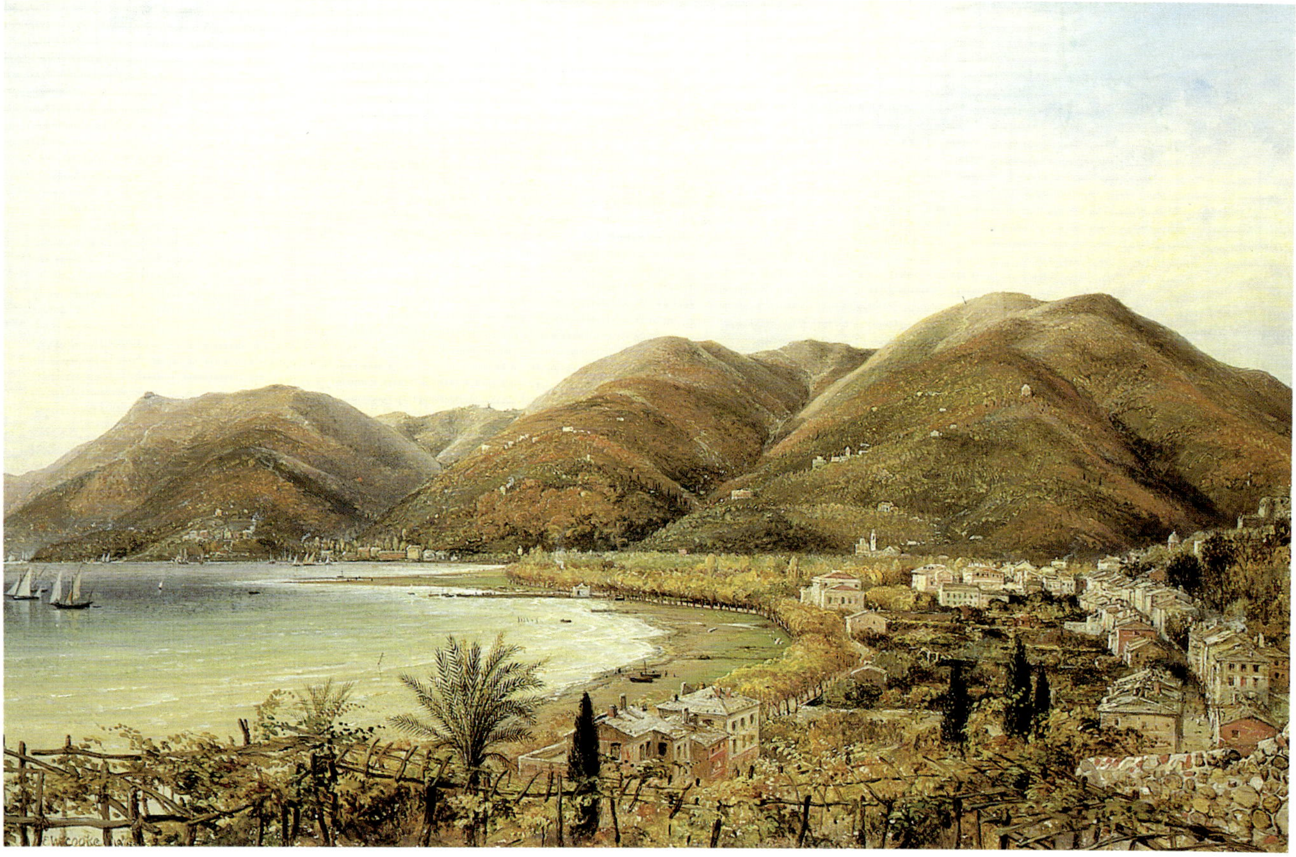

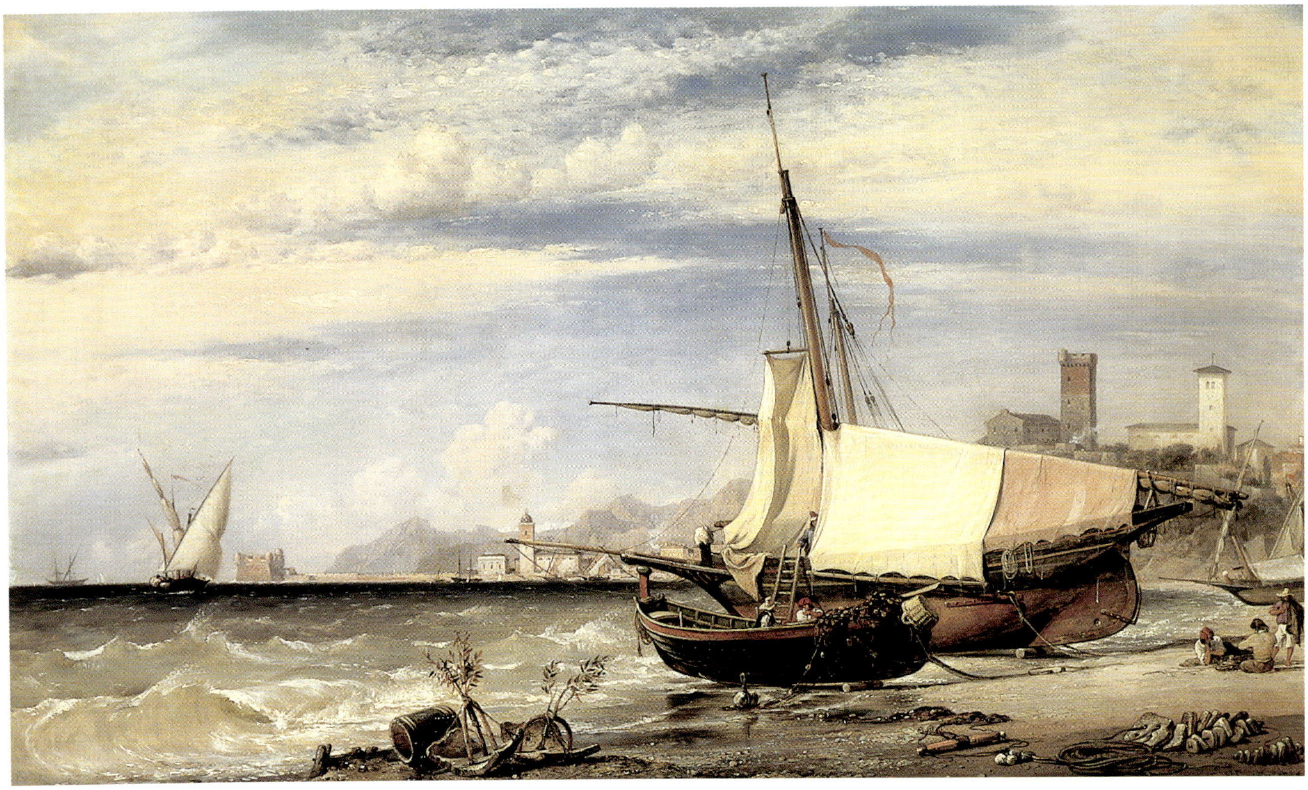

Colour Plate 83. 46/39

Oneglia, a group of feluccas on the beach, Porto Maurizio in the distance

Elaborated from a sketch on the spot, there is much satisfying comment on the local fishermen's gear, cork net-buoys etc. Photo courtesy Sotheby's. Private Collection

The letter continues, cross-written in pencil:

> *You had better not send this letter away as it is full of business. I will write soon with a full account of all we have seen. Tell Harriette that I have bought for her a work of 44 plates, Views of Rome, very good considering, which I am sure she will as a great*

Colour Plate 84. 46/7

Rome, the Neronian acqueduct from its specus or water-channel: the montains of Tivoli (and the Villa Adriana) in the distance Photo courtesy Christie's

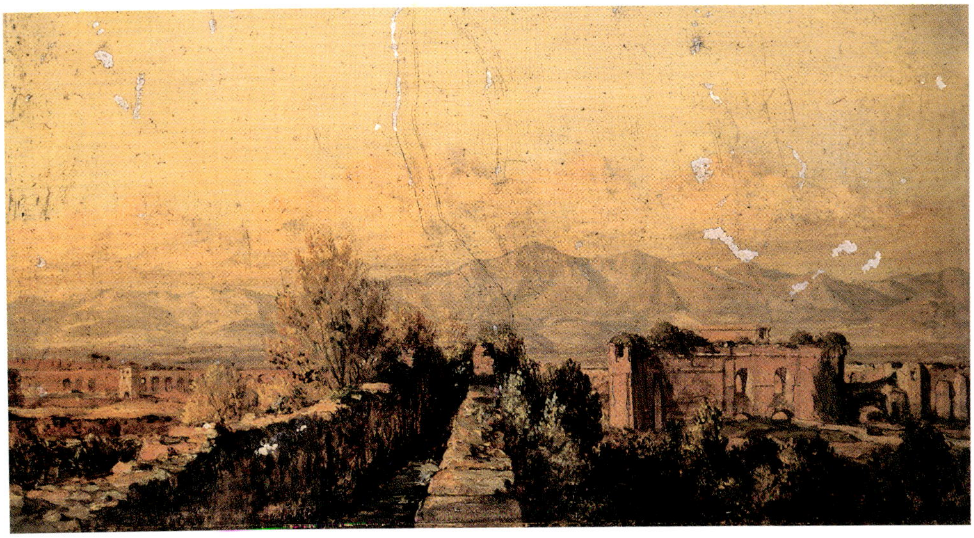

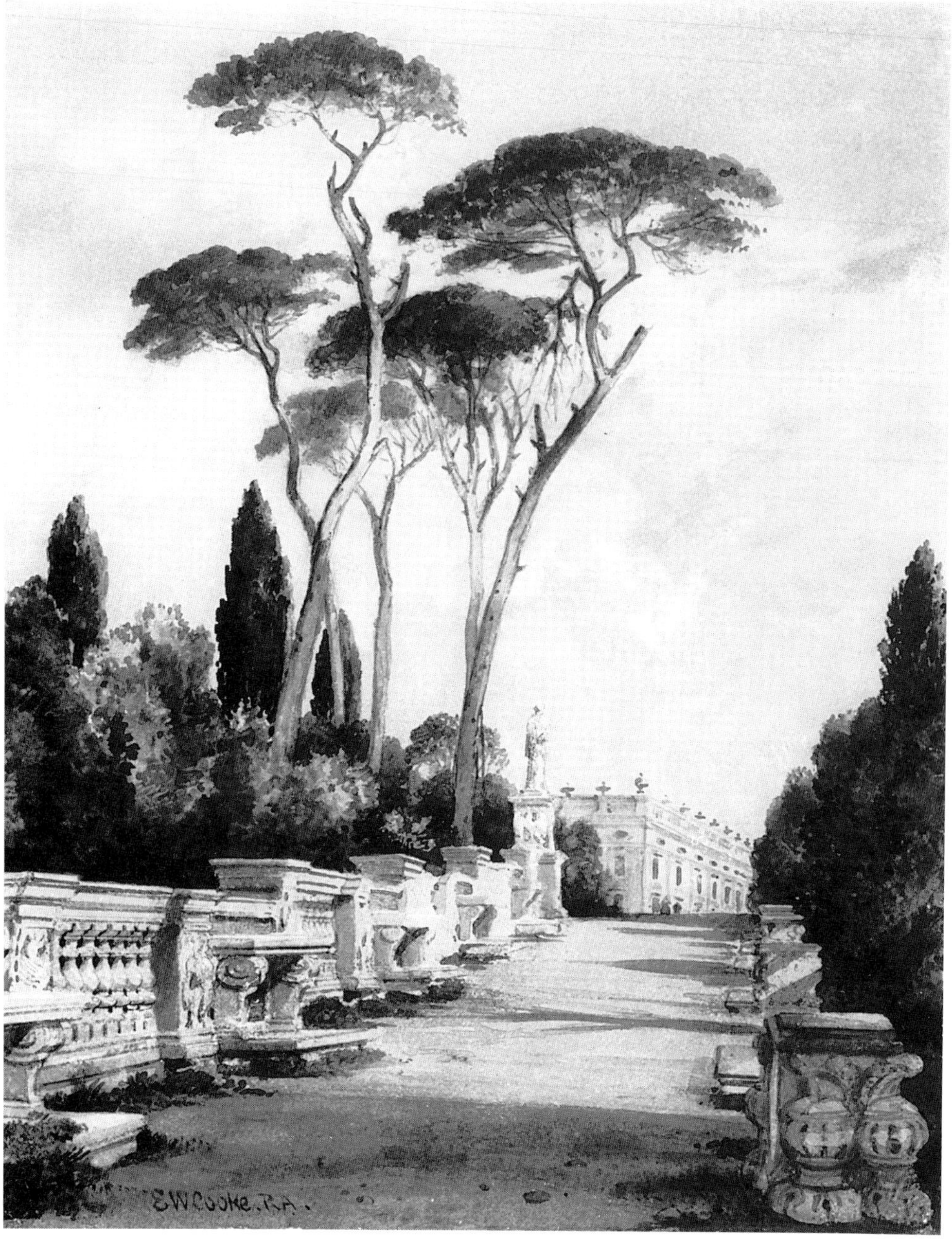

Plate 114. Watercolour
In the gardens of the Villa Borghese
Engraved and printed in *Leaves from my Sketch-book*, John Murray, 1876.
Photo courtesy Agnews. Private Collection

Archaeologist, appreciate. The weather is truly glorious, it is as warm and bright as April & May. Indeed since Xmas we have had a continuous [ ] of fine days. Today Sunday I feel so well that I think I am clear of any more boils. I shall be delighted to get to work again from Nature. This is the true place for an artist to study in. The treasures of Art are beyond everything fine and the Wonders of Nature abound in every direction... Mr Coplestone told me that Fanny Price & her companion are thrown out of work, if they are distressed I should wish to assist them a little, as you deem best.

The letter ends with a flurry of questions and instructions:

I should like to know how the plants do, if any new orchids have bloomed, also what

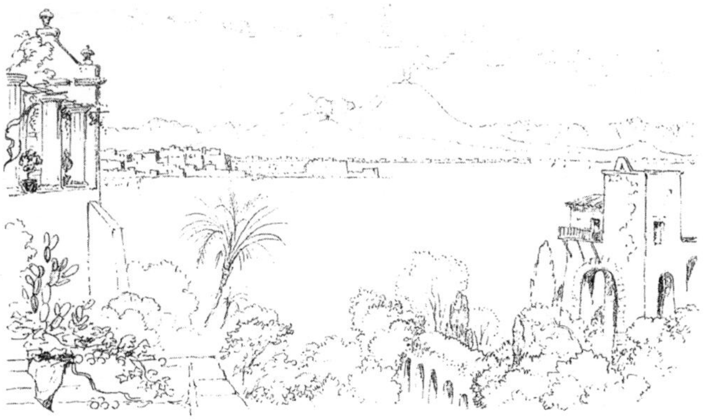

Plate 115. 48/18
Bay of Naples from the Villa Cedroni, Posilippo
A *camera lucida* record; the completed picture, which was small, is not known to have survived.

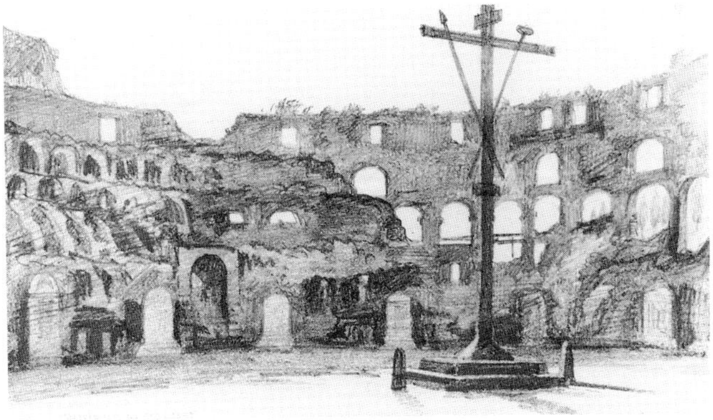

Plate 117 Pencil drawing
Rome, the Coliseum by moonlight, 1846
Photo courtesy Martyn Gregory

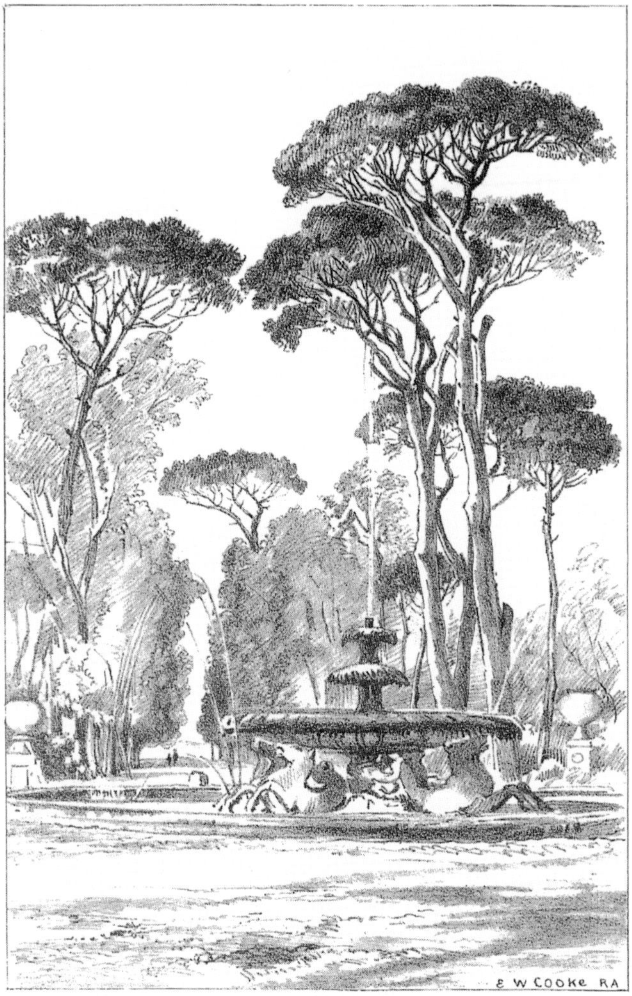

Plate 116 (Above). Engraving
In the Gardens of the Villa Borghese, Rome
Cooke used lines from Nathaniel Hawthorne's *Transformation* on the stone pines that 'lift their dense clump of branches upon a slender length of stem so high that they look like green islands in the air, flinging down a shadow upon the turf so far off that you hardly know which tree has made it'.

Georgie has done in the portrait way and the plant way. Tell Mary to continue to draw and to study that she may be proficient in grinding ultramarine ash &c &c &c. Tell me if our letters seem to have been opened... Let me know in your next how about much cash there will likely to be left when the principal things are paid, as I must arrange accordingly as to my future movements, at any rate I can renew my request to Mr Wells if absolutely necessary. Tell Mr Whitelock I hope to have a letter from him shortly, tell him to direct simply Edward Cooke – Roma. The Carnival will shortly begin. We have an invitation to a window in the Corso, but it is a nonsensical thing. I shall not trouble it much....

Laura Cooke's letter of the same time adds a little to the picture:

Edward was not very well... he never entirely recovered the cold caught at Pisa... Dr Deakin who is a very great botenist [sic] and a very nice man when Edward offered him his fee he refused to take anything, saying that he made it a rule never to take a fee from an artist.[1]

The doctor's art collection, one might guess, was interesting and varied.

The famous Roman Carnival may not have appealed to a serious-minded Protestant Englishman but there were others in whose company the festivities could be enjoyed, including the Elhanan Bicknells from Herne Hill who were touring.

Enjoying and discovering Rome and working to capture in his way the scenery which caught his fancy, Cooke also visited the studios of resident artists of several nationalities, working in different media. As well as T.H. Cromek, who was resident with his wife and small children, he notes Robert Hannah, painter (Plate 112), who became his Executor

1. Cooke MSS.

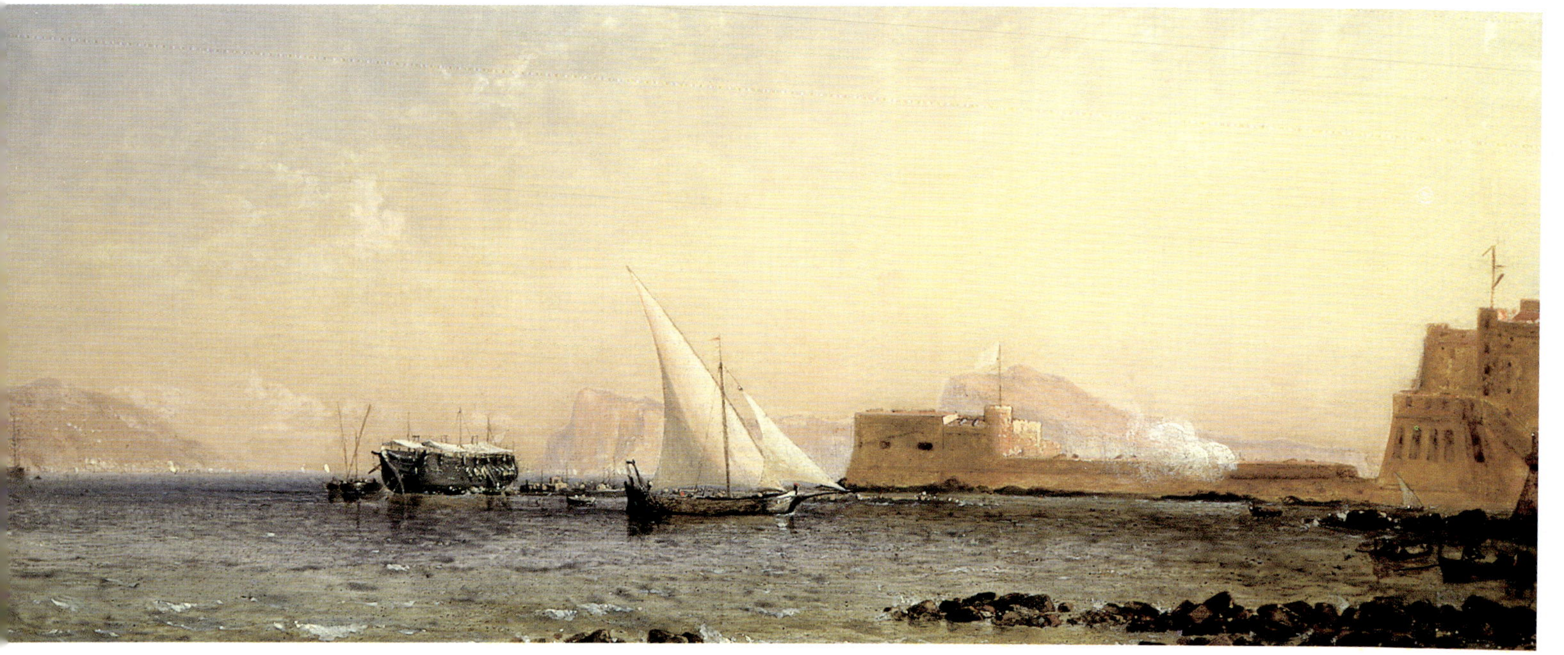

Colour Plate 85. 46/34
The Evening gun, Castel dell'Ovo, Naples. Capri in the distance Photo courtesy Private Collection

and is remembered best for his picture of 1848, *William Harvey demonstrating to Charles I, the circulation of the blood*, J.D. Glennie, S.J. Ainsley, who collaborated with George Dennis on *Cities and Cemetaries of Etruria* 1848, Penry Williams, J.G. Strutt, Charles Vacher, the sculptors R.J. Wyatt and John Gibson, Robert Smith, Hiram Powers, Ludwig Gurlitt. Then J.F. Overbeck, founder of the Nazarene group of painters, showed them his *Pieta* with which Cooke was not impressed.

Colour Plate 86. 46/32
Vesuvius and the Bay of Naples from off Castellamare Photo courtesy Private Collection

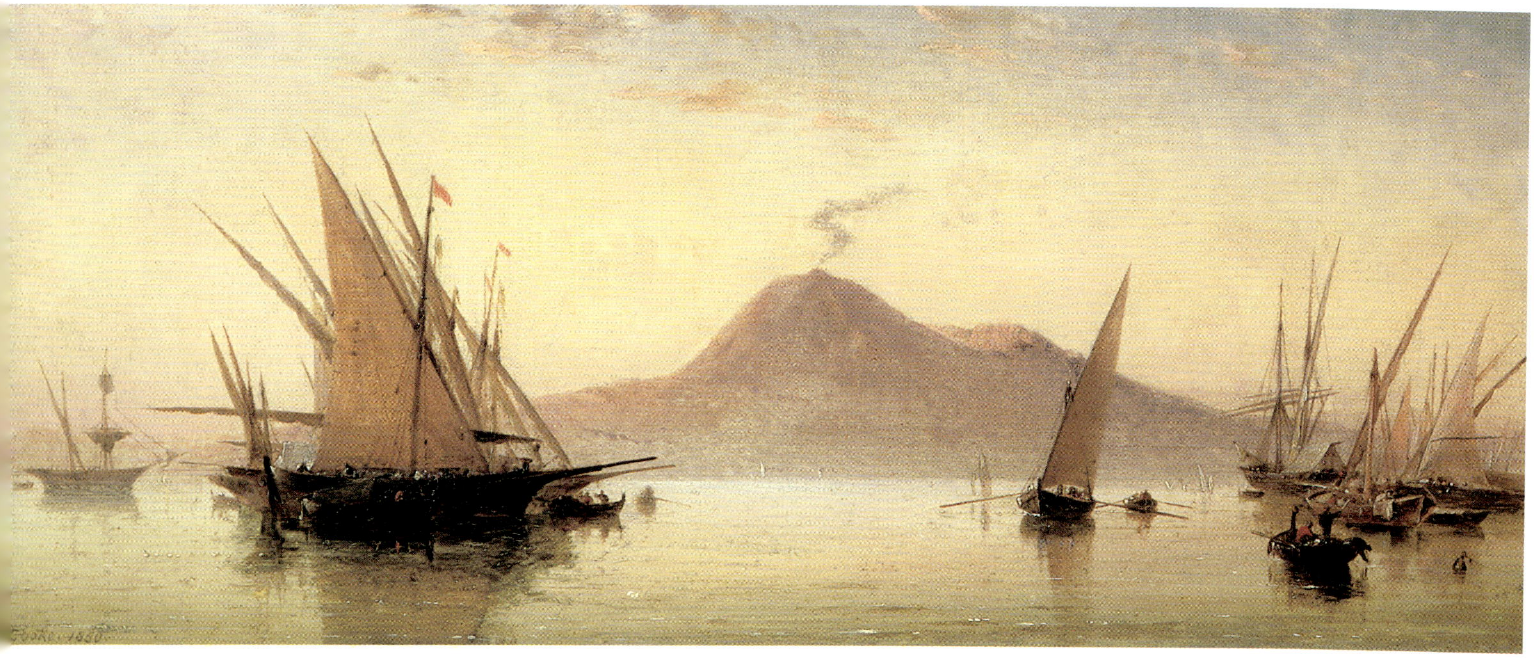

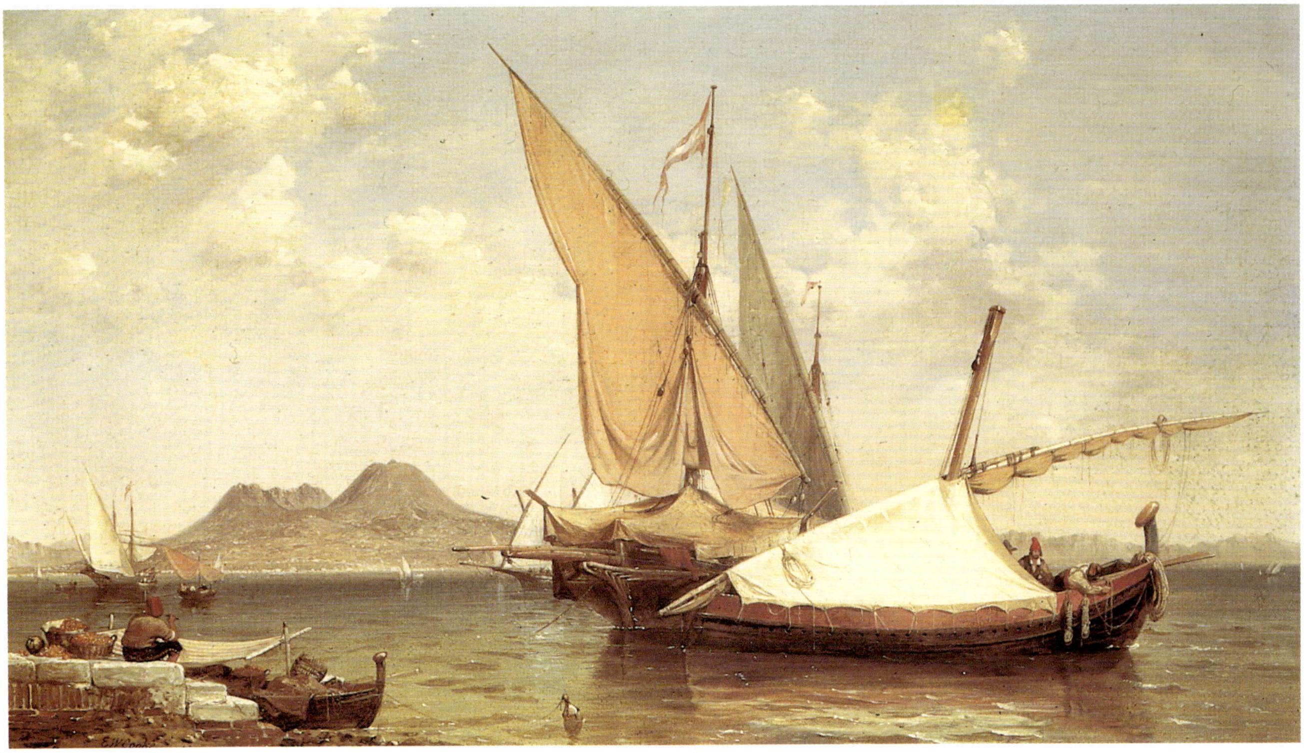

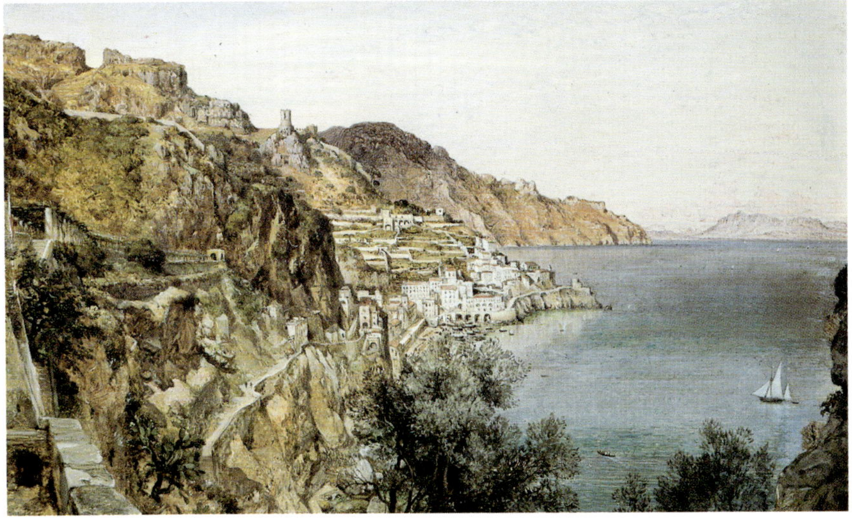

Colour Plate 87. 47/3
Mount Vesuvius, catalan & paranzella
Photo courtesy Sotheby's

Colour Plate 88. 46/16
Amalfi from the Convent, the promontory of Capo Dorso and the Paestum mountains in the distance
Photo courtesy Sotheby's

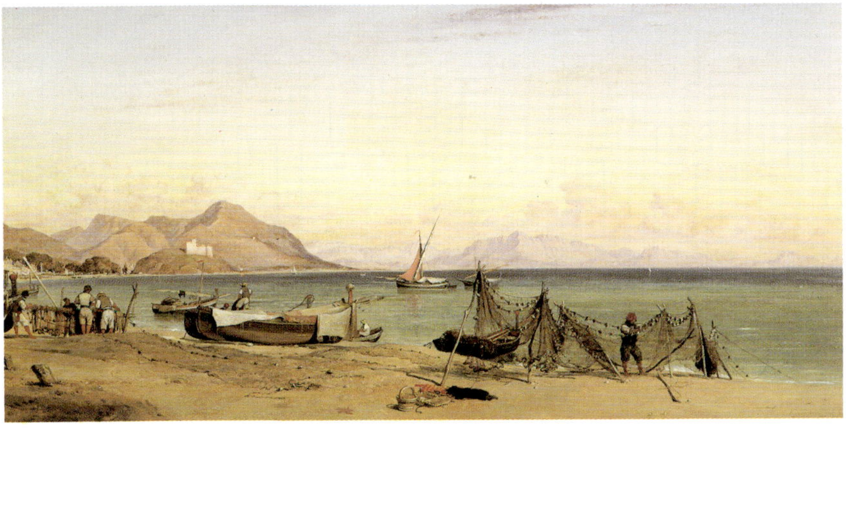

Colour Plate 89. 46/13
Salerno, drying nets, mountains of Paestum in the distance
The pictorial possibilities of draped nets, sails and awnings were thoroughly explored by the artist on this tour.
Photo courtesy Agnews. Private Collection

The visual impact of the city on a stranger was infinitely greater then, more striking indeed than it can ever appear now; even as late as the 1860s it was a majestic weed-grown ruin, with comparatively few inhabitants for its size. The monuments of antiquity were set among market gardens; the great white oxen with sweeping horns and their country carts, seen against temples and fountains, were captured in Cooke's drawings (Plate 114). They were also to be seen in the early photographs taken but a few years afterwards. Vineyards stretched in front of the church of St John Lateran; decorative decay had not yet begun to be replaced by development. Henry James was there in 1869 and found *an antique Queerness and richness that ekes out the reduced state* but returning on a visit in 1872 found black, narrow, crooked, empty streets with new gas-lamps sprouting in the Piazza Barberini.[2]

A camera bought at Flacheron's, the French artists' supplier, for Robert Hannah was probably a version of Cooke's favourite *camera lucida* in the use of which he seems to have been ever ready to instruct.

Evening sessions at the Life class of the French Academy gave him practice in drawing the male nude, but a few of the formal, stiff studies which survive cannot have encouraged him; his supposition that he was rather old to learn was probably well founded. In a letter to his sister Harriette, he confided: *I have made my début in the Life Academy and shall not lose one evening while I stay, and trust I may yet learn something of the figure though it is rather late in life to begin.*

There are colourful notes in the diary of their Roman sojourn; during Holy Week Mr Cooke aimed to see as much pageantry as he could, but was disappointed in trying to see the Pope waiting at table on the pilgrims on the Thursday before Easter, the crowd was too great. Such a round of sightseeing was by no means exceptional; avoiding work on the Sabbath left them free for other favourite activities wherever they were. He witnessed an assassin seek sanctuary and made a sketch, while the guillotine set up for a public execution was viewed after the event. On an early April morning they drove out into the Campagna to an Artists' Festa among the tombs where they found a large assembly of French and German artists, in costume; there was eating and singing and they witnessed *a curious incantation scene of the Sybil in a large cave – very well managed.* His interest in trees is shown by studies of palms and pines and notes on their age and significance. There were a few misfortunes – in the best (or worst) tradition, he had his white painting umbrella stolen from his side as he worked. It was to be his only visit to Rome but some of his sketches were produced in later years in his published collection, *Leaves from my Sketchbook.*

They left on 4 May with the Hannahs for Naples where they again found Elhanan Bicknell and his wife. They visited the museums, churches and beauty spots, ascended Vesuvius and finally departed for Salerno.

Calabrian boats on the sandy beaches were excellent subjects and the fishermen washing, drying and mending their nets, with spread awnings and miscellaneous gear, were colourful. The geological features were also recorded, sometimes appearing to conflict with boats and buildings.

Before leaving home Cooke had noted the ill health of George Loddiges and in a letter to T.H. Cromek[3] he intimated that the sad news of his father-in-law's death shortened their tour. They turned homeward, in a leisurely retreat, viewing Sorrento, Pompeii, Castellammare and visiting Ainsley who was at the Villa Cedroni (Plate 115), Posilippo. Boats in Naples Bay and other enticing views, including moonlight studies of Vesuvius, swelled the number of his paintings. Going by sea from Naples to Genoa and on to Milan which they found, almost with a sigh of relief, *most cheerful & pleasing and clean*, they saw San Carlo Borromeo in his crystal sarcophagus and Leonardo's *Cenacolo* The Last Supper – *a wonderful thing tho' so sadly injured.*

2. 'The Rome of Henry James', J.Fleming, *Country Life* 19 Jan 1951, and *Italian Hours* by Henry James, 1909.
3. B.Dobell, Catalogue 289,No 11. 1911.

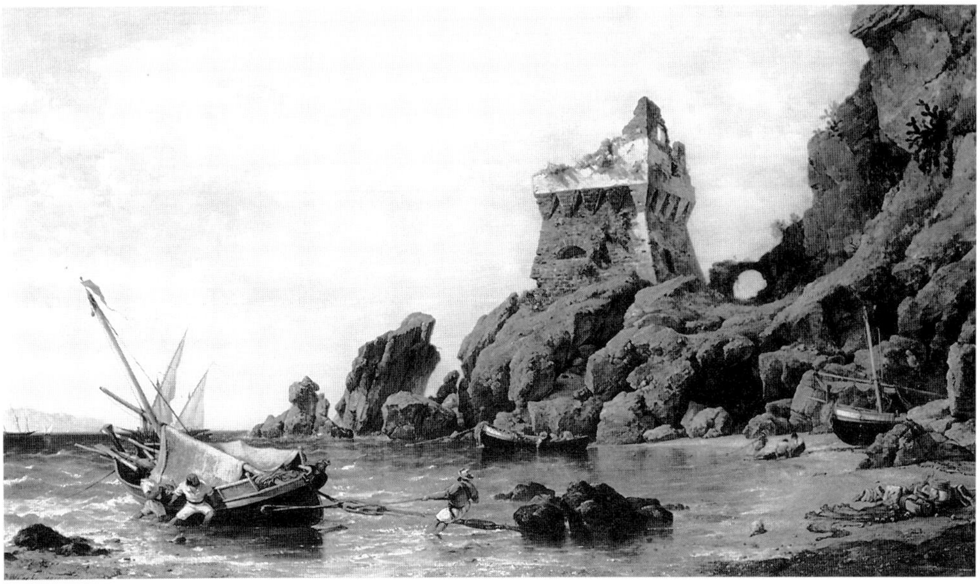

Plate 118. 47/1

Martello Tower, Erchia: Gulph of Salerno

The gentle painter expresses his admiration for the landscape, the ancient monuments, the fishing boats, the men and the way they worked. Capri in the distance.

Photo courtesy Guildhall Art Gallery, Corporation of London

To Lucerne they went by the St. Gotthard Pass and the Lake, drawing all the while, with views from the hotel window, sketches at Schaffhausen Falls, Freiburg, the quay at Cologne, punctuating their return journey. They landed at Blackwall on 30 July and the following day he called on his widowed mother-in-law at Hackney and once more visited the family tomb in St John's churchyard.

Picking up the threads he dined with Sir William Hooker at Kew, visited N.B. Ward and saw his ferns, and displayed his Italian oils to friends and family. William Wells received him once more at Redleaf, where he began painting, enjoying the gardens, noting particularly the Fern Glen and searching for specimens in the surrounding country as far as Eridge. It is of interest that when he came to select a site for his own country place after casting all about Surrey and nearer Sussex, Cooke found something not unlike Redleaf, near Eridge.

A new picture of Italian boats was composed from his sketches and while under Wells' roof he copied a Richard Wilson in the collection, *Italian Lake scene with Anglers*.[4] He showed his paintings to visiting neighbours, Lord De L'Isle, Lord Harrowby and Lord Hardinge, and to house guests including 'Mr Stokes' (probably Charles Stokes) He noted the arrivals and departures – *Sir Walter & Lady James and a snob came*. The identity of the unpleasing individual is not revealed but Sir Walter MP, later 1st Baron Northbourne of Betteshanger, near Sandwich, became a patron and friend. Cooke began a new picture of a Martello Tower (Plate 118), a commission from Wells, and made a sketch of yew trees for him, noting also progress on a picture of Salerno Bay. He went down to Penshurst Place and found abundant specimens of *Ruta & Trichomanes* on a wall in the gardens and noted talking with Mr Rebecca, the architect who was working there for Lord De L'Isle. Ferns were indeed a ruling passion and he was pressing them to form a collection of dried specimens. Later he told Ruskin that the Tunbridge Wells area was the finest in England for them. Once home he was busy potting the live specimens he had acquired on his travels and making up dried sets.

In Barnes he was now painting canvases from his Italian studies for the Exhibitions: *Oneglia looking towards Porto Maurizio* (Colour Plate 83, 46/39) and *Porto Maurizio with palms and a distant view of Oneglia* (Plate 119, 46/44).

David Roberts and his daughter Mrs Henry Bicknell came with her little boy and looked at pictures, but there is no word of the RA's opinion of Cooke's new subjects. Mediterranean light and colouring were challenges of which he was fully aware and, as he seems to have suspected, the critics in their conservatism (which extended to their

4. Christie's sale 22 May 1880,.Lot 130.

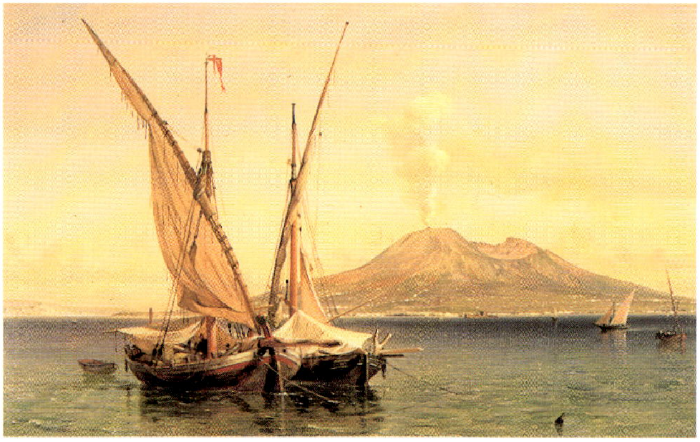

Colour Plate 90. 46/38
The Bay of Naples
Photo courtesy Private Collection

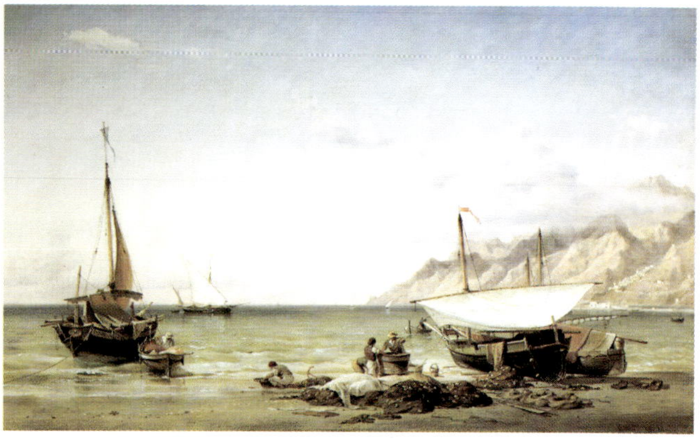

Colour Plate 92. 47/7
Mountains capped with cloud Salerno, morning mist clearing off from the Mountains
This is the studio version of his sketch on the spot, made in the previous year. Photo courtesy Arthur Ackermann & Peter Johnson

vocabulary as well) were not in favour of his change of scene and palette. Some of the notices are worth quoting since they illustrate various of Cooke's strengths amid expressions of personal preference. In the 1848 British Institution show the *Art Journal* declared of No 21 *...From the garden of the Vigna Celimontana.*(47/6): *This type of subject is by no means suited to the known powers of this artist...* while, on the other hand, No.54: *A Zuider Zee Botter working off A Sandbank, Marken in the distance* (47/11, Plate 86) the critic was clearly relieved:

Colour Plate 91. 47/2
Mediterranean craft, Gulf of Genoa
Photo courtesy Private Collection

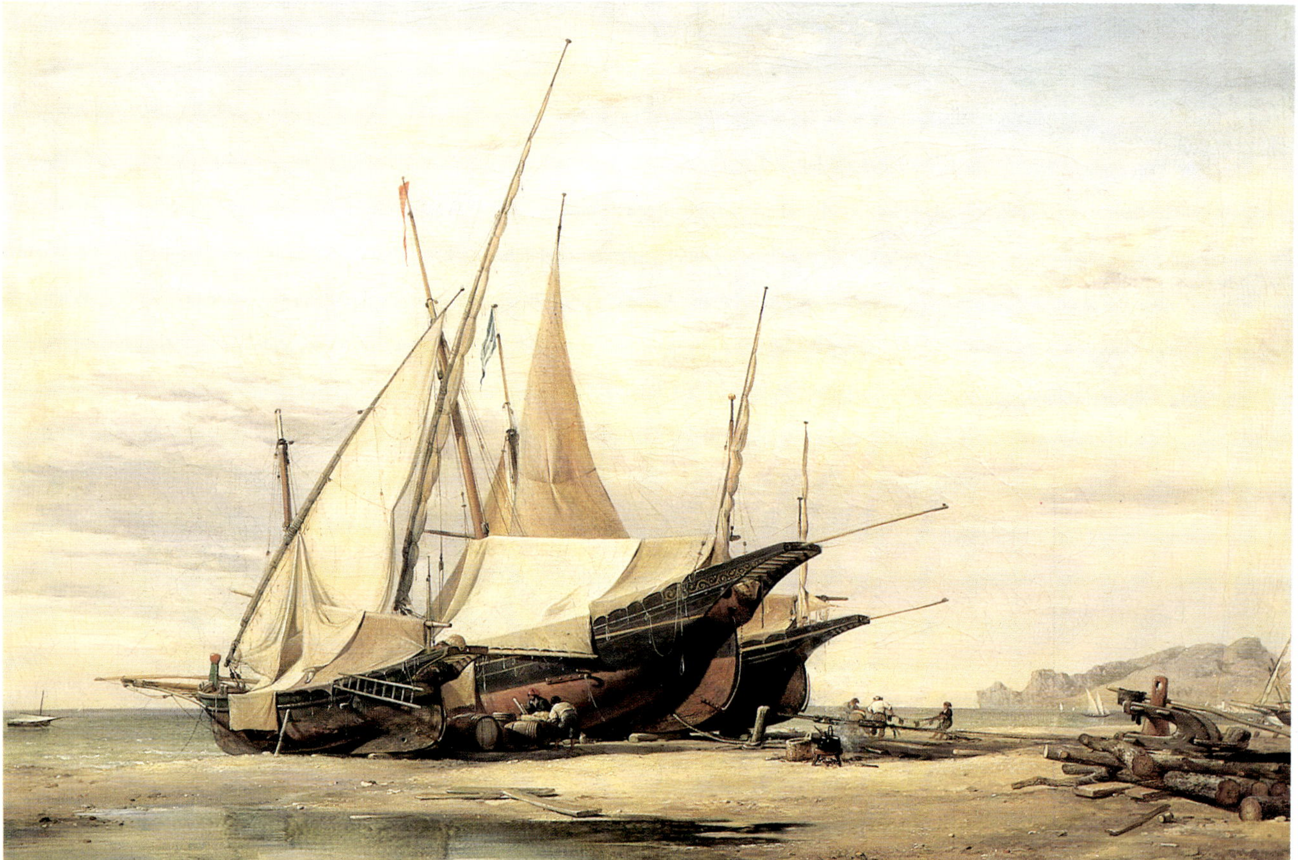

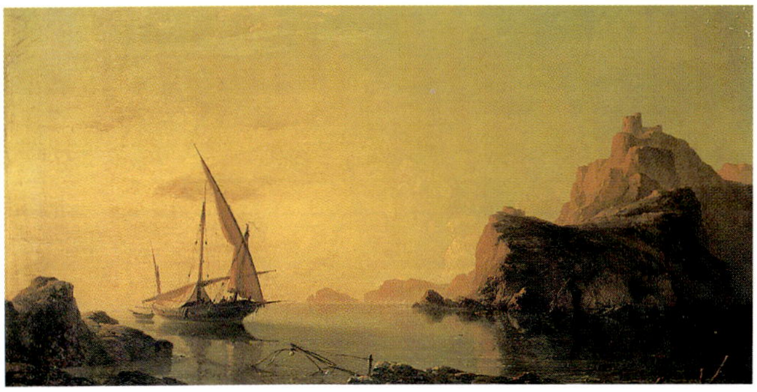

Colour Plate 93. 48/7
Sunset Capo di Misena.'O'er the hush'd Deep...'
Photo courtesy Sotheby's. Private Collection

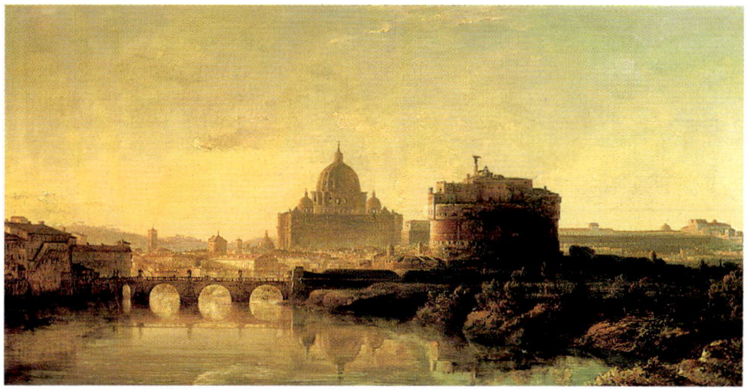

Colour Plate 94. 49/1
Rome & S.Angelo: Thou hast the sunset's glow Rome, for thy dower...
Photo courtesy Christie's

Happy are we again to meet this painter on the green 'glad waters' of the North Sea, the home and temple of all the most 'felon' winds of the compass. We find the unshapely craft sticking on a head of sand, and are rather at a loss to know how she got there. This is an admirable picture, but it supplies evidence that it will be some time before the artist is able to shake off the bilious contamination from which his artistic system so severely suffered in the 'warm south'!

No 223 *Cannes, South of France (47/8); The eye, on a close inspection, discovers much that is truly beautiful in this picture, though, as a whole, it is inferior to his earlier works. The scene lies on the shores of the Mediterranean, presenting in the foreground some boats drawn up on the beach; in the back-draught of the broken*

Colour Plate 95. 68/8
Mending nets, Bay of Naples
This was his return to a remembrance of 1846 and his last Vesuvian picture, backed by copious sketches.
Photo courtesy Richard Green Fine Paintings. Private Collection

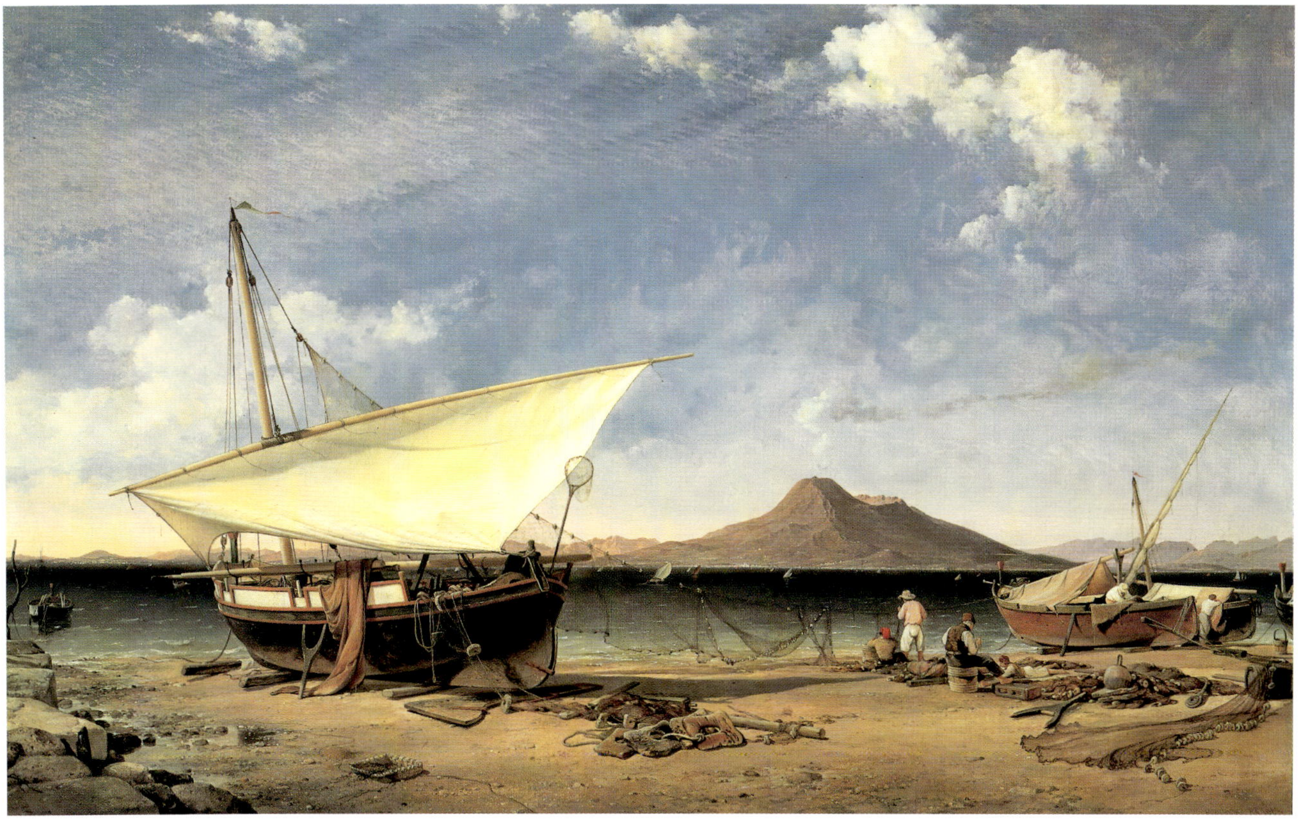

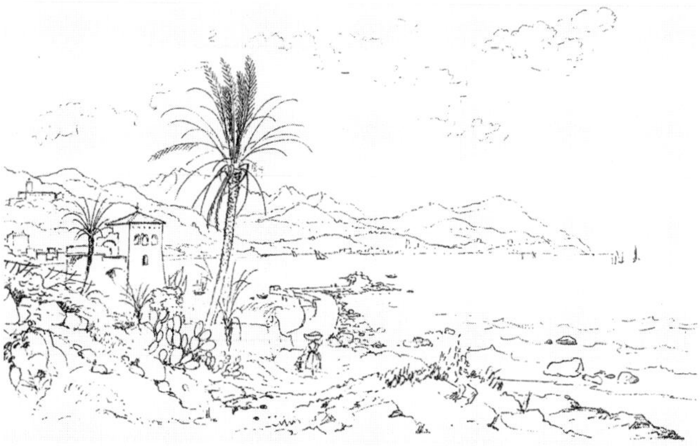

Plate 119. 46/44
Porto Maurizio with palms & distant view of Oneglia
A *camera lucida* record of a completed oil painting, yet to be sighted.

wave, in the sea, and in the sky, there is abundant truth, but it is pronounced with hardness and severity.

No 139 *Italian fishing-craft off the Torre del Marzocco - Leghorn (48/2); A large picture, partaking more of the feeling of the artist's earlier works than we have seen in any of his Mediterranean or Adriatic subjects.*

No 153 *'Thou hast the sunset's glow Rome for thy dower...'* [49/1, Colour Plate 94]; *These lines stand in the place of title to this picture, which presents a view of a portion of Rome, with the Tiber in the centre of the composition on the right of which are seen the Castle of St Angelo and the Vatican. The time is evening and the buildings tell in strength against the warm sky which by the way is charged with clouds in greater number than we think is generally found over Rome. This is the best we have seen of the Italian subjects of the artist; it is a picture of great interest, but the comparison between these Southern subjects and those gathered on the shores of the North Sea, is not a little instructive to the reflective mind.*

E.W. Cooke doubtless reflected upon these strictures, the charge of hardness of outline being by now expected, but his documentary treatment of the new sailing craft and unfamiliar scenes in his view required it. The advent of photography had demonstrated that here was a rival to the recording pencil, and even Turner had exclaimed *This is the end of Art.*[5] However, there is little doubt that Cooke regarded the new science – or art – as no threat, but rather an aid to his work.

For Northern European critics the impact of his Mediterranean light and colour was, as he had feared, a big challenge, but critical acceptance of his 'southern' work was eventually forthcoming. That his Tiber view was painted from sketches made in December, and that his observance of meteorological detail was also strict, would indicate that the criticism of his Roman clouds was probably wide of the mark.

A postscript to this foreign painting tour, which was the longest of his career, is provided by the title of a Christie's sale catalogue, *Ninety Finished Pictures in Oils... most of which have been Painted from Nature,* 26 June 1863. The artist furnished notes to many of the titles, drawing on his arboricultural and historical knowledge. The occupation of Rome by the French three years after his visit had resulted in several memorable losses:

Lot 38. *Rome: Stone Pines, 100 feet high, at the entrance of the Villa Pamfili Doria, on the Janiculum Hill: destroyed by the French, 1848.* [Colour Plate 165.]
Lot 44. *Rome: This Palm was brought from the Levant in 1490 by the 'Passionista' monks of the Convent of SS Giovanni e Paolo, on the Coelian Hill. It blew down the day before the French commenced the bombardment of the city in 1848. It was the oldest palm in Italy.* [Plate 120.]

His habit was to sign and date paintings only when sending them for exhibition, or when

5. A.M.W. Stirling, The Richmond Papers, 1926.

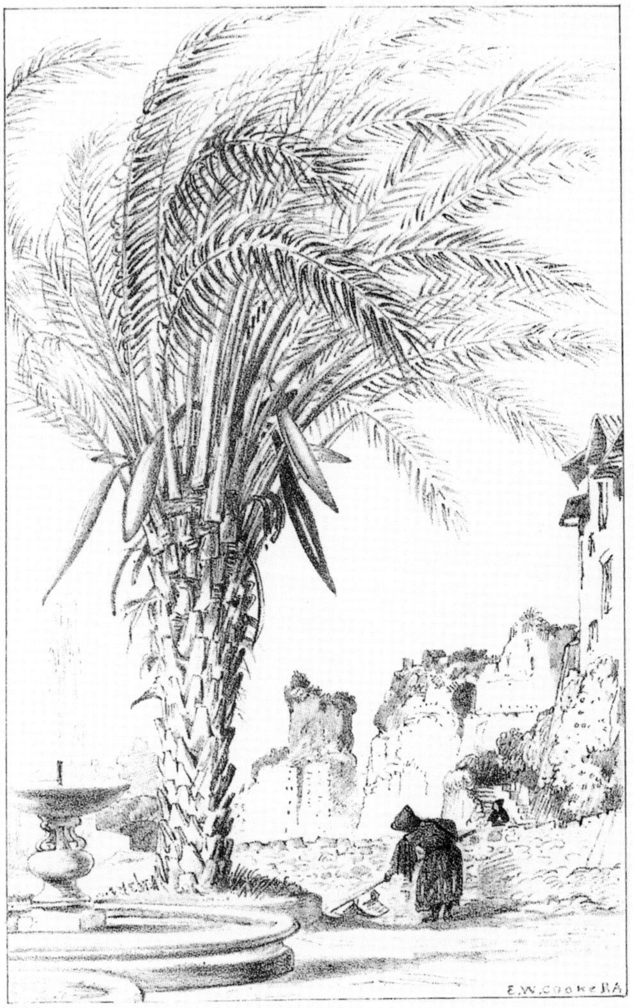

Plate 120. Engraving
Palm in the Villa Bonaventura Rome
'Rome' says Madame de Stael in *Corinne* 'has but two palm trees and both these are in monastic gardens... and there is always a feeling of pleasure in the sight of this representative of Africa... which awakens so many new ideas and sensations.' The artist quoted the author and noted that the Convent of St. Buonaventura was on the highest part of the Palatine Hill.

selling them, so it is possible that some pictures from this trip will bear his signature with 'ARA' and the date 1863.

Cooke returned occasionally to his western Italian sketches for subjects, the last of which was the Academy picture No. 204 of 1869, *Mending Nets, Bay of Naples* (Colour Plate 95) on which the *Art Journal* critic pronounced:

> *We are glad to come upon a more than usually sparkling and vivid scene by E.W. Cooke RA an artist who may have suffered degeneration under over-zealous attempts to paint unpaintable scenes. This artist naturally becomes more vivacious and sensitive to beauty when he nears the coast of Italy, than when he dwells on the stagnant coasts of Holland... a picture which awakens even into poetry under the brilliance of the Italian sky. Admirable too for truth is the modelling of form in the mountain group of Vesuvius, and equally literal is the study of detail on the Neapolitan shore, familiar to every tourist.*

The critic, probably not the same as he who had written twenty years before, unless it was S.C. Hall himself with a reformed opinion, seems now actually to prefer the Mediterranean Sea to the German ocean and the acknowledgement of a poetic feeling is rare. However one is left reflecting on the location of the *unpaintable scenes*, which would imply failures in choice of subject rather than in execution. Holland and Venice with their local sailing craft had been received with due acknowledgement if accompanied by a hint of slight boredom, the 'geological' coastal views drew nothing but admiration and his shipwreck scenes did not fail to impress. Perhaps the stranded whale of 1867 was the culprit, but in its absence, judgement must be reserved!

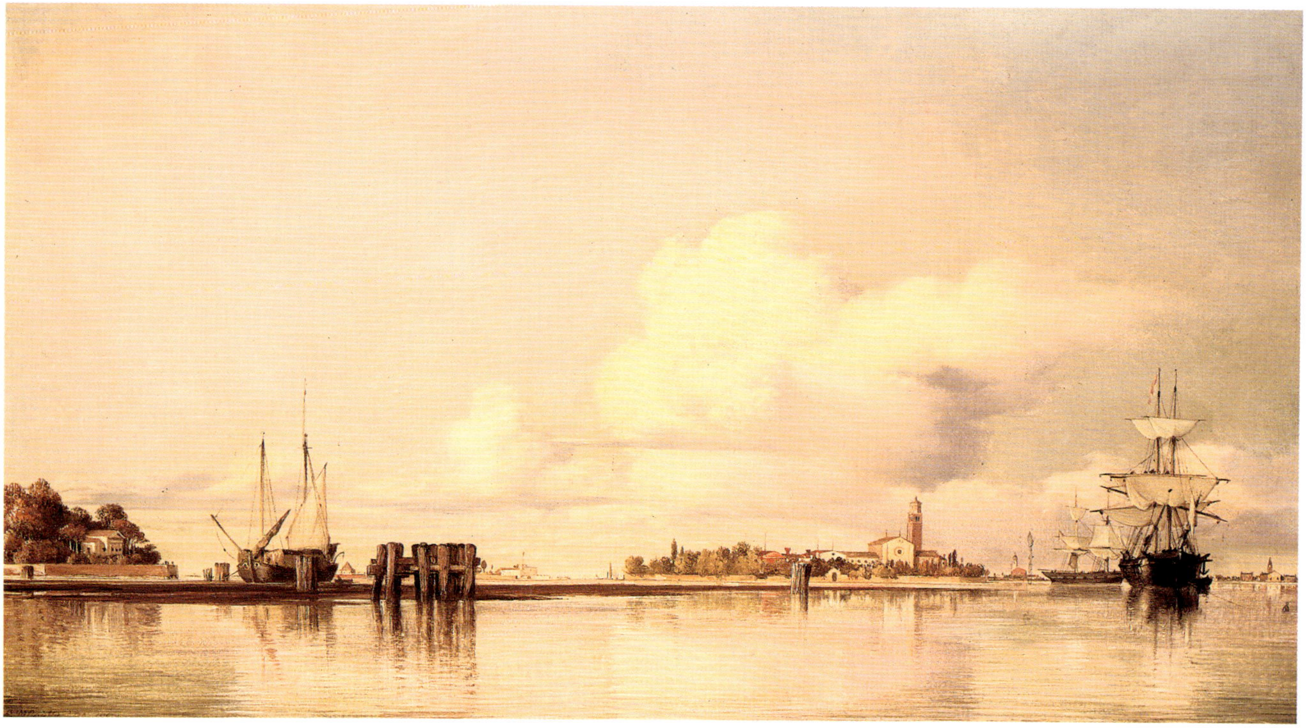

Colour Plate 96. 57/6

Shipping in the Venetian Lagoon

Exact locations are sometimes difficult to fix on account of the similarity of island churches and the changes due to later development. Photo: courtesy Spink & Son Ltd. Private Collection

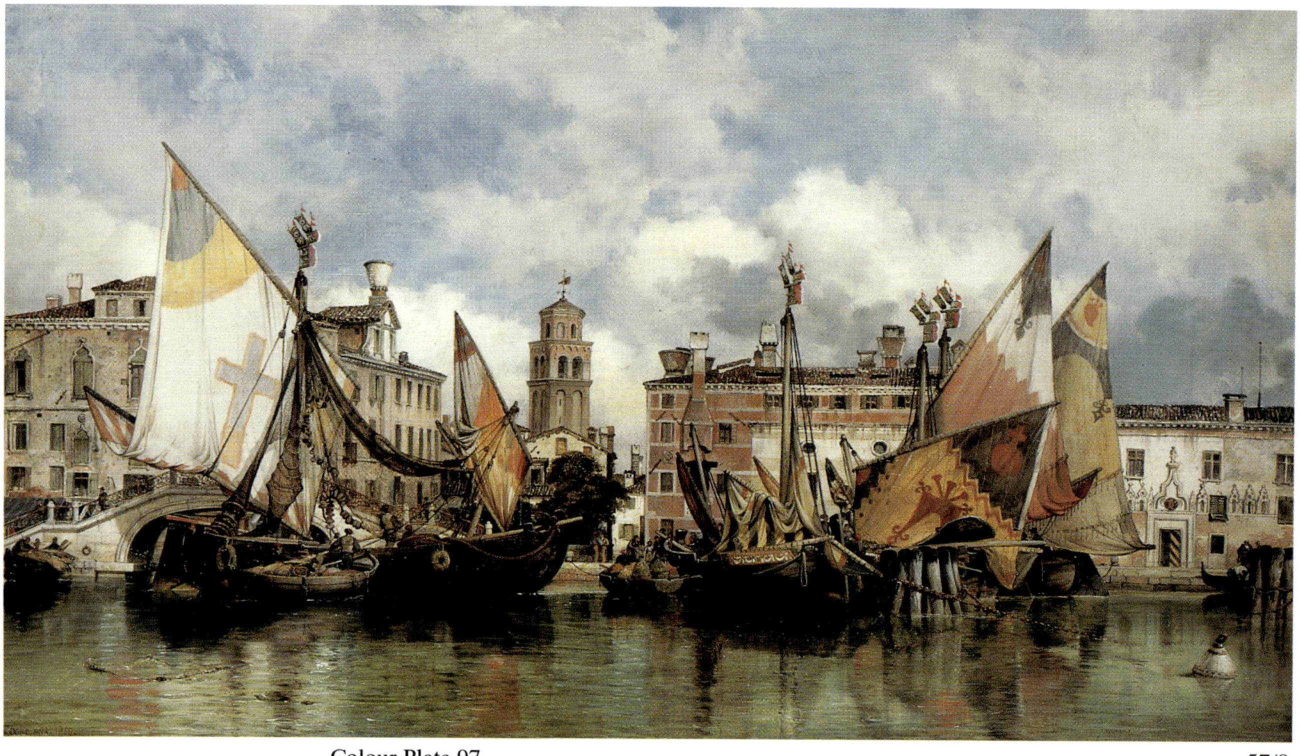

Colour Plate 97. 57/8

Bragozzi off the Ponte Ca di Dio, Church of San Martino

Eastward along the Riva, Cooke found the places where the colourful craft were moored; here, off the Ponte della Veneta Marina and off the Giardini, the Public Gardens, and he returned often to savour them. Photo courtesy Sotheby's. Polak Gallery

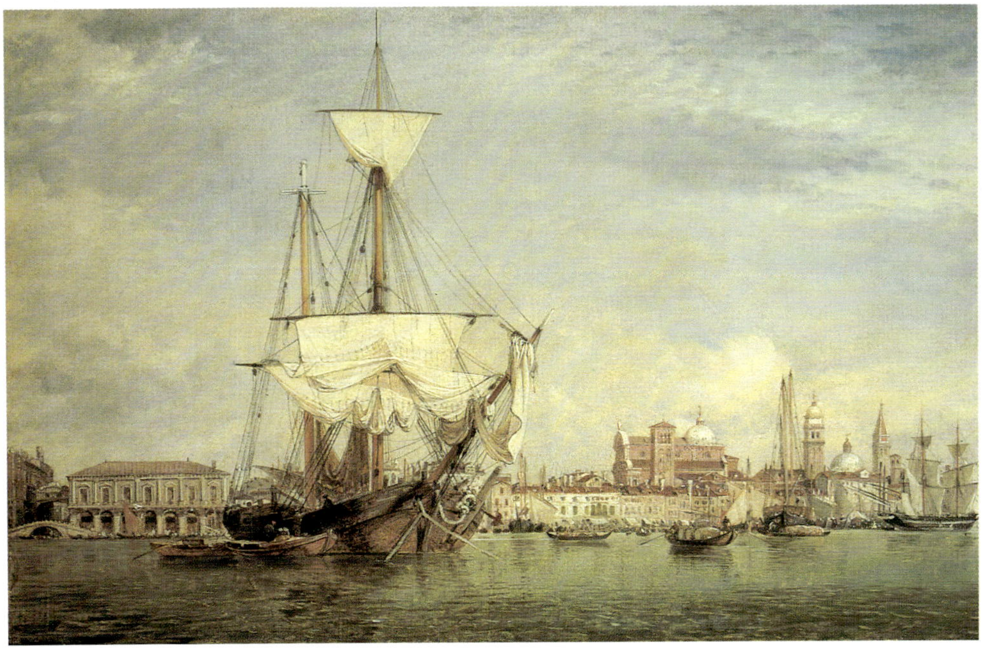

Chapter 9

VENICE AND IL LAGUNETTO

It is the Lagoon – neither lake nor sea, but partaking of the nature of both – which makes Venice unique, not only because it surrounds the City on all sides but also because of its characteristics compounded of mystery and melancholy and constant movement. Sir Ashley Clarke, 1976.[1]

What marine painter, worth his salt, could ignore the call of the Serenissima? Certainly not Edward Cooke, for her waterways fringed by palaces and churches of a unique style reflecting moving colour and light were thronged by a fascinating variety of working craft. Further, the islands in the lagoons were set against a mountainous backdrop and were subject to atmospheric effects which could be theatrical. What more, to his taste, could any place offer?

The city's waterborne economy with its attendant craft of all sizes, propelled by oar and by sail, represented a vast store of interest, most of it showing decidedly exotic characteristics. To a northern eye the costume, the complexions and even the actions of the boatmen were, for those used to Dutch trawlermen and English fishermen, also totally new. The challenge offered by Venetian buildings, even to a draughtsman used to architectural subjects – the churches and palaces in all their varied states of repair seen in sunlight and in mists, early and late – was equally powerful.

Canaletto, Bellotto, Guardi and their imitators were represented in the English art collections which Cooke had seen. For Giovanni Antonio Canale himself the draughtsman of *Shipping and Craft* can have had only admiration. He would have seen prints by Piranesi and the black and white work of Canaletto in both John Sheepshanks' and William Wells' collections and it is significant that on his first visit he took for presentation to the Library of St Mark a copy of his etchings of London Bridge, that powerful study of architecture spanning the waters.

There is an assured grace and reality in the assorted vessels which crowd Canaletto's

1. *Ruskin's Venice* edited by Arnold Whittick, 1976.

Colour Plate 98. 50/23
Venice, the Bacino, Brichepala [L] Riva, Prison, Church of S.Zaccaria
Photo courtesy Martyn Gregory. Private Collection

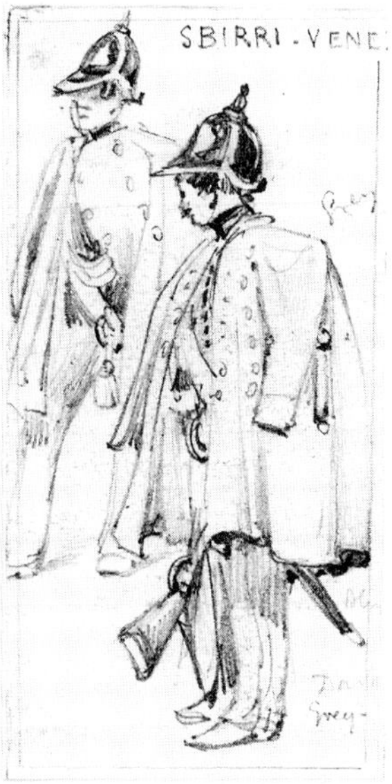

Plate 121. Pencil drawing
Sbirri Venice
Policemen in an occupied city.
Photo courtesy The Trustees of the National Maritime Museum, Greenwich

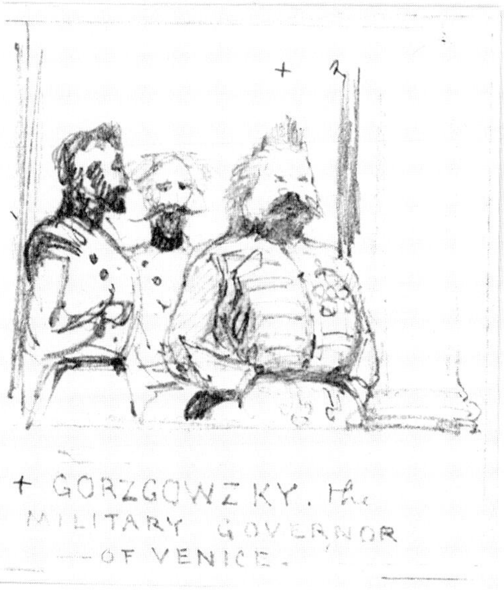

Plate 122. Pencil drawing
General Charles Gorzkowski
A Polish officer, Austrian civil and military Governor, besieger of Venice, who received its surrender in August 1849. Effie Ruskin was on good terms with him. 'A huge man and as popular with the Italians as any Austrian could be' (Lutyens p.215). This sketch of a buttoned-up military notable verges upon caricature.
Photo courtesy The Trustees of the National Maritime Museum, Greenwich

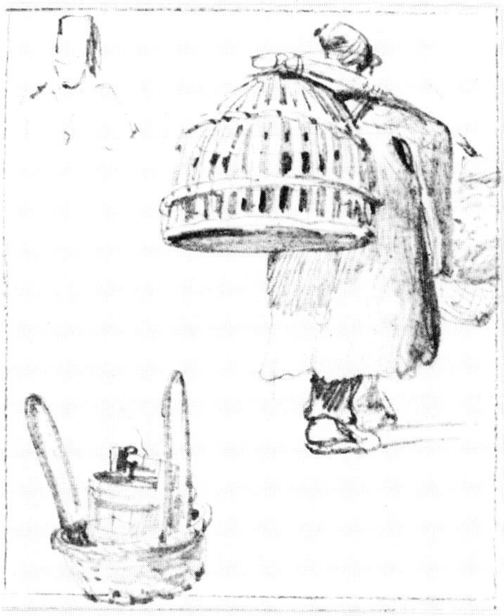

Plate 123. Pencil drawing
Porter & baskets Venice
The well-known amateur of baskets samples the Venetian style with a note of exotic Turkish headgear top left.
Photo courtesy The Trustees of the National Maritime Museum, Greenwich

canvases; the dressed gondolas and other boats processing up and down the Grand Canal in carnival time, or clustered round the Doge's palatial state galley, the *Bucintoro,* are a familiar aspect. The small British and Greek traders, the Adriatic coasters and the Lagune market boats swarming in the Bacino di San Marco[2] are another feature, perfectly delineated and perhaps less often remarked upon.

In the last few years up to the exhibitions of 1850, Cooke's pictures had been mainly Dutch and French with Italian subjects from his 1845-46 tour. Concern to find new ones led him, as before, to follow a well marked trail, over the Alps into northern Italy, through the Veneto and, with high expectation, to the *...glorious City in the Sea.*[3]

It was less a question of viewing new shorescapes than of exploring the shipping and craft. Venetian pictures by Bonington from his brief 1826 visit, which appeared in his sale and his posthumous exhibition of 1834, were among the works greatly admired by Cooke. Also in the 1830s and 1840s the London exhibitions saw Venice according to Turner, Stanfield, Prout and Roberts, as well as through the eyes of J.F. Lewis, W.J. Müller and James Holland. William Wyld had been there in 1833-4 and William Callow, Cooke's contemporary, in 1840.

It should be said that the *character* as conveyed by the intimate details of Venetian water-craft appears to have raised no great enthusiasm in many visiting artists. There is rarely an indication of their having made a close study, such as Cooke was bound to do. Turner's *The Sun of Venice going to sea,* for example, which Cooke doubtless saw in the Royal Academy in 1843, shows only a rather unconvincing approximation *pace* John Ruskin.[4] What at first appears to be a stately craft, a-flutter with flags and painted sails, the *Sol di Veneza* [sic] on closer inspection proves to be a small crowded boat, with but one mast and unusually three flags, given dignity by another larger vessel sailing in her wake. Perhaps she is a *topo*; it is difficult to identify the type and remains a vision, sufficient for Turner's London purpose, but lacking truth to the model. John Constable, writing of the 1828 Royal Academy exhibition, had said *Turner has some golden visions, glorious and beautiful. They are only visions but they are still art....*[5] It is not without the

2. Museum of Fine Arts, Boston, Mass.
3. *Italy* by Samuel Rogers, 1828.
4. Letter of 14 September, 1845.
5. Leslie op.cit., p.166.

bounds of possibility that Edward Cooke, standing before this poetic *Sun of Venice* did not quite believe it and determined to go and see for himself.

He knew how Stanfield the seaman took such things in his stride, of course, and the cosmopolitan William Callow, born in Thames-side Greenwich and bred in Paris, could be relied upon to absorb the essentials and details of rig, build and behaviour, just as he himself had been trained to do. With other artists, however, there is often an uncertainty about all of these points which, to a discerning eye, no amount of painterly bravura can redeem. As was often demonstrated, the generalisations, understatements and inventions which might pass in landscape were fatal in pictures containing shipping. Philip Hamerton, artist and critic, could write *Studies may be accurate... noble pictures are never accurate* and *a painter is an author and likes to move his public and topography moves nobody.*[6] One can be certain that Cooke was moved by J.M.W. Turner's Venetian pictures which began to appear in the Academy from 1833. Although radically different in approach, the younger man admired the senior Academician's visions, as diary references undoubtedly show. It was Stanfield who said, in relation to criticism of the elements in Turner's marine paintings, *I side with the sailors as far as his actual knowledge of the construction and working of a ship but he possessed a wonderful discrimination and power in the character of the craft he depicted....*[7]

Cooke's sketch-book activity in recording everything he saw must have matched Turner's, although his method of dismembering sketchbooks and filing his drawings in classified order, now dispersed, has destroyed the possibility of such a comparison. Further, his copious sketching was only occasionally accompanied by watercolour notes for he relied as usual on oil sketches made on the spot.

He was at Elhanan Bicknell's on 24 April 1841: ...*went to Herne Hill at 4, dined at Mr*

6. Hamerton, *Thoughts about Art,* 1889, p.216.
7. Letter to C.R. Leslie RA, 1859, quoted Van der Merwe, op.cit., p.145,

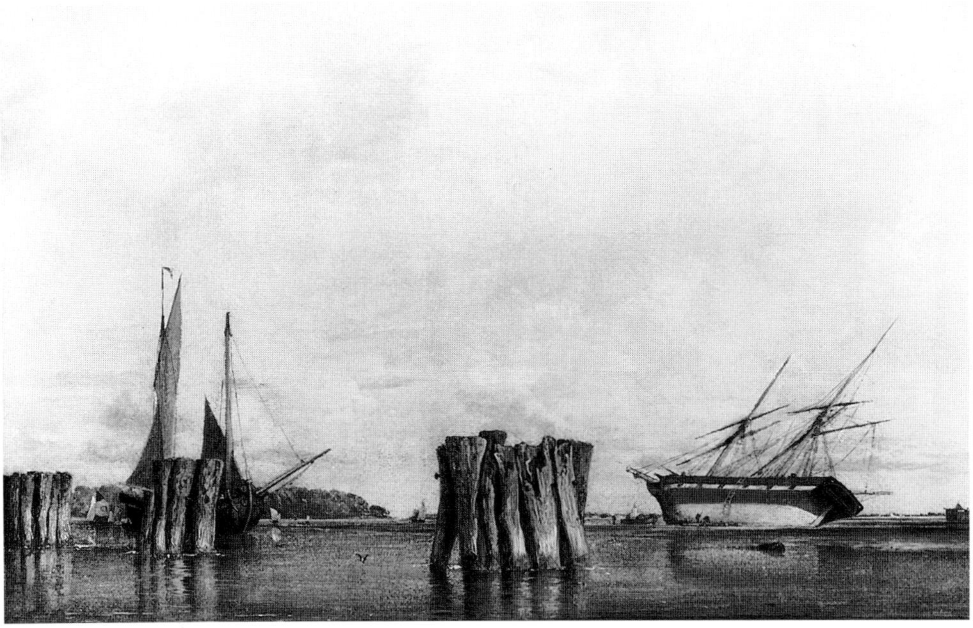

Plate 124. 50/25
Vessel hove-down
Cooke, 'who must see everything' as John Ruskin reported, was as eager to record the life of the shipping community as their splendid surroundings. Repairs or maintenance to this vessel at low water is a perfect example. Photo courtesy Martyn Gregory

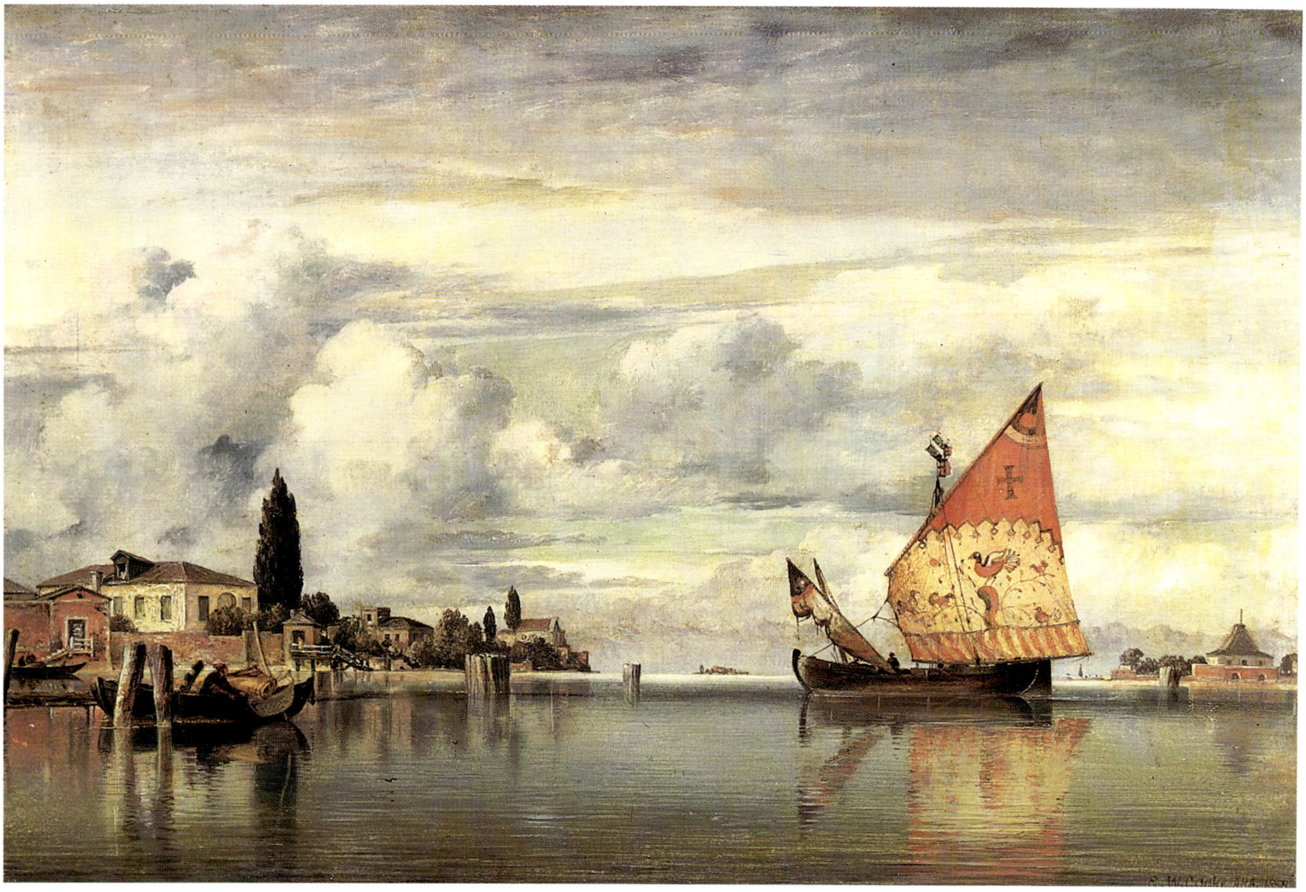

Colour Plate 99. 58/5

On the Lagune of Venice

A bragozzo in a calm among the islands with the impressive mountainous background not often visible today.

Photo courtesy Sotheby's. Private Collection

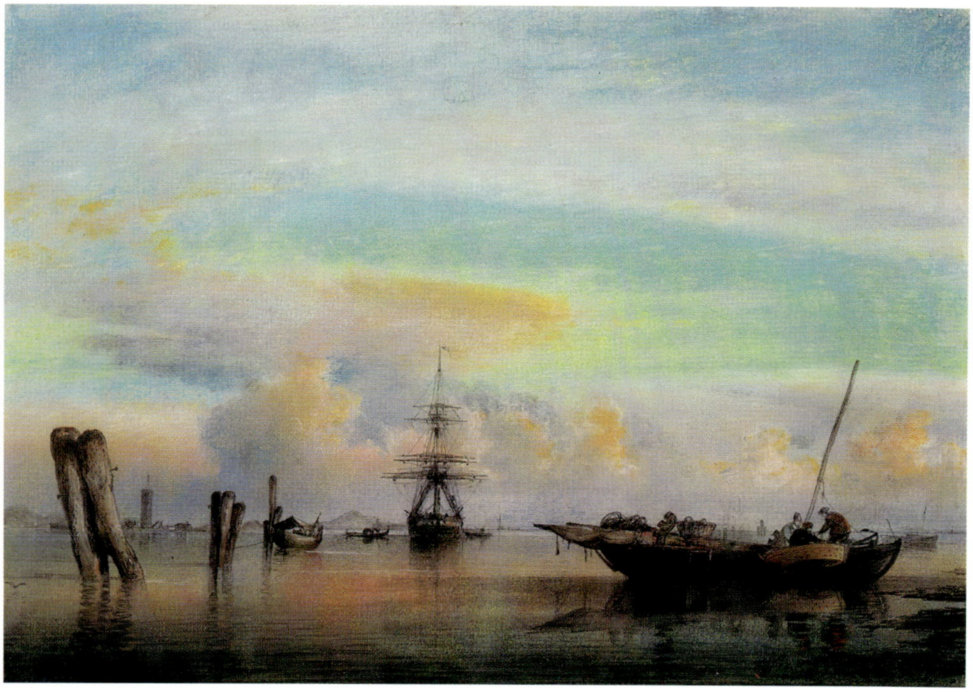

Colour Plate 100. Chalk

Vessels in a Calm; sunset on the Lagune 1870

In a soft atmospheric drawing the interesting details of the fishing craft, including the *burchiello* slung over the side, are not ignored.

Photo courtesy Private Collection

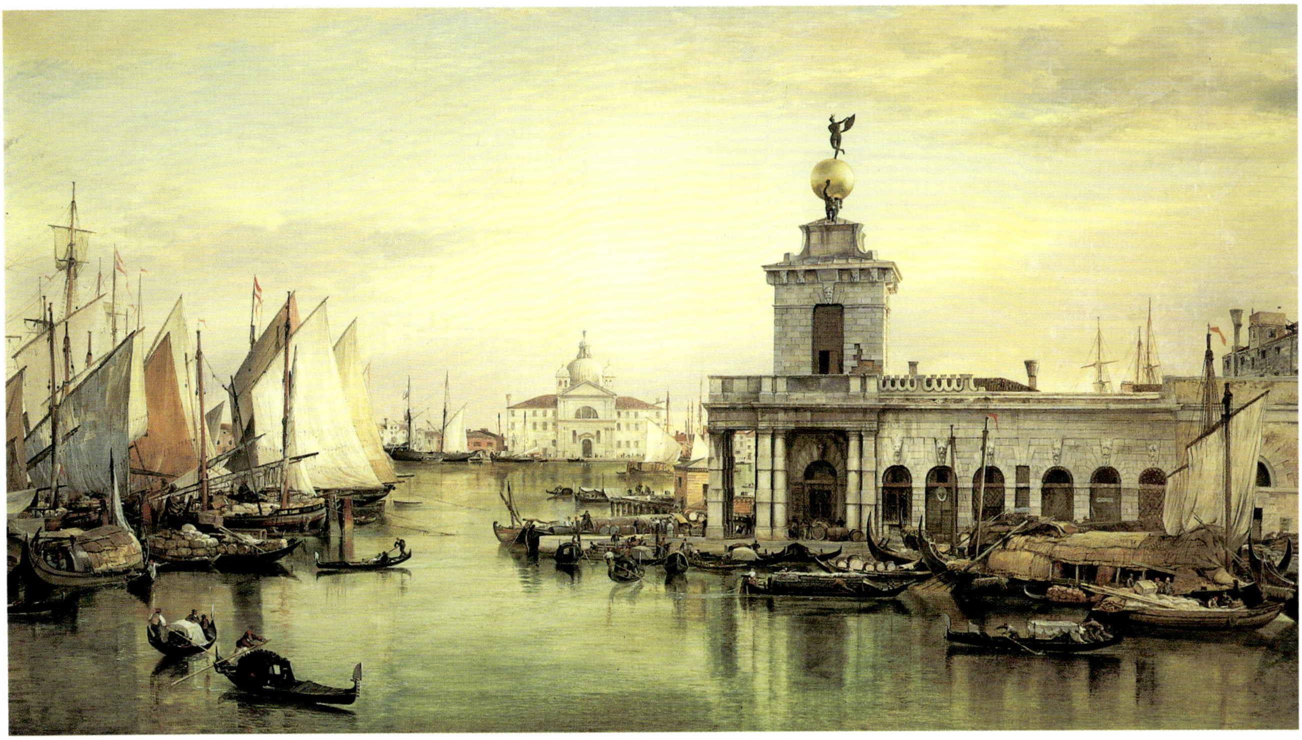

Colour Plate 101. 50/27
Dogana di Mare & Church of the Zitelle Photo courtesy Arthur Ackermann & Peter Johnson Ltd. Private Collection

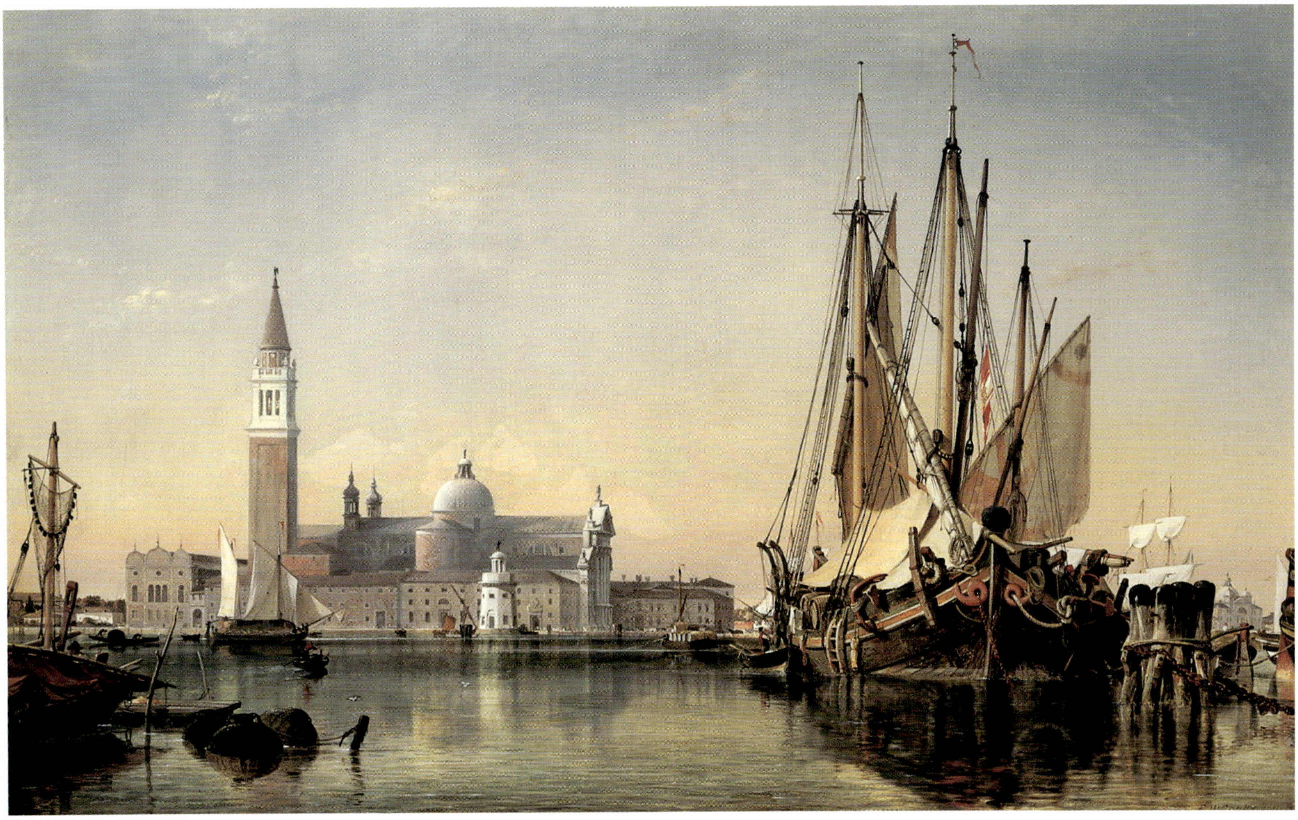

Colour Plate 102. 53/11
S.Giorgio & trabaccoli [1862]
Softly atmospheric, this speaks of the autumn weather which was the artist's favourite time for visiting Venice. Photo courtesy Martyn Gregory. Private Collection

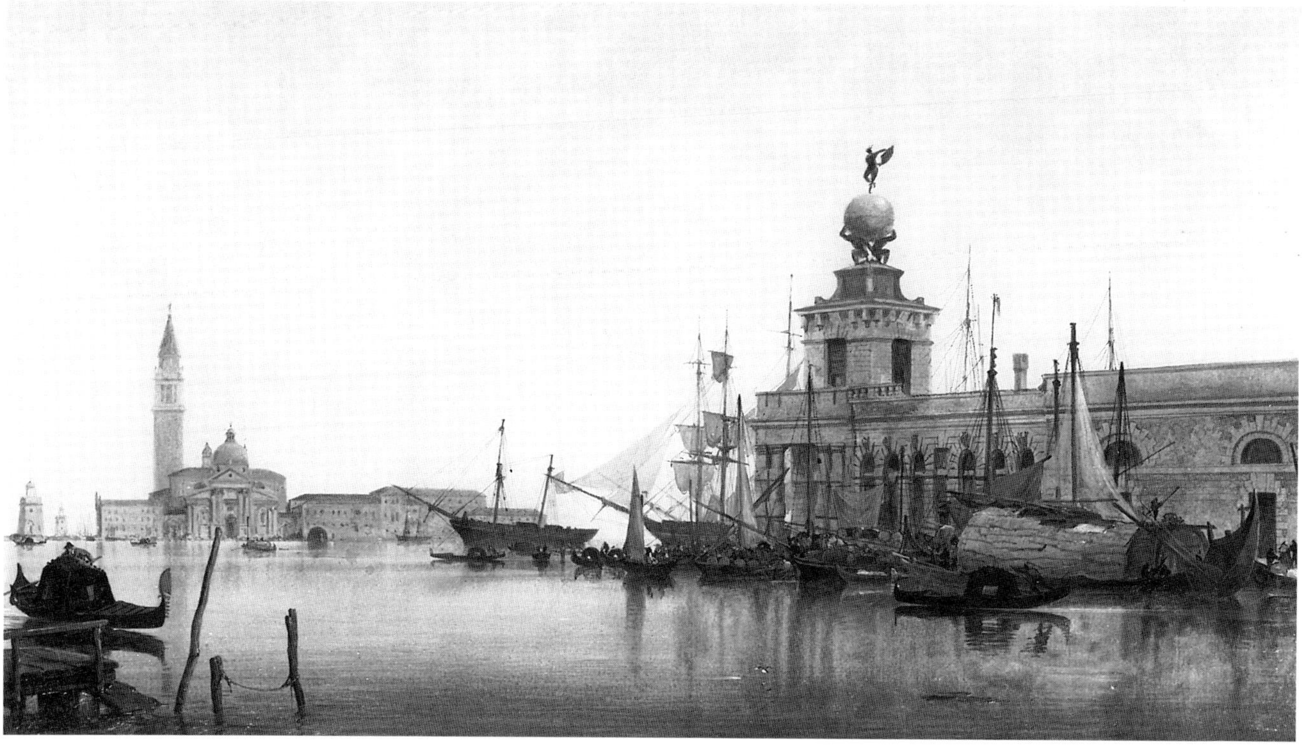

Plate 125. 62/18
The Dogana di Mare (Customs House) with San.Giorgio Maggiore beyond
Photo courtesy Arthur Ackermann & Peter Johnson

Bicknell's met Messrs. Turner RA, Stanfield, Roberts (and Christine), Collins, Phillips, Denning, Gastineau &c &c after a pleasant evening left at 10... but the diarist is as usual silent on topics of conversation. It was not always possible to hear what was being said down the table, especially at a convivial board, as was also noted by Ruskin.[8] In that year's RA.exhibition Turner's *Giudecca, Salute & S.Giorgio* was bought by Bicknell.

A desire to emulate in his own style such exciting pictures – but more, one suspects, a determination to bring his own *particular* brand of observation to bear on these colourful craft, just as he had done in his youthful etchings – must have been a prime reason for Cooke's turn to the Adriatic. The political upheavals, the revolt against Austrian domination, the siege of the city, its bombardment and its surrender in 1849 had been reasons enough for postponing a visit. In the summer of 1850. however, he was evidently ready and the diary entries illustrate the occupations of an industrious resident of Victoria Road, Kensington:

On 6 June he potted all the new water plants, painted on a picture of Vesuvius and at 3 Mr Heathcote, Mr Beckford, Mr Selwin and Mr Lawrence came and looked over his Italian sketches.

He had already begun to collect calotypes, which new photographic marvels were shown to visitors who also inspected the contents of the glasshouses. His friend Cundell, not to be confused with the publisher and photographer Joseph Cundall who was also an expert in the new art or science, took away his little *Zaandam* to calotype, marking his use of photography for recording his paintings instead of his usual *camera lucida* drawings.

Robert McInnes, whom Cooke had last seen in Florence, came to supper and talked about Venice; among his recent pictures had been *A Summer's Afternoon on the Lido near Venice* which was described as the celebration of a festa by a party of peasants and approved of by the *Art Journal: ...we rejoice thus to welcome home the accomplished painter from his long sojourn in Italy.*[9] Each day while Cooke painted, his mother read aloud from John Ruskin's *Seven Lamps of Architecture* (1849) and he was able to record meeting the author at Mr Cheney's at luncheon in the company of Heathcote and Beckford. They drove to Russell Square afterwards and viewed Mr Holford's pictures – which Cooke pronounced very fine.[10]

8. Ibid.
9. *Art Journal* 1848, p.166.
10. Herrman op.cit.

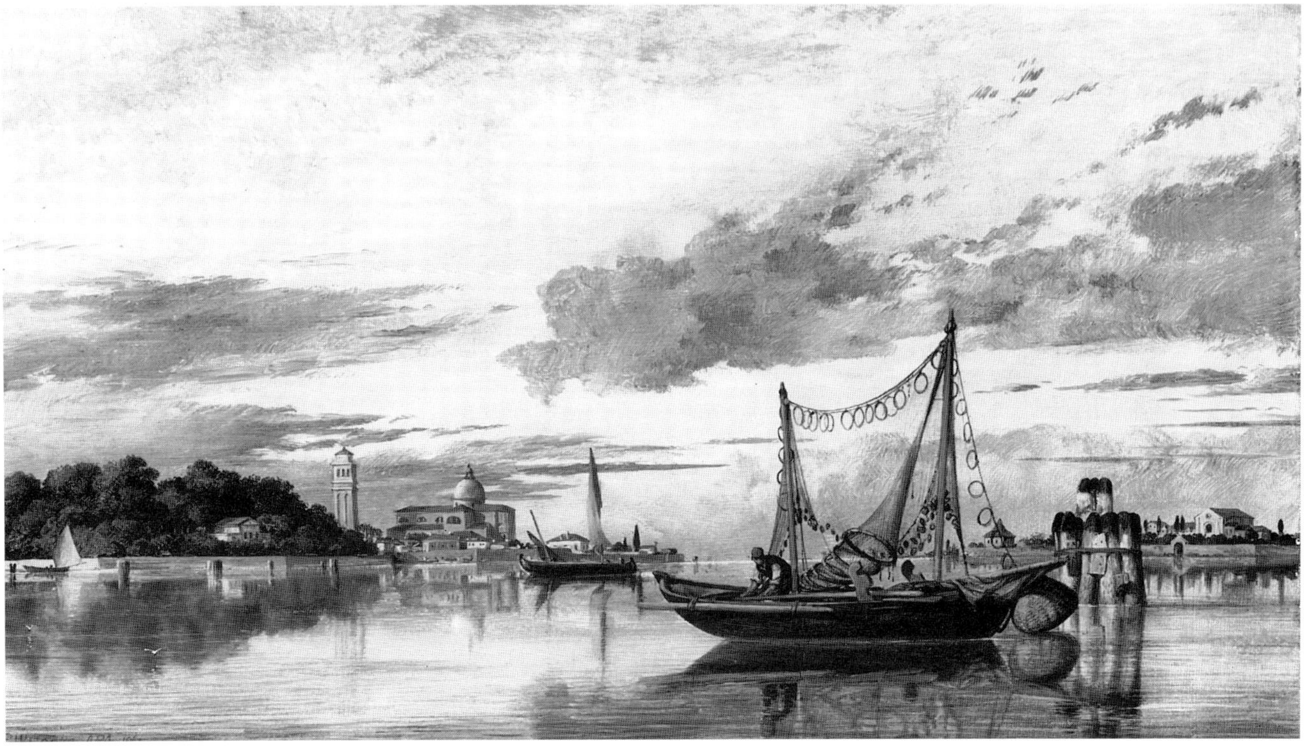

Plate 126. 62/21
The Venetian.Lagoon at Sunset
The location, the time of day and the tender depiction of the topo with its fishing gear show 'Il Lagunetto' at his contemplative best. This may be a study noted as *Evening San.Pietro.*
Photo courtesy Hazlitt Gooden & Fox

At age thirty-one, as against Cooke's thirty-nine years, John Ruskin was writing *The Stones of Venice*,[11] having already been there in 1835, 1841, 1845 and 1846. He had immersed himself in his great study of architectural history and married the nineteen-year-old Euphemia Gray from Perth, known as Effie, in 1848, now bringing her to help him. Young Mr and Mrs Ruskin called at The Ferns, Victoria Road, and looked at Italian sketches, he with a critical eye, but doubtless passing on hints and names of use to an intending visitor. They had returned from Italy in April and would not set out again until the following August, 1851, meeting Cooke there on his, and their, second visit.

He mentions having a case made to house his oil canvas block. For outdoor painting he provided himself with two blocks of oil sketching paper, one thick and the other thin, which he had found satisfactory on his earlier Italian tour and the resulting paintings were usually laid down on canvas when he reached home. The block of canvas was presumably on the same principal, with rectangles of prepared canvas which could be, as it were, peeled off. All this indicated great care and consideration for an important aspect, comfort and ease of operation while painting, for there were distractions and difficulties enough.

He travelled, sketchbook ready, through France, Belgium and Germany, meandering almost to Munich and down the Danube to Linz, thence via Salzburg, Innsbruck, across the Brenner to Bolsena and eventually to Padua. And so, jotting notes (see below, page 295) as typical as any on a tourist postcard, he began his Venetian period which was to last, in fact, almost to the end of his life.

Under an Austrian military governor (sketched by Cooke, Plate 122), there was still a tourist trade with many visitors and also foreign residents like Rawdon Lubbock Brown, an essential contact. Brown who devoted himself to transcribing important documents from the Venetian archives relating to English history, lived there for fifty years and bought and restored the Palazzo Dario. He is not to be confused with Horatio R.F. Brown who succeeded him in the archival work and was known for his entertaining books about life in his adopted city.

11. Volume I published 1851, Vols II and III,1853.

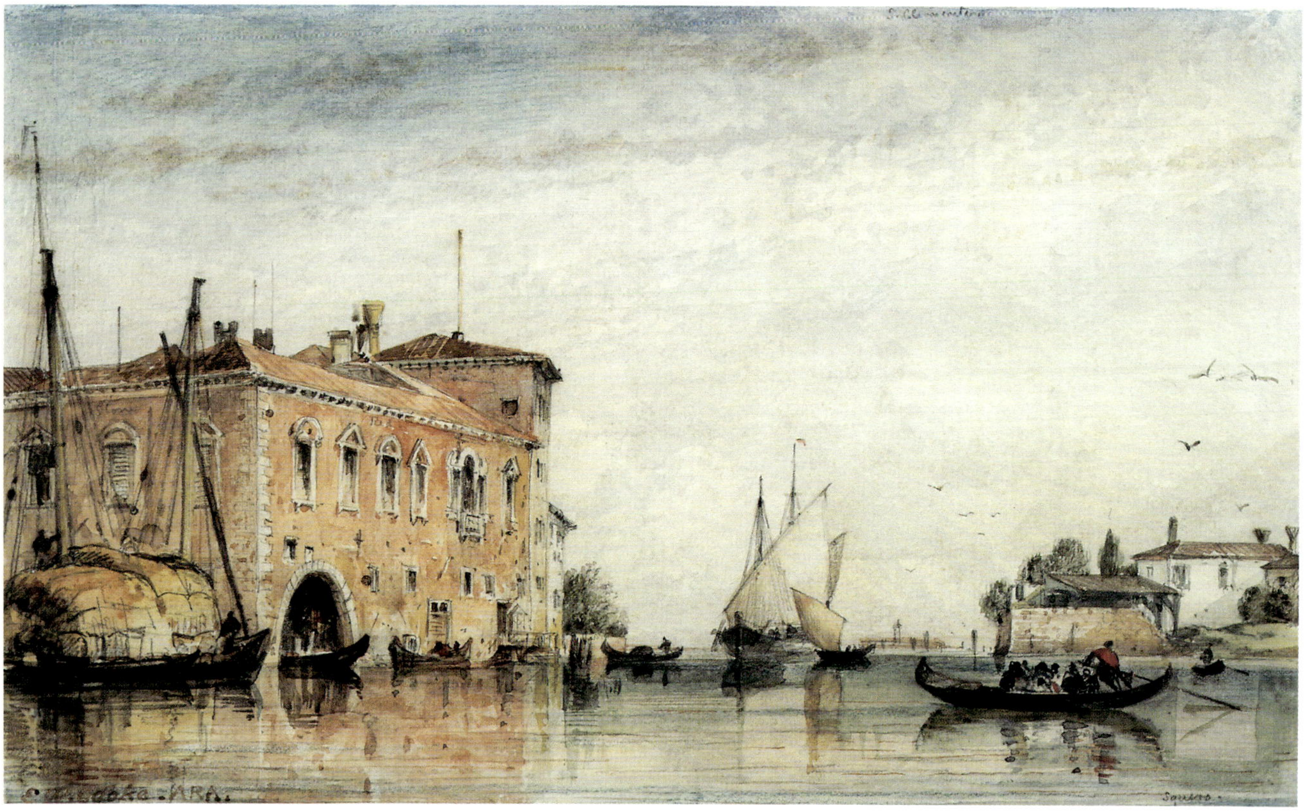

Colour Plate 103. Watercolour

Island of San.Giorgio Maggiore with San Clemente in the distance

A 'squèro' where gondolas were built and repaired is indicated at right. Photo courtesy Private Collection

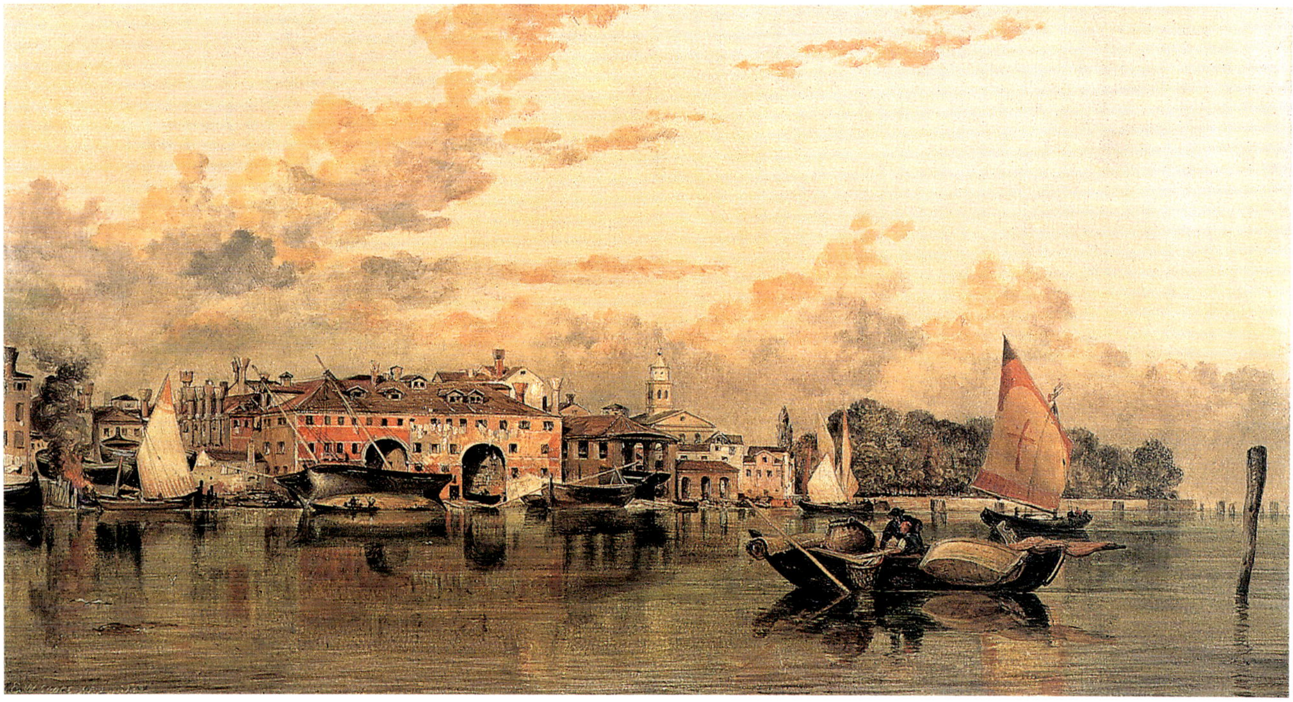

Colour Plate 104. 62/11

Venice, Squèro near the Ponte Veneta Marina, a vessel careening

A boat yard where the accumulation of weed etc. was being burnt off a hull; it had formed a subject for the painter in England, Jersey, France and elsewhere. Photo courtesy Private Collection

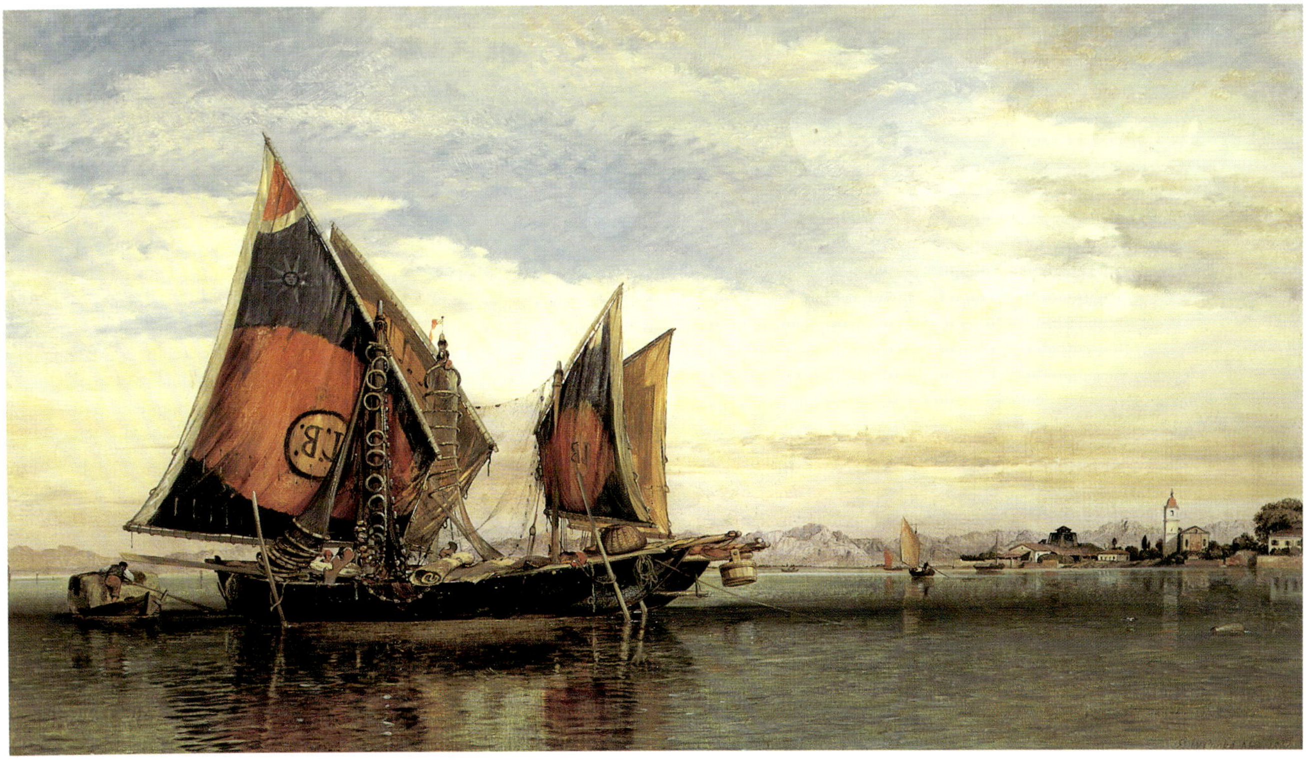

Colour Plate 105. 57/10
Two topi near Murano
Cooke noted in October 1857 painting on the rich coloured sails.The clear autumn air revealing the splendid distancȩ was one reason for his continued visiting at that time of year.
Photo courtesy Private Collection

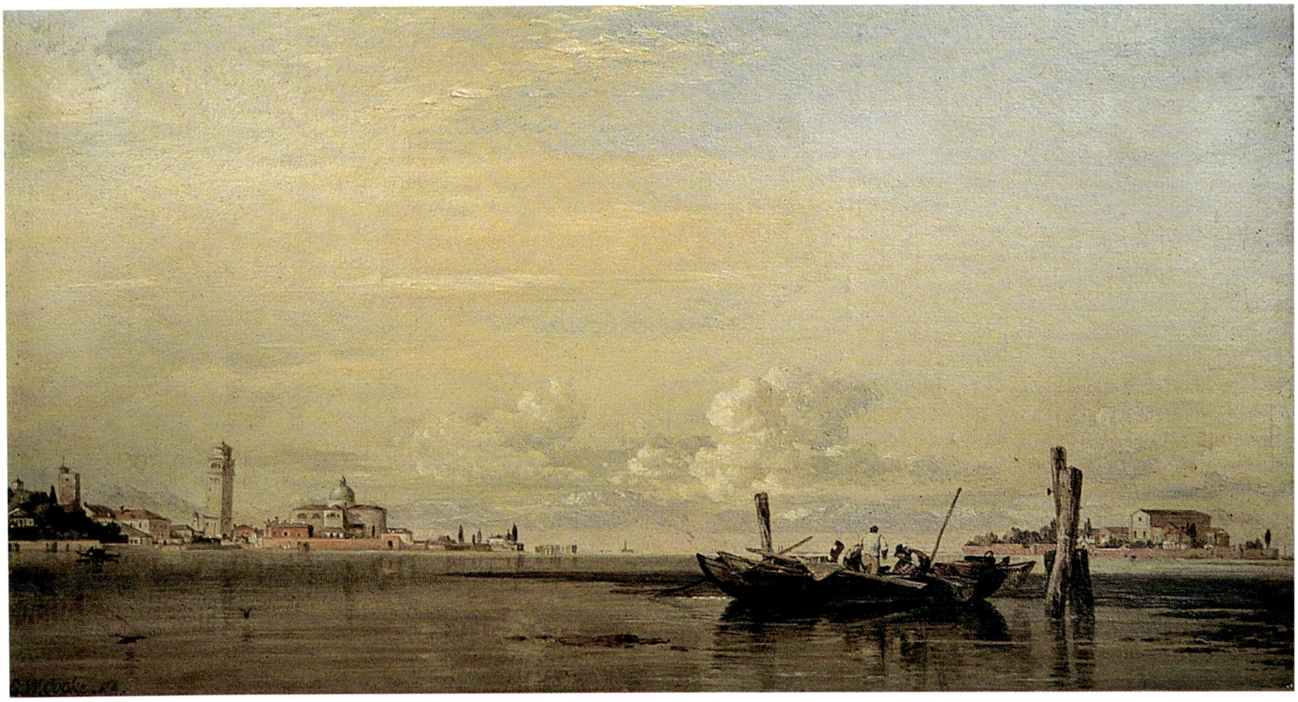

Colour Plate 106. 67/6
On the Lagune of Venice, evening before bad weather
The small tranquil picture reveals distant snow-capped mountains, the Julian Alps. It belonged to his friend, the great gardener Harry Veitch. Photo courtesy Agnews. Private Collection

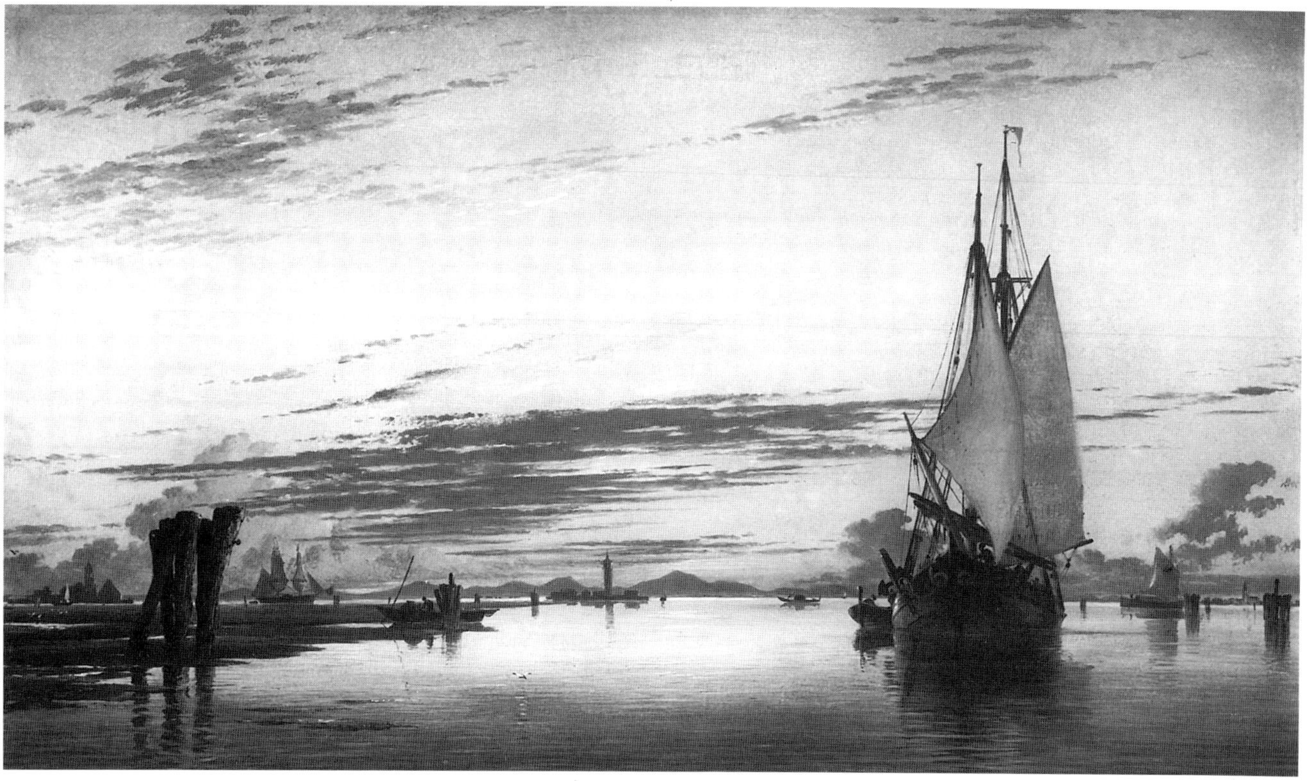

Plate 127. 63/16

The Euganean Hills & the Lagune of Venice – Trabaccolo waiting for the tide, sunset

A faint inscription on the stretcher has enabled this, the painter's original title, to be preserved.

Photo courtesy Martyn Gregory

The hire of a gondola for his stay was essential and the same gondolier, Vincenzo Grilla, was to serve Cooke faithfully through all his Venetian visits. It was necessary to be completely mobile in order to select a satisfactory marine view, one without too much of the familiar skyline from too familiar an angle. Cooke, anxious to produce his own Venice, was able to anchor among the shipping, to paint and return on subsequent occasions having taken appropriate bearings. Seasickness was a distinct possibility in such a floating studio and occasionally some mishap occurred like a foul anchor, which had to be buoyed, slipped and recovered later.

On more than one occasion it has been remarked that a Venetian view by Cooke must be a *capriccio* on account of an unusual spread of familiar landmarks. However in all cases it is possible to fix his position by reference to those marks, and to find the exact stretch of water in which he anchored! One may be permitted to observe that there was very little caprice about Mr Cooke.

The *felze* or cabin top of the gondola, which is not often seen today, could be unshipped in fine weather, but it was a trifle low for comfortable painting and later in 1852 Cooke arranged to have Vincenzo's *felze* raised by 12in. (30.5cm) to allow more room for his operations. Whether this affected the gondola's performance is not recorded, but the artist also designed some additional nautical carvings further to beautify his personal boat. Since he records that the work was undertaken by Fassi, at one of the well-known gondola yards or *squèri*, all was doubtless entirely satisfactory.

The locations in which the various types of craft congregated and could best be seen at work, loading or unloading, repairing, drying nets and sails or awaiting the tide, soon became known to him and their pictorial possibilities fully explored. The Giardini Pubblici or Park, with terrace and steps, was a good vantage point, but he was more often to be found afloat, just offshore.

At the entrance to the Grand Canal the Bacino di San Marco, central anchorage and roadstead backed by the Ducal Palace and the great campanile and bordered by the Molo and the Riva degli Schiavone, had long been 'centre stage'. Opposite, the Dogana di

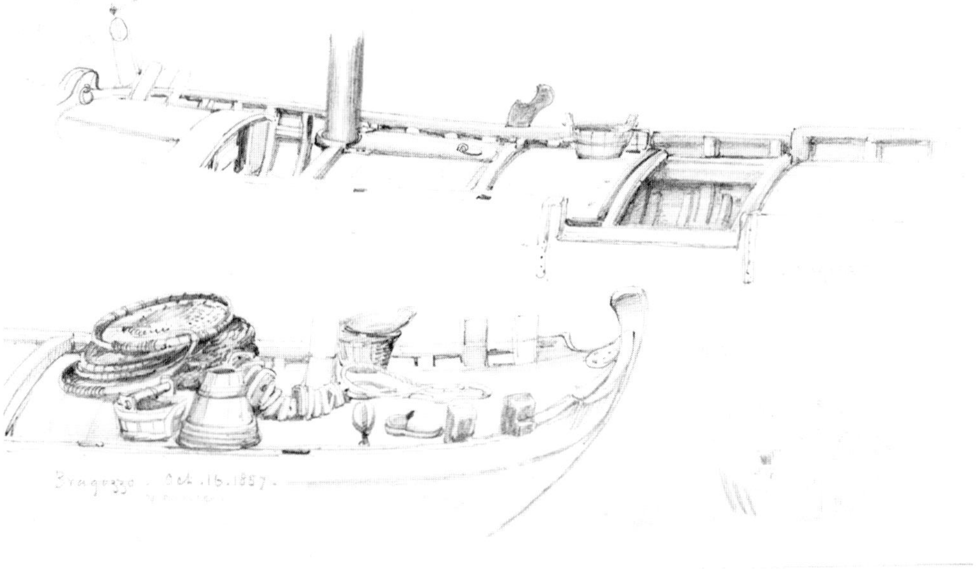

Plate 128. Pencil drawing
Deck details of a bragozzo.1857
Photo courtesy The Trustees of the National Maritime Museum, Greenwich

Mare, the customs house and the great baroque church of Sta Maria della Salute were two more essential ingredients while beyond them San Giorgio Maggiore on its island completed a famous and unique scene.

By 1850 there were already considerable photographic records, daguerrotypes and calotypes of the architectural wonders, but artists of every degree and nationality continued to flock there, intent on sampling these wonders and carrying off their own impressions.

The various bridges going eastwards along the Riva, like the Ponte Ca' di Dio and Ponte della Veneta Marina, where the sailing craft were moored, afforded architectural accents. The lesser domes and spires showing above the waterside palaces were a useful feature permitting identification of the scene among the spinneys of masts and yards.

The boat-building and repair yard, the *squèro,* was marked as a scene of interesting activity, but in a city under foreign military rule it was wise to procure the necessary sketching permits, as he found out!

As one who from early years had been interested in rendering climatic 'effects' – even unusual varieties – he painted in Venice with a new palette. This eventually developed a tendency to the over-ripe in treating the spectacular evening skies and sunsets. In a letter to John Murray, the publisher, he explained that *...the Exhalations from the Palludi ascending to the cold stratum of air (in late Autumn) form the most exquisite cirrhous....*[12] The absence of industrial pollution, which nowadays robs landward Venetian views of their mountainous distance except after high winds have driven away the *smog,* meant that there were attractions in the later part of the year such as snow-capped peaks in the distant Julian Alps which provided Cooke with spectacular backgrounds.

Frequently he noted painting a succession of small sketches of a sky in a chosen view as twilight approached and deepened into night. These sky studies would have the land and water, domes, spires, boats and fishermen painted in at a later sitting.

It is intriguing to find the painter being shown off to distinguished visitors by the resident Rawdon Brown, and Cooke was of course delighted to display his work.

A new set of sea-terms, learnt from his gondolier tutor, was entering his vocabulary. *Bragozzo, Ruscono* and *Trabaccolo, Topo* which means 'mouse' and *Brichepala* which in English would be called a hermaphrodite brig, these now became part of his picture titles.

Sometimes, with an interesting group of boats, the background was of little consequence. His more general views often had a note of the principal buildings in the sub-title for he was conscious that his pictures were in the tradition of the *vedutisti* painters of views which could be carried home to serve as colourful reminders of the

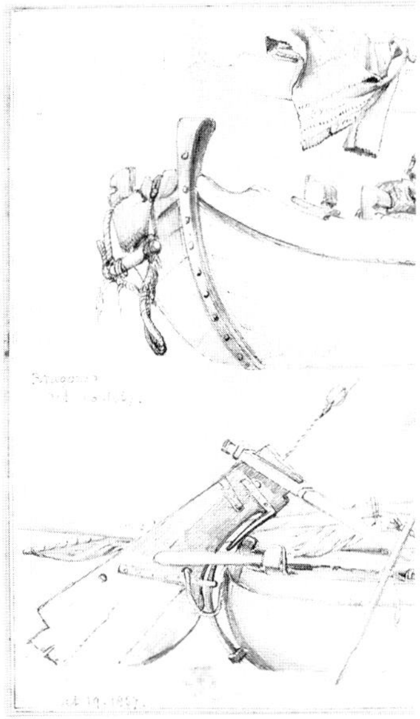

Plate 129. Pencil drawing
Bow & stern of a bragozzo 1857
Photo courtesy The Trustees of the National Maritime Museum, Greenwich

12. John Murray Archives.

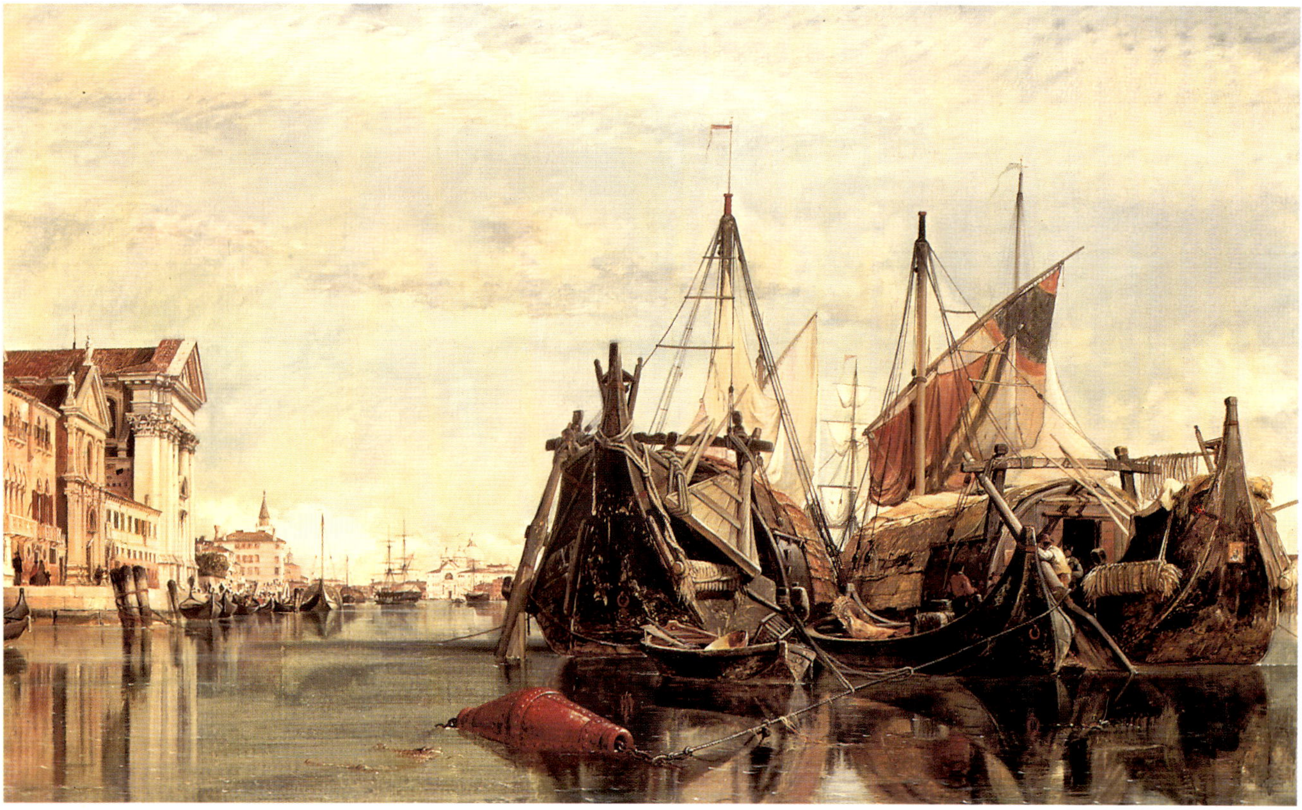

Colour Plate 107. 58/25

Rusconi off the Riva delle Zattere, Venice

Lumbering cargo carriers of strange design were as much to Cooke's taste as were the gaudy fishing craft of the region. Photo courtesy Sotheby's. Private Collection

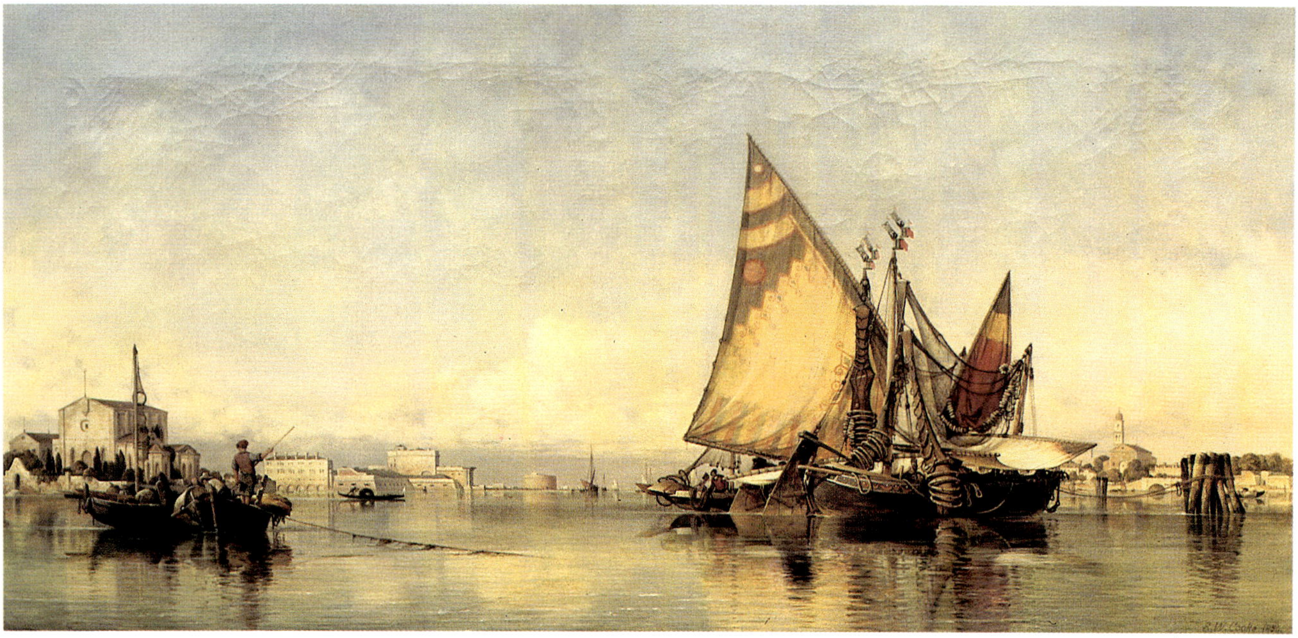

Colour Plate 108. 54/8

Porto di Lido

Cooke painted more than one version of this picture of the gateway to the Venetian Lagoons as shown in his photo-portrait of 1857. Photo: courtesy Bury Art Gallery

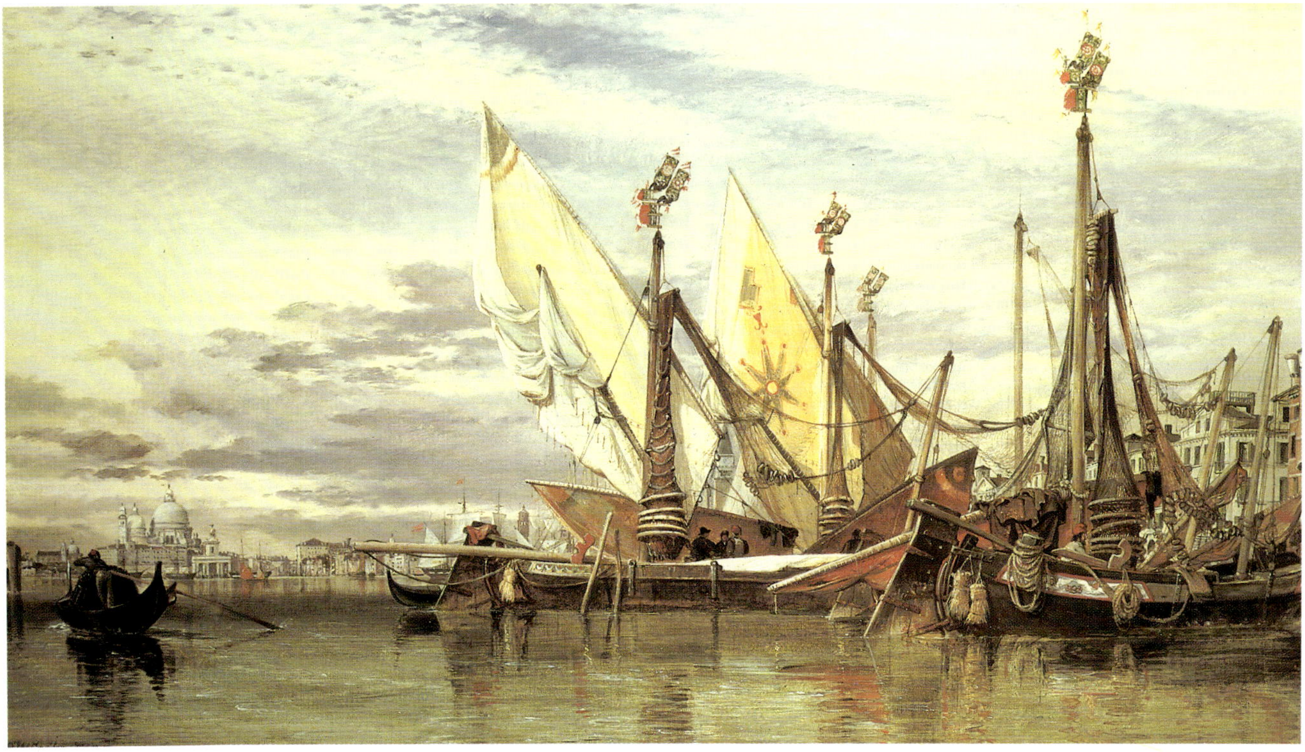

Colour Plate 109. 57/5

Bragozzi off the Riva degli Schiavone

Garlanded with their nets, their elaborate masthead vanes, the *penelo* or *pinella* (see page 165) being clearly shown, the careless group of bragozzi had come to typify Cooke's devotion to Venetian fishing boats. Photo courtesy Martyn Gregory. Private Collection

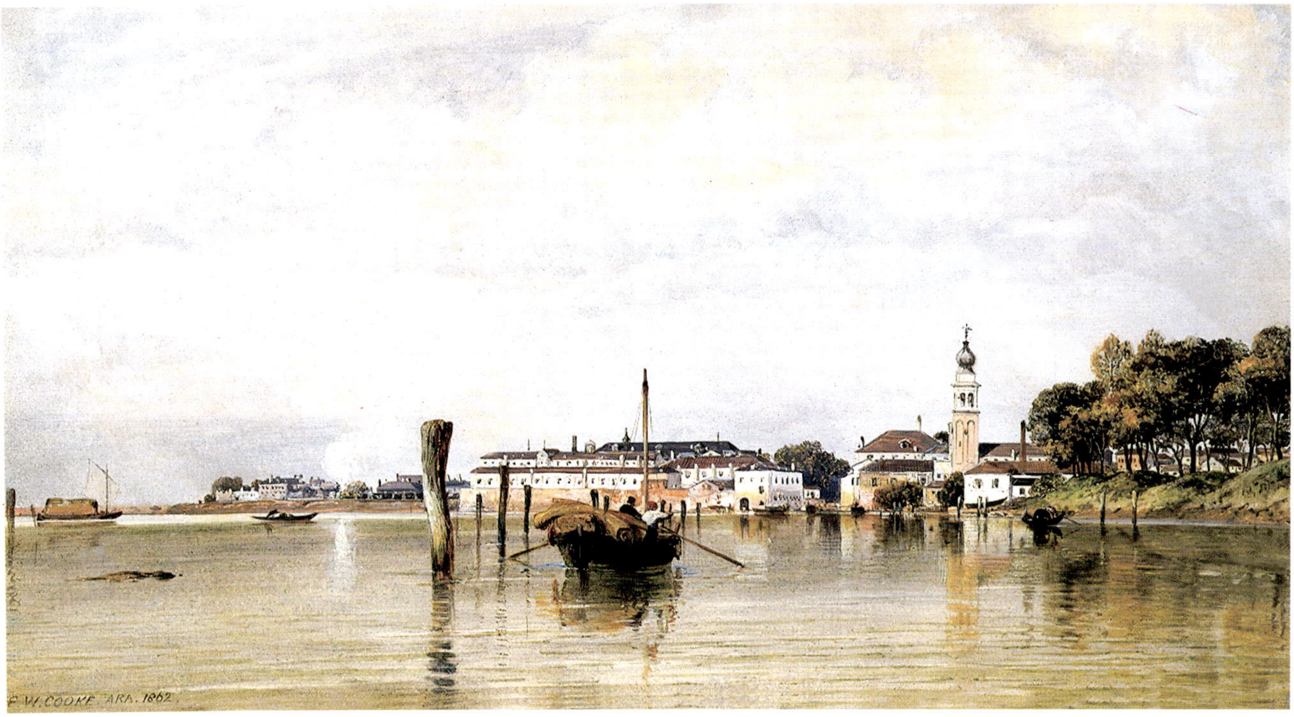

Colour Plate 110. 57/7

Church of the Armenian Convent on the Island of San Lazzaro

An exquisite moment captured in Cooke's gondola perambulations.

Photo courtesy Martyn Gregory. Private Collection

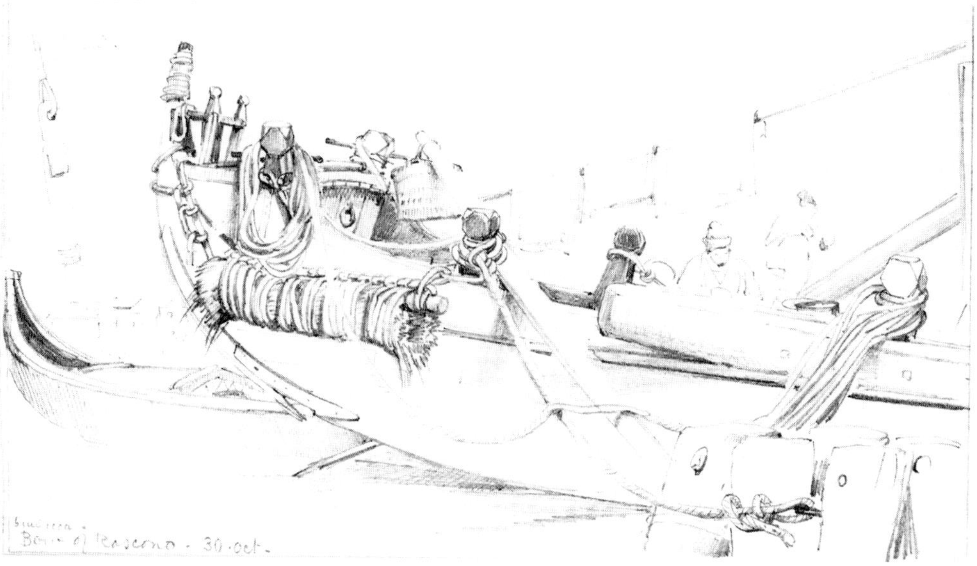

Plate 130. Pencil drawing
Bow of a Rascono 30th Oct.
Photo courtesy The Trustees of the National Maritime Museum, Greenwich

beauties of city, sky and lagoons. Venice's landmarks, and indeed her sea-marks, are her churches which permit, if their similarities can be disentangled, a clear identification of the viewpoint. The Riva delle Zattere on the Canale della Giudecca with its laden lighters, the clustered hulls in the Porto Franco beyond the Dogana di Mare, the *Porto di Lido* meaning in this instance the entrance from the outer sea, these became tried and popular subjects for pictures. The Canale della Giudecca, which lies east-west and so presents a daily sunset scene, was much frequented by the Cooke gondola. The islands of San Michaele and Murano between the city's northern quays, the Fondamente Nuove, and the distant shore, were set in fishing grounds. Further off were the islands of Torcello, Burano, Mazzorbo and San Francesco del Deserta, each a centre of particular interest, each with its church and bell tower.

He was careful to select lodgings with good views so that his operations with the graphic telescope were simplified. However, the age of photography having arrived, the production of calotypes of Venetian scenes by Carlo Ponti,[13] the first to establish a studio in Venice as early as 1852, was greeted by Cooke as a great blessing and he amassed a large collection of Ponti prints. His sale at Christie's ended with five lots of Venetian photographs, in batches of forty. Ruskin initially used daguerrotypes as the base for illustrations to his *Seven Lamps...* and other works and was considering using calotypes for illustrations to *The Stones of Venice,* but found a lack of detail in the shadows.[14] Philip Hamerton thought that the photograph's *literalness and incapacity for selection and emphasis are antagonistic to the artistic spirit.*[15]

Artists could joke about the 'foe-to-graphic' art, the famous quip which seems to have originated with Charles Landseer, an old friend of Cooke's and of whom W.P. Frith said

13. *Vedute e Dettagli...* University of Michigan, Museum of Art, 1992.
14. *Art & Photography,* Aaron Scharf, 1968, p.721.
15. Hamerton, *Thoughts about Art,* 1889, p.64.

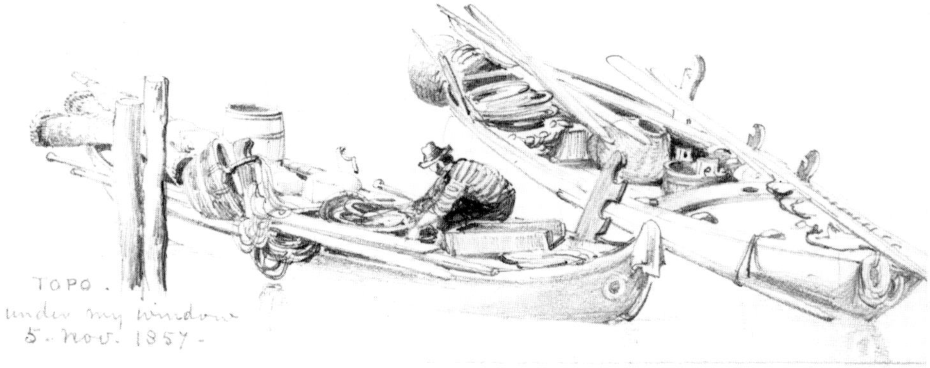

Plate 131. Pencil drawing
Topi, seen from the window, 1857
Photo courtesy The Trustees of the National Maritime Museum, Greenwich

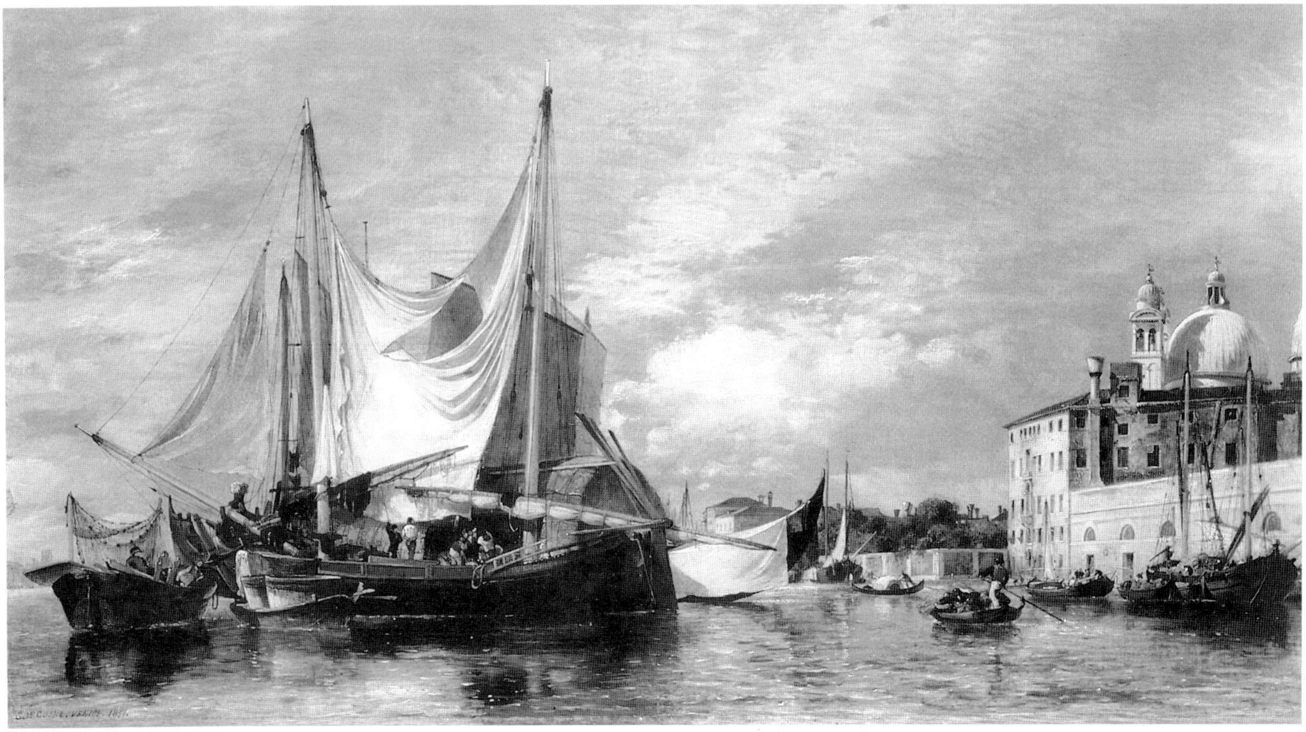

Plate 132. 50/14

Trabaccolo unloading into a Rascono

Painted in the Porto Franco, on the Giudecca Canal behind the Dogana di Mare. and furnished with a variety of craft. 'Il Lagunetto' is painted on the trabaccolo. Photo courtesy Christie's

that he made better puns than pictures,[16] while the picture dealer Louis Victor Flatow, astute but illiterate, spoke of the 'fogey-trapper'![17] According to family tradition Cooke used to refer to the 'fauxtographic' but he nevertheless recognised its utility as a time-saving reference for architectural detail.

He drew with his accustomed insight all the details of the different craft, their construction, the fitting of rudders, masts and yards, the rigging and sails, fittings, equipment, fishing nets and all the working gear needed to paint their portraits (Plates 128 to 131). He had little need of photographic aids for shipping and small craft although his use of the *camera lucida* continued.

A lengthy note in his hand describing the *bragozzo's* elaborate masthead wind-vane demonstrates his enquiring approach to detail:

Pinella or Vane of a Bragozzo or Fishing Craft of Venice

These curious ornaments are carved by the fishermen of Chioggia near Venice, they are invariably of the same general form although they may vary in detail. They represent the Emblems of the Passion of our Lord and date from the period of the Holy Wars when the Venetian Galleys joined the 3rd Crusade. These vessels returned with their Sails, Boats etc covered with the Armorials of the Holy Land, which have been handed down with religious scrupulosity to the present time. Hope is standing on the rostrum of a vessel [her feet on an anchor] as guiding the ship of the Church. The lower portion which hangs on the spindle of the mast is in two parts – in the upper part the cross is the principal object, it has the label for the superscription and the circle representing the universality of Christianity – The Spear – Sponge – Ladder – Lantern – Hammer – Nails – Dice – the Cock – the Coat and the Volto Santo or handkerchief of St Veronica. The Lower Compartment represents Pilate and Herod in armour, each holding a palm of Peace, as having become friends & above and between them is the Roman Eagle. A cross and stars decorates the red banner, below is probably the star of Bethlehem. The small square compartment above contains Justice with her Scales and Sword trampling underfoot

16. W. P. Frith, *My Autobiography and Reminiscences*, Sixth Edn; 1888, p. 142.
17. Ibid, p.142.

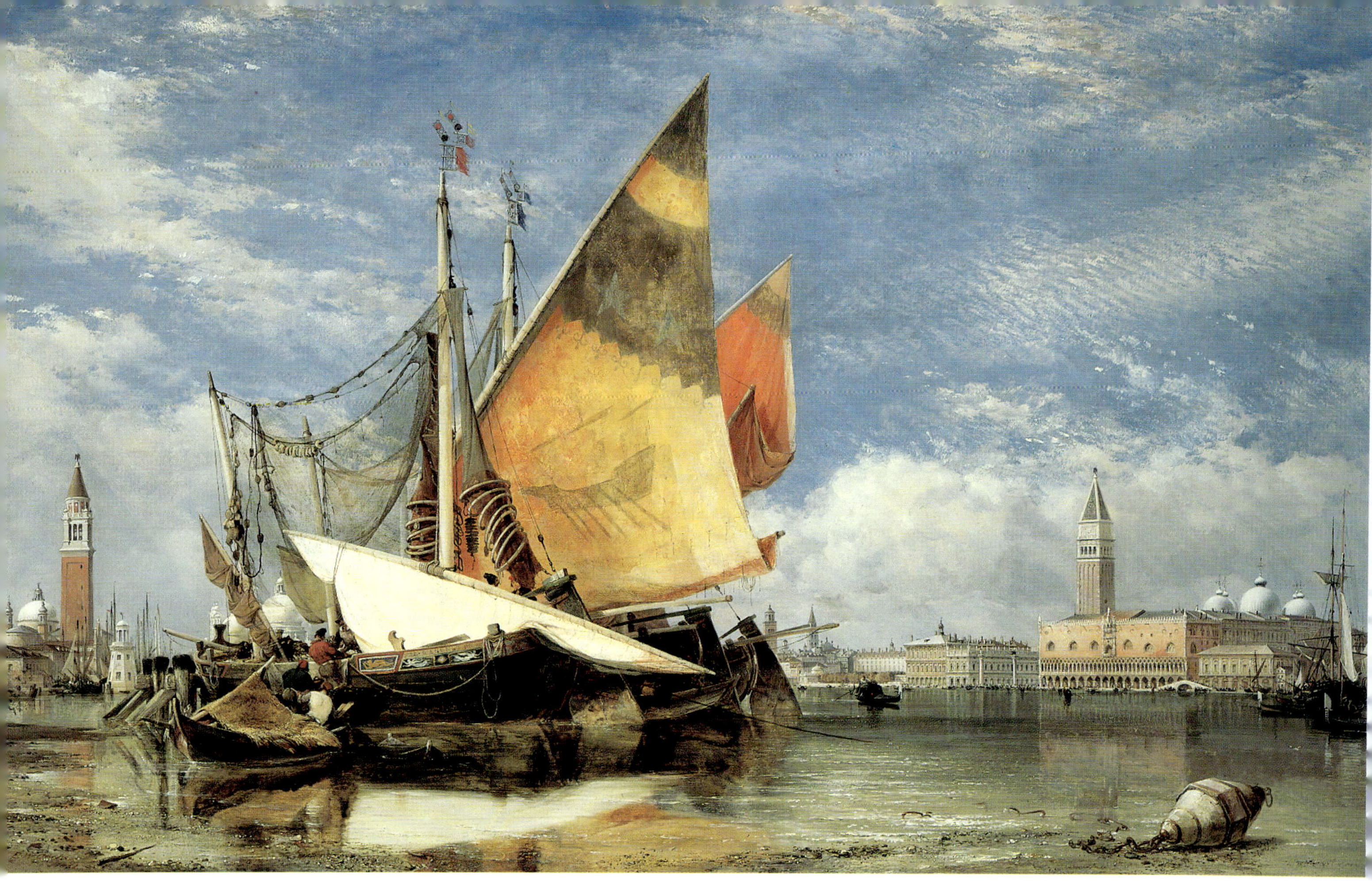

Colour Plate 111. 51/2
Bragozzi, the fishing craft of Venice
Waterborne splendour in the contemporary scene: Cooke records the glories of the local type in this monumental group, the painted sails denoting ownership.
Photo courtesy Richard Green.Fine Paintings. Private Collection

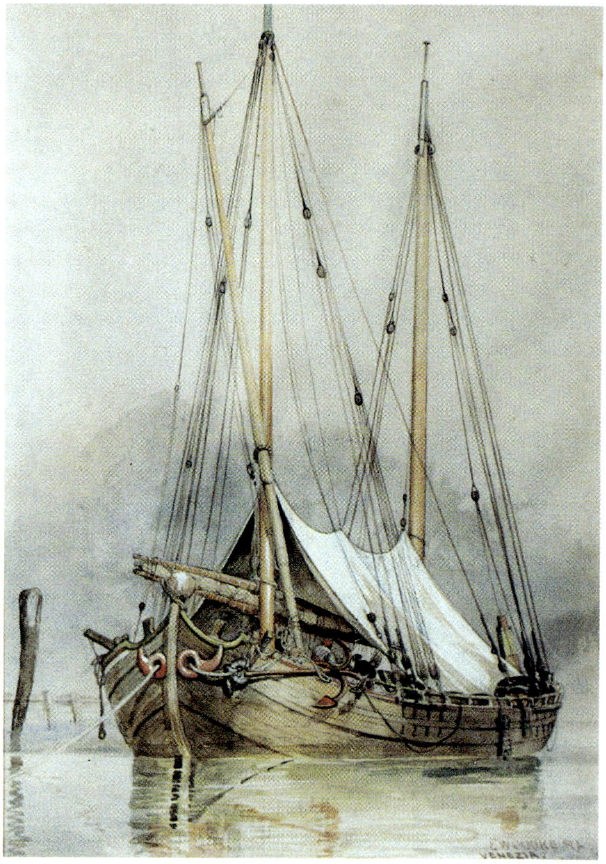

Colour Plate 113. Watercolour
Trabaccolo
A careful portrait of the Adriatic craft which would doubtless stand him in good stead.
Photo courtesy Private Collection

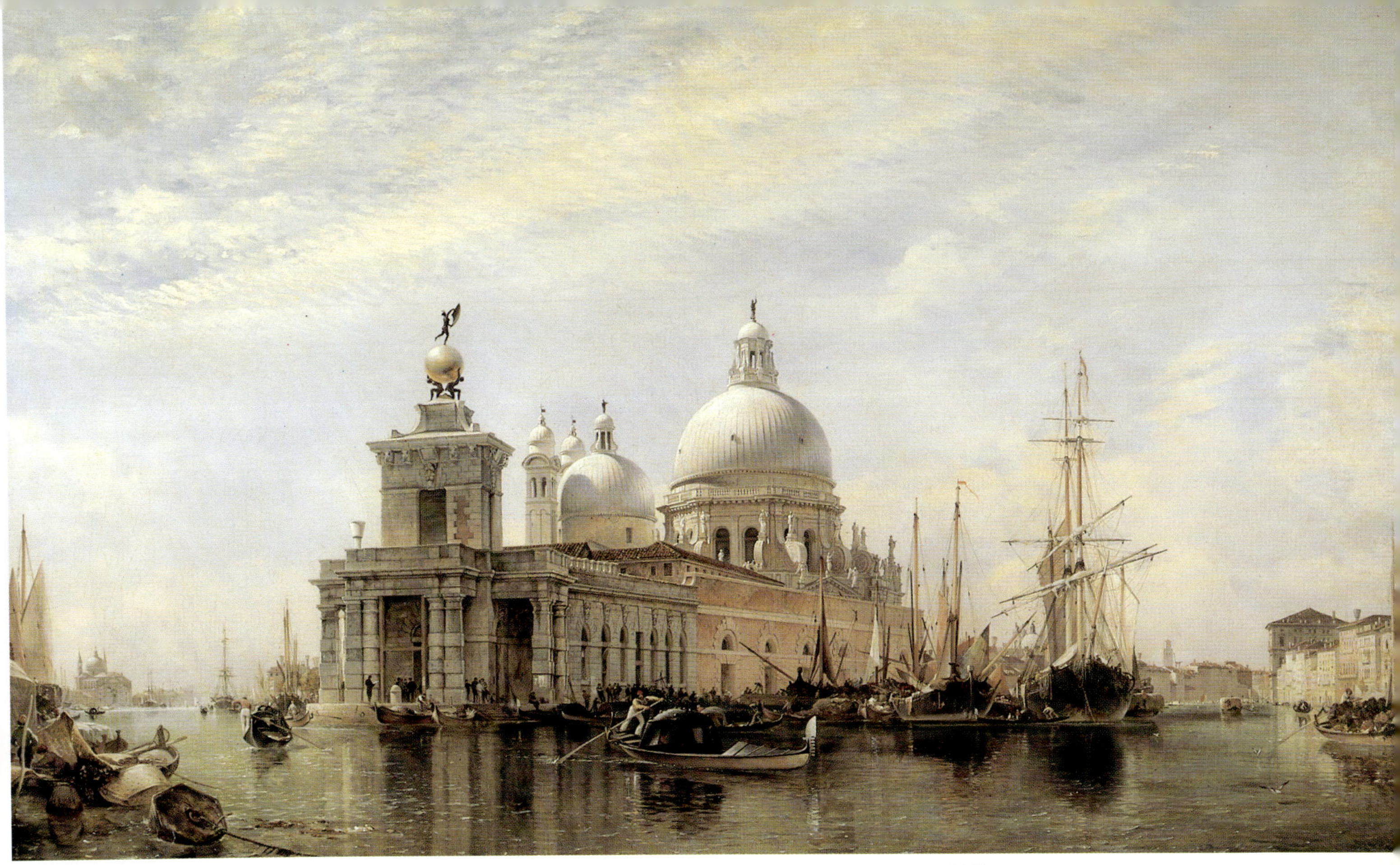

Colour Plate 112. 51/3

The Church of the Salute, the Dogana etc.

There is a magical quality about this realisation of a view which most visiting painters sample. The artist chose this as a representative illustration for his *Art Journal* biography in 1869 and it was reproduced resoundingly for the 1857 Art Treasures Exhibition in Manchester. It had a narrow escape from destruction in the Second World War. Photo courtesy Martyn Gregory. Royal Ocean Racing Club Collection

Colour Plate 114. 50/28

On the Lagune opposite Venice, San Servolo & the Armenian convent in the distance, evening, low water

The craft it is that dominate the distant landmarks. For the inscription discovered on the stretcher see page 168 and Catalogue page 345. Photo courtesy Polak Gallery. Private Collection

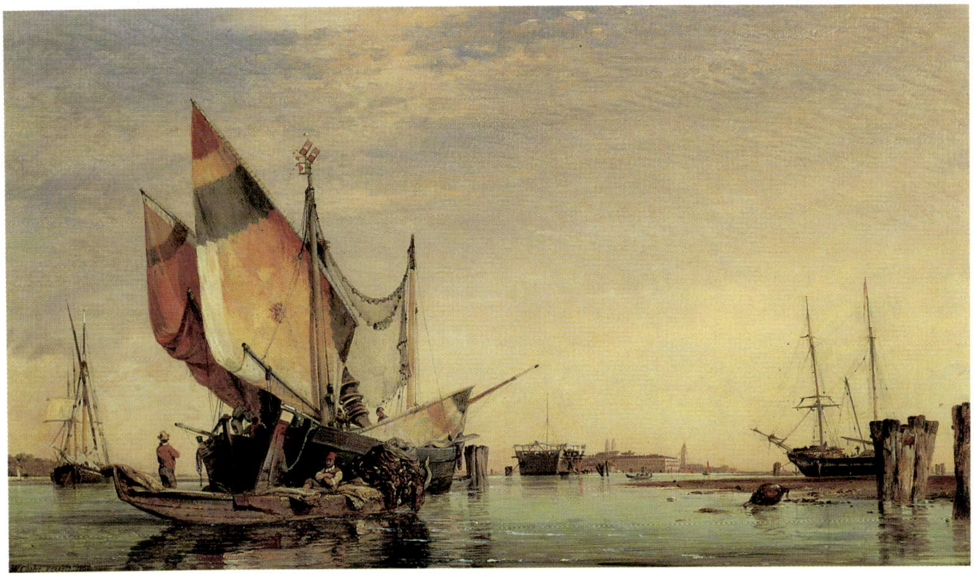

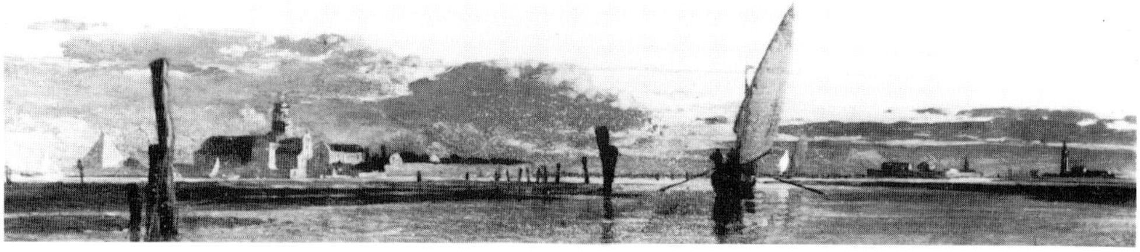

Plate 133. 50/16
Sunset San Clemente after stormy day. Inscribed *Il Lagunetto.*
This vibrant little sketch was a gift to the wife of a friend. Photo courtesy Sotheby's

the horned Demon of Sin. The two parts which point to the wind contain the earliest known carved representation of the Wheel within Wheel of Ezekiel – emblematic of the old and new Covenants, the centre being the Sun of Righteousness its rays extending to the second wheel which is the same but more comprehensive as the Gospel & absorbing the lesser wheel – these are each supported by ring doves with extended wings – here Justice is represented as pursuing the Evil One – above each are crosses with the Archangels wielding their swords & blowing the trumpets. Small pennons are attached in every direction wherever they could be introduced. The whole has a very striking & singular effect.

The harvest of his industrious first visit of twelve weeks, the number of oil paintings, sketches and studies totalled some two dozen. It is not possible to estimate the number of pencil sketches which he produced but many, of varying elaboration, have survived from this and later visits.

Watercolour studies he also recorded having made, but comparatively few have been found. His Academy pictures of 1851, the first fruits of his Venetian experience, were *Bragozzi, the Fishing Craft of Venice* (Colour Plate 111) and *The Church of the Salute, the Dogana &c* (Colour Plate 112). Canvases were rolled for transit and re-stretched on arrival home while the sketches on oil paper were lined by Brown of High Holborn. Cooke enlarged by means of the *camera lucida* – which permitted reduction as well – his sketch of the church of the Salute for the Academy picture.

Some of this first crop of Venetian pictures can be seen to have the added inscription *Il Lagunetto* appearing as a name on the gunwale of a small boat or on the side of larger craft (Plates 132 and 133). In one instance it is painted as an inscription on an awning and in another it is simply beside his signature. Since he had a liking for putting a personal reminder on his vessels, as with *Van Kook* in his Dutch subjects, it appears that he now adopted a Venetian sobriquet. Presumptuous though this may appear, the name seems to be a direct imitation of Giovanni Antonio Canale's *Canaletto.* It demonstrates his determination to make his work remarkable among the vast quantity produced by so many other painters; most looked inwards, hardly venturing beyond the Bacino and Grand Canal, but Edward Cooke was continually looking out across the lagoons. Confirmation of his deliberate use of the nickname has been provided by a painting which passed through the salerooms in 1992, *On the Lagune opposite Venice, San Servolo & the Armenian Convent in the distance. Evening, low water* (50/28, Colour Plate 114). The artist's inscription on the stretcher includes *by E.W.Cooke detto Il Lagunetto*, 'detto' meaning 'called', in this case self-styled!

Chapter 10

EDWARD COOKE AND JOHN RUSKIN

His second Venetian tour in 1851 was also industrious and full of interest while his diary account is amplified by the letters of John and Effie Ruskin who were also there.

It was an occupied city with a strong military presence and the young Emperor of Austria, Franz-Josef I, came to inspect his forces; the feelings of the native Venetians can well be imagined, but there were now many foreign visitors for the tourist trade. Cooke arrived towards the end of August, picking up the threads at once, seeking out Rawdon Brown at the Frari Archives and engaging Vincenzo the gondolier.

Strolling on the Piazza he could meet friends and contacts like Edward Cheney and his nephew Capel Cure, the Turner collector B.G. Windus and his daughter and Mr Francis Barchard of Putney Heath, a friend of William Wells' who evidently owned 'Canaletti' and built Horsted Place in Sussex, 1851-52. Italian lessons from a Mr Merryweather were begun and for an exercise the artist noted that he gave his master a lecture in botany in Italian! The diary records a restless round of activity; making time to read Ruskin's latest pamphlet, *Pre-Raphaelitism,* lent him by Effie, meant perhaps that he was unable to spare a moment to record a verdict. Did the author's views find approval only – it would have been interesting to know whether Cooke echoed Ruskin's prefatory exhortation (quoting his own *Modern Painters*): *...go to nature... having no other thought than how best to penetrate her meaning; rejecting nothing, selecting nothing, and scorning nothing.*

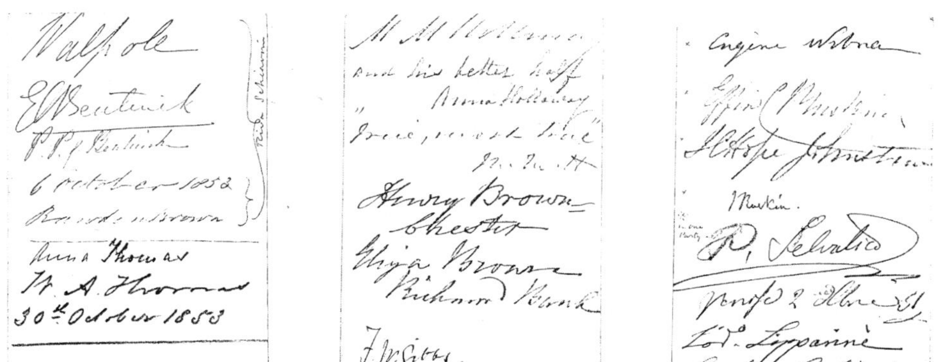

Plate 134. Collection C.R. Cooke, OBE

Visitors to Venice; signatures from the artist's autograph book

In 1851 Cooke recorded the visits of John Ruskin and his wife with Mr Hope Johnstone and General Count Eugene Wrbna, ADC to the Austrian Emperor, to view his pictures. Dott. Selvatico of the Accademia, Prof Lipparini, Sig. Carlini. also called. The 1853 names are noted by Cooke Riva Schiavone which presumably means that they signed his book 'on the march' as it were!

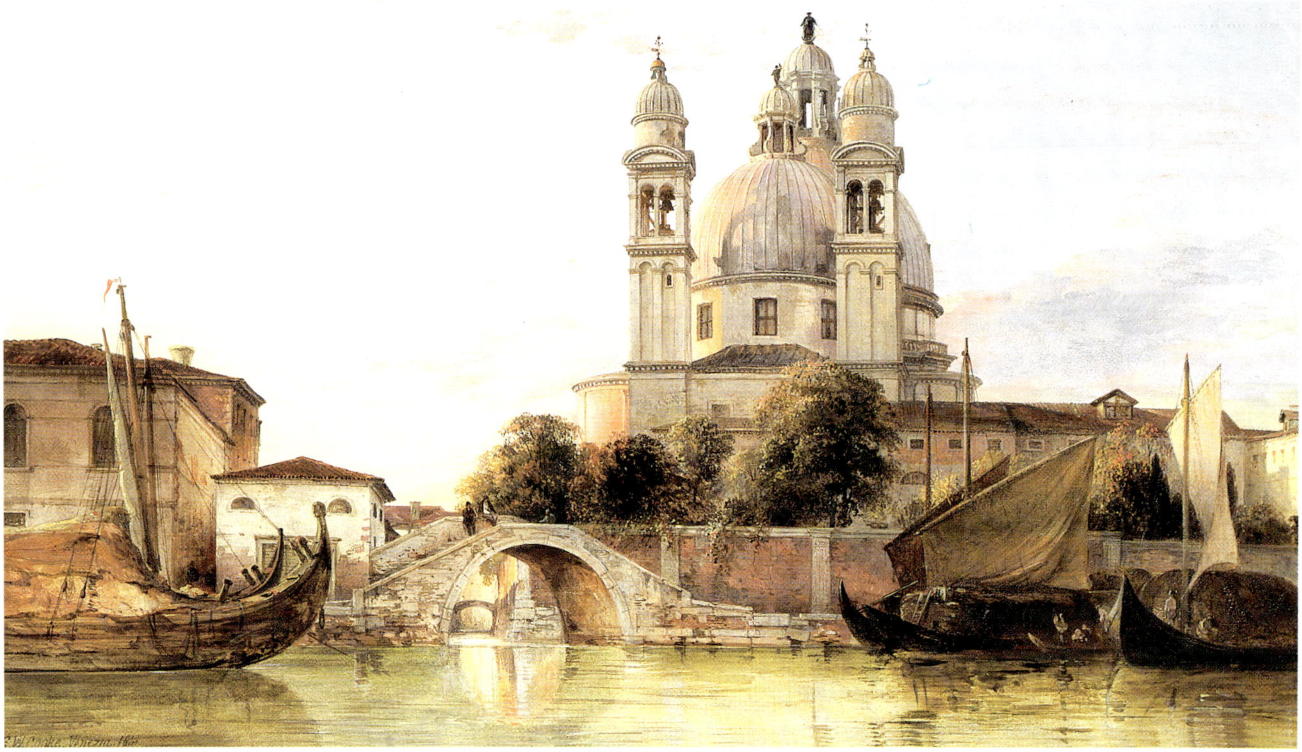

Colour Plate 115. 51/14

Santa Maria della Salute from the Canale della Giudecca

Most *vedutisti* approached Longhena's masterpiece from the Grand Canal but Cooke steered his gondola round to the back where working boats furnish his picture.

Photo courtesy Martyn Gregory. Private Collection

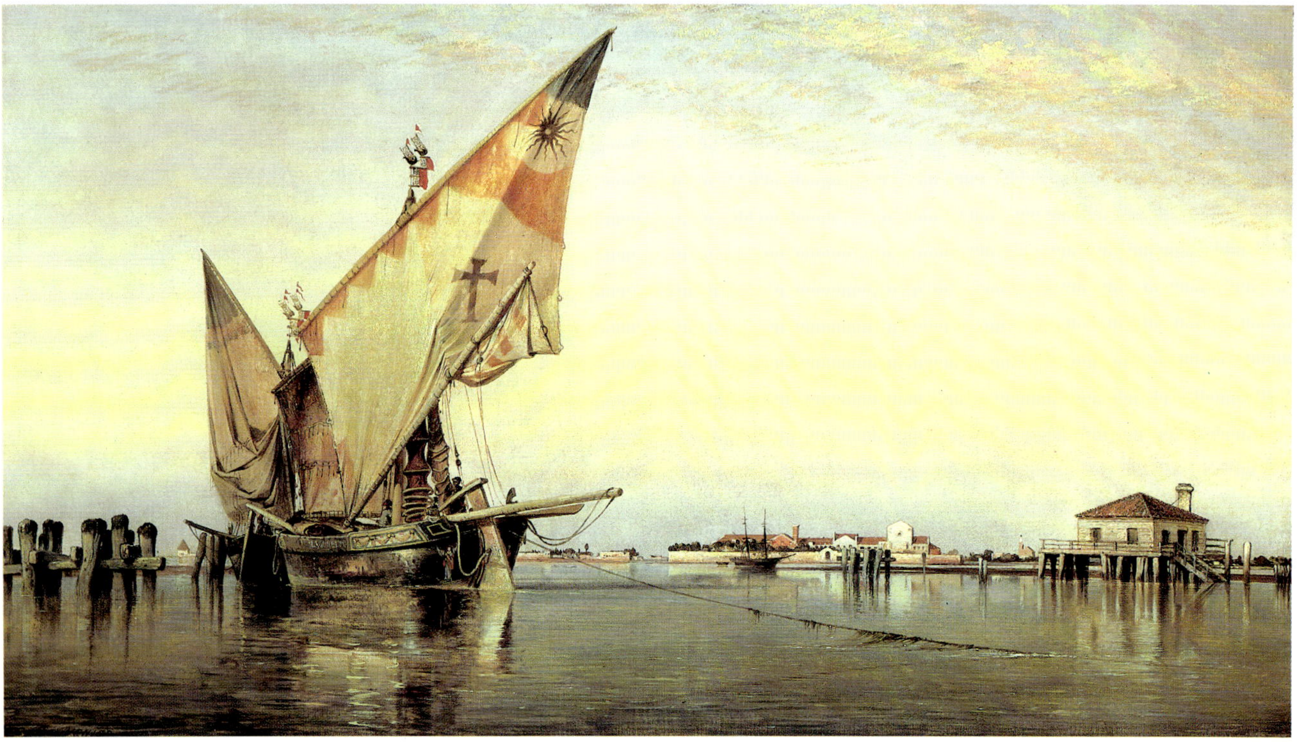

Colour Plate 116. 51/20

Sta Elena, Venice, just after sunset, looking East, waiting for the tide

Photo courtesy Arthur Ackermann & Peter Johnson Ltd. Private Collection

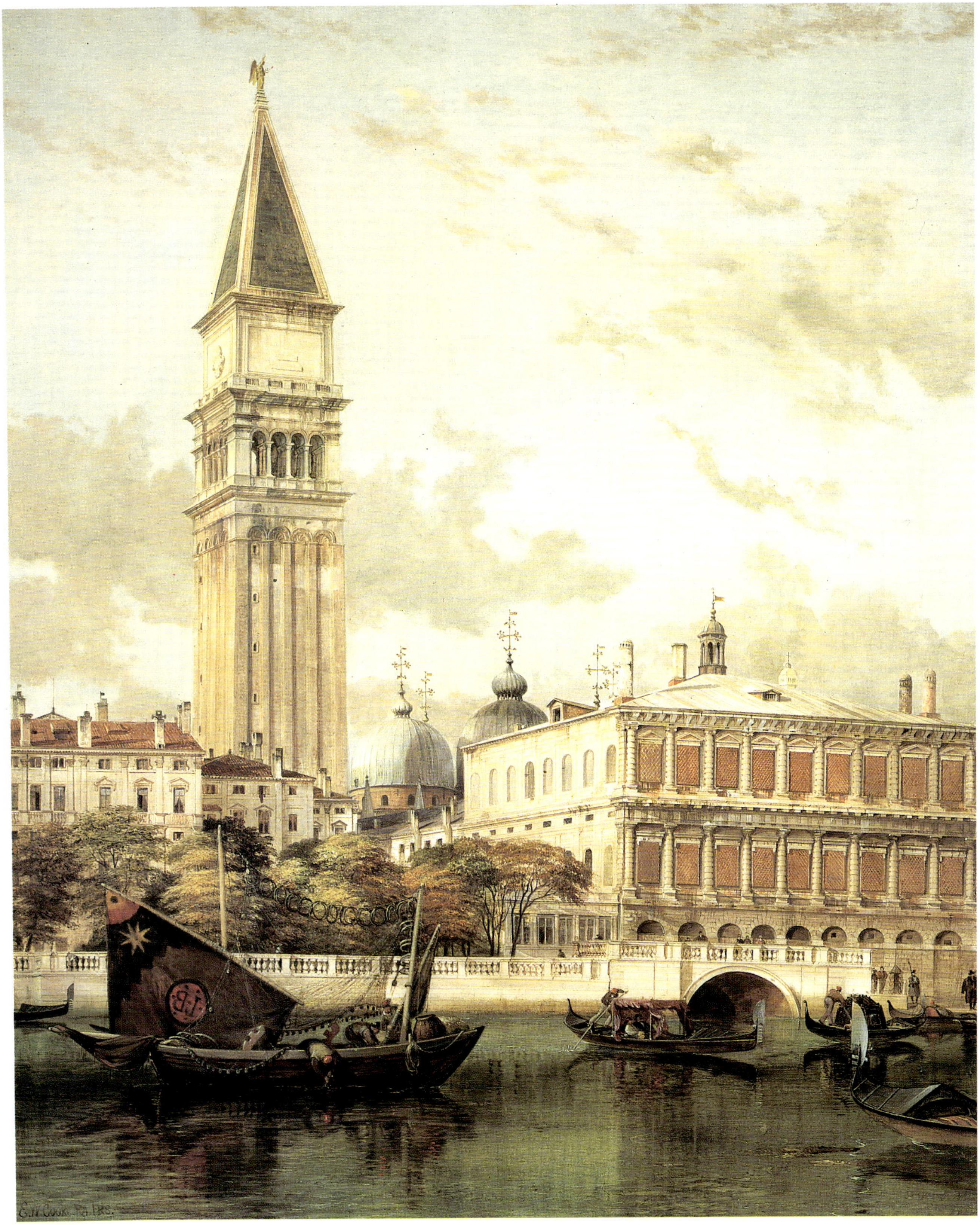

Colour Plate 117. 66/1

The Campanile, Zecca, part of San Marco and the Giardini Reale, Venice

One of a group of 'portrait' shape canvases portraying the central area, the Piazzetta and surrounding buildings. Photo: courtesy M.A. Appleby. Private Collection

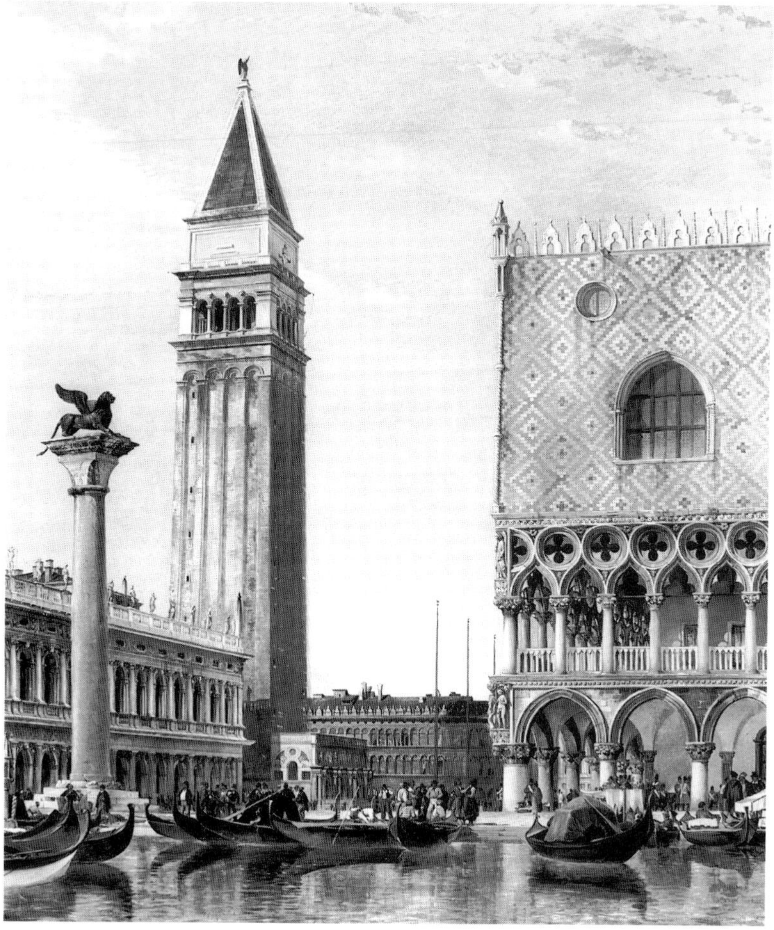

Plate 135. 51/24
The Piazzetta, Venice, with the Lion column
Photo courtesy City of Aberdeen Art Gallery & Museum Collection

The title-page gave it as *By the Author of "Modern Painters"* and being just published the preface was dated Denmark Hill August 1851. Its sixty-eight pages, more than half of which were in fact about that awesome figure Joseph Mallard [*sic*] William Turner with 'the eye of an eagle', contain Ruskin's current thoughts on artistic achievement and capacity. It was in Venice that the author later received the news of the death of Turner whom he called his 'earthly master'. Some of the theories put forward are interesting in view of Ruskin's recorded opinion of Cooke. 'Great' and 'small' people are contrasted – and the ease with which 'great' people accomplish great things – *no great intellectual thing was ever done by great effort.* Ruskin wrote *if a great thing can be done at all it can be done easily... without more trouble than it costs small people to do small things, nay, perhaps with less.*

There is an extraordinary digression on a painter's ideal mission – *the faithful representation of all objects of historical interest, or of natural beauty...* – down the ages, resulting in a vast corpus of documentation – *how content he would become, how earnest, how full of all accurate and noble knowledge....* Ruskin, advocating the value of archaeological recording, *...if every building destroyed in the French or any other subsequent revolution had thus been drawn in all its parts...,* must have had a fervent supporter in Edward Cooke whose systematic classifying of his sketches was to reach library proportions.

W.M. Rossetti wrote a complaint against Ruskin's pamphlet some years later, *an unfortunate and misleading phrase,* he called the remark about non-selection, which for an artist is *impossible... stupid and wrong.* The Pre-Raphaelites he wrote, aimed at reform in the *conception and calibre of subjects quite as much as a reform in the*

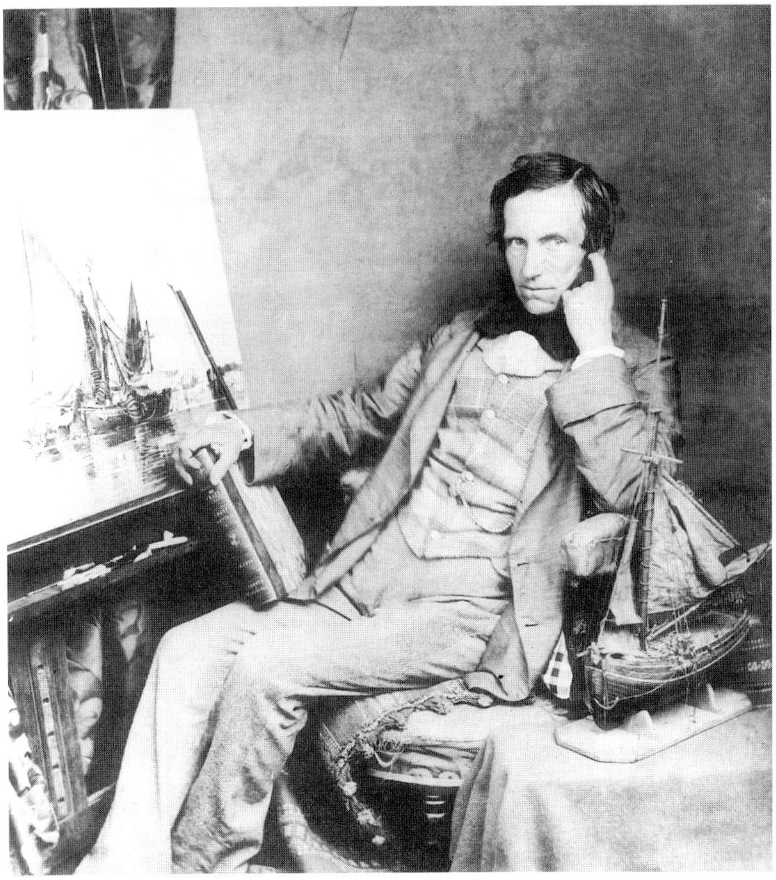

Plate 136.
E.W. Cooke ARA by W. Lake Price, 1857
Price, watercolourist and photographer, took a series of portraits of RAs which was published in 1859, but this one does not appear to have been included. Photo courtesy C.R. Cooke, OBE.

realizing representation of objects... the dullness and frivolity. with which the living men then in repute chose or treated... the sloppy, perfunctory and feelingless way in which they represented the appearances of nature....[1]

Edward Cooke's approach to his art seems to have been already on a course parallel to that adopted by the younger men whom Ruskin now rushed sweepingly to champion, but the *Art Journal* delivered the barbed comment *Much of it is sensible and judicious but it abounds with those singularities of thought and diction which have made the productions of this learned gentleman remarkable, and which, unquestionably, prevent his being an authority.*[2]

Ruskin's praise included Prout with his short sight and his on-the-spot recording of Continental ruins in the nick of time, and J.F. Lewis who had *done more justice to all his powers (and they are magnificent ones,) than any other man amongst us... The value... of his works, as records... is quite above all estimate.* Of William Mulready he wrote – *in delicacy and completion of drawing and splendour of colour, he takes place beside John Lewis and the pre-Raphaelites....*

This is significant as Mulready is indeed often spoken of as a precursor and Cooke was indebted to him for guidance and helpful criticism in his early years as a member of Sheepshanks' circle.

Intensity of observation, the search for the essential character – if that was a Pre-Raphaelite pre-requisite – was evident in Cooke's every mark of pencil and stroke of brush. It was in the choice of subject matter that they differed. On the human side Cooke illustrated labour and the laborious – working fishermen and their boats. His attention at the same time to various branches of natural history proclaim him a polymath typical of

1. *Ruskin, the Critical Heritage,* ed. J.L. Bradley, 1984, p.326.
2. *Art Journal,* 1855, p.219

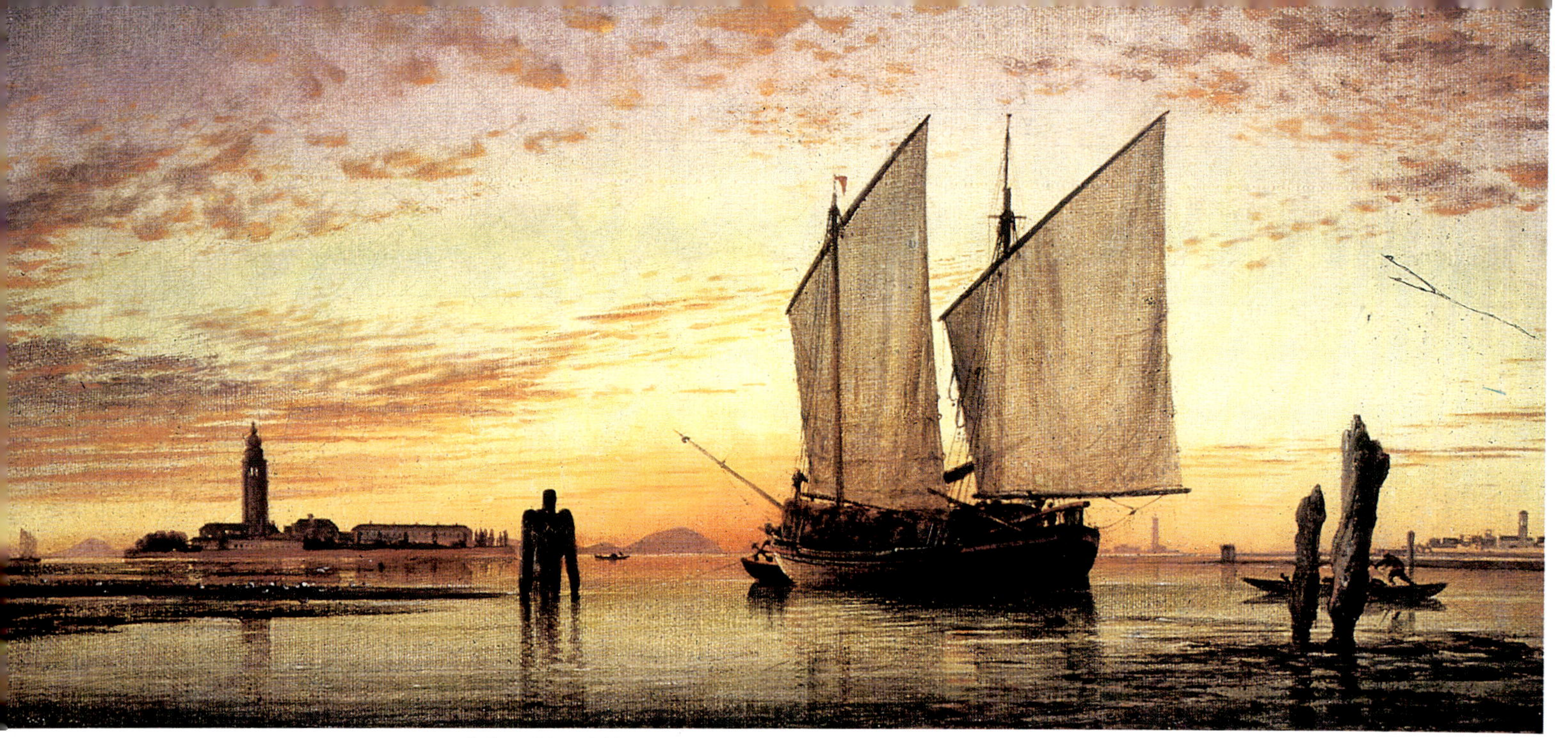

Colour Plate 118. 62/24

Trabaccolo waiting for the tide off the Armenian Convent, Lagune of Venice, Sunset

The Armenian friars were a friendly community, their campanile with its onion dome was a little exotic and their island abounded in the picturesque. It also gave interesting views of the main islands. Photo courtesy Arthur Ackermann & Peter Johnson Ltd

Colour Plate 120 (above right). 62/20

Venice, sunset after rain

The precise location is not known but it could be nowhere else but the Lagune and his painting of the entrancing distance and luminous air is masterly. Photo courtesy Private Collection

Colour Plate 119. 57/11

Sunset on the Lagune of Venice, S. Giorgio in Alga & the Euganean Hills in the distance

Photo courtesy Sotheby's

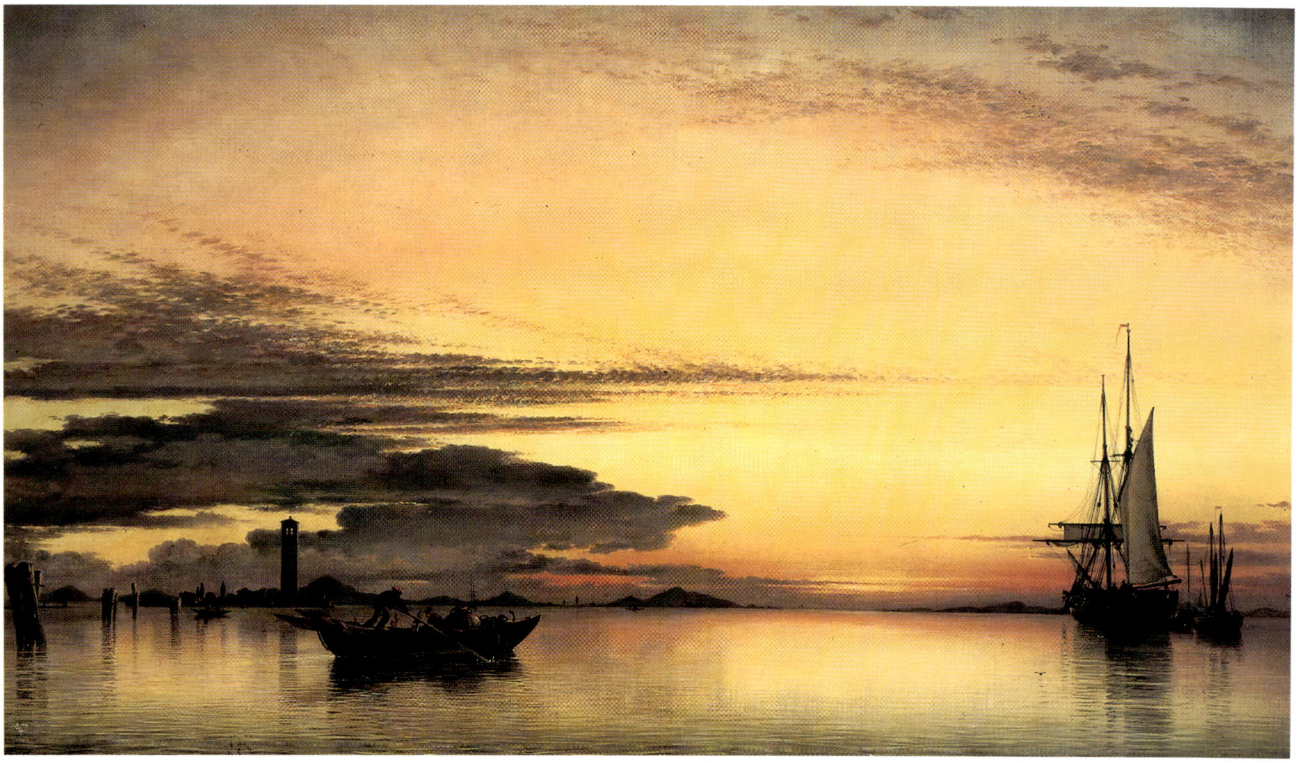

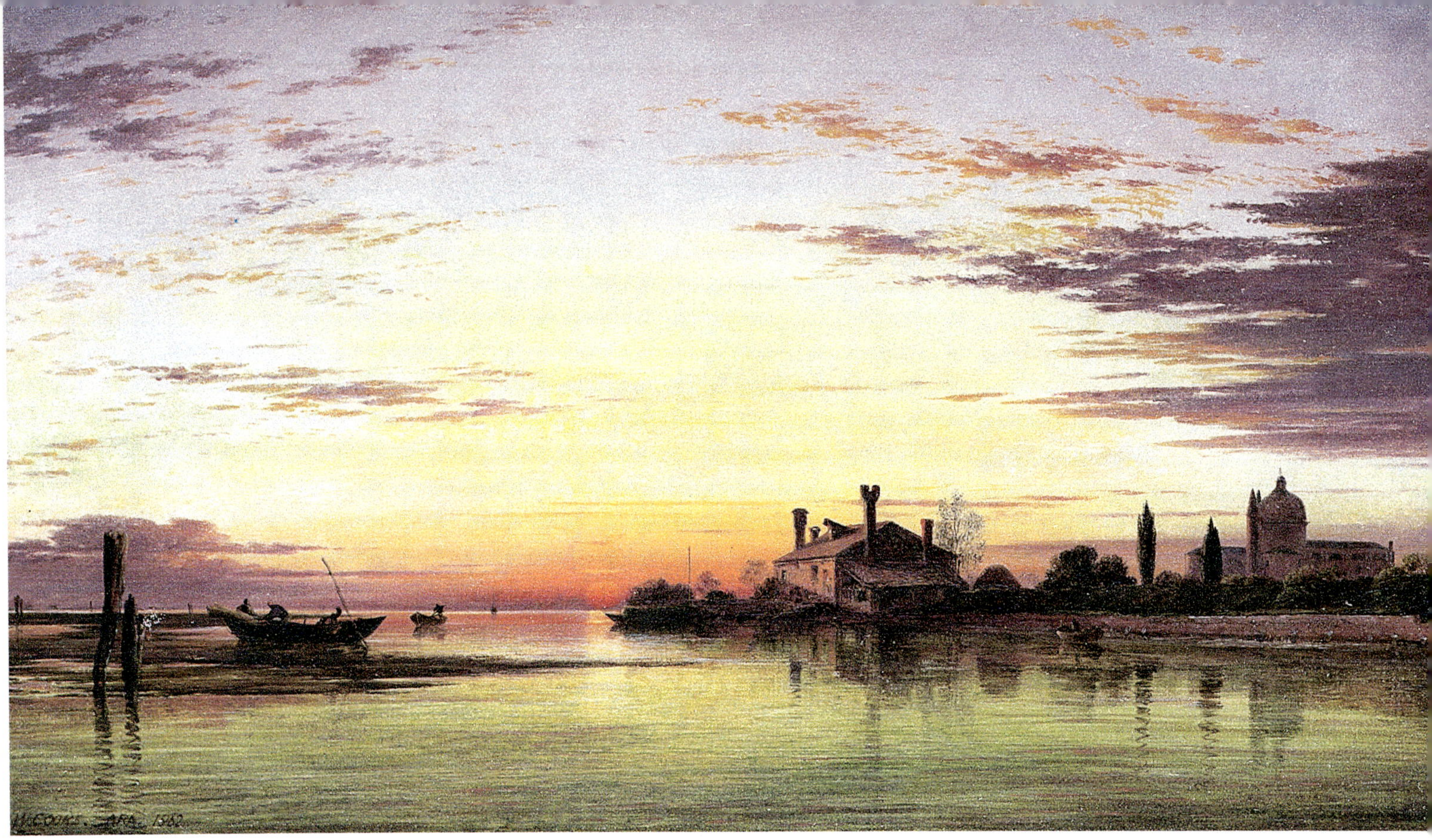

Colour Plate 121 (below). 56/3

Chioggian fishing vessels running into the Lagune of Venice on the approach of a borasco, or violent squall on the Adriatic

The pious inscription on the vessel's quarter, *Noi stiamo sotto Divina Providenza,* is matched by the writing on the *forcola* floating by – *Il Lagunetto.* A commission from a noble collector, this view off Fort Sant'Andrea shows a bragozzo with reefed sail running before the approaching storm. Photo courtesy Sotheby's. Mariners' Museum, Newport News, Va., USA

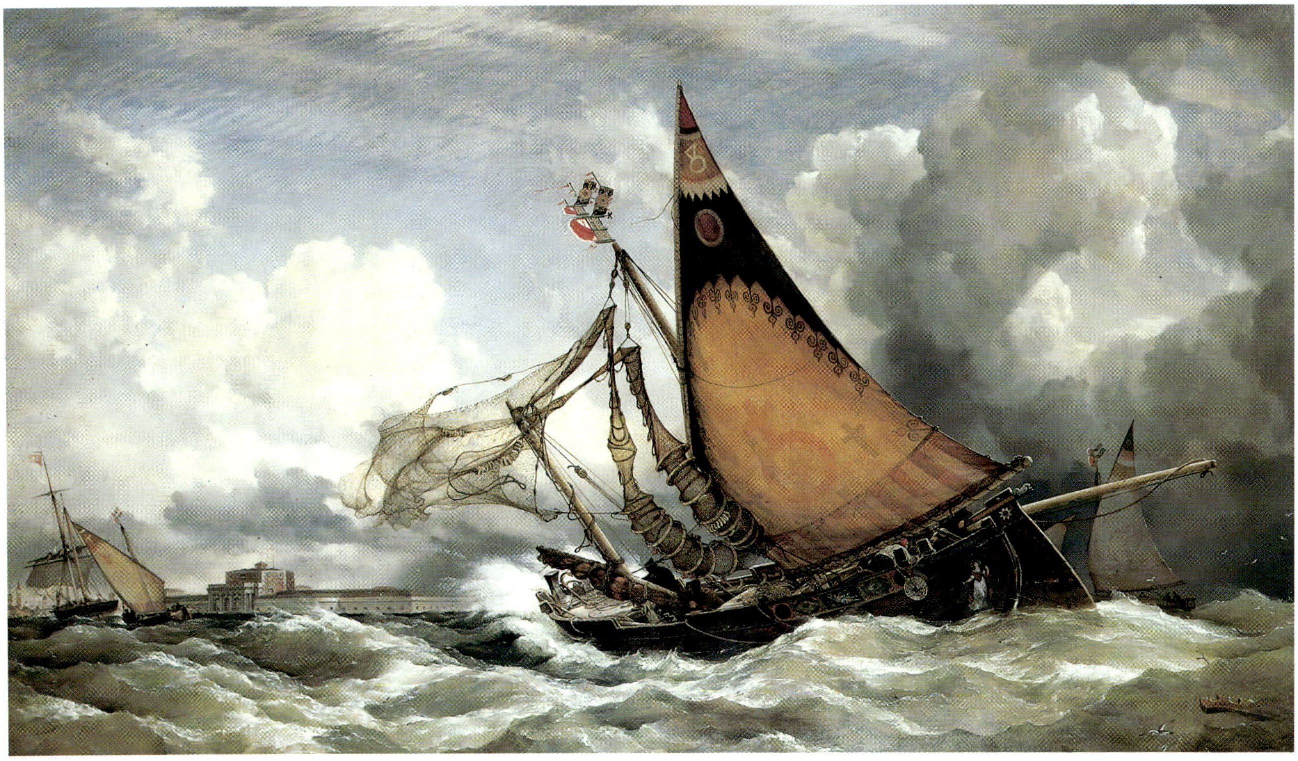

the Victorian age.

Revealing comments by John Ruskin in letters to a fond parent give what his editors are pleased to call a character-sketch of E.W. Cooke. Ruskin's opinion at any one moment could be subject to revision at the next and might be, according to his mood, fanciful and dogmatic by turns.

> *You will see in the Papers that Mr Cooke has been elected ARA. I never saw a man so pleased – but he is pleased with everything. A most curious small man. Good – and kind-and pious – but with a perpetual buz from one thing to another – I never saw such restlessness – or such activity. You will have the Exhibition full of Ducal Palaces next year – such as they may be. But Cooke has taken great pains – and though raw and cold and mean looking – his paintings will be more accurate in detail, than any that have yet been taken. I have led him to look into the detail – and he is as enthusiastic as I am – but his chief failing is that he can never see a dark side – of anything – I see too many but I see the lights stronger for them.*[3]

This is further elaborated by another letter, after the artist's departure:

> *I miss today at my morning prayers, Mr Cooke – who used to make the responses in a most serious and earnest manner. The smallest clever man I ever knew – a man who could be best defined – just as I said above of a truly great man that he could not be abridged – so Mr Cooke is so truly small that nothing could ever enlarge him, and yet full of affection – most unselfish – ready to help all the world, and full of accurate and valuable knowledge in natural history – with which he is always overflowing at wrong times, flying perpetually from one thing to another; and yet if you ask him a plain question about something which you really want to know, you get no answer. He knows a thousand things apropos of it, but not It.*
>
> *If you would like to see some very curious and laborious sketches of the Ducal Palace, and will just send a line to The Ferns, Victoria Road, Kensington to know when he would be at home, he would be delighted to see you and will tell you a great deal about us. He is the most curious mixture of conceit and humility I ever met with.*
>
> *They have just made him an associate R.A. Now, he has as good a right to be R.A. as anybody – far better than Lee, Creswick – or Roberts; but he felt it such a high honour that it quite threw him into a fever of excitement, which I in vain endeavoured to allay by informing him that it was no honour at all – unless to the Academy. But his tiny self-importance and affectionateness came out, in his telling us the next day that 'all the artists in London had been quite in a state of excitement about it (his election),' and that their sympathy was most gratifying!*[4]

This is both amusing and, as a rare personal comment on Cooke the man, most valuable. It is doubtless fair comment though there is clearly a hint of exasperation, but it also requires elucidation. Ruskin, that figure approaching genius, made pronouncements which were quite often reversed by his later judgements and he is using some of the language and thoughts of his recent pamphlet.

Following tradition and normal practice, Edward Cooke had signed his name in the Book at the Royal Academy as a candidate for Associateship at the end of May 1841 before the election but, not having gained it, signed again on 31 May 1849. He would have had tactical advice, support and canvassing from friends like Clarkson Stanfield and David Roberts, who had invited him to the Council's dinner in the previous year. This was a customary 'introduction' of a promising artist, as mentioned by Richard Redgrave,[5] *each member was entitled to bring with him any one exhibitor, for whom he was charged a guinea. He was supposed to select a painter who was rising into fame.* After dinner the very appropriate toast *Honour and Glory to the next Exhibition* was

3. *Ruskin's Letters from Venice,* ed. J.L. Bradley,.1955, No.56, 15 November 1851.
3. Ibid. No.77, 7 December 1851.
5. *Richard Redgrave, A Memoir,* 1891, p.347.

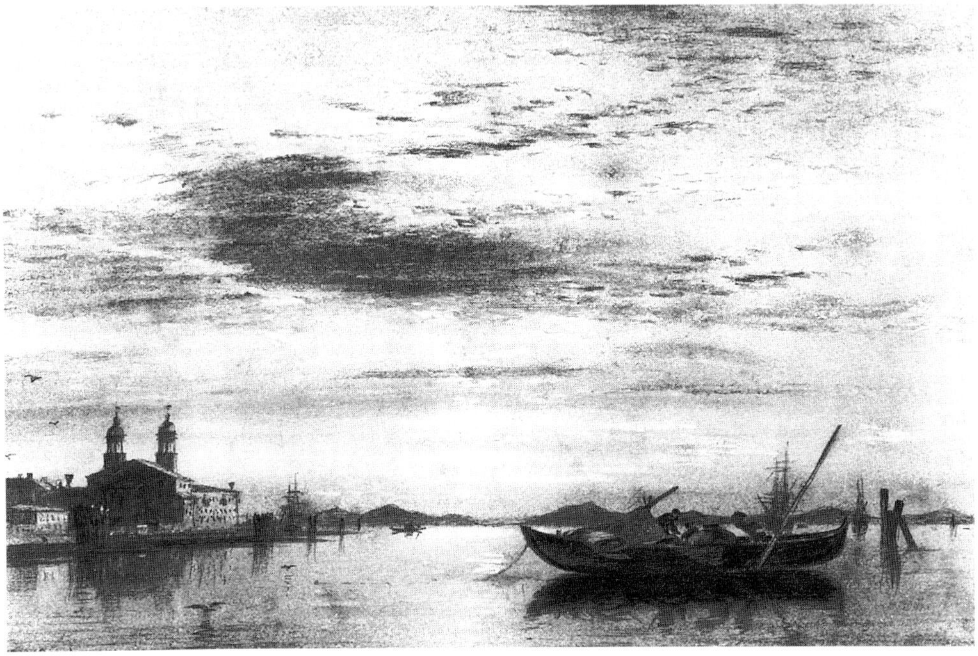

Plate 137. Chalk
The island of San Servilio, called by the Venetians San Servolo, at evening with the distant Euganean Hills.
Photo courtesy Arthur Ackermann & Peter Johnson

traditionally given, following the Loyal toast. Cooke was probably quoting from his sister's letters (which have not survived) the news of his election and good wishes from all the members of his artistic circle. Supporters tended to call on the successful candidate, who in turn went the rounds of his known supporters to offer thanks. This, which was indeed his world, though a small world to Ruskin, would signify 'all London' to the painter. He naturally could not conceal that it was a long-desired honour which had taken ten years, at least, to achieve; election was recognition not only of talent but of faithful support and adherence as well and it merited seven exclamation marks in his diary. It was a major stride on his chosen ascent, something the independent Ruskin could hardly appreciate.

However, we learn from him that here was someone small of stature, a fact which has not emerged from portraits or other sources and may well have to await the discovery of a standing group photograph of RAs of the period for confirmation! A warm kindly man very well informed, who at the age of forty was, one suspects, sufficiently secure and confident of his prowess to be able to hold his own with John Ruskin in practical matters relating to his art. Cooke, the boy found by Pugin to be in need of no instruction, on his part noted that he had an argument with Ruskin about perspective, but alas neglected to record either details or outcome.

One can imagine Cooke's chat about his interests in botany and geology, interspersed perhaps with anecdote, for which according to Redgrave he was renowned, cutting into Ruskin's scholarly concentration, or indeed into his careful drawing. Allowing for some passing irritation which caused Ruskin's verdict and of course for the very considerable difference in background, comments by the *Graduate of Oxford* are intriguing.

Coming from a large and devoted family circle, a hard-working group of artist-craftsmen who had seen tragedy enough in the short lives and deaths of many of its members, including his own wife, Cooke surely had a more varied experience of life than John Ruskin, if on a more mundane level. Money matters too, the economics of family living and questions of 'adequate provision', were outside the latter's cossetted upbringing. With his specially designed travelling carriage and means of purchasing Turner watercolours, it was hardly surprising that he found Cooke 'small'.

Cooke's inability to answer Ruskinian posers while knowing a great deal of relevant detail perhaps lay in the form of the questions. The mental powers of one of the outstanding figures of the century might be expected to produce questions of some obscurity and complexity.

Where then should one look for 'smallness'? Was it perhaps that he voiced no theories of aesthetics and artistic philosophy and had as a member of the realist school no time for fancy? Businesslike singlemindedness and down-to-earth practicality with little pause for reflective contemplation evidently grated on Ruskin. With such a breadth of interests, however, Cooke can hardly be labelled 'small' in the sense of *narrow*.

He shared Ruskin's enthusiasm for geology and one wonders whether thc unanswered questions may have belonged to that field: *Every class of rock, earth and cloud must be known by the painter with geological and meteorological accuracy* proclaimed the *Stones of Venice*

Cooke was also a gregarious animal while the same can by no means be said of his friend. Ruskin's verdict is the comment of a lofty intellect, the view perhaps of a gentleman *amateur* speaking of the working professional, who, when all was said and done, lived by his hand and eye and had at all times to be gainfully employed.

In a perceptive note on Clarkson Stanfield, which must equally apply to E.W. Cooke, P.G. Hamerton in his periodical *The Portfolio* said that he never attempted to *poetize about nature or set the facts he tells us in a subjective light... he did not trouble much about soul, indeed, nor as Goethe puts it 'think much about thinking'. He was not oppressed like Turner by the sadness and mystery of the Earth.*[6] However, it must be said that neither Stanfield nor Cooke was oblivious to the mighty strength of the sea!

The powerful voice of Sir Herbert Read commented *Good art criticism is rare in England. We have had Reynolds and Ruskin... But there has been no real tradition... at once well informed and vigorous and restricted to its proper sphere. The weakness... has been due to two causes: to the low place which the visual arts have occupied in a puritanical scale of values, and to an innate English inability to philosophise about an abstract quality like beauty.*[7]

In any event Ruskin wrote of 'dear old Edward Cooke' many years later when in a gloomy London on the first day of January 1878 and after a period when he had indeed been seeing the 'dark side of things' they met in the Grosvenor Gallery and talked fondly of the Venice they had known and shared and loved. The year before in that same gallery Ruskin had looked with contempt at a canvas by J.A. McNeill Whistler and went into print with his indignation, but that is another story. The libel lawsuit was heard in November 1878 with its famous farthing damages for the painter, but meantime the critic Ruskin had experienced the first of his mental breakdowns. It is odd that the admirer of late Turner should have been blind to the beauty and imagination in Whistler. What is fairly likely is that E.W. Cooke would probably have shared his view of the new style in painting.[8]

During this visit to Venice in 1851 the architectural subjects seem to have predominated. Whether it was the use of the graphic telescope in conjunction with work by candle-light that produced forms and colours which Ruskin called 'raw, cold and mean-looking', that critic was not alone. Others found some of Cooke's pictures 'hard to the last degree' and they were also ready to complain at his Adriatic colours. However, colour in Venice at a particular time of year could strike a painter as not unlike that of the North. Eugène Boudin, the French marine master, visited in 1895 and noted storm conditions, grey vapour and Adriatic waters which were sombre *but these waters, which don't resemble those of the Mediterranean, are mostly green and do not differ from our waters of the Channel....*[9] Concentration on structure was however Cooke's delight and his strength and we can see with what effect the brush succeeded the etching needle. He varied the atmospheric settings for his craft as well as the architectural background, even achieving one canvas of the Dogana in a fog (62/15, not traced). On dull days and wet days too he painted and there is sometimes a sombre brownish tinge to the lagoon, denoting perhaps water as dirty as that of Holland! Cooke may have consciously avoided the popular, bright sunlit scene and one title only refers to the 'blue' lagoon (51/23, not traced).

On the other hand his 'Dutch' love of cloud formations, of sunset skies, approaching storms and the fine colour of the fishing boats enabled him to bring warmth and richness

6. *The Portfolio,* 1869-.
7. *The Works of Man* by L.M. Phillips, Introduction by Herbert Read.
8. *Diaries of John Ruskin,* ed. Evans & Whitehouse, 1956. *The Wider Sea* by J.D. Hunt, 1982, p.367.
9. *Venice Rediscovered,* Exhibition catalogue, Wildenstein, 1972.

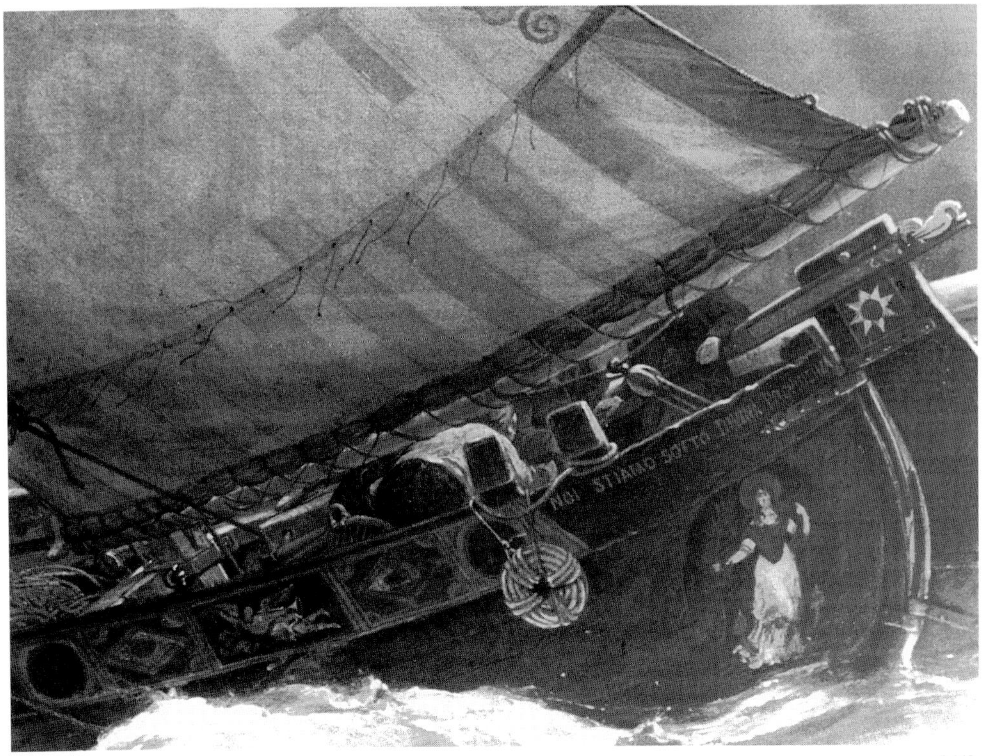

Plate 138. 56/3
Detail of the Chioggian bragozzo Photo courtesy Mariners' Museum, Newport News, Va., USA

into many of his pictures.

Mrs Ruskin in writing home to Scotland mentions these 1851 paintings shown at one of her soirées at which were present:

> *Count Wrbna, madame Pallavicini, Count Falkenhayn and General Reischach, Mr Hope Johnston... also Princess Jablonowska... they are oil paintings of different views here and very beautiful. The Austrians and the ladies were delighted with them and I have since asked Count Falkenhayn to get me an order from the Governor for Mr Cooke to take his paintings out of Venice without being searched which will save him much trouble and a good deal of money too.*[10]

Of that evening Cooke, who was not good at names and often left blanks to be filled in later, noted:

> Nov.26th: *Mr Ruskin called for me and we went together to see the two columns. Went out at 12 and painted boats, figures &c in No.12.Capuchins. Took all pictures and sketches to Ruskin's at 6. Very foggy at intervals all day...Went to R's at ½ p 9. Met Whiston, Generals —and —, Count and Countess Palavicini, and shewed them my pictures.*

When John Ruskin began to publish his *Notes on the Principal Pictures in the Royal Academy* in 1855, the days of his close association with Cooke were past but he noted several of his works, writing in 1858 (Colour Plate 119), *S.Giorgio in Alga, I can answer for the truth of his study, representing one of the calm sea glories of Venice which painters are too apt to despise, though poets never. Both Shelley and Byron seem to have loved these Euganean Hills and the sunsets behind them more than Venice itself.*

The fact that Petrarch lived and died at Arqua in the hills doubtless centred a poet's devotion there and while gazing westwards the effects which Cooke recorded were similarly absorbed. P.B. Shelley in 1818 had composed *Lines written among the Euganean Hills* and the following year *Julian and Maddalo* which contained another reference to the distant peaks which evidently intrigued E.W. Cooke:

10. *Young Mrs Ruskin in Venice* by Mary Lutyens, 1965, p.222.

...Looking upon the evening and the flood
Which lay between the city and the shore,
Paved with the image of the sky; the hoar
And aery Alps, towards the north appeared,
Through mist, an heaven-sustaining bulwark, reared
Between the east and west; and half the sky
Was roofed with clouds of rich emblazonry,
Dark purple at the zenith, which still grew
Down the steep west into a wondrous hue
Brighter than burning gold, even to the rent
Where the swift sun yet paused in his descent
Among the many folded hills – they were
Those famous Euganean Hills, which bear,
As seen from Lido through the harbour piles
The likeness of a clump of peakèd isles –
And then, as if the earth and sea had been
Dissolved into one lake of fire, were seen
Those mountains towering, as from waves of flame,
Around the vaprous sun, from which there came
The inmost purple spirit of light, and made
Their very peaks transparent.

George Gordon, Lord Byron – who was Shelley's Maddalo – gave in his *Childe Harold's Pilgrimage* a line which several painters were to grasp:

The moon is up, and yet it is not night –[11]
Sunset divides the sky with her – a sea
Of glory streams along the Alpine height
Of blue Friuli's mountains; Heaven is free
From clouds, but of all colours seems to be –
Melted to one vast Iris of the West,
Where the Day joins the past Eternity;
While, on the other hand, meek Dian's crest
Floats through the Azure air – an island of the blest!

Ruskin further commended his small acquaintance:

1856. RA No. 583. *Chioggian fishing vessels &c running into the Lagune of Venice on the approach of a borasco or violent squall on the Adriatic:*
Another instance of the extraordinary good fortune which characterises the Exhibition this year is possessing the happiest efforts of almost every master. Do any of us recollect so impressive a study of shipping as this by Mr Cooke, much as he has hunted such quarries across the foam? It is admirably true to the Venetian boat – and the Venetian boat and all the ways of it are beautiful.

Other critics felt differently. The *Art Journal,* having no particular love for the Venetian boat, wrote: *A large picture showing principally a fishing boat making for Venice. We have observed lately that the seas of this painter have become very sketchy; this is markedly exemplified here; the waves want roundness, volume.* [Colour Plate 121 and Plate 138.]

Cooke spent six seasons painting in Venice during the 1850s, pursuing his own quest of the superlative among the shipping as well as paying tribute to the architecture and the climate!

11. This line was used as a picture title by Cooke in 1870, as it had been by J.M.W. Turner and J.D. Harding.

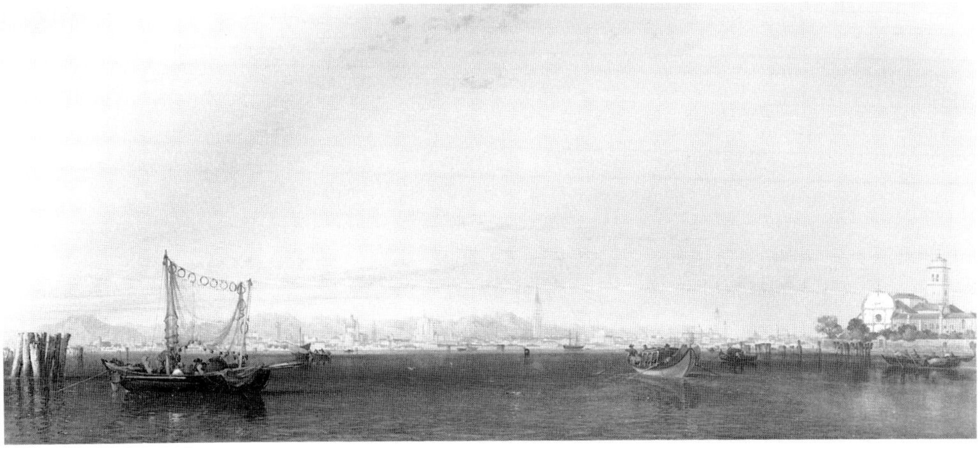

Chapter 11

BELLA VENEZIA

The painter's method and progress is neatly summarised in a Memo at the end of the 1852 diary; would that he had repeated this check annually for it is useful to compare it with the list compiled from available external sources as well as his daily entries:

Memoranda.

No.1. [small] Bragozzi, evening effect, Sta Elena. Begun 1st Sept on large bl[oc]k canvas, Finished it 12 Oct. 52/13
No.2. San Giorgio from Giudecca [with trabaccolo, evening] full moon rising. Begun 1st Sept on large canvas. 52/14
No.3. Topi, San Giorgio & Salute.On large canvas, begun 10th Sept. 52/15
No.4. [Large] Salute, begun last year, canvas. 52/16
No.5. Bragozzi – Redentore.[from Giardino] begun 14th Sept. on large canvas. 52/17
No.6. Small sunset effect, S.Giorgio in Alga. Begun 14th and finished 15th on dark paper block. 52/18
No.7. Small evening sky on dark paper block (narrow) near San Servolo. Put in topo and palli on 25th Sept. 52/19
No.8. Small sky on thin block paper. Stormy effect in Giudecca. 52/20
No.9. Calm silvery [hazy] effect. [Campanile & Ducal Palace] Trabaccoli. Begun 28th Sept. Large canvas. 52/21
No.10. Evening view of Sta Chiara and Sant Andrea Apostoli and part of Campo di Marte. 52/27
No.11. [Glorious] Sunset ptd 4th Oct put in Salute and back of Giudecca on 7th. Thick paper. 52/23
No.12. Sunset from Canale di Giudecca with dark clouds. Sky ptd 6th Oct. Paper block. 52/24
No.13. [small] San Giorgio at sunset, shadow of dome on campanile. Begun on 7th Oct on thin paper block. 52/25
No.14. Salute and Dogana, twilight on small millboard, begun 9th Oct. 52/26
No.15. San Pietro in Castello, begun 15th Oct on canvas block, evening effect. 52/22
No.16. Small twilight on paper, with Brigantine. Young moon setting behind Salute. 52/28
No.17. Dogana and Zitella from window; trabaccolil, rasconi, large canvas. Begun Oct 26th. 52/29

Plate 139. 58/26
Venice from the South off San Clemente, evening
An unfamiliar distant view with alluring mountain peaks. His friend Robert McInnes had exhibited *A Fiesta, scene on the Lido* in 1848, with a similar skyline (Christie's sale 11 March 1995, lot 88).
Photo courtesy Courtauld Institute of Art. Makins Collection

No.18. Zecca, Palace and Campanile from SW. on square large canvas. Begun 28th Oct. 52/30

One of Edward Cooke's rare surviving family letters, written at Hamburg in 1853 on his way from Scandinavia to Venice, likewise reveals the man and his method:

> *...You cannot imagine how sadly I yearn to be there and can scarcely tolerate the time till I arrive there. In Sweden I could not enjoy as I ought the last fortnight in Stockholm when once it was thought of to go to Venice. My heart beat high in anticipation and the days were truly irksome, scarcely redeemed by good friends. The truth is as you well know I could not endure the loss of time and do nothing. Life, feeling well and not at work is torment to me and I want to redeem lost time and cover all expences at the Sale and those of travelling also. I shall however take it very much more easy now, in fact I shall only get studies of interesting bits for pictures and with the exception of San Marco and the Rialto shall work more among the shipping. The San Marco I shall blot in colour of the different parts, all the details I have in those glorious Calotypes. Thanks to them for I could not paint that subject on so large a scale at Venice as I should like, so shall get the colour of the parts and general blottings of effects roughly... I should not do so much nor so well during the beastly dull foggy days in England so shall save time by working there besides on my return so much takes off my attention and it is difficult to begin directly.*

Another part letter reads:

> *...delicious days, quite warm and brilliant and fine freshness in the morning and evening air, in fact perfect in every respect only that the sun sets at ½ p 5 therefore my evening's work is much curtailed. I am in most excellent health and in full swing of work, 13 subjects in progress, many very elaborate but not that architectural parallel line sort of thing like those before, but distant views of the great group, Salute, S.Giorgio, Port of Lido, Riva &c., rather popular subjects I think, though much smaller than usual. I hope I shall make them worth from 80 to £100 apiece... while here in good weather I can do much more than I could in the dark foggy atmosphere of London. I want to begin a long view of Venice from perhaps San Clemente or S.Lazzaro with the mountains seen over, which look most glorious.*[1] (See Plate 139.)

His stay that year, after a long Scandinavian tour, was of twelve weeks wherein he rejoiced in better health for in the previous season he had been confined to his couch with boils behind the knee!

The next visit was in 1858 when he went via Switzerland with a pause in the Alps. A comet which appeared in the Venetian sky was incorporated into a twilight scene (58/32) in November. Named after G.B. Donati, its first observer, it was the same that William Dyce introduced into his famous *Pegwell Bay, A Recollection of Oct 5th 1858,* at which time in England it was at its brightest.

On only one occasion does Cooke seem to have undertaken an elaborate church interior, in the style of David Roberts, and this also in 1858, *The Interior of San Marco from the Baptistry* which was noted as 'looking across the Nave to the Chapel of the Crucifix' (58/30). It appeared in his studio clearance sale of 1863 at Christie's, Lot 89, and a copy of the catalogue exists with an MS note: *NB The most elaborately finished EWC has executed.* There is also inscribed *if sold req[uir]e the pur[chaser] to sign the Regn papr & the note to EWC*, which perhaps related to copyright.[2]

He painted a larger version (59/1) exhibited at the Academy in 1864 but whether the

1. Cooke MSS.
2. Cooke MSS. Copy formerly belonging to Jas. Wyatt Junr of Oxford.

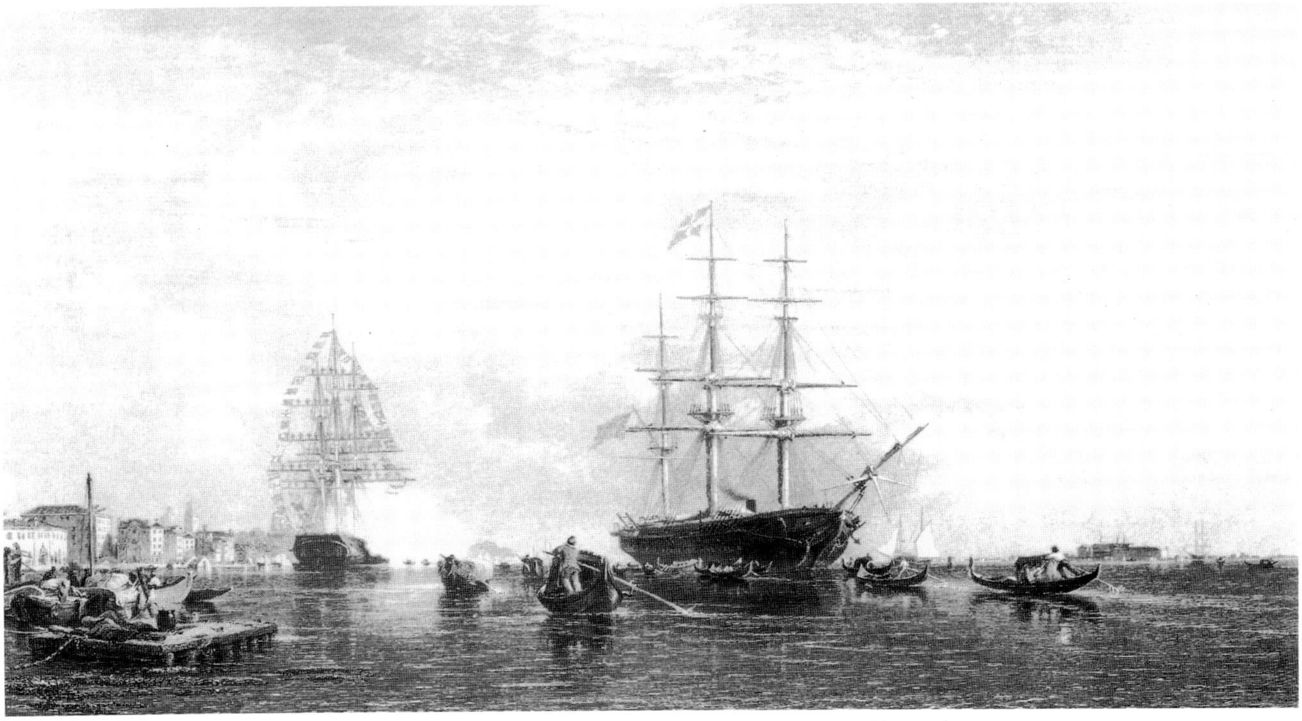

Plate 140. Engraving
Engraved from 62/26 *The Arrival*
The sound of the gun salute brought Cooke out to see H.M. Ship bearing the deposed King of Greece, Otho of Bavaria, anchoring off the Riva. Flag etiquette is observed with the ex-King's standard still flying at the masthead. See Diary Extract Venice 1862. Photo courtesy Private Collection

'finish' of this one surpassed the picture painted on the spot is not known, for only the latter has been seen (Plate 173).

Occasionally an essay in topical journalism enabled him to introduce a new element in his paintings of fishing craft and traders in their extraordinary setting. The deposed Otho of Bavaria, King of Greece, had received asylum on board HMS *Scylla,* a screw corvette commanded by Captain Rowley Lambert RN, and she steamed into the port on 29 October 1862. Cooke visited the ship and later composed a picture from his sketches which was engraved and published in the *Art Journal* with the title *The Arrival.* Due ceremony with the firing of a salute and the dressing of ships overall with flags made a spirited picture which, when exhibited at the British Institution in 1866, bore an explanatory note: *The view comprises the Riva degli Schiavone and the Giardini Pubblici, Lido and San Servolo* (Plate 140)

Ranging round the lagoons he visited the Armenian convent on the island of San Lazzaro near the Lido and made friends with the brethren. The distant view of the city was unusual and he made use of it on more than one occasion. The island looking west in the glow of a sunset made another memorable picture for the tall campanile was topped with an onion dome.

The island of San Clemente noted by Ruskin *...to the south of Venice, from which the view of the city is peculiarly beautiful...*[3] also appealed to Cooke for it too gave a different view of the famous skyline.

A meteorological phenomenon, the Bora or Borasca, a sudden Mediterranean storm, gave him a good subject which on two occasions he developed into a dramatic composition. *Chioggian fishing vessels running into the Lagune of Venice on the approach of a Borasco or violent squall on the Adriatic* (56/3, Colour Plate 121) showed a bragozzo storming along off Fort Sant'Andria with the dirty weather hard on its heels. The painting, the same that Ruskin had praised in *Academy Notes,* was made for Lord Londesborough and was later sold to Sir Julian Goldsmid. After the dispersal of his collection it surfaced occasionally until sold in recent times to the important collection at

3. *Ruskin's Venice,* ed. Arnold Whittick, 1976, p.38.

the Mariner's Museum, Newport News, Virginia, USA. There it provides an admirable introduction to the art of E.W. Cooke and a good example of the English marine painter's interest in showing fishing craft under stress of weather. He returned to the subject with a different composition in 1873 where his bragozzi are *...caught in a Borasco* (73/2, Plate 290 – see also Plate 141).

Perhaps the most unusual of his Venetian pictures was painted for William Duckworth of Orchardleigh Park, near Frome, a Somerset mansion which was designed in the fashionable style of 1858. The painting was to form the back-board to an amboyna wood side cabinet made by the firm of Morant, Boyd & Morant in 1859.[4] The evening view is taken from an anchorage off Sta Elisabetta on the Lido and embraces the incomparable skyline from the islands of Sta Elena on the right to San Servolo on the left, a triptych reposing behind glass in a carved surround with an alabaster medallion representing the personification of Venezia, set above it (57/9, Colour Plate 125). Letters show the artist in the role of salesman:

20th April 1859
Dear Mr Duckworth

Perhaps you will let me know when you desire your picture to be sent to you, if you do not wish it to be sent to your house in Town, it can remain here until you return to the country, for as it is considered my Capo d'opera a great many people have been and some are coming – to see it.

I shall be happy to do anything that may improve it that you may suggest – altho' I cannot see where to put another touch – I never executed a more difficult or laborious work – to produce variety with unity – minute finish with breadth of effect. I worked over it – during the two years it was in hand, with real buon gusto for I loved the subject for its own sake. How I sigh over Bella Venezia when I hear how it is swarming with Austrian troops. I much fear I may not be able to paint there this year.

I beg to acknowledge your kindness in sending me by Lady Coltman a blank cheque to fill up.I could not however at that moment confer with nor detain her as my house was full of visitors & Lady Coltman considerately entered into my difficulty. The sum of 250 Guineas will I think meet your approbation, that being the amount I received for those much smaller pictures of Venice exhibited during the last four years and which occupied me less than half the time devoted to the long panel. Trusting the picture will be a source of increasing gratification to you & your family at Orchard Leigh & with kind compliments to your circle,
Believe me, Dear Mr Duckworth, Yours very truly
E.W.Cooke.[5]

In 1862 he travelled out with Thomas Wyatt, the architect whom he had consulted in the design of the setting for the Duckworth picture. In this year he noted briefly the days spent on thirty oil pictures in hand and also noted are *New Subjects* which were numbered later, presumably in order of priority or preference: 2. Dogana from South, 3. Armenian Convent from Sta Elizabetta. 1. General view of Venice from near Lido. 4. General view from near Murano. 5. View of Ducal Palace and Campanile from West end of Porto Franco (Plate 142). 6. Rialto – sketch cage baskets for poultry, Rialto.

In 1863 he travelled with another companion, Robert Bateman, artist son of his friend James Bateman, the owner of Biddulph Grange, for whom he had made elaborate garden designs.[6] They returned home via Trieste in the SS *Malta* to Ancona and overland to Marseilles etc. Of the ten or so paintings resulting from this trip one (63/12, Colour Plate 126) took an unfashionable look along the Canale della Giudecca with the tower of San

3. *Ruskin's Venice,* ed. Arnold Whittick, 1976, p.38.
4. Sold Christie's 1987.
5. Courtesy Christie's.
6. 'Robert Bateman, a true Victorian', by Amanda Kavanagh, *Apollo,* September 1989, pp.174-9.

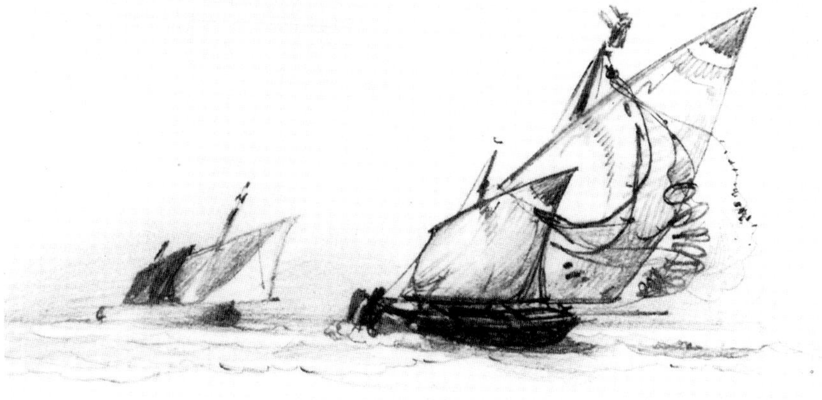

Plate 141. Pencil drawing
Bragozzo with nets flying, running home
The approaching storm in 73/2 (Plate 290) must have resulted from this small sketch.
Photo courtesy Martyn Gregory

Nicolo Tolentino and a merchantman moored in mid- stream.

The following year, 1864, he went all-out for old Venetian glass, the collector taking over from the painter and the latter recording only half a dozen pictures in hand while the former studied and purchased by turns. Once back in London he went round to the British Museum and the South Kensington Museum to look at glass.

Cooke was well able to rely on his great stock of Venetian drawings from his dismembered sketchbooks for the series of views which he continued to paint and it was not until 1877 that he once more set out. On 19 September, travelling with his sister Mary, after delays with lost luggage on the journey he noted at Mestre a glorious sunset and a fine moon over the swampy margin of the lagoons.

They arrived in Venice by rail at 5.30 a.m., took an omnibus to the Hotel d'Angleterre at 6.00 and went to bed immediately. They were up at 10.00, Vincenzo the gondolier came and was engaged. One senses the pleasure in picking up where he had left off, even after such an interval: the 'drive' in the gondola, the dishes at the favourite restaurant, taking coffee and watching the passing crowds to the music of a military band in St Mark's Square. He must soon have learnt that they were almost following in John Ruskin's wake, for after a long stay of nine months that sad figure, nervous and depressed, had returned home in May.

Edward Cooke had made his last gondola painting trip and strangely enough he never began another major Venetian subject. His last had been exhibited in 1873 and there were perhaps half a dozen oils only from this visit (Colour Plate 127). His last Royal Academy picture was a small evening view of Torcello, exhibited in 1879.

He noted at the end of his 1877 diary a list of things – and the old canvas portmanteau – which he was leaving behind in Venice at the British Vice-Consul's and it reads like the catalogue of a village sale by auction:

Mahogany case to hold oil pictures.
Enough oil blocks for 2 journies [sic]: 4 oil blocks, (one Wavy) leave all.
2 Palettes – mall stick – bag of rag
Tin box, japanned. Oil colour box and open wood case for palette.
2 Palette knives (one bent)
1 Deal case. 1 Mahogany with stop (?)
A lot of brushes (leave some)
Roll of canvas, and roll with Riva on.
Guida di Venezia Otto giorni
Conversation book
Roan Prayer book

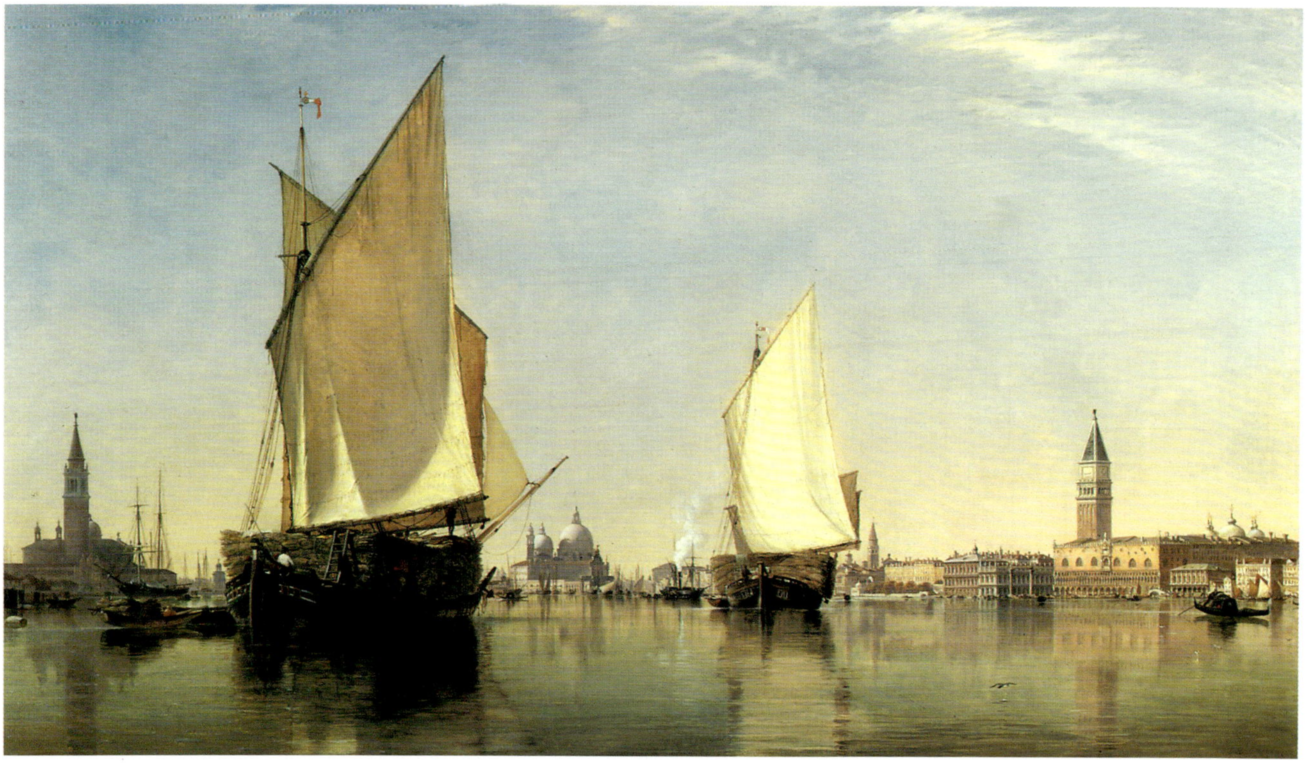

Colour Plate 122. 52/17

Vinegia, Vinegia...

Cooke's Shakespearian quotation came perhaps from having the Works read to him while painting, but the *trabaccoli* are about their mundane tasks laden with wood.

Photo courtesy Spink & Son Ltd. Private Collection

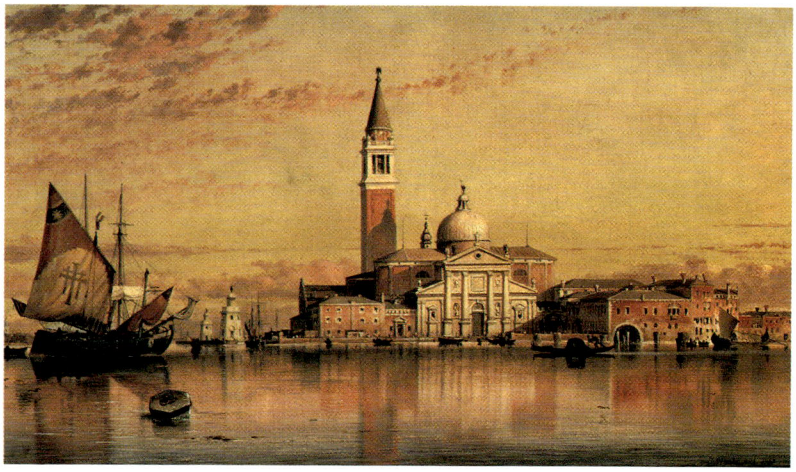

Colour Plate 123. 57/18

San Giorgio Maggiore at sunset: shadow of dome on campanile

Not so much a title as the painter's note identifying this view among his season's work.

Photo courtesy Sotheby's

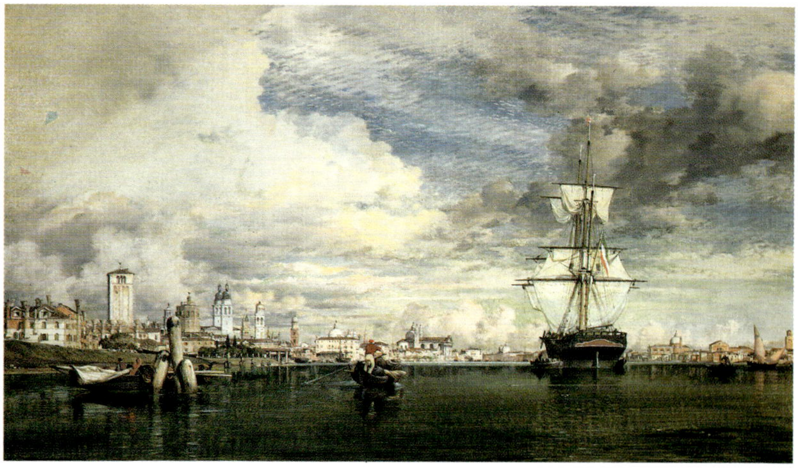

Colour Plate 126. 63/12

S.Nicolo, Venice

A view which the artist labelled as 'off Santa Marta'. The church and Monastery of Santa Marta, in a quarter inhabited by poor fishermen, is today in large part the maritime railway station! Cooke painted a merchantman, with possibly an Austro-Hungarian ensign, lying in the stream off the Churches of San Nicolo dei Mendicoli, with the Redentore, Gesuati etc. in the distance.

Photo courtesy Richard Green Fine Paintings. Private Collection

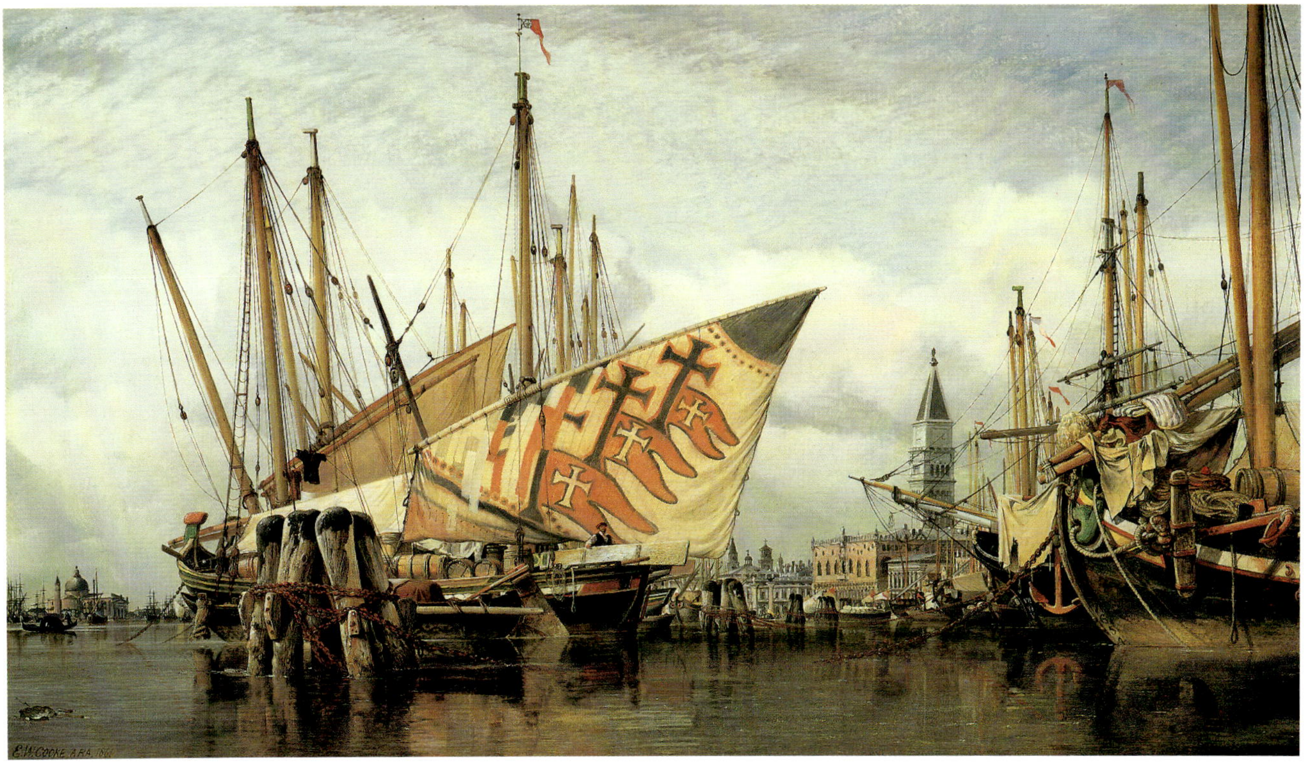

Colour Plate 124. 60/3

Porto Venezia

This was the artist's title while he noted 'View of Venice between tiers of trabaccoli'. When the picture appeared in the salerooms in this century it was called *Port of Venice with Trabaccoli or wide vessels of the Adriatic.* It should doubtless have read 'wine vessels' with their deck cargo of barrels. It is a particularly triumphant celebration of the seaport which he wrote of as 'Dear Old Venice' with, as usual, the working craft as the real subject. Photo courtesy Richard Green Fine Paintings, 1996

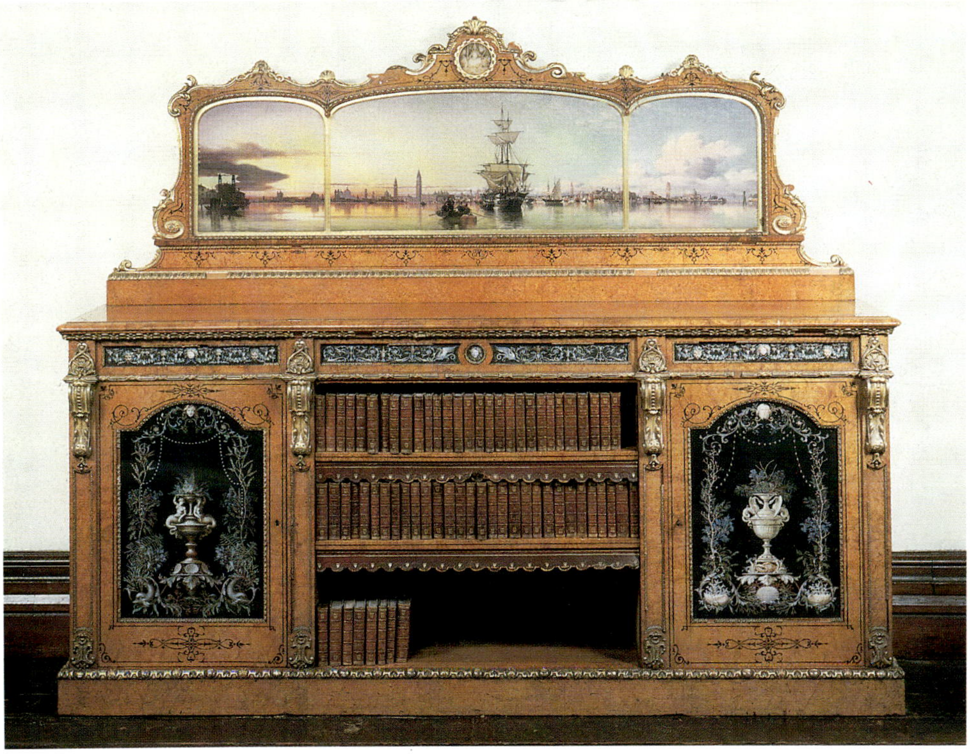

Colour Plate 125. 57/9

Near Sta Maria Elisabetta, Lido; distant view of Venice with S.Pietro in Castello and S.Servolo

Without a title, this painting was noted in the *Ledger* as *View of Venice in three compartments for cabinet.* The wide angle embraces the whole of the famous skyline. It was incorporated into the back of the cabinet or sideboard made by Morant for William Duckworth's house, Orchardleigh Park, in Somerset. Photo courtesy Christie's

Paper of Gum (not powder). Journal.
Map of Venice (in case)
A large lot of tacks. Pot of gall.
Glass muller and 1 slab. One square slab.
2 pieces of cuttle bone. 1 other piece
Large lot of wedges.
A few small tacks. 3 finger stalls.
2 Watercolour boxes = Montagu's box. 1 Sketch book. 1 large block and 1 of Mary's.
Tin flat box for palette. 1 smaller block. Small tin box for oil bottles.
Metallic book and pencils.
Rule with corks. 1 T-square, 1 set square, 1 set square small.
Buff thick block of paper and sheets of ditto.

His wardrobe too was detailed, some for leaving:

Pr. black trousers.1 Black vest embroidered
Goggles. 3 pair Specs – 1 Pr smoky. Eye glass. Opera glass.
To take home: Great Coat. Thick surtout. Thin ditto.
Light overcoat – drab. Drab wideawake. Fez. Silk cap. White hat (new).
Black wideawake, thin bought in Venice. Shooting Jacket, Vest and trousers.
3 Pr/ light grey trousers. Green spotted Vest. Blue cloth boots. Buff ditto boots. Light shoes. White canvas boots. Railway rug. Blue comforter.
Pr. Muffettes. Dressing case with brushes. Pomade. Clothes brush small.
Green gloves. Grey kid. Grey cotton. 2 Pr yellow cotton.
Tea equipage, bottles for spirit. My new metal bottle. Small flask.
2 thick woollen Drawers.3 cotton ditto. 2 thick wool vests.
All shirts. Striped red Ditto & collars. Green stock, green tie, green spotted tie, black tie, old crimson tie. 2 boxes of collars. 1 shirt front.
2 thick grey wool Vests. 1 greenish drab Vest. 2 white Ditto. 2 Pr. socks. 1 thin Pr white Cotton. 1 red gorget. Belt.

In all Cooke had spent ten painting seasons in Venice from 1850 to this final pilgrimage and from the large number of paintings made 'on the spot', as he noted, there were many others, larger, devised in the studio. The Catalogue lists over 190 Venetian subjects, but, as has been indicated elsewhere, while some references are likely to be duplicated there is evidence that his daily notes do not contain a mention of every picture he painted.

The Venetian Pictures and the Critics

Critical notices of his pictures enter not only into their subject and treatment, drawing and colour but also his painting techniques. In the absence of anecdote and overt moral content upon which to comment, the writers on art with an audience to instruct and entertain could also question the artist's veracity. It is not surprising to find them ready to be wearied of the Venetian skyline for an unending succession of views, the *'vedute'*, had started almost when the Academy first exhibited to the public and is yet in progress!

Of his *Bragozzi on the Lagune of Venice* at the British Institution in 1853 (51/25) the *Art Journal* said, after compliments, *We presume a fact is here asserted, but it is almost incredible that a boat apparently so heavy as is the principal, should show the bend of her keel.* It was a question of knowing your *bragozzo* – where the boat's stem ended and her keel began, something rather far from metropolitan awareness.

RA 1853 No 143 (52/22) *San Pietro in Castello, Venice, and the Julian Alps on a November evening. The spectator is placed here at a distance from the church over the lagune. The whole of the intermediate water and objective is kept down in order*

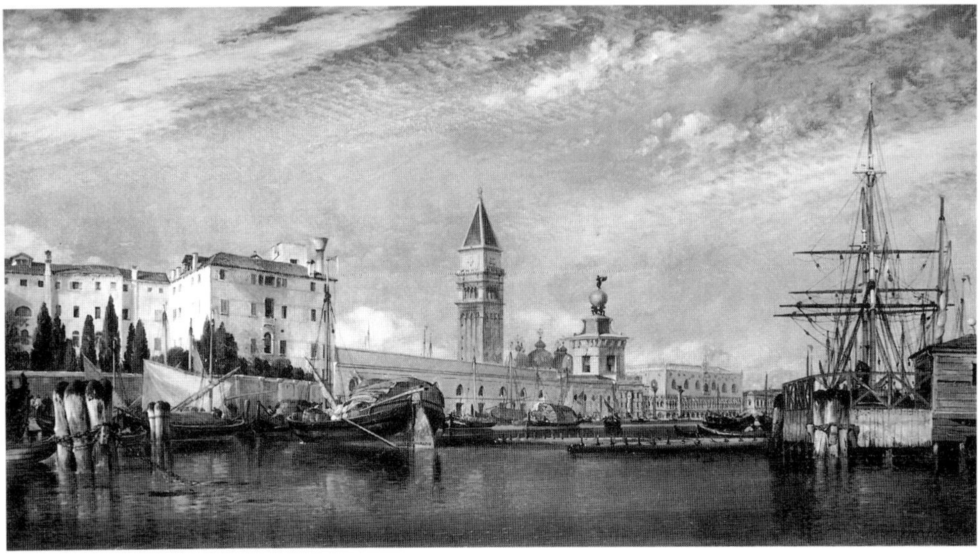

Plate 142. 63/15
Porto Franco, Dogana & Campanile
It was always a busy scene which combined the famous architecture with the serious commerce of the port and Cooke was often a delighted spectator. Photo courtesy Polak Gallery

to force the lustre of the buildings which are lighted by the sun; but the shades of the buildings have no degree of gradation relative to the nearer shades – this we submit the picture wants. It is worked out in all its parts with the utmost nicety.

No 282 in the RA Catalogue was untitled " + + + " but in the *Ledger* appears as *Vinegia, Vinegia, Chi non te vede, ei non te pregia* (52/17, Colour Plate 122) which is a quotation from Shakespeare's *Love's Labour's Lost* (Act IV Sc.ii). The *Art Journal* again:

This is a view of Venice from a point on the water, whence is seen the whole line of buildings from San Marco to S.Giorgio Maggiore, showing between these extreme points, the ducal palace, the piazetta, the campanile, the library and every point of interest in the line – and in order to give distance to these, some heavy boats are introduced near the spectator. This picture is in a very different feeling from that of antecedent Adriatic views. It is a return to that earlier view of nature upon which the reputation of the artist is based.

No 293 (52/16, Colour Plate 128) *San Giorgio Maggiore and the Salute, Venice with fishing craft. The dispositions here are similar to those in the picture by this artist already mentioned – that is, the buildings are secondary. The fishing boats with every peculiarity of their form and equipage, are studiously detailed, and the buildings are not less detailed.*

The entertaining mix of the serious and jocular is admirably illustrated by the same critic's treatment of two pictures in the following year.

1856 BI. No 17 (53/13, Colour Plate 129) *A Cool Day in Venice, Painted on the spot.*
There is for the painter an endless festival in Venice, but it should be remembered that spectators do get tired of the everlasting Ducal Palace the columns, the Campanile, the Library, the Dogana and the Church of San Giorgio; we have not, like the Doge, married Venice and her sea forever; 'sempre Venezia' is as bad as 'toujours perdrix'. It is true we know of nothing characterised by the venerable majesty of the City of the Sea, but nevertheless its luxuries pall upon the appetite. To say that the buildings are the same as we have seen them a little short of a thousand times, is true; but it is not true to say that they are always painted thus; we have here an extraordinary finish, worked out in part "on the spot" everything being sharp and palpable, because the atmosphere is here like a lens. Farewell ye storied palaces till we meet again, on the side wall here, and in the next ensuing ten

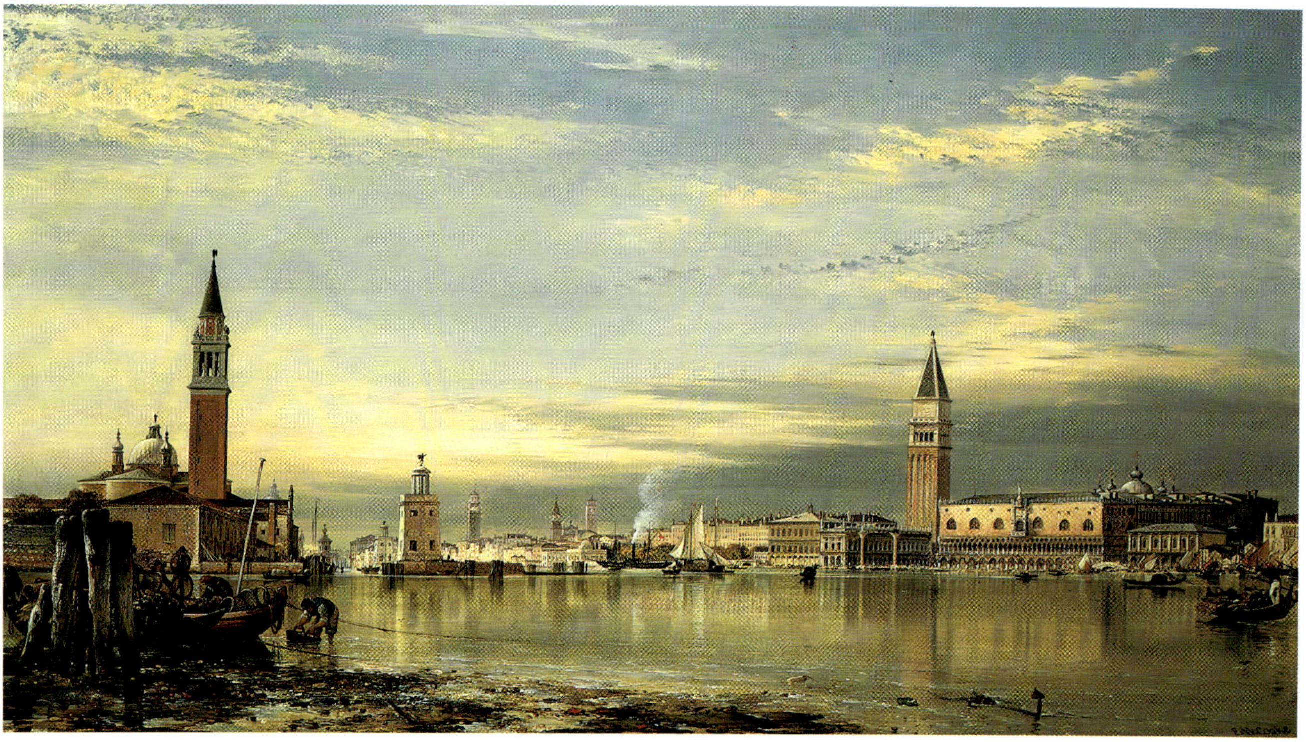

Colour Plate 129. 53/13
General view from Canal of Orphans: *A cool day in Venice*
This *serenissima* view was branded as a capriccio when it appeared in the saleroom in 1980 but it is far from fancy, as the artist's note shows.
Photo courtesy Richard Green Fine Paintings. Private Collection

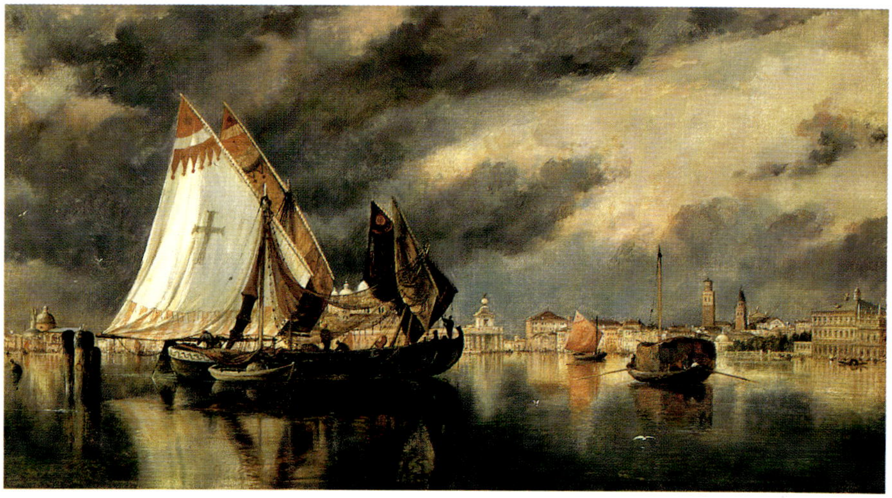

Colour Plate 127. 77/14
Porto di Venezia, Stormy effect
Product of his last visit, this lyrical and dramatic small canvas can serve as his farewell – his bragozzi obscuring most monuments save Fortune's golden ball on the Dogana di Mare!
Photo courtesy Sotheby's. Private Collection

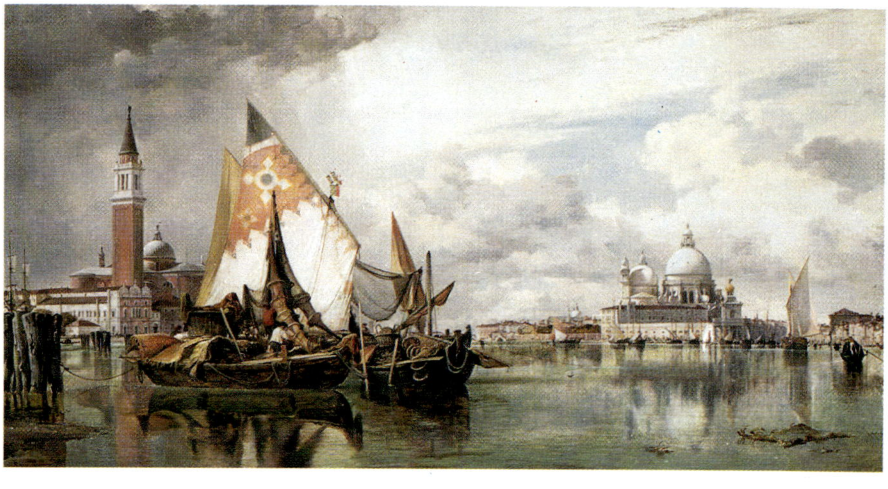

Colour Plate 128. 52/16
San Giorgio Maggiore and the Salute, Venice, with Fishing craft of Chioggia and the Lagune
Bought originally by a Lancashire industrialist, this picture had canvas additions by the time it appeared in the saleroom in 1980. It is now restored to its original proportion.
Photo: courtesy Private Collection

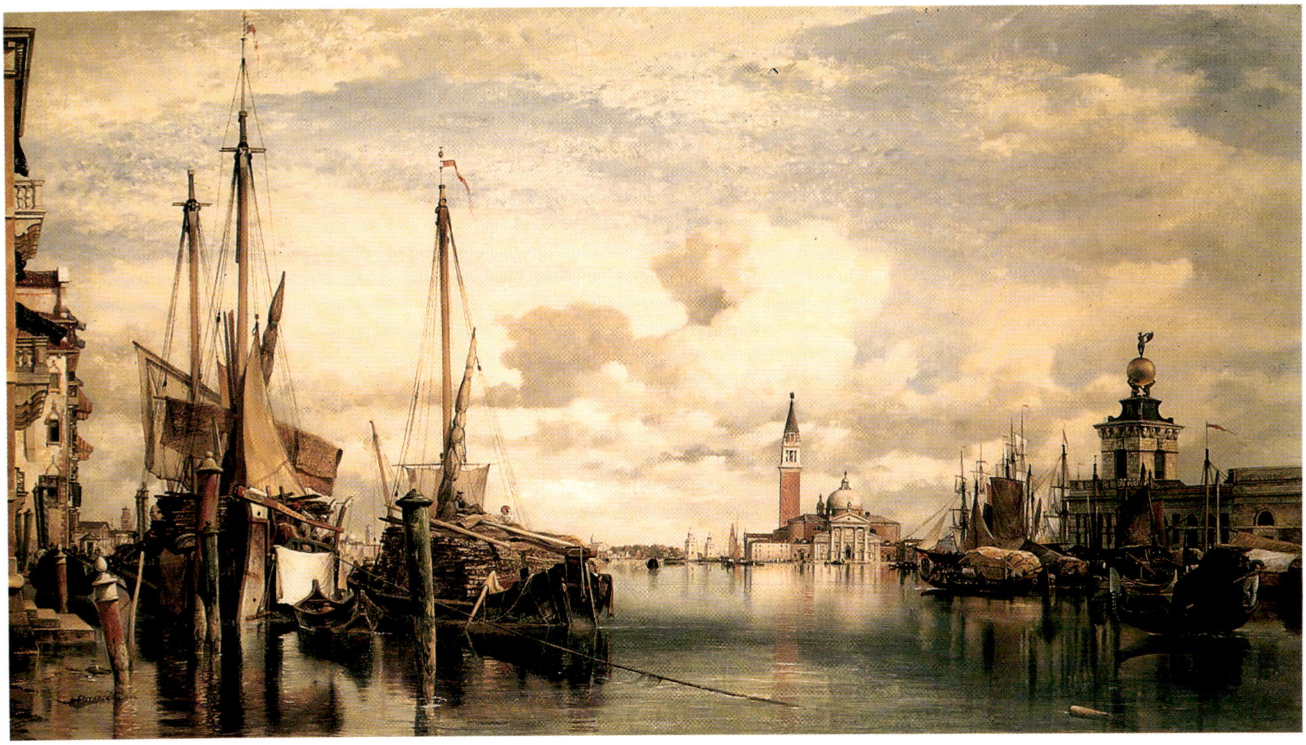

Colour Plate 130. 58/21
Venice, trabaccoli with wood, San Giorgio & the Dogana
Fuel had to be imported into Venice in large quantities, giving Cooke serious subject matter in these bulky vessels.
Photo courtesy Arthur Ackermann & Peter Johnson Ltd. Private Collection

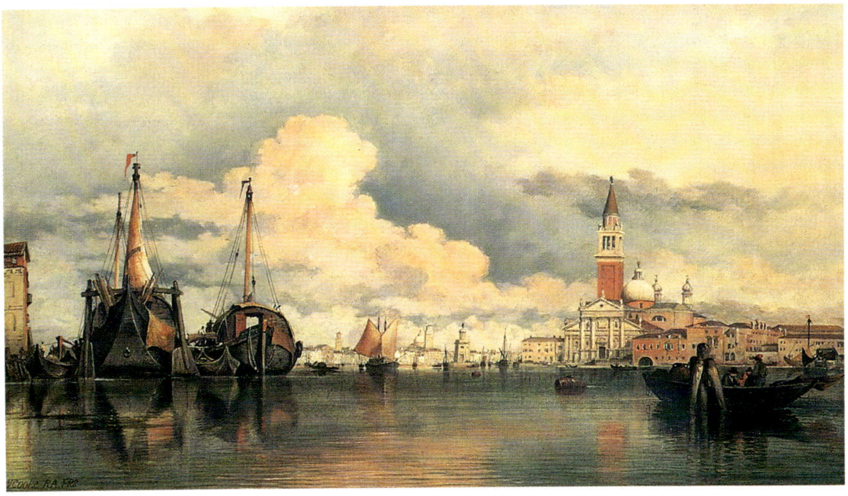

Colour Plate 131. 63/11
The Church of the Gesuati & Riva delle Zattere, with San Giorgio Maggiore, looking East Photo courtesy Justin Lang

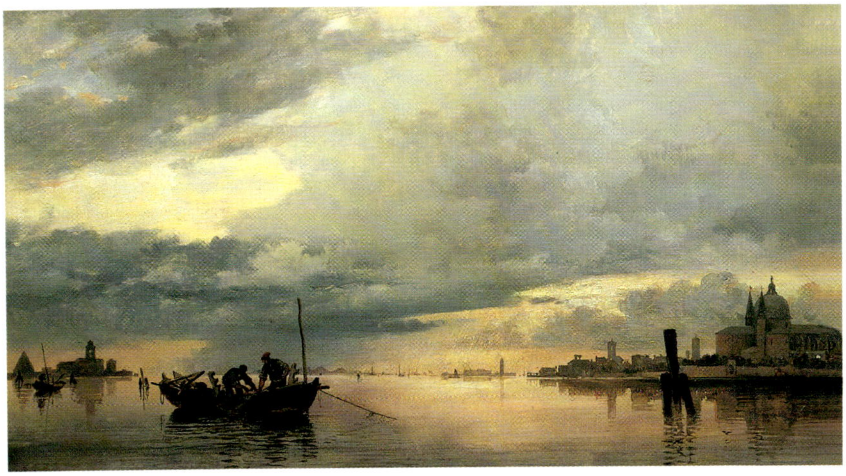

Colour Plate 132. 52/2
A Rainy day on the Lagune of Venice
Photo courtesy Private Collection

Plate 143. 63/13
Bragozzi off the Giardini Pubblici
A good place to see the painted sails of the fishing boats had early been discovered and very often visited, both on foot and by boat. San Servilio (called by Venetians San Servolo) in the distance.
Photo courtesy Arthur Ackermann & Peter Johnson

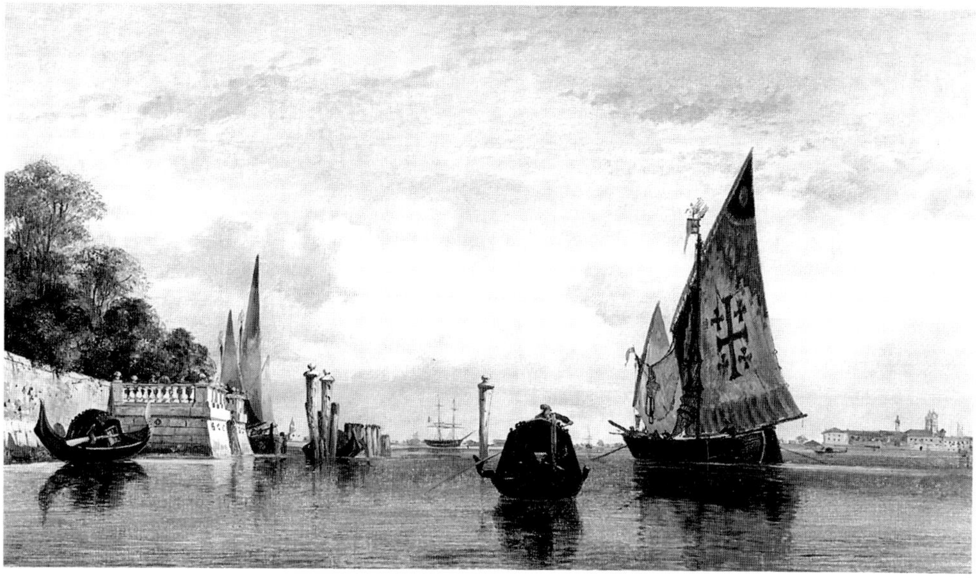

exhibitions of the season, under many a various aspect. This is a cool impression. "Marry ! we shall have hot days enow!"

No 127 (52/2, Colour Plate 132) *A Rainy Day on the Lagune of Venice, a Sketch on the spot.*
Under every phase, hot and cold, wet and dry, have these buildings been served up; and there is perhaps nothing impresses the mind of an observer so sensibly with the bewildering variety of appearance that excellence in art may assume, as to see a hundred different versions of the same subject, all more or less distinguished by valuable quality. The aspect of the scene is according to the description of the title. We have long been weary of speaking of the weather-worn bricks of Venice; we turn therefore with some relief to the sky, of which nothing otherwise than respectful can be said.

No 489 (55/4) *San Giorgio Maggiore, Venice, View looking East, effect immediately after Sunset. – We need not describe this church, everybody knows it as well as St Pauls but it becomes more and more apparent that buildings are the least successful portions of the works of this painter.*

RA 1859. No 262 (58/21, Colour Plate 130) *Venice – In all that appertains to effect, colour, and the fulness of the composition, this picture resembles those that have preceded it, but in manipulation it is manifestly different, being, in comparison with other Venetian subjects by Mr Cooke, but as a sketch...*

This is a 24in. x 40in. (61cm x 101cm) canvas which belongs to a small group in which the emphasis is on the commercial life of the port and the cargo boats. 'But as a sketch' perhaps refers to thinly painted passages and the remarks levelled at another Venetian subject that year point perhaps to a belief that large oils should carry an appropriate weight of paint!

BI 1859 No 3 (57/23) *Bragozzi-Fishing craft of Venice, off the Giardini Pubblici. We observe some change in the convictions of this painter. Look into that sky, ye who are philosophic in airy expression, and tell us if that be anything more than the thinnest wash of turpentine. We notice it simply because we fear it will not stand. The boats are certainly much less severe and therefore, in execution, more agreeable than others that have gone before them.*

The Institution catalogue adds 'Painted on the spot' which probably indicates a size of 11in. x 17in. (28cm x 43cm), perhaps on paper, which would explain a certain thinness of paint. This painting has not so far been sighted. Cooke's habit of 'working-up' his open-air studies sometimes resulted in a more weighty finish (Plate 143).

Chapter 12

SUBJECTS AT A DISTANCE: LATER PAINTINGS

In the year 1854 widespread interest and concern was shown on the arrival in London (brought home by Dr Rae of the Hudson's Bay Company) of pathetic and grim relics of Captain Sir John Franklin's lost Arctic expedition. His two ships *Erebus* and *Terror* failed to return from their 1845 expedition in search of the North West Passage linking the Atlantic with the Pacific across the north of the American continent. Their fate had never been known and it remained a question at the back of the public consciousness, if not in the public eye. The Admiralty, which had offered £10,000 for the discovery of the Passage, now offered an equal reward for proof of Franklin's end. This was claimed by Dr Rae.

What awakened Cooke's desire to paint a subject which was his nearest approach to a historical piece is not clear. The news which suggested his picture of *HMS Terror in the Ice of Frozen Strait* (Plate 144) might have been that Franklin's wife, who would not believe that she was a widow, financed a last searching expedition in 1857 in the hope of finding proof. Jane Lady Franklin lived in Park Place, Kensington. She purchased the screw schooner yacht *Fox* and the Admiralty had co-operated, permitting Captain F. Leopold M'Clintock RN to command an expedition to seek firm evidence on the fate of Sir John.

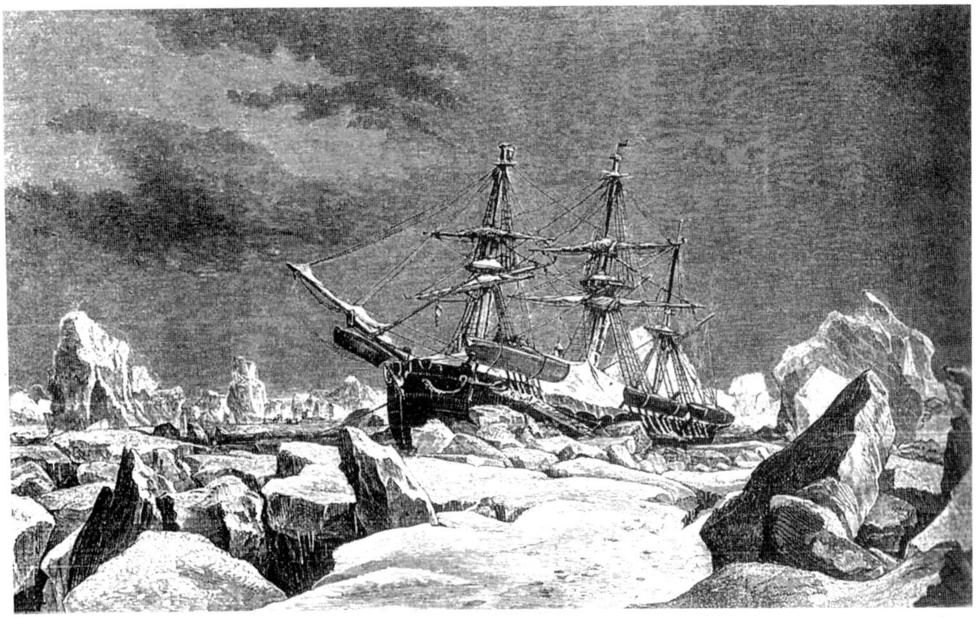

Plate 144. Engraving

HMS Terror *in the ice of Frozen Strait, 1837*

The frightening picture of Captain George Back's exploring ship wintering in the Arctic was painted under the eye of Rear Admiral Sir George Back who had become a neighbour of the painter. An Academy exhibit in 1860, the picture is not known to have survived.

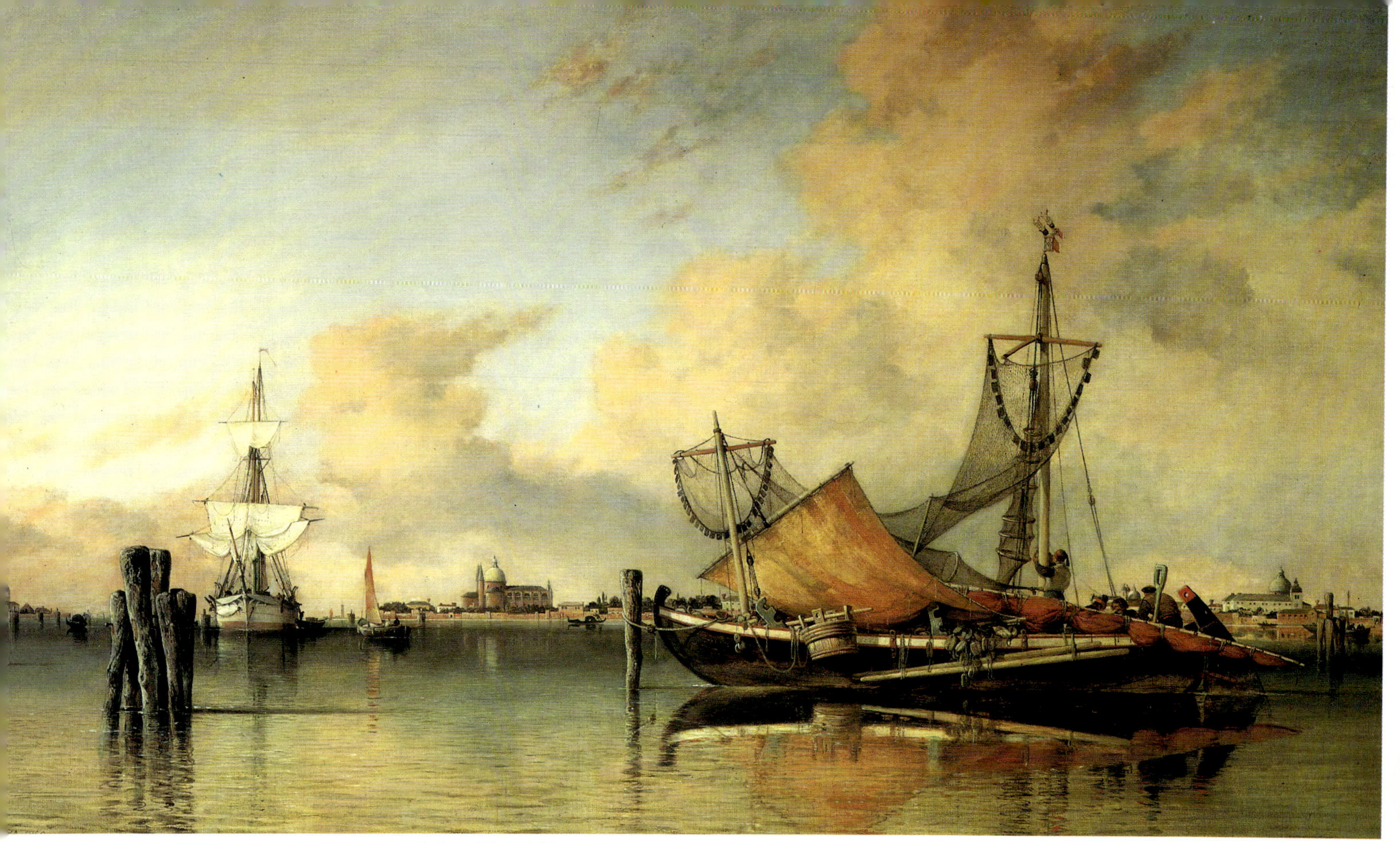

Colour Plate 133. 69/3

On the Lagune, Venice; evening before bad weather

This large Academy picture shares the title of the small 67/6 (Colour Plate 106) and its air of calm with the hint of coming storms. Cooke studied the weather and recorded cloud formations.

Photo courtesy Arthur Ackermann & Peter Johnson Ltd. Private Collection

For such a painter as Cooke there could be no imaginative rendering of an Arctic scene, the like of which he could never have seen, but he did have contacts and could call upon first hand eye-witness accounts and sketches. He was also a frequent traveller through Switzerland and had looked at Alpine glaciers!

Rear-Admiral Sir George Back FRS lived in Kensington, though Cooke had originally met him at a Graphic Society meeting in January 1838. As well as having earlier sailed with Franklin, Back published his own *Narrative of the Arctic land expedition to the mouth of the Great Fish river... 1833-35* (Murray 1836) and his account of the voyage, *Narrative of an expedition in HMS Terror undertaken with a view to geographical discovery on the Arctic shores... 1836-7,* was published by Murray in 1838.

As an aid to painting the Arctic ice floes, there were the plates in the printed account from drawings by Back. Cooke's picture showed the 326 ton ex bomb-vessel which had been converted and strengthened to withstand the stresses of Arctic ice and was a veteran of Polar exploration. On the voyage under Captain Back RN in 1837 they had endured months in a perilous situation.

The evidence and relics gathered in previous searches indicated that the Franklin expedition had perished, but the *Fox* party returned in 1859 having found written proof that Franklin himself died in June 1847. The indomitable Lady Jane had been a widow for twelve years.

In January 1858 Mary Cooke read from Captain Robert M'Clure's *Discovery of the North-West Passage* (1856) while her brother painted on a picture of Bonchurch beach with a rough sea. He was clearly steeping himself in the chill atmosphere and the recorded facts, for this book claimed that the Passage had indeed been found, but by M'Clure sailing in HMS *Investigator* from the Bering Strait.

The diary entries for March provide an entertaining chronicle of Kensington artistic life in the period when the Royal Commissioners for the 1851 Exhibition were buying up

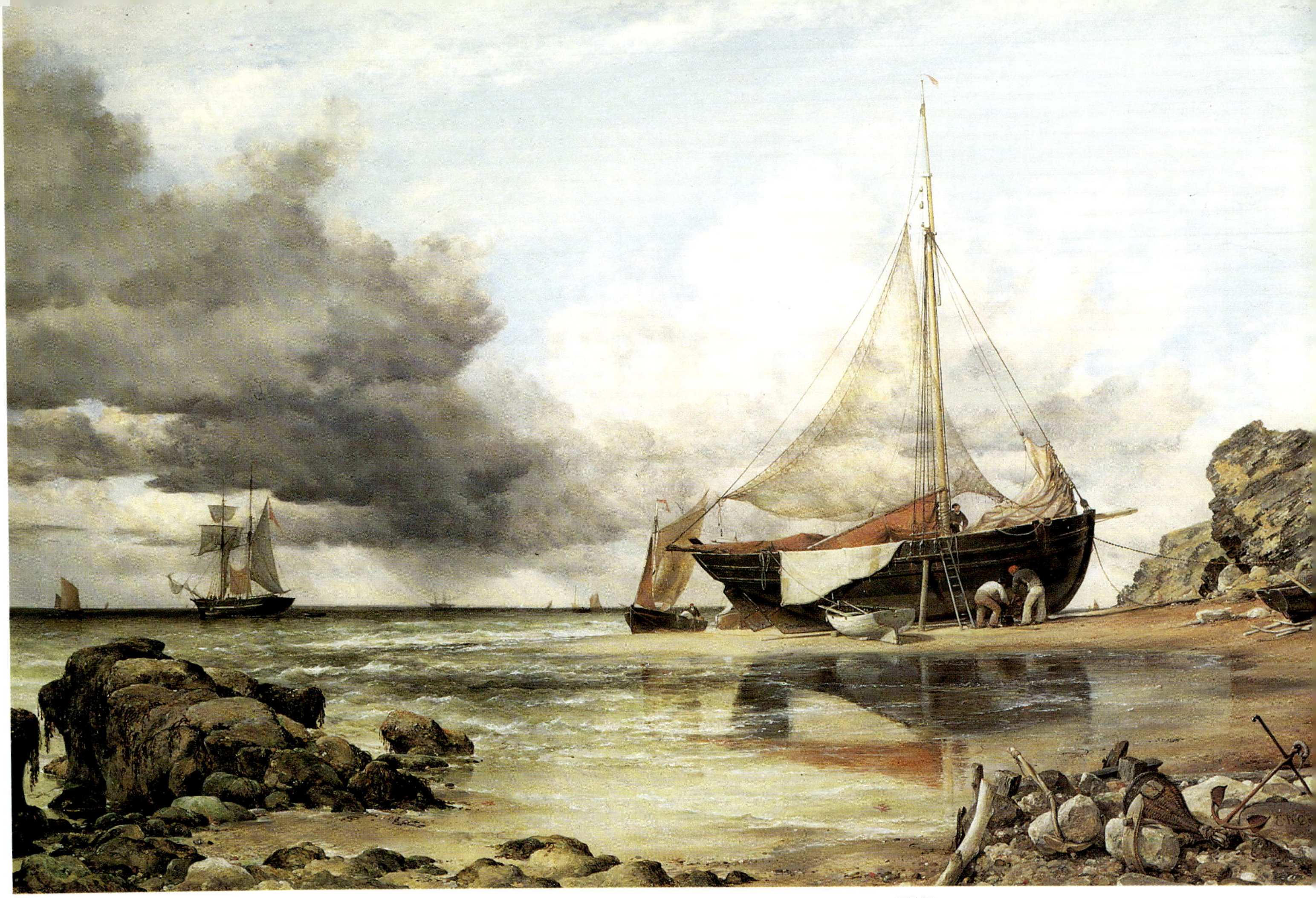

Colour Plate 134. 75/7

Chalk and firestone rocks, forming part of the Undercliff, Isle of Wight

A picture with the same title had been at the RA of 1872 but neither the size nor its present whereabouts are known. The shipping, a far from negligible element, gives way to the geology!

Photo courtesy M.A. Appleby

land in the vicinity, with the Crystal Palace now removed to Sydenham heights. Their Chairman, Albert the Prince Consort, had plans for a grand development scheme, a kind of *quartier latin,* of which only a small part was realised.[1]

After church at St. Paul's Knightsbridge Cooke called on Sir George Back and spent three hours discussing the Northern voyages. Eatwell, the supplier whose name is found stamped on the backs of some of Cooke's canvases, brought a length to *The Ferns* and stretched it on a frame for the Arctic subject. Having drawn in his design of the *Terror* with oil colour on 19 March, he was visited by Admiral Back and they consulted together about it.

It was near sending-in day for the Academy and Cooke had evidently arranged to handle Robert McInnes' picture of a shrine. The brothers Theo & Arthur Burnand, neighbours and patrons, called one afternoon to see the picture and Cooke then went with them to see also J.C. Hook's pictures on Campden Hill, at Tor Villas, which he had built. This studio visiting was a feature of the season and Cooke made extended use of the fashion while the Redgraves remembered the line of carriages which waited until their occupants could enter Sir Augustus Callcott's Kensington house to view his latest pictures.[2]

Admiral Back, with the sailor's concern that his old command should appear correctly, stayed for two hours giving hints. Rising at 7 to paint on the *Terror's* rigging, the artist also needed further references so from Waterloo by train to Weybridge and by fly to Byfleet Cooke journeyed to inspect George Chambers' picture of the *Terror* at Mr Back's.[3]

1. *V & A Album* II, 1983, p.367.
2. Redgrave 1947, p.375.
3. *Early Views of British North America,* Ian G.Lumsden, Beaverbrook Art Gallery Fredericton 1994, p.17.

Other mens' versions of the Arctic scene could be taken into account so he arrived at a compromise in having Admiral Back's detailed directions and the illustrations from his published account and also inspecting Chambers' canvas which was based on drawings by William Smyth, Back's First Lieutenant.

By visiting the Alps in September that year for his ice he was doing his best for an 'on the spot' reference and Cooke had also been reading M'Clintock's *Voyage of the Fox* published by Murray in 1859

It was not until February and March of 1860 that Cooke returned to his Arctic picture with more help from Admiral Back. It was destined for that year's Royal Academy and he noted inside the cover of his diary: *Captain Back started in Terror from Chatham 14th June 1836.*

He went to a reception at Earl de Grey's, encountering a great throng where he met Captain Young of the *Fox*. Lord de Grey had been First Lord of the Admiralty, Lord Lieutenant of Ireland and was the first President of the Royal Institute of British Architects with which Cooke was associated. He also wrote to Captain Hobson and got a reply... and one evening made designs in chalk of Franklin's boat and two skeletons....

A new memorial canvas was evidently in mind with the human figures in outline only, as it were. This calls to mind Edwin Landseer's *Man Proposes, God Disposes* of 1864, commissioned by E.J. Coleman, which showed hungry Polar bears and was understandably not liked by Lady Franklin. The subject was hardly E.W. Cooke's style, and nothing more is heard of it although Captain Hobson came one afternoon and consulted about the new Franklin picture.

In the middle of all this Cooke went to the Royal Institution to hear T.H. Huxley on the origin of species. He met at dinner at Dr. Lancaster's Professor Huxley and Mr Jukes and they all went at 9 to Mr Brodie's Soirée at the Royal Society where they met a great many celebrities including Prince Albert, Dr Walker and Professor Wheatstone.

Of domestic stress there is the occasional hint: *our kitchen chimney was on fire in aft: I got out on roof and we covered it over.*

Sir George Back called and Cooke again worked over the ice under his direction. *Fredk Schuckard came to tea and Tom and Burford in evg. – left at 11. I walked with them for ½ an hour. McInnes arrived at Hannah's. Mrs M. sent us a ham – My birthday.*

The 1860 Royal Academy exhibition catalogue has No 248:

> *HMS Terror in the ice of Frozen Strait, April 1837, when under the command of Captain, now Rear Admiral Sir George Back. (from whose sketch the vessel was painted.) The Terror was abandoned with Sir John Franklin's ship the Erebus in 1848 to the westward of King William's Id. "The whole scene indeed as far as the eye could stretch, was confusion worse confounded, &c."*

The purchaser was Samuel Gurney Esq, price 450 guineas. Perhaps in the *Terror* there was continuing ill omen. In 1866 the private banking house of Overend and Gurney failed hugely, and the calamitous effects were widely felt and for a long time. The auctioneers Robinson's sold pictures belonging to the firm in 1867 and *Terror* now fetched 400 guineas.

The whereabouts of the picture is unknown at the time of writing. It was bought at the sale by the Earl Grosvenor who wrote to the artist to tell him so. The painting was several times lent by him for public showing, the last occasion at a Wrexham Art Treasures Exhibition in 1876. An illustration of it from a drawing by E.M. Wimperis, engraved by J. & G.P. Nickols, accompanied the *Art Journal* biography of the artist in 1869, as one of his major works.

In arrangement of materials and truth of execution the picture is a master-work the Editor declared, leaving a later generation to ponder over his exact meaning.

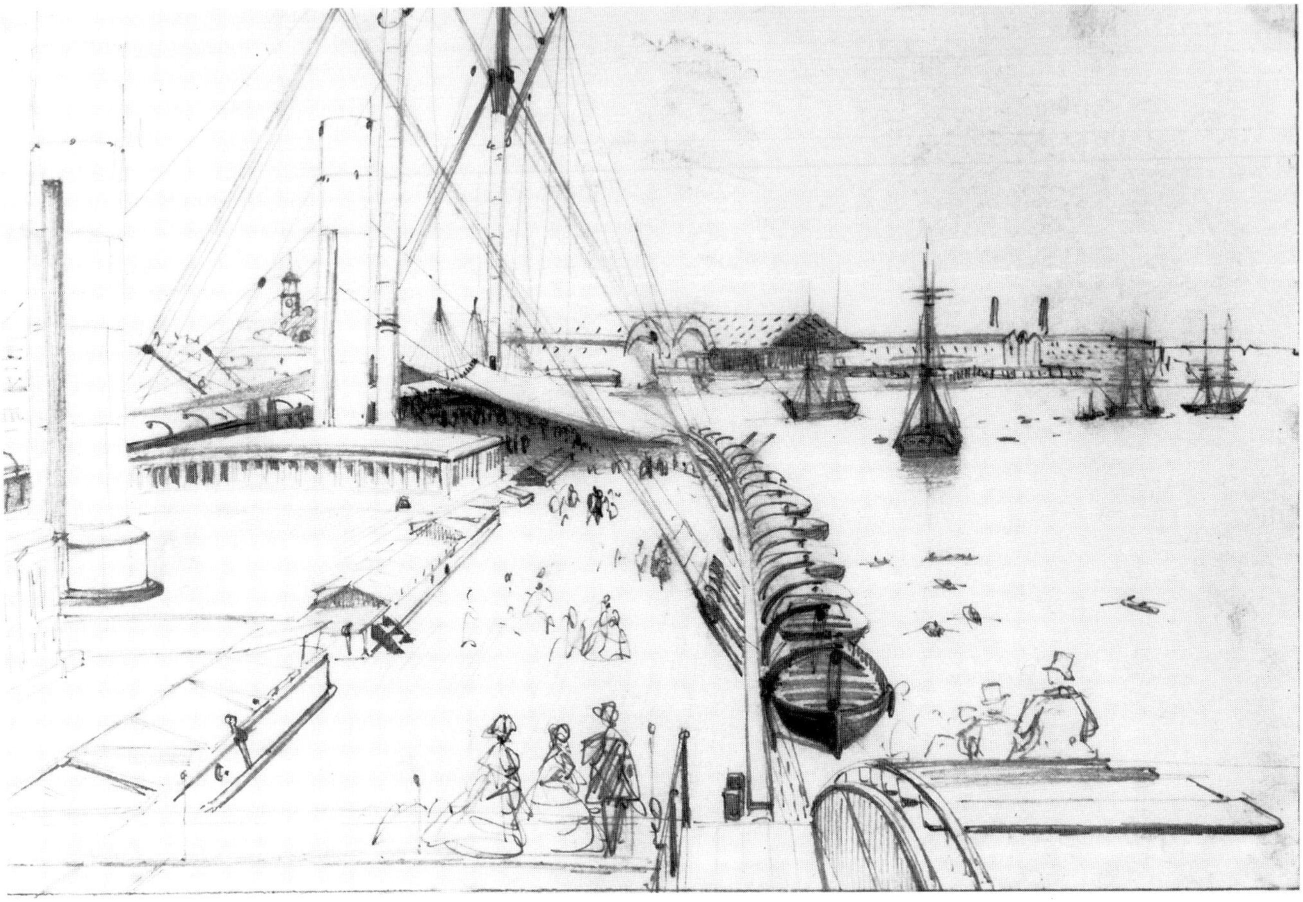

Plate 145. Pencil drawing
Deck of the Steamship Great Eastern. *1859*
View looking aft from the port paddle box of I.K. Brunel's huge screw-and-paddle vessel at first called *Leviathan* which Cooke viewed on her launching cradles at Millwall in December 1857. On 10 August 1859 he went on board with friends and *saw all over the vessel: at 4 sat down to a splendid collation.– dancing to the Artillery Band.*
She lies off Greenwich with Deptford Royal Dockyard in the background. Cooke's perfect sense of scale is shown in his drawing of the spread of the vast awnings over the upper deck, with the crowd beneath them. He had also drawn on board Brunel's *Great Britain* in the Thames in 1845, but none of those sketches is known to have survived. Photo courtesy Christie's

We know what the actual painting looked like for a photograph was taken of the completed canvas by Joubert in 1864 and a print, inscribed by the artist in that year to Lady Franklin, has survived. It is in a collection bequeathed by her husband's great-niece Miss Jessie Lefroy to the Scott Polar Research Institute at Cambridge.

Spain and North Africa

David Roberts had shown them in 1833 the fruits of fourteen months in the Peninsula; J.F. Lewis' drawings of the colour of Spain were admired by Cotman with the Cookes at a Conversazione at the Thatched House Tavern in 1834; John Phillip exhibited regular glimpses of Spanish life and Edward Cooke's occasional meeting with notables like Penrose Mark, HBM's Consul at Malaga, at the Bicknells with Roberts in 1841 helped to kindle his awareness. The attractions of coast and climate, shipping and architecture, mountains and gardens would have seemed eminently worth recording. Richard Ansdell, the animal painter, had collaborated with Phillip in 1857 and he was a close friend and neighbour in Kensington.

He chose the Mediterranean seaboard to visit, bought maps at Stanford's and called for guidebooks at John Murray's. He got the latest edition of *Spain* in sheets, presumably before publication, and later offered observations and corrections on his return in May 1861.[4]

4. John Murray Archives.

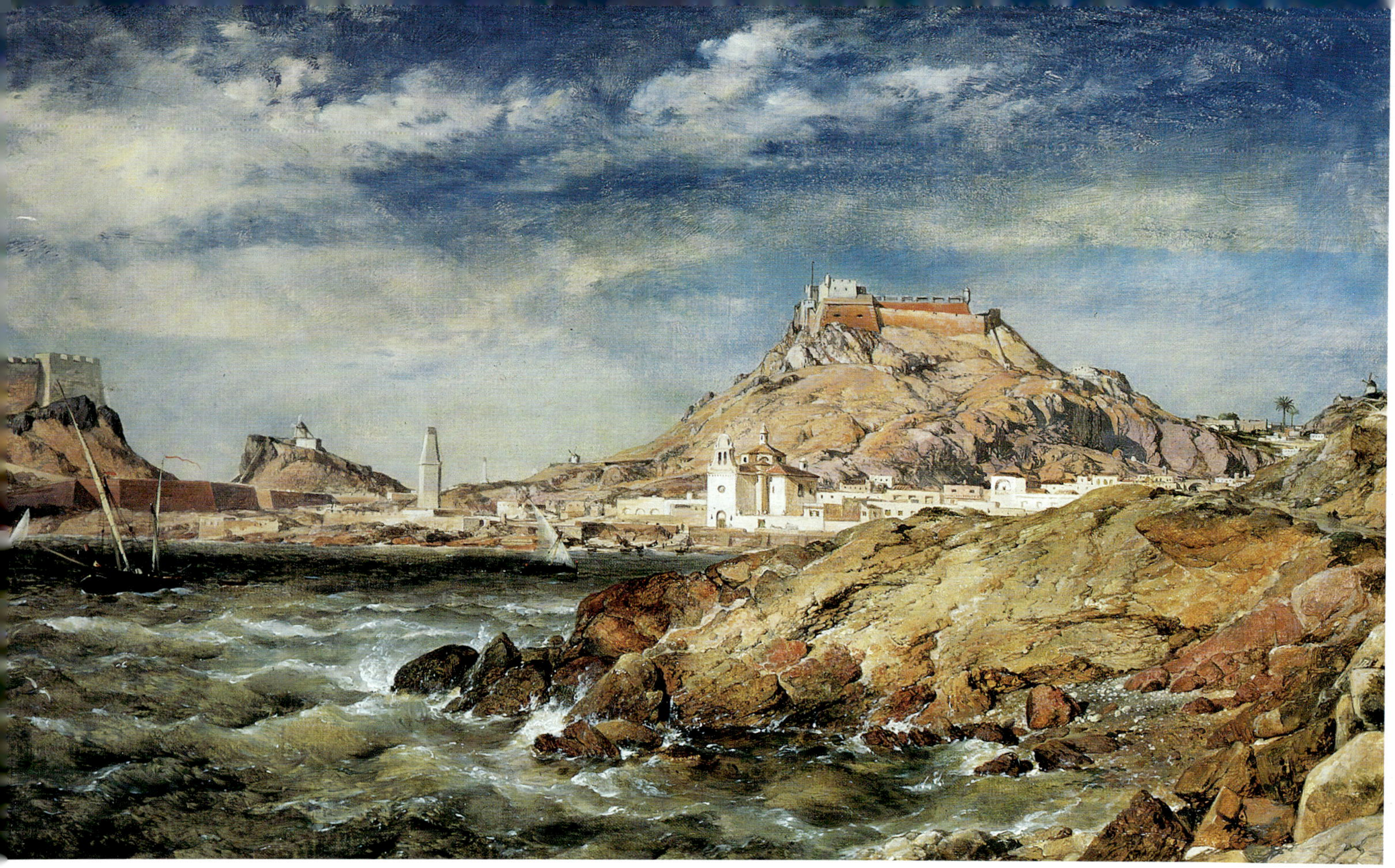

Colour Plate 135. 60/9
Cartagena. Rocks and castle, Sta Lucia: Santa Lucia, Port of Cartagena; East coast of Spain
Photo courtesy Sotheby's. Private Collection

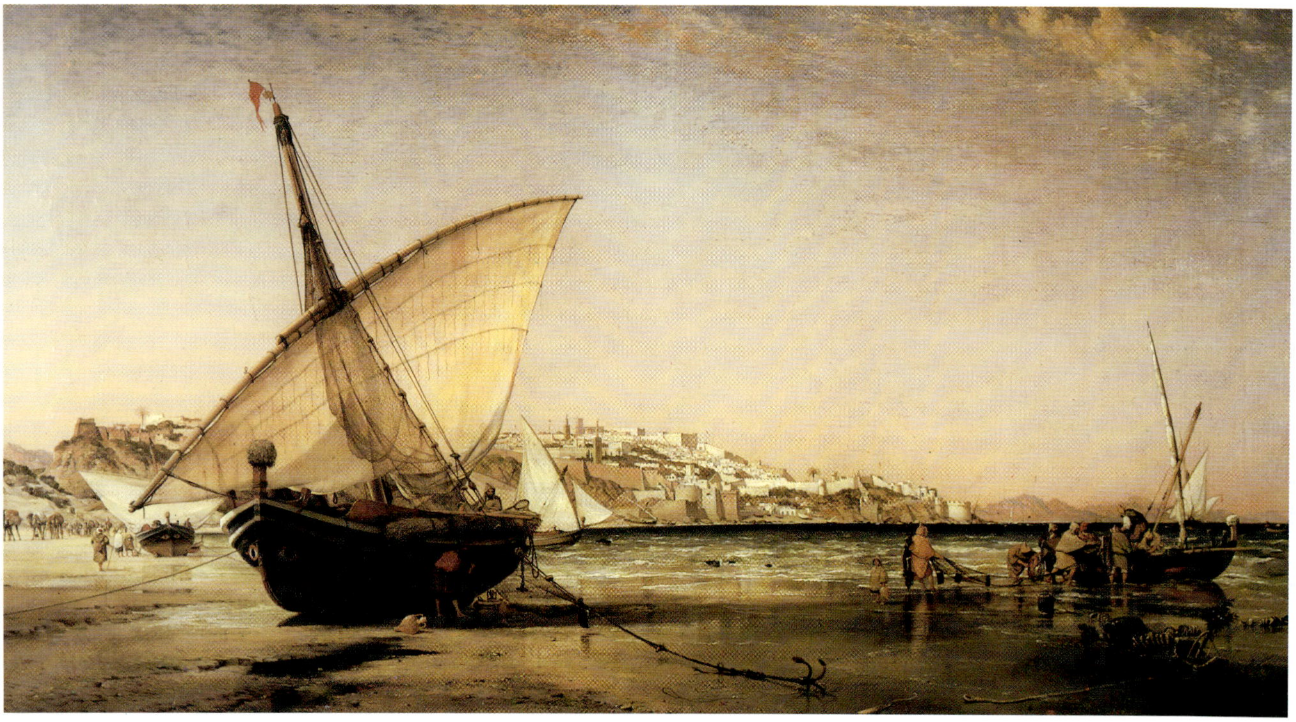

Colour Plate 136. 62/2
The Bay of Tangier, Morocco; the mountains of Spain and Gibraltar in the distance
Photo courtesy Salford Art Gallery

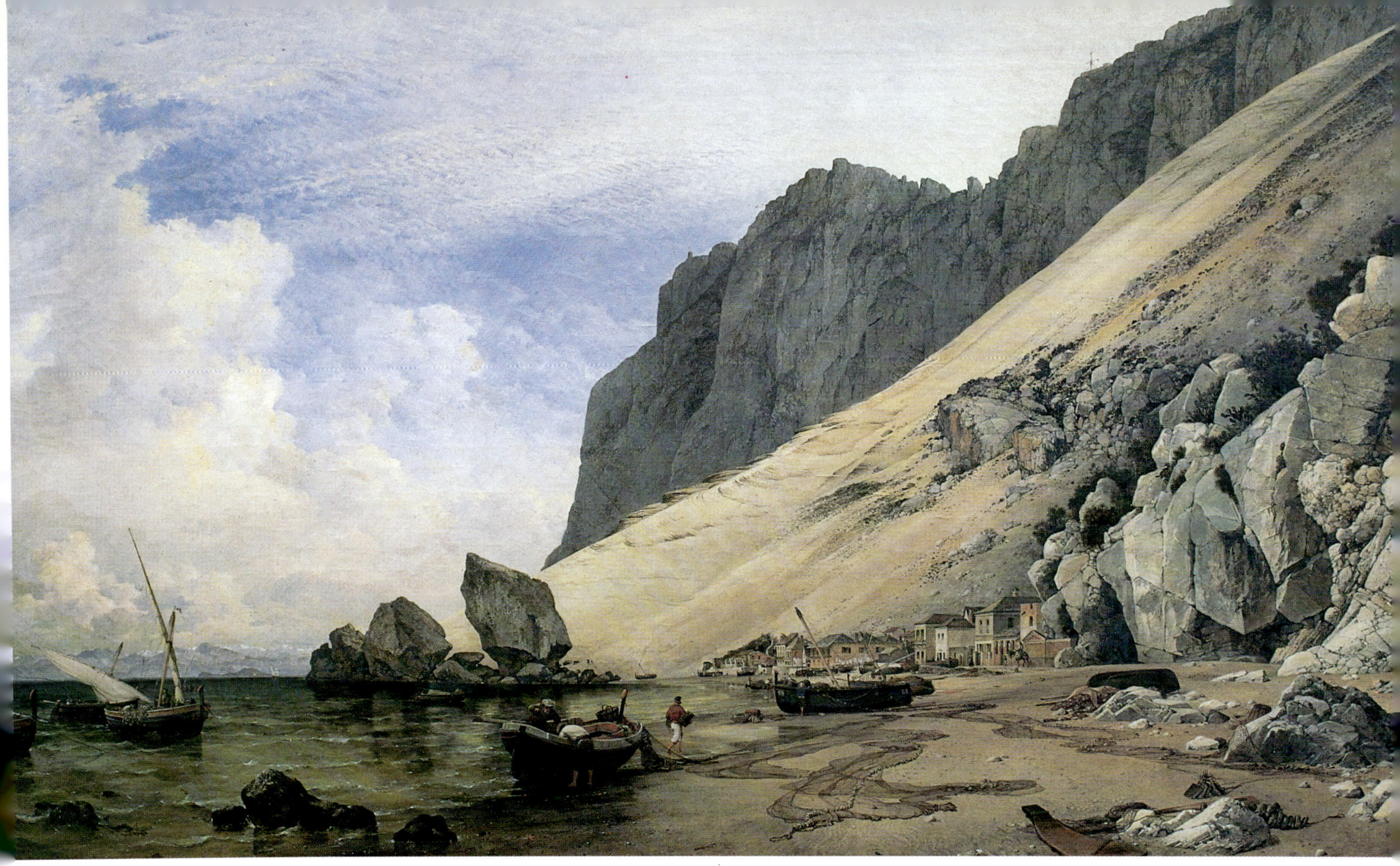

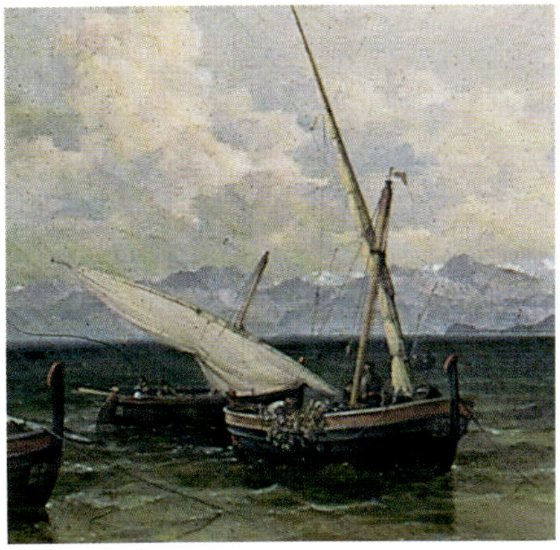

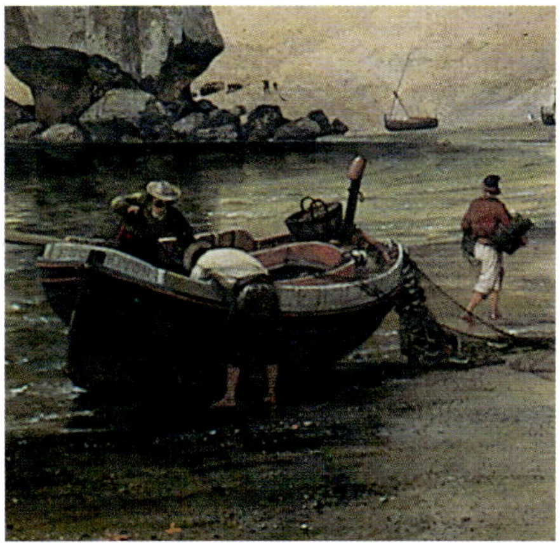

Colour Plate 137. 63/2
Catalan Bay on the East side of the Rock of Gibraltar; the African coast, Ceuta and the Mountains of Atlas in the distance
An undoubted *tour de force* which again embraced a fishing community at work and a geological marvel, this painting secured for Cooke his scientific reputation and further public acclaim.

Photos courtesy Private Collection

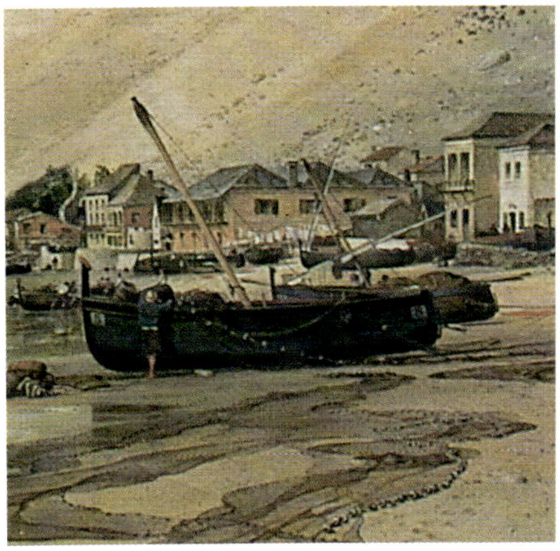

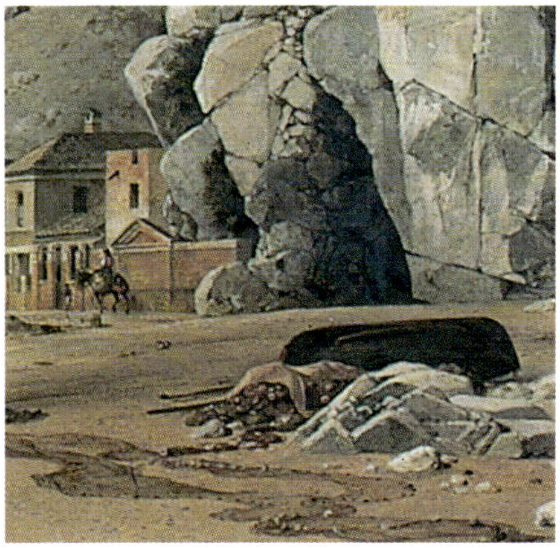

Colour Plate 137A. Detail left
Colour Plate 137B. Detail left centre
Colour Plate 137C. Detail right centre
Colour Plate 137D. Detail right

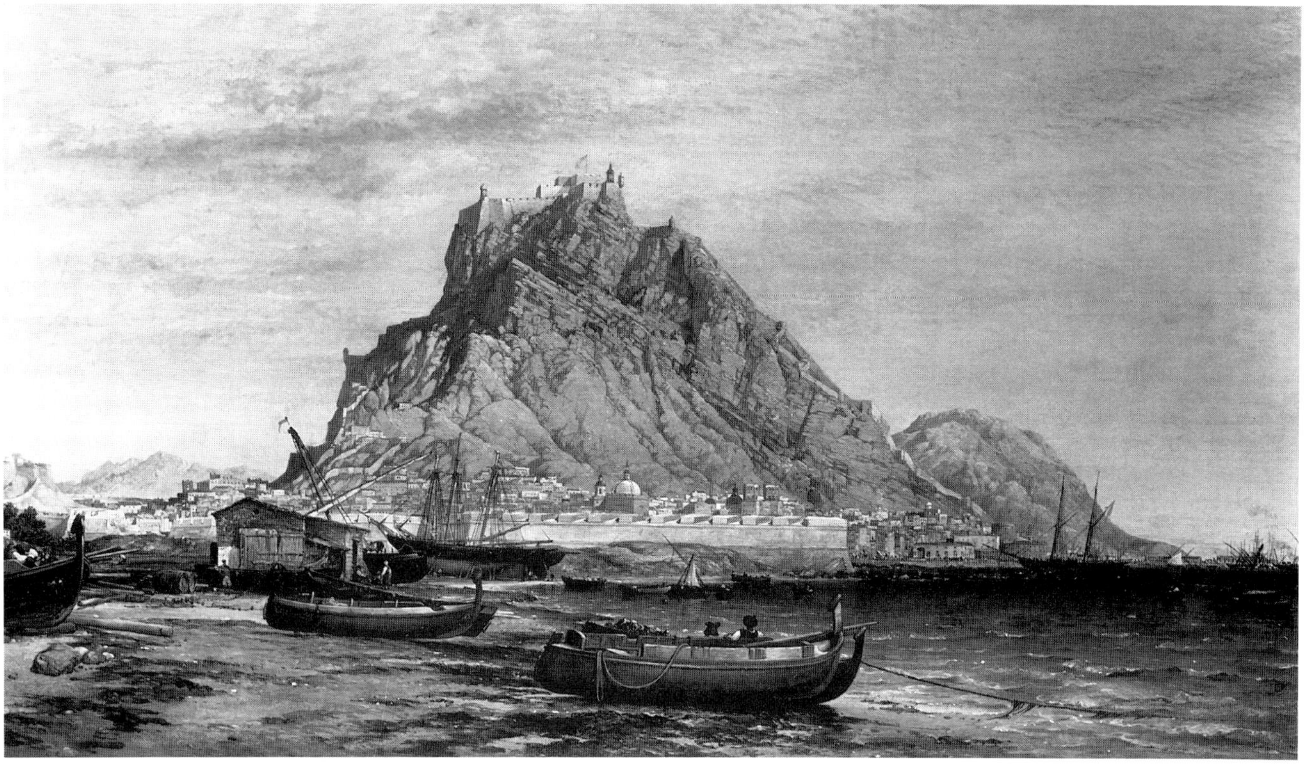

Plate 146. 60/6
The Rock & Castle of Alicante
Several versions of the title occur but this is the sole representative found to date.
Photo courtesy Agnews. Private Collection

In September 1860 he went with Robert Cooke, who was no relation but a cousin of the publisher's, to Wimbledon by bus and was delighted with John Murray's lovely house and grounds which he noted as *A perfect Gem.* Numbers of letters of introduction from his friends, the vintner Charles Gassiott and the orchid grower Sigismund Rücker. for contacts in Spain were forthcoming.

Edward Cooke started off with Robert Bateman, painter son of his friend the squire of Biddulph, through France to Marseilles where they called on Edward Mark, the British Consul; then to Barcelona by the *Marcella* steamer which thumped her way across the Gulf to the discomfort of her more discerning passengers.

Arrived in Spain his attentions were first of all directed to the local craft, going down to the harbour where they took a boat and got a large sketch, partly in watercolours, of Tartanos and Catalans. Cooke spent a long day on the deck of a Felucha drawing a general view of Barcelona with the statue of Neptune and boats.

They moved onwards in their planned route with colourful if annoying diversions. The *Tarragonensa* was a very small dirty steamer and after three-quarters of an hour the cylinder got damaged, as the diarist recorded, and it was opened up while they had to anchor for three and a half hours on a very hot day and calm. The fore deck was covered with peasants and wives and doubtless Cooke drew the groups. Tarragona's cathedral demanded sketches, *...columns and arches, we drew several. The effect of the aisles, transepts and stained glass most superb – we remained there till dark..*

They went to the cloisters and began watercolour drawings of the Patio and part of the Apse of the Cathedral while in the evening Cooke copied a photograph of the façade of it, lent to him by a confectioner opposite the hotel!

The fact that next day there was no boat till night meant that they drew all day at the cloisters and went on board the *Ebro* at six in a lovely sunset. They remained on board below until the captain came and started at one o'clock in the morning for Tortosa. They rested well on sofas while a conjurer and ventriloquist amused them.

Travelling on land was irksome discomfort 'rammed in with two strangers' in the

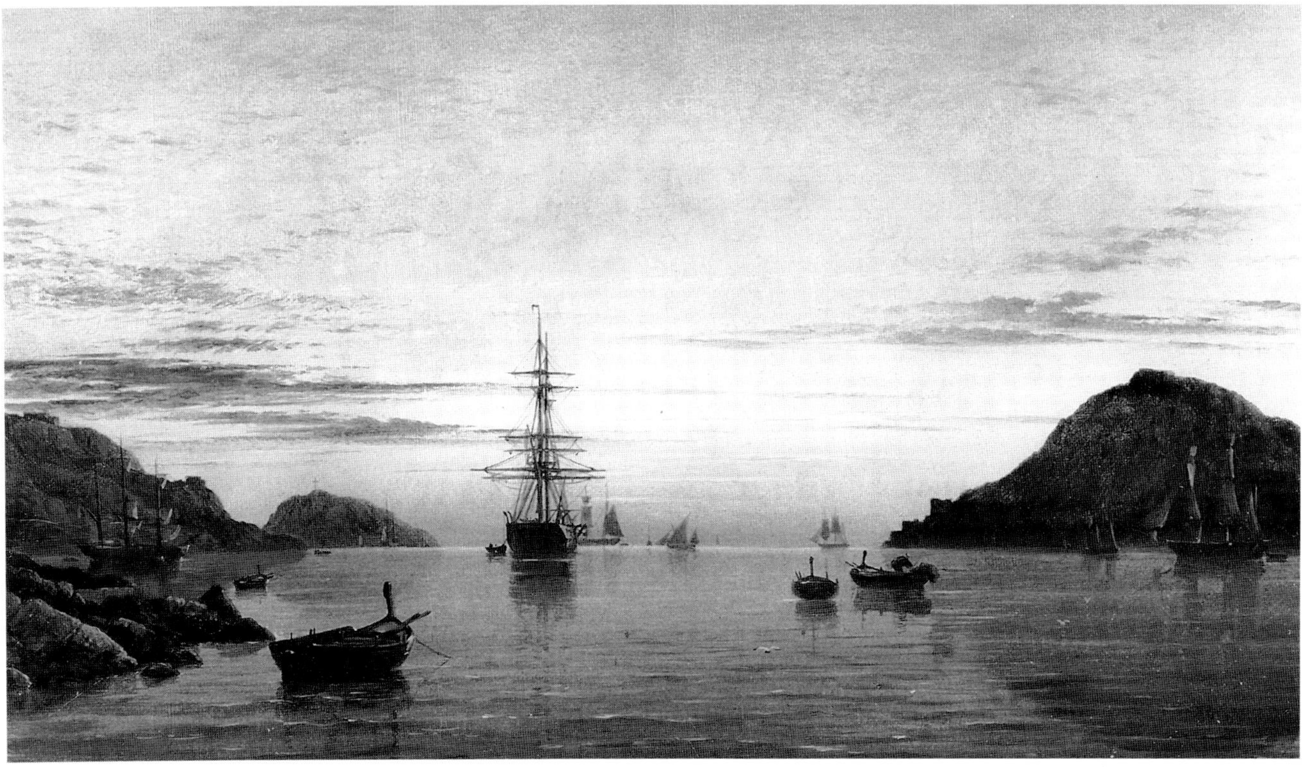

Plate 147. 61/1

Sunset, Bay of Cartagena, with the island of Escombrera in the distance

As was often the case, the Academy picture was four times the size of the painting made on the spot. Photo courtesy Arthur Ackermann & Peter Johnson

cabriolet of the diligence from Tortosa to Valencia. They went to Madrid where they met John Phillip RA who was painting (his 'man' got them into the Prado on a 'closed' day) and Cooke recorded their delight with the assembled works of Velasquez, Titian and Veronese and also enthused about the collections of the *Real Armeria*, making a few sketches.

Back they went to Valencia and on to Alicante (Plate 146) where, armed with a permit to sketch from the Governor, they unpacked oil colours, dined and got a sketch from the deck of a new dredging machine, till darkness fell.

At Cartagena, their next stop, their mail was collected at the Consul's and they met Dr Dalgairns who dosed an Edward Cooke evidently in dire need. Later he introduced them to his family and to the Casino where the English papers were taken; he also found them a lodging and a studio. Cooke painted the view, leaving his traps at a friendly priest's house overnight. The connoisseur of western skies reported *the most wonderful sunset I ever saw* (Plate 147).

Early in 1861 they sailed down to Malaga on board the *Mercurio,* seeking out on arrival the British Consul, William Penrose Mark, elder brother of the Consul at Marseilles and head of an interesting family, long resident in Spain. His father, William Mark Wardlaw, had run off to sea under the name of William Mark and after a career as a purser in the Navy became a Secretary to successively Lord Nelson, Lord Exmouth and Sir Charles Vinicombe Penrose.[5] He had been Navy Prize-Agent at Gibraltar and obtained the post of Consul at Malaga in 1816.

In 1833 David Roberts had experienced much kindness at their hands on his travels and British visitors gravitated towards their house. The provision of a burial ground for Protestants in that Catholic country was one achievement of old Mark's. Cooke had met two of them at dinner at Elhanan Bicknell's, Herne Hill, where David Roberts had introduced them in 1841. There was a large family and of seven girls two, Robina and the youngest Christina Isabel, were still living at home. There were echoes of a violent past: William Boyd Carpenter, later Bishop of Ripon, had an uncle Robert Boyd who

5. *At Sea with Nelson,* W. Mark, 1929.

was shot with General Torrijos in 1831 after an unsuccessful *coup* in spite of Mark's efforts to obtain clemency.

Cooke had been a widower for seventeen years, was almost fifty and his diary notes make it clear that he found in Christina a young woman – she was twenty-seven – whom he could see as his wife. His references to her become more frequent and detailed; he gave her drawing lessons, bought art materials for her and seems generally to have tried to win her by his attentions. Meantime his own painting continued but by the end of a month he was deeply involved and was writing home to his lawyer about a marriage settlement.

Cooke and Bateman went off to Gibraltar continuing their painting expedition, which may have been a mistake. Crossing to Africa he made drawings, painted a coloured sketch of Tangier port from the beach, bought Arab souvenirs in quantity, wrote to Christina and viewed a memorable dragon tree, *Dracaena*, which he drew in the garden of the Swedish Consul's house.

The unfortunate man seemed doomed to receive bad news by post when away on painting tours. Fifteen years back Capri had seen him saddened by the death of his father-in-law and now in Tangier he heard that his youngest sister, Georgiana, Mrs Stephen Ward, had died, not long after the birth of a daughter.

To make matters worse, his hopes of married bliss with Christina Mark were dashed; she in his absence had time to reconsider her feelings and now wrote to end it all. Later she married the Rev Hunt Holley and their daughters presented some of Cooke's drawings to the Victoria and Albert Museum with notes on the artist.

There was evidently still a programme to follow: when he could get a passage from Tangier, Cooke went back to Gibraltar, finished an elaborate drawing of the remarkable geology of Catalan Bay and the Mediterranean side of the Rock and was off to Cadiz where illuminations marked the opening of the railway to Seville.

He then made his way back to Malaga but was greeted on arrival by a letter delivered on board the packet from Penrose Mark and Christina that dashed any hopes he may have retained and made him 'miserable indeed'.

All his gear was sent from the Mark house and he began packing up. His fiftieth birthday on the day following saw his homeward journey begun. A stop in Gibraltar where he went on board HMS *Ariadne* and *Immortalité* provided another useful opportunity for a topical sketch (Plate 148).

Here was a return to normality and on arrival home via the P & O steamer he soon began to pick up the threads of his London life.

His use of the Spanish sketches was not extensive and understandably he never returned to those shores where even the superb sunsets could not obliterate memories of disappointment.

The artist's *Ledger* shows in its later pages blank columns for 'Purchaser' and 'Price'. This proves to be not slack book-keeping but the reflection of a nation-wide recession in trade and a resulting slump in picture buying which caused consternation in the artist communities.

Confirmation of this is found in a letter from Cooke to Sir Joseph Hooker in 1878,[6] saying that he had not *parted with a picture for three years owing to the depressed state of the Trade of the country.* Similarly, to his publisher John Murray he says that he can bear any disappointment after having had eight of his large Royal Academy pictures returned unsold, *...but how fearful to those of my profession who have to depend on the ready sale of their works – such as have their fame and name to make.*[7]

Further confirmation of the state of things is provided by William Holman Hunt's correspondence with John Lucas Tupper, March 1879, in which he reports that painters

6. Royal Botanic Gardens, Kew, Director's Correspondence.
7. John Murray Archives.

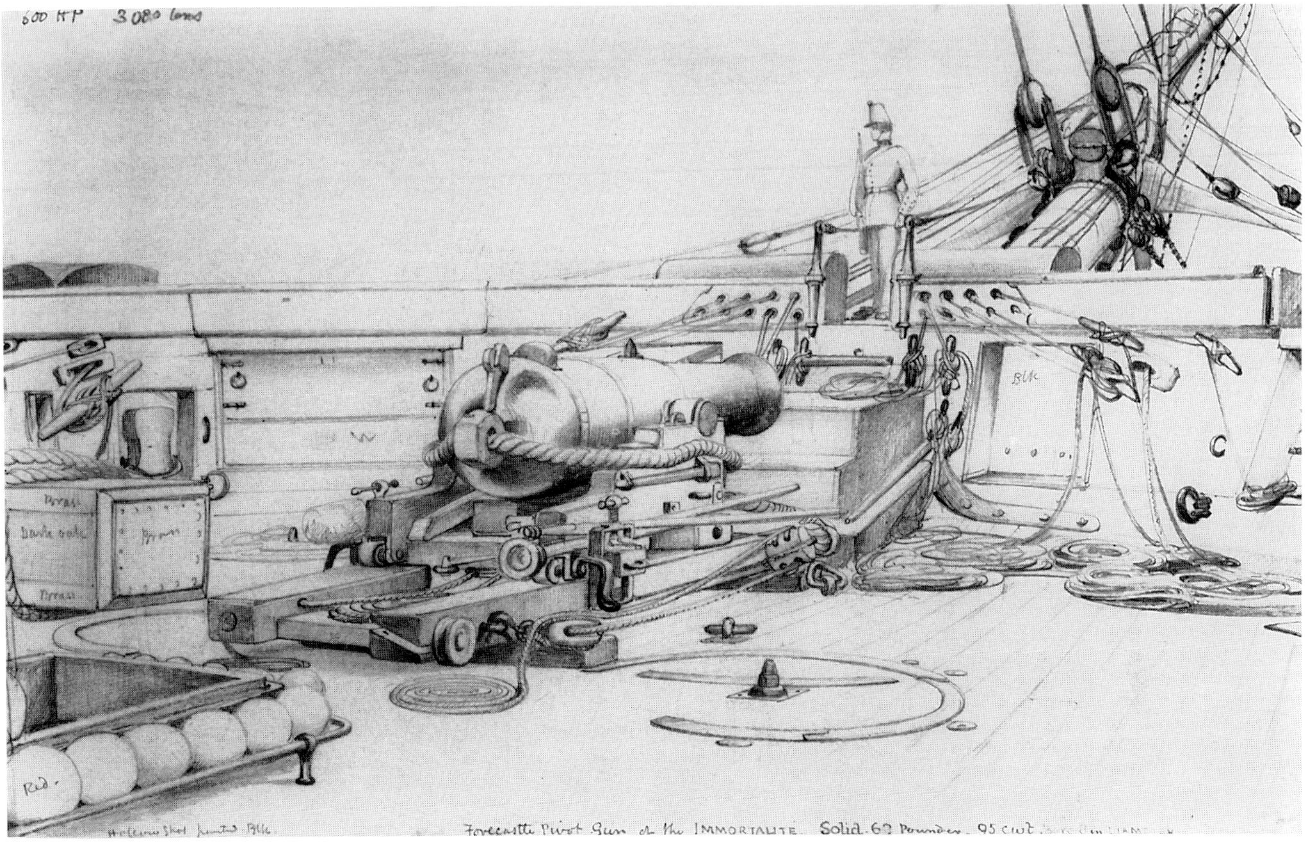

Plate 148. Pencil drawing

The fo'c'sle pivot gun of HMS Immortalité 1861

Cooke went on board at Gibraltar and witnessed the guns' crews at exercise. This 68 pounder fired solid shot as well as explosive shell and he was evidently charmed by the cradled monster and all its fittings, here recorded admirably, as was his habit.

Photo courtesy The Trustees of the National Maritime Museum, Greenwich

of the St John's Wood clique had held a meeting to try to devise some way out of the depression and continues *even the very worst artists for the last year or two have failed to sell any pictures Ansdell to whom such a thing had never happened had all his works sent home unsold, and Cooke did not sell a single picture.*[8]

Richard Ansdell RA, a lesser Landseer and Cooke's friend, is now remembered chiefly for his *Stag at Bay,* 1846. He was a prolific exhibitor of animal subjects and collaborator in supplying furry detail for other painters like John Phillip and Thomas Creswick. ... *his colour was not good and his finished works lack what the painters call 'quality'* recorded Redgrave.[9] Success, too easy success with the animal-loving public, doubtless categorised him as a bad artist in Holman Hunt's view; it is perhaps understandable. The gulf between religious and history painting and lesser profane subjects yawned wide at this time.

Subject apart, the reasoning and the implication that bad artists sold easily comes from one who devoted long hours to the realisation of elaborately detailed passages, for Hunt took several years to complete a major canvas. *Every thoroughly good picture finds a purchaser* wrote Philip Hamerton hopefully,[10] ... *and many pictures that are not good find purchasers also... The kind of art which sells most readily in the exhibitions is not that which carries a great artistic nature highest or farthest, though it is conveniently adapted to the capabilities of a small one.*

Again, shipping and craft and coastal geology, the lack of poetic imagination or moral content in Cooke's marine pieces, failed to interest the serious Pre-Raphaelite. Cooke's close absorption in the essential character of his subjects however, put him on a parallel course with Hunt.

8. *A Pre-Raphaelite Friendship,* UMA Research Press, Ann Arbor, 1986, p.263.P.
9. Redgrave 1947, p.420.
10. Hamerton op.cit., p.139.

They both sold to the gallery owner and publisher, the dealer Ernest Gambart, that major force in the art world, though Hunt was much more closely involved through the great business of engravings from his pictures. Gambart's relinquishing his picture dealing in 1871 was widely felt by many of the artists whose works he handled. During his thirty years of princely retirement in Nice at *Les Palmiers* he saw this demonstrated, for example in the decline of the fortunes of Frederick Goodall, much of whose work had passed through the old Belgian's hands for high prices. Cooke however was not so dependent on one purveyor.

Later, in 1879, Holman Hunt stayed with Cooke in the country at *Glen Andred* for a week-end in June in the company of Professor Richard Owen (whose portrait Hunt painted) and the American landscape painter Albert Bierstadt. It would be interesting to know what he thought of his host's establishment and life-style, and also of his fellow guests. Owen certainly admired the garden, sending a note to Cooke in 1877 to introduce a friend *as great (almost) an admirer of Flora as yourself. He much wishes to see her as dressed by your handiwork.*[11] In Hunt's letters to Tupper the names of Hook and Cooke occur almost as though they were a pair of inseparable oddities. Sea-shore scenes dominated their paintings, although human interest and anecdote from the daily lives of fisherfolk and their children are prominent in Hook's pictures. Both were indeed a far cry from the Dead Sea shores of Holman Hunt's *The Scapegoat,* although its geological background must have woken a response in Cooke.

The *Art Journal* in 1870 said:

> *James Clark Hook and E.W. Cooke have been studying in the land of these Dutch and Flemish painters and are not one whit behind the best of them... Nothing in Dutch art more real or picturesque than No.189 E.W. Cooke, Calm. It has finer qualities than the Calm by Mr Clays now in the French Gallery. Compare the water surfaces in the two pictures. Clays' water has no surface. There is certainly nothing more true or beautiful in the Academy than the study of these bright slumbrous reflections cast in the transparent depth of the tranquil sea.*

11. Cooke MSS.

Chapter 13

THE MIDDLE ORIENT

Apartments at 22 Pall Mall were rented for the finishing and display of Cooke's three Academy pictures in 1873 and as usual invitations were sent to friends and patrons for his private views. These social occasions which usually ran for five days at the end of March allowed Cooke to work on the last stages of his paintings, though the arrivals and departures, the chat and chatter must have made concentration difficult. Since he now lived in the country the temporary move to town was necessary and his club the Athenaeum was near at hand for meals and an evening's reading or a talk with friends. His display of pictures bore fruit, and he recorded a sale to Mr and Mrs Bolckow who came and chose either the Kynance Cove subject or the Dutch one (Colour Plates 139 and 138).

He sent instructions by letter to his sisters on house and garden matters for he was detained in Town by having this year to serve on the RA selection and hanging committees. With evening Council meetings as well it was hard work, from ten in the morning until half past five. Club dinners and Society meetings which occupied his evenings were interspersed with private dinner-parties in celebration of the RA Exhibition, which had become regular features of the season. At Mr Matthews' (Charles P. Matthews of Hertford Street and Havering atte Bower, a brewery magnate, purchaser of his Catalan Bay picture and also of Holman Hunt's *The Finding of the Saviour in the Temple*) he met at dinner F. Toulmin, another patron, Mr and Mrs Ind-Coope, Holman Hunt, young Matthews and Thomas Barlow, probably Thomas Oldham Barlow RA, the engraver.

Even on Good Friday after the service in the Chapel Royal where Dean Stanley preached a most glorious sermon – and luncheon at the RA – they worked at hanging till six. By the 22nd they had reached the watercolours and the drawings were hung by four o'clock on 24th. He then dressed and went at eight to dinner at Sir John Pender's where he met the Duke of Sutherland, Bishop of Winchester, Lords Lyons, Wentworth, Beaumont, Houghton and a great many RAs. Cooke went upstairs for half an hour to a reception after dinner and at eleven pm to a Royal Society Soirée where he found, unsurprisingly, very few people left. There is a determination not to miss any interesting event and one is reminded of Ruskin's jibe about the man who must see everything. Academy dates included 1 May when the Royal Family came (this year with the King and Queen of the Belgians, the Duke and Duchess of Teck, etc.) and the dinner on the 2nd. Having with the rest of the Council arranged the tables and seats, Cooke dressed and returned at half past three. He had as his guests Cyrus Field and Henry Bessemer on either hand and there were Messrs. Poole, Hawkesley and Matthews opposite. He could record excellent speeches and after tea and coffee admirable music which made a very successful occasion. George Dunlop Leslie RA[1] had much to say about the mechanics and protocol of Academy dinners as well as the functioning of the various committees – as a regular attender from the first when made an Associate he regretted not having kept a diary and remembered only the famous names; his father, C.R. Leslie RA, had however left memoirs, although there is nothing on E.W. Cooke.

The State visit of Nasr ed Deen, the Shah of Persia, to Queen Victoria in 1873 included a Review of the assembled British Fleet on 23 June at Spithead, the traditional fleet

1. *The Inner Life of the Royal Academy*, G.D. Leslie RA, 1914.

anchorage off Portsmouth where, since the previous century, ceremonial Royal Reviews had taken place. Thc artist went afloat in Mr Thomas Brassey's yacht *Livonia,* having boarded her in the harbour; they saw the Shah sail out in the Royal Yacht and followed her in tow of a tug. Up and down the lines of ships they passed all morning and after luncheon boarded the men of war *Devastation,* the *Sultan* and the *Hercules.* Well might Cooke record *a most glorious day*.

The Royal Yacht steamed along the lines of anchored warships to the deafening accompaniment of royal salutes and cheers from the ships' companies. The old sailing navy was slowly changing into a force of ironclad ships of war (Plate 149), and HMS *Devastation,* launched in 1871, was the first mastless steam battleship (Plate 150). She was an extraordinary shape, devoid of grace, low in the water, menacing, but a superb symbol of sea-power.

Perhaps Cooke had in mind the cry of the Rt Hon George Goschen MP, First Lord of the Admiralty, at the Royal Academy banquet in 1871: *I will ask the Academicians here present that if this year they have painted The Wooden Walls of Old England* [The *Art Journal* said this was a poor painting by C.E. Johnson[2]] *they will paint next year – if their genius be equal to it, the iron bolts which are as necessary to our security, as were the wooden walls... they are the types of science and strength.*

The *Art Journal,* in reporting this, begged to differ and saw few pictorial possibilities in the 'navy of the future' while observing that *with the destruction of the wooden walls, the art of marine painting seems to have likewise perished... remarkable especially when we remember that a few years since our English painters, Neptune-like, held dominion of the ocean.* Here was a challenge and Cooke designed a large picture to record this modern vessel amid the animation of Spithead. The squat black hulled 'turret sea-going monitor', sometimes derisively called a flat-iron, dressed overall with the coloured bunting of her signal flags, is in a central position with the billowing smoke from her gun salute almost obscuring the fleet to leeward. The Royal Yacht flying the Shah's standard is seen in the distance, in weather which appears to have been anything but bright. When the painting was shown at the Royal Academy the *Art Journal,* in a moment almost of critical indecision, pronounced:

> No. 232 Devastation. ...*we are much pleased but with the exception that the smoke from the muzzle of the great gun disperses itself too soon. A longer continuation of the outline would have conveyed more completely the idea of the irresistible swiftness of the death dealing messenger. Mr Cooke is generally speaking so accurate and so scientific an observer that we almost feel inclined to question our own judgement....*

2. *Art Journal,* 1871, p 174.

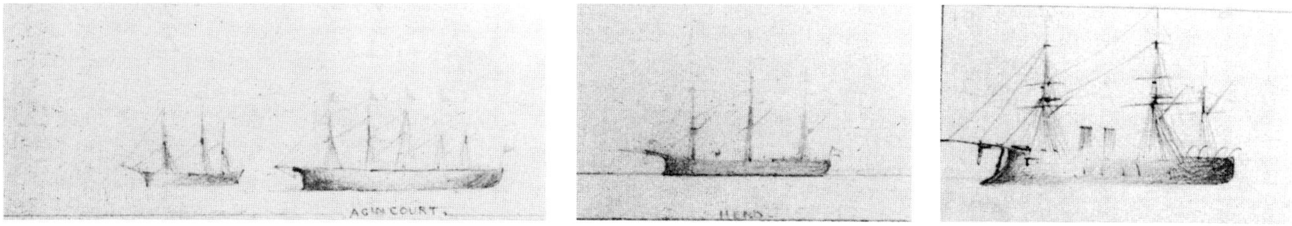

Plate 149.
HMS Agincourt. *and others*

Pencil drawing

Cooke acknowledges the 'new Age' of the sinister iron steam warship. She and her sister, the *Minotaur* of the mid-1860s, were the only five-masted ships of war ever built; funnels were retractable!

Photo courtesy Clarges Gallery

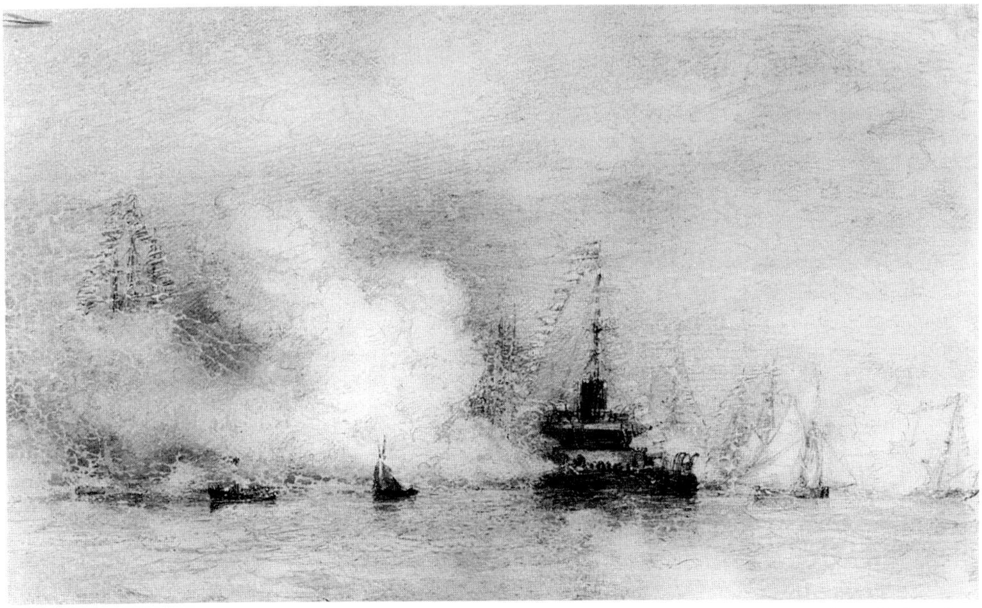

Plate 150. Pencil drawing
HMS Devastation *firing a royal salute.[23] June 1873*
The Naval Review at Spithead in honour of the Shah of Persia was the subject of his painting (Colour Plate 140) in which the centre of interest is the Navy's first mastless battleship. The drawing on a patent coated paper has suffered, possibly from damp, but is the only related study known.
Photo courtesy Martyn Gregory

One answer to the dilemma might be that the ship is firing saluting charges, blanks not shot! The painting was bought by his host on that occasion, Thomas Brassey MP, later Earl Brassey KG, who presented it to the newly founded Royal Naval College at Greenwich 'The University of the Navy' (Colour Plate 140). There is surely an echo of earlier paintings here – *The Temeraire at Sheerness*, the watercolour, and the early oil *Gosport, Flagship Saluting* of 1836, engraved by Finden. It is tempting to conclude that Cooke was consciously repeating a theme: the Gosport and Spithead scenes are set within a mile of each other and there is in each a barge or small boat bearing a senior officer, smartly pulled in the forefront. While the wooden three-decker in the early picture was the symbol of the Navy's fighting force at the dawn of the Victorian age, the same is also true of the *Devastation* some thirty-five years later.

Egypt 1874

After his short visit to North Africa in 1861 Cooke evidently hoped to re-visit Morocco, but plague and bandits amounted to unacceptable risks according to a letter to his publisher John Murray.[3]

Among Cooke's contemporaries there were British painters who had been drawn to Egypt and had voyaged up the Nile; W.J. Müller and J.F. Lewis were two and his friend Frederick Goodall went in 1858 armed with letters of introduction from David Roberts RA who had been *seeking novelty in more distant lands*[4] twenty years before.

Goodall was perhaps the most devoted with his long series of paintings which showed Bedouin and their camels watering at the Nile. Edward Lear, whom Cooke had often met over the years, was much nearer with his interest in geology and his striking drawings of the topography.

It seems likely that Cooke, remembering his own drawings of the massive Egyptian statuary which Royal Engineers moved to a new gallery in the British Museum in 1834, had resolved to go and examine the famous sites for himself. In early 1872 he was invited by a Mr Byass who lived nearby to accompany him to Egypt at rather short notice. Cooke declined but evidently lent him maps and a couple of months later heard, with what feelings one can imagine, of that gentleman's death in France from cholera. The widow returned the maps and presented him with a memorial ring.

He visited Goodall at his great Norman Shaw house, *Graeme's Dyke,* near Harrow,

3. John Murray Archives.
4. Redgrave 1947, p.405.

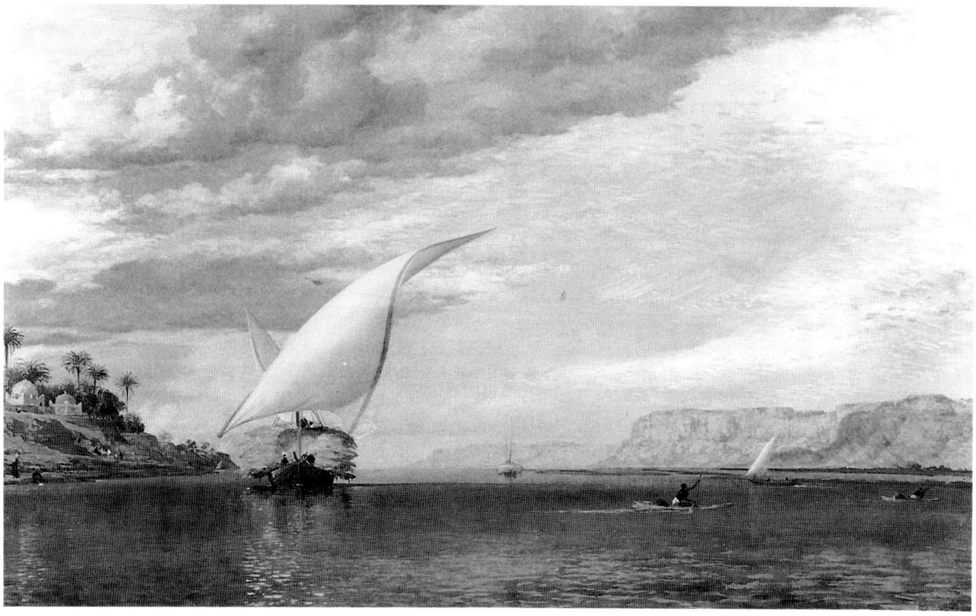

Plate 151. 74/5
Boats on the Nile
The artist's admiration for the graceful sweep of the huge lateen sails was as here and in print (page 274) frequently stated. Photo courtesy The Fine Art Society

viewed his Egyptian paintings and talked of travel in that fascinating land. His own expedition early in 1874 was to be a geological-horticultural-antiquarian excursion as well as a painting trip afloat on the Nile.

To visit the surviving wonders of ancient Egypt meant going overland to Brindisi and by the *Simla* P & O steamer where he found himself in the company of Professor Richard Owen and Mr John Fowler, engineering adviser to Khedive Ismail Pasha. On 5 January 1874 the artist noted a fine streak of bright gold in the sky before sunrise and first Corfu and then the Greek mainland in sight all day. He kept the deck until evening, reading Herodotus – Salamis and Thermopylae! The wind was dead ahead and freshening and the *Simla,* which he found perfect as to her internal arrangements, rolled and pitched fearfully, making his head very bad and giddy and allowing no sleep.

On reaching Alexandria they witnessed the arrival of Hussein Pasha, Minster of Marine, who came off to the ship with '2 galleys and 12'. Accompanied by Owen, Cooke strolled into the fish market, made a sketch of Cleopatra's Needle, took a donkey to Pompey's Pillar and got a sketch of that too. The artist then had a shave and hair cut in the bazaar and drew a minaret, acclimatising himself, as it were.

Travelling with Fowler involved some state. On arrival in Cairo a Khedival carriage took them home with two running footmen preceding. He went to Boulak and got his first sketch of a Nile boat. So began a tour in which his favourite palm trees were found in profusion and the colour of Egypt delighted him. But he heard that Howard Goodall, second son of Frederick RA, was seriously ill at Shepheard's Hotel after an operation, and called to see him.

With Fowler and Owen he went to the Gezeereh Palace and inspected its lovely gardens, spending all day there and making a sketch of palms etc. He met two young men, Mr George and *Mr Malowsky a Russian Painter a pleasant man.* It was a lovely day and Cooke was also impressed by rare trees in the Garden, of which he took the names. Owen called and asked him to make a drawing of the palms and giraffes in the Khedive's garden so he worked all day on it. They mounted the drawing which he named Trop[ical] J[ungle] and it was taken to the Khedive.The painter then set to work on a study of the Pyramids of Memphis and the Great Pyramid with the sun setting between them.

On 8 January the death of young Goodall was announced to him by Mr George. Fowler, Owen and Cooke attended the funeral at the English Cemetery later that day and

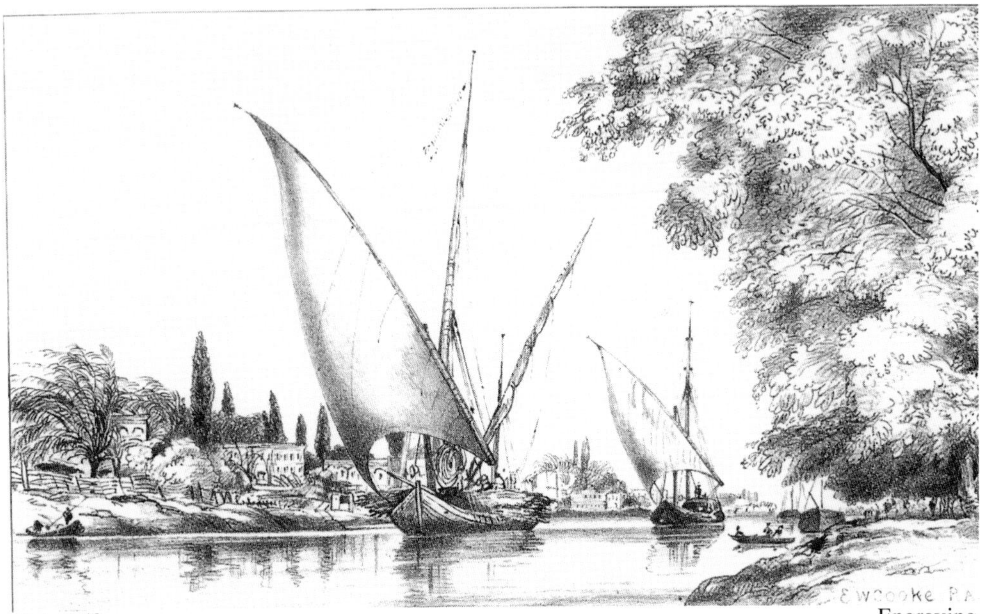

Plate 152. Engraving
The Mahmoodeeah Canal Alexandria
Fifty miles long and said to have been excavated with the loss of 20,000 lives, Cooke however noted that here at the Alexandrian end there was a fashionable promenade amid luxuriant gardens. From *Leaves from my Sketch-book,* John Murray, 1876.

Cooke planted a palm at the grave. They drove to Carl Haag's with Lord Clarence Paget, Fowler and Owen and saw his sketches. The hire of a tourist *dahabijah* or, as Cooke spelt it, *dahabeah* named the *Queen Victoria* belonging to one Watson was achieved for £100 down and the contract signed at the Consul's. His dragoman was noted on the fly-leaf of the diary as Carlo Nicola, and the second or assistant as Lorenzo Galea from Valetta, Malta. Mr Gay, an American painter Winkworth A. Gay, later referred to as 'Gay Bey', and a Mr Scott, whose identity is not revealed, were his fellow subscribers to the expedition. Briefly at Luxor and on in increasing heat to Assouan, Cooke sketched and painted hills, skies, trees, river and boats, often making separate studies of each and combining them at a later stage.

A letter from on board the *Queen Victoria*, ten miles from Assouan, to John Murray indicated that he was already planning another Egyptian painting trip, and he hoped to start next time from Cairo by the first week in December. It was a question of the height of the river. Clearly the pleasure of a voyage under sail, even with the perils of strong winds, sandbanks and hordes of flies, appealed to him. The great temples were visited and other British visitors encountered. Professor Flower, the Lainsons, Mr Brabazon (presumably Hercules Brabazon Brabazon) and the de Launes. In rising temperatures Cooke recorded the life of the river people as well as the monuments, the trees and plants which interested him and of course the atmospheric effects – *worked up Karnak sunset glow.*

Pencil studies of Egyptian subjects (there is a good sample in the Royal Academy collection) show his careful assembly of references, the architecture, palm trees, grouping of figures, camels, boats and landscape, are of course drawn with possible future needs in mind. He worked at his oil sketches in uncomfortable conditions and his scientific interests dictated some of the subjects.

On the return, while awaiting his luggage in Paris, he made sure that he looked at the Egyptian collections and went to the Louvre and the Musée de Cluny as well as the Jardin des Plantes. There were an estimated thirty oil sketches made on the spot and four major paintings completed at home and exhibited in London during the last years of his life. Pictures of the Nile do not seem to have sold readily, nor have they appeared often in the salerooms. His studio sale in 1880 listed them but only two have been seen in recent years, *The Mountains and Plain of Denderah, on the Libyan bank of the Nile; Doum and date palms, sont trees &c* (75/4, Colour Plate 143) and *Pigeon Houses,*

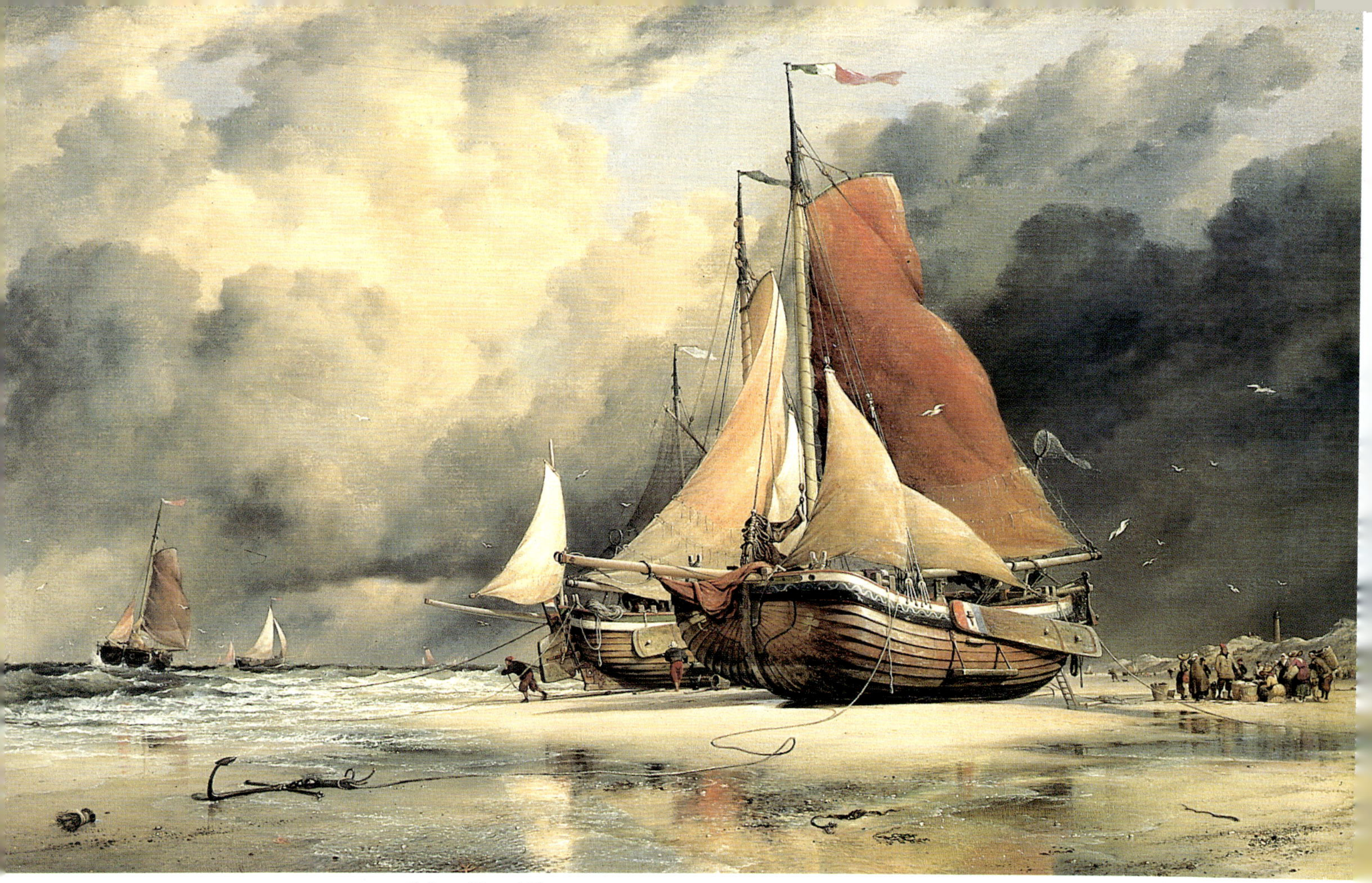

Colour Plate 138. 72/7

Dutch pincks drying sails & nets: Egmont aan Zee – tide coming in

Photo courtesy Private Collection

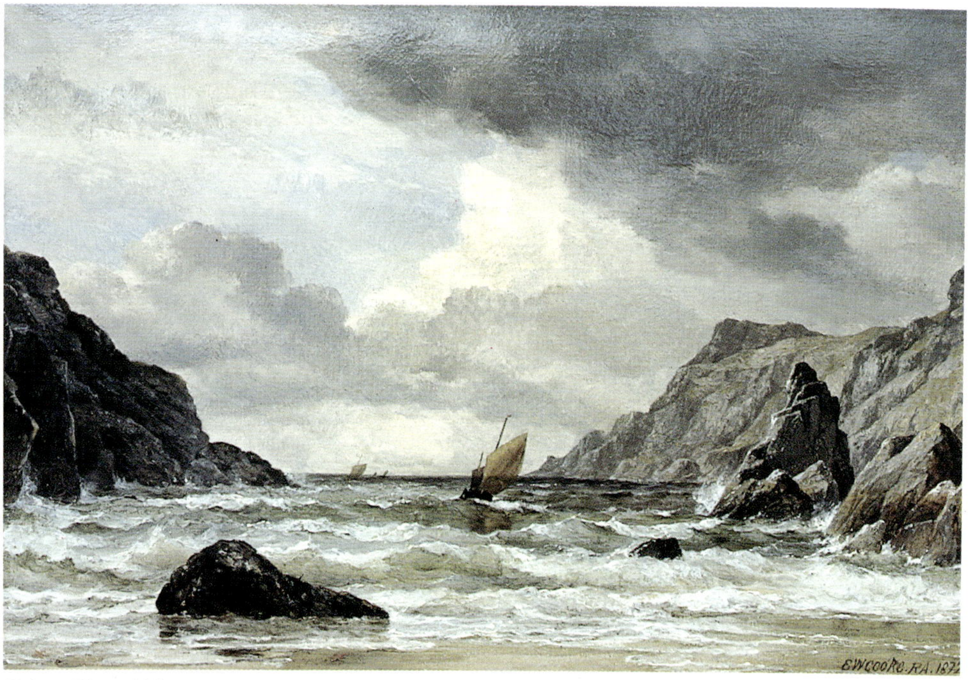

Colour Plate 139. 71/6

Kynance Cove

Larger pictures of this celebrated coastal feature are recorded, but so far not encountered.

Photo courtesy Russell Cotes Art Gallery, Bournemouth

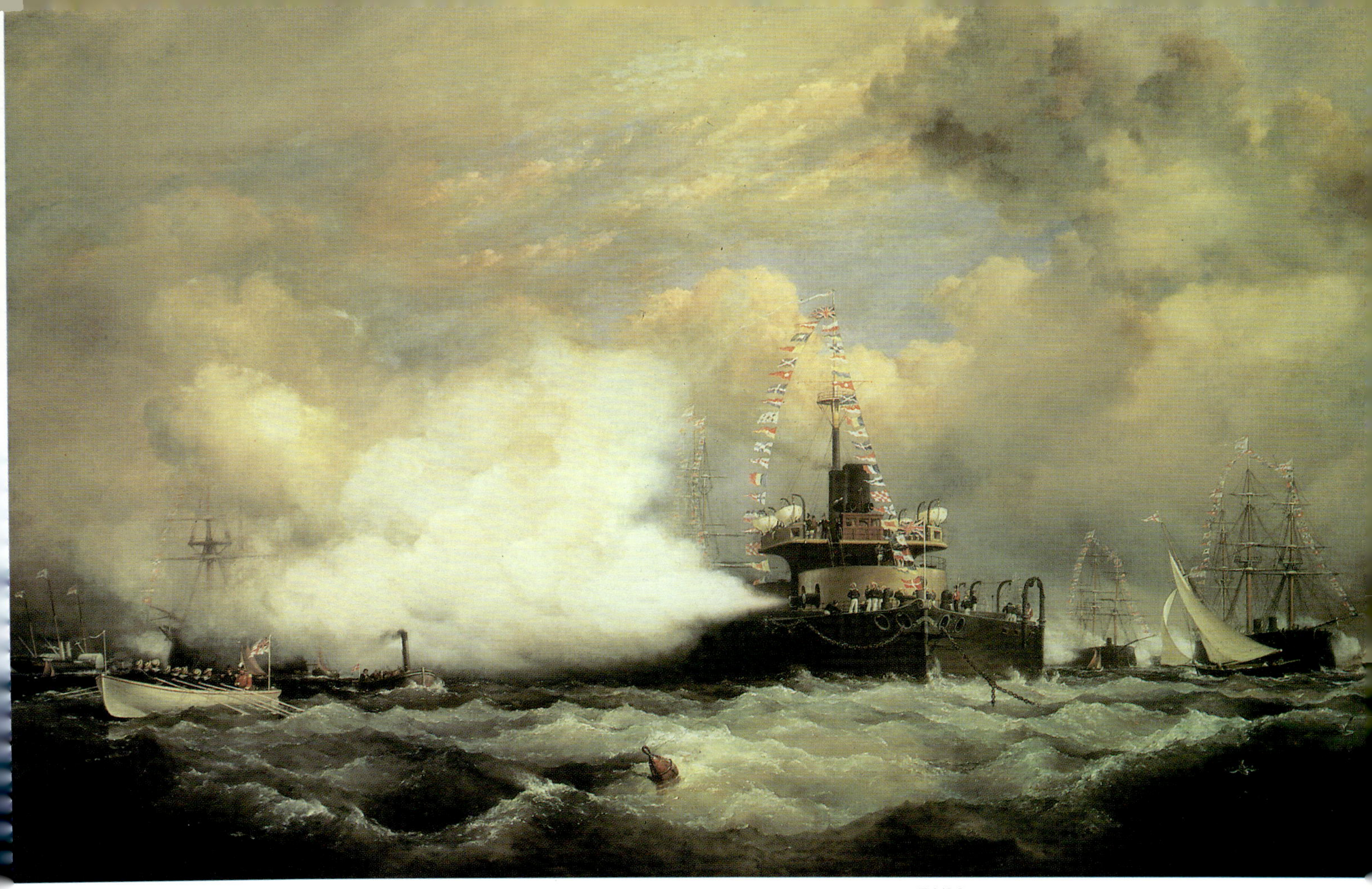

Colour Plate 140. 74/30
H.M. Turret ship Devastation *at Spithead...the Naval Review in honour of the Shah of Persia...July 1873*
Cooke doubtless recalled the First Lord of the Admiralty's exhortation at the Royal Academy banquet in 1871, to paint something modern. Brassey presented the picture to the newly opened 'University of the Navy', the Royal Naval College, Greenwich. John Ruskin in his *Academy Notes* found it *somewhat sable and lugubrious as a national spectacle...*
Photo courtesy The Trustees of the National Maritime Museum, Greenwich

Mutaneh (74/18, Colour Plate 144). The critics of the 1875 Academy exhibition quipped *We have no hesitancy about the truth of Sandy cove, tide flowing and if we fail to pronounce an opinion on the verisimilitude of ... Denderah ... it is simply because we are not familiar with the Libyan or any other bank of the Nile.* John Ruskin, with a gracious gesture in the direction of Cooke's other fields, commended it in his *Academy Notes* of 1875:

> *I may direct attention to the exquisite skill of delineation with Mr Cooke has finished the group of palm trees in his wonderful study of sunset at Denderah. The sacrifice of colour in shadow for the sake of brilliancy in light, essentially a principle of Holland as opposed to Venice is, in a great degree, redeemed in this picture by the extreme care with which the relations of light are observed, on the terms conceded.*

The lawyer, collector and writer Harry Quilter liked the *Date palms and Banana trees in the gardens of the Khedive's Palace...* (76/6) in the 1877 Academy, calling them *a magnificent study.*[5] Whether, had he lived, further pictures from other visits would have established Cooke as a popular painter of Nile boats and temples is idle speculation. Frederick Goodall, a younger man who was at work for many more years, was still painting Cairo in 1901 (*The Snake Charmer)*, though in unmistakable decline.

At the end of 1876 a chance remark in a letter to John Murray indicates that a painting of the Arctic expedition of 1875 was contemplated. He had visited Portsmouth and made

5. *Preferences in Art, Life & Literature* by Harry Quilter, 1892.

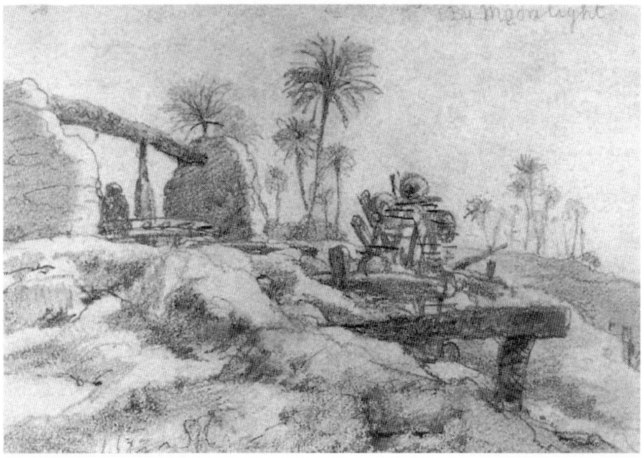

Plate 153. Pencil drawing
By Moonlight, palm trees and well Photo courtesy Martyn Gregory

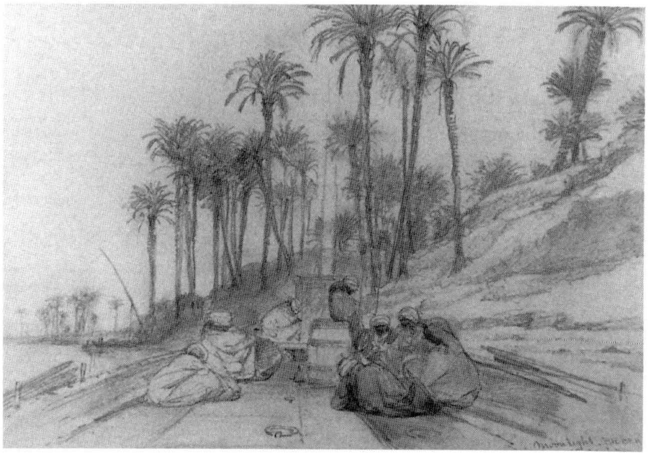

Plate 154. Pencil drawing
Moonlight, Bibbeh, shrouded figures on deck. 26th Jan.
Photo courtesy Martyn Gregory

studies of the two ships *Alert* and *Discovery* and had useful discussions with the leader, Capt Sir George Nares RN, and his officers. There is no evidence of his having started a picture, even of working up sketches, although some pencil studies of the ships have survived.[6] The results of the expedition were perhaps lacking in dramatic interest although in anticipation, it seems, John Everett Millais made a memorable figure piece which was titled *The North West Passage* in 1874. Into this he introduced a portrait of E.J. Trelawny, friend of Byron and Shelley, with flag, chart and telescope and a glass of grog, which latter annoyed the abstinent sitter.

In January 1878 Egypt came at long last to London and it would have arrived before that, had it not been abandoned in the Atlantic and salvaged by a British steamer which took it into Ferrol! It was Thothmes III's obelisk, mis-called Cleopatra's Needle, the same rose-red syenite monolith which Cooke had drawn on his 1874 visit (Plate 161). It appears in his published album *Leaves from my Sketchbook* 1876 with the note:

> *It was given by Mohammed Ali to the English and was to have been removed to England as a record of their success at the beginning of the century, but the project was abandoned and though often renewed of late years has never been carried into effect. Were it erected, as has been suggested on the Thames Embankment, it would be as much out of place and out of keeping with the surroundings as would a camel laden with palm branches – an ordinary and harmonious sight on the banks of the Nile – in a London street.*

This he proceeded to illustrate, to prove his point, but for one with considerable architectural knowledge it is odd that Cooke should have had a blind spot for the classical shape. It was carved with hieroglyphs from two periods of ancient Egyptian history and the Romans had wanted it, getting it from Heliopolis to Alexandria, near the shore. There it remained until in 1877 the Khedive again offered it to Britain and the successful surgeon Mr, later Sir James Erasmus Wilson's determination to bring it to London extended to a donation of £10,000 to make the operation possible. John Dixon and his brother Waynman Dixon designed a strange vessel to float the obelisk; the English engineers framed up the 180 tons of granite and it was sealed into a compartmented cylindrical container of wrought iron plates, pointed at the ends, with thirty tons of ballast to counter the obelisk's taper. This was rolled into the sea. On top was built a cabin and a bridge; there was steering gear and a mast and she carried a captain and crew. The motive power was a steamship which was to tow the *Cleopatra* towards England.

Fired to paint a memorial to the enterprise, Cooke seized upon the moment in the voyage of the strange 90ft. (27.5m) vessel when things began to go wrong; they got into difficulties during a storm in the Bay of Biscay, when the *Cleopatra's* ballast shifted and gave her an extreme list.

To avoid a possible collision in the storm – the weight of the steel towing cable was

6. National Maritime Museum, Greenwich.

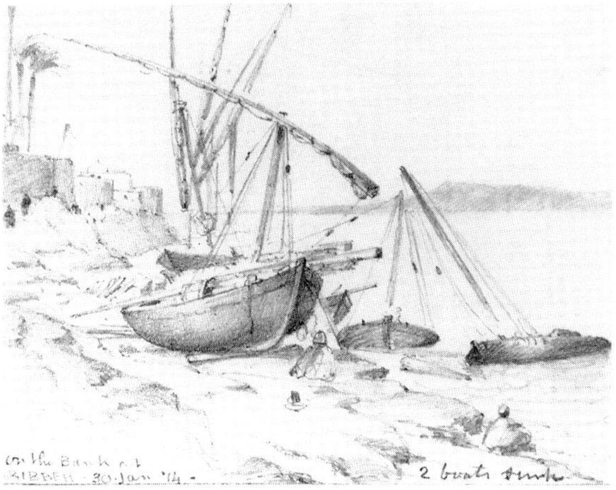

Plate 155. Pencil drawing
Bibbeh, two boats sunk after a storm, 30th Jan.
Photo courtesy Martyn Gregory

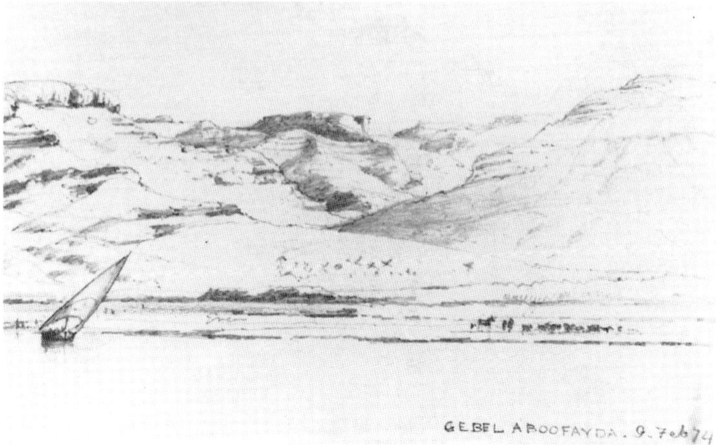

Plate 156. Pencil drawing
Gebel Aboofaydah, 9th Feb.
Photo courtesy Martyn Gregory

likely to draw the vessels together if they were not making way through the seas – she was turned adrift and later during a lull a boat went to take off her men. Tragically the boat and its six occupants was lost before they reached the *Cleopatra* although the rescue was completed later. The pictorial possibilities of the situation perhaps belong more to the journalistic woodcuts of the *Illustrated London News* but there was the strong human interest in the sad loss of life during the voyage. Cooke was as usual following his own interests – he had met Waynman Dixon in Egypt in 1874 but whether the obelisk was mentioned is not recorded. It was, however, a topical subject and a minor triumph of engineering, so characteristically he relished the somewhat bizarre scene. He evidently considered that it was something in his line for he produced a large canvas which was shown at the Royal Academy in 1878, No 330. (77/9, Plate 162) *The Cleopatra Cylinder vessel – containing Cleopatra's Needle, in a hurricane in the Bay of Biscay, 14th October 1877, signalling the steamship Olga to cast off the tow-rope: 'Staunch and Strong the goodly vessel &c.'*

The optimistic quotation was from Longfellow's *The Building of the Ship,* 1849, and it continued ...*That can laugh at all disaster, And with wave and whirlwind wrestle....*

Among his notes is a sketch of the signal flags, and the diary reveals that he received a crated scale model of the vessel from her builders, from which to draw. This illustration of a contemporary incident, or rather an accident, and the significance of the cylinder's contents gave his picture topical interest for the very ancient monument might well have gone to the bottom of the sea. The awkwardness of the strange vessel, an unlovely contrivance, serves in a way to heighten the drama. However the picture did not sell,

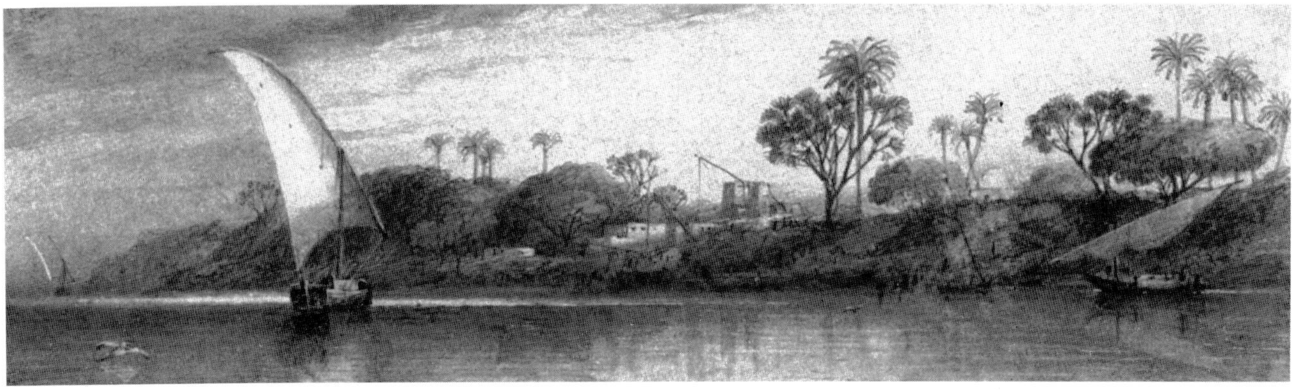

Plate 157. Pencil drawing
Evening on the Nile opposite Keneh Libyan bank.
Drawn on the prepared coated paper which he used latterly, this is inscribed to Decimus Burton FRS, his old friend the architect. Photo courtesy Martyn Gregory. Private Collection

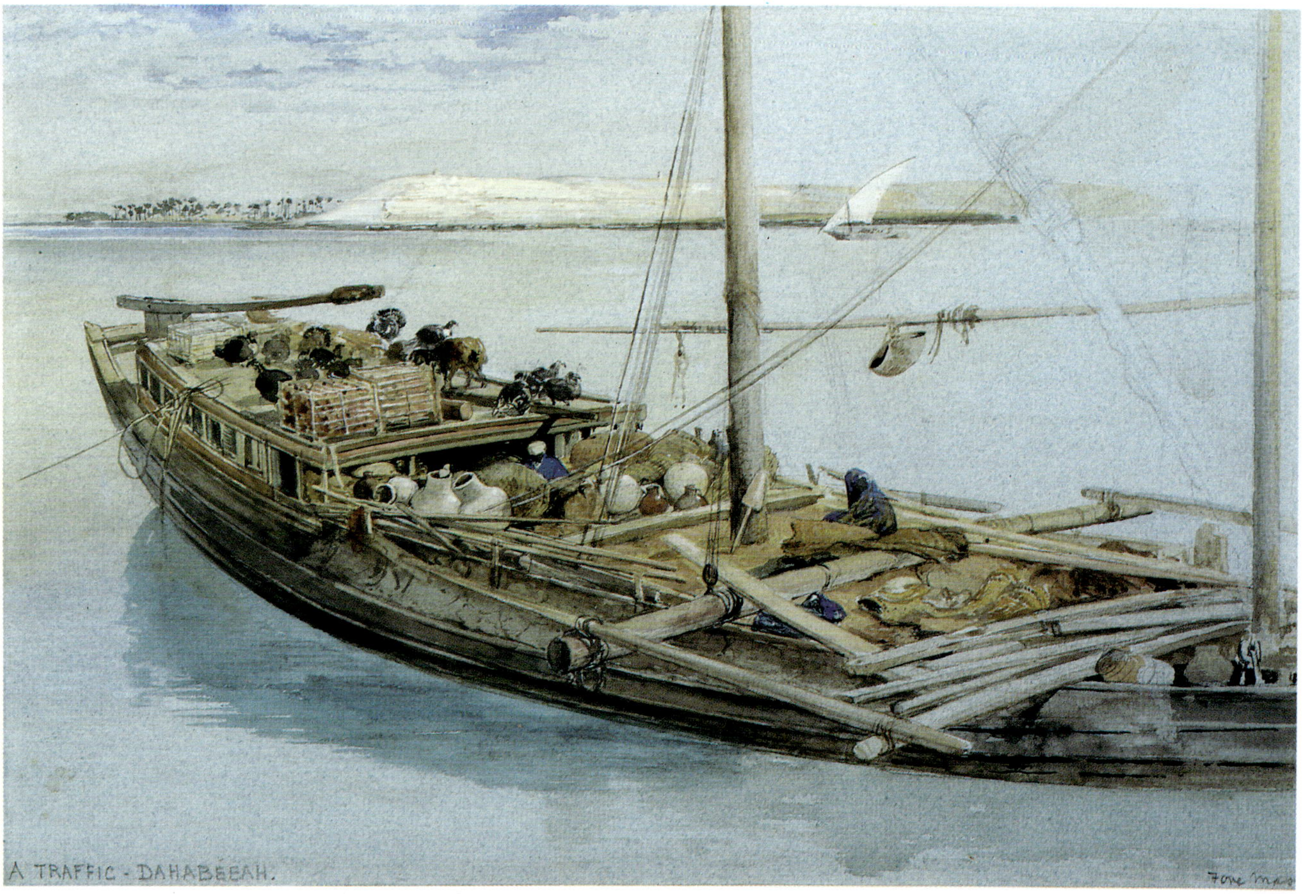

Colour Plate 141. Watercolour

Old Dahabeah with jars and turkeys. Here on the Nile Cooke reasserts his belief in the pictorial qualities of everyday working craft and makes a fascinating drawing. Photo courtesy Private Collection

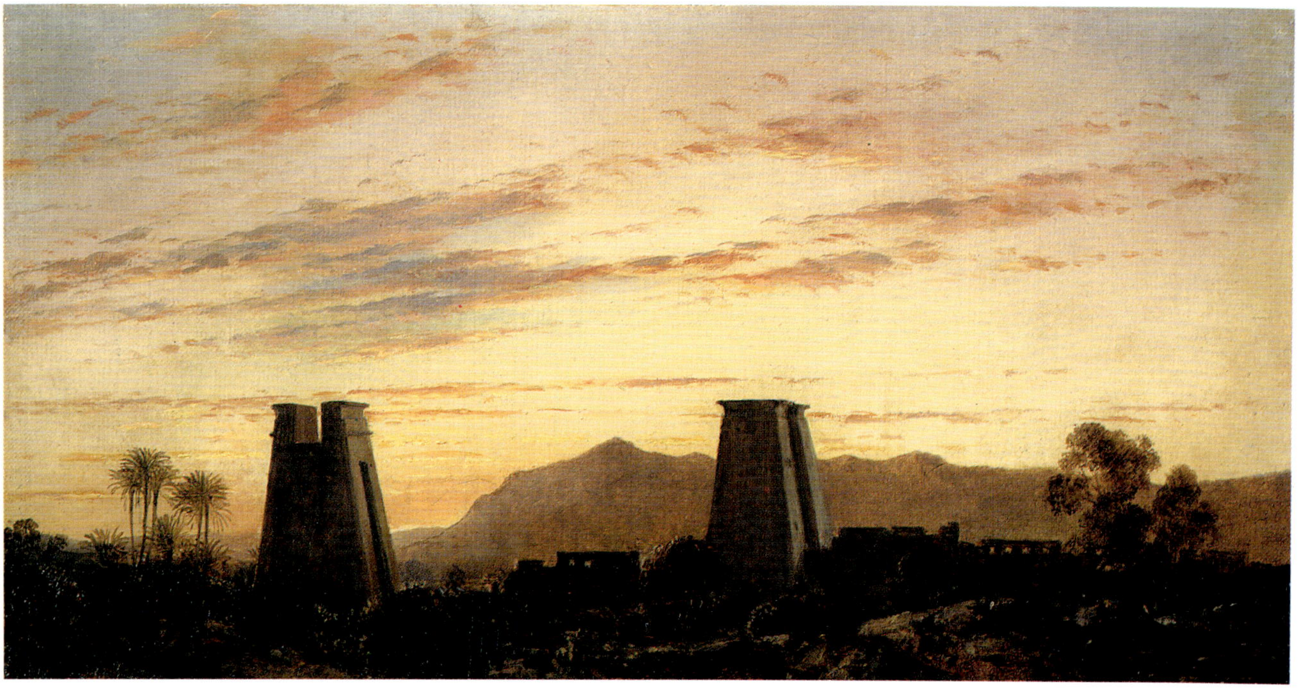

Colour Plate 142. 74/23

Karnak, the Pylon and Propylon looking West

Photo courtesy Private Collection USA

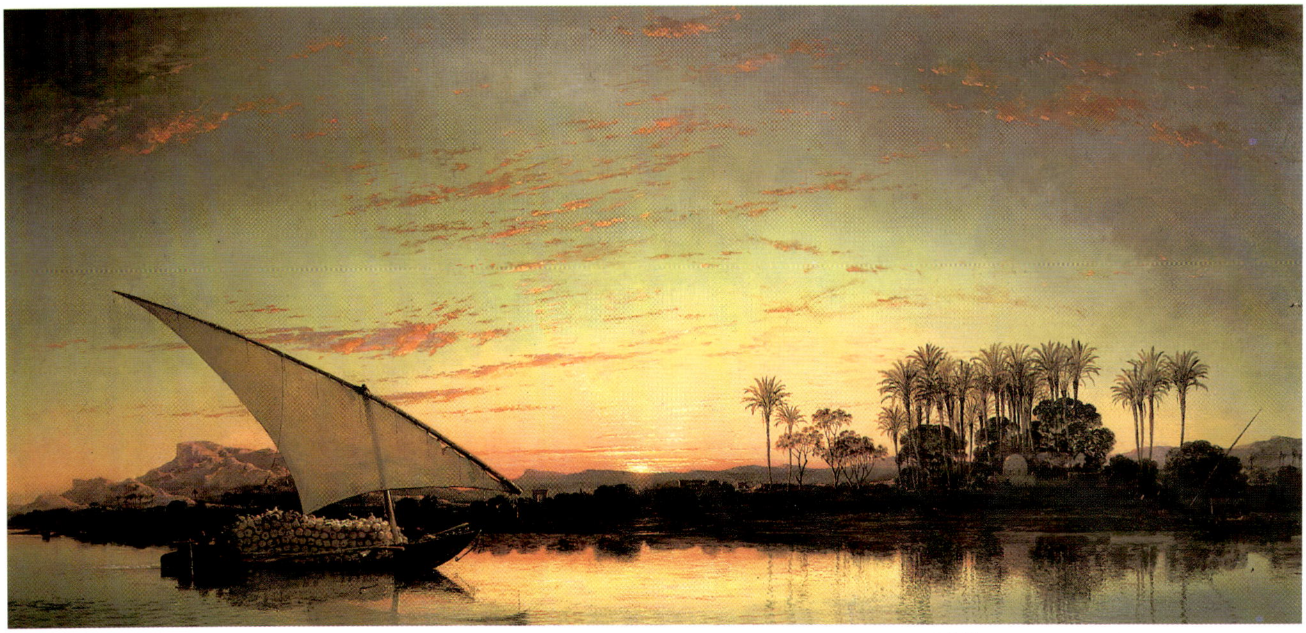

Colour Plate 143. 75/4

The Mountains and Plain of Denderah on the Libyan bank of the Nile; Doum and date palms...

John Ruskin praised the light in this painting in his *Academy Notes,* 1875.

Photo courtesy Mathaf Gallery. Private Collection

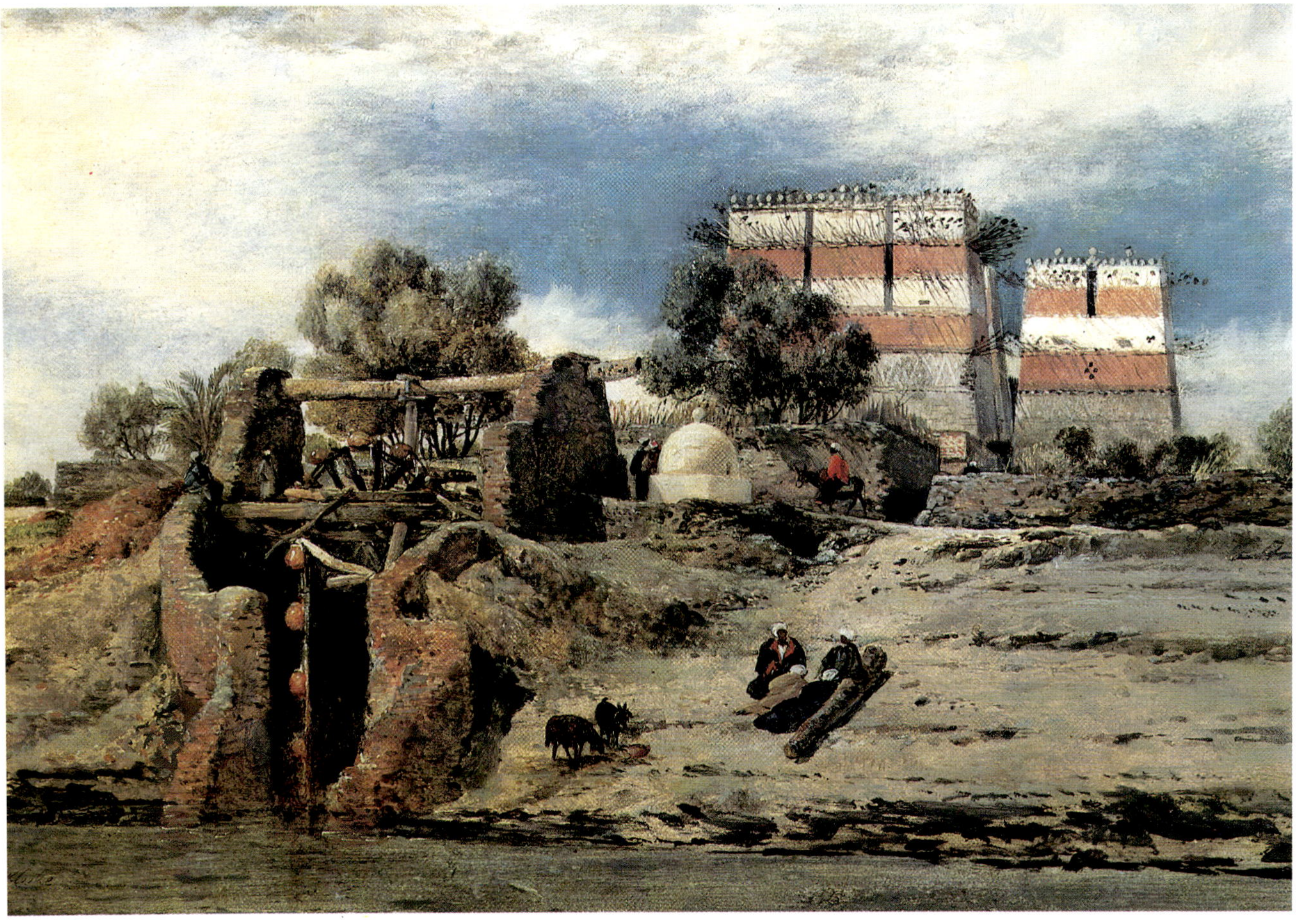

Colour Plate 144. 74/18

Pigeon Houses, Mutaneh near Esneh on the Nile

Photo courtesy Park Gallery, London W2

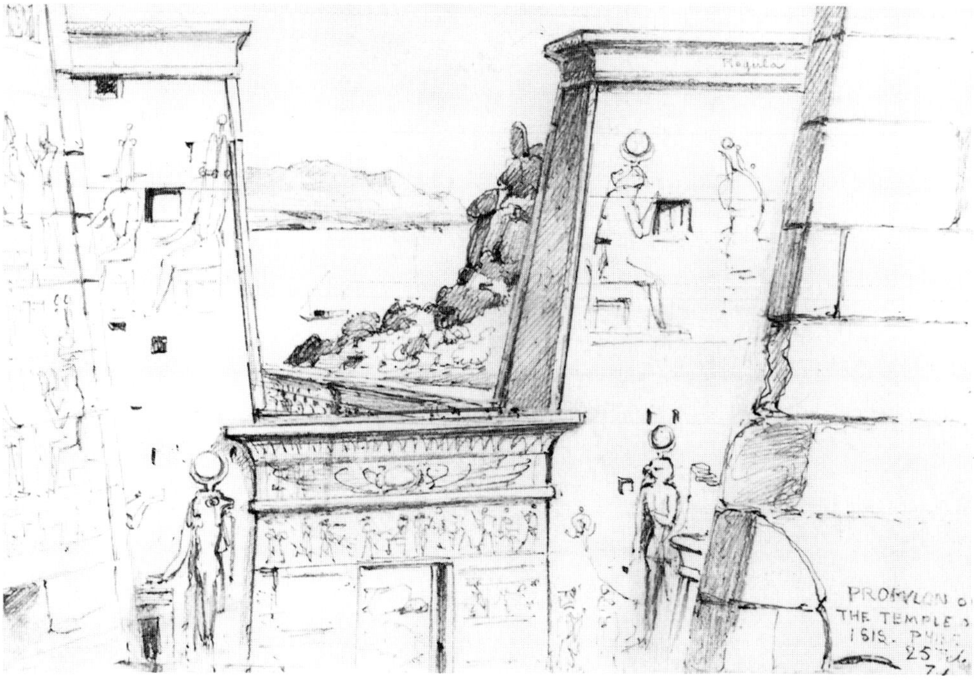

Plate 158. Pencil drawing
Propylon of the Temple of Isis, Philae (before lunch 25th Feb 1874)
Photo courtesy Martyn Gregory

although it travelled to Australia for the International Exhibition at Sydney in 1879. It may not have arrived home before he died, for it was in the second sale of Cooke's paintings, Christie's 1882, bought by the dealer Vokins. Erasmus Wilson FRS was knighted in 1881 and acquired the picture which he bequeathed to the nation; it is now in the Victoria & Albert Museum.

In doubting the Needle's architectural suitability for the Embankment Cooke was not alone. Frederick, Lord Leighton thought it was sited in the wrong place and Frederick Goodall, who quoted him, wrote that it should have been placed in front of the British Museum.[7] However with its attendant sphinxes and bearing a memorial inscription to those who died during the voyage, as well as scars from bomb blast in the First World War, it is still one of the sights of London, even if E.W. Cooke's canvas of a crucial moment is not so accessible.

7. Goodall op.cit., p.325.

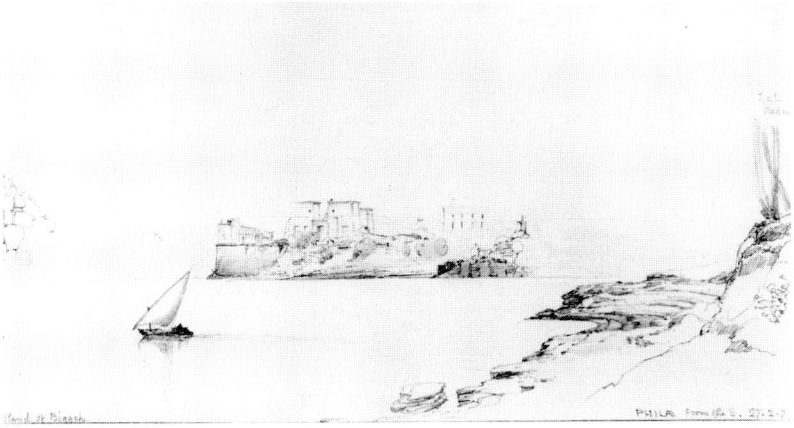

Plate 159. Pencil drawing
Philae from the South, 27th Feb.
Photo courtesy Martyn Gregory

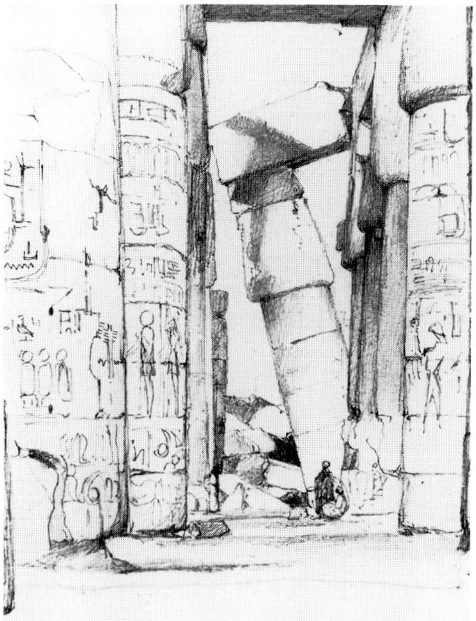

Plate 160. Pencil drawing
Karnak, leaning column, 9th Mar.
Photo courtesy Martyn Gregory

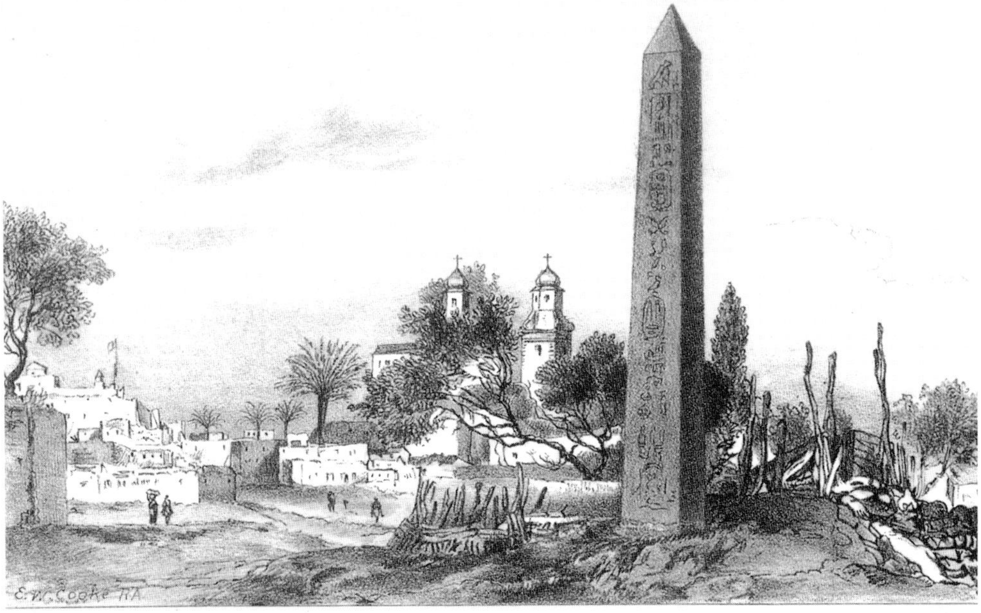

Plate 161. Engraving

Cleopatra's Needle Alexandria

This has a special significance in view of his painting 77/9 (Plate 162). From *Leaves from my Sketch-book,* John Murray, 1876.

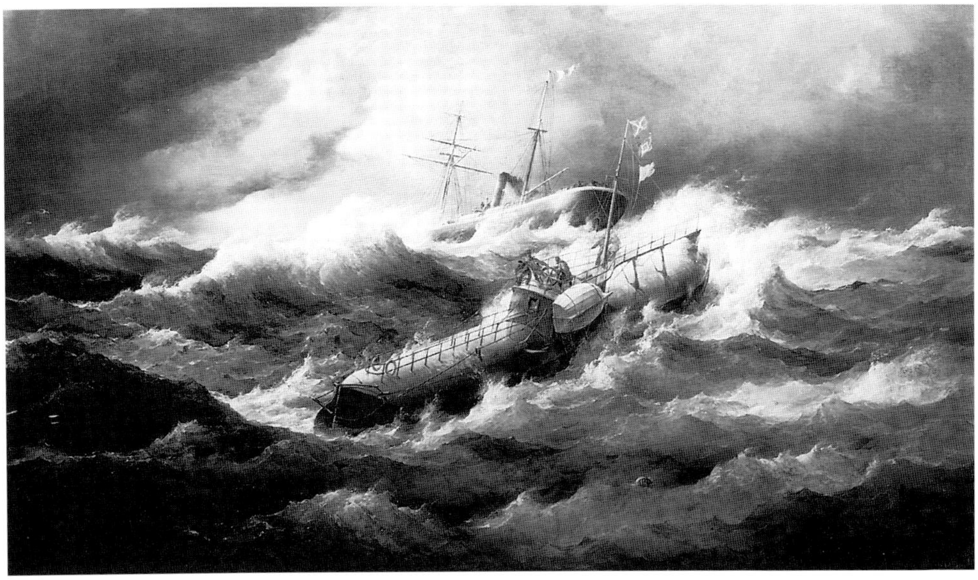

Plate 162. 77/9

The Cleopatra Cylinder Vessel-in the Bay of Biscay

The tramp steamer *Fitzmaurice* salvaged the derelict after the tug *Olga h*ad been forced to let go the towing cable in a storm (see page 213). Cooke's devotion to this famous piece of Egyptian antiquity did not extend to approving the choice of its site on the Thames Embankment. Exhibited RA 1878. Photo courtesy The Board of Trustees of the Victoria & Albert Museum

Where else might the artist have painted, had he lived? A return to Morocco was mentioned and a proposed trip to Sicily with George Dennis occurs in correspondence with John Murray, the same source that reveals a hope for further Nile expeditions. The old marine subjects in Holland and Venice, as the critics were pointing out, had become rather well worn and the barbaric touches of the Nile obviously appealed to Cooke who could turn his searching eye on new boats, new shores and ancient civilisations.

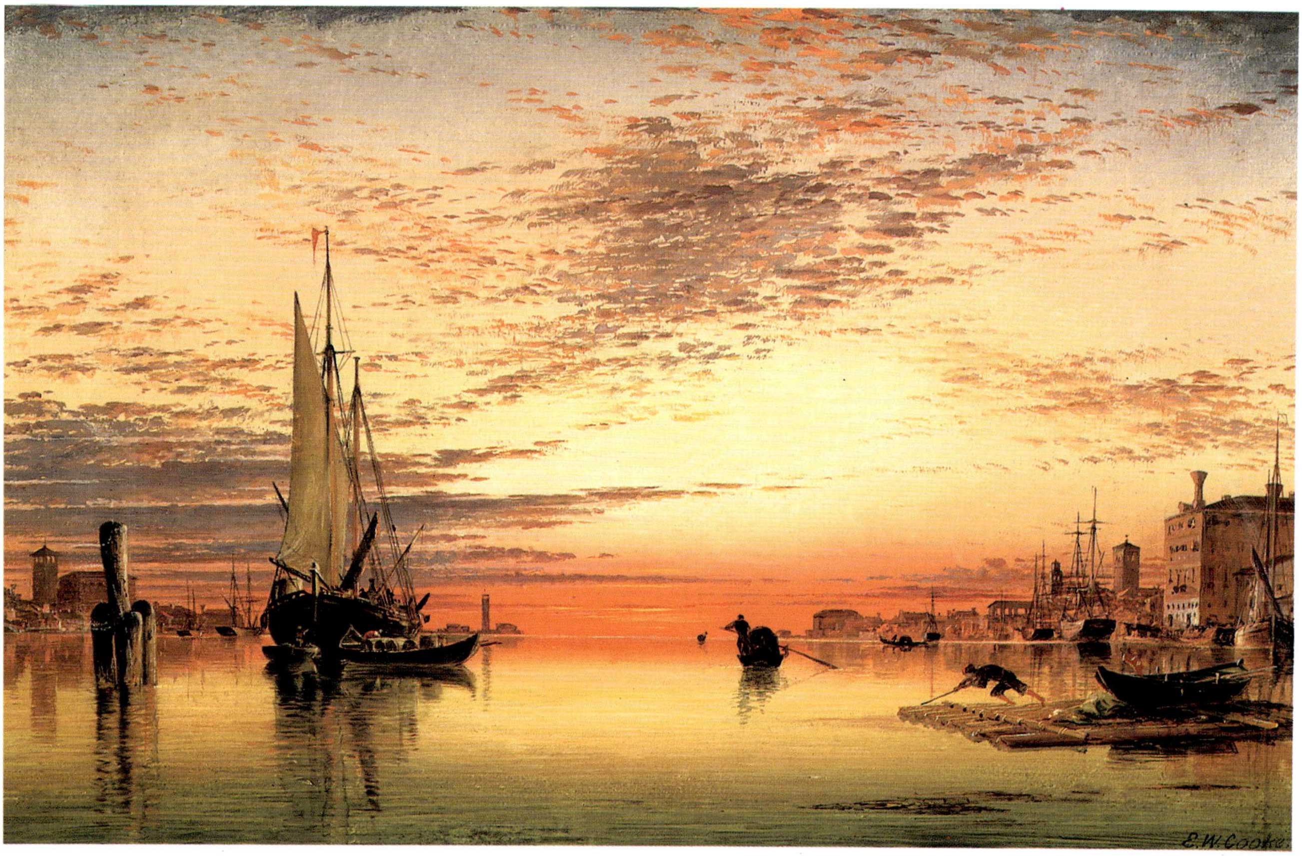

Colour Plate 145. 63/14

Evening sky looking west out of the Canale della Giudecca

Photo courtesy Richard Green Fine Paintings. Private Collection

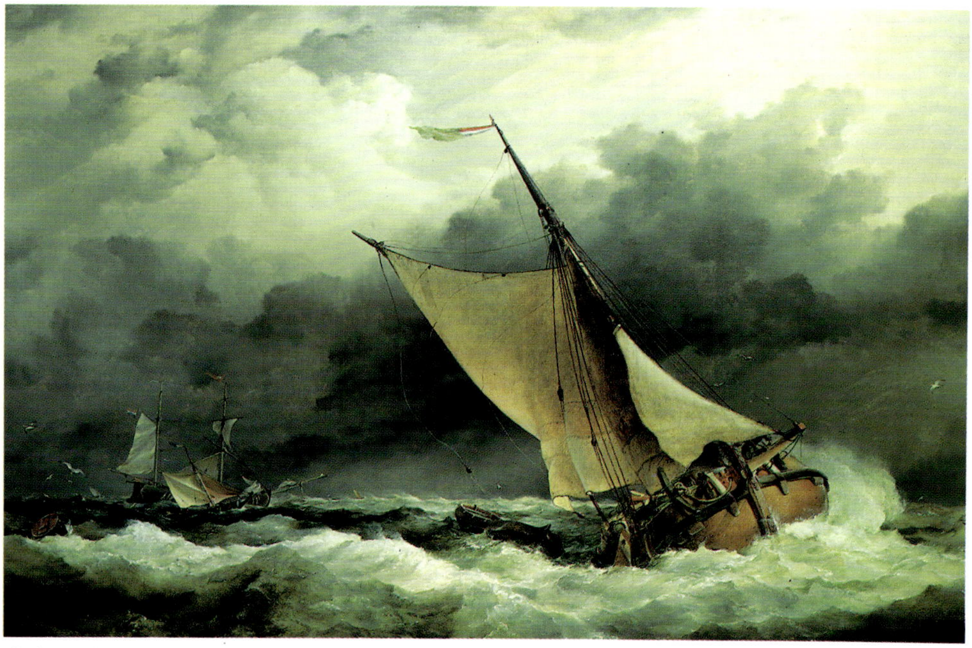

Colour Plate 146. 66/2

Dutch boats in a breeze on the Dollart Zee

The artist had been up near the German border and this stormy picture helped advertise *Van Kook's* familiarity with many types of Dutch craft.

Photo:courtesy Arthur Ackermann & Peter Johnson.Ltd. Private Collection

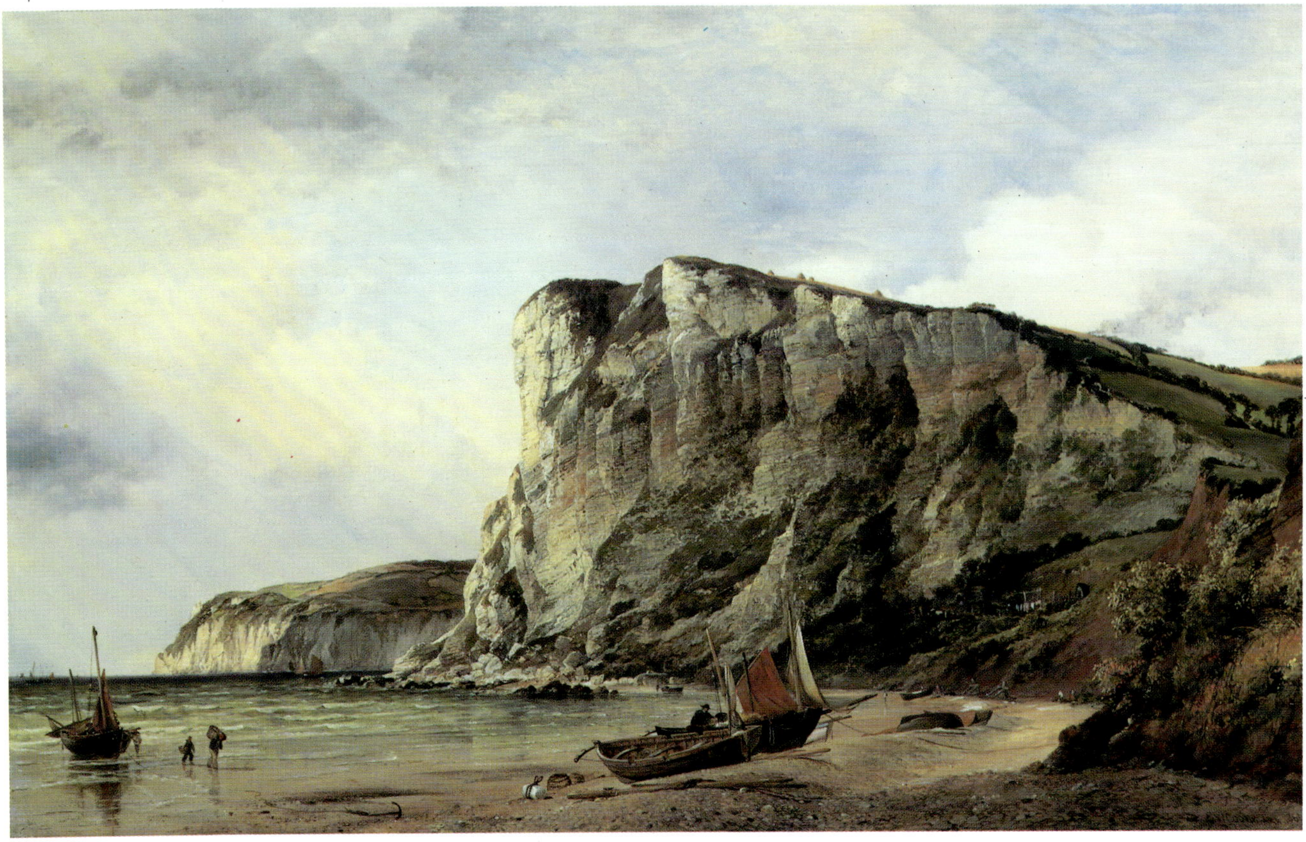

Chapter 14

THE ACADEMICIAN

The *Illustrated London News,* in marking Cooke's election as Academician, wrote of his Venetian pictures that they were *...when compared to the illusory idealisations, more or less of Prout, Turner, Holland and some others, very remarkable for their matter of fact truthfulness and serviceable for their corrective reality....* The journal went on to list the strong points of the new RA's art and made a fervent apologia, opening once more the old questions of prose versus poetry in paint.

> *The prime characteristic of Mr Cooke's art is literal fidelity to nature. He is probably the most scientifically accurate painter we possess. His pictures not merely gratify the lovers of realism in art by the exact reproduction of the outward aspects of the natural world, but they satisfy the geologist, botanist, meteorologist, architect and shipbuilder... Mr Cooke's conscientious and scrupulous respect for the facts which he set himself to record has led to his sometimes being described as a 'topographical' painter, or, with Stanfield, Creswick and David Roberts (especially in their early and more careful styles) as a 'prosaic' painter... True it is that his works are accurately descriptive of the topography of a scene, and hence they have the simple directness and comparative want of suggestiveness of prose; but then they have many indications of artistic feeling in the choice of subject and point of view, but above all in the selection of effect... is there no sweet sentiment of Nature's loveliness and glory in some of this painter's later versions of the glowing sky and golden sea, where the sun sinks beneath the glittering domes and campanili which fringe the Venetian lagune?*[1]

1. 1864.

Colour Plate 147. 58/18
Distant view of Beer Head and white cliff at low water
Many drawings of the rock formations and sketches on the spot resulted in a pair of paintings, one looking east (58/16, Colour Plate 153) and this westerly view. Photo courtesy Richard Green Fine Paintings

Art criticism in the public press followed the pioneer writings in specialist periodicals. The *Literary Gazette* weekly from 1817 had reviewed published, etched and engraved works, prints as well as illustrated books, and contained all manner of news about the art world. Meetings of the Conversazioni were reported with sales and exhibitions also.

The *Athenaeum* had begun in 1828 – a journal of the newer breed which had by mid-century become one of the most powerful literary and artistic forces, catering for the growing cultured classes. It brought integrity to reviewing, in the words of one modern authority,[2] and carried brief and to-the-point notices in keeping with the more urgent tempo of life, as against the long essays in such older publications as John Murray's *Quarterly Review*. George Darley, Irish poet and writer. was the *Athenaeum* art critic. F.G. Stephens, the failed Pre-Raphaelite painter, ... *windy and wordy,*[3] had the job from 1860 until 1901.

Samuel Carter Hall, the founding Editor of the *Art Journal* (as the *Art Union Monthly Journal* 1839-1848), claimed in a farewell article in 1880 that he *saw an Art-public grow up round us and presently the daily press took upon itself those functions so long peculiar to ourselves*. The journal seems to have been an admirer, if occasionally a somewhat condescending admirer. S.C. Hall and his Irish authoress wife were well known to the Cooke family and his obituary notice of the painter, speaking of *a special excellence* in his productions, continued rather curiously with the words, perhaps with a deferential bow to the surviving members, *The family has been always and all of them emphatically good.*

The reception by the critics of Cooke's first exhibited oils must have given him great satisfaction and, although not all the papers would be laudatory all the time, he was hailed from the first as a very promising artist. The fact that his pictures sold fairly readily at the annual London and provincial exhibitions encouraged him to produce further versions of successful subjects but he was at the same time intent on exploring to the full their possibilities as well as looking for new ones.

Pictures 'being bred from', the quip attributed to Ary Scheffer, indicated the near replication of subjects which had already been acclaimed. Richard Redgrave, whose output was modest and whose other activities, such as looking after South Kensington and the Queen's pictures, made demands on his time, remarked in his monumental survey of English painters that when A.W. Callcott's works were in great demand *he was obliged to produce them by system rather than by immediate reference to nature.*[4] Discovery of telling formulae, whether for subjects or in handling paint, led easily to the establishment of what might be called a 'picture manufactory' in the hands of an artist who was concerned primarily with profit. It was ever so: there were those who painted to live and those who lived to paint, but mouths had to be fed – and probably only portrait painters were free from such a supposed distinction. Joseph Farington summed it up: *Portrait painting undoubtedly offers more certain employ than any other branch... landscape painting is not so much encouraged as it has not the advantage of being supported by self-love... there is a sort of Landscape Portrait Painting by which a good deal of money is got, viz painting views of Houses &c but where the picture will only be purchased for its intrinsic merit few will be found to command an income.*[5] This is all familiar country subject-wise and Cooke's note about making his pictures *worth 80 to £100 apiece* shows that he was conscious of his increasing responsibilities.[6]

Writing of the career of Claude Monet, who painted at Etretat on the Normandy coast a year or so after Cooke's last visit in 1879, Professor Robert L. Herbert noted that an artist did not live independent of dealers, clients, exhibitions and *his thirst for success, all of which form a complicated dialogue with society.*[7] It is also clear that Cooke aspired to Academic laurels at their current valuation; it had always been his aim to be a member of the RA, to join the elect, and his approach, as a landscape painter, was uncomplicated

2. *Early Victorian England*, 1934.
3. *Gambart, Prince of the Victorian Art World,* by Jeremy Maas, 1975, p.115.
4. Redgrave, 1947, p.377.
5. Quoted *Constable, Paintings, Watercolours & Drawings,* Conal Shields, Tate Gallery, 1976, p.13.
6. Cooke MSS. Letter of 1853 from Venice.
7. *Impressionism, Art, Leisure & Parisian Society* by R.L. Herbert ,1988, p.299.

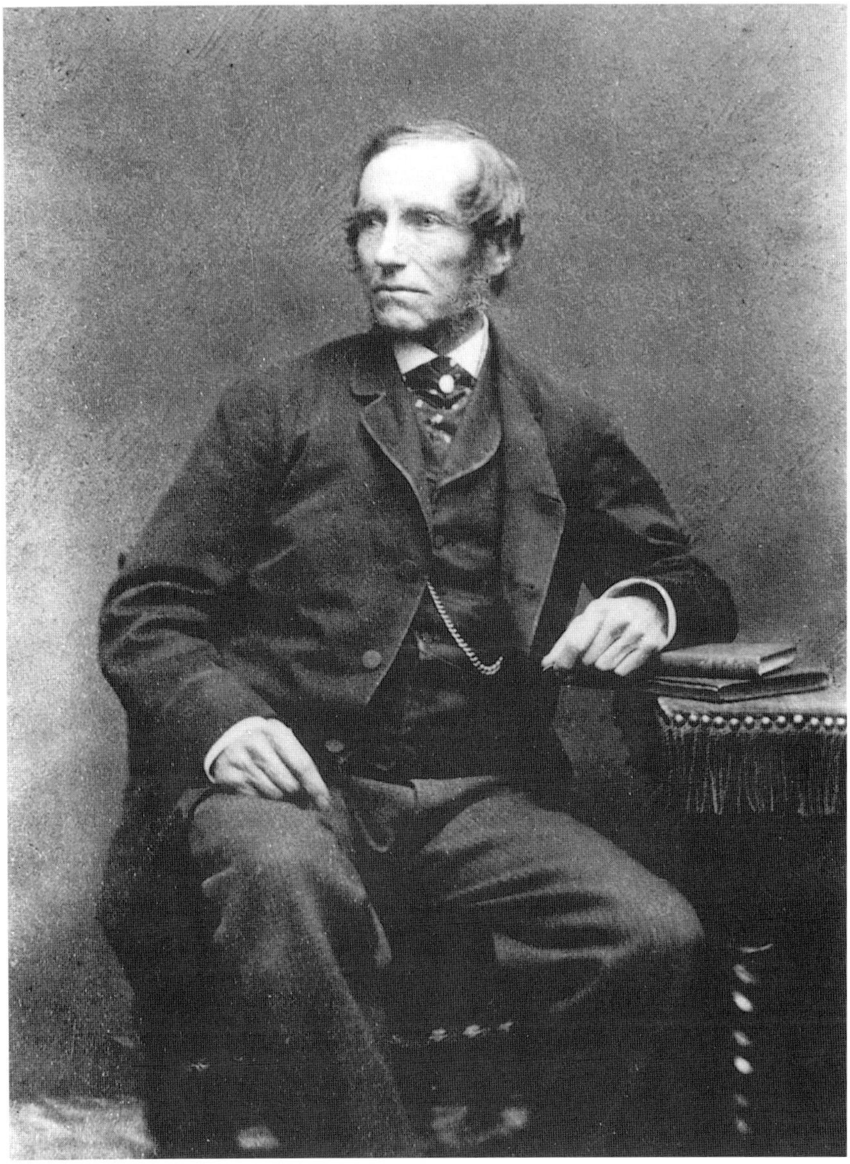

Plate 163.
E.W. Cooke RA by Charles & John Watkins, 1864
An engraving from a slightly different exposure on the same occasion was published with the *Illustrated London News'* notice on the artist's election as RA in this year.
Photo courtesy C.R. Cooke, OBE

by religious, moral, social or other such considerations. The standard of Truth to Nature, as he saw it, was always his leading mark. 'Truth' is a word which frequently appears in the short notes with which the critics mention his pictures in the exhibition reviews: *...there is abundant truth, but it is pronounced with hardness and severity. ...the foreground and middle distance are full of truth. ...there is great truth in this picture but the sky wants depth. ...there is too much of cutting outline about them; otherwise these and their gear, with every incidental item, are made out with microscopic truth. ...is made out with photographic truth.* Usually a negative observation accompanied the word 'truth', evidence that the complete and finished image no longer satisfied. Nor did it, in fact, entirely fulfil the aims of the painter, dedicated though all knew him to be. As he grew older it is evident that the balance between his painting of boats, of sky, of sea and coastal formations was occasionally disturbed, perhaps by his eyesight, for which he consulted one of his patrons, Sir William Bowman, the celebrated opthalmic surgeon.

There is unfortunately no evidence of what E.W. Cooke thought of these strictures or that he took any of it very much to heart. Long ago he had decided that there was only one way to paint his subject, boat or cliff, tree or basket, still water or wild, and that was in a faultless rendering from which everything, including its essentials of formation and construction, might be read. John Constable reckoned that seascape and seashore

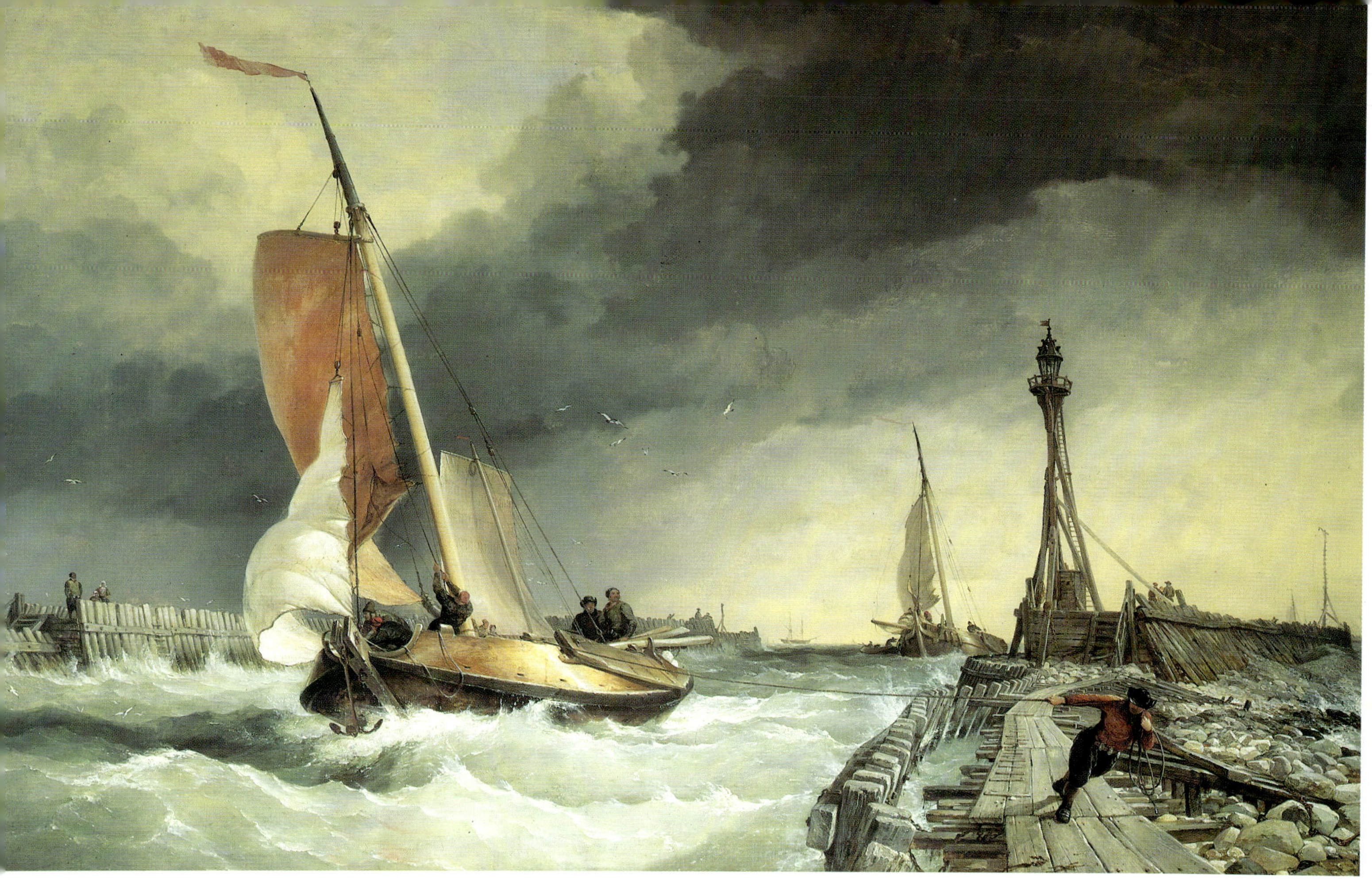

Colour Plate 149. 54/3
Zuider Zee botter returning to port
The *Illustrated London News* published an engraving of this picture with another of his paintings of a French boat but in transposing the captions provided pitfalls for later generations of readers! Medemblik is lettered on the bow of the boat.
Photo courtesy Arthur Ackermann & Peter Johnson.Ltd. Private Collection

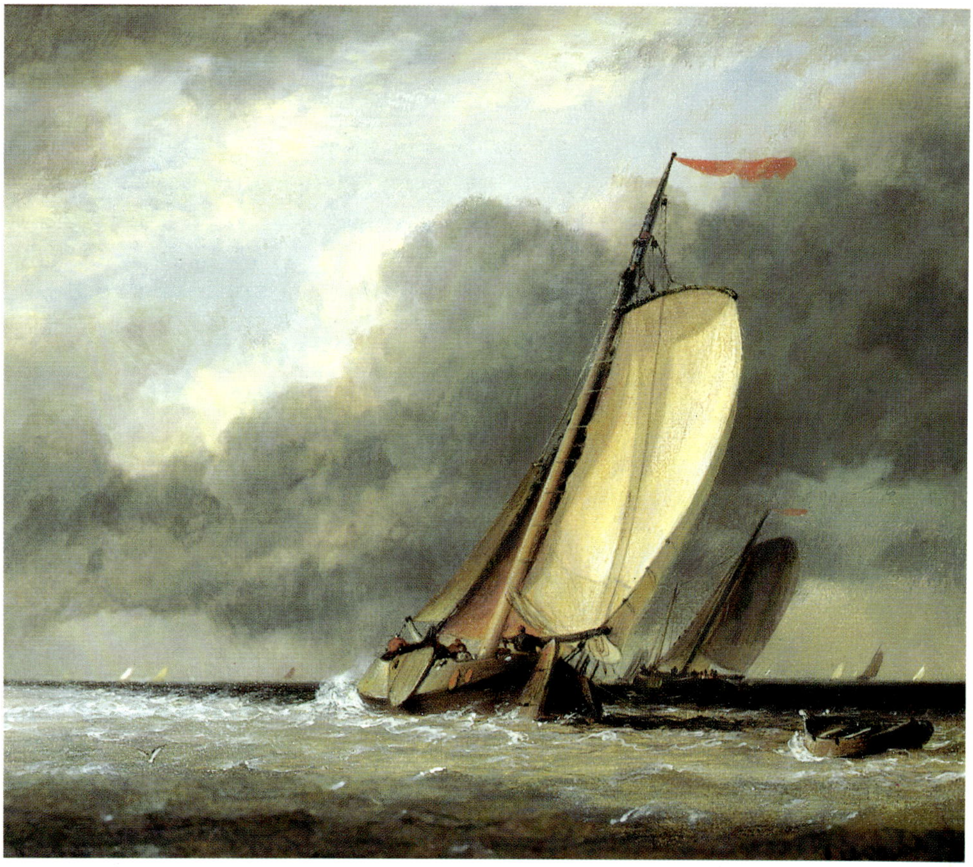

Colour Plate 148. 66/8
Small version of *Dutch boats Hugging the shore.*
Photo courtesy Martyn Gregory

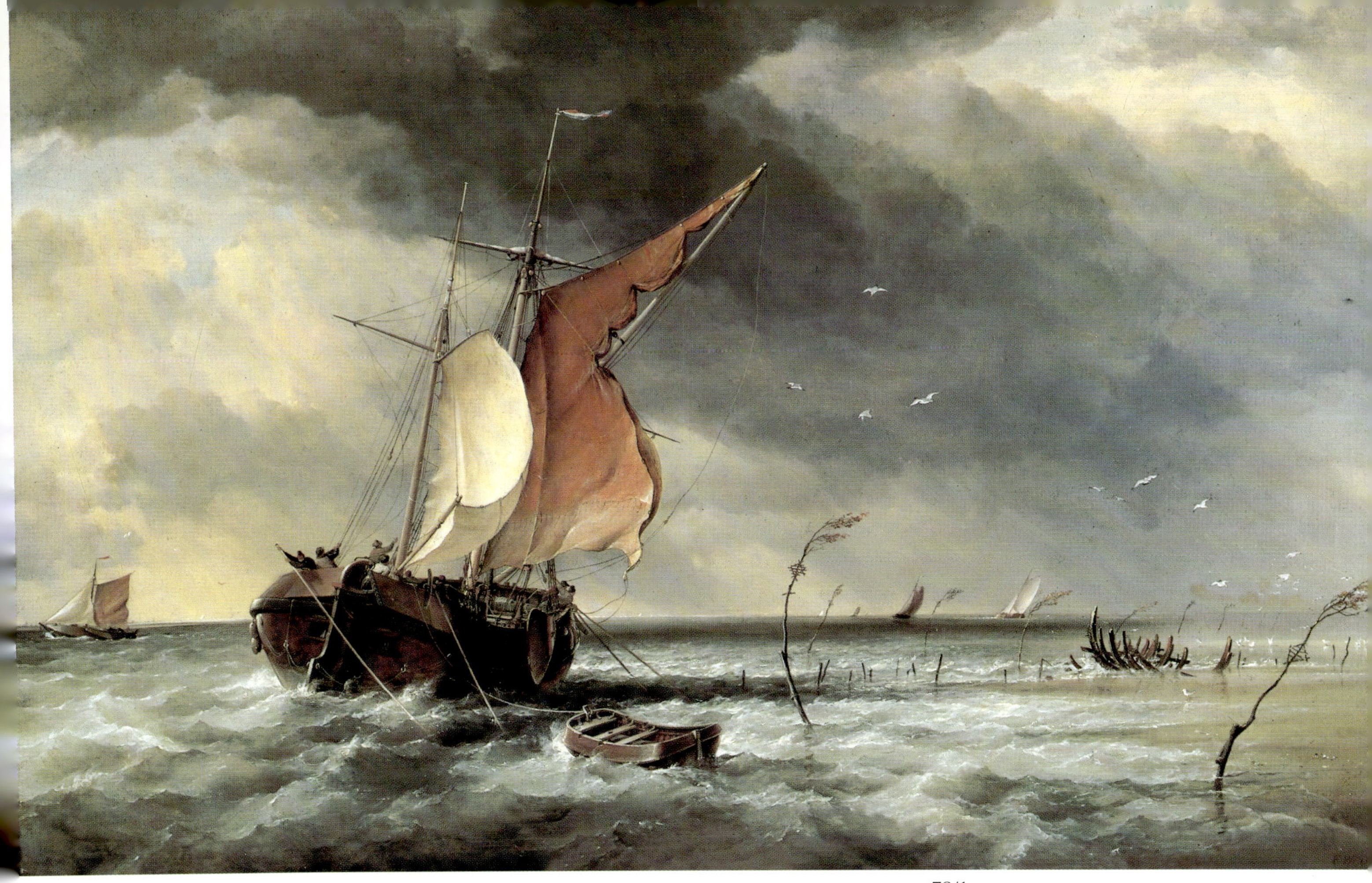

Colour Plate 150. 78/1

A Dutch galliot aground on a sandbank; low water on the Bies-Boshe, Holland

The banks and islands of the Rhine estuary provided settings for everyday navigational mishaps. This is not a wreck but the final return to a subject which had first occupied Cooke in the 1840s.

Photo:Bridgeman Art Library. Cheltenham Art Gallery, Thomas Rishworth Collection

subjects were much easier than the pastoral and were popular, so diverting patronage from his preferred art of landscape. The rendering of the sea, however, was fraught with difficulty and rarely approached a satisfactory solution, according to the painter-critic Philip Hamerton. *Who can paint a wave, who can even draw one? Stanfield and Turner have given us two interpretations of waves which do indeed render some of the facts and are full of honest intentions; but if you want difficulties, even the elementary ones are as yet unconquered.*[8] Edward Cooke with his Dutch sympathies in painting was following in the tradition of the seventeenth century Hollanders for once a painter had made a name as a master of a particular genre that is what he would succeed in selling – painting with a virtuosity which would put a more universal master to shame *...painters of seascapes became proficient not only in waves and clouds, but were such experts in portraying ships and their tackle that their paintings are still considered valuable historical documents... these Dutch artists could convey the atmosphere of the sea with wonderfully simple and unpretentious means [to] transform the commonplace into a vision of restful beauty.*[9] Eventually his exhibition pictures began to seem repetitious to some of the critics; the Dutch shore scenes, his love and delight, were greeted with some hilarity as time wore on.

Technicalities

In the engraver's studio optical aids were everyday objects, and there were inventions which could lessen the strain of drawing detailed subjects, whether landscape or architecture, boats, farm carts or *objets d'art*.

Early diary references to drawing with the *camera* in 1829 might indicate the *camera obscura,* a contrivance which the Cookes certainly possessed, but it is more likely to

8. Hamerton op.cit., p.215.
9. Gombrich op.cit., pp.312-3.

mean the use of Wollaston's prism, a patented invention[10] which was produced for sale in 1807 as a *camera lucida*. William Hyde Wollaston MB, a physician turned chemist, had evidently tried to make drawings of landscape but found his skill wanting. His invention, a four-sided prism mounted at the end of an extending brass rod with a G clamp at the other end for attachment to a drawing board or table, was a fairly simple device although needing application and skill for successful use. The patent specification declared *any person may draw in perspective or may copy or reduce any print or drawing*. Newman in Soho Square, P. & G. Dollond in St Paul's Churchyard and W. Cary in the Strand were suppliers and years later Lechertier Barbe of Jermyn Street, London, who were one of Cooke's colourmen, marketed an imported French version by P. Berville. A boxed version and also one contained in its own sketching case are recorded; the latter, patented by Samuel Parlour in 1836, was inspected by Cooke at Reeves' in June of that year – *new Instrument for Drawing* he called it, without noting his verdict. E.W. Cooke's instruments have not survived.

References to drawing through the telescope might conjure up a picture of sea-side contortions but in fact instrument-makers and others were quick to see the use of Wollaston's prism in contact with the eye glass of an ordinary terrestrial telescope for drawing distant objects. One of W.B. Cooke's engravings, published in March 1844, is *A Telescope View of Windsor Castle* from a drawing made by E.W. Cooke and this has the encircling dark tone suggesting an eyepiece view which may well have been made in that way. However, another drawing aid, by the artist and inventor Cornelius Varley, was patented in 1811 and called the *Graphic Telescope*. One of these had been given to J.S. Cotman, departing for his first tour in Normandy in 1817, by Sir Henry Englefield Bt, the *amateur* who was a confirmed user. It seems likely that his Isle of Wight drawings which George and W.B. Cooke engraved had been made with its aid and this could have been the family's introduction to an instrument which E.W. Cooke is thought to have used frequently. Not only was it an aid in drawing complicated subjects, architecture or sailing craft, particularly those somewhat distant, but with it he could even make enlargements of his paintings. The principle was the same as Wollaston's, and though it was not so simple in use it was capable, especially by 1840 after Varley's various improvements, of a wider application. With a cumbersome tripod stand and drawing table, however, it required a stable foundation and, although portable, was bulky.

By means of two mirrors angled at 45°, one at each end of an astronomical or Keplerian telescope, it produces a correctly aligned image which can be traced by looking into the small eye-piece mirror and simultaneously at the paper below. A print showing it in operation looks somewhat strange for the user peers into an eyepiece at the 'wrong' end of a three-draw telescope.

It gave a characteristic hardness of outline and a resulting lack of depth, according to a note in a display of examples at the Science Museum, South Kensington, although of course this depended very much on the skill of the draughtsman. There were other limitations, as in 1829 when Cooke complained to his diary that he was unable to finish a camera sketch looking along Hammersmith Bridge – the 700ft. (213m) of the original 1827 suspension bridge – because it shook so much. This would have applied equally to prism and graphic telescopes. Varley made use of it for portraiture, producing striking likenesses of an unposed, unsophisticated and almost unflattering kind. Sir Francis Chantrey the sculptor is recorded as having made preliminary portrait drawings with it,[11] and the Cooke brothers' 1818 *Peak Scenery* was based on drawings by Chantrey which, it seems likely, were also made with its aid.

There is here an interesting link with photography which was about to astonish the world of art. The Cooke family with their botanical and geological connections – and both Loddiges and Pye Smith were receptive to importations and new ideas – were often

10. British Patent 2993 of 1806.
11. Hammond op.cit., p.101.

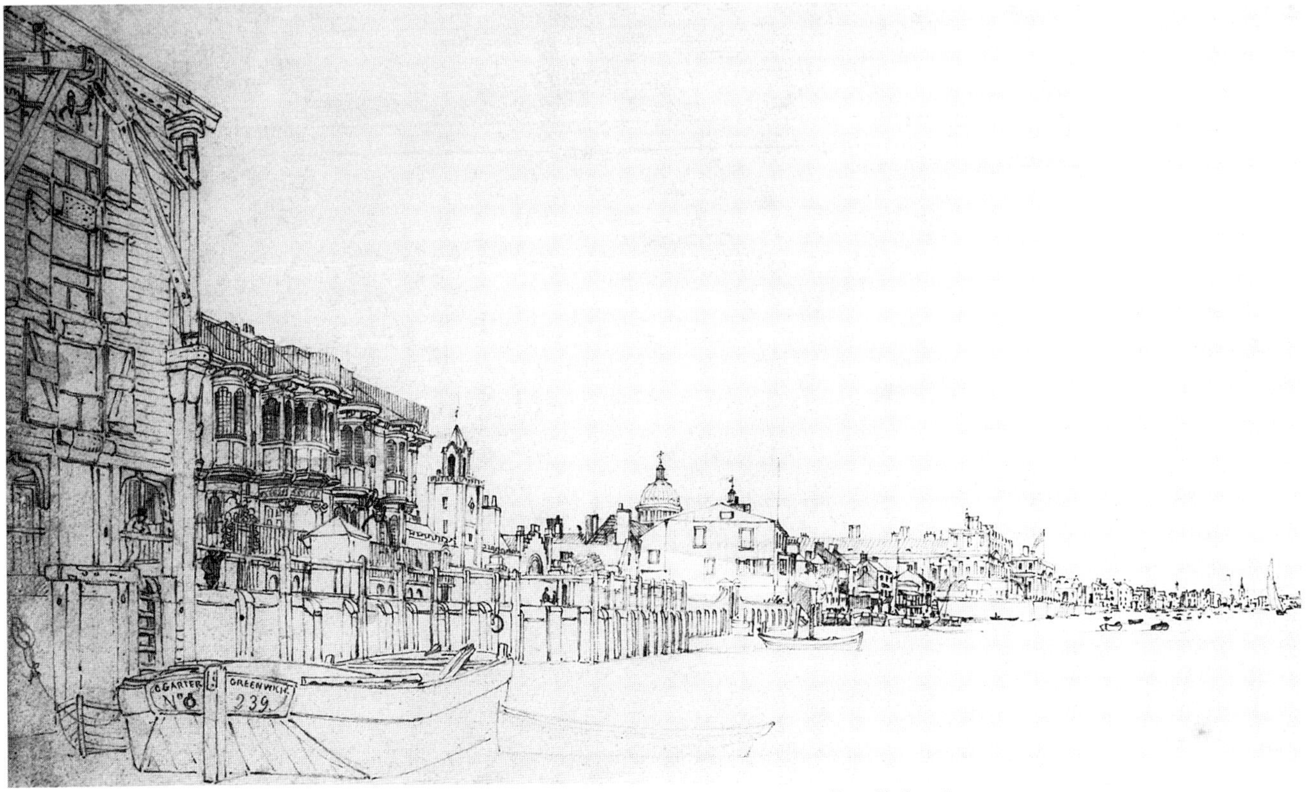

Plate 164. Pencil drawing
The Waterfront at Greenwich. 1836
Drawing made with the aid of a *camera lucida*. The view may well have been for a background to river traffic, but is a valuable record. The warehouse with its cranes has long since disappeared and 'Crowley House', the Tudor building beside it, was demolished in the 1860s. The small gothic building with square tower and belfry is the Earl of Northampton's Almshouses, called also Norfolk College and Trinity Hospital, which still exists in the care of the Worshipful Company of Mercers. Riverside inns give place to Wren's superb group of the Royal Hospital buildings beyond. Author's collection

at the Royal Institution in London to witness demonstrations and hear scientific papers.

One can only conjecture how word of the extraordinary discoveries of Mons. Niepce might have reached the Cookes, but Dr Bauer of Kew, the botanical artist whom from diary references they evidently knew, was also Secretary of the Royal Society and the Frenchman had written to him in 1827 about his silver chloride discoveries and his paper negatives. Sir Humphry Davy FRS collaborated with Thomas Wedgwood, son of Josiah, in his experimental copying of paintings on to glass and wrote on the light sensitivity of silver nitrate in 1802 while professor of chemistry at the Royal Institution. Sir John Herschel at Slough, the astronomer with a keen interest in photochemistry, had found out hyposulphite of soda as a fixative and is credited with coining the word *photography* – his father Sir William was born in Hanover in 1738 so was a contemporary of both the Cooke and the Loddiges grandparents. This surely opens up a possibility that among the ex-Hanoverian residents of the environs of London there may have been some exchange and intercourse. Cousin William Shuckard, whose father was from Frankfurt, became Librarian of the Royal Society in 1835. Niepce went into partnership with the scene painter Louis Daguerre in 1829. T.S. Boys had been back and forth from Paris at that time; John Pye of the Associated Engravers was in correspondence with Daguerre in 1839 and in that year the *Art Union Journal* reported that the Graphic Society had seen at one of its meetings M. Niepce's *light paintings* from which M. Daguerre had brought 'this most extraordinary discovery' to such perfection. Cooke it would appear, had missed that meeting.

There had indeed been experimenting in all quarters and it was dissatisfaction with his efforts to draw with Wollaston's *camera lucida* in 1833 which drove W.H. Fox Talbot

MP FRS to try a *camera obscura* containing sensitised paper and allow sunlight to print the image. Cooke experimented with 'photogenic paper' in May 1839, soon after the publication of Fox Talbot's article *Photogenic Drawing*, but without bothering to record the details or express an opinion to the diary. He was staying with the Loddiges and the microscope had just been demonstrated to his great delight; while in scientific mode, as it were, they were probably trying direct contact reproduction in sunlight, as Fox Talbot had shown with lace, leaves, etc. Another trial of the paper later that month, with Jane Loddiges his future wife and her brother Conrad, involved the use of seaweed which was appropriate for a marine painter.

The *foe-to-graphic art* was Charles Landseer's pun which greeted the invention among the artists in Cooke's circle, but rapidly growing evidence of the new medium's capability carried the latter along. As distinct from the daguerrotype, which was a unique image, the talbotype, soon named by its inventor the *calotype* from the Greek word for beauty, could reproduce itself. It was not until he removed to Kensington in 1849 that Cooke was really in touch with the practitioners and saw exhibitions, collected calotypes and displayed their wonders to friends and visitors. Its utility for recording completed pictures was demonstrated and from 1850, having ordered a calotype camera and lens from Ross, he no longer made outline sketches of his paintings with the *camera lucida* before sending-in day. However, Cooke's description of taking 'another shy' indicates that he had not mastered the techniques and so, his operations being still tentative, he got others to take the necessary photographs. A Calotype Club was founded in 1847 and although Cooke seems not to have joined, among his photographic acquaintances was one member, Joseph Cundall, a well-known figure, publisher in New Bond Street, who it is claimed introduced the first Christmas cards in 1846. He wrote in 1854 *The Photographic Primer* and published several other manuals.[12] There exists a confusion among diary entries with Mr Cundell, so spelt, and his wife, both also taking photographs, portrait and record, who frequented the Kensington soirées and parties. It seems possible that he was the Manager of the Stratford Place branch of the London and Westminster Bank, mentioned as a friend by W.P. Frith,[13] who however reverts to the other spelling. Cooke used the bank and also stood sponsor to Cundell's son Herbert Stewart Cundell in 1850, while Joseph had a son, Herbert Minton Cundall, who became a well-known writer on art and artists. J.F. Joubert de la Ferté, engraver and patentee of acierage (steel facing of engraved plates), a naturalised Englishman, spent time and money on a process of permanent photographic printing and he took plates of several of Cooke's paintings including HMS *Terror*. D.O. Hill of Edinburgh, the painter and pioneer portrait photographer, was known to Cooke and they visited when in each other's capital city. In 1850 he noted that a meeting of the Graphic Society saw calotypes of Rome, Angers and Arles.

W. Lake Price, who took the fine portrait of Cooke at his easel in 1857 (Plate 136), which was one of several made at the same time, also wrote a *Manual of Photographic Manipulation,* 1858, and produced a series of portraits of RAs, published in 1859. Cooke records having his likeness taken in the early years by Cundell, by Rippingham and by Watkins, and also a jolly calotyping session where Robert Hannah and others dressed up in period costume for the occasion.

Other drawing instruments are mentioned and their purpose can be guessed, even if they have not survived in use; the Perspectograph is one and the Apograph (the dictionary definition is 'an exact transcript') in its original case by the maker Smith featured in the sale of George Cooke's studio effects in 1834. An Alethoscope from αληθεια, the Greek for Truth, bought in Venice was another instrument which the diary records, although this seems to have been little more than a parlour toy. A surviving example, Naya's *Aletoscopio,*[14] demonstrates changing effects – day turned into night –

13. Frith op.cit., p.261.
14. *Veduti e Dettagli – The Photography of Carlo Naya,* University of Michigan, Museum of Art, 1992.

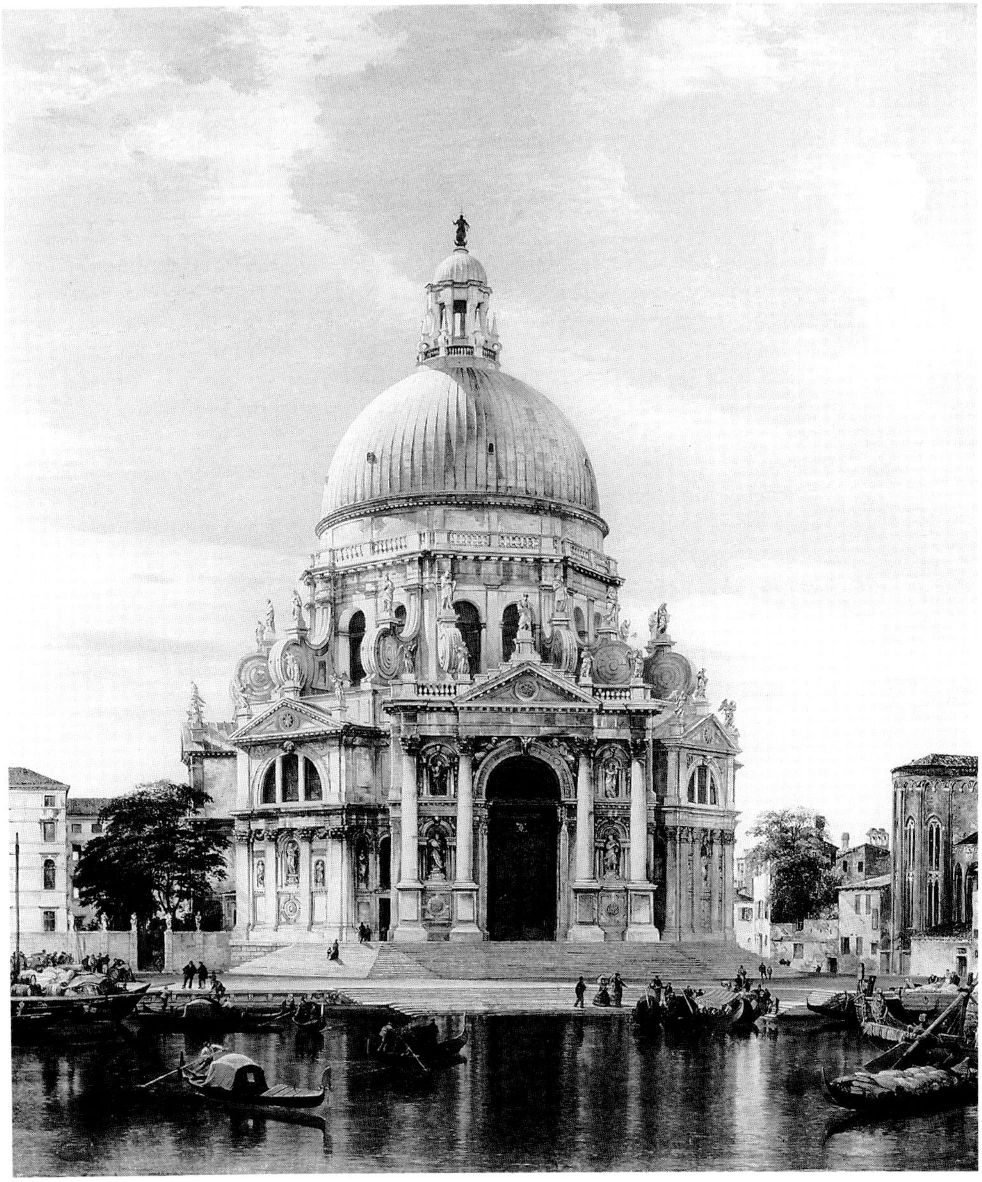

Plate 165. 57/20
The Church of Santa Maria della Salute Photo courtesy National Gallery of Ireland, Dublin

using multilayered photographic prints and mirrors within the device. Carlo Ponti, Cooke's supplier of calotypes from 1851, was eventually eclipsed by Naya. Aaron Scharf's *incredible plethora of contraptions... the diagraph, the agatograph and the hyalograph, the quarréograph, pronopiograph and eugraph, the graphic mirror and the periscopic camera, the solar megascope... the physionotrace...* indicate the range available.[15] As well there arose a scientific application of Wollaston's prism as an attachment for a microscope enabling specimens to be drawn. In Holland in 1837 Cooke recorded demonstrating this to a Dutch gentleman in Leyden.

Artists' Suppliers

The gift of 'capital' oil painting brushes from T.S. Boys in 1830 was followed by his earliest purchases of oil colours and boards from an unnamed supplier, indicating a determination to try his hand. Brushes and a palette he had from James Stark, who 'set him up' for his lessons. Later from Brown of High Holborn he bought canvases, oil

15. Scharf op. cit.

colours and palette knives. Various artists' colourmen in London were patronised by Cooke over the years. Winsor and Newton, the celebrated firm established in 1832, were concerned by 'earnest enquiry and research' to improve the permanence of their watercolours. He bought a set of *colour syringes* from them in 1836 and had a box made to contain them as well as a cover made for the box, but it was not until 1840 that their invention of grinding machinery for oil colours was in production.[16] In that year Cooke noted buying their 'new colour tubes'. Collapsible tubes were patented by John Rand and sold in 1841 by Thomas Brown, High Holborn, one of the chief suppliers of canvas to painters from Constable and Turner to Landseer and Millais; they lined and mounted the oil paper and canvas block paintings which Cooke brought home from his foreign tours.

The firm of Barbe, to whom Cooke also went for materials, for example, *a bladder of colour* in 1844, began with Charles Barbe, musical instrument maker at 60 Quadrant, Regent Street, in the 1820s. About 1835 he appears in the directories also as 'Importer of French painting brushes and colours'. Partnership with Lechertier with additional premises at 7 Glasshouse Street came in the 1860s and the firm existed until 1979 in Jermyn Street, St James's, London. In 1850 Cooke equipped himself for his first Venetian trip at Barbe's but lists Newman as altering his white sketching umbrella and supplying a case for his canvas sketching block, while moist colours (watercolours) were bought from Winsor and Newton. An interesting studio memo, including notes of other suppliers like Charles Roberson, is found at the end of the 1855 diary:

Jan 2. Johnstone sent me India proof of Turner's Cape Colonna – present.
5. Zuijder Zee Botter came back from Liverpool & Miss Mutries Orchids.
8. Ordered canvasses of Roberson: One 42½ x 27 [108cm x 68.5cm]. One 26 x 16¼ [66cm x 41.275cm] and one about 66 x 41 [167.5cm x 104cm]. Also 4 flake white & 1 Ivory black.
8. Ordered of Criswick one frame 42 x 26½ [106.5cm x 67.3cm] sight – one 25½ x 16 & one 52⅝ x 32⅛ [133.6cm x 81.6cm].
10. Roberson sent 2 canvasses (& colors) one for Mr Arden and Mr Burnand
10. Frame for small Venice came from Foords.
18. Roberson sent large canvas 42½ x 27 [108cm x 68.5cm]& colors.
20. Woolly sent 4 doz mounts.
27. Green brt back Calm Zuijder Zee from Liverpool unsold.
Feb 5. Criswick sent 4 frames Viz. Mr. Theop. Burnand's – Mr Arden's & 2 for Schevg. pictures.
5. Woolly sent 8 doz mounts
13. Leighton sent 2 new Solander cases.
Mar 2. Criswick sent frame for Snow pic & 2 small back (?) ogee for Venice.
14. Sent Mr Arden's picture of Venice home (the Riva Schiavone) by Eyles.
15. Sent Sunset picture on Lagune as present to Alderman Salomons.
Apr 10. Pd Crocker for taking pictures to R.A. 8s.0d.

Studio records were evidently kept; some pages in the hand of one of his sisters for the year 1849 have survived,[17] but no more.The names of his framemakers, Criswick and Foord, bookbinders and stationers, Leighton, and Woolly, carriers, Crocker and Eyles, are revealed as well as the names of patrons and of a neighbour, one of the Mutrie sisters, Martha and Annie, flower painters.

His selection of seemingly arbitrary canvas sizes and frames to match is curious. The specification of odd quarter and even eighth inches makes it appear as if his sketches for new compositions were very precisely designed. Cooke at work can be glimpsed from the diary and from the occasional comment by contemporaries. *Gave canvas two coats of cream colour to lose the coarseness of the ticken* refers to a more expensive type of

16. Advertisements to Winsor & Newton's series *The Art of Painting...*, n.d., c.1870.
17. Cooke MSS.

canvas, perhaps the same as ticking, mentioned in 1867, confirming the Redgraves' note: *He delighted in a smooth surface and an almost mechanical correctness of outline.*[18] His palette is mentioned, *always most carefully set, and every colour was well-ground and in its proper place, and he kept them very fluent by adding oil with his brush as he painted.* However he left no indication of his choice of pigments and only the occasional mention, such as reminding his sister Mary that she should become proficient in the grinding of ultramarine ash. This was the remains of the lapis lazuli from which the ultramarine had been extracted *...extremely useful pigments affording greys much purer and more tender... suited to the grey of skies... delicate and very tender azures... where hazy greys are required.*[19] Redgrave further wrote that there was scarcely any impasto in Cooke's painting, *his skies he never permitted to dry while he painted on them and he was careful therefore to finish if possible in a single day.*[20] The skies of his larger studio pictures were indeed painted in one session, which would be a long one. Assisted by one or other of his sisters, who prepared his colours, he would rise early and work all day while the light lasted. Presumably he thus avoided such devices as the wet sheet hung over the canvas at night to retard drying, mentioned as the habit of William Collins by the Redgraves[21] and of W.J. Müller by A.G. Temple.[22] To have been thus mentioned by Redgrave, Cooke's insistence on 'one-shot' sky painting may well have been regarded as somewhat idiosyncratic, but his belief in its necessity is evident, assuring homogeneity of texture, colour and treatment, and in this he was evidently not alone. One must recall the critic's complaint about his 'wash of turpentine', for his oil sketches made in the open air are often very thinly painted and have even been occasionally catalogued as *gouache*, but they are precisely drawn and with gusto. His studio pictures show a light impasto, almost a modelling in paint, of ropes, baskets, foam, stones etc. It is clear that he painted with care and considerable relish for the medium, which must recall John Opie's retort on being asked with what he mixed his paints – *Brains!*.[23]

In 1840. when commencing his *Mont St Michel* (40/6, Colour Plate 44) he recorded *Uncle ground lead for sky and helped me painting it.* In general the labour of preparing colours, before the introduction of ready-ground pigments in oil, was such that painters more prolific than Cooke employed a studio hand or student for the purpose; a supplier, Curtis in the City, ground colours for him.

In his evidence before the Royal Commission of 1857 on the question of the new National Gallery, Cooke declared, in relation to the pollution in London's air which was harmful to oil paintings, that he had a sad experience and had been lead into great error when commencing to paint by using thick Megilp. This, also spelt variously McGilp, Meguilp, Macguelp, a word of unknown origin, was given to a convenient medium of drying oil and varnish.[24] This he employed not only as a medium but also to varnish his early pictures, which were by that date so brown that he declared he could hardly bear to look at them and would gladly paint others to replace them! The diary reveals that on at least one occasion he also 'baked' his pictures in front of a coke stove, to dry them for transport. Since 1842, he reported, he had used only copal and was satisfied with the unimpaired brilliance of his colour. The offending dark varnish was in fact removed from two of the Sheepshanks pictures under Richard Redgrave's eye by one Bentley – as Cooke noted with some satisfaction in his diary for 25 June 1857. *Craquelure* is still found on his early *Mending the Bait Net,* No.40 in the Victoria & Albert Museum Collection, and in *Portsmouth Harbour,* No.49, which may indicate the use of the dread asphaltum, or possibly undiluted copal varnish.

18. Redgrave, 1947, p.424.
19. *The Art of Landscape painting in Oil Colours* by J. Edwards for Winsor & Newton, n.d., p.23.
20. Redgrave 1947, p.424.
21. Redgrave 1866, Vol II, p.418.
22. *The Art of Painting in the Queen's Reign* by A.G. Temple,1897, p.35.
23. Redgrave 1866, p.594.
24. *Art Union Journal,* 1845, p.143.

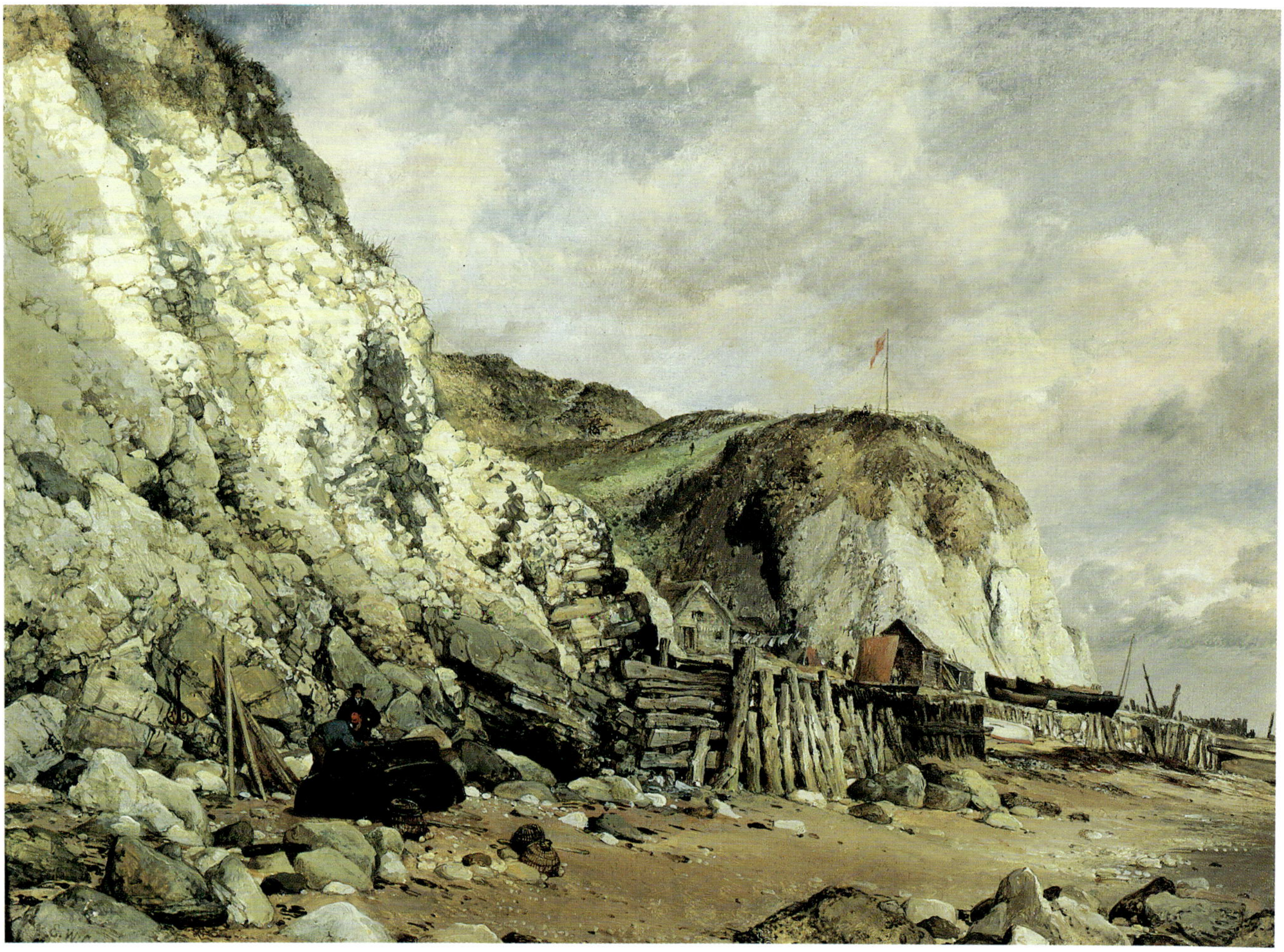

Colour Plate 151. 56/9

Bonchurch pier & cliffs

The massive timber constructions attracted Cooke here and in other parts of the English coast as well as on the Continent. A wooden pier was frequently the subject of a detailed drawing.

Photo courtesy Arthur Ackermann & Peter Johnson

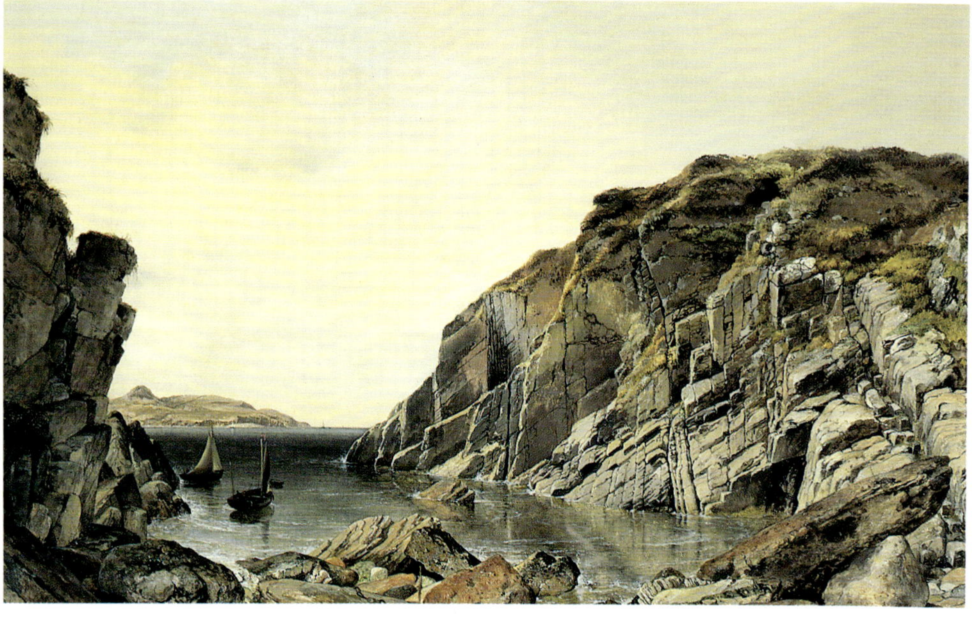

Colour Plate 152 58/10

Slate rocks Valentia Id.

This portrait of the geology of County Kerry began his series depicting features of the British coasts.

Photo courtesy Martyn Gregory. Private Collection

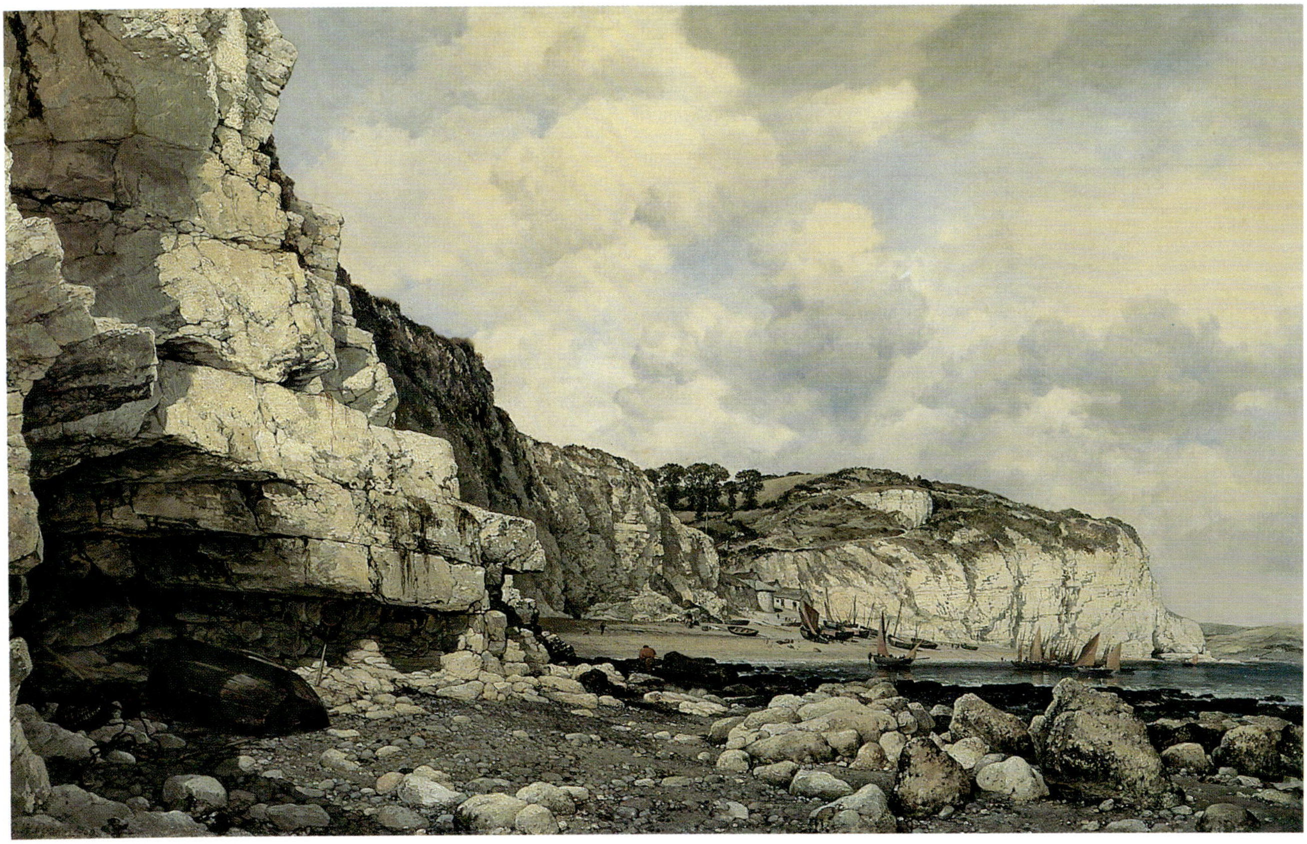

Chapter 15

THE FELLOW: MAN OF SCIENCE

It was in the south-west of Ireland that Cooke ...*commenced his series of highly-finished pictures in oil to illustrate the chief geological features of the British coast,* according to the *Art Journal* of 1869, surely quoting the artist himself. Whether he would have a gallery of his completed rock and cliff paintings or simply accumulate his sketches does not appear, but over and beyond this scientifically angled work can be sensed the *éminence* of J.M.W. Turner who, in the year Cooke was born, had gone off on tour to begin the series of coastal watercolours which were engraved by W.B. and George Cooke. The drama of these views, taken if not with 'the eye of an eagle', in John Ruskin's phrase,[1] then certainly from view-points borrowed from a sea-bird, does include much of the geology even if it is not specific. The pictorial possibilities of such coastal scenery having been thus demonstrated in the *Southern Coast* series, Edward Cooke took careful note as well as making actual copies. His own short-lived series of three plates, later added to *Shipping and Craft*, was to have been *The British Coast,* although the absence of text makcs it impossible to determine whether *Kemp Stairs near Kingsgate; Folkestone harbour, low tide* and *Dover cliffs* were intended to represent the Kent chalk. Clarkson Stanfield worked upon the Dover and also on a Ramsgate which was not used. The series, had it prospered, might have formed a noteworthy example of the genre, although at least one critic saw evidence of the older painter's feeling for stage scenery overwhelming Cooke's 'more subtle approach' and that the three steel plates *anticipate the trivialisation of the traditions of the Topographical school which worsened as the*

1. *Pre-Raphaelitism by the Author of "Modern Painters"*, 1851, p.31.

Colour Plate 153. 58/16
Beer Beach No 4. *Fishing Cove of Beer*
Another of his British coast geological series, but the fishermen and boats were never far from his interest.
Photo courtesy Private Collection

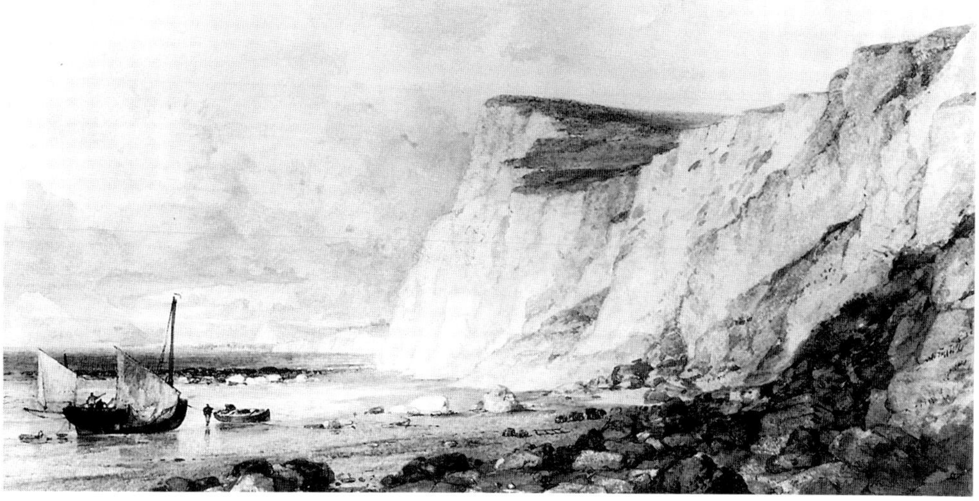

Plate 166. Watercolour
Chalk cliffs, Isle of Wight
Photo courtesy Martyn Gregory

19th Cent wore on.[2] Dramatic coastal erosion witnessed and recorded at Hastings in 1834 might be a beginning of the painted series with further subjects in the Isle of Wight in the following year (Plate 166), but Bonchurch with its cliffs of chalk and marl, for example the views of 1856, seem to have been the first to have notes of the rock formations appended to the titles.

A visit to southern Ireland in 1849 was marked by fern hunting with the habitual sketching rather than any concentration on rocky landscapes. The glory of the sunsets from Bantry Bay were noted but he was not equipped for painting which had to await a later visit in 1858 when he went to record the Atlantic submarine cable operations. Studies of the slate rocks of Valentia Id. off the Kerry coast (58/10, Colour Plate 152) were followed by a group of pictures on the south Devon coast, the *lower chalk* at Beer, later that same year (58/16, 58/18, Colour Plates 153 and 147 and Plate 244), but the cable operations did not inspire him to paint them.

Some surviving pictures bear his inscription on the stretcher with subtitles describing the geology, which are presumably part of the series. Bonchurch, the early favourite, was followed by the triassic cliffs near Watchet and boulders of grauwacke at Porlock in Somerset in the early 'sixties (62/6 and 62/9, Plate 167 and Colour Plate 155) which competed with the serpentine of Kynance Cove in Cornwall. Catalan Bay, Gibraltar, stretching a point to include overseas territories subject to the Crown, was perhaps his geological masterpiece (63/2, Colour Plate 137).

One of his father's works had been the large plates from drawings by Sir Henry Englefield Bt. for *A Description of the Principal Picturesque Beauties, Antiquities and Geological Phoenomena of the Isle of Wight. With Additional Observations on the strata of the Island by Thomas Webster.* This included as well several views of the Dorset coast and the large handsome book was published in 1816 – *In no instance has accuracy been sacrificed to the effect of the engraving* Sir Henry was careful to insist. As a user of Varley's Patent Graphic Telescope his interest in topographical accuracy was maintained. W.B. Cooke had also engraved and published his own views of the island, in 1808. It seems therefore very likely that the delights and unusual features of the island landscape were familiar to young Cooke, if only from proofs pinned up in the studio. Although only five when Englefield was published, he habitually learnt much by copying. In July 1831, aged twenty, he found himself gazing at Shanklin Chine – *most glorious place, made sketch, had tea at the Chine Inn, slept there,* he noted. Exploration of what was to become a favourite stretch of coast continued with short spells for sketching at Niton, Puckaster and Steephill; he bathed and walked along the beach to Luccombe, getting a fisherman to carry the luggage. He walked to Bonchurch (Plate 168) which he thought a lovely place, and so to Ventnor where tea at the *Crab & Lobster* Inn

2. Finch op.cit.

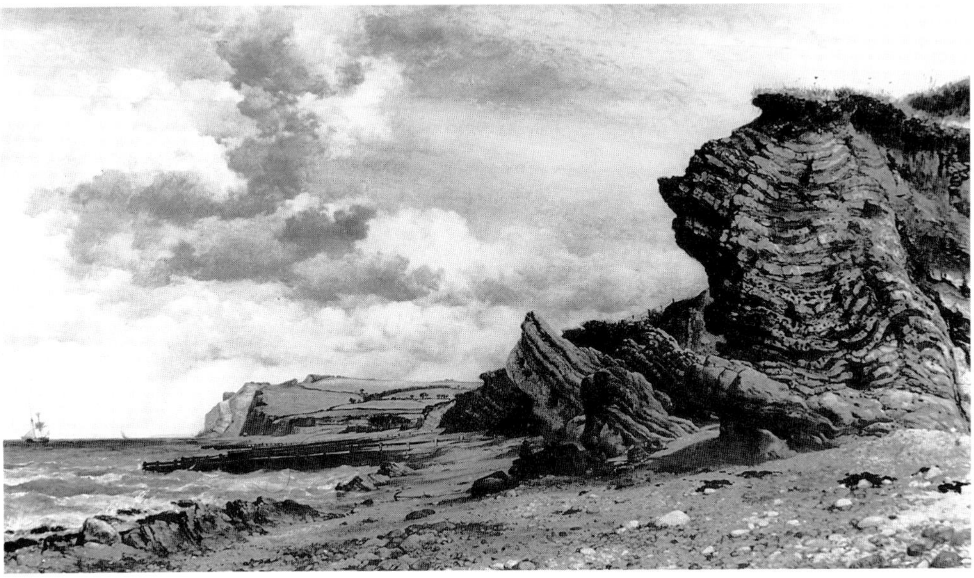

Plate 167. 62/6
Triassic rocks, near Blue Anchor, North Somerset, looking towards Watchet
Blue limestone and clays at the improbable sounding hamlet which perhaps took its name from the local inn; the artist noted 'Bunter' sandstone, which was evidently red and white and fossil-bearing beds. He collected the fossils and spent rainy evenings indoors sorting them.
Photo courtesy Guildhall Art Gallery, Corporation of London

was followed by a walk down to the cove and further drawing. In 1835 he returned, now emerged as a painter in oils, and with the firm purpose which marked his entire life and work he set out to explore and learn about the boats and gear of the local fishermen, recording them as carefully as if he fully realised that they would one day be objects of curiosity. Dyer, a fisherman, made a model of a lobster pot for him which the artist drew in the evening! The *Victoria County History* notes that the entrance to the old village of Bonchurch is marked by a ponded water, the site of a former withy bed. The fishermen wove their pots and baskets from willow saplings known as withies; in *Beach Boats of Britain*[3] it is noted that a wood of willows used to be rented by Bembridge fishermen along the coast and the use of withies is traced into Dorset as well, bringing these activities down to the present day. St Boniface Down above Bonchurch and Ventnor is the highest point in Wight. Englefield's opinion was *the extremely steep chalk down beautiful indeed only by its contrast with the surrounding scenery, but not extensive enough to be, like most of the chalk hills, displeasing from its unvaried surface*. Medieval shipmasters lowered their topsl's in salute as they passed, reverencing the Saint's holy well which was visible from the sea. Below, the extraordinary tumbled landscape and its vegetation, as well as the contorted strata underlying it, were in Englefield's time little known. *No Guide takes notice of it* he says of the rugged paths, springs and thickets of Luccombe.

It was the sea-shore which most attracted Cooke, for there were fishermen's shacks and boats and rough piers or breakwaters, made much as in mediaeval times from lines of tree-trunks infilled with boulders. Also there were the endlessly fascinating 'props', fishing gear, nets, floats, baskets, creepers etc., around the boats. His titles included 'Cliffs of disrupted chalk and marl' and 'Chalk and firestone rocks forming part of the Undercliff, Isle of Wight' (75/7, Colour Plate 134). John Brett ARA had a similar interest and the Ruskinian enthusiasm for rocks and minerals glitters through here also. Parts of the French coast were geologically memorable, Etretat, Blanc Nez, chalk and marl cliffs again, but Holland had few points of geological interest for him save its sand dunes, nor had Venice, apart from the prospect of distant mountains. Other parts of Italy, however, had intrigued him – the mountains of Carrara, a favourite subject for painters were in one of Robert McInnes' 1848 pictures, showing bullocks carting blocks of marble. While on the Riviera Cooke painted *Ventimiglia – masses of fallen conglomerate on the shore* and *Finale, promontory of Lumacella marble: Varigotta in the distance*, titles of pictures from his 1845-46 tour. Vesuvius was ascended and the volcano appears in a number of his Neapolitan coastal studies; the steeps of Amalfi, the Capuchin Convent painted on the spot and views of precipitous Capri have all a strong geological interest.

The glaciers of Switzerland, the breathtaking heights of Gibraltar and the mountains fringing the Nile valley all saw him diligently recording and noting their colours and

3. *Beach Boats of Britain* by Robert Simper, 1984.

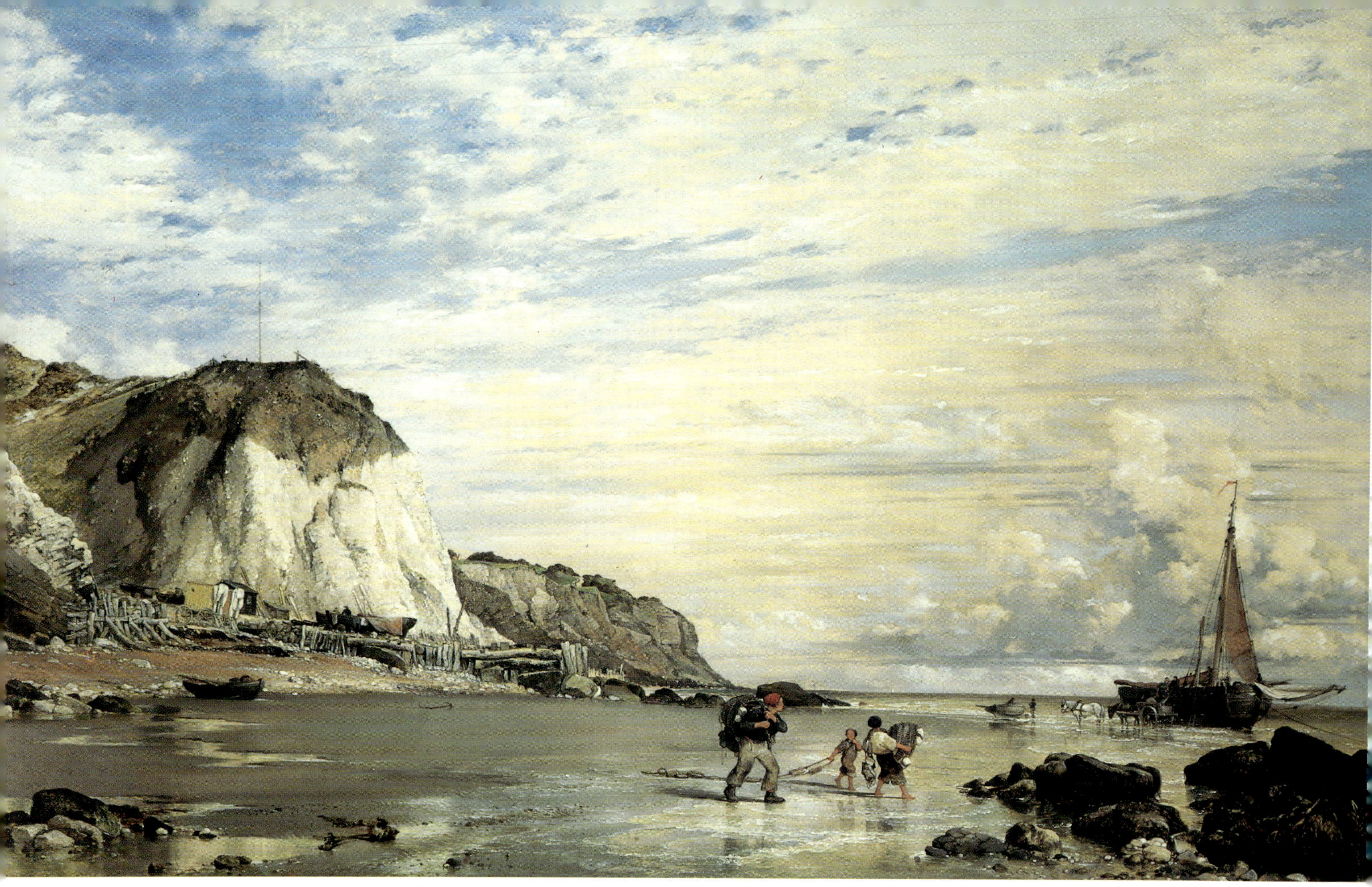

Colour Plate 156. 56/14
A Crab & Lobster shore
The name of a Ventnor Inn gave this title to a beach scene of an almost Pre-Raphaelite quality which the critics declared 'surpasses photography'. Photo courtesy Richard Green Fine.Paintings

Colour Plate 154. 62/7
Minehead & Dunster from Blue Anchor
The pair to his geological Blue Anchor picture (Plate 167) looking west. Cooke perhaps had Turner in mind, whose drawing *Watchet* he possessed, but this is very much his own statement.
Photo courtesy Arthur Ackermann & Peter Johnson

Colour Plate 155. 62/9
The Breakwater, Porlock Wier, coast of Somerset
Inscribed reverse *The shore is composed of huge boulders of Grauwacke.*
Geology vies with the splendour of sea-washed primitive timber defences. The English word Greywack denotes this Silurian conglomerate which Cooke was evidently pleased to record for his series of geological portraits. Photo courtesy Private Collection

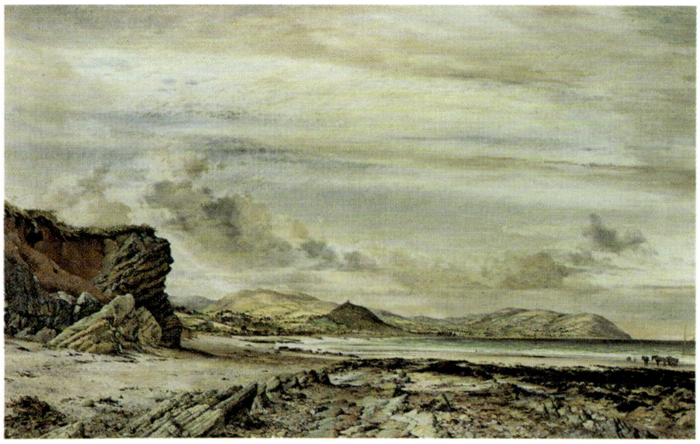

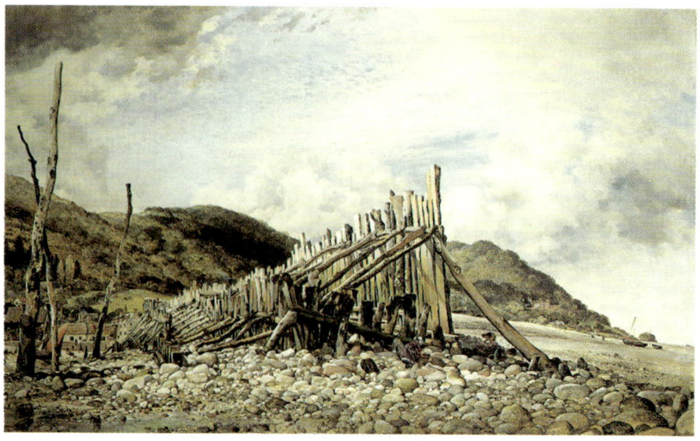

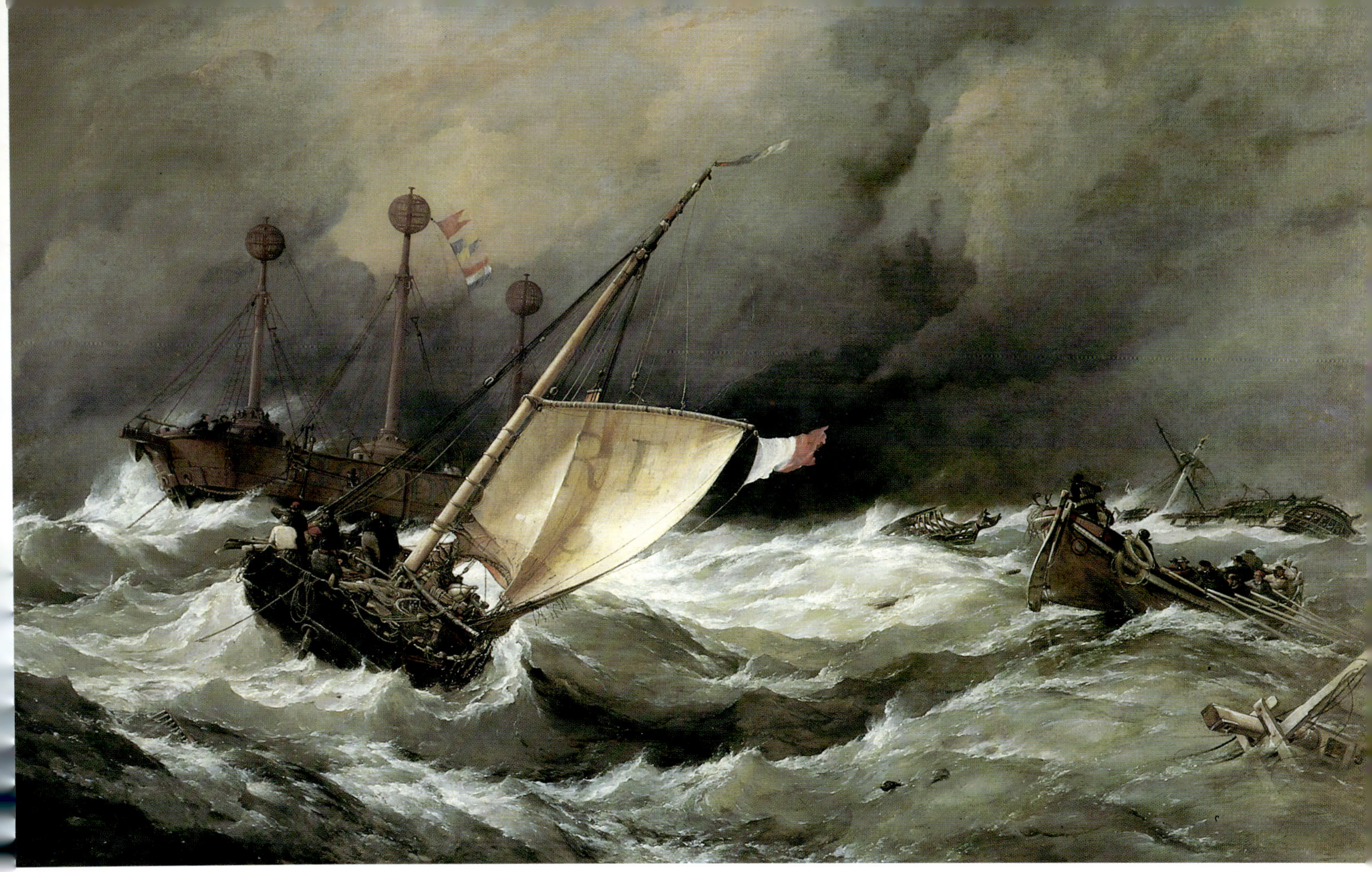

Colour Plate 157. 57/1

Wreck on the Goodwin Sands: *Morning after a heavy gale, weather moderating*

With the example of Clarkson Stanfield's celebrated *The Abandoned* (1856) before him, Cooke evidently hastened to attempt an echo of its pathos. His long addition to the title does not indicate whether it was an imaginary scene, but it won John Ruskin's approval and remains his most dramatic picture.

Photo courtesy Private Collection USA

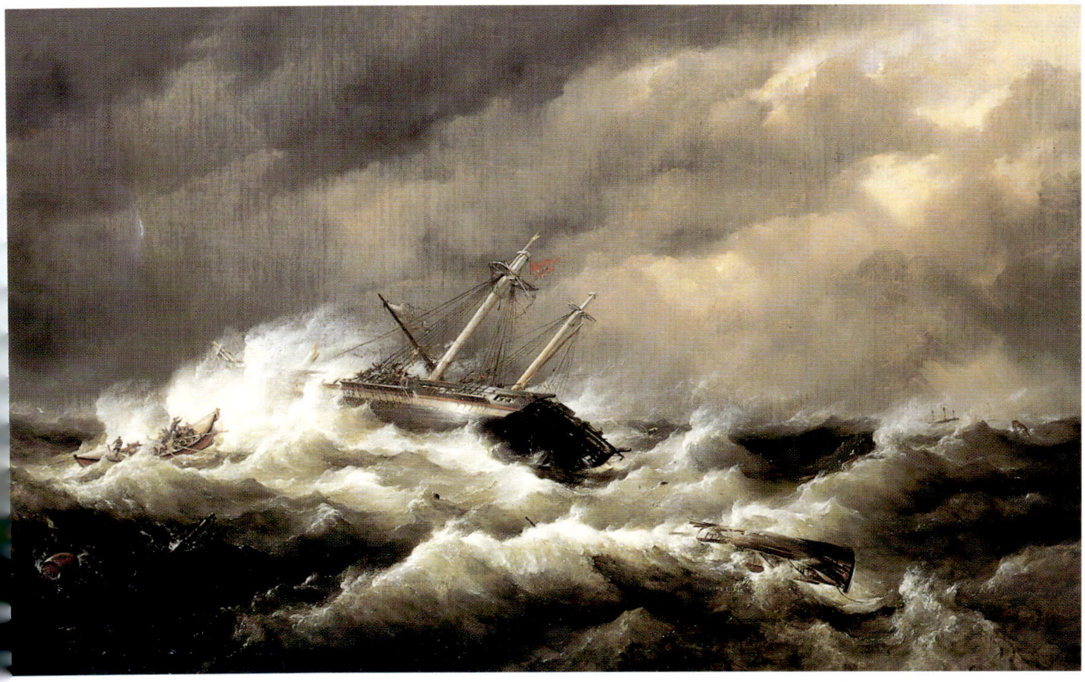

Colour Plate 158. 66/4

Rescue of the crew of a barque on the Goodwin by the Van Kook *North Deal Lifeboat*

His new lifeboat had performed a noteworthy rescue and the picture was calculated to advertise the work of the National Lifeboat Institution.

Photo courtesy Christie's. Private Collection

scientific significance. Baron Alexander von Humboldt, whose passion for scientific observation was kindled by a friendship with one of Capt James Cook's circum-navigating scientists, Georg Forster, and the paintings produced on those epoch making voyages by painters of the calibre of William Hodges RA, had begun the publication of his monumental *Kosmos* in 1845. He expressed thoughts which were welcomed enthusiastically by the *Art Journal* (probably S.C. Hall himself) in 1848, on a page entitled *The Fine Arts Considered as Aids to Science* which was not so much a review as applause for the ideas which addressed the history of landscape paintings and indicated a way forward to large depictions of exotic scenes:...*the engravings which accompany and too often only disfigure our books of travels, have yet contributed not a little to our knowledge of the aspect of different zones, to the predilection for extensive voyages, and to the more active study of nature.* The Baron's enthusiasm suggested ...*Barker's panoramas by the aid of Prevost and Daguerre be converted into a kind of substitute for wanderings in various climates ...enchanting effects might be obtained by ... studies sketched on the rugged mountain... and still more so if these were aided by photographs.*

Large panoramas attached to every city museum would be a means, he explained, of rendering the sublime grandeur of Creation more widely known and felt!

The Lifeboat

Though not a habitual sea voyager, Cooke frequently crossed to France and had on more than one occasion witnessed accidents at sea. The cross-Channel packet in which he was travelling in 1858 ran down a French fishing lugger, which carried no lights on a November night, with the loss of two men and a boy and the artist had been much moved by the occurrence.

In the RA exhibition of 1854 Clarkson Stanfield had shown *The Last of the Crew* (now at Manchester), a ship on the rocks with a lone, crouched survivor. Two years later appeared his well-known *The Abandoned,* a mastless derelict on a heaving stormy sea (present whereabouts unknown). These, greeted with critical acclaim, may well have suggested to Edward Cooke a new class of subject but he was also very much aware of Turner's shipwreck paintings for on a visit to Appuldurcombe House in the Isle of Wight he noted the *most marvellous wreck.* This was the *Wreck of a Transport ship* of 1811 which belonged to Lord Yarborough and was seen by Cooke again in July 1849 at the Old Masters exhibition in the British Institution gallery. In October 1856, when visiting Yarmouth, he found the wreck of the *Coromandel,* a former East Indiaman, but lately 'from the Baltic in Deals' (timber) stranded on the shore. He made detailed studies from every angle, inside and out, with drawings of the wreckage scattered around (Plate 169).

Early the following year he began to design a picture which he called simply 'Goodwin': he visited the Trinity House wharf on the Thames to draw a three-masted light vessel which was there for repair (Plate 170) and, completing his design, drew in the other boats using his Yarmouth sketches. The hull of the *Coromandel* serves for the Goodwin wreck (57/1, Colour Plate 157); one of its boats, almost skeletal after its battering, is taken from one of hers. The floating wreckage, a topmast and cross-trees, is also among the surviving pencil sketches of the group.[4] The following week he was at the Lifeboat Institution, consulting the Secretary, making a drawing of a model lifeboat, and also bringing one home.

For the Royal Academy annual exhibition sending-in days were towards the end of the first week in April and in 1857 Cooke as usual had his own 'Private View' of the paintings he was exhibiting in his own house in Hyde Park Gate, Kensington, where scores of people, friends and patrons, came to admire. These visits to artists at home were a regular feature of the social scene. The Exhibition opened early in May and the Goodwin picture, 51in. x 78in. (129.5cm x 198cm), No. 442 in the Catalogue, had the

4. National Maritime Museum, Greenwich.

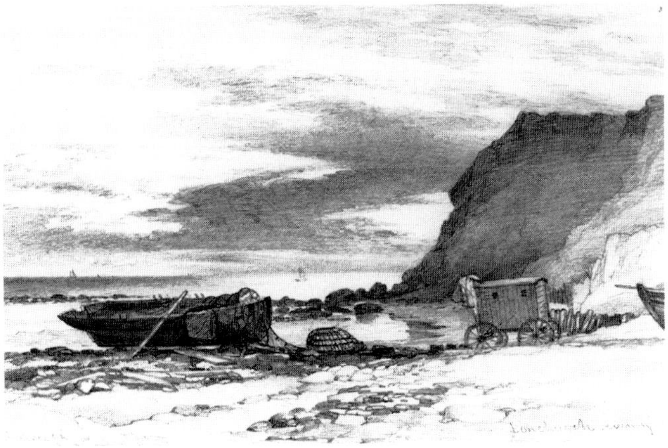

Plate 168. Pencil drawing
Bonchurch evening
Mastery of black-lead pencil is demonstrated by this subtly lit beach scene of his favourite fishing village at his favourite time of day. It was now a resort and a bathing machine, the polite essential, is perhaps the same from which he painted there with dry feet at high tide. Photo courtesy Martyn Gregory. Private Collection

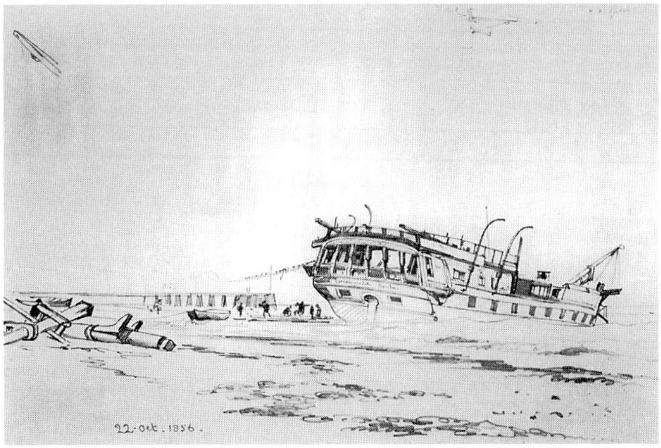

Plate 169. Pencil drawing
The *Coromandel* wrecked on Yarmouth sands
The ex-East Indiaman, then trading in timber from the Baltic, came ashore and was sketched in 1856. His painting of the wreck on the Goodwin Sands (57/1, Colour Plate 157) owes something to this study which is one of a group.
Photo courtesy The Trustees of theNational Maritime Museum, Greenwich

title *Morning after a heavy gale, weather moderating* and a long note:

> *The crews of a pilot boat and lifeboat hearing at daybreak signal guns from the Goodwin floating light vessel, and after communicating with it "bear up" for a waterlogged Indiaman, the crew and passengers perished during the night, the boats having been knocked to pieces; the captain, who would not desert his ship, was rescued by the lifeboat just before the vessel foundered on the north sand head of the Goodwin.*

John Ruskin, that most influential art critic, praised the picture in his unique style among his *Academy Notes* for 1857:

> *Very awful after we have looked at it for a little while; at least that bronze vessel is to me – a ship that is not, and yet is – the true spectre ship, whose sight is destruction. Nor less so the skeleton of the boat with the wild waves sifting through the bones of her, and the single figure waiting on the desolate ship's deck and saved by its faithfulness.*

The *Illustrated London News* remembered this picture in its notice of Cooke in 1864:

> *...what 'topographical' painter could paint the terror of tempest as Mr Cooke has done? Is there, to muscular Christians, no poetry in this painter's representations of the fierce north-easter of the German Ocean with its black storm cloud pinions, driving through maddening waves the dancing life-boat, the drifting galiot or dismasted Indiaman foundering within sight of shore?*

Here the critic as inspired columnist is taking the part of the seaman. The Rev Canon Charles Kingsley's name springs first to mind at the mention of Muscular Christianity, a term coined by some unknown writer for the types who were represented in his books, *athletic, upper-middle class somewhat Christian young men,* rather to the clerical novelist's indignation.[5]

The picture was purchased by Sir Culling Eardley of Belvedere, Kent, and when his collection was sold by Christie's in 1860 it went through several hands including the collector E.J. Coleman's. It was later in the possession of Thomas, first Earl Brassey, the Naval reformer and MP. It appeared in many important exhibitions – in 1862, 1887, 1890, 1891 and 1901. In 1971 it was appropriately shown in London in aid of the Royal National Lifeboat Institution and now rests in a private collection in the USA.

5. *The Dust of Combat – A Life of Charles Kingsley* by R.B. Martin, 1959, p.220.

It is one of Cooke's most important paintings, chiefly because of its dramatic content and his complete realisation of an involved and turbulent scene, but also on account of size and general excellence of execution. It seems that he is here using an unusual degree of imagination in that the wreck is not identified, but is symbolic of the hundreds lost on those hungry sandbanks over the centuries. Cooke, living and working in London but frequently crossing the Channel, became keenly interested in the work of the Lifeboat Institution. The treacherous Goodwin Sands off the east Kent coast extending from Ramsgate almost to Dover had claimed a huge toll of ships down the ages, indeed an entire squadron of warships under Rear Admiral Beaumont had been lost on them in 1703 during the great hurricane in Queen Anne's time. The waters inshore of the sands provided a relatively sheltered anchorage known as The Downs, wherein at any one time – when the winds were contrary – hundreds of sailing vessels might be anchored awaiting a change in wind direction which would enable them to proceed round the 'corner' through the Dover Straits and westward down the English Channel. Cooke had noticed the phenomenon while staying at Hastings when a vast concourse of shipping was released from The Downs. In storm conditions the fate of anchored ships was in the balance – they dragged their anchors, cables parted, they ran foul of each other and in general provided a good livelihood for the Deal boatmen in rescue and emergency supply operations.

Special life-saving boats were not thought of until the last century:

> *the first boat of the locality was placed in Walmer by the Royal National Lifeboat Institution in 1864, a cotton ship with all hands having been lost on the southern part of the Goodwins in a gale from the N.N.E., which unfortunately the Walmer lifeboat, being too far to leeward, was unable to fetch in that wind with a lee tide... another boat was placed in North Deal.*[6]

The *Lifeboat Journal* reported that such a boat, to cover the north part of the Goodwins, *running through the Swashway could reach distressed vessels in positions which the Ramsgate and Walmer lifeboats could not.*

The *Illustrated London News* in 1864 revealed that Cooke had painted the Goodwin picture *with the express view of advancing the objects of the R N L I. He has more recently shown the interest which he takes in those objects by a donation of £200 to pay for a new life-boat. It is called the Van Kook.*

The operation was in fact a joint one, for Cooke had a collecting box in his studio alongside the model lifeboat and visitors – friends and patrons – were invited to contribute towards the cost of the new boat. Thereby another £231.15.0d. was donated. The *Van Kook* was a 40ft. (12.2m) boat, 10ft. (3.05m) in the beam, built expressly for the job by Forrestt of Limehouse. There were of course no powered lifeboats at this time and she was reported to be very fast under sail, manageable under oars and with great stability. She was also noted as *the largest self-righting boat of the Institution* and was on station in May 1865 when Cooke, who was staying at Broadstairs, came across to Deal to look over her with R. Wilds, the coxswain. Robert Wilds was her coxswain for many years and died as a result of exposure and injuries after rescuing the crew of the Danish *Fredrick Carl* in 1885.

The choice of name is typical; *Van Kook* is the playful sobriquet introduced into many of his Dutch sea-shore subjects as the name of a fishing *pinck*, painted on bow or quarter. He evidently also chose the colours in which the lifeboat was painted.

At the end of February 1866 he abandoned painting on his current picture – extraordinarily a stranded whale on a Sussex beach (66/3, present whereabouts unknown) – to begin something more dramatic, having heard of his lifeboat's rescue of the crew from another wreck on the Goodwin sands.

6. *Heroes of the Goodwin Sands,* T.S. Treanor, 1893, p.56.

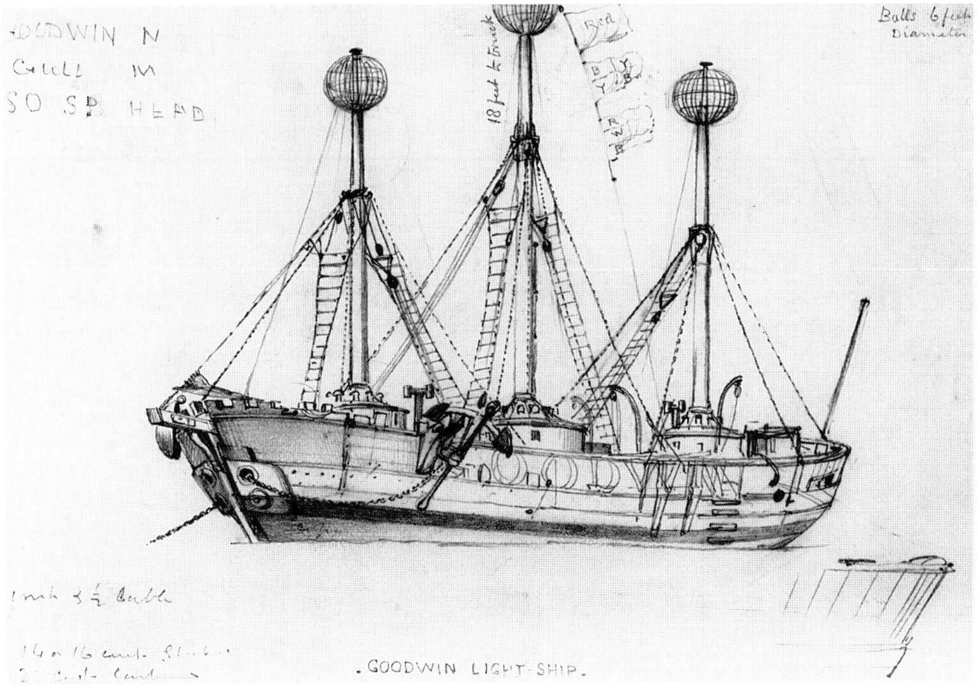

Plate 170. Pencil drawing
The Goodwin Light Vessel
To be sure of his drawing, Cooke visited the docks where the vessel was undergoing refit.

Photo courtesy The Trustees of the National Maritime Museum,Greenwich

The picture was entitled *Rescue of the crew of a barque on the Goodwin by the Van Kook North Deal Lifeboat. 'Through the wild surf they cleave their way, Lost in the foam, nor know dismay, For they go, they go, the crew to save'.* It measured 40in. x 54in. (101.6cm x 137cm) and was in the 1866 Royal Academy Exhibition, No. 139 (66/4, Colour Plate 158). It was bought by Ernest Gambart MVO, Belgian-born print publisher and picture dealer who descended from time to time upon Cooke in his studio and purchased or occasionally commissioned works for show in his large London gallery. His business devolved through his assistant and successor F.J. Pilgeram and his nephew Leo Lefèvre who formed a partnership with the Glasgow Scot Alexander Reid to become Reid and Lefèvre, which are all names woven into the history of the art world.[7] In this picture the position of the barque, with only main and mizzen lower masts standing and the main yard down on deck, is similar to that of the *Coromandel* in the earlier painting, viewed from the port quarter. The ensign is reversed as a distress signal and survivors are clustered in the main shrouds as the lifeboat approaches stern-to. A heaving line has been thrown to the ship and the wrecks of two of her boats appear almost as a warning of the fate of small craft in such a sea; one of the Goodwin lightships is in the distance. A floating spar and a barrel, the great sheets of spray breaking over the fore-part of the stranded vessel and the generally wild water over the Sands make a dramatic scene. The crescent-shaped lifeboat's cautious approach, perilous though it is, seems to be the one controlled feature in the chaos.

Later he noted *The Van Kook lifeboat saved the crew of a schooner wrecked on the Goodwin this morning* and he had an account of the lifeboat's exploits printed. The lifeboat house was later moved a little to the southward but, with its medallions at each side of the doorway, still survives although without its cupola or belfry, or its lifeboat, as the Deal Sea Angling Club.

These are, so far as is known the only 'action' pictures produced by Cooke on the life-saving theme, apart from the later *Cleopatra*. There is a chalk drawing in the Henry Huntingdon collection which relates to sea rescue and is perhaps a preparatory study. Several other pictures of sailing craft in perilous positions have been seen, French, Dutch and Venetian, and he was fond of painting boats under a press of sail entering or leaving harbour, possibly as an illustration of daring seamanship, which in following his cult of the superlative he undoubtedly admired, while the art critics tended to have reservations!

Scientific soirées and lectures, interesting meetings and conversazioni were features of the London season. Private dinner parties and dinners held by learned societies, where conversation would be informed and entertaining, were also much to Cooke's taste. He

7. Maas, op.cit., p.288; *Art & Audacity*, T.J. Honeyman, 1971.

was elected a Fellow of the Geological Society in 1862, of the Royal Geographical Society in 1863 and of the Zoologicial Society in 1865. Attendance at meetings in the Royal Institution, where the great names of the scientific world could be seen and heard in action, had long been a family pleasure and Cooke introduced his sons to these gatherings in due course. Meetings of the British Association for the Advancement of Science, which first attracted him in 1859 when they gathered at Aberdeen, saw him at its other venues over the years: Plymouth, Manchester, Belfast, Dublin, Newcastle and Brighton. The Geological sections were his chief interest but he entered into the round of visits and functions. He was a member of the dining club, named the Red Lions.

He was introduced at a meeting of the Geological Society by Mr Paulet Scrope, otherwise Poulett Thomson, his Kensington neighbour and son-in-law of his old patron William Scrope. The writings and lectures of Rev Dr John Pye Smith from the Hackney days, already noted, had been an important part in his early interest while the works of the geologists Sir Charles Lyell and Sir Roderick Murchison were read and the authors encountered at scientific meetings and at the dinner table; the latter was placed next to the artist at the RA banquet in 1869, doubtless by design.

Expeditions which were part sketching trips and part holidays included scientific collecting, searching for new exhibits, as in 1863 to the French coast looking for ammonites at Cap Blanc Nez. This entailed borrowing hammer and chisel and a handbook from the British consul in Calais but these were relaxations from the concentration of studio work; it was the year of his Catalan Bay picture (63/2, Colour Plate 137) and his election as FRS. The impact which this painting made is well summarised by the *Illustrated London News*[8] which was not only reporting the RA exhibition and its banquet, but also indulging in art criticism:

> *Mr E.W. Cooke does not by mere indecision or inadequacy of execution stimulate the imagination to supply more than he literally gives, but this is from no insufficiency or want of keeping and completeness that makes itself felt as in 'topographical' painters. On the contrary it seems to arise from his omitting nothing – from his giving the facts before him with the most satisfying and absolute fidelity. Mr Cooke is one of the greatest 'realistic' painters now living. He has surpassed all previous efforts in his large and most elaborate representation of Catalan Bay (415) on the east of the Rock of Gibraltar with its vast slope of sand driven up by the easterly winds from the coast in a sheer acclivity of 600 feet in height – here round and over Titanic masses of fallen rock, there taking the form of the finely laminated strata of sandstone, and above, resting against the precipices, towering twice as high, of Signal Station Hill; these again carrying the strained and excited attention to the still loftier sugarloaf hill of secondary limestone, with its caves and fissures, containing Bone Breccia and thence conducting to the African coast of Ceuta and the far-off snowy range of Atlas. When the eye returns to the poor men repairing their boats and spreading their nets in the fore ground, and to the small village of the Genoese colony of fishermen then it is that their relatively insignificant size is fully apprehended, and the stupendous grandeur of the surrounding scenery fully realised. Sir Roderick Murchison might well compliment the painter on the geological accuracy and knowledge here displayed; but as a work of art it is equally admirable – the sea, the boats, the village, the sky are quite equal in drawing and painting to the rocks.*

Elsewhere it was said that many well deserved compliments were paid to the landscape painters of England by Sir R. Murchison and Lord Palmerston in their speeches at the banquet.

8. 23 May 1863, p.105.

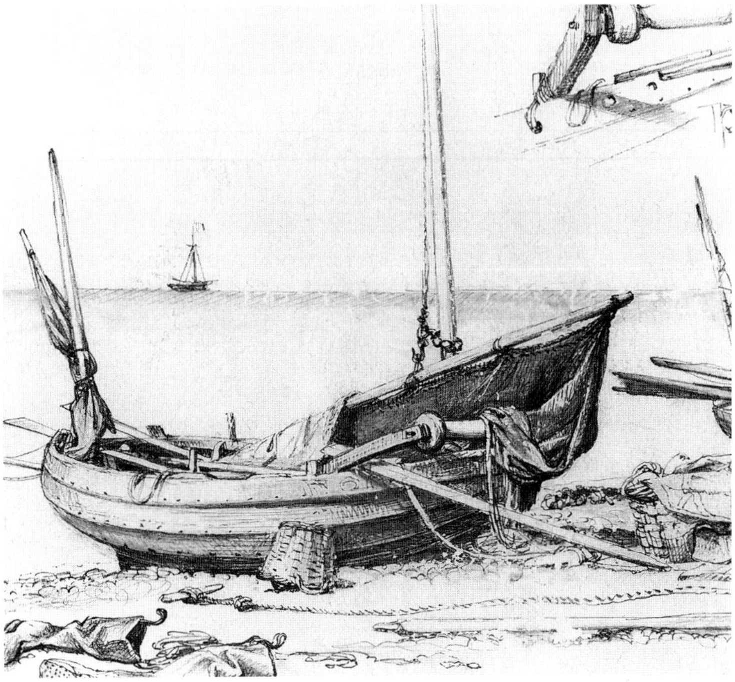

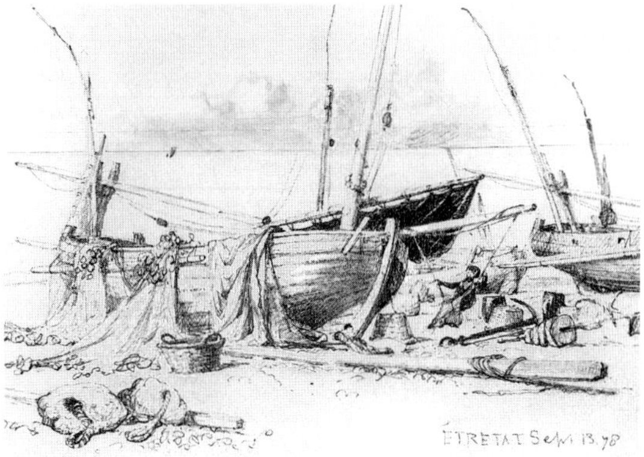

Plate 171. Pencil drawing
Etretat, *canots* on shore 1878
Photo courtesy Arthur Ackermann & Peter Johnson

Plate 172. Pencil drawing
Etretat, 1878
The assiduous recorder quickly became familiar with the fishing *canots* of this community which had also become a resort by 1840.
Photo courtesy Arthur Ackermann & Peter Johnson

It was his father-in-law George Loddiges who introduced him to the microscope, possessing, it is said one of the finest instruments available at that time, by Mr. Tully the innovating London maker. With this in 1835 he showed an attentive and appreciative Edward Cooke numerous wonders of natural history. The Quekett brothers (Edwin, the surgeon, neighbour of N.B. Ward in Wellclose Square, and John, the histologist at the Royal College of Surgeons) were both founder members of the Microscopical Society of London, the first meeting of which was held in Edwin's house on 29 January 1840. Cooke, George Loddiges and his son Conrad were present among a large company which included J.S. Bowerbank, Edgar, Linton, Lister, Owen, Renton, Solly, Ward and many others known to them, as he was pleased to note. He was elected a member in 1852 and purchased a good instrument from Smith & Beck. His 'disc of ferns' which he showed at one soirée in 1853 was, he wrote, *much noticed*. At the Apothecaries' Hall there was a meeting at which 150 microscopes, Wardian cases and fine flowers were on display, a typical scene of enthusiastic participation in 1855. N.B. Ward had served as Master of the Company and a commemorative portrait of him was subscribed for, painted by J.P. Knight, the Secretary of the RA.

In 1878 a painting holiday at Etretat on the Normandy coast, which he had already visited years before, resulted in one Academy picture for the following year, *Falaises en amont d'Etretat,* one of his last group, and a number of others which were in his sale. The distinctive stretch of coast with its chalk cliffs, differing only in aspect from the English side of the Channel, had featured in earlier paintings, for example 44/11. The fishing *canots* and their gear, the beach capstans, floats and *caloges*, old boats roofed over for stores, were unfamiliar and of different construction and therefore worthy of recording (Plates 171 and 172). Gustave Courbet had found the geology and the fishing scene sympathetic some ten years earlier and the chalk cliffs were painted from 1868 by the Impressionist Claude Monet as well. For Cooke the beached boats and the capstans, as well as the catches destined for the Paris market, were the chief source of attraction, although he was keen to make studies of the geological features as well.

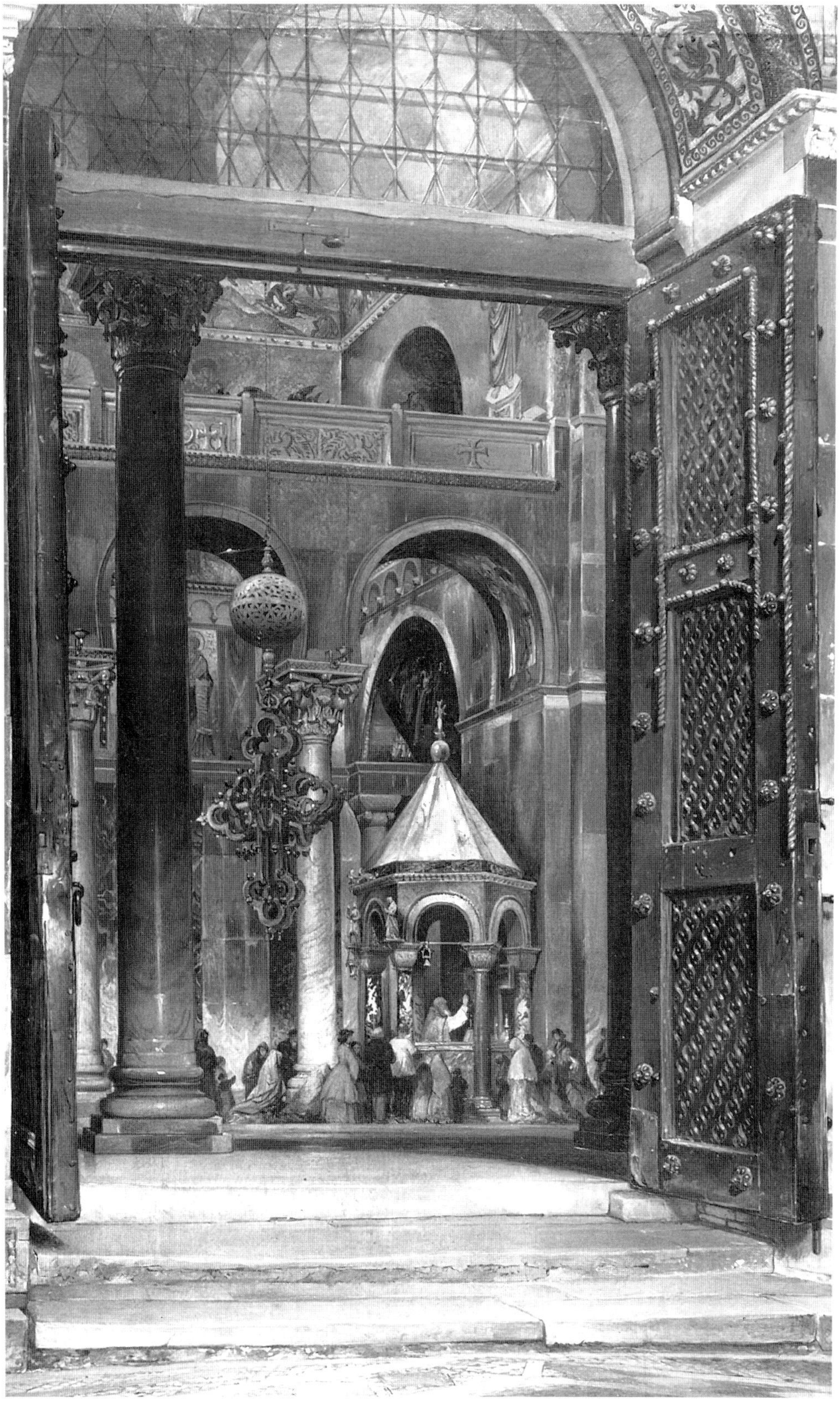

Plate 173. 59/1

Interior of San Marco: Looking across the nave from the Baptistry

His sole venture into church interiors, although there was another version, at present untraced.

Photo courtesy Christie's

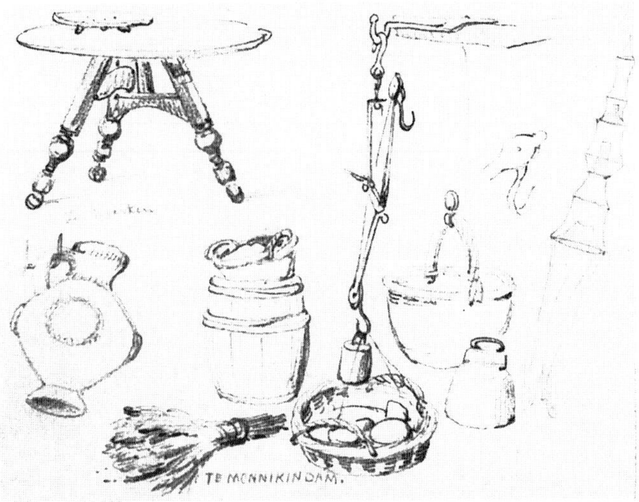

Chapter 16

CABINETS OF CURIOSITIES

Royal and noble collections were renowned, publicised and much visited, while in more modest houses people of education and culture maintained family collections, smaller in extent and in rarity. The cabinet for them was not a small gallery or treasure room, but a piece of furniture housing casts of antique gems, coins, medals and antiquarian relics. That was on the art side, whereas geological specimens, polished stones, fossils, indeed a bewildering variety of 'objects of natural history', dried, bottled or mounted, would reflect a scientific interest. Animal heads and horns including also skulls were displayed, not necessarily as hunting trophies – but there were also ethnological items, tokens of the Noble Savage, weapons, head-dresses, shields and paddles which were also hung as decoration. These constituted in fact a private museum and the Cooke family, maintaining one such accumulation, was evidently well informed about the contents.

In a surviving note carefully penned to his sisters at school, Edward in 1822 wrote: *I must inform you that my Father has had great additions to his cabinet this week composed of valuable Peruvian curiosities, presented to him by General Paroissien.*[1]

George Cooke left a brief *Journal of a Trip to Paris* 1825,[2] evidently his first visit, made in the company of friends including his collaborator George Loddiges and also General James Paroissien who had been envoy to England for Chile-Peru. Watercolour drawings now in the collection of the Liverpool Museums by E.W. Cooke, T.S. Boys and J.P. Heath show these pots which are to be found today in Sir John Soane's Museum. Peruvian vases lent by Cooke to the Art Treasures exhibition at Manchester 1856-7 are probably traceable to General Paroissien. Visiting the Louvre and Bibliothèque Nationale, admiring cameos, sculpture, paintings and globes, the elder Cooke also recorded a gift of 'autographs' indicating another of his collecting interests.

In providing plates for books of travel and exploration, the engraver would have before him not only drawings and paintings of exotic scenes but also in some instances objects from far places as well. Souvenirs brought home by travellers evidently reached the receptive hands of George Cooke since his interests seem to have been well known. Engraved plates for the *General Collection of Voyages and Travels,* nineteen volumes published 1808-1813 by John Pinkerton, must have put him in contact with many

1. National Maritime Museum, Greenwich.
2. Cooke MSS.

Plate 174. Pencil drawing
Dutch gear Marken, Monnikendam &c
Perhaps as an aid to acquiring 'Dutchness' Cooke drew what he found of interest on his travels.
Photo courtesy Clarges Gallery

sources. One of the brothers Kernot (engravers) brought them a club and a New Zealand Patapatoo in 1829 and further clubs from the same place in the following year. Later *a curious dagger and a sponge* and a *shawl from New Zealand* which may have been a Maori feather cloak came from the same source. In July 1833 a parcel and notes came from their friend Richard Rosier containing *a curious drum from Owhyee* while *another curious drum from Otaheite* is recorded as a present in December the same year. 'Curious', the qualifying adjective, admitted these exotic objects to the Regency interior of Albion House, as one of Edward's paintings, for him a rare study, clearly shows (36/10, Colour Plate 159). Pacific explorers' booty seems to have been in circulation; New Zealand and Hawaii as well as Tahiti might indicate relics from Capt James Cook's voyages. A Barnes neighbour, Dr Palin, who kept a boarding school for boys, presented a Chinese waterman's cloak, and at half past eleven at night George Cooke walked home in it! George Eglinton, Mrs George Cooke's brother, who spent some years in Peru and Chile, returned in 1830 with chests of costume, pottery and silver. After his father's death in 1834 Edward Cooke disposed of parts of the collection, the autographs, the coins and also an eighty volume *Cyclopaedia*, possibly that of Dr Abraham Rees FRS who had been tutor in Hoxton and Hackney and which was exceptionally well illustrated with engravings by their friend Wilson Lowry. On the other hand it might equally well have been Diderot's illustrated *Encyclopédie Methodique,* however bound. Christie's held a three day sale of prints from 30 April 1834 which included a number of the copper plates and the original drawings for *London,* Lots 572-592 and Lot 609, an Apograph by Smith, new in the maker's case. This was presumably a device for copying, an *apograph* meaning an exact transcript. The widow, who was named as the publisher of the final part of *London,* retained many sets of engraver's proofs of this and other publications for nearly half a century and these were finally dispersed in 1883.[3]

Presents from friends and well-wishers, often noted in the diary, range from the utilitarian to the historic and were added to the collection. A turned cup made from wood of Shakespeare's mulberry tree was brought by a Mr Shorter while Cooke was staying at Hastings in 1836. A pair of razors made from the iron which shod the piles of Old London Bridge, a gift from John Sheepshanks, might sound less than keen, but Mr Weiss, Cutler in the Strand, found that the metal which had long been in the river bed produced steel infinitely superior to any he had ever met.[4] Rubens' beautiful painting box, which had also belonged to Richard Cosway and then to Sir Thomas Lawrence, it was said, came as a gift from Mrs Scrope. William Scrope, author and artist, his old patron, had died the year before and his daughter Emma became Mrs Scrope when her husband George Poulett Thomson FRS MP, politician and geologist, assumed the family name; they were Cooke's neighbours in Hyde Park Gate. Engraved glass goblets, relics of the Coronation banquet of George IV, were presented by G.S. Marshall, another buyer of his pictures. Indian gods, unspecified, were acquired at the sale of Charles Stokes' effects and Indian swords were a gift from Col Cunningham, one of the sons of Allan Cunningham. Two bronze elephants given by William Wells of Redleaf in 1839 were perhaps souvenirs of his eastern voyages.

The Prince Consort's rooms at Osborne House contain to this day a rack of assorted walking sticks, something which most gentlemen possessed, for it was to appear undressed if one took a stroll without a cane or staff of some sort. Palm sticks were a favourite of Cooke's and he seems to have had a supply from which he could give specimens as presents; there was also at *The Ferns* a rack for his own collection of curious sticks. On Christmas Day 1863 a Mr Walton made him the present of a gun, three hundred years old! A small mahogany cabinet of drawers, itself a conversion from some other piece of furniture, has survived with a representative cross-section of the 'omnium gatherum' of Cooke's time. Casts of medals, seals, engraved gems, reliefs and

3. Sotheby's 12 July 1883.
4. *Curiosities of London* by J. Timbs, 1855, p.58.

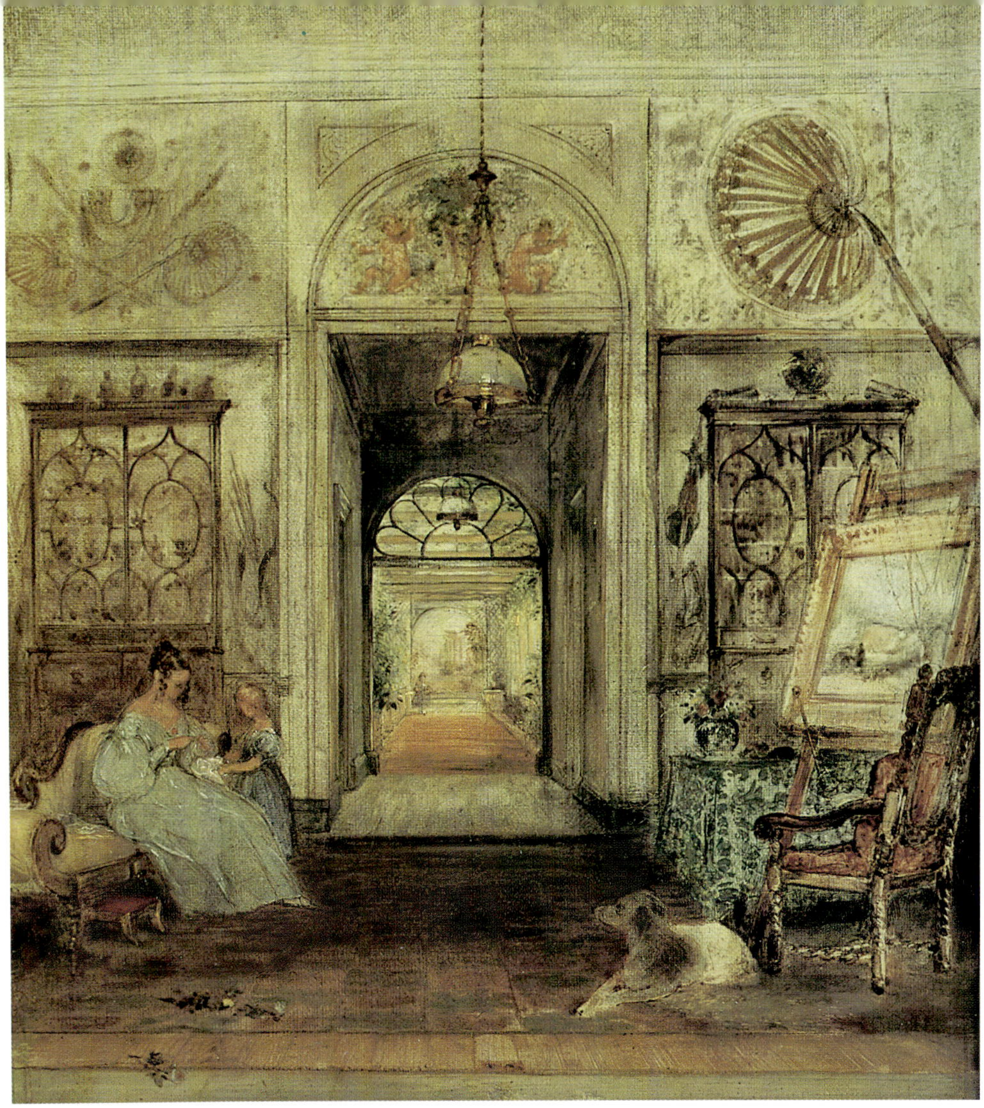

Colour Plate 159. 36/10
Saloon and Conservatory from the Lawn. Albion House
The elegant riverside house at Barnes also contained the family's collection of curiosities and specimens of natural history.
Photo courtesy Private Collection

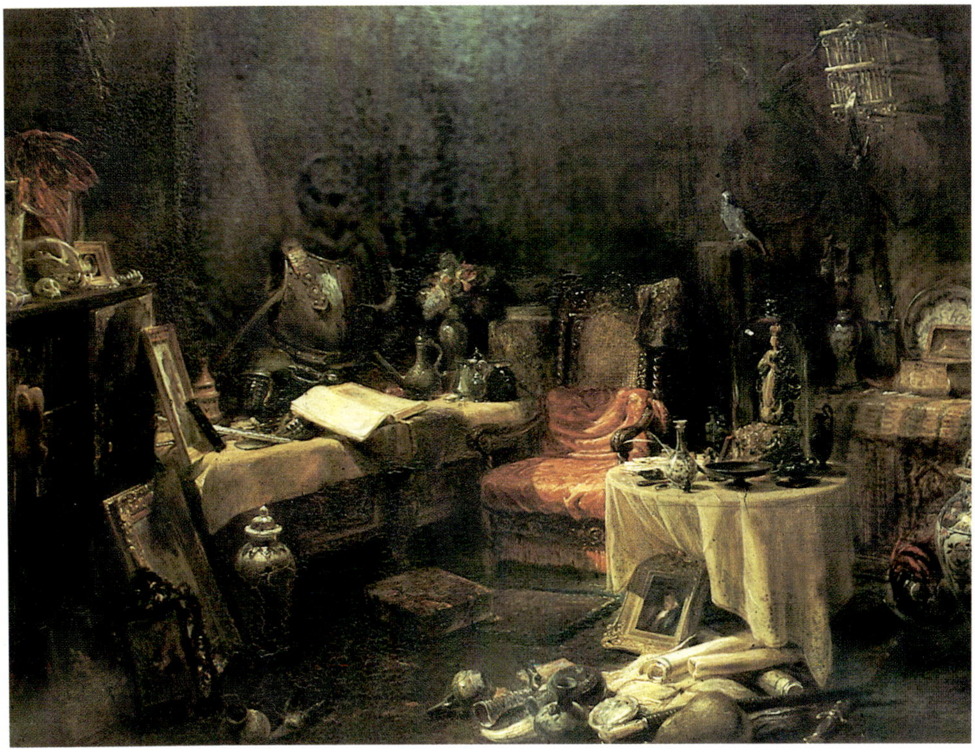

Colour Plate 160 35/7
The Antiquary's Cell [L.] *The interior of my own study at Barnes*
An elaborate still-life which the painter assembled, curtaining the window, borrowing china from neighbours, exchanging old pictures and clothes for armour and antique furniture from the Soho dealers and making studies of the lighting. His mother read to him from Sir Walter Scott's *The Antiquary*.
Photo courtesy The Board of Trustees of the Victoria & Albert Museum

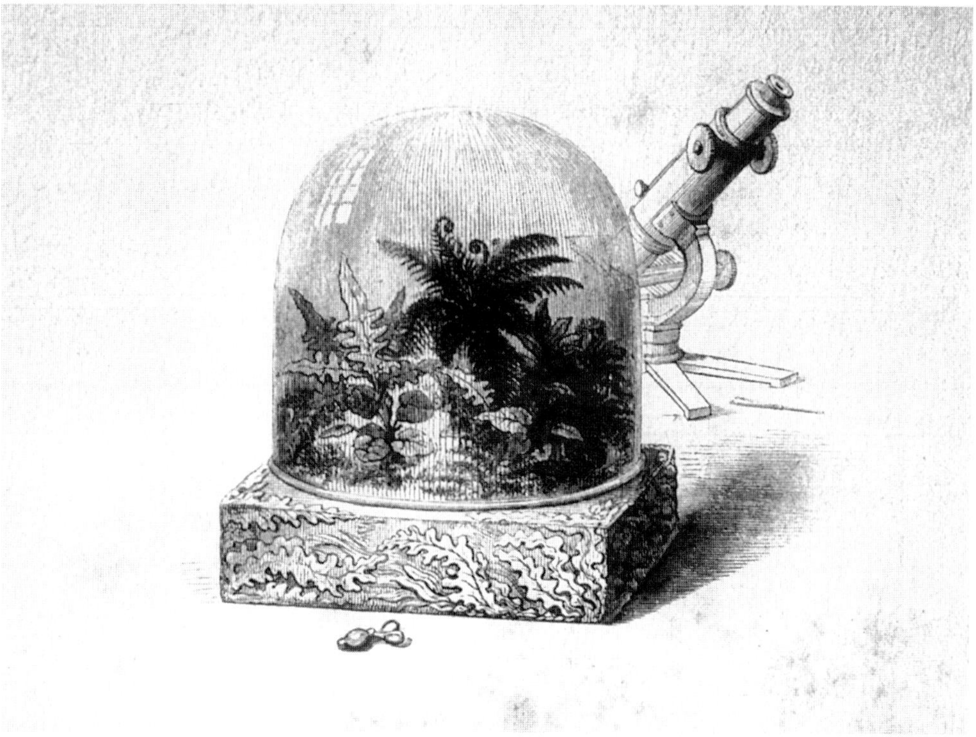

Plate 175. Engraving
Ferns growing under a glass dome with microscope
Another form of 'wardery' with the instrument to which Cooke and N.B. Ward both were devoted.
Photo courtesy Peter Hayden

a few actual fragments of originals are stored with examples of polished agate, a prehistoric bronze *celt* and an adzed sliver of oak from HMS *Royal Frederick*, clearly a relic of his tour of the Royal Dockyard. This is inscribed: 'the largest ship built in England Portsmo: 18 Sept 1835 E.W.C'. Natural crystals, ores, a piece of mosaic with here and there a faded label, these are all that now remain of their 'curiosities' which later necessitated the addition of another room to the Kensington house, *The Ferns,* and the provision of similar space in his country place, *Glen Andred,* to form what the artist proudly called his Museum.

The catalogue of his Sale of Decorative Objects at Christie's 21 May 1880 comprised 'Majolica, Oriental and other Porcelain, Bronzes, Carvings in Ivory, Old Dutch and German Silver, an Old Carved Cabinet, Venetian Leather Screens &c &c'. There was a small group of ship and boat models including an East Indiaman and inevitably a Venetian gondola in a glass case, as well as a group of model buoys. Possibly also there was the rigged smack which is shown in his 1857 photo portrait (Plate 136) given by an Eglinton cousin and owing its sails to the dainty needlework of his sisters and some of the young ladies at their school. On the sale of Sir A.W. Callcott's effects[5] Cooke had acquired five models of boats and he noted other occasional acquisitions such as a model of the *Emerald* cutter from George Wyatt and one of a Singapore boat from the Bishop of Labuan in 1860!

There was also a sale of his *Objects of Natural History* in the year after his death.[6] Over 250 lots embraced *Curiosities from the South Sea Islands &c., Natural History Specimens; Skulls &c; Shells, Fossils, Agates &c; Eggs ; Insects (in store boxes) some rare species and in good condition, principally from East Peru; &c.* The furniture of his Museum was also there – a pair of mahogany framed glass cases of stuffed birds, 8ft. (2.5m) high, and half a dozen counter showcases which were matched with cabinets of drawers. Horned heads were ranged with pairs of horns alone – and heads alone: *Lot 49. Head of an Egyptian mummy, with long hair attached, Lot 50.Very fine specimen of a tattooed New Zealand chief's head.* Lot 36 *Skull of a mule which perished in 1856 with*

5. Christie's 15 May 1845.
6. J.C. Stevens, King Street, Covent Garden, 25 February 1881.

two persons near the summit of St Theodule, found embedded in ice at an elevation of 11,080 feet by Mr E.W. Cooke. Other animal heads had been the gift of W. Cotton Oswell, trophies from his own gun which Cooke had admired in his friend's Groombridge house. The generous hunter made a sacrifice: *He took them over himself and a few days later Mr Cooke brought three exquisite sketches as a thank-offering.*[7]

Venetian Spoils

Far outstripping his miscellaneous collections, the impressive results of years spent in pursuit of old Venetian glass also demanded space for display. There had been moments between spells of painting in Venice when, among the visitors, Cooke could stroll about the city, often guiding friends, and his knowledge of the best shops and his acquaintance with reliable dealers therefore grew. His gondolier Vincenzo Grilla was a good and trusted go-between – if from time to time somewhat unpunctual – but since Cooke hired him season after season there was understanding and continuity.

With Henry Christy, the ethnologist and collector, he went in 1853 on a picture and antiques-buying tour to Holland and Germany and to Sweden where the Bystrom Collection was being dispersed; they travelled on via Hamburg visiting the local 'Curiosity' shops, and across Europe to Venice. This seems to mark the beginning of his interest in the fragile products of Murano.

The diary records his excitements and evident satisfaction as his collection grows. Some plates brought to him by Vincenzo the gondolier were purchased but he found others too highly priced and Christy meantime was buying quantities of 'Persian things'. Cooke added to the luggage on the way home with bronzes and vases bought in Paris. Delft jars bought in Hamburg on the tour arrived eventually in Kensington, as did his

7. Oswell op. cit., Vol. II, p.96.

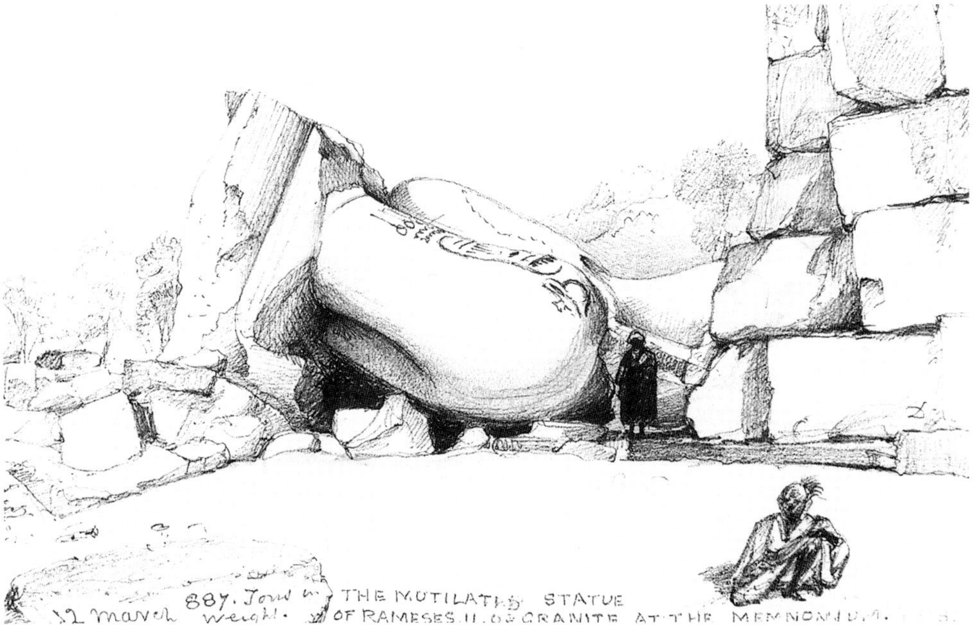

Plate 176. Pencil drawing

Thebes, Mutilated Rameses. 12th Mar.

There is an extraordinary feeling for volume in his pencil line, even if the crouched figure appears somewhat bizarre.

Photo courtesy Martyn Gregory

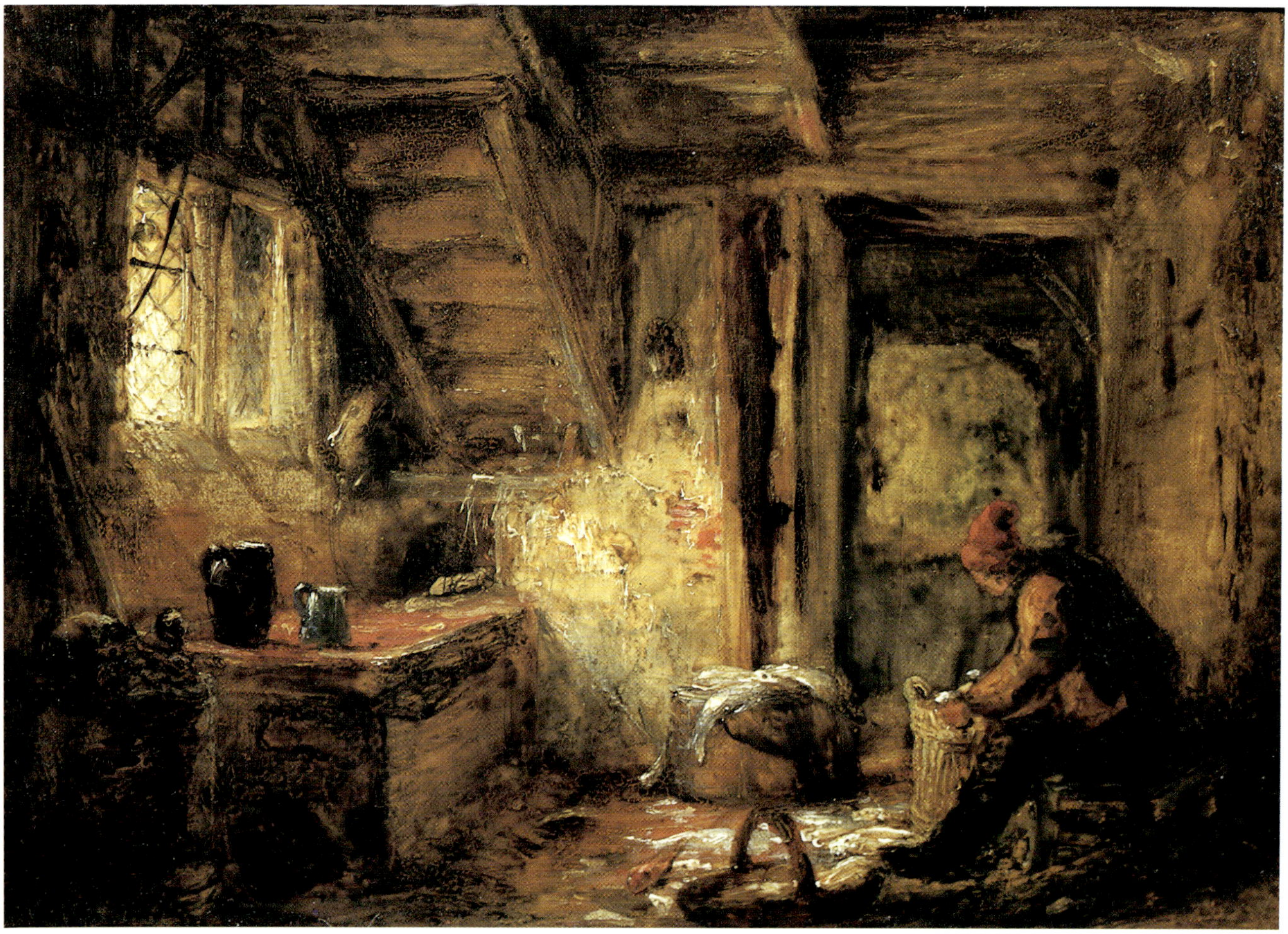

Colour Plate 161. 39/3

Interior with fish

A cottage or outbuilding on the Redleaf estate with fish imported from the coast and caught in the river. Photo courtesy Private Collection

Swedish purchases including a small Correggio *Agony in the Garden* and a study for a 'plafond' by P. Veronese, *The Adoration of the Magi* for a ceiling in a private room of the Ducal Palace at Venice.[8]

Having now the means to indulge his fancy for collecting, he saw the gradual increase in the ranks of fine and fanciful objects which demanded proper stowage. It was in fact at home in London that he found a most fruitful field for collecting old glass. Once it became known that he was in the market, the trade brought desirable pieces to his door. Soon his relations with the antique dealers took on an interesting aspect – barter. The exchange of what Cooke notes as a 'small old picture' (perhaps one of his own) for 'several pieces of Venetian glass' is typical. He records transactions with dealers named Sampson, Attenborough, Niell or Neale, Falcke in Bond Street, A. Myers, Zimmerman, Durlacher, Jacobs, Frederick Davis, Mr Waters and Mr Webster of whom, on 31 May 1864 Cooke wrote: *he took a small sunset picture, Lagune, framed, and I finished up a drawing of Scheveling pincks for him in exchange for 15 pieces of Venetian glass.*

He was also acquiring groups and small collections of glass at auction, as well as a considerable quantity of majolica. With Felix Slade, who bequeathed to the British Museum his glass collection and endowed the Fine Art Professorships, to whom he had been introduced by Edward Blore the architect, Cooke went round Christie's looking at the glass for sale and comparing notes.

In Venice, between forays into the dealers' shops, he painted on a Dutch sea-piece. That there were Dutch vessels on the Canale seems highly unlikely, so one is forced to conclude that from his vast familiarity with the subject he was throwing off a small

8. Included in his sale, May 1880, lots 194 (now Cooke family collection) and 197.

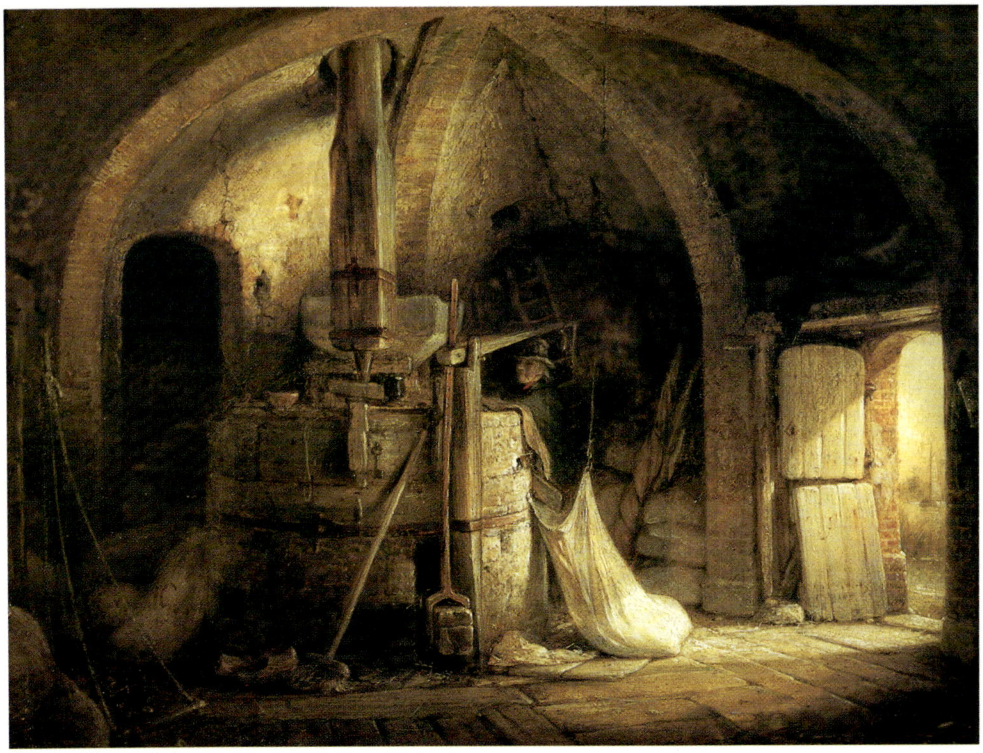

Colour Plate 162. 37/21
Interior of Rembrandt's father's mill, Koukerk near Leiden; lower chamber
A larger version was exhibited at the British Institution, 1839. Although pointed out to travellers as the Rembrandt family mill, it has subsequently been shown that this was not so (National Gallery of Scotland, Edinburgh 1991, *Sunshine & Shadow* exhibition catalogue).
Photo:courtesy Private Collection

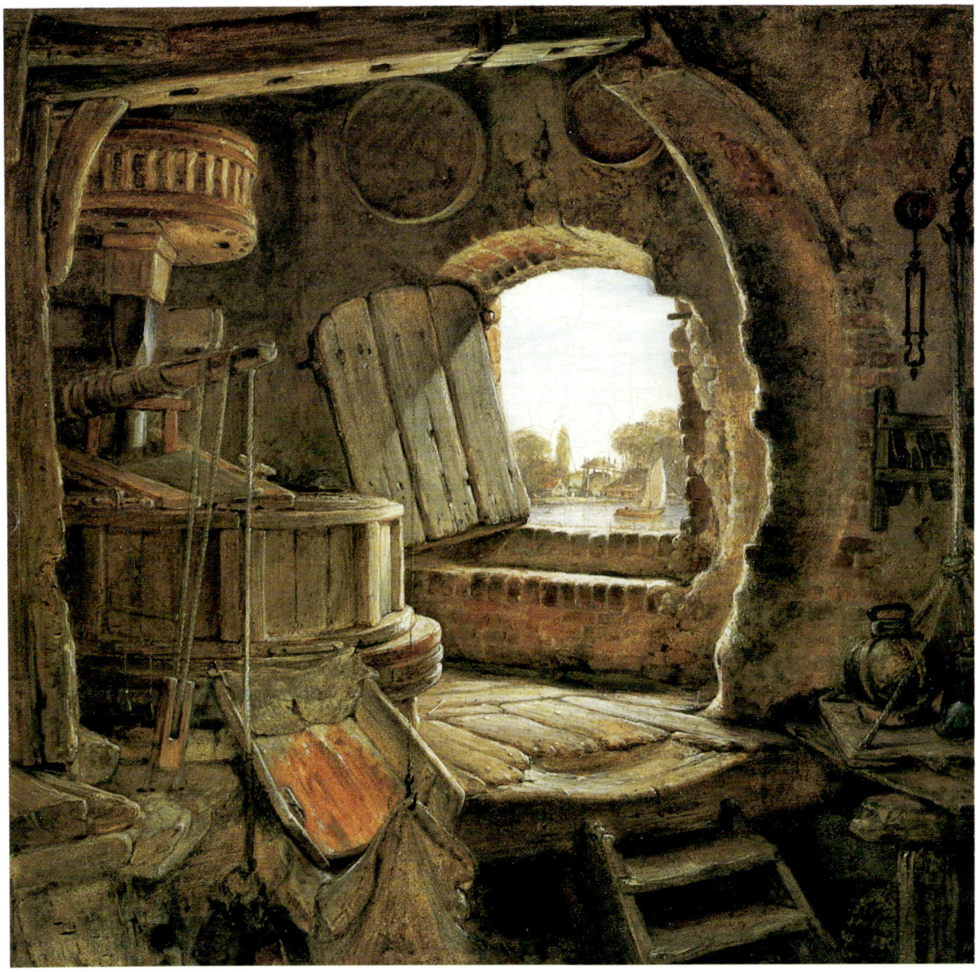

Colour Plate 163. 38/4
Interior of Rembrandt's father's mill, Koukerk; upper floor
'Employing the idiom of the picturesque in the decaying brickwork, scarred wood and deeply worn tread above the ladder, Cooke stresses the passage of time and the continuity of human usage' – Edinburgh 1991, No.3.
Photo:courtesy Private Collection

Dutch picture as a gift to a friend resident in Venice. Mr. Valentine, the recipient, was British Vice-Consul who one evening helped Cooke translate the Venetian terminology of glass into English, from the Catalogue of the Museo Correr.

The diary provides many notes of his glass collecting mixed with other matters:

29th June 1864 : Mr and Mrs Falcke came at 9 and brought a van with the Glass case and 111 pieces of Venetian glass (old). They unpacked and set it up by 3 o'clock. Porter brought me my Diploma of R.A. Painted on Venice sunset. Mr Gambart called and took his Dutch Calm home. Roe came with Clemens to arrange about the new Tree Fern House.

25 July: Glorious rain in night ... Painted on Gambart's Venice. Mr Falcke called & brought fragments of old Roman glass. Lord Grosvenor called and wished to have a picture, also General Codrington, Lady and Miss C., saw glass, pictures, ferns... Lord Grosvenor wrote and bought my Roman Bridge picture.

For the 1867 Paris Exposition he was appointed a Juror, as indeed was W.E. Gladstone.[9] Cooke was in the Glass section, Class 16, with Henry Chance from the Lighthouse Works, Birmingham. Their energies concentrated on judging, they toured Bohemian and Austrian manufacturers' exhibits and the Baccarat and the Powell collections. They viewed stained and painted glass, Pelligot's and Marechal's and Salviati's and Michieli's as well as Chance's own offerings which tended towards lenses for ships' navigation lights. Cooke was eventually awarded a Juror's medal, but while in the circulating throng there had been time for enjoyment of dinner in Russia and *zuppa* in the Italian *caffe* and coffee in the Bey of Tunis' *Kiosque*.

The Venetian glass collection must have outstripped the space in his Kensington house for he lent most of it for a time to the South Kensington Museum. Naturally his treasures had to be shown to the best advantage in his new house and he evidently designed one room around the glass collection. R. Norman Shaw, his architect, tactfully put forward his suggestions:

I see my way quite well to make a very picturesque hall for you admirably adapted to your own requirements, and also convenient for any successor, who may not be fortunate enough to have a large Venetian glass case.

All this to be done nicely if you will let me – as follows – I should make a large bay window (say 13 feet wide) at one end of the side – and next to that put the fireplace – also to be large and deep, so that you could go into it and sit down on the settles at the side and warm your toes and look out at [sic] the windows at the same time – and then the remainder of the wall wd. have a smaller window in which the smaller case wd. stand – this wd. be a rational disposal of the wall space, in accordance with your requirements – and if you will let me, the fireplace may be made lovely, and without running into any very great cost – picture to yourself some little bits of sparkling stained glass in the upper part of the upper parts of the small windows in great fireplace!! wouldn't it be grand. I should only propose to put stone mullions to the principal rooms and not up stairs at all or at most perhaps to one or two windows.[10]

Cooke got to know well Dr Antonio Salviati, proprietor of a Murano glassworks who was also a mosaicist and reviver of that ancient craft. He worked in St Paul's Cathedral and his firm had London links with a depot in St James's Street for table glass. In the establishment of the latter Sir A.H. Layard, who had a house in Venice, Sir William Tite, the architect, and Sir William Drake, collector, had been active. According to C.L. Eastlake,[11] *Dr.Salviati has done his best to produce good designs (some of which have been furnished by Mr Norman Shaw), and old examples for the men to copy.* Copies were also made of items in the Slade collection.[12] Just how deep was Cooke's knowledge of

9. British Museum, Addl MSS.
10. Cooke MSS, Shaw letters.
11. *Hints on Household Taste* by C.L. Eastlake,.1868, p.224.
12. *Magazine of Art,* Vol. IV, 1881, p.23.

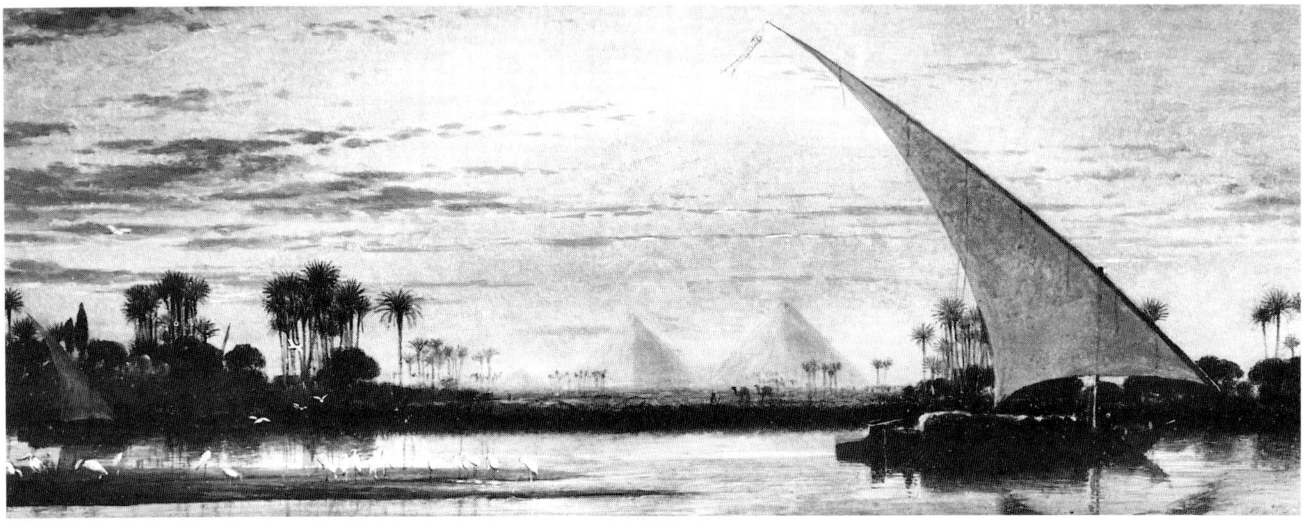

Plate 177. 76/3

The Pyramids, sunset

Just after Christmas 1875 he noted 'I designed 2 little Nile subjects...' and in early January 1876 recorded that he had finished Sunset Pyramids – 'except for pelicans'.

Photo courtesy Hazlitt, Gooden & Fox

old glass is difficult to judge, but among the massed ranks there were evidently some rare and interesting pieces. He had certainly studied and drawn interesting specimens wherever he met them, in Paris, the Hotel Cluny, the Sauvageot Collection, and in the private collections of Thomas Adolphus Trollope in Florence, brother of Anthony the novelist, and Robert Napier at Shandon in Scotland. However there is no record of his having written or spoken in public on the subject.

The dispersal of his glass collection took place at Christie's six months after his death (15 and 16 June 1880: *Collection of Venetian Glass of the Late E.W. Cooke RA, The greater portion of which have been exhibited at the South Kensington Museum*). There were 550 lots and a further sixty of other glass, bits and pieces of ceramic and miscellaneous objects. The collection realised £697.8.0d and over forty pieces were purchased by the British Museum. They now rank in the catalogue among glass bequeathed by Felix Slade, Baron Ferdinand de Rothschild and Sir Wollaston Franks, while occasionally identifiable pieces from his collection appear in the salerooms.[13]

In the London of the 1860s the meetings of the Fine Arts Club, held at members' houses, gave opportunities for display and admiration. At Thomas Baring's and at the Marchese D'Azeglio's they saw superb collections; at Mr Moffat's, Eaton Square, at Miss Burdett Coutts', Mr Spottiswood's, at Mr Tomline's and in other fine town houses, they gathered to view and discuss. Cooke records getting Chaffers to pack early silver and majolica to be sent to Mr W.E. Gladstone's for an evening meeting in May 1867. The Chancellor of the Exchequer, soon to become Prime Minister, had an interesting collection of English porcelain. Reminiscences by the poet and book collector Frederick Locker-Lampson reveal something of the spirit of the Club: *It is not a misfortune to be born with a feeling for association... I am nearer to Titian when I have one of his masterly sketches in my hand... believe me there is exhilaration in collecting. I would call it a perennial joy, if it were not so often pierced by despair.* He notes that this group was *the 'cunabula Romae' the cradle of art-collectors and developed into the Burlington Fine Arts Club in Savile Row.*[14]

Cooke was elected a Fellow of the Society of Antiquaries rather late in his career and does not appear to have read any papers before them, although he 'exhibited' an old ivory cross for discussion in May 1878.

He was evidently not averse to lending items to provincial museums; the City of Nottingham collection which opened in 1878 had three items including a fifteenth century Venetian bronze knocker and a carved ivory jug of Louis XVI, which after his death were sent to Christie's for his sale.

13. *The Golden Age of Venetian Glass* by Hugh Tait, British Museum, 1979, No. 101, pp.73 etc.

14. *My Confidences* by F. Locker-Lampson, 1896, p.189.

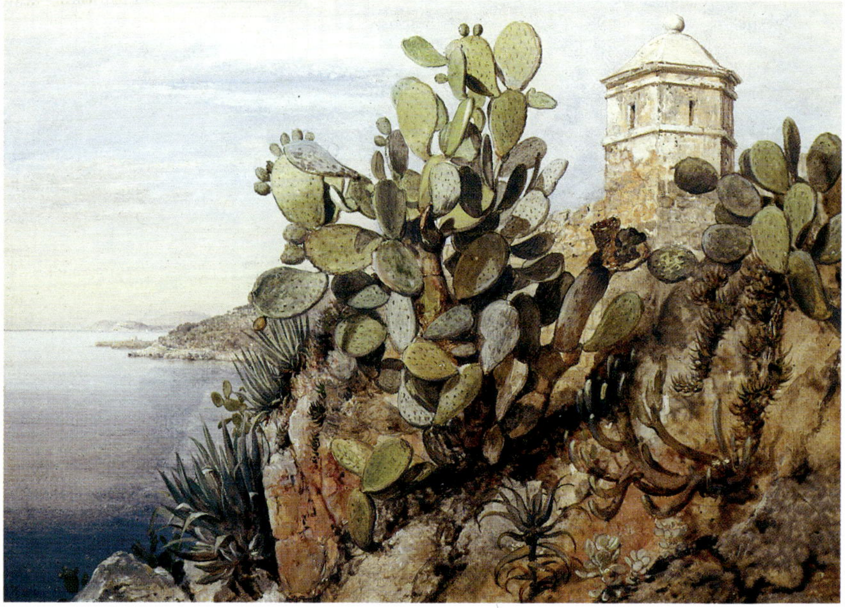

Colour Plate 164. 45/12
Cactus Opuntia Monaco
The artist's delight at his first sight of this cactus is recorded in his diary and, as a keen botanist and dedicated gardener, he sat down and painted it!.

Photo courtesy Arthur Ackermann & Peter Johnson

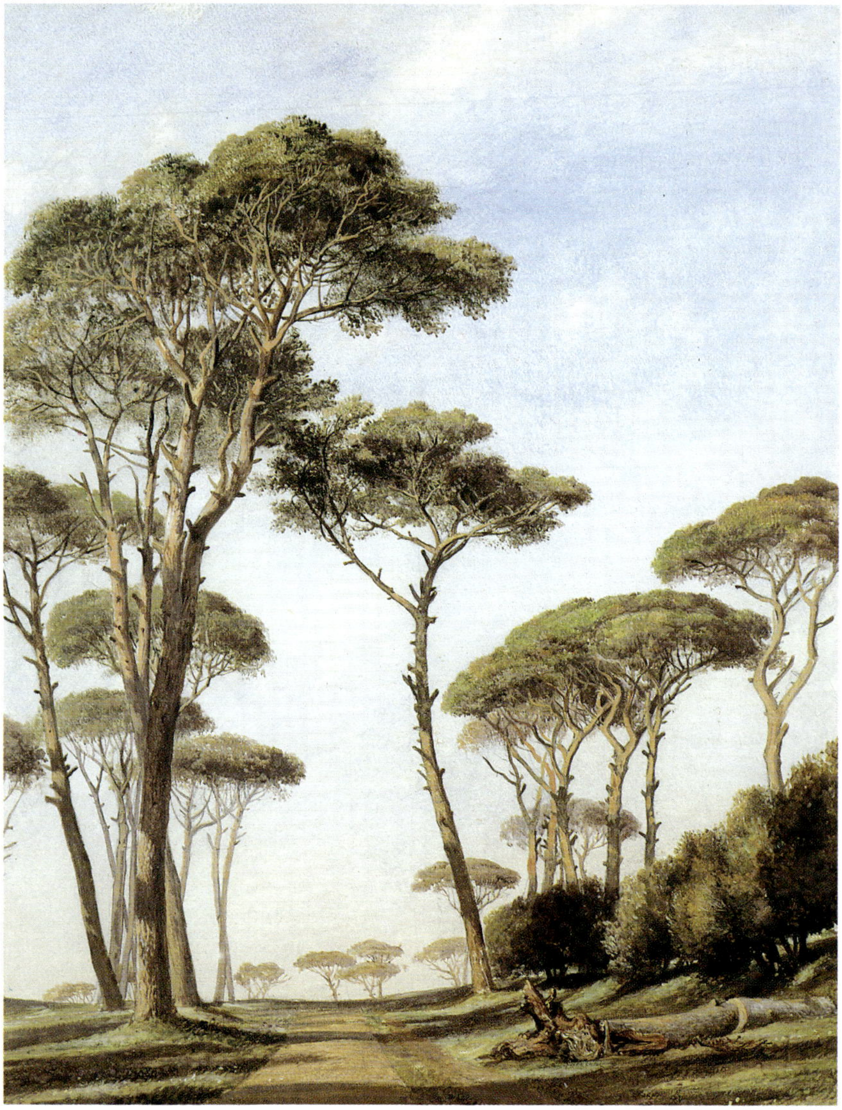

Colour Plate 165. 46/7A
Rome. Stone pines, 100ft high, at the entrance of the Villa Pamphili Doria on the Janiculum Hill; destroyed by the French in 1848 [sic].
An arboriculturalist of part-German extraction might be expected to deplore the destruction by the forces of le Général Ouditot, 2nd Duc de Reggio (who reached Rome in April 1849), of some noteworthy specimens, presumably for camp fires!

Photo courtesy Private Collection

Chapter 17

HOUSE AND GARDEN

The artist at home became a favourite topic with the journalists, for successful painters and sculptors led a gentlemanly existence and the *vie de bohème* was for most a thing of the past. A studio, or more than one, tall windowed and rug-strewn with room to house the obligatory collection, whether blue and white china or 'props' such as old armour or costume, these became part of the plan – 'palatial caricatures of the top-lit bohemian attic'.[1]

Portrait painters needed to occupy good addresses: their sitters expected some style and Reynolds, Gainsborough, Lawrence and the sculptor Chantrey lived in Town. Landscape painters had more choice – John Constable preferred the Hampstead heights but still lived (and died) in Charlotte Street and J.M.W. Turner's various establishments were such as befitted that rare being. Modest Callcott lived and died in Kensington, the Old Court suburb, Prout lived in outer Clapham and Camberwell and Stark in Chelsea. Of Cooke's contemporaries, Hook was in Camden Hill, the Redgraves and C.W. Cope, Samuel Palmer and Richard Ansdell in somewhat different establishments, were in Kensington and there were many others in the area. Noting the passing of Palmer in 1881, the *Magazine of Art* said that he *lived before this time of luxe when painters of powers far more moderate than his exist in a kind of paradise of bric à brac* and there are photographs to prove it.[2]

History painters and those requiring the services of models could not afford to live at a distance, as Frederick Goodall discovered. The palatial residences built by the later generation like Leighton, Millais and Alma-Tadema belonged to an affluence as yet unknown; W.P. Frith noted wryly that they were *pretty decently lodged*.[3]

Engravers in their modest way were little different in their requirements – workrooms and studios had to have good light, there was a need for reception rooms where business might be discussed and visitors entertained.

Although it seems that George Cooke was frequently pressed for time, and sometimes for money, his surroundings in 4 Loddiges Place, Hackney, must have been interesting and colourful. George Loddiges' own home next door was remarkable in several ways. It was heated from the same furnaces as served the hot-houses, his large cased collection of humming birds – which went inevitably with orchids – was tastefully arranged in the four quarters of his drawing room (it is now in the British Museum Natural History). He possessed a chamber organ by Father Smith and one of the finest microscopes made to date, as well as large collections of casts of antique gems and polished specimens of wood from all over the world.[4] These treasures were familiar to the young Cooke.

When his family removed to set up the boarding school at Albion House on riverside Barnes Terrace, their establishment became positively noteworthy (36/10, Colour Plate 159) It was rented from early 1829, a commodious residence with a cottage in the grounds. There was also room for their collection of curiosities to be displayed to advantage. With the knowledge and expertise of the Loddiges nursery behind them, the problems of stocking a garden and hothouses were much simplified. It would have been indeed remarkable if Edward Cooke had shown no interest in growing things; the occupation and activities of his future father-in-law, noted for his scientific leanings, a Linnaean, Council Member of the Royal Horticultural Society and a sympathetic teacher, was calculated to fire the enthusiasm. The value of pleasant and interesting surroundings – indoors and out – in which to work and to show his finished works was therefore an

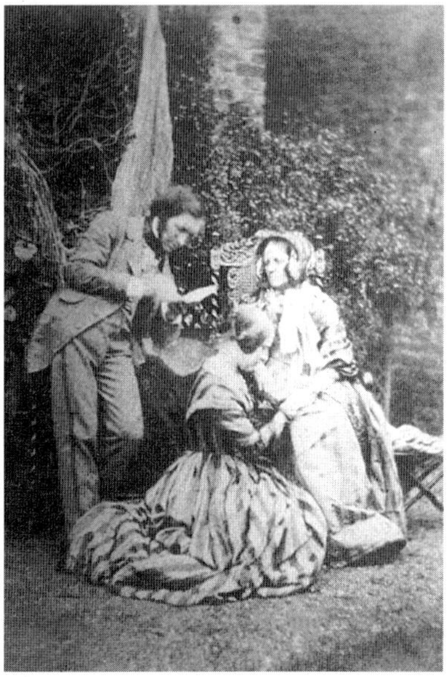

Plate 178.
Garden Group. Kensington, 4 Sept 1849
George Cooke's widow, her son the artist and Mary her youngest daughter. The photographer was possibly Robert Hannah who got *negatives by the camera* on that occasion. Mr Cundell, a friend and neighbour, expert in calotypes was also present. The 'old chair' in which Mrs Cooke is seated was likewise mentioned.

Photo courtesy C.R. Cooke, OBE

1. *The Pre-Raphaelite Dream* by William Gaunt, 1943.
2. *Magazine of Art* Vol. IV, p.xxxvii ; p.169 (Lord Leighton), p.290 (Sir J.E. Millais).
3. Frith op.cit., p.355.
4. *Journal of the Horticultural Society of London,* Vol I, p 224.

early consideration. The family liked a well stocked garden and had some knowledge of propagation; their new house had a fine conservatory with other glasshouses and hothouses. They grew camellias, had grape vines, and could call on expert advice and help from neighbours like the Breffit family whose expertise in pruning and whose gifts of fine fruit in season perhaps point to another firm of nurserymen. Excellence in cultivation brought visitors to admire – Easter was the time to see the camellias – and even passing gentlefolk in carriage and on horseback, strangers, had been known to call for that purpose. The presence of works of art near at hand for viewing must soon have established a discreet method. Buyers of pictures could be conducted round the displays of blooms and regaled with fruit, while those who came to see the latter could also view the prints and pictures in what amounted to gallery surroundings.

After his father's death a room was altered to form a studio, the 'painting room' he called it. Refurbishment in 1840 to receive his young wife and the acquisition of certain lots of furniture from local house sales followed. They went along to view the dispersal of Horace Walpole's collection at Strawberry Hill in 1842, but evidently acquired nothing.

Cooke's patron John Sheepshanks formed a garden at Park Cottage, Blackheath, which was a source of interest. John Constable had been somewhat caustic in his comment on the collector's disposal of his print collection and embarkation on gardening plans – *invested in flower pots* – but the old Yorkshireman was also a member of the Royal Horticultural Society and was often encountered at their shows. Edward Cooke helped with sketches and suggestions for the improvement of the new garden.

In the course of time their distance from the centre of Town and the end of Mrs Cooke's boarding school venture decided them on removal from Barnes. Bayswater, Maida Hill and St John's Wood, where an artist community already existed, were all considered, but they fixed on Kensington where villa gardens and glasshouses were still possible. In late 1848 a new-built house was leased in Victoria Road and its adaptation to the specific requirements of Cooke, the painter and gardener, followed immediately.

He clearly had his own ideas and further was able to express and illustrate them. The Redgraves were called along for an opinion, as was his brother-in-law Conrad Loddiges II from the Hackney nursery; the diary noted *made model of my new garden in clay*.

The visits of the tradesmen, gas-fitters and paper hangers, grainers and painters, are recorded, as too the planning of the heating apparatus. One room was allocated as the *Museum* to house the multiplying successors to the Cabinet of Curiosities – the expanding range of antiquities, objets d'art, glass and specimens of natural history. Camellias in variety from Barnes (although many were sold), a hothouse, a gated part of the garden named The Wilderness, and – even in Victoria Road – a load of logs for a rustic bridge are noted. The deodar and a glycine, wistaria, were transplanted from Barnes with loads of stones and loam; meanwhile in further planning he *stuck out garden with sticks for digging*. Evergreens from Hackney were also delivered and on 8 March 1849 he recorded *First day of painting in the new house – The Ferns*.

As a recognised fern expert and collector he provided himself with a symbol: *I drew a large fern to be done in glass for my hall,* presumably for the entrance door. Early in April 1849 he began a new picture, *Fern Cave – Mounts Bay* from sketches of his west country tour of the previous autumn.

The experts recognised his achievements: *The small gardens attached to his residences in Kensington were models of what small town gardens might be, made by one who combined artistic power of grouping and genuine love of plants* (Plate 179).[5] He wrote letters to patrons and friends, inviting them to view his pictures in the studio before sending-in for the Academy. This was a feature of the exhibitor's year, referred to by W.P. Frith and G.D. Leslie as 'Show Sunday', and although Cooke never painted on the

5. *Gardener's Chronicle*, 10 January 1880.

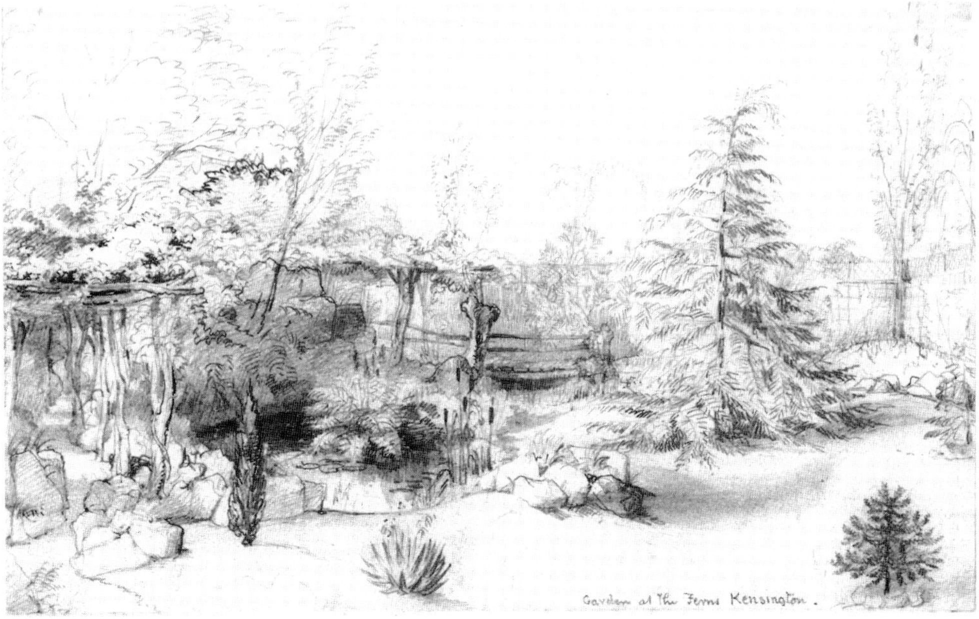

Plate 179. Pencil drawing
A Kensington Garden
It is not clear whether this is Victoria Road or Hyde Park Gate South. However, all agreed it was a model of what a town garden could be – with his encyclopaedic knowledge and the importation of tons of rock, tree stumps and timber for the rustic bridge! Photo courtesy C.R. Cooke, OBE

Sabbath (*colour,* observes Anthony Bertram, *was carnal*),[6] at other times he worked over his canvases while visitors were present, holding his 'views' on weekdays. Dealers and patrons made the rounds of the studios on these pre-private views, and pictures were sometimes bought unfinished, on the easel.

For some reason Victoria Road did not suit him – probably the house was too small with seven in the family without servants – and so in August 1854, a year in which he returned his income for tax purposes as £650, he signed a forty-two year lease on a house in Hyde Park Gate South. At once he began to plan additions and alterations. A new hothouse, a new painting room, a bow window on the drawing room, and in the gardens at front and back stonework by James Pulham and his workmen.[7] This was also to be *The Ferns* and he was later able to purchase the freehold; it was No 9, but no longer exists although a house R. Norman Shaw designed for him which was built in the garden in 1871 (after he had moved to the country) is still there; No. 18[8] was later occupied by Solomon J. Solomon RA, who added a studio at the rear, and then, for some thirty years, by Sir Jacob Epstein.

A fern design in copper was made for the front gate – 'The Ferns Hotel' was ever open to friends to stay a night, as he wrote to James Wyatt Junr, of Oxford![9]. Entertaining, evening parties, microscope soirées, conversazione and the private views at home are detailed in the diary pages. Of his three sisters, Laura was often away from home, as a governess. Harriette, the eldest, seems to have been the housekeeper while Mary, the youngest, who was an asthmatic, often helped in the studio. His mother, presiding over the industrious family, aged splendidly. In spite of ceaseless activity in his garden in Kensington, making the most of the town plot, he began yearning for a broader landscape, in particular a rocky landscape, with room to spread and to try out ideas, plants and trees; also he wanted to be out of the grimy polluted air of London. The movement of painters away from the soot of metropolitan streets and garden plots had begun as early as the 1850s. Thomas Webster, John Callcott Horsley, James Clarke Hook and Myles Birket Foster all decamped. Richard Redgrave had a cottage at Abinger and John Linnell spent thirty years at Redhill after leaving London. Frederick Goodall similarly established a large estate near Pinner, where his Egyptian sheep could graze near the studio window. However, it was not permanent, for his pictures also depended largely on the human figure, Bedouin though they might appear, and Harrow was too far

6. Bertram op.cit., p.56.
7. *Biddulph Grange, Staffordshire. A Victorian Garden Rediscovered* by Peter Hayden, George Philip/The National Trust, 1989, p. 137.
8. *Survey of London,* Vol. 38.
9. Cooke MSS.

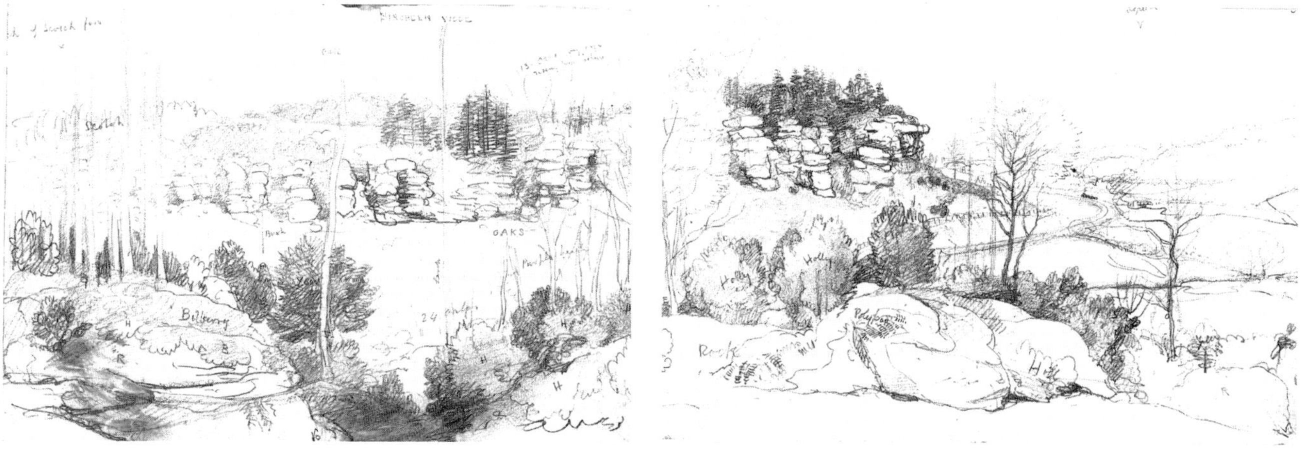

Plates 180 to 183 (Above and opposite). Pencil drawings
The View from *Glen Andred*
Observed by the artist as landscape-gardener in 1867 who was also now a landed proprietor. The features viewed from his chosen site are still evident today. The railway had arrived.

from Town to get willing professional models.

Urban gardens were all very well but by September 1865 Cooke was writing to his publisher John Murray *I am suffering from Earth Hunger and am seeking a pleasant spot where I can have a garden and grow conifers and roses to my heart's content without London smoke.*[10] His searches ranged across the southern shires within easy railway reach of London and he finally settled on a site near Groombridge on the Kent and Sussex borders. He had in fact been there on a fern hunting expedition in 1848 when his friend the Rev Whitelock from Barnes had moved to that parish. It was he who now told the artist about the land: the area had many attractions – Ruskin reported to his father that Cooke advised that the area was the best in England for ferns. The Hamsel Estate belonged to the Worshipful Company of Goldsmiths, possessed commanding views, was rocky, well treed and altogether presented the sort of challenge which Cooke was seeking. The absence of a water supply was a problem of a different sort. A branch railway line was also projected; he was one of the first tenants and reckoned that his house and grounds would attract the attention of others seeking the country and so aid the Company's development of their land.

He bought the book by Robert Kerr, architect, *The English Gentleman's House,* in 1865 that he might be well informed on current trends. Another contributor to the 'revival' was Charles Lock Eastlake II who published his *Hints on Household Taste,* a guide to furniture design and furnishing, in 1868. Cooke's own design for a country house to accommodate not only himself but his mother and the three sisters, to provide studios and to house his collections of Venetian glass, *objets d'art*, horns, heads and Polynesian paddles, as well as comprising the usual offices, began at once, with a bedroom plan. In January 1866 he was staying at St Leonard's on Sea where lived his old friend Decimus Burton FRS, architect of the Athenaeum club building. He was the son and successor of James Burton, born Haliburton, who had been a builder and what is now called a developer, particularly of that coastal resort. The grand house they built – The Holme, Regent's Park[11] – had featured in George Cooke's *London* as a fine example of the latest in the classical style. Now he and Decimus pored over the plans and drew new ones; Cooke with Kerr's book in one hand, was also looking up Vitruvius in the library! No sketches survive of his first essay in building, which was perhaps therefore in the classical style. He showed his completed plans to James Bateman FRS of Biddulph, whom he met one day in the Athenaeum, and took him down to Groombridge to fix the site and aspect. The lease was signed, the plans re-drawn, tinted, shown to friends and then early in May, after the opening of the Royal Academy exhibition and the dinner, he called on Mr Richard Norman Shaw, a young architect in Argyll Street. Two days later he had a new plan and a letter from Shaw to which he swiftly replied 'with objections'. A week later there was another letter and a revised plan; *I studied and improved it* noted Cooke.

10. John Murray Archives.
11. Now Bedford College, London University.

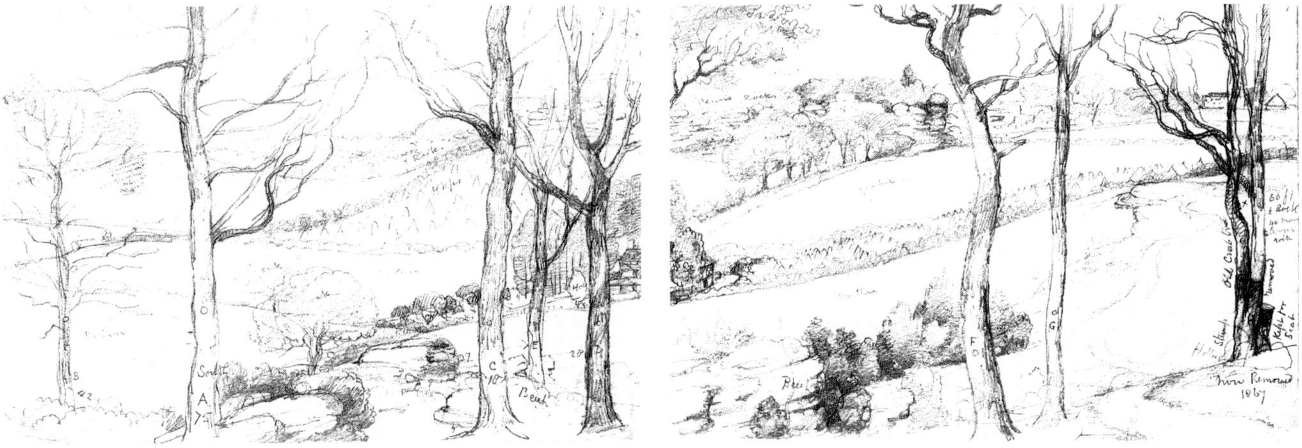

The process of collaboration between client and architect is exemplified in a surviving batch of letters from Shaw, the first of which is memorable. The young designer of houses, with definite convictions, treads dangerously near the brink in referring to the 'incapacity' of whoever put Cooke's plan together – perhaps well realising it was the very fish he was about to play to a successful landing!

30 Argyll St. Regent St. W. May 9th 1866
My dear Sir:
As I have made a sort of rough plan, embodying various suggestions I think I may just as well send it to you and as you are down on your back, which I am very sorry to hear, it may help to amuse you and set you thinking a bit.

There really are so many points about your first plan that I don't like, that I hardly know where to begin, but perhaps on the whole the most objectionable point, is the extremely weak and ineffective arrangement of the Entrance Hall, Principal Stair and Corridor. These occupy a very considerable space – about 60 feet super more than the revised plan I have made, and what do they present – simply a succession of mean places, nowhere more than 8 or 9 feet wide – most troublesome to keep clean, and impossible to furnish – how I do dislike this style of plan entirely – and I am quite sure it arises from pure incapacity on the part of whoever put the various parts together. Then look at the extreme awkwardness, and clumsiness of plan (Pray excuse me if I am very plain spoken on the subject of the plan) in putting the W.C. &c close to the principal entrance door !!!

There can be no doubt that it ought to be near the back exit into the garden, in a position where you can take gentlemen after breakfast, and stroll out into the garden – and also where it would be handy for washing hands &c after dinner, and before going into the drawing room...

By having a fair sized Hall and Staircase – see what a handsome feature you would get into your house and how very charming it would be to see from the Hall and Stairs into the Fernery – not down a long narrow passage – but through a place of considerable width. Then I think the bedroom floor landing might be very delightfully arranged, so that you might see into the Fernery – by keeping the roof at that part a little higher...

Then as for the centre room (in which the glass case stands) – I understand your arrangement for that viz to heat it with hot water only – and have no fire – but this is but a dismal business, and in this climate, and with our ways of living makes a room of that kind very useless – in fact it degenerates instantly into a kind of vestibule, and viewed from that point comes to be a tremendous waste of room – I think a fireplace would be a vast gain, not merely for your own comfort, but for that of any successors.

I hope you will like the proposed arrangement of Dining room and Drawing room – bay window in the position shewn, always makes a room look large, and it is also so extremely comfortable for sitting in, and as in the case of the Drawing room the fire place were kept up at the end, where it is quite out of all draughts from Doors etc.

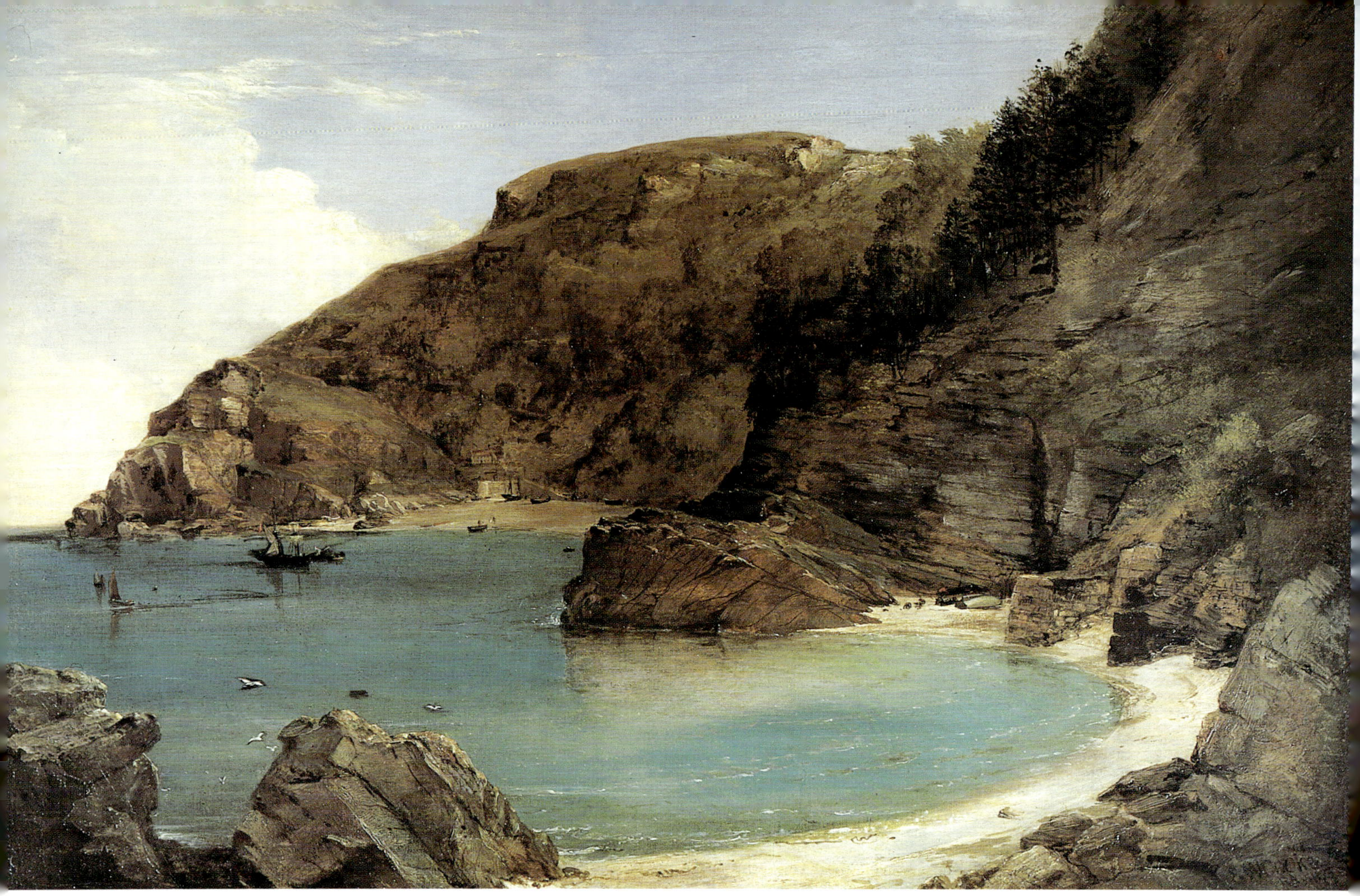

Colour Plate 166. 75/9
Fisherman's Bay and Babbacombe Rocks
Cooke recorded painting the pine trees from those on his Kent property.
Photo courtesy Martyn Gregory. Private Collection

Colour Plate 167.
Glen Andred, Groombridge
The garden from the house. Photo courtesy Peter Hayden

Colour Plate 168.
Glen Andred, Groombridge
His rocks, and perhaps some of his intentions, survive in the Glen. Photo courtesy Peter Hayden

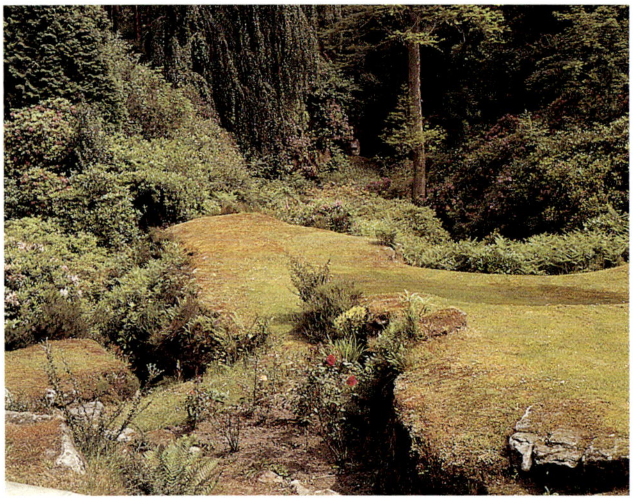

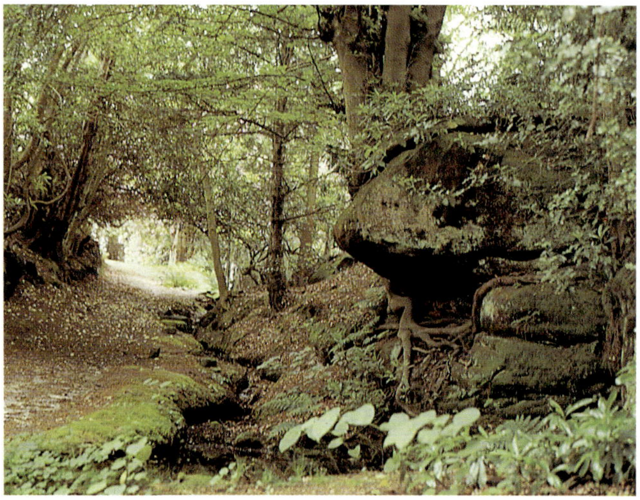

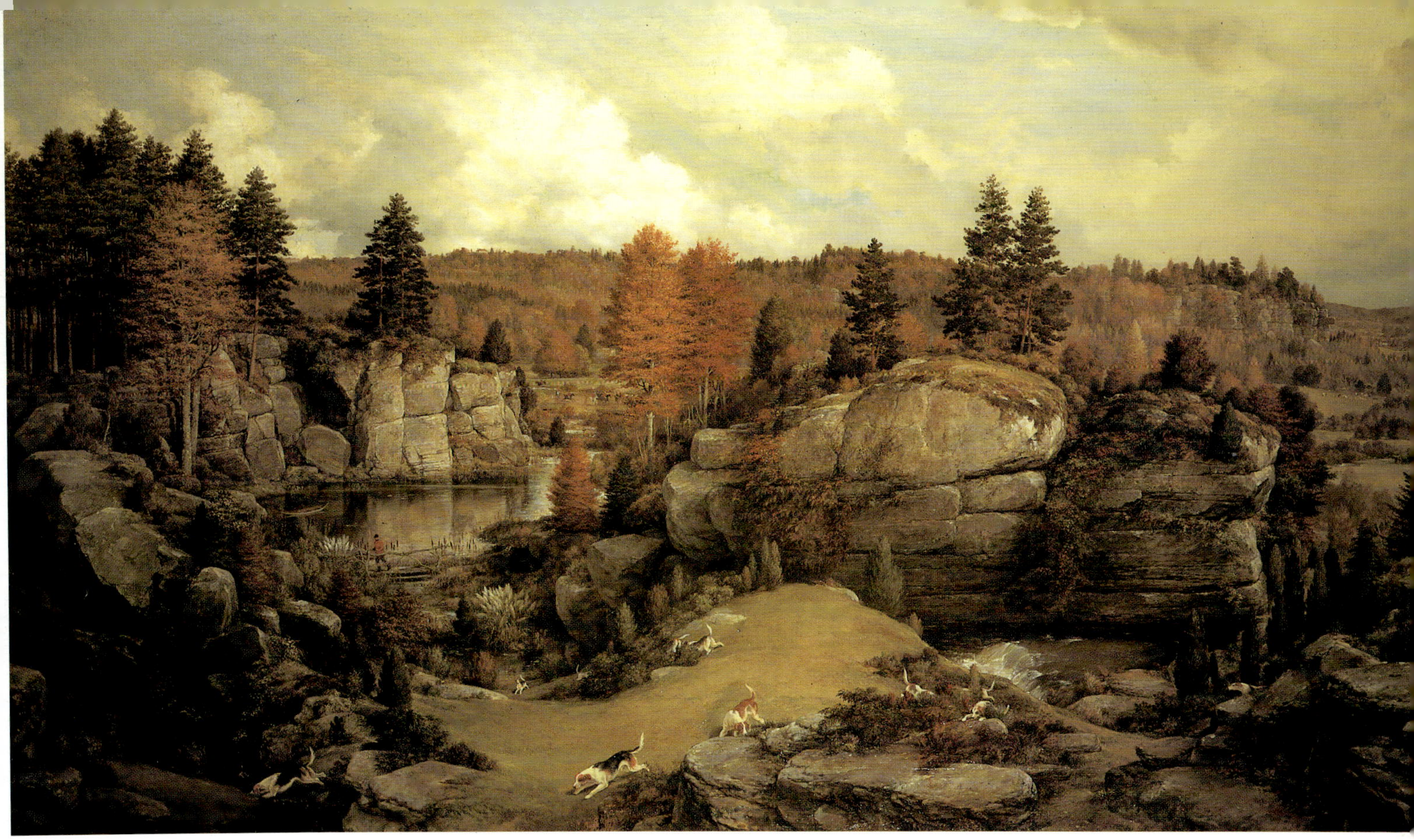

Colour Plate 169. 75/12

View from the Drawing room at Glen Andred– *A Sussex garden glen; late autumn: unexpected visitors*

After eight years' intensive work, planting, baring the rocks and moving mature trees, Cooke had made his beloved garden a great attraction for visitors, but the hounds of the Eridge Hunt were unusual!

Photo courtesy Martyn Gregory Private Collection

Colour Plate 170.

Glen Andred, Groombridge

Cooke laboured mightily over his grounds and more than a century later, with recent proprietors more or less active, the gardens still have a considerable attraction. Photo courtesy Peter Hayden

Colour Plate 171.

Snow in China, in Staffordshire

The gardens at Biddulph Grange which Cooke helped James Bateman to design included the Chinese Temple, Terrace and Water. William Alexander (1767-1816), draughtsman to the first British embassy to China, was a colleague of George Cooke's and the family possessed Chinese 'curiosities', including a portrait of the Emperor. E.W. Cooke's familiarity with Chinese design could be thus explained. Photo courtesy Peter Hayden

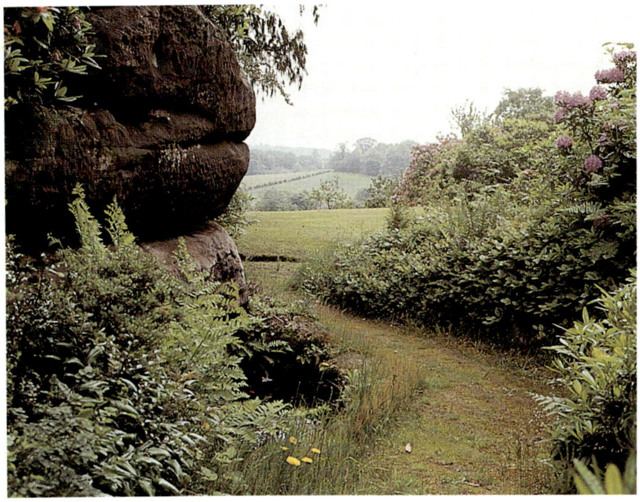

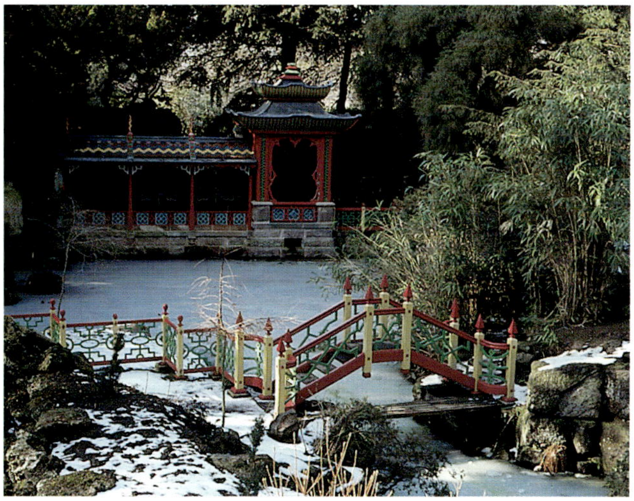

The two Loggia would also be nice, as you might have sun blinds on the outside, and so secure a charming shady place to sit in with lots of room –

As to style I have no fear but that we shall be able to arrange about that very soon – but the first point is the plan – and this it is absolutely necessary to get right, as if you start with a bad plan, you never can possibly get a good house, so I hope you will weigh all this carefully, and jot down all your objections – and if convenient for you I'll come out on Thursday afternoon about 4 o'clock, and we'll have a serious go in at it,

Believe me to remain Yours faithfully R.Norman Shaw[12]

Only by co-operating with a client, and artists were often difficult clients, could the architect obtain work in those days.[13] These letters from Shaw illustrate his psychology in the approach to such a client as Cooke and his winning mixture of enthusiasm, familiarity, flattery and expert opinion.

Shaw had already worked for one painter and the introduction may well have been from J.C. Horsley RA. At Willesley, near Cranbrook, Shaw's additions to his old farmhouse were counted a success. Cooke was also on the Council of the Architectural Museum, Jermyn Street, and numbered many of the profession among his 'circle'.

In his most perceptive and monumental study of the great Victorian architect, Andrew Saint[14] reveals much about the vernacular building style emerging at this time, and about Cooke who turns out to have been a key figure in Shaw's early career. Harking back to William Wells of Redleaf, Saint traces the interest of his painter guests in the old houses of the neighbourhood, from Hever castle, Ightham Mote, Knole, to Penshurst itself, and there was also South Park, where lived General Hardinge whose step-son Sir Walter James (later Lord Northbourne) was to occupy Redleaf itself and became a patron of Cooke's. The architects and patrons in the pages of Cooke's diary are intriguing: – J.B. Rebecca was working for Lord de L'isle when Cooke was painting for Wells; Anthony Salvin was restoring Scotney Castle for Edward Hussey at the same time and rebuilt South Park for Lord Hardinge. He was an old friend and was encountered in Venice. George Devey, architect nephew of Augustus Egg RA, former apprentice to J.S. Cotman and J.D. Harding – the latter a close link with W.E. Nesfield, Shaw's partner – explored the fundamentals of Kentish cottage building and the attractive materials in use. He too worked for Lord Hardinge at South Park (which incidentally replaced Redleaf as Edwin Landseer's second home) and then on the Penshurst estate for Lord De L'Isle. In the early 1850s the painter F.R. Lee RA, another of the Redleaf circle, had Devey enlarge his nearby cottage Culver Hill into the residence Hammerfield. By 1862 young Shaw was drawing Penshurst Place and its outbuildings and went round Sussex with Nesfield filling sketchbooks with the characteristic manor houses, cottages and farmhouses. The old Wealden features – tile-hung upper parts, massive chimneys, mullions and leaded lights, and such roofs – were much admired and a return to an Old English style of building was beginning. Horsley's commission was Shaw's first major house-building task and, as Andrew Saint observes, it was the making of him, for others soon followed.

Shaw's cousin J.W. Temple, a Director of the family shipping company Shaw Savill, bought a Hamsel plot and had the architect build a huge house, Leyswood, there.

Cooke's house, Glen Andred, which still stands, is a large one and has much of the vernacular about it (Plates 184 to 186). Tile hung elevations there are, and gabled roofs, for the revivalist in Shaw provided Cooke with good honest local building materials, a return to an older English type; indeed one is left wondering about his allegiance to Decimus Burton and Vitruvius! In writing to W.E. Gladstone,[15] Cooke called his house *a thoro' Sussex or rustic Elizabethan structure surrounded by wonderful masses of rock and woods of oak, fir, holly and yew. I have a truly lovely spot of about 40 acres. The*

12. Cooke MSS, Shaw letters.
13. *Dictionary of National Biography*, Shaw, R.N.
14. *Richard Norman Shaw* by Andrew Saint, Yale U.P., 1976.
15. British Museum, Addl MSS.

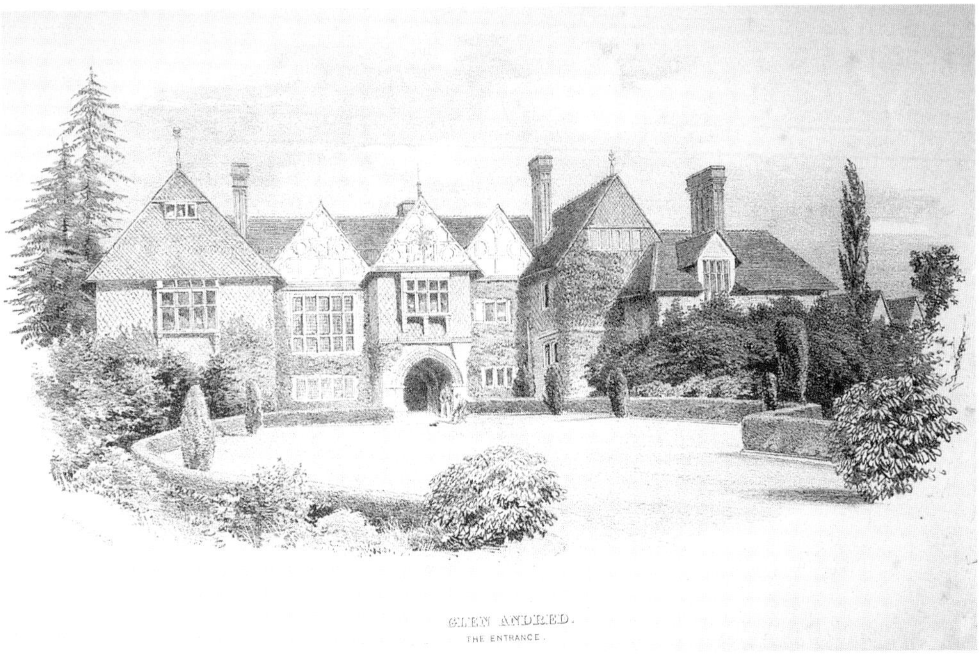

Plate 184. Engraving
Glen Andred, Groombridge showing the intended development.
In 1867, inviting W.E. Gladstone to visit him, Cooke extolled *...its picturesqueness – a thoro' Sussex or Rustic Elizabethan structure.*
Photo courtesy C.R. Cooke, OBE

Medway, here a rapid brilliant trout stream running through.

The name he eventually chose, Glen Andred, was a reference to Andrede's Wolde or Wealde, the great forest which anciently covered that part of England.

Andrew Saint has it that Shaw's buildings have frequently been likened in their stance to ships – *Glen Andred recalling a long trim Vessel athwart the escarpment's edge...* while his cousin's house was *the mighty stranded ark* which is now no more.[16]

Gardens

Cooke, with his coat off, sprang into action at the first opportunity: he had men fell trees and transplant holly bushes into the road hedge, probed and had pits dug to try the depth of soil over the rocks to find how near the surface the desirable formations might be. William Wells had done the same at Redleaf where the gardens included the Rock Walk, the Rocky Lawn and the Rocky Hollow, for the Sussex Weald sees a sandstone outcrop. He also boasted a Dutch Garden and an English Garden and some extraordinary structures such as a rustic orangery, all designed by himself. The enticing approach was described in the *Gardener's Magazine*:[17] *...the eye may detect between the trunks of some large trees just as much of the commencement of the valley as to set the imagination at work to guess its extent.*

Cooke's choice of site for his own country retreat, on the same rocky outcrops to the south-east at Groombridge, also reflected his long interest in and taste for geology. When first at Biddulph in Staffordshire he noted *noble rockwork and giant proportions.* The development of his own site is indicated by the bestowal of names on the different features: Mons Insignis (for a flagstaff), Ward's Rock for his friend N.B. Ward, Bamboozlum, also the title of a comic song, Eagle Rock, perhaps from its shape, Crinkum-Crankum, an eighteenth century term for something twisting and intricate, Greene Alleye, perhaps a quotation from Milton's *Comus,* Bellosguardo, the hill above Florence, Loddigesia, from his wife's family, Scotland, otherwise the Pinetum, Fern Glen and Polypody, Owen's Seat (after Sir Richard), May's Mead and the Milky Way, a path from the meadow to the dairy! His friends, his travels and his sense of humour were all commemorated.

16. Saint. op.cit., p.43.
17. *Gardener's Magazine,* July 1839.

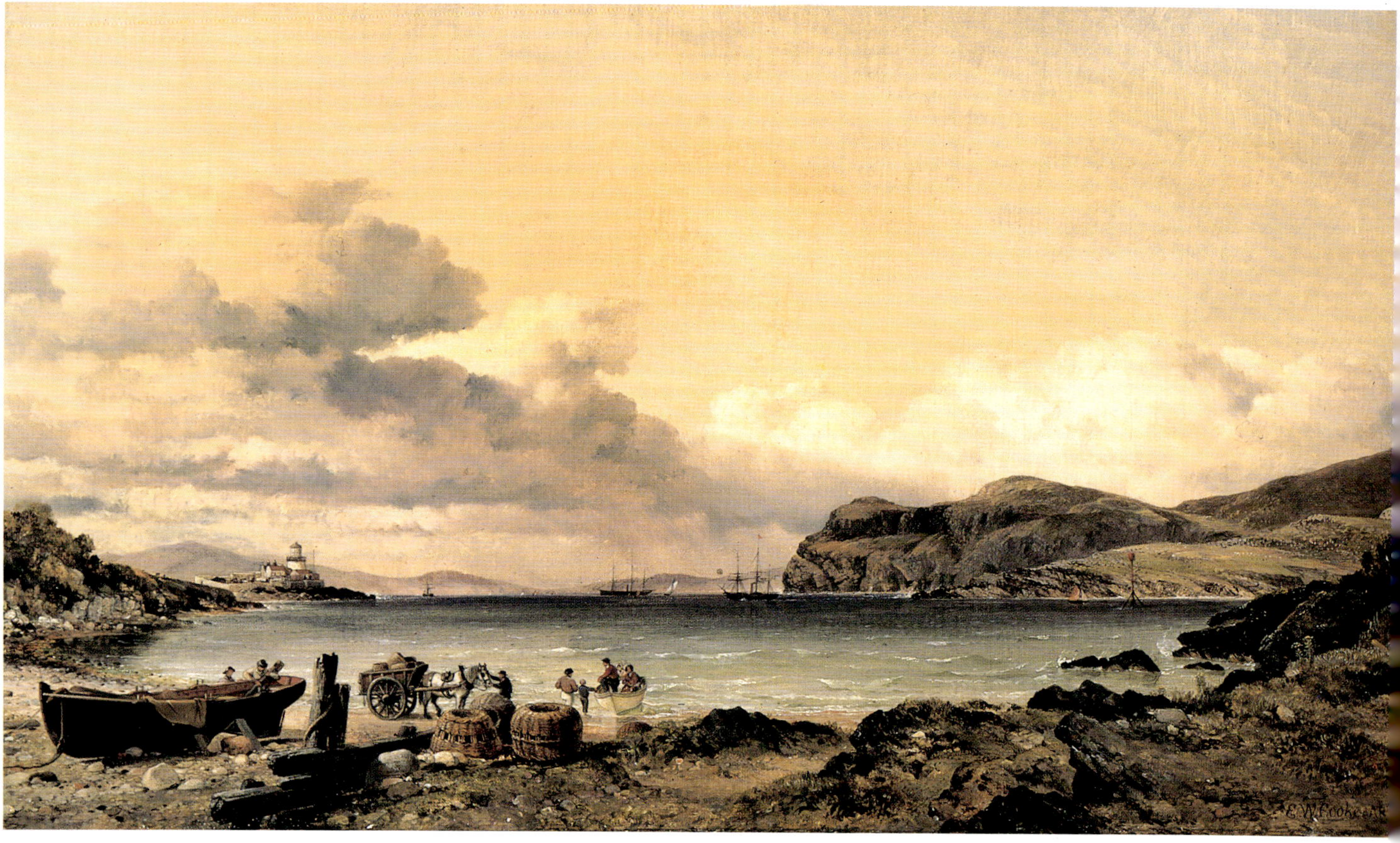

Colour Plate 172 58/11
Glanbane Bay, Valentia Harbour
Photo courtesy Bury Art.Gallery & Museum

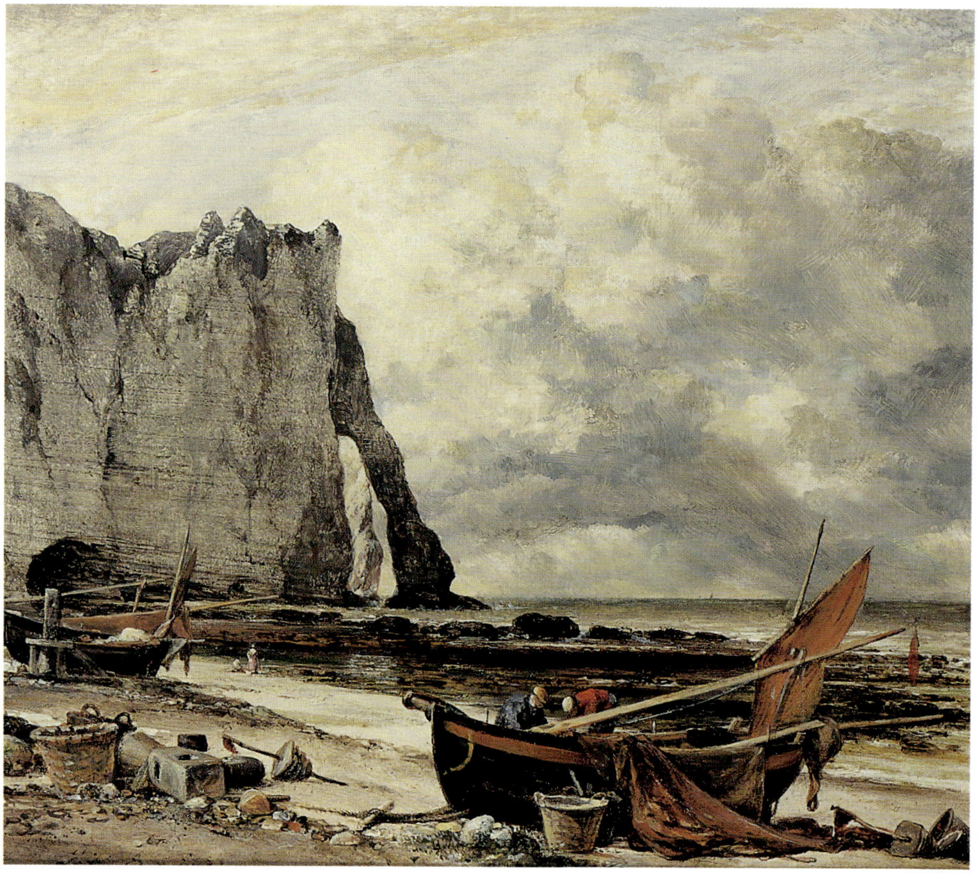

Colour Plate 173. 78/10
Etretat
Late in life Cooke revisited the fishing village which charmed generations of painters before and after him. The cliffs gave geological satisfaction while the *canots* and *caloges* were of a new and different breed, worth study.
Photo courtesy Arthur Ackermann & Peter Johnson

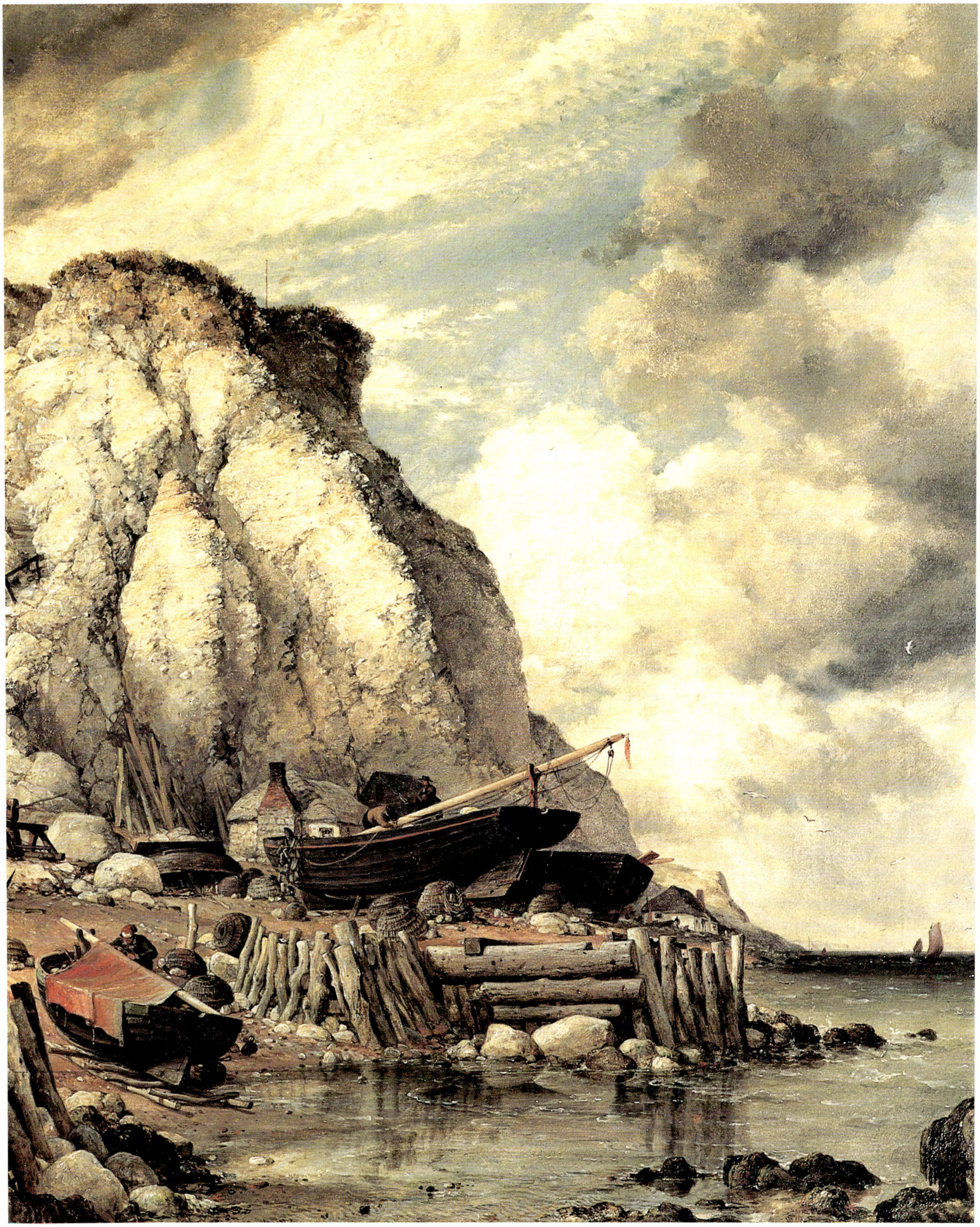

Colour Plate 174. 76/10
Bonchurch in the Olden Time
In twenty years it had been 'improved away' according to John Ruskin in his *Academy Notes* for 1877. The artist evidently agreed. Photo courtesy Private Collection

There was also a kitchen garden which all required much thought, planning and labour and Cooke seems to have worn out a succession of gardeners, not all of them satisfactory. The removal of trees and large shrubs from one place to a more telling position kept the men occupied and loads of plants arrived at the railway station from nurseries near and far. Harry Veitch was a helpful friend who also acquired some of Cooke's paintings. The artist was often working on his land as well as directing his men; in glasshouse and among his rocks the earth-stained proprietor was frequently to be found. A family story of the visiting coachman who called peremptorily to the grimed figure to hold the horse's head and was suitably discomfited by his lady's affectionate greeting of the 'gardener' is cherishable.

A large painting of the scene from the drawing room windows was exhibited at the Academy in 1877 as *A Sussex garden glen, late autumn; unexpected visitors* (75/12, Colour Plate 169). The dramatic landscape which Cooke had developed is shown at a time of year in which he delighted; a brief article in *The Garden* in late 1874 is a glowing catalogue of his planting in its autumn colours. The visitors in this picture, unlike most of his callers, had not come to admire but were on business – they were the hounds of the Eridge Hunt!

The Wider View – Landscape Gardening

If Lancelot Brown was 'Capability', Edward Cooke, who was fond of nick-names, might well have seen himself as 'Potentiality Cooke' for with his rapid pencil and gardening knowledge the development of an existing vista, earth-moving and the planning of terraces, walks and rockwork could be powerfully and rapidly illustrated for the owner.

Visiting his patrons, the enthusiast with sketchbook in hand was always ready to offer illustrated suggestions for improvements and it is clear that numbers of them were indeed adopted. Radiating, as it were, from the houses of his principal hosts were neighbouring

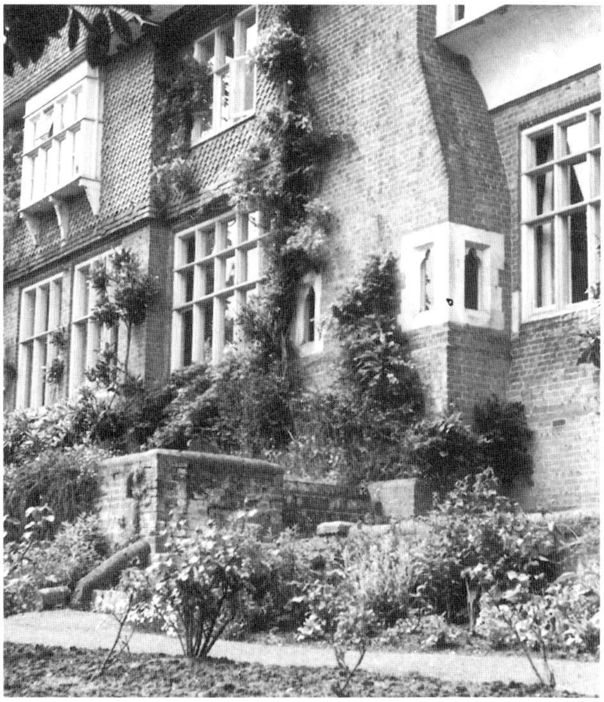

Plate 185.
Glen Andred, Groombridge
The garden front, showing Norman Shaw detail; the small windows are in the drawing-room inglenook.

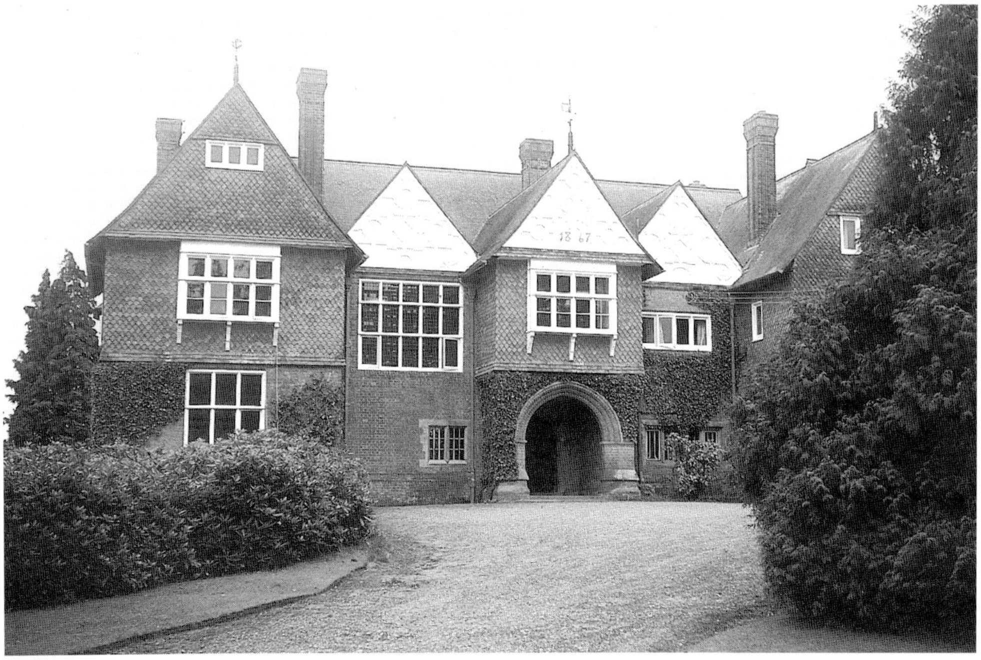

Plate 186.
Glen Andred, Groombridge
A century later and enduring: the sweep of gravel drive and the broad welcoming entrance arch are topped with an ornamented centre gable. It bears the date 1867 and a stylised palm tree. The roundels once held the initials E-W-C.

estates belonging to friends and relations, dinner guests or callers whom Cooke met. From these in turn he often received invitations; a random list is impressive, ranging through Kent with Lord De Lisle at Penshurst, Herbert Field at Ashurst Park, Sir David Salomons at Broom Hill, Sir Walter James at Betteshanger and Sir Culling Eardley at Belvedere. Further afield Gambier Parry at Highnam Court which is in Gloucestershire, Henry Gaskell at Kiddington Hall in Oxfordshire, Lady Dorothy Neville at Dangstein in Sussex, J. Heathcote at Conington Castle in Cambridgeshire, Sir William Armstrong at Cragside in Northumberland, Sir William Duckworth at Orchardleigh Park near Frome in Somerset and Sir William Bowman at Joldwynds in Surrey are joined by numerous others. The artist with full sketchbooks was a welcome guest, after-dinner showing round of the fruits of recent sketching tours with, one imagines, an appropriate and amusing commentary was pleasant entertainment besides which it might well produce a commission for a painting.

The most noteworthy example of his design co-operation still exists in restored glory among the North Staffordshire moors. James Bateman's gardens on his estate at Biddulph Grange north of Stoke-on-Trent are a remarkable survival, now under the care of the National Trust. An enthralling account of its origins and of Cooke's part in its formation, written by Peter Hayden, distinguished garden historian, has unfolded the elaborate story of its development against a horticultural background studded with famous names and illuminated by extraordinary attainment.[18] Various threads in Cooke's life here come together in a most interesting way. The exotic stock in the Hackney glasshouses of Conrad Loddiges and Sons and the transportation of tropical plants by his friend N.B. Ward were both familiar to Bateman who, as a wealthy Oxford undergraduate, had been a plant collector and orchid fancier with wide contacts. The artist first mentions calling on him in London in 1848; they were exactly the same age but with a coal and iron fortune behind him and a very considerable achievement in publishing a huge work on orchids, Bateman, already a Fellow of the Royal Society, was also a man of mark. The house had been designed by him in much the style of the Italianate Osborne House, the Queen and Prince Consort's beloved Isle of Wight palace. Cooke's introduction may well have been through N.B. Ward at a conversazione of the Botanical Society and in September 1849 Cooke visited Biddulph itself, entering upon a

18. Hayden op. cit.

remarkable association. From admiring Bateman's new fernery and its rockwork, 48ft. x 36ft. (14.6m x 11m), an iron, wood and glass structure destined to be a prize-winner at the Great Exhibition of 1851 – although still capable of improvement – Cooke quickly moved into action with pencil and sketch pad. Every sort of design work, beginning with a church and parsonage for the estate, was meat to him! There was a Fern Dell outside too, containing most of the varieties of British ferns and some hardy exotics as well, so he was perfectly in his element. There is hardly any evidence of the processes of co-operation between owner and artist but there were no fewer than seven articles on the gardens in the *Gardeners Chronicle*,[19] so unusual and full of interest were they. The planting of rare imported trees and shrubs and the devising of suitable settings in a somewhat bleak landscape was part of the story, but unfortunately there are only rather meagre diary entries and no drawings to supply the desirable background details.

The later story of the estate, which was sold by Bateman's son after his parents had moved south for his mother's health, is chequered. The auction catalogue of 1871 details the layout of the grounds and acknowledges the part played by Cooke and by Waterhouse Hawkins, the sculptor, in their wide celebrity. 'China', the secret garden with more than a nod in the direction of the willow pattern plate, with pavilion or temple, bridge and lake, remained difficult to find in the folds of the landscape, but was a triumph of ingenuity and while Cooke must have drawn up the elevations, if not the plans, one is left wondering at his sources. William Alexander, who illustrated the account of Lord Macartney's Embassy to China in 1792, had worked with George Cooke and there were Chinese items by him in the family cabinet of curiosities. 'Egypt' had stone sphinxes and clipped yew pylons but, apart from his drawings of the British Museum's Egyptian antiquities in the hands of the Royal Engineers, Cooke was not especially familiar with the civilisation of the Nile valley until a much later date, though he may have known Decimus Burton's elder brother, James Burton Junr, the Egyptologist who in 1838 resumed the original family name of Haliburton by which he is best known.

Biddulph's Italian Garden with its small lake, islands and richly planted margins, perhaps the finest collection of Araucarias in England, the Great Wellingtonia Avenue, The Pinetum, The Rhododendron Ground, The Glen, The Stumpery – *Old Roots., Rugged Stems and Stumps of Trees in all their gnarled, contorted and varied forms, well appreciated home for Ivies, Creepers and Trailing Plants* – were some of the features. The Parterres, the Arboretum, the Rose Garden, the Dahlia Walk, the Cheshire Black and White Timber Cottage, the Lime Avenue, the Bowling Green, the Quoit Ground, the Five's Court and the Music House were all listed in the illustrated sale catalogue. Although the estate failed to sell at auction, it found a buyer the following year in a local magnate, Robert Heath MP. The mansion was rebuilt after a fire in 1896, the year before James himself died at Worthing, having outlived his artist friend by some eighteen years.

There is no indication that Cooke ever returned there after receiving what he noted as a sad letter from Bateman in September 1869, doubtless with news of their decision to sell up. In his posthumous sale there were batches of drawings of gentlemen's seats, and some of Biddulph, but nothing is known of their fate, nor do any of his garden design drawings seem to have survived.

19. Reprinted as *Description of the Gardens at Biddulph Grange* by Edward Kemp, Landscape Gardener, Birkenhead Park, London, 1862.

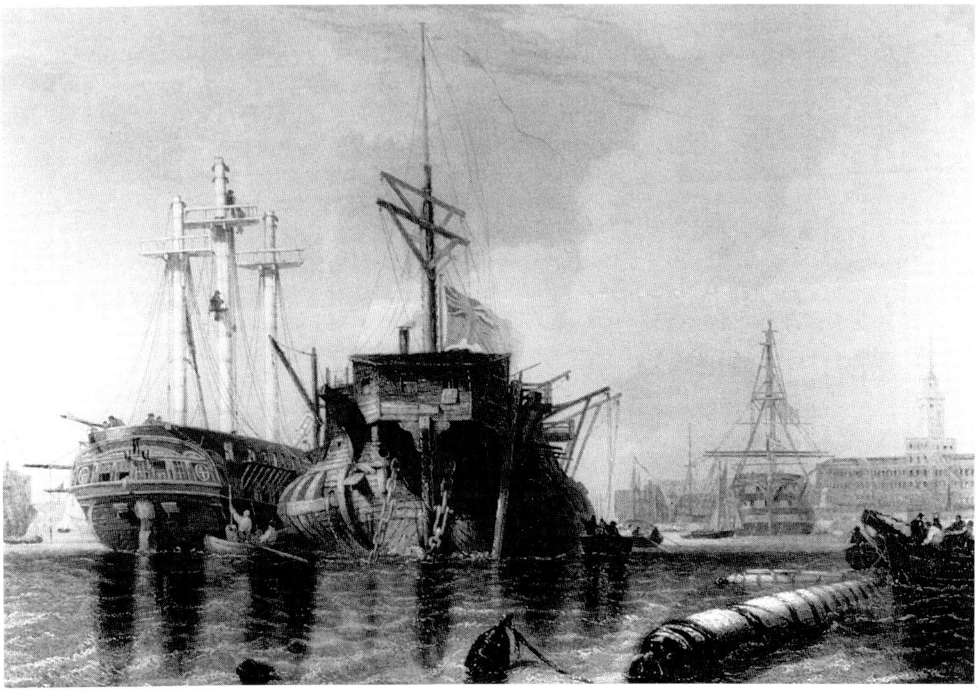

Chapter 18

THE PRINTED PAGE AND OTHER PROOFS

There is a gap of forty years between appearances of E.W. Cooke's name on a title page and then only the later works have text from his pen as well as drawings from his pencil. His early published series of etchings, *Shipping and Craft, Old and New London Bridges* and his contribution to his father's *London* had put Edward Cooke's artistry squarely before the public by the year 1834 and had been greeted with critical acclaim. Thereafter his name occurred only beneath reproductions of his paintings and occasionally as illustrator to other men's books, until the 1870s.

In recent times versions have been printed of the complete *Shipping and Craft* which because of the printsellers' habit of 'breaking' volumes is now rare and quite costly. In 1970 appeared what is to date the best facsimile, furnished with a very interesting and informed commentary on the vessels depicted, recording their outstanding interest to maritime historians. This was written by the marine artist and writer Roger Finch whose remarks on Cooke's approach and technique form a most valuable critical addition.[1]

In 1983 a French publisher at Douarnenez printed *Les Marines de E.W. Cooke* as one of a series on marine artists, with commentary and additional illustrations.[2]

In 1989 an American company produced a facsimile edition of *Sixty Five Plates...* with the title *Sailing Vessels in Authentic Nineteenth Century Illustrations* in their Pictorial Archive series, designed as a reference source.[3] Claiming it as both unabridged and unaltered, they however reproduced from an unbound copy in the Hart Nautical Collection of the Massachusetts Institute of Technology which lacks two plates and includes two which are not by Cooke.

1. Finch op. cit.
2. Editions de L'Estran.
3. Dover Publications Inc., Mineola, New York.

Plate 187. Engraving

Rigging Hulk, Portsmouth Harbour

Engraved and published by the Finden brothers from the painting 36/9, exhibited at the British Institution in 1837 and acquired by J. Sheepshanks. Compelled, it seems, by the apparatus of dockyards, Cooke selected this old French prize *Topaze,* in use for rigging and unrigging ships of war, to represent the Royal Navy's principal establishment in *Ports, Harbours & Watering Places,* 1838.

In 1970 a selection from the original pencil drawings of Old London Bridge in the collection of the Corporation of London at Guildhall was published as a portfolio of seven collotype plates with a title piece.[4] The drawings date between 1826 and 1832 and are an admirable record, showing the unmistakable progress of the draughtsman between the ages of fifteen and twenty-one.

Cooke also etched two somewhat larger individual plates, HMS *Victory* in Portsmouth Harbour, 1830, and a broadside view of HMS *Dreadnought,* 104 guns, the hospital ship moored off Greenwich, a commission for the Seamens Hospital Society in 1831, which was seemingly used for publicity purposes.

There are well-known plates by other engravers after Cooke's paintings and drawings, those made for book illustrations and other publishing ventures.

William Finden and his younger brother Edward (the former a member of the Associated Engravers) established a large studio and their joint output made them one of the best known, with many apprentices and assistants. Edward Cooke encountered one of the brothers at Hastings while the guest of John Sheepshanks in 1835 and a short time later, at Barnes, they selected suitable studies for paintings to be engraved. These were chiefly Portsmouth views representing the Royal Navy and home surroundings, in a proposed series on sea-ports:

Rigging Hulk and Frigate (36/9, Plate 187)
Portsmouth, Entrance to the Harbour (36/12)
View from the Saluting Platform: The Semaphore at Portsmouth (36/21, Plate 60)
Gosport, Flagship Saluting (36/22)
Ships of War at Spithead (36/24)

but there were also

Ramsgate, Kent. Entrance to the Harbour
Yarmouth, Norfolk

The plates were about 6in. x 8in. (15cm x 20cm) and the originals were not of large size. Taken from his own sketches on the spot, the first five were oils and the others watercolours. The Finden brothers' *Views of the Ports Harbours and Watering Places* began to be published in 1838 but they were forced to sell out, *the remuneration accruing from the sale being found inadequate to defray the expenses* according to their successors – further evidence if such were needed of the uncertainty of fine art publishing.

Whatever fee he received from the engraver-publisher, Cooke was able to dispose of his originals elsewhere. A study for this series, the rigging-hulk in Portsmouth Harbour, was shown to John Sheepshanks who bought it on the spot. The next day Cooke carried the painting to the engraver Finden and looked at the works in progress. Several of these were acquired by John Sheepshanks and are now in the national collections.[5] Unused sketches of subjects for *The British Coast* were probably the starting point, for there was a view of the port of Ramsgate which had been begun and furthered with Stanfield's help. Inevitable comparisons arise with Turner's watercolour coastal views and the Finden *Ramsgate* is a case in point. Turner's *Ramsgate* of 1824, which Cooke may well have known, reveals a similar treatment. Both are taken from the seaward side of the lighthouse, off the harbour mouth, providing dramatic interest in the sailing vessels negotiating a narrow entrance. Cooke's picture is without the high piled sea and precariously perched brig seen in Turner's view but, since it would appear from the diary that Cooke had not been afloat, his observations may well have been aided by a memory of the Turner. Ruskin wrote sweepingly that *The lifting of the brig on the wave is very daring... which no other painter than Turner ever represented.*[6] That placing was in fact

4. London Topographical Society, No.113, 1970.
5. e.g. Victoria & Albert Museum, National Maritime Museum.
6. *The Harbours of England,* John Ruskin, 1856.

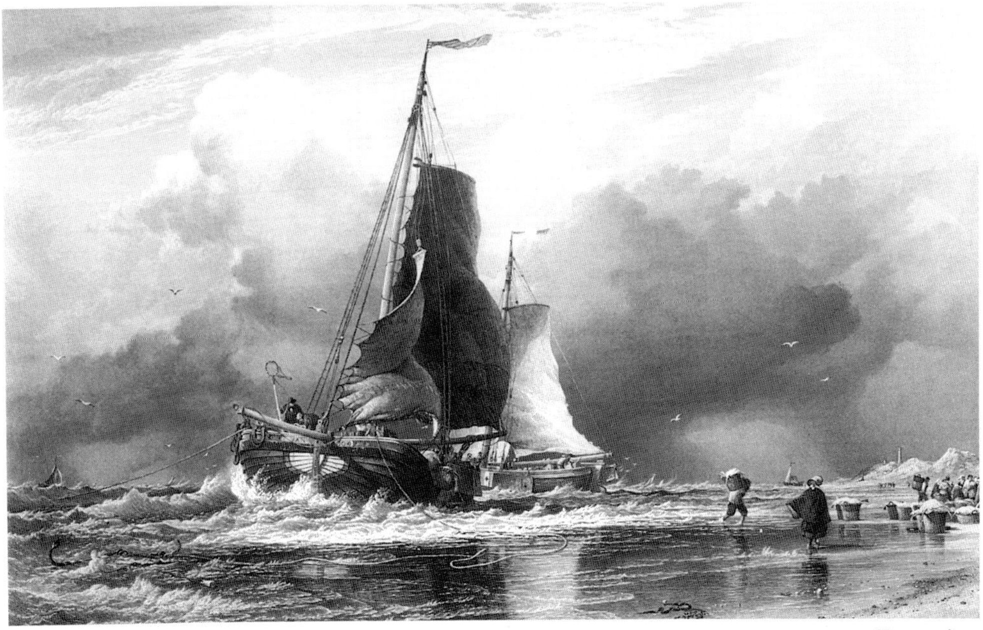

Plate 188. Engraving
Dutch trawlers landing fish at Egmont
Published by the *Art Union,* a large steel engraving by Arthur Willmore. 1874.

well used by seventeenth and eighteenth century marine masters, but here the scale of the vessel appears wrong, it is more like a model boat, an example of the great painter's regard for drama at the expense of mere accuracy.

Samuel Carter Hall who conducted the celebrated *The Art Journal* had obtained from Robert Vernon the rights to engrave and publish all the paintings in his collection which became part of the National Gallery, now the Tate Gallery.

Dutch Boats in a Calm – From the picture in the Vernon Gallery, engraved by Thomas Jeavons (Plate 85), is probably the best known reproduction of any of Cooke's paintings, having appeared in Volume XI, 1849. It was the engraver's only contribution to that publication as well as probably his largest plate according to a recent authority.[7] He brought the first proof to Cooke in Victoria Road for 'touching' and duly collected the corrected copy as noted in the diary.

The Boat House (35/21, Colour Plate 45A), another painting in the Vernon collection, rejoices in a punning title, showing a cave in the chalk cliffs of the Isle of Wight sheltering a fisherman, his craft and gear. It appeared in the *Art Journal* for 1854 with the title *Fisherman's Cave* engraved by Samuel Bradshaw who had married Cooke's cousin Jemima in 1834.

The Arrival, after his painting of Otho ex-King of Greece reaching Venice on board a British man o' war, was another *Art Journal* plate, 1862, engraved by John Cousen who had produced a number of plates after Turner. The Art Union of London published in 1872 a large steel engraving by Arthur Willmore, *Dutch trawlers landing fish at Egmont* (17¼in. x 25¾in – 44cm x 65cm). This picture was evidently painted to order and Willmore's plate can be taken as a faithful translation of Cooke's Dutch sea shore compositions of this breezy type, giving subscribers the authentic *Van Kook* (Plate 188).

Cooke was from time to time asked to provide illustrations to books by a variety of authors. Col Mark Beaufoy, the son of a Quaker brewer in the Barnes area, had scientific interests and money enough to indulge them. A pioneer in the study of floating bodies leading to a better understanding of ship resistance and consequently of hull design, his *Nautical & Hydraulic Experiments,* published by his son Capt Henry Beaufoy in 1834, is a ponderous technical volume which bears a small engraved vignette by Cooke of a natural history subject, a Nautilus or argonaut (a small cephalopod) inscribed 'Learn of the little Nautilus to Sail', a quotation from Alexander Pope which in fact continued *Spread the thin oar and catch the driving gale.*[8]

7. Hunnisett op.cit., p. 92.
8. *Mark Beaufoy's Nautical & Hydraulic Experiments* by Dr Thomas Wright [in] *Mariner's Mirror,* Vol. 75, p.313.

William Scrope,[9] a keen sportsman and an able amateur artist, was author of *The Art of Deerstalking,* 1838, illustrated by various artists, and *Days and Nights of Salmon Fishing on the Tweed,* 1843, with a third edition 1846. Cooke visited him at his house, Wherstead Lodge, south of Ipswich, in 1841 to make drawings. Scrope's daughter and heiress married George Julius Poulett Thomson MP, geologist, who took her ancient family name. His brother Charles Poulett Thomson, afterwards Lord Sydenham, economist, died as Governor General of Canada, news received during Cooke's visit. A Miss Poulett Thomson had been at Mrs Cooke's school. George Julius was the intimate friend and ally of the geologist Sir Charles Lyell, with whom he was joint secretary of the Geological Society, 1825, and was the author of *Geology of the Extinct Volcanoes of Central France,* 1827 and later editions. George Cooke had engraved the plates for the first five volumes of the Society's Transactions[10] and also plates to John Pinkerton's *Petralogy or a Treatise on Rocks,* 1811, so here again was an element of familiarity. Edward Cooke, early acquainted with such things and moving among such figures, was becoming increasingly interested.

John Butler, Earl of Ossory who succeeded as 2nd Marquess of Ormonde, published *Autumn in Sicily, Being an Account of Remains of Antiquity,* 1850. Cooke was engaged to make plates from the author's drawings in which he enlisted the help of his cousin, W.J. Cooke.

A Turnerian watercolour of a sunset scene, *The Funeral of Cowley,* was made for S.C. Hall, also engraved by W.J. Cooke and appearing in *The Gem* for 1838, the same annual in which the engraver's plates after R.P. Bonington had appeared. Abraham Cowley the poet died at Chertsey and the subject of a solemn waterborne funeral procession with black barge at close of day was very much in the Thames-side artist's line. He made in fact a second version of the subject, less reminiscent of Turner and differing in detail from the first; this was the one engraved, while the earlier drawing survived in the family collection.

Nathaniel Bagshaw Ward, botanist, sometime Master of the Apothecaries' Company, was the inventor of the Wardian Case. This very popular piece of equipment or furniture originated in the chance growth of a fern in a closed bottle which he kept for three years – a revelation dating from 1829. He designed larger glazed receptacles and with the help of George Loddiges in 1833 successfully sent plants to and from Australia. He wrote *On the Growth of Plants in Closely Glazed Cases,* 2nd edition 1852, to which Cooke and his sister Georgiana, the author's daughter-in-law, supplied the drawings for the woodcut illustrations (Plate 189). Ward exhibited the cases at the Great Exhibition of 1851 and Cooke assisted in their arrangement. A fashion for Wardian cases or, as the artist called them, *Warderies*, either as glazed window-boxes or free-standing plant cases in the Victorian living room, grew apace (Plate 190). Today modern equivalents have been reintroduced.

Contributions from Cooke's pen, but without illustrations, appeared in *The Garden – The Bronze Pine in the Vatican Garden,* 1872, *Orchids in Dwelling Rooms* (in a regular feature 'The Garden in the House'), 1873, *My Garden in Autumn*, 1874 and *Venice and its Gardens*, 1877.

Published books

A departure from his usual vein, but again demonstrating his natural history interests as well as his sense of fun, was entitled *Entwickelungsgeschichte – Grotesque Animals* (Plates 191 to 193). With illustrations reproduced by the Autotype Company, this was an album published by Longmans/Spottiswoode in time for Christmas 1872. The drawings had begun as pencil sketches, amusing exercises which he referred to as 'Comic Animals' and made in 1861 on a wet day passing through Malvern. He was on his way to

9. Burke's *Landed Gentry:* Scrope of Castle Combe.
10. Christie's 30 April 1834, Lot 229.

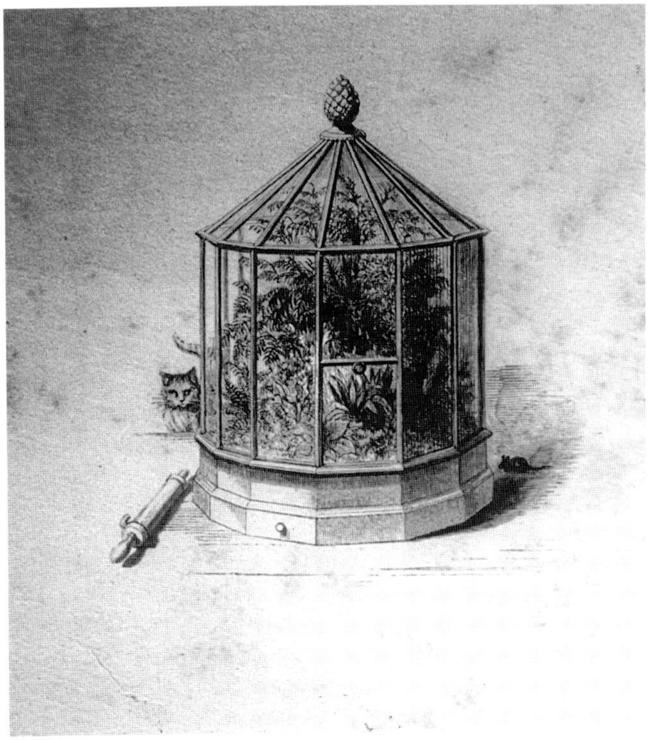

Plate 189. Engraving
Wardian case with syringe, cat & mouse
Woodcut after Cooke for N.B. Ward's *On the Growth of Plants in Closely Glazed Cases.* 2nd edition 1852
Whimsy is at work again; the pine cone on the finial was a favourite *motif* of Cooke's. Photo courtesy Peter Hayden

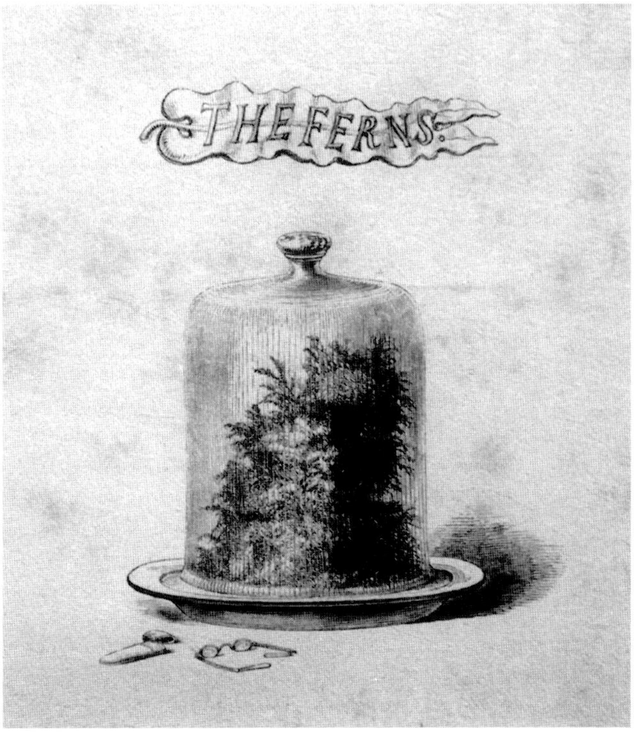

Plate 190. Engraving
The Ferns
Plants growing under a bell-jar. Perhaps intended for a letter-heading since Cooke gave the name to both his Kensington homes. Photo courtesy Peter Hayden

Minehead and Watchet in Somerset and his preface claims he was enjoying a seaside break after the taxing sessions of the British Association meetings in Manchester. He would have heard papers read by leading scientists and these had doubtless turned his thoughts to evolution, fossils and a coastline with which he was not yet familiar. J.M.W. Turner's watercolour vision of Watchet had in fact been Cooke's twenty-first birthday present from his father so that it had doubtless remained in mind for a visit. In this book his imagination, his knowledge and his irrepressible sense of humour combined to give the light to weird combinations of animal, vegetable and mineral features. Charles Darwin's *On the Origin of Species by Means of Natural Selection* had appeared in 1859 and aroused great controversy; his *The Descent of Man* appeared in 1871. Cooke's humorous set was gradually expanded; he began referring to them as his *Darwin Animals,* and later *Queer Animals* and in one instance as *The Varmints.* Shortly before publication he was writing to one contact promising him a view of *Animals from the Moon!!!*

A series of pencil drawings, carefully executed, in which curious combinations of bone, shell, feather, tusks, scales and human limbs were grafted together into terrifying monsters, were each given names and attributes. Couched in archly erudite terms, with Latin mottoes, the captions to these offspring of his invention combined to provide a set with which he was in the habit of entertaining his hosts and their friends, particularly after dinner, on his town and country visits.

'My Odd Animals' he called them finally and they are immediately reminiscent of the demonic figures and monstrosities in the paintings of Hieronymus Bosch and 'Hell' Brueghel, Pieter the Younger. There is something undeniably medieval in these grotesques, springing perhaps from deep in Cooke's European ancestry. The Darwinian controversy made it all topical and the artist's habit of acquiring objects of natural history provided a fruitful reference collection. His accompanying text had the advantage of revision by Professor Sir Richard Owen of the British Museum of Natural History, the

Plate 191. Autotype

Grotesque Animals, 1872 Plate XIX

Complete with translations of their Latin mottos, these are decorative pieces in a collection consisting otherwise of rather nasty creatures:

1 *Swimming at Ease in the Vasty Deep: 2. Safe on the Waves*

No. 1 'This PIG-FACED LADY has the good taste to clothe herself in that most elegant of BIVALVES, HIPPURIS MACULATA (or CLAM-SHELL). She has a scaly CAUDAL extremity, with HANDS OF PORK, and Pigtail. She wears Specs, from being NEAR-SIGHTED only, not from AGE,'

No 2..'Rather CALIBAN-ISTIC, this denizen of the "VASTY DEEP" belongs to no particular genus or species, although doubtless related to the SEA-SERPENT...'

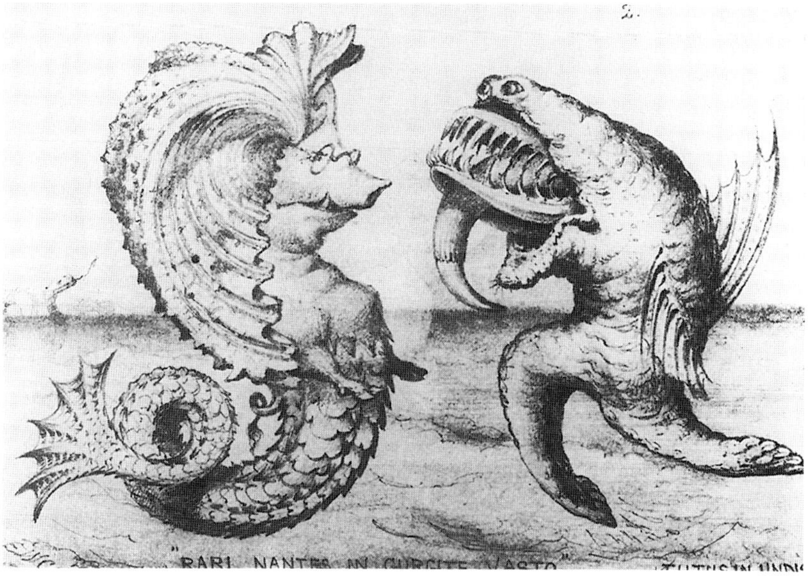

Plate 192. Autotype

Grotesque Animals. Plate VIII

1. *Let us leave off Foolery: 2. Many Heroes lived before Agamemnon*

No. 1. 'This TADPOLE-LOOKING FELLOW has great regard for the safety of his NOSE; unlike a retriever he can neither fetch nor carry, nor would he be a pleasant animal to ride, as he can only 'hop, skip & jump' and his movements are retrograde.'

No. 2. 'This complicated monstrosity combines the head of an ELEPHANT with EAGLE & SERPENT TUSKS... As he divides the hoof, he probably chews the cud also, but is scarcely a true RUMINANT.'

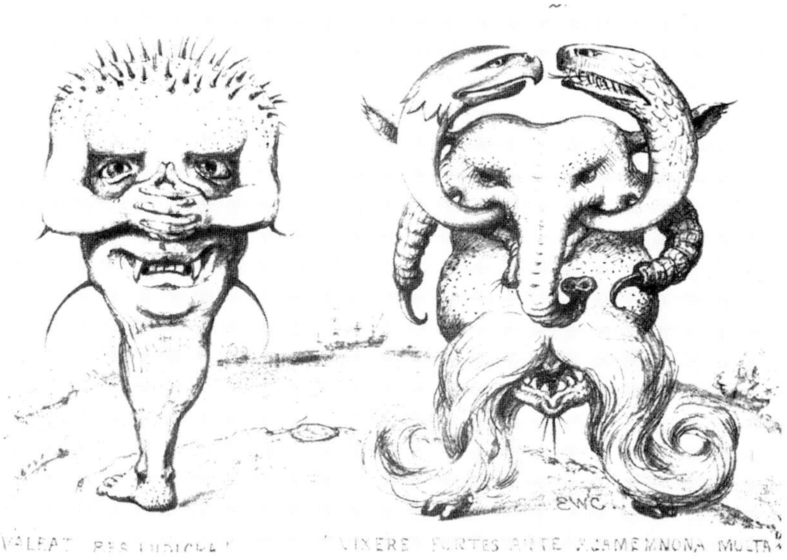

Plate 193. Autotype

Another design from a number not used for the book

His title-page carried the quip about 'natural selection' and on every page the humorous artist vies with the serious scientific observer. One can hear Cooke's after-dinner commentary, punctuated by polite laughter, admiration for his ingenuity and even mild expressions of horror.

Photo courtesy C.R. Cooke, OBE

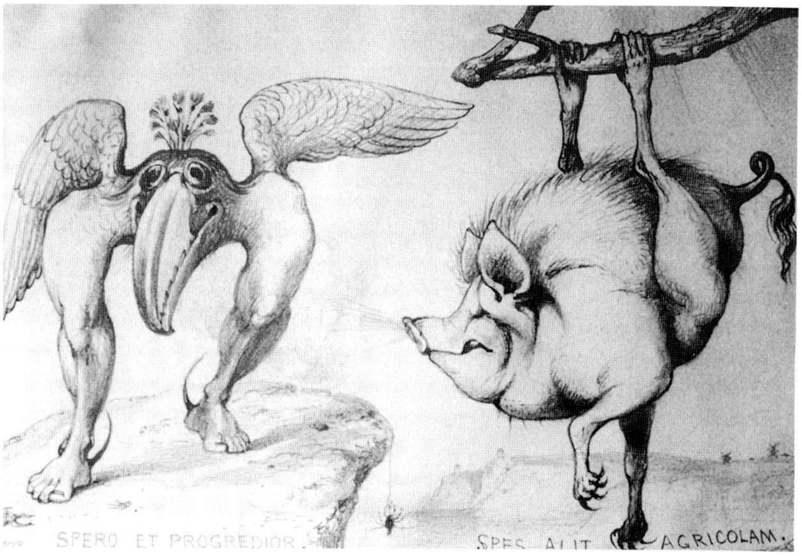

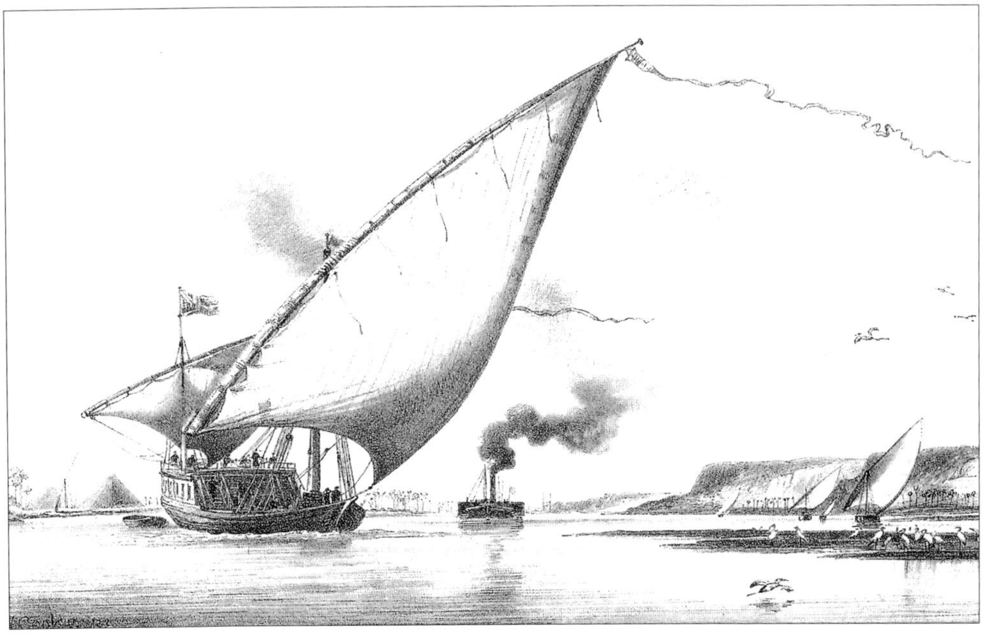

Plate 194. Engraving
Dahabeeah in full sail up stream off Toorah
From *Leaves from my Sketch-book,* John Murray, 1876.

famous zoologist, comparative anatomist and old friend, as well as from other scientists. His title-page bore the tongue-in-cheek verse:

These oddities, from fancy drawn
May surely raise the question
Will Darwin say – by chance they're formed
Or Natural Selection?

The title was probably borrowed from a learned work, Kolliker's *Entwickelungs-geschichte des Cephalopoden* and not all his grotesques were selected for publication, the remainder being in the family collection.

Landscapes, British and Foreign, engraved by Charles G. Lewis after E.W. Cooke RA, thirty plates, oblong quarto, The Art Union of London, 1874, were slight etchings of small size from a selection of his pencil sketches. These range across his favourite places but this volume again unfortunately lends itself to breaking up for the plates, so is not common.

In July 1875 another publication was in mind: writing to the publisher John Murray, Cooke said he possessed *more than 20,000 mounted drawings, many very highly finished* from which to choose.

Leaves from my Sketchbooks, Murray, December 1876, comprised twenty-five subjects: France three, Germany two, Holland one, Switzerland two, Rome eight, Venice two, the rest of Italy two and Egypt five (Plate 194). The title-page bore the Dryden quotation *The pencil speaks the tongue of every Land,* the same thought that decorated the title-page of William Powell Frith's *Autobiography* some years after Edward Cooke's time; even if the poet actually meant paint-brush rather than graphite, the sentiment agrees. The prefatory notice says that his drawings *often served to recall to friends pleasant memories of happy days and sunny climes, and excite a wish to visit places alike remarkable for natural beauty and historic interest.* That it was published by Murray, whose famous *Handbooks* accompanied generations of travellers, is appropriate. The author promised, if his work was well received, to publish another consisting chiefly of scenes on the Nile. In the event the make-up of the second series which appeared in December 1877 was Egypt sixteen plates, Venice five and the Naples area four. The two-tone plates are faithful reproductions of his pencil sketches, an added faint buff tint complements the black-lead and the white of the paper is left in places to heighten the effect. There are a few engraved blocks in the text, which is called on the title page 'Descriptive Letter-Press'. This is an entertaining antiquarian-guidebook recital with useful notes on all Cooke's favourite subjects and some of his opinions as well: *A steamer is not a beautiful object anywhere, but when contrasted with a Nile boat, which*

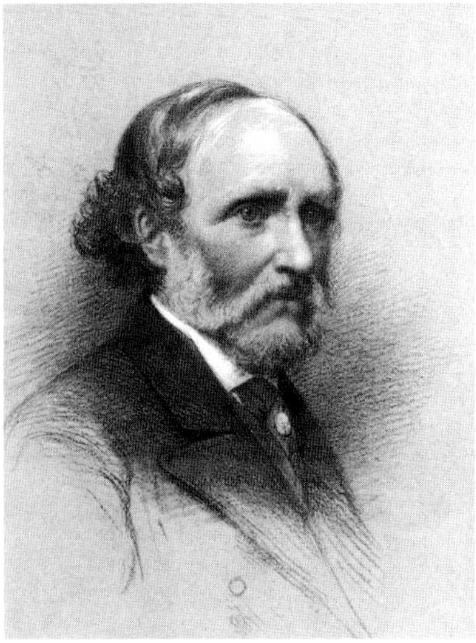

Plate 195.
E.W. Cooke RA
Drawing, unsigned and undated, of a somewhat older man than the Cooke shown in Plate 7. Softer, contemplative, it could be in the last year of his life. The artist has not so far been identified.
Photo courtesy J.D. Cooke

no matter how shabby, always looks well by virtue of the graceful shaped sail, it seems a more panting, puffing, screaming, smoke-ejecting monster than ever. The words could have been written by the late Charles Dickens himself.

Oddly, the plates in the first series are numbered from 1-20 and 30-34, but there are still only twenty-five although one contains two views. There is also known a variant title-page with 'gothic' illuminated capital letters but since that gave his name as William Edward Cooke it was doubtless suppressed. The author must also have gnashed his teeth on finding his beloved Venetian fishing boats appearing as 'paragozzi' when proof reading should have detected the compositor's error in taking a manuscript *Br* for *Par*! The engraver was one Cooper. A contrite letter from Cooke to John Murray[11] dated February 1878 indicates that the second series of *Leaves* was not yet a success, in fact that the publisher had not recouped his outlay: *Doubtless much is attributable to the Severe state of Trade throughout the country and which has so seriously affected we Artists... I do trust that the publication, which has been so generally spoken of in the most flattering terms, will revive with better times... I must confess that I do not remember that you ever warned me of the fact that Illustrated works never succeeded with you...* His private reaction had been firmly recorded on the last day of 1877: *...Saw in evening for the first time the second part of "Leaves from My Sketchbook" all printed and published without my being consulted as to the Plates or the Descriptions – all horribly bad and so black and coarse and vulgar.* He had been concerned that the considerable tonal range of his black-lead drawings should be faithfully reproduced, something not easily accomplished even at that time.

George Dennis, whom he had met in Rome in 1846, was author of *Cities and Cemeteries of Etruria,* 1848, with drawings by S.J. Ainsley, and Murray was advertising a new edition in two volumes as 'in the press' in 1877. Dennis was writing in 1878 a new work on Sicily, and illustrations from Cooke's sympathetic pencil had been suggested. There were still dangers for travellers; back in 1860 when considering the island as a painting ground he had joked to Murray about there being *queer brigandish sort of fellows about who might perhaps spoil a careful sketch in oil by the finishing touch of a stiletto!*[12] but in spite of his earlier Sicilian work for Lord Ossory, which might have indicated his sympathy for the subject, nothing came of it.

For the National Lifeboat Institution's journal he drew for reproduction illustrations of the lifeboats in action. *The Ramsgate life-boat – A Night on the Goodwin Sands* of 1862 and *Wreck of the SS "Stanley" – Position of the "Constance" (Tynemouth) Life-Boat on the Night of the 24th November 1864.* Both emerged as highly dramatic woodcuts underlining the dangers of the service. Several others of his paintings were engraved on wood for the *Illustrated London News* and for the *Art Journal* in 1869.

Had he lived there would doubtless have been other published collections of his drawings. In a review of his *Leaves* the magazine *The Garden* said: *A selection from Mr Cooke's immense library of sketches, made with a view to illustrate vegetation specially could not fail to be both interesting and instructive.*[13]

11. John Murray Archives.
12. Ibid.
13. *The Garden,* Vol X.

Appendix 1

EXTRACTS FROM THE ARTIST'S DIARY

Illustrative of matters artistic and domestic
Selected from the original MS.
1828-1879

[Accompanied by his maternal grandfather, Thomas Eglinton Senr., the retired officer of Customs, Cooke went down to Portsmouth in search of further subjects for *Shipping & Craft* and also to gather subscribers from booksellers & print dealers.]

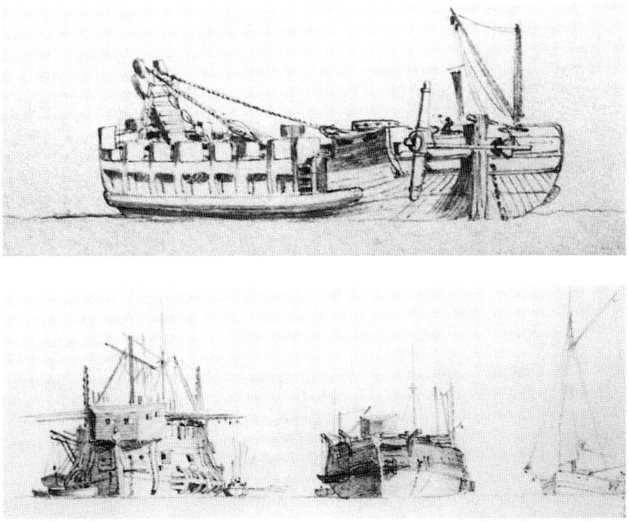

Plate 197. Pencil drawings
Portsmouth harbour, hulks &c
Unlovely though the subject may be, these tiny drawings of working craft are superbly *right.* Photo courtesy Clarges Gallery

1828. Wednesday 4th June Rained very hard. Got outside the Norwich coach and rode to the City perfectly dry. Remained in the Coffee Room at the Spread Eagle till ½ p 7 when we mounted the Southampton Coach and with the Wind in our teeth all the way we encountered a heavy Rain for 45 miles ...to Basingstoke, here we Lunched after a tedious Overland-through-Water journey. Here the Sun appeared through a Cloud and with the Wind soon dried our drenched cloaks and Weather beaten Mazzards. [Mazzard: mazard, mazer, bowl, cup, skull, head.]
We next arrived at Winchester, a most delightful place, stopped ¼ of an hour - most exquisite country - beautiful views - in sight of the Southampton Water - arrived at Mr Guy's at 6 PM.- very glad to see me - made a capital meal- went to the Bookseller Mr Fletcher's - liked the Work -took a long walk about the quay - Itchin Ferry &c - sketched some bits - Supped with Mr Guy - Mrs Guy very nice woman - slept well.
5th June Up before 5 in the morning -sketched the Gate in the High St.,- made hearty breakfast; settled with Booksellers. Mr Guy introduced me to Mr Buchan, printseller, subscribed to *Shipping* Went to the Quay Steamer ready to start, roused myself to't - water very rough,- Wind due E. and blowing very hard.- embarked safely - weighed anchor & off we started in fine style.The wind being *right aft* we hoisted our fore trysail, Jib and sail. Got a scrap of Southampton, Callshot Castle &c, sea tremendously rough. Captain said he never saw it so boisterous in that part before. I must say I never enjoyed anything so much as this voyage - the vessel rocked very much- fine food for the fishes. Got to Cowes in 70 min. Landed on the W. side, walked a long way and returned along the beach to West Cowes Castle, made sketch, dined and boarded the Portsmouth steam packet. Again we tasted salt water, for a very large Wave struck the Vessel's bows where I was standing, completely drenched and almost capsized me, but soon swab'd myself dry again When we reached Portsmouth I was very much gratified with the sight of a 74 and 3 frigates riding at Anchor at Spit Head- they looked magnificent and far surpassed the Ideas I had formed of these Beautiful Vessels. Portsmouth, (which we entered at about ½ p 6) looks very grand at the Entrance, the fortifications extend a long distance especially on the Eastern side which is bounded by South Sea Castle a very strong Bastion the great guns present their Muzzles on every side. I'm sure the very Smell of them would strike terror into the Enemy. We next entered the Port (now comes the treat) that fine ship the *Victory* in which our gallant Nelson was shot in the service of his country) extended her huge Sheer across the Harbour and contrasted well with the minor craft around such as Colliers, Sloops, wherries &c the other Men of War lying up in Ordinary - the Hulks- Prison Ships - Navy cutters- Pilot boats - Luggers- Steamers- dredgers- mooring lighters &c &c altogether presented a most novel and interesting appearance. The immense ranges of building in and connected with the Royal Dock Yard formed the background and finished a very beautiful picture. So much for a first glance of P.- in returning from the Steamer I looked out for a good house wherein to rest my Hide and soon Prog'd [Prog: to poke about] one with a circular stern which overlooked the harbour. There we went and found it was the Still Tavern,

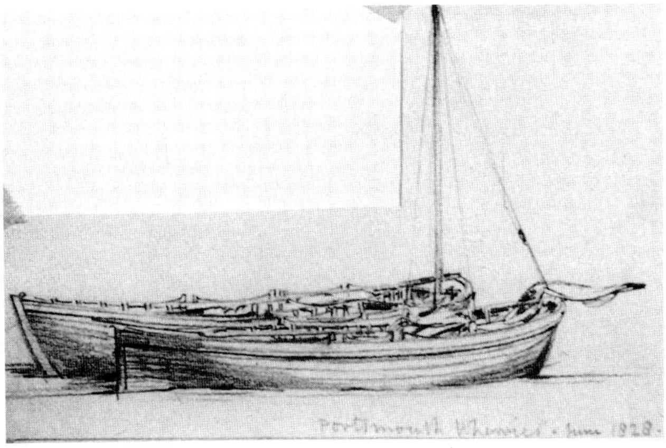

Plate 196. Pencil drawing
Portsmouth wherries 1828
Another type of small craft which has not survived; the first- and second-class Portsmouth wherries were a feature of the busy naval and mercantile port and adjacent waters. Photo courtesy Clarges Gallery

situate at the Point, at the entrance of the Port & commanding a full view of the Sea - Isle of Wight - Gosport- the whole of the Dock Yard & Harbour with the perspective line of battle Ships (housed over) & terminating with the Portsdown Hill & the surrounding country - not forgetting the view of a Most beautiful sunset every evening. After a safe Anchorage & a good laying in of Provisions, we retired to our Hammocks & enjoyed a comfortable share of balmy sleep.

[Later sea voyages and the motion of more advanced ocean-going steamers were to strike the painter far less favourably, but the pleasure in the rough crossing, heightened by the Captain's assurances (doubtless given on all such occasions) indicates that this was his first open-sea excursion.]

June 6th: Rose at 7, Reconnoitr'd the Harbour Wall with my telescope, did not discover any Smugglers (great pity) Breakfasted & set out on my first voyage of discovery with my fellow traveller Grandfather.We first steered for the Royal Dock Yard where we gain'd admission, went all over it, saw that exquisite piece of Mechanism the Block machinery [Sir Mark Isambard Brunel's woodworking machinery for making ships' rigging blocks, 1806], and ultimately saw Mr Gaze, the second Master Attendant to whom I had a recommandatory letter from Mr Stokes. This gentleman was very glad to see me - approved of my work and took me to his office from whence there is a fine view of the Vessels in the Harbour. Here he gave me permission to come whenever I liked. He was about to send off his Lugger (a beautiful boat) to the Galatea frigate lying at Spit Head... and he asked me if I would like to go out in her, which offer I readily accepted, and indeed we had a most delightful sail, with 6 fine old Sailors we cut through the water excessively quick. We had not gone above two miles out when a terrific Thunder storm came on, the Sailors quickly smugg'd on their rough coats and we our canvas Cloaks and fishermens Breeches, then down it came thick and strong, but we did not care a jot.The sailors said it was a brisk Gale & the swell afterwards was delightful.

When we reached the frigate & were made fast to the Guest-warp boom, some of our men went aboard & I (of course) wished to follow but the Lieutenant said he could not allow me, as they were swabbing the decks & in a nasty mess. So I was obliged to put up with the disappointment. Off we went again & soon landed in the Dock Yard for in less than an hour we had been there & back.I returned to Mr Gaze and after to Mr Nolloth the Master Shipwright who said he would be glad to see me on Monday, and then to Mr Schetky, a famous old Naval Officer and drawing master to the Royal Naval College of Portsmouth [John Christian Schetky (1778-1874), marine painter, was not an old naval officer, though he dressed like one]. *He* was very much pleased with the Numbers of *Shipping*. Said it was the most correct work of the kind he had seen, and no doubt he should give me some commissions, he wished to show them to the Governor and Admiral of this Port so I left them...

We went (in a wherry) over the Harbour to Gosport. Fine view of the *Victory* began to sketch it. Had not done much when I looked at my Watch - it was ½ p 6 an the post goes out at 7, no time to be lost so we leap't in a boat & back we came again to the Point. Just had time to scrubb up my letter, gallop'd off & got it to the box in time. Then I wished myself back at Gosport, but it was too late.

Saturday June 7th. Set off to the Dock Yards, saw Mr Gaze, took me to his office, Sketched the Sheer Hulk. Went on board the Tribune frigate which was going out for three years that afternoon. Never was so delighted in my life upon going up the Gangway.

[It is the first fragment of the Diary but the excitement evident in his use of nautical terms and this first sight of the Navy in a spectacular setting, can still be felt.

Cooke next went to Norwich and then visited the Norfolk beaches to sketch the distinctive fishing boats, to be etched as subjects for *Shipping & Craft*.]

October 4th. Started at ¼ before 6 o'clock AM from London, passed through a most delightful country. Breakfasted at Ingatestone, passed through Bury &c and arrived at Norwich ½ p 8 PM. Saw Mother and Mr and Mrs Stark at Cotman's.

5th Went with Edmund [Cotman] to the Cathedral &c and took walk towards Thorp. Drank tea with Mr Stark in the evening, saw Mr Carmichael and Grandfather there.

6th Accompanied Mrs Stark, Mama and Edmund to Mr Hodgson's and the Museum, saw a beautiful mummy &c &c after dinner went with Edmund and took a sailing boat and went down to Thorp. Wind blowing very hard, 2 hours and ½ coming back as we had to beat all the way, got home at 9.

8th. Etched my plate and wrote to Father [his father's letter, see page 28, refers to this visit]. Packed up and went with E.C. to the Aylesham coach at 3 o'clock - had a pleasant ride and set off at 5 o'clock to walk to Hanworth, arrived at Mr Hicks'... [One of Mrs Cotman's sisters (née Miles) married Captain Hicks (a natural son of William Wyndham of Felbrigg Hall), who was naval provost marshal of Norfolk and farmed on the Gunton estate (Kitson, op. cit.)]

9th Walked with E.C to Cromer (5 miles) beautiful Spot, took a - lunch and went upon the beach, sketched several bits and a view of Cromer, dined and nearly lost ourselves coming home, being quite dark.

11th. John Hicks drove me in his pony gig to Cromer. Sketched several things. Took a boat and went off to sea which was rather rough, had a most delightful row about 3 miles out, got home quite safe, without the least sickness.

12th Took a long walk with John Hicks and E.C. to Gunton Park, Lord Suffield's...

13th ...to Cromer, took a machine and had a most delightful bathe, water rather cold though. Sketched some bits and walked along the beach to Runton (a little fishing town) Sketched some boats &c, returned to Cromer. Went up the lighthouse and then went to Mr Earl's at Cromer and drank tea there, after which went... to the Theatre, never laughed so much in my life. Saw the —-

Christmas Day 1828. Mr Cotman was with us who came about the 16th Decr. Assembled a great many - all or own family & Uncle & Aunt Thomas Eglington & theirs, In the evening exhibited a Christmas Tree (very pretty). The 3 Misses Gillham, Misses Loddiges & Hawkins, Mr's Richard & William Rosier & Lindsey came in the evening to see it, enjoyed ourselves very much.

Fri. 26th. Drew a Plant &c.

Sat 27th. Went with Father & Mr Cotman to town, first to Crosby Hall, then took Brixton coach & called on Prout, saw glorious sketches, returned to Mr Cox's, saw more beautiful drawings &c, then to Mr Hixon's where Father bought 2 beautiful drawings by Cox. Next called at Roberts's Abingdon Street Westminster & had another treat of Works of Art & after calling upon Stanfield (who was out) returned home about 11 pm.

Sun. 28th. Attended the Schools Morning & Evening. Mr James Rosier called & looked over Mr Cotman's beautiful Sketches in the evening. Mr Knight & 2 daughters called in the Morning & looked at the Drawings.

30th. Drew & traced (Colliers in a Calm) a subject for *Shipping*. Spent a very pleasant evening, Miss Bennett, Miss & Miss Jane Loddiges & Miss Gillham came, heard Music & danced &c, sung &c in the character of a Sailor.

31st. Etched in the morning, in the eveng. went with Aunt, Mama, Mr.Cotman, Tom & 6 sisters to Mr. Rosier's. Delightful evening. Dressed with John Rosier in the characters of a Sailor & Fisherman & frightened the little ones. Got home at 1 am.

1829

Thurs. Jan 1st. Etched my Plate &c. Mr Cotman went to Mr Loddiges' and sketched some of the Palms. Mr Boys dined with us, went to Covent Garden Theatre in the evng. with Father & Mr Cotman where we met Aunt Needham & Mrs Roberts Went in the Boxes, saw "Woman's Love or the Triumph of Patience" after which the New Pantomime, very well entertained....

2nd. After breakfast went with Mr Cotman to see the beautiful collection of drawings at Mr Windus's at Tottenham... Mr Cotman was delighted-lunched there & took Stage to the City, walked down to the New London Bridge, saw Mr Knight, went all over the works, all the arches cover'd, grand sight. Retd. to the Exchange & rode home...

3rd. Etched in the morng. Mr Lewin called. Bit the *Dutch Galliots* in the eveng. Reduced & traced the *Discovery* Captain Cook's ship. Mr Cotman made me a present of a capital Drawing Rule.

Mon. 5th. Etched *Discovery* &c. Mr Cotman brought us a large Cake.

6th Twelfth Day. Mr Cotman staid at home & drew on a lithographic stone. Father very poorly with Cold & Rheumatism all day.

9th ...Mr Thomas Lewin & Mr Barnard (of the [British] Institution) called. Recd a basket from John Hicks (Hanworth) with a Turkey & Hare. In evng. Father went to a meeting at Mr Doo's. Charles Cooke came.

10th. Mr Cotman went to sketch Crosby Hall. I went about an hour after. Sketched some bits & then went to the Thames Tunnel Office, Walbrook, saw Mr Birkett who accompanied us to the Tunnel (Grand sight) Returned up the river to St Catherine's Docks. Saw Mr Henley who shewed us all over the Warehouses, Vaults &c.- retd to Hackney about ½ p 4 pm. Dined & went with Father & Mr. Cotman to the Conversazione at Free-Masons Tavern - very full meeting. Saw Sir Thos. Lawrence, Mulready, Stanfield, Prout, Harding, Cox, &c &c &c. Rode back to Shoreditch Church & got home about ½ p 1.

Tues 13th Jan Father got up very unwell with bad head ache. Mr Cotman went to Mr Prout's. I went over to Lindsey's - Mama went to town- About 4 o'clock Messrs Cotman Prout Cox & Cox Jnr came, after which Stanfield & Robson, then Mr's Upcott & Burnett. Dined about ½ p 5... Thos. Boys came... Mr & Mrs Gillham came. All put our autographs in Mr Upcott's book. About 11 all the Artists left. Spent a very pleasant evening.

14th: Took plate of Dutchman [*Dutch Galliots*] over to Lindsey for the sky.

February 2nd: Mr Hay accompanied me to Blackwall to sketch an East Indiaman, it was a beautiful day but very cold, the river was grand, being high water, a great deal of ice floting [*sic*] down with the tide. Saw three fine East Indiamen, sketched the *Thames* (1330 tons) which was just going off. Walked home (by Canal) about 5, dined &c. After Tea Mr Boys and Mr West came, they had been to the British Gallery and were much pleased. Mr W. brought a beautiful little picture by Bonnington [*sic*] as a present to My Father who was (of course) delighted. Thos.Boys also promised him a drawing by the same artist. They went away early. I gave Mr West a quarto copy of *Shipping*.

4th: ...we received a basket from Mr Stark with 3 drawings for *London* and one ditto for his own work: viz. Kew Bridge- Paddington Church and Regent's Park for *London* and Yarmouth Bridge of which I etched the shipping. Kew Bridge and Yarmouth ditto were traced during the week. I made two small sepia drawings on Friday and Saturday. Finished all the Plates for No.9 *Shipping*.

March 14th: ...Lindsey came over and etched sky to *Fishing boat Arrived.*

May 28th: Got up early and went to town with Tom by first coach, went to Mr R.Rosier's at the Adelphi Terrace, took breakfast there. Went with him and Mr William to City, went down to see a ship the *Caroline* at St Catherine's Docks with Mr R. and Mr James, and after to Greenwich by boat - walked about the park and dined there (capitally) had Whitebait &c &c. Returned by boat in evening. Got back to Tower 'bout 8. Afterwards got on a Paddington coach & called on T.Boys and Cousin Bill, walked from there to Mr Roberts's in Percy St, he was out. I then walked back to Uncle Tom's, slept there (very tired).

31st: Had breakfast early and went to London Bridge with Mr R. and Wm. Rosier. Walked to St Catherine's Dock and boarded the *Caroline* which was working out into the River. About ½ p 9 off we went - band playing - down the Pool as we were towed all the way to Gravesend by the *Mountaineer* steam vessel. Had a most delightful voyage, a great number of vessels were on the River. On arriving at Gravesend I went in the Pilot's boat and Sketched the Vessel while at Anchor, and afterwards returned (with Friends) in the Steamer to the Tower...

April 16th: Raining all day. Etched plants &c and finished the East Indiaman. James Hennell called. In evening I went up (by Oxford St. coach) to Hawkins and got a proof of the East Indiaman, returned by the same coach. Got hair cut.&c.

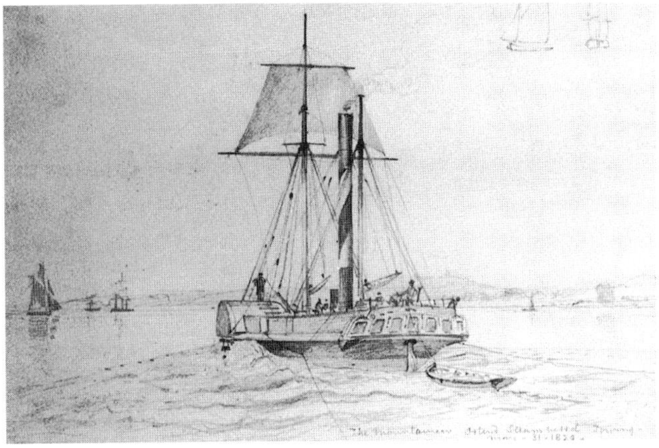

Plate 198. Pencil drawing
The Mountaineer Ostend Steam vessel Towing, May 31st 1829
The barque *Caroline,* with the artist as an excited passenger, was towed from St Catherine's Docks down to Gravesend by this elegant early steam paddle packet. Mention of a band playing on her departure may indicate a maiden voyage. Photo courtesy Clarges Gallery

17th Good Friday ...I finished the E.I.M. and it went to Print. At home by self in eveng. (Dull, very)

9th May: Got Aqua-tints laid by Hawkins... Lindsey came to help us. In evening I went to Hawkins's for proofs of Plants &c & walked from thence to Cousin William's and saw him & Thos. Boys also some clever drawings & pictures by the latter; agreed to go with him to the coast (Hastings) in about a fortnight.

12th June: Father very unwell with rheumatism... I began to Etch the shipping in Mr Stark's plate of *Yarmouth Bridge*. Father took a ride with Dr Palin in his gig being the first time of his going out since his arrival in Barnes. I went out with Mr Hay & had a bathe in the aftn. After tea I made a study of trees &c on the road to Chiswick. Dr Palin supped with us. We bit in the Aqua- tint grounds of plants.

13th Sat. I etched Mr Stark's plate. I made study of Weeds &c in the evng. Grandfather bought 2 pigs which were sent in the afternoon

15th Etched Stark all day... I took a walk in evening towards Chiswick and made a study of weeds. Met Mr Hay, took a row with him and he bathed. Had Shads for supper which Mr H bought on Sunday.

20th: Etched plants &c. In evening Tom came in a four oar'd cutter, accompanied by Mr Henley and Mr Taylor Woodhouse and young Thomson rowed up with them but did not come in... Tom and I rowed back with them as far as Hammersmith Bridge.

23rd: Got up at 4 o'clock and etched plants. I went to town by Hilliard at 10. Got out of boat at Hungerford and went to the Exhibition of the Royal Academy (a Very Grand one) dined near Temple Bar, went to Messenger's and then to Tom in the City. Made several purchases, ordered Trowsers &c, got ticket from Jennings's for an Exhibition of Turner's drawings at the Egyptian Hall but did not go then. Went from City to Hawkins's by Paddington coach, walked from there to Piccadilly and came home at 9 o'clock by Ayling. Father dined at the Star and Garter with the members of the National Gallery, it being their Anniversary. Had an invitation to dinner from Mr Wadmore of Paddington for Sunday. Father took a warm bath at the S & G.

30th: I went to town with Father by West, got down at Somerset House and saw the exhibition. Met Stanfield, Mr Marshall & Lambert, Mr and Mrs Geo.Loddiges there, after which we went to Sotheby's Sale Room where the Bonningtons were selling. Saw T.Boys &c there. Rained tremendously when we came out. Dined and saw the exhibition of Turner's Drawings at the Egyptian Hall and retd. home by West in the evening from Piccadilly...

July 4th: Stopped out plants and bit them all day. Carpenter finished job in the Study. Tom came by West. Saw a grand Boat race in afternoon, it passed our House...

7th. Mr Hay out of his time !!! I etched Plants, fixed up large table in Study storeroom in evening...

8th. Etched 5 Plants in the Morning. Mr Landseer Senr came before dinner and returned after tea. I went to town after dinner pr. Hammersmith. Got down at Piccadilly, bought oils, colours etc. Called at Moon and Co's, walked to Hawkins's for proofs of Plants...

Sunday 12th: Dreadful storm of Rain in morning. We had a letter from Uncle George in Peru... Uncle Kramer came over in his gig and took Father a ride round by Kew and Hammersmith and called at their house in evening. Mr Werner from Berlin called and brought a letter from Mr Kresar to Father. I walked with him as far as Hammersmith Bridge Rd.

13th: I went to Kew by a Passage boat and called on Mr Bauer and took a set of *Shipping* for a friend of his. Went over Kew Bridge and rode to town by a Brentford, called on Tom. saw Captain Burton who had just arrived fr. the West Indies. Dined at the Virginia Coffee House, called on J.Rosier at the Sun Fire Office. Took places in Brighton Coach (at the George & Blue Boar) for Father & Harriette to go on Weds. for their health. Saw Miss Linwood's Exhibition in Leicester Square. Called on Mr Werner & brought a box from Mr Kuger [?Kreser] for Father containing a beautiful bronze statue of Frederic King of Prussia

16th: ...after dinner I walked to Richmond, hired a boat and sketched the Stationers' Barge which was moored off Hill Ferry, then walked to Twickenham and sketched the Navigation and Fishmongers' Barges which were lying off Pope's Grotto. Saw some fine effects at Richmond in evening. Sunsets Glorious !!!!!!!! Walked home in evening and saw the Barges returning & pass our House.(about ½ p 9)

Fri. 24th Had a letter from Father, he wished me to do down to Brighton on Saturday, he was getting better. I went to Richmond to take my place, sent letter off to Father, packed up in evng.

August 13th. [Brighton] Sketched in morng on beach with Tom Shuckard, went to the Coach office (after a good lunch of mock Turtle) accompanied by Cousins Anne & Tom & Harriette to see me off at 12 o'clock, started by the Age Coach & arrived in Piccadilly (London) at ¼

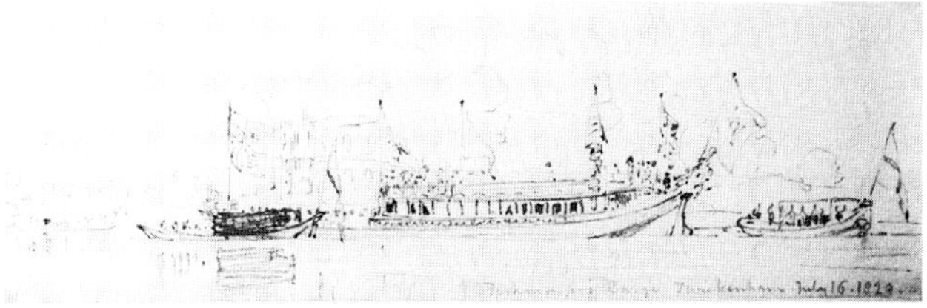

Plate 199. Pencil drawing
City Livery Company barge, the Fishmongers at Twickenham
A minute or so would have sufficed for this slight sketch off Pope's Grotto, but the floating banners of the great gilded ceremonial craft on a festive occasion are nicely shown. Photo courtesy Clarges Gallery

p 5 precicely [*sic*], very quick as we had 6 horses for 20 miles over the Hills - rained more or less the whole way. I had a most uncomfortable ride being stretched out on the Roof all the time as there were such fat (?Brunks) passengers...
17th Made design of Hog boats for *Shipping*. Lindsey came & dined here & went away by Steamboat - he was quite delighted with our "Shop". He brought some of his sketches to show us, as he had left engraving...
Sept 15th Re-bit Dutchman in morng., about 12 T.Boys came to make a sketch of something, dined with us after wh. I accompanied him for a stroll, walked by the river side towards Kew - when about ½ way a most Terrific Thunder & Hail Storm came on & as the tide was so Tremendously High & cover'd the Towing Path on each side the Bridge - where we were - that we had no shelter & got drenched completely - after waiting a long time we saw a boat & hail'd him which took us to Kew. I rowed all the way. At Kew we took some Brandy & water & biscuits which prevented any cold, we then walked home thro' the meadows - saw some most Prodigious effects. Tide unusually High. Mr Lambert & Geo., came just before we left & staid till we retd in evng. After tea T.Boys made a capital Drawing by Candle light - he slept with me in Grandpa's room, we had our Supper in Study.
17th: Up early. Father went to town with me by Akers' coach ¼ p 8 in Morning. Got down at Princes St, called on T.Boys in Greek St. I left Father there and went up to Hawkins's to get proofs of the Berlin Plate. Father went to Cousin Bill's. T.Boys came to me at Hawkins's and we went together by stage to City. Called on Tom (out) and at Bell's. Then to Tower stairs, got into a passage Boat and had a most delightful row to Greenwich. T.Boys sketched in the Park after which we took a boat and I made sketch of the Floating Dock, then returned to Greenwich, had some ale & took a walk over the Park and had tea near the Hospital and retd. by passage boat about dark...T.Boys and I called at Shirley's and looked over some fine Prints. He bought several, we parted in St John's St & he went home.
21st: I traced the *United Kingdom* on copper & etched on it in evng. Mr Roberts (of Percy St) & another gent. called in morng. Mr Kernot also called & brought Father a club & a Patapatoo... A barge was aground all day towards Chiswick. I made Camera sketch through telescope of it.
22nd I etched *United Kingdom* all day. Father worked on my plate of Yarmouth Herring boat... The barge still aground, not Tide enough to get her off, most likely to stay there some time.
23rd I etched during morng. We Packed up some Grapes for Dr. Palin. Grandfather went to Brighton (from St John Street) Mr Smith came about 1. Father & I went to town with Dr Palin in his Phaeton about 2. Went per way of Hammersmith, Shepherd bush to Paddington & the Regent's Park. I called on Hawkins & left Plates (of Dutch boat & Yarmouth boat) for proofs & then went to the Colosseum & met Dr P & Father there.Saw the Magnificent Panorama of London, a most Grand & Stupendous work - we were very much delighted. We also saw the Saloon where we had something to eat (I was very hungry, not having dined) & went out on the outside... The barge aground got off by the morning's tide.
24th: I finished etching the U.K. Father did the tints on it in evening and finished the 2 PLates, Yarmouth and Dutch boats.
29th: ...to the Tower Stairs & got into a Passage boat and Proceeded down the River as far as Limehouse, opposite which I landed and saw a vessel about to be launched at High water. Did not stop to see the Launch, walked a long distance at the Back of the River, made sketch of a Merchantman (aground) opposite the Commerciall Docks, from whence ferried over to Mill Wall , then took boat to Horse Ferry near Greenwich. Made 3 or 4 sketches of *Grampus* and retd. by passage boat to the tower after a very long and tedious row at about ½ p 7 (quite dark from Deptford)... (An Unlucky day, did hardly anything, supped with Mother &c). Before I left sent off Plate of U.K. to Prove, by Hollis [carrier].
November 8th. Sunday. Got up at 6 with Grandfather got breakfast over by 7 & set out for Chatham Dr Palin's chaise met us on the Terrace & took us to Tooley St (London). Went to the Custom House Stairs & went a'board the *Kent* Steamer, started at 9 & arrived at Gravesend at 12 after a pleasant voyage. Took refreshment at Gr[avesend] & proceeded by coach to Chatham thro' Rochester &c, went to the Sun Tavern. After dinner I took a boat & sketched a frigate in ordinary.
9th. Mon. Took a walk over the Lines &c till 7, went to the Globe, took some rum & water & hired the boat again. Proceeded down the Medway 4 or 5 miles as far as the *Hastings* 74, made sketches of it as also of Cutters &c Rowed part of way home. Made sketch of *Dolphin* hulk & returned, landed at 12... left... walked all through Chatham & Rochester over the Bridge & through Stroud [*sic*] [Strood] on the road to Gravesend. Took Refreshment at a house on the Gr.Road, got into coach... went on board the *Kent*... home at ¼ to 10 PM being very tired.

1830
Jan 1st New Year's Day. My Father (who went to town yesterday) returned about 2 to dinner, he brought home the 2 last No's of *Shipping* Plates for retouching, also Burnishers, scrapers &c, steel pens. I proceeded with the etching of Pool for *London* during day. Did not work after dinner. In evng. we played at chess, draughts & Pope with the Children. (Davis measured me for a suit of clothes). Mother called on Captn.Cleveland to invite him to dinner on Sunday. Father recd. letter from Mr Roberts.
March 31st Father watered the whole of the lawn before Bkfst. We worked on Plants &c. Miss Waring sent us some pretty plants for our Conservatory At work in evng. leveling the yard in the front Court... First rain (in evening) during the month, having been bright sunny weather all the time. We had a prime fire in the hothouse flue in the evening. Another Sub[scriber] for *Shipping* pr. Mr. Havell.
April 1st. Snowed during the night, rainy all day. We etched Plants &c. Father attended a Vestry meeting at Barnes in morning... we had strong fire in hothouse flue all day & one in Conservatory in evng...
2nd Went to Town by 9 coach. Left Cloak at Glover's, called on Wilson, Jas & Richd Rosier, Mr Brown & Tom. Bought Stilton cheese for Grandfather, Pigs' Chaps, oranges &c &c and returned home at 2 o'clock terribly wet, being outside [coach] all the way. Etched plants in eveng. - repotted the plants which Miss Waring sent us.
3rd Saturday. We bit-in 9 of the Plants, I traced & etched one. Glover sent basket of fish. 2nd No. of "Cities" came from Moon, Boys's per West. Tom came in eveng & brought drawings &c from Mr Loddiges. I pricked up the hothouse, the borders each side the path for planting &c &c &c.
4th Sunday Grandfather went to Church in morng. About 12 my Uncle Shuckard, George & Anne & Miss Cordwell came in Landau from Windsor where they had been spending a day or two, lunched, & dined at 4. All returned to London in Glass coach at 9. I went to Mr Breffitt's with Cousins to see his grapes.
5th Mr Cowles sent us several very fine plants which we placed in the Conservatory. Father went to Town at 2 o'clock & dined with Mr Bovinet. I cleaned & dusted out the study & storeroom... Mr Lowry called in morng.
6th: Father returned home at ½ p 8 to breakfast, he brought me some capital (oil) painting brushes as a present form Thos. Boys. We etched & finished plants during day. A new music master came in evng in lieu of Mr Knowles, he being too unwell to attend. Bought some river fish just caught & we had them for supper. Grandfather at work recovering chairs... Glorious fine day.
7th. Finished plants during day, went to Town by 7 coach in evng. Took the Duke of Clarence's Copy of *Shipping* with me- got down at Fleet St., and went to the Sussex Hotel to see my Uncle Shuckard, waited there ½ an hour - bought oil colours &c at Curtiss' & went to Uncle Thos. Eglinton's & slept there.
8th Left Uncle's at 8 (took the No.'s of *Shipping* for Subs[cribers] at the Mint) & breakfasted with Uncle & Cousins at the Sussex. George Shuckard accompanied me to the Royal Mint where I left the No.'s, and went with him to the St. Catherine's Docks, met Henley - (made sketch of a Dutch galliott) who took us about the Vaults, Ships &c after which he accompanied us per Boat to Greenwich. Glorious Vessels, Craft &c upon the River, saw the *United*, took "Snack" at Greenwich returned to tower per passage boat. I called again at the Mint & then returned with George to the Sussex to Dinner. Mr Notz, Mr Taunton, Coz. Wm

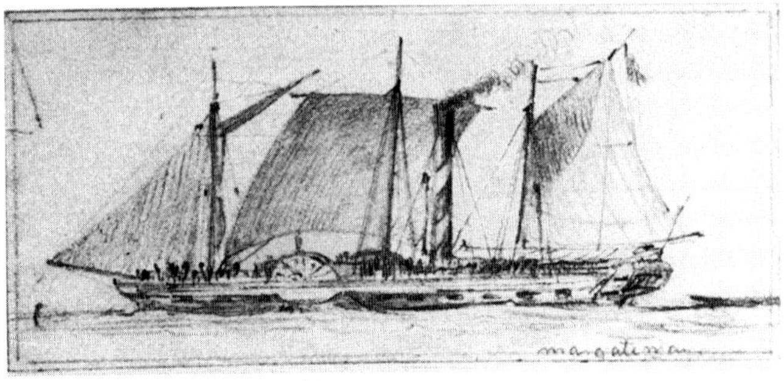

Plate 200. Pencil drawing

Margateman

The touch of humour in naming this small steamer as in 'merchantman' or 'Indiaman' seems typical Cooke, though it may have been in common use on the river. Photo courtesy Clarges Gallery

Shuckard, & Uncle William were there... A new gardener came to work, sent by Mr Cowles (clever fellow).

10th Sat. Went to Mr Gibson's in morng & got my drawing stick - prepared every thing to go to Hastings, went to town with Father after dinner missed the Coach so walked to Ham[mersmi]th. Richard carried the Portmanteaux Bag &c. Got to town per. Speed, first took place in the Hastings coach at the Cross, Charing + Bought new sketch book at Hull & Smarts also a new hat at Pitt's. Father went up to Uncle Wm's I went up to Col.Batty's, took tea & walked with him as far as Soho Sq. called on Thos. Boys went to the Conversazione. Met Col.B. there & also Coz Wm Shuckard & Notz & Dick Rosier. Grand evening, being the last after wh. went with Father to Uncle Tom's, supped & slept there.

11th Sunday Got up & started at ½ p 6 to the coach office Charing + took breakfast with Father there & boarded the Hastings Coach at 8. & continued our way through Bromley, 7 Oaks, Tonbridge & Battle & arrived at the Hare & Hounds (Fairlight) at 5. Dr.Batty's servant met me with the gig & drove to to his house. Din'd, tea'd &c & went to bed at 10. The country was most beautiful but the journey uncomfortable it having rain'd almost all the way.

12th Got out of bed at 6 & discovered it was a dreadfully wet morng. so slept till 8. After Bkfst Dr B. drove me to Winchelsea & Rye where I made several sketches - dined (at 3 o'clock) at the Cinque Port Arms & started for home at ½ p 4 had a delightful ride back arrived at 7 took tea & touched up sketches in eveng. Retired to Nidus at 10. Very pleasant day, delightful country.

13th Rose at ¼ to 7. Fine morng took walk to Gover's Glen (Glorious Spot!) made sketch, returned to bkfst. after which Dr Batty walked part of way with me to Mr Planta's, where he called. I proceeded to Hastings, felt very unwell. Delightful entrance to the town. Beach fine & bustling. Cliffs grand beyond description. I made a sketch or 2, had a bad head

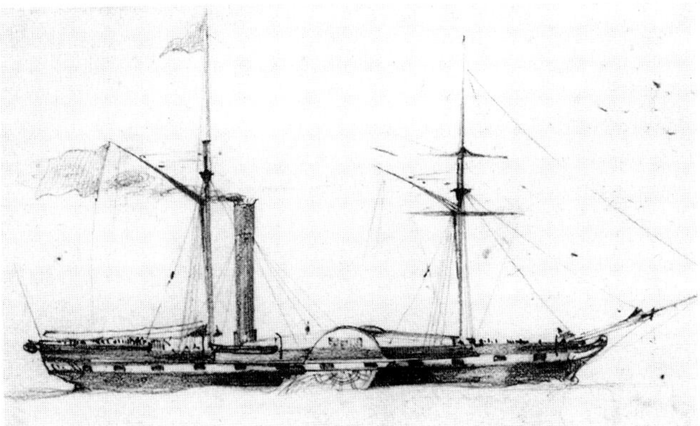

Plate 201. Pencil drawing

Paddle steamer

One imagines the artist must have been afloat and on a parallel course with this lovely vessel to have been able to jot down so much so correctly, adept though he clearly was. The 'frigate' hull with its steam appurtenances and schooner rig is a charming reminder of the 1830s, perhaps running down the Thames. Photo courtesy Clarges Gallery

ache all day. Dr B came down to & shewed me about the Place, called here & there, saw the baths, took lunch at Mrs Bland's. Wrote long letter to Father in Mr Breed's office. Dr B's gig met us at 4 & we drove back to Fairlight, din'd, tea'd & retired to bed at 10. Head much better after tea.

14th After breakfast set out for Hastings. Dr. B's man carried my drawing apparatus, went pr. way of Ecclesbourne gap, beautiful spot. First made sk.of Hastings from the east Rocks (it being low water) & made 2 or 3 other sketches on beach - walked up to Fairlight at 4. Mr & Mrs Savory & Mr Day dined with us & returned to Hastings after tea.

15th Dense mist with rain, got up at 7. After Bk. went to Hastings made 3 sketchcs, saw sloops go off also several fishing boats - drisling rain all day. Retd. to Fairlight at 8, Dr. Batty was out dining at Mr North's...

16th Mr Thorpe took Bkfst with us & accompanied me down to Hastings & remained sketching with me...

17th Saturday Took Bkfst by self (Dr B came home during morng.) We stayed in doors all day & made Col[oure]d drawings (rainy day) At 6 in evng we went in gig to Mr Planta's to dinner. Met Mr Oom there, spent a pleasant evng., returned at ½ p 10. Mr.P subscribed to *Shipping*

18th Sunday... drew &c till 5. Went with Mr Batty to Lover's seat (exquisite spot) & then to Mr Planta's & dined with Mr Oom (Mr P's secretary) (Mr Planta left his house this morng. for Brighton). After dinner Roper the celebrated ex-smuggler came in & smoked Segars with Mr Oom & told us some interesting stories of his life - had a pleasant evening.

19th ...Mr Thorpe came after bkfst & accompanied me down to the beach & returned with me after sketching to Fairlight & dined with us. 3 sloops on beach, sketched 1 - all boats out but 2. Beautiful clear eveng. distinctly saw pr. Telescope, Shakespeare's Cliff,Dover, Hythe, Folkestone &c &c & a vast no. of vessels on the sea - went to bed at 10.

20th Terribly wet morng. went at ½ p 1 pr. Gig with Dr Batty to Hastings. he called & left my India copy of *Shipping* at Mr North's and then went on to Mrs Bland's where we dined, after which went out & made 2 or 3 sketches, retd. there to tea... Wind very high, blew a gale, sea very rough, no boats out...

21st Rainy & foggy morning, went down to Hastings after Bkfst. made 4 or 5 sketches. John Thorpe came down & sketched with me. I fell down & cut my hand - had it strapped at Chemist's. At 4 took a warm bath at Pelham's., met Dr Batty there & we went together to the Rev. Mr Borrowdaile's to dinner (pr invitation). Gig came for us at 8, dreadful wet eveng. Packed up sketches on return. Dr Batty obtained another subscriber to "Shipping" viz. Mrs Benson. He paid me for her & Mr North.

22nd Rose early, got ready & packed up all my things, had bkfst at 7, took farewell of Dr Batty, his servant drove me down to Hastings, got on board the Brighton coach & started at 9 - had a most disagreeable ride through Pevensey, Eastbourne, over Beachy Head, Seaford (near here one of the horses drop't down dead) Newhaven & Rottingdean & arrived at Brighton at 3. rained the whole way- found all pretty well at the Old Ship. Took soup, Chops &c for dinner. In evng. wrote letter to Father, had some capital fun. Went to bed at 11 in No 13.

23rd ...got fine in aftn. went out & got 3 or 4 sketches. Bought a pair of fisherman's boots off a boy on beach. Lieut Williams came in evng staid to supper. Cordwell dined with us. Prime fun.

27th Tues. After breakfast went out with Tom on beach & made sketches. Called on Mr Willm Scott he paid his bill (of *Shipping*) & also Chas Scott & shewed him my sketches...

September 16th Tom came down & helped with luggage to St Katherine's Wharf, got on board the *Columbine* steamer started at 10 & had a delightful passage to Margate, arrived at 5pm & went to the King's head Hotel.

17th Very wet mng. till 2 oclk. Made sketches from the balcony of Hotel all mg: after dinner got finer & went out & sketched Pier &c. Met cousin Emma Cooke. Retd to Inn & wrote to Father - took walk in evng.

18th. Up at 7, beautiful mng.: sketched view of Town & retd. to In to Bkfst after wh: sketched again. - hired a fly, left Margate at 11 went to Kingsgate rained nearly all day...walked over to Broadstairs, man carried luggage, got there at dark, took tea & slept at the Tartar Frigate Inn.

19th Sunday ...made sk. of Town & Harbour before Bkfst after wh: drew 2 others of Pier ...to Ramsgate, had tea & slept at the Royal Oak Hotel, took walk on Pier in evng. Blew gale of wind.

20th. Beautiful day made sketch before breakfast after wh: went out again & sketched till 6 in evng. (a long spell) after tea took walk on cliffs.

21st Went out on Pier Head after Bkfst. tremendous wind & rain all the morng. (great storm at sea in the night) Saw Brigs, sloops, schooners &c

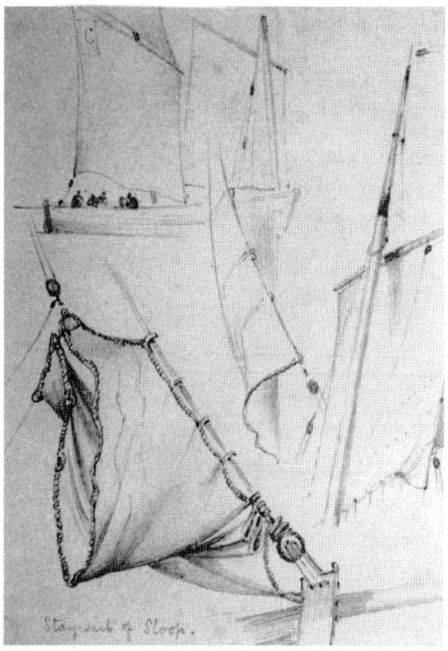

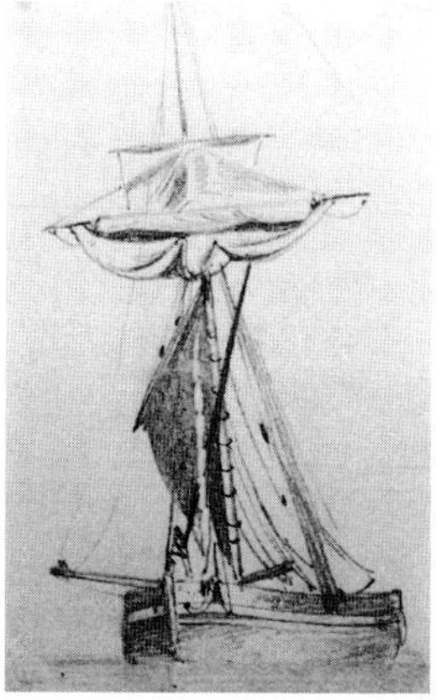

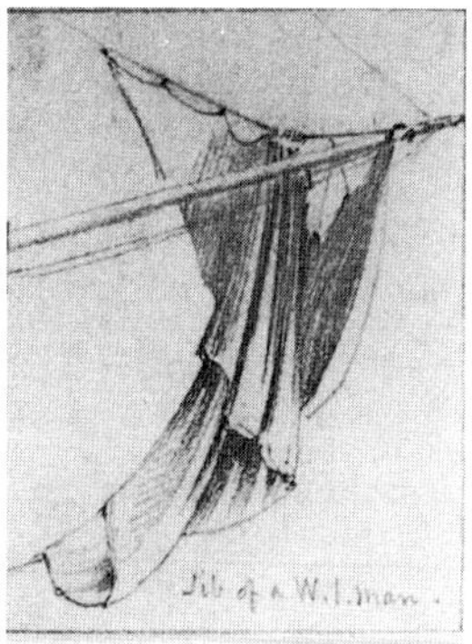

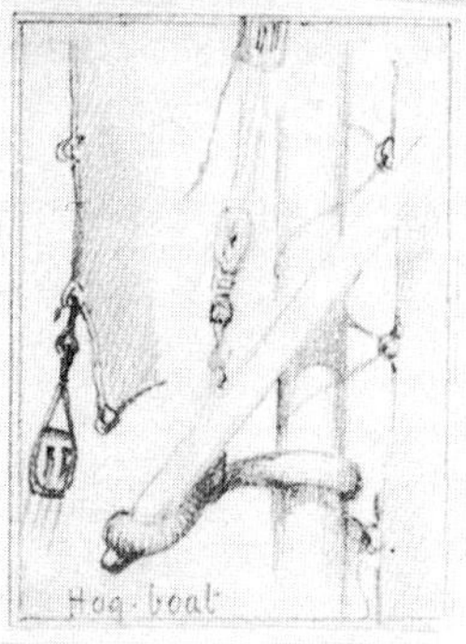

Plate 202. Pencil drawings
Studies in drapery
Three widely differing bits from his sketchbooks, as mounted for future reference. The staysail of the sloop, triced up, is backed by a handsome lugger, possibly a French *chasse marée.* The West Indiaman trading sugar from Jamaica was a big ship and the little Brighton fisherman, the hog boat, reveals the peculiarities of her rig.
Photo courtesy Clarges Gallery

come into the Harbo. most of them damaged more or less. Sea very rough. After dinner went out & sketched...
22nd. ...sketched 2 or 3 views of Sandwich- went to Deal in evng. had tea & slept at the 3Kings Hotel opposite the sea. Took walk on beach by dark. Glorious fine day.
23rd Very wet squally day. Collier stranded on the beach (fine) made sketch of it.
24th Went out after B.to Walmer Castle & Kingsdown & Old Stairs Rained heavily most part of the Time, very rough wind. Made 4 or 5 sketches...

1831
June Sunday 26th. Very stormy rainy day. Mr Cotman, Edmund & John came (à la nautical) per. boat to dinner. Mr Geo. & Edgar Breffitt dined with us.
27th ...went to London Bridge & made skch. ...got ready *Shipping* for Portsmouth, walked to St Paul's & retd home by last coach at ½ p 10. Unlucky day lost gloves, handkerchief &c.
29th. Went at 7 to Putney, Wm. carried bag, rode by the Reform Coach to Portsmouth. Fine weather to Portsdown Hill where it rained heavily - got in at ½ p 4 had tea at the Still. Called on Frank Waring at South Sea- had a capital cruize out to Spithead in his boat wh: he built - took tea with him & he walked home with me to the Still at 10.
30th. After Bk. called on Publishers &c & went to Royal Dock Yard, saw Gaze, went over the *Victory*. Called on F.Waring (& wrote a letter to Father at the Custom House). Went home with him & dined there. Had a cruize round the fleet. Retd. to tea with F.W.
July 1st. After Bk. went over to Block House Fort & made sketches, called on Hinton who paid £5.8.2 as per.Bill. I left him *Victory* proofs. Dined at Still. Met F.W. at the baths & had a cruize with him to Spithead & retd to tea at the Still at 9. Met him at the Assembly Rooms heard music, won a bottle of Eau de Cologne at a raffle. Glorious fine day.
8th ...met Dr Palin & dined with him & Mrs Palin at the Quebec Hotel. Went with them per steamboat to Ryde at 2 oclk.& left them there. I took donkey chaise to Brading, made sk. of Harbour. walked over to Shanklin in evg. (a boy carried luggage) "most glorious place!!" made sk. had tea at the Chine Inn & slept there.
9th. ...made sk. all about the Chine, had dinner at the Inn - bathed in morng. walked along the beach to Luccombe Chine (1 mile) & made sks. Retd. to Shanklin, got Fisherman to carry luggage & we walked along the beach to Bonchurch (lovely place) & on to Ventnor. Had tea at the Crab & Lobster & went down to the Cove & skd. & retd & slept at the Crab.
14th [Southampton] Went to Mr Shayer to Bk. at 8. He walked with me to Mr Ogle's at Millbrook, saw him, his pictures, his Steam Carriage.!!! returned & dined at Mr Shayer's. He took me over the Hants Picture Gallery. Made sks. in boat of South'ton. Met Dr Palin at the Sun. who had been to Netley. Called on Buchan & Fletcher (who paid!!) Mr Shayer sent me a basket of Prawns to bring home...
October 3rd. Etched London Bridge. Mr J.Allen (engraver) came in aftn. & brt. some proofs for father, he returned after tea...
6th Made tracing of "View between the 2 London Bridges" during day. Father went to town pr. stage at 2 oclck. to Hackney where he slept, to arrange as to the completion of the *Botanical Cabinet*.
8th: Finished tracing of London Bridge. Made coloured little drawing of Sunrise &c. Father worked on London Bridge... My eye very bad. Reform Bill thrown out by the Lords !!!... Tom came in evng & brt. a set of drawings from Mr Loddiges: shocking wet day & stormy. Mr Cowles sent us a pig as a present.
13th: Began reducing Copley Fielding's drawing of Southampton John Cowles at work on the new garden...
18th. I reduced Southampton & traced plants. Made daubs of sunsets in eveng. Father finished set of plants. Mr Topham (Brewer) called in morng.... I wrote to Joe Lowry...
19th. Went to Town per West, called on Mr Barnard B[ritish] I[nstitution] saw Capt. Burton there painting. Took cab to Hawkins's left Plates &c there, called on Stanfield, Doo (dined there) & Coz. Bill. Went to Zoological Gardens, much pleased...
November 23rd. Finished the 10 plant plates. I went to Town pr. Hammersmith, left Album at Leggatt's, called on Tom & Jas Rosier, rode to Hackney, called on Mr Loddiges, saw Mr George, (Mr W. out), left plates. Called on Archer, left watch to be repaired, went to Mr Rosier's at ½ p 4 Dined there, saw Mr & Mrs R. Misses Anne, Elizabeth & Charlotte & Mr Jas. In evng. I made 2 portraits of Mr Jas Rosier while he played the violoncello. We had some delightful singing & music. Slept there after a very pleasant evening.
24th. rode to town with Mr Rosier & Jas. Made portrait of Mr Bob Hearne at W.Rosier's office - called on Mr Burton & Leggatt. Went with Bob Hearne to the W[est]I[ndia] Docks pr. Coach & on board the *Thetis*,

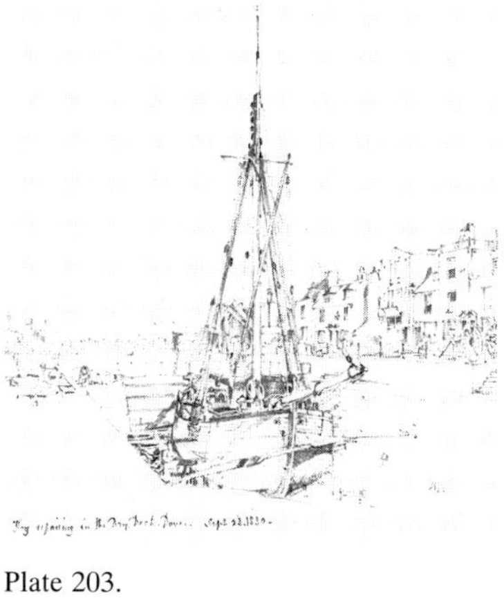

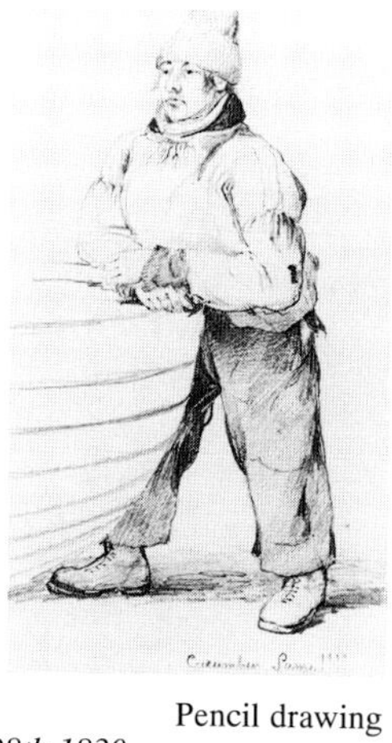

Plate 203. Pencil drawing
Hoy repairing in the Dry Dock Dover Sept 28th 1830
This drawing is a delight in its completeness and, though faint, is a direct and unlaboured statement. Photo courtesy C.R. Cooke, OBE

Plate 204. Pencil drawing
Cucumber Sam!!!!
The careful artist forgot to mention this character, boatman or fisherman, in his daily entries – perhaps a cool customer!
Photo courtesy Martyn Gregory

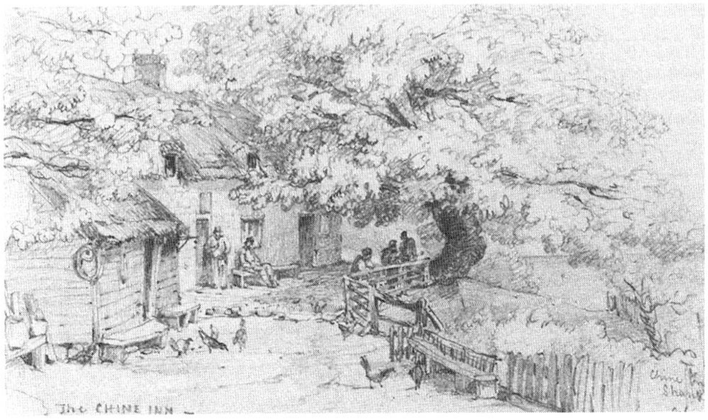

Plate 205. Pencil drawing
The Chine Inn, Shanklin, Isle of Wight
In 1831, on his first visit, he proclaimed *most glorious place* and made sketches on the shore etc. This drawing, dated Oct. 9, must be from his later visit in 1856 on a painting tour.
Photo courtesy Martyn Gregory. Private Collection

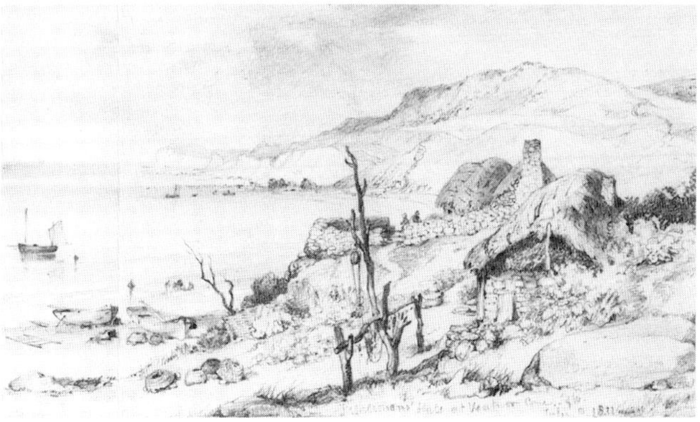

Plate 206. Pencil drawing
Fishermen's huts at Ventnor Cove, Isle of Wight 1831
His first stay on the east side of the island provided so many paintable scenes and so many instances of the colourful but hard life of the fishermen that Cooke was, to coin a phrase 'hooked'. The 'gallows tree' in the forefront, with the means of raising nets to dry, is a kind of archaeological comment and the wicker lobster pots he was soon to learn to make under the guidance of one of the fishermen. The coast was, moreover, a geological curiosity. Photo courtesy Martyn Gregory. Private Collection

dined on board, (Capt Burton did not come down), made sketch or two went to Blackwall…

25th Started after Bk per 1st coach to Town went down to Tooley St aboard a schooner lying at the first wharf from the Bridge & made a sketch of the Old Bridge (the 2 first Arches) introducing part of the delapidations which only commenced this week. Finished it at 3… on our return we found that Grandfather had returned from Norfolk, looking very well…

December 10th John Cowles brought down more plants from Harley & we planted them. H came himself & brt. some peonia roots. Father went to town with me pr. Coach at ½ p 11, went to Brown's, left Argand lamp for him (he out) went to Leggatts' left 6 Drawings in colour on cards, for sale. Bought there Stanfield's *Annual* for Lindsey Aspland and sent it to Hackney by Mr Ford. We then went to London Bridge and over the Old one (which is being pulled down fast)… walked to Dr Batty's Russell Square and left him proof of Frontispiece *Shipping*, bought Ale cock at Pontifex's… called at Hawkins's for parcel containing a netted boa from Cousin Mary Cooke as a present for Mother… Hilliard fetched a basket from Tom's office containing 9 bottles of Rum Shrub, also he brought Grandfather's Duffle coat… Gibson sent home 6 frames for my Diorama also a new Drawing stick for Camera. New coat for me and suit for Father sent from Davis.

28th: I went to Hawkins's, left parcel to be sent to Coz Bill's of 2 sets of Plant Plates & called on Aunt Kramer while Hawkins took off 4 etchings of Father's plate of Southampton. Took soup at the Cock and tea at Brown's. Called on Tilt, brt 2 Ind[ia] Copies of the Water Colour work from him and left 1 at Mr R.Rosier's Adelphi… bought different papers at Creswick's & retd. home pr. Stage at ½ p, 8.

31st. Old Year's Day. Mr Carmichael & Mrs Baker his sister came over in Study & we shewed them various things. I bottled off Ale &c in morng. Father graving on Southampton: sharp Frost all day. Tom came abt 5, had a pleasant evng. singing &c, staid up till 2 o'clk. I began a little drawing on a card (- sea view-) A parcel came from Mr Hollis containing a fine set of Barry's etchings, and a set, 30 in number, of Coignet's studies of trees &c.

1832

January 14th: Finishing Arch of London Bridge …to town, took tea at Mrs Drew's… Went to the Conversazione at the Freemasons Tavern. Met a great many distinguished artists, fine Turner's drawings…

19th Finished plants during day. Laid three large grounds in morng. Coz Bill came at 11 and brought his plate of Calais & Father worked on it all day, he dined here. Mr Geo. Breffitt came and pruned our vines in Vinery & Conservatory & dined here. In evng completed pencil outline of Lond. Bridge subject.

20th Finished Plants. Made tracing of L.B.subject viz. Steps, St Magnus &c… Mr Hollis came in evng & looked over Lysons, took notes & return to town after tea by stage. Father at work on Bill's plate. Hollis took it to town in evng.

23rd I went to Town -walked to Putney, rowed in skuller to London Bridge & sketched the Old Bridge all day: dined near the Monument, called on Brown & took tea there.

27th Horribly snowy rainy morng - cleared up at noon . Went to City in coach with R & W Rosier & sketched at Old London Bridge till 5. Dined at the Commercial, took tea at Brown's, went to the City Theatre with him at 9 & saw the *Beggars' Opera*, went to Uncle Tom's slept there.

February 2nd …called on Mr H. Bennett who paid his bill by cheque which I recd. Dined off pie &c at Wm Rosier's. Went to 5 Adelphi Terrace to meet Father who did not come, so went by self to Drury Lane Theatre, saw *The Rent Day; Turning the Tables & The Pantomime*, with Stanfield's Diorama of Venice - much pleased…

9th. Worked on London Bridge plate in morng. Mother cleaned all the pictures & frames in drawing room… I went to Uncle Tom's, met Tom there, dressed & went up to Coz. Bill's at 9.Met a large party of Ladies & Gentlemen, 60 in all: danced till 1, sumptuous supper. Danced Quadrilles &c till after ½ p 4 when we left & walked to Uncle's (after a very delightful evening - very tired). Father slept at Mr Doo's, sisters slept at Cousin's. Met there the families of the Griffith's, Boys', Graves', Clints', Cumberlands', Rutters' Messrs Goodear, Engleheart, T.Raimbach, Kernott, Sad, Bradshaw, Evans, West, Conrad Cooke & wife, Aunt J.Cooke & 3 cousins.

10th Friday. Up at 10, walked to City, called on W.Rosier for 2 hours looking at Casts, moulds &c, dined at Brown's, walked to B[ritish] Institution, saw Barnard & the Exhibition. Glorious pictures- saw there Sir R.Peel. Earl Grey, Lords Sefton & Wharncliffe, Duke of Norfolk, Mr Watts, D.Roberts & Mr Mrs & Miss Rutter. Met Stark at Piccadilly, he rode with me to Chelsea…

June 5th Mr Cowles called. I trac'd Lond. Br. subject " pile drawing". Father etched L.B. & gave drawing lesson in aft. Mr Stark came & brought a picture to engrave for his work, he left after tea by stage. Nasty dull day. I fixed weights on ropes in Conservatory in… Reform Bill Passed!!!!!!!!!!

15th We etched Lond.Br. & plant plates. Mr Burnett came in morng & fetched Miss B. away [from School]. Mr W.Havell & his brother came in morng. & left after dinner to hunt for a house at Richmond. Mrs Turner fetched Miss T. in evng. Miss Weiss left, also Miss Payne. Rainy day, fine effects, Rainbow &c.

Sept. 11th Mr Raimbach & his daughters came per Steamboat to dinner after which Father & I accompanied them & Harrie & Clarie to Richmond… I took sisters for a row & walked home at 7. Mr Smith (Uncle) came to dinner & slept here. Mr J.B.Allen came in evmg & brt. a Drawing by Turner for me to etch shipping of. He took 4 numbers of my work for Birmingham.

13th. …Mr Roberts came in evng & touched on my proofs of Lond. Br., he left at 8 by stage. Mr Harris brt. critique of *London Bridge* from *Bell's Weekly Messenger* very good!!

15th Saturday. We worked all day on Lond. Br. plates, re-bit them & laid 4 grounds. Mr Wyld called in morng an artist from Paris & a friend of Thos Boys who sent a letter by him…

19th. Very busy all day finishing Lond. Br. plates for Part 2. Mr Wyld came to Dinner at 2 & brt. a folio of drawings sketches &c... Mr Wyld left at 10 I walked part of way with him.

22nd ...Tom attacked with Chicken Pock & confined to his bed. I traced off Christ's Hospital plate also made reducing of Turner's Upnor Castle for Mr Allen's plate as his tracing was damaged... in evng according to ye Prescription of Mr Hutchison I was inflicted for an hour with a mustard poltice round my throat - endured the greatest agony!!! till asleep.

23rd. Sunday Throat very bad all day from effects of the mustard, Mr Kernott came to dinner & brought 3 beautiful carved clubs which came from the South Sea Islands, he left after tea... most glorious fine day splendid sun set!!! River very full of boats, tide Sunday.

27th. Up early, finished 7 plants. I went to Town by Akers, called on Wm, Wyld (Boro') gave him Coast Sketches. also on Brown, Arch, Mr Ford (out)... Dined at Wm Wyld's with his Uncle &c & left at 7. W.W. walked to Brown's with me, home by last stage at 10. During my absence Mr T.Lewin & Mr Roberts called.

28th Etched vessels in J.B.Allen's plate also continued copy of the [Turner] Drawing... I wrote to T.Boys per W.Wyld. Made moonlight drawgs. in evng with smoked paper.

October 1st Monday. Sent off remaining plant plates for Mr Loddiges to Brown, by Hilliard. Made copy of Turner's drawg. all day, in evng pasted paper on the back of the great canvas for Roberts to paint on. Father all day arranging & sorting mildew'd prints of *Shipping*.

December 24th Christmas Eve, finished plant aquatints. Lindsey Aspland came down in morng to dinner & left at 5. I gave him India copy of Lond. Br. work. Mr Stark sent us a Turkey & sausages from Norfolk. Tom came down in evng. Had music &c. Edgar Breffitt brt. in Ale...

1833

July 1st. Made drawing of "Temeraire off Sheerness" during day - Mr Jas Brown & wife of Brighton & Fred. Mahomed called & lunched here. ...Mr Geo.Loddiges & Conrad came in aftn. & left after tea pr. Fulham. I gave Con the Steamboat... we sent off parcels of prints to Christie's for Sale. Fine day

2nd. Finished drawg. & framed it. Began drawg. of plant, Laura went to a fancy fair (with Mrs Cross) at Putney. I went to town in aft. - left my drawing at Boys' for exhibiting at the Conversazione - called on Cox at Kennington - fetched drawings, he gave me one for my Work of L[ondon] B[ridge] - called on Brown, met Father there - arranged prints (from Mr Loddiges) for sale... I called and supped at Salmons, saw Harrie[tte] there. Hungerford market open'd balloon ascended great crowds. I took tea at Mr Arthur Arch's at Kennington.

3rd ...I went to town by bus called Hixon. R.R[osier] & I went to Moon Boys' met 150 first rate artists & Noblemen -Turner &c - splendid evening. Father came at 10 & walked home at 1. I slept at R.R.'s Adelphi (New Coat!).

4th. After Bk. went over Hungerford market - Watercolor Ex[hibition]., called for drawings at Boys'-home at 1 by Coach. Messrs Callow & W.J.Cooke came to Dinner at 4. Thos.Wyld [younger brother of William] drove down in aft. & slept here...

5th. Thos Wyld left at 9 & drove Grandfather to town in his gig-I began drawing of Hay barge and finished it in evening. Mr Stark and A.Priest called in evg: on their return in boat from Twickenham. I rowed them as far as Chiswick - beautiful evening: City barges came by...

7th. Sun ...Mr Austen & Mrs Curran drove down in aftn. & Mr A subscribed to L[ondon] B[ridge] - order'd 2 drawgs... Mr Watts sent a Melon.

8th. rainy day Mr Aggutter called & paid for L.B. I made drawg. of barges at anchor all day. Wrote letter to T.Boys in evng.

9th. Went by first coach to town left things at Salmon's. called on R[ichard].R[osier].(Adelphi) rode to City with him, took 3 drawgs with me shew'd them to Bidden Brown &c R.R took them to Mr Harman [Jeremiah Harman lived at Woodford where Cooke visited and saw both his picture collection and admired his grounds] to see. I called on Gillham, Tom, &c, cab to Mr Austen's Guildford St, shewed me his pictures & very kind [Benjamin Austen, solicitor, uncle of Austen Henry Layard]. Took 3 drawgs and a copy of L.B. paid me 18 guineas- went to City (bankers)... called on Carpenter and Callow, Christie - had tea at Salmon's took bus to Stark - on the water. I took boat and rowed to Putney in search of him & back at ½ p 9, home by stage at ½ p 10.

10th. Began drawg. of Hastings fish market. Uncle Shuckard & William & Aunt Kramer came in a carriage & dined here. Father went to town with them at 5.

11th. Penned in the figures of Hastings & commenced colouring, Father went to town by West & took 2 drawgs to R.R[osier]... Mr Stark came at 6 to tea with Mr Payne & Priest - left at 9...

12th Grandfather went to town by bus to Father's sale which took place at Christie's. I went on with Hastings all day - muddled it !! at 8 walked with Father to Richmond & saw the splendid fireworks opposite the Duke of Buccleugh's, Grand fete - The King there, grand sight.

13th Father & Mother went to town by bus. M went to Mr Stanfield's... I went on with drawg. of Hastings all day.

14th ...rode to Hackney to Mr Aspland's Chapel... dined at Mr Geo. Loddiges with all the family... (The Gillhams Mr.G.Loddiges & Jane all going to Italy on Wednesday - I bid them good-bye).

15th ...I began a copy of Hastings fishmarket. Had letter from Mr Cotman.

16th ...I went on with my drawg. of Hastings... City barges came up.

17th Made studies of fish in morng. Made drawg. of Convict ship & another. Glorious day. The Stationers' barge came up...

22nd. I went on with Hastings fish market & Dutch fishing boats during day.

24th Up at ½ p 5 with R[obert]Smith, he went fishing (& I sketching) & caught a fine perch &c. I made a drawg. of it in morning. Mr Stanfield brought back his daughter to school. Mrs S. & Henry came also, they dined & left at 6. E.Breffitt sent a fine Salmon as a present. Mr Windus called in morng. Had a row with Robert in evng. up the creek.

August 3rd. Mr Cromek came in morng. & brought his sketches at Rome & Italy, most splendid works of art, he dined here & left after tea. F[ather] gave him a set of *London* & I gave him proofs of *London Bridge*. Miss Leishman, an M.P. & a young Gent called in evng. Mr Britton drove his wife down in evng.& had tea here, much pleased with our house...

5th I made drawg., copy of Turner's *Hythe* Mr Graves (colorer) & lady came to dinner... fine day, party came up swan hopping, I sketched them.

6th Went to Mr Loddiges at 9 & made the 2 last drawings for the *Botanical Cabinet* (making 2000 [plates) Dined & took tea with Mr. W.Loddiges...

8th. Father went to town to Brown's by bus, I sent plate to proove by Hilliard, finished copy of Hythe all day, made studies of baskets in evening. Mr Bonnington came to tea & took back my Father's picture by his son, for exhibiting.

14th Etched plants in morng. Tom left at 8. Aunt left by Mr Whiskin's chaise. Mother went to Mrs Bray's with her & took little Mary. Father & I walked to Stark's, he called here during our absence & back to see us - he is off to Hampshire tomorrow

15th Went by bus to town, called at Moon, Boys's - left proofs at Rennie's - called on Mr Sparrow - & Mr Carpenter, who shewed me splendid drawings. Went to City, called on Mr Burton & Tom, dined at Nash's, called on Salmon Botolff Lane & Mrs Hollis in Walworth -called for proofs at Sparrows - and Mrs Salmon's, home by bus, bought colors, palettes &c at Newman's. Had sore throat in evening.

19th ...in eveng. traced figures from the work of Canova...

20th Finish'd drawing of sunset "Bugsby's reach"... I made several effects in eveng. in color - began drawg. of our conservatory in morng. & it took me all day to draw the outline in, very difficult. Edgar Breffitt came in to see me in aftn. - better. Poor Mr Keall called & I relieved his distress. Fine day.

24th Sat. Walked to Pall Mall, saw the Exn. of the 3 Presidents' Pictures. Called on Boys & Colnaghi, Mr C. bought 3 drawings of me, called on Tom, dined at Nash's. Retd home from Hungerford (where I bought a fine salmon) with Tom in the Putney steam boat at 8. - made up my mind to go to Havre, this evg.

Sunday 25th. Went to Coz.Bill at 11 & dined there, called on Mr Bonnington and saw the fine Exhn. of his son's drawings &c- home at 7
26th Went to town by 1st coach called at Colnaghi (Mr C, senior died this morning). Mr D.Colnaghi gave me a letter to Mr Utterson at Ryde. Went to the Passport office... bought sketch-bk & colors at Newman's, called on Mr Taunton - bought trousers - Umbrella & called on Mr Wild, Mr Clarke & Brown, walked to Mr Boys who gave me two letters to gentlemen in Ryde and Havre - called on Mr Bonnington - went to Uncle Tom's to fetch Tom's portmanteau and cloak - returned by coach from St Paul's at ½ p 6 - called at Mr Salmon's he gave me a letter to gentn. at Havre. F[ather] & Laura were there - they came up to see Bonnington's drawings and the British Museum.

27th. Packed up and left Barnes at 11 by stage... called on Mr Clarke who gave me letters to Havre - on Arch (who gave me a commission for 6 drawings in Normandy). Father went to Mr Windus in mg. - at 8 in evg. started from the Belle Sauvage by the Rocket night coach to Portsmouth. F. rode with me to Putney on his way home. Had a pleasant journey, fine night, arrived at Portsmouth at 6 o'clk.

28th. Took warm bath first thing - took bkfst at the Quebec Hotel - called on F.Waring at the Custom House. Made sketch or two - went by Steamer

to Ryde called at W.Rosier's ...sketched about Ryde till 5... Dined with [Rosiers] then strolled about Ryde à la guitar and slept near them.
29th. ...called on Mr.Moon, sketched his cottage, Called on Mr Utterson. Mrs U. very polite and paid me much attention; shewed me most magnificent collection of drawings, pictures & works of art.-wonderful antiquities, armour, carvings &c... back to Portsmouth by the Steamer, dined at the Quebec, called on Mrs Waring, very glad to see me. Wrote letter to Father, left after tea and went off to the *Camilla* Havre steam packet at 8 with luggage - no berth 120 passengers & among them Percy Heath - we spent the night very uncomfortably in a dark hole among the luggage - rough sea -decks drenched, arrived in Havre at 8 o'clock on...
August 30th [France: Le Havre] Friday morning- most extraordinary sight all new & wonderful - such a harbour and Quais - first went to the Hotel des Indes on the Grand Quai and had my first French bkfst. (capital!) Sketched figures on quai, cleared luggage at the Douane, dined at the Table D'Hote at 5 - sketched till dark - went to Café & returned at 8 very tired and sleepy to bed.
31st. Up at 6 went to Pier tremendous wind and awful sea after the storm of the night, saw vessels come in in fine style - bkfst. at 9, sk'd all day till 5... began letter to Father, bed at 11, very tired.
Sept. Sun. 1st ...took walk all about the Piers Docks &c finished letter, dined at Hotel du Bresil, took walk about the Heights till dark. Rained hard in evg. had cafe au lait at Hotel with P[ercy] H[eath].
2nd. Up early sk.'d on the Quais, Hotel de Ville, Port &c.
3rd. Tues Very wet morng... went out & sk'd Tower (?Town) from the opposite Pier. M. Frissard the engineer very polite. I sk'd from his window during the rain... went to the Theatre in evng. with P.H. saw *Napoleon little Corporal* home at 11, bad day & windy.
4th. Sk'd before bk.the tower &c, so wet in morng. till 3 that I stayed in & sk'd baskets &c then made sk. of Market place & voiture, dined at Restaurant with P.H. at 5. Sk'd crane &c in evng.took café at Hotel.
5th. ...P.H. started with me at 3 to Ste Adresse, most beautiful spot. I called on Mr Cundell, he invited me to dinner -Champaigne!! Beautiful house & garden. At ½ p 8 started to return, obliged to go back after a mile & a half walk for my sketch book which I left. Retd. to Havre after a wretched walk in the dark, thro' winding lanes knee deep in mud. Had cafe at Hotel bed at 12 o'clk., tired.
6th Up early, coloured sk. of Market before Bk after which went by steamer to Honfleur - most extraordinary place for picturesque effect - wonderful streets of old houses. Harbour full of vessels & fishing craft, plenty of diligences, carts. Sk'd Church, charette &c Dined at Hotel Cheval Blanc opposite the Harbour, sketch'd fort & Piers in evng. Paraded the town & slept at the Cheval Blanc.
7th. Sat Up early sk'd old Tower in colors before bkf. then sk'd figures in the Market, horses &c & the Church of St Leonard... on the Pier till dark... the Caen & Paris Diligences came in at 8 in the evng. - good fun the emptying out of Passengers.
8th Sun. Heavy rain all day, up at 6 saw 3 steamers come in, 1 full of Troops & cannon. Sk'd a few soldiers & figures from my window. Soldiers & drummers paraded the town all day & made a horrible hub-bub, at 3 went out & saw the King of the French Louis Phillippe & retinue come through the town on their way to Pont au de Mer...
9th. Up early sk'd baskets before bkfst. then sk'd groups of vessels drying sails &c in harbour - fine day, plenty of vessels came in in the evg.

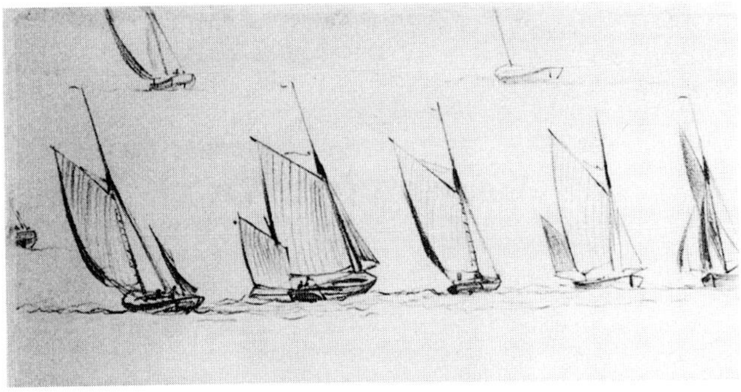

Plate 207. Pencil drawing
Sailing boats
One is reminded of Claude Monet's sketchbook capturing small sailing craft in their element and absorbing the characteristics of outline and also movement. Photo courtesy Clarges Gallery

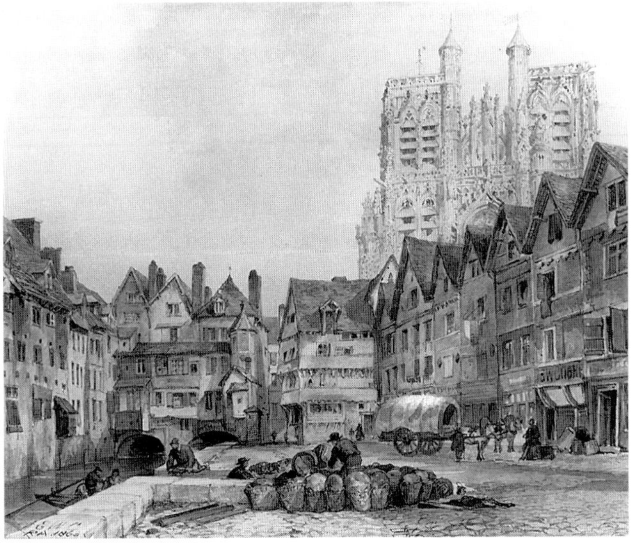

Plate 208. Watercolour
Abbeville
His first French tour of 1833 produced many sketches which pleased his father and were later used for more elaborate drawings.
Photo courtesy Spink & Son Ltd

Dutchmen &c - beautiful effects on the Seine...
10th. Sk'd bell tower, figures &c before bkfst. colord Church view, sk'd vessels, dined at Cheval Blanc, met an English artist !! beautiful effects in evng.
11th Sk'd tower, rain'd hard. Mr Smartly took me to his house, saw his pictures!! Drew baskets & dined at 7. Had bkfst with 2 English ladies -
12th ...left Honfleur by the Steamer with P.H. rough passage to Havre... looked at Prints in the Bibliothec... started at ½ p 2 in a voiture & after a 6 hour journey thro' Harfleur, Montiviliers &c &c arrived at Fécamp, fished out a house, Café de la Marine, opposite the Harbour, had café au lait, took walk on pier, very great sea, slept at Café. Recd. letter from Father which was at the Post office Havre.
[His progress on this first foreign tour can be traced in the Itinerary, and his surviving drawings show his enjoyment of the novelty of the scene. Occasional descriptions are graphic enough to bring instantly a suggestion of a painting.]
[Abbeville] Sunday 13th October: Up early and finished a letter to Mother and posted it by 8 o'clock. Walked all about the fortifications and ramparts, all round the town walls, gates &c. Clever pictures in the church of St Jacques. Made sk. of the Marché au Blé & back view of the church with the Pont D'amour (?) & anr. pencil sketch of market &c - splendid masses in the Cathedral & chaunting, took walk along the river & sketched bits - returned to dinner at 5 then went to the Cathedral and witnessed the fete of St Wilfran [Vulfran]- most splendid sight, all lit up by immense candles, saw the Procession of the Host - very grand hundreds of men & boys carrying torches - had the honor of kissing the bones of the Saint for which I paid 1 lion (?). Splendid liveries of the Priests & incense bearers - an odd old beadle with hooked nose- large white moustachios, red shoes - halbert - Cocked hat with immense red feather - Priest with blue stockings & muddy shoes under a splendid silk damask cassock - I staid there till it was all over then took café and eau de vie & retd. to the Hotel - sat by the first fire this season & very comfortably.

1834
February 12th Painted in morning. At 12 went to town with Father & Mother in coach. Saw the panorama of Captain Ross and Boothia, and then to the private view of Bonington's Exhibition, Regent St. Met a great many first rate artists there. Beautiful pictures and drawings. Then to the British Institution Exhibition. Dined at the Adelphi. I bought canvases and oil colours, palette knives &c at Brown's. At 8 went with Father to the Graphic meeting at the Thatched House. Mother called (at 10) for us and we all returned in coach at 12 o'clock after a delightful day.
13th. At work on large picture all day. I set my palette !!

15th. All day working on large picture. Mr Gibson called and took measure for a new easel and other things for my painting room.
16th. Sun: Read sermons to Grandfather. John Le Keux Junr and his intended called in morning and we took them to see Mr Breffit's vines. Mr Finden and Mr Cousens came. Mr C. staid and dined with us. Mr and Mrs Austen called and brought some fine pieces of coralline. Mr Cotman and John came to tea and left by coach at 8. Mr Doo came to tea and left with Cousens at 9.
18th. ...Father seemed pretty well and improving but suffered dreadfully during the night. A letter came from Uncle Henry Cooke announcing the death of my Uncle Kramer which took place at his house in Huntly St., yesterday...
20th Walked up to Mr Lewin's Regent's Park and made portrait of his little son in colour. Left at 4 and walked to Cousin Bill's. He shewed me beautiful sketches by T.Boys... called on R.Rosier (out) bought palette, oil colours, "Digestive" bread &c &c retd. home by bus. Found Father most dangerously ill with inflammation of the Brain. Dr Scott had been 3 times and bled him in the afternoon... [George Cooke died on 26 February.]
28th ...Coz. Wm Cooke and George Rosenberg came, also Mr Hollis... I made an outline of the profile of my beloved departed Parent (& drawings of the hands). His countenance was most Heavenly and mild, not in the least unpleasant. Poor William and Hollis were much affected at seeing him...
March 2nd. Cousin Wm Cooke came and I assisted him in making a plaster mould of my poor Father's right hand. An operation of 3 hours...
March 6th. Arranged various things, refreshments, wines, &c with Mother, sisters, for the Funeral. At 11 all our mourning family and friends began to arrive. At 1 the procession started ...Hearse & feathers, 1st Coach, Tom, myself, Uncle T. Eglinton, Wm.John Cooke... 4th Coach Mr Callcott, Mr Stark, Mr Hollis Mr R.Rosier then the artists kind friends of my poor Father's who voluntarily came forward at their own expense to pay the last tribute of respect to his remains. 5th Coach Messrs Stanfield, Burnett, W.Finden and [G.T.] Doo - Pall bearers - after which 3 more coaches containing Messrs Pye, Goodall, Watt, Cousens - Humphrys, W.R.Smith, Willmore, Cotman & Gibbon. A great many friends and artists were at the churchyard though not invited. Mr Jeffreys performed the ceremony and my poor Father's remains were laid on the coffin of my lamented Sister Clarinda. After this last melancholy ceremony was concluded we returned slowly to the House and all partook of refreshment, luncheon &c. Mr Callcott and Mr Stanfield saw my first picture...
6th April: Sun. Went to Chiswick and called on Mr Tierney Clark, he shewed me the fine drawings, plans of the Gravesend Pier - went to Mr Callcott's, saw his splendid pictures for the Academy - met Mr Wadmore there - called on Mr Webster (next door) [T. Webster RA] retd. home at 4 to dinner. Mr P.Smith dined with us. S.Hawkins and Mr Zeitter came at 5 and looked over my sketches; they left at ½ p 9 to walk home!...
8th. very busy all day with Mother arranged curiosities, minerals &c and arranging cabinet...
9th April ...to town and left drawings at Christie's. Went to Robson's sale [sale of the remaining works of George Fennell Robson] - met many Patrons and buyers- called at Boys', rode to Hawkins' and left plates for proofs. Rode to Paddington and dined at Mr. Wadmore's Met there Messrs. Fox, Nash, Brown [John Louis Brown] and Martens. Spent a pleasant evening, saw Mr W's fine collection of drawings. Slept there. Mr W gave me a commission for two drawings.
10th ...called on Mr Brown (Prince of Wales's Hotel) He shewed myself and Mr Nash his wonderful collection of Bonington's drawings, truly splendid and surprising works of art !!!! nothing in art so much affected me before. Attended Robson's second day's sale, met many artists and friends. Had surprising luck, met Mr Sheepshanks there who gave me a commission for an oil picture and invited me to Hastings for a few days. Carpenters commenced alterations in my study. Saml. Rogers Esq., called during my absence. He wrote to me also.
May 26th. I began for the first time for three months to persue my art. Worked on the plate of Chiswick & finished it in evng...
27th. Called on Christie. Went to the British Museum,- Engineers removing the Egyptian Antiquities. called on Hawkins for proofs & brought home 2 large Maple frames of ours.
29th Called on Prout at Brixton, went to the Surrey Zoological gardens - much pleased. Went to the British Museum & began drawing the removal of the Memnon for Mr Hawkins [Edward Hawkins].
30th. At the Museum at 8, took breakfast with Mr Hawkins. Staid there till 6 in evng. Many knobs there to see the operations -Lord Farnborough &c &c. Met Mr Watts & Mr Corbould. Home at 8 very much fatigued with my day's exertion. During my absence Thos. Wyld called with M. Thienon a french engraver.
June.13th Made copy of Turner's Picture of Moffat's house during day George Rosenberg went town with Tom at ¼ p 8 he returned to dinner in eveng. Geo & I were introduced as 2 ladies - very ridiculous and then grandfather gave us a very interesting lecture on Philisophy... Mrs Powlett Thomson called.
Sat 21st. Longest Day!!! Up early & pruned & thinned vines in Conservatory, finished picture of *Grass Boat & Weedy Cot* began another of *Coast of Boulogne*. Mr Currie & a gentleman called to see my pictures.
23rd. Messrs Doo, Pye & Watt called & took me with them to Richmond where we dined at the Star & Garter with the Associated Engravers. There were present Mr Doo (Chairman) Mr J.Le Keux (Vice Chairman) & Messrs H.Le Keux, J Le Keux Junr, J.Pye, Watt, Burnett, Wadmore & myself. After a sumptuous Champaigne Dinner we had some Good songs & speeches. At 10 had coffee & Mr Wadmore brought me home...Most splendid evening sky.
28th. To town by first coach, had bkfst at Mr Hullmandel's, met Monsieur le Baron Taylor & Mons. Dauzat a french artist. I made trial of lithography & am much pleased with it. Then went over the Pantheon called on Mons. Thiénon [Claude Thiénon 1772-1846, influenced R.P. Bonington], saw Mr Doo there -Called on Hawkins, left *Chiswick* to print.
July 2nd. Took bkfst at Mr Hullmandel's with Baron Taylor & M.Dauzat. The Baron took copies of *London Bridge, Shipping*. Called on Mrs Austen & left Normandy sketches there. Called on Percy Heath & Coz.Bill... Took coach to Blackwall (Baron Taylor invited me to dinner there) met him, M. Dauzat, Mons. Haghe & his brother, Messrs Hullmandel, Harding Gale & Barnard at 6 sat down to a glorious dinner, whitebait &c &c champaigne &c &c. Then took boats to Greenwich, most glorious effects of twilight from the top of the Hill in the Park. All left Greenwich by stage at ½ p 9. Met Fredk Smith there.
4th. Re-bit the Nautilus plate. Mons Thienon came at 2 & spent the day here.In eveng. we took a walk & saw glorious subjects, he left at ½ p 8, splendid day & effects.I fixed up the camera obscura on lawn.
7th Made drawgs. all day -in evng packed up a great many tools, frames &c for Coz.Bill, also the little tracing press. I put in the figures to a little picture by Uncle Wm Cooke of the interior of the Collosseum.
8th. Went to Mr Hullmandel's to bkfst. Arranged business with Baron Taylor about Spain plates. Went to Brit. Inst. Saw Exhibition of Old Masters. Met 2 Wylds there. Took them to Mr Lewis Brown's & saw his superb collection of Bonnington's drawings. (Baron Taylor & Mr Hullmandel there also)... Bought canvases, colors & saw Madme Tussaud's Exhibtion of Wax figures...
Aug.1st. to Town called on Colnaghi, ordered colors at Winsor & Newton's. Called on D. Roberts, Coz. William Cooke. We re-bit the Fleet Street plate...
2nd. Called on Britton, S.Hawkins, Stanfield, saw glorious pictures, called on Uncle Wm Cooke, dined there, he gave me a picture by Creswick. Got canvases at Brown's, met there Mr Callcott.
5th town in morng. called on Rutley & got frames, order'd more. Called on Green, Chas. St., gilder, also on Mr Stanfield, saw him paint - Mr Doo & Coz. Wm Cooke also on Mr Colnaghi, he paid me for drawings.
Sept.24th. I went to Mr [S.C.] Hall's (he unwell in bed) he corrected the MSS of *London & Vicinity*
Oct. [Hastings], 9th. Walked to the White Rock with Mr Sheepshanks & saw the workmen blast the cliffs. -began picture on the spot of Hastings from the Minnis Rock
14th. Mr Gibbon left for London at 9. Mr Stark called on me in morning and Mr Sheepshanks invited him to spend a week or two with us. Went to St. Leonard's with friend Stark and called on Mr Bland. Saw fine pictures by Crome. Met Mr Brandard and his wife. Spent the evening at Mr Frend's with Messrs. Sh. and Ro. Home at 11. Made sketch of Moonlight and vessels on my return.
16th. Storm brewing up and heavy sea, Fine sight to see the boats running in throught the surf. Met Mr Hodgson, made drawing of boats coming through the breakers. Lieutenant Hawkins called.
17th High wind & tide went with Mr.S. to see the Havock made by the night tide at the White Rock. 2 houses undermined. made sk. or two - in evng Brandard came & Mr S. shewed us more fine prints.
20th. Very rainy day. Mr Stark made sketches of mill and pond. I made sketch near the Fish market... I commenced drawing of end of boat with figures under it. Got measured for Chamois skin boots and Stark also, at Mr Sh.'s expense.
21st. Made sketches of Castle and Pevensey Bay before Bksft. Also sketched about the Mills, most bitter cold day - north wind. I took bad

cold. Champaigne wine at dinner - good Physic for it. Mr Brandard called in evening and brought the drawing for Mr Sh. who shewed fine prints in evening.
22nd. Sketched on the beach. 5 sloops and a brig unloading on shore at once. Heavy sea and Strong wind. Great difficulty in getting off. One vessel broke her warp and was terribly battered by the breakers. Went to Page's the basket maker's, while he made two small baskets (miniatures) I made sketch of interior of his shop. Met Mr Mann, he took me home and shewed me a fine collection of Marine Botany, sea weeds &c.
25th Fine sight on the beach - Herring Fishery, 50,000 washing and sending off to Brighton... in evening made Sepia sketch of basket shop, interior. Mr Sh. gave me a pair of razors made from the iron and piles of Old London Bridge.

1835
February 5th. Varnishing Day Thursday. Up early went to British Institution Pall Mall to varnish pictures. All three hung pretty well for first essays - saw Turner painting on the Great Fire! Callcott, Landseer, Collins, Etty, Chalon, Howard &c &c. At 7 called on James Herring and took him with me to the Historical Academy. 2nd night of Brigand. Bought quire of drawing paper at Winsor's in evening.
12th: Mr Jno.Turner of Clapham came and looked over all my things. He gave me a commission to paint two pictures. I bought panel and began picture of Peter Boat. In evening went to Parriss's and finished Greek female. Met Mr Corbould there.
19th. Painted all day. Finished *Peter Boat* and began another same size of boat coming ashore in a gale. Went to Historical [Academy] in evening- Murillo girl, fine.
20th Went with Uncle to Mr. Lupton's to see Turner's grand picture of Calais Pier. Called on Hawkins. Went to British Institution and saw there Mr and Mrs Windus.
21st. Called on Mr.Stanfield with my little picture, *Peter Boats* for his remarks. Bill returned and looked over sketches. I touched on Rome view. Called on Hullmandel, he paid for the three plates for Baron Taylor.
25th. Mr Cromek [Thos. Hartley Cromek 1809-1873] came to breakfast and spent the day looking over sketches. Painted all day.
March 3rd Painted on pictures, took both to shew Stanfield and Roberts who criticised them. After dinner took the picture of *Peter Boats* to Suffolk Street for the Exhibition. In evening went to Parriss's with Fredk Smith and drew Orange woman. Home at 10. During my absence Lord Ossory called and sent more drawings of Cicily [*sic*] to be engraved.
13th Cromek went with me in afternoon to British Museum and to a great many old furniture and Armour dealers. I bought a pair of Gauntletts and he bt. a helmet. Order'd frame at Creswick's...
16th ...went with Cromek to Parriss's in evening, Made pencil sketch of Cavalier, Cromwell's time, in ten minutes, did not stop. Then went to the Phrenological Society meeting, met Wm Hering and Herbert...
Fri.20th: Painted all day. The Marquess of Lansdowne called and gave me a commission for a picture. Collyer sent home a splendid frame which he gilt. In evening went to Rustic [Academy] and drew fisherman. Cox Junr there.
21st: Painted all day. Mr Cox Junr called and also friend Stark in evening. Went to Artists' Fund Meeting at Freemasons Tavern for an hour, then home to Barnes.
[The Royal Academy sending-in day was early in April: Cooke took along his entries and two of T.H.Cromek's also.]
Apr.11th. I called on Mr De Wint and took him a copy of *London Bridge* (Boards) and he paid for it. He shewed me his fine large drawings for the next Watercolour exhibition. Touched proofs of Lord Ossory's plates. After dinner left Uncle's... attended the sale of Lord Charles Townsend's pictures. Met Mr Wadmore there &c &c. Mr Sheepshanks bought *Duncan Gray* by Wilkie. Returned home with Tom at 7.
May 4th Mon. I went to town with E.Breffitt in his boat, called on Mr Rainy & at the British Institution - went with Mr & Miss Sheepshanks to the Royal Academy first day - most tremendously crowded - met all the artists there also Mrs Gillham & daughters. Left at 5 dined at Newton's walked to City, called on French & Brown (took coffee there) & home by bus in evng. Tom was upset in going to town by Seeley's coach which turned over. Fortunately he escaped injury except a sprain in his back: he retd. home at 4...
5th. I went to town by bus in mng. called on Mr Sheepshanks, met Gibbon there - we all three went to Greenwich by stage & walked over to Blackheath & saw his beautiful new house & grounds at Blackheath Park. (Mr Dyer came there while we stayed) Called on Mr Wyon & walked back to Greenwich, rode to City, dined with them at Williams's Old Bailey & then chose several stove grates at Faulkner's also range &c for Mr S. Walked home with Mr S for ½ an hour, called on Mrs Rd. Rosier & retd. home by Portsmouth Mail to Putney by ½ p 9 very tired.
7th Went to town at 10, called on Barnard & Hodgson. Went to the Water color Exhn., very fine met Nash there. Called & lunched at E.Breffitt's - he gave me Seed. Went to the Royal Academy, met Mr C.Stokes & Mr. Windus. Walked to City called for boots at Gage's... Mrs & Thomas Cromek came for a few days.
8th Made sketches with Camera with Cromek - drawing of my old chair &c. Took walk, music in evng. Miss Etherington went to town, she has a bad cold. Hilliard fetched basket from E.Breffitt's with Marmalade & seed for me.
11th. Cromek & I drew a group of armour in morng. Mr Rainy called to look over the House. -at ½ p 12 after an early dinner Cromek & I went to Hampton Court by the german Barouche, saw all the fine pictures, china &c - maze- Bushy park &c...
13th. Went to town by stage at 10 called on Mr Sheepshanks but he had gone to Hastings Went with E.Breffitt to Blackheath by bus & looked over the garden, vines &c - laid out beds. Very soaking wet aftn. Dined at Princess of Wales Blackheath & left by stage at 6.
14th called on Henry Eglinton to see a picture - rode to Roberts's, called there & at Stanfield's. Dined at Coz. Bill's, met there Coz. Caroline. Rode to Uncle Wm's, took tea there, packed up things. he walked with me to Tiffin's. I went to several Jews' shops & bought silk for my old chair. Called on A.Graves for my sketchbook...
15th Friday. All day arranging an Antiquary's room with armour & curiosities in my study. Made a sk. in color in evng. by candle light. Mr Stark came in evng & left at 8.
16th Completed the arrangement of my room & commenced the outline of a picture of it in evng. Miss Waring called to see it & I called there, they lent me China jars to group with the rest & paint... Mr J. Cadogan came in evg. & dined with us; he took Miss E.Needham home by bus in evng.
18th Mon. ...Painted all day on Picture Uncle Wm Cooke & wife came to tea & left at 8½ to Hammersmith (they much pleased at my room,) Mother read *The Antiquary* to me ... Mr Popinjay Prigg - a Mann came in evng....
23rd Felt better this morng. painted on Picture all day. Fredk. Smith came down at 1 with proofs to touch: left after dinner. Tom came in evng & brought John Eglinton with him.
28th. Went to town with Mother by stage, I took up old pictures & old clothes, made exchanges &c with Jews in Princes St, for China Jar, Carvings, Helmet &c. Bought Tea boards &c...
June. 4th Painted on Picture in morng. Mr Sheepshanks came down at 12 to see it. I walked with him (on his way home)- to Chiswick
10th Painted in morng, went to town at 5 & took tea at Rosenberg's, went with him to the Graphic: very good meeting. Mr Doo sent me a beautiful proof of the etching of John Knox, as a present: I slept at Rosenberg's...
July 2nd. to town at 9 Called on Mr Sheepshanks. (he bt.drawings of me) called on Tiffin (sold him drawgs) Hodgson. Sold drawgs to Colnaghi & Holloway. Called on Leggatt, Arch, Tom & Shirley. Took tea at Uncle Tom's.
4th.Sat Called on Mr Austen, he bt. 4 drawgs. Called on Mr Wadmore (out) & on J.H.Robinson - called on Fuller bought colors &c at Newman's & Winsor's. Called on Colnaghi, Hodgson & Tiffin - & on Mr Wadmore. Retd home at ½p 8.
10th. Sent off my picture of "Olla Podrida" to Mr Sheepshanks. Dr Scott called, also Miss Waring. Packed up things all day...
11th. Up early, Post carriage came for us after bkfst at 7 & took us all to Hammersmith. Tom accompanied us - at ½ p 8 the Birmingham Tantivy coach took us all aboard & we had a pleasant ride at a very quick pace to Oxford thro' Henley arrived at ½ p 1... called on Mr Wyatt who let us have his handsome apartments in the High Street...
30th ...the girls made preparations for Gypsying tomorrow - at Nuneham - most terribly hot day.
31st: Friday. Sketched arms of Magdalen College in the Schools gate-way before breakfast. At 9 started with all our family and Mr Wyatt's to the River, and met on board the House Boat 4 Miss Winstanley's, Messrs G & J.Bridges, Perkins, Paine, Mrs Hickman, Miss Boxall, Mrs Fussell, about 25 in all and we had a delightful voyage to Nuneham. Some went on first in the cutter and the rest followed after lunch I made sketch of the Party amusing themselves in various ways !!! then dined capitally and danced under the trees till tea time. Some of the gents bathed and we danced again till 8. Mr Harcourt and 2 ladies came and looked at us. Had a pleasant ride home but were detained an hour at Sanford at the Lock, the water being very low....
1st August, Saturday Made caricature of a party on their voyage to

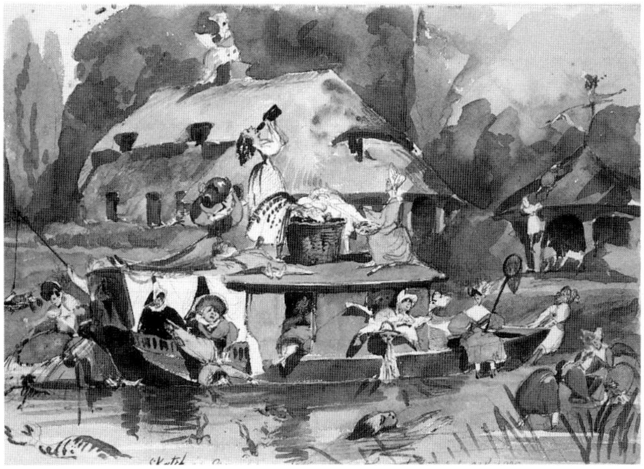

Plate 209. Watercolour, 1835
Sketch at Nuneham taken on the spot July 31st 1835...
Another sketch from Elizabeth Wyatt's album, of the party's 'gypsying' expedition. Photo courtesy Martyn Gregory. Private Collection

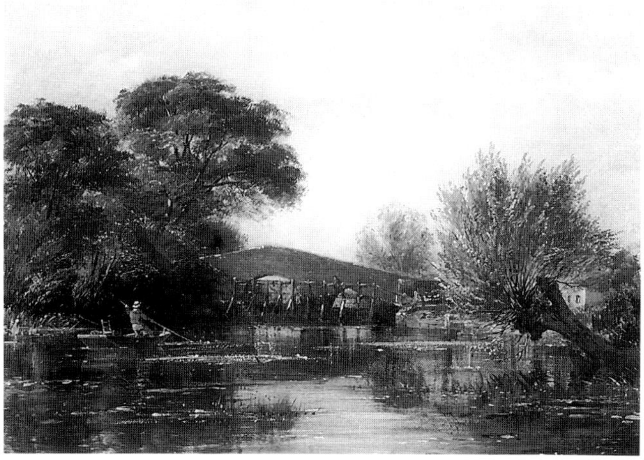

Plate 210. 35/10
Godstow bridge
Water, fresh or salt, was never far from Cooke's consciousness. Staying with the Wyatts, Oxford picture dealers and frame-makers, Cooke produced some fresh, telling studies of river landscape and riverside buildings. Photo courtesy Yale Center for British Art

Nuneham with part of their provisions. In afternoon went with George Wyatt to Christ Church College and saw the Anatomical Museum -also the great Kitchen. We went into Corpus College also. After tea went out to Oseney Mill and sketched it with the Lock. G.W Accompanied me and then went afterwards to Mrs Hickmans, with Sisters and Miss Wyatt also. J.Wyatt and Mr Perkins were there, went for a call and staid for a ball, for we knocked up a dance with Highlander in costume &c, home at 11.
2nd Went to Ch.(All Saints) with Mr Wyatt. Took walk round Wadham College gardens with Mother & back to dinner after which wrote long letter to Tom - & in evening took walk to Hinksey Ferry with Mother & Mary - we all supped with Mr Wyatt. I gave Miss Wyatt the sketch of "Nuneham Party".
4th Tues. Went to Oriel College with Mr Wyatt in morning: then went to Drewitt's Mill and made several sketches of it - very hot day, bathed on my return. Mrs Wyatt had a party in eveng. which we all joined - viz. the Misses Winstanley, Mrs Hickman, Miss Boxall, Miss Bridges and her brothers. Mr Jno. Bridges came down today and spent the eveng. also Mr Perkins. Had dancing in the great room and music afterwards, much amusement from some verses on our Nuneham trip by Miss Winstanley.

1836
April: 1st Good Friday. Most rainy & dark & cold day we have had- F.& Geo Smith called in the mg: on their way to Richmond. I arranged sketches in ev: F.Smith returned in ev:
2nd. Sat. I finished pictures of *Hastings sands & Mending bait net* - F.Smith at work on *Shipping* plates - very rainy cold day.
4th. F.Smith came before bkfast. I went with Mother & Laura to town in fly, took my two pictures shewed them to Mr Callcott, saw his fine pictures & also called on Mr Webster & saw his. Called on Robinson met Mr Sheepshanks there. Mother left pictures at Tiffins & went on to Hackney. I went with Mr S.& Mr R. to Mr E.Landseer's, saw his glorious pictures. Called on Gibbon & on Stanfield, saw his large picture of Trafalgar- rode to City, dined, called on Harwood & Tom & went to Hackney.Took tea with Mrs Geo.Loddiges, saw the camellias. Left in fly at ½ p 8 & came home at 10 -very fine day...
5th. Went to town with Harriette pr.Ham[mersmi]th. Went to the British Inst[itutio]n. I went to Tiffins and painted on pictures there- returned to Instn. for Harriette & met Mr. Geo.Loddiges & Conrad there. Went also to the new Nat: Gal: & saw the Designs for the new Houses of Parliament. Mr.L went to see my pictures & I took them to the Academy.- called on Foord for small frame & returned home at 7 by bus. Had bad sore throat in ev: very wet aftn:
6th. Made drawgs: all day for Jas Wyatt & wrote to him in ev:
8th. Fri. Made drawgs: all day. Mr Watts, Fred: & Mr Peacock called in m: I wrote to Mr Wells, prepared parcel for Oxford. In ev: Mrs Angell returned home. F.Smith gave us some capital songs & recitation.
9th. Fin[ishe]d drawgs: went to town at 1 called at Winsor's, Brown's, R.Rosier's, Harwood's, Tom's &c. Went to Blackheath in ev: & slept at Mr Sheepshanks'.
10th. Sun Took walk with Mr. S all round by Greenwich, Blackwall [*sic*] & Woolwich. In aft: 3 Gents came & left after tea. During my absence from Home Jas Wyatt & Jas Bridges went to Barnes also Henry Eglinton. I slept at Blackheath.
11th. Mon. Jas Wyatt came down while we were at bk: at 11 went to town with him & Mr Sheepshanks by the Greenwich railway. Called on Brown & R.Rosier (just returned from a tour). Bought knife, india rubber, shoes &c, called at Winsor's for color box. Took tea at Bridges', returned home at 9. [P.A.] Mulready came in ev: & slept here. Had letter from Mr.Wells.
12th. Arranged & worked on Drawgs: Went to Mr Breffitt's in aft: with F.Smith beetle hunting!! In ev: George B[reffitt] & Miss E.B. came in & we had a few good things by F.Smith. Mulready left after tea.
13th. Packed up things & left Barnes at 1. -booked luggage at the British Hotel: called on Hodgson to see a picture by Isabey. Met Wyatt there & went with him to the Brit: Inst: called on Sowerby at Lambeth & also on Edgar Breffitt, saw the panorama of "Thebes". Took tea at Bridges' with Wyatt, Fox & Jas B came in & we all went down to the Graphic meeting at 8. Had a good & full meeting. Returned at 12 to Uncle's & slept with Tom.
14th Thurs. Went to City called on Brown - Stark- Harwood, E.Breffitt: went to the Nat: Gall: for an hour and left by the Tonbridge Wells coach at 2, very wet for an hour, got outside at Bromley and had a pleasant ride to Redleaf at ½ p 6. Mr Wells received me most kindly also Mr Lee. Mr Jno Wells dined with us; saw some of the splendid collection of Mr Wells and some fine sketches by Landseer &c
15th After bkfast Mr Wells shewed me his splendid collection of Pictures and then went all round the Gardens and grounds, most beautiful place & glorious plants and houses - took a stroll all round the park by the river, took some beetles. Saw Mr Lee paint a Grebe and went with him for a walk before dinner. Mr Jno Wells left in m[orning]: very fine warm day. In evening Mr W. shewed me drawings by Pocock.&c &c.
16th Mr Lee commenced another picture of birds - I made sketch of Summer house in garden. Looked over 2 or 3 cottages on Mr Wells's estate. Went out to the river with Mr Lee after lunch and he took a Jack. Mr Pickance dined with us and left at 10 -most beautiful day.
17th. Sunday. Went to Penshurst Ch. with Mr. Wells and back through the Park, took stroll round the Garden and grounds Mr Streatfeild and a gent called in m[orning] on Mr Wells. In evening we had the Hall lighted up and sat there for some time enjoying the fine pictures. Very cold damp foggy day. Wrote to Harriette.
18th. Made sketch of a Ram's head from a picture by Edwin Landseer before bkfst then finished sk[etch] of summer house and drew baskets and horn seats. Went at 12 with Lee to a trout stream and he caught 4 fine fish. I made sketches about and a study in colour of Barden Mill. Home at 6 to dinner. Misses Bouveur[?] & Rey dined with us.
19th. After bk. went out with Lee, drew ploughs &c, back to lunch and then went down to the river and set trimmers, threw cast net and fished;

caught 3 Jack and some perch also made sketch of waterfall before dinner; in evng drew Cottages (model) & shells with camera.
20th. Drew ferns in garden, also Plough on Canvass, made sketch of the old well and bucket and painted it in oil on Panel. Very dull cold day. Lee painted horses and plough. In evening we drew shells by the camera.
21st. Up early and made sketches before bk. of Lodge and Cottage. Painted on picture of Well on the spot. Lee painted figures in his plough subject, took walk with Mr Wells to some fine sand rocks on his estate before dinner - in ev. drew Landseer's sketch of deer. Had letter from Harriette and wrote to Mr Mann.
22nd. Made drawings from Landseer's pictures before bk. -painted on Well picture. Lee and David went out with nets and tackles in morning to fish. I joined them at 2 & we caught some fine perch and Jack, back at 6 I sketched the sluices. In evg. sketched pictures by E.Landseer (in my book) of Roebuck & Tarmagon [*sic*]
23rd. Made drawing of Wild Duck from Landseer's painting. Painted a fine large Chub in mg. At 4 went with Mr Wells to see men barking trees. Lee fished below the lower fall and I made two sketches of it. Tremendous storm came on, in ev. made drawing in Asphaltum of an Oxford scene for Mr Wells's Scribblers book [British Museum].
24th. Sunday. Most terribly wet all day. Lee left Redleaf at 1 in Mr Wells's carriage. for town. In ev. made drawings of vases, rustic cups &c, packed up.
25th. Up early made sketches of the House from the Lawn &c Left Redleaf after bk at 9, rode Pr. Penshurst coach to Watts Cross. Made sketches about Holland Den while waiting for the stage, at 12 it came up and had a capital ride to Hastings, most delightful day. Mr & Mrs Man received me most kindly. Dined at 6 took a stroll in ev: with Mr M. Mrs Reynolds & Mrs Fry called. I brought some Jack and a wild fowl from Redleaf.
26th. Made sketches in mg: & took a bath after dinner. Strolled on beach, wrote to Harriette. At 7 Mr Palmer, Mrs Fry and Mrs Reynolds came & spent the ev: here, looked at sketches, marine botany &c. Gave Mr Mann a copy of *London Bridge*.
27th. Went on board the *Adelaide* cutter, saw Captain Eyre. Went in Mr Mann's galley to Bulver Hythe with Mrs Fry & Mrs Reynolds, they went digging for shells. I called at 42 tower to see Mr Mitchell who was out. Bought prawn gins & nets &c. After dinner took walk with Mr M & called on Mr Buchannon & saw his plants. Mr & Mrs Shorter came to tea and spent the evg: I looked at objects with the microscope
28th. Thurs. Went out before bk: bought "pannier" from french fisherman. After bk: went with Mr Man aboard a Dutch galliott and also aboard a french lugger: bought an old jacket and cap of the captain. Made sketches of rocks &c at Ecclesbourne, drew baskets &c in afternoon - had letter from Harriette in mg: Met Mr Hebden & Mr Mc Clure.
29th. After bk: went in the galley to St Leonards & fetched Mrs Fry & Mrs Reynolds, took them aboard the *Rob Roy* cutter. Mr McClure run us down to Beechey [sic] Head - had a capital breeze from the North, made sketches, had lunch and retd. at 5, delightful sail. Dressed and went with Mr & Mrs Mann to dine at Mr Shorter's, met Mr Scrivens & Mr Phillips, home at 11, glorious moonlight night.
30th.Sat. Went with Mr Mann in the Galley to 41 Tower. Mrs Fry met us and looked over the Martello tower, I made sketch of the interior also of an old lime kiln at Bulver hythe - dined with Mr Mitchell & returned home to tea- met Mr McClure and gave him some proofs of shipping. In evg: Mr Mann looked over the Algae and Corallines & gave me some specimens. Cold windy day.
May 1st. Went after ch[urch]: on board the *Rob Roy* cutter and sailed with Mr McClure to 46 Tower near Bexhill, walked back to 41 and called on Mitchell. Met Mr Shorter and returned to Hastings to dinner. Called on Mr Shorter for an hour or two in aftn: Mr Savery took tea with us: very windy cold day. Went out with Mr Mann for a turn by moonlight at 10.
2nd. Took breakfast with Mr Savery & he took me to Maxfield a curious old farm house near Guesling - made sketch of an old kitchen there. Back to Hastings at 2. Most soaking rain all day. Went with Mr Mann along the beach and bought several marine Stores, nets, dresses of Fishermen &c - called on Mr Hawkins, - had warm bath - Went with Mr & Mrs Mann in fly to spend the evg: at Mr Hardman's - met there Drs Harwood &c &c &c, had music, home at 11. Mr Shorter called and brought me a cup made from Shakespeare's mulberry tree as a present. In ev: packed up things.
3rd. Up early left Hastings at 10 by the "Paragon" coach through Tunbridge Wells, returned home from St Paul's by bus at 9, found all well. Gave Mrs Mann a drawg: in mg: of the Shore near Hastings.
4th Completed drawg: of Martello tower &c arranged sketches and nets &c &c.
5th. Went to town by bus at 9, called on Mr Wells who invited me to dine there in the ev: Called on Lee and Wm.Hering and also at Dr Eliotson's with him to see his pictures. Went to the Institution to fetch picture of *Marine Stores*, but found it was sold - introduced to Mr Seguier. Bought camera at Watkins's and wrote & sent it off to Mitchell at St Leonards - called on Foggo, went to the Academy, met Mr Wells there, staid till 6 & rode with him to Fladong's Hotel. Dined there at 7 and met Lee and Landseer, delightful meeting, left at 11 & rode to Uncle Eglinton's and slept there. Soaking rain.
6th. Gave Aunt a drawing of *Pilot boat in stays*. Called on Brown, met R.Rosier - went to Harwoods for books, rode to Blackheath - Mr S[heepshanks]. and Mr Fox were out, I went also and met them in Lewisham. Mr E.Landseer and Mr W.Allan came in afternoon and dined there & left at 9. Fox & I slept there. Mr Horsley Junr called in ev: beautiful day.
7th.Sat. Left Blackheath in mg: with Fox. Called on Brown and Wm Rosier & went to Hackney. Dined at Mr Geo.Loddiges', he shewed me his fine microscope. Returned to town with Conrad and met Mrs Loddiges & all the Young ladies at the Academy in aft: then went with Conrad, Jane & Helen to see the industrious fleas. Called on Mr Wells in evening, met Lee there, left my sketches with Mr W. amd also 2 copies of *London Bridge* and one at Glynn's for Mr Seguier: returned home by bus at 9. Tom came by last bus at ½ p 10, very unwell. Had letter from the Earl of Winchelsea - fine hot day.
9th. Tom left at ½ p 8. I went to Wilton Crescent at 11 and called on the Earl of Winchelsea, who gave me a commission for a new picture. Left *Shipping* at Mr Seguier's - called on Burnett, saw Fox, called on Percy & Lucy. Rode to town, called on Mr Wells (out) & on Bridges(out) - bought brushes at Brown's. Dined with Uncle William Cooke, called on Mr Finden, went to the Academy, met Roberts, Stark, A.Clint & Knight also Mr Wells he walked with me to Piccadilly - returned home pr.Hammersmith at 9, saw [P.A.] Mulready on my return - he slept here. Brought Capt. Glascock's book of the *Naval Service* from Rosenberg's. Fine day. Mrs Angell left us & went to Mrs Rosenberg's to board there.
10th. Harriette arranged sketches &c. I commenced a picture for Mr. Wells, - painted the sky from Nature. Miss Barke spent the aft: here, Miss E.Breffitt called in evg:
11th. Painted on picture of tarring. Fredk. Smith came in mg: & worked on *Shipping* plates. At 6 went to town, bought hat at Pitts's, called on Foord, went to the Graphic at 8 introduced Paul Mulready. Had a full meeting, met Mr Wells, E.Landseer, Sir John Swinburne &c &c &c Returned with Brandard to Islington slept at Uncle's. Very fine day.
12th. Went with Tom to City to buy boots! Called on Foord and returned home at 12 -painted all day on picture of *Tarring the Boat*. Man brought in evg: my large frame from Foord's for the picture of *Pilot Boat*. Very hot day.
13th. Painted all day on picture of "Tarring". Mr Wm Finden came in aft: & left after tea - he selected sketches for drawings. Jno Eglinton came in mg: for a few days. W.Ratcliff & his sister called in evg:
14th. Painted in mg: at 12 went with Mother & Harriette in fly to Horticultural Gardens - the first show of flowers - met there Messrs Sheepshanks, Fox, Wells, Griffiths, Mr & Mrs Gillham, Miss G., also Mr & Mrs Geo. Loddiges, Conrad, Jane, Helen, Mrs Wm L[oddiges], Miss Maria, Miss Bowes,& Mr. Sheffield - also many other friends. Had a most delightful day, glorious weather - the show of flowers very fine; three bands were stationed & played very finely. We left at 6 and returned by water.Tom came at 3. Eliza went to town and returned at 10.
15th. Went to Mortlake Church with Jno Eglinton. Mrs [S.C.] Hall & a lady called in ev: In the aftn: we saw the eclipse of the Sun very finely. Most beautiful day. Made sketch of picture for Mr Wells in pencil
16th. Went to town at 10 called on Bridges & Lee & on Mr Wells, fetched pictures & sketches from there. Went to Blackheath met Messrs Wadmore, Burnett & Fox who dined there. They left by stage at 8 I shewed them my Chub [V&A 48] & other sketches & slept there. Mulready came while I was away. Mr S[heepshanks] paid me for picture.
17th. Rode to the City with Mr S. Recd cheque at Salt's, called and fetched sketch books at Harwoods.[J. & F. Harwood, 26 Fenchurch St., Stationers, printers & publishers]. Called on Tiffin, Watkins & Hill, Foord. Went to the Water Color Ex[hibition]: & Academy. Dined with Jas. Bridges at the York, called at "Devilles", home at 7 by stage. Had music in ev: called on Mrs Breffitt.
18th. Wrote letters in mg: painted on Picture in aftn: Wm. Hering and Mr Elliott called in aftn: & looked at sketches. Gents came to look at the house. In ev: took stroll with Fred. and Jno - beetle hunting. Sketched weeds. Called on Gibson & ordered portable easel &c.
19th. Up early and took walk with Fred & John, beetle hunting; painted

all day on large picture of sea piece. Mother Harriette & Eliza went to town by bus and returned in ev: Mr Hamilton called in mg: Lord Winchelsea and his son Lord Maidstone called & looked over sketches in aftn:
22nd. Mr Thiénon came in mg: & shewed me sketches & etchings & looked over mine. Mr & Mrs R.Rosier & little ones came down in a britzka [open carriage with room to recline] & dined with us, after wh: Harriette, Mary & I went with them to Hampton Court, walked about the grounds and returned to tea, left at 7. M. Thiénon & two friends called again, gave me a sketch of our house which he had made. E.Breffitt took tea with us. F.Smith left us in mg: having fin[ished] the plates.
24th. Painted on pictures. P.M[ulready] fin[ished] portrait of Mrs Needham. At 1 Mrs Angell & Lucy came, dined here & left after tea, Mrs A. took Poll back with her. I packed up colours & panells to go to Blackheath for a few days. Eliza went to town. P.M. left in aft: Hilliard brought tea from R.R[osier].
25th. Went to town with John Eglinton in mg: left luggage at Charing X. Called on Deville, bought tubes for oil color, called at Brown's (colourman) & at Uncle W.Cooke's (out) went to the Academy for 5 minutes, saw Fred.Smith. Rode to Blackheath met Messr Burnett & Fox there. Fox went with me to Greenwich Fair before dinner. Etty came at 5, dined with us and left at 8 with Fox. Burnett and I slept there.
26th. Mr Burnett painted on Hastings picture, I made drawing of Brugmansia. Mr Streatfeild called on Mr S after dinner. We took a walk to Greenwich Park: cold easterly wind
27th. Commenced two little pictures. Burnett painted on Hastings. Took walk with him down to the water walk below Greenwich.
28th. Painted & drew on Brugmansia. Mr Streatfeild called, I went home with him & he took me all over Mr Brandram's grounds at Lee, most beautiful place… Back to dinner. Party of ladies called here to see the pictures &c. Burnett finished his picture & left after tea, by stage.
30th. Started after bk: to the Water Side and painted on a view of Blackwall from near Enderby's works, back at 3. Mr Gibbon came & brought a proof of *Suspense*. I walked over the Heath on his way back with him.
31st. Up & made sk: of Park Cottage before bk: after wh: started for town. Called on Holland & saw Mr S. there, called on Tiffin, bought colours & panels at Brown's. Brought back picture of *Lobster Pots* from Tiffin to Blackheath, rode to Greenwich by steamer from Hungerford. Made outline on Millboard of view of Greenwich from the East & returned to Blackheath at 5 by stage. Holland dined with us. Stark came at 5 & left after tea. Harriette sent parcel to me of Palette, Camp stool &c. Mr Mann also wrote to me in frank to Mr S. Holland left at 11. Fine day, river splendid.
June 1. Painted on small picture and on Lobster Pots Mr S[heepshanks] went to town & retd. at 2. Paul Mulready came at 1, dined with us & left at 9. Mr Courthope came in ev: Made pen & ink sketch in ev: of Mill Wall & vessel.
2nd. Painted on Blackwall. Mr Wyon sent over to me to make a drawing of the Menai bridge, which I did. Gibbon & Mr Joubert dined here
3rd. Rode to the Lime Kilns, walked to Greenwich & went to town by steamer, landed at St Katherine's, called on Mr Wyon at the Mint, took his book back of Menai Bridge also drawing. He shewed me over many parts of the Mint and presented me with a proof impression of his double sovereign in gold. Called on Henley at the Docks, dined with Tom: called on Brown, Jas. Rosier, at Reeves's to see Mr Parlour's new Instrument for Drawg: called at Stark's, Foord's & Sampsons & returned to Greenwich by the steamer from Hungerford. Made sk: of *Dreadnought* & part of Deptford. Walked home at 8 to tea, rainy day, drew mills in sketchbook from little picture
4th. painted on Blackwall picture. Mr & Mrs Gray, his two daughters & Dr Ruppell came to see the pictures &c & were much delighted. Fredk.Smith called in aft: & left after tea. I called on Mr Gray in ev: & he shewed me many interesting specimens. Home at 10, made study of French fishing boat - wrote to Harriette.
5th.Sun. Went to the New Church in m: Mr W.Finden came at 2 & dined with us, left at 9 by coach, dull day rather rainy. Made sketch of my picture of *Hastings from the Minnis Rocks*.
6th. Mr Jas.Bridges came while we were at Breakfast, he brought basket with 12 fine Chrysanthemums from Oxford for Mr Sheepshanks. I walked to Eltham with him at 11. Made small drawg: of E.Landseer's picture of Comical Dogs. Finished drawing of Brugmansia. Painted on *Antiquary's Cell* & Blackwall. At 9 went with Mr S. to Greenwich with Bridges on his way to town. Harriette wrote to me in ev: I wrote to W.J.Cooke & Horwood the printer.
7th. Assisted Mr Sheepshanks to Hang & rearrange his pictures -packed

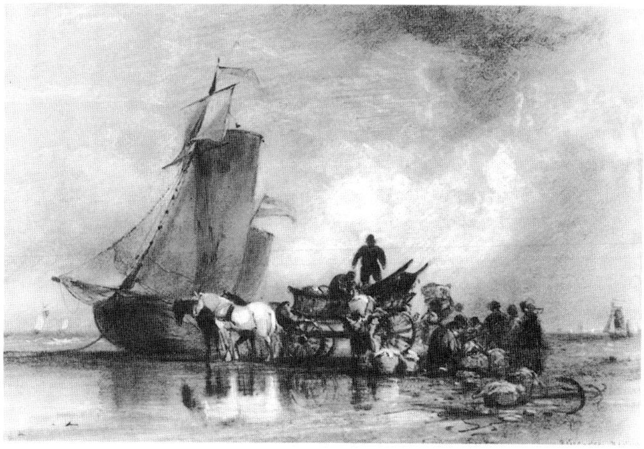

Plate 211. Chalk drawing
Scheveling, cart loading fish. Inscribed Redleaf
Perhaps study for 38/5 *Dutch fish waggon,* Wells Collection.
Photo courtesy Martyn Gregory. Private Collection

up things dined at 1 & left Blackheath at 2 by coach to Charing Cross, cabbed it to Sampson's for trousers, Foords, Kilner's, Brown's in Holborn & St Pauls. Home by coach at 6 to tea, found all better & preparing for the festival of Thursday. [His brother's wedding.]
10th. Fri. Bridges wrote & I answered him. Uncle left in mg: & Aunt staid. I began a picture of *Hulks in Portsmouth Harbour* for Mr Finden. Stormy day.
11th.Sat. Jas Bridges - his sister & Misses E.& S.Wyatt came in fly at 10 oclk: & looked at sketches &c &c. At 12 had cold collation & at 1 started to the Horticultural Gardens, the second Fete. We went in two carriages, Mother, Harriette, Laura, Miss Roberts & self, the Bridges &c, met at the Gardens all the Loddiges & Gillhams - a wedding party - Miss Emma married this morng: to Mr Henry Winsor: - met there also Mr Sheepshanks & Mr Fox: the Flowers were very fine & the company very numerous- windy but fine day. Left at ½ p 6 & returned to Barnes to tea. Bridges & party left at ½ p 8 for town. Uncle came in ev:
July 6: Gibson sent home my new painting box. Harriette made a cover for it and also for the easel. I arranged all my colours and packed up. Davis [tailor] sent home my sketching equipment, Plaid, Peruvian hat also. to Redleaf:
8th July. Up early and unpacked pictures, strolled about the Garden… Mr Wells very poorly with swelled face… I made study in oil of shed… looked at drawings in evening. Most delightful day, I feel quite enraptured with this most glorious place. The flowers and plants are truly magnificent and the views most beautiful in every direction.
August 5th: Painted sky from Backhuysen before breakfast. Painted basket and fish in picture of kitchen at Bellinghams farm, (Packing Fish).
6th: Had an accident by throwing down the Ostade- but not much injured- made me feel quite feverish all the rest of the day.
13th: …Collins and Lee went a stroll with me in Penshurst Park. I drew Armour at the Castle. In the evening lit up the Murillo and sat enjoying it.

1837
30th August: …aboard the *Columbine* [Rotterdam] packet at 7… very rainy and squally all day. Left the Foreland about 2… took to my berth about 5 and stayed there until 5 the next morning. Terribly shaken, no sleep, headache. Tremendous squalls of rain with waterspouts.
31st: On going upon Deck saw the low flat coast of Holland with the Sand ridges of Goree, the high land mark and church just ahead, at 6 the Goree Pilot came aboard and we run over the bar and into the Flakee to Helvoetsluys. here we stopped ½ an hour- (officers cleared the ship) our Post Office courier took the bags ashore to proceed by land to Rotterdam for as we could not enter by the Brill we were obliged to make 70 miles extra voyage - passing Willemstadt thro' the Kell- near Dort. The Old Maas, Vlardingen -Schiedam to Rotterdam …after clearing luggage went to the Pays Bas Hotel, then strolled about the town and into the Great Church. Went up to the Top of the Tower with a gent and had a delightful view of the Town -sketched bits… took stroll in evening. Met Mr Lewis and his daughter - saw Donaldson and J.Bailey
5th Sept: [The Hague] After bk. called on Mr Procter (with letter) met

there Dr. Tuke (a friend of W.Hering's) who accompanied us to the gallery of fine pictures at the Museum - highly delighted with many glorious things - called at Baron Verstolck's and saw some of his superb pictures - then went in carriage to the Palace in the Wood [Huis ten Bosch]- much gratified by the tasteful and ornamental style of the decorations - particularly with the room of pictures by Jordaens. Drove from thence to famous fishing village of Shoeveling [Scheveling, an older name for Scheveningen] - a most interesting spot to me: the beach covered with fine picturesque boats and figures, with a profusion of flags and pennants glittering at the mast heads....

6th: ...dined and made sketches on beach, fine subjects for pictures ... glorious sunset -shrimp boats coming in- very fine.

10th: Heavy sea on beach, 80 boats hanging by their anchors, just afloat, having come in, in consequence of the brisk breeze in the night. Went to the Hague at 11 and to the English Church ...on coming out was compelled to go to the commissary of Police, where I was kept nearly an hour till they had obtained my passport from the English Ambassadors - called on Mr Bodein (out) went with Mr Thomas Proctor to the Wood and was highly delighted with its beautiful character - its fine trees and sheets of water & shady walks - the band of the Grenadier guards was playing opposite the Society or subscription room of the nobility and gentry) - surrounded by thousands of the most respectable classes of the Hague - promenading amongst the trees, sparkling in the sun and reflecting in the quiet lakes, a beautiful sight. At 4 o'clock all had left for dinner...

11th. Painted on picture, sketched &c: fell in with a German Painter on the beach, making a study in oil...

14th: ...Painted on second picture- beach very interesting, crowded with figures & boats &c. A severe gale commenced at 12 o'clock and continued all day and night - from the West. The sea was tremendous and the boats coming in all day - 8 large Hering boats left Scheveling on their cruize - made sketches of figures &c on beach...

18th: Painted during day on a new subject which I commenced this morning as a study for a large picture - selling fish. Dr Tuke came over from the Hague at 8 and took breakfast with me... The beach in a tremendous bustle all day, the fleet of Herring Boats going off, it blew half a gale from the S.W. and the flood tide rolled in very heavily. About 4 o'clock the whole 45 boats got clear away and stood to Nor'rd. The beach was thronged by several thousand people, women and children taking farewell of their husbands and Fathers - the shore was left quite deserted, only a few trawlers remaining- very wet eveng.

22nd: 40 trawlers came in early and the shore was a mass of Fish and Fish women. Very fine. Painted on Fish arrived- all day. Sketched shrimp boats. Glorious day and sunset.

24th: called on Mr Bodein who introduced me to Mr Van Heun an amateur painter...

26th: Beach very full and interesting, early in morning 30 pincks came in - great deal of fish, particularly skate, carts fetching the fish up, very good subjects. Sketched before bk. then painted all day on Sorting Shrimps, sky from nature. Wind in the North - dirty weather brewing -but glorious day - napped for 3 hours after dinner.

October 3rd: Hazy morning but most beautiful effects on the Shore - a glorious day. Several Hering boats came in with a million fish also trawlers. Stark calm in evening - sea exquisite at sunset. Painted on dark picture all day. Mr de Haan and family came up to see my pictures in morng. Wrote to Mr Wells...

4th: ...Mr Procter and daughter - a lady and Sir William Johnstone came over to see my pictures in morning for an hour. I took a walk through the village with Mr de Haan to see the smoking houses for the Hering and also to the basket maker's for models.

5th: Out before bk. sketching. Went to basket makers... called on Mr Procter and went with Richard P. to the Exhibition of modern pictures - no great thngs... Went to Mr Van Heun's at 4 to dinner. Met Messrs Bodein ...&c who all made a great deal of me. Looked over prints &c. M ... prepared a large bowl of English Punch and at 10 they all rode to Scheveling to see me safe home...

6th: ...went by self to see the collection of M. Steingraghts... rode back with Mr de Haan at 5, dined with him and spent a pleasant evening. He gave me a letter of introduction to his Brother at Leyden... aurora borealis very fine in eveng.

Saturday 7th Oct: Out on beach, very fine, plenty of Fish, went to the basket Maker's, ordered a new model to be made. Called on Mr de Haan and sketched from his window - he came to see my pictures. Mr van Heun came also. Packed up my traps and left Scheveling after a month's visit... Went to the Treckschuit to Leyden, a most delightful trip, made sketches all the way. Stopped at Liedshurdam for a snack and a sketch. Passed many curious and beautiful mills...

9th: After breakfast Mr Fleming called and we went to call on Mr de Haan. Shewed him the Camera in application to the Microscope. He then took me to the Museum where I staid an hour or two lost in wonder and admiration at the superb collection of comparative anatomy, insects &c and natural History in general.Then went to the Botanic Garden and was much pleased...

10th: Up early, after bk: walked to Hazerswoude about 4 miles on the road to Utrecht to see Rembrandt's mill which I found to be a most interesting old structure, made a sketch or two inside. Mr Braat the owner was very polite and I took some coffee with him, walked back at 2... went to Raadhuis & saw the pictures &c - some curious specimens, then made a few sketches about the Gates and moats. Mr Fleming called to see my pictures in eveng. He painted an interior view and made more sketches from across the river, leaving his 'traps' at the mill overnight and continuing next morning.

13th:[Haarlem, Logement of the widow de Boer] Called on Mr de Haan living in a splendid house in Smeestraat with fine garden who was kind enough to procure me admission to the Teylerian Museum, he accompanied me there and I was much gratified with the fine collection of Minerals (and Pictures, modern but good) he then took me for a delightful stroll round the Boulevards of the Town and came to my hotel to see my pictures. I then made several sketches of Poorten and Schuiten on the Spaarn. lovely boat with green mast... took a long stroll by the brilliant light of a most lovely moon - back at 10 to tea...

17th: after bk. went to the Museum at 10, saw Mr. Apostool, returned to Hotel with Mr Klinkhamer - shewed him pictures and sketches... at 2 Mr Apostool paid me a visit and seemed much pleased with my pictures and sketches. I lent him my small books to look over.

18th: Went to the Palace but as the Queen was not yet buried I could not be admitted to see it. Went to the Museum and Mr Apostool went with me to Mr Six's to see his truly superb collection of pictures. Staid there some hours and had the greatest feast of art I had ever enjoyed. Mr A then introduced me to the Society Doctrina for an hour or so.

Nov. 1st Painted copy at Museum [Ostade] Began a copy of a beautiful Vandervelde. Painted in the sky Saw Mr Lamberts & gave him small sketch of Ship Canal. Long expected parcel arrived from London with letter from Harriette... recd. copies of *London; Shipping & London Bridge* works. Called on Mr Maes & shewed him & then on Mr. de Haan...

13th. Went by Steamboat to Zaandam. Made a few sketches & walked a long distance amid a myriad of Mills. Most extraordinary sight altogether - the place having the appearance of a Chinese town, so many bridges & canals. Visited the house of Peter the Great & sketched the chair he made use of. Retd. to Amsterdam at 4 by the sailing schuit. Spent the eveng. at Mr Apostool's met Messrs Six, Taurel, Lamberts, Cranenburg & a great many strangers. After coffee we looked over some of the finest prints of Rembrandt, Backhuizen, & also some by modern artists to wit views of London Bridge, Shipping & Craft!

15th. Mr Luden went with me to Mr Van Loon's & saw his glorious collection of pictures. Splendid Backhuizens, Rembrandt, Wouvermans. He then introduced me to Mr Van der Hoop who politely shewed me his superb collection of pictures, some grand works of the greatest masters. He also has two excellent Schotels.

17th ...called on Mr Proctor & left some prints for him. Went to bootmaker & bought Scheveling slippers. Called on Mr Steengraght on the Vyberburg, who introduced me, after I had seen his pictures, to Baron Verstock's collection of Pictures. Packed up Model !! Baskets !! &c & at 4 dined with Mr Proctor & family & also Sir Wm Johnson & Dr Tuke - left them & bid adieu to the beautiful village of The Hague (at present looking most miserably dull & dirty) Packed up & went by diligence to Rotterdam & staid at the New Bath hotel...

18th. Up at 6 & left Holland after a delightful cruize of three months by the *Attwood* packet at 2 o'clck. Head wind the whole voyage, took to berth until 9 AM

19th Sunday morning off Margate, glorious morng. bright & fresh Delightful voyage up the river meeting hundreds of vessels of all classes going out with wind & tide. Arrived at Custom House at 4. Went immediately to brother Tom's, dined with him & spent the evng. there Slept on the sofa very soundly...

1838

June 29th: [The Hague.] Went after bk. at ½ p 10 to the Baron Verstolck's & looked again at pictures - he shewed me some wonderful drawings by Rembrandt - Vandervelde &c. ...after dinner went again to the Baron's met there Mr. Mazel, looked over some of the Baron's most choice etchings, perfectly unique - a most rare treat...

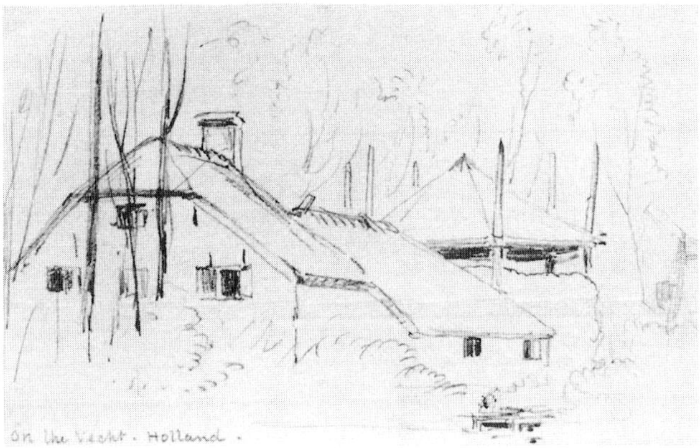

Plate 212. Pencil drawing
On the Vecht
Dutch farms and their buildings as part of the landscape were sympathetically embraced by Cooke when guest of his friends the Maes family at Nieuwer Hoek, Loenen, on the Vecht.
Photo courtesy Clarges Gallery

30th: ...went with Mr Marlton to see Kruzeman's picture of the Prince of Orange. Called on Mr Mazel and he took me and introduced me to several Dutch Painters viz. Mr Van Hove- Van Oss - Backhuysen - Bosboom - Shelfhout - Rosenboom - Eeckhout and saw all their ateliers and pictures. They all called in evening, Mr Kruzeman also, to see my pictures and works & they were much pleased...
[Here Cooke was rubbing shoulders with significant figures and noting doubtless their strengths and peculiarities. Andreas Schelfhout was in touch with French artists, Gudin and Isabey and one of his pupils was J.B. Jongkind. H. van de Sande Backhuysen bore a good marine name but was a landscape painter, but it was Johannnes Bosboom (1817-1891) who is reckoned among the first of the renascent Hague School landscapists.]
July 30th: Painted all day - Mr Brondgeest called to see my sketches at 2 - posted Jane's and Laura's letters by Batavier dined at Cattermole's - very wet in ev. Klinkhamer took tea with me and smoked a few cigars - in evg. made designs for new pictures. Cramp very bad in both legs in the night.
31st: Painted all day. Mr Maes called and invited me to go with him to Loenen tomorrow - to his country seat-...
August 1st: Packed away things and at 12 went to Mr Maes'. After luncheon we went in his elegant carriage to Loenen on the road to Utrecht to his country seat on the Vecht river - called Nieuwer Hoek - arrived about 3 after a most delightful ride through Abkower and Baambrug by the canals.
4th: ...painted on picture of the Spaarn & made a sketch picture on paper of the Molen van Van Dam at Loenen under the effect of rain & storm - completed it in 4 hours.

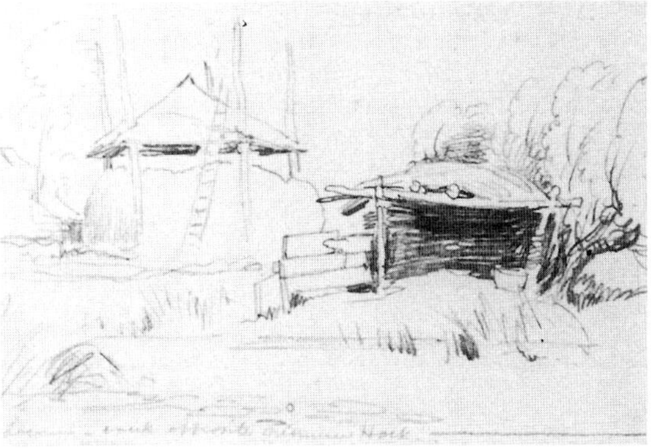

Plate 214. Pencil drawing
Loenen Creek, opposite Nieuwer Hoek, on the River Vecht
'In former times one of the favourite resorts of wealthy Hollanders' (Guidebook).

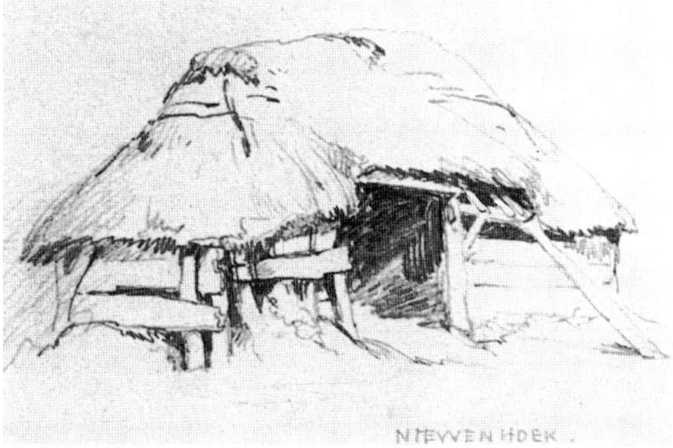

Plate 213. Pencil drawing
Barn, Nieuwer Hoek
Photo courtesy Clarges Gallery

6th: ...looked over and made sketches from Zeeman's [R. Nooms'] etchings. Saw Lamberts and Klinkhamer, commenced a study in oil on paper of new subject a *beurtman* on the Y... took stroll by the Stadts Herberg - got sk. or two - very fine again in aftn.
11th: Took bkfast with Mr Hitchcock, sketched eelboats (by his house), bought oils & colors &c. at Portman's. Painted on Amsterdam picture. Mr Curtis the banker friend of Geo. Rennie's called to see me & my pictures. Dined at Peters' at 5 and then went over to the Tol Huis & sketched the Holle Sloot &c, home at 8 to tea... beautiful effects on Y. Hitchcock lent me Rademaker's etchings of views in Holland.
13th: Painted all day on picture - Mr Curtis called- Mr Lamberts came also- Klinkhamer procured for me the 2 Vols of Rademaker's etchings, 300, for 7 Gulden. Wrote to Jane in ev.

1843
August 18th: After Bkfst went in Schuit with Jane to Rembrandt's Mill, saw Mr and Mrs Braat and family, made sketch and retd. to Leyden at 12, packed up- Dr Molkenboer called to see my pictures at Smit's. Left L by diligence at 1 and arrived at Hague at ½ p 2. Wrote to Mr Loddiges with Rodbard's list of plants [note in Diary: J.C.Rodbard, Flora's Lusthof by de Rynsburger Poort, Leyden] & posted it - dined at Old Doelen & left for Scheveling by omnibus at 6 - took luggage to Loghers' & slept there - took stroll on sand, hundreds of fashionables & boats - glorious sunset - & clear weather. Met Mr Weimar, saw the Queen on sands.
19th: Out early, plenty of boats, began picture of Scheveling for Mr Stokes [43/6], sketched it in. Took stroll on sands and in town - went at ½ p 5 to Bad House, dined and sat for a couple of hours on the Esplanade. Saw the Princess of Orange and other élite of the Hague - very fine bright day. Took tea at B.H. and retd on Sands to Loghers - 100 boats arranged in a straight line along the shore. Wind NE.
29th: Rainy morning but soon changed to a warm but grey day - out before bk., sketched - painted on view from window, sea, sand &c all day

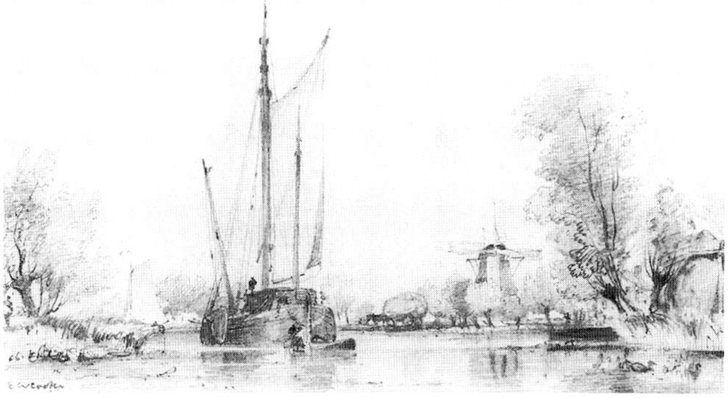

Plate 215. Pencil drawing
On a Dutch river
It is tempting to suggest the River Vecht at Loenen, but no related titled work has appeared. Photo courtesy Martyn Gregory

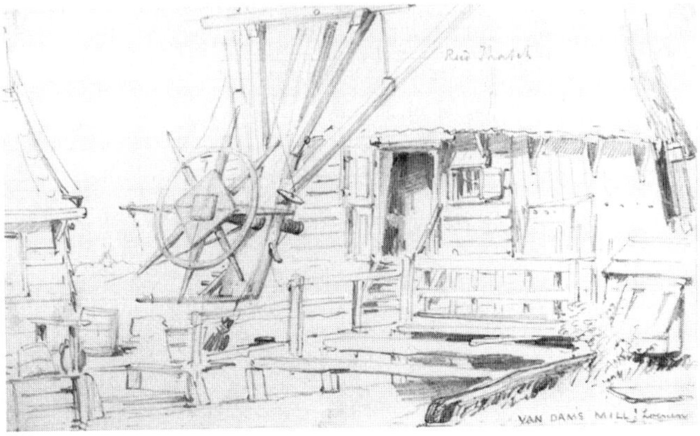

Plate 216. Pencil drawing
Van Dam's mill
Both watercolour and oil studies of this windmill on the River Vecht were made in 1838 but have not been sighted.
Photo courtesy Clarges Gallery

- in evg. a great many boats came in late. We went out and saw the sales going on by twilight with lanterns. A vast quantity of fish arrived - Jane better.
Sept 1st: Out early - got sketch of repairing mast-head. After bkfst sketched view near Koepel- painted on view from window till 4... after dinner I went to Hague posted letters, called on Mr Weimar - bt. colors and canvass at van Gogh's - walked back at 8 to tea- very fine day, quite a calm sea.

1845
[FRANCE]
10th August [Avignon] Felt better. Went to the Grand Mass at the Cathedral (saw the Arch Bishop) then to the Papal Palace and examined the interior - to the ruined church of the Convent of the Cordeliers (& saw the tomb of Laura) in the Rue des Tanneurs - a curious street with a narrow stream full of waterwheels - first saw *Adiantum Capillus Veneris* in the walls of the stream -in great profusion...
15th [Arles] After Bkfst went down to the Quai and saw a latine [lateen] sail for the first time,- made sketches on the river and perambulated the town, saw Tower of Constantine -the Cathedral & its Cloisters (fine) the ancient Theatre (sketched) and the grand Arena - mounted to the top, superb view - saw the procession of a Fête de Localité - girls and children dressed in white... I sketched fragment of Forum adjoining the Hotel.Very hot day.
17th. Sunday. About 6 we had the first view of the Mediterranean and

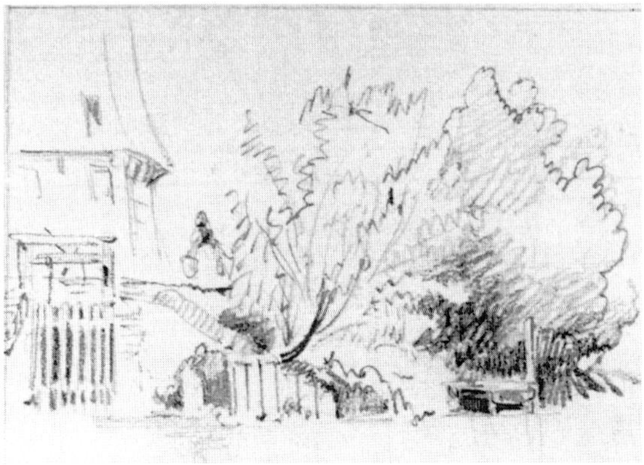

Plate 217. Pencil drawing
By Van Dam's mill
Photo courtesy Clarges Gallery

the port & city of Marseilles gloriously lighted up by the rising sun. Arrived at the Hotel des Empereurs at 7 to Bkfst, then went to the French Protestant church at 10 - & afterwards visited some of the other churches... in evening took walk round the Harbour - to the mouth called the reserve- saw a glorious sunset and wonderful effects of Blue sea.
18th. After Bkfst went round the Harbour sketching boats &c - crossed at the entrance fort and made coloured sketch of the lighthouse &c from the rocks... after dinner went to La Reserve and back by water & strolled about the Prado &c...
21st [Toulon] Up early & out in market. Left by 9 o'clock boat for La Seyne across the Harbour, a most lovely ride amidst the men of war- glorious scenery all round the Rade - sketched about there all day (dined at Hotel d'Europe) and returned by 6 o'clock boat (two pence each) the hottest day we have had. Laura troubled with nettle rash, my throat better.
22nd. George's birthday - 3 years old - up early left by diligence at 8 o'clock in coupée for Nice- very fine and lovely road to Draguinan passing thro'... on to Fréjus by moonlight, glorious scenery, fine pass of L'Estrelles - arrived at Cannes at 5 in morning and at Antibes at ½ p 6 to Bkfst. -saw Date palm first time growing naturally- very brilliant morning.
25th. Up early and sketched in harbour before bk. - and boats on beach before our hotel, then commenced a picture of Toulon from La Seyne - painted till 6 and took a stroll. Met Mr & Mrs Barchard on the promenade, walked ½ an hour with them- took an ice and home at 9 - very fine and cooler day. Got letter from Georgie and Mary with good news.
28th. Sketched hauling in net &c before Bk. Bought bottles for ferns, re-arranged <u>A.Petrarchae</u> for Mr Barchard to take to England. Painted on rocks from windows...

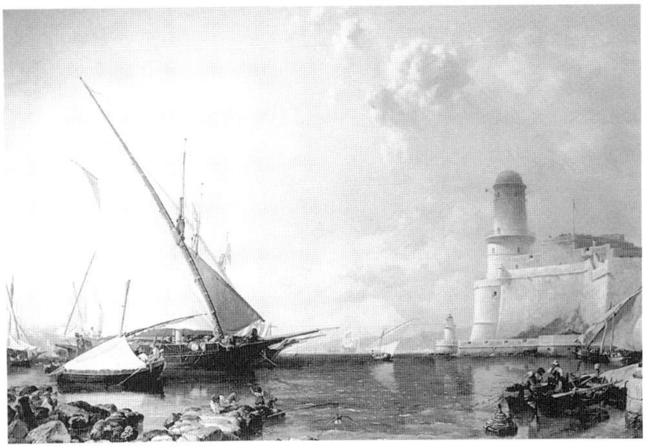

Plate 218. 50/3
The Port of Marseilles
The lofty lateen yard and sail of the Mediterranean xebec has an exotic appeal to the English artist who also noted for future reference the spread of awnings in hot weather. Photo courtesy Michael Appleby

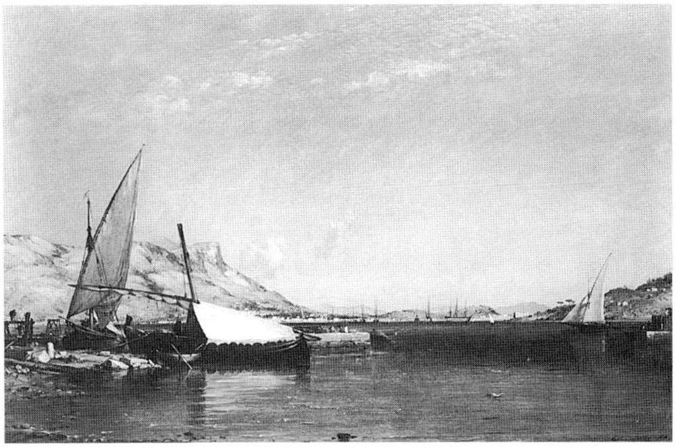

Plate 219 45/7
Toulon, the Rade
Crossing the roadstead to La Seyne he sketched the imposing scene and delighted in the varied shipping encountered on the way. In fact the painting was begun a day or so after he had left but while still fresh in his mind. Photo courtesy Yale Center for British Art

29th. Sketched on beach before Bk, painted till 1 o'clock on Rocks from my window- Mr Barchard and Mr Harvey called for me amd we went in boat to Villa Franca [Villefranche] - a curious little town in a deep bay next to Nice on the E. Walked about the place and into a lovely private garden, sketched &c -Went to Beaulieu through beautiful orange and olive groves- saw the great olive tree 40 ft in circumference ... saw 2 palms...

Sept.2. Tuesday Sketched before bk. at Port, then packed up and made sk. from window of Nice. Went to Consul and Police about Passport- hair cut- bought articles, dined at 1 and after some trouble about a permit to leave the Port and hiring a boatman we started in a boat with 2 men at 3 & left Nice reluctantly - Napoleon & son rowed us and we arrived at Monaco at 7 after a pleasant passage, sea calm at first but a little swell came on after. On approaching the place much struck by its extraordinary character. Rocks & bastions & towers - cactus &c. Baggage just looked at and went to Hotel des Colleges, very comfortable - took coffee and a stroll. Lovely day & night.

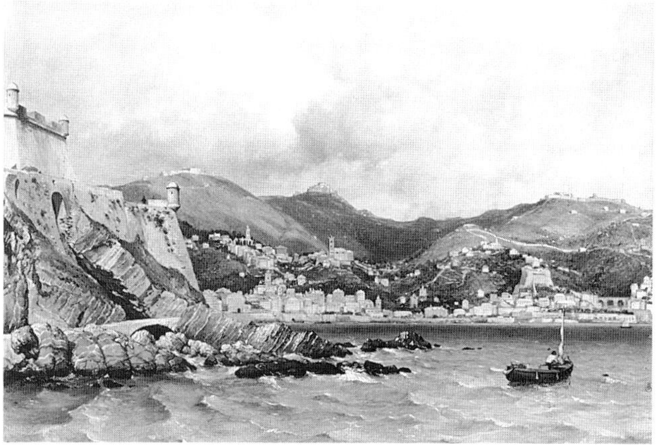

Plate 220. 45/11

Mountains of the Riviera & little Bay of Monaco

Early in his first Mediterranean tour the excitement of new things was fresh; geological features vied with botany, the landscape and fishing boats for his attention. Photo courtesy Michael Bryan

3rd. Went down to Port and sketched Tartano and back to Bk. at 9. Set palette and went down to the Port and painted a view of the bay and part of the hill & Towers- boat &c from under the arch - then went round the rocks and sketched Town - back at ½ p 6 to dinner then took stroll round the wood and plantations opposite the sea - men fishing among the rocks with a fire burning - very fine cool day.

7th Sunday. After bk. we took our books and went to the West, sat under Olive tree and read the service of the Church, also sang hymns under a grand Carob tree- wandered along the sea shore among olive groves - most enchanting spot - Sea very fine and more agitated.

9th. Painted new subject on walls, of Opuntia [cactus] & then began another view of Monaco with Arch & Palm on left till 4 & then went down to Port & worked on old sketch of Mountain and sea - back to dinner at 7 - finished Laura's letter to Harriette in evening - glorious day. A young Priest came & looked over my sketchbook while I painted - Laura drew in water colors.

12th. Finished sk. in oil of Aloes, cactus &c before bk.- packed up and left Monaco at 11½ in boat - had pleasant row, sea very fine and blue to Mentone. Landed at the little fort and had luggage searched, went to the Hotel de la Poste - nice rooms overlooking the Sea - sketched fort and boats & dined at 4, then took stroll on beach - fine Sea and breakers -

13th. Went down on rocks and sketched-in subject on Block, of Fort before bk. Painted sky from my window & then (at 2 o'clock) went down again and painted it with sea & rocks and retd. at ¼ to 7 to dinner, very tired. Very fine not too Bright nor hot. Moon greasy for Italy - Laura terribly bitten by B flats F sharps and Musquitos - my hands also bitten a few [times] by the latter.

[Their onward travels coastwise into Italy are recorded with much of the same detail and delight.]

19th. Began sk. before bk. of Palms hanging over a rivulet- after bk. completed picture of San Remo from pier - painted till 5, then completed sketches in book - visited churches &c, took stroll out of the W. gate & back by the Sea Shore - at 7 to dinner - in evg. very heavy shower of rain, wrote letters - next morning quite bright & sunny - & warm.

20th. Saturday Wrote before bk. then went up to the Madonna della Costa & painted a view of the church with the tall Cypresses. A very kind Gent - a painter lent us a chair & staid all the time by me - he showed me his Atelier & his pictures (in a large building formerly the palace of the Bishops of San Remo) - in evg. went to a Chymists close by - whose son makes models of birds most beautifully - he showed us his collection of Natural History - curious ceremony on completing a Bridge.

21st. After bkfast. Mr Lorenzo Martini the painter came & looked at my pictures & sketches also the London Bridge work. We went to the Jetty and read the church service &c - went into the fort and saw the huge skeleton of a whale - after dinner Mr Martini came and conducted us to L'Arma on the Sea coast about 4 miles to the E, saw the curious little chapel in the cave under the rock, retd. at 8 to coffee, most pleasant walk - fine & cool.

November 4th. Made sketches of Porto Fino from Ricco and as there was no vehicle to be had, we awaited a *vetturino*. Met with a good one at 2 and went on box. Laura inside with pleasant companions, Signor Gervigno & wife. Stopped for 2 hours at Rappallo. I made 2 or 3 sketches of old tower. Lovely road and views of Genoa - horse nearly tumbled over precipice - arrived at Chiavari at 6, very cold evening, dined at 7 & slept at the Hotel de la Poste very comfortably - fine bright day.

5th. Went to the Post - no letter - after bk. went to Lavagna (2 miles off) & sketched. Called on Sig. Gervino at his Palazzo Franzone who was very glad to see us. I saw a fine view from his window so returned to Chiavari for colors & tools & went back. Commenced a small picture at 4 and finished it by 6 - sun setting over sea - Laura made 2 sketches for his wife and he gave us a cameo and a glass seal of Petrarch. We left at 6 and back at 7 to dinner...

11th. Took bk at 8 & at 9 the Frate Signore Buonaventura called to see pictures with which he was pleased. I went up to his convent and painted all day from the Loggia, a view of the Town & Port of Spezzia - the monks sat around me and conversed all the time - Laura staid at hotel and wrote to Aunt - in evening she read *Athenaeum*, very dull & cloudy all day with misty evening,

15th. Very wet indeed in morning...went up to convent & painted a dingy sketch of the hills to the Eastward of Gulph, the Carrara mountains quite lost in the mist & clouds. Retd. at 2 and worked on picture of Sestri - went out with Laura at ½ p 3 to the Westward and sketched 2 subs in the rain - saw the outline of the marble mountains - back at ½ p 5 to dinner - in evg. L. read History of Italy in Italian - I worked on sketches. Settled for 1 weeks lodging.

18th Very bright & fine all day & hot sun. The Carrara mountains I have now seen for the first time & most lovely they are in form & color... after bk. went to the convent & painted view of the mountains - at work all day till 5... most superb effect of warm light on mountains in evg. - just before sunset....

December 8th. Went to the Church of Santa Croce at 11. A most extraordinary fine building for monuments, sculptures, pictures & frescoes. Michaelangelo's tomb, Dante's, Galileo Etc, very fine. Pictures by Agoli & others by Sassoferato and Allori. Curious frescos and pictures

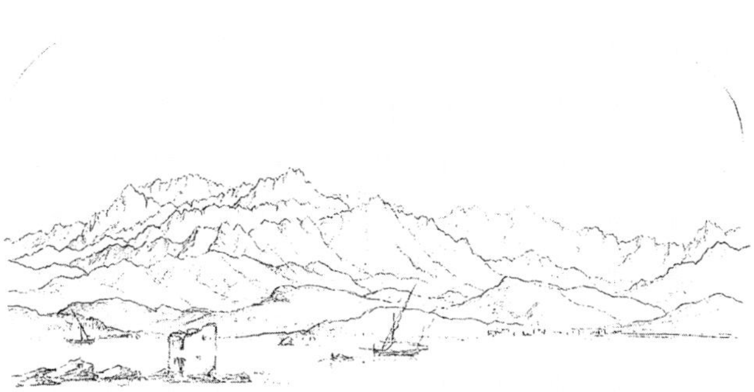

Plate 221. 46/47

The marble mountains of Carrara from the Capucin convent, Spezzia, sunset effect

Camera lucida record of a painting made from a sketch of the previous year. There is an element of geological study in this monumental landscape.

by Cimabue and Giotto and Gaddi - in Sacristy, some on large Crucifixes - altogether a great treat. Cloisters interesting, made 3 sketches of towers &c from the Piazza - looked into other churches - in evg. I called on McInnes for an hour...
18th. Painted till ½ p 12. Mr and Mrs Gorton & Mrs McInnes called. L & I accompanied the latter and called on Mr Woodburn (out) then on Powers the Sculptor [Hiram Powers (1805-1873) American sculptor, established from 1837 in Florence. His *Eve before the Fall* was much reproduced.], saw his *Eve* & other fine works then called on McInnes. Visited the church of Santo Spirito, very fine, made sketches of Ponte Trinita & Uffizi, till dark. Spent the evg. at home writing...
20th ...went to the Carmine, saw the Masacchio fresco. Packed up & dined at Luna. Bought articles. Left Florence by diligence at 2, Mr & Mrs McInnes came to see us off in the heavy rain which began at 12 and never ceased all day and night. Proceeded very slowly, the roads being very heavy and did not reach Siena till past 1 o'clock in the morning. Staid there to supper. Felt great regret at parting from McInnes & his family, sorry also to leave Florence. Sleepless night. [The floods were out and their way south was full of perils.]
22nd ...Passed another very tedious sleepless night and proceeded very slowly with 8 horses and 2 oxen.
23rd (My beloved Conrad born, 1843). Still rain & gloom - passed some curious remains of antiquity on the road side and crossed part of the Campagna, very beautiful country. As soon as daylight dawned saw the Eternal City for the first time about 7 miles off. Most interesting approach, St Peter's and the Tiber on the right - entered the Porto del Popolo at 8 o'clock and went to the Dogana, luggage visé and we secured apartments at 14 Via Monte Brianzo, removed luggage there and took bkfst. Rested a few hours (having head ache). At 2 went out in the rain and wind to the Post Office & on to the Capitol & Forum and to the Colosseum &c - wonderful scene beyond all expectations !!!!...
24th. Called on Mr & Mrs Radford, went with him to the Police Office and got pass for 12 months stay. Called for Laura and we went over the Bridge of St Angelo to St Peter's - wonderful pile, went into part of the Vatican, took luncheon at Mr Radford's, he accompanied us to Cromek's who with his wife and mother were truly delighted to see us. I saw some sketches in Greece...
Rome, Christmas Day: Went to the English Church, heard Mr Hutchinson preach from 2nd Luke 13 & 14 Very fine Sermon. Communicated with 100 others, 4 clergymen officiating at Altar. Called on Mr Radford, went with Laura to the Forum & Coliseum At 5 we went to Cromek's to tea spent a pleasant evening with his family. Looked at sketches. Saw his sweet children dance the Tarantella.
26th Called on Cromek & he accompanied us to see lodgings. Saw very comfortable ones on the Pincian Hill. Called on Mr & Mrs Hannah & met there Mr & Mrs Bicknell. Began sketch from our lodgings of St Angelo.
31st. After bk. went with L & met Cromek at the Trinita di Monte & he accompanied us to make the arrangements about lodgings - settled all with him. I rec'd note at Torlonia's. Packed up & left the Casa Ranucci at 12 with baggage and removed to our new apartments 13 Piazza della Trinita di Monti, got in wood. At 3 went with Mrs Cromek to the Gesu Church and heard the Te Deum sung most exquisitely in the presence of the Pope & a great many Cardinals . The organ music was most grand, 3 organs in the church. Returned at 5½ Passed the magnificent fountain of Trevi... bought various things for housekeeping - sketched Claude's house from my window.
[He made one note of current finances: Left England with Circular notes £150; Sovereigns £53; Bank of England note £10; Silver - 15s 4d. Also letter of credit on Torlonia £300. Expenses to Oct.11 evening - £62. There is far too much to print - the tourist's delight and the artist's education is revealed on every page of a tiny pocket notebook *H.Penny's Second Quality Metallic Books - Warranted if written on with the -Prepared Pencils- To be as plain & durable as Ink.*.]

1846
[Rome] Jan 2nd Cromek called at 10 & looked at my oil sketches. I painted on St Peter's & St Angelo. At 3 took stroll with Laura. Found letter at P.O. with good news of home.Visited the Forum of Trajan saw beautiful column, back at 5. I took a turn in evng. dull & cold.
3rd Sat. Bought colours at the French shop. Painted boats in view of St Angelo. Mr Radford called & looked at oil sketches also Mr & Mrs Hannah & Mrs R. Cromek came to tea for 2 hours & looked at sk. books. Very cold day.
5th. Mr Newton called & looked at oil sk. Went at 1 to the Vatican & drew from sculptures in the long gallery- went to St Peter's & heard Vespers in the Capella del Coro - most exquisite music & voices. The gorgeous building increases in size & beauty every time I visit it. Left at ½ p 4 & retd to dinner at 6. Mr Radford called for me left Laura at Mrs Hannah's & Mr H accompanied us to the Academy - made my first drawing from the life. Called for Laura on my return at 8 & we wrote letters in evng. Cold & raw day tho' sunny & bright.
7th. Painted on 2 Monaco subjects. Mr Newton came for 3 hours looking at skts. &c... sketched a wine cart, went to the Forum saw the Temple of Janus Quadrifrons, House of Rienzi, Temple of Vesta, Ponte Rotto, T. of Fortuna Vir? the island or ship of Aesculapius, fish market T. of Octavia & called at P.O & back at 4. Robert Smith called. Academy in eveng. During my absence Cromek called for an hour or two & brought us books. Bright but cold day.
9th Called on Robt.Smith at his studio & saw his models & sculpture. Ariel very clever. Went also to see another Sculptor adjoining. Painted on 2 or 3 pictures. At 2 Mrs Cromek came to see my sketches... Cromek called & I took walk with him on Pincian till dinner. Academy in evng. Read Donovan's *Rome* . Most clear & beautiful day & mild.
10th Called on Glennie saw his beautiful drawgs. of Pola & about Rome...
11th Sunday. Heard Mr Hutchinson in morng. preach... & also in aftern... went to the studio of Overbeck (between the two Services) saw his beautiful designs & a large picture of a Pieta - not so good. In evng we took walk in the gardens of Villa Borghese.

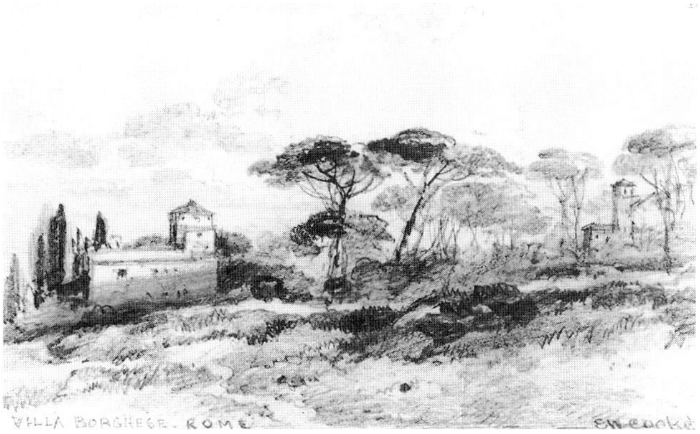

Plate 222. Pencil drawing
Villa Borghese, Rome.1846
Trees and gardens here captivated him no less than the ruins of antiquity. This sketch is clearly part of the painting 49/10 (Plate 283).
Photo courtesy Martyn Gregory

14th. Drew models of Baskets with camera. Called on Mr Newton, on my return found Mr Vivian & a lady looking at Pictures. Went at ½ p 1 to Sta Maria Maggiore & on to St John Lateran - very interesting - fine cloister of the House of Constantine- curious fragments mosaics-relics-pictures, Chapel & tombs - Bernini's *Dead Christ* View from the Façade very fine over the Campagna with the ruins of the great aqueducts & walls with Santa Croce in Gerusalemme & the distant Sabine & Alban Hills. Staid 2 hours & retd. at 5. Academy in evng. Mr Radford & Robt Smith spent the eveng with us & looked at pictures & sketches. Very warm day.
Feb 5th ... called on Ainsley & saw his oil sketches &c. L & I went to Vatican saw sculpture & Egyptian & Animal rooms &c then to St Peter's home by fields & ferry by ½ p 5... Mr Newton lent me Piranesi's work on Antiquities of Albano to look over. Glennie spent the evng.(after 8) with us.
6th. Laura took lesson in Italian in morng. I drew from Piranesi, retd Mr Newton's book.-went with him to see a fine collection of Piranesi's works. At 2 called on Ainsley and he accompanied us on a stroll, first to the Colonna Gardens saw the fine Pine tree planted on the day of Rienzi's death - also the huge marble fragments of the Temple of the Sun - also ruins of the Baths of Constantine then to the Forum, Coliseum & to the little church of San Clemente with curious mosaics & a Chapel decorated with frescos by Masacchio- then to the Baptistry of St.Jno Lateran & to the Scala Santa. Retd at 5, dull day but mild. Academy Library in evng. Mr Newton & Ainsley spent the evng here & left at 12.
7th Sat. Drew at French Academy till 12. Bought drawng board for camera stand. Ainsley called for us at 1 o'clk & we took Mr Newton on

our way & went to Mr Strutt's, saw his pictures & sketches also those of his Son. Etchings also, very good things - then to Gibson's very much pleased with his beautiful sculpture & models...

10th Painted on Avignon Bridge in morng. After dinner we called for Radford... to the Villa Doria Pamphili outside the Porta San Pancrazio the gardens are most superb consisting of fine undulations & noble terraces -Fountains, cascades, grottos, shady groves and alleys of Evergreen oak & above all the most magnificent Stone Pines -in great masses of the finest growth. The terrace garden under the Villa is laid out with parterres exhibiting various arms & insignia of the Doria family - & bordered with Orange trees full of fruit. From the Upper terrace the finest view of the Vatican & St Peter's with Monte Mario & the distant —- Mountains is obtained

Saturday Feb 14th. Cromek called early, we went with the Hannahs & Mr Bicknell to the Corso at 12 and saw the opening of the Carnival by the troops of the Pope & the Senators. Towards the close Hannah & I went to the starting point in the Piazza del Popolo. Met Ainsley there, saw the start of the Horses which went off at full speed. The Carnival was a most poor & miserable affair.

17th. Went to the Vatican to draw but the Order was not signed by the Director so I could only contemplate. Staid 2 hours then went to St Peter's and sketched Lions... dined and we went with the Hannah's to Mr Bicknell's in the Corso, saw the tail of the Day's carnival... felt poorly.

19th. Called on Mr Newton (out) went to P.O., bought *confetti* for the little Cromeks. Ainsley came and brought Geo. Dennis who has just arrived from England... Hannah & I walked through the Carnival, met Ainsley & Dennis, we all four went down through the motley groups to the Piazza Venezia, got a seat on the stand and saw the horses come in, and the winner receive the prize of the flag...

24th ...Laura went to Mr Bicknell's to see the last of the Carnival. I dined and then went with A., D., and H. to see the *Mocoletto* [moccoletti] a curious and pretty sight & a most amusing scene, home at ½ p 7. In evg. wrote to McInnes...

March 2nd. Went with Hannah to choose a Camera [lucida] at Flacheron's, which he bought, then called on Geo Dennis (out) & sketched from St Angelo - waited until ½ p 1 for him & retd. home - met him and we started for a stroll first to the Arch of Galen- saw a man take Sanctuary at the door of the adjoining church - he had stabbed another man. Then to the Porta San Lorenzo and along the walls (inside) to the Porta Maggiore & examined the baker's Tomb and the aqueducts near also the Temple of Minerva Medica - a grand ruin in a vineyard. Home at ½ p 6 to dinner - spent a pleasant evg. at Ainsley's, met Mr & Mrs Hannah, George Dennis, Mr & Mrs Strutt & Son and Mr Ewings. We looked at his new sketches in Etruria - glorious day - my cold bad.

14th March ...went to see the Coliseum by moonlight. Most glorious sight, heard some Germans sing in concert under one of the great Arches of the Temple of Peace. Made sk. of the C. by light of a taper.

Sunday 15th. Heard Mr. Hutchinson in morning preach from V. Mark 56 v. Called on Radford after dinner & we went for a walk to St M.Maggiore and St J.Lateran, heard Vespers, went to the Colisseum & saw a curious sight, a number of people worshipping at the altars, the officiates, about 30 in number each wearing grey gowns with hoods on their heads with small holes cut for the eyes. Spent the evg. at Cromek's he shewed us drawings & relics - he gave me a stick of cedar from Mt. Lebanon and some ochre from Sienna.

16th. Cromek called and took me to Colman's, saw his pictures and sketches of Buffaloes & animals also on Mr Gurlitt a Danish painter, saw his fine pictures of the Campagna, very well-colored and grand scenes. Called for Hannah and we went to the Pamphili Gardens & painted all day on 2 sketches - a most glorious day, went to Academy in evg. - had letter from Harriette with good news.

17th. Mr Colman came to see sketches. We went for a stroll, sketched Arch of Galenius[?] - had my sketching umbrella stolen from my side. Drew about St John Lateran. aqueduct &c along the Coelian to Sta Maria di Navicella, drew the galley - returned to Colisseum - & up to S.Pietro ad Vincoli, sketched Palm &c there.

21st. Cox and D[igby] Wyatt came to see sketches... I went to the Tarpean Rock... we went down to see the guillotine, an execution having just taken place. I sketched the Temple of Vesta, Cloaca Maxima, carts & oxen, Parts of Arch of Titus...

March 22nd Sun. Went with Ainsley & Laura to the Sistine Chapel & heard Mass before the Pope & Cardinals. Very fine effects of light & color, rich dresses of the Priests &c. Then to St Peter's and after parting with A. we walked to the top of Monte Mario into the Villa. Glorious view of Rome. Returned at 3 to English church, a stranger preached 13 Heb 14 v, very good. Then called on Hannah & heard the benediction of the Virgin at the Church of Sta Trinita di Monti, most exquisite singing of the nuns - in evng. Cromek came also Watt & Hannah: dull & grey day.

23rd Went with Hannah to the Colonna gardens, got some of the wood of the Pine, thence to the Villa Volskonski [*sic*] by the aqueducts near the Scala Santa. Drew in a subject for painting & began another with Wolf &c Back at ½ p 6; L dined at Mrs Hannah's, I at (Li—-'s) Went with L & Mr & Mrs H. to the Church of —- Illuminated for 40 hours prayer Took coffee at Nuovo, very warm scirocco wind, dull & grey.

24th Went with Hannah to the same villa & we painted all day. Mrs H. & Laura joined us there at 3 & we returned together at ½ p 6. Mogg, Geo Dennis & Cox called in evg., I called on Radford in evg and met Mr & Mrs Barrington there. A most lovely day, bright & lovely effects on aqueducts & mountains.

25th Went with the Hannahs to the Aqueduct & sketched panoramic view from the Loggia on top of Villa —- He left at 5 & I painted oil sketch from the specus of the aqueduct, home at ½ p 7 to dinner Met Ainsley at Nuovo & went to the Ch. sopra Minerva & saw the Pope & Cardinals. We shewed my sketches to Mr & Mrs Barrington. Most lovely day bright & warm

26 Glennie & Hannah came at 9 & we started for a sketching stroll, very gloomy morng. We began painting from the garden of the Convent of St John & St Paul on the Coelian with the cypresses. At 3 it began to rain & continued all the aftn. We sketched under cover & home at ½ p 6 Cromek & Ainsley called during my absence. Laura went out with Mrs Radford, she got letter from Mrs Bicknell.

27 Fri. Gloomy dark day. Went with Mr & Mrs Hannah & Laura to the Sciavia & Doria Palaces to see the pictures, then went to the Borghese Villa & painted one of the small fountains till dark. In evg. Cox called; felt very poorly. My birthday.

28 Sat. Better. Called on Ainsley & Hannah. Met Boddenham. Went with H to the Villa Borghese & we painted fountain &c near the Casino. Academy in evg. Bought paper &c. Dull & lowering day but sunny eveng. L posted letter to Georgie.

30th. Called on Glennie, out, bkfst at Nazzari, made sk. from window. Mrs Cromek came to see sketches. C. came also, Hannah called. Laura had lesson. Cox called, we went to Ranucci & then to Post Office & got letter from Mama, good news. Called on Torlonia & on Geo. Dennis (on Tarpeian Rock) he shewed us up to the Loggia, glorious clear view. Called again on Ranucci & on Glennie. Dined early went to Borghese Villa drew terrace & pines after 5 o'clock. called on Ranucci again and in evg. packed up plants & roba for our departure tomorrow. A glorious bright day. G.Dennis called.

31st Tues. Finished packing, called & secured apartments, also on Glennie. Ainsley called. Left the Trinita di Monti at 12 & removed to Casa Ranucci. Dined & called on Wyatt (architect) saw his sketches & drawings, very clever then to the Villa Borghese for an hour & made sketch. Called on Hannah Laura went with them to Cromek's to see his drawings, she felt poorly from her nose bleeding profusely. Took coffee at Nuovo & went to Academy for an hour. Glorious fine day.

April 1st. Bkfst at Nuovo - on Glennie, out - Set palette & went to the Convent garden of St Bartolommeo, made sketch of the ship of Aesculapius & ponte Quattro Capi. Began oil sk. of Ponte Rotto & Temple of Vesta from garden. Back at 7 to dinner, Geo.Dennis called in evng. A glorious bright day & lovely eveng. sky.

5th Palm Sunday. Went to St Peter's, Laura went into one of the Ladies galleries, I got a good place near the Baldachino and saw the whole splendid ceremony of blessing the palm branches (which were most tastefully plaited up into ornamental forms) Grand procession round the building. Retd. at 1 & in afternoon went to Church. Mr Hutchinson preached from Rev. Went after into the garden of the Hotel de Russie on the Pincio & into the Medici Villa, then to the Ch. of Trinita di Monti & heard the fine singing. Spent the evg. with Mr Hannah - fine but cool day.

30th ...Started at ½ p 7 with Cromeks in carriage to join the Artists' Festa in the Campagna. About 3 miles out we arrived at some very fine ruins of Tombs where we found a large assembly of German and French artists in costume, many on horses, they encamped and took breakfast, then sang in one of the Tombs. After about an hour's stay they all moved on to the Farm of Cervaro, curious incantation scene of the Sybil in a large cave, very well managed. They then distributed the Orders and insignia of the Mezzo-bajocco, they all then retired to the quarried caves of Tufo to dinner. We were joined by Mogg, ate our repast and started to return at 3. Met a vast number of carriages on the road, going to join the party. Took tea at the Cromeks, then went to the Colisseum, went over the upper part, got a sketch or two.

June 11th Amalfi Painted in house and sketched baskets &c in morning.

At 1 we went up to Grotto and painted till 6. An old man (out of his mind) came up & preached a sermon - in derision - rainy day, glorious sky in evg.- painted by candle light.
Sun 21st. Longest day. Up at 3½, left Amalfi after bkfst. with 4 men in a boat and had a most pleasant passage to Capri in 5 hours, arriving at 10 o'clock. Passed the finest coast scenery, glorious rocky islands, towers &c. White column of smoke from Vesuvius very fine indeed. Glassy calm all the morning. Steep ascent from Marina to the town of Capri. Went to Hotel de Londres in the midst of orange, vines & fig groves and distant peeps of the sea.
22nd. Went down to the Marina before bkfst. Very toilsome walk up the hill back at 12.-took roba down & began 2 pictures, one a view looking out of a fisher's house & another of rocks &c at Capri - back at ½ p 8 to dinner, terribly hot day.

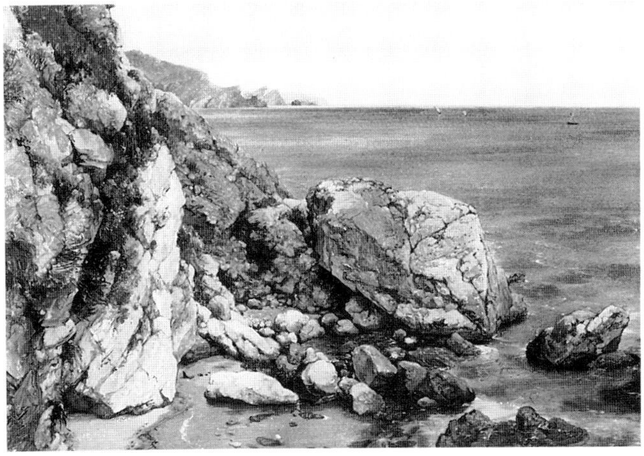

Plate 223. 46/28
Rocks at Capri, Capo di Campanello in the distance
Photo courtesy Spink & Son Ltd

26th. Worked on Palm and on other subjects before brfst. We went at 4 down to Marina and painted on Cliffs. Boatman brought us 7 letters from Naples. 4 from home contained the most bitterly distressing news I have ever had - announcing the death of my most beloved friend and Father Mr George Loddiges, who expired after a lingering illness on Friday 5th of June, we returned to Hotel with breaking hearts & passed a sorrowful evening & night. May God in his Mercy grant consolation & comfort to the bereaved family. Other letters from Cromek, Mr Stokes and Mrs McInnes.
July 21st …at 2 started by steamer passing the most grand & sublime scenery, particularly when looking back towards the St Gotthard Alps. Passed Tell's chapel at Schwyz. Mr & Mrs Barrington & Daughter came on board, a most agreable meeting. Wonderful effect of sunset color on the richly mantled slopes & mountains. Arrived at the Zwaan Hotel at Lucerne at ½ p 8…

1850
June 27th [London]. Called on F.Hering (out) & on Henry H[ering]. Saw Roberts's *Jerusalem*-called on Newman about Camera stand - home at 2 to dinner. Wrote letters & arranged prints &c. Tom Shuckard called and took tea here. I went to Italian Opera with him, *Le Prophète* very fine. The Queen and Prince &c came (she was struck at just before) and was greatly cheered. Home at ½ p 12. Very fine day, cooler.
28th …met Brockedon - called on Cromek, home at 5, & on Ansdell. Mr & Mrs Pryor & his brother called to see his picture in eveng. Ross sent my Calotype Camera & he came in evg.to arrange the fitting up the inside - Cundell called. Hook & his wife called in evng. Thunder storm.
July 2nd: Began painting little panel of Castel dell'Ovo. Called on Ansdell at 5 and consulted about chemicals for Calotype - called on Bell. At ½ p 7 went with Mama & H & M to a large party at Redgrave's. Games in garden and then acted charades very clever, home at 2, pleasant evening. 9 R.A.'s. Lady K. Wigram sent me (from Lady Selkirk) a plant of *Adiantum* from Man, alive.
Sat 6th Painted on Castel dell'Ovo. Mr & Mrs Ruskin called in aftn. & looked at Italian sketches…
24th: Portmanteau sent home. Wrote letters. Town at 11. got Passport, took it to be visé at the Austrian Embassy. Called on H.Hering, Medwin, Barbe, home at 2 attended the ceremony of laying the first stone of our Church, a large concourse assembled - a sharp shower followed. Terrey called in here, Cope also, went to the Vicarage to luncheon, met a large Party… returned with Peter Cunningham & Le Grew to Uwins, took coffee there. Arthur Glennie & his 3 nieces came at 7 to tea, Uwins came in also- shewed them Italian sketches. Walter Hawkins called in evg…
25th: Cut down Rucker's Scheveling picture (man with anchor). Wrote letters. Took picture in cab to Rucker's and he gave me cheque… called on Tom Shuckard at Clayton & Co's, signed Lease and paid for it. Called on Cundell, drew cheque - called on Watkins for camera, -not done- at Winsor and Newton's for moist colours. White Umbrella stick altered at Newman's. Bought colours at Barbe's and a mackintosh seat. Home at 8 to tea. Cundell call'd and brt. Circular Notes and Banker's book- very wet day.
Aug 3rd. [Nürnberg] Up early Mr Ellis & I went to St Lawrence Ch., beautiful Gothic spire like pinnacle - in the Ch. fine stained glass &c saw the picture Gallery of Early German Masters - the market &c & back at 9 to Bkfst. Then went to St. Sebald - fine tomb of Saint by Visscher, then to Albert Durer's House & to the Castle, fine view over town. Got 2 sketches & started by ½ p 1 train thro' Augsburg to Munich, arrived at 9, drove to 4 Hotels all full & back to Golden Sun, dined & slept there.
Sun 4th. Mr Ellis read prayers & preached to 9 English people - he & I retd. to Maulick's Hotel, took walk in aftn. saw Ludwig's Ch… No letter at Post Office. Met Mr & Mrs Barclay at Table D'Hote - & Mr Crofts & Brother.
17th [Insbruck] Went to the Custom House & passed my 2 trunks (which had been sent from Munich)- back to Bkft. saw Cathedral & took place in Stillwagen for Sterzingen & at 12 started by it & had a delightful view of the country from the Coupée. It cleared up in the aft. & we crossed the Brenner Pass Ascended for 4 hours thro' glorious ravines & rich valleys River dashing along at ones feet…
Aug. 26th: [Padua] …went all over San Antonio, very fine shrine of *il Santo* then to Giotto's Chapel of the Arena, full of Divine compositions …remained there 2½ hours… left at 7 by train & entered the glorious Venice at ½ p 8. When the boat entered the Grand Canal, after passing the Salute the Moon rose and revealed the glories of the scene, but the Piazza exceeded all that I could possibly have imagined. Left Roba at Danielli's and walked on Piazza till 12 o'clock, a glorious promenade.
27th: First thing after breakfast I went to San Marco. Met Mr Holloway and his cousin and a Mr Rathbone of Liverpool. Agreed to join them in seeing some of the wonders, took guide and a Gondola-first saw the Doge's Palace, Dungeons &c, full of fine pictures &c. Belle Arti (Titian's *Assumption* &c &c. Church of Salute, Giovanni & Paolo, then to the Armenian Convent at S.Lazzaro, conversed with Padre Pasquale - saw the printing. In evening went up the Campanile and walk in Piazza. A Glorious day in Venice, Called on Mr Brown (out). Got letters at P.O.
28th. Bkfst at ½ p 7 with Holloway & his 2 friends - saw the Scalzi, very rich in marble - little picture by Bellini, Church of the Frari, Titian, Peter Martyr - Titian's tomb - Canova's monument. Outside is the Equestrian figure of Bartolomeo Colleoni, very fine. Crossed the Rialto they bought articles of shells &c. I called for an hour on Mr Brown. Went in gondola to the Giardino with H. Dined with them at Restaurant & took a *giro* round by San Girogio & Giudecca & took an ice at Florian's. Band playing, out till 11 on Molo. Slept at Danieli's again.
29th: Went in Gondola to Breakfast with Mr Brown- he shewed me beautiful things. Hired my own boatman, we went to secure apartments, did not succeed at Casa Angelini, took others close by. Paid 6 weeks to Sig. Marzo, the Commissary of Police. Went to Jew's, hired furniture with Mr Brown, it was sent in in afternoon, beds put up etc…
30th: Could not sleep from Zanzari - men came and fixed mosquito net. Breakfasted at home and made my own tea with my spirit machine. Made camera outline of Santa Maria della Salute from my window …went to San Giorgio and began sketch: terrific thunder, lightning & rain for 2 hours. Dined at 4½ & returned till 7 & had tea. Mr Brown called in evening and staid till 10 telling me capital stories. I shewed him my *London Bridge work*. Felt better, cool day.
Sept.4: Went with Mr Brown to different offices about an Order to Draw. Saw no one. Prepared a new subject, first in oil. Set palette then called at Archives, Frari, for Mr Brown and went to Palazzo Reale, General not there. Dined and in afternoon painted first sky in Venice. At 6 rowed to Mr B's and we went to Piazzetta and walked till 9; read *Galignani* till 10.
Sept 7th: Wet morng till 12 then very fine & glorious evg. & sunset. Painted on boats till 1 & then went in Gondola & painted Campanile &

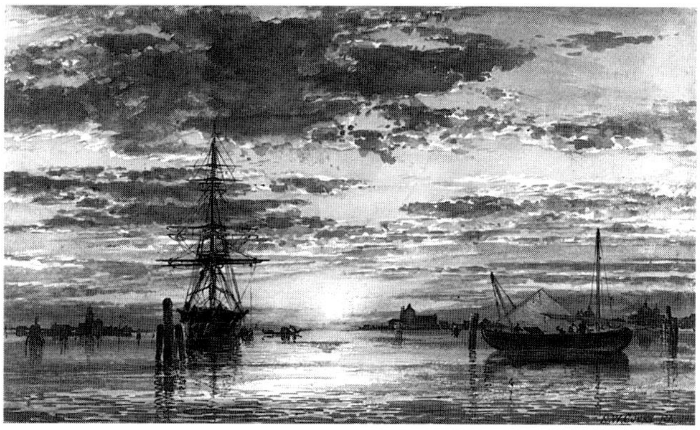

Plate 224. Watercolour
On the Lagune, Venice, sunset
Instructive comparisons can be made with the oil sketch of 1866 (66/10, Plate 289) which is the same scene in dull weather. The date 1864 could indicate an item prepared for his clearance sale of 19th June 1865, perhaps Lot 83. Photo courtesy Arthur Ackermann & Peter Johnson

Ducal Palace from nature in small picture. Back at 3 & dined in Restaurant with Charles Hardinge (who called on me in morng.) At 5 I took him in my boat to Murano & we got a sketch or two. Rowed a good deal. Back at ¼ p 7 to Molo & took promenade. Met Mr Brown & Mr & Mrs Smyth & Mr & Mrs Bentinck. No letter.
9th ...went off Royal Garden & began new subject of Zecca & Ducal palace. Terrible thunder storm came on while I was in boat - got oil study of stormy sky. Fine Bragozzi tacking out near Giardino. In evng walked on Piazza & wrote to Laura. Wonderful effect of setting sun on dark sky - claret color.
14th: ...to the Giardino &.painted on group of Bragozzi lying off the wall. Most superb colour and effect. Mr B[rown] hail'd me. Back at 3½ to dinner. At 5 started again rowed out close to Lido, following and sketching bragozzi going out. Sketched the two forts at entrance. & rowed back- most marvellous rich sunset - at ½ p 7 to tea. Painted rigging in picture in evg. A charming day.
18th. Dull dark day, painted on Bragozzi at home in morng. Dined at 3 & went at ½ p 4 to San Giorgio & painted on first picture with the Trabaccolo till dark.After tea went to the Teatro Apollo. Took walk on Piazza & Molo. Home at 12 very mild night.
October. 2nd Count Erdody called at ¼ to 10 & I went with him to the Arsenale & drew the model of the *Bucentaur* till ½ p 2 (boat waited). Retd. at 3 & soon after Lady Francis Hope & Miss Lascelles, Lady Grey & Daughter, Count Erdody, Mr Brown & Mr & Mrs Bentinck called to see my pictures...

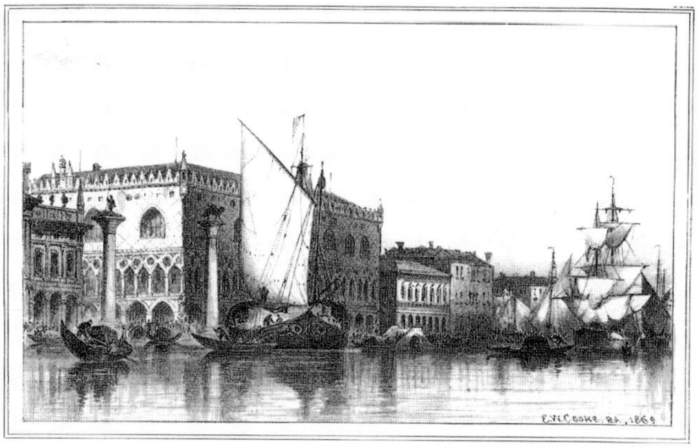

Plate 225 Engraving
Bella Venezia
This was the title of one of his RA pictures in 1860, but whether it is the same subject is not known. His caption was pure guide-book with quotations from Samuel Rogers and Lord Byron, but also claiming that of late years (1876) the decay of the city had been alleviated, which might be an acknowledgement of John Ruskin's efforts. From *Leaves from my Sketch-book,* John Murray, 1876.

26th: Exceedlingly wet all day till 4 oclk - read *Othello.* Painted new subject sky and Brichelapa till 5 then went for a Giro. Pulled up to the Giardino - glorious sunset, fine coloured clouds near horizon - grand effects of stormy sky to the East. Sketched War trabaccolo and had a hard pull against a swingeing tide back at 6. Dined at ½ p 6 with Phillips and joined him at Gallo in eveng. Heard *Don Pasquale* again. He retd with me and had some grog. fine eveng.
27th: Called on Brown. He and Phillips took me to Mr E. Cheney's house [Palazzo Soranzo-Piovene]. Highly interesting and full of beautiful objects of taste and art. They came to see my display of pictures.
28th: Made camera sketch of Danish brig off Salute. Drew Gondolas etc... Painted from 12 to ½ p 4 on picture of Brichepala, put in Riva, Prison, Church of San Zacharia &c. Very fine bright day but cool. Mr Brown hail'd me. Rowed up the Giudecca, sketched Redentore, very fine sunset indeed, ...in evng wrote long letter to Rucker. Wonderfully fine colour in clouds at Sun set.
Nov 8th: ...went out off S. Giorgio & painted on general view of Venice, evng effect-drew Tartana. Mr Brown boarded me and we pulled to Lido. Walked with him on sands, drew Fort St Andrea. Then in evng. painted on Sta Elena & another, dined by invitation with Phillips and Berg, a Norwegian painter, at the Cafe Français.
[Cooke and Brown walked where Shelley and Byron had ridden and the

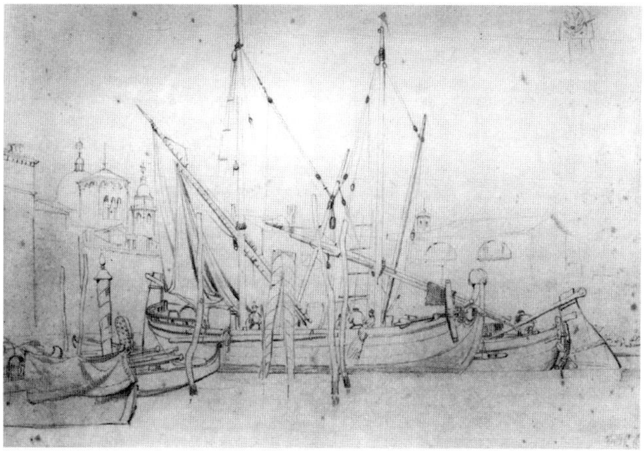

Plate 226. Pencil drawing
Venice, trabaccolo lying stern-to the Riva
This drawing bears an impressed EWC stamp, as occasionally found.
Photo courtesy The Trustees of the National Maritime Museum, Greenwic

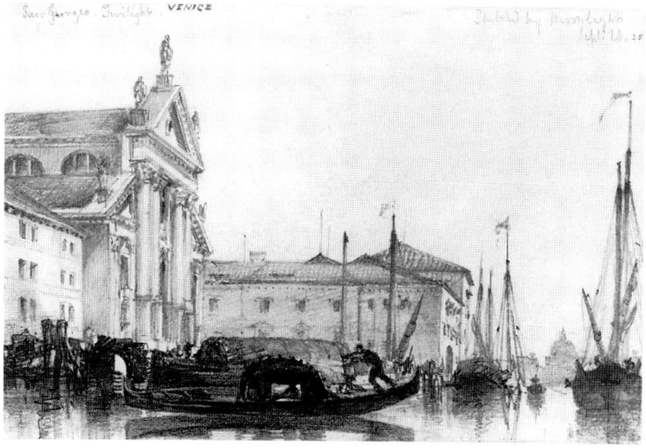

Plate 227. Pencil drawing
San Giorgio Maggiore, Twilight/Moonlight Sep 20 1850
The great island church gave subjects from all angles and evidently at all hours. Illustrated in *Henry James on Italy, Selections`from 'Italian Hours'.* 1988. Photo courtesy Martyn Gregory

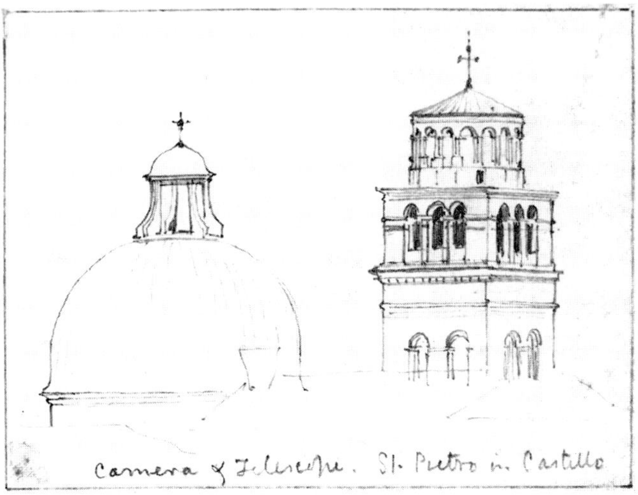

Plate 228. Pencil drawing
San Pietro in Castello
The former cathedral of Venice; reference details of dome and campanile drawn with the *camera lucida* and telescope, perhaps Cornelius Varley's instrument.
Photo courtesy The Trustees of the National Maritime Museum, Greenwich

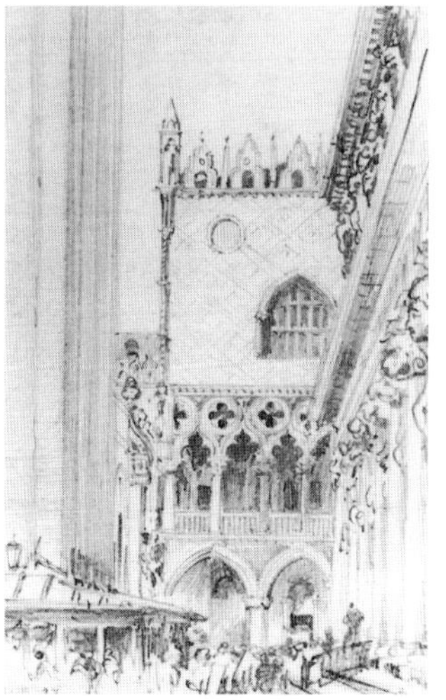

Plate 229. Pencil drawing
Corner of the Doge's Palace seen between the Campanile and the Procuratie Nuove Aug. 27 Photo courtesy Martyn Gregory

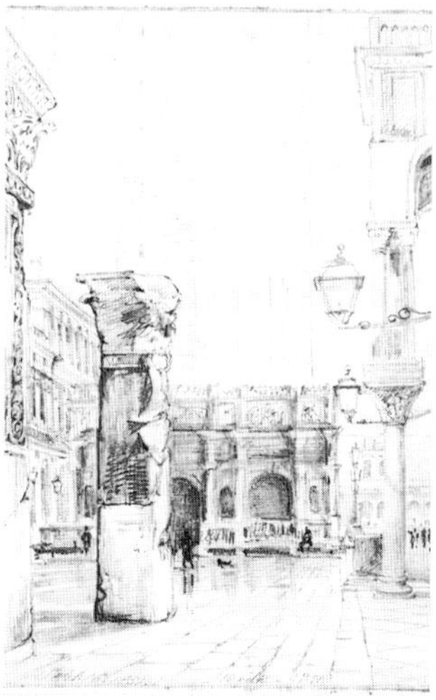

Plate 230. Pencil drawing
The Piazzetta by gas light- 10 o'clock at night, Sept. 16 1851
The short, square carved 6th century.pillars from Acre at left with Sansovino's Loggetta beyond and the Campanile lightly indicated. This is a tourist's souvenir with a dash of artistic bravura.
Photo courtesy The Trustees of the National Maritime Museum, Greenwich

painter was fortunate in having the society of this knowledgeable expatriate.]
9th: Very foggy all morng. At 10 Mr Berg with Phillips and Clark the Architect came to see sketches &c .I made camera drawing of Henry VIII's seal for Brown. Took a long time and made my head ache. At 3 went out and painted sea from Canale S.Giorgio. ...dined at 6 with Phillips then bought 3 wooden Persian spoons in Merceria.
15th: ...set palette and went to S.Michaele, painted and drew chain of Julian Alps, most lovely and clear. Brown came up in a sandolo and we went to Bersaglio and got into the garden amongst the cypresses, fine view...

1851
Sept.19th Called on Ruskin, he out.. She lent me his *Pre Raphaelitism* which I read. At ¼ p 11 I went to call on Mr Cheney (out). Went in gondola and worked on Ducal Palace... at ½ p 8 went to Ruskin's to tea. Met Lady Sorrell and daughter. R[uskin] shewed me his two Turners.
20th: After [Italian] lesson Mr Ruskin called and we went together to Murano in both boats and studied the old —- full of rare beauties. I got sketch of boats and began a sky. Very lovely effect and on return painted another of stormy effect. Home at 7 to dinner, very tired. After d. bought Calotypes on Riva...
26th: ...saw Roberts and Cotterell at the Europa and dined with them at Table d'Hote at 5. Met also there Jones and Bicknell. Took the latter a giro to Porto in evening. Had walk and café with Roberts. Painted all morning on Rie of Palazzo Ducale and had a lovely sunny day at last
30th: Saw the Emperor leave by steam for Trieste. Gunboats firing etc... Sent for Roberts and Cotterill in my boat and we all went to Ruskin's to dinner. Pleasant evening. Left at 10. I painted and read till 1.
Oct 4th: After lesson, Roberts called with Salvin. I called on Ruskin, we went with an extra man to Murano and saw the churches and on to Mazzorbo and Torcello. Made sketches of the pulpit in Duomo Sta Fosca and on Canal. Got a snack and retd. at 5. Glorious fine day... Had a chat with Salvin at his hotel, brilliant moonlit evening.
7th: After breakfast went out with new canvas and began Piazzetta with Lion column, Campanile and Ducal Palace. Salvin sat in my boat and sketched. At 4¼ we returned and dressed. Dined at Ruskin's with Roberts. Met Nerly and wife, Mr Gibbs, Lady Sorell and Mr Cure. Left at ½ p 10.
10th: Holloway and wife called. Took coffee on the Piazza and went with them for a row on the Canale. Brilliant moonlight.
13th: Mr Brown of Chester and Kilburn called with wife and brother. He gave me a commission. Painted sky at home in No.8... Met Roberts on Piazza and

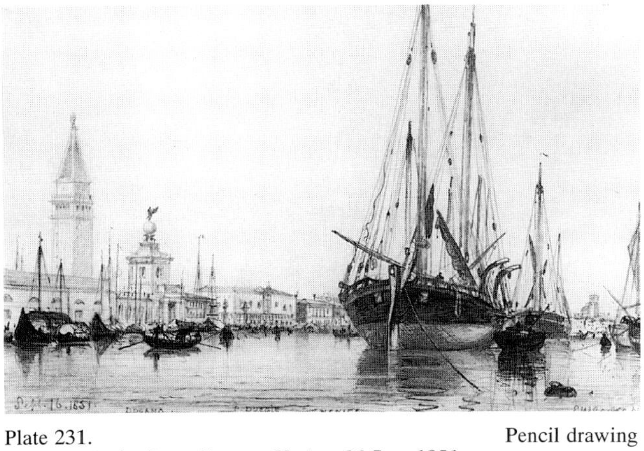

Plate 231. Pencil drawing
Shipping in the Porto Franco, Venice. 16 Sept 1851
Drawn on the same day as the Acre pillars (Plate 230), it was signed later as the news of his election as ARA did not arrive until November. Illustrated in *Henry James on Italy, Selections from 'Italian Hours'*, 1988. Photo courtesy Martyn Gregory

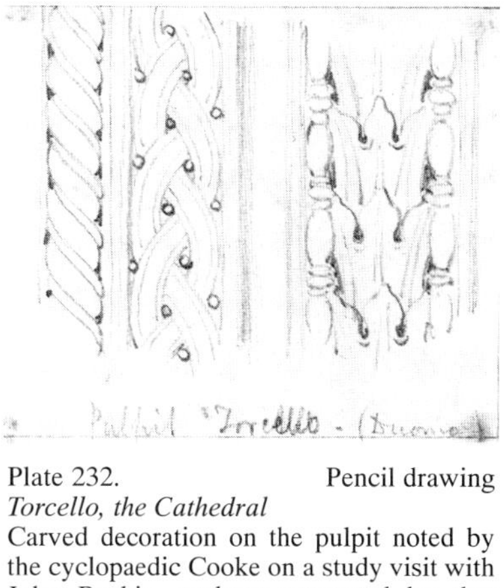

Plate 232. Pencil drawing
Torcello, the Cathedral
Carved decoration on the pulpit noted by the cyclopaedic Cooke on a study visit with John Ruskin, perhaps prompted by that architectural historian. Saturday 4 October 1851.
Photo courtesy The Trustees of the National Maritime Museum, Greenwic

went at 9 to Lady Sorrell's Soirée. Met Messrs. Gibbs, Campbell, Mr and Mrs Dawkins [Consul].
14th: Lord Overstone called with Holloway at 9... Dined at Danieli's with Lord and Lady Overstone and daughter and Count Strelitzki. Took my sketches to show them.
15th: ...Painted on Bibliotheca till 3. Saw Roberts painting in San Marco. Lord and Lady Overstone accompanied me to several shops. Had a row and got a sketch of Rascono. Dressed and dined at 6 at Mr Dawkins... Mrs Loudon sent me a note on her departure.
23rd: Ruskin called and asked me and Roberts to dine there, R called with me on them in morning. I painted all day until 4 on Campanile. Took a row, saw a Greek Bombard come in. Dressd and fetched Roberts in boat and we dined at Ruskin's at 5. Met Lord Dufferin. Very pleasant evening, Farewell to Roberts. At 11 took him on board the Trieste steamer. Glorious day and evening. Very low at parting with R[oberts].
24th: Arranged and cleaned new colours which Roberts left me. Very high East wind but brilliant day and superb evening. Got camera sketches of Salute from Belle Arti...Painted a little moonlight bit by candelight
Nov. 1st: Drew with Camera and Telescope the Bronze figures and Ball of Dogana. Drew in with Camera the Salute from my window, canvas on ground and drew with a long stick, worked on it till 3½ then called and saw Nerli. Met Ruskin, finished sketch of San Giorgio and at 6 dined at Gallo.A most boisterous evening, heavy gale
11th: Went to the Post and got two letters from Mary announcing my election as ARA !!!. Bought 2 books on architecture for 8 Zwanzigers at a stall. A most glorious day, bright and pleasant. Painted on Bibliotheca and S.Marco till 5. Got 2 sketches of San Giorgio. A marvellously glorious evening and effects of warm light... dressed and went to Ruskin's Music. Made drawing of the buildings of Piazzetta for Mrs R., and gave her a moonlight sketch. Wrote ARA for the first time!... got sketch by moonlight on Piazza.
December 6th ...went with Commissioner to get passport visé...took stroll about Turin... Took place in Dilijog. Started for Lyons in Coupé, had a Sardinian as a companion. Arrived at Sousa at ½ p 9. Had coffee and began to ascend Mont Cenis. All snow.
7th: Changed to Sledges with 8 Mules. All night on the mountain... reached Chambery at 8 o'clock.
8th: Arrived at Lyons at 12, found the place invested with troops. Cannon planted on the Bridges and fires and bivouacs in all directions. Dined at the Hotel des Beaux Arts. Went to the Cathedral and pottered about till 6 when I started in Diligence for Chalons with 2 sailors from Malta and an Officer, Mr Hill from Corfu. Also a fat Frenchman and a woman.
11th: [Paris] ...went to the Louvre. Met Mr Marlay, enjoyed the glorious pictures more than ever. Bought A.Durer's prints. Took stroll to Bronze shops with Mr Marlay.
12th: Bought toys, ivory carvings etc... met Mr and Mrs Gambier Parry at a Bronze shop. Dined at Table D'Hote, packed up, read news.

1852
Aug.28th: ...hired a suite secondo Piano at the Casa Pacchierotti... felt

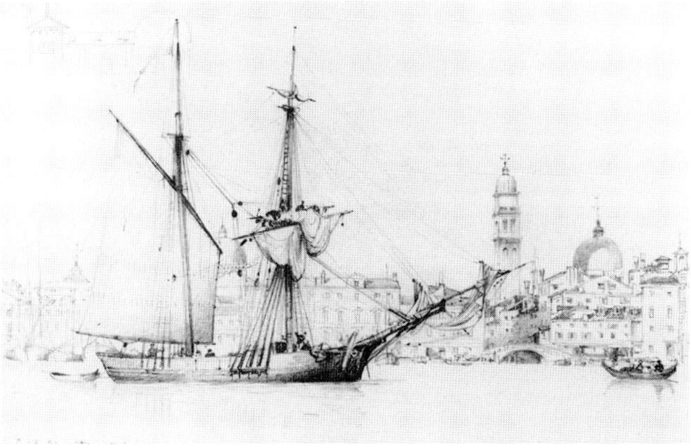

Plate 233. Pencil drawing
A Mediterranean brigantine off San Giorgio Maggiore
Looking towards the Riva with the tower of San Giorgio dei Greci, evidently drawn in September 1852 – after 8 pm (diary) – *We took a giro about the Porto in the evening and got 2 sketches.*
Photo courtesy Martyn Gregory. Private Collection

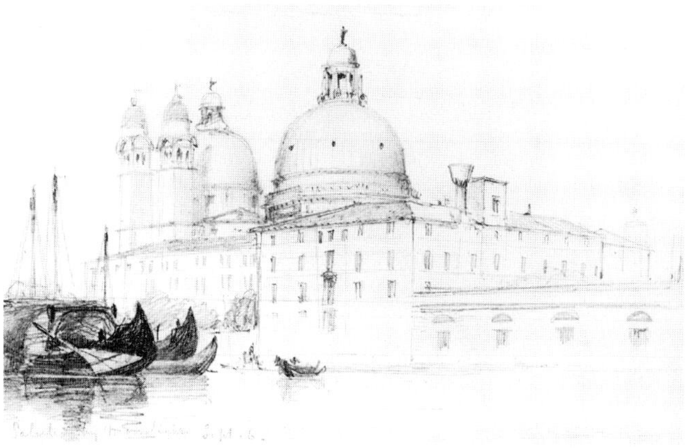

Plate 234. Pencil drawing
Santa Maria della Salute by Moonlight
The strange, dark shapes of the *rusconi* lying in the Porto Franco allow an ethereal quality to the domes of the church in spite of the paleness of the sky. Photo courtesy Martyn Gregory

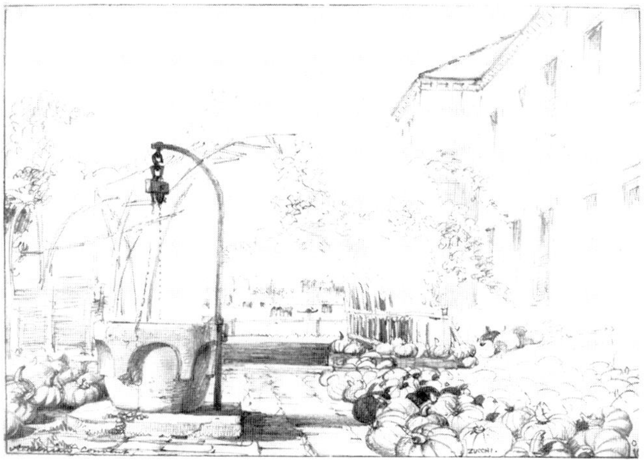

Plate 235. Pencil drawing
Courtyard and well in the Armenian convent on the Island of San Lazzaro
The view under the trellis reveals not only the lagune of Venice but the city and, on that day, the line of the distant Alps.
Photo courtesy The Trustees of the National Maritime Museum, Greenwich

very comfortable, a glorious view from window, S.Giorgio, Dogana, Zitella, Porto Lido and Salute.
Sept. 2: ...Mr Harding called, he sent man to make stretchers for canvases. I drew in S.Giorgio all day at home. Laura read *Bleak House.*
25th: Called on Lady Eastlake before breakfast and lent her my new calotypes to look at.
Oct. 5th: ...painted domes, towers &c of Salute (back of Dogana subject)... in evening went to Creek of San Giorgio and put in distant water to two little skies viz. S.Servilio and S.Lazzaro - and La Grazia.

1853
26th: June [London] ...H.Christy and I went by the *Batavier* to Rotterdam. Dull day, no sun but hundreds of vessels in river. Wind right aft. At 10 laid down on couches and got some rest. Rolled very much but quiet easy passage.
27th. Overtook the *Lord Auckland* off the Brille entered the Maas at ½ p 5, Rotterdam (after bkfst on board) at 8. Cleared at Custom House, coach to Rail. started at ¼ to 10, arrived at the Hague at ½ p 10, coach to Scheveling at 11. Took rooms at Mr. Maas's Badhouse. Stroll on shore, a great many boats aground and fish sales going on; got sketch, dined at 2...
28th. Very rough sea and wind S.W. by S. Some boats came in all the

others remained ashore. I made Camera and Telescope sketch of a Pink from my window. Took warm bath. H.Christy went to the Hague to Picture Museum. He bought some pictures. Dined at Table d'Hote at ½ p 4, then lounged on Dunes till tea - al fresco - good band, lots of company.
July 1st: Out on Sands before Bkfst for ½ an hour. Plenty of fish in. After B. went to Hague, called on M. Mazel for ½ an hour then to Exhbn. of Modern Masters [the Tentoonstellingen van Levende Meesters]. Walked about and bt. wares in two or three shops - hair cut- back to Schevg. to dinner at ½ p 4. Out on Sands for 2 hours, got 2 sketches - & in Town went to see Model- tea up in my room and arranged with H.C. for our journey. Most lovely day but cool evening. No letter at Post.
2nd: Out before Bkfst. H.C.went to Hague and bt. pottery &c, back at ½ p 4. I drew with Camera from window and then went out and got sketch in water colors of Pink, back at ½ p 4. Mr Kasteele dined with us then we took a walk to the New Bath house and had some Curazoa. Got sketch of sands. Back to coffee. H.C walked back to Hague with Mr K. A club dined here and made a great row very late.
1st Sept Arrived at Dear old Venice
21st. Stroll before breakfast. 2 Gents brought 2 Vols of Tiepolo's sketches. H[enry] C[hristy] and I bought 1 Vol. I went out and painted till 4 in Giudecca. Painted Zitella & houses on Riva and towers of Gesuati. Called on Ponti and got new calotypes. Dined at Vapore, H.C. called for me and we drove to Ghetto, Jews not at home. Then round by the Lagoon… Cafe and Galignani at Café François
Oct 23rd: Took walk before breakfast then drove with H.C to Brown's. Saw the Tintoretto in private room at the Belle Arti with Harding, then went to Europa. Coffee at Vapore and at 3 started with 3 men to Torcello. Saw both buildings. Dog eat up our luncheon. Left at ½ p 4 and back to SS Giov. and Paolo… walked about Rialto and dined at Vapore with the Thomases
24th: Sig. Giordani called in morning, also Mr Merryweather. I went to Ponti's and paid him by cheque £21 for Photos.[?]. Got letter from Scott with 5£ note. Got £10 changed into Napoleons at Shielin's. Brown called and saw pictures, I took zuppa and went out and got sketch of boats off Prigione…
25th: Drove to Belle Arti, saw Harding. Drove to Mudie, Giordano and Brown. Brought Sig. Tagliapietra and man from Belle Arti and they saw me pack pictures and put the seal on… called on Lady Sorrell… took place in Diligence. Harding called in evening and paid me 2 Napoleons. Met Burnett at Florians.
26th: …I left Venice by rail at 11, a most lovely day. Pleasant journey to Verona, read Ruskin… at 4 started in Diligence, arrived at Breschia about midnight
29th …At 5 AM in Diligence, had a most delightful journey over the Splugen, warm and brilliant all the way and wonderful icicles.

1855
October 10th: …started at 11 by the Rainbow for Rotterdam. River looking lovely, so many vessels beating up. Tide against us to Gravesend, got clear of land before dark, sea and wind increasing all night to a gale. Vessel rolled dreadfully. Turned in on couch at 8.

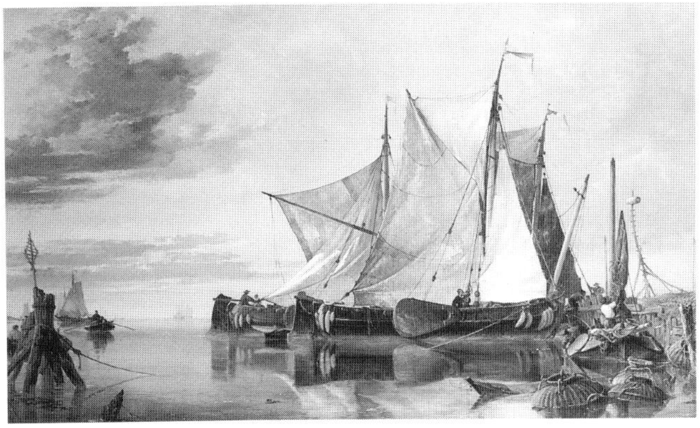

Plate 236. 58/6
Dutch boats in a calm, evening on the Zuider Zee
Here Cooke seeks to repeat his success with the Robert Vernon picture of 1843 enlarged (Colour Plate 57). The critics thought such close detail on so large a scale was harmful to its qualities. In reproduction harmony is restored. Photo:courtesy Phillips Fine Art Auctioneers. Private Collection

11th: At 5 heard soundings and went on deck. A sea of foam and breakers all round. We were crossing the bar at the Brielle - inside smoother water. Cast anchor for daylight. At ½ p 7 weighed and stood into the River Maas arrived at Rotterdam at 8… coach to Scheveling, Sea very rough.
12th: Sea very rough and stormy, high wind. Brig off the coast in peril. She anchored two miles away. No boats able to go out. I pottered about the strand, got some sketches. Went to the boat builders to see about a model. Boils very painful.
13th: Very fine brilliant day. Wind and sea somewhat abated three boats hauled down by 12 horses to the water level and prepared for sea. 2 went off. I got some sketches. English brig weighed, and we thought she was going to beach here, but she went to the Northward; she seemed waterlogged.
15th: Wind shifted from NE to S., three boats put off, a shrimper trawled all day and brought in a large quantity in afternoon. I drew pinck with Camera and telescope.

1857
June 1st: Wrote letters and arranged business for Eatwell [framer]. Left at 11 met Mr and Mrs Hannah and Mr and Mrs McInnes at Stephen's at ½ p 12, all went with him and Georgie to *Great Eastern*, then to *Dreadnought* and then to Greenwich Park. Saw Kiss in the Ring, back by rail at 7 to the Circus… Agnew sent a case with my picture of St.Andrea Venice to be repaired.
4th. Waterhouse Hawkins sent 4 Goldfish and a model of Saurian reptiles, busy completing cabinets in morning and arranging- went to South Kensington, saw Redgrave & Smith. Mr Finch called with —- at

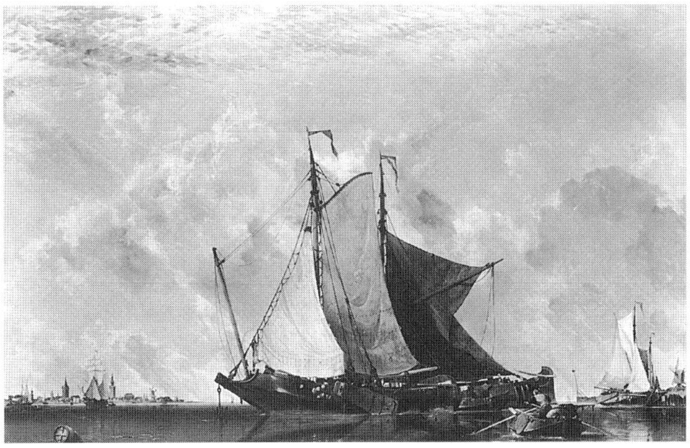

Plate 237 65/3
Zuider Zee schuits in a calm (Hollandsche kust windstille)
Photo courtesy Hamburger Kunsthalle

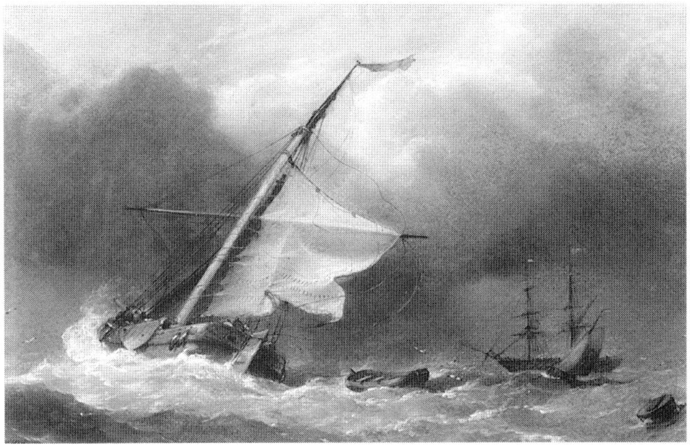

Plate 238. Chalk drawing
Dutch craft in rough weather
There is a distinct similarity to the poon off Harlingen, 59/2 (Colour Plate 70), but on closer examination it is only a similarity. Cooke seems to have liked this geometric stance with the big sprit of the mainsail now horizontal. Photo courtesy Martyn Gregory

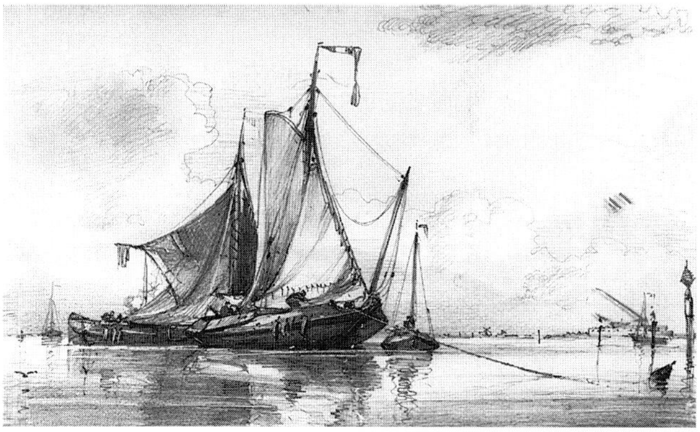

Plate 239. Pencil drawing
Botters off a fort
Possibly a scene in the Scheldt, it has the feel of a finished picture, as yet unidentified. Photo courtesy Martyn Gregory. Private Collection

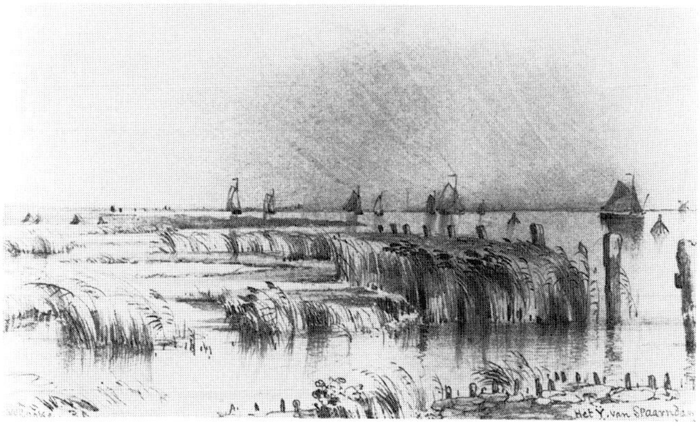

Plate 240. Pencil drawing
Het Y van Spaarndam Photo courtesy Martyn Gregory. Private Collection

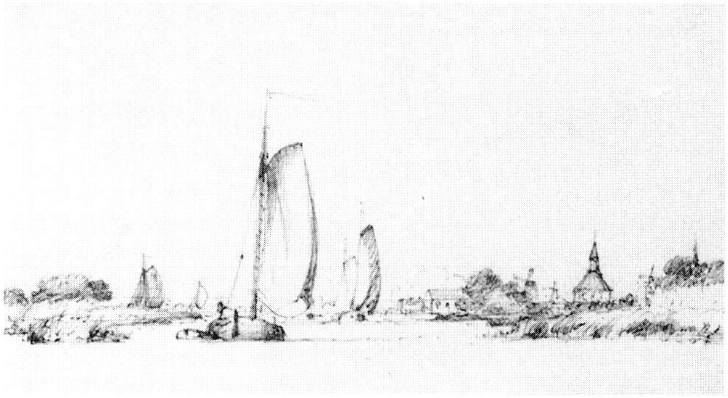

Plate 241. Pencil drawing
On a canal Photo courtesy Clarges.Gallery

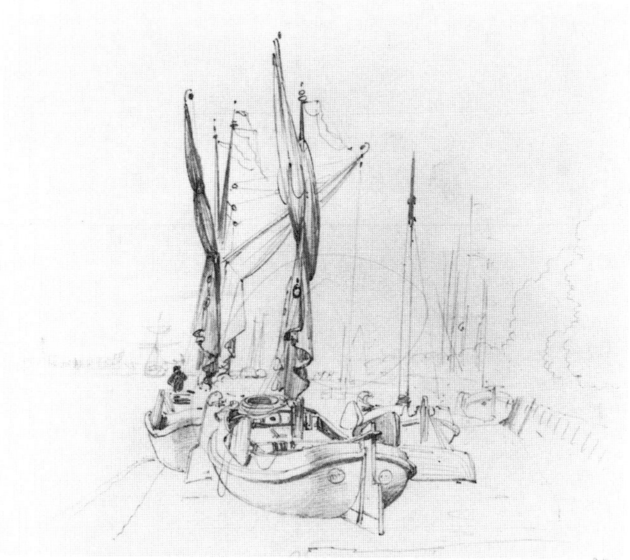

Plate 242. Pencil drawing
Belgian craft 1855
Inscribed in Cooke's hand *Kanooten op de Scheldt te Antwerpen.*
Photo courtesy Martyn Gregory

3 to look at Garden and then Sir Wm Ross. In evening a garden and bowls party. McInnes, Hannahs, Browns, Barlows, Redgraves, Copes, Cropseys, 2 Cundells, Ansdell and Phillip came from Spain, Mrs and Miss A, Knights & Miss Saml and Miss Redgrave, Georgie, Stephen, Roe, Mutries, Barwell, nephew of Redgrave's, Baxter - We had Charades (& dancing after supper) Very merry.
5th: ...Henry Bicknell took my P.Veronese and H. Christy's Correggio to British Institution for Exhibition. Painted on small Bonchurch. Eatwell came and I ordered new cabinet... Mrs Marryatt & 2 ladies came in aft. to see Garden. Waterhouse Hawkins came at 6 to tea and we settled about Mr Bateman's frog. Very hot indeed all day. Wrote to Mr Bateman with sections.
10th: Man fixing rustic work in Stumpery. Painted on Lancaster ['s picture]. Uncle Tom came to dinner. I went to Greenwich by water at 6, dined with R.A. Club at Trafalgar. Met Marshall, Thorburn, S.Cooper and Son Boxall and Mr Coleridge, Cousins, Stocks, Egg, Elmore, Stone, Wilmore, Weekes &c. Pleasant evening. All left by bus at ½ p 10.
12th: ...went to Royal Society, heard Faraday - last - I sent some Carpology & cones & Fossil Palms.
13th: Painted on and finished Lancaster. Potted orchids and new ferns. Gas fitted in Studio. Man altering carved form. Painters at work... to Private View of Brit Inst Old Masters - Met Lady Eastlake and Dr Waagen. They took me to P.View of the Turners at Marlbro Ho.- marvellous collection... Wm Hering and Sophy & niece came to tea, also Mr and Mrs Bond - bowls, sketches etc, W.H.left at 10. I gave him a drawing...
15th: Painted till ½ p 11 on Mr Cressingham's picture. Peter Cunningham called for me and we drove to Norwood Cemetary and attended the funeral of Douglas Jerrold. A vast number of persons present. Mitchell drove me to town, home at 4 to dinner - painted till 7. Left after tea for Brit Arch -last- Chas. Barry read account of Scaffold and Machinery of Victoria Tower...
16th: Painted on Cressingham... Uncle Geo. brought a Dr. — Spaniard to see me & Uncle took tea here. Mrs Ridgeway brought a Caique for my Museum. Went to the Linnaean in evg. at Burlington House - proposed as a Member - Left at 10 and home, dressed and went to Ansdell's party. Dancing till ½ p 2. Pickersgill elected R.A.
18th: Called on Cope. Voted for Mantell at Dispensary, went in cab to Lake Price's, took picture, sketches and Model. He took 3 Collodion portraits of me. Home at 2. Mr Bateman called, & I helped him at China. Dined and attended Committee at Arch. Mus. Mr W.Hawkins took me to Antiquarian Society meeting - Mr Morgan brt a collection of watches. Mr Ashpitel ? read paper on Cumae, home at 11.
20th: Painted on Cressingham -...Mr Merli and daughter came to see Garden... Went to S.Kensington at 9 & joined the Committee of the Architectural Museum & received the Queen and R.family. Home at ½ p 11 with Redgrave and Mulready. Very hot day and rain in evening.
25th: Banana coming on to fruit. Redgrave called for me at ½ p 9 & we went to the Museum. Saw my 2 pictures, Bentley having cleansed off the McGilp. Went round Museum, home at 12, painted till 7 on Cressingham. Sent proofs of London Bridge to Mr Palmer and Mr Ridgeway [Samuel Palmer lived in Rd.]... worked all evng. in Garden.
26th: ...by water to London Bridge, left by ¼ to 4 Express to Reigate. Met a large party 60 - Entomologists, at the White Hart Hotel - dined

there at ½ p 5. Entertained by Wilson Saunders. Left at 9, home at 11, with F.Smith.

July 2nd. Potted orchids - painted on and finished small Ventnor picture & worked on small Bonchurch. Mr Miller came with proof which I touched - he dined here. Dr Waagen, W. Hering, Mr and Mrs Hannah dined here at ½ p 6. Pleasant evening. Mr Palmer came at 8 & looked at Cornwall sketches. Georgie came in eveng. and slept here. Cool grey day.

4th: Eatwell and man fixed the new Cabinet and Painted it - & then french polished Sideboard. I arranged study and re-hung frames - put Orchids in baskets &c. Smith & Beck sent new Gas lamp for Microscope... my object case fell on my toe, very severe pain. Mama paid many accounts. Arranged ferns in eveng.

8th: Sent to Ruckers for flowers in morng. All day arranging house and garden. Arthur Burnand called also Sir Charles Barry. Criswick sent glass for back of sideboard. At 5 my friends came viz: Yates, Busk, White, Owen, Ansted, Back, Fellows, Playfair, Percy, Dickson, Chapman, Deane, Ward, Steve, Warrington, Gray, Myers, Marshall, Roper, Furze, Burchell, Mitchell, Kippist, Smith, Layard, Bowerbank, F.Smith, Queckett, Bell, Barlow, Glaisher, Sir Charles Eastlake, Lady Dorothy [Neville?]

14th: Busy arranging for party. Mr Pye Smith called in morng. also Ainsley. I went to town in morning, got grey straw hat also tickets for "Frozen Deep" etc. back at 4. At ½ p 6 Sir Wm Ross came also Chalon, Frost, the Friths, Hannahs, Browns 3 - C. Marshalls, Geo Stanfields, Donaldson, Sants, Jno Birkett, Scoles, Alderman Salomons, A.Burnand, Ferreys, Radford, Rankley, Ansdells, Phillip, H.Herings, W.Hering, Lovers, Jas. Rosier, Fairholt, Waleys, Steve & Georgie, E.Field. Elmore. Hart, Falkener, Stones

15th: Painted on Thunder cloud and arranged room - Went to Haymarket in evening - Douglas Jerrold night. Saw the *Housekeeper* and the *Prisoner of War*. Home at 12, hot day. Le Grew called on his return from Nice.

16th: Painted boat and net of small Thundercloud all day. Mr Cressingham called & gave up the picture - Mr and Mrs Heathcote and a lady called. I went to Bowerbank's at 6, met at Dinner Sir R. Schombergk Mr Ward, Morson, Yates, Hudson, Dr Lethby, Young, Grant, McAndrew. Left at 10 with Sir Robt & we came to Town together in cab - sharp rain in eveng and cool air.

18th: Finished small Thundercloud and began new Scheveling on old Sky, calm. ...Went to Committee at 7 at S.K.Museum - took the Chair. Lord de Grey came at 8 & at 9 we went up to the General Meeting, which went off excellently well at the new place, met many friends. Walked home with Harriette at 11...

20th: ...Painted boats &c very hot and sleepy all the aft. Went to Legrew's after bkfst - he gave me fine lion's skull and others, and horns for Museum. Went to Hannah's at ½ p 6. Met Phillip, Frith, Egg, Pickersgill Thorburn, Ansdell, Stone, Rankley, Brooks and Lewis...

July 23rd: ...went to Erith by train - at 2, carriages met us and drove up to Belvedere to dine at the great feast given to the officers of the *Agamemnon, Niagara & Susquehanna*- and Directors of the Submarine Cable for the Atlantic. The fete took place in a grand marquee - Excellent speeches, music and dancing by sailors. Left by 6 train home at 8.

[The following day he visited the ship at Greenwich and noted that he was preparing for a journey to Ireland.]

29th: (Bristol) Started by steamer *Juverne* from the Basin at 11, after Bkfst. Lovely scenery down the Avon and thousands of vessels on the Bristol Channel - off Cardiff- all day steaming in sight of land (S.Wales). Dined and turned in at 10. Very smooth passage all night crossing the Irish Channel.

Aug.1st. Went off with luggage to *Agamemnon* and got a nice berth - No. 2 Port side. Lunched and dined on board. Went to the *Niagara* and got sketch from poop. Saw Capt. Hudson and Mr Morse. Lieut Brown took me over the *Susquehanna* and sent me back to the *Agamemnon*. Pleasant evening, slept on board.

3rd: Made sketches of deck of *Agamemnon* with the machinery &c also some from stern gallery. Afternoon very wet and misty. The *Cyclops* and *Leopard* sailed out of harbour at 5 & we weighed at ¼ past and followed them, the *Niagara & Susquehanna* - after clearing the lightouse we went to dinner - I changed berth to Captain's cabin.

4th: No sleep all night from fearful rolling of the vessel and the great swell of the ocean. I laid down all day on Sofa in Captain's [state?] cabin - he reminding me of the Skerrigs [Skelligs] and other things which I sketched. Arrived at 4 at anchorage off Valentia - dined early and came ashore with luggage and 2 others in cutters - touched at *Niagara & Leopard*. Had tea at Hotel and went up to — to sleep. Same room with Mr Isaacs.

5th: Went with Mr Isaacs to Begnis Island & got sketches. Then to *Niagara* - lunched on board. Sketched the cable paying out on boats and Tug - went with the cable to the shore- first to hand it to the trench amidst thousands of people - the Lord Lieutenant spoke and after prayers and speeches & great cheering all dispersed - we came home with the 3 ladies in boat to dinner tea- I went up with Isaacs to sleep at Shanhanes.

7th: Went off with Mr Stephen in boat to *Niagara* with provisions and got sketches of gear. Tug took in a mile of thick cable & I went with C.Field, Mr Stephen with Capt Wainwright's gig and saw the joining of the cable on the paddle box boat, then dined with the officers of the *Leopard* - back at 6 dressed and walked up to Glanleam. Shewed the Knight my sketches...

8th: Went to breakfast at Mr Leckey's, he drove me and his son up to the Quarry - and then walked to the top of the hill & saw the Squadron out of Sight - got sketches of distant panorama and Airey's cairn.

11th: News of the cable having broken- no communication -went up to Glanleam to luncheon and went with the Knight & Mr Fitzgerald &c to see the Cave & on to the Tents, returned with Mr Stephen to Knight's Town and got seedling Osmundas. Dressed and went to see Miss FitzG's new house. Took tea spent the evening at the Watch room, back at 2 to bed.

17th: Started in car with Mr and Miss Statham, Mr and Mrs Fugeon, T.Peyton, Mr and Mrs Biddulph to Gap of Dunloe. Rode the ponies to the Lake and then over to Dinas Island to our cold collation. Very many songs and glees, -Bugles and echoes, fired guns &c. Rowed through Middle Lake and Lower Lake. Got sketches and ferns. Landed at Ross Castle and the car met us and drove through Lord Kenmare's estate. Home to Hotel, took tea with Mr. Fugeon. Most delightful day I ever spent as a pic nic. Packed ferns &c. [Killarney]

18th: Started after Bkf.at ¼ to 9 by train ... to Limerick Junction & on to Waterford. Nearly lost my passage - got a boat and followed the steamer. Our vessell the *Camilla* full of oxen, pigs, poultry, sheep and very few passengers but several soldiers. I got a great many sketches. Lay to for water off the mouth of the Avon - slept well, very calm passage indeed.

19th: Up at 8 after good rest, shave and breakfast off fresh mackerel. Went on deck coast not visible from Haze. Wrote two letters, got sketches on board, arrived at Bristol at 5... left by fast train at 6.10, in town at 10.10...

1858

[Further cable operations took him to Valentia Island again, and this time he painted; it was an extraordinarily active year]

June 14th Painted on 2 Scheveling pictures all day. Intensely hot. Wrote several invitations & had replies. Doncaster came in evng. & we made garden Rough log Seat. Mr Bateman came in eveng. about 8, stroll round the Garden & left after tea.

15th Painted on & finished Scheveling - worked on long Venice. Hottest day we have had. Miss E.Wyatt, niece & friend came & lunched with us. Went at 5 & took tea with Mr Ward (in Garden) & drove with him to

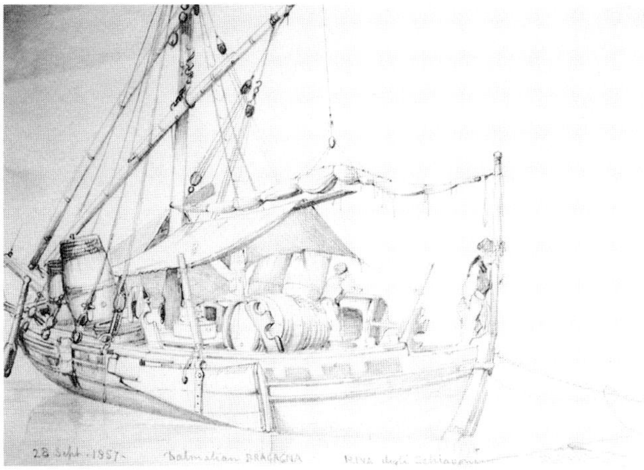

Plate 243. Pencil drawing

Dalmatian bragagna 1857

Moored on the Riva dei Schiavoni, Venice The careful observer records the vessel's rudder slung over the side to avoid damage against the stone quay.

Photo courtesy Clarges Gallery

Mr.Gassiot's - met many friends - invited several - Mr May brought me up to Gt.Geo.St., home at ¼ p 12. Thermometer 88 in the shade

16th Painted on vessel in long panel - Mylne called. Laura came with Miss Portmans to see Italy sketches. Went in evng. to soirée at St Bartholomew's Hospital - a large number present. Mylne brt me home at 1. Intensely hot day & evng.

17th. Grey & cool day threatening rain. Painted on Greek vessel. Mr & Mrs David called also Laura... dined at Mr & Mrs Jno Thomas's with H.& Mama. Pleasant cool evng. Letter from Hopgood about the payment of House...

18th. Went to Hannah at 10, we went to Clutton's in the Boro', met Mr Hopgood & settled about the purchase of my house. We called on Tom - out. Went to the London & Westminster Bank, home at 5 to dinner. Gardened in evng. Mama & H went at 9 to Mr Westmacott's after a dinner party!!! I went at 10, home at ½ p 11.

Sat 19th. Started early with Mary & Conrad to Blackwall Rail & on to Thames Haven - boat to Margate at 3 dined at the Pier Hotel. Drove to Kingsgate & walked home along the cliff & beach at ½ p 8 to tea & lobsters - slept at Pier Hotel...

20 We went to Margate New church in mg. & after dinner took a stroll towards Mutrix farm & along the Parade. Met Read - back to tea & slept at Hotel.Very fine day.

21st Packed & started at 11 oclk. by steamer & had a very delightful passage up to London Bridge against tide - breezy & pleasant, arrived at 5 & home at ½ p 6 to tea. Worked in garden watering &c till dark.

22nd Arranging garden, altering pictures in mng. Went to town, signed Deeds of purchase of Freehold at Hopgood's. Bought cartridge paper at Hodges', called at Barbe's for color box, Medwins's, F & Mason's, home at ½ p 5. Hannah called, he sent his man to fix his tables & Ansdell's in my studio. Worked late in garden with lad, watering, arranging seats, planting &c. Hannah called. Busy all morng. At 5 our visitors came viz. Capts. Pim, Collinson, Drs. King, Wards, Percy, Burchell, Gray, Professors Tyndall, Ramsay, Frankland, Bell Queckett, Wheatstone, Huxley, Playfair, Scott ARA, Westmacott RA, Appold, Bentham, Bowerbank, Furze, Glaisher, Warrington, Marshall, Miers, Ward (Nat.), Bennett, Loddiges, White, Mummery, Grove, Fergusson, D & T Wyatt, Burkett, Waley, Mays, Cockerell, Webster, Mayo, Tifft, Barry, Lawless, Christie, Brett, Clarke, Saward, Mylne, Thomas, Uncle - Wright - & 43 ladies also.

25th Mr & Mrs McInnes called. We packed up all the morng., canvases, colors, Roba &c, started at ¼ to 5 from Paddington & arrived at Milford Haven at ½ p 12 at night, Went im[mediatel]y on board the *Malakoff* steamer & had a fine passage to Waterford- wind & tide against us, 11 hours sail, landed at ½ p 12. Breakfast at the Adelphi Hotel.

26th. Stroll, met Mr Hall he took us to see his friend Mr Arden. Mary very poorly. We started by the 3 oclk train from Waterford to Limerick Junction, on to Mallow & Killarney at 9 oclk. Had tea at the Kenmare Arms, took places in the Mail Car for Valentia & slept there.Very lovely day & delightful journey. Met Miss Fitzgerald en route on the rail.

Sun 27th Up at 6, left after bk, at ½ p 7 by the Killarney Mail car & we had a most delightful journey by Dingle Bay to Cahir, went on to Valentia at 2½. Mr Lecky & daughter received us most kindly. After luncheon strolled in garden, dined at 6 -strolled up the hill, met Mr & Mrs Whitehouse, Saward, &c &c.

28th Unpacked painting Roba, set up easel. Col Vandaleur & Mr Keane took me in their boat to Beginus, we studied its geological character, got ferns & plants, landed at 6, dressed & drove up with Mr Lecky to Glanleam to dinner. Met there Mr & Mrs Whitehouse, Mr Cippy, Miss Bailey & the family. Most agreable eveng. Drove back at 11 with Mr Saward. Fine breezy day- E.Eardley bt. my *Goodwin*.

29th At 11 had car, Mr & Susan Lecky, Mary & John drove up the Hill visited ... & then to the Quarry, got a sketch, lunched there. Ladies drove home. Mr. L & I went down to the Lighthouse & walked round by Glanlearn, home at ½ p 6 to dinner. Mr Gurney, Mr Fry & Mr Whitehouse took tea here. We all went to see the people dance jigs on the Quay

30th Face much worse & head bad. Laid down & slept in morng. Capt & Mrs Lyons & Miss L. called also Mr Cane & Mr Cippy. The Knight sent down for me- in aft. Mary went for a Sail. I got sk. of the *Black Eagle* - the Prince came ashore - not out all day, better in evng.

July 2nd, Went after bk. at 11 with Mr Gurney, Fry, Brooking, Saward, Stephen, F.Logie &c on board the *Comet* to the Blasquetts, landed & mounted to top, got sketches, returned to Valentia at 4 to dinner. At 5 two boat races took place - the Valentia boat beat the *Black Eagle's* I laid down till 9. Mr Lecky took the Ladies for a sail in evng.

3rd Went in boat round the rocks & painted till ½ p 5 on Spot. Mary read. Johnny helped me home tea-dinner at 7. Stroll with Mr Lecky & Mr Saward towards Port Magee - saw Mr Whitehouse fixing wire across the Harbour for Dublin. Spent an hour with Miss Fitzgerald in evng. Letter from H.

Mon. 5th. Heard by Telegram that the cable parted after 150 miles were paid out Mr Gurney & Mr Fry left at 4. I went on board the *Black Eagle & Shamrock* gunboat, saw Capt. Petley, Lieut Cowell went up to Glanleam to dinner at 5 to meet the Prince & Party. I showed him my sketches - we all had great fun among the Hay Cocks & all went down to the boat to say Adieu. We then went to the lighthouse & saw the *Black Eagle* steam out of the Harbour - we cheered them - great sea running. Tea at Glanleam, walked home at 11. Painted sky in rocky subject.

7th. Went over to Kilellan with M & Miss Susan Lecky in boat. Painted till ¼ to 6 Johnny left us & came in evng for us, sailed back. The Knight called. Stroll in evg. with Mr L. to Lagganeersk[?], found out subjects for painting.

8th Very strong North wind all day, could not go out. Painted at home on Rocks in No.2.

9th Went in car with M & Miss Susan to Runagiveen, painted till ¼ to 6. John fetched M & Miss S in boat at ½ p 2 & came again for all the traps... The Knight & family came to see me paint.

10th. Sat Went after bk. to Runagiveen & worked on picture. Miss S. came also - Jno, Mr L. & Miss E came at 2 in boat for me & we retd. to dinner - in aft.went in boat to Beginnis & got sketches on the sandbanks, home in a mist at ½ p 7 to tea. The Steamer *S. Western* came in & lay aground. Letters from Laura. Mild day.

13th Very wet & driving mist all day, blew very hard, brisk sea running. Not out all day. Painted sky on new canvas & put in sky to Runagiven picture... I made drawg. in evng for Mr Lecky.

14th Most lovely day calm & mild. Went in car to Lagganeesk & painted rocks. Miss Leckys read & drew there. All the Fitzgeralds came down to see me at work... my parcel came from Harriette, canvass &c with letters...

17th. Threatening morng. Went in boat to Runagaveen & worked on picture. Painted lighthouse, Begnis &c. Miss L. came, rain set in at 3 & John came for me in boat Heavy squall of rain coming home. wet eveng... Wrote to Bateman, Nicholson, Miss Coutts.

19th Went out to Lagganersk in covered car with John, fixed it up on a bank, painted on Donlas, Begnis & Lighthouse in continued heavy squalls of rain till 3. The horse was taken out & came again for us after dinner. Mr Whitehouse shewed me all his apparatus for Electric signals - in evng made 2 drawgs for Mr L.

20th Went to Lagganeesk & painted on Donlas Head & the Glanleam rocks -from beach... most lovely day & calm...

23rd. Packed up pictures till 12, drove with Mary & Miss L. to say goodbye at Glanleam - they went to Lighthouse & Miss Mary Fitzgerald went with me to the Coombe - saw rare ferns, drove back to dinner. Went out for Osmunda & blechnum...

Sat 24th. Left Valentia in boat with 4 men to Cahirciveen - Miss S.Lecky & John came with us to the car- wet journey to Killarney...

28th [Chester] Up at 6 went at 7 to Service at Cathedral & round the walls, back at 8 to bkfst. Went at ¼ to 9 by rail to Crewe & Harecastle, waited 2½ hours. Wrote to Geo. Wyatt & Tom, arrived at Biddulph at 2¼. Mrs Bateman absent but retnd with Miss Egerton from Cheshire in aftn. I went up to the Moor & planned a bridge & returned thro' China.

29th Got letters from home. All day busy with Mr Bateman at Chinese temple &c and Garden. We had the painter to try colors. In evng wrote to Mr Lecky. M. poorly yesterday, better today.

30th All day at work for Mr B about China. Mrs B. drove I & Mary to Knypersley in aftn. We did not dress but went out after dinner till 10. Most lovely day.

Sat 31st. Hard at work till 12 at China. Left with Mary at ½ p 12 in Chariot with Mr & Mrs Weston to Congleton Station - arrived in London at ½ p 7 & home at 8 to dinner-tea - found all well - pictures & plants arrived.

August 3rd Busy all morng. writing letters & sending off Hymenophyllum &c &c preparing pictures to be sent home . Went to town in aft. & called at Lees, Mr Hopgood's, Watkins & Hill. Home at 5. Miss Hawkins brought home George in aft. I went with L & H to Princess's with the Hannahs to see *Merchant of Venice*.- Hannah sent a superb painting box in eveng., in case.

4th All day writing titles, letters &c for pictures for the Provincial Exhbns. Guillet called, Mr Westmacott also. Mr & Mrs Hannah came at 6 also Mr Lecky & Steve & Georgie - we opened the new beautiful painting box & all were delighted with it. Mr Mummery came in evg. All left at 12.

5th Very busy all morng. arranging pictures, went to town got cash at

Bank. Bought color box at Barbe's & coat at Hyams. Mr Furze took tea with H & I he bought my Scheveling Thunder cloud picture & took it with him. Hannah called in eveng. & explained his new color box he gave me.

6th Aug ...Left home with Mama & George & Con by 10.30 train from Paddington, arrived at Bridport at ½ p 2. Went to town & waited for Stage Coach at ½ p 6, drove to Lyme Regis at ½ p 8.Took run round the Cobb, took tea & slept at the Cups Hotel. Lovely country. Mr White of Bonchurch, rode to Charmouth in coach. He was going to visit Macready there.

7th After bk. took boat & 4 men with G & C & went to Beer, took lodgings & returned at 3¼, dined at Cups & all left by large boat - lovely eveng. - to Beer. Mama at lodgings & we next door at the Dolphin Inn.

8th Sunday Heard Mr Glaskett at the Church in aftn. & Mr — in evng. I took walk to Seaton with Con & M. to Axmouth pier by cliff & back by road. Stroll with Mama in aft & evng. on cliff.

9th Began a picture at low water & painted till tide had come up. Home at 4 to dinner & at ½ p 5 went again & painted another beginning on beach. Very lovely day lobsters & crabs in plenty. Stroll on beach by starlight...

11th Painted sky & on rocks while tide is out till 4. Mama & Con went in donkey car to Seaton & saw lodgings... at 6 started with Geo & Con for Branscombe shore over the clifs, made sk. & a dense Sea fog came on & we returned at 9 to tea & prawns.

13th Went after bkft. & painted on view from Shingle till 1. Lieut. Davis came to see me. Con sent to Seaton to bathe. I began new picture of arched rock & painted on it till ¼ to 7 when the tide came up & drove me in to dinner. Stroll in evng.- cooler day pleasant breeze.

14th.Sat ...I sketched on beach till 1, dined at Dolphin with George & painted all the aft. till 7 on caverned rock. Arranged everything & walked over to Seaton at 9 to tea - Tremendous rain all the aftn. Beer flooded - painted under an overhanging rock in rain.

16th. Walked after Bkft. with Geo to Beer, got 3 letters & 3 newspapers. Geo read them to me painted on Beach subject sitting in the White boat. Dined al fresco & painted on arched rock till ½ p 6 & till tide flowed. After cleaning palette Geo & I walked to Seaton to tea. Very high wind & sea but mild & pleasant.

17th. Soaking wet all morng. Wrote to Dr Hooker, Nicholson & Laura. Dined at Seaton & went at ½ p 3 along the Shore to White Cliff & tried to get round among the rocks - heavy Sea & Water too high. Took off clothes & waded in great peril -got thro' the Arched rock at ¼ p 4. Took tea at Capt Davis's with Mrs D & her Daughter. Took stroll to see Variegated Elm. Left Beer at 9 & walked home to supper.

18th. ...set palette, got sketches on beach at Beer till 1½ then we all three took *roba* down to beach at White Cliff & endured 2 heavy squalls of rain. Conrad went home to dinner & back to help me. Painted White Cliff, back at ¼ to 6 to dinner-tea. Got sk. of Lobster pots in evng.

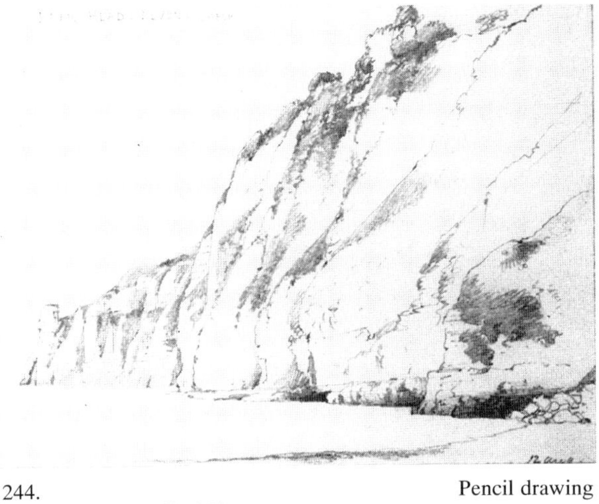

Plate 244. Pencil drawing
Beer-Head. Devon Chalk 1858
Significant in his coastal series, for these are the last of the white cliffs which began in Yorkshire; westward the cliffs are red sandstone. His paintings of Axmouth harbour and Beer cove are from this same visit. See 58/16, 58/17, 58/18 and 75/10 – Colour Plates 147, 153 and Plate 245). Photo courtesy Clarges Gallery

20th ...Set palette & went after dinner to Axmouth Ferry - began new picture on large canvas. Mama came & she sent tea. Miss Davis, Mrs Smith came to see me. I & Geo walked to White Cliff with them by moonlight.Wrote to Alderman Salomons & Mary.

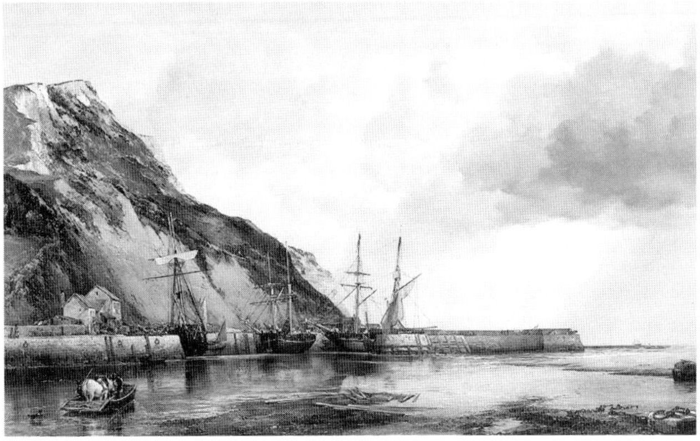

Plate 245. 58/17
Axmouth Ferry: Axmouth Harbour
A topographical painting with serious mercantile marine overtones. The scene today is little changed. Photo courtesy Christie's. Private Collection

Weymouth 25th. Boys bathed & we walked over to Sandsfoot Castle & back to dinner at 2. At 3 drove there with large canvas &c, & began to paint it. The tide came up & drove me up to the cliff. Donkey chaise came for me at 7 - most lovely day. stroll in eveng.

28th Painted water & distant cliffs from window till 3. Mama & boys went to meet the Hannahs at ¼ p 1 at Station (not there). They came by train at 3 to dinner. Took walk on the Nothe & on to Sandsfoot Castle, back to tea. Mr Furze spent the evng here. Hannah brought letters, Map of Schweitz, Newspapers &c. Lovely day

Sept.7th. Packing up, writing letters. Making Will &c all day with Mary. Uncle Geo. came to dinner & went to Station with me & saw me off at ½ p 8 by Mail to Dover. Went to Ansdell's to sign my Will at his house. Went by *Alliance* steamer. Met Scott at Calais.

Sept. 10th. [Switzerland -Sallanches: St. Martin] Scoles & Son started to walk to Chamouni [Chamonix]. I & the 2 gents took carriage together at 8 & drove through lovely scenery of the Arve to Les Ouches - often passing the Scholes's, arrived at Chamouni at 2. Started with a Guide after Luncheon to the Cascade du Dard & Cascade des Pèlerins & then across the Glacier du Bossons & descended to the base, returning by the main road to Chamouni. Supped at Table D'Hote. Prof. Tyndall called to see me. [Professor John Tyndall (1820-1893)]

Sat.11th Started at 6 with 2 guides, Scoles & 3 gents & walked to the Montanvert to breakfast. Got sketch & started at ½ p 10 by the Ponts on the Mer de Glace, 6 miles. ascended the Couvercle & round the Egralets-to the Glacier du Talefre, crossed it, very wet indeed with some snow-crossed the Morains & reached the Jardin. Dined, sketched & at 3 descended to the Glacier - passed the Mauvais Pas- at 8 quite dark- to Le Chapeau (to coffee) Lanterns to Les Tines village in the Valley. Got a carriage to return to Chamouni at 11 to supper.

12th Sun. Went with Mr Gainer (a Friend) to the English Service at Hotel Royal. Mr Eardley preached very fine sermon. Met Mr & Mrs Jas.Bell. We went with them in aftn. at ½ p 4 to the G. Du Bossons & retd. at 8 to dinner. Most lovely day. Tyndall & Mr Willes started at 7 to ascend Mont Blanc.

13th Scoles & Gainer started at 8 by Tete Noir walking to Martigny. I finished sk.of Chamouni & started at 12 with Knapsack & colors to G. Du Bossons. Boy carried Roba, painted till 6. Rained & I went under the Glacier. Very fine - exceedingly cold on the Moraine - home at ½ p 7. Tyndall called on me after his ascent & safe return.- It was fearful weather for snow & cold -One guide frost bitten & returned. (Very hot day.)

Sat 18th. Met Dr.Manheimer. Mr Williamson & I ascended the Gorner Grat at 11 & staid on summit till 1. Got a panorama of Monte Rosa, Breithorn Riffelberg & Matterhorn, Gorner & the glaciers & the St Theodule Glacier. Dined and descended to Zermatt. Got sketch of

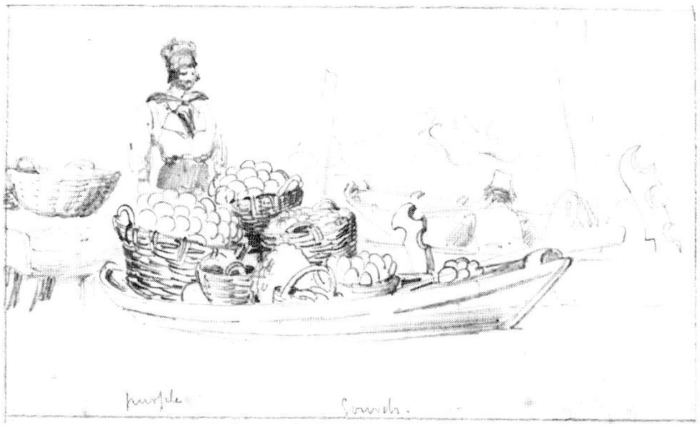

Plate 246. Pencil drawing
A market boat with Gourds &c
Photo courtesy The Trustees of the National Maritime Museum, Greenwich

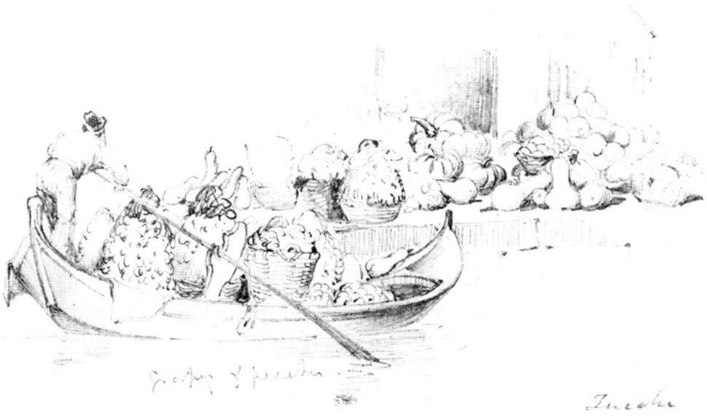

Plate 247. Pencil drawing
A fruit boat, grapes & peaches
Photo courtesy The Trustees of the National Maritime Museum, Greenwich

Matterhorn from near the —- Glacier..
20th. Up at ½ p 3 & at ½ p 4 started with Mr MacDonald, 3 ladies & Mr Sercombe, 2 Guides, 4 mules & 4 porters. Ascended to the snow of St Theodule at 9. Left the mules, got sketch & crossed the snow 2½ hours. Reached the Hut- highest in Europe. Coffee & rest & descended 1 hour & at 1 reached Breuil, they [?] remained, S & I walked on to Tournanche at 5 I got mule he went on with 2 porters for luggage. I followed by moonlight thro' glorious valley. Arrived at Chatillon at 10, very tired - supped & slept at Leone d'Oro.
22nd Railway to Caluso on main line & on to Novara & Ticino. No baggage arrived -sent Telegram - 2 trains came in without it. I dined & slept at Hotel nr. Station. Finished letter & posted it there. Lost another day - my luggage sent to Turin in mistake.
24th Sept. Arrived at ¼ p 4 AM Venice took roba to Albergo della Vapore, Stroll to San Marco & Riva Schiavone. Enquired at 7 places for Rooms. Back to bkfst. Got letter from Mary (sent to Visp) at P.O. Wrote to Sig. Pacchierotti. Met Cockerell on Piazza & Leighton. Dined & slept at Vapore.
25th ...got Portmanteau from Brown's, saw Vincenzo - saw Apartments. Spent evening with Cockerell & Leighton &c. Met Brown, Bentinck & Cheney on Piazza. Very hot day & evng.
28th. Removed down to new quarters, excellent rooms & riva for boat - arranged all & after dinner at ½ p 3 started to begin first picture *viz* The Zitella & Redentore & Giudecca. Drew it in & began sky in color, back at 7. Walked with Vaughan in evng saw in *Galignani* reference to me. Got letter from Harrico. Made sketch of wood trabaccoli from window & Salute by moonlight.

1860
[Alicante] Nov. 26th. After Bkfst went out to Palm tree and painted on small oil picture of Alicanti then to boats and painted the foreground, sea &c. Had the ill-luck to break the mahogany frame for the canvas block...
28th Up late. Bkfst at Cruz de Malta. Called on Consul. Miss Barrie mended my specs. A most truly lovely brilliant day... went off to the grove of Palms, made sketches there all day, and of the Stone pines...
Dec.5th ...The Colonel called for us in his Tartano and drove us to his country house. I sketched a young Palm in fruit.
8th Up at 3 AM and started by Diligence at 4. At about ½ p 7 reached Elche a wonderful place for Palms, whole forests and groups. Had Chocolate there...and went on to Orthuela, a beautful road and a very curious picturesque town. Got sketch of the River and Falls - of muddy water. Started at 3 through the fertile Huerta for 15 miles. Curious mud and thatch cottages. Arrived at Murcia at 6, wheel nearly off at Gate to city. Went to the Posada de Telegrafo got a bad supper and worse beds. Felt very much prostrated with Diarhoea. Took Laudanum and slept well.
Christmas Day. Still blowing hard but fine. Went to Muralla and read the Service. Then returned and dressed and went to Doctor D's at 2 and dined there. Excellent Christmas fare including a plum pudding &c. Saw the servants dance and sing to guitar, tambourines and castanets. Very pleasant day and evening.
29th Read news before Bkfst. At 11 went to Mole and tinted in general view. Then to S.Lucia and got sketches on shore. A most superb sunset, rosy, rotten sky.

1861
Jan 9th Called on Mr John Mark, saw the Ladies and Miss Christina shewed me her sketches of portraits. I bought her a box of chalks. Ordered hat, bought wares. Painted on sunset sky, called on Mr Clemens. At 8 went to spend a pleasant evening at Mr Powley's, met Miss Mark, Miss Christina Mark, Captain Hamilton, Mrs Smith and family. Shewed them my sketches. Nice music by the Ladies...
10th. Painted in morning... spent a few most agreable hours at Mr Mark's...
14th. ...Painted on large sunset Cartagena. Spent a pleasant evening at Mr John Mark's. Made drawing of sunset with Miss Christina Mark's chalks...
28th Called on Mr Boylan and Penrose Mark. We all met together at John's at ½ p 11 and consulted about the business of settlements. Lunched at ½ p 2. I wrote to Hopgood and H. Bicknell in afternoon and spent a delightful evening with Christina.
[Expeditions intervened]
30th Up early, packed all and removed things to John's. Called with Christina on Mr and Mrs Penrose [Mark] and Mr and Mrs Holley. Made drawings and took them to Mr Powley's. Dined early and met Mr Boylan at office of Diligence. Mr and Mrs Penrose met us and at 4 started with 14 mules - for Granada. Broke our pole and lost 1½ hours repairing it...
31st. Arrived at Granada at 9½ went to the Fonte del Alameda to breakfast. The Marquis conducted us to the Alhambra - went all over it and after to the ? Carmera de las Torre Beramejas, got sketch from the lovely garden.
[They were there until 6 February, Cooke having written at least one very long letter to Christina. Back in Malaga he gave the young woman a lesson in drawing in water-colour "on view of Dresden." More subjects presented themselves]
Feb. Sun 10th: A schooner was cast ashore just below on the sands

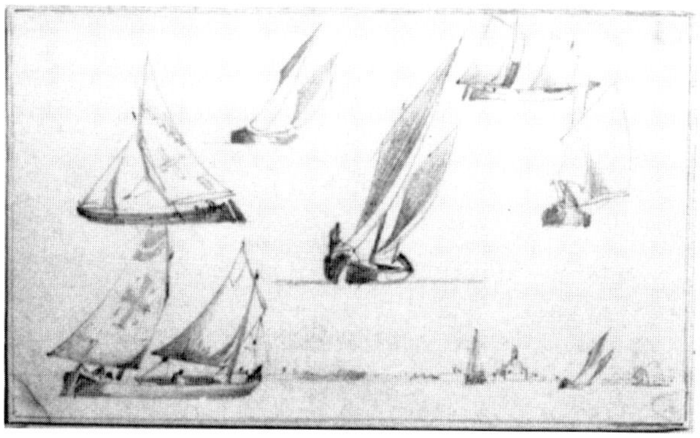

Plate 248. Pencil drawing
Venetian boats under sail
In his gondola he followed the departing fishing boats, sketching.
Photo courtesy Clarges Gallery

during the heavy gale in the night. Attended the Service and remained all day at Jno Mark's...
11th: Got sketches before Bkfst of wreck, began new picture of wreck off Malaga. Drew it in. ...I spent the evening at J. Mark's- perspective lesson
12th: After Bkfst sketched vessel ashore and then to Consul's terrace, got sketch of Sant Anton and mountains from Battery. Drew-in picture at Jno. Mark's till 3. Christina read letters from her brother Edward and from friends in England. All most satisfactory.
13th: Ash Weds. Attended Service in morning. Went home with Penrose and Mr Holley- signed an application for a licence- drew-in picture at John Mark's made sketch also. Christina not very strong today... I dined with family in evening.
[Gibraltar] 20th Feb: ...I went round the North side of Catalan Bay and got some sketches - and got arrested. Sent on by Orderly, met the Officer, Mr Hill who released me - having sketched without an order...
[He obtained the necessary paper next day and proceeded to sketch]
23rd. Read news. Mr Powell left for Malaga, he took a letter from me to Christina. Walked with Robert to Catalan Bay and worked on sketch. Rain drove me under the shelter of Lieut. Hill's house. Had luncheon with him and returned before gun-fire to dinner at Hotel. In evening Mr Morse [perhaps S.E.Morse, d.1871?] shewed me and Mr Boylan his photos.
Sun 24th: Mr Power called for us and took us to his pew in the Cathedral. Lady Codrington shewed us her superb *Dracaena Draco* in fruit. Then took luncheon with Capt. Freeling... called in evening on Sir Alexander and Lady Dunbar. Wrote to Christina.
25th. Packed up early and went on board the *Adelia* at 11, got sketch of Gibraltar. We took in tow a felucca so proceeded slowly against a strong wind & tide. Passed Tarifa and arrived at Tangier at ½ p 5. A fearful conflict of Turks, Jews and Infidels took place on landing to get our luggage carried ashore...
March 5th: Met Mr Reade who took me to the old Fort with guns which I sketched. Went to dinner with him. Got two letters, one from home and one from Chrisina which made me very wretched and miserable. Mary's announced the death of poor dear Georgie on 25th Feb. Left very soon, came home and wrote to Christina.
14th: Got sketch on quay. Left by train at ¼ to 1 and arrived at Jerez at 3. Called on Mr Gordon who shewed me his Botega and different wines. Then conducted me to the outside of Town and I got sketch... left by rail for Seville.
15th: After Bkfst called on Phillip (out). Saw the Museo, Murillos and the Caridad pictures. Also met Sir A. and Lady Dunbar... went to see Alcazar... and Cathedral... went up the Giralda - lovely view, made sketch of it. Dined at 6. J.Phillip called on me at Hotel.
16th: Went to meet Phillip and Deane at Cafe Francais and then to Tabacco Fabrica, with the Dunbars and Lady Abercrombie. Then out the Puerta and round the walls... Went off to Cordoba by rail at 6.
Sunday 17th: Went to the Mezquita Mosque, a most wonderful building. Met a pleasant man who accompanied me all over it, saw everything...
26th: Went to Church in morning and drove with Mr Powley in Calesa to Torre Molinos and said A Dieu to Christina in the garden of the Fonda de Parody, Hacienda de San Miguel. Drove back at 6 very wretched. Tea and dinner at Mr Powley's. Called to see John Mark and left Malaga at 9 by steamer.
April 4th: ...went with Capt Freeling, joined the Governor, Compte d'E and his friend, and Mr Hood on board the *Immortalité*. The yards were manned and a salute fired. After going round the vessel the drums beat to quarters and every man was at his post in 7 mins., every gun manned. After several rounds at the target 1,000 yards off, the pivot 82 pounder was fired several times and then a broadside. We returned at 5 to dinner. No signal for the *Delta*. In evening made sunset drawing of Cartagena for Mrs Freeling also one of Venice for Mr Power.
5th: Packed up, bought gaiters, Fez, rug, Sombrero and called with drawing on Mr Power. Made sketch of Convent garden, also drawing for the General and one for Mr Hood. Called on the latter and he gave me photos. Packed, dined at 5 and left Capt. Freeling's at ½ past. Boarded the *Delta* and got an excellent berth with Mr - an Officer of the Royal Navy. Tea at 8. Grog at 10. Slept very well, smooth water. Begun drawing of Dutch boats.
May 4th:[London] ...Went to R.A at 3, felt better. Met all my friends - very interesting speeches - remained till the last. Home at ½ p 11.
13th: ...Went to Christie's and Forster's and with Major Boileau to see the Gorillas. Also had a peep at the new rooms at the National Gallery - very fine...I attended General Meeting at the Athenaeum - stormy debate not over till 5. Dined and sat with Hart, Boxall and Percy till ½ p 8. Went to hear Smyth finish Geological lecture at Jermyn St and then to the close of the paper on Japan at the Geographical. Home at 11...

1862
Oct.3rd: ...by train from Bergamo at 7.20. Mr Herbert and Miss Duckworth came into the same carriage with us at Dezenzano and left again at Piacenza. We arrived in Venice at 4.45... took apartments at Barbesi's opposite the Salute for Wyatt and I. Washed and dined at Vapore... coffee at Florians. Finished letter to Mother and strolled about Piazza with Wyatt.
4th: Went early and found Vincenzo at his Traghetto. He fetched my Roba from Brown's and we took Breakfast at Vapore. Then to Shielins, got £10 cashed. Took Wyatt to Sta Maria Formosa... met the Duckworth's on Piazza... bought new hat and had other repaired. Ordered wine and ale at Trauner's
17th: ...painted on Dogana in a Fog till ½ p 10 then worked on Squero & on S.Pietro in Castello & on sky of Squero and Giardini Pubblici. Glorious sunset, clouds - cumulus.
23rd: Called at Post and for Mr Layard, but he could not come. Went to Mr White and brought his whole party to Ca Cuculo and went with them to the Salute. I said adieu and went out to the Lagune but had forgotten oils and returned and painted on San Giorgio No 3., and the sunset Giudecca. Dined at Vapore with Inchbold and met Layard on the Piazza. Called and saw Decimus Burton at Europa. Dull day.
29th: Very dull morning. Felt poorly, took stroll. Painted at home till 2. Heard guns - a salute to the ex-King of Greece just come into Port in the *Scylla* English screw sloop-of-war. Yards were manned and colours dressed on the Austrian sloop. I went out but the ex-King did not disembark. Retd. at 4 and painted skies till dark...
30th: ...went out to S.Servolo at 12½ and began Wyatt's little picture, drew it in and painted sky, also a small sky with rays of sun - put in Topo to Sunset Salute. The ex-King of Greece disembarked and left by rail in evening. The *Scylla* fired a salute.

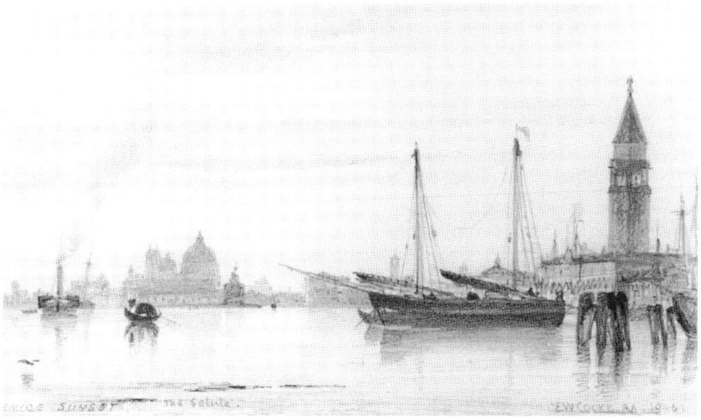

Plate 249. Pencil drawing
Sunset Salute
A hurried sketch, yet full of atmosphere, this has been signed and dated, perhaps as a gift, in 1864. Photo courtesy Martyn Gregory. Private Collection

Nov.1st: Heavy rain, stormy wind and rough water prevented my leaving home till 2. Went out and drew the *Scylla* view in pencil. Then on the new canvas began to paint it. Afternoon tolerably fine. Worked till dark. Took stroll on Piazzetta and Molo. Dined at 7 at Vapore with Inchbold [J.W.Inchbold (1830-1888), painter in the Pre-Raphaelite circle, continental traveller, lived in Switzerland 1877-87]. Caffe and Galignani at Specchi. Stroll and home at 10. Read *Illustrated News* in evening. After Bkfst stretched new canvas on one of the old stretchers.
2nd: ...Went with Valentine on board the *Scylla,* took Lieut., Challis and the Asst. Surgeon to the Belle Arti. Brought Mme Salviati and family to see my pictures. Band in Piazza in afternoon. Dined at 8 on board the *Scylla*...
7th: Went up the Campanile with Mr and Mrs Calvert Toulmin then called on Mr Perry [British Consul-General] he and daughter shewed me their Palace, they called to see my paintings at 3. Went out in boat to Canal of San Clemente and painted 3 sunsets... In evening read and copied out Bologna and Ferrara from Murray's Handbook.

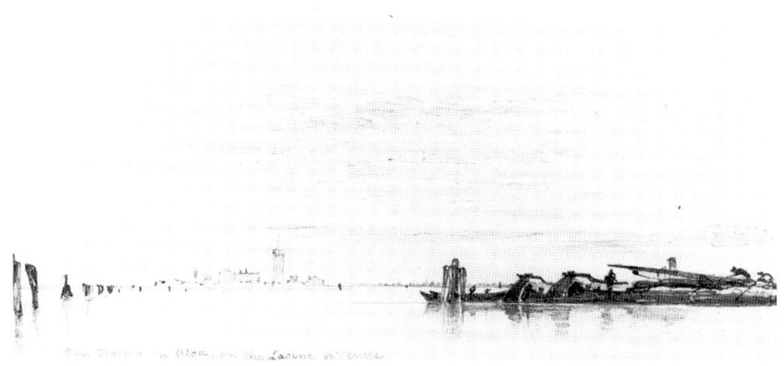

Plate 250. Pencil drawing
San Giorgio in Alga on the Lagune of Venice
The artist working quickly against evening light has just time to block-in the dark shapes of laden lighters and the lonely island of 'St George in the Seaweed'. Photo courtesy Martyn Gregory. Private Collection

1863

Oct 2nd: Vincenzo came early with boat. Bkfst at home, prepared for painting and set palette. Went out and began No 1, picture of Ponte della Veneto Marin- painted till dark, R.Bateman with me. Dined at Vapore - ices at Suttil. Valentine sent Papers. Vincenzo got my trunk, canvas and stretchers from Consul's (no key). Showery day.
7th: Painted at home till ½ p 1. Went to Vapore and dined there, and then to Santa Marta and painted on new picture, larger size, of the buildings on the North of the Canale della Giudecca, till dark. Glorious sunset. Put in purple cloud to a prepared sky. Mr Crace and Mr Bicknell arrived at the Europa. Heavy rain at night.
21st: George Stanfield called while we were at Bkfst. Dense Caligo till 11. Went over to Dogana and sketched a group of Rasconi with mats &c. Then worked on Porto Franco subject till dark. Glorious sunset. Stroll and dined at Vapore.
24th: After Bkfst we went out with both men to Giudecca and after a walk on Zattere got sketches of brigs, then to the Canal of the Ponte Lunga and got sketches of fish baskets. Then on board the *Tripoli* steamer. Painted on 2 small sunsets.
26th: Cold morning, called on Valentine and Mr Perry. Got sketches of Burci off Danieli. Painted a beginning of a small Dutch picture at home. After dinner at Vapore we went to Ponti's, selected Photo's. Met Capt Fowke and Messrs Pattinson & friends, shewed them many things about San Marco, back at 10 to tea. Brilliant moon.
Nov.2nd: Went to Ponti's at ½ p 9, met Lady and Miss Rennie, bought photo's.Then bt. glass, bottles &c, then shewed them the Scala. Packed trunk to go to England and Portmanteau to stay here.

1864

April 7th Painted on & finished small oil picture of Zuider Zee, Diploma pic. came from Joubert's & I painted on it for two hours -Guillet took it & letter to R.A.in aftn... Men brought glass cabinet from Durlacher's & broke a large pane. Mr Waters called & brt. Onyx cup &c...
8th Finished little wee Dutch picture & gave it & an oil picture of the Bay of Naples for a great many Venetian things brought by Mr Waters, also 2 Camei, very fine, several Onyx charms, a ring, two brooches, a Vidicombe onyx cup &c. 2 men came with glass to replace broken one - all the morning at it - had to change more glass. Verity came to repair different gas burners. Went to town in aft. to Christie's to look at Brett's bronzes &c Tea at Athenaeum & read - called at Colnaghi's, met Mr Bowman there. Got new watch at — heard Dr Percy on Iron at R[oyal] I[nstitution].
9th Sat Finished San Giorgio- sent it to Joubert's & frame to Guillet - Find: Sunset Lagune. Mr Cole & Mr Durrell called. Went to Town & called on Mr. B[eresford] Hope & on Alderman & Mrs Salomons, called at Nixon's, home at ½ p 7. Touched on photos in evng & arranged Venetian glass in case. Warm day. Joubert sent photos of Diploma [picture] - lost chased steel snuffbox.
11th. Worked all morng. on Venice from Giudecca. After dinner (early) went to Athenaeum & waited all aftn. till 7 to see Garibaldi. Many ladies there in balcony, Prof. Ansted took tea with me, home at 11. Very cold but bright day. Garibaldi met with a most enthusiastic reception - dense crowds everywhere.
12 Finished Venice & Giudecca. M read account of Garibaldi's entry - Called on Sige Marras. Went to Town at ¼ to 1 bought 2 little Lots, Roman Bronzes at Brett's Sale - went to Brit. Inst. Dined at Athenaeum - ordered at Green's coat & other things. Coffee at Athenm & took Richmond & Herbert to hear Cardinal Wiseman lecture at S.Ken.Mus, Architectural Museum Met H[arriette], M[ary], young Ingelow & Creswick... A.Burnand sent subscription to Lifeboat £12.10.0d.
13th Finished Venice from Giudecca. Guillet brt home Naples framed & mounted. I worked on it & Con took it to the Duke of Sutherland's for Garibaldi with letter. I went to see Mulready's pictures at S Ken. Mus, called for John & Bessy Hannah back thro' Gardens, ...A Myers came with 4 pieces of Venetian glass & took a drawing of Honfleur back.
14th. ...to Rye, left our luggage there & on by rail to Winchelsea. Saw church &c, walked in aft. to Rye & strolled till 5½. Dined at Cinque Ports Hotel ...wrote to Sir W.James, and Mother, after tea slept there...
15 After bk drove in Dogcart with Con to Lydd - 11 miles across the Marsh. Took a gig to the Sea & got sk. of Dungeness lighthouse thro Telescope. Con went to it across shingle 1 mile & ½... left by 5 train to Deal at ½ p 7, went to Royal Exchange Hotel, Mrs Cork's, to tea & supper. Sir W.James sent his groom with a letter to say how ill he had been.
16 Wet morng. we went to Sandown Castle & then called on Capt Nott who took us to see Capt.Cannon at Walmer - looked at the Lifeboats. I called on Mr Cavell the Mayor...
21st Went to see Garibaldi at Mr Seely's, met Hope Johnstone there, shook hands with the General. Mr Myers brt my Greek fragments of glass & the Majolica dish. Arranged all the Venetian glass, Greek glass, majolica &c. Mr & Mrs Nicol & Mrs Jno. Webster came at 3 & looked at pictures. Mr N. wishes for a sea piece. Mr Felix Slade called & saw glass, he drove me to Christie's, saw China & pictures of Mr Herbert's.
25th ...went to R.A., large picture badly hung above the line. Went to Athenm. wrote letters, met Dr Acland. Home at 10, cold E. wind chest very bad...
26th. Wrote letters, went to Academy, painted all day there on 2 pictures. Met Doo, tea at Athenm. read *Times, - Globe...*
27th. Painted on Bay of Monaco (for Myers) & on Evng. cloud, Venice... I dined at Sir John Rennie's, 7 Lowndes Sq. Sat by Lady Head & Mrs Morrell...
28th ...went to Christie's & bt. 2 Mulready sketches
29th Mr Myers called & took pic. of Bay of Monaco. Sigmd & Wm Rücker called also Capt. Englefield [Inglefield] Mr Northcote sent cheque for his picture & also £10 for Lifeboat... C.Landseer called for me & we went to Alderman Salomons' to dinner - met Sir Edwin, Lord Hardinge, Hart, Lee, Knight, Stanfield, Roberts, Herbert, Mr Wragg, Mrs Salomons home with Redgrave.
30th. Painted till ½ p 1 on sunset sky - called at Royal Society, left cheques at Bank, went to R.A. at 3¼ - had a good muster of grandees. I sat at the head of the table. Mr Brand on my right - delightful music & fine speeches. Took Gambier Parry to the R.Society, Con there, pleasant hour-*Sculpture by Photography* ...Vokins called to measure frames for Rücker.
May 4th Dear Mother's Birthday. Worked on Naples during day & on Watercolor Drawings Mr Webster came at 5 & brt. 4 pieces of Venetian glass - man sent another one from Oxford St., dined up in Study. Mr & Mrs Newton came also Mrs & Bessie Hannah & Robt. Bateman, had great fun all the evening. Mr Bateman called here in aftn. before his lecture at the Horticultural Soc.
9th Worked up several watercolor & pencil drawings for the Fancy Fair of French Protestant Schools...
10th Sent drawgs to Mrs Frith for the Sale. Paid Joubert, dined at Mr Fearon's, met D.Burton, Miss Wood, Mr Lewin, &c &c pleasant dinner party...
12th. worked up drawgs sent 5 more to Mrs Frith for Bazaar... went with Mr D.Burton to see Herbert's great picture at H[ouse] of Lords & also Designs for Museums. Dressed at Athenaeum & dined at Mr Anderdon's. Went with Cope from there to S.Ken Mus to meet the Prince & Prcss of Wales, Lord Granville's party.
16th After bk. designed in Charcoal my Life-boat picture on Dining Room wall, till luncheon then painted on chalk cliffs Tréport...
17th Ptd on White cliffs all day Mr Webster came & brt 3 Venetian pieces, pink & white. He took his Drawg of St Heliers Harbour & 2 pencil sks. of Dutch views.
30th Worked a little on Venetian pictures... Sir W.James came & drove me up to town, gave me a cheque for £25 for the Life boat Called to see Venetian glass at Webster's, drove to Conduit St., met the Committee of Architectural Education Scheme...
31st Mr Webster called & he took a small Sunset picture framed, & I finished up a drawing of Scheveling pinck for him in exchange for 15

pieces of Venetian glass.
June 11th Worked up Drawg of Oxford Mill & sent it by Geo. to Falcke. Worked on Topaze hulk... I called on Falcke Bond St & saw a superb collection of Venetian glass, 120 pieces then went to see De La Rue's collection at Willis' Rooms... went with Geo to De La Rue's Astronomical soirée. Con came.
18th Mr Falcke called also Mr Hartshorne & Son, they staid 2 hours.
20th ...by train to Dartford. Mr Matthews joined at Lond. Bridge. Mr Cosier's carriage took us to Wilmington Hall, saw his Mediaeval *objets d'art*, very fine, stroll in garden till 7. J.Gilbert, Mr C's nephews & Manson dined there...
27th Painted on Gambart's picture of Dutch calm & on small Venetian sunset. Mr Falcke & Mr Miers called... Mr Jacobs came twice brt a Majolica vase & 3 wine decanters, a Venetian glass & an old German ribbed bottle also 2 large Kylins. Lady Abercrombie & son called...
28th. Went to Town, called on E.Falcke & settled about glass. Brt home a fine collection of ancient fragments of iridescent glass. Painted all day on Venetian sunset for Falcke. Rob Bateman came to dinner, Miss Lyon called. Mr Joubert brought Mr Powell the Glass Manufacturer to look at the Venetian glass...
29th Mr & Mrs Falcke came at 9 & brt a van with the Glass case & 111 pieces of old Venetian glass. They unpacked it & set it up by 3 o'clk. Porter brt me my Diploma of R.A.... Painted on Venice sunset Mr. Gambart called and took his Dutch Calm home.
October [Venice]
Oct. 5th: Went to Post with Vincenzo, then to R.Brown's, met the Bentincks - went over to the Correr Museum and saw the Glass, crossed to Richetti's and spent 2 hours looking over things - home at 3 and began small picture of Dutch calm...
7th: ...called on Leighton (saw him take a header into Canal)- sat while he dressed - he drove me home. Went to Nani's, met Brown and the Bentincks, staid three hours there bargaining for things. Bought M o Pearl box and some old Glass, Iron work &c.he took me to a man to pack them...
8th: Called on Rietti, bought several pieces of old Glass, also on Bianchi (out) Got at a small shop some fragments of an old Mistura Vase, to put together at home. Returned at 3 and finished small Dutch picture for Valentine.called at Zen's and bought 5 Nap[oleon]s worth of Glass.Got letter from Harriette in afternoon, much warmer today.
12th: Lovely day. Out before breakfast went in gondola to Ricchetti's, bought 17 pieces of glass. Went to Blumenthal's for cash. In afternoon Ricchetti brought them home and I paid him. Brown & Bentinck called. Painted in afternoon on Dutch boats...
19th: Out before breakfast, very warm all day Scirocco. Painted all morning on water and mountains of big cloud subject, then stroll on Zattere - went over the Hotel Calcina. Worked on Dutch boats till 5, stroll on Piazzetta...
24th: Very soaking rain all day. Painted a new sky copy of Salute picture lent me by Brown. At 3 called on Valentine and we went to Palazzo Ducale to see Lorenzo, next to San Marco & I went to Ponti's selected Photo's, back at 6- in evening V. helped me translate terms of Venetian glass from Catalogue of Correr Museum
26th: Rainy and dark all day. Tide over the Piazza in evening. Got change of £10 at Blumenthal's and paid Dina for the glass, maiolica, silver cups &c I bought. Painted on small Salute. Called on V. at ½ p 2 and we went to the Correr museum and got catalogue. Home at 4 and painted till dark...
28th: Got shave before Breakfast. At 11 Brown brought Sige Tagliapietra, Cecchini and — to see my pictures and to tell me I was to be one of the Members of the Accademia. Went to Ducal Palace with Brown to see Lorenzi and bronze Cavedoni. Then to Dina and bought a great many things. Painted till ½ p 3. Got cash at Blumenthal's and paid Dina 50 Napoleons for all my purchases. Brought home small things and a Giotto picture...
29th: Went to Dina's, bt set of Glazed Tiles and 2 Gatti di Occhi [?] in glass and a Crystal snuff-box - back at 12 and painted on small Salute till ½ p 4. Then with V. to S. Giorgio Schiavone - shut, then to carpenter - bt a Venetian plate and a Beer mug like Capo di Monti ware - back to dinner, at 8 went to tea at Mr Howells [Wm.Dean Howells, U.S.Consul] - met a painter Mr Baldwin (American) there - home at 1.
2 November: Carpenter came at 1 and I paid him 18 Florins for case and 2½ for 2 old pictures and packing. Went to Vincenzo and he took me on board the *Atlas*... very wet and cold all day- called for Cash at Blumenthal's, paid 18 francs for 12 Photo's. Left pictures and books at Brown's and saw him. Then to Murano, sketched old glass. Saw the Director of the Museum. Back at 5 went with Valentine to dine at Mr Perry's. Met Mr Lytton Bulwer and Bride and Mr P Junr... and Mme Hurtado and the Marchesa. Drew Glass, home at 11¼, packed.
3rd: ...Vincenzo brought a large Bacchetta and we saw the four cases on board the *Atlas* by 12. Called for and took Mr Bulwer to see the Scala, S.Giov Crisostomo...&c Then to Rieti's and bought 3 Naps worth of 7 pieces of old glass. Packed them and took them to the Agents and got Bill of Lading. Called on Mme Salviati and at Accademia... dined with V and he went with me to Station, left at 4.40, supper at Pedrocchi, bought glass plate and left Padua by mail at 10½.
[The collector's urge took him by way of Florence, his packing cases having gone by sea.]
Nov. 5th ...went to Post and Uffizi Galleries. Staid till ½ p 2; Caffe and went to 2 Antiquarians, the second Ribblets. Selected about 9 or 12 pieces of old glass, Venetian... worked out trains in evening and list of glass.
Sun.6th: Read Service. Heavy storm all day, gale. Moved to 20 Lung'Arno. Went about City to churches. Dined at Hotel. Read news. Arno enormously swollen, 9 miles an hour.
7th: Called at Post - breakfast at Luna, went to Duomo and Battisteria. Bought 5 Palm [walking] sticks - 15 Fl. Then home and to French the Bankers. Changed £20 notes, then to Ribblets, bought 10 objects of Glass Ivory and Majolica- Pd £20. Called on Mr [Adolphus] Trollope- out and Mr Matthews - out. Went to Ch. of the Annunciata. Very cold all day. No rain. Arno less swollen. Dined at Luna, coffee at Doneys - read News at Club.
10th: ...went to — bought a few things of him, packed them in little square portmanteau. Left *Murray* [Guide-book] at Mr Matthews', called on Mr Trollope, saw his lovely house, garden and collection of antiquities. Drew a Venetian vase and cover... bought a 2nd hand portmanteau which just holds my *roba*...
11th: ...got to Leghorn at 3, called on Mr Bean our Consul, took berth in the *Isere* (Caird's building) dined and strolled about till 5½ went on board... left at ½ p 7, wet evening, very steady vessel, no motion, smooth water. Wrote long letter to A.Burnand to insure my pictures.
[In Genoa where they paused, he met Mr Rücker, his sister and 2 nieces in the Duomo: then on to Marseilles, on a fine moonlight night and a smooth voyage on which he and a Spanish Engineer were the only passengers.]
15th: [Paris]...left me drawing Venetian glass in the Sauvageot collection, then went to 3 Antiquarians on the other side of the Seine, bought 2 Ures of old Venetian, one Purple with metal lid. Read news in eveng. in Saloon - met a Mr Dutton.
16th: Went up to Exhibition building with Barlow and to a shop where I bought a fine Ivory carving of Bacchus. Bt. 6 sticks, palm, & drew at Louvre. Mr B went with me - sat with him while he dined & saw him off to Marseilles, he lent me £10. Drew in eveng. dined at ½ p 7. Read news. Mr Puxley here, we had a chat together.
17th Got a shave & bkf. at Cafe, Stroll round Palais Royale, went to Louvre, drew more glass. Left at 2, called at 3 Antiquarians, bt. 3 pieces of glass at one shop & 2 at another. Went to Hotel Cluny, drew 3 pieces of glass & saw the Glorious old Murano plates with enamelled pictures on them...
19th: Carpenter came at ½ p 8 and packed the Glass in 2 boxes. Bought a Bronze for Steve in Rue Lafitte - went to Hotel de Cluny and drew several more Glasses- called at shops - dined at Hills. Bought a curious kind of animal of dark glass - Venetian. Worked up drawings till 12...
Dec.1st. [London] Painted all day on Venetian sunset & on Myers' picture, put in new sky. Mrs Barlow called. Mr Myers came & brt. 4 pieces of Venetian glass & a crystal tazza. Went with Mary in fly to dine at Mr Henry Wigram's
Sat 3rd. ...Falcke's man brt 2 ruby cups which I bought 15/-.
31st Finished pencil drawg for Mr Webster & drawg of Pilot boat off Dover, sent it to Guillet's. Myers took his picture of Scheveling sands & a drawing of Schevg. pincks for a Venetian glass bowl in *or molu* stand. Joined with the old & new Councils at the Academy, home at ¼ to 12. Ushered in the New Year with the 100th Psalm.

1868
Tues 24th Nov. Election at East Grinstead. Left by ¼ to 8 train with Mr Saint & Whitelock & Mr Jeffery. Voted for Liberals and saw Sackville College. Left at 10. Voted for Liberals at Charing Cross. Went to Burlington House, met the President & members & saw all the grand new Galleries. Dined at Athenaeum at 3 & home by the Express at 4 Able met me with Pony, lovely day. Bought colors at Barbe's. Made drawing of Sackville Coll. in chalk in evng.
25th. Finished chalk drawg in morng for Mr Jeffery. He drove me to

Goodman's at 1, to choose a horse, saw a dark brown Guelding & a grey Mare - drove home at 3. Wrote to Mrs Glendining, Punnett, Nesfield, Veitch & Black.- cold day. Men carting stone & getting in Hop bincs.

28th Worked on Goodwin in morng. drove to Station at 2 & brought back Laura. Cart fetched luggage & case of frames. The Oswells called in morng. Mr Lutwidge came to luncheon - gave me a commission for a large picture. Mr Jeffery sent the new carriage from Mr Read's... Men got up stone.

30th Prepared for Veitch. He came by 2 train & after luncheon we strolled all over garden & settled no end of positions for plants Dined at ½ p 5, in evng made lists over plans of ground. I gave him the small picture of Scheveling. H & L went to see articles at a Sale at Tunbridge Wells. Case came from Barbe's.

Dec.1 After Bk we went into garden & made plans for plants all over ground & rocks till 11, then I drove him to Station. Miss S.Saint called with a Lady. I worked in garden removing plants with Carde, Yucca, Cryp &c. In evng made chalk drawg. of Dutch botter in calm. Dull & mild. Laura read Tallyrand.

2. Worked with men in garden till 12 planting Rhodos & removing plants. Men brought loam. arranged Clumps. Wrote to Veitch, Bateman, Jeffery - mild soft day. Servants & Laura went to penny reading in eveng. Letter from Helen, in evng hung drawgs in various rooms. Worked up large Goodwin, wrote to Robinson.

4th. All day with men preparing for planting, making holes, removing loam & sand, fixing up trees, root upwards, Stumps, removing Hollies &c. Mr Jeffrey & Miss B called & took H to the Wells. Sands came & fixed curtains &c. Heavy rain in evng. Finished Goodwin & framed it in eveng. & the 2 small drawgs of Zuider Zee & Scheveling. L read Tallyrand to us in Study.

Mon 7th. 3 large Scotch firs blown down in the night. All the men cut them up & placed them upside down - we built up Stumps, removed large Hollies, planted other things, made holes for Conifers, carted loam. Veitch sent Goode this morng. he pruned fruit trees in K. garden. [Rev.] Mr Reed called. Goodman rode over. Wrote to George & Nicholson. Men glazing broken squares in Fernery. Fine mild day.

8th sent for 3 heavy loads of plants from Station-from Veitch. We planted all day. Irish Yews & conifers, Yews & Box &c. Men digging holes & getting loam, fixing Stumps &c. Very heavy rain indeed. In evng made drawg, of Bay of Naples in chalk... strong wind all day.

9th all day planting conifers, Irish Yews, Araucarias, Arbutus &c with 4 men & Goode. Wrote to Veitch for more plants... change of wind & weather cool but dry. Got up 4th load of plants from Station & got loam carted.

10th. All day planting with 4 men & Goode. Got in the conifers - the Court Yard plants, aucubas & box. I planted ivies & V[irginia]. creepers on Stumps & placed aucubas. Stevens & 4 sons at work grubbing stumps & cording them in Wilderness... Goodman fetched my cart mare & brought the Brown Guelding used him in Cart for sand & mould. In evng worked up Dutch Calm.

11th Very strong wind & tremendous rain very difficult to plant. We sent 3 times for a second consignment of plants from Veitch. In evng completed drawg of Dutch boats Calm & framed it & another. Wrote to put off Nesfield & Goodall coming tomorrow.

12th Sat. Very hard at work all day planting with Goode & 4 men. Wren bringing up Loam. Mr Jeffery called & brt. us Cod fish &c. Goodall came by the 2 o'clk train. After luncheon we went all over the garden & helped planting conifers. Men at work grubbing roots of trees all day. A very charming day. Shewed Goodall plans of house & lists of plants in evng.

13th Used the carriage the first time to go to Withyham Church with Goodall & Laura. Mr Read preached, home at ½ p 1 Very dark & dull day but no rain. Able & Wren drove - Goodall left by 6 train. He took walk to Mr Temple's in aft. & went over the house.

15th Very mild pleasant day We planted a great many things, raised the Wellingtonia &c. In evng. worked up Bay of Naples, small one. Laura read Hood to us all. Mr Jeffery came & saw our Pig, Tomsit cut him up.

16th Veitch sent a large quantity of plants, 2 loads, we appropriated all & planted a great many. Took on 2 more men. The Stevens's finished 7 cords of wood stubs & stacked them. In eveng worked up chalk drawing of Vesuvius

17th Men planting Poplars &c.&c.&c. all day... sent fly for Mr F.P.Barlow at 6. He dined here & slept. I shewed him a great many sketches in evng. to select subjects from, for drawgs.

18th Busy all day. Mr Barlow left in pony chaise at ½ p 7 after Bkfst for London. Sands came & began hanging the Vandeveldes on Staircase. Stevenses at the pond & digging up immense Hollies which we planted about Stumps & in Wilderness. Very fine morng. but wet aftn... In evng Fulman came with Richd. Parker & I engaged him as Gardener & Coachman to live in Lodge.

19th Lovely sunrise & such a glorious warm day. 2 butterflies out.We planted all day - finished Hollies & Laurels about Lodge & entrance. Did the Irish Yews. Stevens got up very large Hollies which we placed in front of Stumps. We planted the Araucaria on top of rock & Stump near Newton's Appletree with great effect. Men digging out pond. Sent carriage to Station at 2 to meet L. & M. Mary very unwell with Asthma & head ache. In evng made drawg. of Dort in chalk.

23rd. Sent for last batch of plants, 2 Araucarias Euonymas & Aucubas - we planted them Goode at work pruning fruit trees in K garden. Men puddling ponds & planting Hollies. Mr Jeffery called & drove me to the Wells. Called at Durrants, Trices, Hair cut. Got pickle fork from — Mr J drove me back at ½ p 3 a most gorgeous sunset, fine all the way home. In evening made drawing of it with a view on Lagune. Moon fine.

24th Goode pruning in K garden & planting the rest of the things. We got all the 4 pools puddled & full of water. Men bringing loam & peat to fill up - we planted large Hollies. Cart fetched up old Fernery & gratings & took Crates back for Veitch. Got horse shod. Brt up 2 limes from Mr Saint. I sent 2 drawgs to Mr & Mrs Whitelock & wine to Fulman. In eveng I made drawg of Rome for Mrs Jeffery. George came by last train & walked up at ½ p 10.

25th. Christmas Day Drove to Withyham Church with Aunt Eglinton. & George & staid to communicate. Sent 2 drawgs of Rome & Lagune to Mr & Mrs Jeffreys as a present. Spent a very pleasant day. Mary came down. Great fun about a wig & pig-tail for me & the live chicken on table. Mr Goode came up & dined here. Mr Currie & Archie drove over in morng.

26th Men bringing peat up to Heather Hill, grubbing hazels & clearing away wood &c. Goode finished pruning & nailing up ivies. Mr & Mrs J.Field rode over Mr — called. Oswell brought his children. Parker & wife came to see cottage & saw garden. 2 loads of old Fernery came from Station. Mr & Mrs Whitelock & Mrs Woolf called. Made 2 chalk drawgs in evg. L & Geo read. Goode left at 5¼, sowed Mahonia.

28th Tremendous gale 2 Scotch firs blown down near Yew. The Stevens's cut them up & began to form Bridge to K. garden. Awful rain all aftn. Parker & wife came with their furniture into Lodge. Alderman Salomons came with Mrs Wragg & Hart, terribly dark & wet when they called in aft: great floods out all over Meads & river. In evng worked up drawing of Rome from Tiber... Mummers came in evng & sang

29th Awful steady rain all morng. Floods higher this eveng. the Meads like a grand lake. I worked up drawg. of Scheveling for Mr Barlow & in evng made drawing of Bragozzo in a Borasco. Very fine & sunny aftn. & superb effects, full moon today, brilliant night. Parker & Carde fixing stakes to newly planted trees

31st Worked on smaller Bay of Naples & began large picture of Vesuvius. Men filling up abt. Bridge & bringing up Peat for beds. Most brilliant day & superb moon. H & Geo drove to Station to bring up C.Loddiges, but he did not come. In evng worked on large drawing of Vesuvius. Ushered in the New Year with the 100th Psalm. George walked to Mr Jeffreys & back.

1874

January Weds 28th [on the Nile] A very strong mistral wind ahead of us and a horrible sand storm, blinding at times. Made colored Drawing of an old Dahabeah with Earthen pots Turkeys &c, then went to the Mud Village Bibbeh - all on big mounds with Dove Cots - tombs & thousands of Palm. Railway & Sugar house - got sketch of Palms by Moonlight with Deck figures.

29th. Blowing all day ½ a gale from the S; remained at Bank all day. Got sketches in the Mud Village of Dove Cots & two of Palms, Boat building &c. Very cold early, warm day but bitter wind & awful sand & dust in morng worked up sketches in Watercolour & oil in aft got large sketch of Palms nr. Mosque. Awful gale all the aftn & eveng. our Dahabeah in some danger close under the bank which kept giving way - could scarcely rest or sleep with the movement. In morng it blew a perfect Hurricane of wind, rain, dust & dirt filling every place - continued all the morning, 3 vessels sunk close to us, above & below, awful scramble for bundles of sugar cane. Wrecked Rudder cast up close to us. We collected Palm sticks & got some sketches - wind got to S. & in evng came strong.

February Mon 9th Posted letters at Rhoda after bkfst & immediately set sail. Fine N.Wind all day went up abt. 42 miles. Passed superb cliffs of limestone on R.Bank - got several sketches - painted on two half pictures, put in boats. Superb sunset, glorious scene on river with boats. Saw an enormous number of Fellaheen going on board boats & steamers for Cairo.

10th Left our anchorage at 8 & had a fine N.Wind all day 7 hours passing

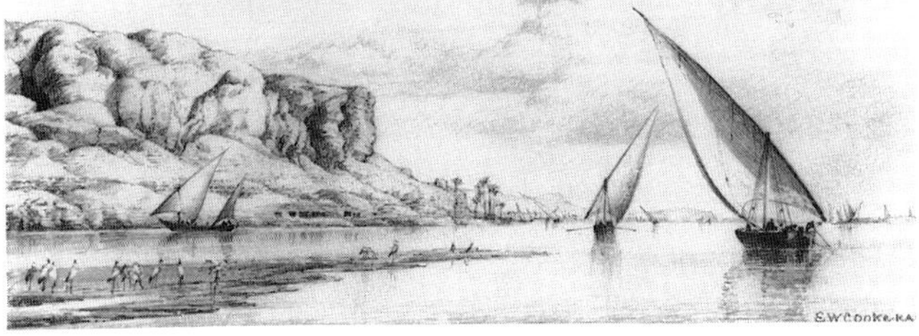

Plate 251. Pencil drawing
Cliffs of Gebel Sheykh, Nile.1874 Photo courtesy Martyn Gregory

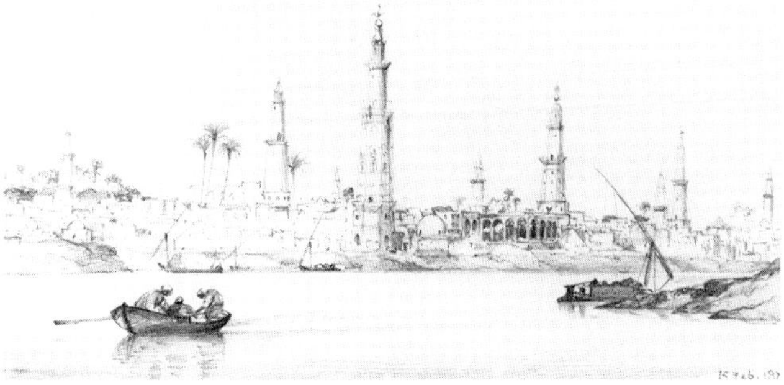

Plate 252. Pencil drawing
Girgeh, minarets. 15th Feb. Photo courtesy Martyn Gregory

under the Cliffs of Gebel Aboofayda. Glorious. Passed Manfalool at sunset & went on till 10 when we anchored. I painted Sunset sky & worked on other pictures. Got 14 sketches of Cliffs, boats &c. Most lovely day but cold evening. Gout bad.

Sunday 15th. Began to sail before Sunrise & had a light wind NW all day. We passed Girgeh at ½ p 11 a large Town with many mosques & minarets then passed by Bellianeh a large village with nothing but Dove Cots like Towers. Very soft mild evening, wind dropped & we lay to at Bank at 9, below Farshoot.

16th Very lovely mild morning superb sky all day Blue & curdled with white cirrhi. Started early & trecked a good deal but a capital wind got up about 11 and we passed Farshoot (Left Bank) & Sahib Bajoora On each side superb Doums & Dates [palms], lovely banks fine view of grand range of mountains - all day, I painted them & sky on large canvas - in evng most glorious view with groves of Palms. Hard on a shoal for 70 mins. I sketched the mountains.

17th. Sailed at 5 AM got aground 3 times, 1 hour in the morng. & in evng at 5, couldn't get off. Carlo went to a Village & saw the Sheikh who sent 5 men & after 20 min got off & sailed. I painted all day on mountains & Earthenware Boat. Got sketches of Doums & Camels in a boat &c. Very fine breeze & clear sunset. Mild. Lost 4 hours, got Doum fruit ashore.

18th Got aground soon after starting & anchored in the stream till 6 AM when we sailed, fine wind brought us along fast & we reached Luxor at 5. Glorious sunset & lovely new moon. Called on American & English Consuls- pipes & coffee. Gay dined on the *Griffin* with American friends, Scott spent eveng. there. Wrote long letters till 1 o'clock. Painted cliffs & water in two pictures all day. Warm. Saw the Great temples.

19th Up early called at Post Office & on Mustapha Aga - no letters . The *Griffin* sailed off early - we left at 10 & had a good wind all day which carried us 40 miles - most lovely warm day, passed glorious Rocks close to Water Gebelayn. I painted on 3 pictures in my cabin. Lovely moon & stars. Felt over-done, very warm.

20th Began to move soon after 6 & had a fair wind all day. Passed Esneh abt. noon & sailed by moonlight. Passed 3 dahabeahs coming down. Glorious rocky knolls on our left. I painted on several small pictures, began Sunset in evng & a rocky hill from Nature on Deck. Very hot, 72°. Glorious sunset behind Palms & trees. Passed Edfou by moonlight.

25th. Left at 9 on Donkeys with Lorenzo over the Wilderness to Philae. Crossed in the big boat. Got sketch from Propylon of Temple of Isis, then had luncheon in the small temple - on Pharoah's Bed. got sketch of part of it & another from Pylon of T. of Isis & distant views also got Palm branch, Took the Donkeys to Mahalla. Lots of Dahabeahs. Saw the Duke of Hamilton's D- being hauled up by 100 men. We descended in our own boat sent to meet us, home at 6. Got sketch of figures at Assuan

26th. After bkfst set new palate [*sic*] scraped off the sand of Gizerah subject opposite & painted all morng till 2 upon it, then went with Gay to the Sakir against the lofty stone wall. He painted it in oil & I got two

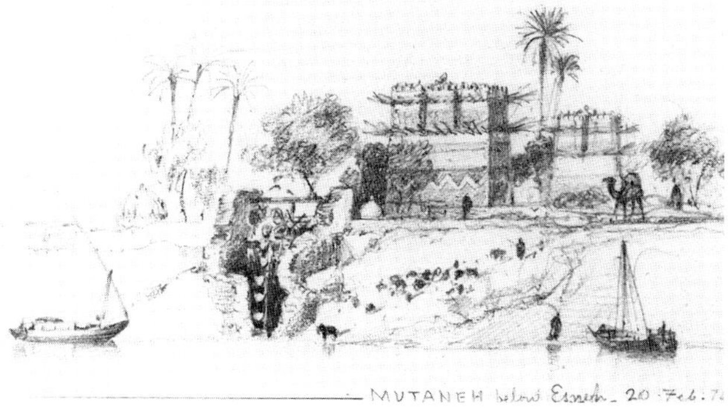

Plate 254. Pencil drawing
Mutaneh, below Esneh. 20th Feb.
Compare the painting 74/18 (Colour Plate 144), Egyptian pigeon houses, which was done from the ship's deck on the return trip in March.
Photo courtesy Martyn Gregory

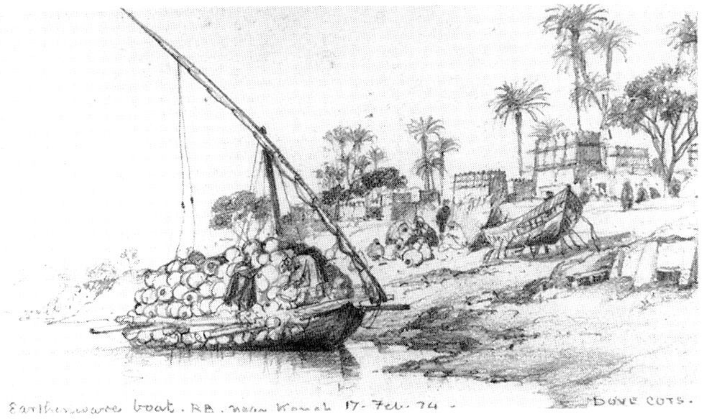

Plate 253. Pencil drawing
Earthenware boat, R[ight]B[ank] near Keneh 17th Feb.
Photo courtesy Martyn Gregory

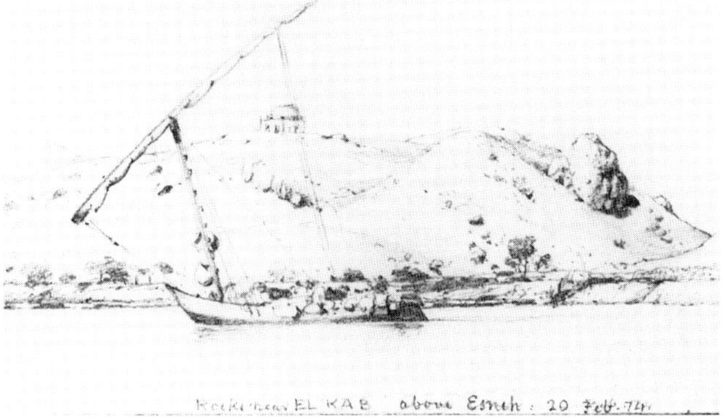

Plate 255. Pencil drawing
Rocks near El Kab, above Esneh 20th Feb.

sketches of it & also two others on the Island - boat fetched us at 6. Windy N all day 2 steamers left, the German Dahabeah came.
27th. Started with Lorenzo on Donkeys across the Desert to Philae, went thro the Village on East & got some sketches of the Island temples &c & a Sakir; then round to the N.West, got sketch of Doum & rocks, rode thro' Mahalla, the old ruined burial ground: rode a camel, sketched a dead camel, back at 6. 2 Americans called upon us in eveng. Cool grey day till 4 then Glorious Sunset.
28th. Worked up sketch from Deck before bkfst. After bkfst went on Donkeys with Gay to the Great Quarries, drew obelisk, then to Bazaar bought Pottery &c. Mr Brabazon called on me from the — After luncheon went [over?] & painted Zakir & tall Wall. Met Mr Willinck, went to the — Dahabeah, back at ½ p 6. Too windy to leave Assuan - fine moon.
March 9th. Up early set palette. Young Mustapha Aga called & brought me a whole packet of letters. Gay & I took a stroll outside, all round the village. At 11 began oil study of a Sheykh's tomb close by. At 1 had luncheon & at 2 all went on Donkeys to Karnak. The road beautiful, made 4 sketches. Met Mr & Mrs De Laune there. I staid till sunset. After dinner went to American Consul's. Dancing women.
16th. After Bk. got sketches from M.Ghudis garden. Helped to dig out a young Doum Palm & polled it. At Luncheon Mr & Mrs Willinck came in. I went to the Temples & got 3 camera sketches of T. of Amunoph II & Propylon of Temple of Ramises & the Minarets. Awful dust storm all day. I got sketch from the *Fostat*. Lent Mr. Scott £2.
17th. Up & out at 7 finished 3 sketches about Luxor before Bk.then at 9 went on Donkeys with Gay to Dahr el Bahren Temple, most interesting - got sketch of fish then saw No 35 Tomb, & on Dahr el Medinet- a pretty little Temple - back at ½ p 2 Donkey to Karnak, got 3 sketches, back at ½ p 6. We left Luxor at 8 PM.
19th Moved very slowly in night & twice in morng, tried to go against wind which was high. Fixed the boat at Ballas and sketched boatmen loading it with Ballassee or Water Jars. Painted in Cabin all day finished 2 pictures of Gebelayn, finished long evening scene of Karnak looking E.. & began a Karnak of Pylon & Propylon looking W. Very cold indeed.
26th. At 7 we were passing the bold bluffs of Gebel aboo Fayda. Most glorious, got sketch before Bkfst then arranged & packed up all the fragments & relics till luncheon, then finished Philae & prepared two sunset skies. Copied Luxor from photo. Very hot in day & flies intolerable. Cool eveng. went on sandy shore for a stroll.
27th My Birthday. arrived at 7 at Rhoda & made fast. Got letter from Bank of Egypt Walked up to station, got sk.of lovely palm. Painted view of Cairo & began one of Luxor. Very strong North wind, quite a little sea Could not get our parcels from the Station, got down to Beni Hassan.
April 2nd. Strong wind against us as we dropped down all day- passing the Pyramid on the left Bank of Maydoom a squall blew us on to a bank close to a lovely domed (fluted) tomb among palms. Got 3 sketches. Made finished sketch of Boat entering Calais for Mr Rogers.
3rd. Calm morng. arrived at Cairo L[eft] Bank among 22 Dahabeahs at ½ p 1.

1877
Sept. 21st [Venice]: Up early & went with M[ary] in gondola to Blumenthal's, got 2 notes cashed, chat about Valentine, now consul at Azores, then to Mr — our Consul here, got my Portmanteau and picture commenced [?] - back at 1 to luncheon-set palette, unpacked old Portmanteau full of Painter's Roba, went out at 3 began new subject from Steamboat pier of view towards Grand Canal. Got sky palette and began new subject close to San Giorgio of Zitella and sunset on Giudecca... met A.Burnand and 2 nieces at Florian's.
22nd: Found out church of San Giovanni in Bragora. Met Arthur Burnand. I and Mary went with him and party to the spot whence I took his picture [Arthur Charles Burnand was a Lloyd's Underwriter and he and his brother Theo., Underwriter to the Marine Insurance Co., Old Broad St., were uncles of Sir Francis, Editor of *Punch* and patrons of Cooke and several other Academicians]. Then to Arsenale, saw Cats and I drew in new view from boat. A.B. and niece called on me and M. Went with them to see several churches, and back at 5. I went to S.Giorgio Maggiore and tried to paint, but only had big brushes. Back just before an awful thunderstorm with heavy rain came on. Wonderful effects of sky. Cleaned up and we dined at Cavalletto. M. poorly. I took Val to Dr Salviati, walked to his new shop in Piazzetta. Coffee at Florian's...
29th: Vincenzo never came all day. Mary went to Ponti's and got 2 Photo's. I painted from them, Campanile and part of Ducal Palace, all day in house...
Oct.1st: ...painted water in Molo picture at home - took short walk had luncheon at 2½ then out in boat and worked on Salute Scuola subject till 5 then painted on S.Giorgio picture a glorious sunset, streaky cirrhi... lovely day fine delicate clouds.
Oct.2nd: Very lovely early morning, hazy and grey, painted on Molo picture till ½ p 1... we had a short stroll before lunch then drove to Lido, got sketch of Jews' Burying Ground. Met Mr Brown, walked across to the Adriatic... found Oenothera on Lido.
6th: Very strong wind, we went and saw the Carpaccios at San Giorgio dei Schiavone and to San Francesco della Vigna, San Martino, then painted at home. Vincenzo came to see us. After lunch we went on foot with Mr and Mrs Gould and Miss Thornton to San Crisostomo and on to the Madonna del Orto, all restored, saw the superb Tintorets. Walked back at 6, blowing a gale all day. Dined at Cavaletto, caffe at Florians. We bought two wire breadbaskets and a black wideawake.

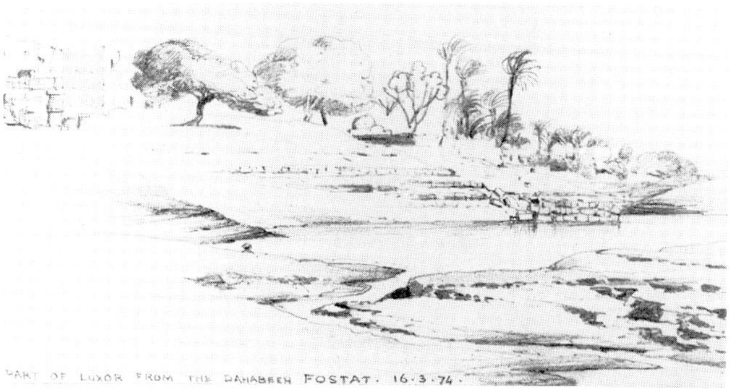

Plate 256. Pencil drawing
Part of Luxor from the Dahabeeh Fostat 16th Mar
Photo courtesy Martyn Gregory

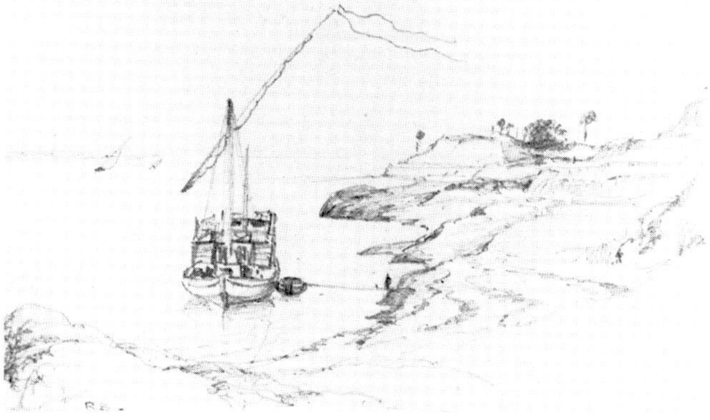

Plate 257. Pencil drawing
Dahabeah R[ight]B[ank]
Perhaps the good ship *Queen Victoria*. Photo courtesy Martyn Gregor

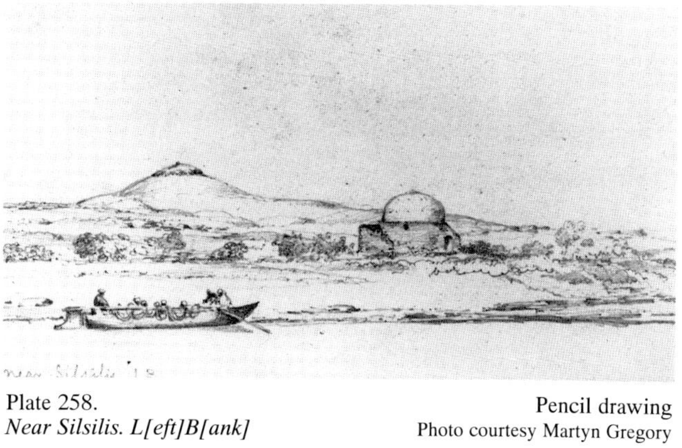

Plate 258. Pencil drawing
Near Silsilis. L[eft]B[ank]
Photo courtesy Martyn Gregory

9th: Went out alone to Canal of San Giorgio and worked on wall and trees, also on storm subject. Back at ½ p 12. Went with Vincenzo to Dr Salviati's and went with him and son and a stout party to Murano, to his works, saw some lovely things made. Left at 5 in great peril from the huge waves crossing to San Michaele di Murano. Dined alone at Cav. Poor Mary at home with cold.
10th: Packed up with Vincenzo till 12. Luncheon. Met Mr Brown. Col. de Horsey, Miss Lee Smith and a friend called to see sketches. Mary called on Mr Bunney [John Wharlton Bunney 1828-1882 had been a clerk in Smith, Elder's (John Ruskin's publishers) but took to painting, lived in Italy from 1863 and in Venice from 1870. He exhibited views of the city at the Royal Academy from 1873 but for the last four years of his life was engaged on painting for Ruskin a 7ft. x 5ft. view of the west front of St Mark's basilica (now St George, Sheffield)]. Met Mr A.Trollope. ...Mr and Mrs Elze came in evening, also Mr and Mrs Bunney, he shewed me lovely drawings of vessels.
13th: went after brkfst and visited 4 churches for Tintorettos... Market crowded and then to S.Marco. Gave Miss Thornton a lesson in perspective... Started at ½ p 3 to San Giov e Paolo and to the Fondamenta Nova. Got sketch of Murano saw the Gesuiti church and then to Miracoli, shut up, and San Bartolommeo. Spent the evening at Mr and Mrs Bunney's, saw lovely things, Turners &c. Mr and Mrs Trollope and Mr and Miss Smith.
19th: Mary better. I went to the Ponte della Ca di Dio and sketched Bragozzi and Topo. Took Mary to see some small apartments close to bridge, she walked out for first time. After luncheon went over to Giudecca and made elaborate sketch of Salute, Dogana and distant houses. Back at 5, saw Bunney on Piazzetta painting... Miss Thornton came in to see the fireworks opposite our hotel. The Singers came and sang opposite.
20th: Went after bkfst to Ponte Ca di Dio and got sketch of Bragozzi &c... callled on Mr Malcolm, he gave me card to see Palazzo where I saw Layard's lovely pictures. Got sketch of M[arco] Polo's house. M called on Mme. Elze, took book. The Patriarch [of Venice] came in. Packed up all the evening.
22nd: Up at 6, left Venice after Bkfst by ½ p 8 train. Vincenzo took Mary and I and Miss Thornton to station. Most lovely bright day and the scenery exquisitely beautiful, colour of trees so golden. Arrived at Turin at ½ p 8. Tea dinner at Hotel Suisse and slept there. I took stroll and heard the Band at Caffe. Mary keeping well.

1878 [France, Etretat]
September 15th: Very ill in night, not up till 11. M went after déjeuner to the English service, I read it at home. Took stroll under the East cliffs. Quantities of Chelcedony. Became acquainted with Mr Hawksley, lent him my *Leaves*. Getting rough weather, we took long walk over Down on West.
Mon 16: Very heavy gale and a grand sea, huge breakers on the beach. Got sketch and painted from window on boats and gear. M read *Graphic & Daily News*. After Déjeuner all had coffee in small room with Mrs Hayter and family, sons and daughters. Good fun over lessons in drawing I gave them. Fine struggling moon.
Tues 17: After Bkfst went out and painted a study of Malm cliff... less wind and sea, no boats out...
26th: Out sketching with the Heatons after Déjeuner. Went with Mary to see Sig. Boldini at his large studio, charmed with his pictures; he lent me his folding Easel which I used. Painted boats in Caloge pictures till 5... Gave Mr Heaton a good lesson in the use of the Camera; a truly lovely warm day.
30th: Blowing half a gale all day. Immense breakers. 8 boats came in early & a large lot of fish, Conger &c. Got sk. after bkfst of Fish & baskets for Paris. At 12 went to Balcony room and worked on 1st subject on millboard. Mary read *Pall Mall*, she called on Mme Vatinel, I lent her 1st Volume of *Leaves*.
October 2nd: Painted boats of East Cliff before Déjeuner and afterwards painted canots in 2 millboard pictures on beach. Mild and calm. Pleasant painting... wrote long letter to Conrad... Mr Rich (American artist) and Mme Vatinel and M & I dined together.
3rd. After Bk got Camera [lucida] sk. of the W, Cliff from Malm rock. After Déjeuner painted from balcony - E.Cliff & then on Foreground & boats from beach. Mary read & walked with Mme Vatinel. A vast lot of fish sent to Paris. Cool evng. after lovely day...
8th. After Bk worked over the Malm rock at home, then on beach till 12. After Déjeuner out again working at the Rock & Summer House till ½ p 5. M went with Mme.V. & Mr Rich to see Merli' pictures of Moses in the bull rushes & Rebecca at the Well. Got stroll before dinner, 2 English folk dined here. Truly lovely day & bright moonlight. Had hair trimmed. Mary got sk. of ornament on Church door.

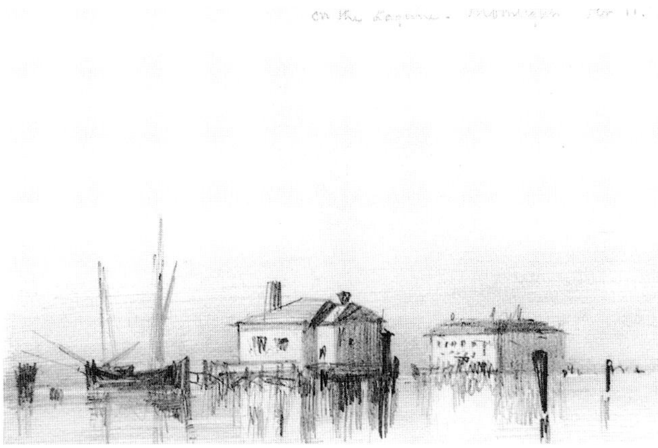

Plate 260. Pencil drawing
On the Lagune, moonlight.
Sketchbooks (later dismembered) full of notes such as this held Cooke's memoranda. Their appeal and potential for picture-making, even in monochrome, is remarkable. Photo courtesy Martyn Gregory

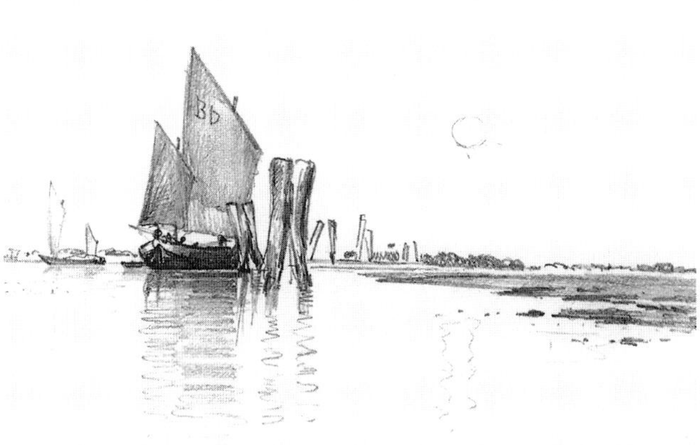

Plate 259. Pencil drawing
Moon rising over the Lagune
A rapid sketch which provides everything for a superbly tranquil evening study – but did he ever use it? Photo courtesy Martyn Gregory

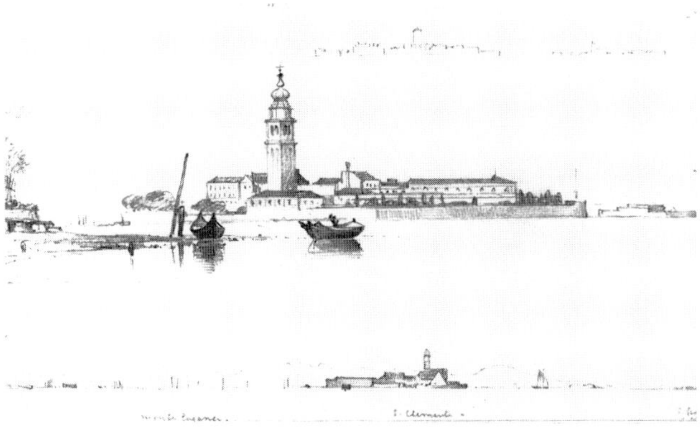

Plate 261. Pencil drawing
Islands of San Lazzaro, San Clemente and San Giorgio in Alga
Topographical sketches, made with no time to lose, show the artist's grasp of essentials. The grace of the small Venetian boats adds much charm. Photo courtesy Martyn Gregory

10th: Tremendous sea and blowing a gale all day; painted at home on 3 pictures, began new rough sea before Déjeuner... fine moon through heavy clouds. All the boats drawn up to the Capstans.
14th: Went out after bkfst & ptd on Malm rock, figures &c till Déjeuner then put in foreground baskets &c to picture of West Falaise. Mr & Mrs Hawthorne came and sat by me, M shewed her my pictures and sketches. At ½ p 3 went down low on shingle and began a canot covered with sails and cloths & nets till ½ p 5. Took stroll on Esplanade. We 4 dined together in small Annexe. Glorious day & moon.
16th Packed up all the pictures & luggage. Met Rich & Mme V. at Déjeuner, took places in Bus, returned candlestick, wrote to Col.Grant. M. wrote home - got sketch of view between the Caloges. Left by bus at 4 arrived at Havre at 7. Supped & slept at the Hotel L'Amirauté. Took stroll to Pier, café & back at 9.
21st [Paris] At 10 went with Mary to the Trocadero & spent 2 hours in the garden & at the Chinese & other Houses & shops. Bought stick & other things. At 12 we went to the Exhibition, lovely garden in front. Walked thro' the Avenue des Nations & back outside. Got café, saw Salviati's Colln. & Michieli's Bronzes. Walked at 5 to Troc. I got sketch. M went home, all dined together in a small room. I laid down. Con called on us. Laura, Miss B.Drummond & Mary walked to the Arc de Triomph, lovely Day.
Sat 26th. Went early to Exh. to Wills' plants. the French Chamber of Commerce, Ports of France, then Bath apparatus - Spanish Pavillion. French machinery. Pullman Car, French pictures then to the East Wing of the Trocadero, a wonderful collection of the finest Mediaeval Art, flint implements... home at ½ p 5, very heavy gale & drenching rain.
Nov. 4th. Up late, Bkfst at Restaurant Place Royale, boat to Champ de Mars, saw the Iron works of Schneider & several new Courts. Made sketches of Venetian glass. Went to Italian Restaurant, met Dr Salviati & Giulio, we re-arranged some of his glass. Saw Mr Webb & Mr O[sler?] his designer who shewed me some exquisite things. I took notes. Saw Doccia & Turin ware. Back by boat at 6 dined at — bought wares...
6th. Bkfst at Hotel at ½ p 8 boat to C. de Mars at 10 m to 10: spent 3 hours in Picture Gallery. Met Harriette at 2 & we went about a little together. I went to Queensland, New South Wales, Webb, G... & Osler & other things. Met Salviati & went to Egypt & back by 6, dined at — called to see Laura, Harriette & Miss D[rummond] in evg. read *Galignani...*
13th [Glen Andred] Went by 10.7 train to Victoria, called on D.Keys & got my watch repaired, left bag at Athenaeum, got cheque at Bank. Opened case at Barbe's exchanged Portable Easel - repacked it, called on Thierry, luncheon at Club. Ordered Claret at Durand's. Dined with Webster at Club, went to R.A. & elected Leighton President. I gave him a beautiful Palm Stick Back to Club by 10 & went by rail to Cannon St. & slept at Steve's.
19th. Letters from A.Little & I replied, from W.Hayter, Mary came down to late dinner with me. I painted all day on two skies & on boat (last) & in evng. while L. read News.
20th. ...painting all day on small picture. Mr Caird & Finna & wife & 6 others - Sir — & Lady Outram called in aftn., saw Houses & Library. They drove from Tonbridge Wells in aftn... Cold & dull sky...Sent cheque to Wonfor Fund, 2Gns.
December 5th. Wrote several letters & packed up. Left by 1.15 train from Groomridge thro' to Charing X, arrd. at 4. Boy carried bags to Scammells, got hat, left bag at Pickersgill's, took grapes & Flowers. Took Grapes to Hulke, dined at Club at 6, went to R.A.meeting, went thro' the Visitors in the several Schools. I brought forward my motion as to the Architect. Retd. with Hook to the Keeper's: grog. cigars & we both slept there.
6th. Called on Mr Hulke, went to Christie's wrote to Eyles & Mr Drummond. P.Hardwicke & Con. Luncheon at Club, went by Metrop[olitan] to Mr Burton's (away at St. Leonards). Called on Mrs Percy, went to Stores, met Con. Called on Mr Dredge. Dressed at Pickersgill's, drove with Hook at ¼ to 8 to Sir Fredk Leighton's. Met at dinner Calderon, Faed, Sant, S.Cooper, Horsley, Wells, Poole, Hook, Millais. Excellent dinner & all very jolly. Went to Painting room, saw charming studies & crockery. Superb house. Brilliant day but snow in eveng. Slept at Keeper's again.
10th. Up early Bkfst at 8, at ¼ to 9 drove to Swalelands at ¼ to 10. Mr & Mrs Drummond at Bkfst. At ½ p 10 Mr Eyles came from Penshurst Station. We both went with Mr D. all over his ground, East, West & North, planned a good deal & marked trees to be felled & lopped. Luncheon at ½ p 1, Mr E & I left at ½ p 2, arrived here at 3¼. We went with Legge also round grounds & settled many alterations & removals of oaks & conifers. In evng on sketches. Murray sent me G.Dennis's 2 new Vols on Etruria.
11th. Jonthan felled the tall Larch, nearly 60 ft long & sawed it up into 3 lengths & felled a tall Birch also, close to Pool. I painted on Malm Rock, Etretat in day & at night. Mr Drummond sent my Goloshes by Post...
25th. We had a great many Christmas Cards - severe frost but bright sunshine. Dear Mother had 46 cards, sent several. Took stroll in Pinetum with Steve. A grand shew of presents at 4. Laura gave me a new Dinner service. Harriette gave me an Arab lantern from Algiers. Dear Mother repeated Pope's *Messiah* before dinner. A nice party, whist, music & sketching in eveng.

1879
[Cooke visited France, Belgium, Germany and Holland but from the middle of this year made increasing mention of pain and sleepless nights. By the end of the year he was failing fast.]
18th Dec. [Note] R.A. Election. ½ p. 7.
Not a wink of sleep all night. Lucy rubbed my back and removed the severe pain... attended me & read nearly all day... at 5 went into the Whale room. Lucy read to me & Mother. Severe frost all day. Made lists of sketches for the different Societies. I felt easier during day. William Breffit sent us a superb Crimp'd Cod... Whitelock called to see me.
19th Dec. Had a very good night, more sleep less pain. Eatwell sent the picture back, stretched. Mr H. Willett sent a large Turkey to Mother. At 2 carriage fetched Mr Hannah who consulted with me. Mr Wallis called, also Dr Satchell. Still cold & frosty. Felt easier during day.
20th Frost continuing. Mr Wallis called in morng. Carriage fetched at 2 Con[rad} & Laura. She brought my Will from Mr Hopgood & we went through it together and consulted as to a Codicil to be added. Laura sat up all night. Had a restless night.

[Diary ends. He died on 4th January 1880.]

Appendix 2

CATALOGUE
of Paintings in Oils
by

EDWARD WILLIAM COOKE, RA FRS
(1811-1880)

Compiled from the artist's Diaries and his Ledger, from Algernon Graves's *Royal Academy Exhibitors, British Institution Exhibitors, A Century of Loan Exhibitions* and *Art Sales.* George Redford's *Sales of Pictures* &c. *Art Prices Current; Art Sales Index.*

Geographically arranged in chronological order

Great Britain, Channel Islands, France, Netherlands, Germany, Italy, Venice, Spain, Egypt.

Titles in *italics* are as Exhibited or Sold; other notes towards identification are as mentioned in the artist's Mss, above. [D] Diary; [L] Ledger. Picture size followed by F indicates overall frame size. CL where a pencil outline drawn with a *camera lucida* exists.

Abbreviations

Dates of Auction sales in the 19th Century eg 22.1.67, 14.7.92. 20th Century sales are given in full, eg 22.1.1967, 14.7.1992.
Names of auction houses : B, Bonham's; C, CNY, Christie's and branches; S, SB, SBT, &c. Sotheby's and branches; P, Phillips &c.
The artist's sales at Christie's: EWC 63/, EWC 65/, EWC 80/, EWC 82/. The catalogue of the 1970 Exhibition at Guildhall in the City of London is referred to as EWC 70/
Exhibition references: the last two digits of the year, the catalogue number, if known, followed by an indication of the artist's showing in that year, eg RA 79/461/2.3, the Royal Academy annual exhibition 1879, No 461, which was the second of three works hung.

Year/No.	TITLE/Signed	Price	Size/Exhibited	Collections	Sales
GREAT BRITAIN					
29/1	*The Lucy Anne 74, running into Portsmouth* [sign for the Old Ship Inn Brighton, painted there]		Panel	Pres. Mr J.L.Shuckard Cooke Colln.	
30/1	Sky from nature		small [D]—		
33/1	*The Portrait of a horse;* [J.Biggs's, Barnes]			Mr Ratcliff	
34/4	Grass Boats : *Scene on the Thames near Barnes*	10Gns.	18x23 (45.5x58.5) F. BI 35/78/1.3	Jacob Bell	
34/5	Weedy Cot			—	
34/6	Twilight Effect: Windmill, river scene			R.Rosier	
34/8	Vessels off Portsmouth in a Storm			—	
34/9	Sunset, River scene… Find.21.1.35		small	Pres. G.T.Doo	
34/10	*Pier at Broadstairs* Find.30.1.35	12Gns.	Birm.34	Jas.Wadmore	C.5&6.6.64.
34/11	*Pilot boat entering Dover*		12x16 (30.5x40.5)	Pres. Conrad Loddiges	
34/12	Hastings beach & East cliff. Ptd. on spot		12x16 (30.5x40.5) 11x15 (30x38) panel	— Mrs J.A. Baker F.Sabin	 C.22.11.1963/29

Year/No.	TITLE/Signed	Price	Size/Exhibited	Collections	Sales
34/13	Luggers: *Hastings storm, boats coming in*	£25	14x21 (35.5x.53.5)	Dr Pinckney	
34/14	*Ecclesbourne Gap from the Hill*			—	
34/15	*Hastings from the Minnis Rock.* Ptd. on spot.	£21	V & A No 46	J.Sheepshanks	
34/16	*Coast scene, sunrise*		12x16 (30.5x40.5)	Rowland or Shepherd	
34/17	*Hastings boats.* Ptd. on spot	35Gns.	12x16 (30.5x40.5)	Daubigney	C.20.4.43/46
				Lord Normanton	
35/1	Copy of WJ Cooke's R.P.Bonington [Shipping]		9½x13½ (24x34)	—	
35/2	*Peter boat on the Thames*	£15	14x21 (35.5x53.5)		
			Suffolk St./35	Jno Turner of Clapham	
	as ditto *evening*		13x19 (33x48)	Shepherd	C.20/1/1912/68
35/3	*Boat coming ashore in a gale-Hastings*				
			14x21 (35.5x.53.5)	Jno Turner	
35/5	*Hay Barge off Greenwich*	£21	14x21 (35.5x.53.5)		
			RA 35/350/2.2	Miss Ann Sheepshanks	
				Miss Ruth Garwood,	
				1984 Pres:	
				National Maritime	
				Museum	
35/6	Hastings panorama: *Hastings Beach,*		20x25 (51x63.5)		
	painted on the spot		BI 45/24/1.5	Chas.Oddie	
35/7	*The Antiquary's Cell*	45 Gns.	35x42 (89x106.5)		
	[The interior of my own study at Barnes]		F 22½x29½ (57x75)		
			BI 36/24/1.5	J.Sheepshanks	
				Sheepshanks Gift 1857	
				V & A No.42	
			EWC 70/131		
			Whitworth Art Gallery 1984		
			Wm Morris & the Middle Ages		
			Essen *London* 1993		
	Illust. *The Romantic Interior*				
	Clive Wainwright.1991				
35/8	small interior; (probably a		—		
	reduced version of 35/7)				
35/9	Willows, Magdalen water Oxford:		9½x13½ (24x34)	John Hillersdon	
	On the Cherwell, Mag. Coll. Oxford				
35/10	*Godstow Priory bridge & Weir, Oxford*		9⅞x13 (25x33)	—	
				Stephen G.Holland	C.25.6.1908/
	s&d. 35	20Gns.		Permain	
			9½x13½ (24x34)	W.Pearce, Eastbne	C.5.12.1913
		7Gns.		Permain	
	cf. 35/11		9½x13½ (24x34) bd.	S.4.6.1969/	
		£1000		Agnew	
				Paul Mellon Colln.	
				USA	
35/11	Another (from other side) Godstow Priory bridge	£10	9⅞x13 (25x33)	T.Creswick	
35/12	Ferry Hincksey House & river Oxford		9½x13½ (24x34)	—	
	Ptd. on the spot				
35/13	Drewitt's Water mill: *Wiers paper*				
	Mill near Oxford	6Gns.	9½x13½ (24x34)		
	Sold Dec 42 to			Henry Vaughan	
	cf. 48/14	Panel	Tate Gallery.1900	H.Vaughan Beq.	
35/14	Blackheath, windmill:				
	Find. 4.9.35.			Pres. J.Sheepshanks.	
				V & A No.47	
35/15	Copy of J.Constable, *Hampstead Heath*	2Gns.		W.Bowman	C.24.3.93/57
	belonging to John Sheepshanks			Quilter	
35/16	Lime kiln Woolwich [Charlton]			—	
35/17	Baskets from models, Ventnor			—	
35/18	Interior of fisher's hut: I.o.W.			—Probably a sketch or	
				beginning for 35/29	
35/19	Beezley's Oxford shed. ?			—	
	Marine Stores see 35/22				
35/20	*Lobster pots, Ventnor*	25 Gns.	15½x21 (39.5x53.5)		
			BI 36/307/3.5	Sheepshanks.	
				V & A No.39	
35/21	*Undercliff Cave,Ventnor.*	30 Gns.	27x31 (68.5x79) F;		
	also called *The Boat House*		16½x20½ (42x52)		
			BI 36/440/5	Robt.Vernon	
			Tate Gallery		
	(Engraved S.Bradshaw as *Fisherman's*				
	Cave Art Journal 1854) cf. 66/9				
35/22	*Marine Stores, Steephill, Ventnor*	30 Gns.	29x32 (73.5x81) F.		
	cf. 66/9		BI 36/55/2.5	Earl of Winchilsea	

Year/No.	TITLE/Signed	Price	Size/Exhibited	Collections	Sales
35/23	River scene Find. 20.1.36.		6x8 (15x20.5)	Pres. W.B.Cooke	
35/24	*Mill, Barnes Common*		9½x11 (24x28)	Pres. Georgiana Ward Conrad W.Cooke Marjorie Loddiges Private Colln.	
35/25	*Old shed, Barnes*		10x14 (25.5x35.5) board	— R.A.Lee Martyn Gregory Private Colln.	EWC 80/128
35/26	*View on the Isis near High Bridge, Oxon*	30 Gns.	24x26 (61x66) F BI 36/438/4.5	W.Wells	
35/27	Wiers paper mill near Oxford sketch		—		
35/28	Felled tree Blackheath			Pres.—	
35/29	*Mending the Bait nets, Shanklin* s&d. 36	20 Gns.	14x21 (35.5x53.5) RA 36/208/1.2 16¾x21 (42.5x53.5) EWC 70/14	Sheepshanks. V & A.No.40	
35/30	On the Thames, Millwall			—	
36/1	*Hastings sands*	£20	14x21 (35.5x53.5) RA 36/434/2.2	Jno.Turner Clapham	
36/3	picture for Mr Bowling		[small]	—	
36/4	Old well and bucket. Redleaf		[L] in Studio		
36/5	Lord Winchilsea 's new picture. cf. 36/15				
36/6	Tarring the boat: *On the Beach, St Lawrence, Isle of Wight*	£60	32 x 41 F 21 x 30 BI 37/40/3.5	Wm.Wells	
36/7	Blackwall from Enderby's works	—			
36/8	Greenwich from the East [Blackheath from Greenwich] On the spot. Fin. 13.6.38	5Gns.		John Hunt Esq.	
36/9	*Rigging Hulk and Frigate at Portsmouth* [The Topaze hulk with frigate alongside] Engraved: Finden's *Ports, Harbours.&c....*	£30	12x16 (30.5x40.5) BI 37/19/2.5	Sheepshanks V & A. No.43	
36/10	Saloon and conservatory from the lawn, Albion House, Barnes		c.12x10 (30.5x25.5)	Private Colln.	
36/11	Brig on Sands: *Vessels on the sands at Hastings*	£60	32x41 (81x104) F. 21½x30 (54.5x76) BI 37/42/5.5	W.Wells	C.10.5.90/11
36/12	*Entrance to Portsmouth Harbour* Engraved: Finden's *Ports...*	25Gns.	12x16 (30.5x40.5)	Sheepshanks V & A. No 49	
36/13	sky from Bakhuysen			—	
36/21	*Semaphore at Portsmouth* Engraved: Finden's *Ports...*	20 Gns.	12x16 (30.5x40.5)	W.Finden National Maritime Museum	
36/22	*Gosport. Flagship at Portsmouth, Victory Saluting* Engraved: Finden's *Ports...*	20 Gns.	12x16 (30.5x40.5)	W.Finden Theo Burnand Arthur Burnand	C.25.2.88/60 C.26.3.92/25
36/24	Seventy-four at Spithead: *Spithead, a 74 drying hammocks* Engraved: Finden's *Ports...*	8 Gns.	5x8 (12.5x20.5) vignette	W.Finden	
36/25	Martello Tower			—	
36/26	Fishing subject: *Chub*		15x20 (38x51)	Pres: J Sheepshanks. V & A No.48	
36/27	*An Interior with Fish*	£80	20x24 (51x61) BI 37/41/4.5 Manch. 57/411	W.Wells Vokins	C.10.5.90/10
37/4	*Mackerel* s&d. 37		7x10 (18x25.5)	Pres: J.Sheepshanks. V & A No.44	
37/20	Group of Fish			Jacob Bell	
37/5	*Rouge et Noir* (second version of *Lobter Pots*) Fin.29.12.38 cf. 35/20, 38/7		14x19½ (35.5x49.5) Manch.57	W.Wells Agnew	C.10.5.90/9
37/6	*Net Profit, a scene on the Thames* ,Putney	£20	14x19½ (35.5x49.5) BI 41/13/2.6 Liv.41/59	Shepherd	
37/7	*Brighton hog-boat on the sands* s & d 37	50Gns.	32x41 (81x104) F. 21½x30 (54.5x76) BI 38/68/2.6 EWC 70/20	Sheepshanks V & A No.41	
37/8	Old pollard oak Forster's farm Redleaf [Doubleton Farm]		31x 40 (79x102) F. 21½x30 (54.5x76) BI 43/381/4.4	W.Wells	Sales
37/19	Sketch of Jane with white lilac in her hair 2nd June		12x10 (30.5x25.5)	Private Colln.	

Year/No.	TITLE/Signed	Price	Size/Exhibited	Collections	Sales
38/3	Stumps and old pieces of wood. Painted Redleaf				
	[for inclusion in -?]				
38/6	Evening effect on spare canvas			—	
38/7	Copy of lobster, Sheepshanks, for Darby of Colebrookdale				
38/8	Blackwall		small	—	
38/9	Jane Loddiges, sketch portrait.			—	
39/3	Copy:interior with fish		6x8 (15x20.5)	For J.Bell	
	cf. 35./18, 36/27			Private Colln.	
39/15	Copy: the same. [Fin. 19.3.39		6¼x8⅜ (16x21)	Pres. G.Loddiges	
40/1	*The pilot boat lying-to; Pilot going on board*		54x72 (137x183)	M.Bernard 1970	
	a frigate s&d. 40		RA 40/427/1.1.	Hahn	
			Liv.41/357.	Private Colln.	
41/6	Redleaf rocks, cave. *A Fisherman's Cave.*	40Gns.	21½x30 (54.5x76)		
	Ptd. on spot.		RA 42/253/2.3	W.Wells	
	As *The Smuggler's Cave*		Liv.42/54.		
43/1	Hay barges; *Mouth of the Thames,*	£20	35x47 (89x120)		
	vessels off the Maplin lighthouse		F: ? 24x36 (61x91.5)		
			BI 43/39/1.4	Lord Charles	
				Townshend	
				O & P Johnson	
43/2	new Vessels in Thames. *The Thames: Whose ample*		35x47 (89x120)		
	breast displays unfurl'd... mis-quote, T.L. Peacock:		F: 24x36 (89x120)		
	The Genius of the Thames Thy spacious breast displays		RA 43/577/2.2	Mr Rowland.	
	unfurled/The ensigns. of th' assembled world...				
	as *The River*		BI 44/105/2.5.		
43/11	Brig in a gale.*The Sea: heavy squall clearing off,*	£70	55x70		
	Bass Rock		(112x178)		
			F: 40x55 (102x140)		
			BI 44/130/3.5		
	as*Vessels scudding nr Bass Rock*			Laurie	1873 (James)
		315Gns.		Anon	C.30.6.83/223
		200Gns.		Grindley	
				H.Steven	C.10.5.84/97
		125Gns.		Mappin	
	as *Rough weather off Bass Rock*		35½x52½ (90x134)	Miall	C.9.5.1969/72
		£399		Agnew	
44/2	Barges in Medway:*The Medway with*	100Gns.	24x48 (61x122)		
	Upnor Castle, evening		RA 44/304/1.2	David Barclay	Sale
44/6	*Pilot boat coming out of Dover*	13Gns.		Conrad Loddiges, Pres.	
	? as *Dover pilot boat returning*		11½x16 (29x41)p.	Carey	C.29.6.1923
47/4	*Opposite my house at Barnes*		9x12 (23x30.5)	—	S.10.7.1973/107
					S.20.11.1973/3
				Agnews	
47/5	Dumbarton rock		4½x7 (11.5x.18)	—	
				Private Colln.	
47/9	*The Rock and Royal Castle of Dumbarton*	£150	68x88 (173x223.5)		
	on the Clyde		(F): 53½x72 (136x183)		
	s&d. 47		BI 48/389/5.5	J.C.Harter	
	as *Dumbarton Castle*				C.26.4.90/25
	(Graves: '1851')	390Gns.	53x71 (135x180.5)	Percival [?Harter}	
	as *French herring boats Havre*			Anon	C.5.5.1900/113
	s&d. 47	£210	53x71 (135x180.5)	Burton	
				Anon	C.23.3.1901/75
	nd	105Gns.	53x71 (135x180.5)	Webster	
	as *Havre herring boats*	200Gns.		[P.Harter]	C.8..6.1901/94
				Blakesley ?Black.	
				Exors. Dowager	
				Lady Pease	C.20.7.1979/85
				bt. in.	C.29.2.1980/158
	as *French herring boats running into the port of*				
	Havre de Grace				
	cf. 40/2 (France)			Christopher Wood.	
				Private Colln. USA	
48/14	*Wiers paper mill Oxford*		9⅜x13¾ (24x35) board		
	s&d. 48	£20	Norwich.1848	John Hillersdon	
				Richard Green	
	cf. 35/13 Tate Gallery [different view]			Agnews	
	cf. 35/27			Private Colln.	
48/15	Beard's Mill Oxford	£20	9½x13½ (24x34.5)	John Hillersdon	
	s.			Agnews	
				Richard Green	
				Private Colln.	
48/22	Interior of Martello Tower. see 78/4				

Year/No.	TITLE/Signed	Price	Size/Exhibited	Collections	Sales
49/3	*A Fern cave- a scene in Mounts Bay Cornwall*		17x22 (43x56)		
			RA 49/436/3.3	Llewellyn	
			Manch.1849 Glas.		
			1850 Ipswich.1851		
	Camera lucida pencil outline			Martyn Gregory 1992	
53/2	*The pier and Bay of St Ives, Cornwall*	£294	34x49½ (86.5x126)		
			RA 53/448/5.5	Aldmn.Salomons	
			Manch.1857		
53/3	Rock-strewn beach		12x19 (30.5x48.5)		C.1.2.1978/115
53/4	Hastings, collier on shore	£20		W. Hirons	
55/7	Snow scene: *Winter, a scene on the Fens of Huntingdonshire,old draining mills, now disused*		RA 55/645/4.4	J.Heathcote	
56/5	The Thames Millwall, barges		19½x3 (50x8)	John Morley	
	s&d. 57			F.W.Cozens	C.17.5.90/127
				Agnew	
56/7	Ventnor cliff & beach 1.			—	
56/8	Breakwater at Bonchurch 2.		small	Robt. Hannah (present.)	
56/9	Bonchurch pier & cliffs 3.		11¼x14 (29x36)	John Morley	
	s&d. 57			O & P Johnson	C.10.5.1985/34
56/10	Old Breakwater 4.			J.Montefiore	
				[Returned 1859]	

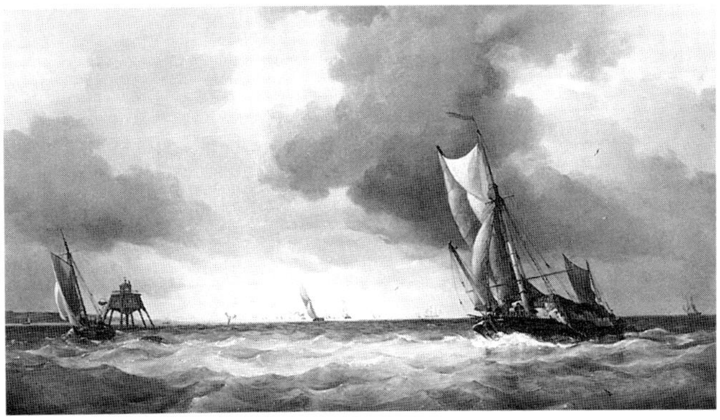

Plate 262. 43/1

Mouth of the Thames, vessels off the Maplin lighthouse

The typical swim-headed spritsail barge laden with hay figured in many drawings and paintings, as was appropriate for a craft which swarmed on the London river . Photo courtesy Arthur Ackermann & Peter Johnson

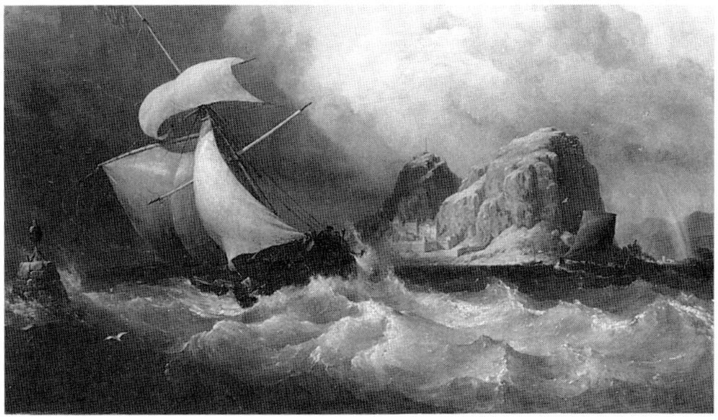

Plate 263. 47/9

The Rock & Royal Castle of Dumbarton on the Clyde

Masquerading in several sale catalogues as French herring boats entering Havre, this picture may still bear that incorrect title. It was one of only two Scottish subjects which he painted. Photo courtesy Christie's

56/11	Bonchurch cliff & rocks 5.		—		
56/13	Old bathing Cove pier from nature 6.		9x12 (23x30.5)	G.Wyatt	
				Gilbert Standen, 1937	
56/14	*A Crab & Lobster shore.* 7.		27½x42 (70x107)		
	s&d. 57		RA 57/28/1.4	G.C.Dewhurst	
			Manch.1887/567		SB.20.11.1973/5
	as *Near Lyme Regis*			Richard Green	
					C.13.5.1977/85
					SBT.13.6.1978/96
	as *A Crab & Lobster shore*			Owen Edgar Gallery	
56/15	Under West cliff Ventnor cove 8.		11½x15½ (29x39.5)	FJ Nettlefold	C.5/6.6.1913
		9 Gns.		Carey	
56/16	*A Bit of English Coast.* 9.		27x41 (68.5x104)		
			RA 57/500/3.4	Duncan Dunbar	
	as *Undercliff, Isle of Wight*				C.5.5.94/88
				Vicars	
56/17	New little Bathing bay & jetty with Dunnose Head 10.			Pres. H.Bicknell	
	as *The White Cliffs with Fishing Craft*				Grogan, Boston, Mass., USA 10.1995/457
	as *The Seashore at Bonchurch Isle of Wight*				
	s&d. 61		7⅝ x 13¾ (19.3 x 35)	Quilter Colln	
				Spink, The Small Picture Show 1996, No. 22	
56/18	*Shrimpers.* 11		11x16 (28x40.5)	–	C.Scotland 19.9.1985/429
	s&d. 56		10¼x15½ (26x39.5)	Richard Green	C.16.5.1986/107
	as *The End of the Day*			Agnew	
	cf. 56/19 (detail)				

Year/No.	TITLE/Signed	Price	Size/Exhibited	Collections	Sales
56/19	General view, Ventnor cliffs 12.				
	s&d. 66		22x38 (56x96.5)	Private Colln	
	see 66/10				
57/1	Wreck on the Goodwin Sands: *Morning after a*		51x78 (129.5x198).		
	heavy gale,weather moderating		RA 57/442	Sir Culling Eardley	
	inscr. Ramsgate	730Gns.		b.i	C.30.6.60/16
				Thos Haigh	
		405Gns.		b.i.	C.13.6.68/79
	C.Cat.note "Send to Mr Cooke"			E.J.Coleman	C.1.5.69/78
				Agnew	
				Earl Brassey	
		£1050			P.14.12.1970/60
			N.R.Omell 1971		
			Marine paintings by		
			British Artists18th &		
			19th Cents	John W.Rollins	
			Guarisco Gallery,		
			Washington DC USA		
			No.106		
	as *The Ramsgate Life-Boat and Pilot-Boat Going*				
	to the Assistance of a Foundering East Indiaman				
	on the North Sand-head of the Goodwin Sands				*C.*26.11.1982/25
				Private Colln. USA	
	Sketch: RA 70/582 Watercolour/pastel				
57/24	Rough Sea [Bonchurch] *A Sniff of the Briny,*		27¼x41¾ (69x106)		
	day after a gale		RA 58/447/4.6	Joseph Hill	
58/2	*The Undercliff at Bonchurch*				
	s&d. 58		27½x42 (70x106.5)		
			RA 58/530/5.6	Aldm. Salomons	
			26¼x41 (66.5x104)	O & P Johnson	
				Private Colln.	
58/7	*HMS Terror in the Ice of Frozen Strait, April 1837*				
	when under the command of Captain, now Rear				
	Admiral Sir George Back...	£472	RA 60/248/3.5	Samuel Gurney	Robinson & Co.,
					Old Bond St
					14.3.1867/284
				Earl Grosvenor	
				Marquess of Westminster,	
				later Duke of Westminster	
			Int.Exn 62/668;		
			Leeds 68/1397;		
			Int Exn.73/1018;		
			Wrexham 76/488.	Present whereabouts unknown	
58/9	Ireland. Rocks, Laggan. No 1.			—	
58/10	Runagiveen *Slate rocks,Valentia Harbour* No 2				
	as *On the Kerry coast*		16½x26½ (42x67.5)	Lecky	C.24.4.1909/50
	Finished Jul.1867?			Martyn Gregory	
	s.		17x26½ (43x67.5)	Private Colln.	
58/11	Donlas, Begnis & lighthouse. No 3		—		
	inscr. *Glanbane Bay, Valentia Harbour, Kerry, Ireland.*		15½x25¾ (39.5x65.5)	Wrigley Beq 1901	
	s&d. 60				
	Gallery title *Valentia Bay, Ireland.*			Bury A.G.	
			EWC 70/23		

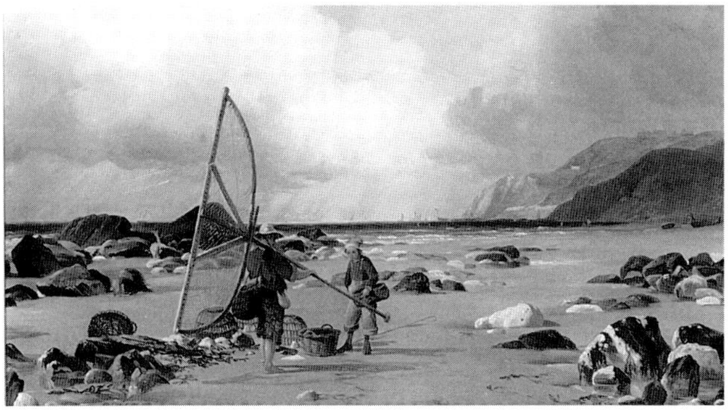

Plate 264. 56/18
Shrimpers. Isle of Wight
A rare surviving example of an oil sketch later incorporated into a picture. See 66/10, Colour Plate 9). Photo courtesy Agnews

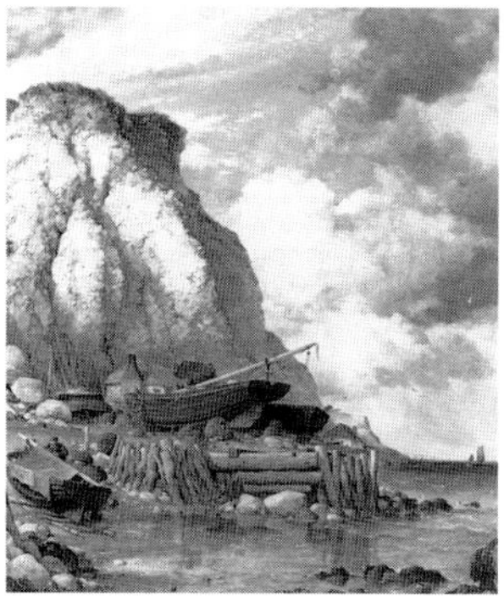

Plate 265. 58/2
The Undercliff at Bonchurch
Photo courtesy Arthur Ackermann & Peter Johnson

Year/No.	TITLE/Signed	Price	Size/Exhibited	Collections	Sales
58/12	N.E., rocks of Big Innis. No 4		No 4—		
58/13	Beer at low water		17x26 (43x66)	Jas Wyatt (by exchange)	
	as *Beer Cove, Devon*				C.17.2.83/103
				Misses Standen 1937	
58/14	Beer.			—	
	bought 1861	£225		W.Agnew	
58/15	Arched rock Lower chalk, Beer Head		—		
					EWC 80/137
		47Gns.		Robt.Hannah.	
58/16	Beer beach *On the Coast of Devon*				
	s&d. 61		17¼x26 (44x66)		
			BI 60/129/	—	
	as *Fishing Cove of Beer*			Anon	C.20.6.76/93
				Price	
	as *Seaton Bay*			Private Colln.	
58/17	Axmouth Ferry:*Axmouth Harbour Devon,*				
	low water		24¾x40¾ (63x103.5)	Jas. Coulson	1873 R.N.James
	s,d & i. 64 [?61]	£330.15.0		Albert Grant	C.24.7.77/156
		£346.10.0		Broadhead, Leeds (Dlr)	
				R.Worthington OBE FRCS	
		£8,500			C.6.6.1980/253.
				Private Colln.	
58/18	Distant view of Beer Head & White cliff		17x26½ (43x67.5)	—	
	Beer Head coast of Devon			Private Colln. London 1960	
	s&d. 61				S.29.3.1995/
				Richard Green	
58/19	*Sandsfoot Castle, Weymouth*		25½x41 (65x104)		
			RA 59/539/3.3	Wallis.[?Dealer]	
				T.Ball	C.14.5.60/199
				J.Graham	C.30.4.87/61
				Permain	
		34Gns.	25¼x41½(64x105.5)		S.10/11.7.1922/135
				Wilson	
59/8	*Repose on shore near Hastings* (inscr. on reverse.)				
	'end of boat turned up' [D]		7x10 (18x25.5)	—	
	s&d. 60				
	as*Fishermen resting on Bonchurch Beach,*				
	I.of Wight with Freshwater Bay & the Needles beyond				C.12.5.1990/200
				Stephen Garratt	
				Private Colln.	
60/2	*A Dutch galliott running into the port of Aberdeen*				
	during a heavy gale	500Gns.	42x66 (106.6x167.6)		
	s&d. 60		RA61/175/1.1	Duncan Dunbar	C.5.5.94/90.
				Sir Jas. Laing	
					C.2.12.1911/146
		30 Gns.	41½x66 (105.5x167.6)	Sampson	
				Wilfred Vere Doughty	
				Beq.1941	
				Great.Grimsby Museum	
				& Heritage Service	
62/6	Blue Anchor.Lias rock:*Triassic rocks,near Blue*				
	Anchor, North Somerset, looking towards Watchet		17x27 (43x68.5)		
	s.		BI 66/112/2.3	—	
	as *On the Bristol Channel*		16½x26½ (42x67.5)	David Price	C.2.4.92/45
				Agnew	
				John Byram 1963 to	
			EWC 70/18	London, Guildhall A.G.	
62/7	Blue Anchor: from laminated rocks [L] Minehead		16½x26½ (42x67.5)		Putticks
	and Dunster with banded cliffs. inscr. on reverse:				31.5.1927/
	Minehead & Dunster Castle from Blue Anchor				
		30 Gns.		Ottway	
	inscr.'Painted on the spot		17x27 (43x68.5)	O & P Johnson 1989	
	by E.W.Cooke RA'		*E.W.Cooke RA & his*		
			contemporaries No.38.		
62/8	Old pier Porlock Wier: ?*Porlock Wear [sic]*		17x34 (43x86.5)		
	Sloop unloading		Edinburgh 1863	E.Gambart	
	Ptd.on the spot				
62/9	*The Breakwater, Porlock Wier, coast of Somerset,*			—	
	inscr. rev.*The shore is composed of huge boulders*		17x27 (43x68.5)	—	EWC 80/133
	of Grauwacke: painted on the spot.			Private Colln.	
	s&d. 64				
62/10	*Cottage at Porlock with breakwater* (small)		Gassiott Junr.		

Year/No.	TITLE/Signed	Price	Size/Exhibited	Collections	Sales
62/14	Porlock weir		9x14 (23x35.5) [L].	—	
63/19	'Touched on Sky of Goodwin.' [57/1] (possibly				
	repair or freshening.)				
64/7	Lifeboat.'Design on wall' see 66/4		—		
64/20	*Pilot boats off the North Foreland Going to a brig*		40x55 (101.5x139.5)		
			BI 65/139/2.3	W.Leaf	C.7.5.75/
				W.Leech	C.21.5.87/122
		£178.10.0		Tooth	
64/21	*Pilot boat off the North Foreland*				
	s&d. 65		7x11½ (18x29)	Private Colln.	

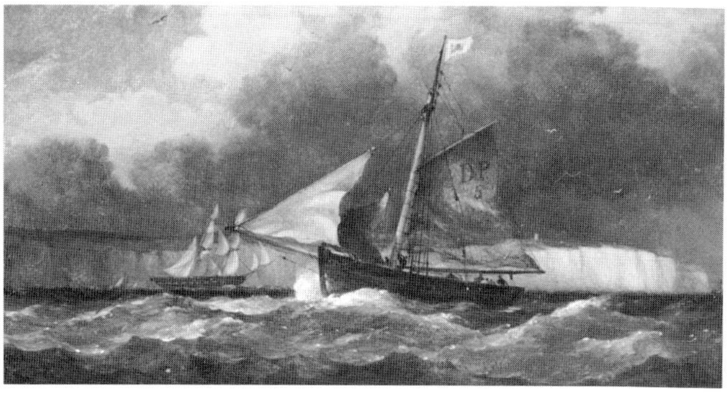

Plate 266. 64/21
Pilot boat off the North Foreland
A small picture which may have been painted twenty years before when the pilots were his subject in drawings and paintings.
Photo courtesy J.Collins & Son, Bideford

Year/No.	TITLE/Signed	Price	Size/Exhibited	Collections	Sales
66/3	Skeleton of whale:*A Visitor from High Latitudes*		—		
			41x66 (104x167.5)		
			RA67/512/3.3	—	
66/4	*Rescue of the crew of a barque on the Goodwin*				
	by the Van Kook North Deal Lifeboat		40¾x66 (103.5x167.5)		
			RA66/139/1.5	E.Gambart	
			Bradford 70/116,		
			Leeds 75/2,		
			Manch.87/604	Henry Dewhurst	C.19.4.90/60
				Earl of Swinton	C.21.10.1975/466
				Anon	C.3.5.1985/159
				Private Colln.	
66/9	Chalk Cave, baskets:*Marine Stores*		16½x20 (42x51)	—	
	s.		RA 66/497/5.5	George Boulton, Eastbourne	
			16½x21 (42x53.5)		S.Pulb. 1992
	cf. 35/21 & 35/22			Martyn Gregory	
				Private Colln.	
66/10	General view, Ventnor Cliffs *Bonchurch shore*				
	looking towards Ventnor		22x38 (56x96.5)		
	s&d. 66		BI 67/28	Private Colln.	
	commenced on spot 1856 (56/19 renumbered)				
67/9	Rocks, Laggan, 2nd version of 58/9 (or the same		—		
	worked over).				
67/10	Slate rocks,Valentia. 2nd version of 58/10,(or the		—		
	same worked over).				
71/3	Bonchurch: *A Bit of English Coast*				
	title as used for 56/16		31x53 (78.5x134.5)		
	s&d. 71		RA71/224/1.2	Andrew G.Kurtz	
	as *Off the Isle of Wight*	315 Gns.		Agnew	C.9.5.91/71
71/4	*Pulpit rock Kynance*. 1. on spot		—		
71/5	Lion rock and Lizard Pt. 2.		small	—	
71/6	*Steeple rock Kynance* (Low water, sketch):3.			—	
				Bournemouth Russell	
	see also 73/1			Cotes AG	EWC 80/138
71/7	Study of sea looking out towards Bill. 4.		—		
71/8	Looking out of cave, Kynance 5. small		—		
72/1	*Hastings luggers coming ashore in a Breeze*	619 Gns.	RA72/246/2.4	Col.Holdsworth.	C.30.4.81/64
			34x54 (86.5x137)	bt.in.	
				Chas Churchill 1897 (Temple)	
				late of Weybridge Park	
			34½x54½ (87.5x138.5)		C.16.2.1917/73
		£78.15.0		Cassell	
	as *Strong breeze off Hastings*			Polak, 1960	
72/2	Steephill :*Chalk and firestone rocks forming part*				
	of the Undercliff, Isle of Wight		34½x54½ (87.5x138.5)		
	s&d. 72		RA 72/540/3.4		
				late Percy Marsden	C.18.6.1926
	cf. 75/7	22Gns.		Horsley	

Year/No.	TITLE/Signed	Price	Size/Exhibited	Collections	Sales
72/3	Sky from nature for large picture small.		—		
72/8	Hastings lugger running ashore				
	s&d. 73		7¼x12 (18.5x30.5) millbd.		
				Arthur Jackson	C.30.11.1928
		22Gns.		Brook St Gall.	
73/1	*Steeple Rock (of serpentine) Kynance Cove,*				
	Lizard, Cornwall, low water		35x51 (89x129.5).		
	[D] 'put in wreck'		RA73/419/2.3	-Bolckow Esq	C.2.5.91/92
		400Gns.		Stern	
			34x55 (86.5x139.5)	Lord Michelham	Hamptons 24.11.1926/
73/3	HMS *Captain* in portrait of young Baring by Hon H.Graves.				
73/4	Glen Andred rocks from nature			—	
74/30	Ironclad:*H.M.Turret ship Devastation at Spithead, on the occasion of the Naval Review in honour of the Shah of Persia, 23rd July 1873* "Presented to the Naval University, Greenwich by Thomas Brassey Esq.,MP"		55x81 (139.5x205.5) RA 75/232/1.3	R.N. College,Greenwich. on loan to National Maritime. Museum.	
75/3	Scotch firs from nature.			—	
75/7	*Chalk and firestone rocks forming part of the Undercliff, Isle of Wight)*		28½x41 (72.5x104)		S.17.11.1971/144
	s&d. 1876			Appleby	
	(as "Edward Wake Cooke")			Private Colln.	
75/8	Wyatt's picture, Bay with donkeys,.small				
75/9	Wyatt's picture, Bay with fir trees:*Fisherman's Bay and Babbacombe Rocks*		21x27 (53.5x68.5)	James Wyatt Junr.	C.17.2.83/104 SB.24.6.1982/172
	s&d. 75				
	as *Sandy cove-tide flowing.* RA75/369/2.3 ie May exhibition but 75/9 first mentioned in Diary. in July.)			Martyn Gregory Private Colln.	
	s.				
75/10	*Beer Head, sea-piece.*				
	s&d. 75		30 x 40 (76x101.5)	—	
	as *Beer Head Devon with Axmouth in the distance*	130 Gns.			C.17/19.2.83/107
	as *Bury Head Devon*			XNY.2.5.1979/222	
	s&d. 76(?)	£1345	28x39 (71x99)	Martyn Gregory Private Colln.	
75/11	Ward's rock [Garden scene]		small	—	
75/12	View from Drawing room: *A Sussex garden glen; late autumn:unexpected visitors*		54x80 (137x203) RA77/1341/4.4	—	
			Brighton Pavilion 1878; Crystal Palace 1879	E.V.Cooke Spink Martyn Gregory	
			English Romantic Landscape 1992,No.1	Private Colln.	
76/5	*A Bit of Bonchurch in the Olden Times*		23¼x14¼ (59x36)	Charles Gassiott	
					C.19.5.1978/116
				O & P Johnson	
76/10	Another *A Bit of Bonchurch in the Olden Times*		23½x17½ (59x44/5)		
	s&d. 76		RA 77/320/2.4	Broadhead, Leeds (Dlr.)	
		11Gns.		Brocket	C.2.2.1923/
				Private Colln.	
77/1	Rough Sea:*A Fishing lugger coming ashore in a gale*	£150	26x42 (66x106.5) RA 78/502/3.3		
			Brighton 78	Mr Arthur Tooth	
				Henry Lovatt	C.21.5.81/110
		290Gns.		Tooth	
				Martyn Gregory	
77/10	Rock study Glen Andred		small	—	
77/11	Man of War schooner in the Hamoaze, Plymouth		upright	—	
78/4	*Interior of Martello Tower,Pevensey. Morning after a capture of smugglers by coastguards*		17x21 (43x53.5)		EWC 80/127
				E.W.Grindley	C.8.1.87/599
	Old picture, 48/22			Martyn Gregory.1979	
				Private Colln.	

Year/No.	TITLE/Signed	Price	Size/Exhibited	Collections	Sales

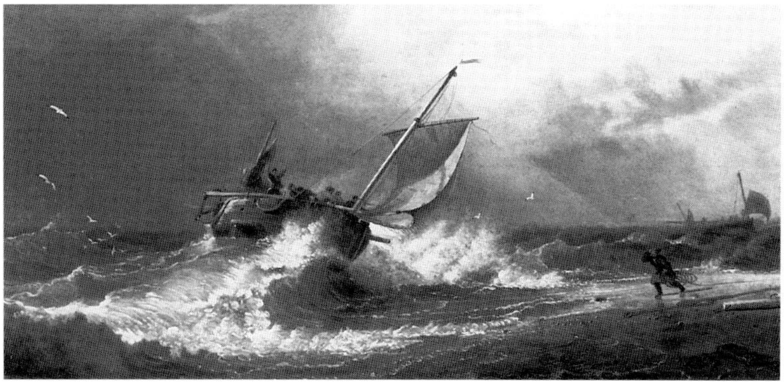

Plate 267. 77/1
A fishing lugger coming ashore in a gale (Hastings)
This was the ageing painter's reminiscence; one of his first sketching tours was as the guest of Dr Batty, a well-known London gynaecologist who had a house at Fairlight, Hastings, in 1830. A series of etched *Coast Sketches* of Hastings was planned but never executed, although in 1834-35 several paintings similar to this are recorded.
Photo courtesy Martyn Gregory

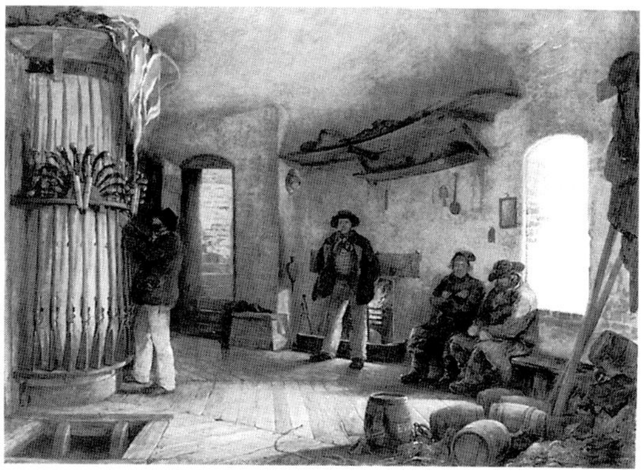

Plate 268. 78/4
Interior of Martello Tower, Pevensey. Morning after a capture of smugglers by coastguards
In the 1830s these Napoleonic defences were the base of the Preventive service against smuggling which was still rife. In a nostalgic look at a past age, Cooke brought out a painting begun thirty years before and carefully finished it off. A watercolour is known which includes a female figure.
Photo courtesy Martyn Gregory

CHANNEL ISLANDS

Year/No.	TITLE/Signed	Price	Size/Exhibited	Collections	Sales
36/14	Sloop sunk in St Brelade's Bay:			—	
36/15	Gathering vraic [pronounced *wrack*]:		18x24 (45.5x61)		
	Collecting seaweed, St Aubin's Bay, Jersey		RA 37/491/2.2	Earl of Winchilsea	
36/16	Guernsey pier with sloop coming in:		26x33 (66x84)		
	Pilot boat running into St Peter's Port Guernsey		F. 18x24 (45.5x61)		
			BI 37/3/1.5		
	inscr.on rev.Feb 23rd 1838		Liv. 37/216	Rev.Dr Pinckney	
	cf. anr. version Graves Sales			Jon.Peel Colln.	C.11.3.48/61
				Morgan	
					S.31.5.1989/
				Private Colln., Guernsey	
36/17	*Dutch Galliot, St Peter's Port,Guernsey*		23x18 (58.5x45.5)		
			upright		
			Liv. 37/157	Rev.Dr Pinckney	
			O & P Johnson	Private Colln.	
			E.W.Cooke & his		
			Contemporaries 1989 No.6.		
36/18	Breaming a schooner.			—	
36/19	Greve de Lecq: on the spot [Perhaps a watercolour]		8½x12 (21.5x30.5)	A.C.Burnand	C.26.3.1892/3
	cf. 36/25 & 48/12				Tooth
36/20	Brig entering St Helier's in a gale			—	
36/25	Reserve				
38/1	Mont Orgueil Castle Jersey			Sheepshanks [?]	
39/9	Burning seaweed:*Burning vraic Jersey*				
			31x42 (78.5x106.5)		
			F; 21½x31½ (54.5x80)		
			BI 41/185/6.6	C.W.Packe	
	Ptd.Redleaf, Barnes		Birm.1839		Los Angeles, USA
					27.6.1996/4190
40/5	St. Aubins Bay Jersey		12x16 (30.5x40.5)	Mr Wadmore	C.5.6.64
40/8	[Copy] Finished.6/42			C.Loddiges.Pres.	
41/1	*Elizabeth Castle, Jersey, from the Causeway;*				
	Low Water	£200	55x71F (139.5x180.5);		
			41x56 (104x142)		
			RA 41/810/1.1	Marq. of Westminster	
	s&d. 41		BI 42/116/4.6.		
			Manch.57/537		
				Dowager Duchess	
				of Westminster	
				Major Sullivan	
				Private Colln.	

Year/No.	TITLE/Signed	Price	Size/Exhibited	Collections	Sales
41/2	Sketch for above [?Watercolour]		—		
43/5	*Wreck of a sloop on the Hemitage Rocks, Jersey*				
	[? anr version of 36/14]	£25	17½x23½(44.5x59.5)		
			BI 44/89/1.5	G. Shipley	
	CL			Liv.1844/44	
48/12	Jersey,Grève de Lecq. Martello tower				
			11½x17½ (29x44.5)	—	
			Manch.49. Carlisle 50		
	CL		Newcastle sold.		

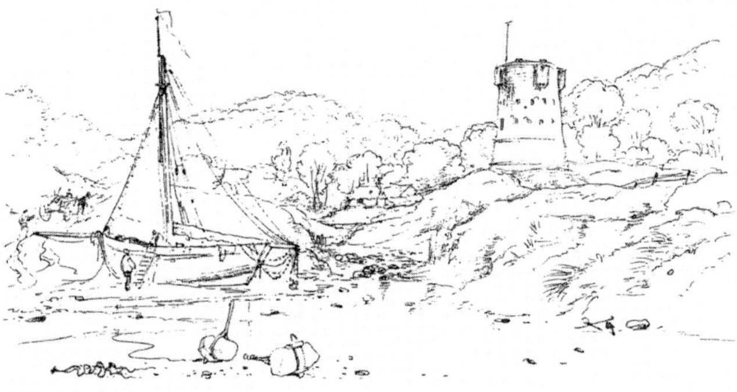

Plate 269. 48/12
Grève de Lecq, Jersey
Camera lucida record of a painting exhibited in the provinces in 1849 but noted *At home June 1850.*

FRANCE

Year/No.	TITLE/Signed	Price	Size/Exhibited	Collections	Sales
34/1	Fishbaskets at Honfleur		oil sk	—	EWC 65/215
34/2	*Trouville fishing smack entering the Port of Havre*				
	de Grace		27x36 (68.5x91.5)		
	[L.] Fin. 19.2.35.	35Gns.	BI 35/490/3.3	W.Walker, Nottingham	
	cf. copy Perkins Colln.				
34/3	Began another [Honfleur/Havre calm]		large		—
34/7	*Scene on the coast of Normandy*		19x23 (48.5x58.5) F.		
		10Gns.	BI 35/95/2.3	D.Hodgson	
	[L] Coast of Normandy near Boulogne				
35/4	Fishing boats on the Seine: *Honfleur fishing*				
	boats becalmed				
	[L]French fishing boats in a calm off Havre		14x21 (35.5x53.5)		
		£21	RA 35/2/1.2	Lord Lansdowne	
	Ptd. London.				
36/2	French pilot boat				
	[same as 37/1 off Granville?] large		—		
36/23	Mont St Michel.				—
37/1	Granville from the sea:[L.] Pilot boat off Granville.		36x50 (91.5x127)		
	French sloop etc. off Granville in Normandy	£50	RA37.471/1.2	F.Stock, Liverpool	
			Liv.1837/8		
37/2	*Mont St Michel, Normandy*		32x42 (81.5x106.5)		
			F; 21¾x31½ (55x80)		
		60Gns.	BI 38/78/3.6	J Sheepshanks V & A. No.42	
	Painted Barnes & Redleaf (Cart in centre, receding)				
37/3	new long Mont St Michel				
39/6	Mont St Michel figures and horses:large				
	see 40/6.				
39/10	*Calais Sands with Shrimpers*		17x31½ (43x80)	C.Baring Wall .No.283	
	Ptd. on spot & Barnes			Lord Northbrook	
	s&d. 42		16¾x31½ (42.5x80)	Countess of Northbrook	C.12.10.1945/5
39/11	*Calais from the Sea*		35x47 (89x119.5)		
			F; 24x36 (61x91.5)		
		50 Gns.	BI 40/391/5.6	Thos. Baring	
				Appleby Bros.	
				Musée de la Ville de Calais	
39/12	Boulogne fisherwomen:*Fish Arrived, Boulogne*		36x48 (91.5x122)		
	Ptd. on spot		F; 24x36 (61x91.5)		
		£80	BI 40/406/6.6	Wm.Wells.	C.27.4.1860/?
39/13	Trouville boat- on an old canvas [L.]Trouville:				
	French fishing boat on larboard tack in rough sea.				
	Trouville fishing boat in a fresh Breeze		56x71 (142x180.5) F;		
	Ptd. Barnes & Redleaf		41x56 (104x142)		
		£130	BI 40/71/2.6	Lord Northwick	

Year/No.	TITLE/Signed	Price	Size/Exhibited	Collections	Sales
39/14	*Calais Pier, sloop returning to port*				
	Ptd. Redleaf		56x71F (142x180.5);		
			41x56 (104x142)		
		£130	BI 40/44/1.6	Wm.Wells	C.27.4.60/7
		350Gns.		Flatou	C.23.3.61/45
		350Gns.		Rhodes	
				Martyn Gregory	
39/15	Reserve				
40/2	*French Herring-boat running into the port of*		67x86F (170x218.5);		
	Havre de Grace		54x72 (137x183)		
	Ptd. Barnes.	150Gns.	BI 41/175/5.6	Gretten [Gritten]	
	As *Off the Port of Havre*		Glasgow 1901/558		
			1925, British Empire		
			Exhbn.Wembly		
				Alexr. Dennistoun	
		285Gns.			C.9.6.94/35
			EWC 70/12	Jas.Kenyon MP, pres. 1901	
				Bury Art Gall.	
			No.17*Spirit of the Sea*		
			Bury, Preston, Oldham		
			1982		

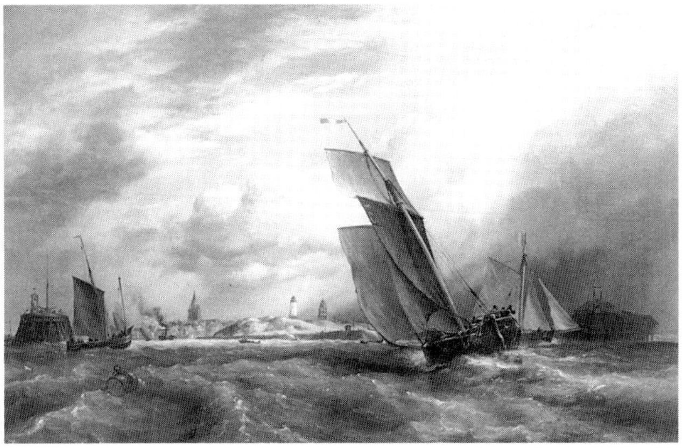

Plate 270. 39/11
Calais from the Sea
The cross-Channel passenger's view of the port, following in astern of a trawl-boat while a pilot cutter heads out past the famous Fort.
Photo courtesy Appleby Bros. Musée de la Ville de Calais

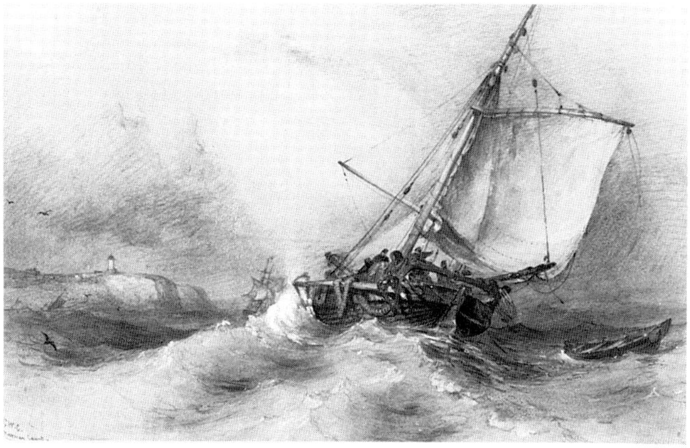

Plate 271. Watercolour
Trouville fishing boat on larboard tack in rough sea
Inscribed 'E.W.C.Norman Court Oct 1839'. Given to W. Baring Wall when staying at his country house. The diary notes, 30 October, *Made drawing of French fishing boat (same as large picture).* The large picture then in progress has the above title in the *Ledger* but was shown, British Institution 1840, as *Trouville fishing boat in a fresh breeze* (39/13, present whereabouts unknown).
Photo courtesy Martyn Gregory. Private Collection

Year/No.	TITLE/Signed	Price	Size/Exhibited	Collections	Sales
40/6	*Mont. St.Michel, Peasants returning to Pontorson*				
	on the approach of the tide		55x70 (140x178) F;		
	Ptd. Barnes & Redleaf		41x56. (104x142)		
		160Gns.	BI 41/41/4.6		
				Marquess of Lansdowne	
			B.I.Prize of 50Gns.		C.4.11.1994/163
				—	
42/1	*Shrimpers and Montois on the sands of*		41x56 (104x142)		
	Mont St.Michel, Normandy	160Gns.	RA 43/432/1.2	Jas.Edwards	
	Ptd. Barnes.				
			38x55½ (96.5x141)	Wm.Leech	C.21.5.87/121
		290Gns.		Agnew	
				Sydney Art.Gall., NSW.1887.	
42/9	Breaming Boulogne (same as 42/10 ?)				
42/10	Portel for Mr Vernon: *Portel, coast of France*		39x50F (99x127);		
			28x40 (71x101.5)		
			BI 43/109/2.4	Mr White [Dlr]	
	as *Portel beach with stranded boat & fisherfolk*				
		11Gns.	25½x39½ (65x100.5)	Sampson	C.20.4.1925/
		20Gns.		Sampson	C.6.7.1928/

Year/No.	TITLE/Signed	Price	Size/Exhibited	Collections	Sales
43/10	*French Pilot boat rounding Calais Pier* s&d. 44		14x18 (35.5x45.5), board BI 46/23/1.2 22x26 (56x66) F.	—	S.10.6.1965/155
43/12	*Calais harbour* CL as *Sloop entering Guernsey Harbour* Graves's *Art Sales* which dates the sale incorrectly as 1847 cf. 36/16 (Channel Is.)	£54 42Gns.	14x18 (35.5x45.5)	Spink Jonathan Peel Morgan	C.11.3.48/61
43/13	*Pilot boat rounding Calais Pier* On board marked *Brown Holborn.& G.H.Pinckney, Tawstock Ct, Barnstaple* label on rev.& [gothic] EWC in black wax.		14 x 18 (35.5 x 45.5)	Mrs Kirkpatrick Martyn Gregory	

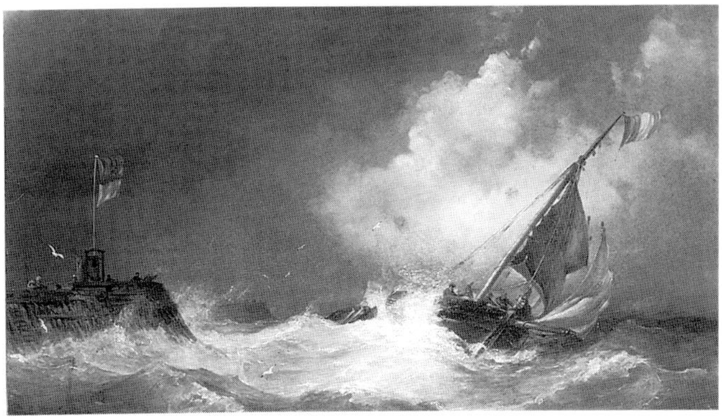

Plate 272. 43/13
Pilot boat rounding Calais pier
The spirited behaviour of small boats handled by experienced seamen of whatever nationality drew Cooke's admiration. 43/10 is almost a replica, exhibited at the British Institution. Photo courtesy Martyn Gregory

Year/No.	TITLE/Signed	Price	Size/Exhibited	Collections	Sales
44/4	*Shrimpers on the sands of Mont St Michel*	50Gns.	Liv.1844/177 Birm.Glasgow	George Bowes	
44/9	French fishing boats becalmed on the Seine: *Sandbank near Quilleboeuf on* the Seine, craft waiting for tide and wind arched top CL	£60	36x48F (91.5x122); 23½x35½ (60x90) BI 45/70/3.5	Lord Wharncliffe	
44/11	*Fécamp herring boats going to sea; Etretat in the distance* Copies seen O&PJohnson file; S file. cf. Diary p.805	£20	28x40 (71x101.5) BI 45/104/5.5	Mr Sheppard	
44/12	*Mont St Michel, misty morning* (arch top frame)	60 Gns.		Wm. Wells	Sales 1848,-57,-60
45/6	Avignon, remains of old bridge		panel	—	EWC 63/7; EWC 80/99
45/7	*Toulon, the Rade* s. RA sold 16.1.1864 cf. small version 62/5		12x18½ (30.5x47) panel	Theop. Burnand [not his Sale] Mellon, Yale Center for British Art	
45/8	Nice, aloe from back window of hotel			—	
45/9	Monaco,view from under arch: hill, towers, boats &c.			—	
45/10	Monaco, looking towards palace and mountain [or 45/13?] as *Palace of the Prince at Monaco*		9⅛x12 (24x30.5)	Decimus Burton Spink C.R.Cooke OBE Private Colln.	John P.Fearon C.25.2.1977/90
45/11	Mountains of the Riviera and little bay of Monaco			Michael Bryan	
45/12	*On walls,Monaco, cactus opuntia.* s&d. 45		9½x13½ (24x34.5) paper on board	— Ackermann & Johnson.	EWC 80/92 S.3.3.1993/64
45/13	Monaco with arch and palm on left [see 45/10]				
45/14	Cactus and aloes			—	
45/15	Port			—	
47/8	*Cannes, south of France*	£120	27x39 (68.5x99) F. BI 48/223/3.5	Mrs Bates	
48/9	sky Boulogne fishing craft ashore small			—	

Year/No.	TITLE/Signed	Price	Size/Exhibited	Collections	Sales
48/11	*Breaming a Calais lugger, low tide*				
			17⅜x23⅜ (44x59.5)	—	
	s&d. 48	£25	Liv.1849/13		
	Bt.Feb.50. with Art Union prize by Council of				
	Liverpool Academy			Liverpool Royal Institution	
				Walker Art Gallery 1948	
			Walker A.G. 1960/56,		
			150th Anniversary of		
			Liverpool Academy		
			EWC 70/15		
48/13	S.Valery , retouch of old picture, which fell and				
	was ruined: *Squally weather St Valery en Caux,*				
	coast of Normandy				
	CL	£40	Liv.1848/274	C.Prater	
48/16	Trouville boats: *A Squall, French fishing boats*				
	making for Calais				
	s&d. 48	£120	Liv.1849/69		
	cf. 50/4		Glasgow 1859	Llewellyn	
	as *Seascape with Shipping*?				
			36½x50½ (93x128.5)	Sir W.Leese	S.4.2.1931
	as *Off Calais*	£18	35 x 49 (89x124.5)	Brittan	S.11.6.1931
	as *Trouville fishing boats making for Calais*				
			36½x50½ (93x128.5)		S.6.11.1991/18
48/23	Pilot boat: [L] Boat entering Calais, pierhead on left		7x9 (18x23)		
		10Gns.	Glasgow 1849	Duke of Hamilton	Sale 1882
				H.Dewhurst, Huddersfield	
	as *Trouville boat*		8x10 (20.5x25.5)		C.19.4.90/27
			Agnew	ex Hamilton Palace Colln.	
50/3	*Port of Marseilles* [L] Mediterranean craft in				
	outer harbour		35x51 (89x129.5)		
		200Gns.	RA 50/1262/4.4	Henry Christy	
			Manch.1851		P.28.2.1977/29
		£3,800		Private Colln.	
50/5	Squall, Calais.			—	
54/2	French lugger entering Havre: [altered]	£400	40x65 (101.5x165)		
	French lugger running into Calais		RA 54/394/2.4	A Burnand	C.26.3.92/59
	s&d. 4	700Gns.		Clarke	
		230Gns.		Bromhead & Co.	C.29.1.1926
	as *Shipping off the Dutch Coast*				C.29.11.1985/9
		£21,000	41x65½ (104x166.5)	Guarisco Gallery,	
				Washington DC.	
	Illust: *I.L.N.* Jun 1854. p.513 & *Art Journal* 1869				
54/4	*Quillebeuf*		8½x11½ (22x29)		
	s&d. 54	£30		A.C.Burnand	C.26.3.92/26
				Vokins	
	as *Beached fishing vessels*				P.20.11.1990/222
56/4	Calais sands, sky ptd. before:[L] Boats coming				
	out of Calais			John Montefiore	
62/5	Toulon copy		small		
	cf. 45/7		6¾x14 (17x35.5)	G Wyatt	
				G.Standen 1937	
62/31	*A Calais fishing boat aground at the mouth of*		4½x8½ (11.5x21.5)	—	
	the harbour		BI 63/420/2.2		
	s&d. 63		10Gns.		C.2.5.1924/
64/4	*Trouville fishing craft off Cap la Hève. The Havre*		?37x55 (94x139.5)		
	lighthouses on the cliffs at Ingouville in the distance		RA 64/12/1.4	C.J.Northcote	
				see C.J.Palmer	C.16.5.68/104
				Agnew	
		£446/5	36x54 (91.5x137)	Edwin Dixon	C.21.3.73/94
		575Gns.	36x54 (91.5x137)	A.Wigram	
					C.11.3.99/69
		270Gns.		McLean	
64/6	*Chalk cliffs.Treport, Normandy.*		12x16 (30.5x40.5)	Price	C.21.3.73/38
64/22	*French fishing craft, mouth of the Seine*		6¾x11¼ (17x28.5) board		
	(Quillebeuf)		BI 65/150/3.3	Clarke	C.16.5.85/57
	s,d&i. 64			F.J. Sumner	
					SBT.13.6.1978/97

Plate 273 68/3
French sloop entering the harbour of Tréport
Photo courtesy Martyn Gregory. Private Collection

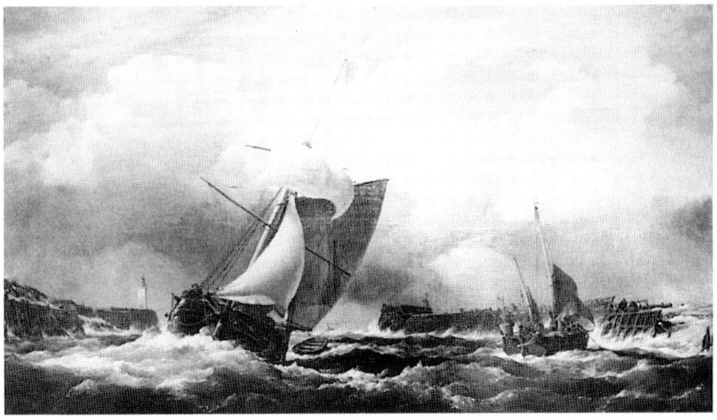

Year/No.	TITLE/Signed	Price	Size/Exhibited	Collections	Sales
68/3	*French sloop entering the harbour of Treport*		31x52(78.5x132)		
			RA69/863/3.4	Lutwidge [Commission]	
			31½x52 (80x132)		C.17.12.1910/28
		44Gns.		Vicars	C.3.4.1922/117
		44Gns.		Pawsey & Payne	
				J.MacMillan, Kensington	
				Ch St 1969	
				Hahn 1970	
				Private Colln.	
71/12	Trouville boat at mouth of Seine.		7½x11¾ (19x30) panel		
	cf. 35/4, 44/9				
	also watercolour drawing. William Drummond Advt.				
	Connoisseur Jul/1976				
72/9	Calais on panel		small	—	
75/5	*Calais Harbour, view of Old Pier and Fort Rouge*		24x35 (61x89)	A.Warren Smith	
	with Sloop entering			[Commission]	C.24.9.76/57
				E.W. Cooke	
				George Boulton	C.13.12.1902/52
				Miss Louisa Cook	
				A.W.M. Marshall	
				Private Colln.	
77/9	*The Cleopatra Cylinder vessel - containing*				
	Cleopatra's Needle, in a hurricane in the Bay		34½x54 (87.5x137)		
	of Biscay, 14th October 877, signalling the		RA 78/330/2.3	(E.W.C)	C.11.3.82/150
	steamship Olga to cast off the tow-rope	155 Gns.	Liverpool.79.	W.Vokins.	
	s&d. 78		Sydney NSW, 79	Sir Erasmus Wilson FRS	
				V & A Mus.Beq. of above,1886	
			E.W.C. 70/13		
78/5	*Beached fishing vessel, Etretat, Normandy.*		10x13 (25.5x33) board—		EWC 80/117
	s&d. 78			George Loddiges	
	inscr. on rev. with title & address			D.Brandon	
				Martyn Gregory	
				Private Colln. Germany	

Plate 274. 78/5
Beached fishing vessel at Etretat, Normandy
The *canots,* their beach capstans and gear all distinctive, provided Cooke with a new genre which he clearly relished.
Photo courtesy Martyn Gregory. Private Collection

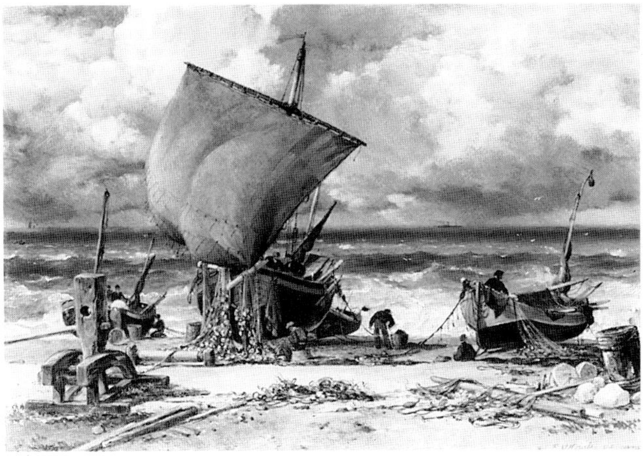

Year/No.	TITLE/Signed	Price	Size/Exhibited	Collections	Sales
78/6	West cliff				
78/7	View from window		small on millboard	—	
78/8	Malm cliff, study		millbd.	—	
78/9	No 1. caloge [D] *women making nets...put in fish*				
			block	—	
78/10	East Cliff, Etretat		10½x14¾ (26.5x37.5)		EWC 80/125
		36 Gns.		Robt.Hannah	C.4.4.1910/8
		3½Gns.		Lister	
78/11	West Cliff, Etretat, from balcony	—			?EWC 80/124
	s.		10x11 (25.5x28)	Julian Senior[Dealer]	
			'square half picture'		C. 28.4.1906/
		8Gns.		Huggins & Co.	
				PrivateColln. Sussex 1943	
				O & P Johnson 1991	
				Private Colln.	
78/12	New E.Cliff		—		cf. EWC 80/123
78/13	Malm rocks and green downs above		—		
78/14	Rough sea			—	
78/15	Rocks at low water with West Falaise				
	as *Etretat cliffs and boats*		9½ x 12½ (24 x 31.75)	Robt. Hannah	EWC 80/122
				Robert Middlesex	C.6.11.1995/166
78/16	Low on shingle, *canot* covered with sails, clothes				
	and nets.			—	
78/17	Malm rock with brick arch			—	
78/18	Old caloge, Etretat				
	as *Stranded boat Etretat*	2½Gns.	7x10½ (18x26.5)	Robt.Hannah	C.4.4.1910/9
				Leger	
79/2	Etretat: *Falaise en amont Etretat; coast of Normandy*		27x42 (68.5x106.5)		
	s&d. 79		RA 79/461/2.3	Charrington	C.9.6.1911/27
		38Gns.	26 x 42 (66x106.5)	Ansdell	
					C.24.1.1975/146
79/4	Glen Andred evening sky on a small rough				
	green sea of Etretat				
	cf. 78/14.				

NETHERLANDS

Year/No.	TITLE/Signed	Price	Size/Exhibited	Collections	Sales
37/9	Scheveling: [Scheveningen] fine evening effects.		13½x20 (34.5x51)		
	Dutch shore still day after stormy weather	£115/10-		David Price	C.2.4.92/44
				Agnew	
37/10	*Selling Fish Scheveling*	40Gns.	18x26 (45.5x66)		
			BI 39/53/1.6	Jno. Dawkins	
	Ptd. Barnes and Redleaf. ?s & d 38				
37/11	Study for selling fish: *Dutch fishermen selling*	20 Gns.	12x18 (30.5x45.5)	Lord Wharncliffe	
	Thornback			[Pair]	SB.15.12.1981/44
					CSK.5.5.1994/132
				Canon Gallery	
				Private Colln.	
37/12	Fish arrived,with figures:*Dutch fishermen at*	£70	28x45 (71x114.5) F:		
	Scheveling, selling thornback		18x36 (45.5x91.5)		
			BI 38/79/4.6	Jno.Harris	
				T.Holloway	
				Royal Holloway College	
37/13	*Sorting shrimps*	20Gns.	20x26 (51x66) F:		
			12x18 (30.5x45.5)		
			BI 38/194/5.6	Lord Wharncliffe	
	Scheveling, On the spot.			[Pair]	SB.15.12.1981/44
					CSK.5.5.1994/132
				Canon Gallery	
				Private Colln.	
37/14	Sky of stormy subject: *Dutch boats on the Ij*		20x26 (51x66) F:		
	near Spaarndam		12x18 (30.5x45.5)		
			BI 38/201/6.6	—	
	cf. also 38/2, larger version				
37/15	Interior of Rembrandt's mill: Original picture of				
	the upper floor...			H.M. The King of Holland	
	Ptd. on the spot. Fin. 10.38	£50	24x18 (61x45.5)	Not in Royal Colln. 1990	
37/16	Copy of Ostade. Amsterdam museum		10x12½ (25.5x32)	EWC studio [Ledger]	EWC 80/131
37/17	Copy of Van de Velde, Amsterdam museum:	40 Gns.	18x24 (45.5x61)	Thos Baring	
	[Calm, Rijksmuseum]			Private Colln	

Year/No.	TITLE/Signed	Price	Size/Exhibited	Collections	Sales
37/18	*Scheveling trawl-boats drying nets* with large				
	figures. Ptd. on the spot				
	Find.8.6.38	40 Gns.	18x24 (45.5x61)		
			BI 38/1/1.6		
	[L] at Sale £71		Liv.38/182 (Property of W.Wells Esq)		
37/20	*On the Dutch coast, Zandvoort*				
	On spot. Fin.3.38	£35	18x24 (45.5x61)		
			Suffolk St 38/	Dr J.Hearne Pinckney	
37/21	*Upper floor of 'Rembrandt's Mill'*		9¾x12½ (25x32)	Seguier	
				Private Colln	
38/2	*Dutch boats on the Ij near Spaarndam*	£90	41x48 (104x122)		
	Ptd. Redleaf;		RA 38/562/1.1	Lord Northwick	
	cf. 37/14				
38/4	Interior Rembrandt's mill, Upper floor,		7½x8 (19x20.5) panel	Thos Garbe	C.24.5.62/32
	open window				
	s&d. 43			Smith	
				Mrs AD Cowan	
			8x8 (20.5x20.5)	Agnew	C.25.1.1974/116
					Maas Gallery
	as *Rembrandt's Father's Mill*		Edinburgh N. G		
			Scotland 1991		
			Exhbn. *Sunshine &*		
			Shadow: The David Scott		
			Collection.No.3.		
				Private Colln.	
38/5	Scheveling with cart *Dutch fish Waggon*	£90	28x36 (71x91.5)		
			BI 40/188/4.6	Wm. Wells	C.27.4.60/19
				Wallis	
	as *Schevg. beach: Painted for the Redleaf Colln.*		WJ.Lancaster		C.29.4.82/173
38/10	*On the Dutch Coast, Egmont aan Zee*		55x72 (140x183) F;		
			44x61 (112x155)		
			BI 39/182/5.6	Lord Northwick	
38/11	Sketch of Molen van Van Dam, Loenen.		On paper	—	EWC 65/214.
	as *Dutch draining mill, stormy weather*	12 Gns.	7½x9 (19x23)	R.G.Taylor.	C.4.4.1930
38/12	Amsterdam from the Ferry: looking across the Ij				
	Amsterdam from Buiksloot-Creek		35x48 (89x122)F;		
	Ptd. on spot.		24x36 (61x91.5)		
	s&d. 39		BI 42/44/2.6		
			Liv. 39	T.Baring	
				Countess of Northbrooke	
		20Gns.	23½x35½ (60x90)		C.14.2.1940
				W.Klinkhoff	C.9.10.1970/94(2)
				Appleby see39/1	
				Cooling Gallery, 1972	
				Private Colln.	
38/13	*Dutch draining mill at Nieuwersluis* [near Utrecht;	£25	27x33 (68.5x84) F;		
	Molen van Van Dam with Rainbow]		18x24 (45.5x61)		
			BI 41/11/1.6	W. Bryant (Dlr)	
	Fin. 15.8.39		Norwich 42		
38/14	Boat builders Loenen:*V*	£30	27x33F (68.5x84);		
	iew on the River Vecht near Loenen		18x24 (45.5x61)?		
			BI 42/1/1.6	Wm Wells	C.10.5.90/12
	Ptd. on spot.			W.Vokins (Dlr)	
38/15	*The lower chamber of Rembrandt's mill*	£21	29x34 (73.5x86.5) F;		
			20x24 (51x61)		
			BI 39/141/4.6	Dr Scott MD	
38/16	*Upper floor of Rembrandt's mill*		29x34 (73.5x86.5) F;		
			20x24 (51x61)		
	Ptd. Redleaf		BI 39/131/2.6	Thomas Baring	
38/17	Haarlemmer Meer *On the Lake of Haarlem*	£50	35x48F (89x122);		
			24x36 (61x.91.5)		
	[Diary sold 6.43]		Liverpool 39/186.		
			Norwich 42		
	cf. 41/3				
38/18	*Interior of Rembrandt's mill*		26x30 (66x76) F;		
	Painted Redleaf		20x24 (51x61)		
			BI 39/384/6.6	Wm.Wells	C.10.5.90/8
			19x23½ (48.5x60)	E.I.Nathan	C.20.4.1928
		10Gns.		Williams	

Year/No.	TITLE/Signed	Price	Size/Exhibited	Collections	Sales
38/19	*Rembrandt's Mill* From across the river		31x40 (79x102) F;		
			21x30 (53.5x76)		
			BI 39/132/3.6	Thos.Baring	
				[bookplate on reverse]	
				Guardian Royal Exchange.plc	
39/1	*Zuider Zee fishing boats returning to port*	40Gns.	24x36 (61x91.5)		
	Stormy day		Liv.39 Bir.42	W.Bryant (Dlr)	
			23½x35 (60x89)	W.Klinkhoff	C.9.10.1970/94(2)
				Appleby see 38/12	
39/2	Sky :*with gull & rooks* panel			—	
39/4	Scheveling:	35 Gns.	13¼x19 (33.5x48.5)	Sir T.Baring Bt.	
39/5	Small Scheveling: ['V.small slip']	10Gns.	3⅞x10⅜ (10x26.5)	Pearce Seaman Esq.	
39/7	Scheveling, Cart & Beach:*Scheveling Sands*		37x49 (94x124.5) F;		
			26x38 (66x96.5)		
	s.	£70	BI 40/174/3.6	Lord Northwick	
			25½x37½ (65x95)	Sir J.Fowler	C.6.5.99/52
	as *Unloading catch*				S.18.7.1962/
				P.Polak	
39/8	Scheveling subject cut down		14x19½ (35.5x 49.5) [L]	—	
40/3	Scheveling: sunset for			C.Stokes	
40/4	*Scheveling pinck getting off shore*	£70	37x49 (94x124.5) F;		
	Ptd. Barnes		26x38 (66x96.5)		
	s&d. 40		BI 41/25/3.6	Lord Northwick	
			Glas.78/104	John Graham	C.30.4.87/60
	as *A Lugger Ashore*			Agnew	
					S.25.1.1959/138
					SPBNY.18.6.1982/3
				Martyn Gregory	
				Private Colln.	
40/7	Scheveling with horses			Robert Vernon; commission	
	completed 12/41 [Diary] cf. 42/6				
41/3	Haarlem [re-touch of 38/17, for BI]	£50	24x36 (61x91.5)		
			BI 42/56/3.6	W.Bryant (Dlr)	
	Note: *In Holland July 41:Diary missing.*				
41/4	Dutch fisher's house: On the Vecht *Dutch fishing*	£25	26x33 (66x84) F;		
	house near Vreland		18x24 (45.5x61)		
	Ptd. on spot.		BI 42/393/6.6	Bryant (Dlr)	
			Birm.42.Bradford 73.		
	as fisher's "home"		17½x23 (44.5x58.5)	Mrs.H.J.Mason	C.21.2.1947/40
		£57		Vicars Bros.	
41/5	Zaandam:*Mouth of the River Zaan, with*	160Gns.	55x71 (139.5x180.5) F;		
	Zuider Zee fishing craft &c; Amsterdam		41x56 (104x142)		
	in the distance		BI 42/126/5.6	Sir Chas Coote Bt.	
	Ptd. Redleaf, Barnes. cf. 49/7				
41/7	*On the Vecht*				
	cf. 41/4	£20	small	Thomas Creswick	
42/2	*Broekenhaven a fishing port of the Zuider Zee*	£90	30x48 (76x122)		
			RA 42/510/3.3	Chas. Ainsworth	
			29½x47½ (75x120.5)	Geo. Audley	X.18.3.1932
				Strauss	C.25.5.1979/50
				O & P Johnson	
				Owen Edgar Gallery	
42/3	Scheveling:*Dutch fishing boats on a lee shore,*	£40	16x20 (40.5x51)	Sir T.Baring	
	bringing in the catch			Lady Emma Crichton	
	Ptd. Barnes.			Private Colln.	
42/4	*Dutch boats beating in the Scheldt*	30 Gns.	17x21 (43x53.5)		
			Liv.42/25	George Holt	
			EWC 70/24	Emma Holt Beq.Liverpool	
42/5	Copy of 42/3			—	
42/6	*Scheveling sands.*[Ledger- Shore with cart & nets		29x41 (73.5x104)		
	& 3 horses waiting]		RA 42/28/2.3		
	as *On the Dutch Coast near Katwijck*		43x55 (109x140) F;		
	s&d. Dec 42		29x41 (73.5x104)		
			BI 43/129/3.4	Sir Thos. Baring Bart	
				Townley	S 14.7.1993/1
				Polak	
	label on rev.'Sir T[Baring].Bt.MP 12/6/93/No.44'				
	(C.Sale of Baring pictures on that date, but not				
	this) cf. 40/7				

Year/No.	TITLE/Signed	Price	Size/Exhibited	Collections	Sales
42/7	*Egmondt aan Zee, North coast of Holland*	£50	31x40 (78.5x101.5)F		
	CL		BI 44/212/5.5	Geo. Holt	
42/8	*Scheveling sands*	£65	18x23 (45.5x58.5)		
			RA 42/48/1.3	S. Rücker	
	Ptd. Barnes		Birm.42.Holland		
42/11	Reserve				
42/12	*Fishing boats on the sands at Scheveling*	17Gns.	12x16 (30.5x40.5)		
			Norwich.42	Henry Vaughan	
42/13	*Dutch Pinck ashore at Scheveling*	30 Gns.	18x24 (45.5x61)		
	s&d. 42.		Liv.42	Jas. McMurdo	C.8.6.78/135
		150G		Corbett	
				Auckland AG. ,New Zealand	
43/3	Scheveling		long shape	Geo. Loddiges. Present	
43/4	*Scheveling Herring boat preparing for sea*		18x24 (45.5x61)	Mr White (Dlr)	
	s&d. 43		22x30¼ (56x77)	Hon.F.Baring	
		£120		P.Polak	S.18.7.1962/
43/6	*Scheveling sands*				
	s&d. 43	50 Gns.	17x27 (43x68.5)	Mr Chas.Stokes	C.27.5.1988/69
	Ptd. on spot			Richard Green	
43/7	*Mast down* [Scheveling]			—	
	Ptd. on spot		22x30 (56x76)	—	
				Martyn Gregory	
	s&d. 43			Private Colln.	
43/8	Sky & Sea on strip of canvas			—	
43/9	*Dutch boats in a Calm*		26x37 (66x94) F;		
			16½x27 (42x68.5)		
		50 Gns.	BI 44/205/4.5	Robt. Vernon	
	Ptd. Barnes/Redleaf			Tate Gallery	
	engraved T.Jeavons,*Art Journal* Vol XI, 1849				
43/12	*Dutch boats in a Calm*	36G	Norwich. 45	Phillips Esq	
43/14	*Scheveling, getting off shore*		16½x23½ (42x59.5)	—	
		15 Gns.		Cooling	C.18.3.1932
44/1	*Antwerp from the Scheldt, morning*	100Gns.	24x48 (61x122)		
	s&d. 44		RA 44/469/1.2	Sir J Wigram.Bt.	
	Ptd. Barnes				SB.5.11.1974/167
			20½x47½ (52x120.5)		S.14.12.1983/1
					S.16.7.1993/63
				Private Colln.	
44/3	Boats in the Ij: *Calm, Amsterdam in the distance*	50Gns.	15x27 (38x68.5)	Pearce Seaman Esq.	C.9.7.1954/95
		30 Gns.		Sutton	
44/5	*Nieuwendam*	50 Gns.		Lord Winchilsea	
				[Commission]	
44/7	Calm:Sketch for *Mijnheer's yacht becalmed*		Miss [Helena] Loddiges		
44/8	*Dort, Morning, Mijnheer's yacht becalmed*	100Gns.	27x39 (68.5x99)		
			BI 45/90/4.5	Private collection	
44/10	*Belgic galliot aground in the shallows off Bergen*		26x38 (66x96.5)		
	op Zoom	£75	BI 45/44/2.5	Lord Chas.Townshend 1854?	
	CL	24Gns.		Vicars	C.28.3.1913
44/12	Small Scheveling			Mr Darnell [L]	
45/3	Dutch boats in a calm:*Dutch fishing craft off*	£60	35x47 (89x119.5) F;		
	Fort Lillo,mouth of the Scheldt		23x35 (58.5x89)		
			BI 46/89/2.2	J.Barlow	
			EWC 70/21	C.R. Cooke OBE.	
				Private Colln. N.Z.	
45/4	small copy of same	10Gns.		H.Bicknell	
45/5	Hooft Zaandam [sunset?]	£12	10x17 (25.5x43)		
			BI 48/361/4.5	T.Creswick	
47/11	*A Zuider Zee botter, working off a sandbank;*		53x69 (134.5x175.5) F;		
	Marken in the distance		40x56? (101.5x142?)		
	CL		BI 48/54/2.5		
			Liv 48/116		
48/3	*Dutch Yachting on the Zuider Zee*	£80	23½x38 (59.5x96.5)		
			RA 48/174/2.2	Geo. Marshall*	
	Art Union Prize*			C.F.Dendy Marshall Beq.	
				1955	
				National Maritime Museum	
48/4	*Scheveling*. Sandhills with church, stormy. Mast down	£70	23½x38 (59.5x96.5)		
			RA 48/147/1.2	Geo. Marshall	
	CL			Norwich	P.14.12.1981/44

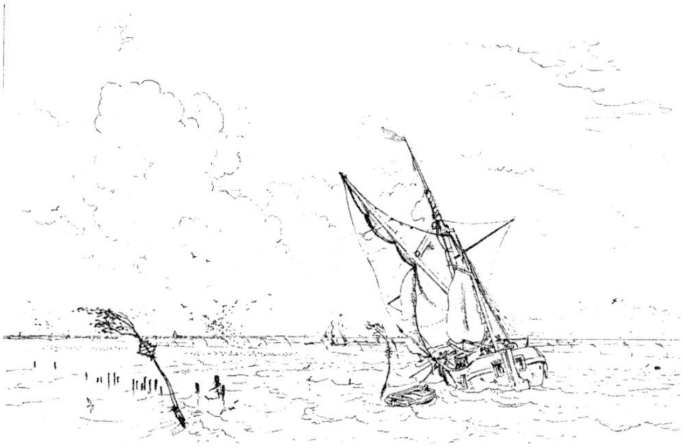

Plate 275. 44/10
Belgic galliott aground...
Camera lucida record of an 1845 British Institution exhibit.

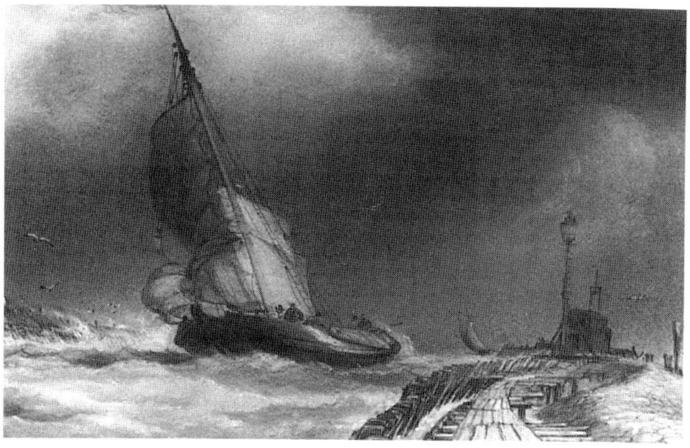

Plate 276. Chalk drawing
Zuider Zee botter entering harbour
Its similarity to his paintings and sketches of Broekenhaven put this drawing into that group; cf. 54/3 (Colour Plate 149).
Photo courtesy Martyn Gregory

Year/No.	TITLE/Signed	Price	Size/Exhibited	Collections	Sales
48/6	*Dutch Boats on the IJ off Amsterdam*	20Gns.	9x18 (23x45.5) F;		
			6x13½ (15x34.5)		
			BI 49/8/1.3	G.Field	C.4.4.1930/
		40Gns.		Gooden & Fox	
48/8	sky Scheveling		small	—	
48/17	*Katwijck Coast of Holland*	£40	14x18 (35.5x45.5)		
			Liv 48/11	John Clow	
		48Gns.			Winstanley, 20.4.52/16
	as Fishing boats at Katwijk		13½x17½ (34.5x44.5)	C.Butler	C.17.4.1964/56
		140Gns.		Gooden & Fox	
48/20	*Beurtman passing the Booms, Amsterdam*	£15	4x9 (10x23)		
			Not Exhibited	T. Sidney Cooper, RA.	
48/21	On the Dutch Coast near Scheveling: cart & men gathering seaweed.	£35	11½x17½ (29x44.5)		
			BI 49/365/3.3	H.Smith	
48/24	Beurtman off Amsterdam, Ransdorp Tower	15Gns.	4x9 (10x23)	Lord Chas TownshendSale	
48/25	*Vessels off Amsterdam, Ransdorp Tower in distance*	15Gns.	4 x 10 (10x25.5)		
			Manch. 48	Boden	
49/2	*On the Scheldt.*			—	
		£80	41x54 (104x137) (?F)		Foster's15.2.55/33
				W.Llewellyn	Foster's 4.4.55/48
	Not in Ledger.	£58.16	40 x 57 (101.5x145)	—	
49/5	Dutch River: *A Dutch Calm.*	100Gns.	17¾x35¾ (45x91)		
			RA 49/130/1.3	T.Horrocks Miller	
	s&d. 49		18x36 (45.5x91.5)		
			RA[OM] 1889/24	same owner	
				Thos Pitt Miller	C. 26.4.1946/68
		£68.5.0		Sutherland	
					CSK.17.5.1990/199
		£24,000		Martyn Gregory	
				Private Colln.	
49/5A	*A Dutch Calm, Zuider Zee fishing craft* with white buoy on sand on left	100Gns.	17½x35½ (44.5x90)		
			Manch.49	F.Pryor	C.15.5.85/64
		160Gns.		Agnew	
49/7	*Dutch boats on the Zaan, Amsterdam in the distance*	110Gns.	21x34 (53.5x86.5)		
	CL		Birm. 49.	H.Farnum, Philadelphia	
49/8	Spaarendam for Liverpool:*Zuider Zee fishing craft drying nets in the harbour of Spaarndam*	100Gns.	17¾x35½ (45x90)		
			Liv 49/52	S.Rücker sold Christies[L]	
				Richard Lloyd	
	as *Dutch boats becalmed on the Zuider Zee*				C.27.4.1923/
		58 Gns.		Banner	
				Jas.Dugdale	C.24.6.1927/
		78Gns.		Agnew	
			18x36 (45.5x91.5)		C.22.11.1991/141
				Burlington Paintings	

Year/No.	TITLE/Signed	Price	Size/Exhibited	Collections	Sales
49/9	*Dutch pilots warping their craft out of harbour in*	150Gns.	35x49 (89x124.5)		
	rough weather		BI 50/45/1.4	John Barlow	Sale 1858
		£200	36x50 (91.5x127)	Robt Kirkham Hodgson	
			35x48½ (89x123)	Lady Norah Hodgson	C.21.11.1924/
		85Gns.		Amor	
				Cdre.Chas.C.P.Noble	
		£11,500			C.13.10.1978/11
					SB.15.5.1979/80
					S.24.6.1982/149
49/11	Dutch calm: *Dutch fishing craft off the Booms,*		24½x39½ (62x100.5)		
	Amsterdam		RA 50/315/3.3	Francis Barchard	
			Manch.50		
			Brighton 84 lent	ditto	
				P. Polak 1965	
49/13	*Dutch Boats on the Ij* [L] Amsterdam in distance	50Gns.		Mr Heathcote	
			15x27 (38x68.5)	Sutton	C.9.7.1954/95
		30Gns.			
49/14	Katwijck		small	Glasgow	—
50/1	Dutch boats on calm river: *A Bit of Holland*				
	s&d. 50	20Gns.	10x15 (25.5x38) F;		
			5⅜x11½ (13.5x29)		
			BI 50/352/3.4	Sir William Tite	
				National Maritime Museum.	
50/2	*Dutch Fishing station*			George S.Marshall:Present.	
	s&d. 50		6¼x8½ (16x21.5) panel	Richard Green	
	as *Dutch Fishing boats up river*. Cat/ 29.				CSK.5.5.1994/131
				Royal Exchange AG.	
50/4	Dutch calm: *Dutch sawmill and Zuider Zee craft*	£25	18x22 (45.5x56) F;		
	on the Ij, Zaandam in the distance		11x15 (28x38)		
	s&d. 50		BI 51/101/1.1	George S.Marshall	
				W.E. Williamson Colln.	
				Deal	
				Dover Museum	
50/6	*Scheveling sands, tide making in*	£100	18x36 (45.5x91.5)		
			RA 50/93. Manch.50	F.Pryor	C.15.5.85/65
		160Gns.		Agnew	
51/7	Sky, copy of Bergen op Zoom [?44/10]		—		
51/9	*Scheveling shore, low water* [L] Schevg.pincks	£120	29x47 (73.5x119.5) F;		
	drying nets and sails, low water, tide coming in		18x36 (45.5x91.5).		
	s&d. 52		18x36 (45.5x91.5).		
			BI 52/90/1.1	C.Delafosse	Fosters 15.2.55/48
		£76		Leggatt	
		£126			C.14.5.98/17
				Agnew	
			18¼x36 (46.5x91.5)		S.10.6.1964/152
				Royal Exchange Art	
				Gallery 1993	
				Private Colln.	
52/4	*Zuider Zee fishing craft returning to port*	£280	35x49 (89x124.5)		
	s&d. 52.		RA 53/347/4.5	S.Wheeler, Brunswick Tce,	
				Brighton	
	as *Fishing craft returning*			Vicars 1936	
	Note: Begun as *Medemblik*; called *Enkhuizen* in				
	Feb./Mar 53.when bought Mr Starkey, but later				
	'given up'.Called *Zuider.Zee*,March 53.				
	as *Dutch pincks entering Zuider Zee.*				C.19.5.1978/170
52/5	*Dutch fishing craft, Katwijck*	40Gn	21½x37 (54.5x94)		
	s&d. 52	£136	21x36½ (53.5x92.5)	David Price	C.2.4.1892/46
		370Gns.		W. Vokins	
				Lord Amherst of Hackney	
			21x37 (53.5x94)		C.12.12.1908/
				Vicars Bros.	W.H. Lane
					17.2.1983/394
		£15,500		Richard Green	
52/6	*Dutch pincks off Katwijk*		21¾ x 37 (55x94)		
	s&d. 53		BI.53/136/2.3	J.Barlow	C.6.11.1995/150A
52/7	*Dutch craft on the Zuider Zee*	60Gns.	Manch. 52 [n.t.]	J.Barlow	Sale 1858
		£136 [L]			
	? as *Boats on the Zuider Zee*			Thos.Ball	C.14.5.60/196.
52/8	*Scheveling pincks ashore low water, tide coming in*		Liv.52/92	F.N. Johnstone	

Year/No.	TITLE/Signed	Price	Size/Exhibited	Collections	Sales
52/9	Egmond for Mr Davis. *Dutch Fishing boats*		large	John Davis	C.25.3.65/216
		630Gns.		Agnew	
52/10	Dutch calm.			—	
52/11	[L] Shore at Scheveling- on the spot 1838	£60	Liv.52/81	S. Rücker	
52/12	*A breezy day Scheveningen, unloading the catch*				
	s.ARA	£42	18x24 (45.5x61)	—	
	as *Breezy day,Scheveningen*		17½ x 23½ (44.5x59.5)		C.16.3.1934/
		18Gns.		Vicars Bros.	
				Martyn Gregory	
				Private Colln.	
52/31	*Fishing boat ashore, waiting for the tide*				
	s&d. 53.		24x18 (61x45.5)	—	
	Find. 4th Jan.			Alexr. Russell	
53/1	Enkhuizen. begun Feb.8th			—	
	Scheveling beach, selling fish				
	s&d. June 54	£40	13x19 (33x48.5)	Joyce Esq	
	?as *Low tide, Scheveningen,landing fish.*				C.27.3.1909
				Gooden & Fox	
				Lady Caroline Salt	
			13½x19½ (34.5x49.5)		B.12/1/1989/350
		£12,000			
53/6	*Scheveling shore, low water, Pincks preparing*	£125	BI 54/29/1.1	Arthur Burnand	not in his Sale
	for sea				C.26.3.92
54/1	*Dutch fishing pincks off Egmond aan Zee, hauling*	250Gns.	30¼x47¾ (77x 121.5)		
	off shore		RA 54/526/4.4	Robert Hudson	
				Bromhead	C.29.1.1925/
54/3	*Zuider Zee botter returning to port*	300Gns.	34x53 (86.5x134.5)		
			RA 54/264/1.4	Wm Edgar	
			Manch.54	Mrs.F.Edgar	C.15.6.89/116
	Illust: *I.L.N.* (captions reversed), Jun.54 p.513	200Gns.		W.Vokins	
				O & P Johnson 1970	
			O & P Johnson		
			E.W.Cooke RA & his		
			Contemporaries 1989/24		
	inscr..*Medemblik/Van Kook* on bows of boat.			Private Colln.	
54/9	Calm.*Shallow water, shores of the Zuider Zee*		21x36½ (53.5x92.5)		
			Liv.54/191	Jacob Bell	
				Colln Mrs Spencer Bell	
				1893	
	s&d. 55			Lady Poë	C.1.5.1936/83
				Vicars	
54/10	*Still Water, a creek of the Zuider Zee*	£25	5x13 (12.5x33)		
	s&d. 54		BI 55/7/1.3	Chas Warner	
		16Gns.	5½x13½ (14x34.5)	C.B.O.Clarke	C.8.5.1936
					S.Billingshurst
				Richard Green	24.5.1995/321
54/12	*Scheveling sands, tide making in*		9½x14 (24x33.5)	Mr Stitt	
	s&d. 55		board	Royal Exchange Gallery	
	inscr.on rev.				
					SB.18.3.1980/11
					?lot 9, 58/21
55/1	*Dutch Boat getting off, Scheveling sands, low*		16x24 (40.5x61)		
	water, tide making in		RA 55/323/2.4	Alderman D. Salomons	
	s.ARA				
	as *Scheveling shore from my window*				C.28.5.1926
		15Gns.	15½x23½ (39.5x59.5)	Carey	
55/8	Scheveling boats, rough sea: *A North Sea Breeze*		42x65 (106.5x165)		
	on the Dutch Coast: fishermen hauling the "pinck"		RA 55/269/1.4	Calvert Toulmin	
	out of the surf		Interntl.Exh.1862/693		C.26.6.86/43
	s&d.				
	as *Sea Breeze,Scheveningen*	470 Gns.			S. [*sic*]
		30 Gns.	42½x68? (108x172.5?)		
				Camerons	C.1.3.1929/
		£370	42x66 (106.5x167.5)		B.8.9.1966/1
				Sabin Galleries 1966	
				National Maritime Museum	
55/9	*Thundercloud on the Dutch Coast*	small	John Furze		
55/10	*Thundercloud passing over Dutch coast -*		18x24 (45.5x61)		
	tide on the turn		RA 57/535/4.4	Jas.T. Caird, Greenock	
	s. ARA	£33		Collings	C.27.4.1923/
				Martyn Gregory	P.14.12.1981/44

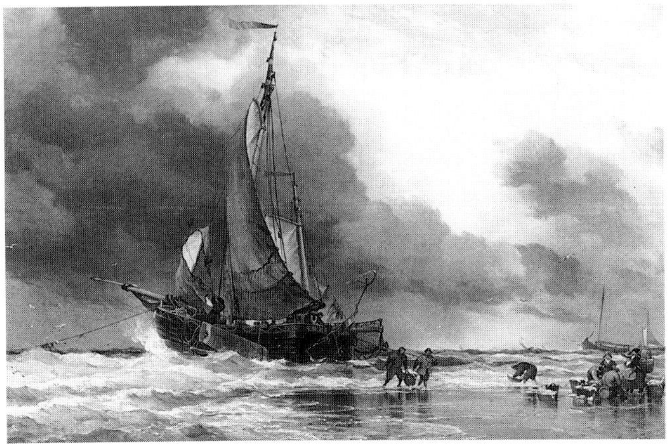

Plate 277. 55/10
Thundercloud passing over the Dutch coast; tide on the turn...
Photo courtesy Phillips Fine Art Auctioneers

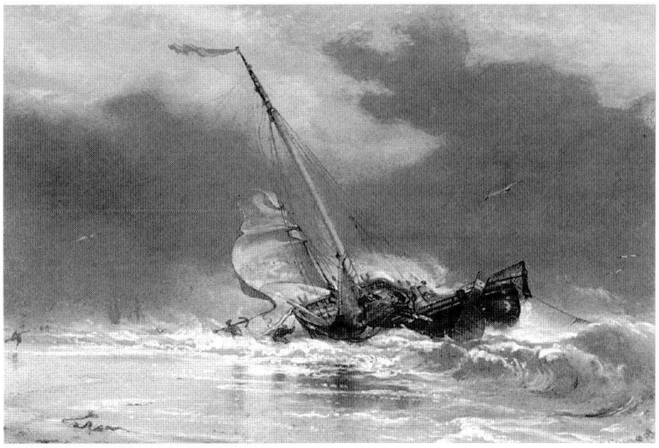

Plate 278. Chalk drawing
Beaching a Dutch pinck
The design, dated 1868, is very near several of his popular exhibited paintings. Photo courtesy Phillips Fine Art Auctioneers

Year/No.	TITLE/Signed	Price	Size/Exhibited	Collections	Sales
56/1	*The Port of Delfzijl on the Dollart, an inland sea of Holland.*		26x42 (66x106.5)		
			RA 56/433/2.5	Joseph Arden.	C.26.4.79/52
				Agnew	
56/2	Scheveling: *Dutch pincks arriving and preparing to put to sea on the return of the tide*	400Gns.	41½x66½ (105.5x169)		
	s&d. 56		RA 56/53/1.5	Theo Burnand	C.25.2.88/6
			Victorian Era Exhibition.1897	Lord Burton	P.27.9.1976/45.
			Royal Exchange Art Gallery	Private Colln. 1989	
			Royal Exchange Art Gallery 1994	Private Colln.	
56/6	Dutch calm: painted at Ventnor			—	
56/20	Scheveling		8x14 (20.5x35.5)	James Wyatt	
56/21	*A Pinck or Scheveling trawler hauling her head to wind through the breakers, during flowing tide*		32x55 (81.5x139.5)	—	
			Crystal Palace 57. Liv.58		
			32½x53 (82.5x134.5)		C.25.1.1924/57
		18Gns.		Sampson	
57/2	Scheveling calm, on old sky: *Dutch Shore, a still day after stormy weather*	50Gns.	13½x20 (34.5x51)		
	s&d. 58		BI 58/121/2.3		
			Glasgow Art Union 59		
		17Gns.			C.22.7.1927
	(Witt:1938)			Burton Jones	
57/25	Scheveling:				
	s&d. 58		11½x17¾ (29x45)	Lyme Gallery	
57/26	second Scheveling: *Landing Catch on a Lee Shore*		18x28 (45.5x71)		
	[L] Dutch Trawler preparing for sea (?)		Birm 58	H.Criswick	
	s&d. 58			Richard Green.	SB.25.10.1977/2
57/28	New Scheveling *Dutch fishing boats, tide flowing, wind off shore*		BI.58/23	—	
58/6	*Dutch boats in a calm, evening on the Zuyder Zee*		35x54 (89x137)		
			RA 58/282/1.6	Mr Reiss, Manchester	
	as *Barges moored in calm water near a jetty*				C.10.2.1961/135
			35½x54½ (90x138.5)		P.15.12.1992/25
				Private Colln.	
59/2	*A Dutch peon* [sic, poon] *running for the port of Harlingen, is driven in a heavy squall outside the south pierhead*		42x67 (106.5x170)		
			RA 59/388/2.3	Henry Berger	
				Mrs Berger	C.5.3.1900/8
	Ptd. in studio			Vicars	S.3.6.1987/-
				Owen Edgar Gallery	
				Colln. P.G. Gallichan Esq.	
59/4	*Dutch Pincks, Scheveningen*	£230	26½x42½ (67.5x108)	E.Gambart	
	s&d. 60			Charles Gassiott; Beq.to Guildhall, City of London.	
			EWC 70/17		
			Bury *Spirit of the Sea* Exhn.1982/15		

Year/No.	TITLE/Signed	Price	Size/Exhibited	Collections	Sales
59/9	*Scheveling,tide coming in*			G. Hilditch	C.27.7.1934
	s&d. 60			Leggatt	
60/1	*Zuider Zee fishing craft in a calm*		RA60/34/1.5	J. Webster	
62/1	*Hoorn on the Zuider Zee; a fishing sneb leaving*		41½x55 (105.5x139.5)		
	the port		RA62/408/1.5	Wm.Phillips	
	(Chalk sketch for painting				EWC 65/108
				Private Colln.)	
62/3	*Dutch trawlers at anchor off Scheveling, waiting*		34x53 (86.5x134.5)		
	for the tide		RA63/230/1.3	Mrs L-Henry Woods	
	s&d. 63		36x54½		C.5.5.83/142
					SB 9.4.1974/37
	as *Van Kook and other Dutch fishing smacks*			Brian Goulder	
	trawling off shore			Private Colln. Holland	
				Martyn Gregory, 1994	
63/1	*Dutch boats on the Zuider Zee*		6½x11 (16.5x28)	—	
	s&d. 63	6½Gns.		Pinto	C.11.3.1912/125
63/18	*Dutch fishing craft on the Ij off Ransdorp* [L]	40Gns.	10½x14 (26.5x35.5)		
	near Amsterdam		BI/64/36/2.2	J.Hill	
	s&d. 64		O & P Johnson 1989/10		
				Private Colln.	
64/1	Diploma picture: *Scheveling Pincks running to*		35½x54 (90x137)		
	anchor off Yarmouth...		RA 64/223/2.4		
	s&d. 64		Royal Academy,		
			Diploma Gallery		
			Leeds 1868/1485;		
			Bournemouth 1957		
			EWC 70/11		
			Clarkson Stanfield,		
			(Tyne & Wear) 1979		
64/2	*Scheveling pincks, low water*		23x34 (58.5x86.5) [L]		
			RA 66/411/4.5	Sam.Mendel	C.24.4.75/419
		850Gns.	35x54 (89x137)		
			[saleroom]		
64/9	*Dutch fishing craft off Dordrech*		6¾x11¾ (17x30) board*t*		
	s&d. 64		BI 65/133/1.3	—	P.22.3.1976/34
					SB.6.12.1977/3
		£800	6¾x11 (17x28.5)		
64/11	Dutch calm for Vice Consul [Venice-Mr. Valentine]		small		
64/12	*Dutch boats on the Zuider Zee*		16x25 (40.5x63.5)	Capt. D.Galton RE	P.24.5.1971/58
	s & d 64	£2,500		Polak Gallery	
	63/15 pair				
64/17	Dutch boats with rushes. as *Dutch fishing craft*		9½x14¾ (24x37.5)	—	C.4.12.1911/153
	on Zuider Zee	12½Gns.		Sampson	
64/19	Scheveling boat on sands		4¼x9½ (11x24)	—	
	s. initials			Arthur Kennedy	C.20.5.1912/73
	as *Anchoring the Lugger*			David Messum, 1985	
	frame title *Anchoring the lugger*				
	Pair to 68/7				
65/1	*A Dutch Beurtman aground on the Terschelling*		42x66 (106.5x167.5)		
	sand (North Sea) after a snow storm		RA 65/595/1.1	W.Leaf	C.7.5.75/509
				Edw. Hermon	C.13.5.82/50
				T. Holloway	
				Royal Holloway College	
			Brighton: *Painters of*		
			the Sea 1979		
			Greenwich:*Art of the*		
			Van de Veldes 1982/153		
			National Maritime Museum		
65/2	Gambart's Dutch boats: *Rough sea with Scheveling*		24x35 (61x89)	Ernest Gambart (Dlr)	
	pinck getting off shore			Snowdon Henry	C.13.3/97/83
	s&d. 66			Miller	
	cf. Temple.'Sir Wager Watson of Victoria St' 1897			J.Snowdon Henry	C.27.5.99/124
		160Gns.		McLean	
		25Gns.		Mitchell	C.26.4.1935
	as *Beaching the pinck in a strong breeze*				P.14.12.1981/446
65/3	*Zuider Zee schuits in a calm*		24x34 (61x83.5)	Wilkinson	
	as *Windstille Hollandsche kust*			G.C.Schwabe stiftung	
				Hamburger Kunsthalle 3366	
65/4	Calm Scheveling [D]			—	

Year/No.	TITLE/Signed	Price	Size/Exhibited	Collections	Sales
66/2	Rough sea [at St Leonards] *Dutch boats in a breeze*				
	on the Dollart Zee		36x54 (91.5x137)		
	s&d. 65		RA 66/218/2.5	Jas. Hopgood	C.27.3.97/122
				Charles Goldsmith,	
				New York.	
				O & P Johnson	
				Private Collection	
66/5	Dutch boats on Ij.		small	Agnew	
66/6	Dutch boat on sand: *Fishing "botter" aground in*		23½x33½ (59.5x85)		
	the Scheldt		BI 67/453/3.3		
	s&d. 67		Man.87/716	H.W.F. Bolckow	C.5.5.88/30 &
					22.5.91/
	Vicars advert 1936; ex coll.Bolckow.			C.24.6.1983/76	
	not in *Ledger*			Private Colln.	
66/7	*Dutch boats in a calm* (with windmill)		6½x9¾ (16.5x25)		
	s&d. 66		BI 67/298/2.3	George Field	
				Barclay Field	C.10.6.93/3
				Agnew	C.23.5.1924/11
					Knight, Frank &
					Rutley
					25.5.1960/109
				Polak	
66/8	*Dutch boats Hugging the Shore on the Zuyder Zee*		7¼x9 (19.5x23()	—	
	s&i. on rev.			Martyn Gregory	
				Private Colln.	
67/1	*Dutch boats "hugging the shore", Amsterdam in*		41x66 (104x167.5)		
	the distance		RA67/479/2.3	Jos.Fenton	C.5.5.79/153
	as *Dutch fishing boat*			Capt. Robt.B.Brassey	C.14.2.1940/-
		7Gns.		Mitchell	ST.12.6.1979/74
				Kenulph Gallery,	
				Winchcombe	
67/4	Scheveling, mast-down			—	
67/5	Another ditto				—
68/1	*A Scheveling trawler preparing for sea*		35½x54½ (90x138.5)		
			RA68/626/2.2	—	
		60Gns.		Stephenson Clarke,	
				Haywards Heath	C.11.7.1922/149
				Clark	
68/2	Scheveling: *Dutch pincks beached on a shoreline*		9¾ x15¾ (25x40)	—	
	s&d. 68				P.9.7.1985/28
				Owen Edgar, Cat 85-6/37	
68/4	*On the Dutch coast, Egmont, tide making in*	large			
			RA68/7/1.2	—	
68/5	Katwijk		small	—	
68/6	Scheveling: *On shore for a tide, coast of Holland*		35x53 (89x134.5)		
	s&d. 69		RA 69/116/1.4	—	Dreweatts
					10.1980/738
				Richard Green	C.26.3.1982/68
				Owen Edgar Gallery	
					CNY.13.4.1995/375
68/7	Dutch boats in a calm		4½x9½ (11.5x24)	—	
	frame title *Dutch craft on Zuider Zee* (arched top)				
	s&d. 70			Arthur Kennedy	C.20.5.1912/73
	Pair 64/19			David Messum,1985	
68/9	*Dutch pincks at Scheveling*		4½x9½ (11.5x24)	—	
	s&d. June 70		board	Polak	C.26.11.1982/322
69/1	Scheveling:*Landing Fish, Coast of Holland*		37½x55 (95x139.5)		
	s&d. 69		RA 70/365/4.6	H.A.Brassey	C.23.2.01/139
		620Gns.		Agnew	
	? as *Scheveling harbour, lighthouse &c*				Knight, Frank& R.
		26Gns.	36 x 56 (91.5x142)		25.11/1929
	as *Landing fish*		37½x55 (95x139.5)	Capt.Robt.B.Brassey	
					C.14.2.1940/220
		9Gns.		Cooling	
69/2	New picture for Art-Union Perhaps *Dutch*				
	Trawlers Landing fish at Egmont				
	Engraved Arthur Willmore, 1872. see 70/4 below				
70/3	*A Calm day on the Scheldt*		38x55½ (96.5x141)		
	s&d. 70		RA70/189/2.6	Lord Brassey	
			Whitechapel 1890/43.	Private Colln.	

Year/No.	TITLE/Signed	Price	Size/Exhibited	Collections	Sales
70/4	*Landing fish at Egmont*		31x48 (78.5x122)		
	s&d. 70		Intl.Exh 1871/121		
			Geo Boulton		
		300Gns.		J.Grant Morris	C.23.4.98/74
	as *North sea pincks landing fish at Egmont coast*				
	of Holland				C.15.5.1935
		38Gns.		Vicars Bros.	
				O & P.Johnson	C.28.1.1972/59
	begun as 'Scheveling'			Private Colln.	
71/1	*Dutch boats in a calm off Den Helder*		RA71/1078/2.2	—	
71/2	New picture on panel, as sketch for large picture.	—			
71/9	*Dutch calm*		11¾x16 (30x40.5)		
	s&d. 71		?RA 72/208/1.4	[D]-Banbury 1967	
				City Gallery	
				Gooden & Fox	
	Apollo 5/67				
71/11	*Dutch pincks in a stiff breeze off the coast at*		5¾x18¾ (14.5x47.5)	—	P.12.7.1982/31
	Scheveling				
	s&d. 72	£4000	6x19 (15x48)		
72/4	Scheveling: *On the Shore,low water*		9⅛x12⅜ (23x31.5) board		
	s&d. 71		EWC 70/28; Manchester		
			AG; J. Blair Beq, 1917		
72/5	Sky for John Murray's Dutch Calm.		—		
72/6	Decimus Burton's calm		small	—	
72/7	*Dutch pincks drying sails and nets:*		32x49 (81.5x124.5)		
	Egmond aan Zee, tide coming in		RA73/921/3.3	Agnew	
				Baron Albert Grant.1873	
					C 28.4.77/142
				Agnew	
				Sir W.A.Rose, 1877	
				Private Colln.	
75/13	Broekenhaven: *A Port on the Zuider Zee*		RA 76/573/4.4		EWC 80/141
		390Gns.		Agnew	
76/2	Calm on Zuider Zee: *A Zuider Zee fishing haven*		35½x54½ (90x138.5)	—	
			RA 76/223/2.4		EWC 80/142
		460Gns.		Agnew	
				Grogan, Boston USA	
					8.10.1992/-
				Private Colln.	
76/9	*A Scheveling pinck preparing for sea*		36x54 (91.5x137)		
			RA 77/288/1.4	Broadhead.Leeds [Dlr]	
	Illust.*Academy Notes* H. Blackburn,1877				
78/1	Beurtman *A Dutch galliot aground on a sandbank;*		35x54 (89x137)		
	low water in the Bies-Boshe, Holland		RA 78/182/1.3	—	
	s&d. 78		Australian Int.Exhn.1879		
				Brig.Gen.Sir J.Laycock	
				1946	
		£47.5.			Spencer Retford
			EWC 70/16	Cheltenham A.G.	
78/2	*Dutch pincks unloading their catch at Egmond aan Zee*		24¼x36 (61.5x91.5)	—	C.26.10.1979/156
	not s or d. similar to *Art Union* Engr. 1874,				
	possibly a forgery.			Private Colln.	
79/3	*On the Dutch coast at Camperdown ; a squally*		RA 79/262/1.3		EWC 80/144
	day, tide out.	410Gns.		Agnew	

GERMANY

Year/No.	TITLE/Signed	Price	Size/Exhibited	Collections	Sales
45/1	*Cologne from the South*	100Gns.	RA 45/333/1.2		
			Liv. ?Sold there.		
			23¼ x47 (59x119.5)		C.4.6.98/99
				Maj. Poulton	
			23½x47 (59.5 x119.5)	Grant	C.22.4.1912
		£23.2.0			
45/2	*Coblenz & Ehrenbrietstein*	£105	RA 45/365/2.2	Lady A.Paget	
55/13	*Danish fishing craft on the Elbe at Blankenese,*	80Gns.	16x25 (40.5x63.5)		
	low water				
	sold 2/57		BI 56/245/4.5	John Dryden	

Year/No.	TITLE/Signed	Price	Size/Exhibited	Collections	Sales
71/10	*Danish fishing craft on the Elbe off Blankenese, low water* s&d. 72	700Gns. £103	34½x53½ (87.5x 136) RA 72/643/4.4 Manch.1887 33x53 (83.75x134.5)	— W.Wells Agnew Mrs T.Agnew Thos. Agnew Liverpool Brown & R. 19.3.1909 Rochdale Art Gallery	C.9.6.1877/86 C.16.6.1906/80

ITALY

Year/No.	TITLE/Signed	Price	Size/Exhibited	Collections	Sales
45/16	Ventimiglia: sea dashing with great force over rocks as :*Ventimiglia - masses of fallen conglomerate on the shore. Above on the right is the frontier fortress of Italy, towards Nice*				EWC 63/12
45/17	*San Remo Gulf of Genoa* s.		9x14¼ (23x36.2) Spink, The Small Picture Show 1996, No. 23	Private Colln.	EWC 80/100 S.16.7.1975/128
45/18	Madonna dell Costa with tall cypress.*Church on the summit of the City Hill, San Remo*			Private Colln.	EWC 63/84
45/19	View of street from window, *From the Loggia of the Hotel, San Remo.*				EWC 63/85
45/20	Porto Maurizio with palms and distant view of Oneglia see 46/44, studio version.				
45/21	Reserve.				
45/22	Distant view of Porto Maurizio from jetty Oneglia, feluccas on beach see 46/39 studio version				EWC 63/17
45/23	Linguella, church on shore, distant view of Alassio				
45/23A	*Alassio - the island of Gallinaria in the distance, famed among the ancients for its breed of fighting cocks*			Russell Cotes A.G. bt Earl Grosvenor 1868	EWC 63/16 Bournemouth,
45/24	*Finale, promontory of Lumacella marble: Varigotta in the distance*				EWC 63/14
45/25	Rock and tunnel. *Rock at Finale, pierced by Napoleon I for the Cornice road* s&d. 60		9½x13½ (24x34.25)		EWC 63/13 P. Sevenoaks 5.4.1995/124
45/25A	another with boat in foreground 'on this side'; sunset effect *Finale, Breccia and Limestone cliff, tunnelled for the Cornice road*				EWC 63/5
45/26	Genoa, evening effect, moon, sky and mountain... from the Lanterna looking east;the promontory of Porto Fino in the distance.Full moon rising			Martyn Gregory Private Colln.	EWC 63/21
45/27	Genoa, early morning	3Gns.	5½x18½ (14x47)	B.J.Hudson Humbert Guarisco Gallery Washington DC	EWC 63/18 C.31.3.1913/ S.29.3.1983/9
45/28	Genoa, sun setting over sea. *Genoa with its hill-fortifications; the rocks below are now covered by an immense coal-depot for the use of vessels of war*				EWC 63/20
45/29	Genoa, from hotel room: *Mountain of Porto Fino, Sta. Marherita, Chiavare and Lavagna, across the Bay*				EWC 63/23
45/30	*La Spezzia, view of port and town from loggia of the Capuchin monastery* inscr. on verso ...*from the refectory of the Convent* s&d. 45		11½x18 (29x45.5)	Martyn Gregory Private Colln.	EWC 63/24 S.16.3.1988/14
45/30A	La Spezzia: *Carrara Mts from the Convent of the Capuchins* cf. 46/47 studio version				EWC 63/26
45/31	Little chapel; ? Carrara Mts, sunset.				EWC 63/27
45/32	Gulf with olives. *Gulf of Spezzia, Oratory and young olive trees; Lerici the residence of Byron and Shelley in the distance.*				EWC 63/25
45/33	*Leghorn from Punta del Molo. The ancient Roman towers and the Carrara mountains in the distance*			T.Hughes 1868 [D]	EWC 63/28

Year/No.	TITLE/Signed	Price	Size/Exhibited	Collections	Sales
45/34	*Florence, the Arno & S.Frediano, ponte della Trinita from hotel window*		7½x12½ (19x32)	Spink 1978	EWC 63/29 Anderson & Garland 1994/
45/34A	*Ponte della Trinita*		10x11¾ (25.5x30)	Spink Mrs Penn	C.6.5.1912/17
45/35	View down the Arno *The Pitti Palace in the Boboli Gdns Florence; the tower of the Palazzo Ducale and Fiesole in the distance*				EWC 63/30
45/36	*Rome, The bridge and castle of St.Angelo, St Peter's, Hospital of Spirito Santo &c the Janiculum Hill in the distance*		8¼x14 (21x55.6)	Spink, The Small Picture Show 1996, No. 24	EWC 63/42 CSK.3.1995
45/37	Reserve				
45/38	Genoa, part of harbour with bastions. *The Port of Genoa. Departure of the Empress of Russia for Sicily, 1845*				EWC 63/19
45/39	Roman fruit baskets				EWC 65/220
46/1	*Rome, ruins of the Temple of Venus Erycina, near the Porta Pia (adjoining the spot where the Vestal Virgins were bricked up alive) the buttresses on the right are the substructure of the House of Sallust*				EWC 63/43
46/1A	*Group of the Amalthea in the Villa Borghese, Rome*				EWC 63/33A
46/2	*Rome. Fountains and stone pines in the Villa Doria Pamphili,the encampment of the French in 1848.*		11¼x16½ (28.5x42)	Agnew (C. Morland Agnew & by descent to H.L. Agnew) Hazlitt,Gooden and Fox, Private Colln.	EWC 63/39 EWC 80/104 C.32.5.1910/34 S.20.6.1978/51
46/2A	*Rome, the cypresses on the Coelian Hill, the Via Sacra &c &c.*				EWC 63/35
46/3	*Rome the Palatine bridge now the Ponte Rotta: Temple of Vesta, tower of Sta Maria in Cosmedin, the mouth of the Cloaca Maxima &c*				EWC 63/36
46/3A	*Rome. Fountain at the entrance of the Borghese Villa*				EWC 63/37
46/4	*Rome. This Palm was brought from the Levant in 1490 by the 'Passionista' monks of SS Giovanni e Paolo on the Coelian Hill. It blew down the day before the French commenced the bombardment of the City in 1848. It was the oldest palm in Italy*				EWC 63/44
46/4A	View from Volskonski Villa with Wolf				
46/5	View of Forum from Coelian Hill			—	
46/5A	*The Campagna and Walls of Rome, with the Church of Santa Croce in Gerusalemme...* The walls of Honorius, the Campagna and the Monte Albano		c.7x10 (c.18x25.5) BI 47/198/3.6	Lyle 1980 Private Colln NZ	EWC 63/31

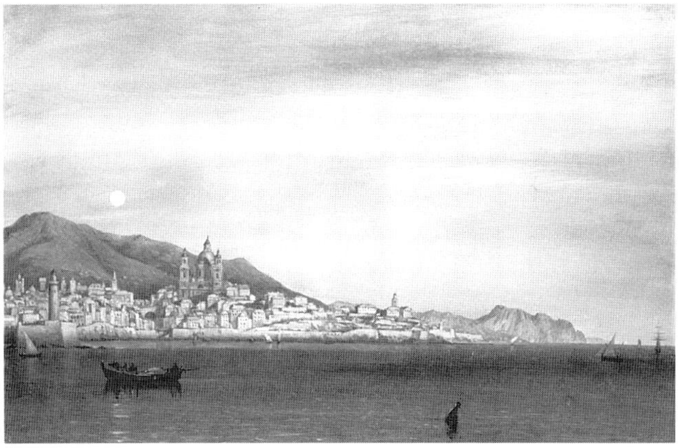

Plate 279. 45/26
Genoa, evening from the Lanterna, the promontory of Porto Fina in the distance, full moon rising Photo courtesy Martyn Gregory. Private Collection

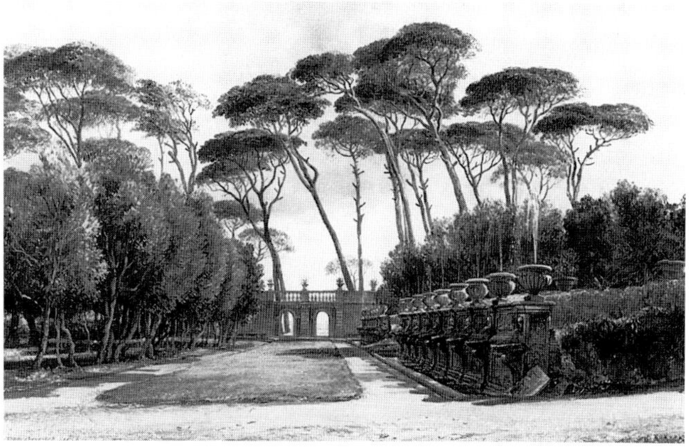

Plate 280. 46/2
Fountains and stone pines, Villa Doria Pamphili, Rome
Photo courtesy Hazlitt, Gooden & Fox. Private Collection

Year/No.	TITLE/Signed	Price	Size/Exhibited	Collections	Sales
46/6	Dark grove of Ilex from ditto. *Rome. Group of evergreen oaks, Convent of SS Giovanni e Paolo. A portion of the Colosseum* [sic] *seen through the opening*				EWC 63/34
46/6A	Copy made for Dr.Deakin (Rome).			—	
46/7	*Rome. The Neronian Aqueduct, from its specus or water-channel: the mountains of Tivoli in the distance* s&d. 46 as *Ruins of Villa Adriana*		6½ x10¼ (16.5x26)	—	EWC 63/32 C.10.3.1995/84
46/7A-	Group of Stone Pines, Villa Pamphili, *100ft high, at the entrance of the Villa Pamphili Doria on the Janiculum Hill in 1848. they were destroyed by the French*			Private Colln.	EWC 63/38
46/8-	*Rome. Part of the ruined aqueduct of Nero*			Martyn Gregory	EWC 63/33
46/8A	Tivoli,*Temple of Vesta, nearly undermined by the great inundation of the Anio in 1826. Monte Catillo in the distance*				EWC 63/41
46/9	*Villa d'Este, Tivoli: fountain of Neptune*			—	
46/9A	*Villa d'Este, Tivoli: the magnificent cypresses are the oldest and finest in the world; their height is 125 feet*				EWC 63/83
46/10	Sybil's temple.			—	
46/11	Calabrian boat. *Salerno, unloading in hot weather.*	11Gns.	Japan Exn.1910 8½x17 (21.5x43) 8½x17½ (21.5x44.5)	W.S. Hoare,Highgate Walter Spink	EWC 63/62 EWC 80/97 C.17.2.1912/87
46/12	View from window *Salerno, hauling in the seine net; Monte St Angelo in the distance*				EWC 63/81
46/13	General view *Salerno, drying nets, the mountains of Paestum in the distance.*		16⅞x28 (43x71) Agnew *Images of Victorian Life* No.80, 1990	Agnew 1990	EWC 63/61 U.S.A.
46/14	Mountains capped with cloud *Salerno, morning mist clearing off from the Mountains* cf. studio version 47/7				EWC 63/60.
46/15	Amalfi, from loggia of hotel, *Shore of Amalfi, washing nets in the stream from the Valley of the Mills which passes under the Hotel*		11x17 (28x43) Annual Marine Exhibition 1986, No. 10	Royal Exchange Art Gallery	EWC 63/52
46/16	Capuchin convent, rocks and sea:*Amalfi from the Convent, the promontory of Capo Dorso and the Paestum mountains in the distance* paper on board (cf. Anr. version 46/42		10½x15 (26.5x38) Exhn. 1978; *Victorian Ideal*	Mr Thomas 1864 Roy Miles	EWC 63/56; S.14.2.1978/51 S.24.6.1982/162 C 4.10.1980/77a re-offered C 8.5.1981/ 90.
46/17	Calabrese boat. *Shore of Amalfi from the Hotel, storm brewing*				EWC 63/53
46/18	Amalfi looking East under cliff. *Amalfi from below the Convent*				EWC 63/54
46/19	Flying fish		paper	National Maritime Museum	
46/20	Atrani			—	
46/21	Gothic ruin on beach. *Ruined church on the shore at Amalfi*				EWC 63/57
46/22	View from grotto of Convent *Cappucini convent Amalfi from the shore*				EWC 63/58
46/23	In cellar			—	
46/24	another			—	
46/25	Rocks below *Convent at Amalfi* s&d. 46 inscr. 'on spot July 1846'		11¾ x 17½ (30x44.5) paper on canvas		S.10.7.1991/84
46/26	Old watch tower, Erchia. see 47/1 studio version			—	EWC 63/59?
46/27	Capri, looking out of a fisher's house		Hillersdon		
46/28	Rocks and cliffs. *Rocks at Capri, Capo di Campanella in the distance*		9¼x13½ (23.5x34.5)	— Spink	EWC 63/55

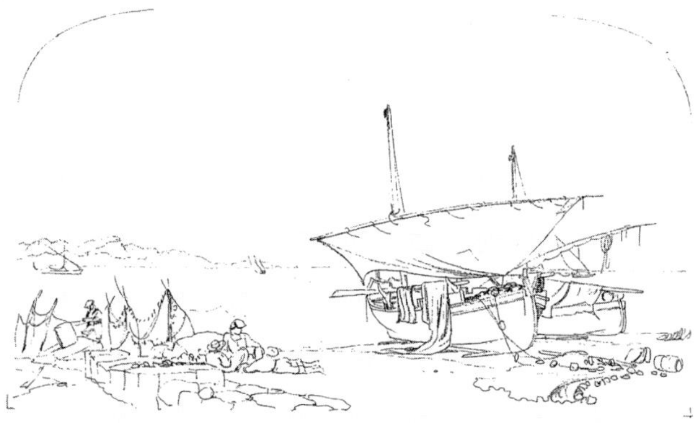

Plate 281. 46/42
Salerno Bay and the mountains of Paestum from Amalfi
Camera lucida record of a painting in the British Institution exhibition of 1847.

Year/No.	TITLE/Signed	Price	Size/Exhibited	Collections	Sales
46/29	Palm subject: Capri & Bay of Naples				
	Studio version 48/1				
46/30	Vesuvius from Sorrento			—	
46/31	*Castellamare, Marina and lighthouse - formerly*				
	the residence of the ex-King of Naples, the Arsenale				
	&c, Ischia in the distance				EWC 63/51
46/32	*Vesuvius and the Bay of Naples from off Castellamare*		5x13 (12.5x33)	H.Pryor	
	s&d. 50			Martyn Gregory	
	inscr. on rev.*Evening, Vesuvius....*		5¾x13½ (14.5x34.5)	Private Colln.	
46/33	Naples. lighthouses from window *Bay of Naples,*				
	Monte St Angelo, Lanterna, Castel a Mare, Vico,				
	Piano of Sorrento &c				EWC 63/46
46/34	*The Evening gun, Castel dell'Ovo, Naples. Capri in*				EWC 63/82
	the distance, sea breeze set in		5x13 (12.5x33)	H.Pryor	
	s&d. 50			Martyn Gregory	
			5¾x13½ (14.5x34.5)	Private Colln.	
46/35	Boats from Villa Cedroni, Posilippo				
	cf. 48/18, 48/19				
46/36	Vesuvius by moonlight			—	EWC 63/67A
46/37	ditto		small	—	
46/38	*Bay of Naples, Vesuvius from Castellamare*		11x17 (28x43)	Mrs E.Penn	C. 6.5.1912/18
				Sampson	
	s.				P.23.10.1972/223
				Spink	
				Private Colln.	
46/39	[at Redleaf] Italian boats *Oneglia, a group of*				
	feluccas, Porto Maurizio in the distance				
	as *Bay of Capri*		18½x29½ (47x75)		C.23.10.1981/49
	s&d. 47	£2900		Owen Edgar Gallery.	
	cf. EWC 63/17			O & P Johnson 89/22	
				[as Porto Maurizio	
				see 46/44]	S./3/1994/
				Private Colln.	
46/40	copy of small [Richard] Wilson (of Wm.Wells's)			—	
46/41	Martello tower; at Mentone near Monaco [L]				
	commission W.Wells			—	
46/42	*Salerno Bay and Mountains of Paestum from*				
	Amalfi		18x29½ (45.5x75)		
	CL		BI 47/254/4.6	F.W. Newton	
46/43	*Vesuvius and Bay of Naples from off Castelamare*				
	s&d. 46		46x50 (117x127) F;		
			23½x39 (59.5x99)		
	CL 'Dr,Ward'		BI 47/115/1.6	Pres. Mrs Georgina Ward	
				(sister)	
	as *Fishing boats in the Bay of Naples.*				C.21.4.1961/47
					C.24.2.1961/12
				Meatyard	C.16.3.1962/63
	as *Trading vessels in the Bay of Naples*		23½x39 (59.5x99)		SB 20.11.1973/4
				Dr. David A. Fermont	SB 25.7.1974/142
46/44	*The Bay of Porto Maurizio in the Gulph of Genoa,*				
	Oneglia in the distance				
	CL		37x51 (94x129.5) F		
	cf. 45/20.		BI 47/321/5.6	Charles Stokes	

Year/No.	TITLE/Signed	Price	Size/Exhibited	Collections	Sales
46/45	*Temple of Fortuna Muliebris*			—	
46/46	*Temple of Minerva Medica*			Harriette Cooke. Pres.	
			3½x5¼ (9x13.5)		P 12.7.1982/104
	anr. version?		5¼x 7½ (13.5x19)		
46/47	*The marble mountains of Carrara, from the Capuchin*				
	convent, Spezzia, Sunset effect				
	cf. 45/31 sk.		27x38 (68.5x96.5) F;		
			17½x29 (44.5x73.5)		
	CL	£45	BI 47/427/6.6	Geo.Greenhill Esq.	
46/48	*Bridge of Caligula, Posilippo & coast of Baiae in*				
	distance				EWC 63/80
46/49	*Capo di Sorrento, Ischia, Procida and Baiae in*				
	distance; fishing Gozzi on the shore				EWC 63/79
46/50	*Capri & Mts. of Sant Angelo, Bay of Naples, on*				
	right is Tiberio a cliff 1000 feet in height, from				
	whence criminals were precipitated by Tiberius				EWC 63/50
46/51	*Island of Capri from Naples, storm coming on*			—	EWC 63/48
46/52	*Vesuvius from Capri, the New Crater hiding the*				
	centre of Monte Somma				EWC 63/49
47/1	Martello Tower,*Tower of Erchia: Gulph of Salerno.*		24x39½ (61x 100.5)		
	s&d. 49[?]	£120	RA 47/318/3.3	Lord Northwick	
	cf. 46/26.		Liv.1847/39;Birm.1849.		
			EWC 70/6	Guildhall A.G., London,1902	
				Chas.Gassiott Beq.	
47/2	Italian craft:*Mediterranean craft, Gulf of Genoa*		21x29½ (53.5x75)		
	CL.	60Gns.	RA 47/105/1.3	W.Barchard	C.19.7.1909/91
		18Gns.		Leger	
	Illust: J. Roundell, *TSBoys* Leger Gallery 1971			Private Colln.	
47/3	*Vesuvius, Catalan & Paranzella* [L]				
	CL	35Gns./	14½x22½ (37x57)	Jno.Hillersdon	
	s&d. 47		14x22 (35.5x56)		SB 29.6.1976/2
	as *Vesuvius and Bay of Naples*; sealed on stretcher.			Polak Gallery	
	pair to 48/1				
47/6	*Rome. View from garden of Vigna Celimontana,*	60Gns.	F.22x30 (56x76)		
	looking towards Tivoli		BI 48/21/1.5	C. Stokes	
47/7	Salerno, clouds over mountains:*Fishermen sorting*				
	catch		18x28 (45.5x71)	—	B.1.3.1973/85
	s&d. 47			O & P Johnson	
	cf. 46/14			Private Colln.	
47/8	Reserve				
47/12	Calabrian mountains *Coast of Calabria from*				
	Salerno	50Gns.	RA 47/136/2.3	E.Ford	
48/1	Capri with palm: *Capri & Bay of Naples*				
	s&d. 48		14x22 (35.5x56)	Jno Hillersdon	
	CL		14½x22½ (37x57)		SB 29.6.1976/3
	cf. 46/29 sketch. Pair 47/3.				
48/2	*Italian Fishing craft off the Torre del Marzocco,*				
	Leghorn		54x69 (137x175.5) F;		
			40x55 (101.5x139.5)		BI 49/139/2.3
			Manch.49	S. Rücker	C.28/9.1.1930
		18Gns.		Mills	C.1.5.1931/
		11Gns.		W.E.Preston	
				Bradford AG	
	rejected by RA. See also drawing:				C.1988
			O&PJohnson 1989/-		
48/5	*Sorrento, afternoon*	£20	9x14 (23x35.5)	Mrs Bates	C.9.7.1954/233
	cf. 46/49.		8½x14 (21.5x35.5)	Agnew	
			9½x14½ (24.5x37)		S. Billingshurst
					30/1/1996/131
48/7	Evening effect with rocky promontory on right:				
	Sunset, Capo di Miseno	40Gns.	Man 48	J.Barlow	
48/10	[Copy of] Baiae sunset	30Gns.		G.Twining	
	cf. above 48/7				
48/18	*Bay of Naples from Villa Cedroni, Posilippo*		5x9 (12.5x23) [L]		
	CL		Glasgow 49	Laura M.Cooke, Pres.	EWC 63/47
48/19	Another		1¾x4 (4.5x10)	Mary N.Cooke, Pres.	
49/1	Rome & S.Angelo: *Thou hast the sunset's glow*		17½x35½ (44.5x90)		
	Rome for thy dower	150Gns.	RA 49/153/2.3	S.Rücker	
	cf. 45/36			Miss Harriet Rücker	C.18.3.1932/34
	as *Rome from the Tiber*	15Gns.		Illingworth	

Year/No.	TITLE/Signed	Price	Size/Exhibited	Collections	Sales

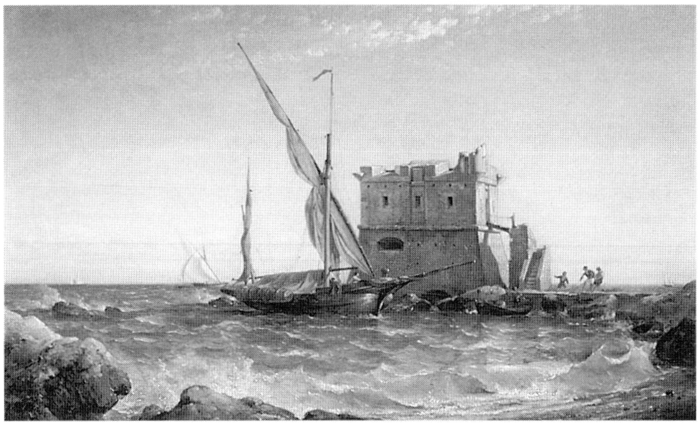

Plate 282. 49/4
Evening, A Scene on the Riviera di Ponente, Gulph of Genoa
Photo courtesy Sotheby's

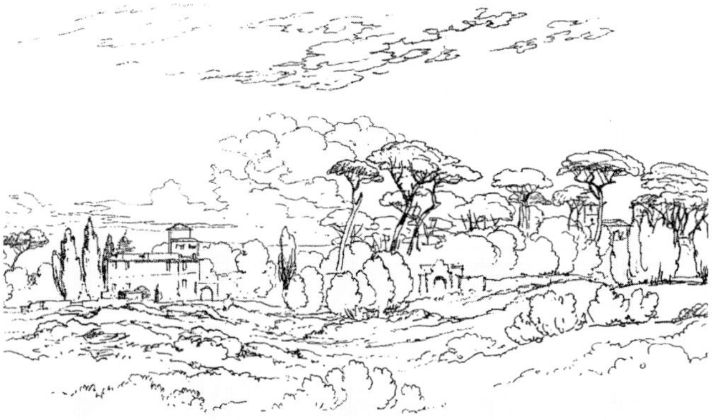

Plate 283. 49/10
The Villa Borghese from the walls of Rome
A *camera lucida* record of his British Institution exhibit of 1850.

49/4	*Evening, A Scene on the Riviera di Ponente,Gulph*		17½x30 (44.5x76)		C.30.11.1990/40
	of Genoa		RA 50/58/1.4	Conrad Loddiges, Pres.	
	as *A Felucca by a tower on the Mediterranean Coast*				
	as *Felucca entering harbour...*		18x28½ (45.5x72.5)		S.13.6.1990/5
49/6	Palace of Caesars with Palm		small	Lady [Walter] James	
49/10	[L] Raphael's villa : *The Villa Borghese from the*				
	walls of Rome		15x27 (38x68.5)		
	CL		BI 50/369/4.4	G. Pritchard	
49/12	*Capo di Miseno* [repetition of 48/7]		BI 50/87/2.4		
	s&d. 49		25x37 (63.5x94) F.		
	CL	45Gns.		G. Delafosse	
	with quotation from Byron *The Corsair* as title.		14⅞x26⅞. (38x68.5) [L]		
	O'er the hushed deep the yellow beam he throws/				
	Gilds the green wave that trembles as it glows				S.1.10.1986/217
63/5	Bay of Baiae from Posilippo, on old sky			—	
63/6	*Bay of Naples*		17x35½ (43x90)	S. Rücker	
				Miss Harriette Rücker	C.18.3.1932
64/5	*Naples* presented to Giuseppe Garibaldi in London				
	perhaps 46/ series				
68/8	Vesuvius;*Mending nets, Bay of Naples*				
			35x55 (89x139.5)	—	
	s&d. 69		RA 69/204/2.4		C. 11.1992/
				Richard Green	

VENICE

50/7	Venice: Salute. Dogana and part of Palazzo Ducale				
	[L] *Venice from S.Giorgio with trabaccolo*		15x25 (38x63.5)	Lady F. Hope.	
	Copied large 59/6				
50/8	Zecca, Doge's palace.		11x17½ (28x44.5)	—	
50/9	S.Giorgio, stormy sky		10x17 (25.5x43)	—	
50/10	Looking East.[L] San Giorgio, gray morning, from window		9x17⅞ (23x45.5)	Pres. R.Ansdell RA	
50/11	Salute and Dogana from gondola				
	as *Il Lagunetto*	£80	15x25 (38x63.5)	Delafosse	Sold July 51
			14½x25¾ (37x65.5)	Mrs A. Venables Brunton	
					C.8/9.5.1914/123
		18Gns.		Cassell	
50/12	Sunset with trabaccolo [L] Salute	£20	10x14 (25.5x35.5)	Hugh Owen	
50/13	*Sunset, Lagune of Venice façade of S.Giorgio*		11½x17½ (29x44.5)		
			12x18½ (30.5x47)		C.7.5.75/508.
		63Gns.		Dowdeswell	
	Mr Delafosse had a copy, Jan 56. [55/12]				
50/14	*Trabaccolo unloading into a rascono*				
	s&d. 51	£60	15x25 (38x63.5)	W.C. Sole	Sold Feb 52
	as *Sailing barges on Venetian canal*		14x25½ (35.5x65)		
		£231		Willmer	C.14.10.1960/111
				Polak	

Year/No.	TITLE/Signed	Price	Size/Exhibited	Collections	Sales
50/15	*Salute & Dogana at sunset*				
	Ptd. Kensington	£25	6x12 (15x30.5)	T.Wyatt	
50/16	Evening sky towards S.Clemente [L] *Sunset San*		5x13 (12.5x33)	Pres. Mrs Pryor	
	Clemente after stormy day				B.2.11.1978/37
	inscr.HMP ex dono EWC, also *Il Lagunetto*				
	cf. 62/21		4¾x13¼ (12x33.5)		SB.2.10.1979/14
50/17	Sunset S.Servolo, various craft. [L]		5x13 (12.5x33)	Pres. R.Ansdell RA	
50/18	Sant'Elena evening effect.	25Gns.	4x9 (10x23)	Benson Rathbone	
50/19	Distant view of Front of Ducal Palace		11x17 (28x43)	—	
50/20	[L.] small sunset La Grazia.		4x9 (10x23)	—	
50/21	[L.] small sunset S.Servolo.		4x9 (10x23)	—	
50/22	*Giudecca Sunset* [L] Gesuati church Evening		8¾x17¾ (22x45)	Pres. S. Rücker	C.17-20.2.1912/86
	s&d. 50	9Gns.	9x17 (23x43)	Vicars	
			9x18 (23x45.5)		SB.20.10.1981/28
50/23	Brichepala [L] Riva, Prison, Church of San		11¼x17¼ (28.5x44)	—	
	Zaccaria. *The Bacino*			Ionides	SB28.11.1972/12
	s&i. Venezia 50			Watson	C.20.6.1986/35
				Martyn Gregory	
				Private Colln.	
50/24	S.Michaele with Murano in distance		9x17 (23x43)	—	
50/25	Brig hove-down [L] Palli, vessel hove down, Venice	£25	9x14 (3x35.5)	—	
			Glasgow 51		
				Martyn Gregory	
				—	
50/26	Bragozzi, fishing craft off the Giardini pubblici, Venice	100Gns.	15x25 (38x63.5)	Jos Miller	
				O. Coope	C6.5.1910/9
		£38.17		Eyles	
50/27	Dogana di Mare with church of the Zitelle		26¾x42 (68x106.5)	—	
	s&d. Venezia 50			Sir Godfrey Llewellyn	C.10.7.1970/105
			O & PJohnson 1989/32		
50/28	General view, evening effect. *On the Lagune*				
	opposite Venice, San Servolo & the Armenian				
	convent in the distance. Evening, low water		15½x26¼ (39.5x66.5)		
	s&d. 50			F.N. Johnstone	
	ins. on reverse as above &*E.W.Cooke detto il Lagunetto*				C.14.6.62/38
	sold 9.8.51	£45		W.Vokins	
			15x25¾ (38x65.5)		C.20.6.1924/115
		70 Gns.		Sampson	
				F.T.Sabin 1969	
			EWC 70/9	Richard W.D. Copeland	
	Illust: J.Maas,				S. 20.1.1993/111
	Victorian Painters p 62		14¾x25½ (37.5x65)	Polak Gallery	
				Private Colln.	
				Spink, The Small Picture	
				Show 1966, No. 25	
50/29	Evening off Giardino, half-Trabaccolo, sunset		11¼x17 (28.5x43)	Richard Barrington	
	inscr.*Il Lagunetto* 1850				
	sold June 1851				
	as *The Lagoon, Venice*				SB.25.11.1975/91
50/30	Sea from Canale San Giorgio.			—	
50/31	[L.] S.Giorgio by moonlight	£26	10x17 (25.5x43)		
			Liv.51	E.Gambart	
51/1	*Bragozzi, San Marco and Doge's Palace*	£25	8x11 (20.5x28)	W.Smith [L] 24.7.51	
	[study for 51/2]				
51/2	Bragozzi & Doge's Palace: *Bragozzi,the fishing*	200Gns.	35x49 (89x124.5)		
	craft of Venice		RA 51/539/1.2	Geo. Pritchard	
		£57.15.0		E.J. Moore	C.2.8.1946/
				Vicars	
			35½x50 (90x127)	Polak, 1948	
					CSK.5.10.1989/136
		£78,000+		Richard Green	
51/3	*The Church of the Salute, Dogana etc.*		32x53 (81.5x134.5)		
	enlarged from small picture (?50/11)	300G	RA 51/732/2.2	Samuel Christy MP	
	Reproduced:(Colnaghi) Catalogue,Plate 85,		Manch. 51;		
	Manchester Art Treasures Exhibition 1857		Manch 57/324		
	Art Journal 1869			Royal Ocean Racing Club	
51/4	*Sunset behind the Salute*	£65	16⅞x29 (43x73.5)	H.L. Gaskell	
51/5	Sunset behind Salute		17x29 (43x73.5)	J.HTurner, Brighton	
	Commission,copy of 51/4			Calvert Toulmin	C.26.6.86/29
				Vokins	

Year/No.	TITLE/Signed	Price	Size/Exhibited	Collections	Sales
51/6	*Venetian fishing boats off the Giardini pubblici*		26½x42 (67.5x106.5)	—	
	d.51			Alex. Young	C.13.3.1913/13
				Cassell	
	cf. 50/26	£136	26x41 (66x104)	Mrs E.P. Wing	C.22.3.1946
				Vicars	
51/8	Sunset effect, Salute- *Venetian sunset*		17x21 (43x53.5)		
	s&d. 51			Mrs Brotherhood	
		21Gns.			C.25.2.1927
				Harrison	
51/10	Reserve				
51/11	S.Servolo and S.Lazzaro from off Giardini.				
	Bragagna subject [D]. No.1				
51/12	*Venice '...whose dear spires Rising at distances*				
	o'er the blue lagoon [It is reward enough for me				
	to view, Once more...]'. No.2				
	s,d & i. 51,Venezia		26½x41 (67.5x104)		
	sold Apr.52	£178.8	RA 52/526/2.2	Joseph Arden,Rickmansworth	
			26½x42 (67.5x106.5)	Park	C.26.4.79/53
		810 Gns.		Forbes	
	As *Venice the Bacino*, 26 x 23[*sic*]			Vicars Bros.	C.10.7.1970/30
		640Gns.		Morrison	
	Sighted 1994: cut down.			Private Colln.	
51/13	*Bridge of Sighs, Venice.* No.3		27x32? (68.5x81.5?)		
	Ptd. from gondola		RA 58/346/3.6	J.Dillon	
				Sewall W.Barker	C.31.5.75/128.
		220Gns.		Teuton	
51/14	*Sta.Maria della Salute from the Canale della*		15x25 (38x63.5)	Lord Overstone	
	Giudecca. No.4			Martyn Gregory	
	s&d. 41[sic]			Private Colln.	
51/15	Giudecca from off La Grazia. No.5.			—	
51/16	sky, very lovely effect. No.6			—	
51/17	Redentore,stormy sky, evening. No.7			—	
51/18	*The Piazzetta, Venice, with Lion column.*		31½x26½ (80x67.5)		
	Campanile & Ducal Palace. No.8		Manch.1887/586	H.W.F.Bolckow	C.5.5.88/32
		600Gns.		W.Vokins	
				Vavasseur	C.23.4.1910/26
		60Gns.		Sampson	
				Alexr.Webster Beq 1921	
				Aberdeen Art Gallery	
51/19	*Sunset behind Salute, with Greek bombardo.* No.9		6¾x13 (17x33) board	W.Hirons	
	inscr. *Lagunetto* 51				Jolly's Bath
					21.3.1977
				Polak Gallery	
51/20	Distant view of Sta.Elena, Lido &c with trabaccolo		15½x26¼ (39.5x66.5)		
	waiting for the tide: *Sta Elena, Venice, just after*	£50	BI 53/4/1.3	Peto	S.13.12.1984/24
	sunset, looking East. No.10		O & P Johnson.1989		
	s&d. 52		*E.W.Cooke & His*		
	boat inscr. *Il Lagunetto*		*Contemporaries,* No 23		
51/21	*Moonlight S.Giorgio* Painted by candle-light. No.11	£26	9x17 (23x43)	S.Rücker	
51/22	Bibliotheca, new from gondola off Molo. San				
	Marco,Campanile, Ducal Palace, capuchins. No.12.			—	
51/23	Salute from window. No.13			—	
51/24	San Giorgio in Alga from Giudecca. small sunset.				
	No.14			—	
51/25	San Giorgio Maggiore from Molo, evening .No.15			—	
51/26	San Pietro twilight. No.16			—	

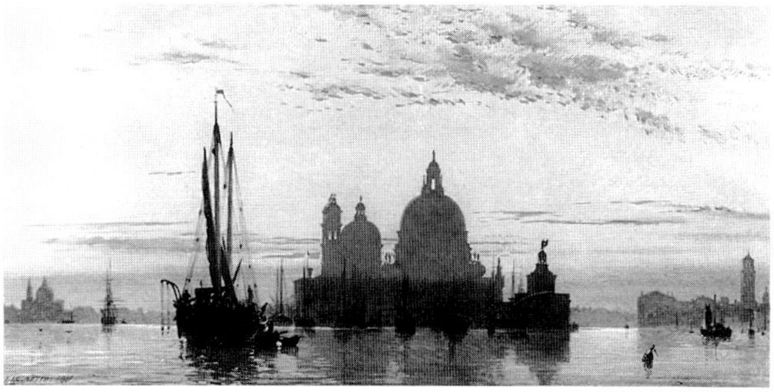

Plate 284. 51/19
Sunset behind the church of the Salute. 1851
Photo courtesy Polak

Year/No.	TITLE/Signed	Price	Size/Exhibited	Collections	Sales
51/27	New large Campanile. No.17			—	
52/1	*'Give me,then, way; This is the Doge's Palace '*		4ft.7x5ft.6 - 55x66		
	[D. Lion picture]		(139.5x167.5)		
			[7½ in (19) frame?]		
		126Gns.	RA 52/405/1.2	Samuel Christy MP	
	less commission £6.18.6		Manch.52 Edin.54		
	as *Doge's Palace & Piazzetta*			Mrs Christie Miller	
			51x40 (129.5x101.5)		
			[*sic*]		C.26.6.1931/158
		22Gns.		Gooden & Fox	
52/2	*Rainy day on the Lagune of Venice*		BI 56/127/3.5	Delafosse	
	s&d. 53	£35	11x17 (28x43)	P.Miller	C.28.1.1972/39
	inscr. on reverse		O & PJohnson		
			E.W.Cooke & his Con-		
			temporaries 1989 No 8		
				Private Colln.	
52/3	San Pietro sunset			—	
52/12	*Bragozzi on the Lagune of Venice near the*		26½x42¼ (67.5x107.5)		
	Giudecca		BI 53/151/3.3	—	C.2.4.1910/126
	s&d. 52,	30Gns.		Vicars	
	inscr. *San Clemente*			Richard Green	
				Agnew	SB.12.7.1977/60
				Private Colln.	
52/13	Bragozzi, evening effect. No.1.				
	Begun Sept.1. Fin. Oct 12.		large block canvas.	—	
52/14	S.Giorgio,evening from Giudecca with Trabaccolo,				
	full moon rising. No.2				
	Begun Sept.1		large canvas	—	
52/15	Topi. S.Giorgio & Salute from window. No 3				
	Begun Sept.10		large canvas	—	
52/16	Salute, begun last year. No.4		26½x41 (67.5x104)		
	San Giorgio Maggiore and the Salute, Venice,	£200	RA 53/293/3.5	W.Bashall, Farington Park,	
	with Fishing craft of Chioggia and the Lagune			Preston	
	inscr. *Cooke Venezia.*			Armstrong heirlooms from	
				Cragside	C.24.6.1910/49
	s&d. 52		26½x42½ (67.5x108)	Agnew	
				Morland Agnew	
			30x42 (76x106.5)		S.9.4.1980/1.
				Owen Edgar Gallery.	
	Extra canvas removed		27x42 (68.5x106.5)	Private Colln.	
52/17	*Vinegia, Vinegia, chi non te vede,ei non te pregia*		26x41 (66x104)		
	[Shakespeare, *Love's Labours Lost,* from Italian	£200	RA53/282/2.5	Jonah Cressingham	
	proverb]. No. 5	£315			C. 27.6.74/129.
	Begun 14 Sept.52			Agnew	
	Sold Mar.53			s&d. 52	
	inscr. *Il Lagunetto*			Sir Francis McClean	CScot.9.6.1994/602
		£44,000		Spink.	
				Private Colln.	
52/18	Small sunset S.Giorgio in Alga. No 6				
	Begun 14th finished 15th.		paper block	—	
52/19	Venice from Lido, near San Servolo, small evening			Private Colln.	
	sky with Topo and palli 25th Sept. No.7		7⅞x13¾ (20x35) dark		
	s.ARA		paper block(narrow)	—	
52/20	Small Stormy effect in Giudecca. No 8		thin paper block.	—	
52/21	Calm silvery effect: Trabaccoli. No 9				
	Begun 28 Sept.		large canvas	—	
52/22	Evening view of Sta Chiara and S.Andrea Apostoli				
	& part of Campo di Marte. No.10		thin paper	—	
52/23	Sunset. Put in Salute & Giudecca on 7th. No.11				
	4th Oct		thick paper	—	
52/24	Sunset from Canale di Giudecca with dark clouds.				
	No 12. Ptd. 6th Oct.		paper block	—	
52/25	S.Giorgio at sunset. Shadow of dome on campanile.		11½x17½ (29x44.5)		
	No 13. Begun 7th Oct		thin paper block		
	cf. 57/18				
52/26	Salute & Dogana, twilight. No 14				
	Begun 9th Oct		small millboard.	—	
52/27	*San Pietro in Castello and the Julian Alps on a*		21x36 (53.5x91.5)		
	November evening. No.15		canvas block		
	Begun 15th Oct.	100Gns.	RA 53/143/1.5	Samuel Christy MP	

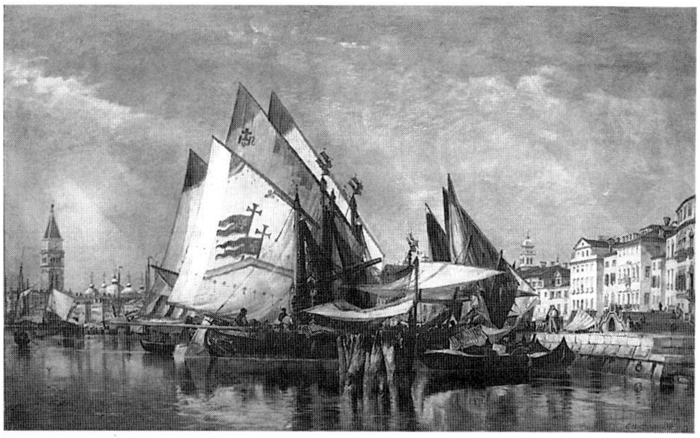

Plate 285. 53/7
The Riva degli Schiavone Venice
The splendour of the painted sails of the vessels lying off the quay within the famous setting was a subject which Cooke returned to several times but never without due regard to their gear and nets – their underlying purpose. Photo courtesy Art Gallery of New South Wales

Year/No.	TITLE/Signed	Price	Size/Exhibited	Collections	Sales
52/28	Small twilight with brigantine. No 16		on paper	R.Armitage	C.8.5.1959/
	s&d. 55			Agnew	
	as *The Armenian Convent*		EWC 70/128	Private Colln.	S.Pulborough1990
52/29	Dogana & Zitelle from our window. No 17				
	Begun 26 Oct		large canvas	—	
52/30	Zecca, Campanile, trees from S.W. No 18				
	Begun 28 Oct		on square large canvas	—	
	cf. 66/1.				
53/7	Venice, boat sails & blue sky. No 1. *Riva degli*	220 Gns.		Anon.	C.5.12.61/276.
	Schiavone		19½x30¾ (49.5x 78)	W.Grapel	C.10.5.84/47
	as *Fishing boats at Venice*			bought in [Graves]	
				W.Grapel	C.4.2.88/96
		140Gns.		Easby	
				New South Wales A.G.	
		£165		Purchased.1888	
53/8	Topo in view of Riva. cf. above			—	
53/9	*Canale of the Giudecca with Turkish vessel;*		18½x29¾(47x75.5)		
	churches of the Gesuati and Redentore	£100	Glasgow Art Union 1855	W.Murdoch, Halifax NS	
	cf. 55/2 & 67/2		EWC 70/125	Sheffield, Graves A.G.	
53/10	Greek bombards off Giardino. No 3		—		
53/11	S.Giorgio & trabaccoli. No		19½x31 (49.5x78.5)	—	C.10-11.7.1922/10
	s&d. 62	31 Gns.		Nicoll	
			20x31 (51x78.5)		S.20.6.1989/25
				Martyn Gregory	
				Private Colln.	
53/12	General view from near La Grazia				
	s&d. 53		11x17½ (28x44.5)	—	
	as *Venice, general view of port*				C.2.4.1910/112
		9Gns.		Roe	
	as *Venetian view looking from the Lagoon*				
	towards the Giudecca		Colnaghi 1959 No.20,		
			ex-Cyril H.Ayscough Colln.		
53/13	General view from Canal of Orfanelli: *A Cool*				
	day in Venice, painted on the spot…		20x35 (51x89)	—	
	s&d. 53				
	as *A Cool day in Venice*		B.I.56/17/1.5	John Morley	
			19½x34 (49.5x83.5)	Agnew.c.1930.	Dreweatts
					22.4.1980/706
				Richard Green	
53/14	S.Servolo			—	
53/15	Salute sunset			—	
53/16	View near Venice with Island of Murano			M.Colnaghi	
	s&d. 53			J.Cressingham, late of	C.27.6.74/118
				the Grove, Carshalton	
				perhaps	P.21.7.1987/-
53/17	Port of Lido and Fort Sant'Andria: *Porto di Lido, the*		19½x34 (49.5x86.5)		
	entrance to the Lagune of Venice from the Adriatic	80Gns.	RA 54/469/3.4	William Herbert Esq	
	s&d. 53	530Gns.		F.T.Turner	C.4.5.78/21
		150 Gns.		Sir H Adair	C.28.2.1903/37
				Sir W Hicking Bt	C.13.6.1919/86
		95Gns.		bought in Hyam	C.11.6.1923/132
	cf. 54/8, anr.version				
	Lake Price photo, 1857 for a third				

Year/No.	TITLE/Signed	Price	Size/Exhibited	Collections	Sales
54/5	*The Molo, Venice*		BI 57/33/1.5	—	
54/6	Sunset, back of S.Giorgio: *Canale degli Orfanelli,*		15x23 (38x58.5)		
	Venice ,Sunset	60G	BI 55/181/3.3	Joseph Miller	
54/7	General view, pifero in centre: *General view of*				
	Venice with pifero waiting for the tide	£220	20x41 (51x104)	Calvert Toulmin	
	as *Midday-Venice*		20x42 (51x106.5)		C.26.6.86/41
		195Gns.		Grundy or Grindley	
	s&d. 1858?		20x41½ (51x105.5)	HMW Oppenheim,	
				Bruton Street	
	as *Mid-day Venice, Pifero waiting for the tide*	60Gns.		Col. Stewart	C.13.6.1913/
	? as *Lagune of Venice*				C.23.2.1940/
		23Gns.	20x42 (51x106.5)	Mitchell	
54/8	*Porto di Lido*		24x48 (61x122)		
			Manch.1854	Bolongaro	
				John Barratt	Capes, Dunn &c
					5.11.89/68.
		£330		Agnew	
	cf. 53/17		EWC 70/4	Bury A.G. from Wrigley	
				family 1954	
54/11	small Salute			—	
55/2	Turkish vessel in Giudecca view cf. 53/9			—	
55/3	*Riva degli Schiavone, Venice, fish arrived.*		RA 55/344/3.4	- Newsham Esq	
			BI 57/181/5.5 ?		
55/4	*S.Giorgio Maggiore, view looking East, effect*		26x42 (66x106.5). 200		
	immediately after sunset	200G	RA 56/489/33.5	Dewhurst	
	s&d. 56				Morrison McChlery
					Glasgow 5.9.1957/60
				Pawsey & Payne	C.10.7.1970/87
				P.Polak	
55/5	Dogana for Alderman Salomons: *The Dogana*		c.26x42 (66x106.5)		
	di Mare, Venice, from the Palazzo Morosini on	200Gns.	RA 56/517/4.5	Lord Mayor Sir David	
	the Grand Canal			Salomons, Bt MP	
55/11	Sky for Charles Warner: *Back of Giudecca and*				
	S.Clemente	£25		Chas. Warner	
55/12	Copy *Façade of San Giorgio Maggiore,a warm*				
	evening		11x17 (28x43)		
	cf. 50/13	£45	BI 56/95/2.5	C.Delafosse	
56/3	Bragozzi running into port: *Chioggian fishing vessels*	400Gns.	41½x66½ (105.5x169)		
	running into the Lagune of Venice on the approach		RA 56/583/5.5	Lord Londesborough	
	of a borasco, or violent squall on the Adriatic			Lady Otho Fitzgerald	
	s&d. 56	£336			C.10.5.84/6.
	inscr. *Il Lagunetto*			Sir Julian Goldsmid	
		£420		Agnew	C. 13.6.96/39.
		20 Gns.	41½x67 (105.5x170)	Sampson	C.1928/
			42x68 (106.5x172.5)	A.C.Nelson	S.4.6.1969/200
				Rutland Gallery	
			EWC 70/3	J.C.H.Bibby	SB.24.6.1982/154
				Mariners' Museum, Newport	
				News Va. USA	
57/3	Sky & sea		18x24 (45.5x61)	—	
			canvas		
57/4	Gesuati church:		small	—	
57/5	*Bragozzi, fishing craft of Venice off the Riva degli*		15x25½ (38x65)	Duncan Dunbar	C.5.5.94/89
	Schiavone			Webly or Welby	
	s&d. 57			Private Colln.	
57/6	Venice:island view. As *Sailing vessels...near*		14¾x25¼ (37.5x64)		C.28.1.1977/46
	Flushing	£2,600		Morton Morris	
	s&d. 57				
	as *Vessels on the Venetian Lagoon*			Spink	
57/7	sky, San Lazzaro				
57/8	*Bragozzi off San Martino, Riva degli Schiavone*		17½x28 (44.5x71)	A.Rogers	
	[Ponte Ca' di Dio]			T.A.Rogers	C.18.4.1913
	s&d. 58	£71.8.0		Roberts	
	'on the spot'		17x29 (43x73.5)		S.31.5.1989/269
		£18,000		Polak	

Year/No.	TITLE/Signed	Price	Size/Exhibited	Collections	Sales
57/9	Near Sta Elisabetta, distant view with S.Pietro in		14x55½ (35.5x141)	W.Duckworth, Orchardleigh	
	Castello and S.Servolo			Park, nr Frome	
	s&d. 59				
	[L] View of Venice in three compartments for cabinet				C.21.9.1987/243
				R.A.Lee	(at Orchardleigh)
			lent for show:		
			E.W.Cooke & his		
			Contemporaries 1989		
			O & P. Johnson. No.28		
57/10	Two topi near Murano: *On the Venetian Lagoon*				
	s&d. 60		16x26 (40.5x66)	—	
	as *Italian Lake scene*				C.23.3.1984/20.
					S.12.10.1986/27
				Martyn Gregory	
				Private Colln.	
57/11	*Sunset on the Lagune of Venice, S.Giorgio in Alga*		26x42 (66x106.5)		
	and the Euganean Hills in the distance		RA 58/557/6.6	Miss Angela (later Baroness)	
	s&d. 57			Burdett Coutts [d.1906]	
			Int.Exhn.1862/653.		C10.7.1922/76
		18 Gns.		Sampson	
	see 52/18				S.20.5. 1992/83
					S.12.11.1992/103
57/12	Brig from off Giardino: long view cf.57/9			—	
57/13	*Venetian fishing craft on the Adriatic shore of Lido.*		25x40 (63.5x101.5)		
	[L] *Bragozzi in the Adriatic*		RA 58/299/2.6	Theo. Burnand	C.25.2.88/62
	s&d. 58	105Gns.		Tooth	
				Lawson	C.15-6.5.91/278
				R.Lawson	C.6.6.1903/32
		125Gns.		Gooden	
		120Gns.		Jos. Gillott	C.30.4.1904/117
		120Gns.		Gooden	C 21.7.1978/155
		£4,500		Richard Green	
				Oscar & Peter Johnson 1979	
			O & P Johnson	Private Colln.	
			E.W. Cooke and His Con-		
			temporaries 1989 No. 5		
57/14	*Boat off Lido*		11¼x17 (28.5x43)	—	
			EWC 70/127	J.N.Mappin	
				Sheffield AG	
57/15	*Sunset on the Lagune,S.Giorgio in Alga & the*		10½x15¼ (26.5x38.5)	Theop.Burnand	C.25.2.88/61
	Euganean Hills	26Gns.		Kitchin?	
	Find. 13.1.58				
57/16	Trabaccoli off Riva:			—	
57/17	Isola S.Pietro, angle of Arsenale:*Bragozzi off the*		11x17 (28x43)	Wallis	
	Arsenale, Venice, Murano in the distance		Birm. 18 58; Bristol 1859;		
	Illust.*I.L.News* 28.1.1869 p 97..		French Gallery 1859.		
57/18	*San Giorgio Maggiore at Sunset*				
	{Shadow of dome on campanile] cf. 52/25				
	s&d. 57		14½x20½ (37x52)		S.12.11.1992/104
57/19	Topo aground near S.Giorgio:*Topo. fishing boat of*		11x15¾ (28x40) [L]		
	the Lagune, aground on Palludi, Venice		11¾x16 (30x40.5)		
	s&d. 58			—	
			Birm.1858; Bristol 1859;		
			French Gallery 1859.		
	Ptd. on spot			Tate Gallery, Chas. Frazer	
				Beq. 1905	
57/20	*Sta.Maria della Salute Venice*		31x26 (78.5x167.5)	H.W.F. Bolckow	
		710Gns.	Manch.1887/652		C 5.5. 1888/31
				H. Brunning	
				National Gallery of Ireland,	
				Beq. Henry Callcott Brunning	
57/21	Morning Venice with Topo: *Early morning on the*				
	Lagune. Presented by the artist		9¾x14 (25x35.5)	A.C.Burnand	C.26.3.92/38.
57/22	Put in Salute and Dogana to sunset sky			—	
57/23	Steps of Giardini: *Bragozzi, fishing craft of Venice,*				
	off the Giardini Pubblici		15x24 (38x61)		
	s. ARA		BI 59/3/1.1	C.F.Lutwidge Esq.	
	Ptd.on spot			O & P.Johnson	
57/27	Bragozzi in a *borasco*		large	[not mentioned again]	
	cf. 56/3 & 73/2				

Year/No.	TITLE/Signed	Price	Size/Exhibited	Collections	Sales
58/1	*San Pietro di Castello evening; Lagune fishing*		15½x26 (39.5x66)	A.Rogers	
	craft waiting for the flood		Manch.58	T.A.Rogers	
	s&d. 58				
	as *Island near Venice, sunset*				C.18.4.1913
		19Gns.		Cassell	
	as *Sunset on the Venetian lagune, S.Giorgio in*				
	Alga and the Euganean Hills in the distance Exh				
	RA 58 (but not this)				
	cf. 57/11, 57/15				S.10.6.1964/251
			14½x25 (37x63.5)	Betts	
	Connoisseur Oct 64. Advt. M.Newman May 66				
58/3	Giudecca at Sunset: Ptd. on spot.			Mrs Boyd	
58/4	*San Giorgio Maggiore, Venice*		15½x26 (39.5x66)	Duncan Dunbar	S.5.5.94/87
	Bought 59.			Webly	
58/5	*On the Lagoon, Venice*				
	s&d. 58		11½x17 (29x43)	—	SBT.12.6.1979/73
	Pair to 63/14			Spink	
				Private Colln.	
58/8	Reserve				
58/19	Glacier du Bossons, Switzerland			—	
58/20	Venice: *Zitella, Redentore & Giudecca*			Geo R.Burnett	C.24.3.60/48
				Agnew	
58/21	Trabaccoli with wood, S.Giorgio & Dogana *Venice*		24x40½ (61x103)		
			RA 59//262/1.3	Arthur Burnand [not his Sale]	
	inscr. *Venezia 59*			Russell Cotes	C.24.11.1916/20
				Cooling	SB 27.3.1973/161
				O & P Johnson	SB 18.3.1980/9
				Private Colln.	
58/22	Gesuati:			—	
58/23	Cloister with tower of S.Lazzaro, Armenian convent				EWC 63/88?
58/24	Sunset sky *Salute and San Giorgio*		12½x22½ (31.5x57)	—	
	s&d. 59			Owen Edgar Gallery	
58/25	Rusconi:*Riva delle Zattere,Venice*		20x31 (51x78.5)	Chas. Warner	
	s&d. 59			Anon	C.10.2.94/60
		95Gns.		Baretter	
				R.Warner	C.2.4.1965
			EWC 70/1	F.Sabin	
				R.W.D.Copeland	SB.20.11.1973/3
					SB.12.7.1977/61
				Owen Edgar Gallery	
58/26	General view: *Venice from the South, off S.Clemente,*		Catalogue *Master*		
	evening		*Paintings from Four*		
			Centuries p.76		
	s&d. ARA 5-		19x42 (48.5x104)		
			Manch.1860	Sir W.Bowman	C.24.3.1893/247
			19½x41½ (49.5x105.5)	Agnew	
				H.F.Makins, Queen's Gate	
			O & P Johnson 1989/4	Private Colln.	
58/27	Moonlight S.Giorgio:			—	
58/28	warm sky:		small	—	
58/29	Campanile and Ducal Palace, with Corvette			—	
58/30	San Marco: interior of Baptistry		25½x17 (65x43)		EWC 63/89
	see also 59/1, begun in England				
58/31	Topo fishing: *Mazzorbo, lagune of Venice*		5x11 (12.5x28)	G.H.Russell	
	sold Dec 64.		panel		
	cf. 59/3			Polak 1960	
58/32	S.Giorgio & Salute from Canale degli Orfanelli, in				
	comet sunset:*Venice with Comet*		£225	20x35 (51x89)	Agnew 1861
	as *Venice Twilight*		19¼x34 (49x86.5)	Charles Skipper	C. 24.5.84/45
	s&d. 'on the spot' 59			Agnew	
		55 Gns.	19½x34½		
			(49.5x87.5)	Leggatt	C.4.4.1930/
				M.Bernard	
	Advts. *Burlington* June 1966,		Arden Gallery,		
	&..*Apollo* Sept 1970		Henley in Arden		
58/33	Mountains and S.Pietro from S.Lazzaro, under the				
	wall:			—	
58/34	*Painted in my Gondola*				EWC 80/107

Year/No.	TITLE/Signed	Price	Size/Exhibited	Collections	Sales
59/1	*Interior of San Marco, Venice from the Baptistry*		25½x17 (65x43)		
	s.		RA 64/635/4.4	—	
	as above, also *Looking across the nave to the*				
	Chapel of the Crucifix	285Gns.			EWC 63/89
			Whitechapel,		
			St.Judes 1887/11		
			lent Sir Wm Drake		
	cf. 58/30			Mrs K A V Waddilove	
		£500		McInnes	C15.10.1976/119
59/3	Copy of small picture of topo fishing with circular				
	net [58/31]				
	Sunrise on the Lagune, Venice		17½x23 (44.5x58.5)	W.Agnew	
	as *Sunrise near Mazzorbo Lagune Venice* from old				
	label on reverse.				C.14.7.1924/
		18Gns.	17½ x23½ (44.5x59.5)	Sampson	
				J.Collins, Bideford 1988	
	s&d. 60		18x24 (45.5x61)		
	cf. 57/21 Mr Burnand's *Morning Venice with Topo*				
	[D. April 59]				
59/5	Venice, Ducal Palace*: Bella Venezia*		35x54 (89x137)		
			RA 60/102/2.5	Arthur Burnand	C.26.4.92/58
	s&d. 60				Agnew
59/6	*The Piazzetta of St Mark, Venice.* (Bibliotheca with		31½x26¾ (80x68)		
	Column of S.Teodoro, Salute, Dogana & part of		RA 60/422/4.5		
	Palazzo Ducale)		Manch.87/586	H.W.F. Bolckow.	C.5.5.88/33
					W.Vokins
59/7	*Venice from San Giorgio with trabaccolo*:[D] Sal.				
	Dog. & part of Duc. Pal. 'Sky copied from				
	Lady Hope's'.(50/7-)		Large		
60/3	View of Venice between tiers of Trabaccoli:[L]	£175	17½x29 (44.5x73.5)	W.Agnew	
	Porto Venezia, *Crosses and banners on sails*	£178/10-		Knowles	C.5.11.61/1059
	s&d. 61			Owen	
				Sir C.Booth	C.13.3.97/19
		115Gns.		C.T. Harris of Denmark Hill	
	Port of Venice with Trabaccoli or wide(sic)				
	[wine] vessels of the Adriatic				C.27.11.1913/79
		32Gns.		Campbell	
		42Gns.	16½x28¾ (42x73)	Visct.Hambleden	C.6.4.1916/
				Red Cross Charity Sale	
		44Gns.		Acland.	
	as *Boats in Lagoon*				
	as *Shipping at anchor...*			Owen Edgar Gallery 1984	CNY.15.5.1995/374
				Richard Green	
62/4	*Sunset: Lagune of Venice.*	20Gns.	7½x14 (19x35.5)		EWC 63/73
				Wyatt	
				Standen 1937	

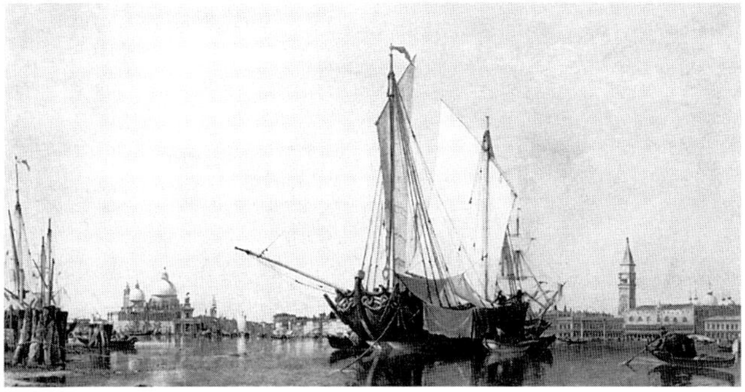

Plate 286. 59/7
Venice from San Giorgio with Trabaccolo
On his first visit in 1850 the artist was clearly fascinated by the characteristic *trabaccolo da trasporto,* here posed against the famous skyline. The awning or sail hung overside is lettered *Il Lagunetto,* his chosen alias. An earlier picture, 50/7, his first completed Venetian subject, is almost identical. Photo courtesy Thos.Agnew & Son

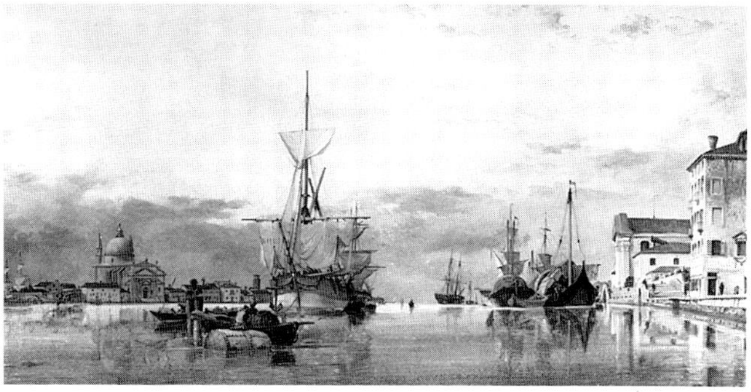

Plate 287. 62/19
Shipping on the Canale della Giudecca
Sanctified by the Churches of the Redentore, left, and the Gesuati on the Fondamenta delle Zattere, right, this picture nevertheless shows the artist excited by work in progress. Sheers rigged on the sailing vessel in the centre are probably to replace a lower mast. There are some very miscellaneous craft.beyond and an unprepossessing riveted mooring buoy near at hand; who else but Cooke would have given significance to such an object? His gondola was presumably anchored. Photo courtesy Arthur Ackermann & Peter Johnson

Year/No.	TITLE/Signed	Price	Size/Exhibited	Collections	Sales
62/11	*Squèro, vessel careening.* No.1 [Diary]				
	s&d. 63		10½x17½ (26.5x44.5)	Private Colln.	
62/12	San Pietro di Castello. No.2 [Diary]			—	
	as *Venetian Lagoon at Sunset.*				
	s&d. 62		11x17¾ (28x45)	Hazlitt Gooden & Fox	
62/13	San Gregorio. No 3 [Diary]			—	EWC 80/114
62/14	*Venice from squero near Giardini pubblici.*				
	No.4 [Diary]				C.23.5.68/119
				Jones Lloyd	
62/15	Dogana di Mare, in fog. No.5. [Diary]				
62/16	Evening sky San Clemente *Venetian Lagoons,sunset.*			—	
	No. 6 [Diary]		7¾x11⅛ (19.5x 28)		
	s&d. 62			Manchester City A.G.1917/206	
	Illustrated *American Light, The Luminist Movement*				
	1850-1875 National Gallery of Art,Washington DC.				
	1980, No.235 as *E.B.Cooke- On the Nile*				
62/17	Venice, general view from San Servolo. No.7 [Diary]				
	s,d&i. 62.			Polak Gallery	Jolly's 21.3.1977
62/18	*Dogana di Mare & San Giorgio Maggiore* No.8		6½x12¾ (16.5x32.5)		
	[Diary]		10¾x17¾ (27.5x 45)		SB22.2.1972/17
	s&d. 63			O & P Johnson	
62/19	*Canale della Giudecca* with part of Gesuati &				
	Redentore. No.9 [Diary]				
	s&d. 63		10¾x17¾ (27.5x45)	O & P Johnson	SB22.2.1972/17
62/20	Canal of S.Clemente,sunset.*Venetian Sunset after*		11x17¾ (28x45)	—	
	Rain (frame title) No.10 [Diary]		10¼x16½ (26x42)	Sir Bruce W. Seton	
	s&d. 62.	20Gns.		Vesley	C.2-4.3.1912/97
				R.Trehearne	X.5.10.1973/165
		£787		Hartnoll & Eyre	
	Ilust.*Country Life*9.5.1974		Saffron Galleries 1974		
			10x17 (25.5x43)		SB.12.12.1978/7
	as *Sunset on Lagune*		10¼x16 (26x40.5)		C.24.10.1980/75
	as *View on Giudecca with Redentore beyond*				C.5.11.1982/43
			11x17¾ (28x45)		
			paper on canvas		
				Owen Edgar Gallery	
	Catalogue *Master Ptgs from Four Centuries* p76-7.				
	[Captions transposed]			Private Colln.	
	Note *Venice, evening after a day of storms*				
			10½x17 (26.5x43)	Mrs T.S.Kennedy,	
				Wetherby	C.26.7.1912/14.
		8½Gns.		Mitchell	
62/21	Sunset Salute No.11		small		
62/22	*Trabaccolo waiting for the tide off the Armenian*				
	Convent, Lagune of Venice, Sunset. No.12 [Diary]		7½x15 (19x38).	—	
	on spot s&d. 62	£35	BI 63/119/1.2		Sale —-/6
					S.22. 3.1977/68
			7x14½(18x38)		S.11.12.1979/91
					S.17. 6.1980/14
					S.11. 6.1986/36
			Oscar & Peter Johnson:		
			E.W.Cooke & his		
			Contemporaries 1989,		
			No. 26		
62/23	Sunset Salute. No.13		small	—	
62/24	View from near San Servolo. No.14. [Diary]		small	for Thos. Wyatt	
62/25	small sunset, rays upwards. No.15 [Diary]				
62/26	*The Arrival of Otho, Ex-King of Greece, at Venice,*		19½x37½ (49.5x95)		
	29 October 1862, in H.M.Corvette Scylla 21 guns,		BI 66/1/1.3	—	
	Captain Rowley Lambert RN. The view comprises			C.J.Northcote	
	the Riva degli Schiavone and the Giardini			C.J.Palmer	C.16.5.68/101
	Pubblici, Lido & S.Servolo. No.16. {Diary]	252 Gns.		Agnew	
		24 Gns.		Mrs Rachel Beer	C.22.7.1927/
	engr. *Art Journal* 1862			Cooling	
	as *The Arrival*				
62/27	Sunset back of Giudecca with churches of Zitelle				
	and Redentore. No.17. [Diary]		long picture		
62/28	Sunset. No.18. [Diary]		large		

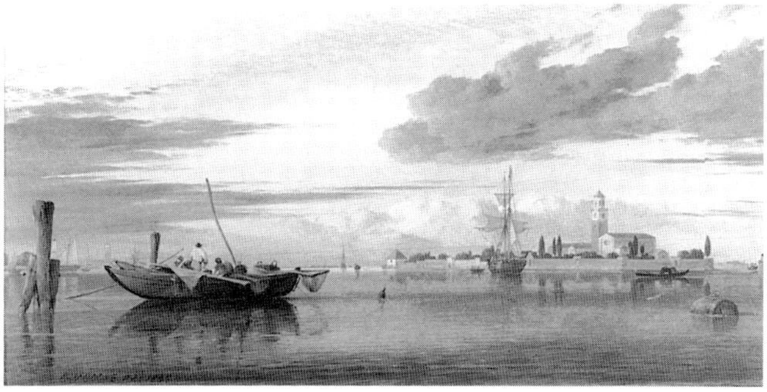

Plate 288. 64/18
Isola della Certosa, evening Photo courtesy Sotheby's

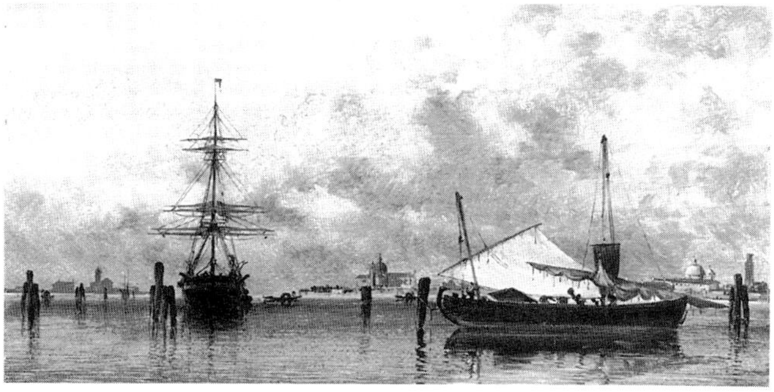

Plate 289. 66/10
Boats on a Venetian Lagoon
An on-the-spot evening study from the south, one of many and now impossible positively to identify. Cf. watercolour Plate 224.
Photo courtesy Spink & Son Ltd

Year/No.	TITLE/Signed	Price	Size/Exhibited	Collections	Sales
62/29	*Armenian Convent, San Lazzaro from off Sta*		10¼x16½(26x42)		EWC 63/88
	Elisabetta. No.19. [Diary]				S.Pul. 1990
	s&d. 62			Martyn Gregory	
				Private Colln.	
62/30	Sunset. No.20. [Diary]		small	—	
63/1	Copy sky		small	—	
63/3	Salute and sunset Dogana: *The Salute, at sunset, Venice*		25x41 (63.5x104)		
			RA63/585/3.3	Sir W. Bowman	
			Leeds 68		C.24.3.93/246
		95Gns.	26x42½ (66x108)	King	
		18Gns.	25½x42 (65x106.5)	Sampson	C.6.4.1916/76
63/7	Venice, Ponte della Veneta Marina			—	
63/8	Luminous evening cloud			Geo. Gurney	C.17.3.83/216
		95Gns.		Agnew	
63/9	*Venice*		10½x17¼ (27x44)	—	
	s&d 63			F.P.Murray, Eaton Sq.	C.30.7.1915/
		13Gns.		Meinertzhagen	
63/10	Buildings to north of Canale della Giudecca				
63/11	Gesuati and Riva looking E.to San Giorgio Maggiore			—	
	s.		11x17½ (28x44.5)	Justin Lang	P.EA.1994/539
63/12	General view off Sta. Marta *S.Nicolo, Venice*				
	s&d. 64		15x27 (38x68.5)		SB.27.6.1978/161
	as *Venetian scene with Merchantman at anchor*			Richard Green	SB.16.6.1981/74
63/13	*Euganean Hills & the Lagune of Venice: Trabaccolo*				
	waiting for the tide, Sunset				
	inscr. on rev. s & d 64		11x17 (28x43)	Martyn Gregory	
63/14	Evening sky looking W. out of Giudecca, with raft.		11x17 (28x43) paper	Mrs Thomas	SBT.12.6.1979/73
	s&d. 64			Richard Green	
	Pair to 58/5				C.11.6.1993/153
63/15	Porto Franco with part Scuola della Salute.		16x25 (40.5x63.5)	Capt D.Galton RE	P.24.6.1971/59
	San Marco,Bacino & Riva	£3,000		Polak Gallery	
	s&d. 64			Private Colln. Australia	
63/16	*Euganean Hills and the Lagune of Venice,sunset,*				
	low water	40Gns.	BI 64/36/2.2	?Veitch	
63/17	Sunset.S.Pietro di Castello for			- Watkins (Photographer)	
64/8	Gambart's Venice [L] from Giudecca			—	
64/10	Sky copy of Venice sunset.			—	
64/13	Huge dark cloud.			—	
64/14	Copy of Salute sky, lent by Rawdon Brown			—	
64/15	Venice on millboard:		7¼x10¼ (18.5x26)	—	C.1.6.1984/24
	Brig at L. church at R.			—	
64/16	*Santa Maria della Salute with the Giudecca beyond*		11x17 (28x43)	—	
	at Sunset.		paper on canvas		C.26.11.1982/246
	s.RA				P.25.7. 1987/
				Owen Edgar Gallery	
64/18	Copy of sky, Sta Elena.*Isola della Certosa, in the*				
	Venetian Lagoon				C.13.5.1977/11
	s&d. 65		12x18½ (30.5x47)	Owen Edgar Gallery	
			12½x19 (31.5x48.5)		
			paper on canvas		SNY.16.2.1994/389

Year/No.	TITLE/Signed	Price	Size/Exhibited	Collections	Sales
66/1	*The Campanile, Zecca, part of San Marco and the*		33x26 (84x66)		
	Giardini Reale, Venice		RA 66/338/3.5	—	
		£892	34x26 (86.5x66)	Mrs E.Clarke	C.28.11.1972/103
				Appleby	
				Private Colln.	
66/1A	Sunset, Venice		6¾x10 (17x25.5)	C.T.Harris, Denmark Hill	C.27.11.1913/80.
		11 Gns.		Merton	
			6½x9¾ (16.5x25)	W.E.Vickers, Ashley Gds.	
					C.27.4.1914/-
		6Gns.		Newman	
66/10	*Boats on a Venetian lagoon*		11x17 (28x43)		S.Chester
					19.10.1989/315
	s&d. 66			Spink	
67/2	*Canal of the Giudecca, Venice; churches of the*				
	Orfanelli, Gesuati, Zitella & SS. Redentore		32½x55 (82.5x139.5)		
	s&d. 67		RA67/223/1.3.	Geo.Boulton	
			35x54 (89x137)	J.Grant Morris	C.23.4.98/75
		£315		Ashbee	
			EWC 70/7	H.S.Ashbee Beq.1902	
			35½ x 55 (90x139.5)	Tate Gallery	
67/6	*On Lagune of Venice, Evening before bad weather*		11x17 (28x43)	[D] Jas. Veitch	
				Royal Albert Memorial	
				Museum Exeter in aid of	
				Sir H Veitch Trust	C.22.10.1954/56
				Curtis	
	cf. 69/3		11¼x17 (28.5x43)		C.5.5.1960/128
		£126		Agnew	
				Private Coll.	
67/7	Topo and vessels, sunset: *A topo or Lagune fishing*				
	boat, Venice		RA70/266	—	
67/8	Gondola.			—	
69/3	*On the Lagune, Venice; evening before bad weather*		25x42 (63.5x106.5)		
	s&d. 69		RA69/885/4.4	W J Lancaster	C.9.5.70/95
				ditto	C.29.4.82/110.
		£378		Broadhead [Leeds dlr.]	
			25¼x42¼ (64x107.5)	Mrs E.Ackroyd	C.10.10.1958/
		£157		Cooling.	C.10.2.1961/98
		100 Gns.		Leger	
			OPJ 1989/27	Private Colln.	
	cf. 67/6				
70/1	Venice by moonlight- *Venice 'The moon is up and*				
	yet it is not night.' Byron: *Childe Harold* IV		RA70/87/1.6	—	
70/2	Hazy day, Lagune of Venice			—	
73/2	*Venetian fishing craft (Bragozzi) caught in a*		34¾x54⅞ (89x139.5)		
	'Borasca' in the Adriatic, off Fort Sant Andrea		RA73/310/1.3.	Agnew	
	s & d 73			H.A. Brassey	C.23.2.1901/140
		220Gns.		Lister	
				Col.R.Montgomery 1906	
				Walker AG- Liverpool.	
			Victorian vision of Italy,		
			Leicester 1968/103		
			EWC 70/8		

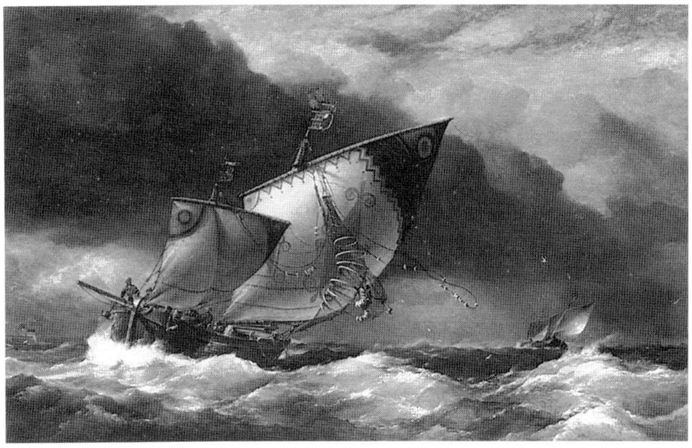

Plate 290. 73/2
Bragozzo caught in a borasco
He had previously painted the flight of the boats before the storm, but here a further stage in the encounter is depicted with dramatic force. See Plate 141. Photo courtesy Trustees of the National Museums on Merseyside, Walker Art Gallery.

Year/No.	TITLE/Signed	Price	Size/Exhibited	Collections	Sales
75/6	Sunset Lagune		small	A.W.Thorold,	
				Bishop of Rochester	
77/2	Venice, Salute from balcony			—	
77/3	Grand canal & Giardini.		—		
77/4	To Palli off Scuola della Salute including Dog. & Duc.		—		
77/5	Ducal Palace and Campanile			—	
77/6	Two Bragozzi at anchor in Porto. *The Giudecca*		10½x17½ (26.5x44.5)		EWC 80/113
	s&d. 77			De Casseres Colln.	
					C. 28.3.1956/15
77/7	Evening sky.				—
77/8	Zitelle, old garden wall				EWC 80/109
77/14	*Porto di Venezia, stormy effect*				—
	s&d. 78		10½x18 (26.5x45.5)		S. 1992/
78/18	*Torcello, evening* with bridge.		small panel		
			RA 79/585/3.3	Sir W.Siemens	

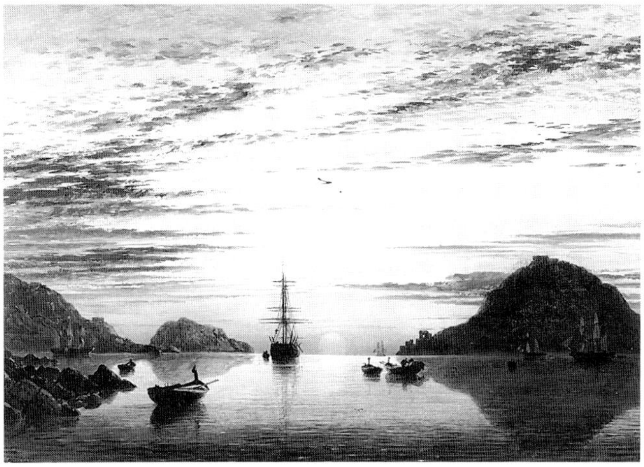

Plate 291. 60/10

Sunset in the Bay of Cartagena

A most wonderful sunset moved him also to paint a larger version for the 1862 RA. Photo courtesy Arthur Ackermann & Peter Johnson

SPAIN AND MOROCCO

Year/No.	TITLE/Signed	Price	Size/Exhibited	Collections	Sales
60/4	Palms and cloister of Carmine. Valencia		—		
60/5	Alicante with palm				
60/6	*Alicante*		14x22 (35.5x56)	W.Agnew 1863 [L]	
	s&d. 60		14½x23 (37x58.5)		C.25.5.1956/170
	Ptd. on spot	30Gns.	EWC 70/10	Agnews	
				Private Colln.	
60/7	*The moon rising behind the rock of Alicante*				EWC 65/218
		25Gns.		Whitehouse	C.16.5.68/79
60/8	Castle cliff from Terrao: *The Rock and fortress*		25x41 (63.5x104)		
	of Alicante; east coast of Spain		RA 62/501/2.5	Sir John Pender	
		235Gns.	25x42 (63.5x106.5)		C.11.2.1955/50
60/9	Cartagena. Rocks and castle, Sta Lucia: *Santa*		15x24 (38x61)		
	Lucia, Port of Cartagena; East coast of Spain		BI 66/245/3.3	George Boulton 1865	C.13.12.1902/53
	s&d. 65	30Gns		H.Newton	
			14½x22¾ (37x58)	Sir H.K Newton Bt 1930	SB.27.10.1978/49
			15½x24 (39.5x61)		C.24.10.1980/77
					C.8.5.1981/89
	?Anr version sd 66			Spink	S.24.6.1982/163
				Hal O'Nians	
60/10	Most wonderful sunset: *Sunset in the Bay of*		7½x10½ (19x26.5)	W.Agnew 1861	
	Cartagena			H.Harvey Frost/Hilda Frost	
	s&d. 60		EWC 70/25	Maurice Bradshaw	
				b i .	C.18.10.1974/33
					C.14.5.1976/179
					B.31.3.1977/178
60/11	Green and gold and purple. *Bay of Cartagena*		17x26 (43x66)		C.1.2.1908/
				Lister	
60/12	Sunset Muralla			—	

Year/No.	TITLE/Signed	Price	Size/Exhibited	Collections	Sales
60/13	Rock & Fortress of Alicante				EWC 63/90
	cf. 60/8			[D] Sir George Lee 1868	
61/1	Sunset Cartagena: *Sunset, Bay of Cartagena; the*		26x42 (66x106.5)		
	Island of Escombrera in the distance		RA62/659/5.5	W.Marshall	
	s&d. Jan 15 61	310Gns			C.8.11.61/1601
		240Gns		J.Marshall	C.28.5.81/41
		230Gns		Vokins	C.5.3.87/161
				O & P Johnaon	
61/2	Cartagena (deep water)[L].		25½x41 (65x104)	- Hill Esq	
61/3	Alicant with palm, new				
61/4	Alicante sunset			—	
			10½x15 (26.5x38)	Sampson	C.24.2.1921/131
61/5	Cartagena		very small	Agnew	
62/2	*The Bay of Tangier, Morocco; the mountains of*		41x65 (104x165)		
	Spain and Gibraltar in the distance		RA62/589/3.5	C. P. Matthews	C.6.6.91/16.
		210 Gns.	42½x66 (108x167.5)		
			EWC 70/5	Salford AG. Pres.1904	
				Sir George.Agnew	
63/2	*Catalan Bay on the East side of the Rock of*		42½x66½ (108x169)		
	Gibraltar; the African coast, Ceuta, and the		RA63/415/2.3	E.Gambart [?]	
	Mountains of Atlas in the distance...		Int.Exhn 1873/743	C.P.Matthews	C.6.6.91/15
				Haigh	
		310Gns		Henson [Graves.Sales]	
				Christopher Russo	
				Private Colln.	
63/4	Bay of Tangier with Apes Hill & Gibraltar in				
	distance				
	see 62/2; a second version or repaint?				
64/3	*Ruins of a Roman bridge.of about the second or*		41x66 (104x167.5)		
	third century, near Tangier, north-western		RA 64/466/3.4		
	Barbary The caravan in early morn, is proceeding			Earl Grosvenor	
	to Tangier from Fez in Morocco. In the distance			Duke of Westminster	
	the Spanish coast, Gibraltar &c.		Leeds 1868/1467	p.w.u.	
67/3	Moorish patio with palms			—	

EGYPT

Year/No.	TITLE/Signed	Price	Size/Exhibited	Collections	Sales
74/1	Egypt. Sunset sky, pyramid and palms				EWC 80/89
74/2	Grey calm sky				
74/3	Steamer on a strip of blue sky, little slip of a subject				
74/4	Stratified cliffs				
74/5	New sky, boat: *On the Nile*				S.15.5.1968
	s&d. 64 [*sic*]	£580	14¾x23½ (37.5x59.5)	Fine Art Society	
74/6	new pic. boat (half)				EWC 80/118
74/7	ditto				EWC 80/120
74/8	Sunset and rocky hill				EWC 80/79
74/9	Karnak sunrise				
74/10	Gezereh				
74/11	Sakir and tall wall				EWC 80/80
74/12	sunset				
74/13	ditto				
74/14	Kom Ombos from sand bank, evening effect				EWC 80/84
74/15	'Three skies on grey paper: preparation'				
74/16	sky				
74/17	sky				
74/18	Scene from deck.*Egyptian pigeon-houses*				
	(7th March, off Mutaneh)				EWC 80/82
	s.		10½x 16½ (26.5x42)		Ewbank,Woking
	as *Middle Eastern river landscape*				9.2.1995/251
				Park Gallery	
					S.6.11.1995/224
74/19	Sheikh's tomb				EWC 80/88
74/20	Young doum palm in Smith's garden				EWC 80/85
74/21	Cactus pilastro				
74/22	Sky in Gebelayn				EWC 80/90
74/23	*The Pylons at Karnak: Theban Mountains in the*				EWC 80/83
	distamce		5¼x13¾ (13.5x35) paper		C.30.6.1981/114
				Agnew	
				Colln Paul Mellon,	
				Upperville.Va	

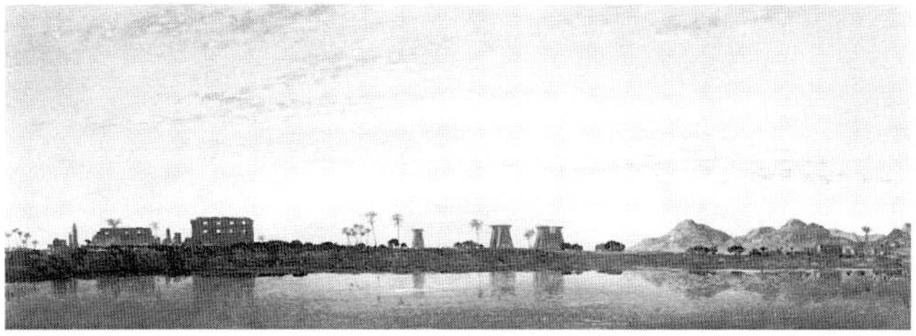

Plate 292. 74/24
Pylons at Karnak, the Theban mountains in the distance
Photo courtesy Agnews. Paul Mellon Collection, Upperville, Virginia, USA.

Year/No.	TITLE/Signed	Price	Size/Exhibited	Collections	Sales
74/24	*Karnak, Pylon and Propylon looking West*		8x15 (20.5x38)	Private Colln. USA.	
74/25	Philae, sunset sky				EWC 80/87
74/26	sunset				EWC 80/74
74/27	sunset				EWC 80/76
74/28	Cairo				EWC 80/119
74/29	Luxor				EWC 80/86
75/1	Nile				EWC 80/72
75/2	Narrow panel sunset sky.				
75/4	*The Mountains and Plain of Denderah on the Libyan bank of the Nile; Doum and date palms...* (Reproduced as colour cover for *Florence Nightingale's travels in Egypt*		27x54 (68.5x137) RA 75/443/3.3	Mathaf Gallery	
76/1	*The ruins of Kom-Ombos on the right bank of the Nile, illuminated by the western afterglow* Illust. *Academy Notes* H.Blackburn 1876	?90Gns.	26x54 (66x137) RA 76/79/1.4	Partington	EWC 80/143
76/3	Study of new sky: *Pyramids,sunset* (Storks at L., dahabeah at R.) s&d. 76. inscr. on rev.		5$\frac{3}{8}$x11$\frac{1}{2}$ (13.5x29) panel	Jonathan Peckover, Wisbech Spink	C.26.5.1972/117 C.6.5.1977/201
76/4	*Philae "the Beautiful" at early morn, looking south* as *Ruins of Philae*	£336	RA 76/493/3.4	Gellatly	EWC 82/151
76/6	*Date Palms and Bananas in the gardens of the Khedive's palace, Gezeereh, opposite Boulak, Cairo.* see 74/10	54Gns.	RA 77/354/3.4 Newcastle 1878; Royal Albert Hall 1879.		EWC 80/139
76/7	Thorold's picture. Thebes			— ? A.W.Thorold, Bishop of Rochester	
76/8	Theban mountains cf. 76/7		small	—	
78/3	Kom Ombo			— (cf. 74/14 & 76/1)	

Appendix 3

RECORD OF WATERCOLOURS

Cooke MSS No.33. Notebook, 9in. x 7½in. (23cm x 19cm) bound – leather spine, marbled boards, plain paper watermarked T. Barratt 1828.

There are 'thumbnail' ink sketches of Nos. 1-82, see Plate 35.

In March 1832 Mr Wm Rosier had of me the following drawings on cards & mounted – the whole of which he had handsomely framed and hung in his drawing room.

1. Old Stairs Blockade Station
2. Boat and figures
3. Ditto Shower of Rain (Newhaven)
4. Kemp Stairs
5. Sunset – galley coming in
6. Snow scene – ice &c
7. Snow scene – sportsman –
8. Composition. Landscape Trees &c
9. Portsmouth (man of war cutter)
10. Moonlight – Putney
11. Twilight river scene – craft &c
12. Sunset rocks Isle of Wight.

W.R. paid me for 10 of these 19 March 1832.

On 16th June 1832 presented W.Rosier with
13.Drawing of Grove House Woodford framed and glazed.
14 Presented him also with a portrait of himself, which he framed.

Presented the following drawings on different occasions -

14+Sepia sketch of vessels unloading at a Pier on cream cold. card – made about the Summer of 1832. Sold Mr Sheepshanks July 2nd 1835 for £1.1.0

15. Coast scene– figures — Miss Bennett.
16. Do. Do. — Richd. Rosier Esq.,
17. Do. horse and figures in — Miss Gillham's album.
18. Recollection of Bonnngton. Pilot boats — Miss E.Gillham's album
19. Coast scene — Miss Whiskin's album
20. Whimsicals, pen & ink. — Miss Whiskin ditto.
21. Ditto. Do. — Miss S Whiskin Do.
22. Snow scene Do. Do.
23. Newhaven — Edgar Breffitt.
23+ Barge aground, Blackwall Reach. — Colnaghi Pd. £3.3.0
24. Coast scene — Miss E.Breffitt
24+ Small drawg on card, Coast scene & figures. — Pres. Mrs Austen on 27 Nov 1833.
25. Collier. Storm coming on. Sk. — Presented to Mr R.Rosier.
26. Sunset. Spithead — Miss Annie Rosier.
27. Do. Coast scene — Miss E Rosier
28. Thames fishermen. Rainbow Battersea, drawn 19th March 1833, now framed in Parlour. A copy of this larger presented to R.Rosier on his Birthday and mine, 27 March 1833.
29. Gypsies 4th June Wimbledon Common &
30. Sea view, cutter &c. — Miss Jane Loddiges.
31. Sea view 6th June. — Mr W.Callow

About 20 very small cold. drawings on card as vignettes to friends assembled for my birthday at Barnes June 1832.

32. Large drawing of Grove House Woodford to Mr R.Rosier as some acknowledgement of his active services as our Hony. Secy.
33. Puckaster Cove, I. of Wight. Drawn April 19 1833.
34. Hay boats off Greenwich 11th April 1833

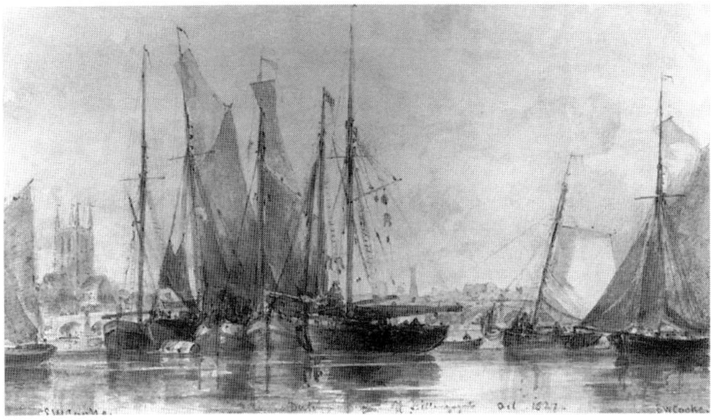

Plate 293. Watercolour
Off Billingsgate Oct. 1827
The group of small fishing boats resembles the plate *Scotch Smacks – Thames* in *Shipping & Craft.* Beyond, the tower of St Saviour's (now Southwark Cathedral) on the south bank. It is commendable work from a sixteen-year-old. Photo courtesy Martyn Gregory

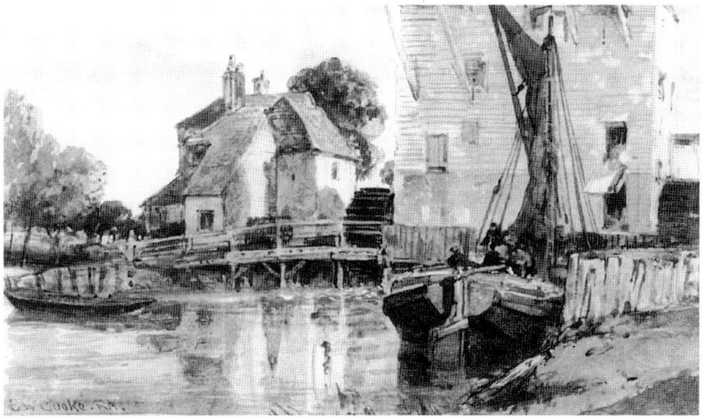

Plate 294. Watercolour
The Mill at Moulsey near Hampton Court. 22nd July 1829
From Barnes he went up river too, looking for subjects – barges – both commercial and ceremonial, at Hampton Court, Richmond, Twickenham, Kew.This drawing was in his 1865 sale, Lot 95 or Lot 133. Photo courtesy Spink & Son Ltd. Private Collection

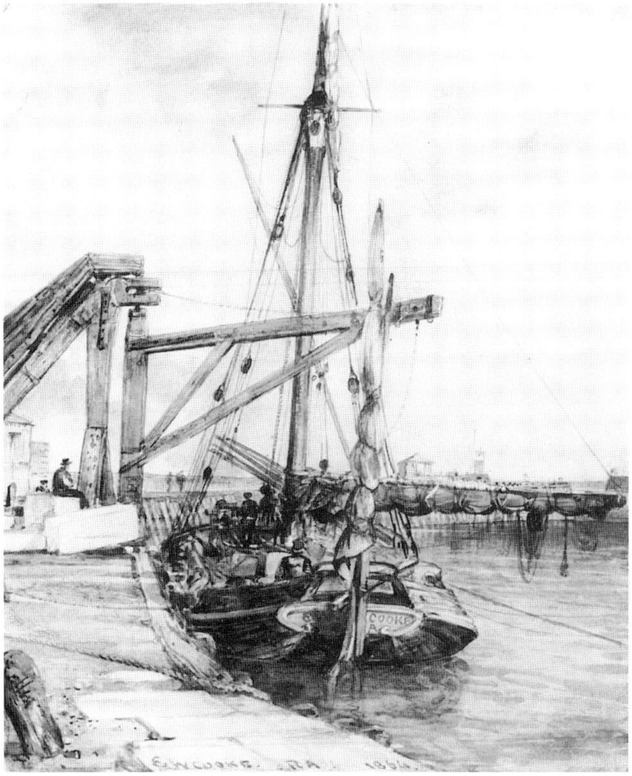

Plate 295. Watercolour
Timber barge Dover
Drawn in 1830 and signed for his studio clearance sale of 1865, this pleasant little commercial dock scene is full of interest and close observation. Photo courtesy Martyn Gregory. Private Collection

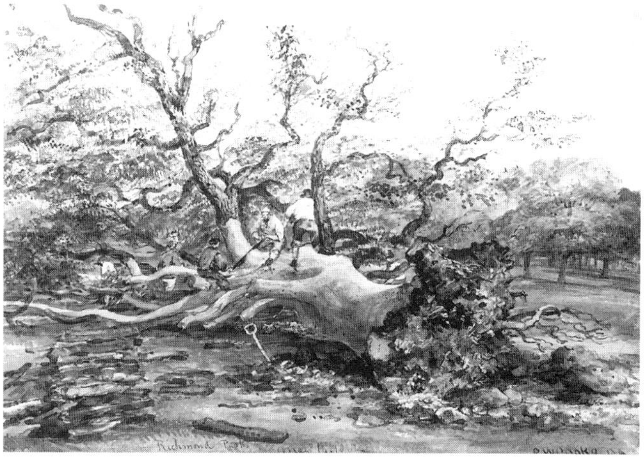

Plate 296. Watercolour
Fallen Oak, Richmond Park
Dated 14th May 1832(?). Probably Lot 2 in his sale of 1865 as *Felling an Oak, Richmond.* Photo courtesy Martyn Gregory

35. The Temeraire, 90, off Sheerness with the Admiral in his gig &c. 1st July 1833
36. Hay boat Chatham - and men of war with Rainbow & stormy effect 5th July.
37. Barges or "tide-waiters" drying Sails (calm) off Bombproof battery Medway, 8 July
On the 7th July 1833 Mr Rosier introduced me to Benjamin Austen Esq., & on 9th July I took 3 drawgs. to him – viz the Temeraire, Puckaster Cove and Hayboats Chatham – & he paid me £14.14.0
On the 11th July Mr Moon had (thro' R.R[osier]) No 34 the Hay boats Greenwich and 37 tide waiters for £6.6.0
38. Fishing boats with trolling nets on the Sands at Hastings – group of fishermen, horses &c drawn 24 July 1833. sold at Sale May 5th 1834 for £4.6.0 framed.
39. Dutch Schuyts off Yarmouth – rough sea. Mr Colnaghi bought it with 23+ for £3.3.0 each.
40. Made copy of my father's beautiful drawing of Hythe by Turner – finished it on 10th August 1833.
Started on 27th Aug. 1833 to Portsmouth on my way to Normandy. Retd on the 17th Oct & made about 300 sketches, including figures, baskets &c.
41. The first drawg. I made on my return from Normandy – entrance to Havre with a French vessel coming out. 8 ins by 5 [20cm x 12.5cm]. Ordered by Messrs. Arch. Delivered to him 20th Nov. (Finished 30 Oct)
42. Grand Quai, Rouen. Looking toward Mont St Katherine. 8 ins by 5 [20cm x 12.5cm]. Made for Messrs. Arch. Sent home 20 Nov. (Finished 7th Nov.)
42 [*sic*]. Trouville fishing boat in a calm, distant view of Havre. 8 ins by 5 [20cm x 12.5cm] for Messrs. Arch. Sent home 20 Nov. (Finished 1 Nov)
43. Dieppe Harbour, morning with fishing boats drying sails & crucifix &c. 8 by 5 [20cm x 12.5cm]. Arch (26 Nov) 44. Rue Guillaume Lion & Rue des Arpents Rouen with tower of St Ouen in distance – soldiers & figures. 8 by 5 [20cm x 12.5cm] for Arch. Sent 20 Nov.
45. Tower at Honfleur with fishing boat aground, low water. For Arch deld.20 Nov.
45+ Copy of 45 larger, made for Mr Jas Baily with 56, 57. He paid £3.3.0 each for them.
46. View on the Seine near Oissel. Drawn 28th Oct and presented to Mr Austen 5th Dec. Twilight effect.
47. A small drawg. of Sunset, vessels in a calm near Havre – the sky from nature drawn 26 Nov. Destroyed X
48. Effect of rain, sky sketched from nature at Barnes 17 Dec.The landscape is flattish country near Neufchatel, mills &c. Sold to Tiffin for £2.2.0 on the 2nd July 1835.
49. Entrance to the port of Havre with a Trouville fishing boat going in – shortening sail &c sea being rough (sketch taken on 31st August the morning after the terrific storm and gale) drawn at the latter end of November – size 16 ins by 11 [40.5cm x 30cm]. Mr Austen purchased this and ordered a companion to [be] made to it of Ramsgate viz. No.
50. Ramsgate Pier and lighthouse – Gale coming on. East Indiaman, Calais lugger and Pilot-boat entering the harbour– very stormy effect – 16 by 11 ins [40.5cm x 30cm] in size. Drawn Dec 4th 1833. Made another 53 and much improved it.
51. Pont Neuf, Quai de Paris & Ile de la Croix Rouen. Noonday effect. 12 ins by 9 [30.5cm x 23cm] (from a sketch)
52. Another view of the same Bridge with a curious effect of light. Stormy dark sky distance & buildings all in bright Red light from the

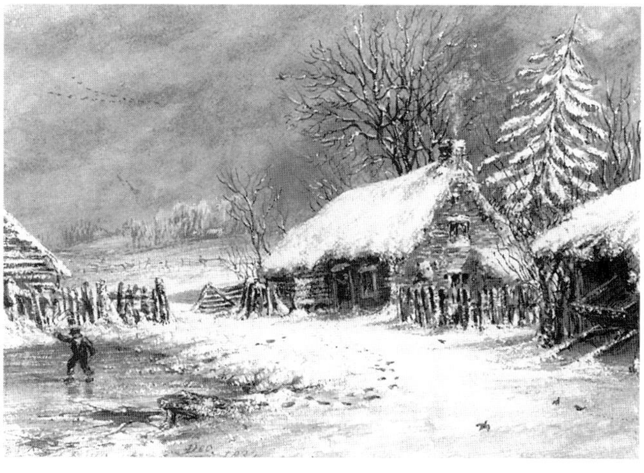

Plate 297. Watercolour
Snow scene with skater, Dec. 1832
Photo courtesy Martyn Gregory. Private Collection

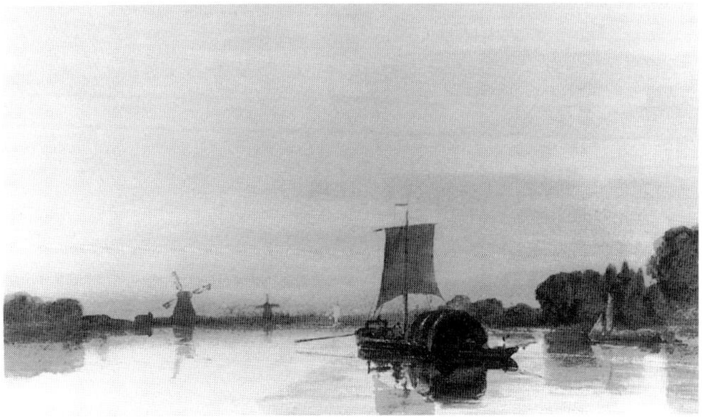

Plate 298. Watercolour
Grey morning, Battersea 1834
This atmospheric drawing of his early Thames period is No 66 in the Liber (MS 33.). See Plate 35. Photo courtesy Albany Gallery

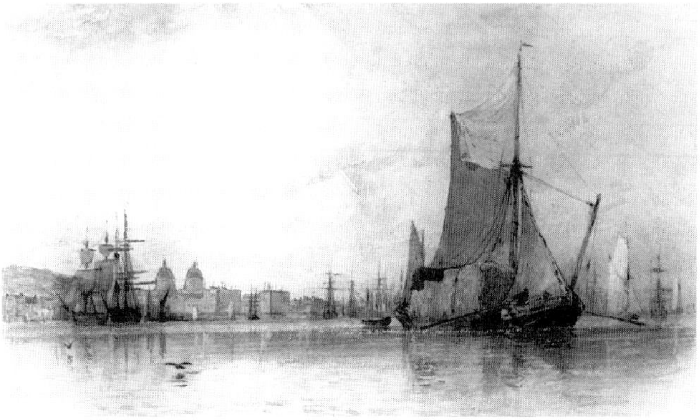

Plate 299. Watercolour
Hay barge, Greenwich 1835
A small vignetted version of Plate 40. Photo courtesy Martyn Gregory

setting sun – boats in foreground in sombre shadow – a Rainbow also – 11 by 8 [30cm x 20cm] – this drawg. with No's 49, 50 & 51 I took home to Mrs Austen as per commission on 20th Decr. with all of which she expressed herself pleased. Mrs A. returned my drawg. 52 of Rouen on the 31st Decr. when I called – the effect being to[o] extravagant !!!
53. Copy of 50 rather smaller made as a pair to No. 49 for Mr Austen 18th Decr. 1833. Brig introduced instead of ship.54. Grove House. Presented this drawing to Richard Rosier Esq on the 26th Decr. 1833 contd.
54.Back view of Grove House Woodford (Finished 24th Decr 1833) evening effect, sun gilding the tops of the gables, middle all in shadow – in this drawing I took the liberty being and old "schoolfellow" of introducing two sleeping lions on pedestals & balustrade – with a Philosophic gent reading.
55. Sunset effect at Feversham with boats lying aground – made about the latter end of July.
56. View on the Seine at Elbeuf among the islands, this with another of the same place
57. were finished on the 4th & 7th Jan 1834, exhibited at the Conversazione on the 11th and taken to town for Mr Bailey (as per commission) on the 25th 1834 with another No 45. Size of each about 8 inches. All 3 Pd. for pr.W.Rosier on 25th March 1835.[*sic*]
58. The *Jupiter* 50 guns shipping an awful sea over her larboard bow in a severe gale of wind, from a bad sketch by a Lieutenant — drawn and finished on 21st Jan and sent to Messrs. Arch (as per commission) on 23rd Jan 1834. Size about 13 ins [33cm] in length (Dec 12 they paid me 3 Gns for it)
59. Sketch for a larger drawing fishing boats in a stormy day rough sea, made on 23rd Jan 1834. Sold to Tiffin July 2nd 1835 for £3.13.6.

60. Composition, Sylvan scene, retired spot, heron in foreground and temple in distance drawn 10th Jany. about 10 inches [25.5cm] in size (upright) Presented to Mrs Angell 18th Jany 1835.61.Facsimile of my original sketch "Rue de la Tuile Rouen with the Cathedral tower" sketch made Oct 1st 1833. Completed the copy Jany 1st 1834. About 8 inches [20cm] in height – Sold to Mr Austen July 4th 1835 for £3.3.0 Paid.
62. Cliffs at Fecamp with the rocks at Low water – sun setting, figures in foreground – 1st drawing made on my return from the Continent – find. 25th Oct 1833.
63. Morning – low water– outside the pier at Honfleur–vessels drying sails –calm. July 7th 1834 – (6 inches) [15.25cm]
64. Fishing boats at Honfleur about 9 inches [23cm] high made 10th July 1834.
65. Grey morning – ploughing 7th & 9th July (5 inches) [12.5cm]
66. Grey morning – Battersea 9th & 10th July (8 inches) [20cm]
67. Design to illustrate Akenside – a vessel dashed against the cliffs & the crew drowning. Jany 22nd 1834.
68. Dover castle and basin from the Custom house Quay – vessels unloading – drawn 8 inches high.
July 12th 1834 Mr D.Colnaghi bought 5 drawings viz. numbers 63-64-65- 66 & 72 . paid 10 Guineas for them.
Made pencil sketches of the removal of the Egyptian Antiquities from the old building to the new Grand Hall on the 29th May, 30th & 31st and on June 2nd, 3rd, 4th, 5th, 7th, 16th & 17th – made about 20 sketches and left them 16th July for Mr Hawkins at the British Museum –
69. Composition River scene. Pagoda at Kew introduced. Made about the middle of January 1834, presented to Miss Etherington 26th Jany 1835.

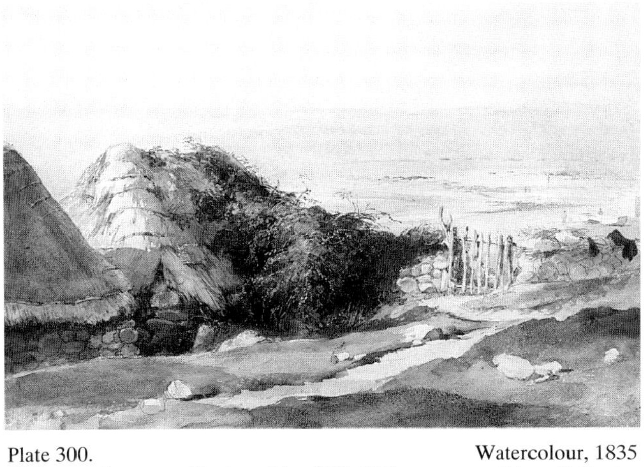

Plate 300. Watercolour, 1835
Fisherman's cottage Ventnor Isle of Wight Photo courtesy Private Collection

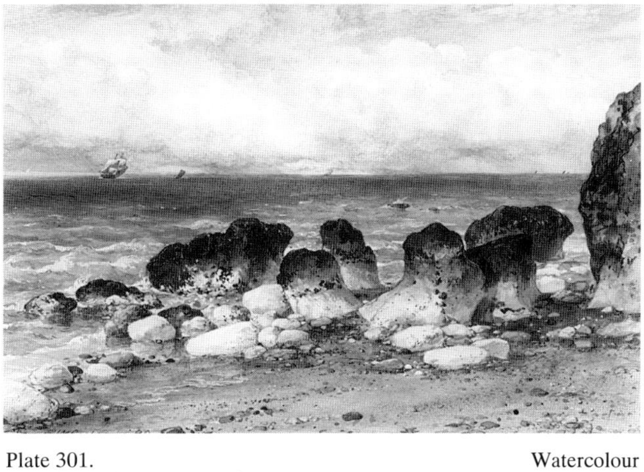

Plate 301. Watercolour
View from shore: strange formations Photo courtesy Martyn Gregory

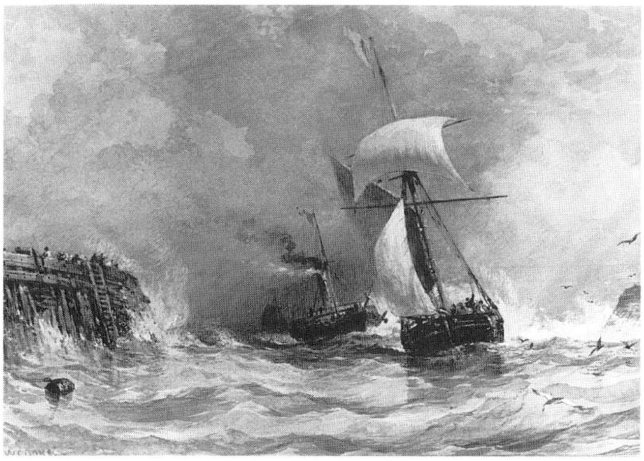

Plate 302. Watercolour
Dover Pier vessels entering harbour. [1837]
Two versions of this subject are recorded (MS 33) – the other is in the British Museum. Photo courtesy Martyn Gregory. Private Collection

70. Hulks at Chatham – effect of storm. Drawn soon after my return from my trip there with Stark in June 1833.
71. Sketch from Nature from our lawn – evening– June 9th 1834 (6 inches) [15.25cm] Sold to Colnaghi July 2nd 1835 for £2.12.6. Paid.
72. Grey coloured – bit on the Thames– Greenwich in the distance – fishing boats &c (6 inches) [15.25cm] 10th July 1834.
73.Rainbow effect on the Seine near Canteleu – Decr. 14th 1834, Given to Jemima Cooke now Mrs S.Bradshaw.
74. Twilight effect on a heath with a Mill. Gipsies returning from their maraudings – July 7th 1834 – 7th July 1834, about 11 inches [28cm]. Mr Holloway bought it July 2nd 1835. Pd. £2.2.0
75. Capstern [*sic*] and Rope House near the fish market Hastings. 2nd drawing made after my return from thence in Octr. Finished on 25th Novr. 1834
76. Ruins of 2 cottages which were undermined by the Sea in Oct. at Hastings near the White Rock brewery – drawing made 29th Novr. 1834. Mr Sheepshanks.
77. View of East Bourne St. Hastings. 1st drawing since my return 24th Novr 1834. This and the preceding drawg. I left at Mr Sheepshanks' on the 26th Novr, 1834 both about 6 inches [15.25cm] long.
78. Sloop coming ashore at Hastings, made 2nd Decr 1834 for Mr Sheepshanks. He paid £6 for four drawings, this and No's 75, 76 & 77.

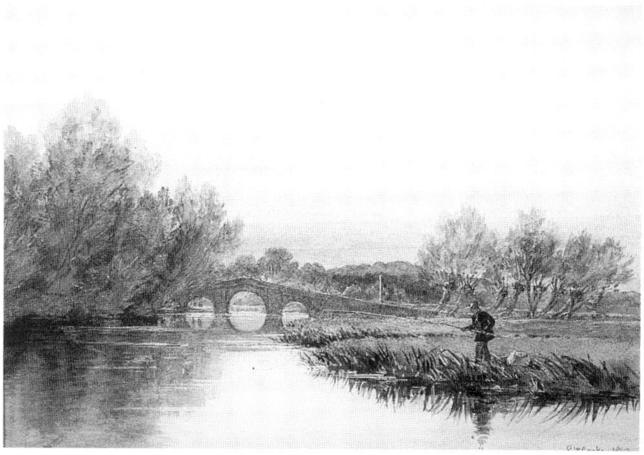

Plate 303. Watercolour, 1840
Fisherman beside a bridge near Oxford Photo courtesy Private Collection

79. New London Bridge – drawg. in Sepia – finished on 30th decr, 1834. Mr Sheepshanks bought it and paid £5.5.0 for it.
80. Copy of 79 for Mr Bovinet – finished on 3rd Jany. 1834. Paid per Mr Greene, £5.5.0 on the 15th Jany 1835
81. First sketch for 79 – gave it to Mr Sheepshanks 31st Decr. 1834.
82. Quai Henri Qtier, Dieppe – drawn on the spot.

[End of illustrations; here Cooke's own MS ends; the remaining entries, un-numbered, are in another hand – probably that of a sister.]

			[ruled column]
[83] Thames near Deptford	June 1835	Mr Sheepshanks	2.2.0
[84] Boats running to port	do.	do.	1.1.0
[85] Armour study	May 1835	do.	2.12.6
[86] Weeds, varnished	1829do.		2.2.0
[87] Boats at Pier. Seppia [*sic*]	May 1830	do.	1.1.0
[88] Punt, Kingston	Aug 1830	do.	10.6
[89] Culver Cliff	do.	do.	10.6
[90] Upnor (Color)	June 23rd 1833	do.	10.6
[91] Near Mortlake	August 26th 1831	do.	10.6
[92] Calais Pilot boat	do.		2.12.6
[93] Fishing boat arrived	do.		1.1.0
[94] Main deck of the *Victory*	April 8th	do.	
[95] Men of war in ordinary	do	do.	

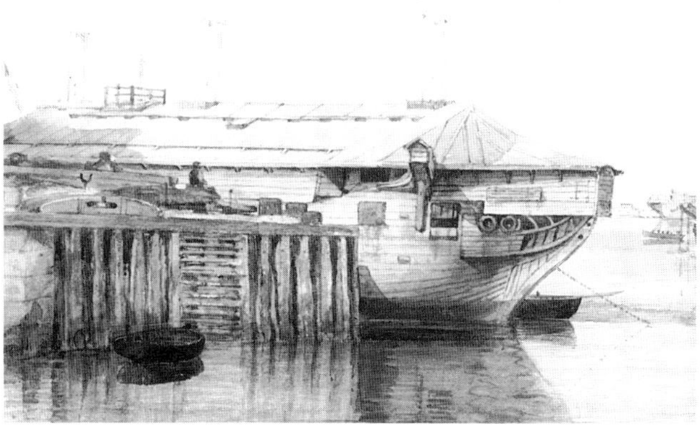

Plate 304. Watercolour
HMS Trincomalee *at Portsmouth*
Cooke's dockyard observations preserved the 46 gun India-built frigate of 1817, later a renowned training-ship which survives into the present time, re-named HMS *Foudroyant.* 'In ordinary' or reserve, with decks housed-over against the weather, she evidently took his eye! The drawing was Lot 85 in his Christie's sale of 1865, sold Gladwell for £2.10s.0d. Photo courtesy Martyn Gregory. Private Collection

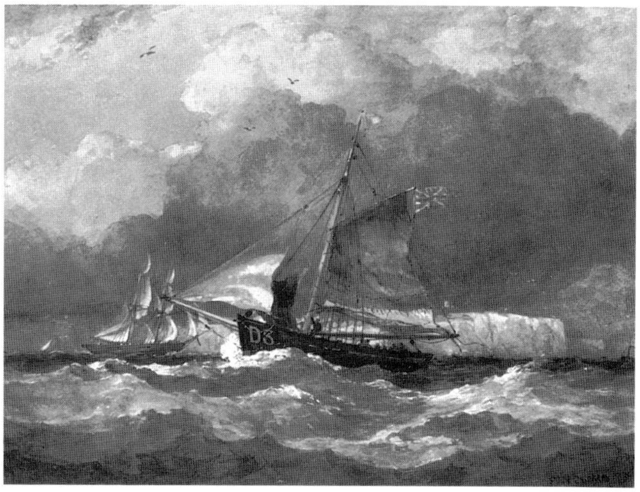

Plate 305. Watercolour
Dover pilot boat off the North Foreland
A small oil version is known, also dated 1864 (64/21, Plate 266).
Photo courtesy Martyn Gregory

[96] View of Chatham with			
Waterloo	do.	do.	
[97] Sketch of Hastings sands			
looking out (pen & ink)	Oct./35.	do.	
[98] Dutch Galliott.			
Mr Colnaghi.	May 1831		1.11.6
[99] Porte Leone Rouen	June 19th	Mr. Tiffin	1.10.0
[100] Gap at Runton -	July 20th 1837	do.	1.1.0
[101] On the Seine near Saumur [sic]	do.	do.	1.1.0
[102] Culver cliffs near			
Bembridge	do.	do.	15.0
[103] Wiers Mill Oxford	April 18th /37	R.H.Solly Esq.	)
[104] do.	do.	do. do.	)
[105] Twilight near Hinksey	do.	do.	)
[106] Barden Mill	do.	do.	)£21.0.0
[107] Redleaf Lake	do.	do.	)
[108] Redleaf	do.	do.	)
[109] Dover Pier.	April 19th 1837	Mr Griffith.	
[110] Cromer	July 1st /35	Mr. Tiffin	5.5.0
[111] Barges ashore Barnes	829	do.	1.1.0
[112] Neufchatel (Rainy effect)	Oct. 1833	do.	2.2.0
[113] Rue de la Tuile	Oct./33	Mr Austen	3.3.0
[114] Peter Boats	do.		1.11.0
[115] Sunset Calais	June /35	do.	2.12.6
[116] Calais sands	Mr.Bell		3.13.6
[117] Sunset Barnes	June 9/34	W.J.Cooke	present
[118] —	July 7 /35	Mrs. W.J.Cooke	do.
[119] Dutch boats.Seppia [sic]	Feb/ 29	Mr Holloway	10.6
[120] Dover	April 19th	Mr Griffiths [*sic*]	
[121] Bridge at Redleaf	do.	do.	
[122] Rue de la Tuile Rouen	Mr. T.Clark		
[123] Rue de la Grosse Horloge		do.	
[124] Gravesend Pier	Augt 21st 1834	do.	
[125] Cliffs, Bonchurch	June 29th /36	Mr.Harman	£8.0.0

[126] French horses	do.	do.	
[127] Richmond Hill	Mrs Glendinning		present
[128] Beach Fécamp	Mrs Hawes		do.
[129] On the Seine	do.		do.
[130] In the Pool	April 16th	Mr. Fuller	1.10.0.
[131] Funeral of Cowley	Feb 26th /35	Mr.[S.C.] Hall	
[132] Yarmouth Herring			
Fishery	April 6th/37	Mr Finden	
[133] Ramsgate fishing boat			
entering the harbour	do.	do.	
[134] Drawing of boats.	March 7th /35	Master Wadmore.	
[135] Vessel on the lee shore			
Jersey, seppia.	Mr Apostool		
[136] Sloop on the beach			
Hastings	Mr Lamberts		
[137] Timber barge Barnes			
(pencil)	March 11th	Mr Hawkins	
[138] Sunset Fécamp	March 27th/39	Mr R.Rosier	
[139] On the coast of Normandy	March 6th/39	Miss Barke	
[140] Vessels at Spithead	do.	do.	
Sent to Mr Griffiths [*sic*] April 12th 1839			
[141] Mont St.Michel with vessel and cart (Sepia)			4.4.0
[142] do.	Street view, looking down		4.4.0
[143] do.	do. looking up		4.4.0
[144] Schooner aground on a lee shore (Sepia)			4.4.0
[145] Vessel breaming St Heliers			4.4.0
[146] do.	do. at night		4.4.0
[147] Brig running into St Heliers in a gale			2.2.0
[148]Part of the Pier St Aubins			3.3.0
[149] Elizabeth Castle & St Aubins sands			3.3.0
[150] Cliffs at Grève de Lecq, Jersey			3.3.0
[151] "Leave not a wreck behind" scene on the rocks of			
Elizabeth Castle [Jersey]			4.4.0

END

Appendix 4

THE ITINERARY 1824-1879

Index to foreign travel

1833	France
1836	France & Channel Is.
1837	Holland
1838	Holland
1839	France
1840	Germany, France
1841	France, Holland
1842	France
1843	Holland
1845	France, Italy
1846	Italy
1847	Channel Is.
1849	Ireland
1850	Germany, Austria, Venice
1851	France, Italy, Venice
1852	Switzerland, Venice
1853	Holland, Sweden, Germany, Venice
1855	Holland, France
1857	Ireland, Venice
1858	Ireland, Switzerland, Venice
1860	Spain
1861	Gibraltar, Morocco, Spain
1862	Switzerland, Venice
1863	Switzerland, Venice
1864	France, Germany, Venice
1867	France
1869	Channel Is.
1873	France, Italy, Egypt
1874	Egypt, Italy, France
1875	France
1876	Holland
1877	Venice
1878	Ireland, France
1879	France, Holland, Germany

1824. **Jun.** Brighton. [evidence of surviving sketchbook.]

1828. **Jun.** 4 Southampton, Cowes, Portsmouth. 6 Portsmouth Dockyard. **Sept.** 15 Gravesend, Rochester, Chatham. **Oct.** 4 Norwich. 8 Hanworth. 9 Cromer. 11 Hanworth. 12 Gunton Park. 13 Cromer. **Dec.** 21 Hackney. 27 Brixton, Westminster.

1829. **Jan.** 2 Tottenham [Windus]. 10 Crosbie Hall, Thames Tunnel. **Feb.** 2 Blackwall. 22 Mortlake. 23 Barnes, Hackney. 25 Exeter'Change. **Mar.** 15 Barnes, Hackney. 22 Woodford Bridge, Hackney. 28 Conversazione. 29 Mortlake, Hackney. **Apr.** 23 Isle of Dogs. 24 Billingsgate. **May** 10 Barnes, resident. 18 Kew. 20 Richmond. 28 Greenwich. 31 St Katherines Docks, barque *Caroline* to Gravesend; return to Barnes. **Jun.** 9 Hackney. 16 Richmond, Teddington, Twickenham. 21 Wimbledon, Roehampton. 23 Royal Academy. 30 Sotheby's, Bonnington Sale, Turner Exhibn., Egyptian Hall. **Jul.** 15 Richmond. 21 London Bridge. 22 Hampton Crt. 25 Brighton. **Aug.** 13 to Barnes. **Sept.** 17 *United Kingdom* steamer, Greenwich. 18 Docks. 29 Limehouse, Greenwich. **Oct.** 17 Pool of London. **Nov.** 8 Chatham, Sun Tavern. 9 Gravesend, Barnes.

1830. **Jan.** 16 Paddington [Wadmore]. **Apr.** 7 Greenwich. 11 Fairlight, Hastings [Dr.Batty]. 12 Rye, Winchelsea. 13 Hastings/Fairlight. 22 to Brighton. 28 to Barnes. **May.** 6 Royal Academy. **Jun.** 7 British Institution. 30 West India Docks, Blackwall. **Jul.** 13, 14, 15 Windsor. 18 barque *Caroline* Blackwall to Gravesend. **Aug.** 25 London Bridge. 28 Greenwich to Gravesend, Royal Yacht Club regatta. **Sept.** 8 National Gallery. 16 Margate, King's Head Hotel. 18 Kingsgate, Tartar Frigate Inn, Broadstairs. 19 Ramsgate, Royal Oak Hotel. 21 Pegwell, Belleview Tavern. 22 Sandwich, Deal, Three Kings Hotel. 23 Sandown Castle. 24 Walmer, Kingsdown, Oldstairs, Deal, Dover, Castle Hotel. 29 Folkestone, True Briton Inn. **Oct.** 1 Sandgate. 2 Hythe, Swan Inn. 3 Barnes. 9 London, St Dunstan's, Greenwich, Painted Hall. 18 Chelsea. **Nov.** 4 West India Docks, ship *Thetis,* Blackwall, Greenwich. 25 ditto. **Dec.** 8. Woodford, Grove House school. 9 do.

1831. **Jan.** 18 Hullmandel's conversazione. 22 Chelsea, James Stark's. 26 Barnes. **Mar.** 12 Conversazione, Freemason's Tavern. 26 do. **Apr.** 5 Hackney. 6 Artists and Amateurs Conversazione, Freemasons' Tavern. **Jun.** 7 Greenwich, Woolwich, 9 Grove House Society, Adelphi. 19 Greenwich. 29 Portsmouth. **Jul.** 8 Ryde, Brading, Shanklin, Chine Inn. 9 Ventnor, Crab & Lobster Inn. 10 Niton, White Lion Inn. 11 Newport, Wheatsheaf Inn. 12 Cowes, Vine Inn. 13 Southampton, Sun Inn. 14 Barnes. 29 London Bridge. **Aug.** 1 do. Adelphi. 14 Richmond, Twickenham. 15 London Bridge. 16 do. **Sept.** 3 Kingston. 8 Westminster, Coronation Day. 22 Woolwich, launch of HMS *Thunderer.* 30 London Bridge. **Nov.** 15 do. 4 Docks, Blackwall. 25 London Bridge.

1832. **Jan.** 14 Conversazione. 22 London Bridge. 23 do. 25 do. 26 do. 27 do. **Feb.** 3 British Inst Varnishing day. 10 B.I. opening. 17 London Bridge. 22 London Bridge. **Mar.** 7 Conversazione. 20, 21 London Bridge. 24 Conversazione. **Apr.** 22 Richmond, Wimbledon, Roehampton. 29 Chigwell Row. **May** 1 Woolwich Dockyard. 20 Teddington, Bushey. 22 Kew Green. **Jun.** 7 Woodford. 14 London Bridge. **Jul.** 1 Richmond, Twickenham, Kew. 7 Herne Bay. 9 Whitstable, Canterbury, Faversham. 10 Canterbury, Herne Bay. 12 Barnes. 31 London Bridge. **Aug.** 1 New London Bridge. 12 Hampton Court. 23 Greenwich.

1833. **Apr.** 11.First conversazione of the Graphic Society. **May** 7 Norwood, Mr Griffith's Turners. **Jun.** 7 Hampton Court. 19 Chatham, with Jas.Stark, Chest Arms Inn. 21 Upnor. 22 Sheerness, Queenboro', Upnor, Jolly Sailor Inn. 24 Chatham. 25 Upnor (first oil from nature). 26

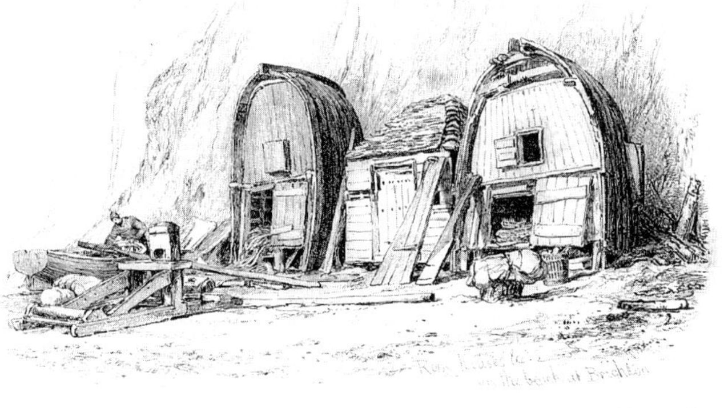

Plate 306. Engraving
Rope Houses, Brighton
One of the twelve *Coast Sketches.* In this Cooke explores the picturesque clutter which was part of the off-shore fishery. These plates formed part of the second edition of *Shipping & Craft.*

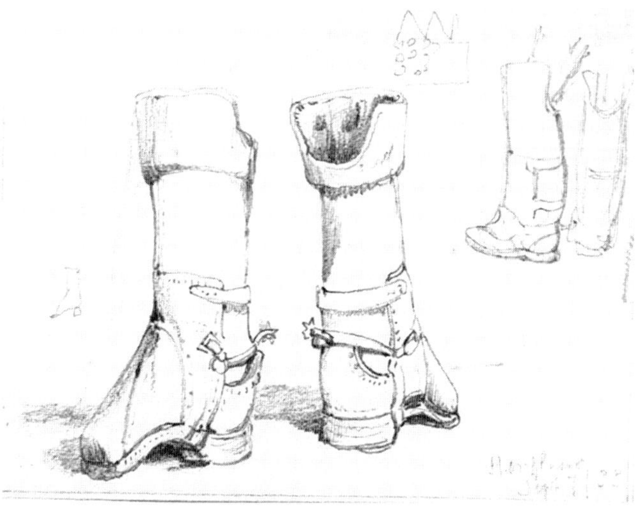

Plate 307. Pencil drawing
Postillion's boots, Honfleur 7th Sept. 1833
Draw everything new and singular his father had advised.
Photo courtesy Clarges Gallery

Chatham, Gravesend, Barnes. **Aug.** 27 Portsmouth. 28 Ryde. 29 Portsmouth/Le Havre./ **Sept.** 5 Ste. Adresse, Le Havre. 6 Honfleur. 12 Le Havre, Fécamp. 15 Dieppe. 20 Rouen. **Oct.** 3 La Bouille. 4 Rouen. 7 Elbeuf. 8 Rouen. 11 Abbeville. 14 Montreuil, Boulogne. 15 Boulogne-Calais. 17.Calais-London. 18 Hackney/Barnes. **Dec.** 4. Conversazione.

1834. **Jan.** 8 Graphic Society, Thatched House Tavern. 11 Conversazione, Freemasons Tavern. **Feb.** 12 Graphic Society. **May** 10 Brighton. 16. Barnes. **Jul.** 16 Deptford Railway. **Aug.** 16 Gravesend. 22 Dover. 27 Barnes. **Sept.** 22 Hastings. **Oct.** 28 Barnes.

1835. **Jan.** 10 Conversazione. 20 to stay for 3 months at W.B.Cooke's. **Feb.** 11 Graphic Society. **Mar.** 14 Conversazione. 20 Artists Fund, Freemasons Tavern. **Apr.** 20 Hastings. 24 Bexhill/Hastings. 26 St Leonards/Hastings. 29 Barnes. **May.** 5 Blackheath. 11 Hampton Court. 20 Blackheath. **Jun.** 8 Greenwich. 25 Blackheath. **Jul.** 11 Oxford. 16 Godstow. 20 Oseney. 21 Wiers paper mill. 28 Cumnor, Stanton Harcourt. 29 Iffley. 31 Nuneham. **Aug.** 3 Ferry Hincksey. 4 Drewitts Mill. 5 London/Blackheath. 30 Greenwich, Woolwich. 31 London/ Blackheath. **Sept.** 5 Woolwich. 10 Portsmouth. 14 HMS *Victory.* 23 Ryde/Ventnor, Crab & Lobster Inn. 26 Ventnor, Rock Cottage. 30 Ventnor, Union Cottage. **Oct.** 13.Portsmouth. **Nov.** 2 Beezley's Oxford. 5 Blenheim. 9 to Barnes. 11 Blackheath/Barnes. 30 Blackheath. **Dec.** 15 Blackheath. 16 London. 19 Conversazione: J.S.Cotman elected.

1836. **Jan.** 20 Blackheath. 23 Conversazione. **Feb.** 4 British Institution/ Blackheath. 6 Barnes. 10 Graphic Soc. **Mar.** 10 Blackheath. **Apr.** 14 Redleaf [William.Wells]. 25 Hastings. **May.** 3 to Barnes. 25 Blackheath. **June** 2 to London/Blackheath. 7 Barnes. **Jul.** 7 Redleaf. **Aug.** 15 Barnes. 17 Blackheath. 29 to Southampton. 30 St Peter Port, Guernsey. **Sept.** 7 St. Heliers, Jersey, London Hotel. 19 Granville, Normandy. 21 Mont St. Michel. 28 Pontorson/St Malo. 30 Jersey. **Oct.** 20 to So'ton. 21 Barnes. 25 Blackheath. **Nov.** 12 Barnes. 15 to Redleaf. **Dec.** 16 to Barnes.

1837. **Jan.** 11 Conversazione, Thatched House Tavern. 12 Blackheath. 14 Barnes. 27 British Inst. Varnishing Day. **Feb.** 8 Graphic Soc. 17 Conversazione. **Mar.** 8 Blackheath. 18 Suffolk St. Private View. **Apr.** 19 Redleaf. 27 Knole/Blackheath. 28 Barnes. **May** 11 Royal Academy. 22 Tottenham [Windus]. 24. Ash Grove. **Jun.** 29 Blackheath. **Jul.** 3. Brighton. 8 Newhaven. 12 Barnes. 26 Redleaf. **Aug.** 22 Barnes. 30. *Columbine* packet to Rotterdam. 31 Rotterdam. **Sept.** 2 Gouda/ Rotterdam. 4 Delft, The Hague. 5 Scheveling, Pays Bas Hotel (Scheveningen). 8 The Hague. 9 Scheveling. **Oct.** 7 Leyden. 12 Haarlem. 15 Amsterdam, Cattermole's English Hotel. **Nov.** 13 Zaandam/Amsterdam. 16 The Hague. 17 Rotterdam, New Bath Hotel. 18 *Attwood* packet. 19 London. 20 Barnes. 23 Blackheath. 24 Hackney/Adelphi. 25 Barnes. 30 Sevenoaks, Glendining's. **Dec.** 2 Redleaf. 23 Barnes.

1838. **Jan.** 10 Graphic Society. 27 Conversazione. 28 Blackheath. 29

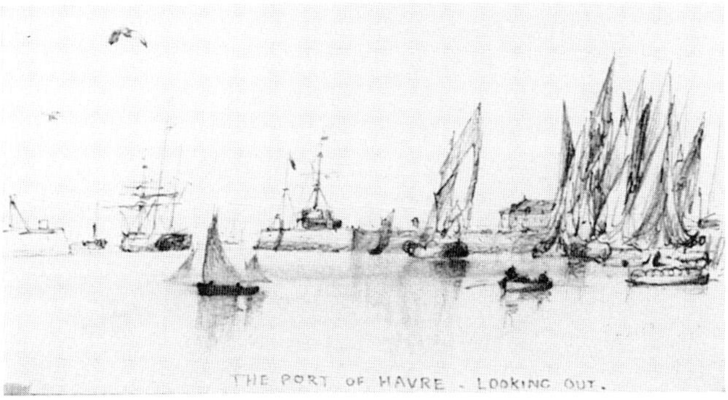

Plate 308. Pencil drawing
Port of Le Havre looking out
A small, slight but deft sketch, everything the painter could want for an evocative harbour scene with shipping. He is not however known to have used it.
Photo courtesy Clarges Gallery

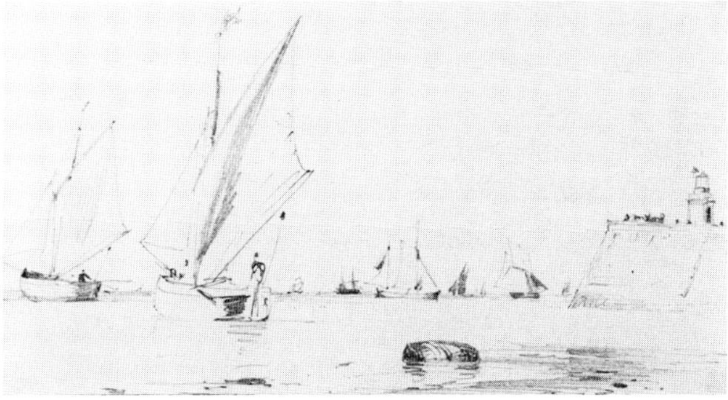

Plate 309. Pencil drawing
Havre de Grace, or Le Havre
Even slighter, but full of movement with fishing luggers setting out at low water and economically stated shipping in the offing.
Photo courtesy Clarges Gallery

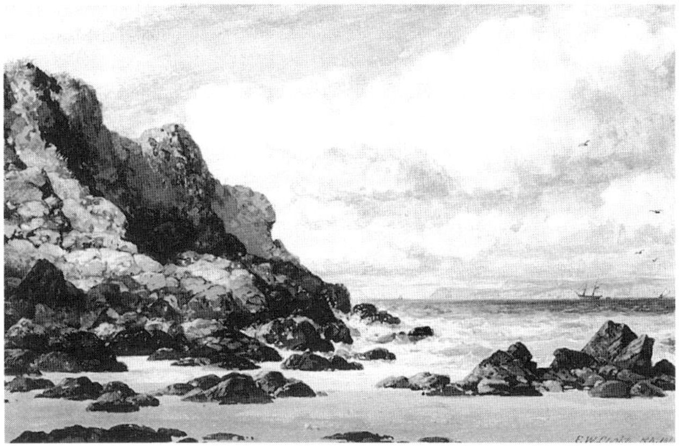

Plate 310. Watercolour
On the South coast, Jersey Photo courtesy Martyn.Gregory

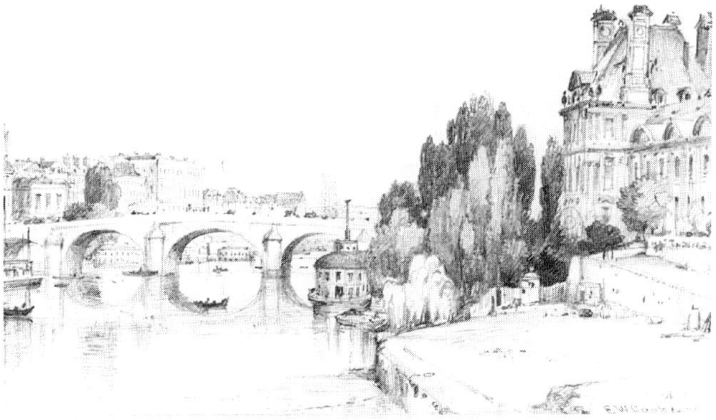

Plate 311. Pencil drawing
Paris, Pont Royale & Tuileries
Diligent even on his honeymoon – which was also his first visit to Paris – in July 1840, he made two drawings of the bridge. A view looking upstream taken at the same time appears in his *Leaves from my Sketch-book* 1876. Photo courtesy Martyn Gregory. Private Collection

Ruins of Royal Exchange. **Feb.** 17 Conversazione. 24 Redleaf. **Mar.** 26 to Barnes. 28 Blackheath. 29 Hackney. **Apr.** 2 Lord de Grey's Conversazione. 5 Freemasons' Tavern; dinner to John Doo. Soirée, London Institution. 19 Redleaf. 30 Ash Grove. Glendining. **May** 2 Chevening, Otford. 30 Woodford, Mr Harman's collection. **Jun.** 9 Dulwich Gallery. 15 Hackney. 19 Redleaf. 25 Rotterdam. 26 Delft. 27 The Hague. **Jul.** 1 Scheveling. 2 Leyden. 3 Haarlem. 4 Amsterdam. 8 Haarlem. 10 Utrecht. 11 Doorn. 12 Nijmegen. 13 Cologne. 14 Bonn. 15 Coblenz. 17 Mainz. 19 Deutz (Cologne). 21 Arnheim. 22 Amsterdam. **Aug.** 1. Loenen on the Vecht. 3 Amsterdam. 16 Loenen, Nieuwersluis. 25 Amsterdam. 27 Loenen, Nieuwenhoek. **Sept.** 10 Amsterdam. 14 Monnikendam, Marken. 15 Edam. 16 Volendam, Hoorn.17 Scharndam. 18 Enkhuizen, Broekenhaven, Medemblik. 19 Kolhorn, Zand, Den Helder. 20 Kijkduin, Nieuw Diep. 21 Camperdown. Alkmaar. 22 Edmond aan Zee. 23 Beverwijk, Wijck aan Zee, Amsterdam. 25 Willemsluis (Amsterdam). **Oct.** 6. Leyden. 8 Hazersworde: Rembrandt's mill. 14 The Hague, Leyden. 21 The Hague. 23 Rotterdam *Batavier* packet. 24 Hackney. 25 Barnes. 27 Hackney. 29 Camberwell. 30 Barnes. **Nov.** 7.Blackheath/Barnes. **Dec.** 8 Redleaf. 22 Barnes. 24 Hackney. 26 Ash Grove. 27 Redleaf.

1839. **Jan.** 1 at Redleaf. 16 to Hackney. 19 Barnes. 24 Hackney. 28 Hackney. 31 Varnishing BI. **Feb.** 1 to Hackney. 4 London BI. 10 to Hackney. 16 Greenwich/Blackheath. 17 Barnes. **Mar.** 13 Graphic Society. 14 Jacob Bell's. 25 Hackney. **Apr.** 11 Hackney. 16 Redleaf. **May** 2 to Hackney. 4 Barnes. 27 Hampton Ct & Bushey. 29 Richmond. **Jun.** 6 Kew. 12 to Hackney. 18. Barnes to Redleaf. 26 to Town. **Jul.** 8 Hackney. 11 at Barnes. 13 Anchorwyke, Mr Harcourt. 16 Windsor/ Hackney. 22 Barnes/Hackney. 23 Barnes. 28 Hackney. 29 Barnes. 30 Hackney. 31. Blackheath. **Aug.** 1 Barnes. 4 Yachting, to Greenhithe, to Woolwich/Hackney. 8 at Barnes. 11 to Hackney. 12 to Barnes. 26 to Hackney. 27 Town. 28 Calais packet. 29 Calais. **Sept.** 20 Gravelines. 23 Boulogne. **Oct.** 7 to Dove 8.. to Town. 26 Basingstoke, Norman Court. 28 Salisbury. **Nov.** 1 to Town. 15 Redleaf. **Dec.** 21 to Barnes.

1840. **Jan.** 22 Stratton Hants. 25 Winchester/Stratton. 27 Winchester. 29 to town. 30 BI Varnishing. 31 Blackheath/Hackney. **Feb.** 1 BI PV. 12 Third meeting of Graphic 15 Hackney. **Jun.** 13 Wedding Hackney/Rochester. 16 Ostend. 17 Ghent. 19 Antwerp. 23 Brussels. 24.Mechlin/Brussels. 25 Waterloo. 26 Aix la Chappelle. 29 **Jul.** 1 Coblenz. 2 Bingen, Mainz, Frankfort. 4 Darmstadt. 7 Heidelberg. 9 Karlsruhe. 10 Baden Baden. 1 Strassbourg. 13 Mannheim. 14 Coblenz. 15 Trier. 17 Metz. 19 Paris. **Aug.** 3 Rouen. 4 Le Havre. 5 *Phoenix* packet. 6 Blackwall/Barnes. **Oct.** 9 Cheltenham/Gloucester. 10 Thirlestaine House. 12 Gloucester/Cheltenham. 14 Northwick. 17 Sezincott. 19 Oxford/Barnes. **Nov.** 14 Artists Fund Mtg. 16 Redleaf. **Dec.** 3 to Hackney. 4 to Barnes.

1841. **Jan** 25 Tottenham, Windus's/Barnes. 27 Barnes. 30 PV BI. **Feb.** 17 Hackney. 20 Barnes. 28 Hackney. **Apr.** 8 Redleaf. 17 to Hackney. **Jun.** 15 in Town. **Jul.** 14 Scheveningen [Missing] **Aug.** 13 to Barnes (On return). **Sept.** 11 Etching club at Barnes. 20 Cheltenham Lord Northwick. 25 Thirlestaine /Barnes. **Oct.** 5 *Orwell* steamer to Ipswich. 9 Holbrook. 14 Do. to Blackwall/Barnes. 17 to Hackney. 18 Hastings, Castle Hotel. **Nov.** 4 to Redleaf. 24 left Redleaf. **Dec.** 8 Barnes.
1842. **Feb.** 3 BI Varnishing. 9 Graphic Society. **Apr.** 7 Strawberry Hill

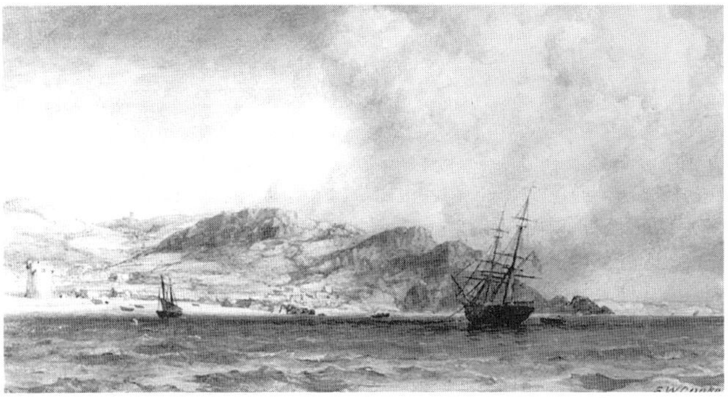

Plate 312. Watercolour
St.Brelade's Bay Jersey Photo courtesy Martyn.Gregory

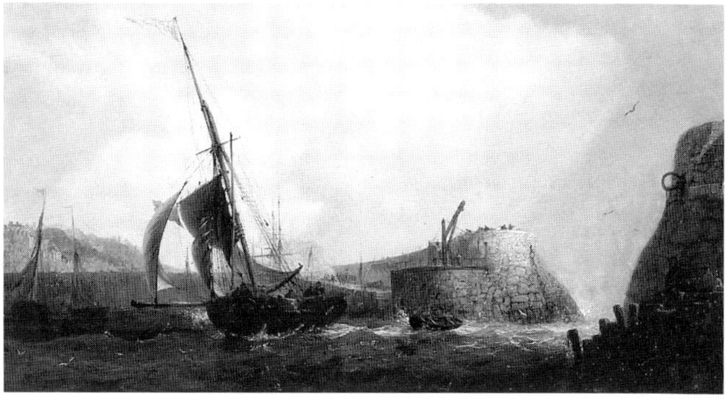

Plate 313. 36/16
Pilot boat running into St Peter Port Guernsey
Studies in seamanship, boats entering or leaving harbour, attracted Cooke's admiring pencil and with him the theme endured.
Photo courtesy Sotheby's

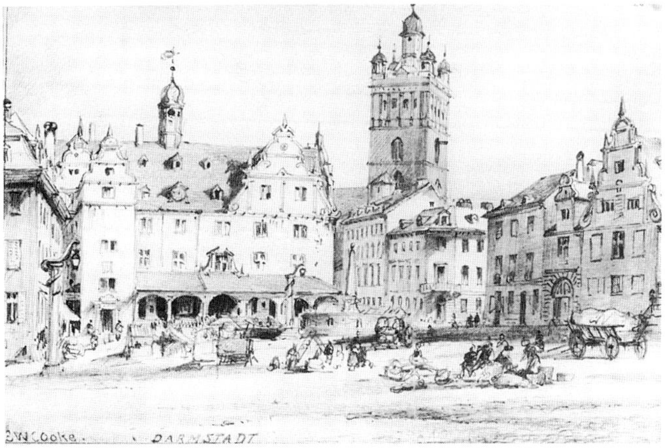

Plate 314. Pencil drawing
Darmstadt – Monday 6 July 1840
On his honeymoon he sketched the Market Place and Radhaus during a visit to his cousin William John Cooke and family, who had recently settled in the city. Photo courtesy Martyn Gregory

Sale. **Jul.** 25 RA Dinner. **Aug.** 25 Brighton. **Oct.** 6 *Royal William* to Herne Bay/Dover. 7 *Royal George* to Boulogne. 16 *City of Boulogne* packet to London. 24 Redleaf. **Nov.** 15 to Hackney. 26 Barnes '8 wks absence'. **Dec.** 14 Graphic Soc.

1843. **Mar.** 1 Greenwich, Woolwich. 15 Hackney. 16 Barnes. **Apr.** 12 Graphic Soc. **May** 28 Hackney. 31 Town/Barnes. **Jun.** 23 Redleaf. **Jul.** 6 to Barnes. 15 Old Jewry 16. Batavier packet. 17 Scheveling. 18 Hague/Schevg. 26 Amsterdam. 3. Zaandam/Amst. **Aug.** 8 Nieur Hoek. 12 to Amsterdam. 16 Haarlem. 17 Leyden. 18 Scheveling. **Sept.** 3 Hague/Schevg. 10 Hague. 11 Schevg. 14 Leyden. 17 Amsterdam. 20 Zaandam. 22 Rotterdam. 23 Dort/Antwerp. 25 Brussels. 26 Waterloo. 29 Ghent. 30 Bruges, Hotel du Commerce. **Oct.** 1 Ostend, *Lord Melville* packet. 2 London/Hackney. 3 Barnes. 28 Hackney. 30.Barnes. **Nov.** 1 Hackney. 10 Redleaf. 28 to Barnes. **Dec.** 13 Graphic Soc.

1844. **Jan.** 5 to Hackney. 8 to Barnes. **Apr.** 18 Redleaf. 20 Tunbridge Wells. **May** 13 Hackney/Barnes. [Missing] **Jun.** 12 Hackney. 13 Barnes. **Jul.** 18 Hackney. 20 Barnes/Greenwich. 17 Redleaf. 31 to Reigate. **Aug.** 13 Barnes/Hackney. 16 Kew. **Sept.** 17 Hungerford, Chilton Lodge [Scrope]. 19 Littlecote. 21 to Barnes. 24 to Redleaf. 25

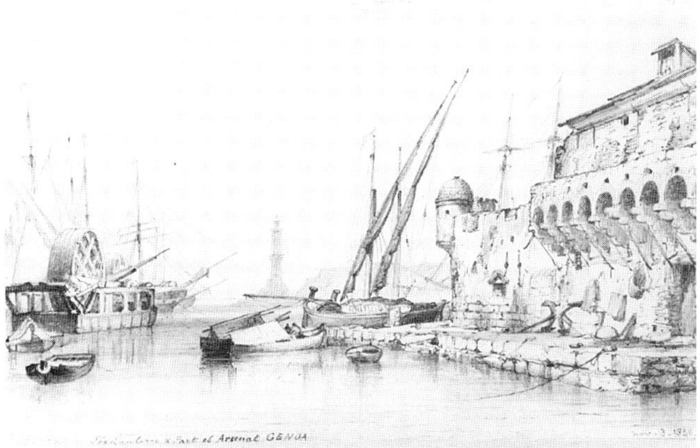

Plate 316. Pencil drawing
Genoa, the Lanterna & part of the Arsenal. Nov.3 1845
In the distance the famous lighthouse which identifies the port. One of his 'finished' sketches combining antiquity, the essential shipping and a lumbering harbour craft such as few artists would care to include. Illustrated in *Henry James on Italy,* Barrie & Jenkins, 1988.
Photo courtesy Martyn Gregory

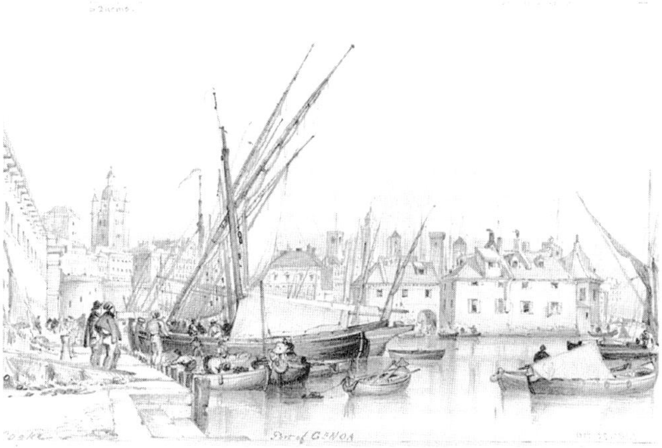

Plate 315. Pencil drawing
Genoa, the port. Oct.1845 Photo courtesy Martyn Gregory

Eastwell Park Ashford [Ld.Winchilsea]. 28 to Redleaf. **Oct.** 3 to Barnes. 4 Hackney. 5 Barnes. 7 Worcester/Barton Court [Peyton]. 18 Ledbury, Highnam Ct. [Gambier Parry]. 22 Barton Ct to Liverpool. 23 New Brighton. 30 Lpool/Birmingham. 31 to Barnes.

1845. **Feb.** 6 BI VD. **Mar.** 11. Hackney/Blackwall *The Great Britain* steamship. 12 Graphic Soc. 21 Hackney. **Apr.** 19 Redleaf. 26 Barnes. **Jun.** 23 Redleaf. 25 to Barnes. **Jul.** 13 Hackney. 18 Brighton/Dieppe /Rouen. 19 Paris. 27 Versailles. 29 Chalons. 30 Lyons. **Aug.** 1. Viennes. 4 Valence. 5 Avignon. 11 Vaucluse. 14 Avignon, Nimes, Arles. 17 Marseilles. 21 Toulon. 22 to Antibes. 23 to Nice. **Sept.** 2 boat to Monaco. 12 boat to Mentone. 15 Ventimiglia. 17 San Remo. 23 Porto Maurizio. 25 Oneglia. 27 Alassio. 30 Finale. **Oct.** 9 Savona. 10 Genoa. **Nov.** 3 to Nervi. 4 Rappallo/Chiavare. 8 Spezzia. 22 Carrara. 24 to Pisa. 26 Leghorn. **Dec.** 2 Pisa/Florence. 20 Florence/Siena. 21 Radicofani. 22 Monte Fiascone. 23 Rome.

1846. **Apr.** 15 Tivoli. 29 to Rome. **May.** 4 to Mola di Gaeta. 5 Capua. 6 Naples. 19 Vesuvius. 20 Salerno. 22 Paestum. 28 Amalfi, Capuchin Hotel. **Jun.** 7 Ravello/Amalfi. 18 Erchia/Amalfi. 21 by boat to Capri. 27 to Sorrento. 30 to Castellamare. **Jul.** 2 to Pompeii/Naples. 8 Posilippo. 13 *Castor* packet to 14 Civitavecchia. 15 Leghorn/Genoa. 16 Genoa/ Milan. 20 to St Gothard Pass. 21 to Lucerne. 23 to Zurich. 24 Freiburg. 25 Strasbourg. 27 Cologne. 29 to Ostend. 30 Rainbow steamer to Blackwall/Barnes. 31 to Hackney/Barnes. **Aug.** 8 Kew. 14 Hackney/ Barnes. 19 Redleaf. 24 to Town. 27 Redleaf. **Oct.** 1 to Barnes. **Dec.** 9. Graphic meeting.

1847. **Feb.** 2 BI VD. 6 BI PV. 10 Graphic. 13 Hackney. **Mar.** 10 Graphic. **Apr.** 7 Kew. 14 Graphic. 15. Redleaf. 24 To Barnes. **May.** 13 Kew. 26 Hackney, Barnes. **Jun.** 4 Folkestone. 9 Hythe, Folkestone. 11 Dover, Sandwich. 12 Canterbury. 15 Ramsgate. 23 Penshurst, Redleaf, Town. **Jul.** 1 Kew. 13 Southampton. 14 Jersey, Granville. 15 Mont St Michel, St Malo. 16 Dinan, S.Brieuc. 17 S.Malo. 19 to Jersey. 20 Guernsey. 21 Torquay, Plymouth. 23 Exeter, Bristol. Bath. 24 to Paddington. **Aug.** 7 York. 9 Castleford, York. 10 Scarborough, York. 11 Newcastle, Tynemouth, Berwick. 12 Edinburgh. 14 Portobello. 17 Stirling. 18 Trossachs Inn. 19 Loch Long. 20 Arroquhar Inn. 21 Glasgow. 23 Ardrossan. 24 Brodick. 26 Ardrossan. 27 Glasgow, Dumbarton. 28 Luss, Dumbarton. **Sept.** 1 Inverary. 2 Oban. 4 *Dolphin* steamer to Staffa, Iona, Oban. 6 Dunstaffnage Castle. 7 Glencoe. 8 Inverness. 9 Cawdor Castle. 10 Culloden. 11 Fort William. 13 to Glasgow. 15 Edinburgh. 22 Dalkeith, Edinburgh. 23 Newcastle, Carlisle. 25 Penrith, Keswick. 26 Ambleside, Bowness. 27 Ambleside. 28 Kendal, Manchester. 29 to Liverpool. **Oct.** 2 to Manchester. 4 Haddon Hall, Rowsley. 5 Chatsworth, Birmingham. 6 to Town. 9 Greenwich. 18 Hackney & the Zoo. **Nov**. 7. Tulse Hill [Bicknell]. 24 Richmond, Kew. **Dec.** 8 Graphic.

1848. **Jan.** 12 Graphic. **Feb.** 2 BI VD. 5 BI P.V. 8 Clapham [N.B. Ward]. 24 Kew. **Mar.** 3 Hackney. 8 Graphic. **May.** 1 RA opening. 10

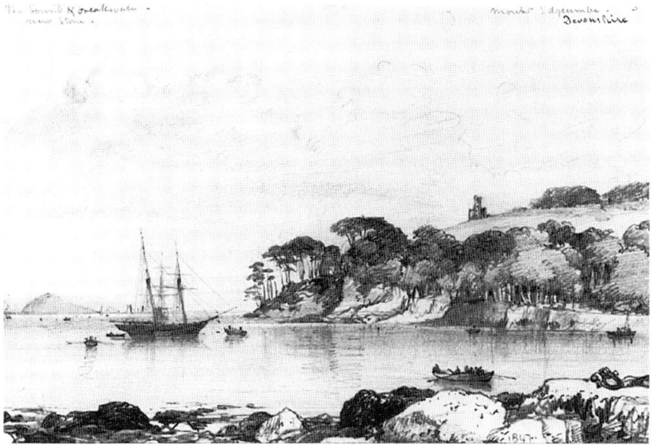

Plate 317. Pencil drawing
Mount Edgcumbe The Sound and Breakwater – Mew Stone. 1847
The Cornish side of Plymouth Sound, a drawing made in the evening of 22 July, when he noted *glorious effects of sunset.*
Photo courtesy Martyn Gregory. Private Collection

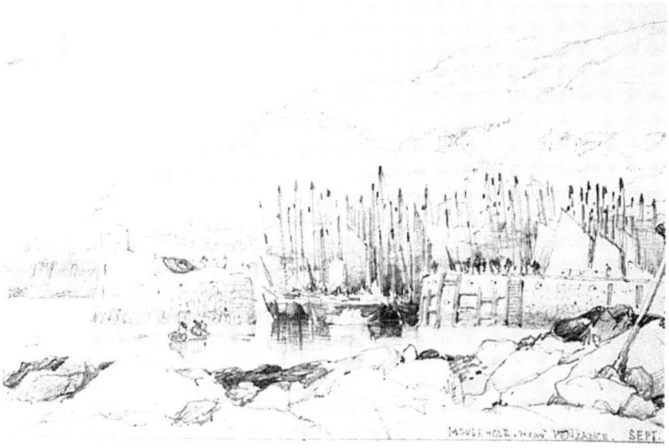

Plate 318. Pencil drawing
Mouse Hole near Penzance. 1848
The tiny Cornish harbour with the fishing fleet in port; 'Mowzle', even in a rapid soft pencil sketch, has all Cooke's fine gradations and would have enabled him to make a pretty little marine picture.
Photo courtesy Clarges Gallery

Graphic. **Jun.** 7 Gravesend, Cobham & return. 17 Weybridge and Send Court. 21 Woking, Egham, Virginia Water. 22 Hammersmith & home. **Aug.** 22 Ramsgate. 23 Broadstairs & back. 24 Canterbury, Redleaf. 25 South Park. 28 Groombridge/Redleaf. 29 Ightham/Redleaf. 30 to Groombridge. **Sept.** 4 T.Wells/Ramsgate. 5 *Eclipse* to Woolwich/London. 6 Barnes. 8.Exeter, 9 Dawlish, Newton, Torquay. 11 Babbacombe. 12 Brixham, Dartmouth, Totnes, Plymouth. 13 Mt Edgcombe/Mt Batten. 14 Tor Point. 15. Tamar to Cothele. 16 to Falmouth. 18 Redruth, Hayle, Penzance. 19 Marazion, St Michael's Mount. 20 St Mary's, Scilly. 21 Tresco. 22 Peninnis. 23 St Agnes. 25 Old Town Bay. 27 Porthellick. 28 to Penzance. 29 Newlyn, Mousehole. **Oct.** 1 Marazion. 2 St Just. 3 Botallack Mine. 4 Cape Cornwall. 5 Lands End. 7 Penzance. 9 Hayle, St Ives. 16 Marazion & Mount. 17 Newlyn, Lamorna & back. 18 Logan Stone. 19 Truro, Exeter. 20 Bath, Salisbury, Wilton House. 21 Old Sarum, Stonehenge. 23 Salisbury/Barnes.

1849 **Jan.** 10 Graphic. **Feb.** 7 BI VD. 8 last day at Barnes. 9 Denmark Hill [GS Marshall]. 10 BI PV. **Mar.** 5.Clapham [Mr Hudson]. 7 to Kensington. 24 Conversazione Freemason's Tavern. **Apr.** 28 Mr Darby's. 29 Kingston on Thames, Claygate. **Jun.** 12. Redleaf. 18 Kensington. **Jul.** 4. Erith, Belvidere. 7 to Kensington by boat. 28 Belvidere. 31 RA closing dinner. **Aug.** 14 Slough [Hillersdon], Dropmore & back. 18 Peterboro: Connington Castle [Heathcote]. 19 Glatton [Mr Wingfield]. 20 Peterborough. 21 Ditto, Eye, Thorney, Crowland. 23 Whittlesee mere. 24 Ely. 25. Cambridge. 27 to Kensington. **Sept.** 1 Woolwich, Erith. 3 boat to N.Woolwich/Hackney. 7 Biddulph Grange. 8 Knypersley/Biddulph. 11 Stoke [Minton's], Trentham & back. 13 Hawarden Castle [Coleridge]. 15 Chester/Hawarden. 17 Tabley Park. 18 Knutsford/Biddulph. 22 Chester, Holyhead/Dublin. 25 Howth. 26 Killarney. 29 Muckross Hotel. **Oct.** 4 Bantry. 5 Cork. Victoria Hotel. 6 Blarney Castle. 8 to Dublin. 9 Bray, Co Wicklow, Barrington. 11 Dublin. 13 Bangor. 15 Conway. 17 to Liverpool, Lynns Hotel. 18 Longsight [Mr Barlow]. 22 Manchester. 23 Birmingham/Gloster/Bristol. Taunton, Barton Grange. 27 to Windsor. 29 to Kensington. **Nov.** 14 Graphic.

1850. **Jan.** 4 Hackney. 9 Graphic Society. 19 Artists Fund Meetg. 28 Barnes. 2 Victoria Rd. **Feb.** 2 PV.BI. 8 Hackney. 9 Victoria Rd. 16 Hackney Mar. 13 Graphic. 23 Artists Fund Dinner. **Apr.** 10 Greenhithe, Dartford. 22 Artists Fund. 24 Erith, Woolwich. **May.** 1 Exeter, Newton, Torquay. 3 Paignton, Bury Pomeroy. 7 Bristol/London. 9 Sion House. **Jun.** 5 Artists Fund. 15 Kingston. 17 Hoddesdon/Kensington. **Jun.** 26.Hackney/V.Rd. **Jul.** 8 Artists Fund. 9 Windsor. 10 Wexham [Hillersdon]. 11 Victoria Rd. 22 Wellclose Sq [Ward]. 23 Penshurst, Chafford. 29 *Undine* packet to Calais. 30 Ghent, Cologne. 31 Mainz. **Aug.** 1 Frankfort, Wurtzburg. 2 Nurnburg. 3 Munich. 7 Augsburg. 8 Ratisbon. 9 Linz. 10 Ischel. 12 Salzburg. 14 Unken. 15 St Johann. 16 Insbruch. 18 Bolsena. 19 Trento. 21 Verona. 23 Mantua. 25 Vicenza/Padova. 26 Venice. **Nov.** 19 Trieste. 21 Vienna. 25 Prague. 26 Dresden. 28 Berlin. 30 Cologne. **Dec.** 2 Aix. 3 Calais. 4 Dover/London. 21 Eton. 23 Victoria Rd.

1851. **Jan.** 25. Conversazione. **May.** 16 Sandwich, Betteshanger. 23 Ramsgate/Betteshanger. 24 Canterbury/Whitstable. 27 to London. **Jun.** 14 Ash Grove. 16 to London. **June.** 27 Wexham Grove/town. **Jul.** 29. Hackney. **Aug.** 11 Folkestone/Boulogne. 12 Paris/Chalons. 13 Geneva. 14 Martigny. 15 Brieg. 16 Simplon. 17 Baveno/Como. 18 to Milan. 19 Bergamo. 20 Brescia. 21 Verona/Venice. **Dec.** 3. to Brescia. 4 Milan. 5 to Turin. 6 to Lyons. 7 Chambery. 8 Lyons. 9 Paris. 15 to Boulogne/Folkestone. 20 Hackney/Kensington.

1852. **Feb.** 11.Graphic. **Mar.** 22 Artists Fund. **Apr.** 13.Kingston/Box Hill. 16 Torquay. 19 Newton/ Ashburton. 20. Crediton. **Apr.** 21 Bideford. 22 Clovelly, Barnstaple, Ilfracombe. 24 Lynmouth. 27 Minehead. 28 Bridgwater/London. **Jul.** 19.Blyth Hall [Dugdale]. 23.Biddulph Grange. 27 Burslem/London. **Aug.** 10 Broom Hill, Tunbridge Wells. 11 London. 18 Folkestone/Boulogne/Paris. 19 Strassbourg. 20 Basle/Zurich. 21 Coire. 23 Chiaverna. 24 Como. 25 Milan. 26 Verona/Venice. **Dec.** 6 [about] leaves Venice-[missing]. 13 Paris. 14 Calais.

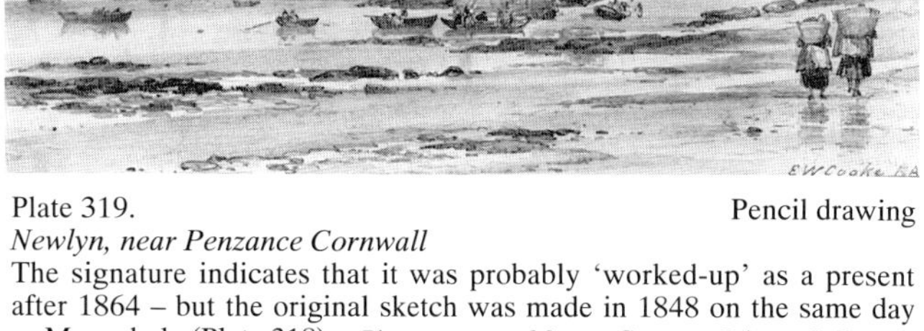

Plate 319. Pencil drawing
Newlyn, near Penzance Cornwall
The signature indicates that it was probably 'worked-up' as a present after 1864 – but the original sketch was made in 1848 on the same day as Mousehole (Plate 318). Photo courtesy Martyn Gregory. Private Collection

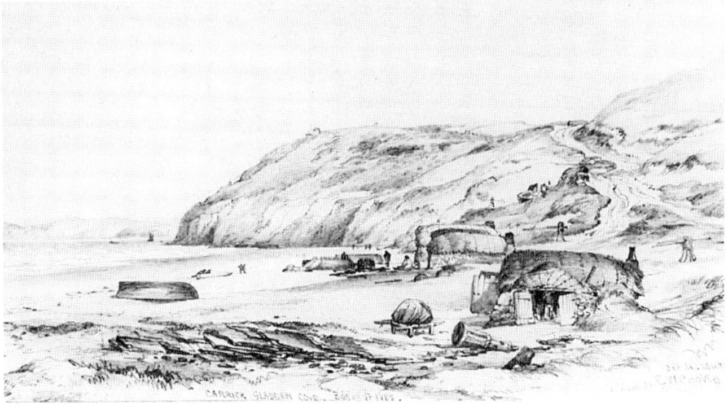

Plate 320. Pencil drawing
Carrick Gladden Cove St Ives Bay. Oct. 11th 1848
Here was a small working community with characterful and unfamiliar features. The thatched fishermen's huts look as if they are based on upturned boats; there are beach capstans strategically placed and a 'stretcher' for carrying nets is carefully observed. Geological features like the layered rock and a feeling for landscape in the view across the bay past the massive headland and the track winding down are very much Cooke. The signature indicates that it was probably 'worked-up' as a present after 1864 – but the original sketch was made in 1848 on the same day as Mousehole (Plate 326). Photo courtesy Martyn Gregory. Private Collection

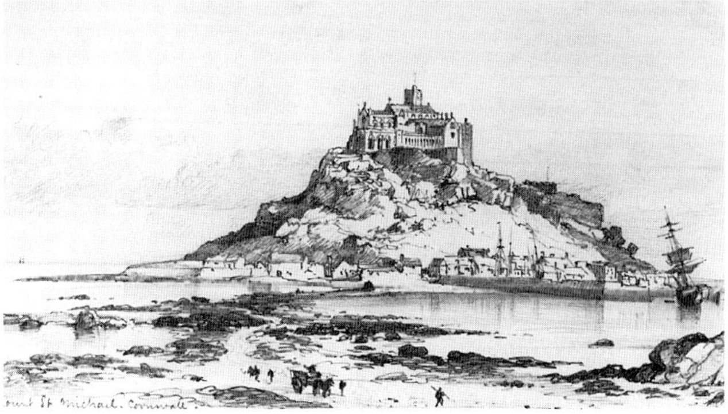

Plate 321. Pencil drawing
Mount St Michael Cornwall
Probably a drawing of 1848; he had been again to Mont St Michel in Normandy the year before, which could explain why he did not write the usual English 'St. Michael's Mount.
Photo courtesy Martyn Gregory. Private Collection

1853. **Jan.** 15.Brighton. 21 Shoreham/Brighton. 25 Kensington. **Apr.** 7.Brighton. 8 Hastings. 9 Ashford/Ramsgate. 11 Broadstairs/Margate. 12 London/Clapham. 13 Kensington. 18 Brighton/Hastings [Albion Hotel]. 19 Tunbridge Wells [Kentish Hotel]. 20 Kensington. 29 PV R.A. **May.** 6.Sydenham Crystal Palace. **June.** 6 Greenwich RA Club. 26 Rotterdam *Batavier.* 27 Scheveling. 29 Hague/Scheveningen. **Jul.** 4 Rotterdam. 5 Amsterdam. 6 Zaandam/Amsterdam. 7 Harlingen/Leeuwarden. 8 Groningen. 9 Delfzil/Emden/Leer. 10 Oldenburg/Bremen. 11.Hamburg. 12 Blankenen/Hamburg. 14 Lubeck/packet. 15 Ystadt. 16 Kalmar. 17 Stockholm (sea). **Aug.** 1.Upsala. 2 Skokloster/Upsala. 4 Stockholm. 13 to Lubeck. 16 Travemunde. 17 Hamburg. 22 to Berlin. 23 Dresden. 25 Prague. 27 Vienna. 29 to Adelsberg. 30 Trieste. **Sept..** 1 Venice. **Nov.** 26 to Verona/Breschia. 27 Treviglio/Milan. 28 Como/Chiaveri. 29 the Splugen. **Dec.** 1 Basle/Strasbourg/Paris. 7 Boulogne/Folkestone/London. 9 Leatherhead/Clapham/Finsbury Circus. 10 Hackney. 28 T.Wells, Broom Hill. 30 London/Finsbury Circus. 31 Hackney/Kensington.

1854. **Feb.** 5 Denmark Hill [Bicknell]. **Apr.** 5 Letherhead/Epsom. 6 Gravesend,Strood, Chatham. 7 Holme, Connington. 8 Glatton, Gt & Little Gidding. 10 Leyton, Hammerton, Sawtry. 11 Fens. 12 Kensington, Graphic. 29 R.A. dinner. **May.** 3 Newhaven. 4 SS *Paris* Dieppe. 9 Eu.Treport. 12 Folkestone, London. **Jun.** 10 Crystal Palace. 12 Greenwich Hosp. Dinner, Crown & Sceptre. **Jul.** 15 Slough, Wexham. **Aug.** 19 Erith. 21 Hackney, Gt Palm, Herne. 22 Kew. 25 Slough, Dropmore. 31 T.Wells, Broom Hill. **Sept.** 1 Redleaf. 2 Bentham Hill. 4 Broom Hill to Kensington. 7 Leatherhead. 8 Hackney. 9 Manchester. 12 Congleton [Batemans]. 16 Manchester. 18 Congleton/ Biddulph/ Knypersley. 21 Kensington. **Oct.** 7 Taunton, Barton Grange. 10 Gloucester, Highnam Ct. 16 Bath. 17 Kensington. 26 Stratford (E). 27 Kensington. **Nov.** 4.Windsor. 7 Kensington. 13 Jury, Clerkenwell. 15 Hackney. **Dec.** 13 Graphic Soc.

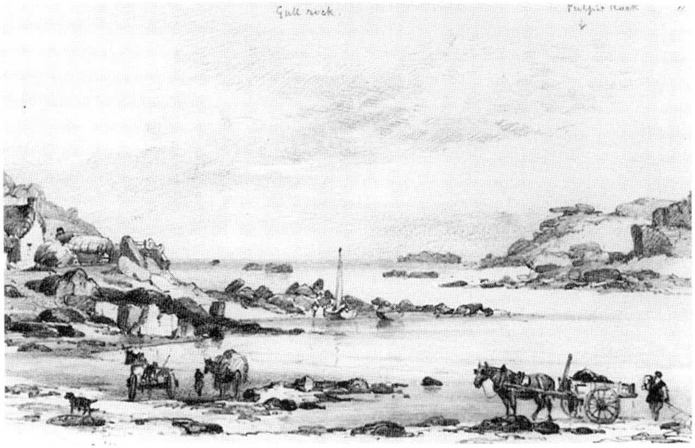

Plate 322. ???
Old Town Bay Scilly Is.
The fishing cove and the seaweed gatherers, as well as geological points of interest, make this calm September scene in 1848 an attractive picture. He also made colour sketches of the rocks and drew the Loggan Stone. Photo courtesy Martyn Gregory. Private Collection

1855. **Jan.** 13 Hackney. **Apr.** 17 Weymouth [Royal Hotel]. 18 Portland. 19 Nothe, Sandsfoot. 20 Portland, Chesil to Lulworth. 23 Wool, So'ton, Kensington. **May.** 10 Woking Waterers. **Jul.** 14 Slough, Wexham Grove. 15 Windsor. 20 T.Wells, Broom Hill. 24 Left B.H. **Aug.** 17. Margate, Minster, Sandwich, Betteshanger. 21 Sandwich, Canterbury, home. **Sept.** 1 T.Wells, Broom Hill [Salomons]. 4 Ashurst Park [Mr Field]. 5 Broom Hill. 8 Holwood, Bromley. 10 Belvedere/Holwood. 11 Kensington. 26 Atherstone, Merivale Castle. 27 Trentham/Merivale. **Oct.** 1. Stoke Biddulph. 6 to London. 10 *Rainbow* packet to Rotterdam. 11 Hague, Scheveling. 17 Rotterdam/Antwerp. 19 Brussels/Paris. 30 to Calais. **Nov.** 2 to Dover. 4 Dover, London.

1856. **Apr.** 11 Woodstock, Kiddington [Gaskell]. 19 Oxford, Wyatts. 22 Southampton SS. *Atrato.* 23 Review, Spithead/Soton. 24 Netley. 25 Soton, Yacht *Sylph.* 26 Newport IOW, [G.Wyatt]. 28 Gosport/Basingstoke/Oxford. 29 London. **May.** 5 Greenwich, RA Club. **July.** 26.Redhill, Woodhatch [Nicholson]. 28 Eastbourne, Anchor Hotel. 29 London. 31 Kiddington Hall. **Aug.** 2 Birmingham, Congleton. 7 Birmingham, Heyford. 9 Oxford/London. 12 Ryde. 15 Freshwater, Albion Hotel. 16 Brixton, IOW. 18 Ventnor. 30 Bonchurch, Bath House. **Oct.** 18 Ryde, Gosport, London. 20 Lowestoft, Royal Hotel. 22 Pakefield/Yarmouth, Victoria Hotel. 23 *Coromandel,* Gorleston. 24 to London. **Nov.** 7 Petersfield. Dangstein [Neville]. 12 New Grove, Petworth [Robinson]. 17 to London. 19 T.Wells, Ashurst Pk. [Field]. 27 Broom Hill. **Dec.** 2 Ashurst. 6 Redleaf. 8 to London.

1857. **Apr.** 9 Ashurst [Mr Field]. 28 to London. **May.** 4 Manchester, Pendleton. 5 Art Treasures Exhn. 9 to Congleton, Biddulph. 13 Merivale. 16 to Oxford. 18 Kiddington. 20 to London. **Jun.** 1 *Great Eastern* steamship, Greenwich. **Jul.** 23 Erith, Belvedere, London. 28 Bristol [Swan Hotel]. 29 SS *Juverna* to 30 Queenstown. **Aug.** 1 HMS *Agamemnon.* 4 to Valentia. 13 to Waterville. 14 Killarney. 18 to Waterford, *Camilla* to Bristol. 19 to London. **Sept.** 3 Bonchurch. 7 to London. 10 Folkestone/ Boulogne/Paris. 12 Strasbourg/Basle. 14 Lucerne/Fluellen. 15 St Gothard to Milan. 17 Venice. **Oct.** 10 Padua. 12 Venice. **Nov.** 13 Verona. 14 Milan. 16 Verona for Passport. 17

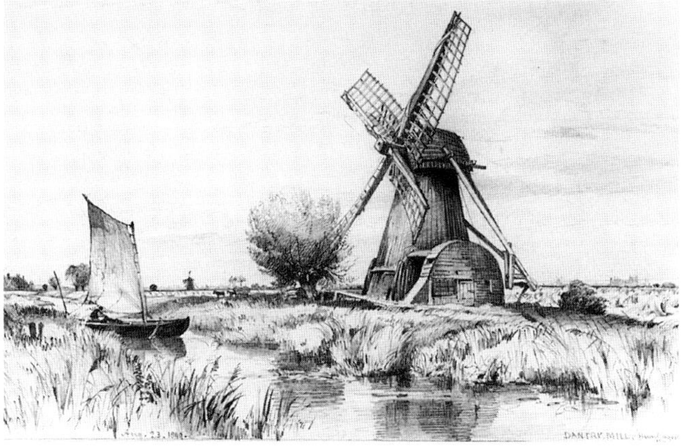

Plate 323. Pencil drawing
Dantry Mill, Huntingdon. Aug. 1849
On a visit to John Moyer Heathcote and his two artist sons at Conington Castle, they went afloat and along the River Nin (Nene) – *dined in the boat and all drew watermills (draining).*
Photo courtesy Martyn Gregory. Private Collection

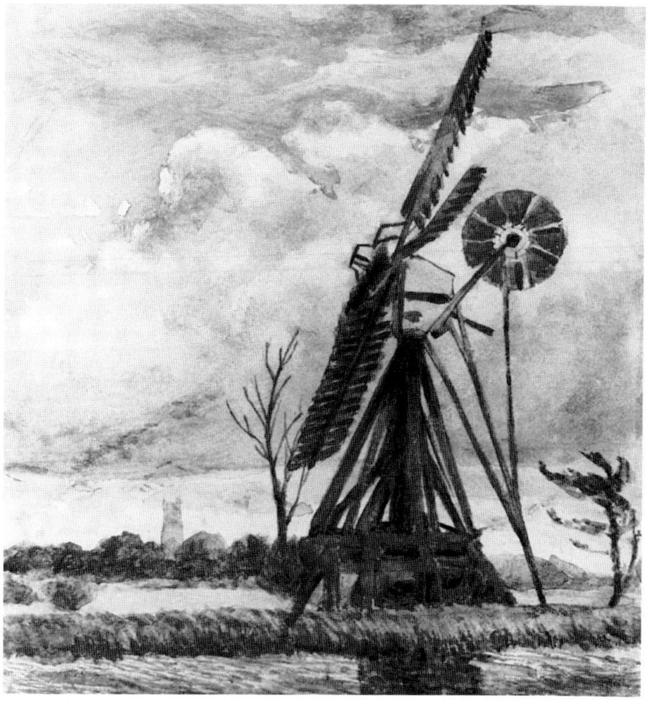

Plate 324 Watercolour
Fen draining windmill Photo courtesy Martyn Gregory

Milan/Turin. 18 Aix/Geneva/Macon. 19 to Paris. 24 to Calais/Dover. **Dec.** 4 Greenwich, SS.*Leviathan.*

1858. **Jan.** 9 Hackney Jun. 19 Margate. 21 to London pr steamer. 25 Milford Haven SS. *Malakoff.* 26 Waterford, Killarney. 27 Valentia. **July.** 2 Blasquetts. 24 Killarney. 25 to Dublin. 27 Chester. 28 Biddulph. 31 London. **Aug.** 6 Bridport, Lyme Regis. 7 Beer by boat. 14 Seaton. 19 Axmouth Harbour. 24 Sidmouth. 25 Weymouth [Victoria Hotel]. 26 Sandsfoot Castle. 30 Portland. **Sept.** 3 to London. 7 Dover/Calais. 8 Paris/ Macon. 9 Geneva/St.Martin. 10 Chamounix. 11 Mer de Glace. 12 Glacier du Bossons. 13 Do. 14 Tete Noir to Martigni. 15 Visperthal, S.Niklaus. 17 Zermatt. 18 Gorner Grat. 20 Ascent/Chatillon. 21 Caluso. 22 Novara & Ticino. 23 Milan/Venice. 24 Venice 4 AM. **Nov.** 19 Milan. 20 Novara, Genoa. 24 Savona/S.Remo. 25 Nice. 26 Marseilles. 27 Lyons. 28 Paris. 29 Calais ½ p 2 AM. 30 Home at 930 PM.

1859. **Apr.** 7 Reigate [Nicholson]. 21 Newhaven. 22 Seaford. 23 E.Grinstead, Redhill. 24 to London. **May.** 2 Greenwich RA Club. 9 Ramsgate. 14 Broadstairs, Kingsgate. 15 Pegwell Bay. 16 Dover/ Folkestone. 17 Shorncliffe, Sandgate. 18 Hastings, Albion Hotel. 20 to London. **Jul.** 12 Ash Grove. 13 Penshurst. 14 to London. 30 Biddulph. **Aug.** 4 Birmingham/London. 6 Wexham, Slough. 10 Greenwich, *Great.Eastern* steamship. 13 Ash Grove. 16 to London. 19 to Edinburgh. 20 Portobello. 21 Leith. **Sept.** 2 Dysart, Wemyss. 3 North Berwick. 5 Greenock [Caird]. 9 to Aberdeen. 12 B.Assn. Meeting. 22 Balmoral, Ballater. 30 to Greeenock. **Oct.** 4. SS *Windsor Castle* down the Clyde. 5 Paisley. 7 Loch Fyne, Callton Mor. 10 Kilmory. 11 SS *Iona* to Greenock. 13 Millport. 17 to Edinburgh. 19 Jardine Hall. 21 to Manchester, Biddulph. 27 Colwick, Cliffords Inn. 28 Merivale. 29 to London.

1860. **Mar.** 31 AGBF Freemason's Tav. **Apr.** 14 Glendining, Ash Grove. 24 to Oxford. 25 Kiddington. 27 to town. **May.** 19 *Magician* to Margate. **Jun.** 15. Biddulph. 20 Merivale [Dugdale]. 21 to town. 27 to

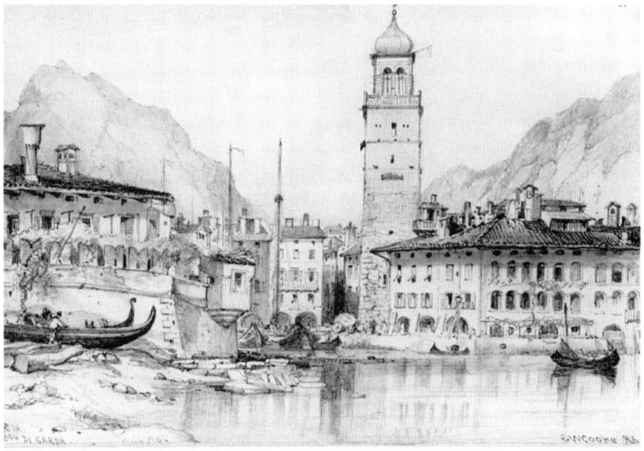

Plate 325. Pencil drawing
Riva, Lago di Garda. August 20th 1850
On his way to Venice, staying at Riva overnight, Cooke found time for three sketches about the lakeside town, in a strong southerly wind he noted. Photo courtesy Martyn Gregory

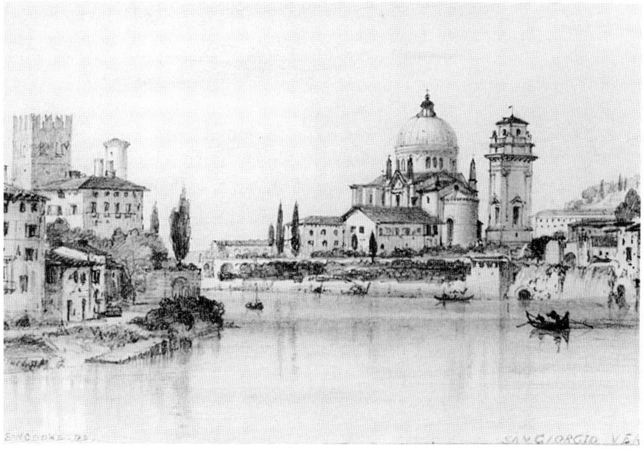

Plate 326. Pencil drawing
San Giorgio Verona
Photo courtesy Martyn Gregory

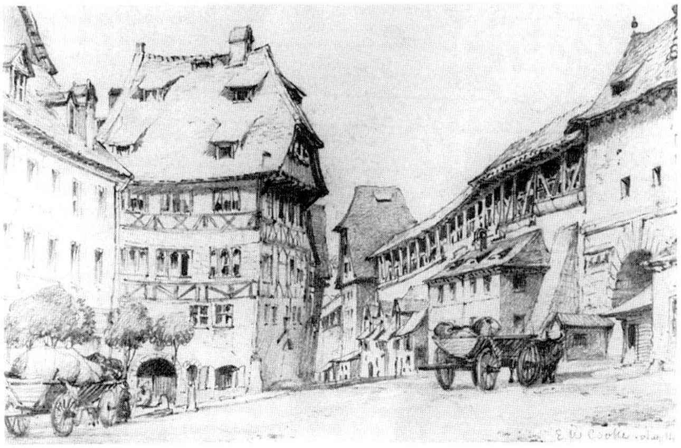

Plate 327. Pencil drawing
Albert Dürer's house Nürnberg [1850]
This drawing from sketches made at the scene on his only visit to the city was published in *Leaves from my Sketch-book,* 1876, with appropriate notes on the *Dürerhaus.* Photo courtesy Martyn Gregory

Oxford (British Assn.) **Jul.** 5 home. 12 The Cedars [John Penn]. **Aug.** 21 Poole [Jas Salter]. 23 Swanage. 25 Shanklin, Daish's Hotel. 28 Portsmouth, home. **Sept.** 7 Wimbledon [J. Murray]. 26 Dover-Calais, Verviers. 27 Cologne. 28 Dresden. **Oct.** 4 to Scheveling. 8 Antwerp, Ghent, Calais, Dover. 9 home. 20 Folkestone-Boulogne-Paris. 22 to Marseilles. 24 Barcelona. 28 Monserrat. 30 Tarragona **Nov.** 4 Tortosa. 5 Valencia. 10 to Almansa. 11 Madrid. 16 Valencia. 17 Alicante. **Dec...** Murcia. 9 to Cartagena.

1861. **Jan.** 3 *Mercurio* to Almeria. 4 to Malaga. 30 to Granada. **Feb.** 19. Gibraltar. 25 to Tangier. **Mar.** 8 Gibraltar. 13 to Cadiz. 14 Jerez, Seville. 16 to Cordoba. 18 to Seville, Cadiz. 21 to Algeciras. 22 Gibraltar. 23 Malaga. 27 Gibraltar. **Apr.** 1 HMS *Ariadne* 2 Immortalité. 5 SS *Delta.* 10 Southampton & home. **Jun.** 8 Rosherville. 10 Kew. 15 Biddulph. 19 home. 21 Reigate. **Jul.** 6 Southend. 7 to Kensington. 24 Peterborough. Connington. 25 Oakham, Stamford, Connington. 27 Mr Smyth's, Billing Road. 29 Castor, Peterboro, Houghton. 30 Northampton/Houghton. 31 home. **Aug.** 3 Ash Grove. 5 Seven Oaks, home. 24 Frome, Orchard Leigh, Duckworth. 27 Longleat/Frome. 28 Home. **Sept.** 2 Congleton. 6 Manchester, BA meetg. 16 Worcester [Sir C. Hastings]. 20 Witley [Lord Dudley]/Worcester. 21 Malvern/Worcester. 23 Bristol/Taunton/Barton Grange. 24 Minehead. 25 Blue Anchor. 27 Watchet. 28 Barton Grange. **Oct.** Home. 15 Hastings, St Leonards. 16 Eastbourne. **Nov.** 25 to Brighton, Eastbourne. 30 to Town. **Dec.** 7 Eastbourne. 9 home.

1862. **Apr.** 14 Eastbourne. 19 Pevensey, Hurstmonceux, Eastbn. 21 Brighton/Eastbn. 22 home - Dangstein, Liss. 24 home. 27 Dartford/home. **May.** 5 Greenwich. 6 home. 24 Oxford. 27 home. **Jun.** 21 Penshurst/Redleaf. 25 home. **Jul.** 7 Reigate, Wallfield [Hughes]. 9 home. 12 Brentwood [Lovell Reeve]. 14 home. 26 Watford [Longman]. 28 home. **Aug.** 16 Hunstanton to Cromer. 21 to Ipswich. 22 *Alma* to Harwich/home. 28 Watchet, Blue Anchor. **Sept.** 8 Porlock Wier. 17 Ilfracombe, Britannia Hotel. 18 Combe Martin. 20 left Porlock Wier, Taunton/home. 27 Dover, Calais, Paris. 28 to Basle. 29 Zurich/Char. 30 Splugen. **Oct.** 1 Como. 2 Bergamo. 3 Venice. 11 Padua. 14 Venice. **Nov.** 17 to Padua. 18 Ferrara. 20 Bologna. 21 Modena. 22 Parma. 24 Milan. 25 Certosa/Milano. 26 Turin, Susa, Lans le Bourg. 27 Culoz. 28 Paris. **Dec.** 1 Calais Dover/Victoria.

1863. **Jan.** 16 Eastbourne. 20 Hastings, St Leonards, Victoria. **Apr.** 10. Dover. 14 *Maid of Kent,* Calais. 21 Dunkerque/Calais. 25 Dover/ Folkestone. 26 home. **May.** 4 Greenwich, dinner. 9 Kings Langley. 11 to Town. 15 Tonbridge, Horsmonden [Austen]. 16 Leigh Park, Redleaf. 18 to Town. **Jul.** 2 Crystal Palace Hotel. 4 Home. 7 Greenwich. 9 C.Palace Hotel. 14 Pulborough, Storrington. 15 Parham. 16 Worthing, Littlehampton, Storrington 17 Petworth/Town. 20 *Engineer* to Tilbury & retn. 25 Romford [Dr Newman]. **Aug.** 1 Strood, Rochester. 2 Sheerness and back. 3 Preston Hall. 4 Bedgebery. 5 Scotney. 6 Bayham Abbey. 7 Bodiam Castle/home. 10 Biddulph. 15 Holyhead HMS *Majestic.* 21 Warrington. 24 Newcastle upon Tyne. **Sept.** 2 Tynemouth, Cullercoats. 4 Marsden, South Shields. 5 Durham. 7 to Lincoln. 8 to Hull. 9 Beverley, Hull, Lincoln, Peterboro/Home. 19 to Eastbourne. 21 home. 24 Dover/Calais/Paris. 26 to Basle. 27 to Lucerne. 28 via Lugano. 29 Milan. 30 Venice. **Nov.** 3 to Trieste. 4 Malta to Ancona. 6 to Rimini. 7 Ravenna. 8 Bologna. 11 Piacenza/Genoa. 13 via San Remmo. 14 Mentone, Nice. 16 Marseilles/Paris. 19 Boulogne/Folkestone/home.

1864. **Apr.** 14 Rye, Winchelsea. 15. Lydd, Dungeness, Deal. 16 Sandown, Walmer. 18 to Canterbury, Penshurst. 20 to Town. 22 Stratford on Avon. 25 Warwick-Town. **May.** 19 Broadstairs. 20 Ramsgate & back. 21 Margate & back. 25 to Town. **Jul.** 2 Romford, Havering. 4 in Town. 16 Streatham [Mr Leaf]. 23 Reigate. 25 to Town. 30 to Easthbourne. **Aug.** 1 to Town. 5 at Hackney. 6 Dartford [Mr Cozier's]. 13 Abbot's Langley, Nash Mills. 20 T.Wells, Groombridge. 22 to Town. 27 Petworth, Robinson. 29 to Town. **Sept.** 5. Wexham Slough/home. 10 to Storrington. 13 Petworth/ home. 16 to Congleton, Biddulph. 20 to Town. 28 Dover, Calais, Paris, Strasbourg. Karlsruhe. 30 Munich. **Oct.** 1 Dresden, Insbruck. 2 Bolsena, Trento, Verona. 3 Venice. **Nov.** 4 Rovigo, Bologna, Florence. 11 Leghorn, SS *Isere.* 12 Genoa. 13 Marseilles (by sea). 14 Paris. 21 Calais, Dover, home.

1865. **Jan.** 14 St Leonards. 18 to Town. 19 Hastings. 22 to Town. **May.** 5 Broadstairs 13. Deal/Ramsgate/Broadstairs. 17 to Town. **June.** 17 Kings Langley. 24 Haslemere, Midhurst. **Jul.** 1 Billing Road, Mr Smyth. 4 Blisworth and to Town. 8 to Wm Longman's (?Ashlyns). 10 left Ashlyns for Town. 22 Oxford. 28 in London. 29 Tonbridge, Horsmonden [Mr Austen]. 31to Redleaf/Broomhill. **Aug.** 1 to Town. 16 to Poole. The Hive, Parkstone. 19 Blandford & Durweston. 21 The Hive. 22 Sailing off Old Harry. 24 to Town/Reigate/Home. 26 Redleaf. **Sept.** 2 Redhill. 4 Gomshall, Abinger. 7 Birmingham. 9 Colebrookdale. 14 Cannock Chase. 15 Worcester/Colwall. 18 Biddulph. 20 Arley Hall. 21 Warrington/Euston, home. 23 Alton, Selbourne. 25 Farnham, Waverley/Wycke. 29 Burford lodge, Box Hill. **Oct.** 7 Back again. 12 Greenwich [Mr Mathew]/Dorking. 14 Haywards Heath. 18 at Petworth. 19 Petworth House. 23 to Redhill/Reigate/Dorking. 24 Pulborough/ Petworth. 27 in Town. 28 Haywards Heath & back. **Nov.** 2 to Balcombe. 4 Haslemere. 6 Lurgishaw, Black Down. 7 to Town. 21 Haslemere, Weycombe & home. 25 Lewes/Isfield & back. 29 Haslemere, Hoebourne Farm. 30 Friday Hill/home. **Dec.** 1 Eastbourne. 4 Uckfield. 5

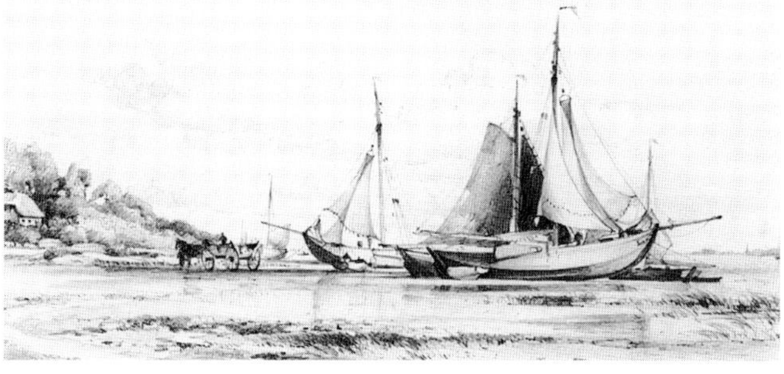

Plate 328. Pencil drawing
Blankenese on the Elbe, Denmark, near Hamburg
This view, from the opposite direction to 71/10 (Plate 101), may be that of 55/13, the other Blankenese title, exhibited at the British Institution in 1856. Photo courtesy Martyn Gregory

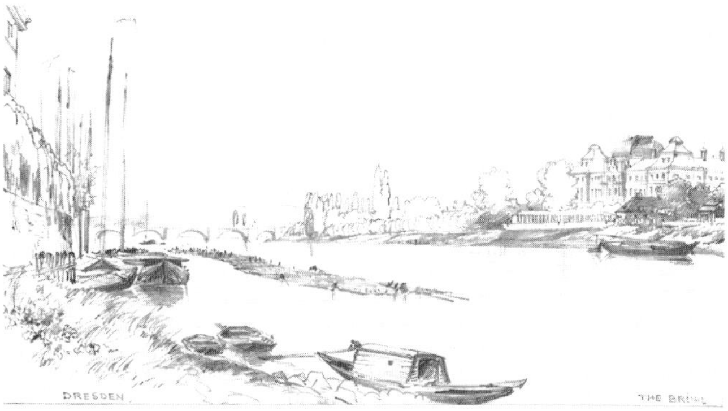

Plate 329. Pencil drawing
Dresden. The river & The Bruhl
The view from the Augustus Bridge towards the Albert Bridge with the snaking raft of timber on the River Elbe was probably drawn in 1853.
Photo courtesy Martyn Gregory

Pevensey Bay. 6 in Town. 7 to Eastbourne & back. 15 Groombridge. 16 in Town. 19 to Groombridge (GB). 20 to Town. 28 to GB. 29 to Town.

1866. **Jan.** 1 At St Leonards/Town. 4 St Leonards. 23 to Town. 25 St Leonards. **Feb.** 1 to Town. 6 T.Wells. 7 in Town. **Apr.** 14 Penshurst/Redleaf. 18 GB. **May.** 2 Kensington. 22 GB. 31 In Kensington. **June.** 26 Dulwich. **Jul.** 2 to GB. 3 to Town. 16 to GB. 20 to Town. **Aug.** 15 to GB. 28 to Town. **Sept.** 1 to GB. 7 to Kensington & Congleton. 11 to Town. 12 to GB. **Oct.** 13 to Kensington. 16 to GB. **Nov.** 17 to Eastbourne. 21 at GB. 27 in Town & back. **Dec.** 1 to Town & back. 10 to Town. 11 to GB. 18 to Town. 19 to GB. 21 to Kensington.

1867. **Jan.** 24. to St Leonards. 29 Lealands.GB. 31 Town. **Mar.** 30 GB & back. **Apr.** 10 to Paris [Int. Exhib.]. 29 to London. **May.** 1 GB. 2 to Town. 23 at GB; back to Town. 26 Blackheath. **June.** Mitcham, GP Bidders. 3 to Town. 14 to GB. **Jul.** 11 Margate /return. 15 Southampton, Bidder's yacht *Mayfly*. 19 to Portsmouth/Petworth, 22 to Town, 29 GB/return. **Aug.** 3 Wexham, Slough. 4 to Town. 5 to GB. 8 at Kensington. 10 to Ramsgate. 11 to Town. 17 Windsor. 19 to Kensington. 24 to Margate. 28 GB/return. 30 to Edinburgh. 31 Portobello. **Sept.** 3 to Dundee. 11 Perth and Stirling. 12 Shandon .16 Greenock/Town. 20 to GB. 21 Havering. 26 at GB. **Oct.** 8 Brambletye/ret. 15 to Town. 16 GB. **Dec.** 10 at GB. 24 to Kensington. 26 to Grbdge.

1868. **Jan.** 1 to Town. **Feb.** 21 to Summerford. 22 to GB. 24. Kensington. **Mar.** 11 Graphic & Fine Arts Club. **Apr.** 9 GB & back. 23 GB, Summerford. 25 to Town. **May.** 6. to GB. 9 to Town, Slough [Hillersdon]. 11 to Town. 13 to GB. 16 to Kensington/Penshurst. 18 to Town. 19 at Edmnton. 20 Kensington. 29 to GB/Summerford. 30to Kensington. **June.** 4 to GB/ Summerford. 17 to Town, Fine Arts Club. 30 last night at the *Ferns*. **Jul.** 1 To GB, 1st night in *Glen Andred* (GA). 7 Lower Sydenham. 9 to Town, Langham Hotel. 10 to G'bridge. **Nov.** 24 East Grinstead, to vote/to Town/and back.

1869. **Jan.** 25. To Southampton, *Normandy* to Guernsey. 29 *Waverley* to So'ton. 30 in Town. **Feb.** 5. at GA. **Mar.** 18 to Town, Grosvenor Hotel. 19 at GA. **Apr.** 5. to Town, Athenaeum. 8 to GA. 24 to Town. Kew. 30 New Royal Academy PV. **Sept.** 4 to Brighton. 5 to GA. 9 Sevenoaks. 10 to GA. **Oct.** 11. to Town/Pinner. 12 to Hull/Bridlington, Britannia Hotel. 13 Filey, Crescent Hotel. 14 Scarborough/Whitby, Rly Hotel. 16 Middlesborough. 18 Marton Hall [Bolckow], Fountains Abbey/ Harrogate, Prospect Hotel. 19 York. 20 to Town. 24 at GA. **Nov.** 11 to Town at Goodall's. 12 to GA. 19 Redhill. 26 at GA. **Dec.** 15 to Town, RA Election. 16 to GA.

1870. **Jan.** 1 to Town & back. 25 to Town, RA Election. 26 to GA. **Feb.** 7. to Redleaf & back. **Apr.** 1 to Town (RA). 4 to. GA. 14 to Town & back. 16 to St Leonards. 21 Normanhurst [Brassey]. 25 to Town, R.A. VD. 27 at GA. **May.** 2 to GA. 28 to Town/Kings Langley. 30 to Graemsdyke, Pinner. **June.** 1 to Town/GA. 16 to Town, Gomshall & back. 23 to Crystal Palace/Town. 29 to GA. **Jul.** 9 to Town, Dickens' sale. Oxford. 20 to Slough/GA. **Aug.** 2 to Town & back. **Sept.** 8 to Town via Sevenoaks. 9 to Rowsley, Stancliffe. 11 Matlock/Darley. 12 to Chatsworth. 13 to Liverpool/New Ferry. 14 Rock Ferry/L'pool, B.A.Meeting. 21 to Newcastle, Benwell Hill. 23 Cragside. 26 to Morpeth/Newcastle, Jesmond. 27 Jarrow & back. 28 to Middlesborough [Bolckow]. 29 York, Station Hotel. 30 to Town/GA. **Oct.** 13 to Cranbrook. 15 to GA. 29 to Town, Wandsworth. 3 to Town. **Nov.** 1 GA. 2 Crowboro'/Withyham. 7 at GA.

1871. **Jan.** 7 to St Leonards. 12 T.Wells/GA. **Feb.** 10. to Town. 11.Reigate. 14 at GA. 27 to Town & back. **Mar.** 30 to Town (RA). **Apr.** 1 to GA. 18 to Town & back. 20 No. 22 Pall Mall. 25 to GA. 26 to Town. **May.** 6 to GA. 8 to Town. 25 to GA. **June.** 8 to South Ken. 10 at GA. 22 to Town. 23 in Town. 24 at GA. 28 in Town, RA soirée. **Jul.** 1 at GA. 10 to Penryn. 11 Constantine. 12 Conrad's wedding. 13 at the Lizard. 15 Kynance cove. Helston. 17 Kynance. 19 Landewednack. 21 Bumble rock. 24 Marazion [Mrs Warrington Smythe], Penzance, Newlyn. 25 Kynance. 26 Kynance. 27 Constantine. 28 Penryn. Paddington. 29 to HPG & GA. **Aug.** 11 Town, Newcastle, Rothbury. 12

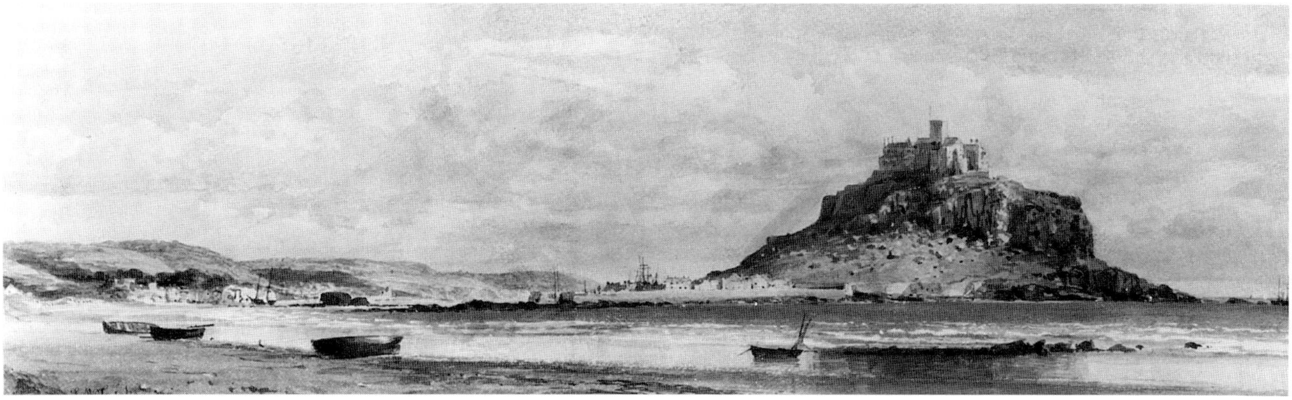

Plate 330. Watercolour
St Michael's Mount, Cornwall 1858
This drawing has the air of a seventeenth century topographical view.
Photo courtesy Martyn Gregory

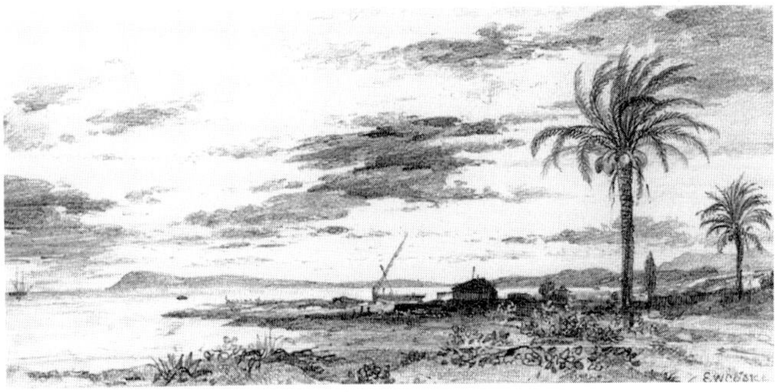

Plate 331. Pencil drawing
Near Alicante, Spain [1861] L32
A westward evening sky, a lateen-rigged fishing vessel and a palm tree could be said to summarise Cooke's delight in Mediterranean scenery.
Photo courtesy Martyn Gregory

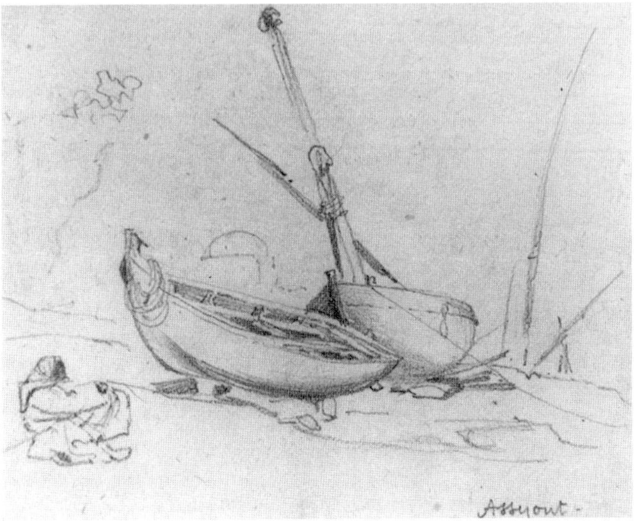

Plate 332. Pencil drawing
Assyout. 25th Mar. [1874]
Photo courtesy Martyn Gregory

at Cragside. 18 Brinkburn. 22 Bamborough. 24 Dunstanburgh, Warkworth. 25 Cragside. 29 to London. 30 to GA. **Sept.** 27 Possingworth [Huth]. 28 to GA. **Oct.** 21 Battle, Normanhurst Ct. 23 to GA. **Nov.** 9 Uckfield [Dr Bennett]. 10 to GA. 16 to Town. 17.Clapham [Conrad's]. 20 Pinner [Goodall]. **Dec.** 9 at GA. 20 to Town. 25 at GA. 30 to Town PV OM RA. 31 to GA.

1872. **Jan.** 28 to Town [Con's]. 30 to GA. **Mar.** 19 to Town [RA]. **Apr.** 7 to GA. 25 to Town, RS Club. 26 RA VD. **May.** 5 Mortlake [Prof Owen]. 7 to GA. **June.** 20 in Town [RSClub]. 21 to GA. 26 to Town. 29 at GA. **Jul.** 3 in Town, to GA. 15 to Town & back. 27 Findon, Brighton [Willett]. 30 to GA. **Aug.** 8 to Brighton. 9 to Town. 10 to Brighton. 11 to GA. 13 to Brighton [B.Assn Meeting]. 17 to GA. 19 to Brighton. 23 to GA. 28 to Chilworth [Austen]. 29 Joldwynds, Gomshall [Bowman]. 30 to GA. 31 Uckfield, Newick Pk. [Sclater]. **Sept.** 2 to GA. 4 to Brighton & back. 6 to Town, Pampesford [Hamond]. 9 to Cambridge & back. 10 to Royston/Clapham. 11 to GA. 24 to Town. 25 Highnam Ct [Parry]. 26 in Gloucester. 27 Berkeley Cas & back. 28 to Worcester/Ironbridge. 29 at Benthall Hall [Maw]. 30 Stafford/Town/GA. **Oct.** 7 St Leonards. 8 to GA. 19 to Town. 21 at GA. **Nov.** 5 to Town. 6 to GA. 30 Buxted, Oldlands [Nesbit]. **Dec.** 2 Lewes to GA. 5 to Town, RS Club, RA. 6 to GA. 12 to Town. 16 at GA. 27 Penshurst, Redleaf & back. 31 to Clapham.

1873. **Jan.** 1 at Clapham to GA. 7 to Town. 8 to GA. 17 to Eastbourne/St Leon. 21 St Leonards to Town. 23 at GA. **Feb.** 11 to Town. 13 at GA. 15 to Town. Stephens. 17 to GA. 19 to Town. ***2. GA,*** to Town. 27 at GA. **Mar.** 1 to Town. 5 to GA. 14 to Town. 18 to GA. 25 to Town. 27 at 22 Pall Mall [RA hangng.]. **Apr.** 28 to GA. 29 to Town. **May.** 7 to Farnham [Hook]. 8 Fernhurst [Dobson]. 9 Petworth [Upton]. 10 Whitley [Foster]. Town. 31 to GA. **June.** 7 to Uckfield, Newick Pk.[Sclater]. 10 GA. 17 to Town. 18 to GA. 20 to Portsmouth/Ryde [Gassiotts]. 21 Portsmouth Dockyd. 22 at Gassiott's. 23 Spithead Review [Shah]. 25 Bonchurch. 26 to Town. 27 to GA. 28 to Seven Oaks [Prestwicks]. **Jul.** 1 in Town. 3 to Portsmouth Ryde. 7 Ryde to GA. 10 in Town. 11 to GA. 12 to Uckfield [Nesbit]. 15 in Town. 16 to GA. 28 to Battle, Netherfield. 29 Netherfield, Boring, to GA. **Aug.** 8 to Town. 9 to Bayfordbury. 12 to Hertford/Town. 26 to Combe Pk., Seven Oaks. 28 to Uckfield/GA. **Sept.** 12 to Brighton .13 to GA. 14 to Town. 15 to Barmouth. 16 to Portmadoc, Penryn. 22 to Llanfarfechan. 24 Llandudno, Conway/back. 25 Bettwys, Capel Curig. 26 to Warwick. 29 to Town/GA. **Oct.** 3 to Town. 4 to GA. 11 in Town/Farnborough [Mongredien]. 13 Town. 15 at GA. 28 to Town. 29 to GA. **Nov.** 8 to Town. 11 at GA. 22 to Town/Pinner. **Dec.** 1 G A/to Town. 3 at GA. 5 to Town. 8 at GA. 11 in Town. 13 to GA. 16 to Town. 22 GA/to Town/back. 28 to Town. 29 to Paris. 31 Versailles.

1874. **Jan.** 1 Paris to Culoz. 2 to Turin. 3 to Bologna. 4 to Brindisi SS *Simla.* 9 Alexandria. 10 to Cairo. 14 to Heliopolis & back. 15 to Tourah & back. 21 boarded *dahabeah.* **Feb.** 2 at Feshan. 5 at Abooseyeh. 11 Siout. 14 Sohag. 18 Luxor. 21 Karnak. 23 Assouan. 27 to Philae & back. **Mar.** 1 left Assouan. 2 Kom Ombos. 3 Edfou. 5 Esneh. 7 Mutaneh. 9 Karnak. 15 Tombs at Thebes. 17 left Luxor. 20 Keneh/to Denderah. 25 Assiout. 27 Rhoda /Beni Hassan. 29 Minieh. **Apr.** 3 Cairo. 5 Alex. 6 SS *Simla.* 10 Brindisi/Ancona. 11 Bologna/Turin. 12 Paris. 16 Calais. 17 Dover/London/Clapham. 18 to GA. 22 to Town. 25 at GA. 27 to Town VD RA & back. 30 Royal PV RA to Town. **May.** 11 GA to Town, Upper Tulse Hill. 12 [Huggins] to Town. 14 at GA. 27 to Town. 28 Gomshall & back. 29 to GA. **June.** 2 to Town. 13 Uckfield [Sclater]. 16 GA. **Jul.** 2 to Town. 3 to GA. 11 to Redhill/Reigate, Colley Manor. 14 G A to Town. 17 GA. 19 St Leonards. 21 to Crystal Palace /Town. 22 to GA. 26 at H. Bicknell's. 27 to GA. **Aug.** 1 to Uckfield, Horsted Pl. [Barchard]. 5 to Crystal Pal/Town/GA. 7 to Town, Greenwich. 8 to GA. 18 to Town/Carlisle/Stranraer-Larne. 19 Belfast B.Assn.Meeting. 22 to Portrush, Giants Caus. 24 Ballycastle/Belfast. 27Carlisle. 28 London/ G. **Sept.** 4 to Town & back. 12 Redleaf & back. 14 Bedgebury [Hope]. 16 to Battle, Oaklands [Brabazon]. 17 to GA. 19 to Town/Sittingbourne Sharsteds [De Laune]. 22 to Town. **Oct.** 1 to Town/Stansted [Maitland]. 3 to Town/GA. 5 to. Portsmouth. 7 to GA. 22 to Town/Streatham Hill [Huggins]. 23 to GA. **Nov.** 12 in Town, to Leeds, Farnley Hall [Fawkes]. 13 to Town. 14 to GA. 18 Town/GA. 23 to Town/Crewe, Crewe Hall. 25 to Town. 27 at GA. **Dec.** 2 to Town. 3 to GA. 6 [at Pickersgills] to GA. 31 to Town RA Councils.

1875. **Jan.** 1 in Town [Sopwith's]. 27 to Lewes & back. **Feb.** 6 to Brighton. 8 to GA. 27 St.Leonards. **Mar.** 1 to GA. 4 to Town RSoc Club. 5 to GA. 17 to Town. 18 to GA. 31 to Town. 22 Pall Mall. **Apr.** 3 to GA. 23 to Town VD RA. 24 to GA. 29 town. **May.** 8 in Town/Dover, SS *Bessemer* to Calais. 10 Dover/London. 14 G A /to Portsmouth. 15 to Ryde. 17 to Portsmouth/GA. **June.** 15 at GA. 22 to Town/*Warspite* & back. 23 to Town. 27 at GA. **Jul.** 1 to Town/Birmingham, Litchfield. 5 to Town, RA Elections. 6 GA. 17 to Town. 20 at GA. 24 town/Teynham [DeLaune]. 26 Betteshanger. 27 to Sandwich/Town/St Albans & back. **Aug.** 6 to Town & back. 12 to Seven Oaks, Combe Bank [Spottiswoode]. 14 to Paddock Wood, Capel Manor [Austen]. 17 at GA. 25 to Bristol B.Assn. 28 to Portishead/Clifton. 30 to Tortworth Pk [Ducie]. 31 to Bristol. **Sept.** 2 Stanton Drew, Chedder and return. 3 to Town/GA. 18 to Wisbech [Peckover]. 20 to Peterboro'/Holme [Heathcote]. 21 Holme Wood [Wells]. 23 to Stansted. 25 to Town/GA. **Oct.** 4 to Ryde. 6 to Yarmouth & back. 7 to Town/GA. 9 to Buxted, Old Lands. 11 at GA. 16 Sherwood [Smith]. 17 to GA. **Nov.** 9 to Town. 10 to Hertingfordbury [Baker]. 11 to Bedwell Pk. [Hanbury]/Town/GA. 13 to Brighton. 15 to Uckfield [Bennett]. 16 to GA. **Dec.** 29 to Town & back.

1876. **Jan.** 1 to Town. 4 at GA. 6 at Sopwith's. 8 at GA. 22 Brighton & back. **Feb.** 3 to Town. 5 GA. 19 to Town. 20 to GA. 23 to Town. 29 at GA. **Mar.** 1 to Town. 4 G A, to Town/St Leonards. 6 to GA. 25 to Town. 28 GA. 30 to Town. **Apr.** 4 to GA. 5 to Town. 6 to GA. 8 to

Town. 9 to St Leonards. 13 GA. 21 to Town RA VD & back. 26 to Town. 27 to GA. 28 to Town. **May.** 1 to GA. 13 to Town. 14 to GA. **June.** 1to Town, RS Club. 8 at G A, to Town. 9 to GA. 10 to Town. 12 at GA. 15 to Town. 16 to GA. 17 to Worthing [Wilson Saunders]. 19 to GA. 29 to Town. **Jul.** 1 to GA. 11 to Town. 15 at GA. 22 to Uckfield [Sclater]. 24 to GA. 25 to Town/Clapham [Con.]. 26 to Welwyn [The Frythe]. 27 to Town. 28 to GA. **Aug.** 1 to Town & back. 5 to Town & back. 11 to Town & back. 13 to Eastbourne. 14 to GA. 19 to Joldwynds [Bowman]. 23 at GA. 24.in Town. 25 to Brecon. 28 to Crickhowell/ Raglan. 30.Chepstow/Tintern. 31 Ross/Hereford/Colwall [Peyton]. **Sept.** 1 to Town [Ruckers]. 2 to GA. 8 to Harwich. 9 *Avalon* Rotterdam/ Utrecht. 10 Amsterdam. 11 to Zwolle. 13 Kampen/Amsterdam. 14 Scheveling. 15 Hague & back. 16 to Rotterdam. 19 to Flushing. 20 Sheerness/Town/GA. **Oct.** 9 to Selbourne [Wakes]. 11 to Petworth, Gore Hill [Upton]. 12 to Killington [Robinson]/GA. 14 Lamberhurst Court [Morland]. 16 to GA. 19 to Town R S Club. 22 at GA. **Nov.** 2 to Frome [Orchard Leigh, Duckworth]. 4 to Town/Pampsford. 6 to Town & back. 16 to Town, RS Club. 18 at GA. 27 to Portsmouth. 29 to Worthing/GA. 30 to Town. **Dec.** 1 to GA. 2 T Wells Dornden. 7 to Town, RS Club. 18 at GA. 20 to Town. 21 to GA. 30 to Town PV OM.

1877. **Apr.** 26 VD RA. 27 in Town RA. **May.** 7 to G A [lost Diary]. 12 Old Lands [Nesbitt]. 14 to GA. 16 to Town. 17 to GA. 25 to Town. 27 at GA. 30 to Town, RS Recepn. **June.** 1 to GA. 4 to Town. 9 at GA. 13 to Town, RS.Soirée. 16 Uckfield [Sclater]. 21 in Town. 23 at GA. 26 to Town. 27 to Combe Bank/GA. **Jul.** 4 to Town. 5 to GA. 19 to Combe Bank & back. **Aug.** 1 to Wisbech. 2 to Town. 8 G A to Town/Plymouth. 13 East Looe. 14 Plymouth. 23 Newton, Torquay. 24 to Moor? 28 to Town [Hannahs]. 29 to GA. **Sept.** 4 to Town & back. 6 to Brighton/back. 7 to Lewes, Conyboro [Dodson] 8 to GA. 11 To Newhaven [+ MNC]. 12 *Alexandra* to Dieppe/Paris. 14 Portalier by mistake. 15 Berne/Modane. 16 Turin. 19 to Venice **Oct.** 15 Verona & back. 17 to Conegliano & back. 22 to Turin. 23 to Culoz. 24 Paris. 26 to Chartres & back. 27 to Boulogne *Foam* Do Dover/Canterbury [Fleur de Lys]. 29 to GA. 31 to Town & back. **Nov.** & **Dec.** at GA.

1878. **Jan.** 1 to Town. 2 to GA. 16 to Town, RA Electns. 21 at GA. 29 in Town. 30 in Town. **Feb.** 4 at GA. 13 to Town/Surbiton [Shoubra]. 14 to GA. **Mar.** 9 to Town *[Cleopatra]* Oxford [Wyatt]. 10 to Town/GA. **Apr.** 4 to Town [103 Jermyn St]. 9 to GA. 17 to Town Geolgl Club. 18 to GA. 25 to Town RA VD. 27 to GA. **May.** 1 in Town. 6 to GA. 15 Swaylands/Redleaf/ret. 16 to Town. 17 to GA. 22 to Town R Soc Recep. 24 at GA. **June.** 1 [Sherwood] & back. 5 to Town Geolgl Club &c. 7.Kew/GA. 18 to Town new *Warspite.* 20 to GA. 27 to Town R Soc &

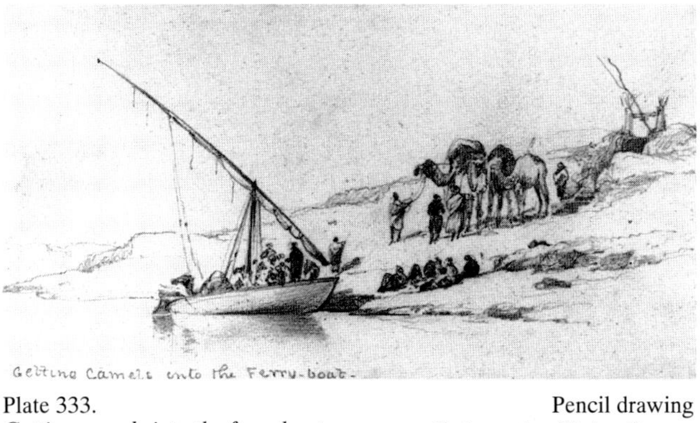

Plate 333. Pencil drawing
Getting camels into the ferry boat
Photo courtesy Martyn Gregory

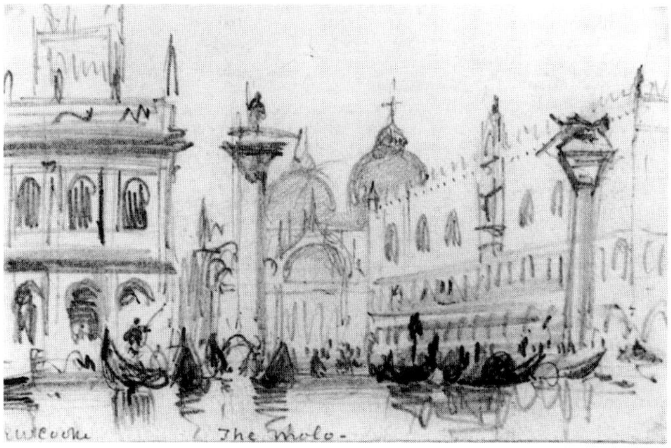

Plate 334. Pencil drawing
Venice: The Molo
Almost a scribble, it appears to record an *aqua alta,* where the lagoon overflowed the Piazzetta.
Photo courtesy Martyn Gregory

RA. 29 to GA. **Jul.** 11 in Town, to GA. **Aug.** 1 to Town & back. 3 to Eastbourne. 5 to Brighton. 6 to Swanage. 10 to GA. 12 to Holyhead SS *Leinster.* 13 Dublin [Arcbp Trench] B.A Meeting. 14 Howth & back. 17 to Powerscourt &c. 21 to Malahide &c. 23 SS *Ulster* to Holyhead. 24 to GA. **Sept.** 7 to Town & back. 9 to Folkestone. 10 *Alexandra* to Boulogne/Rouen. 11 Etretat. **Oct.** 15 to Yport & back. 16 to Le Havre. 17 to Honfleur & back. 18 steamer to Caen. 19 to Trouville. 20 to Paris [Passy]. 21 International Exhn until 31 to Calais/Dover/Town. **Nov.** 1 to G A & back. 2 to Dover *Calais-Douvres* to Paris. 4 Exhibition. 9 to Rheims. 10 to Amiens. 11 to Calais *Foam* Dover/GA. 13 to Town RA Elects. 15 at GA. 30 to Town R Soc. **Dec.** 2 RA/to GA. 5 to Town RA. 6 [Leighton's]. 7 to GA. 10 Swalelands [Drummond] & back. 19 to Town RA Elects. 21 at GA. 26 to Dornden [Eaton] & back. 28 to Town, Grosvenor PV.& back.

1879. **Jan.** 1 to Town Japanese at Burlington F A Club. 2 R A Old Masters. 4 to GA. 16 to Town R Soc Club, Soc.Ant. 18 at GA. 22 to Town RA Electns. 23 to GA. **Feb.** 6 to Town, R S Club. 7 to GA. **Mar.** 27 Speldhurst & back. **Apr.** 2 to Town R Soc Recept. 11 GA. 17 to Town. 19 at GA. 24 to Town RA VD.RS Club. 28 at GA. 30 Town PV Grosvenor, RS Club. **May.** 4 to GA. 17 to Town AGBF. 20 at GA. **June.** 12 to Town RS Club. 13 at GA. 19 to Town RA Elects. 23 GA. 24 to Town. 27 at GA. **Jul.** 3 in Town/to GA. 5 to Town/Foots Cray [Pender] & back to GA. 26 to Broomhill & back [Salomons]. 30 to Town & back. **Aug.** 8 to Town RA/GA. 13 to Dover. 14 *Calais-Douvres* Calais/Amiens/Havre 15 Honfleur & back. 26 to Dieppe/Tréport. 27 Eu & back. **Sept.** 5 to Namur. 7 to Dinant & back. 8 to Cologne. 10 to Bingen. 11 to Oberwesel & back [C.Haag]. 12 to Rudesheim & back. 13 to Dusseldorf. 15 to The Hague. 16 at Scheveling. 19 Delft. 21 The Hague. 23 to Antwerp. 25 to Ghent/Ostend. 28 to Bruges & back. 30 *Cmte de Flandres* to Dover /GA. **Oct.** 9 to Yarmouth. 12 Cromer. 14. Norwich/Lowestoft. 15 to Town. 20 at GA. **Nov.** 19 to Town [HMS Pinafore]. 20 R Soc Club. 21 to GA. **Dec.** 20 at GA –

Diary Ends.

Appendix 5

ACCOUNTS for the year 1849

The only surviving example of the artist's careful recording of daily expenditure. The removal to Victoria Road Kensington took place, his first trip to Ireland, much work establishing his garden and there are occasional notes of artists' colours, clothes and household supplies purchased. Expenditure on travel, tips to servants and pew-openers and pictures sent by his carrier Crocker, are useful indications of a mid-century life-style.

A small sheepskin covered account-book with E.W.Cooke printed label on cover, large part of contents cut out. Pages printed in red columns. Paper watermarked *Lane & Co 1829.*

[Inside front cover:]			
Millboard	18 x 23 3/8	*Getting off Shore*	
Canvas	18 x 23	*Fern Cave* frame 51788	[1849]
Millboard	9⅜ x6	*Katwyk*	[1849]
Millboard	10 x 8	*Boat coming into Calais*	
1st page -[mutilated:]			
call	E.Ford		
	Storr		
	E Sheppard		
send	Plumber		
call	Criswick		
write	Shewin		
call	Mr Moore		
write	Hering		
	Harwood		
send	Artists Fund [deleted]		Paid.
Fox -			[Blank]
call	Leighton		5.0d
call	Etty Sub		£1.1.0
-	Church subscription		
call	Gower thick boots		
-	Johnson -wine		£9.16.0
	Lewis.		
second leaf:			
Nov 30	Burrys' spring cart to V[ictoria R[oad]		6.0
-	Men planting Deodar		2.0
Dec 8	Wigley- carting loam to VR		6.0
-	Do. 1 load of stones to VR		4.0
-	Chant-load of loam from Common		6.6
Nov 30	3 men removing Deodar		10.11
-	Wigley 1 load to VR Stones		5.0
-	Crocker for frames & cases VR		6.0
Jany11	Cord for pictures		11.6
	Henry paid for iron gratings		£5.5.0
12	Crocker for carriage of Do.		5.0
26	Wigley for load of earth		5.0
27	Do.		5.0
30	Do.		4.0
31	Crocker brt load of bricks		1.0
30 & 31	3 load of old bricks		1.6
Feb 2	Double load of Wimbledon peat		£1.1.0
31 & 1	2 loads of Stones -Mr Moore		
-	load of stones Redleaf.		
[3 pp blank]			
Jany 1849.			
1.	Mr Day. Garden		6.0
	Busses to VR & City		1.0
	Bishop Andrews' Devotions (Laura E.,)		4.6
	Hosiery		11.6
2	Busses		1.3
	Dinner, string &c		1.5
	Leighton binding L.B.		£1.8.0
	Servt. Xmas box(Austs)		1.0
	James Xmas box		2.6
3	PDC parcels		1.6
4	Busses to VR		1.0
	Fly man		1.6
5	Crocker for frames coming		6.0
	Rail & cabs Clapham		3.9
6	Busses to & fro		2.0
	Henry		£5.0.0
7	Church		2.6
8	Subscription to Schools. Roseblade		£1.1.0
	Hymn book		1.6
	Fly man		1.6

9	Busses (L & I) to VR & back	2.0
10	Busses to VR & City	1.3
11	Busses Hackney	2.0
-	Cab	2.0
-	Writing paper	£2.0.0
-	Stock 2/6 collar 9d	3.3
12	Henry	£5.0.0
	Busses VR	1.0
-	Fly man	3.6
	Servt 1/- Pikes & Bdge 1/2	2.2
13	Busses to VR	1.0
-	Henry	£5.5.0
14	Church- Propg of Gospel	10.0
15	Busses to VR	1.0
16	Crocker for picture BI	10.0
-	Do. for grating to VR.	
-	Balls bill to Xmas	£5.5.0
17	Buss to VR & town & back	2.6
	Taper	6
18	Busses	1.3
-	Servt Uncles	1.0
19	3 cabs	3.2
	Busses	1.3
-	Gloves, White) & a collar (Beans)	2.0
20	Busses	1.1
21	Busses &c	1.4
-	Sheppard on a/c	£5.0.0
22	Busses	1.0
23	Busses with Laura	2.6
-	Luncheon with Henry	10.0
-	Henry on a/c	£5.5.0
-	Crocker's men beer	1.0
-	P D C	.6
24	Post stamps	1.0
	Busses &c	1.2½
	Crockers men	1.0
25	Busses with Mama to VR	1.6
	Crockers men	1.6
26	Busses	1.0
27	Busses &c	1.4
-	Henry	£4.15.0
-	Crocker's men	1.6
30	Criswick's man Gilder	2.6
-	Busses &c	1.2½
-	P D C curtain VR	.8
	Henry lent me	10/-
31	Busses to VR & City	2.0
Feb 1	Busses to VR & Barnes	1.0
	Notepaper 1/- mem book 6d	1.6
-	Criswick's man. Gilt Mouldg.	1.0
2.	Man for carting Wimbledon peat	1.0
	Busses VR 1/- & memn from Green's with picture 1/-	2.0
	James	.6
31	Crocker on acct & 1/-	£2.1.0
3	Busses VR & City & home	4.6
	Henry	5.0
Feb 4	Church	2.6
5	Henry	£1.0.0
	Uncle for Insurance	£5.0.0
	Mama notes	£135.0.0
	Mary for small bills	£ 40.0.0
	Busses	3.4
	Gas man	1.0
6	Busses to VR & back	1.0
	Bread, butter &c VR	1.1

7	busses 1/5 cab 8d	2.2
-	the porter at Institution	1.0
8.	Busses with Mary to VR	1.6
-	Stamps Hull	1.0
-	beer	1.3
-	Crocker & men	5.0
-	Eggleton	2.0
-	James for board	5.0
9.	Crocker	1.0
-	{Cabs 2/- busses 1/3	3.3
	{Mr Marshall's srvt	1.0
	Goodale's bill	[blank]
10.	Busses	1.0
-	Carrier for 2 doz wine (E.Ford)	£1.4.0
11 Sunday	Busses & bridge with Mary	£1.2.0
12	Bundle of laths	1.8
-	cab 1/- busses to Hanckney 3/-	4.0
-	Br. Inst. Mary	1/-
-	Envelopes (25)	.6
14	Eggleton	1.0
	Busses with Mama	3.0
15.	James	2.0
16.	P.O.Stamps 2/6 Envelopes 3d}	
	Note paper 4d. Ink 6d}	3.7
	2 letters 2d. JAmes 8d	10
17	Busses to Barnes	2.0
	James Flack. Wages &c	£1.10.0
	Crocker on acct.	£3.0.0
	Ditto & men beer	2.8
	Cox labourer 4½ days	13.6
	P.D.C. pattern of paper	4
	Carriage of Sand Stone & men	£1.11.0
	letter	1
	Quick balance of acct	11.6
19.	Busses to & fro	6
-	Cocoa /6 - biscuits /6	1.0
	Mansell for 3 loads Brick rubbish	6.0
20	Eggleton 1/6 Mary 2/-	3.6
21	Bus & cab- Barnes pike 7c	2.5
22	2 letters	2
	Eggleton	1.6
Feb 24	Cox, one week	18.6
Sun 25	Busses to Hackney	2.0
27	Piano men	1.0
-	busses to Clapham	1.3
28	busses	1.3
Mar 2.	busses	1.0
-	Beer. Kilderkin Stout & Cask	£2.0.0
-	Crocker balance	£2.5.0
	Beer, men	2.6
	Cox	1.0
-	P.O.Stamps	1.7½
-	Carpet man	6
3.	Lewis balance	£20.0.0
4.	Busses to Barnes, M & I,	1.0
	Church	2.0
5.	Busses to Clapham	1.3
7	ditto back	1.3
8	Eggleton	1.0
9	Philipson	1.0
10	[blank]	
11	Busses to & from Twickenham	2.0
12	Busses to Hackney & back	2.0
-	figs, dates & cocoa	2.6
13	Fly man from Hackney	2.0
-	Sheppard for glass shades	8.0
14.	bus to town	6
-	Eggleton	1.0
-	Criswick's boy	6
15	Eggleton	2.6
-	Blackman load of plants	2.6
17	Cox. 4 days & 1 hour labour	13.0
-	Tom labour 2 days 2 hours	7.6
18	Church	1.0
19	Busses to Clapham & back	2.6
20	Eggleton	2.0
-	man Venables short day	2.6

-	little box to Conrad Loddiges	[blank]
22	Goodale's man	6
23	Cox 4 days	12.0
-	Venables 2 ¾	8.6
24	busses to & from Town	1.0
25+	Busses to Broadway	1.0
26	Venables ¾ day	2.6
-	Wigley load of things [furniture]	5.6
27	200 turfs & carting	15.0
-	Plants.Frewin	2.0
28	Eggleton	2.0
-	150 turfs & carting	11.10
29	Cox 3 days & ½	10.6
-	Venables 1¼ day	4.0
-	P.O.Stamps 2/6 .envelopes	[blank]
31	Medicine	1.3
-	Paper (note) envelopes	2.11
Apr 1	Medicine	2.6
4	50 turfs	3.9
5	man laying down turf	[blank]
-	P.O.Stamps	do.
7	Man in garden	1.6
8	church	2.6
11	Eggleton acct	£4.1.7
7	cab to Bayswater	2.6
Mar 27[*sic*]	Henry	5.0
-	Grass & clover seed	1.6
-	coffee 2/- Uncle 1/6	3.6
	Nails hooks &c	9.7
12	busses	2.0
-	notepaper 1/ labels 2/2	3.2
-	Gloves 2/6, sweets 1/6	4.0
13	Eggleton- 1 day	4.6
-	Cox ¾ day	2.6
-	Tom. loan	£5.0.0
14	Cox 1 day	3.0
16	Busses to Clapham	2.6
-	marmalade	8
-	Cox 1 day 3/-	3.0
17	Eggleton 1 day	4.6
18	Cox came at 9 Bricklayer at 10 o'clock	5.6
19	Cox & B came at 6 left at 10	2.6
20	Cox & B all day	8.0
21	Pd. Cox 13.6 & B. 14.0	£1.7.6.
-	Lewis's men	1.0
-	Carpenter	6
22	Pew-opener	2.6
23	Brown's boy	4
24	busses	9
-	figs & biscuits	1.2
-	Scizzors	9
-	Envelopes with Initial E	1.0
28	Purday 3 days & extra hour	18.0
-	Cox do. do.	11.0
-	Busses to Clapham 1/-. hair /6	1.6
-	busses home to Hackney	2.0
-	servt Christy's	1.0
May 1	Purday - odd hours	3.6
2	Cox 1 day ½	7.0
-	Mr Higgs for a load of Peat	£1.1.0
Apr 23	Mrs Brown for Cards (altered)	5.6
3	Gardener for box Edging	7.0
-	busses to & fro Wellclose sq	1.6
4	Grant Gas bill	£22.0.0
7	busses & cabs	4.3
-	Maccaroni (Hackney)	2.6
9	cab- my share !	6
-	slippers	[blank]
10	Busses	9
-	2 tubes Jaune brilliant	10
11	busses to & fro	1.3
12	Busses to Kew	1.1
-	carriage of Stone &c	£1.14.6
-	men for do.	1.6
13	Church	1.0
15	Hat Townends	10.6
-	Blackman Plants	2.0

16	Crocker for Pictures	8.0
-	Busses	2.0
18	Young Cox from ½ p 9	4.0
-	Ansdell's boy	1.0
19	Cox 4 days	12.0
-	P.O.Stamps	2.6
22	busses	1.0
23	Young Cox 1 o'clock	2.6
-	Eggleton	5.0
25	Young Cox - carpenter 3¼ days	17.6
-	Venables evening 2 hrs	6
26	Venables 1 day	3.6
27	Church	1.0
28	busses Town	9
29	busses to & from Kew	1.0
30	Egan's bill	£1.4.0
-	Henry for hose	12.6
-	4 plants (Potter) for Henry	4.0
-	H. expenses & sundries	7.0
-	Busses & cabs to Town & back	3.6
31	busses to & fro Ginger beer	1.4
	R A Catalogue	1.0
-	Eggleton	5.0
-	basket from Kew Plants	6
Jun 1	Post Stamps	1.0
-	Busses	1.3
-	5 Plants Hendersons	13.0
-	Venables 1 eveg	[blank]
2	Bus & cab to Ruckers	1.6
3	Church	1.0
4	Wine & brick rubbish men	1.0
-	Venables & boy short eveg	[blank]
	Old Cox eveg	1.6
-	Young Cox from 9 AM to 5	[blank]
5	Kilderkin Porter (Berry)	£ 1.1.0
-	P.O.Stamps	2.6
6	Busses	2.0
-	Alpaca coat Nichols	£ 1.1.0
-	Handkershiefs, gloves, ties &c Beans -	£1.0.0
-	Honey soap	4
4 & 5	Tacks & lamp-black	1.6
6	Colour (Green) & oil &c	2.7½
8	Purday 1 day	5.6
-	Venables 2 days & ½	8.0
-	busses	2.0
-	German elastic lead ?	2.0
-	Paletot Nichols	£2.2.0
-	Paid Holmes Bill	£2.2.0. Harriette repaid me
-	Cox 1 day carpenter	[blank]
9	Cox 1 day paid him for a week	£1.13.0
-	busses to & from Town	1.6
-	Cab to Chiswick	3.0
-	Busses home 4/-	4.0
-	6 Shirts Nicoll	£2.5.0
11	Cox 1 day carpenter	4.0
-	thinnings for color	7
12	Cab & bus & porter & Chronicle	2.11
-	Fare to Penshurst 2nd Class	6.2
16	Servt Mr Whitelocks	1.0
18	Mr Cox for Stone (Redleaf)	£1.0.0
	Do. for Martin for wood	£1.10.0
-	Servants Redleaf	5.0
18	Fare 6/2 cabs & bus home	9.0
19	P.O.Stamps	1.0
19	Hunt bill plumbing pr Mary	£6.15.2
20 June	Gas burnt 3,000 feet	[blank]
20	Artists Fund (30th)	£2.6.2
23	Cox painting trellis 8½ hrs	6.6
-	Pd Mr Moore 1 Qrs Rent	£25.0.0
24	Parcel from H.Eglington	1.6
27	28 pencils	7.6
-	10 plants climbers	4.6
29	Laura for Pomade	1.0
30	Cab to Wellclose Sq	4.6
-	slipper repaired	3
July, 1	Church	1.0
2	hair cut /6 P.O.Stamps/6	1.0
3	Busses 1/- Institution1/-	2.0
4	Emma	2.6
-	cab to Station	1.0
-	Rail & boat to Erith	1.6
-	Porters luggage	1.8
7	Servt.	4.6
	Boat & rail to town	1.6
-	Porters & busses home	2.2
9	Busses 1/3 Cab 1/6	2.9
-	Gloves (thread)	1.6
	Biscuits	3
11	Busses	1.3
12	Leather top Goloshes. Medwin	£1.5.0
-	Writing paper & Envelopes	4.3
-	P.O.Stamps	2.6
-	Sable brushes & tube (Barbe)	3.6
-	Mary	2.6
14	Times (?) 1 week	1.0
-	Brushes &c for Spare room	8.11
15	Busses to Hackney	2.0
17	Pd. H.Hering -bill (Mama)	£15.12.6
18	Pd Criswick bill to Xmas	£21. 6.6
-	Eggleton 1 day extra time	5.0
19	Mama paid Heal for 2 Mattrasses for Spare bed	£2.18.0
20	Subn. to Etty's Exn.	£1.1.0
-	Busses	1.0
22	Cabs to & fro Barnes	3.0
23	Busses to & fro Surrey Gardens	4.3
-	admission & sets for 4	8.0
-	P.O.Stamps	2.6
21	Times 1 week	1.0
25	Busses 1/- cab & pike 3/3	4.3
-	Maps of N. Wales (Letts')	8.6
-	Envelopes	1.0
27	Busses	1.0
-	Gloves (Geo Beans)	3.6
-	letter to Sir C.Eardley (late)	6
-	Waistcoat - buff	9.6
28	Bus & boat 2 boys Erith	1.9
30	boat & bus home (boy) [sic]	1.9
31	busses	1.6
-	Dinner ticket R.Academy	£1.1.0
Aug 1	P.O.Stamps	5.0
-	busses Hackney (?) My & Conrad too	4.0
	spectacles repaired	6
	Boots repairing Medwin	6.0
2	Busses	1.4
3	Busses	1.0
-	boots by P.D.C.	6
4	P.O.Stamps. Writing paper	[blank]
6	1 Kilderkn. of Porter (Berry)	£1.1.0
7	Busses	1.9
-	Servt Mr Edgar's	1.0
8	Gas man	8
9	Christy's servt	1.0
11	Henry for 3½ doz Glass illumination buckets:	7.6
	Do. Expenses	10.0
-	Beazley 2 days & 1 hour	12.0
-	Henry for E.Ford's bill	£10.16.0
-	Return ticket Slough	3.9
-	Dinner at Slough	5.0
-	Fly man 1.0	
15	6 pencils & tube French Ultra (Barbes)	2.4
-	Envelopes & cord for stick	1.6
16	Plant of F. Foena ramousum(?)	2.6
-	Check fishing coat Nicholls	£1.14.0
-	cloth cap	6.6
-	Portmanteau & C. bag repaired	5.0
-	Strap 1/6 Cab & bus 2/-	3.6
17	Busses to Hackney 2/- hair /6	2.6
-	Metallic book for George	1.0
-	Archdeacon Sinclair	£5.0.0.
18	Started for Connington. Cab to Sq	3.0
-	Fare to Peterboro 13/- biscuits 3d	13.3
23-	Mr Wells's gardener	2.0
24	Joseph 1/- Allem 7/6	8.6
-	Rail to Ely 6/3 bus 1/1	7.4

25	Cathedral	1.0
-	Ely. With Mary. Bill & Servts at Lamb	£1.0.0
-	Rail to Cambridge 4/6 bus 1/6	6.0
-	Buns 3d. Bus & porter 1.6	1.9
-	Kings College Chapel	1.0
-	Memo bk.1/- Soap 2d, Sundries 2/8	3.10
26	at Church	2.0
-	letters	3
27	Bill Mrs Smiths 16/1 Servt 2/6	18.7
-	Bus 1/3 Rail 19/-	£1.0.3
-	Cab 4/-pike 3d	4.3
	2 guides 2 catalogues	3.0
-	soda water	5
	Total at Connington, Ely & Cambridge	£5.16.5
28	Eggleton 1 day	5.0
29	Fly man 3/- pikes 1/6 Servt 1/	5.6
30	Poors Rates to L.Day 1850	£7.5.2½
-	P.O.Stamps 2/- Tailor 8/-	10.0
Sept 1	Busses	1.6
-	Rails for M & I to Erith	6.0
3	Servt 2/- boats & Rail 2/-	4.0
-	Bus to & from Hackney	2.0
-	Cabs & Theatre Tempest	6.6
4	Busses to & from Hackney	2.0
5	P.O.Stamps	3.6
	Busses	1.3
	Italian chalk	5
Left home		
7	Cab & pike	3.3
	Express fare to Norton Bridge	£1.11.6
-	Do. to Congleton	3.3
-	Times news & biscuit	7
13	Rail to Chester from Congleton	5.3
-	Do. to Queen's Ferry	1.0
[total b.f.]		£2.4.10
-	biscuits /3 Gig & man, pikes &c	4.3
15	Dinner at Chester	2.6
-	Guide N.Wales	1.6
-	Rail to Q's Ferry	1.0
17	Servt 2/- Coachman 2/6	4.6
-	Rail to Chelford	4.6
-	Gig to Tabley	8.7
18	Servant Tabley	2.0
22	Servant Biddulph Grange	10.0
-	Groom	2.6
-	Washing	3.0
	Rail to Chester	6.0
-	Stokers & Pokers	2.6
	rail to Conway	4.0
	do. to Bangor	2.6
	Bus to Menai	1.6
-	Rail to Holyhead	2.6
	Packet to Kingstown Ireland	11.0
-	Supper on board	2.0
-	Rail to Dublin & porter	1.3
23	Church, cars &c	2.9
25	Rail to & from Howth & car	1.8
-	Dinner at Howth	2.6
-	Exhibition of limestone Man	6
26	Rail to Mallow	18.0
-	Car	1.4
-	Coach 6/- Man 1/6 to Killarney	7.6
[Total b.f.]		£7.5.11
Sep.27	letters	7
-	boat & Car round Lake	10.0
28	lunch & Car	2.0
-	Stick /6 boat /6	1.0
29	Basket 1/4 paper/8	2.0
-	Bill at Hotel	£1.1.0
	Boots & porter	2.0
-	car to Mucross	3.6
	Boot repaired	6
30	Church 1/- car /6	1.6
Oct 2	Car to Police Station	1.0
3	Share of car & boats	8.4
4	Bill at Mucross Hotel	£2.9.9
	The Boots	3.6

-	Car to Bantry 7/- Man 1/-	8.0
	luncheon Kenmare	1.2
5	Mail to Cork	10.0
	Bill at Bantry	7.6
	Coachman	2.4
-	Arbutus ornaments Killarney	18.0
6	Bill at Cork	8.0
	Car to Blarney Castle	3.6
	Steamer & porters to Cove	1.3
	Lunch at Cove	1.6
	Church Cove	2.0
[Total b.f.]		£15.15.10.
Oct 8	Porter, boat & car to Cork	1.9
	Fare by coach Mallow	3.8
	Bateson expenses	10.0
	Guide book	8
-	Rail to Dublin	18.0
	lunch & car	1.4
9	Map of Ireland	4.0
-	Gloves 1/- Cars 1/- hair /6	2.6
-	Rail /10 cars to Bray	3.0
11	Servt	1.6
-	Rail 8 car 1/-	1.8
14	Porter	6
-	Steamer to Holyhead	11. 0
-	H. to Llanfair	3.0
-	bus to Bangor 1/6 porter /6	2.0
13	Bill at Morrison's	£1.9.6
-	Boots	2.6
	cab	1.0
-	rail to Kingstown	8
15	bill at Bangor	18.9
	boots & bus	1.6
	Car to station 2.0	
-	Rail to Conway	2.6
-	Porter & woman at Old house	1.6
16.17.	Servt.	2.0
	Rail to Chester	8.2
[total b .f.]		£22.10.10
17	Do. to Birkenhead	3.0
	boat & porter	10
	cab to Lynn's	1.0
	cab to Rake Lane	4.0
18	boy at St George's Hall & cab	1.6
-	R.Smith (bill at Morrisons)	£2.7.0
	Bill at Lynn's	11.0
	rail to Manchester	4.0
-	cab to Upton House	2.6
19	cab	1.4
21	rail to & from Altringham [*sic*]	2.0
22	Servt	2.6
-	Cabs 3/- & rail to Stockport 1/-	4.0
-	cab to Harter's	5.0
-	Pikes & mill (Stockport)	1.10
23	lad 2/- cab 2/6	4.6
-	rail to Birmingham	15.0
	do. Bristol	15.6
	Do. to Taunton	7.0
-	Bkfst 1/9; Fly to Barton Grange 7/6	9.3
27	Servt	5.0
-	Rail to Windsor from Taunton	£1.3.0
-	Driver & porters	2.0
29	lad, Windsor	2.0
-	rail to Town 3/-, porter /6	3.6
	cab & pike home to The Ferns	2.9
[Total]		£31.1.10
Oct 30	Eggleton	5.0
31	Busses to Hackney	2.6
Nov 1	Bell glass	6.6
-	bus & basket	1.0
-	biscuits, grapes, dates &c	3.4
-	note paper & envelopes	2.6
-	? Leads	1.0
3	Bus & string /8	1.8
4	Church	1.0
-	busses	2.0
5	Kilderkin Porter (Berrys)	£1.1.0

7	Parcels of Hymenophyllum	1.6
-	Cab to Hannah's	2.3
Nov 23	Busses	9
24	Pocketbook for George 2/-busses 2/-	4.0
26	Geo ?sans	2.0
27	Bus /6 biscuits 1/6	2.0
-	Woollens. Beans	14.0
29	Van Voorst for Newman ferns	18.9
-	2 parcels from Van Voorst	8
30	Box Mr Bateman	2.3
-	letter to Mr Bateson (Paris)	10
Dec 1	Bus	6
-	Bronze Grehound [*sic*]	18.0
2	Church	1.0
3	Busses	1.0
4	Busses	1.9
3	tubes Barbes	1.4
8	Busses	1.9
-	figs /10 Blk gloves 2/6	3.4
11	P.O.Stamps	8
	Tailor	[blank]
12	Graphic	£1.1.0
-	cabs &c	4.10
13	Kilderkin Porter (Berry)	£1.1.0
14	Bus & Cab ? Frys	2.6
-	P.O.Stamps	2.6
15	Busses	9
16	Do. & Cab	2.3
20	Cab	1.0
21	Bus	1.0
22	Bus	1.0
24	Busses	3.0
-	Volckman	2.8
-	Oranges /6 Servt.7/	7.6
_	Kilderkin of Stout (Berry)	£1.7.0
-	Church	2.6
27	Busses 1/- tapes /6	1.6
-	Diary & pocket book	2.6
-	Writing paper	2.6
-	Figs	2.8
29	Busses	2.0
-	Black Bordrd paper	8
30	Busses	1.6

STUDIO NOTES – 1849, 1851
From the back of the Account book, 1849

Jan 5th Crocker brought 2 frames from Criswick, one for Livorno & the other for small Sorrento.

- Crocker took to Mrs Bates picture and frame of Cannes & Sorrento & new frame.

16 Crocker took old french frames to Criswick's to be repaired & returned with a new flat

Jan 27th to VR, also a new frame for Erchia from Criswick's same day.

Brown sent 2 canvases.

April 23 Brown sent 1 small panels

28 Brown sent canvas for Conrad's picture.

Aug 4 Criswick sent new frame for Rome to MR S.Rucker nar.

-9 Criswick sent large frame and glass for print of Transfiguration-

Dec.22 2 new frames came from Criswick -

Dec.27 Microscope sent home.

[In centre of book following Cooke's pencilled Accounts: in Ink, in the handwriting of one of his sisters:]

Order sent to Criswick's Dec 31st 1851

4 frames (60195) of [1852 deleted] of following sizes

A - $17\frac{2}{8}$ x $11\frac{4}{8}$

B - $17\frac{2}{8}$ x $10\frac{5}{8}$

C - $17\frac{3}{8}$ x $10\frac{5}{8}$

D - $17\frac{2}{8}$ x $11\frac{4}{8}$

E (60645) - $10\frac{5}{8}$ x $4\frac{6}{8}$

One upright - $31\frac{5}{8}$ x $26\frac{6}{8}$

One ditto - $31\frac{6}{8}$ x $26\frac{4}{8}$

Jan 1852.

1st Criswick sent 3 frames for Venetian subs (on the Spot) Collins pattern.

2. [EWC's hand] Sent copies of London Bridge and Shipping to Leighton.

3. Brown sent 3 Venetian oil sketches home of the larger size - lined on stretchers.

7. [Sister] Brown sent last oil sketch home.

12 Ordered key labels at Stevens's.

-5 small frames came home from Criswicks that were ordered 4h Dec.

- Microscope box came home.

13. Picture of Scheveling (Mr Delafosse's) sent to Institution (Crocker).

- Mounts came from Woolley's (6 doz large and 6 doz small) paid cheque £5

- 2 Upright frames for Venetian pictures from Criswicks

14 Wrote for 2 doz largest mounts.

- Microscope clipper came home.

- Wrote to Smith Rathbone Place for 200 Government enveloppes.

6 Turner's drawings and 33 Ed[ward]s. drawings to the Graphic.

15 Drawings & [&c] came home from Graphic.

- Leighton sent home Ed. two works for Academy - also port-folio (Italy) - also one Solander case (Venezia).

- Ed[ward]. took the works to Academy (present)

15 Paid Hunt's bill £1 .8. 9.

16. Lent Hart 6 drawings with palms. viz 1 pen & ink sk. of palm, 2 Aloe at Monaco, 3 Cactus at Monaco 4 seats in Borghese garden ½ coloured. 2 mounted pencil sketches viz 2 San Remo

- Begun mounting oil sketches (Italy)

17 200 Govenmt. Enveloppes came home. Ordered 100 notes of do.

19 Diploma came from Academy with book.

- Ordered cards at Mrs Browns

- took fish & pencil sketch to Mr Stokes.

- Wrote to Criswick and Green about pictures from Manchester.

22. 100 small enveloppes came. paid bill of others with them £1.11.6.

- sent to Silas Eyles.

- wrote to Green for two tubes of white tubes [*sic*]

- Mr Turner paid £50 on account for "Salute".

24. New double Easel came home.

- Leighton sent "Britain" Solander case.

- same time sent folio for baskets to be covered.

26 Packing case from Glasgow containing 2 small pictures viz."Sunset at Venice" & "Palli Eveng." Ed. took little study of Corner of Ducal Palace to Mr Cockerell, Architect's meeting.

- Sent letter with particulars of Ducal Palace to Mr. Cockerell

- hung Venetian small pictures in back drawing-room making 3 rows.

28 Folio(basket maker) came from Leighton's;

Feby 6 Put up brackes (fern) on staircase

- took Venezia Vol 2 to Sir W.James's dinner party.

7 Eyles brought home Easel from being altered.

- Ed[ward]. went to see Salute picture & send it home to Mr S.Christy.

11 Ordered canvas (Naples yellow tone) of Brown also 1 tube of Vermillion & 2 little pots.

14 Yellow canvas and Vermillion came

March 1 Frame came home from Criswick's for Eastlake's print.

2 Man came from Brown's to lengthen canvas of Upright Venetian picture.

3 . 2 tubes & brushes came from Brown's

15 Laura brought ferns &c for Gardens .

- took two folios to be covered at Brookes Oxford St (2 labels brought home)

17. Eggleton came and Davis (for ½ day) put in new plants and shrubs.

19. Smith & Beck sent home the new slide &c for Microscope.

- Gasfitter brought new arms for gas in Study.

- Hunsford brought home the two columns of Parcheti [?] & put them up.

- Criswick sent home the frame for the large Venice.

- Mr Hannah sent his smalle (r) ? lamp to lend Edward

- reframed and rehung prints in front drawing room.

20 - Gasman finished in Study. Carpenter mended the boards.

Ends

BIBLIOGRAPHY

Manuscripts

Cooke Family

John Frederick Lewis Collection: autograph letters from engravers &c. The Free Library of Philadelphia, Pa., USA

John Murray, Publishers. The Archive…

John Pye. British Library Museum: Addl. Mss. Pye

Royal Academy of Arts: Library MS 405

Royal Botanic Gardens, Kew. Director's Correspondence

Periodicals

Arnold's Magazine of the Fine Arts, 1834, Vol. III, No. VI, p. 557 (obituary of George Cooke by George Hollis)

The Art Journal, 1849-1912

Art Union Journal, 1844-1848

Artists & Amateurs Magazine, Rippingville, E.V., 1843

The Athenaeum

Cobbett's Magazine, March 1833

The Critical Guide 1796, quoted by Peter Cunningham, quoted by Redgrave

The Garden, Vol. X

Gardener's Chronicle, 10 Jan. 1890

Gardener's Magazine, July 1839

Magazine of Art, Vol. IV, 1881

The Portfolio – An Artistic Periodical, edited by Philip Gilbert Hamerton 1869-1894

Journal of the Royal Horticultural Society of London, Vol. I, p. 224

Miscellaneous Works

Blunt, Wilfrid, *Flower Books from the Library of the Society of Herbalists* (exhibition catalogue), The Arts Council, 1953

Clarke, Benjamin, *Glimpses of Ancient Hackney & Stoke Newington,* 1893

Eastlake, Charles L., *Hints on Household Taste,* 1868

Edwards, J., *The Art of Landscape Painting in Oil Colours* for Winsor & Newton, n.d.

Fleming, John, 'The Rome of Henry James', *Country Life,* 19 January 1951

Hammond, J.H. and Austin, J., *The Camera Lucida in Art & Science,* 1987

Hayden, Peter, *Biddulph Grange, Staffordshire, A Victorian Garden Rediscovered,* George Philip/The National Trust, 1989

James, Henry, *Italian Hours,* 1909

Kemp, Edward, *Description of the Gardens at Biddulph Grange,* 1862

Mayhew, Henry, *London Labour and the London Poor,* 1851-64

Rogers, Samuel, *Italy,* 1822

Rubin de Cervin Albrizzi, G-E., *Bateaux et Batellerie de Venice,* Paris, 1978

Ruskin, John, *The Harbours of England,* 1856

Ruskin, John, *The Stones of Venice,* Vol. I published 1851, Vols II and III 1853

Scharf, Aaron, *Art & Photography,* 1968

Simper, Robert, *Beach Boats of Britain,* 1984

The Survey of London, Vol. 38

Tait, Hugh, *The Golden Age of Venetian Glass,* British Museum, 1979

Thornbury, Walter, *Old & New London* 1873, Vol. II

Timbs, John, *Curiosities of London,* 1855

Treanor, Rev. T. Stanley, *Heroes of the Goodwin Sands,* 1893

V & A Album II, 1983, p. 367

Venice, *Venezia E Le Sue Lagune,* 2 vols., 1847, Venezia, Nell I.R. Privil Stabilimento Antonelli

Wainwright, Clive, *The Romantic Interior,* 1989

Walker, Richard J.E., *The Palace of Westminster after the Fire of October 1834,* The Walpole Society, Vol. XLIV

Winsor & Newton. Advertisements to Winsor & Newton's series *The Art of Painting…* n.d., c.1870

Collective Studies

Baldry, A.L., *British Marine Painting, The Studio* Special Number, 1919

Bertram, Anthony, *A Century of British Painting 1851-1951,* 1951

Blackburn, H., *Academy Notes,* 3 vols., 1879

Boase, T.S.R., *English Art 1800-1870,* 1959

Clement, Clare A. and Hutton, Lawrence, *Artists of the Nineteenth Century and Their Works,* 7th ed., Boston, 1894

Cunningham, Alan, *Lives of the Most Eminent British Painters…* 1880, Vol. III, with additions by Mrs. Heaton

De Groot, I. and Worstman, R., *Marine Prints by the Dutch Masters,* 1980

De Leeuw, R. and others, *The Hague School, Dutch Masters of the 19th Century,* 1983

Engen,R.K., *Dictionary of Victorian Engravers & Print Publishers & their Works,* 1979

Finberg, A.J., *The English Water Colour Painters,* 1905

Gaunt, William, *The Pre-Raphaelite Dream,* 1943

Gaunt, William, *Marine Painting,* 1975

Gaunt, William, *Victorian Olympus,* 1952

Gombrich, Sir E.H., *The Story of Art,* 1966

Grant, Maurice H., *Dictionary of British Etchers,* 1952

Grant, Maurice H., *A Chronological History of the Old English Landscape Painters,* rev. ed., 1957

Graves, Algernon, *Dictionary of Artists who have exhibited works in the principal London Exhibitions 1760-1893,* 3rd. ed., 1901

Graves, Algernon, *The Royal Academy of Arts 1869-1904 A Complete Dictionary of Contributors,* 1905

Graves, Algernon, *The British Institution 1806-1867 A Complete Dictionary of Contributors,* 1908

Graves, Algernon, *Art Sales from early 18th Century to early 20th Century,* 1918 (reprinted New York 1970)

Graves, Algernon, *A Century of Loan Exhibitions,* 1910

Grundy, C.R., *Catalogue of Pictures & Drawings in the Collection of Frederick John Nettlefold,* 1937

Hardie, Martin, *Watercolour Painting in Britain,* Vol. III Victorian, 1969

Herbert, R.L., *Impressionism, Art, Leisure & Parisian Society,* 1988

Herrmann, Frank, *The English as Collectors,* 1972

Hind, Arthur M., *A History of Engraving & Etching,* 1927

Hughes, C.E., *Early English Watercolours,* rev. ed. Jonathan Mayne, 1950

Hunnisett, Basil, *Steel-Engraved Book Illustration in England,* 1980

Hunnisett, Basil, *Illustrated History of British Steel Engravers* rev. ed. 1989

James, Ralph N., *Painters and their Works; A Dictionary of great artists... & prices paid for their works at auction,* 3 vols., 1896
Lambourne, L., and Hamilton, J., *British Watercolours in the Victoria & Albert Museum,* 1980
Leslie, G.D., RA, *The Inner Life of the Royal Academy,* 1914
Lister, R., *Prints and Printmaking,* 1984
Lumsden, Ian G., *Early Views of British North America,* Beaverbrook Art Gallery, Fredericton, 1994, p. 17
Oppé, A.P., *Art [in] Early Victorian England,* 2 vols., 1934
Ottley, H., *Biographical & Critical Dictionary of Recent and Living painters & engravers...* 1866
Palgrave, Francis T., *Essays on Art,* 1863
Parkinson, Ronald, *British oil paintings at the Victoria & Albert Museum 1820-1860,* 1990
Piper, John, *British Romantic Artists,* 1942
Pointon, Marcia, *The Bonington Circle: English Watercolour & Anglo-French Landscape,* 1985
Pointon, Marcia, *Bonington, Francia & Wyld,* 1985
Pye, John, *Patronage of British Art* 1845
Quilter, Harry, *Preferences in Art, Life & Literature,* 1892
R. [Ruskin, John], *Pre-Raphaelitism by the Author of 'Modern Painters',* 1851
Redgrave, Richard RA and Redgrave, Samuel, *A Century of British Painters by Richard & Samuel Redgrave,* new ed. by Ruthven Todd, Phaidon Press, 1947
Redgrave, Richard RA and Redgrave, Samuel, *A Century of Painters of the English School...* 1st ed., 2 vols., 1866
Roberts, W., 'John Renton & other Hoxton Nurserymen', *Journal R.H.S.,* Vol. 1938
Roget, J.L., *A History of the 'Old Water-Colour' Society,* 2 vols., 1891
Ruskin, John, *Modern Painters,* 1843-1860
Strutt, Joseph, *Biographical Dictionary of Engravers,* 2 vols., 1785
Sutton, Denys and Sutton, Anthony, *Venice Rediscovered* [Catalogue of a] *Loan Exhibition in aid of the Venice in Peril Fund,* Wildenstein, 1972
Temple, A.G., *The Art of Painting in the Queen's Reign,* 1897
Whitley, W.T., *Art in England 1800-1820,* 1928
Whitley, W.T., *Art in England 1821-1837,* 1930

Individual Artists, etc.
Kavanagh, Amanda, 'Robert Bateman, a true Victorian', *Apollo,* Sept. 1989
Wright, Thomas, 'Mark Beaufoy's Nautical & Hydraulic Experiments', *Mariner's Mirror,* Vol. 75
Roundell, James, *Thomas Shotter Boys, 1803-1874,* 1974
Dubuisson, A. and Hughes, C.E., *Richard Parkes Bonington, His Life & Work,* 1924
Curtis, A., *L'Oeuvre Gravé de Bonington,* Paris, 1939
Peacock, Carlos, *Richard Parkes Bonington,* 1979
Britton, John, *The Autobiography of,* 2 vols., 1849-50
Cundall, H.M. (ed.), *William Callow, an Autobiography,* 1908
Leslie, C.R., RA, *Memoirs of the Life of John Constable,* 1951
Beckett, R.B. (ed.), *John Constable's Correspondence,* Suffolk County Record Office 1962-68, Vol. VI
Tate Gallery, *Constable, Paintings, Watercolours & Drawings* (exhibition catalogue) by Leslie Parriss, Ian Fleming-Williams and Conal Shields, 1976
Cooke, E.W., *A Selection of Drawings of Old & New London Bridge,* London Topographical Society, Publication No. 113, 1970
Finch, Roger, *Shipping & Craft by E.W. Cooke,* a facsimile edition with descriptive notes by Roger Finch, 1970
Fox, Uffa, 'The Marine Artist to whom seamen owe most' (chapter in his *Sail and Power,* 1936)
Howgego, J.L., *Edward William Cooke RA FRS 1811-1880* (exhibition catalogue), Guildhall Art Gallery 1970
Cooke, E.W., *Sailing Vessels in Authentic early nineteenth century Illustrations ('Sixty-five Plates of Shipping and Craft') Edward William Cooke,* Dover Publications, Mineola, New York, 1989
Cooper, Thomas Sidney, RA, *My Life,* 1890
Cope, C.H., *Reminiscences of Charles West Cope RA,* 1891
Kitson, S.D., *John Sell Cotman,* 1937
McLean, Ruari, *Joseph Cundall, A Victorian Printer,* 1976
Dibden, Thomas F., *Reminiscences,* 1836
Robertson, David, *Sir Chas Eastlake and the Victorian Art World,* Princeton, New Jersey, 1978
Farington, Joseph RA, *The Farington Diaries,* 2nd ed., 1978
Frith, William Powell RA, *My Autobiography & Reminiscences,* 6th ed., 1888
Maas, Jeremy, *Gambart, Prince of the Victorian Art World,* 1975
Goodall, Frederick, RA, *The Reminiscences of...,* 1902
Hall, Samuel Carter, *Retrospect of a long life,* 2 vols., 1883
Hart, Solomon Alexander, RA, *The Reminiscences,* ed. Alex Brodie, 1882
Hook, A.J., *James Clark Hook RA,* 2 vols., 1932
Horsley, John Callcott, RA, *Recollections of a Royal Academician,* 1903
Coombs, J.H. and others (eds.), *A Pre-Raphaelite Friendship; the correspondence of William Holman Hunt and John Lucas Tupper,* UMA Research Press, Ann Arbor, Michigan, USA, 1986
Ormond, Richard and others, *Sir Edwin Landseer, RA,* Thames and Hudson in assn. with Philadelphia Museum of Art and Tate Gallery, 1981
Leslie, Charles Robert, RA, *Autobiographical Recollections,* ed. Tom Taylor, 1860
Locker-Lampson, Frederick, *My Confidences,* 1896
Mark, William, *At Sea with Nelson,* 1929
Naya, Carlo, *Veduti e Dettagli – The Photography of Carlo Naya,* Ann Arbor, Michigan, 1992
Oswell, W.E., *William Cotton Oswell, Hunter & Explorer, The Story of his Life,* 2 vols., 1900
Raimbach, Miss, *Abraham Raimbach, Memoirs & Recollections,* 1843
Redgrave, F.M., *Richard Redgrave CB RA, A Memoir Compiled from his Diary,* 1891
Conner, Patrick, *Michael Angelo Rooker,* Batsford
Cook, E.T. and Wedderburn, A., *The Library Edition of the Works of John Ruskin,* 39 vols., 1903-1912
Bradley, J.L. (ed.), *Ruskin's Letters from Venice,* 1955
Evans, J. and Whitehouse, J.H. (eds.), *Diaries of John Ruskin,* 3 vols., 1956
Lutyens, Mary, *Young Mrs Ruskin in Venice,* 1965
Whittock, Arnold (ed.), *Ruskin's Venice,* 1976
Clegg, Jeanne, *Ruskin and Venice,* 1981
Hunt, J.D., *The Wider Sea, A Life of John Ruskin,* 1982
Bradley, J.L. (ed.), *Ruskin, The Critical Heritage,* 1984
Stirling, A.M.W., *The Richmond Papers,* 1926
Saint, Andrew, *Richard Norman Shaw RA,* Yale U.P., 1976
Spanton, W.S., *An Art Student & his Teachers in the Sixties,* 1927
Van der Merwe, P.T., *The Spectacular Career of Clarkson Stanfield, Seaman, Scene-Painter, Royal Academician* (exhibition catalogue), 1979
Finberg, A.J., *Life of J.M.W. Turner RA,* 2nd ed., 1961
Turner Studies, Vol. I, 1981
Shanes, Eric, *Turner's Rivers, Harbours & Coasts,* 1981
Herrman, Luke, *Turner Prints – The Engraved work of J.M.W. Turner RA,* 1990
Uwins, Mrs., *Memoir of Thomas Uwins RA,* 1858
The Art of the Van de Veldes (exhibition catalogue), National Maritime Museum, Greenwich, 1982
Vizetelly, Henry, *Glances back through Seventy Years,* 1893
Hamerton, P.G., *Edward Matthew Ward RA,* 1895
Ward, Edward Matthew RA, *Miscellaneous Reminiscences,* ed. E.O. Darell, 1911

INDEX

Page references in bold type refer to illustrations and captions